Street by Street

GLASGOW

AYR, EAST KILBRIDE, GREENOCK, KILMARNOCK, PAISLEY

Clydebank, Coatbridge, Cumbernauld, Hamilton, Helensburgh, Irvine, Lanark, Largs, Motherwell, Shotts

Ist edition May 2001

© Automobile Association Developments Limited 2001

This product includes map data licensed from Ordnance Survey® with the permission of the Controller of Her Majesty's Stationery Office. © Crown copyright 2000. All rights reserved. Licence No: 399221.

All rights reserved. No part of this publication may be reproduced, stored in a retrieval system, or transmitted in any form or by any means– electronic, mechanical, photocopying, recording or otherwise – unless the permission of the publisher has been given beforehand.

Published by AA Publishing (a trading name of Automobile Association Developments Limited, whose registered office is Norfolk House, Priestley Road, Basingstoke, Hampshire, RG24 9NY. Registered number 1878835).

Mapping produced by the Cartographic Department of The Automobile Association.

A CIP Catalogue record for this book is available from the British Library.

Printed by G. Canale & C. S.P.A., Torino, Italy

The contents of this atlas are believed to be correct at the time of the latest revision. However, the publishers cannot be held responsible for loss occasioned to any person acting or refraining from action as a result of any material in this atlas, nor for any errors, omissions or changes in such material. The publishers would welcome information to correct any errors or omissions and to keep this atlas up to date. Please write to Publishing, The Automobile Association, Fanum House, Basing View, Basingstoke, Hampshire, RG21 4EA.

Ref: MX071

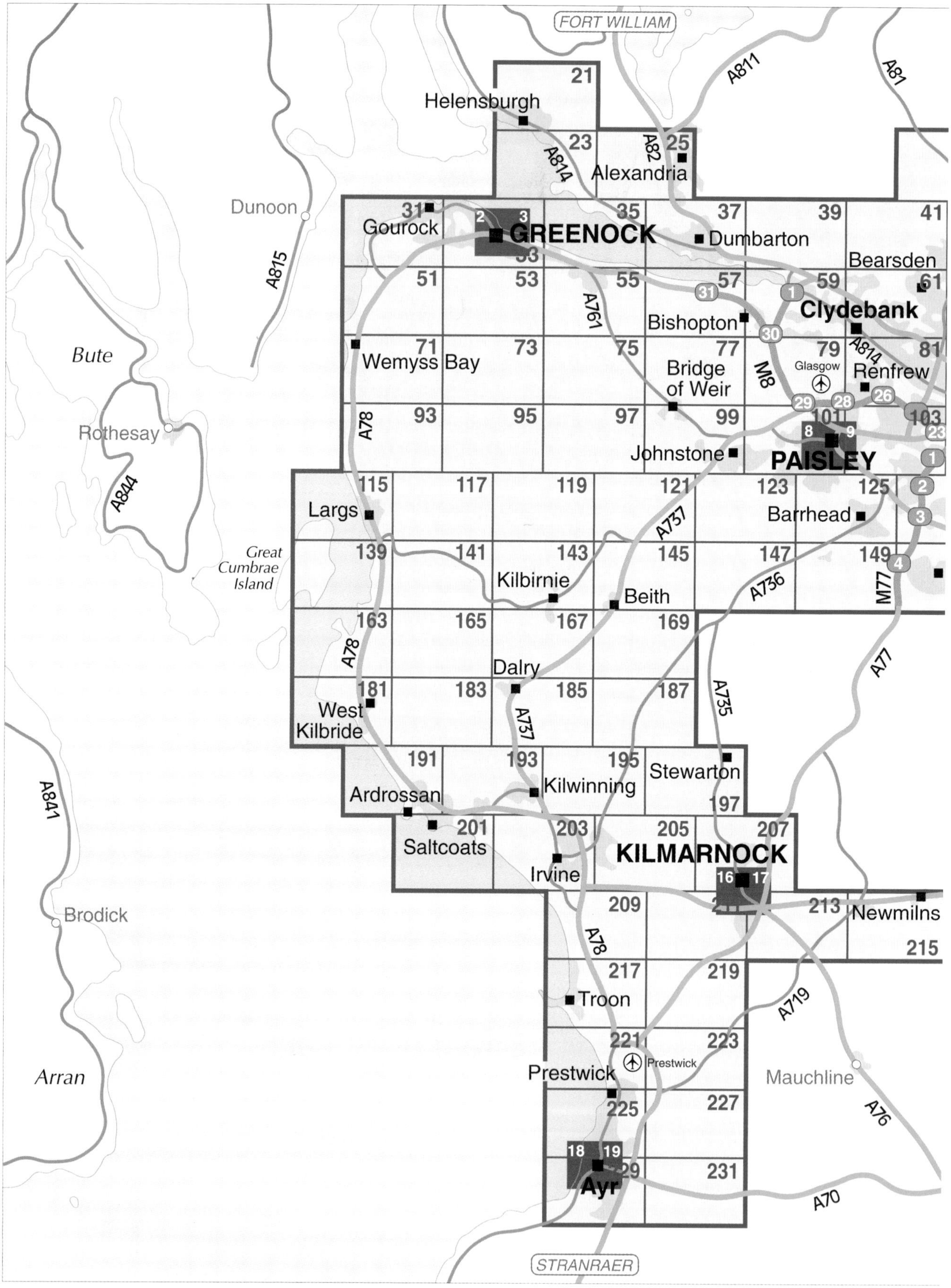
FORT WILLIAM
A811
A81
Helensburgh
21
23
25
A814
A82
Alexandria
Dunoon
A815
31
Gourock
2
3
GREENOCK
33
35
37
Dumbarton
39
41
Bearsden
51
53
55
57
31
1
59
61
Clydebank
A761
Bishopton
30
Bute
Wemyss Bay
71
73
75
77
Bridge of Weir
M8
79
Glasgow
A814
81
Renfrew
26
29
28
Rothesay
A78
93
95
97
99
101
103
23
8
9
Johnstone
PAISLEY
1
A844
115
117
119
121
123
125
2
Largs
Barrhead
A737
3
Great Cumbrae Island
139
141
143
145
147
149
4
Kilbirnie
Beith
A736
M77
163
165
167
169
A78
Dalry
A77
181
183
185
187
West Kilbride
A735
A737
A841
191
193
195
Stewarton
Ardrossan
Kilwinning
197
201
203
205
207
Saltcoats
KILMARNOCK
Irvine
16
17
209
211
213
Newmilns
Brodick
A78
215
217
219
Troon
A719
221
223
Prestwick
Prestwick
Mauchline
Arran
225
227
A76
18
19
229
231
Ayr
A70
STRANRAER

Enlarged scale pages **1:10,000** 6.3 inches to 1 mile

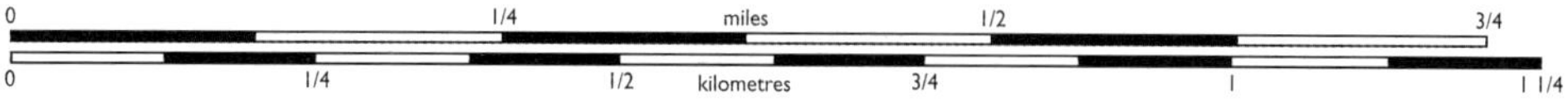
0
1/4
miles
1/2
3/4
0
1/4
1/2
kilometres
3/4
1
1 1/4

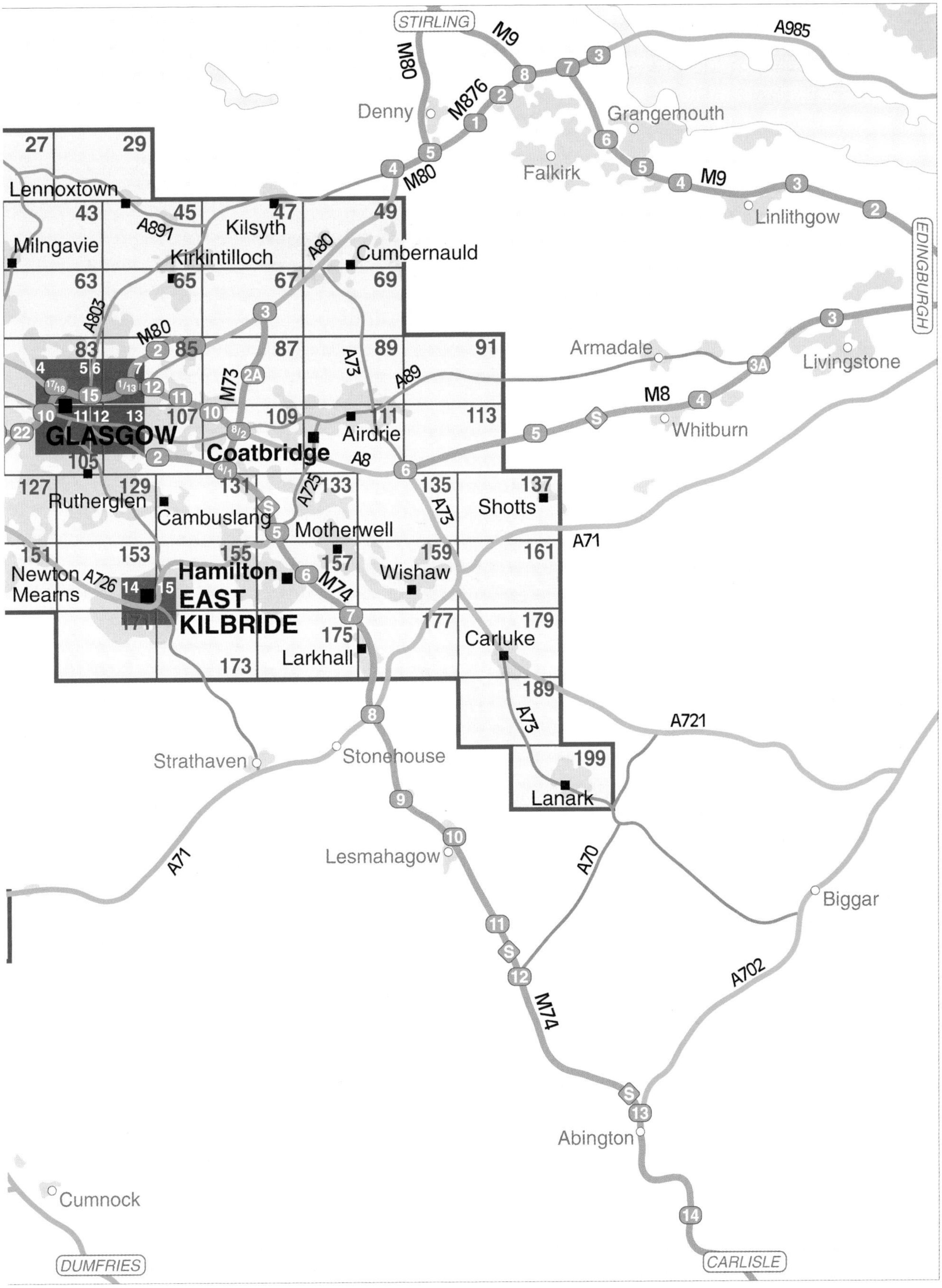

3.6 inches to 1 mile

Scale of main map pages 1:17,500

0 1/2 miles 1

0 1/2 1 kilometres 1 1/2 2

- Junction 9 — Motorway & junction
- Services — Motorway service area
- Primary road single/dual carriageway
- Services — Primary road service area
- A road single/dual carriageway
- B road single/dual carriageway
- Other road single/dual carriageway
- Restricted road
- Private road
- One way street
- Pedestrian street
- Track/ footpath
- Road under construction
- Road tunnel
- P — Parking
- P+ — Park & Ride
- Bus/coach station
- Railway & main railway station
- Railway & minor railway station
- Underground station
- Light railway & station
- Preserved private railway
- LC — Level crossing
- Tramway
- Ferry route
- Airport runway
- Boundaries- borough/ district
- Mounds
- 93 — Page continuation 1:17,500
- 7 — Page continuation to enlarged scale 1:10,000

Symbol	Meaning
	River/canal lake, pier
	Aqueduct lock, weir
465 ▲ Winter Hill	Peak (with height in metres)
	Beach
	Coniferous woodland
	Broadleaved woodland
	Mixed woodland
	Park
	Cemetery
	Built-up area
	Featured building
	City wall
A&E	Accident & Emergency hospital
	Toilet

Symbol	Meaning
	Toilet with disabled facilities
	Petrol station
PH	Public house
PO	Post Office
	Public library
i	Tourist Information Centre
	Castle
	Historic house/ building
Wakehurst Place NT	National Trust property
M	Museum/ art gallery
✝	Church/chapel
	Country park
	Theatre/ performing arts
	Cinema

2
C3 1 Charles Pl
B4 1 Salmon St
A7 1 Merino Rd 2 Wemyss Bay St
A4 1 Orangefield La
C4 1 Buccleugh St
D4 1 Crown St
E4 1 Cathcart Sq
F4 1 Customhouse Pl 2 New Dock La 3 Open Shore
A B C D E F
32
GREENOCK
Central
Strone Farm
Arts Guild Theatre
Secondary School
Ardgowan Bowling & Tennis Club
McLean Mus & Art Gallery
James Watt College
Ardgowan Medical Practice
Greenock West Station
Greenock Health Centre
Highlanders Academy Primary School
Wellpark Clinic
Greenock Central Station
St Patricks Primary School
Notre Dame High School
Drumfrochar Station
Overton Primary School
Whinhill Golf Club
Whinhill Reservoir
Reservoirs
Overton Reservoir
BROUGHAM STREET
DALRYMPLE STREET A770
A78 HIGH STREET
DALRYMPLE STREET A8
INVERKIP ST
NELSON A78 STREET
NEWTON ST
ROAD A78
B7054 CORNHADDOCK STREET
DRUMFROCHAR ROAD
B7054
B788 INGLESTON
BAKER STREET
RUE END
DELLINGBURN ST
Container Way
Roxburgh Street
Regent Street
Wellington Street
Dempster Street
Prospecthill Street
Holmscroft Av
Roxburgh Avenue
Brisbane Street
Finnart Street
Patrick Street
Union Street
Ardgowan Street
Newton Street
Kelly Street
West Stewart Street
West Blackhall St
Cathcart Street
Terrace Road
Lynedoch St
Hope Street
Mearns Street
Bank Street
Duncan St
Murdieston St
Peat Road
Papermill Road
Merino Road
Carvock Drive
Kilmun Rd
Upr Cartsburn Street
Riverside
Lomond
Darndaff Rd
Crawberry Road
Katrine Road
Whinhill Road
Old Largs Road
Beith Road
Brachelston Street
Scott Street
Chapel Street
PA15
1 grid square represents 250 metres

G6 1 Empress Ct

G9 1 Glenbrae La

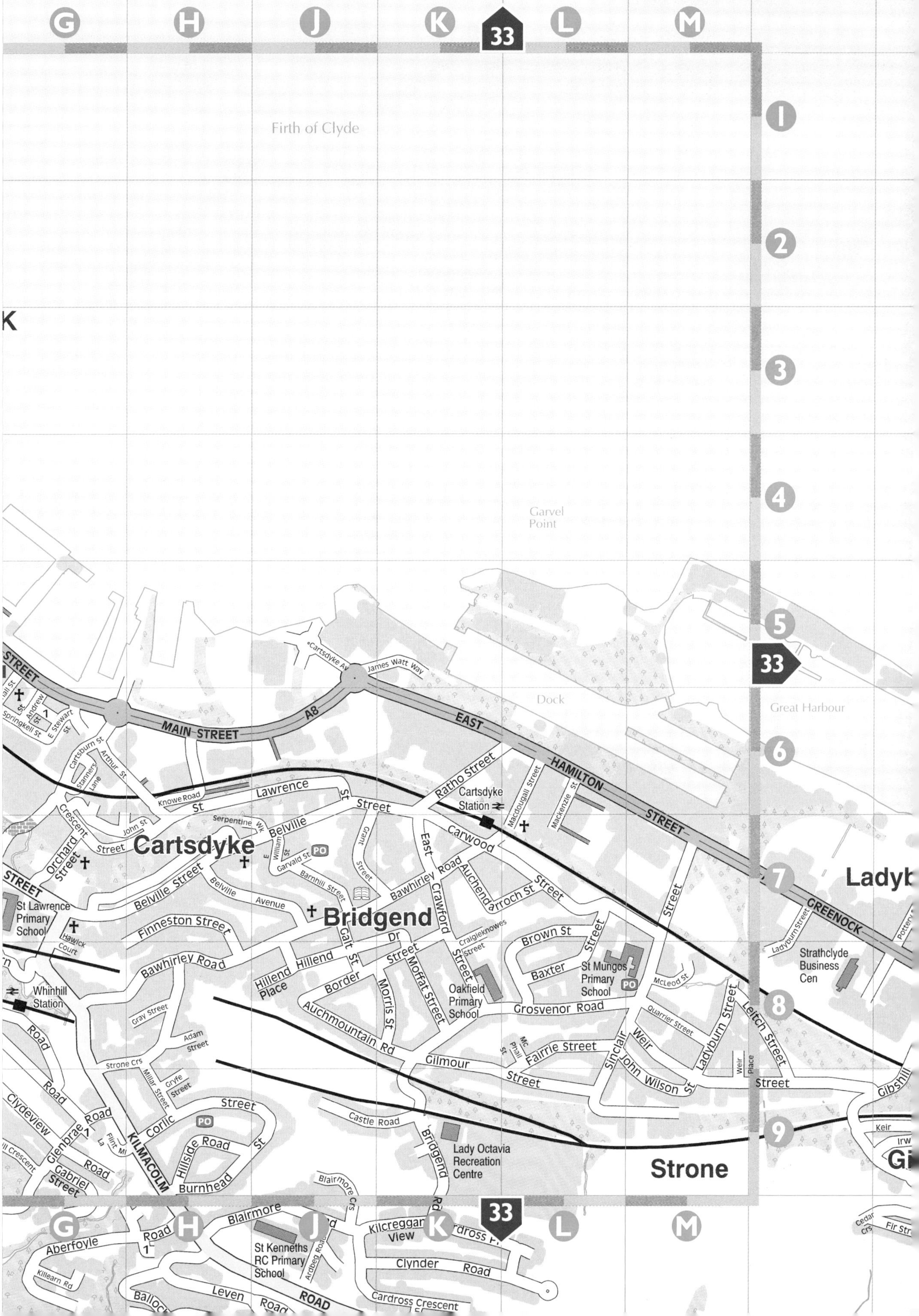
G
H
J
K
L
M
33
1
2
3
4
5
6
7
8
9
Firth of Clyde
Garvel Point
Dock
Great Harbour
Cartsdyke Av
James Watt Way
MAIN STREET
A8
EAST
HAMILTON
STREET
GREENOCK
Springkell St
Andrew St
E Stewart St
Cartsburn St
Arthur St
Stanners Lane
Knowe Road
Lawrence St
Street
Ratho Street
Cartsdyke Station
Macdougall Street
Mackenzie St
Crescent
John St
Serpentine Wlk
Belville
Orchard Street
Street
Cartsdyke
E William St
Garvald St
PO
Grant Street
East Crawford
Carwood Street
Barnhill Street
Bawhirley Road
Auchendarroch St
St Lawrence Primary School
Belville Street
Belville Avenue
Bridgend
Finneston Street
Hawick Court
Bawhirley Road
Hillend Place
Hillend Dr
Galt St
Street
Moffat Street
Craigieknowes Street
Street
Brown St
Street
Baxter
St Mungos Primary School
McLeod St
Ladyburn Street
Strathclyde Business Cen
Whinhill Station
Road
Gray Street
Adam Street
Border
Morris St
Auchmountain Rd
Oakfield Primary School
Grosvenor Road
Quarrier Street
Leitch Street
Weir Place
Weir
Sinclair
John Wilson St
Fairrie Street
Mc Phail St
Gilmour Street
Street
Gibshill
Strone Crs
Millar Street
Gryfe Street
Road
Clydeview
Glenbrae Road
Flint Mi
La
Corlic
Street
Hillside Road
St
KILMACOLM
Burnhead
Castle Road
Bridgend Rd
Lady Octavia Recreation Centre
Strone
Keir
Irw
Gi
Blairmore Crs
Ill Crescent
Gabriel Street
Road
Aberfoyle
Road
Blairmore
St Kenneths RC Primary School
Ardbeg Road
Kilcreggan View
Ardross Pl
Clynder Road
Killearn Rd
Balloch
Leven Road
ROAD
Cardross Crescent
Cedar Crs
Fir St
Ladyb
K

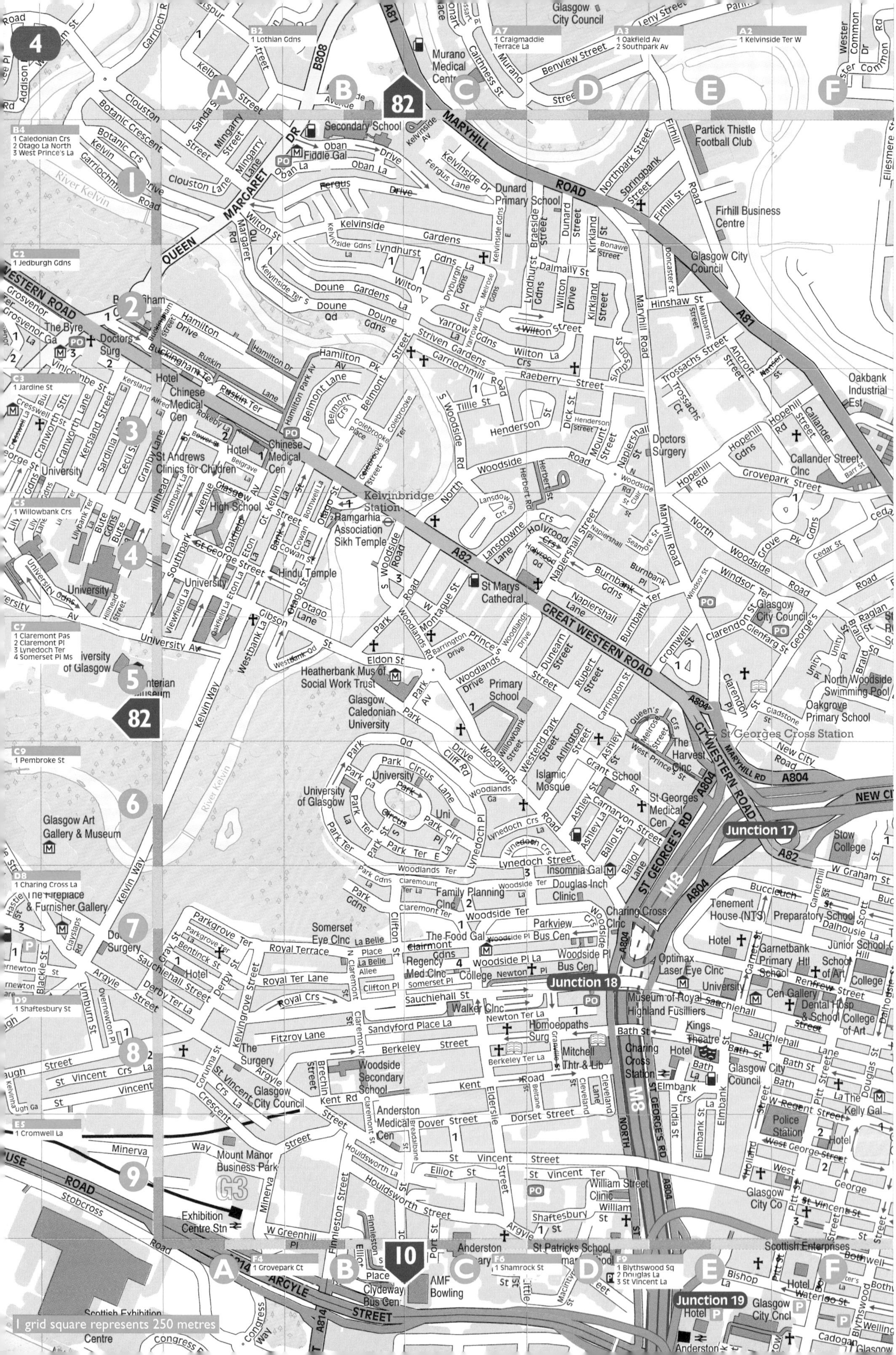
4
B2 1 Lothian Gdns
A7 1 Craigmaddie Terrace La
A3 1 Oakfield Av 2 Southpark Av
A2 1 Kelvinside Ter W
B4 1 Caledonian Crs 2 Otago La North 3 West Prince's La
C2 1 Jedburgh Gdns
C3 1 Jardine St
C5 1 Willowbank Crs
C7 1 Claremont Pas 2 Claremont Pl 3 Lynedoch Ter 4 Somerset Pl Ms
C9 1 Pembroke St
D8 1 Charing Cross La
D9 1 Shaftesbury St
E5 1 Cromwell La
F4 1 Grovepark Ct
F6 1 Shamrock St
F9 1 Blythswood Sq 2 Douglas La 3 St Vincent La
82
10
Junction 17
Junction 18
Junction 19
Glasgow City Council
Murano Medical Centre
Partick Thistle Football Club
Firhill Business Centre
Dunard Primary School
Secondary School
Oban Drive
Fiddle Gal
MARYHILL ROAD
GREAT WESTERN ROAD
QUEEN MARGARET DR
Kelvinbridge Station
Ramgarhia Association Sikh Temple
Hindu Temple
St Marys Cathedral
Heatherbank Mus of Social Work Trust
Glasgow Caledonian University
University of Glasgow
Hunterian Museum
Glasgow Art Gallery & Museum
St Georges Cross Station
North Woodside Swimming Pool
Oakgrove Primary School
Oakbank Industrial Est
Callander Street Clnc
Doctors Surgery
Islamic Mosque
St Georges Medical Cen
Insomnia Gal
Douglas Inch Clinic
Charing Cross Clnc
Family Planning Clnc
The Food Gal
Parkview Bus Cen
Woodside Pl Bus Cen
Somerset Eye Clnc
Regency Med Clnc
Walker Clnc
Homoeopaths Surg
Mitchell Thtr & Lib
Charing Cross Station
Museum of Royal Highland Fusiliers
Kings Theatre
Tenement House (NTS)
Preparatory School
Garnetbank Primary School
School of Art
Optimax Laser Eye Clnc
Woodside Secondary School
Anderston Medical Cen
Mount Manor Business Park
Exhibition Centre Stn
William Street Clinic
St Patricks School
Scottish Enterprises
Clydeway Bus Cen
AMF Bowling
Police Station
The Kelly Gal
Stow College
Glasgow Cncl
Anderston
ARGYLE STREET
M8
A804
A82
A81
A814
B808
River Kelvin
1 grid square represents 250 metres

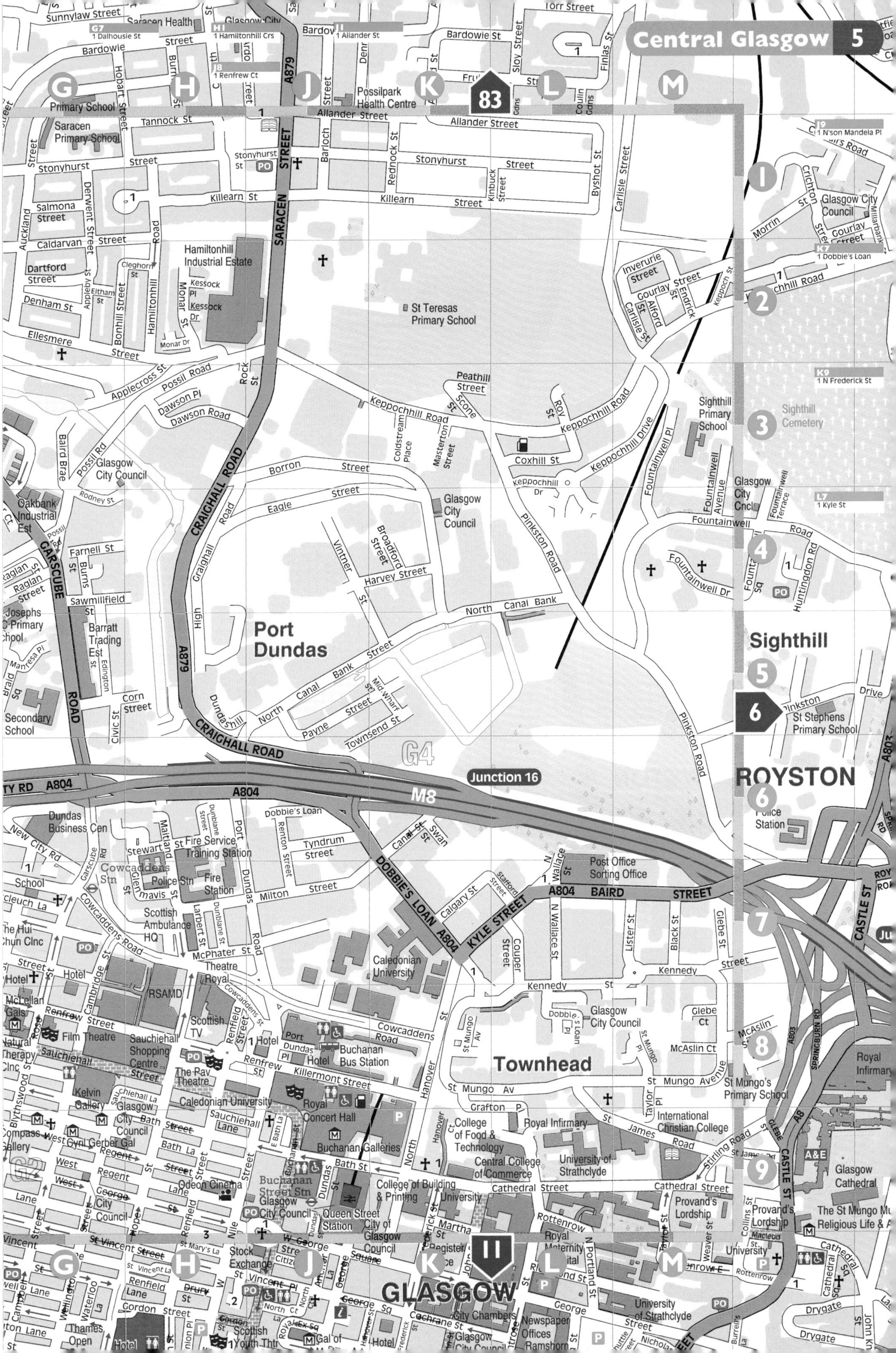
Sunnylaw Street
Saracen Head
Bardowie
Hobart Street
Primary School
Saracen Primary School
Tannock St
Stonyhurst Street
Salmona Street
Caldarvan Street
Dartford Street
Denham St
Ellesmere Street
Applecross St
Possil Road
Dawson Pl
Dawson Road
Hamiltonhill Industrial Estate
Kessock Pl
Kessock Dr
Monar Dr
Rock St
SARACEN STREET
A879
Possilpark Health Centre
Allander Street
Barloch Street
Rednock St
Killearn St
Killearn Street
Kinbuck Street
Byshot St
Carlisle Street
St Teresas Primary School
Inverurie Street
Gourlay St
Endrick St
Keppoch St
Keppochhill Road
Peathill Street
Scone St
Roy St
Keppochhill Drive
Coxhill St
Fountainwell Pl
Fountainwell Avenue
Fountainwell Road
Fountainwell Terrace
Fountainwell Dr
Huntingdon Rd
Sighthill Primary School
Sighthill Cemetery
Sighthill
Glasgow City Council
Morrin St
Crichton St
Gourlay Street
Pinkston Road
Pinkston Drive
St Stephens Primary School
ROYSTON
Police Station
Baird Brae
Possil Rd
Rodney St
Oakbank Industrial Est
GARSCUBE ROAD
Farnell St
Burns St
Sawmillfield St
Barratt Trading Est
Edington St
Corn Street
Civic St
Secondary School
CRAIGHALL ROAD
Craighall Road
High St
Borron Street
Eagle Street
Vintner St
Broadford Street
Harvey Street
Coldstream Place
Masterton Street
North Canal Bank
North Canal Bank Street
Port Dundas
Dundashill
Payne Street
Townsend St
Mid Wharf St
G4
Junction 16
A804
M8
Dundas Business Cen
New City Rd
Maitland St
Dunblane Street
Port Dundas Road
Renton Street
Dobbie's Loan
Tyndrum Street
Canal St
Swan St
Fire Service Training Station
Cowcaddens Stn
Police Stn
Fire Station
Milton Street
Scottish Ambulance HQ
McPhater St
Theatre Royal
RSAMD
Cowcaddens Road
DOBBIE'S LOAN
KYLE STREET
A804 BAIRD STREET
Post Office Sorting Office
Calgary St
Stafford Street
N Wallace St
Couper Street
Lister St
Black St
Glebe St
Kennedy Street
Kennedy St
Caledonian University
Glasgow City Council
Glebe Ct
McAslin Ct
St Mungo Av
St Mungo Avenue
St Mungo Pl
Townhead
Grafton Pl
Royal Infirmary
International Christian College
St Mungo's Primary School
SPRINGBURN RD
Royal Infirmary
CASTLE ST
A8
A803
A&E
Glasgow Cathedral
Cathedral Street
James St
Stirling Road
Taylor Pl
College of Food & Technology
Central College of Commerce
University of Strathclyde
College of Building & Printing
Provand's Lordship
Collins St
Macleod St
The St Mungo Museum of Religious Life & Art
Hanover St
North Hanover St
Cowcaddens Road
Port Dundas Pl
Hotel
Buchanan Bus Station
Killermont Street
Royal Concert Hall
Buchanan Galleries
Bath St
Buchanan Street Stn
Queen Street Station
Glasgow City Council
City of Glasgow Council
George Square
Martha St
Rottenrow
Royal Maternity Hospital
N Portland St
University
GLASGOW
City Chambers
Newspaper Offices
University of Strathclyde
Drygate
Cathedral Sq
Renfrew Street
Film Theatre
Sauchiehall Street
Sauchiehall Shopping Centre
The Pavilion Theatre
Scottish TV
Kelvin Gallery
Glasgow City Council
Caledonian University
Compass Gallery
Cyril Gerber Gal
Regent Street
West George St
Odeon Cinema
St Vincent Street
Vincent Street
Renfield Lane
Stock Exchange
Drury St
Gordon Street
Scottish Youth Thtr
Cambridge St
Renfield Street
Wellington St
Waterloo St
Hope St
Hotel
G2

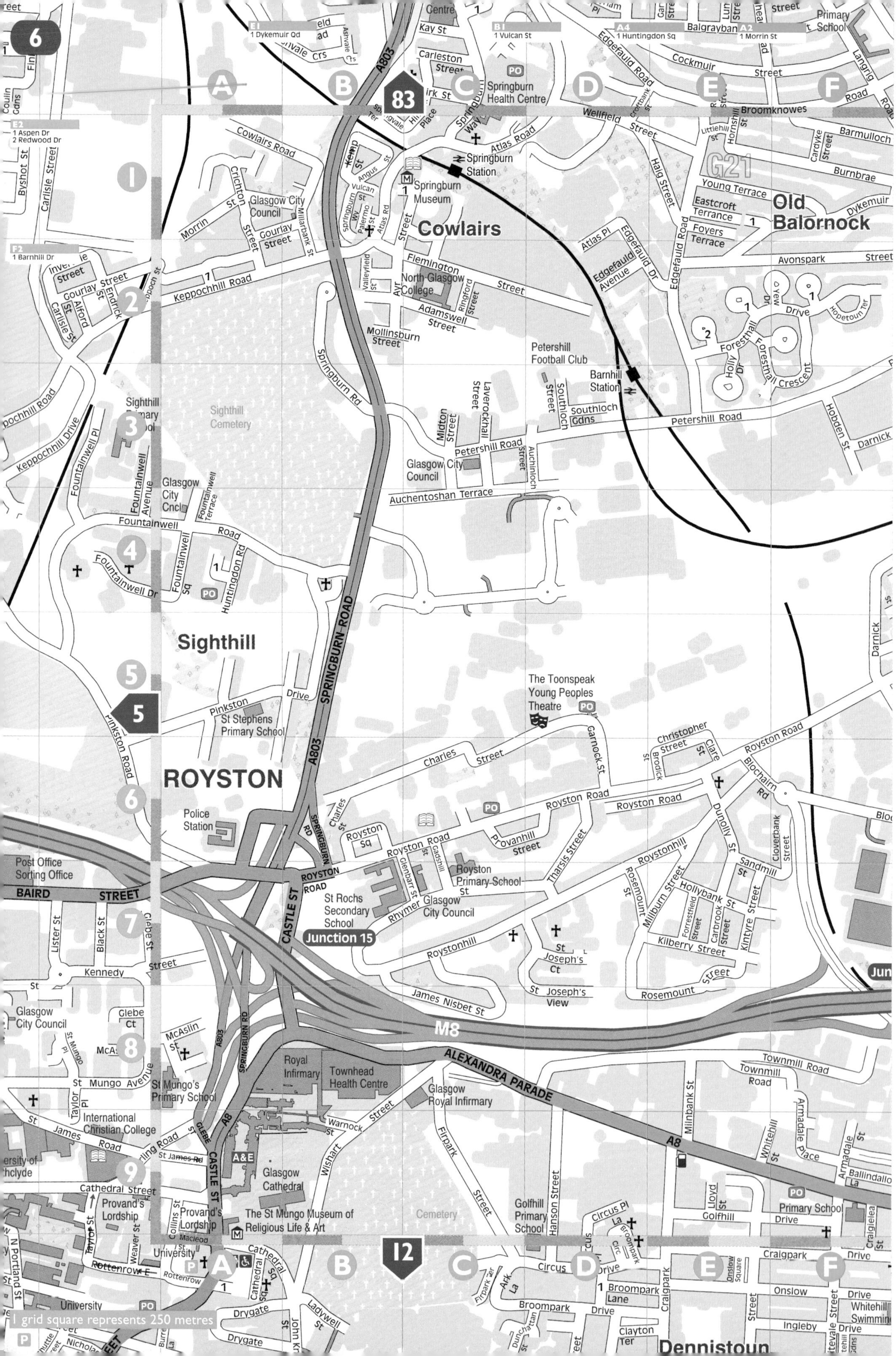
83
Cowlairs
Old Balornock
Springburn Station
Springburn Museum
Springburn Health Centre
North Glasgow College
Petershill Football Club
Barnhill Station
Sighthill Cemetery
Sighthill Primary School
Sighthill
ROYSTON
St Stephens Primary School
The Toonspeak Young Peoples Theatre
Police Station
Post Office Sorting Office
St Rochs Secondary School
Royston Primary School
Junction 15
M8
Royal Infirmary
Townhead Health Centre
Glasgow Royal Infirmary
St Mungo's Primary School
International Christian College
Glasgow Cathedral
The St Mungo Museum of Religious Life & Art
Provand's Lordship
Golfhill Primary School
Primary School
Dennistoun
G21
A803
A8
Springburn Road
Royston Road
Petershill Road
Keppochhill Road
Alexandra Parade
Baird Street
Castle St
Cathedral Street
Wellfield Street
Broomknowes
Edgefauld Road
Fountainwell Road
Pinkston Road
Charles Street
Kennedy Street
St James Road
12
5
1 grid square represents 250 metres

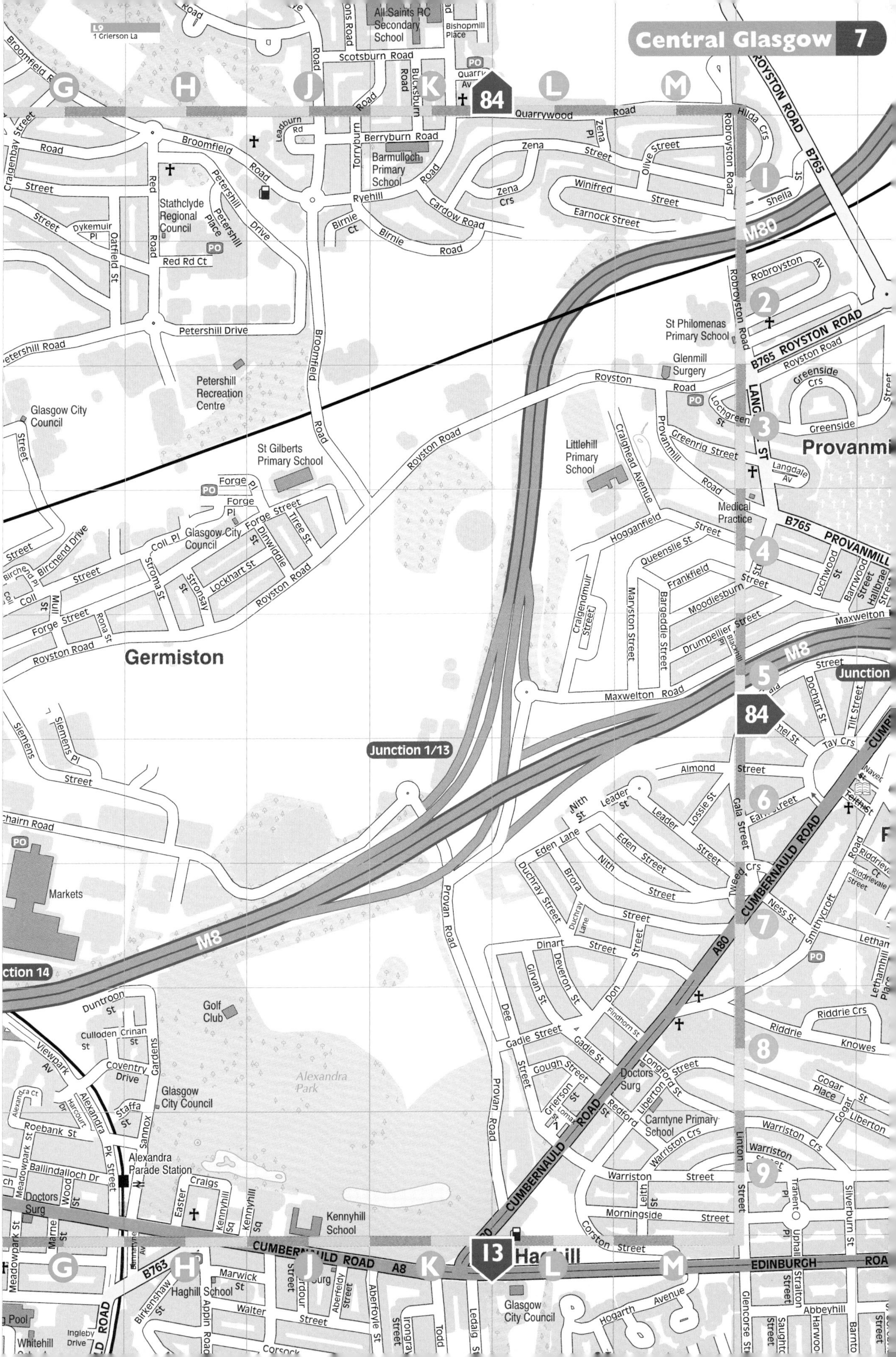

1 Grierson La
Broomfield Road
All Saints RC Secondary School
Bishopmill Place
Scotsburn Road
Quarry Av
Quarrywood Road
Berryburn Road
Barmulloch Primary School
Leadburn Rd
Torryburn Road
Bucksburn Road
Craigenbay Street
Broomfield Road
Red Road
Petershill Drive
Petershill Place
Stathclyde Regional Council
Dykemuir Pl
Oatfield St
Red Rd Ct
Petershill Drive
Petershill Road
Ryehill Road
Birnie Ct
Birnie Road
Cardow Road
Zena Street
Zena Pl
Zena Crs
Olive Street
Winifred Street
Earnock Street
Hilda Crs
Robroyston Road
ROYSTON ROAD
B765
Sheila St
M80
Robroyston Av
St Philomenas Primary School
B765 ROYSTON ROAD
Royston Road
Greenside Crs
Greenside Street
Glenmill Surgery
Royston Road
Petershill Recreation Centre
Glasgow City Council
St Gilberts Primary School
Forge Pl
Forge Street
Glasgow City Council
Coll Pl
Birchend Drive
Tiree St
Dinwiddie St
Lockhart St
Stronsay St
Stroma St
Mull St
Rona St
Forge Street
Royston Road
Germiston
Lochgreen St
Langdale St
Greenrig Street
Provanmill Road
Provanmill
Langdale Av
Littlehill Primary School
Craighead Avenue
Medical Practice
B765 PROVANMILL
Hogganfield Street
Queenslie St
Frankfield Street
Moodiesburn Street
Drumpellier Street
Blackhill Pl
Craigendmuir Street
Maryston Street
Bargeddie Street
Lochwood St
Barrwood Street
Hallbrae Street
Maxwelton Road
M8
Junction
Dochart St
Tilt Street
Tay Crs
Siemens Pl
Siemens Street
Junction 1/13
Almond Street
Leader St
Nith St
Lossie St
Earn Street
Gala Street
CUMBERNAULD ROAD
Eden Lane
Eden Street
Nith Street
Brora Street
Duchray Street
Duchray Lane
Tweed Crs
Ness St
Smithycroft
Riddrievale Street
Riddrie Knowes
Markets
M8
Junction 14
Provan Road
Dinart Street
Deveron St
Girvan St
Don St
Findhorn St
Dee St
Gadie Street
Gadie St
A80
Letham
Riddrie Crs
Riddrie Knowes
Duntroon St
Golf Club
Culloden St
Crinan St
Viewpark Av
Coventry Drive
Gardens
Alexandra Park
Glasgow City Council
Staffa St
Harcourt Dr
Alexandra Pk Street
Roebank St
Meadowpark St
Ballindalloch Dr
Wood St
Doctors Surg
Sannox
Alexandra Parade Station
Craigs
Easter
Kennyhill Sq
Kennyhill School
Gough Street
Grierson St
Lomax St
Longford Street
Doctors Surg
Liberton St
Redford St
Carntyne Primary School
Warriston Crs
Warriston Street
Linton Street
Gogar Place
Gogar St
Liberton Street
Tranent Pl
Leith St
Morningside Street
Corston Street
Silverburn St
Uphall Pl
Marne St
Meadowpark St
Haghill
CUMBERNAULD ROAD
A8
EDINBURGH ROAD
B763
Birkenshaw St
Haghill School
Marwick St
Walter Street
Aberfeldy Street
Aberfoyle St
Irongray Street
Todd
Ledaig St
Glasgow City Council
Hogarth Avenue
Glencorse St
Straiton Street
Abbeyhill Street
Saughton Street
Whitehill
Ingleby Drive
Appin Road
Corsock

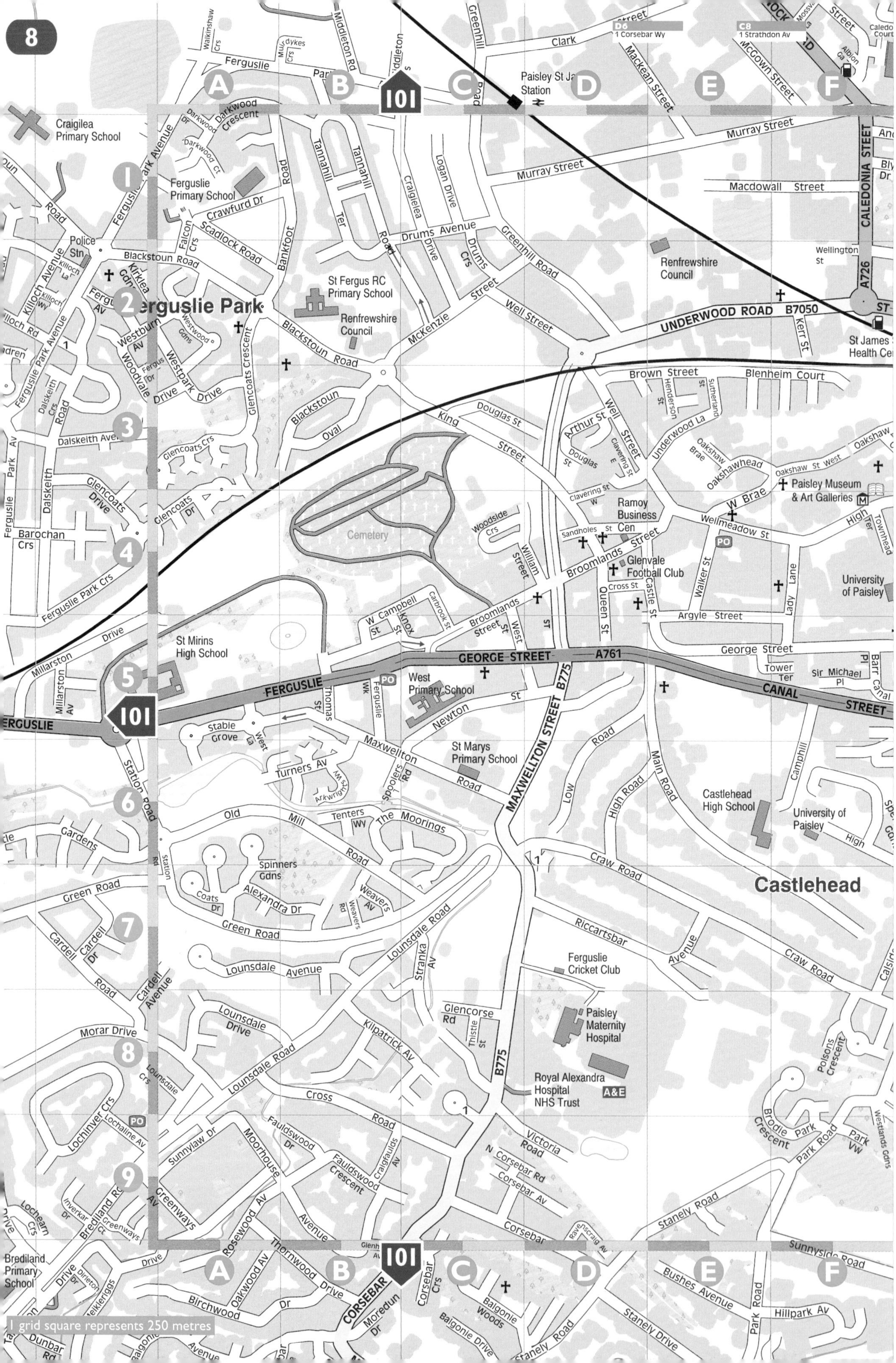
D6
1 Corsebar Wy
C8
1 Strathdon Av
Walkinshaw Crs
Muirdykes Crs
Middleton Rd
Middleton
Greenhill Road
Clark Street
Mackean Street
McCown Street
Albion Ga
Caledonia Court
Ferguslie Park
Paisley St James Station
A
B
C
D
E
F
101
Craigilea Primary School
Darkwood Dr
Darkwood Crescent
Darkwood Ct
Tannahill Ter
Tannahill
Craigielea Road
Logan Drive
Murray Street
Macdowall Street
CALEDONIA STREET
A726
Andrew
Blythswood Dr
Ferguslie Park Avenue
Ferguslie Primary School
Crawfurd Dr
Bankfoot Road
Falcon Crs
Scadlock Road
Drums Avenue
Drums Crs
Greenhill Road
Renfrewshire Council
Wellington St
Police Stn
Killoch Avenue
Killoch La
Killoch Wy
Blackstoun Road
Kirklea Gdns
Ferguslie Park
Ferguslie Av
St Fergus RC Primary School
Renfrewshire Council
McKenzie Street
Well Street
UNDERWOOD ROAD B7050
Kerr St
St James Health Centre
Killoch Rd
Westburn Av
Westwood Gdns
Fergus Dr
Woodvale
Westpark Drive
Drive
Glencoats Crescent
Blackstoun Road
Blackstoun Oval
Brown Street
Henderson St
Sutherland St
Blenheim Court
Dalkeith Crs
Dalkeith Road
Dalkeith Avenue
Glencoats Crs
King Street
Douglas St
Arthur St
Well Street
Underwood La
Oakshaw Brae
Oakshawhead
Oakshaw St West
Oakshaw St
Douglas St
Clavering St E
Clavering St W
Paisley Museum & Art Galleries
Ferguslie Park Av
Dalkeith
Glencoats Drive
Glencoats Dr
Ramoy Business Cen
W Brae
Wellmeadow St
High St
Townhead Ter
Barochan Crs
Cemetery
Woodside Crs
Sandholes St
Broomlands Street
Glenvale Football Club
Walker St
Lady Lane
University of Paisley
William Street
Cross St
Castle St
Queen St
Argyle Street
Ferguslie Park Crs
W Campbell St
Knox St
Carbrook St
Broomlands Street
West St
Millarston Drive
St Mirins High School
George Street
GEORGE STREET A761
Tower Ter
Sir Michael Pl
Barr Pl
Canal
CANAL STREET
Millarston Av
FERGUSLIE
Thomas St
Ferguslie Wk
PO
West Primary School
Newton St
MAXWELLTON STREET B775
Stable Grove
West La
Maxwellton Road
Turners Av
Arkwright St
Spoolers Rd
St Marys Primary School
Low Road
High Road
Main Road
Campbell
Castlehead High School
University of Paisley
High
Station Road
Old Mill Road
Tenters Wy
The Moorings
Gardens
Station Rd
Spinners Gdns
Coats Dr
Alexandra Dr
Weavers Av
Weavers Rd
Craw Road
Castlehead
Green Road
Green Road
Cardell Dr
Cardell Road
Riccartsbar Avenue
Craw Road
Calside
Lounsdale Avenue
Lounsdale Road
Stranka Av
Ferguslie Cricket Club
Cardell Avenue
Glencorse Rd
Thistle St
Lounsdale Drive
Kilpatrick Av
Paisley Maternity Hospital
Morar Drive
Lounsdale Crs
Lounsdale Road
B775
Polsons Crescent
Royal Alexandra Hospital NHS Trust
A&E
Cross Road
Lochinver Crs
Lochaline Av
Sunnylaw Dr
Moorhouse Av
Fauldswood Dr
Fauldswood Crescent
Craigfaulds Av
Victoria Road
N Corsebar Rd
Corsebar Av
Brodie Park Crescent
Park Road
Park Vw
Westlands Gdns
Brediland Rd
Inverkar Dr
Greenways Ct
Greenways Av
Rosewood Av
Avenue
Corsebar
Ravenscraig Dr
Stanely Road
Sunnyside Road
Lochearn Crs
Brediland Primary School
Drive
Dirleton Dr
Meikleriggs
Oakwood Av
Thornwood Drive
Glenburn Av
CORSEBAR
Moredun Dr
Corsebar Crs
Balgonie Woods
Balgonie Drive
Bushes Avenue
Park Road
Hillpark Av
Stanely Drive
Stanely Road
Birchwood Dr
Dunbar Rd
1 grid square represents 250 metres

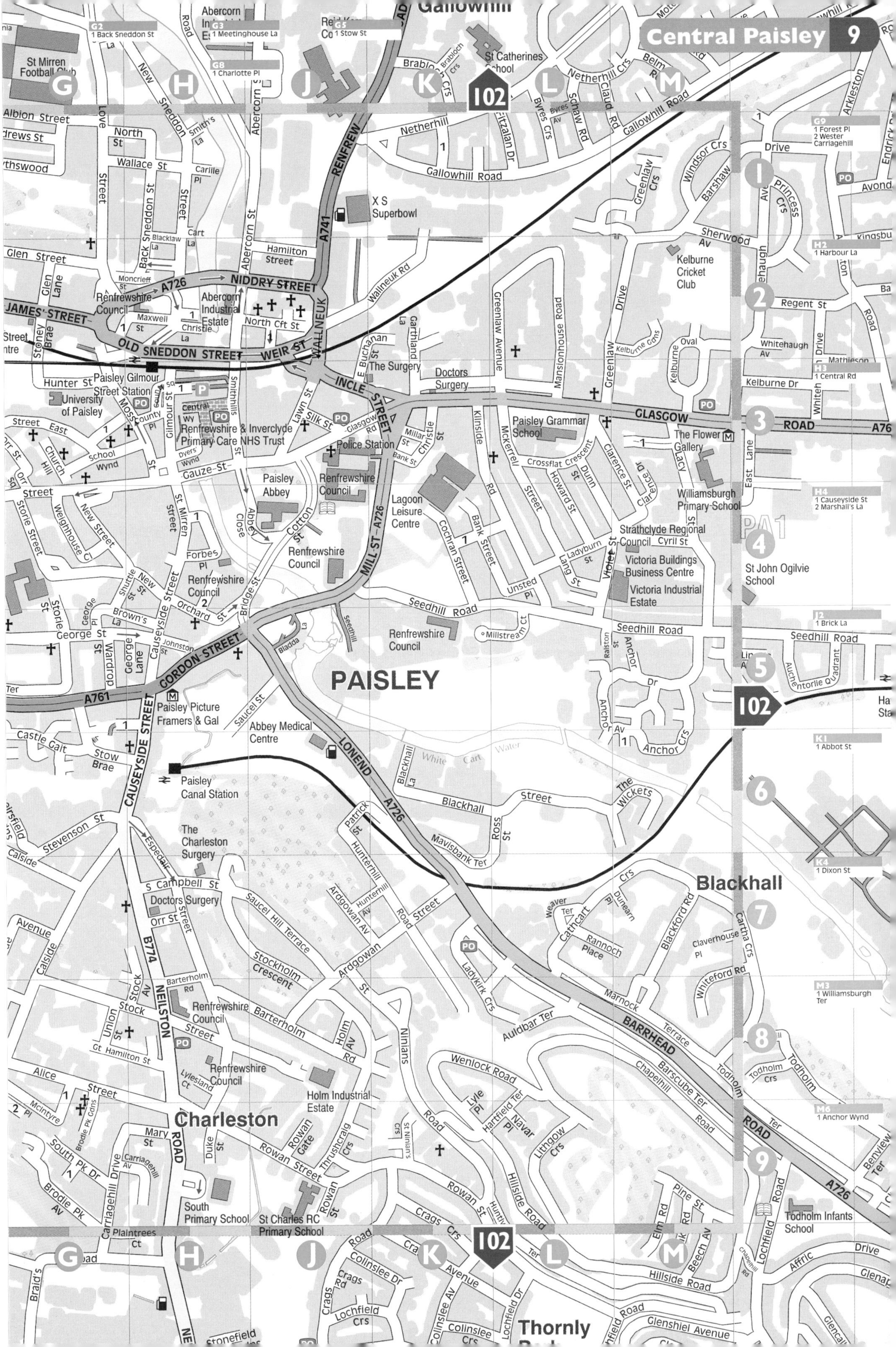
Gallowhill
G2 1 Back Sneddon St
G3 1 Meetinghouse La
G5 1 Stow St
G8 1 Charlotte Pl
G9 1 Forest Pl 2 Wester Carriagehill
H2 1 Harbour La
H3 1 Central Rd
H4 1 Causeyside St 2 Marshall's La
J2 1 Brick La
K1 1 Abbot St
K4 1 Dixon St
M3 1 Williamsburgh Ter
M6 1 Anchor Wynd
St Mirren Football Club
St Catherines School
Abercorn Industrial Estate
Albion Street
North St
Wallace St
Love Street
New Sneddon Street
Smith's La
Carille Pl
Blacklaw La
Cart La
Abercorn St
Glen Street
Glen Lane
Hamilton Street
Moncrieff St
Renfrewshire Council
NIDDRY STREET
JAMES' STREET
OLD SNEDDON STREET
WEIR ST
WALLNEUK
Maxwell St
Christie La
North Cft St
Stoney Brae
RENFREW
A741
A726
X S Superbowl
Netherhill
Gallowhill Road
Fitzalan Dr
Byres Crs
Byres Av
Schaw Rd
Claud Rd
Netherhill Crs
Gallowhill Road
Windsor Crs
Greenlaw Crs
Barshaw
Sherwood Av
Kelburne Cricket Club
Drive
Princess Crs
Avondale
Kingsburgh
Regent St
Whitehaugh Av
Mathieson
Kelburne Dr
Kelburne Oval
Kelburne Gdns
Greenlaw Drive
Greenlaw Avenue
Mansionhouse Road
Wallneuk Rd
Garthland La
E Buchanan St
The Surgery
Doctors Surgery
INCLE STREET
GLASGOW ROAD
A761
Paisley Gilmour Street Station
Hunter St
University of Paisley
Gilmour St
Central Wy
Smithhills St
Renfrewshire & Inverclyde Primary Care NHS Trust
Lawn St
Silk St
Glasgow Rd
Police Station
Millarston St
Christie St
Bank St
Kilnside Rd
Mckerrell Street
Paisley Grammar School
Crossflat Crescent
Howard St
Dunn St
Clarence St
Clarence Dr
The Flower Gallery
Lacy St
Williamsburgh Primary School
East Lane
PA1
St John Ogilvie School
School Wynd
Church Hill
Orr St
Dyers' Wynd
Gauze St
Paisley Abbey
Renfrewshire Council
Lagoon Leisure Centre
Cochran Street
Bank Street
Strathclyde Regional Council
Cyril St
Victoria Buildings Business Centre
Victoria Industrial Estate
Ladyburn St
Lang St
Unsted Pl
Violet St
Storie Street
Weighhouse Cl
New Street
St Mirren Street
Forbes Pl
Abbey Close
Cotton St
MILL ST A726
Seedhill Road
Seedhill
Millstream Ct
Ralston St
Anchor Dr
Anchor Av
Anchor Crs
Auchentorlie Quadrant
Shuttle St
New St
Causeyside Street
Orchard St
Bridge St
George St
Brown's La
Johnston St
George Lane
Wardrop St
GORDON STREET
Bladda La
PAISLEY
Paisley Picture Framers & Gal
Saucel St
Abbey Medical Centre
LONEND A726
White Cart Water
Blackhall La
Blackhall Street
The Wickets
Castle Gait
Stow Brae
CAUSEYSIDE STREET
Paisley Canal Station
Stevenson St
Calside
The Charleston Surgery
Espedair St
Patrick St
Hunterhill Rd
Ross St
Mavisbank Ter
Blackhall
S Campbell St
Doctors Surgery
Orr St
Saucel Hill Terrace
Hunterhill Av
Ardgowan Av
Road Street
Weaver Ter
Cathcart Crs
Dunearn Pl
Blackford Rd
Cartha Crs
Claverhouse Pl
Rannoch Place
Whiteford Rd
Avenue
Stockholm Crescent
Ardgowan St
Ladykirk Crs
Marnock Terrace
B774
NEILSTON
Stock Av
Barterholm Rd
Renfrewshire Council
Barterholm
Holm Av
Holm Rd
Ninians
Auldbar Ter
BARRHEAD
Union St
Stock Street
Gt Hamilton St
Lylesland Ct
Wenlock Road
Barscube Ter
Chapelhill Road
Todholm
Todholm Crs
Alice Street
Mcintyre Pl
Brodie Pk Gdns
Charleston
Holm Industrial Estate
Lyle Pl
Hartfield Ter
Navar Pl
Lithgow Crs
ROAD
Benview Ter
Mary St
South Pk Dr
Carriagehill Drive
Carriagehill Av
Duke St
Rowan Gate
Rowan Street
Thrushcraig Crs
St Ninians Crs
Road
Hillside Road
Pine St
Brodie Pk Av
South Primary School
St Charles RC Primary School
Rowan St
Elm Rd
Beech Av
Lochfield Road
Todholm Infants School
A726
Plaintrees Ct
Crags Crs
Crags Avenue
Colinslee Dr
Crags Rd
Lochfield Crs
Colinslee Av
Colinslee Crs
Lochfield Dr
Thornly Park
Hillside Road
Glenshiel Avenue
Affric Drive
Glenapp
Braid's
Stonefield
102

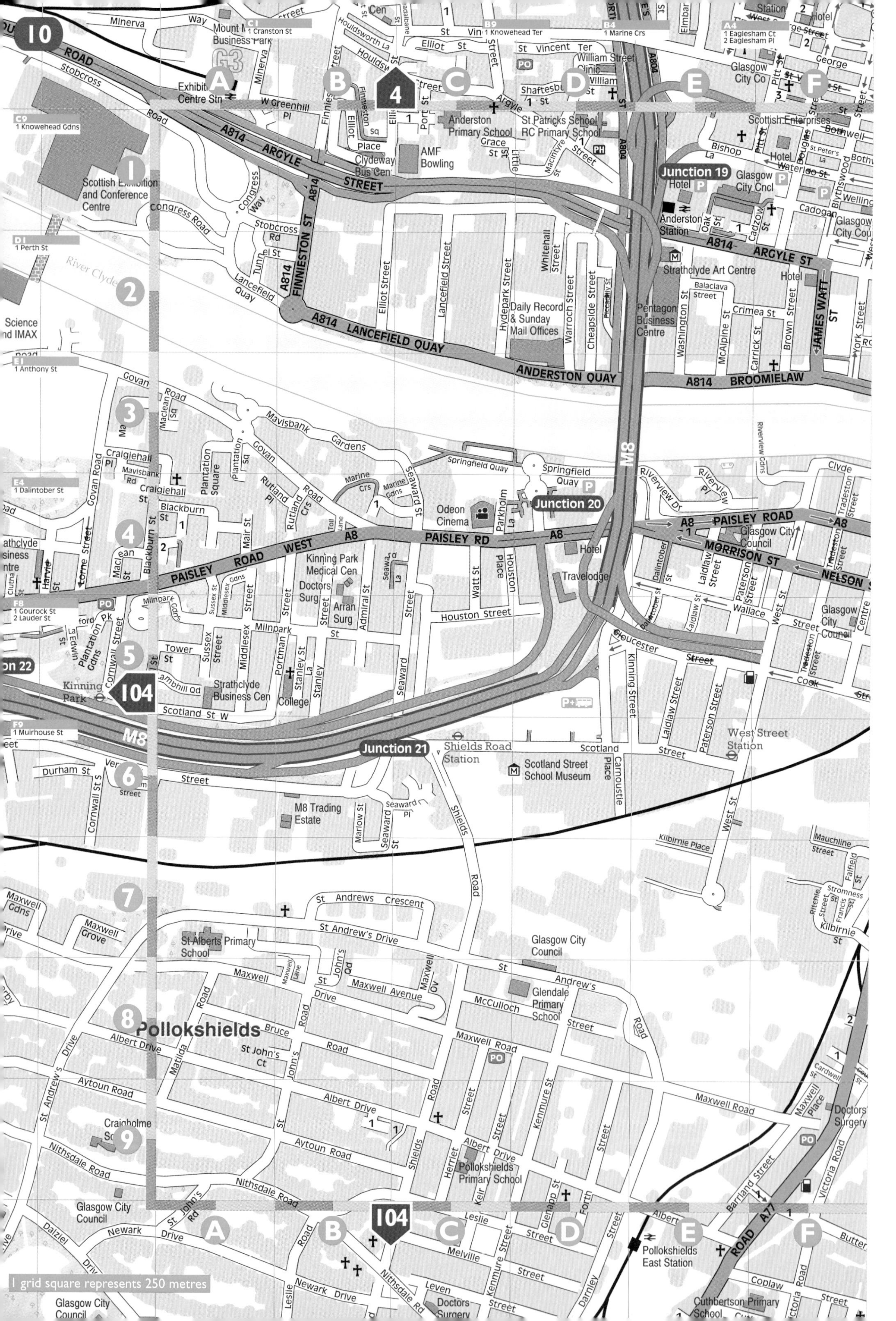

A
B
C
D
E
F
1
2
3
4
5
6
7
8
9
4
104
104
C1 1 Cranston St
B9 1 Knowehead Ter
B4 1 Marine Crs
A4 1 Eaglesham Ct 2 Eaglesham Pl
C9 1 Knowehead Gdns
D1 1 Perth St
E1 1 Anthony St
E4 1 Dalintober St
F8 1 Gourock St 2 Lauder St
F9 1 Muirhouse St
Minerva
Way
Mount Vernon Business Park
Houldsworth La
Elliot St
St Vincent Ter
William Street
Glasgow City Co
George
ROAD
Stobcross
Exhibition Centre Stn
W Greenhill Pl
Finnieston
Anderston Primary School
St Patricks School RC Primary School
Shaftesbury St
Argyle
A814 ARGYLE STREET
Scottish Enterprises
Bothwell
Grace St
Clydeway Place
AMF Bowling
Bus Cen
Bishop La
Hotel
Waterloo St
Junction 19
Glasgow City Cncl
Scottish Exhibition and Conference Centre
Congress Road
Congress Way
Stobcross Rd
Tunnel St
Lancefield Quay
A814 FINNIESTON ST
Anderston Station
Cadogan
Wellington
Glasgow City Council
A814 ARGYLE ST
Strathclyde Art Centre
River Clyde
Elliot Street
Lancefield Street
Hydepark Street
Whitehall Street
Warroch Street
Cheapside Street
Daily Record & Sunday Mail Offices
Pentagon Business Centre
Washington St
Balaclava Street
Crimea St
McAlpine St
Carrick St
Brown Street
JAMES WATT ST
York Street
Science and IMAX
A814 LANCEFIELD QUAY
ANDERSTON QUAY
A814 BROOMIELAW
Govan Road
Maclean Sq
Mavisbank Gardens
Springfield Quay
Springfield Quay
Riverview Gdns
Riverview Dr
Riverview Pl
Clyde
Craigiehall Pl
Mavisbank Rd
Craigiehall St
Plantation Square
Plantation Sq
Govan Road
Rutland Pl
Rutland Crs
Marine Crs
Marine Gdns
Seaward St
Parkholm La
Junction 20
Odeon Cinema
Blackburn St
Mair St
Toll Lane
PAISLEY ROAD WEST A8
PAISLEY RD A8
A8 PAISLEY ROAD A8
Glasgow City Council
MORRISON ST
NELSON ST
Tradeston Street
Harvie St
Lorne Street
Maclean St
Kinning Park Medical Cen
Doctors Surg
Arran Surg
Admiral St
Seaward La
Watt St
Houston Place
Hotel
Travelodge
Dalintober St
Laidlaw Street
Paterson Street
West St
Milnpark Gdns
Sussex St
Middlesex Gdns
Milnpark St
Houston Street
Wallace Street
Glasgow City Council
Centre
Plantation Pk Gdns
Cornwall Street
Tower St
Sussex Street
Middlesex Street
Portman Street
Stanley St
Stanley La
Seaward Street
Gloucester Street
Kinning Street
Laidlaw Street
Paterson Street
Cook Street
Junction 22
Kinning Park
Lambhill Qd
Strathclyde Business Cen
College
Scotland St W
M8
Junction 21
Shields Road Station
Scotland Street
West Street Station
Durham St
Cornwall St S
Street
Scotland Street School Museum
Camoustie Place
M8 Trading Estate
Marlow St
Seaward St
Seaward Pl
Shields Road
West St
Kilbirnie Place
Mauchline Street
Falfield St
Stromness St
Ritchie Street
Francis St
Kilbirnie St
Maxwell Gdns
Maxwell Grove
St Andrews Crescent
St Andrew's Drive
St Alberts Primary School
Glasgow City Council
Maxwell Lane
St John's Qd
Maxwell Avenue
Maxwell Ov
Maxwell Drive
St Andrew's Street
Glendale Primary School
McCulloch Street
Pollokshields
Bruce Road
Albert Drive
Matilda Road
St John's Ct
John's Road
Maxwell Road
St Andrew's Drive
Aytoun Road
Albert Drive
St John's St
Shields Road
Street
Street
Kenmure St
Maxwell Road
Cardwell St
Maxwell Place
Doctors' Surgery
Craigholme School
Nithsdale Road
Aytoun Road
Herriet Street
Albert Drive
Pollokshields Primary School
Keir St
Glenapp St
Forth Street
Victoria Road
Barrland Street
Glasgow City Council
Nithsdale Road
St John's Rd
Newark Drive
Leslie Street
Albert Road
ROAD A77
Butterbiggins
Dalziel Drive
Road
Melville Street
Kenmure Street
Pollokshields East Station
Leven Street
Doctors Surgery
Darnley Street
Coplaw Street
Cuthbertson Primary School
Newark Drive
Leslie
Nithsdale Rd
Glasgow City Council
1 grid square represents 250 metres

GLASGOW
Gorbals
Hutchesontown
Oatlands
Glasgow Green
River Clyde
Glasgow Central Station
High Street Station
Queen Street Station
Bridge Street Station
St Enoch Stn
City Chambers
Glasgow City Council
University of Strathclyde
Royal Infirmary
Glasgow Cathedral
Provand's Lordship
The St Mungo Museum of Religious Life & Art
Central College of Commerce
College of Building & Printing
Stock Exchange
Scottish Youth Thtr
Gal of Modern Art
Stirling's Lib
City Cncl
Argyle Indoor Market
Argyle Street Station
St Enoch Bus Cen
St Enoch Shopping Centre
Police Station
Midland Arches Theatre
Thames Open College
City Halls & Ticket Office
Newspaper Offices
Ramshorn Thtr
Hutcheson's Hall
Sharmanka Gal & Workshop
Transmission Gallery
Brenda Temple Art Exposure Gallery
Tron Thtr
Tron Steeple
Tolbooth Steeple
Mercat Cross
Rangers Football Club
Gallowgate Mkt
Barras Market
Fire Station
St Andrews Cathedral
Open Air Mkt Stall
High Court & Court of Justiciary
Sheriff Court
Central Mosque
St Johns RC Primary School
Florence Street Clinic
Gorbals Health Centre
Blackfriars Primary School
St Francis Primary School
St James Primary School
Butterbiggins Medical Centre
Richmond Park School
Cemetery
BROOMIELAW
CLYDE STREET
ARGYLE STREET
HIGH STREET
GALLOWGATE A89
LONDON ROAD
SALTMARKET A8
BRIDGEGATE A8
GORBALS STREET A8
CROWN STREET A8
BALLATER STREET A74
NORFOLK ST
KINGSTON ST
OXFORD ST
COMMERCE ST A77
BRIDGE ST
EGLINTON STREET A77
CATHCART ROAD A728
LAURIESTON ROAD A728
CALEDONIA ROAD A730
KING'S DRIVE
G5 1 Wallace St
G6 1 Kilbarchan St
G7 1 Abbotsford Pl
H1 1 Gordon La 2 National Bank La 3 West George La
H7 1 Caledonia Rd
J2 1 Springfield Ct
J6 1 Old Rutherglen Rd
J7 1 Cumberland St
K2 1 Brunswick La
K3 1 Melville Ct 2 New Wynd 3 Old Wynd
K4 1 Jocelyn Sq 2 Mart St 3 St Margaret's Pl
K8 1 Cumberland Pl 2 Oregon Pl
L3 1 Chisolm St 2 Parnie St 3 St Andrew's La
M3 1 Spoutmouth
L8 1 Old Rutherglen Rd
L4 1 James Morrison St
5
12
105

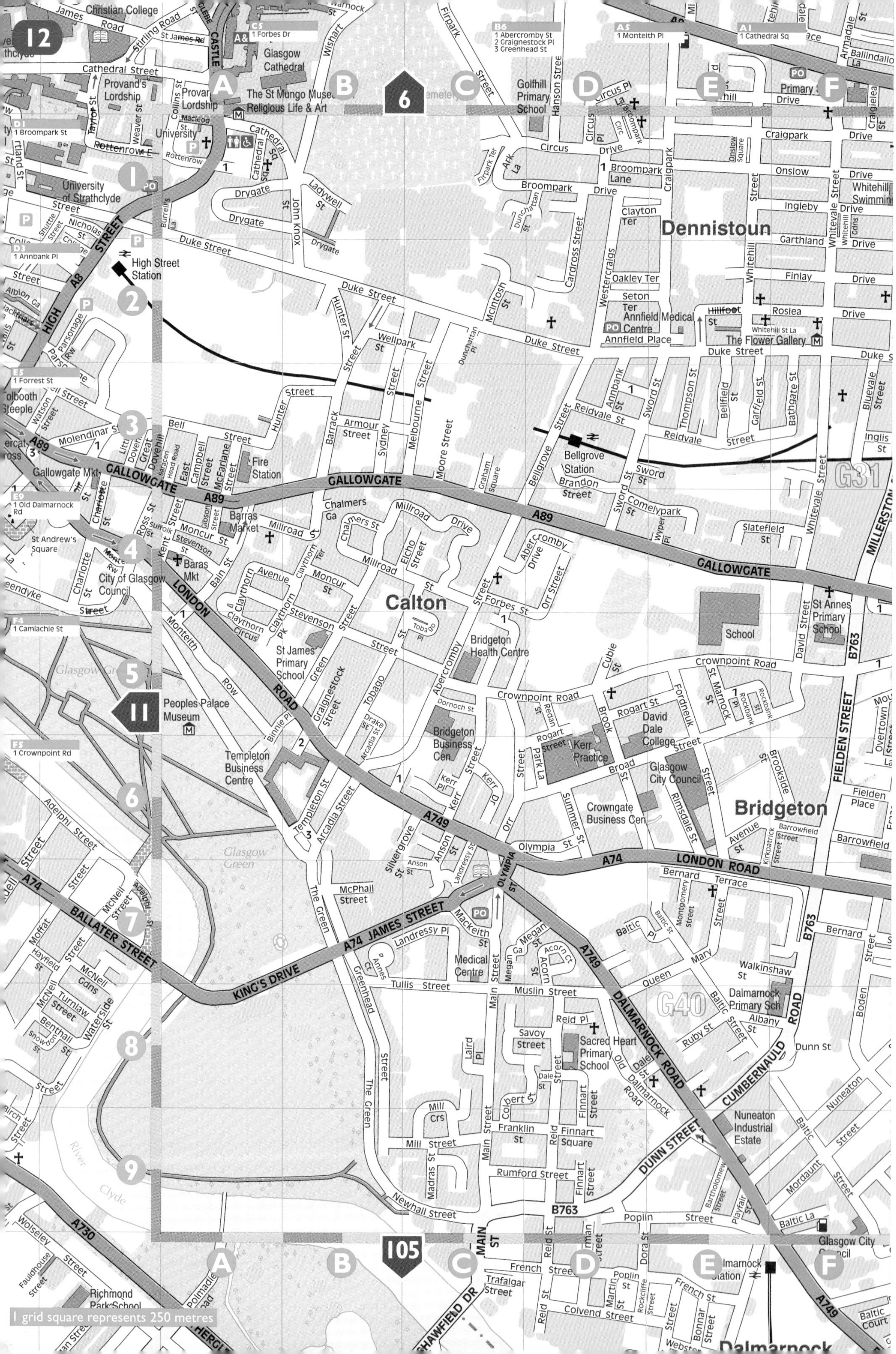

Christian College
James Road
Stirling Road
St James Rd
Cathedral Street
Provand's Lordship
Glasgow Cathedral
The St Mungo Museum
Religious Life & Art
University
Rottenrow
Rottenrow E
Cathedral Sq
Drygate
Ladywell St
John Knox St
University of Strathclyde
Nicholas St
Duke Street
High Street Station
HIGH STREET
A8
Parsonage Rw
1 Broompark St
1 Annbank Pl
1 Forrest St
1 Old Dalmarnock Rd
1 Camlachie St
1 Crownpoint Rd
1 Forbes Dr
1 Abercromby St
2 Craignestock Pl
3 Greenhead St
1 Monteith Pl
1 Cathedral Sq
Firpark Street
Golfhill Primary School
Hanson Street
Circus Pl
Circus Drive
Broompark Drive
Broompark Lane
Craigpark
Onslow Drive
Whitehill Swimming
Ingleby Drive
Garthland Drive
Finlay Drive
Roslea Drive
Dennistoun
Clayton Ter
Cardross Street
Oakley Ter
Seton Ter
Annfield Medical Centre
Annfield Place
Hillfoot St
Whitehill St La
The Flower Gallery
Duke Street
Bellgrove Station
Reidvale Street
Reidvale St
Annbank St
Sword St
Thompson St
Bellfield St
Garfield St
Bathgate St
Bluevale Street
Inglis St
Whitevale Street
G31
MILLERSTON
Wellpark St
Hunter Street
Hunter St
Barrack Street
Armour Street
Sydney Street
Melbourne Street
Moore Street
Graham Square
Bell Street
Molendinar St
Gallowgate Mkt
GALLOWGATE
A89
Fire Station
Barras Market
Millroad St
Chalmers Ga
Millroad Drive
Brandon Street
Comelypark St
Slatefield St
Wyper Pl
Abercromby Drive
Orr Street
Forbes St
St Andrew's Square
Moncur St
Stevenson St
Baras Mkt
City of Glasgow Council
Charlotte St
LONDON ROAD
Claythorn Avenue
Claythorn Circus
Claythorn Pk
Calton
St James Primary School
Tobago Pl
Tobago Street
Bridgeton Health Centre
Cubie St
Crownpoint Road
St Annes Primary School
School
David Street
B763
FIELDEN STREET
Glasgow Green
Peoples Palace Museum
Monteith Row
Binnie Pl
Templeton Business Centre
Templeton St
Arcadia Street
Craignestock Street
Drake St
Dornoch St
Bridgeton Business Cen
Kerr Pl
Kerr Dr
Rogart St
Redan St
Park La
Kerr Practice
David Dale College
Glasgow City Council
Broad St
Crowngate Business Cen
Summer St
Rimsdale St
Bridgeton
Brookside
Fielden Place
Barrowfield Drive
Barrowfield Street
Kirkpatrick Street
Olympia St
A749
A74
LONDON ROAD
Bernard Terrace
Silvergrove St
Anson St
Landressy St
OLYMPIA ST
McPhail Street
The Green
Adelphi Street
BALLATER STREET
A74 JAMES STREET
KING'S DRIVE
Landressy Pl
Mackeith St
Medical Centre
Megan St
Acorn St
Tullis Street
Muslin Street
Main Street
Greenhead St
Moffat St
Hayfield St
McNeil Gdns
Turnlaw Street
Benthall St
Waterside St
Baltic Pl
Queen Mary St
Walkinshaw St
Dalmarnock Primary Sch
Albany St
G40
Reid Pl
Savoy Street
Sacred Heart Primary School
Laird Pl
Dale St
Colbert St
Old Dalmarnock Road
DALMARNOCK ROAD
CUMBERNAULD ROAD
Dunn St
Nuneaton Street
Nuneaton Industrial Estate
Mill Crs
Mill Street
Franklin St
Finnart Square
Finnart Street
DUNN STREET
Madras St
Rumford Street
Newhall Street
B763
Poplin Street
Bartholomew Street
Playfair St
Baltic La
Glasgow City Council
Mordaunt Street
River Clyde
A730
Wolseley Street
Fauldhouse Street
Richmond Park School
Polmadie Road
SHAWFIELD DR
MAIN ST
Reid St
French Street
Trafalgar Street
Poplin St
Dora St
Martin St
Rockcliffe Street
French St
Dalmarnock Station
Colvend Street
Bonnar Street
Baltic Court
Dalmarnock
6
11
105
1 grid square represents 250 metres

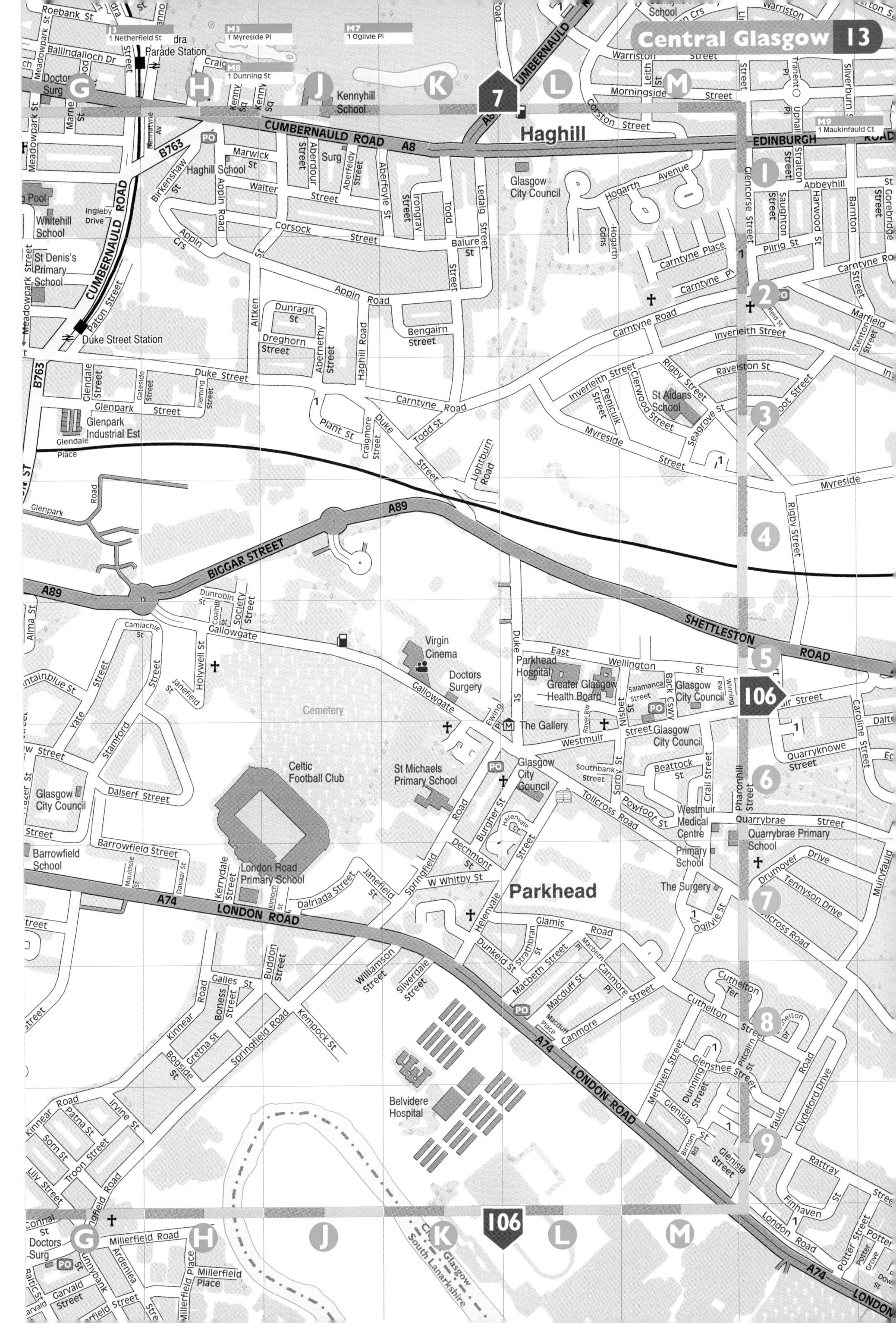
J3 1 Netherfield St
M3 1 Myreside Pl
M7 1 Ogilvie Pl
M8 1 Dunning St
M9 1 Maukinfauld Ct
G
H
J
K
L
M
7
106
1
2
3
4
5
6
7
8
9
Haghill
Parkhead
CUMBERNAULD ROAD A8
EDINBURGH ROAD
A89
BIGGAR STREET
SHETTLESTON ROAD
A74 LONDON ROAD
B763
Roebank St
Meadowpark St
Ballindalloch Dr
Parade Station
Duke Street Station
Kennyhill School
Haghill School
Whitehill School
St Denis's Primary School
Ingleby Drive
Paton Street
Marwick St
Walter Street
Corsock Street
Appin Road
Appin Crs
Birkenshaw St
Aberdour Street
Aberfeldy Street
Aberfoyle St
Irongray Street
Todd Street
Ledaig Street
Balure St
Glasgow City Council
Hogarth Avenue
Hogarth Gdns
Carntyne Place
Carntyne Pl
Carntyne Road
Inverleith Street
Ravelston St
Rigby Street
St Aidans School
Clerwood Street
Penicuik Street
Myreside Street
Seagrove St
Glencorse Street
Abbeyhill
Pilrig St
Saughton Street
Harwood St
Barnton Street
Gorebridge Street
Marfield
Stenton Street
Warriston Street
Morningside Street
Corston Street
Leith St
Dunragit St
Dreghorn Street
Abernethy Street
Aitken St
Haghill Road
Bengairn Street
Duke Street
Glendale Street
Gateside Street
Fleming Street
Glenpark Street
Glenpark Industrial Est
Glendale Place
Plant St
Craigmore Street
Todd St
Lightburn Road
Glenpark Road
Rigby Street
Myreside
Dunrobin St
Coalhill St
Society Street
Gallowgate
Camlachie St
Holywell St
Janefield St
Virgin Cinema
Doctors Surgery
Cemetery
Celtic Football Club
St Michaels Primary School
Parkhead Hospital
Greater Glasgow Health Board
East Wellington St
Salamanca Street
Back Cswy
Winning Rw
Nisbet St
Ravel Rw
The Gallery
Westmuir Street
Southbank Street
Sorby St
Beattock St
Crail Street
Powfoot St
Tollcross Road
Westmuir Medical Centre
Primary School
Quarrybrae Street
Quarrybrae Primary School
Pharonhill Street
Quarryknowe Street
Caroline Street
Drumover Drive
Tennyson Drive
Muiryfauld
The Surgery
Ogilvie St
Stamford
Yate
Dalserf Street
Barrowfield Street
Barrowfield School
London Road Primary School
Kerrydale Street
Mauldslie St
Davaar St
Kinloch St
Dalriada Street
Janefield St
W Whitby St
Springfield Road
Dechmont St
Burgher St
Helenvale St
Helenvale Street
Glamis Road
Strathbran St
Dunkeld St
Macbeth Street
Macbeth Pl
Macduff St
Canmore Pl
Canmore Street
Macduff Place
Cuthelton Ter
Cuthelton Street
Methven Street
Glenshee Street
Dunning Street
Pitcairn St
Glenisla St
Glenisla Street
Birnam Rd
Clydeford Drive
Rattray St
Finhaven St
London Road
Potter Street
Potter Grove
Gailes St
Buddon Street
Williamson Street
Silverdale Street
Kinnear Road
Boness Street
Gretna St
Bogside St
Kempock St
Belvidere Hospital
Patna St
Irvine St
Sorn St
Troon Street
Lily Street
Millerfield Road
Millerfield Place
Ardenlea
Garvald Street
Baltic St
Connal St
Doctors Surg
Glasgow South Lanarkshire
Glasgow City Council
Dalserf Street

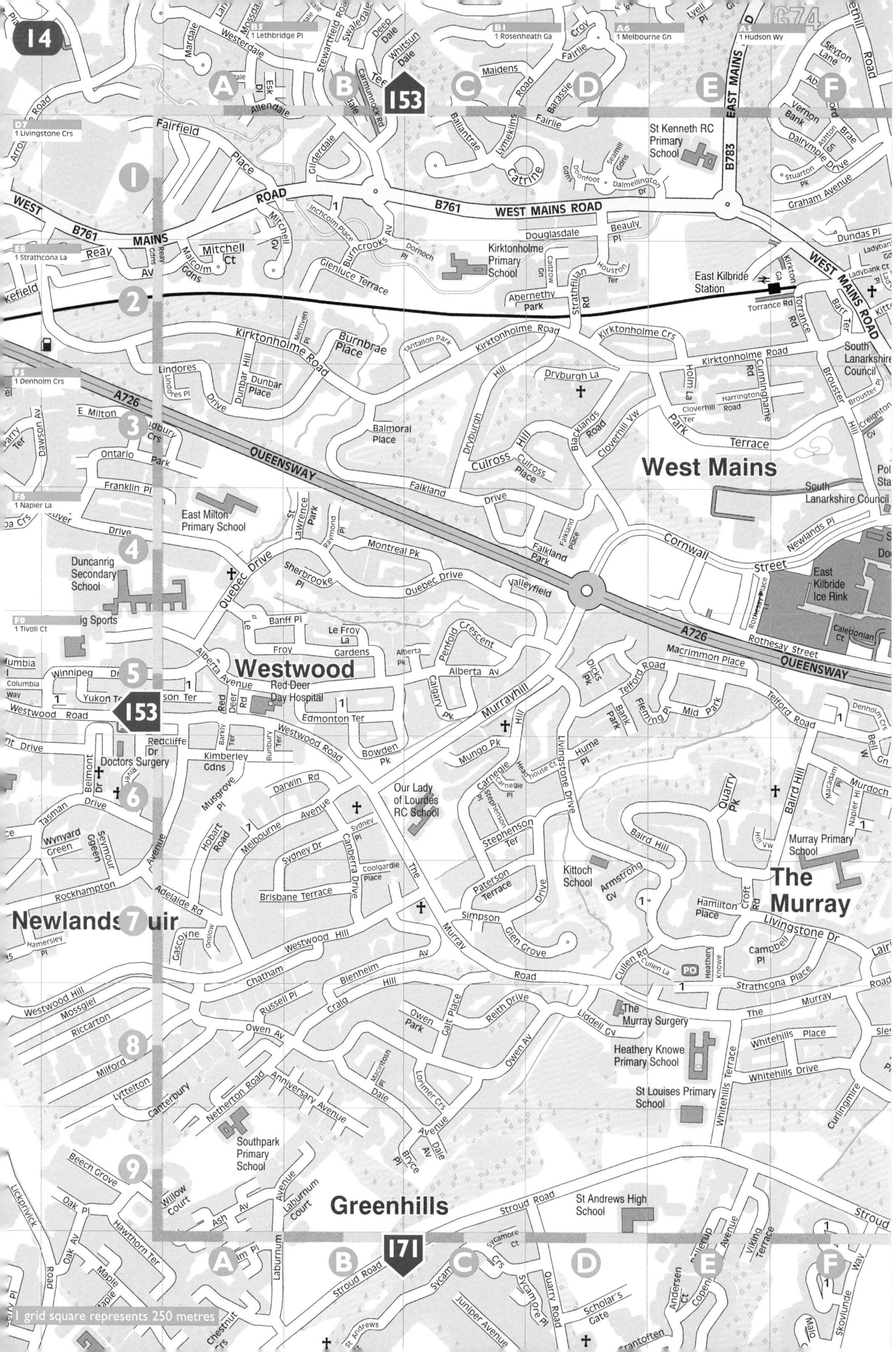
B5 1 Lethbridge Pl
B1 1 Rosenheath Ga
A6 1 Melbourne Gn
A5 1 Hudson Wy
G74
D7 1 Livingstone Crs
E8 1 Strathcona La
F5 1 Denholm Crs
F6 1 Napier La
F9 1 Tivoli Ct
A
B
C
D
E
F
1
2
3
4
5
6
7
8
9
153
171
Westerdale
Mardale
Stewartfield Road
Swaledale
Deep Dale
Whitsun Dale
Esk Dl
Allendale
Camunnock Rd
Maidens
Croy
Fairlie
Barassie
Road
Seyton Lane
Vernon Bank
Dalrymple Drive
Ashton Gn
Brae
Stuarton Pk
Graham Avenue
Fairfield
Place
Gilderdale
Ballantrae
Lymekilns
Catrine
Doonfoot
Seamill Gdns
Dalmellington Dr
St Kenneth RC Primary School
B783
EAST MAINS RD
WEST MAINS ROAD
B761
WEST
MAINS
ROAD
Mitchell Gv
Mitchell Ct
Malcolm Gdns
Reay Av
Reay Gdns
Inchcolm Place
Burncrooks Av
Dornoch Pl
Glenluce Terrace
Douglasdale
Beauly Pl
Kirktonholme Primary School
Cadzow Gn
Strathfillan Rd
Houston Ter
Abernethy Park
East Kilbride Station
Kirkton Ga
Torrance Rd
Torrance Rd
Barr Ter
Dundas Pl
Ladybank Gdn
Ladybank Ct
Kefield
Methven Pl
Burnbrae Place
Tantallon Park
Kirktonholme Road
Kirktonholme Crs
Kirktonholme Road
South Lanarkshire Council
Lindores
Lindores Pl
Dunbar Hill
Dunbar Place
Drive
Dryburgh La
Holm La
Cunninghame Rd
Brouster Hill
Brouster Pl
Creighton Gv
Cloverhill Ter
Cloverhill Road
Harrington Road
Park
Terrace
A726
E Milton
Dawson Av
Ludbury Crs
Ontario Park
Franklin Pl
Balmoral Place
Dryburgh Hill
Culross Hill
Culross Place
Blacklands Road
Cloverhill Vw
West Mains
QUEENSWAY
South Lanarkshire Council
Falkland
Drive
East Milton Primary School
St Lawrence Park
Raymond Pl
Montreal Pk
Falkland Place
Falkland Park
Cornwall
Street
Newlands Pl
Duncanrig Secondary School
Quebec Drive
Sherbrooke Pl
Quebec Drive
Valleyfield
Rothesay Place
East Kilbride Ice Rink
Caledonian Ct
ig Sports
Banff Pl
Le Froy La
Le Froy Gardens
Penfold Crescent
A726
Rothesay Street
QUEENSWAY
Macrimmon Place
Alberta Avenue
Alberta Pk
Alberta Av
Westwood
Red Deer Day Hospital
Telford Road
Dicks Pk
Winnipeg Dr
Columbia Way
Yukon Ter
Red Deer Rd
Calgary Pk
Murrayhill
Bank Park
Fleming Pl
Mid Park
Telford Road
Denholm Crs
Westwood Road
Edmonton Ter
Westwood Road
Bowden Pk
Hill
Hume Pl
Bell Gn
Redcliffe Dr
Barkly Ter
Bunbury Ter
Kimberley Gdns
Mungo Pk
Carnegie Pl
Carnegie Pl
Headhouse Ct
Livingstone Drive
Quarry Pk
Baird Hill
Macadam Pl
Murdoch
Napier Hl
Belmont Dr
Doctors Surgery
River
Musgrove Pl
Darwin Rd
Our Lady of Lourdes RC School
Stephenson Pl
Stephenson Ter
Baird Hill
Hill Vw
Murray Primary School
Tasman Drive
Wynyard Green
Seymour Ggeen
Hobart Road
Melbourne Avenue
Sydney Pl
Sydney Dr
Canberra Drive
Coolgardie Place
The Murray
Paterson Terrace
Drive
Kittoch School
Armstrong Gv
The Murray
Avenue
Rockhampton
Brisbane Terrace
Hamilton Place
Croft Rd
Livingstone Dr
Newlands
Muir
Adelaide Rd
Simpson
Glen Grove
Cullen Rd
Cullen La
PO
Heathery Knowe
Campbell Pl
Lairh
Hamersley Pl
Gascoyne
Onslow
Westwood Hill
Av
Strathcona Place
Road
Chatham
Road
Westwood Hill
Mossgiel
Riccarton
Blenheim
Craig Hill
Russell Pl
Owen Av
Owen Park
Galt Place
Reith Drive
Liddell Gv
The Murray Surgery
The Murray
Whitehills Place
Milford
Macintosh Pl
Dale
Lorimer Crs
Owen Av
Heathery Knowe Primary School
Whitehills Terrace
Whitehills Drive
Lyttelton
Canterbury
Netherton Road
Anniversary Avenue
St Louises Primary School
Curlinghaire
Avenue
Dale
Bryce Pl
Av
Southpark Primary School
Beech Grove
Willow Court
Avenue
Laburnum Court
Greenhills
Stroud Road
St Andrews High School
Stroud
Oak Pl
Hawthorn Ter
Ash Av
Lickprivick
Oak Av
Maple
Laburnum
Stroud Road
Sycamore Ct
Crs
Sycamore Ct
Quarry Road
Scholar's Gate
Andersen Ct
Copen
Viking Terrace
Skovlunde Way
Juniper Avenue
St Andrews
Chestnut Crs
Crantoften
1 grid square represents 250 metres

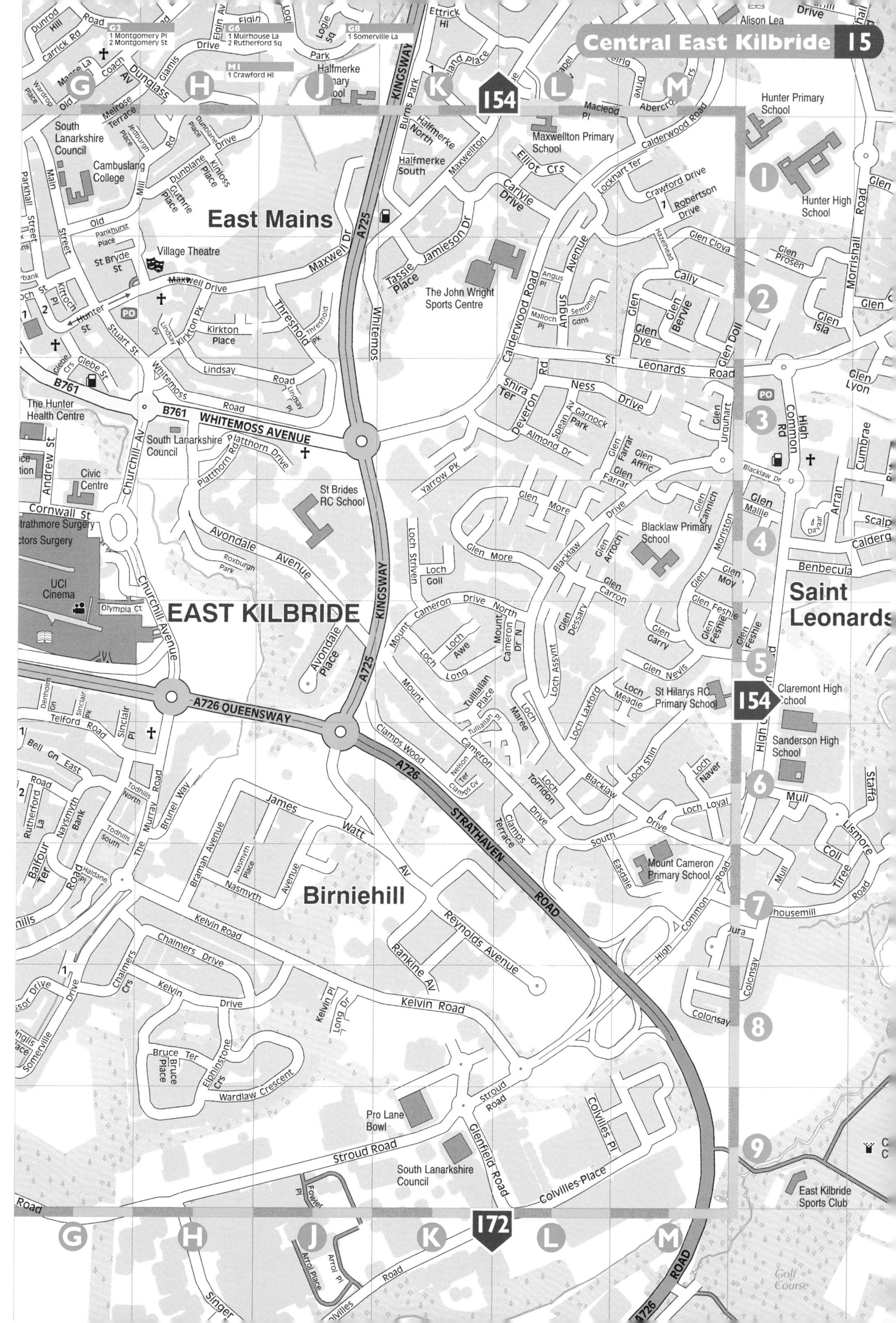
G2
1 Montgomery Pl
2 Montgomery St
G6
1 Muirhouse La
2 Rutherford Sq
G8
1 Somerville La
M1
1 Crawford Hl
G
H
J
K
L
M
154
1
2
3
4
5
6
7
8
9
I
172
East Mains
EAST KILBRIDE
Birniehill
Saint Leonards
South Lanarkshire Council
Cambuslang College
Village Theatre
The Hunter Health Centre
Civic Centre
Strathmore Surgery
UCI Cinema
Olympia Ct
Halfmerke Primary School
Maxwellton Primary School
Hunter Primary School
Hunter High School
The John Wright Sports Centre
St Brides RC School
Blacklaw Primary School
St Hilarys RC Primary School
Claremont High School
Sanderson High School
Mount Cameron Primary School
Pro Lane Bowl
East Kilbride Sports Club
Golf Course
Alison Lea
A725
KINGSWAY
B761
WHITEMOSS AVENUE
A726 QUEENSWAY
A726
STRATHAVEN ROAD
PO
Maxwell Drive
Maxwell Dr
Hunter St
Stuart St
Glebe St
Kirkton Place
Lindsay Road
Whitemoss Road
Threshold
Churchill Avenue
Platthorn Drive
Avondale Avenue
Avondale Place
Roxburgh Park
Cornwall St
Andrew St
Telford Road
Sinclair Pl
Bell Gn East
Naysmyth Bank
Rutherford La
Balfour Ter
The Murray Road
Brunel Way
Todhills North
Todhills South
James Watt Av
Bramah Avenue
Nasmyth Place
Nasmyth Avenue
Kelvin Road
Chalmers Drive
Chalmers Crs
Kelvin Drive
Kelvin Pl
Long Dr
Bruce Ter
Bruce Place
Elphinstone Crs
Wardlaw Crescent
Somerville Drive
Stroud Road
Glenfield Road
Colvilles Place
Colvilles Pl
Reynolds Avenue
Rankine Av
Fowler Pl
Arrol Pl
Arrol Place
Singer
Calderwood Road
Carlyle Drive
Elliot Crs
Maxwellton
Jamieson Dr
Tassie Place
Whitemoss
Halfmerke North
Halfmerke South
Burns Park
Macleod Pl
Lockhart Ter
Crawford Drive
Robertson Drive
Glen Clova
Glen Prosen
Cally
Glen Bervie
Glen Dye
Glen Doll
Glen Isla
St Leonards Road
High Common Rd
Ness Drive
Shira Ter
Deveron Rd
Spean Av
Garnock Park
Almond Dr
Yarrow Pk
Angus Avenue
Angus Pl
Malloch Pl
Semphill Gdns
Glen Urquhart
Glen Farrar
Glen Affric
Glen More
Blacklaw Drive
Glen Cannich
Glen Arroch
Glen Carron
Glen Dessary
Glen Moy
Glen Feshie
Glen Carry
Glen Nevis
Moriston
Loch Striven
Loch Goil
Mount Cameron Drive North
Mount Cameron Dr N
Loch Awe
Loch Long
Tullialan Place
Loch Maree
Loch Assynt
Loch Laxford
Loch Meadie
Loch Shin
Loch Naver
Loch Loyal
Loch Torridon
Clamps Wood
Clamps Terrace
Nelson Ter
Clamps Gv
Mount Cameron Drive South
Easdale
Blacklaw Dr
Glen Mallie
Arran
Davaar
Benbecula
Cumbrae
Scalpay
Calderglen
Glen Lyon
Morrishall Road
Mull
Staffa
Lismore
Coll
Tiree
Jura
Colonsay
Philipshill Road
Mousemill

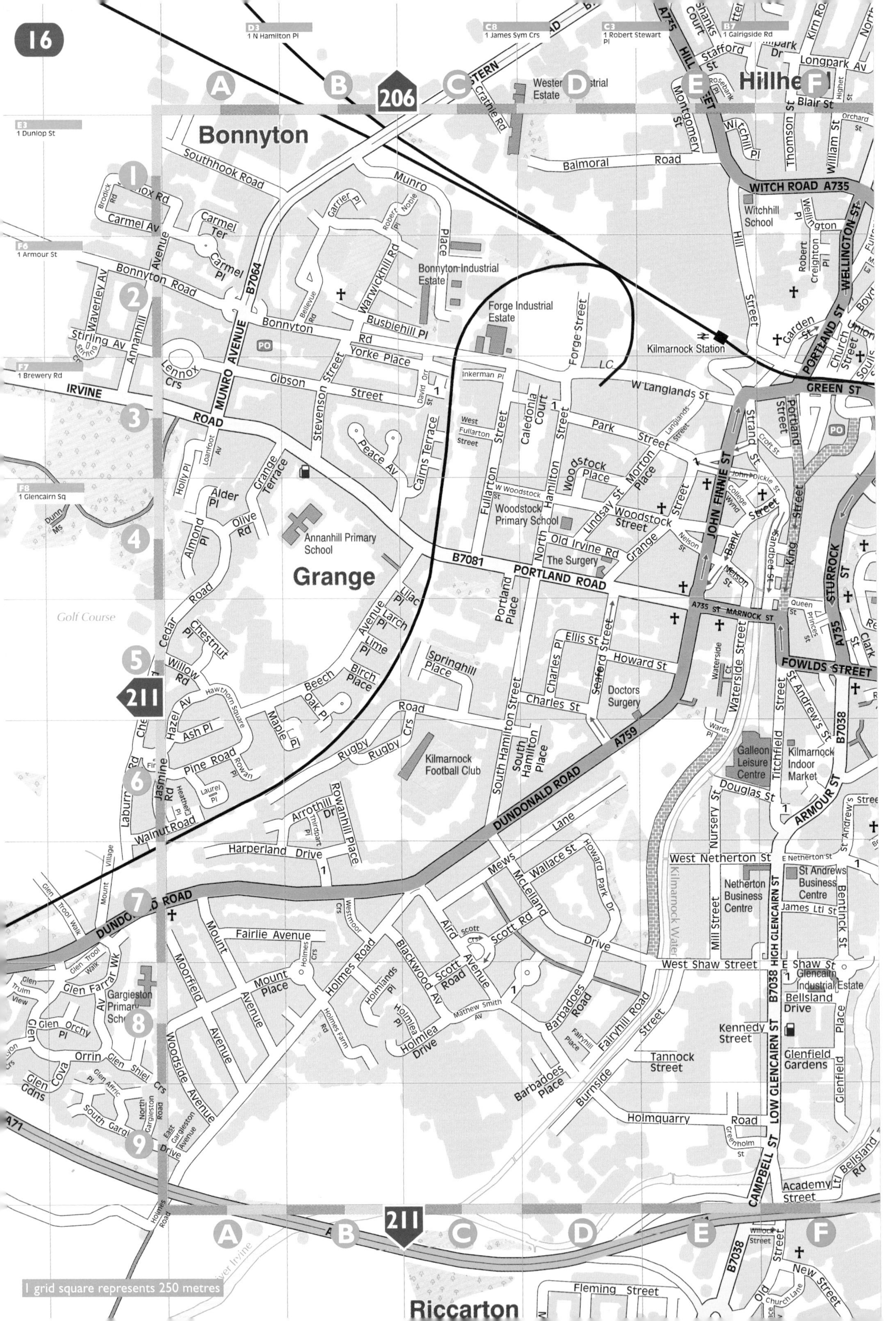
D3 1 N Hamilton Pl
C8 1 James Sym Crs
C3 1 Robert Stewart Pl
B7 1 Gairigside Rd
E3 1 Dunlop St
F6 1 Armour St
F7 1 Brewery Rd
F8 1 Glencairn Sq
A
B
206
C
D
E
F
Bonnyton
Hillhead
Western Industrial Estate
Crathie Rd
Montgomery St
Stafford St
Shanks Court
Longpark Av
Blair St
Orchard St
Thomson St
William St
Witchhill Pl
Balmoral Road
Southhook Road
Munro Place
Lennox Rd
Brodick Rd
Carmel Av
Carmel Ter
Carmel Pl
Bonnyton Road
Waverley Av
Stirling Av
Annanhill Avenue
B7064
Garrier Pl
Robertson Pl
Noble
Warwickhill Rd
Bonnyton Industrial Estate
Forge Industrial Estate
Forge Street
WITCH ROAD A735
Witchhill School
Hill Street
Wellington St
WELLINGTON ST
Robert Creighton Pl
Bellevue Rd
Busbiehill Pl
Bonnyton Rd
Yorke Place
Gibson Street
Stevenson Street
Lennox Crs
MUNRO AVENUE
PO
IRVINE ROAD
Inkerman Pl
David Orr St
LC
W Langlands St
Kilmarnock Station
Garden St
PORTLAND ST
Church Street
Union
GREEN ST
Loanfoot Av
Holly Pl
Grange Terrace
Peace Av
Cairns Terrace
West Fullarton Street
Fullarton Street
Caledonia Court
North Hamilton Street
Park Street
Langlands Street
Strand St
Croft St
Portland Street
John Dickie St
College Wynd
Woodstock Place
Morton Place
W Woodstock St
Woodstock Primary School
Lindsay St
Woodstock Street
Alder Pl
Olive Rd
Almond Pl
Dunn Ms
Annanhill Primary School
Grange
B7081
PORTLAND ROAD
Old Irvine Rd
The Surgery
Grange Street
JOHN FINNIE ST
Bank Street
Nelson St
Sandbed St
King Street
STURROCK ST
Golf Course
Cedar Rd
Chestnut Pl
Lilac Pl
Larch Pl
Lime Pl
Avenue
Portland Place
Ellis St
Charles Pl
Seaford Street
Howard St
A735 ST MARNOCK ST
Waterside Ct
Waterside Street
Queen St
Princes St
A735
Clark St
FOWLDS STREET
Willow Rd
Hawthorn Square
Birch Place
Beech Oak Pl
Springhill Place
Charles St
Doctors Surgery
Hazel Av
Ash Pl
Maple Pl
Rugby Road
Rugby Crs
South Hamilton Street
South Hamilton Place
A759
Wards Pl
Titchfield Street
St Andrew's St
B7038
Galleon Leisure Centre
Kilmarnock Indoor Market
211
Pine Road
Rowan Pl
Jasmine Rd
Heather Pl
Laurel Pl
Laburnum Rd
Kilmarnock Football Club
DUNDONALD ROAD
Arrothill Dr
Thirdpart Pl
Rowanhill Place
Douglas St
Nursery St
ARMOUR ST
Walnut Road
Village
Harperland Drive
Lane
Mews
Howard Park Dr
Wallace St
McLelland Drive
West Netherton St
E Netherton St
St Andrew's St
St Andrews Business Centre
Netherton Business Centre
Kilmarnock Water
Mill Street
HIGH GLENCAIRN ST
Glen Trool Walk
Mount Avenue
DUNDONALD ROAD
Fairlie Avenue
Westmoor Crs
Aird Avenue
Scott Crs
Scott Rd
James Ltl St
Bentinck St
Glen Trool Walk
Glen Farrar Wk
Glen Truim View
Gargieston Primary School
Moorfield Avenue
Mount Place
Holmes Crs
Holmes Road
Holmlands Pl
Blackwood Av
Scott Road
Mathew Smith Av
Barbadoes Road
Fairyhill Road
West Shaw Street
E Shaw St
Glencairn Industrial Estate
Bellsland Drive
Holmlea Pl
Holmlea Drive
Holmes Farm Rd
Fairyhill Place
Burnside Street
Kennedy Street
Tannock Street
LOW GLENCAIRN ST
Glenfield Gardens
Glenfield Place
Glen Orchy Pl
Glen Shiel Crs
Orrin
Glen Cova Gdns
Glen Affric Pl
South Gargieston
North Gargieston Road
East Gargieston Avenue
Drive
Woodside Avenue
Barbadoes Place
Holmquarry Road
Greenholm St
CAMPBELL ST
Academy Street
Ltl Bellsland Rd
A71
Holmes Road
River Irvine
B7038
Willock Street
Old Street
New Street
Church Lane
Fleming Street
Riccarton
1 grid square represents 250 metres

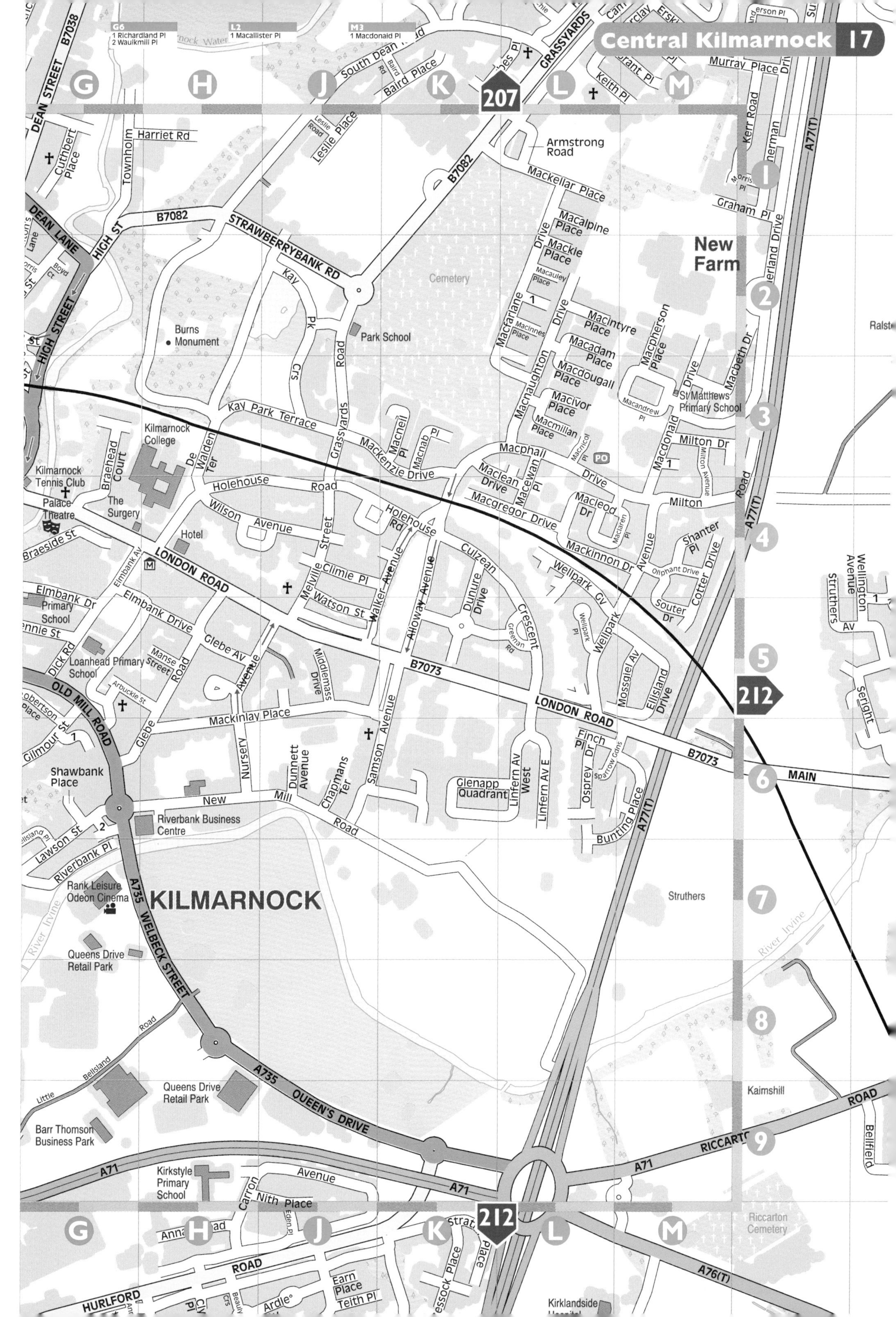
G6
1 Richardland Pl
2 Waulkmill Pl
L2
1 Macallister Pl
M3
1 Macdonald Pl
G
H
J
K
L
M
207
212
1
2
3
4
5
6
7
8
9
DEAN STREET
B7038
South Dean Road
Baird Place
GRASSYARDS
Keith Pl
Murray Place
Harriet Rd
Townholm
Cuthbert Place
Leslie Place
Leslie Road
Armstrong Road
B7082
Mackellar Place
Kerr Road
A77(T)
Graham Pl
Macalpine Place
Mackie Place
Macauley Place
New Farm
DEAN LANE
HIGH ST
STRAWBERRYBANK RD
Kay Pk Crs
Cemetery
Macfarlane Drive
Macinnes Place
Macintyre Place
Macadam Place
Macdougall Place
Macpherson Place
Macbeth Dr
Burns Monument
Park School
Grassyards Road
Macnaughton Drive
Macandrew Pl
St Matthews Primary School
HIGH STREET
Kay Park Terrace
Macivor Place
Macmillan Place
Macdonald Drive
Milton Dr
Kilmarnock College
Macneil Pl
Macnab Pl
Macphail Drive
Macnicol Pl
Kilmarnock Tennis Club
Braehead Court
De Walden Ter
Mackenzie Drive
Maclean Drive
Macewan Pl
Milton Avenue
Milton Road
Palace Theatre
The Surgery
Holehouse Road
Wilson Avenue
Holehouse Rd
Macgregor Drive
Macleod Dr
Maclaren Pl
Shanter Pl
Braeside St
Hotel
Street
Culzean Crescent
Mackinnon Dr
Wellpark Gv
Oliphant Drive
Cotter Drive
Wellington Avenue
Struthers Av
Elmbank Av
LONDON ROAD
Climie Pl
Melville Street
Walker Avenue
Alloway Avenue
Dunure Drive
Souter Dr
Elmbank Dr
Primary School
Elmbank Drive
Watson St
Greenan Rd
Wellpark Pl
Wellpark
Mossgiel Av
Ellisland Drive
Dick Rd
Loanhead Primary School
Manse Street
Glebe Av
Road
Middlemass Drive
Avenue
B7073
Seright
Arbuckle St
OLD MILL ROAD
Mackinlay Place
LONDON ROAD
Finch Pl
Osprey Dr
Sparrow Gdns
Gilmour St
Glebe
Nursery
Dunnett Avenue
Chapmans Ter
Samson Avenue
Glenapp Quadrant
Linfern Av West
Linfern Av E
Bunting Place
MAIN
Shawbank Place
New Mill Road
Riverbank Business Centre
Lawson St
Riverbank Pl
Rank Leisure Odeon Cinema
A735 WELBECK STREET
KILMARNOCK
Struthers
River Irvine
Queens Drive Retail Park
Road
Little Bellsland
Queens Drive Retail Park
A735 QUEEN'S DRIVE
Kaimshill
ROAD
RICCARTON
Bellfield
Barr Thomson Business Park
A71
Kirkstyle Primary School
Avenue
Carron
Nith Place
Eden Pl
Riccarton Cemetery
A76(T)
Place
Earn Place
Teith Pl
Ardle
HURLFORD ROAD
Kirklandside

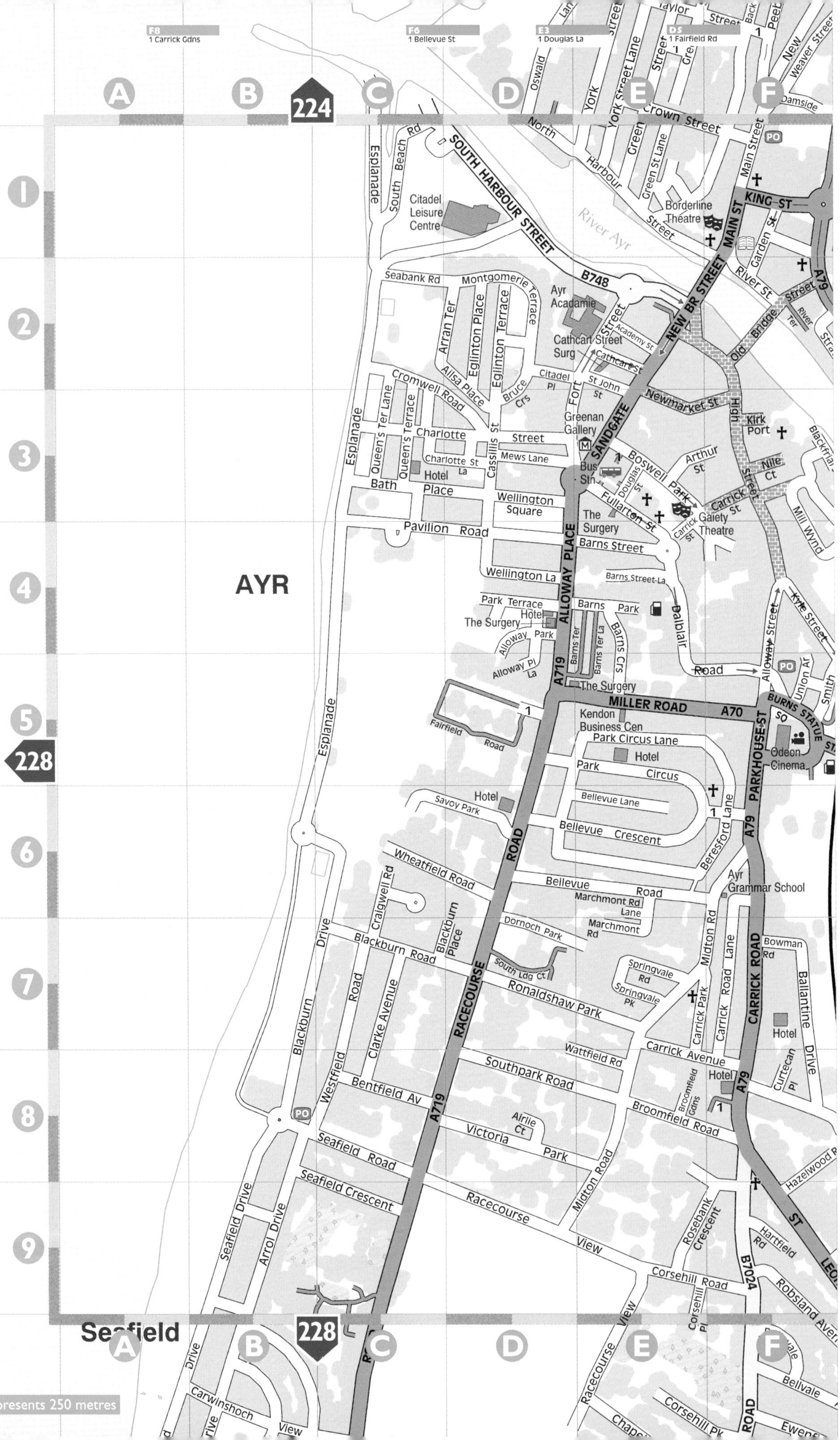
F8
1 Carrick Gdns
F6
1 Bellevue St
E3
1 Douglas La
D5
1 Fairfield Rd
224
228
AYR
Seafield
Esplanade
South Beach Rd
SOUTH HARBOUR STREET
Citadel Leisure Centre
River Ayr
Borderline Theatre
North Harbour Street
York Street
York Street Lane
Green Street
Green St Lane
Crown Street
Main Street
KING ST
MAIN ST
NEW BR STREET
River St
Garden St
Old Bridge Street
River Ter
A79
B748
Seabank Rd
Montgomerie Terrace
Arran Ter
Eglinton Place
Eglinton Terrace
Ailsa Place
Ayr Academie
Academy St
Cathcart Street
Cathcart St
Surg
Cromwell Road
Bruce Crs
Citadel Pl
Fort Street
St John St
Newmarket St
High Street
Kirk Port
Greenan Gallery
SANDGATE
Queen's Ter Lane
Queen's Terrace
Charlotte Street
Charlotte St La
Cassillis St
Mews Lane
Bus Stn
Douglas St
Boswell Park
Arthur St
Nile Ct
Bath Place
Hotel
Wellington Square
The Surgery
Fullarton St
Carrick St
Gaiety Theatre
Mill Wynd
Pavilion Road
Barns Street
ALLOWAY PLACE
Wellington La
Barns Street La
Kyle Street
Park Terrace
Barns Park
Dalblair Road
Alloway Street
The Surgery
Alloway Park
Barns Ter
Barns Ter La
Barns Crs
Alloway Pl La
A719
Union Ar
Smith
MILLER ROAD
A70
BURNS STATUE SQ
Fairfield Road
Kendon Business Cen
Park Circus Lane
Odeon Cinema
PARKHOUSE ST
Park Circus
Bellevue Lane
Savoy Park
Bellevue Crescent
Beresford Lane
Wheatfield Road
Bellevue Road
Ayr Grammar School
Marchmont Rd Lane
Marchmont Rd
Dornoch Park
Craigwell Rd
Blackburn Place
Blackburn Road
South Ldg Ct
Springvale Rd
Springvale Pk
Midton Rd
Carrick Road Lane
CARRICK ROAD
Bowman Rd
Ballantine Drive
RACECOURSE ROAD
Blackburn Drive
Clarke Avenue
Ronaldshaw Park
Carrick Park
Wattfield Rd
Carrick Avenue
Curtecan Pl
Southpark Road
Westfield Road
Bentfield Av
Broomfield Gdns
Broomfield Road
PO
Airlie Ct
Victoria Park
Seafield Road
Midton Road
Hazelwood Rd
Seafield Crescent
Rosebank Crescent
Racecourse View
Seafield Drive
Arrol Drive
Hartfield Rd
ST LEONARDS
B7024
Corsehill Road
Corsehill Pl
Robsland Avenue
Racecourse View
Carwinshoch View
Bellvale
Corsehill Pk
Chapel
ROAD
1 grid square represents 250 metres

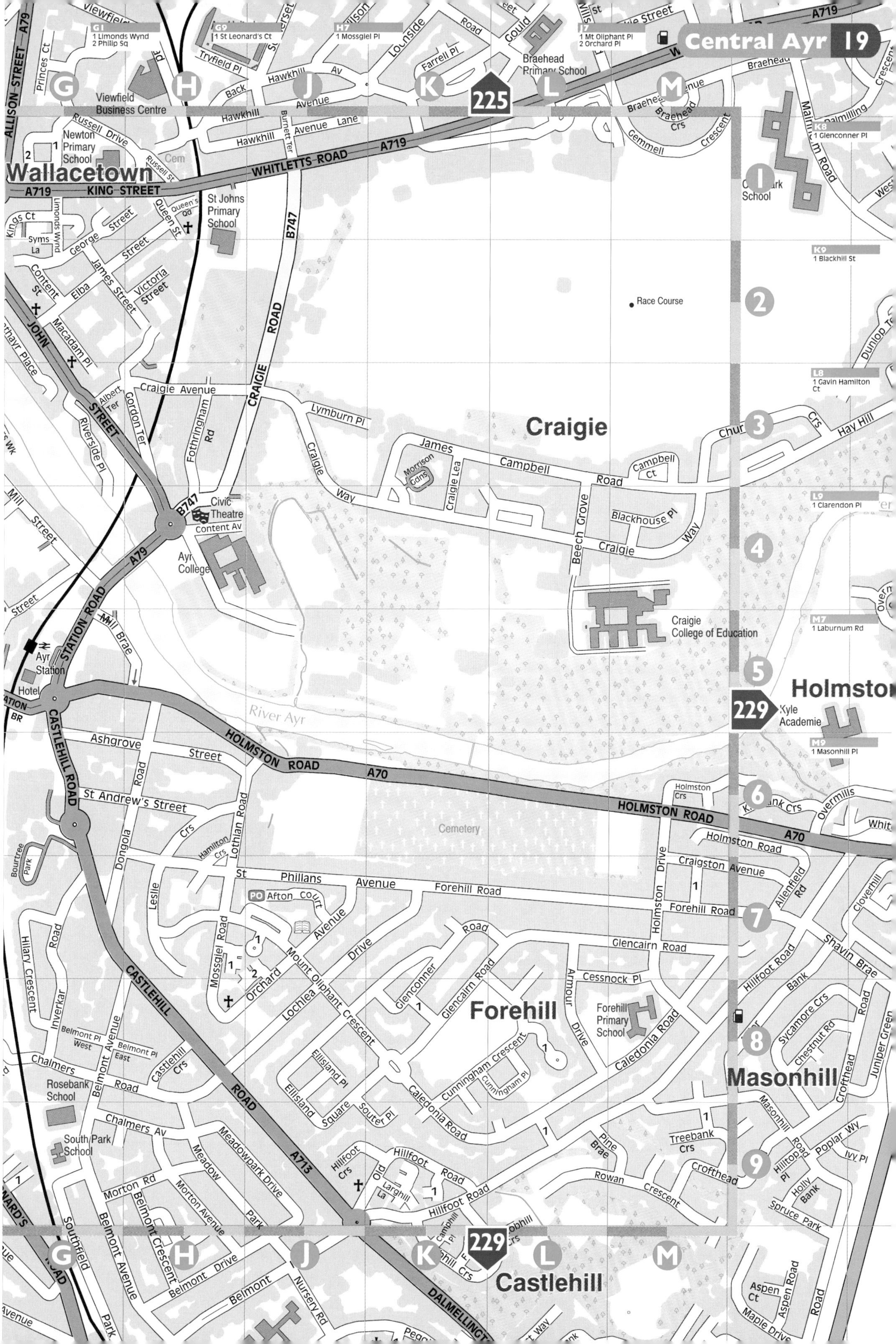
G1
1 Limonds Wynd
2 Philip Sq
G9
1 St Leonard's Ct
H7
1 Mossgiel Pl
J7
1 Mt Oliphant Pl
2 Orchard Pl
K8
1 Glenconner Pl
K9
1 Blackhill St
L8
1 Gavin Hamilton Ct
L9
1 Clarendon Pl
M7
1 Laburnum Rd
M9
1 Masonhill Pl
225
229
Wallacetown
Craigie
Forehill
Masonhill
Castlehill
Holmston
Viewfield Business Centre
Newton Primary School
Braehead Primary School
St Johns Primary School
Civic Theatre
Ayr College
Ayr Station
Hotel
Race Course
Craigie College of Education
Kyle Academie
River Ayr
Cemetery
Forehill Primary School
Rosebank School
South Park School
WHITLETTS ROAD
KING STREET
A719
A79
B747
A70
A713
ALLISON STREET
JOHN STREET
STATION ROAD
CASTLEHILL ROAD
CRAIGIE ROAD
HOLMSTON ROAD
DALMELLINGTON ROAD
Hawkhill Avenue
Hawkhill Avenue Lane
Burnett Ter
Russell Drive
Russell St
Tryfield Pl
Farrell Pl
Gould
Lochside
Braehead Crs
Gemmell Crescent
Limonds Wynd
Kings Ct
Syms La
George Street
Queen St
Queen's Ct
James Street
Elba Street
Victoria Street
Content St
Macadam Pl
Craigie Avenue
Albert Ter
Gordon Ter
Fothringham Rd
Riverside Pl
Mill Street
Mill Brae
Content Av
Lymburn Pl
Craigie Way
James Campbell Road
Morrison Gdns
Craigie Lea
Campbell Ct
Beech Grove
Blackhouse Pl
Hay Hill
Dunlop Ter
Ashgrove Street
St Andrew's Street
Dongola Road
Lothian Road
Hamilton Crs
Leslie
St Phillans Avenue
Afton Court
Forehill Road
Holmston Crs
Holmston Drive
Holmston Road
Craigston Avenue
Allenfield Rd
Overmills
Glencairn Road
Shavin Brae
Hillfoot Road
Cessnock Pl
Armour Drive
Caledonia Road
Mossgiel Road
Orchard Avenue
Mount Oliphant Crescent
Lochlea Drive
Glenconner
Glencairn Road
Cunningham Crescent
Cunningham Pl
Ellisland Pl
Ellisland Square
Souter Pl
Hilary Crescent
Inverkar Road
Belmont Pl West
Belmont Pl East
Belmont Avenue
Castlehill Crs
Chalmers Road
Chalmers Av
Morton Rd
Morton Avenue
Meadow Park
Meadowpark Drive
Belmont Crescent
Belmont Drive
Southfield
Nursery Rd
Hillfoot Crs
Larghill La
Pine Brae
Rowan Crescent
Treebank Crs
Crofthead
Crofthead Road
Masonhill Road
Hilltop Pl
Poplar Wy
Ivy Pl
Holly Bank
Spruce Park
Sycamore Crs
Chestnut Rd
Juniper Green
Aspen Ct
Aspen Road
Maple Drive
Bourtree Park
Cloverhill
PO

D7
1 Columba St

D8
1 Maitland St

D5
1 Urquhart Pl

D6
1 Abercromby Pl W
2 W Abercromby St

C8
1 Colquhoun Sq

B7
1 Bonar Law Av
2 Camsail Av
3 Cove Pl
4 Roseneath Dr

A7
1 Macaulay Pl
2 Strathclyde Pl

B6
1 Rowallan St
2 Upr Sutherl'nd St

A
B
C
D
E
F
1
2
3
4
5
6
7
8
Highlandman's Wood
Ardencaple Farm
Glenoran Road
Kathleen Park
Rhu Road Higher
Dalmore Crs
Cumberland Avenue
Empress Dr
Frazer Av
Mains Av
Jutland Court
Bannachra Drive
Ardencaple Dr
Castle Av
Loch Drive
Kidston Drive
RHU ROAD LOWER
Cairndhu Avenue
Cairndhu Gdns
Ardencaple
West King Street
Baird Avenue
Coulport Place
Ferniegair Av
Courtrai Av
Sutherland St
Woodend Street
Upper Sutherland Crs
Lwr Sutherland Crs
Duchess Park
Duchess Drive
Macleod Crs
Paterson Dr
Macleod Drive
Edward Drive
Barclay Drive
Queen Street
Millig Street
Stafford St W
West Montrose Street
Campbell Street
Suffolk Street
Glasgow Street
West Princes Street
William Street
John Street
John St Lane
Argyle Street West
James Street
Stafford Street
Lomond School
Scott Ct
A814
WEST CLYDE STREET
HELENSBURGH
Helensburgh Swimming Pool
Helensburgh Central Station
Princes Street East
Grant St
Lorne St
Argyle St East
Helensburgh Medical Cen.
King St East
Hermitage School
Parklands School
SINCLAIR STREET
Colquhoun Street
B832
Redclyffe Gardens
Kennedy Drive
Hillview Drive
Blackhill Drive
West Dhuhill Drive
Gillespie Dr
Glen Drive
West Lennox Drive
Upper Colquhoun Street
Douglas Drive
Munro Dr West
West Rossdhu Drive
West Abercromby Street
Helensburgh Upper Station
Hotel
The Hill House (NTS)
SINCLAIR STREET
Sinclair Lane
Dhuhill Dr E
Sinclair Dr
Douglas Dr E
Douglas Dr
Kilbride Drive
Munro Drive
Maclachlan Road
East Rossdhu Drive
Chapelacre Grove
Abercromby Street
St Andrews Wynd
Albert Street
Victoria Road
Charlotte Street
St Michael Drive
Albert Drive
Havelock Street
Havelock Place
Glenfinlas Street
East Montrose Street
Lomond Street
George Street
King's Crescent
East King Street
Henry Street
Adelaide Street
Princes Street
Crawford Drive
Duncan Road
Bain Crescent
Abercromby Crescent
Lever Road
East Lennox Drive
Easterhill Road
Helensburgh Golf Club
Sannox Place
Machrie Dr
Golfhill Drive
Drumadoon Dr
Kildonan Drive
Pladda Way
Lochranza Drive
Primary School
St Josephs School
Granville St
Bell Street
Victoria Infirmary
Cemetery
Garraway Road
Kirkmichael Road
Old Luss Road
Craigendoran Avenue
EAST CLYDE STREET
Talisman
Hanover Street
PO

E6
1 Butt Av
2 Dixon Rd
3 Maclachlan Pl
4 Sinclair Dr

E8
1 Adelaide St
2 Argyle St East
3 Glenfinlas St

F6
1 Boston Dr
2 Brodick Dr
3 Corrie Pl
4 Mcewan Dr

F7
1 Lamlash Pl
2 Mcauslan Pl
3 Pirnmill Pl
4 Shiskine Pl

F8
1 Athole St
2 Johnson Ct
3 Millerslea Gdns
4 Mossend Av
5 Rosedale Gdns
6 Upr Adelaide St

1 grid square represents 500 metres

G6
1 Horton Pl
G7
Street names for this grid square are listed at the back of the index
G8
1 Buchanan Rd
GLEN FRUIN ROAD
A817
G
H
J
K
L
M
1
2
3
4
5
6
7
8
B832
East Kilbride
Fruin Water
Highfields
Inverlauren
Cross Keys
Drumfad
Callendoun
Daligan
LUSS ROAD
B832
LUSS ROAD
Kent Drive
Drive
Kent Drive
Hardy Hill
Winston Place
Camperdown Court
Road
Winston Road
PO
Townhead
Ben Bouie Drive
Colgrain Primary School
Beech
Place
Drumfork Road
Camis Eskan House
23

HELENSBURGH

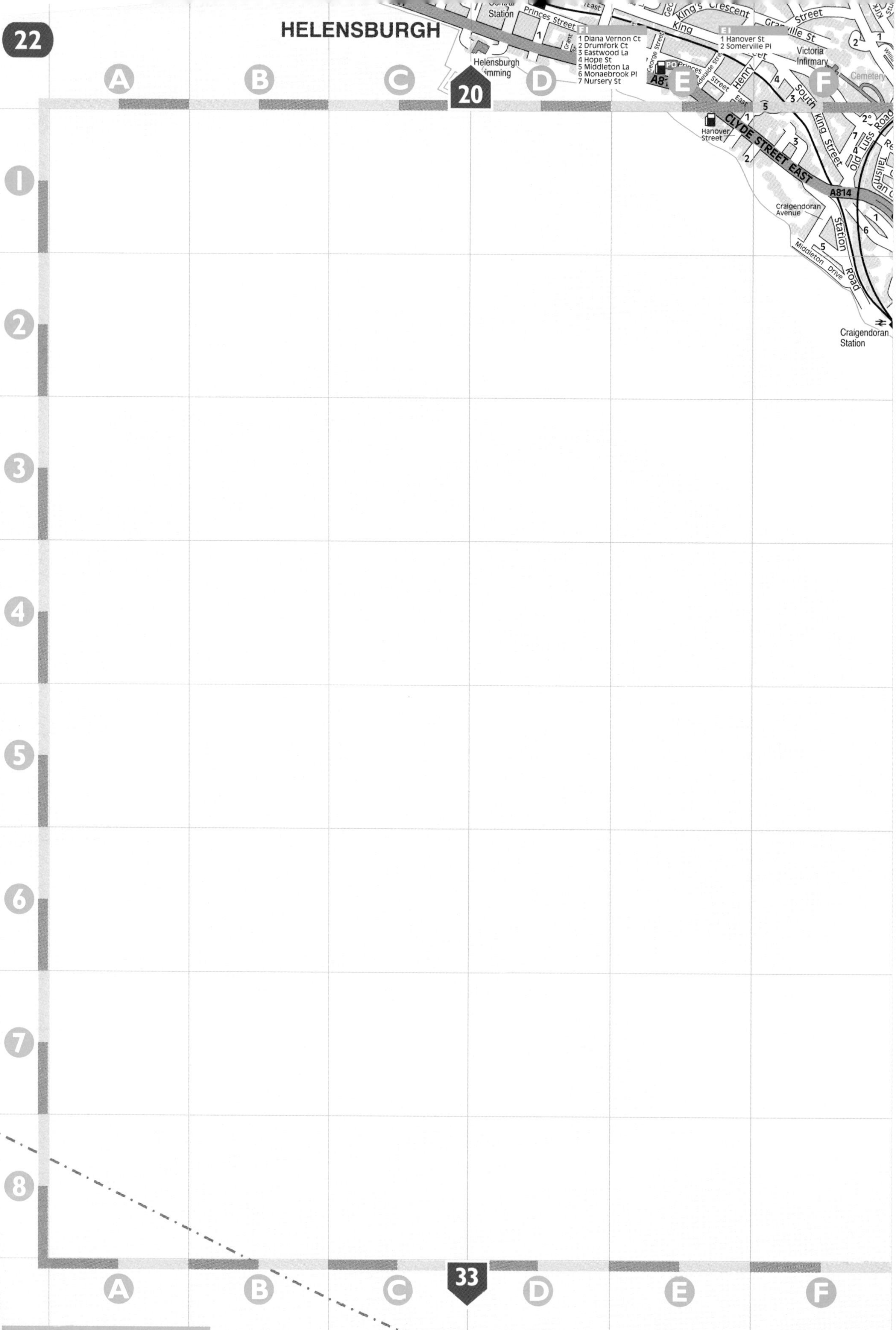

Station
Princes Street
Grant St
F1
1 Diana Vernon Ct
2 Drumfork Ct
3 Eastwood La
4 Hope St
5 Middleton La
6 Monaebrook Pl
7 Nursery St
E1
1 Hanover St
2 Somerville Pl
King's Crescent
King
Granville St
Street
Victoria Infirmary
Cemetery
Helensburgh Swimming
George Street
PO
Princes
Adelaide Street
Henry Street
East
South King Street
Old Luss Road
A814
CLYDE STREET EAST
Hanover Street
Craigendoran Avenue
Station Road
Middleton Drive
Craigendoran Station
A
B
C
D
E
F
1
2
3
4
5
6
7
8
20
33

1 grid square represents 500 metres

G1
1 Armstrong Rd
2 Jeanie Deans Dr
G2
1 Moore Dr
H1
1 Aldrin Rd
Ben Bouie Drive
Colgrain Primary School
Beechgrove Place
Drumfork Road
Collins Road
Ashton Drive
Campbell Dr
Kenilworth Avenue
Waverley Avenue
Drumfork Road
Cardross Road
CARDROSS ROAD
Marmion Avenue
Lawrence Avenue
Dennistoun Cres
Guy Mannering Crescent
Craigendoran
Camis Eskan House
A814
CARDROSS ROAD
Colgrain
Moss Road
LC
Keppoch House
Red Road
Stoneymollan
Badyen Farm
Lyleston
Drumhead
Lyleston Farm
Cemetery
LC
Geilston Burn
Ardmore
Ardardan
Mollandhu
A814 CARDROSS ROAD
Brooks House
Darleith Rd
Smithy Rd
Smithy Ct
BARRS
LC
21
24
34
G
H
J
K
L
M
1
2
3
4
5
6
7
8

Auchendennan Muir
B8
1 Kilmahew Gv
A8
1 Kilmahew Ct
Darleith Muir
A
B
C
D
E
F
1
2
3
4
5
6
7
8
Blackthird
Auchinabreck
Stoneymollan Road
Darleith Farm
West Dunbartonshire
Argyll and Bute
23
Auchensail
Badyen Farm
Cairniedrouth
Asker Reservoir
Asker Farm
Kilmahew Burn
High Milndovan
Kilmahew Farm
Low Milndovan
Wallacetown Burn
Hotel
Kirkton
Cardross Primary School
Darleith Road
Geilston
Hillside Rd
River View
Napier Av
Fair Way
35
Wallacetown
West Dunbartonshire
Argyll and Bute
1 grid square represents 500 metres

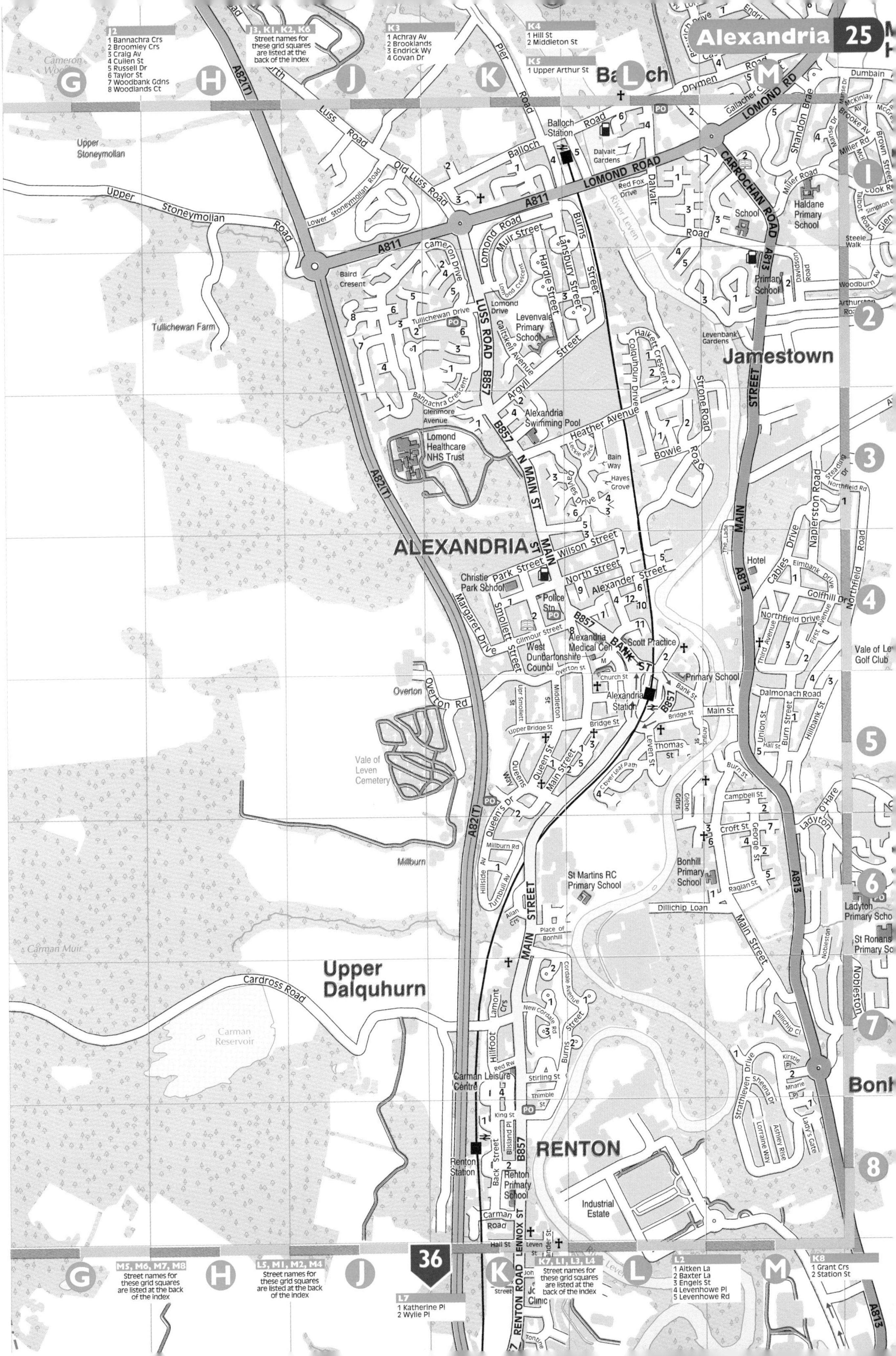
J2
1 Bannachra Crs
2 Broomley Crs
3 Craig Av
4 Cullen St
5 Russell Dr
6 Taylor St
7 Woodbank Gdns
8 Woodlands Ct
J3, K1, K2, K6
Street names for these grid squares are listed at the back of the index
K3
1 Achray Av
2 Brooklands
3 Endrick Wy
4 Govan Dr
K4
1 Hill St
2 Middleton St
K5
1 Upper Arthur St
G
H
J
K
L
M
Balloch
Balloch Station
Upper Stoneymollan
Upper Stoneymollan Road
Lower Stoneymollan Road
Old Luss Road
Luss Road
Balloch Road
LOMOND ROAD
A811
A82(T)
Drymen Road
LOMOND RD
CARROCHAN ROAD
Dalvait Gardens
Dalvait Road
Red Fox Drive
River Leven
Haldane Primary School
School
Shandon Brae
Miller Road
Steele Walk
Woodburn Av
Arthurston Road
Davidson Road
A813
Primary School
Baird Crescent
Cameron Drive
Tullichewan Drive
Tullichewan Farm
Lomond Road
Muir Street
Hardie Street
Lansbury Street
Burns Street
Lomond Drive
Levenvale Primary School
Gaitskell Avenue
Argyll Street
Halkett Crescent
Colquhoun Drive
Levenbank Gardens
Jamestown
MAIN STREET
LUSS ROAD B857
Bannachra Crescent
Glenmore Avenue
Alexandria Swimming Pool
Lomond Healthcare NHS Trust
Heather Avenue
Strone Road
Bowie Road
Bain Way
Hayes Grove
Davies Drive
Leckie Place
N MAIN ST
B857
Steading Dr
Northfield Rd
Napierston Road
Northfield Road
ALEXANDRIA
MAIN ST
Wilson Street
North Street
Alexander Street
Christie Park School
Park Street
Police Stn
Hotel
Cables Drive
Elmbank Drive
Golfhill Dr
Northfield Drive
First Avenue
Third Avenue
Vale of Leven Golf Club
Margaret Drive
Smollett Street
Gilmour Street
West Dunbartonshire Council
Alexandria Medical Cen
BANK ST
Scott Practice
Primary School
Overton St
Church St
Alexandria Station
Bank St
Dalmonach Road
Overton
Overton Rd
Upr Smollett St
Middleton St
Upper Bridge St
Bridge St
Main St
Union St
Burn Street
Hillbank St
Hall St
Queens Way
Queen St
Main Street
Clover Leaf Path
Leven St
Thomas St
Angus St
Burn St
Vale of Leven Cemetery
Queen's Dr
Glebe Gdns
Campbell St
Croft St
George St
O'Hare
Ladyton
Millburn Rd
Millburn
Hillside Av
Turnbull Av
St Martins RC Primary School
Bonhill Primary School
Raglan St
Ladyton Primary School
Dillichip Loan
Allan Crs
Place of Bonhill
MAIN STREET
St Ronans Primary School
Nobleston
Carman Muir
Upper Dalquhurn
Cardross Road
Carman Reservoir
Lamont Crs
Cordale Avenue
New Cordale Rd
Burns Street
Dillichip Cl
Hillfoot
Red Rw
Stirling St
Thimble St
Strathleven Drive
Sheena Dr
Kirstie Pl
Mhairi Pl
Lorraine Way
Ashley Rise
Lady's Gate
Bonhill
Carman Leisure Centre
King St
Renton Station
Back Street
Bilsland Pl
RENTON
Renton Primary School
Industrial Estate
Carman Road
Hall St
LENNOX ST
Leven St
RENTON ROAD
Clinic
Tontine
PO
1
2
3
4
5
6
7
8
36
M5, M6, M7, M8
Street names for these grid squares are listed at the back of the index
L5, M1, M2, M4
Street names for these grid squares are listed at the back of the index
K7, L1, L3, L4
Street names for these grid squares are listed at the back of the index
L2
1 Aitken La
2 Baxter La
3 Engels St
4 Levenhowe Pl
5 Levenhowe Rd
K8
1 Grant Crs
2 Station St
L7
1 Katherine Pl
2 Wylie Pl

Blairquhosh
A81
West Highland Way
Blane Water
Dumgoyach Farm
Duntreath Castle
Craigbrock
Cantywheery
Strath Balne
Middle Ballewan
Arlehaven
Aychengillan
Ardoch
Craigmore Cott
Craigmore
A809
CUILTS ROAD
B821
BALLACHALAIRY
YETT
STATION ROAD
Carbeth Ho
Easter Carbeth
Carbeth Loch
Boards
Cuilt Brae
Stirling
East Dunbartonshire
Craigallian Loch
Craigallian
Allander Water

41

1 grid square represents 500 metres

G5
1 Ballewan Crs
2 Blane Av
3 Blane Crs
4 Blane Pl
5 Cuilt Pl

H5
1 Craigmarloch Vw
2 Wester Leddriegreen Rd

H6
1 Dumbrock Dr

J6
1 Dumbrock Crs

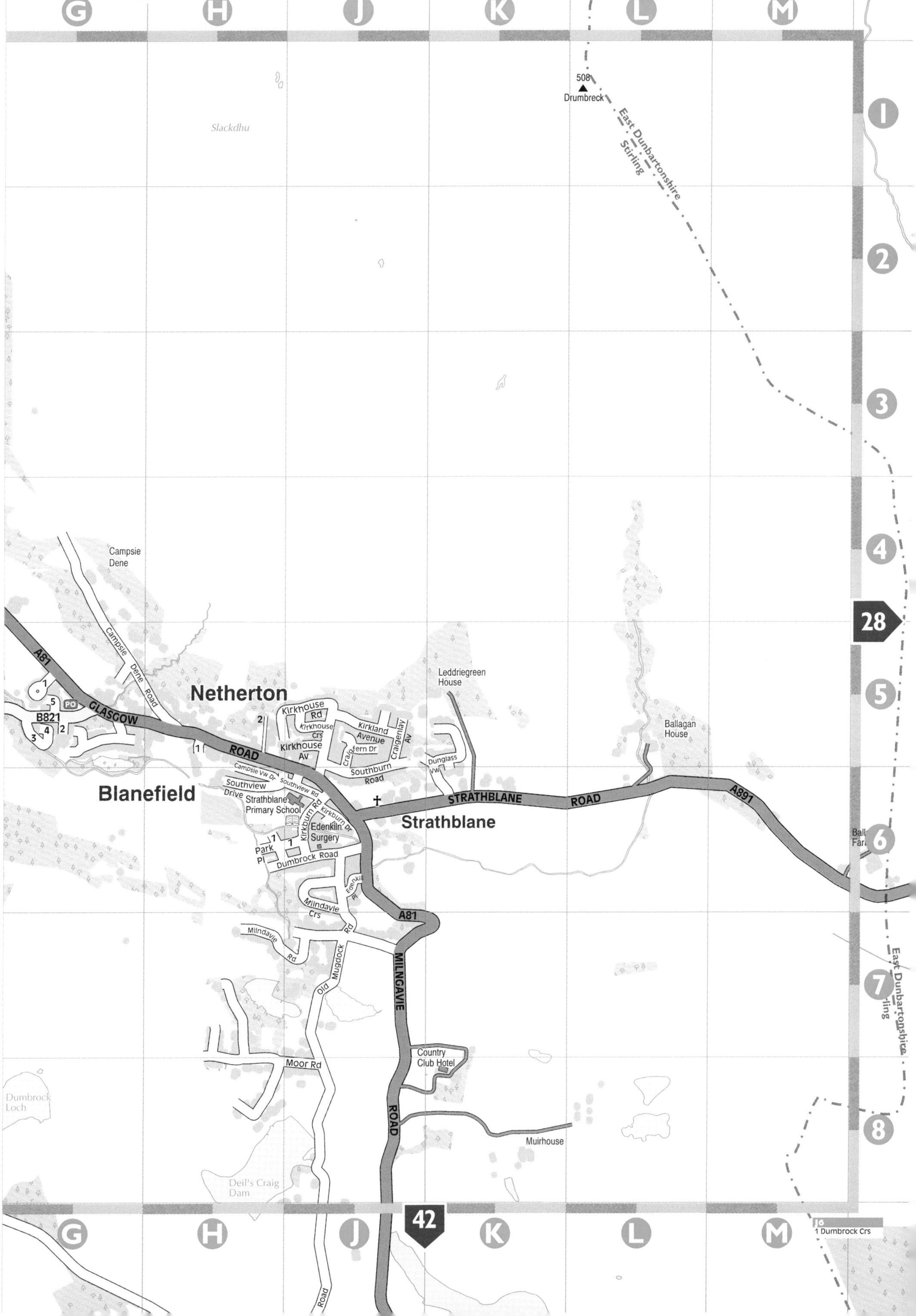

Slackdhu
508
Drumbreck
East Dunbartonshire
Stirling
Campsie Dene
Campsie Dene Road
A81
GLASGOW ROAD
B821
PO
Netherton
Blanefield
Strathblane
Kirkhouse Rd
Kirkhouse Crs
Kirkhouse Av
Kirkland Avenue
Craigenlay Av
Craigfern Dr
Southburn Road
Dunglass Vw
Campsie Vw Dr
Southview Rd
Southview Drive
Strathblane Primary School
Kirkburn Rd
Kirkburn Dr
Edenkiln Surgery
Park Pl
Dumbrock Road
Edenkiln Pl
Milndavie Crs
Milndavie Rd
Old Mugdock Road
MILNGAVIE ROAD
Moor Rd
Country Club Hotel
Muirhouse
Dumbrock Loch
Deil's Craig Dam
Leddriegreen House
Ballagan House
STRATHBLANE ROAD
A891
28
42

A
B
C
D
E
F
1
2
3
4
5
6
7
8
Fin Glen
Finglen Burn
Knocknair
Fassis
27
Knowehead
Knowehead
Ballagan Farm
Blairtummock
STRATHBLANE ROAD
Craigbarnet
A891
STRATHBLANE ROAD
Craigend Farm
East Dunbartonshire
Stirling
Lennox Castle Hospital
43
1 grid square represents 500 metres

J8 1 Crofthead Dr
L8 1 Heather Vw

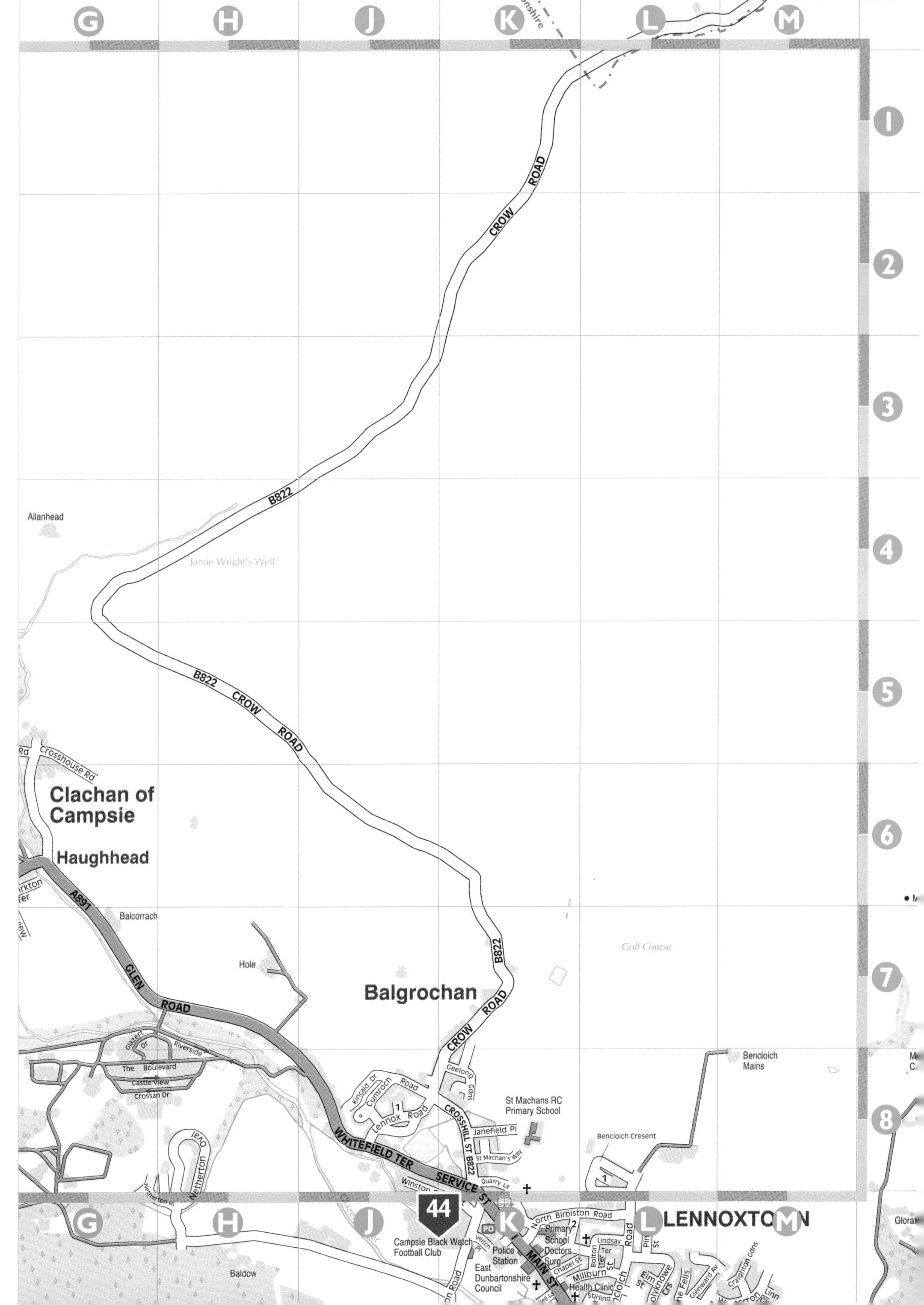
Stirling
East Dunbartonshire
CROW ROAD
B822
Allanhead
Jamie Wright's Well
B822 CROW ROAD
Crosshouse Rd
Clachan of Campsie
Haughhead
A891
Balcorrach
GLEN ROAD
Hole
Balgrochan
Golf Course
Glazert Dr
Riverside
The Boulevard
Castle View
Crossan Dr
Netherton Oval
Netherton Hl
Kincaid Dr
Cumroch Road
Lennox Road
Geelong Gdns
CROSSHILL ST B822
Janefield Pl
St Machan's Way
Quarry La
St Machans RC Primary School
Bencloich Cresent
Bencloich Mains
WHITEFIELD TER
SERVICE ST
Winston
44
Campsie Black Watch Football Club
Baldow
PO
Police Station
East Dunbartonshire Council
MAIN ST
North Birbiston Road
Primary School
Doctors Surg
Lindsay Ter
Bolton Ter
Chapel St
Millburn St
Health Clinic
LENNOXTOWN
Glenward Av
Craighton Gdns
G
H
J
K
L
M
1
2
3
4
5
6
7
8

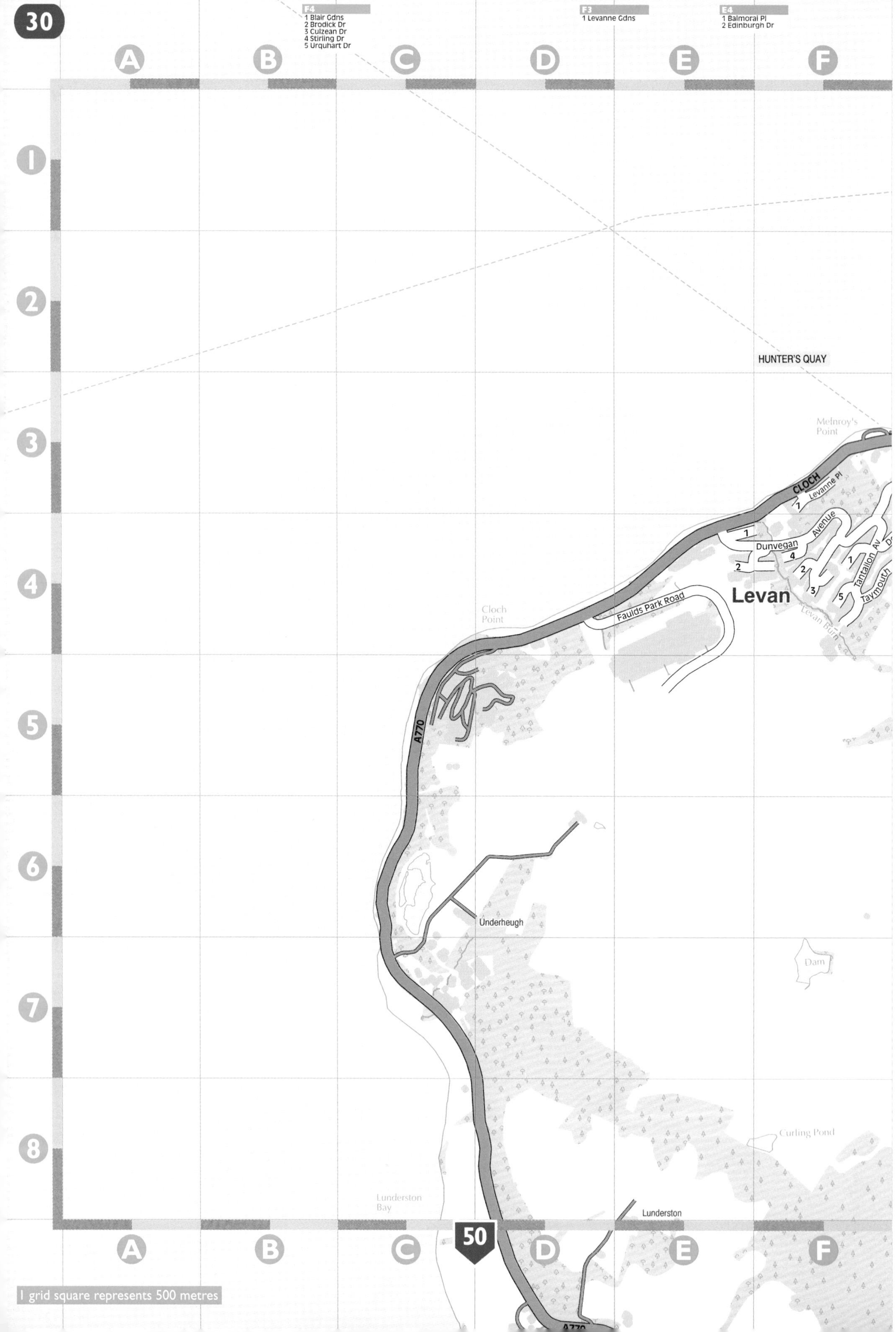
F4
1 Blair Gdns
2 Brodick Dr
3 Culzean Dr
4 Stirling Dr
5 Urquhart Dr
F3
1 Levanne Gdns
E4
1 Balmoral Pl
2 Edinburgh Dr
A
B
C
D
E
F
1
2
3
4
5
6
7
8
HUNTER'S QUAY
Melnroy's Point
CLOCH
Levanne Pl
Avenue
Dunvegan
Tantallon Av
Taymouth
Levan
Levan Burn
Fauids Park Road
Cloch Point
A770
Underheugh
Dam
Curling Pond
Lunderston Bay
Lunderston
50
1 grid square represents 500 metres

G3
1 Dunrobin Dr
2 Rosemount Pl
3 St Andrews La

H3
1 Glenbervie Pl
2 Hawthorne Pl

J2
1 Ashburn Gdns
2 Ashburn Ga
3 Ashgrove Av
4 Ashton Pl

J5
1 Berwick Rd

J3
Street names for this grid square are listed at the back of the index

J6
1 Wellyard La

J7
1 Crisswell Cl
2 Wellyard Wynd

G H J K L M
1 2 3 4 5 6 7 8
Ferry Terminal
Gourock Station
DUNOON
KEMPOCK ST
Pierhead Clinic
Gourock Health Centre
Gourock Bay
West Bay
A770
ALBERT ROAD
SHORE STREET
Bath St
St John's Road
Binnie Street
John Street
Royal Street
Gourock Central Junior School
Barrhill Road
Broomberry Drive
King St
Davidson Drive
TARBET STREET
A771
CARDWELL RO
Cove Road
Cardwell Bay
Caledonia Crs
Lochview Av
Royal Gourock Yacht Club
ASHTON ROAD
Ashton
Victoria Road
Moorfield Rd
Golf Rd
Gourock High School
Avenue
GOUROCK
Manor Road
Clyde Rd
Argyle Rd
Nelson Road
Burnside Rd
Glen Av
Duthie
Oxford
Jacobs Drive
Fletcher
Finnie Ter
Tower Drive
Divert Rd
Iona Crs
Bute St
Allsa Road
Arran Road
Drumshantie Road
Macmillan Dr
Staffa Street
Kirn Drive
Moorfoot Drive
Skye Crs
Finnart Crs
Sycamore Pl
View
Cowal Crs
Firth Crs
Turnberry Av
Cloch Brae
Cowal Avenue
Gourock Golf Club
Belleisle Pl
St Andrews Drive
Gleneagles Dr
Carnoustie Avenue
Ferry Terminal
ROAD
Moorfoot Primary School
St Ninians RC Primary School
George Road
Mathie Crs
Midton
Reservoir Road
Grenville Rd
Garvie Avenue
Hilltop Crescent
Larkfield Road
Hilltop Rd
Coves Reservoir
PA19
Cemetery
Earnhill Road
Fife Rd
Road
York Road
Dartmouth Av
Plymouth Av
Weymouth Crs
Falmouth Dr
Bournemouth Rd
Larkfield Road
Chester Rd
Inverclyde Royal Hospital
A&E
Larkfield Primary School
Sacred Heart Primary School
Westmorland Road
Cumberland Road
Stafford Road
Road
Fancy Farm
Neil
Sutherland
Gleninver Rd
Earnhill La
Banff
Caithness Road
Nairn
Larkfield
Burns Road
Cambridge Road
Devon Rd
Oxford Rd
Angus Road
Lothian Rd
Lincoln Rd
Norfolk Road
Springfield Primary School
Berwick Road
Warwick Rd
Auchmead Road
Ravenscraig Recreation Centre
Branchton Station
Jean Armour Ter
Glencairn Road
Carrick Ter
Ayr Ter
Minerva Ter
Burns Road
Road Primary School
Athole Ter
Kintyre Ter
Kinloch Ter
Kylemore Terrace
Kirkwall Road
Branchton Road
Rothesay Road
Branchton
Cupar Dr
Forfar Road
Banks
Braeside
Davaar Road
St Gabriels RC Primary School
Dalriada Rd
Braeside Rd
Juno Ter
Mars Road
Wellyard Way
Drumillan Hill
INVERKIP ROAD
Alleymill Gdns
Glenburn School
A78
Leitchland
Greenock School
Spango
Flatterton
Spango Burn
INVERKIP ROAD
IBM Station
Chrisswell
32

M2, M4, M5, M6
Street names for these grid squares are listed at the back of the index

L3, L4, L5, L6
Street names for these grid squares are listed at the back of the index

L2
1 Craigmuschat Rd
2 Darroch Av
3 Darroch Dr
4 Drumshantie Rd
5 Mccallum Crs
6 Park Ter

K6
1 Jupiter Ter

K2, K3, K5, L1
Street names for these grid squares are listed at the back of the index

K4
1 Banff Pl
2 Fife Dr
3 Nairn Dr

B5
1 Auchneagh Av
2 Curlew La
3 Delfie Dr
4 Gateside Gdns

B1
1 Battery Park Dr
2 Drums Ter
3 Kincaid St
4 Lylefoot Crs

A5, B4, B6
Street names for these grid squares are listed at the back of the index

A3
1 Falcon Crs
2 Partridge Rd

A4
1 Glamis Pl
2 Rook Rd

A1
1 Lyle Rd

A2
1 Lyle Pl
2 Woodlea La

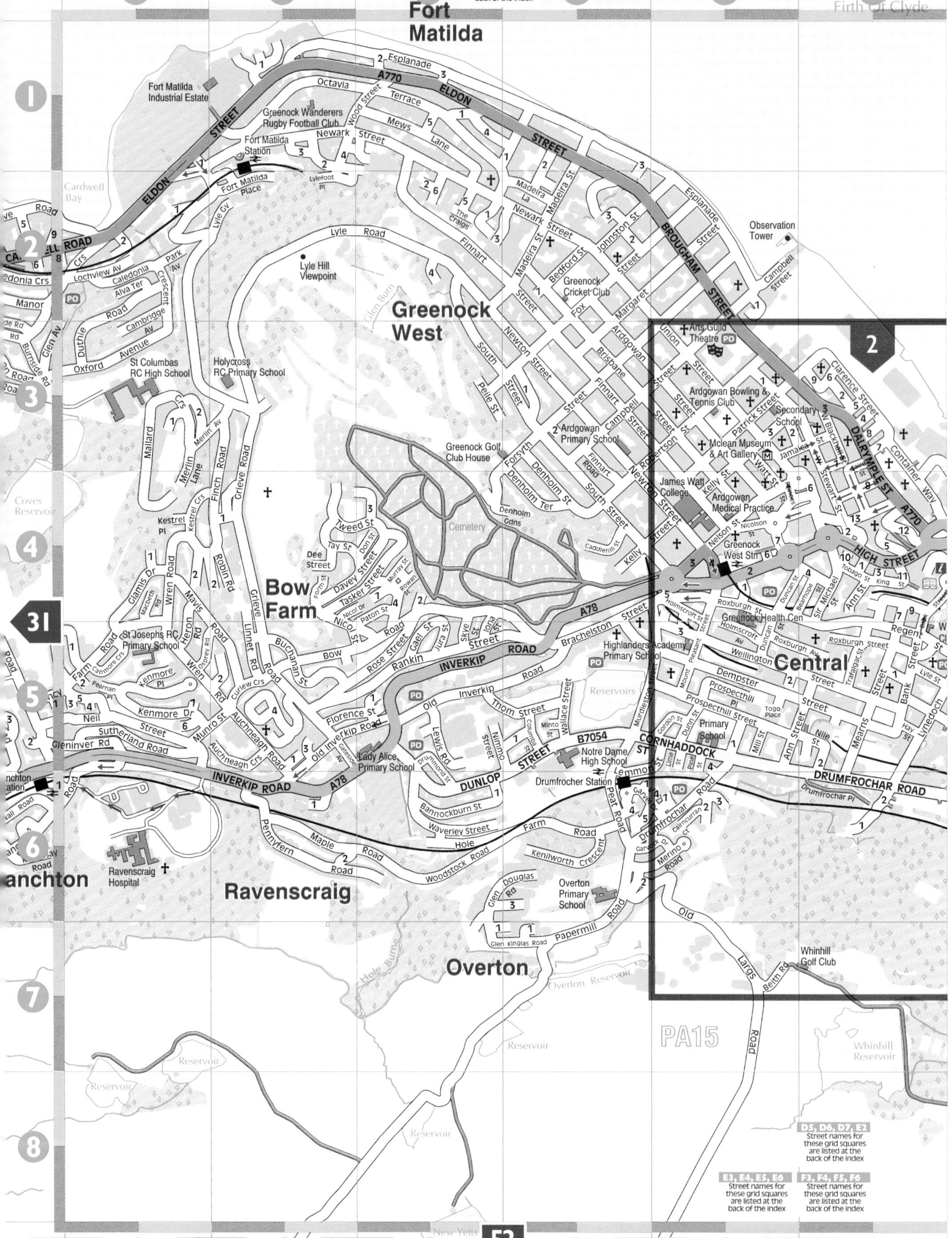

C1
1 Eldon Pl
2 North St
3 Roseneath St
4 Welbeck St
5 Westfield Dr

C2, C5
Street names for these grid squares are listed at the back of the index

C4
1 Brae Vw
2 Graham St
3 Ness Rd
4 Walker St

C6
1 Abbot St

C7
1 Glen Luss Rd

D1
Street names for this grid square are listed at the back of the index

D2
1 Bedford La
2 Glen St
3 Johnston Ter

D3
1 Carmichael St
2 Forsyth Gv

D5, D6, D7, E2
Street names for these grid squares are listed at the back of the index

E3, E4, E5, E6
Street names for these grid squares are listed at the back of the index

F3, F4, F5, F6
Street names for these grid squares are listed at the back of the index

G4, G6, H5, J6
Street names for these grid squares are listed at the back of the index

G5
1 Antigua St
2 Bogle St
3 Dellingburn St
4 Hill St
5 Station Av
6 Virginia St

H6
1 Hawick Ct
2 Kennedy's La

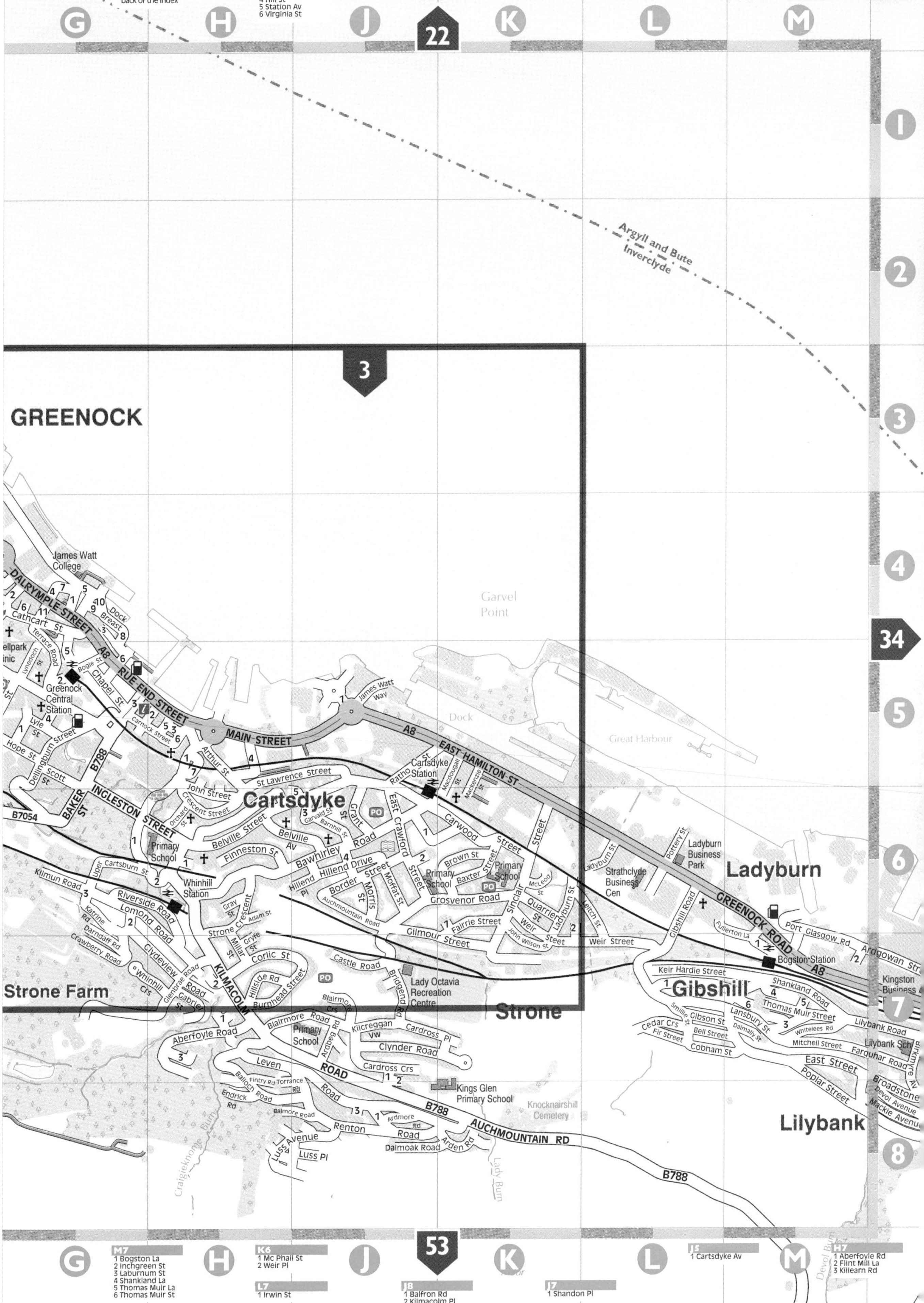

M7
1 Bogston La
2 Inchgreen St
3 Laburnum St
4 Shankland La
5 Thomas Muir La
6 Thomas Muir St

K6
1 Mc Phail St
2 Weir Pl

L7
1 Irwin St

J8
1 Balfron Rd
2 Kilmacolm Pl
3 Leven Pl

J7
1 Shandon Pl

J5
1 Cartsdyke Av

H7
1 Aberfoyle Rd
2 Flint Mill La
3 Killearn Rd

C7
1 Crawford St
2 Falconer St
3 Mirren's Shore
4 Queen St
5 Water St
6 West Quay
B8
1 Alderwood Rd
2 Bogiewood Rd
3 Duncan Rd
4 Ivybank Rd
B7
1 Anderson St
2 Belhaven St
3 Huntly Pl
4 Princes St
A7
1 Chapelton St
2 Glenburn St
3 Mary St
23
33
54
LC
LC
PORT GLASGOW
Ardgowan Street
Kingston Industrial Est
Kingston Business Park
Lilybank Road
Lilybank Sch
Port Glasgow Protestant Athletic Club
St Johns RC Primary School
Farquhar Road
Birkmyre Av
Broadstone AV
Devol Avenue
Mackie Avenue
Glenpark Drive
Rossbank Rd
Ivybank Crs
William St
Jean St
Glen Avenue
Highholm St
Brown St
Balfour St
Shore St
Huntly Ter
King Street
Princes St
Scarlow St
Fore St
Church St
John Wd
Station Rd
Court Rd
A8
Port Glasgow Health Centre
Port Glasgow Baths
Bay Street
Newark Castle
Castle Rd
Highholm Av
Highholm Primary School
Port Glasgow Station
Lochview Rd
Ardenclutha Dr
Hillside Dr
Alderbank Road
Alderbrae Road
Springhill Road
Barrs Brae La
Glenhuntly Road
Glenhuntly Terrace
Angus Rd
Berwick Road
Kinross Avenue
Moray Road
Ardmore Road
Barr's Brae
Bouverie St
Lwr Bouverie St
GLASGOW RD A761
Ashgrove Lane
Wilson St
Bruce St
Wallace St
Robert Street
Clune Park Primary School
CLUNE BRAE A761
Clune Brae
Benclutha
GREENOCK ROAD A8
Fyfe Shore Rd
Fyffe Pk
Kelburn Terrace
PO
Glasgow Road
Cemetery
West Dougliehill
Dougliehill Road
Reservoir
Devol Burn
C8
1 Roseyard Pl
2 Willison's La
D8
1 Caledonia St
2 Montgomerie St
3 Newark Pl
E8
1 Clune Park St
2 Maxwell St
Burnhead Rd
Auchenfoil La
Auchenfoil Rd
Duchal St
Gareloch Lane
Gareloch Road
Muirshiel
Dubbs Road
Devol
Devol Industrial Est
Bridgend Avenue
Boglestone
West Rd
North Road
South Road
Primary School
Brookfield Road
Westfield Rd
Northfield
Mid Avenue
1 grid square represents 500 metres

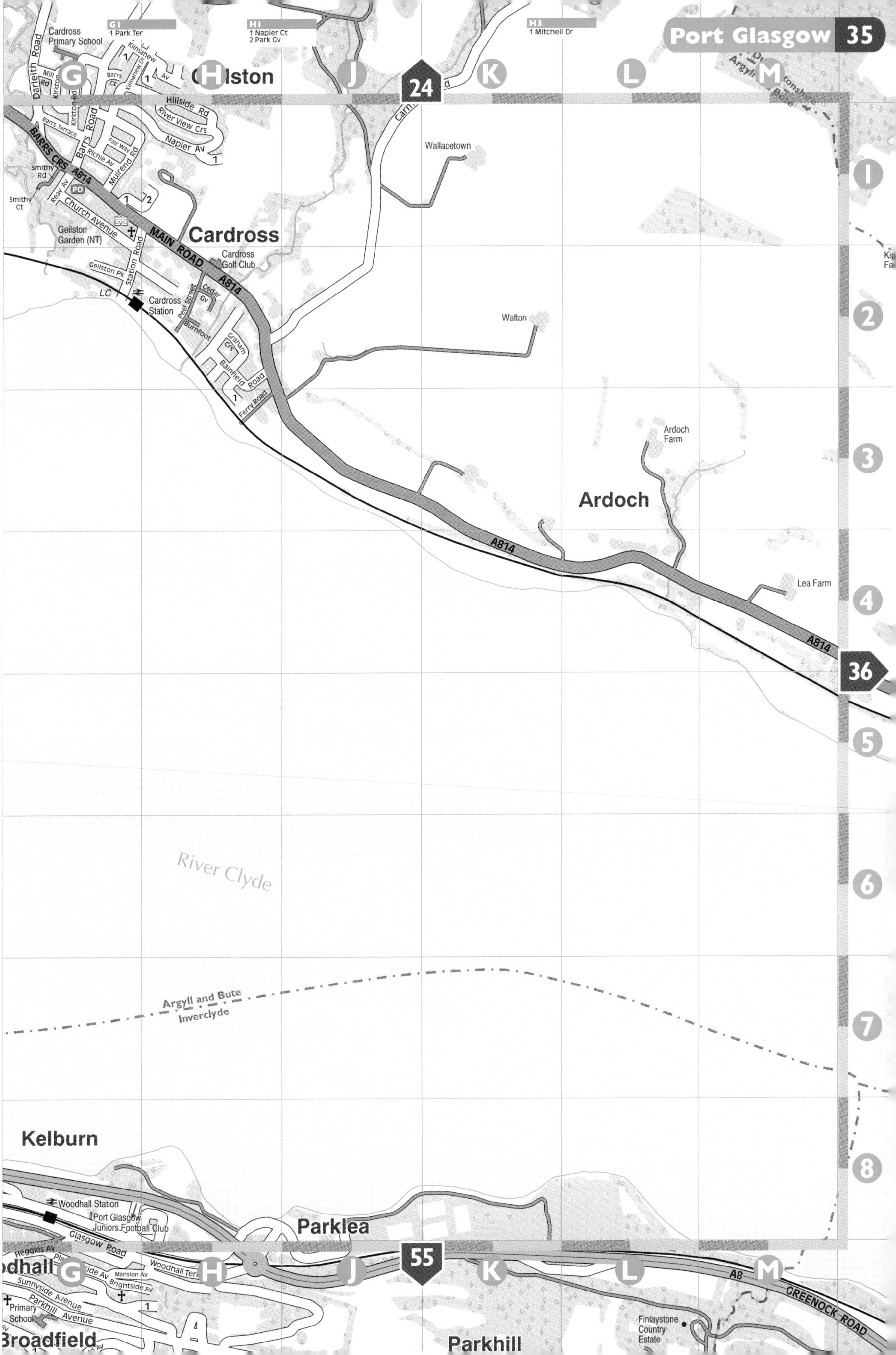
G1
1 Park Ter
H1
1 Napier Ct
2 Park Gv
H3
1 Mitchell Dr
Cardross Primary School
Darleith Road
Kilmahew
Kirkton Rd
Barrs Ct
Hillside Rd
River View Crs
Napier Av
Barrs Terrace
BARRS CRS
A814
Barrs Road
Fair Way Rd
Richie Av
Muirend Rd
Smithy Rd
Smithy Ct
Reay Av
PO
Church Avenue
Geilston Garden (NT)
MAIN ROAD
Cardross
Cardross Golf Club
Geilston Pk
Station Road
LC
Cardross Station
Peel Street
Cedar Gv
Burnfoot
Graham Crs
Bainfield Road
Ferry Road
Wallacetown
Walton
Ardoch Farm
Ardoch
A814
Lea Farm
River Clyde
Argyll and Bute
Inverclyde
Kelburn
Woodhall Station
Port Glasgow Juniors Football Club
Glasgow Road
Parklea
Heggies Av
Mansion Av
Brightside Av
Woodhall Ter
Sunnyside Avenue
Parkhill Avenue
Primary School
Broadfield
Parkhill
Finlaystone Country Estate
A8
GREENOCK ROAD
Argyll and Bute
G
H
J
K
L
M
1
2
3
4
5
6
7
8
24
36
55

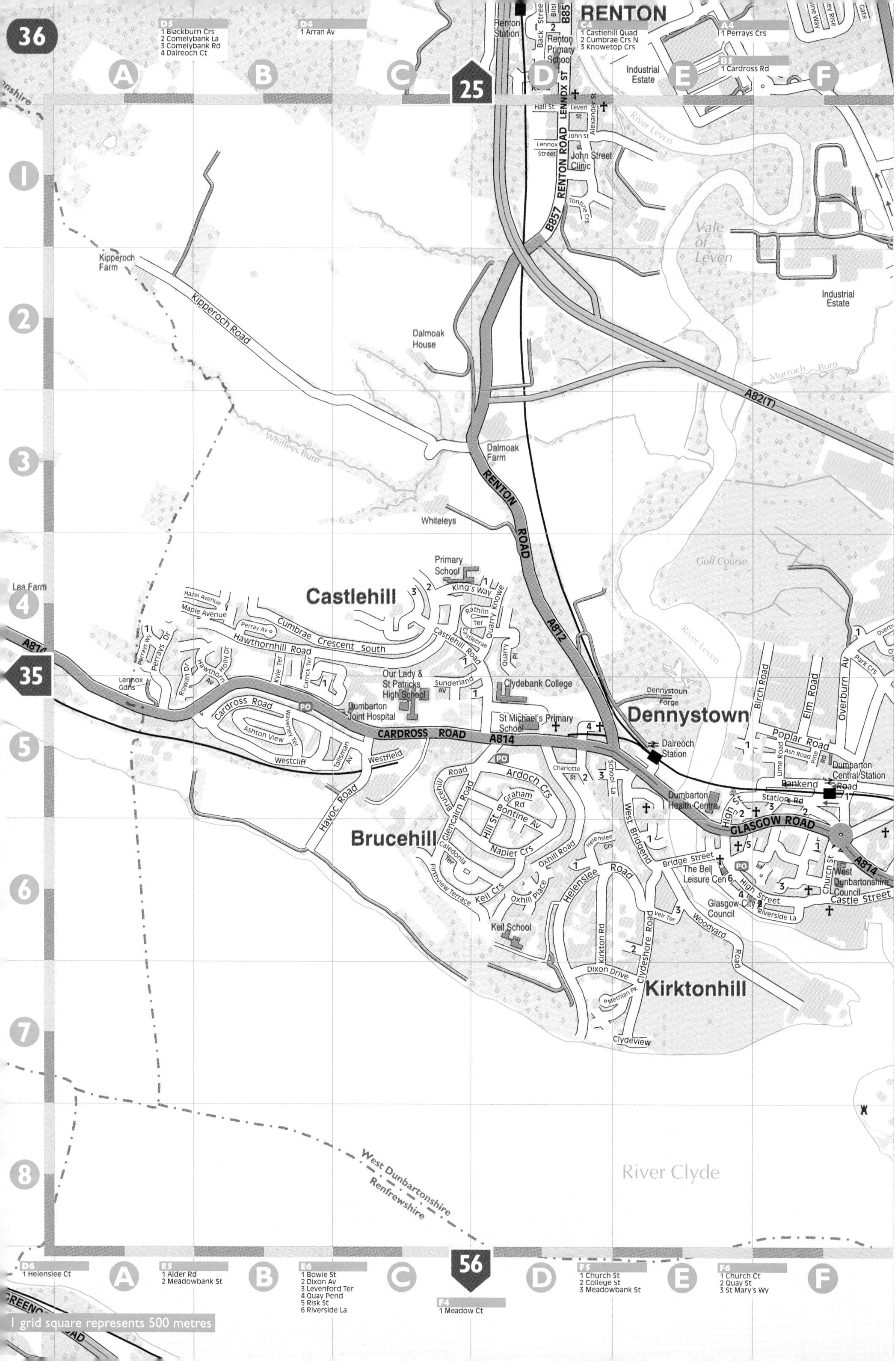
D5
1 Blackburn Crs
2 Comelybank La
3 Comelybank Rd
4 Dalreoch Ct
D4
1 Arran Av
C4
1 Castlehill Quad
2 Cumbrae Crs N
3 Knowetop Crs
A4
1 Perrays Crs
B5
1 Cardross Rd
RENTON
Renton Station
Renton Primary School
Industrial Estate
25
35
56
A
B
C
D
E
F
1
2
3
4
5
6
7
8
Hall St
Leven St
John St
Lennox Street
Alexander St
LENNOX ST
RENTON ROAD
John Street Clinic
Tontine Crs
B857
B85
River Leven
Vale of Leven
Industrial Estate
Kipperoch Farm
Kipperoch Road
Dalmoak House
Murroch Burn
A82(T)
Whitleys Burn
Dalmoak Farm
RENTON ROAD
Whiteleys
Golf Course
Lea Farm
Primary School
King's Way
Castlehill
Hazel Avenue
Maple Avenue
Perray Av
Cumbrae Crescent South
Hawthornhill Road
Rathlin Ter
Quarry Knowe
Castlebrae
Castlehill Road
Quarry Pl
A812
River Leven
A814
Perrays Wy
Perrays Dr
Rowan Dr
Hawthorn Av
Holly Dr
Kyle Ter
Carrick Ter
Lennox Gdns
Our Lady & St Patricks High School
Sunderland Av
Clydebank College
Dennystoun Forge
Dennystown
Birch Road
Elm Road
Overburn Av
Park Crs
Cardross Road
Waverley Ter
Ashton View
Westcliff
Talisman Av
Dumbarton Joint Hospital
PO
CARDROSS ROAD
A814
St Michael's Primary School
Dalreoch Station
Poplar Road
Lime Road
Ash Road
Pine Rd
Dumbarton Central Station
Westfield
Charlotte St
School La
Bankend Road
Station Rd
Havoc Road
Road
Ardoch Crs
Graham Rd
Bontine Av
Glencairn Road
Brucehill
Hill St
Napier Crs
West Bridgend
Dumbarton Health Centre
High St
GLASGOW ROAD
A814
Caledonia Ter
Firthview Terrace
Keil Crs
Oxhill Place
Oxhill Road
Helenslee Crs
Helenslee Road
Bridge Street
The Bell Leisure Cen
High Street
Church St
West Dunbartonshire Council
Castle Street
Glasgow City Council
Riverside La
Veir Ter
Woodyard Road
Keil School
Kirkton Rd
Clydeshore Road
Dixon Drive
Methlan Pk
Kirktonhill
Clydeview
River Clyde
West Dunbartonshire
Renfrewshire
D6
1 Helenslee Ct
E5
1 Alder Rd
2 Meadowbank St
E6
1 Bowie St
2 Dixon Av
3 Levenford Ter
4 Quay Pend
5 Risk St
6 Riverside La
F4
1 Meadow Ct
F5
1 Church St
2 College St
3 Meadowbank St
F6
1 Church Ct
2 Quay St
3 St Mary's Wy
1 grid square represents 500 metres

G4 1 Doveholm
G5 1 Alexander St
G6 1 Knoxland Sq 2 Lennox St

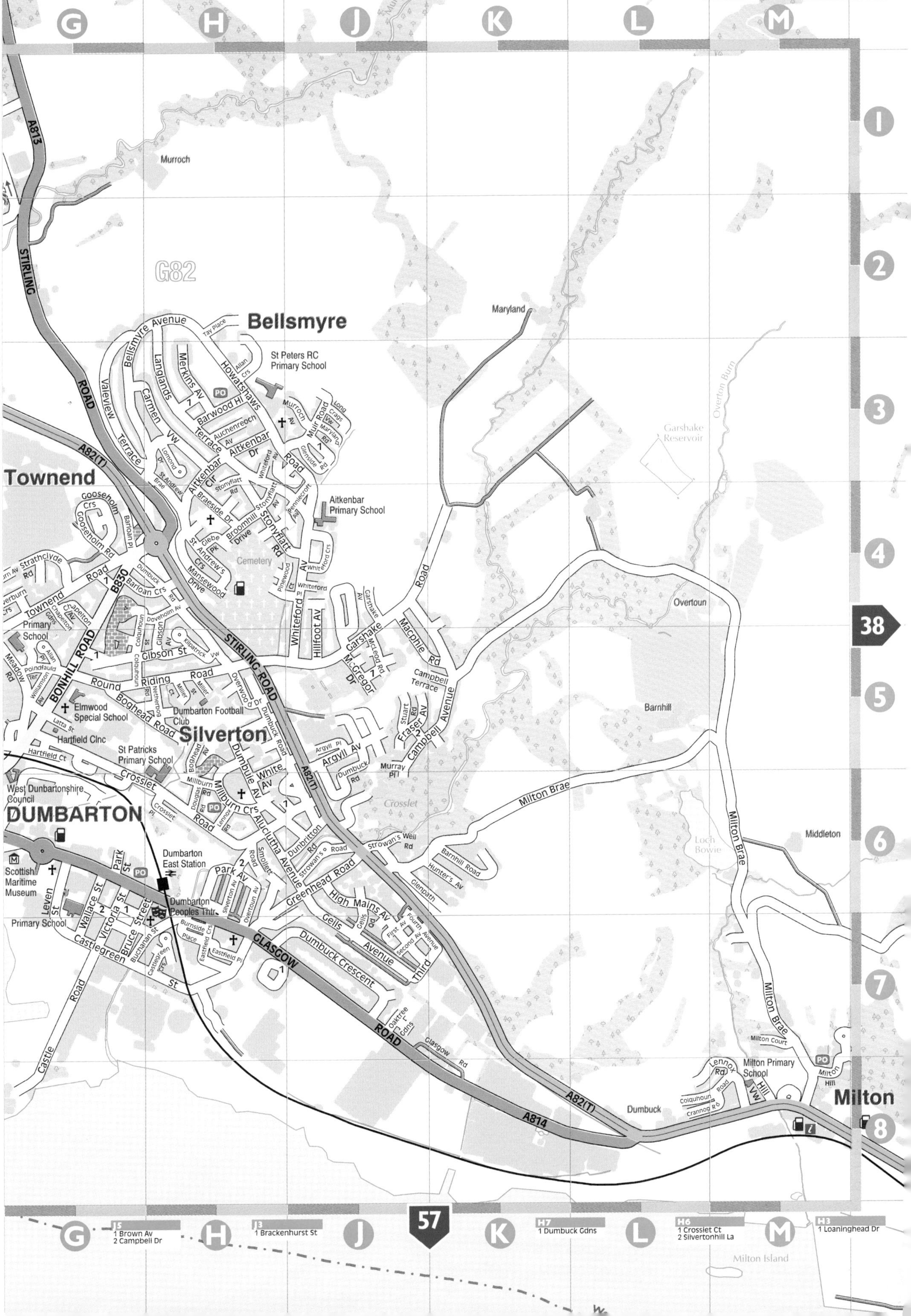

G H J K L M
1 2 3 4 5 6 7 8
38
Murroch
Murroch Burn
A813
STIRLING ROAD
G82
Bellsmyre
Bellsmyre Avenue
St Peters RC Primary School
Maryland
Garshake Reservoir
Overton Burn
Townend
Aitkenbar Primary School
Cemetery
Overtoun
Barnhill
Silverton
Dumbarton Football Club
Elmwood Special School
Hartfield Clnc
St Patricks Primary School
West Dunbartonshire Council
DUMBARTON
Crosslet
Milton Brae
Middleton
Loch Bowie
Dumbarton East Station
Scottish Maritime Museum
Dumbarton Peoples Thtr
Primary School
GLASGOW ROAD
A82(T)
A814
Dumbuck
Milton Primary School
Milton
Bonhill Road
B830
Castle Road
Greenhead Road
Dumbuck Crescent
Strowan's Well Rd
Campbell Avenue
Macphie Rd
Garshake Road

J5 1 Brown Av 2 Campbell Dr
J3 1 Brackenhurst St
H7 1 Dumbuck Gdns
H6 1 Crosslet Ct 2 Silvertonhill La
H3 1 Loaninghead Dr

Milton Island

A
B
C
D
E
F
1
2
3
4
5
6
7
8
37
58
Fyn Loch
Black Linn Reservoir
Lang Craigs
Darnycaip
Loch Humphrey
Creigarestie
Greenland Reservoir
Rigangower
Greenland
PO
Milton Hill
Milton
Auchentorlie House
Kilpatrick Braes
A82(T)
Bowli
GREAT-WESTE ROAD
2
A814
DUMBARTON ROAD
Scott Av
Manse Road
PO
1
Bowling
1 grid square represents 500 metres

G
H
J
K
L
M
1
2
3
4
5
6
7
8
Lily Loch
Saughen Braes
Duncolm
Craighirst
40
Greenside Reservoir
Boglairoch
Loch Humphrey Burn
Wester Cochno
59
60
Craigleith

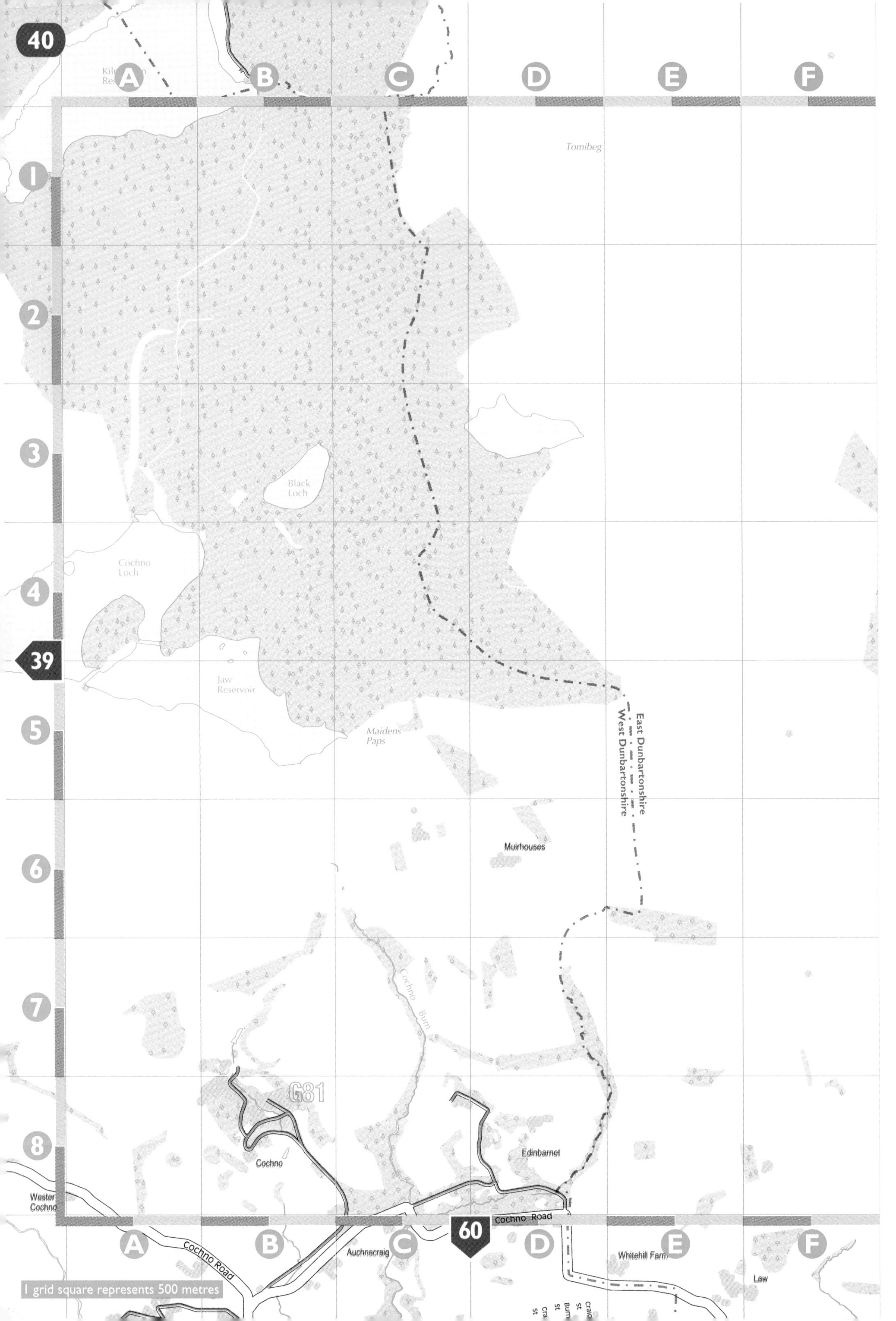
A
B
C
D
E
F
1
2
3
4
5
6
7
8
Tomibeg
Black Loch
Cochno Loch
39
Jaw Reservoir
Maidens Paps
East Dunbartonshire
West Dunbartonshire
Muirhouses
Cochno Burn
G81
Cochno
Edinbarnet
Wester Cochno
Cochno Road
60
Auchnacraig
Whitehill Farm
Law
1 grid square represents 500 metres

J6
1 Douglas Muir Gdns
K7
1 Auldmurroch Dr
2 Craighurst Rd
3 Garvel Pl
L6
1 Clober Farm La
2 Ker Rd
Stirling
East Dunbartonshire
Craigallian Loch
Dumbrock Loch
West Highland Way
26
Allander Water
Craigallian
Visitors Centre
Golf Club
A809
Mugdock Castle
Mugdock Wood
High Craigton
Carneddans Wood
Laighpark
Low Craighton
Milngavie Golf Club
42
The Loan
Carneddans Road
Craigton Burn
G62
Tambowie
Little Balvie
Crossburn
Douglas Muir
School
Craigton Road
Clober Golf Course Club House
Clober Primary School
St Josephs School
Clober Road
B8050
Craigdhu Rd
Stock Road
61
Craigdhu Road
Windyhill
M6
1 Birrell Rd
2 Cloberfield Gdns
3 Clochbar Av
4 Dunlop Pl
5 Stable Pl
6 Watt Pl
L8
1 Cairnlea Rd
2 Cauldstream Pl
Preston field
Keystone
Forrest Dr
Nasmyth Av
Moorfoot Way
Alston Gdns
Rutherford Av
Abercrombie Drive
Kilpatrick Dr
Fintry Gdns
Paterson Pl
Culloch Rd
G H J K L M
1 2 3 4 5 6 7 8

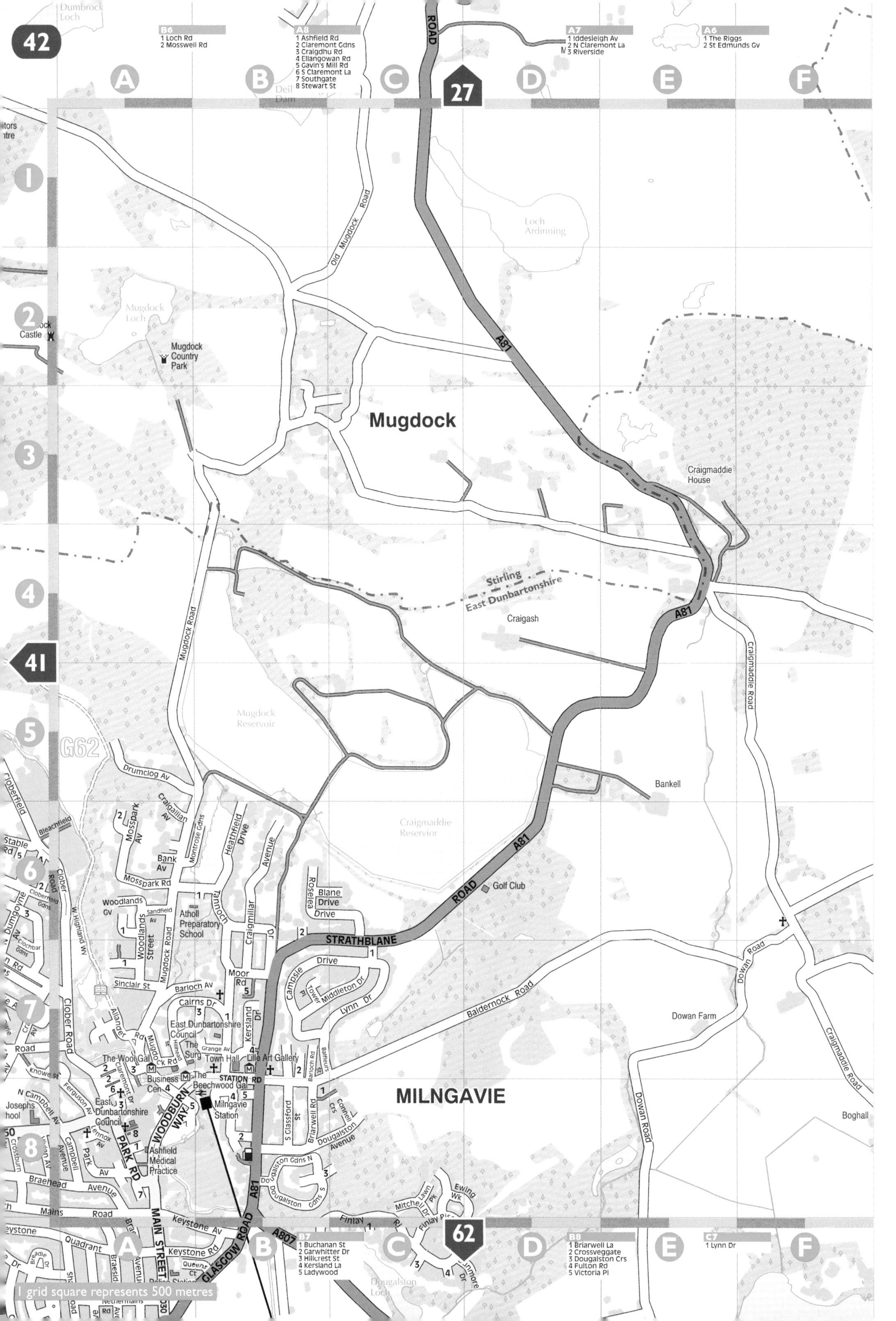
B6
1 Loch Rd
2 Mosswell Rd
A8
1 Ashfield Rd
2 Claremont Gdns
3 Craigdhu Rd
4 Ellangowan Rd
5 Gavin's Mill Rd
6 S Claremont La
7 Southgate
8 Stewart St
A7
1 Iddesleigh Av
2 N Claremont La
3 Riverside
A6
1 The Riggs
2 St Edmunds Gv
27
41
62
B7
1 Buchanan St
2 Garwhitter Dr
3 Hillcrest St
4 Kersland La
5 Ladywood
B8
1 Briarwell La
2 Crossveggate
3 Dougalston Crs
4 Fulton Rd
5 Victoria Pl
C7
1 Lynn Dr
Dumbrock Loch
Deil Dam
ROAD
Old Mugdock Road
Loch Ardinning
Mugdock Loch
Mugdock Country Park
Castle
A81
Mugdock
Craigmaddie House
Stirling
East Dunbartonshire
Craigash
Mugdock Road
Mugdock Reservoir
G62
Drumclog Av
Bankell
Craigmaddie Reservior
Craigmaddie Road
Golf Club
STRATHBLANE ROAD
Blane Drive
Roselea Drive
Heathfield Drive
Montrose Gdns
Craigallian Av
Mosspark Av
Bank Av
Mosspark Rd
Woodlands Gv
Woodlands Street
Sandfield Av
Mugdock Road
Atholl Preparatory School
Tannoch Dr
Craigmillar Avenue
Campsie Drive
Tower Pl
Middleton Dr
Lynn Dr
Moor Rd
Barloch Av
Sinclair St
Cairns Dr
East Dunbartonshire Council
Kersland Dr
Baldernock Road
Dowan Road
Dowan Farm
Craigmaddie Road
The Surg
Grange Av
Town Hall
Lillie Art Gallery
The Wool Gal
Business Cen
The Beechwood Gal
STATION RD
Barloch Rd
Balfleurs St
WOODBURN WAY
Milngavie Station
MILNGAVIE
Dowan Road
Boghall
S Glassford St
Briarwell Rd
Connell Crs
Dougalston Avenue
Dougalston Gdns N
Dougalston Gdns S
A81
Clober Road
Cloberfield
Bleachfield
W Highland Wy
Clober Road
Allander Rd
Knowes St
Ferguson Av
Claremont Dr
East Dunbartonshire Council
N Campbell Av
Josephs
Lennox Av
PARK RD
Ashfield Medical Practice
Campbell Avenue
Park Av
Braehead Avenue
Crossburn
Mains Road
Keystone Av
Keystone Rd
Quadrant
MAIN STREET
GLASGOW ROAD
A807
Finlay Ri
Finlay Rise
Mitchell Dr
Lawn Pk
Ewing Wk
Dunmore Dr
Dougalston Loch
Queens Ct
A
B
C
D
E
F
1
2
3
4
5
6
7
8
1 grid square represents 500 metres

G
H
J
28
K
L
M
1
2
3
4
44
5
6
7
8
Craigend Muir
Craigmaddie Muir
Blairskaith Muir
Newlands
North Blochairn
Blochairn
Blairskaith
Tower Road
Barraston Farm
Baldernock
North Bardowie
Glenorchard Road
Hillhead
Back O' Hill Road
Baldernock School
Fluchter
Fluchter Road
Back O' Hill
Craighead
Barnellan
Golf Course
63
Golf Club
Golf Course Rd
Balmore

E2
1 Argyle Gdns
St Machans RC
Primary Sc
D1
1 School La
2 Statefield
B8
1 Michael
Mcparland Dr
Bencloich Cresent
Castle View
Crossan Dr
Cumrock Road
Lennox Road
Kincaid
CROSSHILL ST B822
Janefield Pl
St Mac
Quarry La
WHITEFIELD TER
29
Netherton Oval
Netherton Hl
Glazert Water
LENNOXTOWN
North Birbiston Road
Campsie Black Watch
Football Club
Veitch Pl
Police
Station
Primary
School
Doctors
Surg
Chapel St
A891
MAIN ST
East
Dunbartonshire
Council
Well La
Lindsay Ter
Bolton Ter
Millburn St
Health Clinic
Stirling Pl
Bencloich Road
Pine St
Elm St
Holyknowe Crs
The Fells
Glenward Av
Craighton Gdns
Linn Gln
Westerton
Glorat Av
Hillview Av
Holyknowe Rd
Ashcroft Av
Benvue Road
Warren Wk
Meikle Bin Brae
Bluebell Wy
Redhills Vw
Campsie
Recreation
Centre
MILTON RD
ROWANTREE
PLACE
Glazert Meadow
Glazert Pk Dr
Morrison Dr
Baldow
Station Road
South Brae
Westerton
ROWANTREE TER
West
Muckcroft
Muirhead
G66
Barrhill
B822
43
Upper
Carlestoun
Kinkell
Langshot
Farm
Whitehill
Barraston Road
Acre Valley
House
Balquharrage
Acre Valley Road
CAMPSIE ROAD
Carlston
Balgrochan
Wardend Rd
W Balgrochan Road
Nevis Dr
Kings Pk
Road
Blair Gdns
Campbell Pl
Maitland Drive
Buchanan Pl
School
Mill Crs
Moray Dr
Atholl Av
Torrance
Primary School
West Rd
Park Crs
Woodmill Dr
Hayston
Golf Course
Torrance
Dalriada Dr
Cormack Av
Hawthorn St
Viola Pl
Guthrie Pl
B822
Tower Rd
Smeaton Av
Dundas Av
Ballencrieff Av
Forth Rd
Clyde Av
MAIN ST
Rosehill
Firbank Av
Kelvin Vw
Allander Dr
Craigmarloch Av
Queens Vw
Firbank Av
River Kelvin
64
A
B
C
D
E
F
1
2
3
4
5
6
7
8
1 grid square represents 500 metres

J8
1 Braehead St
2 West High St

K8
1 Peter D.stirling Rd

L8
1 Broomhill Fm Ms
2 Cleddans Rd
3 Daniel Mclaughlin Pl
4 Hardmuir Gdns

G
H
J
K
L
M
1
2
3
4
5
6
7
8
46
65
Glorat House
Drumairn
Sheilds Cottage
Alloch Dam
Mount Dam
Newmill
A891 CAMPSIE ROAD
Valleyfield
Mount Pleasant Crs
Glazert Water
Lochalsh Crs
Lochiel
Drive
Craighead Rd
Derrywood Rd
Craighead Primary School
Scott Av
PO
Antermony Loch
Greta Meek La
Elizabeth Av
Archibald Ter
Marley Way
James Leeson Ct
Hillside Ter
Laburnum Drive
Cairnview Road
Beechtree Ter
Irvine Gdns
Chestnut
Harkness Av
Montgomery
Kirkton Crs
Camperton
Kincaid Wy
Glenburn Crs
Linden Lea
Blair Dr
Kincaid Field
Redmoss Road
Glazert Pl
Maple Av
Willow Dr
B757
Munro Dr
Alder
Rowan Av
Poplar Dr
Larch Gv
Cedar
Briar Bk
Sycamore Wy
Drive
Cherry Pl
Limetree Walk
Juniper Drive
Hazel Bank
Road
ANTERMONY ROAD
A891
Milton of Campsie
Alton Farm
Redmoss Farm
BIRDSTON ROAD
Glazert Water
Wetshod
Inchbelle Farm
Birdston
Kirkintilloch Golf Course
River Kelvin
Broomhill Industrial Estate
A803
MILTON ROAD B757
Forth & Clyde Canal
Alisa Dr
Pro Bowl
Kirkintilloch Industrial Estate
Harestanes
Kirkintilloch Road
Springfield
Kelvinvale
Eastside Industrial Estate
Arran Dr
Whitehill Av
Campsie Rd
High Street Industrial Estate
KILSYTH RD
Banks Rd
Grahamsdyke Rd
Langmuir Av
Fell Vw
Afton Vw
Burns
Alloway Gv
Alloway
Alloway Ter
Doon Wy
Burns Rd
Road
Eastside
Turret Theatre
Hillhead Rd
Sheils Rd
Merkland School
PO
Hayston
Kelvin Ct
Norwood Avenue
Claremont Avenue
E High St
Canal Street
Redbrae
Meiklehill
Road
St Flannans RC Primary School
Merkland Pl
Auld Kirk Museum
John St
Meiklehill Ct
Highfield
Road
Merkland
A803
York Place Surgery
Town Hall
Waverley Park Day Hospital
Rosebank Av
Newdyke
Washington Rd
A8006
LAIRDSLAND RD
Road
Avenue
GLASGOW RD
Kelvin Wy
Adams
Glasgow Rd
Bellevue Road
Byars Road
Doctors Surgery
Primary School
Southbank Surgery
Marmion Dr
Quarry Drive
St Marys Primary School
Rob Roy Football Club
Fraser Gdns
Coxdale Av
Beaufort Drive
Bellfield Road
Northbank Rd
Victoria St
Alexandra Street
Kirkintilloch Foot Clinic
Waverley Crs
Kenilworth Road
Ivanhoe Drive
Eildon Road
Border Way
Briar Road
Croft
Friars
PO
Barrhill

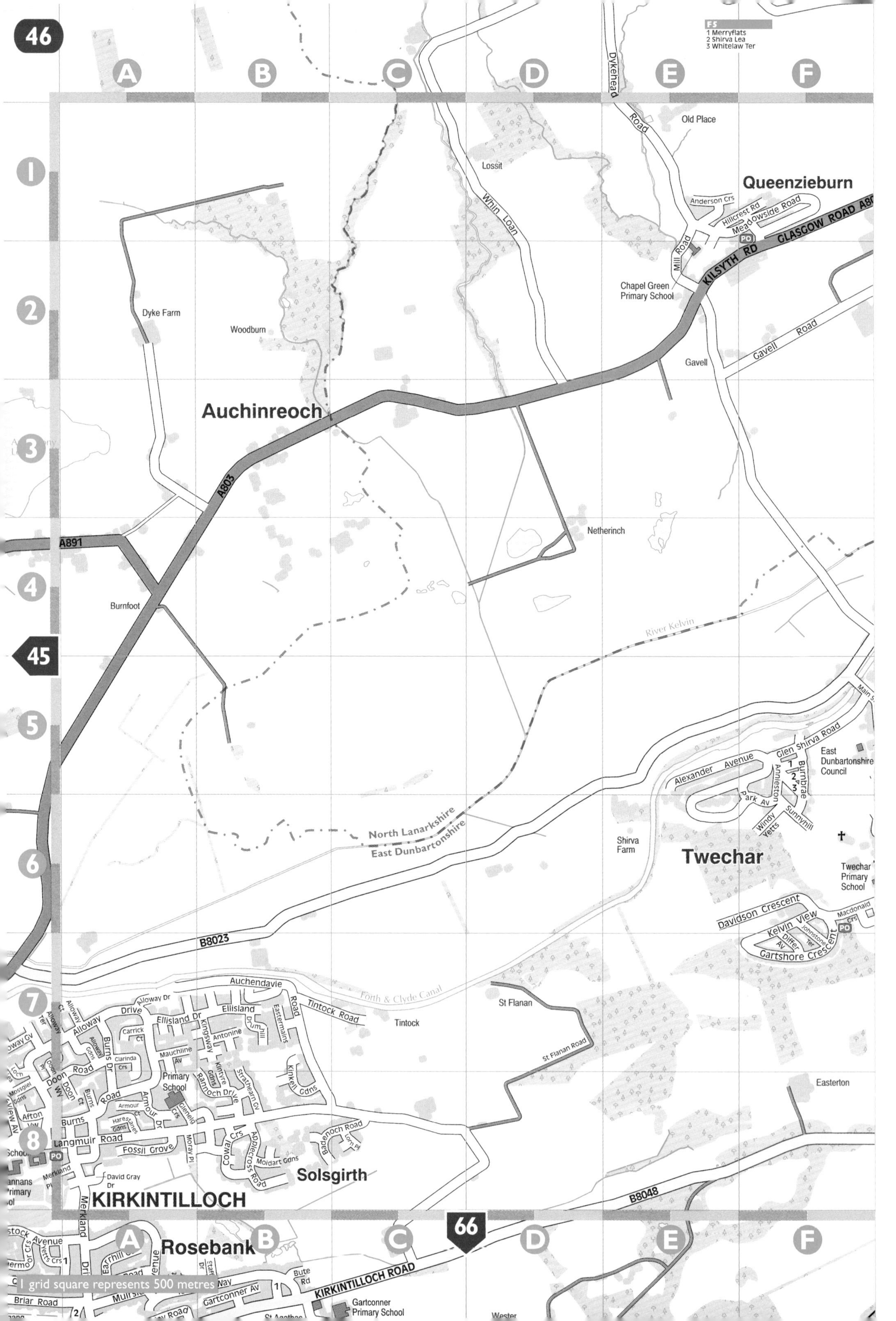
F5
1 Merryflats
2 Shirva Lea
3 Whitelaw Ter
A
B
C
D
E
F
1
2
3
4
5
6
7
8
45
66
Dykehead Road
Old Place
Lossit
Queenzieburn
Anderson Crs
Hillcrest Rd
Meadowside Road
GLASGOW ROAD A803
KILSYTH RD
Mill Road
PO
Whin Loan
Chapel Green Primary School
Dyke Farm
Woodburn
Gavell
Gavell Road
Auchinreoch
A803
Netherinch
A891
Burnfoot
River Kelvin
Main St
Glen Shirva Road
East Dunbartonshire Council
Alexander Avenue
Burnbrae
Annieston
Park Av
Sunnyhill
Windy Yetts
Shirva Farm
Twechar
North Lanarkshire
East Dunbartonshire
Twechar Primary School
Davidson Crescent
Macdonald Crs
Kelvin View
Johnstone Ter
Differ Av
Gartshore Crescent
B8023
Auchendavie
Auchendavie Road
Forth & Clyde Canal
Tintock Road
Tintock
St Flanan
St Flanan Road
Alloway Dr
Alloway Drive
Ellisland Dr
Ellisland
Eastermains
Drumhill
Carrick Ct
Kingsway
Antonine
Burns Dr
Clarinda Crs
Mauchline Av
Primary School
Doon Road
Kintyre Gdns
Strathearn Gv
Kinkell Gdns
Ramnoch Drive
Armour Dr
Glenfield Crs
Afton Vw
Burns Road
Langmuir Road
Fossil Grove
Moray Pl
Cowal Crs
Applecross Road
Moldart Gdns
Badenoch Road
Lorn Pl
Solsgirth
Merkland Pl
David Gray Dr
KIRKINTILLOCH
Merkland
Easterton
B8048
Rosebank
Bute Rd
Gartconner Av
KIRKINTILLOCH ROAD
Gartconner Primary School
Briar Road
Wester
St Agathas
1 grid square represents 500 metres

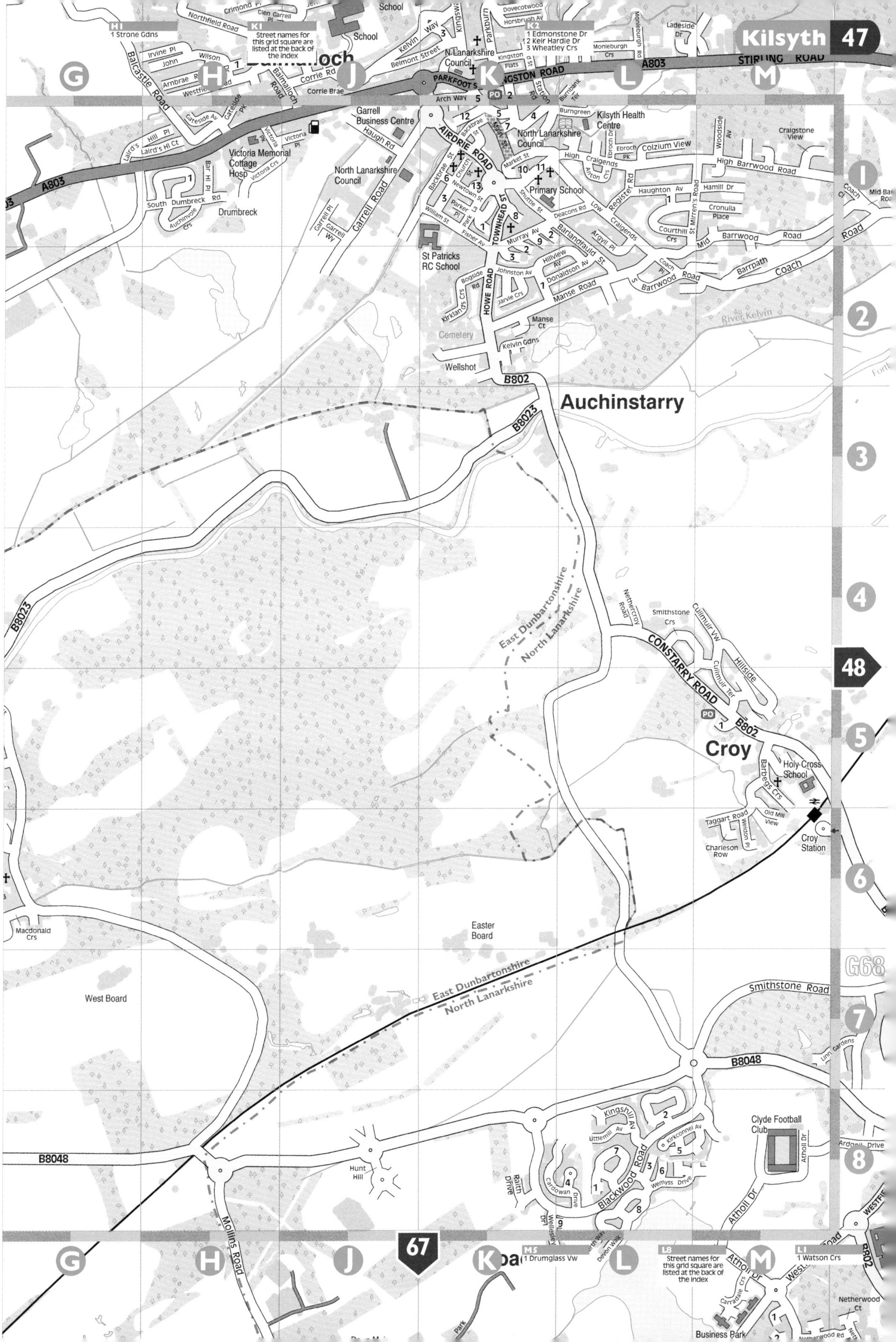
H1
1 Strone Gdns
K1
Street names for this grid square are listed at the back of the index
K2
1 Edmonstone Dr
2 Keir Hardie Dr
3 Wheatley Crs
School
Crimond Pl
Glen Garrell Pl
Northfield Road
Kelvin Way
Belmont Street
Kingsway
Parkburn
Dovecotwood
Horsbrugh Av
Ladeside Dr
Monieburgh Rd
Monieburgh Crs
N. Lanarkshire Council
Kingston Flats
Irvine Pl
John
Wilson
Arnbrae Rd
Westfield Rd
Balcastle Road
Balmalloch Road
Corrie Rd
Corrie Brae
Parkfoot St
Kingston Road
A803
Stirling Road
Arch Way
Station Rd
Burnbank Ter
Burngreen
Kilsyth Health Centre
Garrell Business Centre
Haugh Rd
Gateside Av
Gateside Pk
Victoria Pk
Victoria Pl
Laird's Pl
Laird's Hl Ct
Hill Pl
Victoria Memorial Cottage Hosp
Victoria Crs
North Lanarkshire Council
Backbrae St
Main St
Airdrie Road
North Lanarkshire Council
Ebroch Dr
Ebroch Pk
Colzium View
Woodside Av
Craigstone View
High Barrwood Road
High Craigends
Anton Crs
Market St
Primary School
Register Rd
Haughton Av
St Mirren's Road
Hamill Dr
Cronulla Place
Courthill Crs
Mid Barrwood Road
Coach Rd
Mid Barrwood Road
Bar Hl Pl
South Dumbreck Rd
Auchinvole Crs
Drumbreck
Garrell Pl
Garrell Wy
Garrell Road
Church St
Newtown St
Backbrae St
Parker La
Park Pl
William St
Fisher Av
Shuttle St
Townhead St
Deacons Rd
Low Craigends
Argyll Pl
Barlandfauld St
Murray Av
Hillview Av
Donaldson Av
Manse Road
Coach Pl
S Barrwood Road
Barrpath
Coach Road
St Patricks RC School
Bogside Rd
Kirklands Crs
Johnston Av
Howe Road
Jarvie Crs
Manse Ct
Kelvin Gdns
Cemetery
Wellshot
River Kelvin
B802
Auchinstarry
B8023
B8023
East Dunbartonshire
North Lanarkshire
Nethercroy Road
Smithstone Crs
Cullmuir Vw
Hillside
Cullmuir Ter
Constarry Road
B802
PO
Croy
Holy Cross School
Barbegs Crs
Old Mill View
Taggart Road
Weldon Pl
Charleson Row
Croy Station
48
Macdonald Crs
Easter Board
West Board
East Dunbartonshire
North Lanarkshire
G68
Smithstone Road
Linn Gardens
B8048
B8048
Kingshill Av
Littlemill Av
Kirkconnel Av
Blackwood Road
Wemyss Drive
Cardowan Drive
Raith Drive
Wellesley Dr
Clyde Football Club
Atholl Dr
Ardgoil Drive
Hunt Hill
Mollins Road
Atholl Dr
Westfield Rd
B802
67
M5
1 Drumglass Vw
L8
Street names for this grid square are listed at the back of the index
L1
1 Watson Crs
Devon Wk
Carradale Crs
Netherwood Ct
Netherwood Rd
Business Park
G H J K L M
1 2 3 4 5 6 7 8

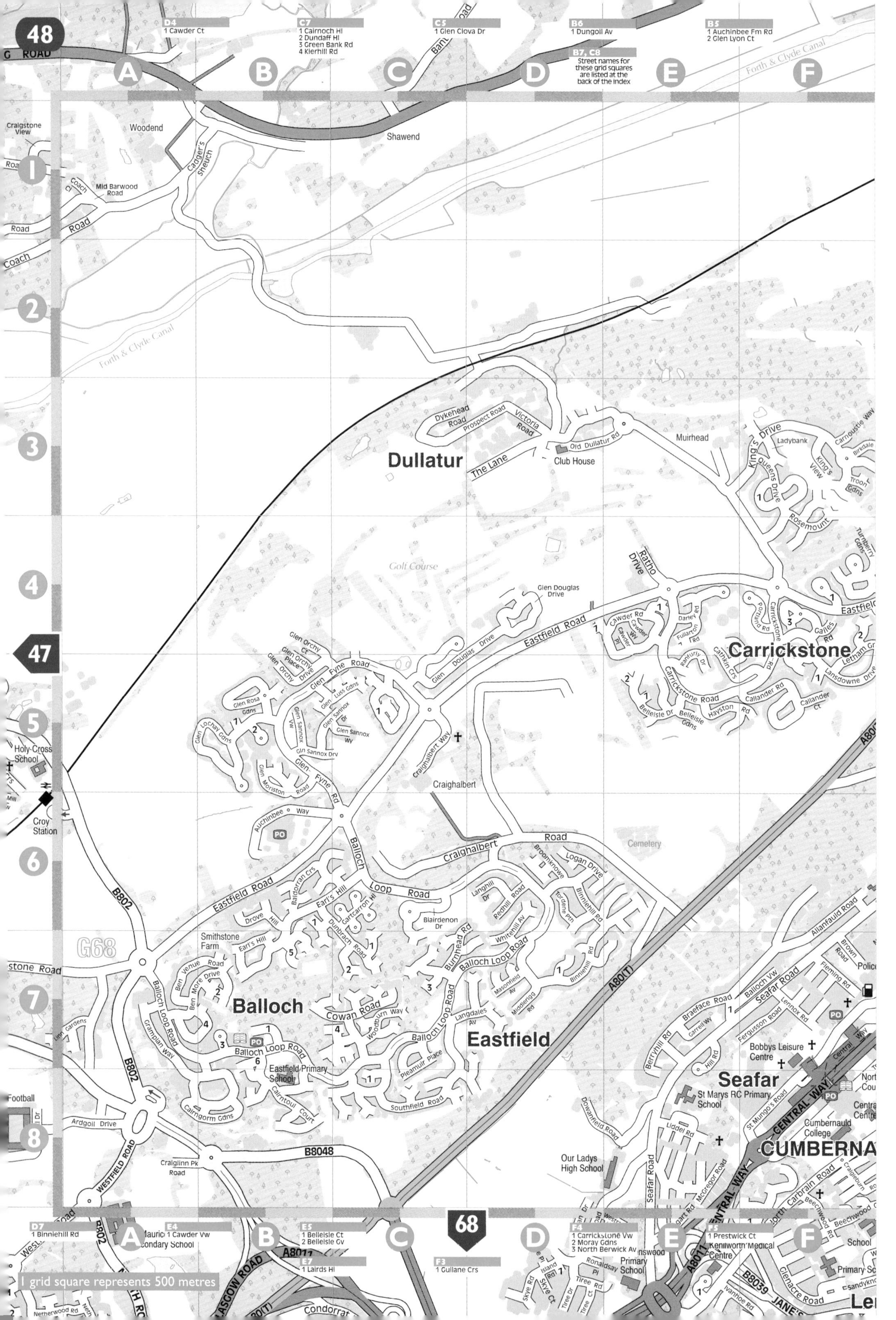
D4
1 Cawder Ct
C7
1 Cairnoch Hl
2 Dundaff Hl
3 Green Bank Rd
4 Kierhill Rd
C5
1 Glen Clova Dr
B6
1 Dungoil Av
B7, C8
Street names for these grid squares are listed at the back of the index
B5
1 Auchinbee Fm Rd
2 Glen Lyon Ct
A
B
C
D
E
F
1
2
3
4
5
6
7
8
Forth & Clyde Canal
Craigstone View
Woodend
Shawend
Cadger's Sneuch
Mid Barwood Road
Coach Road
Dullatur
Dykehead Road
Prospect Road
Victoria Road
Old Dullatur Rd
Club House
The Lane
Muirhead
Ladybank
King's Drive
Queens Drive
King's View
Carnoustie Way
Birkdale
Troon Gdns
Rosemount
Turnberry Gdns
Golf Course
Ratho Drive
Glen Douglas Drive
Eastfield Road
Cawder Rd
Cawder Wy
Cawder Pl
Darley Rd
Fullarton Rd
Banfurly Dr
Cathkin Crs
Carrickstone
Carrickstone Rd
Carrickstone Road
Portland Rd
Gailes
Letham Gr
Lansdowne Drive
Callander Rd
Callander Ct
Hayston Rd
Belleisle Dr
Belleisle Gdns
Glen Orchy Ct
Glen Orchy Place
Glen Orchy Drive
Glen Fyne Road
Glen Luss Gdns
Glen Rosa Gdns
Glen Lochay Gdns
Glen Sannox Vw
Glen Sannox Dr
Glen Sannox Wy
Gln Sannox Drv
Glen Moriston Road
Glen Fyne Rd
Craighalbert Way
Craighalbert
Holy Cross School
Croy Station
Auchinbee Way
PO
Balloch Loop Road
Craighalbert Road
Cemetery
Broomknowe
Logan Drive
Eastfield Road
Baldorran Crs
Earl's Hill
Gartcarron Hl
Drove Hill
Dunbrach Road
Blairdenon Dr
Langhill Dr
Redhill Road
Binniehill Rd
Tordene Pth
Whitehill Av
Burnhead Rd
Balloch Loop Road
Masonfield Av
Middlerigg Rd
Binniehill Rd
B802
G68
Smithstone Farm
Ben Venue Road
Ben More Drive
stone Road
Balloch
Cowan Road
Woodburn Way
Langdales Av
Eastfield
A80(T)
Linn Gardens
Grampian Way
Balloch Loop Road
Eastfield Primary School
Pleamuir Place
Southfield Road
Cairntoul Court
Cairngorm Gdns
Football
Ardgoil Drive
WESTFIELD ROAD
B8048
Craiglinn Pk Road
Allanfauld Road
Brown Road
Police
Fleming Rd
Seafar Road
Balloch Vw
Braeface Road
Carrell Wy
Lennox Rd
Fergusson Road
Berryhill Rd
Hill Rd
Bobbys Leisure Centre
Central Way
Seafar
St Marys RC Primary School
St Mungo's Road
CENTRAL WAY
Cumbernauld College
CUMBERNA
Dowanfield Road
Liddel Rd
McGregor Road
Our Ladys High School
Seafar Road
North Carbrain Road
Beechwood Rd
School
D7
1 Binniehill Rd
E4
1 Cawder Vw
E5
1 Belleisle Ct
2 Belleisle Gv
E7
1 Lairds Hl
68
F3
1 Gullane Crs
F4
1 Carrickstone Vw
2 Moray Gdns
3 North Berwick Av
F5
1 Prestwick Ct
Kenilworth Medical Centre
Primary School
Ronaldsay Pl
Tiree Rd
Skye Rd
Skye Ct
Island Rd
B8039
Glenacre Road
Ivanhoe Rd
A8011
Netherwood Rd
Condorrat
47
1 grid square represents 500 metres

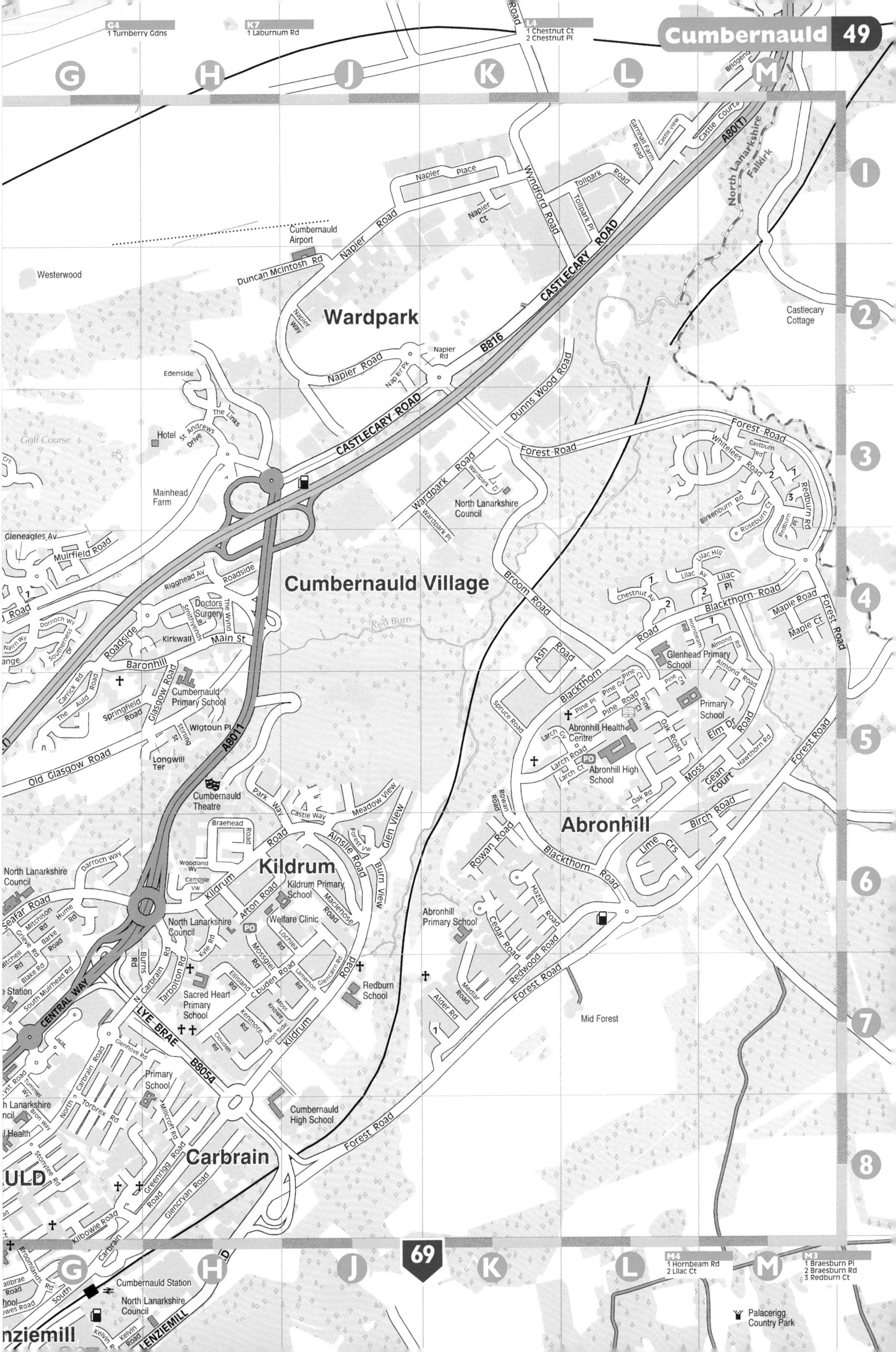
G4
1 Turnberry Gdns
K7
1 Laburnum Rd
L4
1 Chestnut Ct
2 Chestnut Pl
G
H
J
K
L
M
1
2
3
4
5
6
7
8
Wardpark
Cumbernauld Village
Abronhill
Kildrum
Carbrain
Cumbernauld Airport
Westerwood
Golf Course
Hotel
Mainhead Farm
Edenside
The Links
St Andrews Drive
Napier Place
Napier Road
Napier Ct
Napier Way
Napier Rd
Napier Pk
Duncan McIntosh Rd
Wyndford Road
Tollpark Road
Tollpark Pl
Garnhall Farm Road
Castle View
Castle Court
Bridgend
A80(T)
CASTLECARY ROAD
B816
North Lanarkshire
Falkirk
Castlecary Cottage
Dunns Wood Road
Forest Road
Wardpark Road
Wardpark Ct
Wardpark Pl
North Lanarkshire Council
Whitelees Road
Castburn Rd
Birkenburn Rd
Roseburn Ct
Redburn Rd
Redburn Pl
Lilac Hill
Lilac Av
Lilac Pl
Chestnut Av
Blackthorn Road
Maple Road
Maple Ct
Broom Road
Red Burn
Gleneagles Av
Muirfield Road
Rigghead Av
Roadside
Doctors Surgery
Smithyends
The Wynd
Kirkwall
Main St
Dornoch Wy
Nairn Wy
Southerness Dr
Baronhill
Carrick Rd
The Auld Road
Springfield Road
Glasgow Road
Cumbernauld Primary School
Wigtoun Pl
Stirling St
Longwill Ter
Old Glasgow Road
A8011
Cumbernauld Theatre
Park Way
Castle Way
Meadow View
Glen View
Forest Vw
Ainslie Road
Burn View
Braehead Road
Woodland Wy
Campsie Vw
Darroch Way
North Lanarkshire Council
Seafar Road
Mitchison Rd
Hume Rd
Barke Road
Greive Rd
Blake Rd
South Muirhead Rd
Kildrum Primary School
Maclehose Road
Afton Road
Welfare Clinic
Lochlea Rd
Mossgiel Rd
North Lanarkshire Council
Kyle Rd
Burns Rd
N Carbrain Rd
Tarbolton Rd
Ellisland Rd
Cluden Road
Lamerton Rd
Glencairn Rd
Redburn School
Sacred Heart Primary School
Kenmore Rd
Moss Knowe
Doon Side
Cloucen Rd
LYE BRAE
B8054
CENTRAL WAY
Glenhove Rd
North Carbrain Road
Primary School
Torbrex Rd
Millcroft Rd
Bron Way
Stonylee Rd
Greenrigg Road
Glencryan Road
Kilbowie Road
Carbrain
Cumbernauld High School
Ash Road
Spruce Road
Blackthorn Road
Pine Pl
Pine Gv
Pine Road
Pine Ct
Pine Crs
Hornbeam Rd
Glenhead Primary School
Almond Road
Almond Rd
Primary School
Elm Dr
Abronhill Health Centre
Larch Gv
Larch Road
Larch Ct
Abronhill High School
Oak Road
Oak Rd
Moss
Gean Court
Hawthorn Rd
Birch Road
Lime Crs
Rowan Road
Hazel Road
Abronhill Primary School
Cedar Road
Redwood Road
Medlar Road
Alder Rd
Mid Forest
Forest Road
North Lanarkshire Council
Cumbernauld Station
Broomlands Rd
South
Kelvin Road
LENZIEMILL
nziemill
ULD
69
M4
1 Hornbeam Rd
2 Lilac Ct
M3
1 Braesburn Pl
2 Braesburn Rd
3 Redburn Ct
Palacerigg Country Park

E4
1 Alison Ct
2 Glebe Rd
3 Langhouse Pl
4 Primrose Pl

D5
1 Ardgowan Crs
2 Finnockbog Dr
3 Hill Rd
4 Willow Pl

D4
1 Station Rd

A8
1 Broom Rd

30
70
Curling Pond
Lunderston
A770
Bankfoot
Ardgowan
Ardgowan Point
ROAD
Bridgend
Inverkip
INVERKIP
Marina
Main
Street
Millhouse Road
Swallow Brae
Magpie Crs
Swift Av
Primrose Crs
Primrose Av
Langhouse Road
Langhouse Av
Cemetery
Daff Av
Inverkip Primary School
PO
Glen Crs
Bogside
Langhill
Station Av
Commoncraig Pl
Kip Av
Finnockbog Road
Beatock Pl
Inverkip Station
A78(T)
Beatock Burn
Langhouse
Daff Burn
Kip Water
Inverkip Bay
Berfern
Hill
Everton
Finnock Bog Farm
Brueacre Burn
Innellan Rd
Whiting Road
Kilchattan Dr
Ascog Pl
Mt. Dr
Toward Rd
Stuart Rd
Brueacre Rd
Ardgowan Road
Carron Rd
Wemyss Bay Primary School
Castle Road
Sunart Rd
Linnhe Rd
Etive Road
Melfort Rd
Striven Road
Lomond Road
Ryan Road
Leven Road
Katrine Road
Undercliffe Road
Terrace
PA18

1 grid square represents 500 metres

IBM Station
Chrisswell
G
H
J
31
K
L
M
Reservoir
Main Aqueduct
PA16
Reservoir
Dunrod
Dunrod Road
Dunrod Well Reservoir
Majeston
Kip Water
Shielhill
Cornalees Bridge Centre
52
Cornalees
Daff Reservoir
Leapmoor Forest
Crawhin Reservoir
Kelly Cut
Leap Moor
71
Loch Burn
1
2
3
4
5
6
7
8

A
B
C
D
E
F
32
72
51
1
2
3
4
5
6
7
8
Reservoir
New Yetts Reservoir
Whitelees Moor
Old Largs Road
Whitelees Cottage
Darndaff Moor
Killochend
Loch Thom
Compensation Reservoir
Darndaff
Cornalees
Gryfe Reservoir
Gryfe Water
Garvock
Dowries
1 grid square represents 500 metres

Renton
Luss Avenue
Luss Pl
Road
Dalmoak Road
Arden Rd
AUCHMOUNTAIN RD
B788
Craigieknome Burn
Lady Burn
Devol Burn
Lurg Moor
Burnhead Moor
Knocknair's Hill Reservoir
AUCHENFOIL ROAD
B788
Burnhead
Gryfe Reservoir
Garshangan
Garshangan Burn
Mansfield
Dykefoot
Hillside
Green Water
G H J K L M
1 2 3 4 5 6 7 8
33
54
73

E2
1 Barscube Av
2 Farm Rd
E1
1 Braehead Rd
2 Bridge Rd
D1
1 Harelaw Av
2 Lurg St
3 Muirshiel La
4 Rosneath Rd
C1
1 Millbank Rd
2 Millburn Rd
Port Glasgow Station
Springhill Road
Bouverie St
GLASGOW RD A761
Clune Park Primary School
CLUNE BRAE A761
GREENOCK ROAD A8
Kelburn Terrace
West Dougliehill
Dougliehill Road
Reservoir
Devol Industrial Est
Devol
Cardross Avenue
Bridgend Avenue
Boglestone Avenue
Primary School
Merrylee Av
Muirdykes Avenue
Port Glasgow Golf Club
Mid Auchinleck
Bardrainney
Doctors Surgery
Harelaw Reservoir
Devol Moor
Harelaw
Montrose Avenue
Methil Rd
Auchenbothie Road
Marloch Av
Devol Road
Cunston Cott
Crosshill Road
Auchentiber
West Kilbride
Pennytersal
Priestside Farm
High Mathernock
Auchenfoyle
Gryfe Water
Strathgryfe
Gryffeside
Horsecraig
Cauldside
B788
Faulds
Strathgryfe
Cairncurran
Jock's Craig
Dippany
Green Water
F1
1 Bogside Rd
2 Oakbank Rd
F2
1 Crosshill Pl
F3
1 Markinch Rd
2 Maxwellton Rd
3 West Woodside Av
1 grid square represents 500 metres

34
53
74

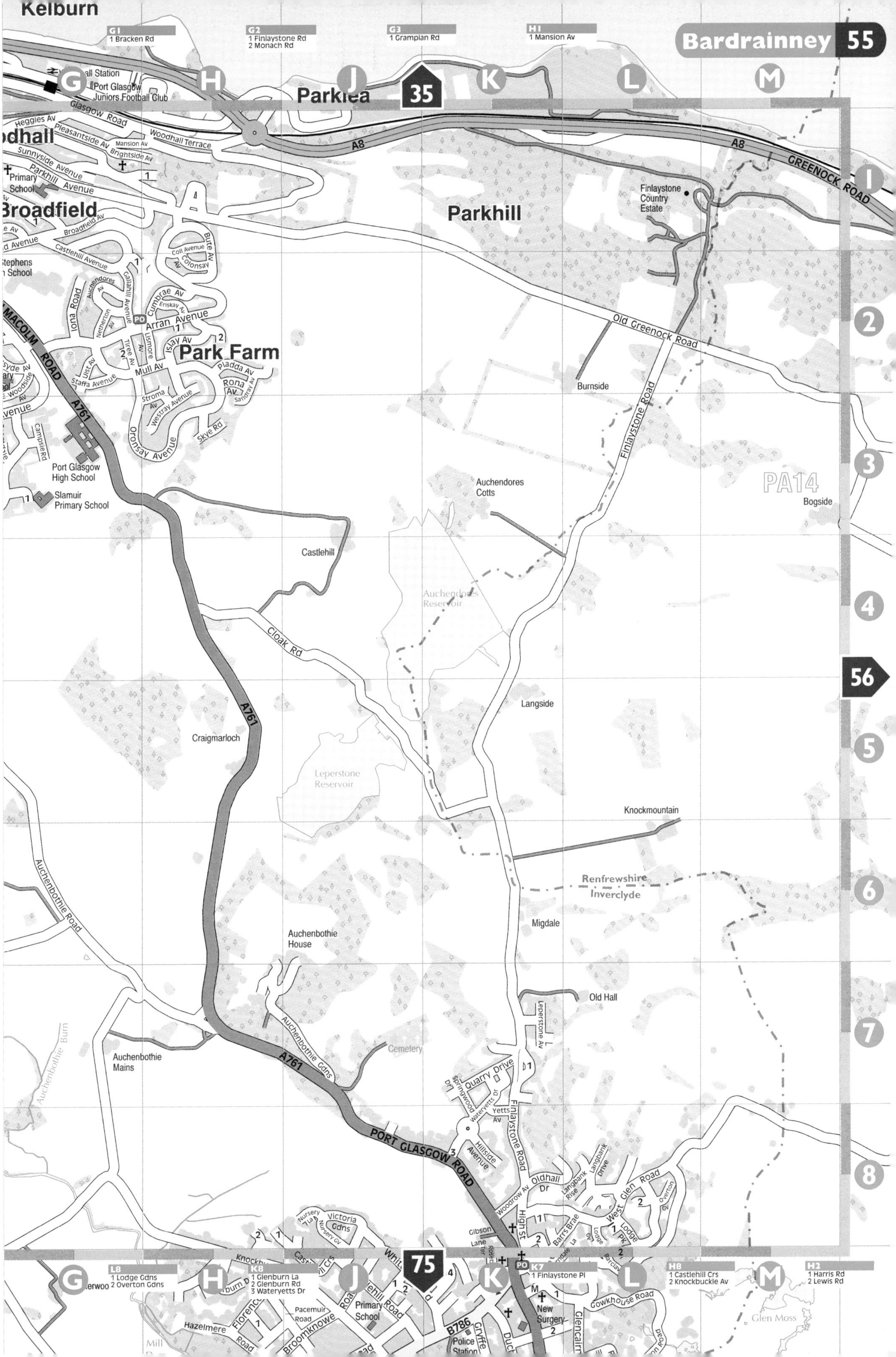
Kelburn
G1 1 Bracken Rd
G2 1 Finlaystone Rd 2 Monach Rd
G3 1 Grampian Rd
H1 1 Mansion Av
Port Glasgow Juniors Football Club
Parklea
35
Glasgow Road
Heggies Av
Pleasantside Av
Mansion Av
Brightside Av
Woodhall Terrace
Sunnyside Avenue
Parkhill Avenue
Primary School
Broadfield
Broadfield Av
Castlehill Avenue
A8
GREENOCK ROAD
Finlaystone Country Estate
Parkhill
Coll Avenue
Colonsay Av
Bute Av
Cumbrae Av
Eriskay Av
Arran Avenue
Islay Av
Iona Road
Auchendores Av
Netherton Av
Callahill Avenue
Park Farm
Tiree Av
Usmore Av
Mull Av
Uist Av
Staffa Avenue
Pladda Av
Rona Av
Sandray Av
Stroma Av
Westray Avenue
Oronsay Avenue
Skye Rd
KILMACOLM ROAD
A761
Campsie Rd
Port Glasgow High School
Slamuir Primary School
Old Greenock Road
Burnside
Finlaystone Road
PA14
Bogside
Auchendores Cotts
Castlehill
Auchendores Reservoir
Cloak Rd
56
Langside
Craigmarloch
Leperstone Reservoir
Knockmountain
Renfrewshire
Inverclyde
Migdale
Auchenbothie Road
Auchenbothie House
Old Hall
Leperstone Av
Auchenbothie Burn
Auchenbothie Mains
Auchenbothie Gdns
Cemetery
Quarry Drive
Springwood Dr
Wateryetts Dr
Yetts Av
Hillside Avenue
PORT GLASGOW ROAD
Oldhall Dr
Langbank Rise
Langbank Drive
West Glen Road
Overton Gv
Woodrow Av
High St
Barr's Brae
Lodge Pk
Victoria Gdns
Nursery La
Nursery Gv
Gibson Lane
75
L8 1 Lodge Gdns 2 Overton Gdns
K8 1 Glenburn La 2 Glenburn Rd 3 Wateryetts Dr
K7 1 Finlaystone Pl
H8 1 Castlehill Crs 2 Knockbuckle Av
H2 1 Harris Rd 2 Lewis Rd
Pacemuir Road
Primary School
Hazelmere Road
Broomknowe
B786
Police Station
Gryffe
New Surgery
Glencairn
Gowkhouse Road
Glen Moss
G H J K L M
1 2 3 4 5 6 7 8

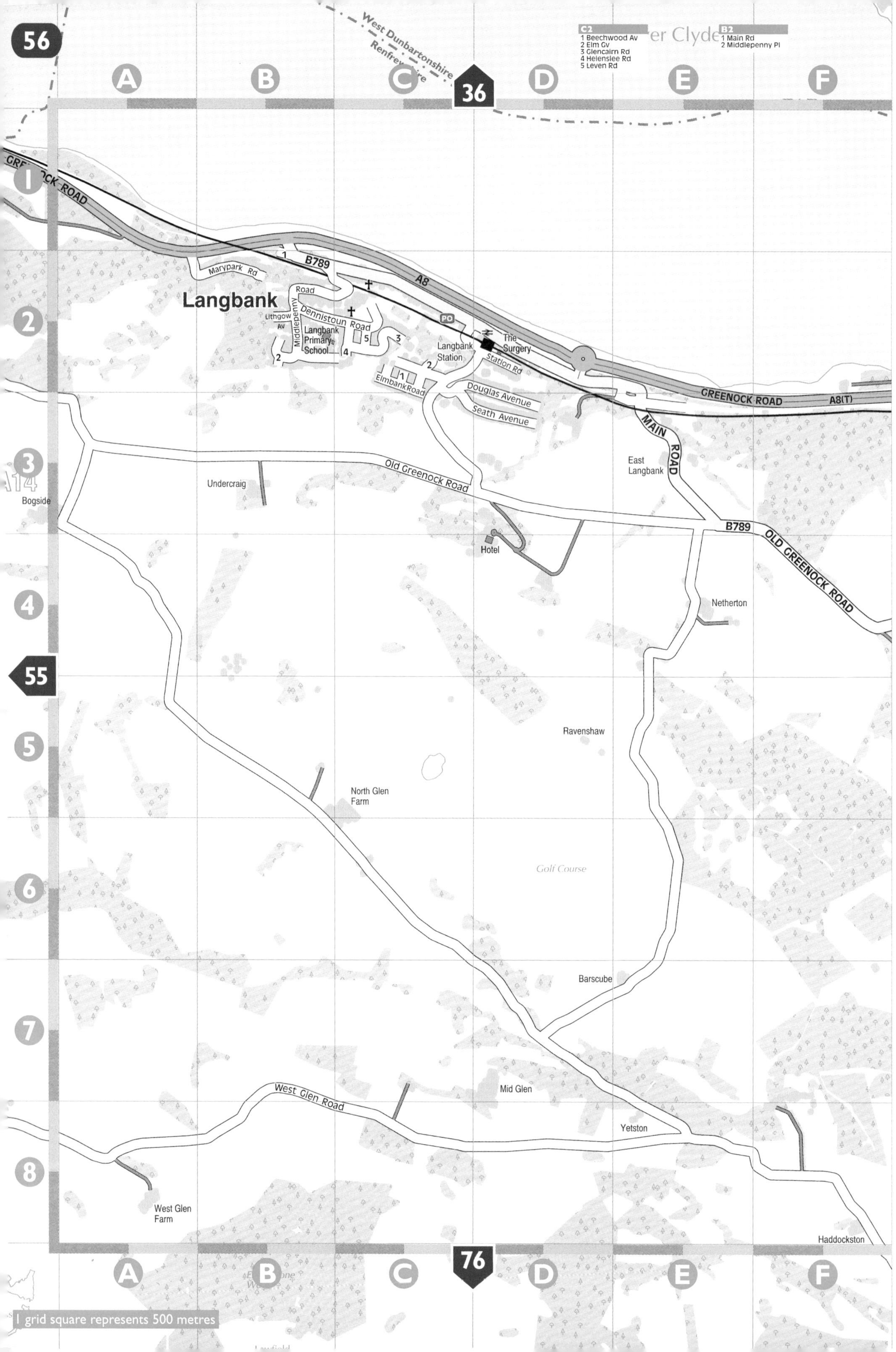
C2
1 Beechwood Av
2 Elm Gv
3 Glencairn Rd
4 Helenslee Rd
5 Leven Rd
B2
1 Main Rd
2 Middlepenny Pl
West Dunbartonshire
Renfrewshire
36
55
76
A
B
C
D
E
F
1
2
3
4
5
6
7
8
GREENOCK ROAD
B789
A8
Marypark Rd
Road
Langbank
Lithgow Av
Middlepenny
Dennistoun Road
Langbank Primary School
PO
Langbank Station
The Surgery
Station Rd
Elmbank Road
Douglas Avenue
Seath Avenue
GREENOCK ROAD
A8(T)
MAIN ROAD
East Langbank
Old Greenock Road
Undercraig
Bogside
Hotel
B789
OLD GREENOCK ROAD
Netherton
Ravenshaw
North Glen Farm
Golf Course
Barscube
Mid Glen
West Glen Road
Yetston
West Glen Farm
Haddockston
1 grid square represents 500 metres

M5
1 Wraisland Crs
Dumbuck
A82(T)
A814
Colquhoun
Crannog Rd
Milton
G
H
J
K
L
M
37
Milton Island
West Dunbartonshire
Renfrewshire
River Clyde
Junction 31
M8
Ferryhill Plantn
A8
GREENOCK ROAD
Old Greenock Road
Hatton
Cora Campus
Chestnut Avenue
Slateford
58
Whitemoss Dam
Whitemoss Farm
B789
Drums
Lyle Crescent
Kingswood Rd
Cemetery
Ingliston Drive
Hamilton Crs
Newton Rd
Ingleston
BISHOPT
PA7
Formakin
West Glenshinnoch
Meiklefield
East Glenshinnoch
77
Towncroft
Reilly Road
1
2
3
4
5
6
7
8

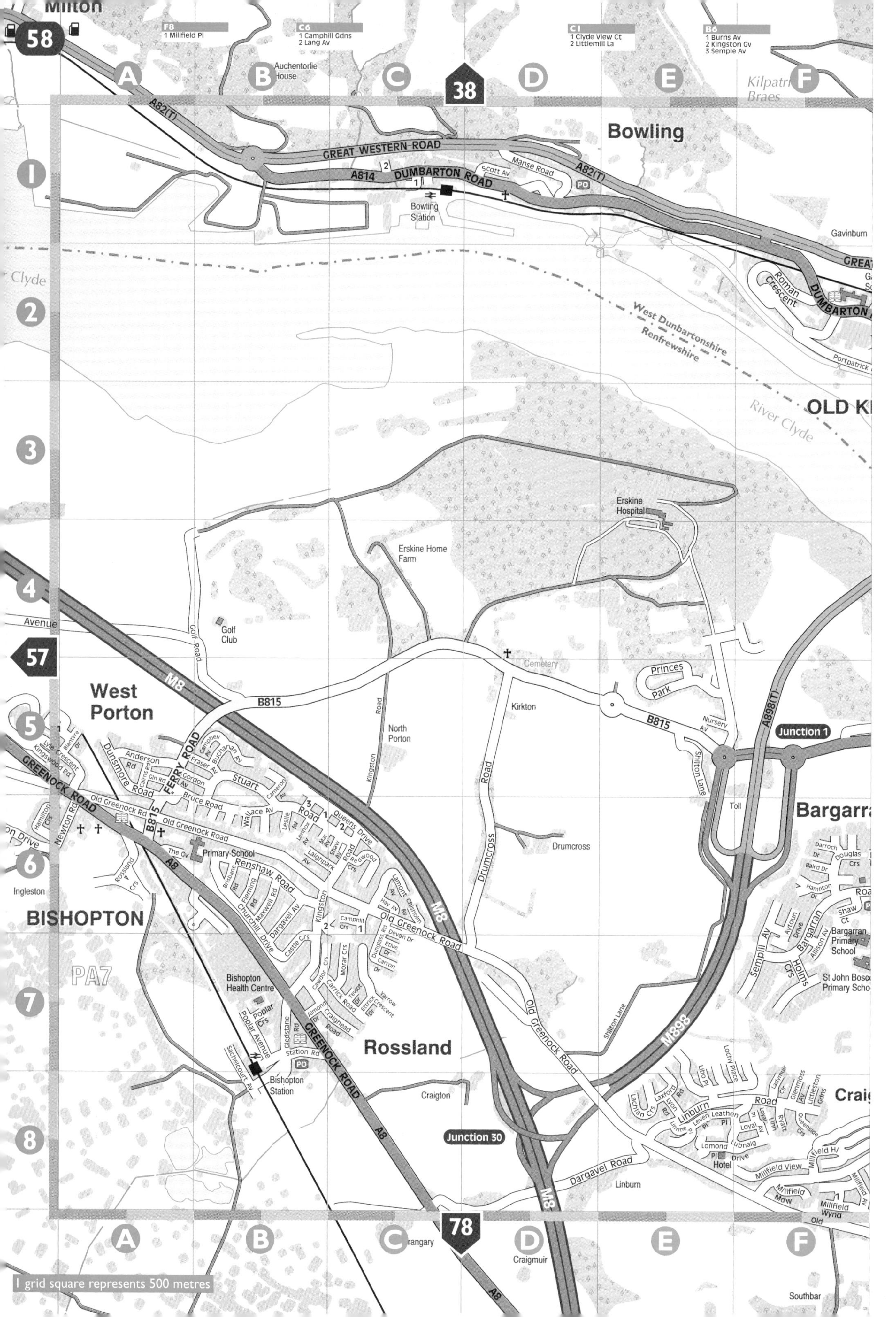

Milton
58
38
57
78
F8
1 Millfield Pl
C6
1 Camphill Gdns
2 Lang Av
C1
1 Clyde View Ct
2 Littlemill La
B6
1 Burns Av
2 Kingston Gv
3 Semple Av
A
B
C
D
E
F
1
2
3
4
5
6
7
8
Auchentorlie House
Kilpatrick Braes
Bowling
A82(T)
GREAT WESTERN ROAD
A814
DUMBARTON ROAD
Scott Av
Manse Road
PO
Bowling Station
Gavinburn
Roman Crescent
Clyde
West Dunbartonshire
Renfrewshire
Portpatrick
OLD K
River Clyde
Erskine Hospital
Erskine Home Farm
Avenue
Golf Club
Golf Road
Cemetery
Princes Park
Nursery Av
B815
Kirkton
A898(T)
Junction 1
West Porton
M8
North Porton
Kingston Road
Shilton Lane
Toll
Bargarran
FERRY ROAD
Campbell Av
Buchanan Av
Fraser Av
Anderson Rd
Dunsmore Road
Cairns Rd
Gln Rd
Gordon Av
Stuart
Cameron Av
Lyle Crescent
Kingswood Rd
Blantyre Dr
GREENOCK ROAD
Old Greenock Rd
Bruce Road
Wallace Av
Leslie Av
Queens Drive
Newton Rd
Hamilton Crs
on Drive
Old Greenock Road
Drumcross Road
Drumcross
The Gv
Primary School
Renshaw Road
Laighpark Av
Redwood Crs
A8
Ingleston
Rossland Crs
Brisbane Rd
Fleming Rd
Maxwell Rd
Dargavel Av
Kingston Av
Lamont Av
Chisholm Av
Hay Av
BISHOPTON
Churchill Drive
Castle Crs
Camphill Crs
Devon Dr
Etive Dr
Carron Dr
Dunglass Rd
Morar Crs
PA7
Bishopton Health Centre
Poplar Crs
Poplar Avenue
Cawdor Crs
Carrick Road
Teviot Dr
Ettrick Crescent
Yarrow Crescent
Almond Dr
Craighead Road
Gledstane Rd
Station Rd
Sachelcourt Av
Bishopton Station
Rossland
Darroch Dr
Douglas Crs
Baird Dr
Hamilton Dr
Shaw Ct
Semple Av
Ayrtoun Drive
Bargarran Road
Allison Av
Bargarran Primary School
Holms Crs
St John Bosco Primary School
M898
Shilton Lane
Lochy Place
Libo Pl
Lachlan Crs
Laxford Rd
Lyon Rd
Linburn Road
Leven Pl
Linnhe Pl
Leathen Pl
Loyal Av
Lomond Pl
Lubnaig Drive
Hotel
Ladymuir Cir
Glenmoss Av
Littleston Gdns
Queenside Crs
Craig
Craigton
Junction 30
Dargavel Road
Linburn
Millfield Hill
Millfield View
Millfield Mdw
Millfield Wynd
Millfield Av
Old
Crangary
Craigmuir
Southbar
1 grid square represents 500 metres

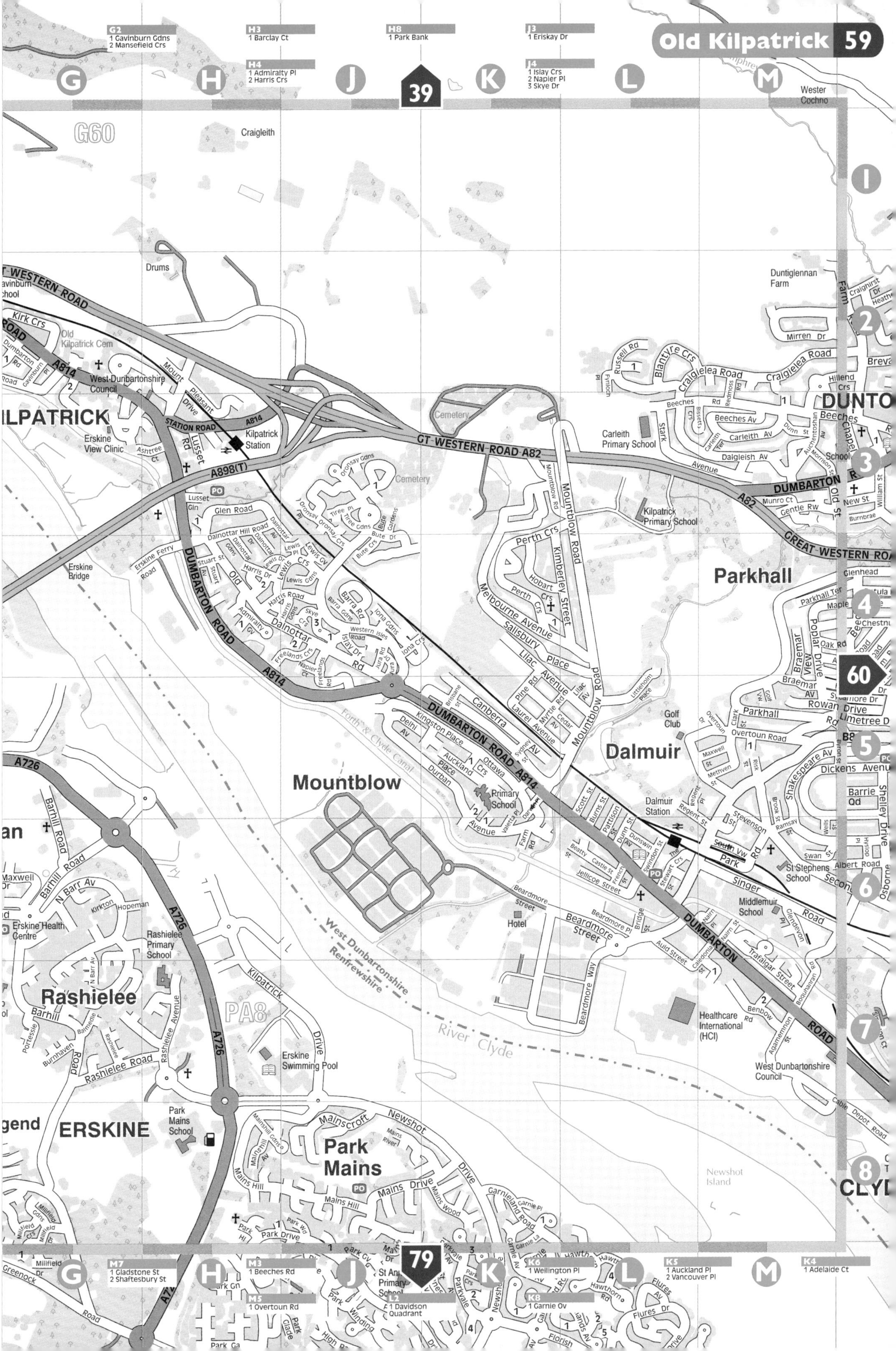
G2
1 Gavinburn Gdns
2 Mansefield Crs
H3
1 Barclay Ct
H8
1 Park Bank
J3
1 Eriskay Dr
H4
1 Admiralty Pl
2 Harris Crs
J4
1 Islay Crs
2 Napier Pl
3 Skye Dr
G
H
J
39
K
L
M
Wester Cochno
G60
Craigleith
Drums
Duntiglennan Farm
GT WESTERN ROAD
Kirk Crs
Old Kilpatrick Cem
A814
West Dunbartonshire Council
KILPATRICK
Mount Pleasant Drive
STATION ROAD
Kilpatrick Station
Erskine View Clinic
Ashtree Ct
Lusset Rd
A898(T)
GT WESTERN ROAD A82
Cemetery
Russell Rd
Blantyre Crs
Craigielea Road
Mirren Dr
Carleith Primary School
Beeches Av
Carleith Av
Dalgleish Av
DUNTOCHER
DUMBARTON RD
A82
Munro Ct
Gentle Rw
New St
GREAT WESTERN ROAD
Kilpatrick Primary School
Glen Road
Dalnottar Hill Road
Erskine Ferry Road
Erskine Bridge
Oronsay Gdns
Bute Gardens
Lewis Crs
Harris Road
Barra Rd
Iona Gdns
Western Isles Road
Perth Crs
Mountblow Road
Kimberley Street
Hobart Crs
Melbourne Avenue
Salisbury Place
Lilac Avenue
Parkhall
Parkhall Ter
Poplar Drive
Braemar View
Rowan Drive
Limetree Dr
Golf Club
DUMBARTON ROAD
A814
Canberra
Kingston Place
Delhi Av
Auckland Place
Ottawa Crs
Durban Avenue
Forth & Clyde Canal
Mountblow
Primary School
Littleholm Place
Dalmuir
Overtoun Road
Shakespeare Av
Dickens Avenue
Shelley Drive
Dalmuir Station
Regent St
Stevenson St
South Vw
Park Rd
Singer Road
St Stephens School
Albert Road
Middlemuir School
Beardmore Street
Hotel
Jellicoe Street
Auld Street
Trafalgar Street
Beardmore Way
Healthcare International (HCI)
Benbow Rd
West Dunbartonshire Council
Cable Depot Road
Newshot Island
CLYDEBANK
60
A726
Barhill Road
Erskine Health Centre
Rashielee Primary School
Rashielee
Rashielee Avenue
Rashielee Road
Kilpatrick Drive
PA8
West Dunbartonshire
Renfrewshire
River Clyde
Erskine Swimming Pool
ERSKINE
Park Mains School
Mainscroft
Newshot Drive
Park Mains
Mains Drive
Mains Hill
Park Drive
Garnieland Road
79
M7
1 Gladstone St
2 Shaftesbury St
M3
1 Beeches Rd
M5
1 Overtoun Rd
L2
1 Davidson Quadrant
K6
1 Wellington Pl
K8
1 Garnie Ov
K5
1 Auckland Pl
2 Vancouver Pl
K4
1 Adelaide Ct
Greenock Road
St Annes Primary School
Flures Av

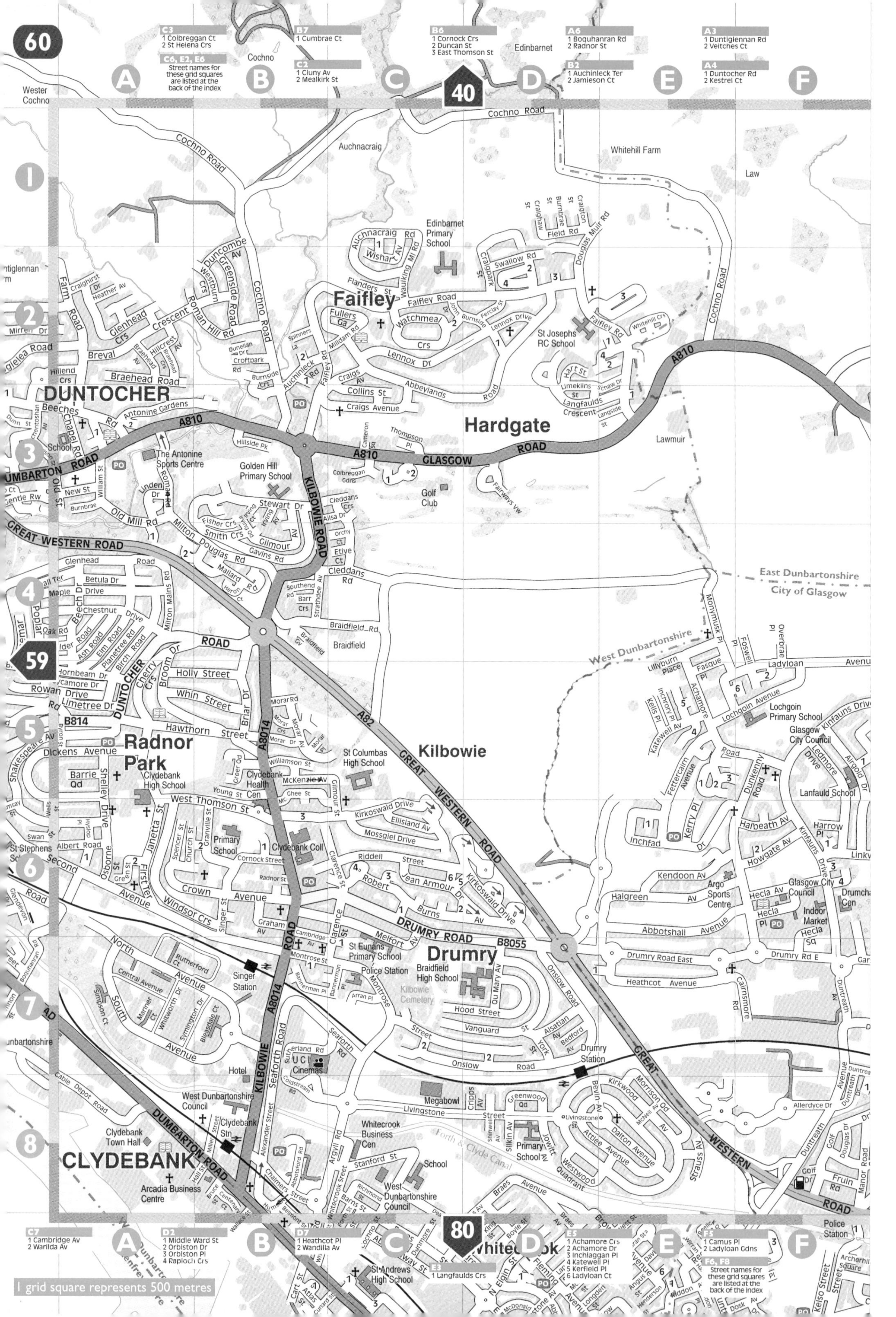
C3
1 Colbreggan Ct
2 St Helena Crs
C6, E2, E6
Street names for these grid squares are listed at the back of the index
B7
1 Cumbrae Ct
C2
1 Cluny Av
2 Mealkirk St
B6
1 Cornock Crs
2 Duncan St
3 East Thomson St
A6
1 Boquhanran Rd
2 Radnor St
B2
1 Auchinleck Ter
2 Jamieson Ct
A3
1 Duntiglennan Rd
2 Veitches Ct
A4
1 Duntocher Rd
2 Kestrel Ct
40
59
80
Wester Cochno
Cochno
Edinbarnet
Auchnacraig
Whitehill Farm
Law
Cochno Road
Edinbarnet Primary School
Faifley
Hardgate
DUNTOCHER
Lawmuir
The Antonine Sports Centre
Golden Hill Primary School
Golf Club
St Josephs RC School
A810
GLASGOW ROAD
DUMBARTON ROAD
GREAT WESTERN ROAD
KILBOWIE ROAD
Braidfield
East Dunbartonshire
City of Glasgow
West Dunbartonshire
Radnor Park
Kilbowie
St Columbas High School
Clydebank High School
Clydebank Health Cen
Clydebank Coll
Lochgoin Primary School
Glasgow City Council
Lanfauld School
Argo Sports Centre
Indoor Market
Drumry
DRUMRY ROAD
B8055
St Eunans Primary School
Police Station
Braidfield High School
Kilbowie Cemetery
Singer Station
Drumry Station
UCI Cinemas
Megabowl
West Dunbartonshire Council
Clydebank Stn
Clydebank Town Hall
CLYDEBANK
Arcadia Business Centre
Whitecrook Business Cen
Primary School
Forth & Clyde Canal
Whitecrook
St Andrews High School
Police Station
C7
1 Cambridge Av
2 Warilda Av
D2
1 Middle Ward St
2 Orbiston Dr
3 Orbiston Pl
4 Rapioch Crs
D7
1 Heathcot Pl
2 Wandilla Av
E3
1 Langfaulds Crs
E5
1 Achamore Crs
2 Achamore Dr
3 Inchlaggan Pl
4 Katewell Pl
5 Kerfield Pl
6 Ladyloan Ct
F5
1 Camus Pl
2 Ladyloan Gdns
F6, F8
Street names for these grid squares are listed at the back of the index
1 grid square represents 500 metres

G6
1 Ardhu Pl

G7, J1
Street names for these grid squares are listed at the back of the index

H2
1 Cairnsmore Dr

H3
1 Lewis Gdns
2 Skye Gdns
3 Tiree Gdns

H5
1 Bankglen Rd
2 Summerhill Pl

H6
1 Jedworth Rd
2 Linkwood Gdns
3 Rozelle Av

H8
1 Keal Av
2 Moraine Pl

J2
1 Auchineden Ct

M3, M4, M5, M6
Street names for these grid squares are listed at the back of the index

L4, L5, L6, L7
Street names for these grid squares are listed at the back of the index

K6
1 Allender Rd

K3, K5, K7, L3
Street names for these grid squares are listed at the back of the index

K1
1 Muirhouse Pk
2 The Poplars

K2
1 Grampian Wy

J3
1 Burnside Ct
2 Dryburgh Rd
3 Kenilworth Crs

J7
1 Bladnoch Dr
2 Rotherwood La
3 Stranraer Dr

C8
1 Drumlaken Av
2 Drumlaken Ct
C1
1 Auchencruive
2 Bridgegait
3 Oswald Wk
4 Virginia Gdns
B4
1 Kenmore Gdns
2 Tyndrum Rd
A7
1 Banchory Crs
42
61
82
A
B
C
D
E
F
1
2
3
4
5
6
7
8
Council
Park Rd
Medical Practice
Braehead Avenue
Mains Road
Keystone Av
Quadrant
Main Street
Glasgow Road
Keystone Rd
Queens Ct
Braefoot Avenue
Braeside Avenue
Shaw Road
Police Station
B8030
Nethermains Rd
Drive
Galbraith
Drumlin Drive
A81
A807
Finlay Rise
Mitchell Dr
Dunmore Dr
Dougalston Loch
Auchenhowie Road
Milngavie & Bearsden Sports Club
Langbank
Dowan Road
Bardowie Loch
Sports Centre
Golf Course
Hazel Av
Mosshead Road
Beech Av
Hawthorn Avenue
Burnbrae Av
Avenue
Carseview Dr
East Dunbartonshire Council
Kilmardinny Crescent
Douglas Park Crs
Reid Av
East Dunbartonshire
City of Glasgow
Boclair
B8049
Boclair Road
Temple of Boclair
A879
Cemetery
Milngavie Road
Hillneuk Dr
Hillside Dr
Golf Club
Hillfoot Station
Birch Vw
Roman Dr
Summerston Farm
Millichen Road
Millichen
Balmore Road
Boclair Av
Aviemore Gdns
Kinnaird Crs
Durness Avenue
Methven Av
Birnam Crs
Boclair Crescent
East Dunbartonshire Council
Doctors Surgery
Glenfarg Crs
Dunkeld Dr
Inveroran Drive
Glendaruel Av
Rannoch Drive
Buchanan Drive
Greenwood Dr
Kessington Drive
Kessington Road
School
Kessington
Brora Dr
Etive Av
Earn Av
Avon Av
Oronsay Crescent
Afton Crs
Clathic Av
Borland Road
Pollock Road
Macfarlane Road
Cameron Dr
Speirs Road
Second Avenue
First Avenue
Golf Course
River Kelvin
Arisaig Dr
Glenfinnan Dr
Albert Drive
Woodvale Av
Killermont Rd
Morar Dr
Carry Av
Lochaber Rd
Hutchison Dr
Cluny Dr
Cluny Av
Killermont Av
Maryhill Road
Hollymount
Coronation Wy
Balmoral Dr
Ballater Drive
Blackhill
G23
Blackhill Road
Cawder Cuilt
Killermont Vw
West Dunbartonshire
City of Glasgow
Acre Road
Acre Dr
Duich Gdns
Shielbridge Gdns
Harburn Pl
Westerkirk Dr
Summerston
Calderculit Primary School
Staffin St
Abercorn Pl
Foxhills Pl
Hoylake Pl
Broughton Rd
Calderculit Road
Arrochar Street
Torrin Rd
Invershiel Rd
Arrochar Dr
St Blanes Primary School
Chatton St
Littleton St
Craigbo Rd
Lambhill Cemetery
D1
1 Murdoch Dr
University of Glasgow
D7
1 Letterfearn Rd
D8
Street names for this grid square are listed at the back of the index
E7
1 Hawthornden Gdns
E8
Street names for this grid square are listed at the back of the index
F8
1 Broughton Gdns
2 Newstead Gdns
Summerston Station
Arrochar Street
St Agnes Primary School
Tresta Road
1 grid square represents 500 metres

Craighead
M5
1 Allander Gdns
2 Calder Ga
M7
1 The Rowans
Fluchter Rd
Parnellan
G
H
J
43
K
L
M
Golf Course
Golf Club
Golf Course Rd
Glenorchard Road
Balmore
I
A807
BALMORE ROAD
A807
Balmore Road
Bardowie
Station Rd
Allander Av
BALMORE ROAD
Balmore Haughs
2
G64
3
River Kelvin
4
Buchley
Balmuildy Road
Balmuildy Road
64
Wilderness Plantation
East Dunbartonshire Council
Forth & Clyde Canal
5
Jellyhill
Hilton Pk
Hilton Terrace
Darnley Cs
Norfolk Crs
Westfields
Stirling Gdns
Stirling Drive
Muirton Drive
Primary School
The Surgery
Heriot Crs
Meadowburn
Teviot Av
Yarrow Rd
Hilton Road
6
Atholl Gdns
Gleneagles
Lomond Drive
Faskally Av
Devon Gdns
Stirling Drive
Tofthill Av
Southesk Avenue
Broadleys Avenue
Balmuildy Road
Marchmont Gdns
Moray Crs
Dalhousie Gdns
Carrour Gdns
Tofthill Gdns
Glenburn Gardens
Keir Dr
7
Dunbartonshire & Lomond Council
ROAD
A879
East Dunbartonshire
City of Glasgow
Forth & Clyde Canal
Lochfauld
Lochfauld Road
Turnbull High School
St Andrew's Av
St Mary's Road
Bishop Gardens
Brackenbrae Avenue
Novar Gardens
Bardrill Dr
Duncrub Dr
Pollok Drive
Eldon Gdns
Brackenbrae Road
Beaufort Gardens
East Dunbartonshire Council
The Fort Theatre
Kenmure Avenue
Kenmure Cres
Kenmure Dr
Kenmure La
Kenmure Gardens
Kenmure Avenue
PO
8
Bishopbriggs Station
Boclair
Emerson Rd
Arnold Av
KIRKINTILLOCH ROAD
Laigh Kenmure
Possil Loch
Castlebay Drive
Clovergate
Heatherbrae
Brackenbrae
Gorsewood
83
G
H
J
K
L
M
A879
Nature Reserve
Sheldaig Rd
Hillswick Crs
Milton Bank Primary School
Cathay St
Skerray St
Castlebay St
Scaraway St
Raasay St
Stornoway St
Egilsay Crs
Street
Scaraway Pl
Shapinsay St
Scaraway Ter
Scaraway Dr
Valley St
Doctors Surgery
Road
Duncryne Place
Colmuir Dr
Viewfield Rd
Colston
KIRKINTILLOCH ROAD
East Dunbartonshire Council
Mungo St
Mavis Bank
Muirpark Dr
Springfield
Avon Rd

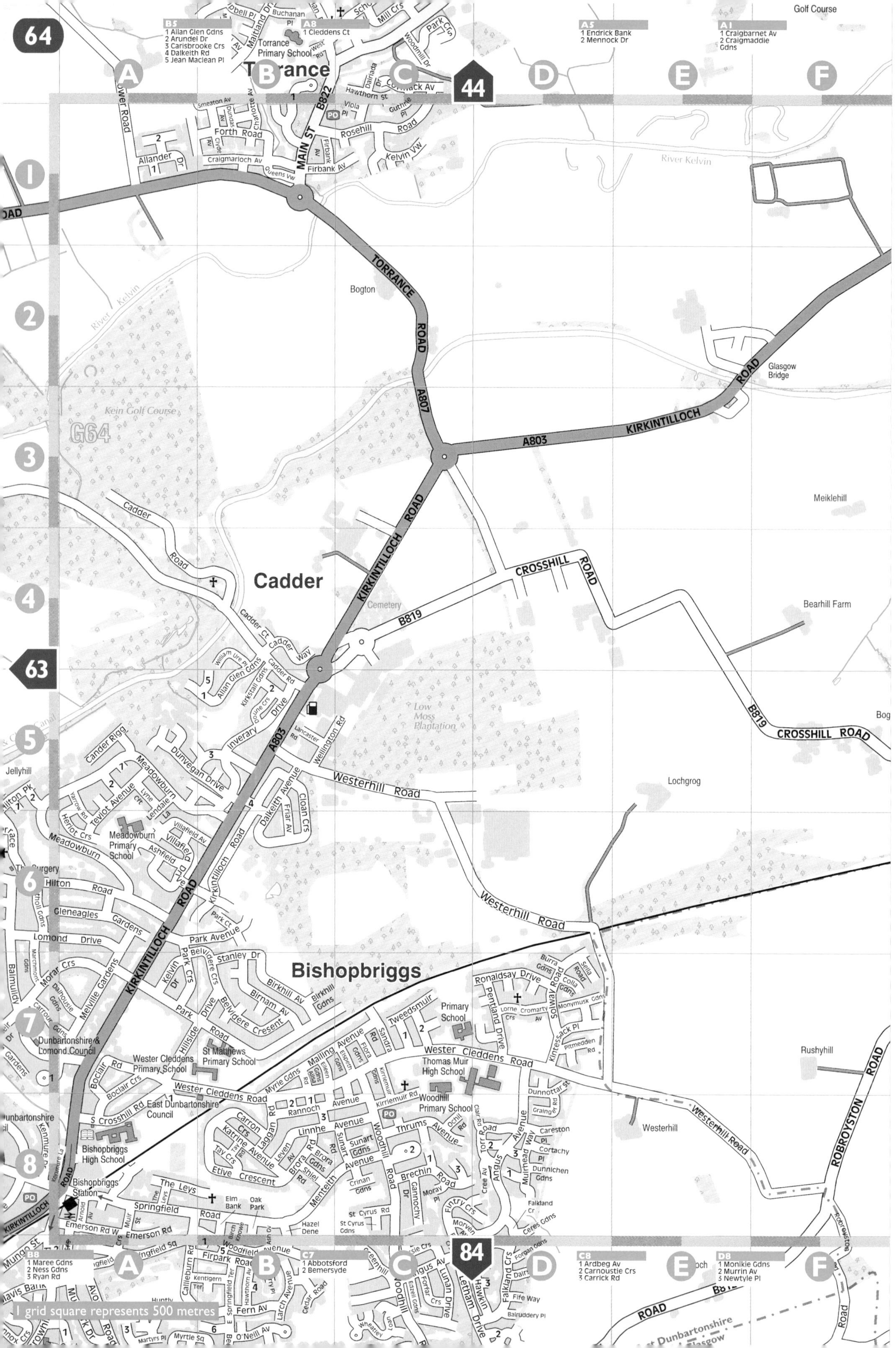
B5
1 Allan Glen Gdns
2 Arundel Dr
3 Carisbrooke Crs
4 Dalkeith Rd
5 Jean Maclean Pl
A8
1 Cleddens Ct
A5
1 Endrick Bank
2 Mennock Dr
A1
1 Craigbarnet Av
2 Craigmaddie Gdns
Golf Course
Torrance
Torrance Primary School
44
River Kelvin
TORRANCE ROAD
A807
Bogton
Glasgow Bridge
KIRKINTILLOCH ROAD
A803
Kein Golf Course
G64
Meiklehill
Cadder
Cadder Road
Cemetery
B819
CROSSHILL ROAD
Bearhill Farm
Low Moss Plantation
63
Westerhill Road
Lochgrog
Jellyhill
Meadowburn Primary School
Bishopbriggs
Dunbartonshire & Lomond Council
Wester Cleddens Primary School
St Matthews Primary School
Thomas Muir High School
Woodhill Primary School
Primary School
East Dunbartonshire Council
Bishopbriggs High School
Bishopbriggs Station
Wester Cleddens Road
Westerhill
Rushyhill
ROBROYSTON ROAD
84
B8
1 Maree Gdns
2 Ness Gdns
3 Ryan Rd
C7
1 Abbotsford
2 Bemersyde
C8
1 Ardbeg Av
2 Carnoustie Crs
3 Carrick Rd
D8
1 Monikie Gdns
2 Murrin Av
3 Newtyle Pl
1 grid square represents 500 metres

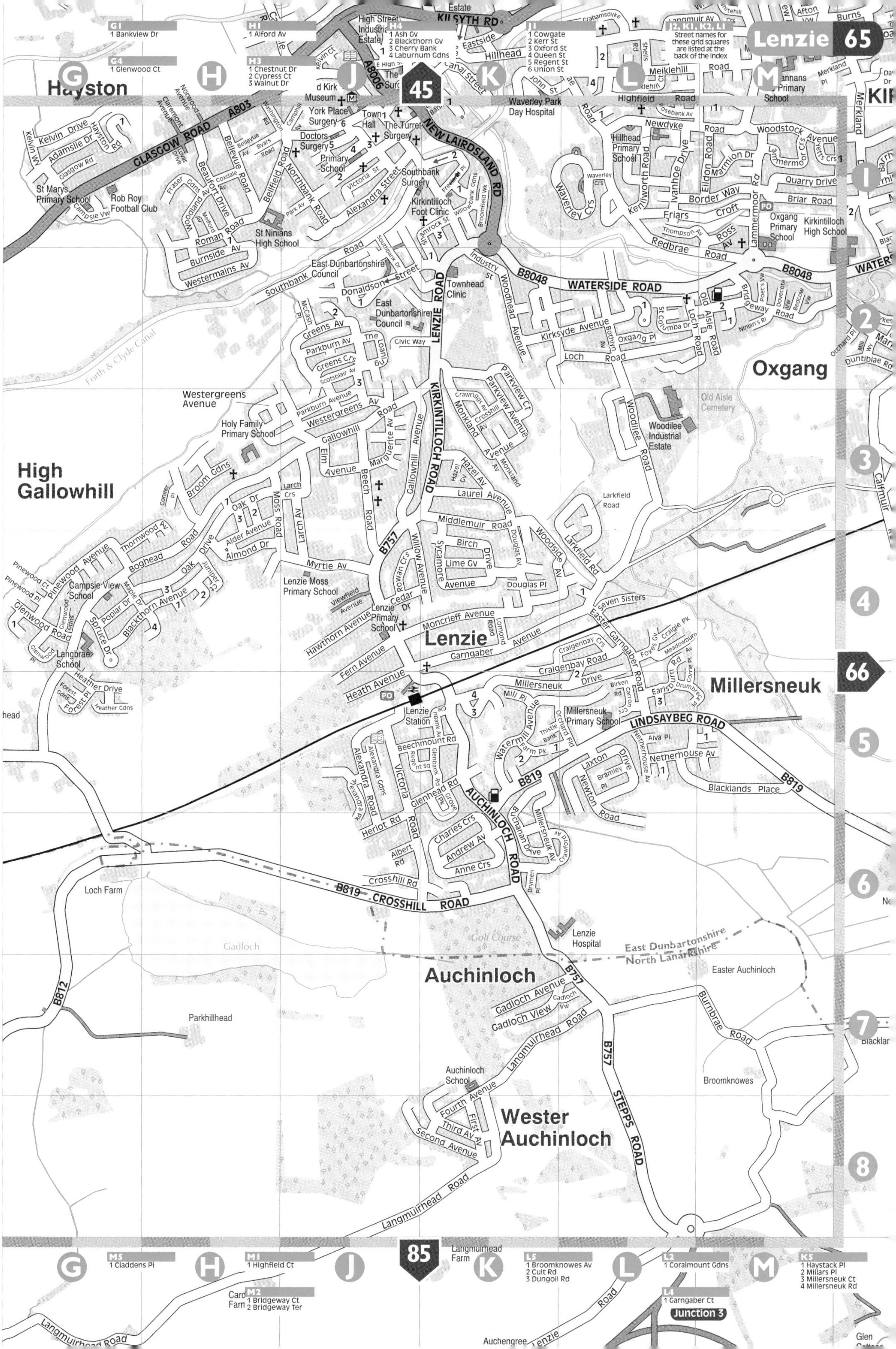
G1
1 Bankview Dr
G4
1 Glenwood Ct
H1
1 Alford Av
H3
1 Chestnut Dr
2 Cypress Ct
3 Walnut Dr
H4
1 Ash Gv
2 Blackthorn Gv
3 Cherry Bank
4 Laburnum Gdns
J1
1 Cowgate
2 Kerr St
3 Oxford St
4 Queen St
5 Regent St
6 Union St
J2, K1, K2, L1
Street names for these grid squares are listed at the back of the index
Hayston
KILSYTH RD
High Street Industrial Estate
A8006
45
NEW LAIRDSLAND RD
GLASGOW ROAD
A803
Waverley Park Day Hospital
Highfield Road
Newdyke
Hillhead Primary School
Kirkintilloch High School
Oxgang Primary School
WATERSIDE ROAD
B8048
Redbrae Road
St Ninians High School
Rob Roy Football Club
St Marys Primary School
East Dunbartonshire Council
Townhead Clinic
Kirkintilloch Foot Clinic
Southbank Surgery
LENZIE ROAD
KIRKINTILLOCH ROAD
B757
Oxgang
Old Aisle Cemetery
Woodilee Industrial Estate
Forth & Clyde Canal
High Gallowhill
Holy Family Primary School
Westergreens Avenue
Campsie View School
Lenzie Moss Primary School
Lenzie Primary School
Langbrae School
Lenzie
Lenzie Station
Millersneuk
Millersneuk Primary School
LINDSAYBEG ROAD
B819
66
AUCHINLOCH ROAD
Lenzie Hospital
B819 CROSSHILL ROAD
Loch Farm
Gadloch
Golf Course
East Dunbartonshire
North Lanarkshire
Auchinloch
Easter Auchinloch
B812
Parkhillhead
Auchinloch School
Wester Auchinloch
STEPPS ROAD
Broomknowes
Langmuirhead Road
85
Langmuirhead Farm
Cardfarm
M5
1 Claddens Pl
M1
1 Highfield Ct
M2
1 Bridgeway Ct
2 Bridgeway Ter
L5
1 Broomknowes Av
2 Cult Rd
3 Dungoil Rd
L2
1 Coralmount Gdns
L4
1 Garngaber Ct
K5
1 Haystack Pl
2 Millars Pl
3 Millersneuk Ct
4 Millersneuk Rd
Junction 3
Auchengree

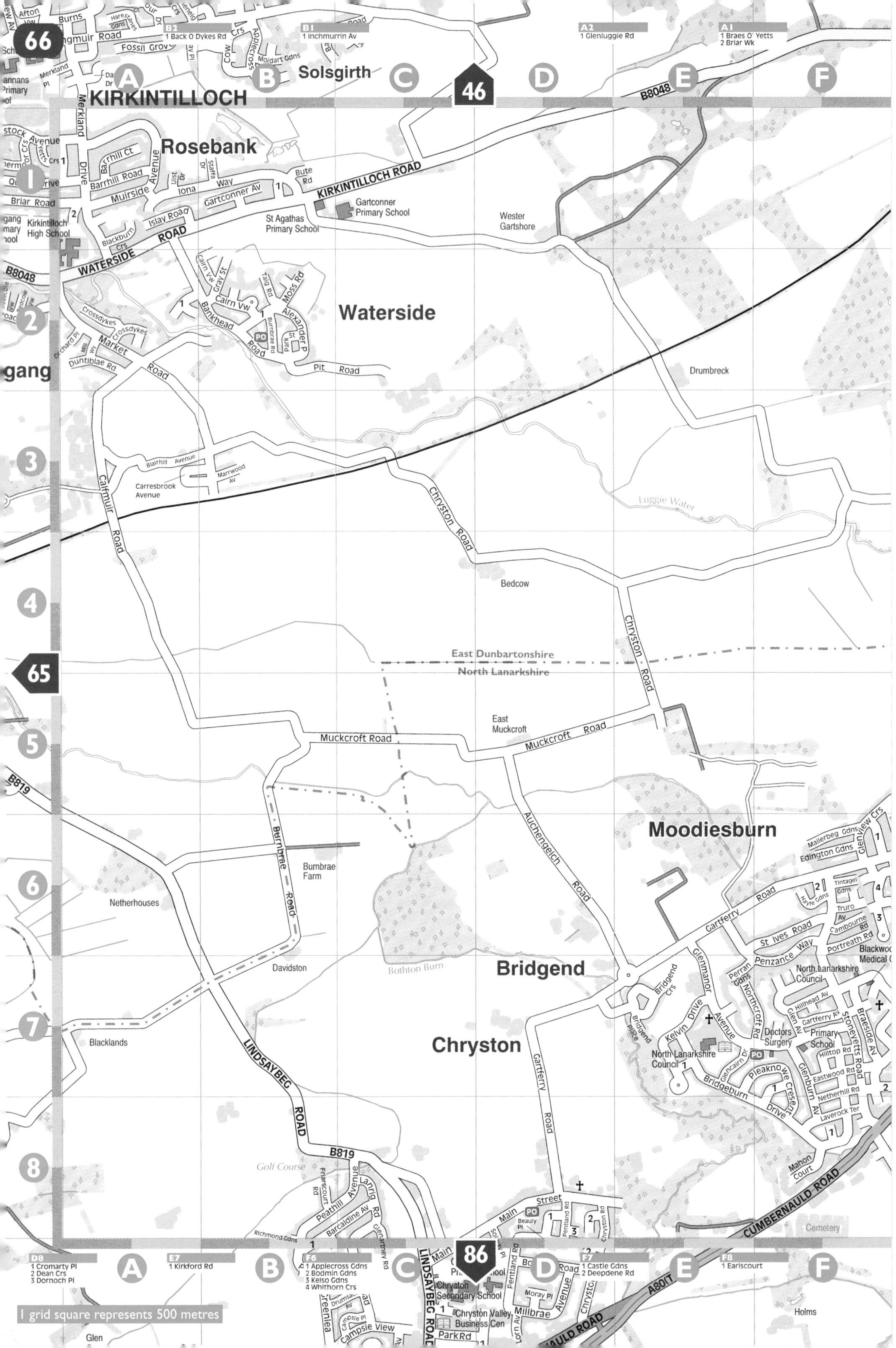

66
46
65
86
A
B
C
D
E
F
1
2
3
4
5
6
7
8
B2 1 Back O Dykes Rd
B1 1 Inchmurrin Av
A2 1 Glenluggie Rd
A1 1 Braes O' Yetts 2 Briar Wk
KIRKINTILLOCH
Solsgirth
Rosebank
Waterside
Moodiesburn
Bridgend
Chryston
Kirkintilloch High School
Gartconner Primary School
St Agathas Primary School
Wester Gartshore
Drumbreck
Bedcow
East Dunbartonshire
North Lanarkshire
East Muckcroft
Burnbrae Farm
Netherhouses
Davidston
Blacklands
Golf Course
Luggie Water
Bothton Burn
North Lanarkshire Council
Doctors Surgery
Primary School
Blackwood Medical C
Chryston Secondary School
Chryston Valley Business Cen
Cemetery
Holms
Glen
KIRKINTILLOCH ROAD
WATERSIDE ROAD
B8048
B819
LINDSAYBEG ROAD
CUMBERNAULD ROAD
A80(T)
Chryston Road
Muckcroft Road
Auchengeich Road
Gartferry Road
Burnbrae Road
Calfmuir Road
Market Road
Bankhead Road
Pit Road
Main Street
Fossil Grove
Merkland Drive
Barrhill Road
Barrhill Ct
Muirside Avenue
Gartconner Av
Islay Road
Iona Way
Blackburn Crs
Crossdykes
Duntiblae Rd
Orchard Pl
Blairhill Avenue
Carresbrook Avenue
Marrwood Av
Calrn Vw
Gray St
Talg Rd
Moss Rd
Alexander P
Park St
Burnbrae Rd
Briar Road
Moldart Gdns
Applecross
St Ives Road
Penzance Way
Portreath Rd
Cambourne Rd
Truro Av
Tintagel Gdns
Mailerbeg Gdns
Edington Gdns
Glenview Crs
Glenmanor Avenue
Northcroft Rd
Perran Gdns
Kelvin Drive
Bridgend Crs
Bridgend Place
Bridgeburn Drive
Pleaknowe Crescent
Glenburn Av
Stoneyetts Road
Braeside Av
Hillhead Av
Gartferry Av
Hilltop Rd
Eastwood Rd
Netherhill Rd
Laverock Ter
Mahon Court
Friarscourt Rd
Peathill Avenue
Lanrig Rd
Barcaldine Av
Richmond Gdns
Glenartney Rd
Pentland Rd
Beauly Pl
Moray Pl
Millbrae Avenue
Park Rd
Campsie View
D8 1 Cromarty Pl 2 Dean Crs 3 Dornoch Pl
E7 1 Kirkford Rd
F6 1 Applecross Gdns 2 Bodmin Gdns 3 Kelso Gdns 4 Whithorn Crs
F7 1 Castle Gdns 2 Deepdene Rd
F8 1 Earlscourt
1 grid square represents 500 metres

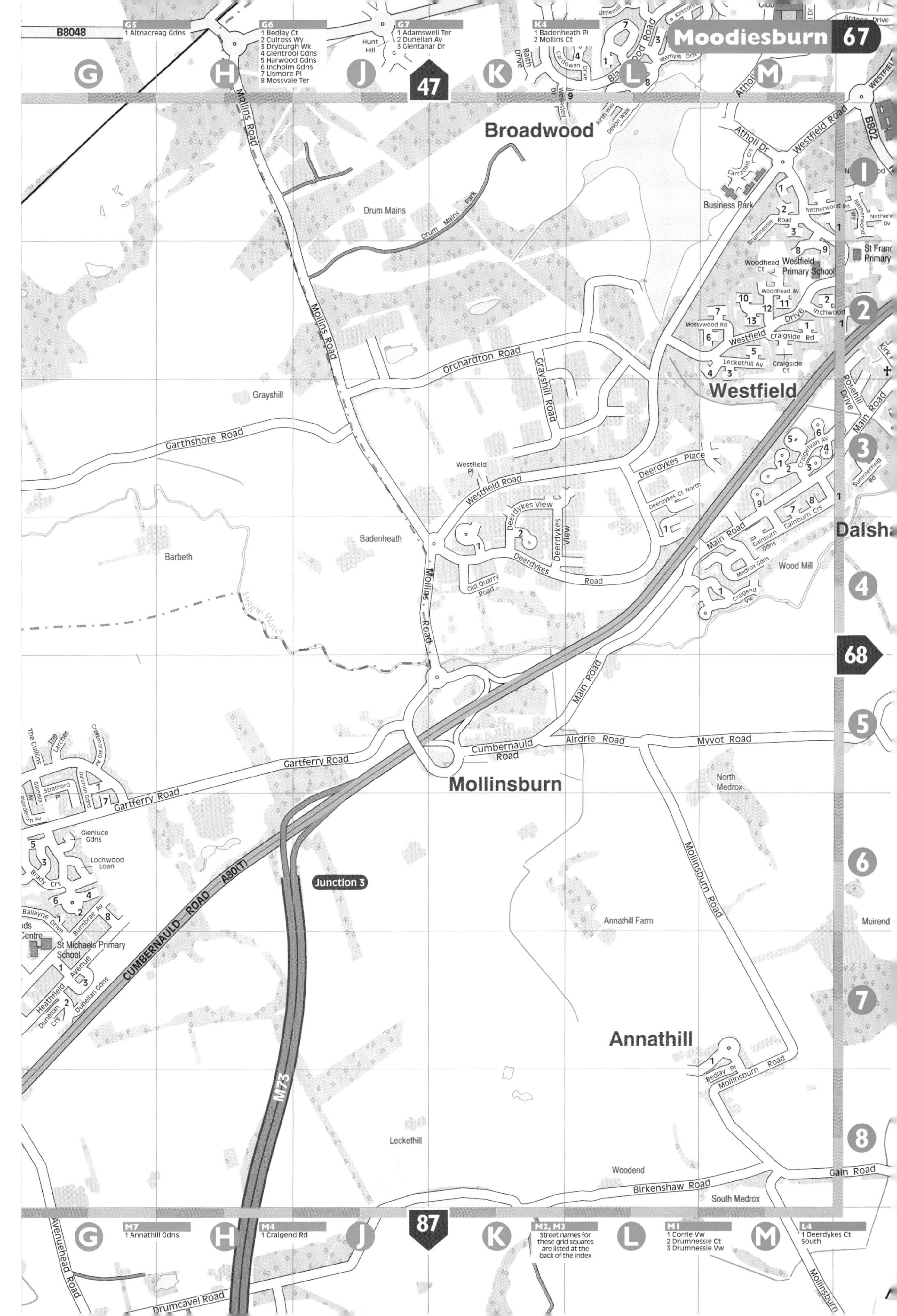
G5
1 Altnacreag Gdns
G6
1 Bedlay Ct
2 Culross Wy
3 Dryburgh Wk
4 Glentrool Gdns
5 Harwood Gdns
6 Incholm Gdns
7 Lismore Pl
8 Mossvale Ter
G7
1 Adamswell Ter
2 Dunellan Av
3 Glentanar Dr
K4
1 Badenheath Pl
2 Mollins Ct
B8048
Hunt Hill
47
68
87
Broadwood
Drum Mains
Drum Mains Park
Mollins Road
Orchardton Road
Grayshill Road
Grayshill
Garthshore Road
Westfield Pl
Westfield Road
Deerdykes Place
Deerdykes Ct North
Deerdykes View
Deerdykes Road
Old Quarry Road
Badenheath
Barbeth
Luggie Water
Business Park
Atholl Dr
Westfield Road
Carradale Crs
Drumnessie Road
Netherwood Rd
Netherwood Wy
Woodhead Ct
Westfield Primary School
St Francis Primary
Woodhead Av
Inchwood Drive
Mossywood Rd
Westfield Drive
Craigside Rd
Leckethill Av
Craigside Ct
Westfield
Rosehill Drive
Main Road
Craigelvan Av
Summerfield Rd
Gainburn Crs
Gainburn Gdns
Medrox Gdns
Craigend Vw
Wood Mill
Dalsh
Main Road
Cumbernauld Road
Airdrie Road
Myvot Road
North Medrox
Mollinsburn
Gartferry Road
The Cuillins
The Larches
Croftmoraig Av
Strathord Pl
Dalcruin Gdns
Glenluce Gdns
Lochwood Loan
Brady Crs
Ballayne Drive
Burnbrae Av
St Michaels Primary School
Avenue
Heathfield
Dunellan Crs
Dunellan Gdns
CUMBERNAULD ROAD A80(T)
Junction 3
M73
Mollinsburn Road
Annathill Farm
Muirend
Annathill
Bedlay Pl
Mollinsburn Road
Leckethill
Woodend
Birkenshaw Road
Gain Road
South Medrox
M7
1 Annathill Gdns
M4
1 Craigend Rd
M2, M3
Street names for these grid squares are listed at the back of the index
M1
1 Corrie Vw
2 Drumnessie Ct
3 Drumnessie Vw
L4
1 Deerdykes Ct South
Avenuehead Road
Drumcavel Road

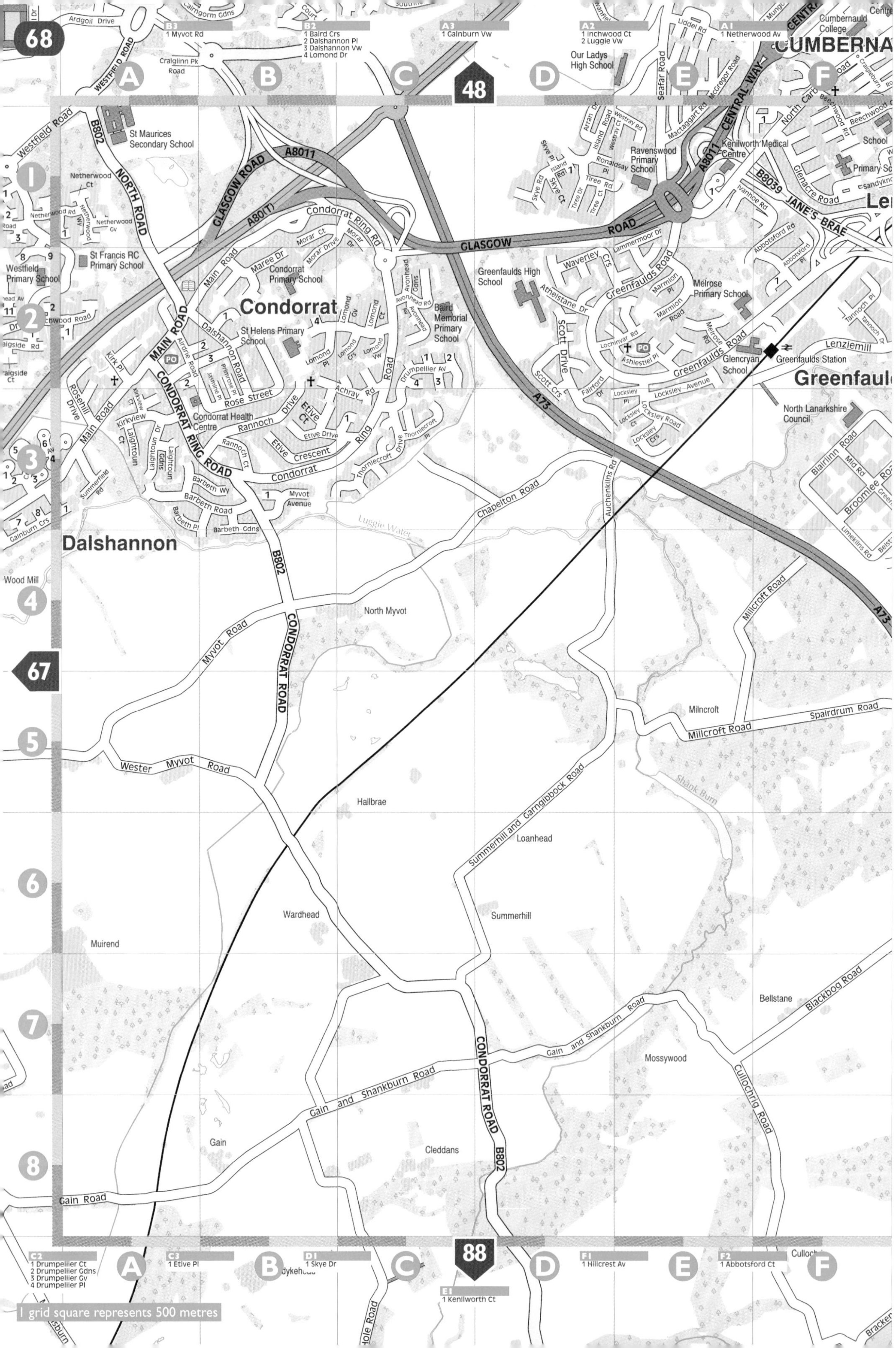
B3
1 Myvot Rd
B2
1 Baird Crs
2 Dalshannon Pl
3 Dalshannon Vw
4 Lomond Dr
A3
1 Gainburn Vw
A2
1 Inchwood Ct
2 Luggie Vw
A1
1 Netherwood Av
48
CUMBERNAULD
Cumbernauld College
Our Ladys High School
St Maurices Secondary School
Netherwood Ct
St Francis RC Primary School
Westfield Primary School
Westfield Road
NORTH ROAD
GLASGOW ROAD
A8011
A80(T)
Condorrat Ring Rd
Morar Ct
Maree Dr
Condorrat Primary School
Condorrat
St Helens Primary School
Baird Memorial Primary School
Drumpellier Av
MAIN ROAD
CONDORRAT RING ROAD
Rose Street
Rannoch Drive
Etive Crescent
Condorrat Health Centre
Barbeth Road
Barbeth Gdns
Myvot Avenue
Dalshannon
Luggie Water
Chapelton Road
GLASGOW ROAD
Greenfaulds High School
Ravenswood Primary School
Kenilworth Medical Centre
CENTRAL WAY
B8039
JANE'S BRAE
Glenacre Road
Waverley Crs
Athelstane Dr
Greenfaulds Road
Melrose Primary School
Scott Drive
Lochinvar Rd
Glencryan School
Greenfaulds Station
Greenfaulds
Lenziemill
North Lanarkshire Council
Locksley Avenue
Locksley Road
A73
Auchenkilns Rd
Blairlinn Road
Broomlee Road
Wood Mill
North Myvot
Myvot Road
CONDORRAT ROAD
B802
Millcroft Road
Milncroft
Spairdrum Road
67
Wester Myvot Road
Hallbrae
Shank Burn
Summerhill and Garngibbock Road
Loanhead
Wardhead
Summerhill
Muirend
Bellstane
Blackbog Road
Gain and Shankburn Road
Mossywood
Cullochrig Road
Gain
Cleddans
Gain Road
88
C2
1 Drumpellier Ct
2 Drumpellier Gdns
3 Drumpellier Gv
4 Drumpellier Pl
C3
1 Etive Pl
D1
1 Skye Dr
E1
1 Kenilworth Ct
F1
1 Hillcrest Av
F2
1 Abbotsford Ct
1 grid square represents 500 metres

Carbrain
1 Greenfaulds Crs
1 Spairdrum Rd
Stonylee Rd
Greenfaulds Road
Glencryan Road
Kilbowie Road
Carbrain Road
Broomlands Rd
South
Cumbernauld Station
North Lanarkshire Council
LENZIEMILL ROAD
Lenziemill
G67
Kelvin Rd N
Kelvin Road
Telford Pl
Telford Road
B8054
Greenside
Waterhead
Road
B8039
Palacerigg Country Park
Tannoch
Luggie Water
Stirling Road
Blair Linn Vw
Tower Rd
BLAIRLINN ROAD
Luggiebank
Blairlinn
Glenhove
Coathill
Fedderland
Wester Glentore
Hulks Road
Millcroft Road
STIRLING ROAD
Muirhead
Boglea
Loanhead
Brackenknowe Road
Windyridge
BLACKBOG RD
Staylee
B8039
STIRLING ROAD - A73
Blacktongue
Greengairs
Whinrigg
Rankin Crs
Hillview
Greengairs Primary School
GREENGAIRS ROAD
PO
Coalburn Street
Laurel Grove
Cameron Road
Cameron
B803
Drumgray House
Wattston
Drumgray Gdns
Drumgray Lane
Hillrigg
Riggend
Mill Road
Meikle Drumgray Road
ROAD
49
89
G
H
J
K
L
M
1
2
3
4
5
6
7
8

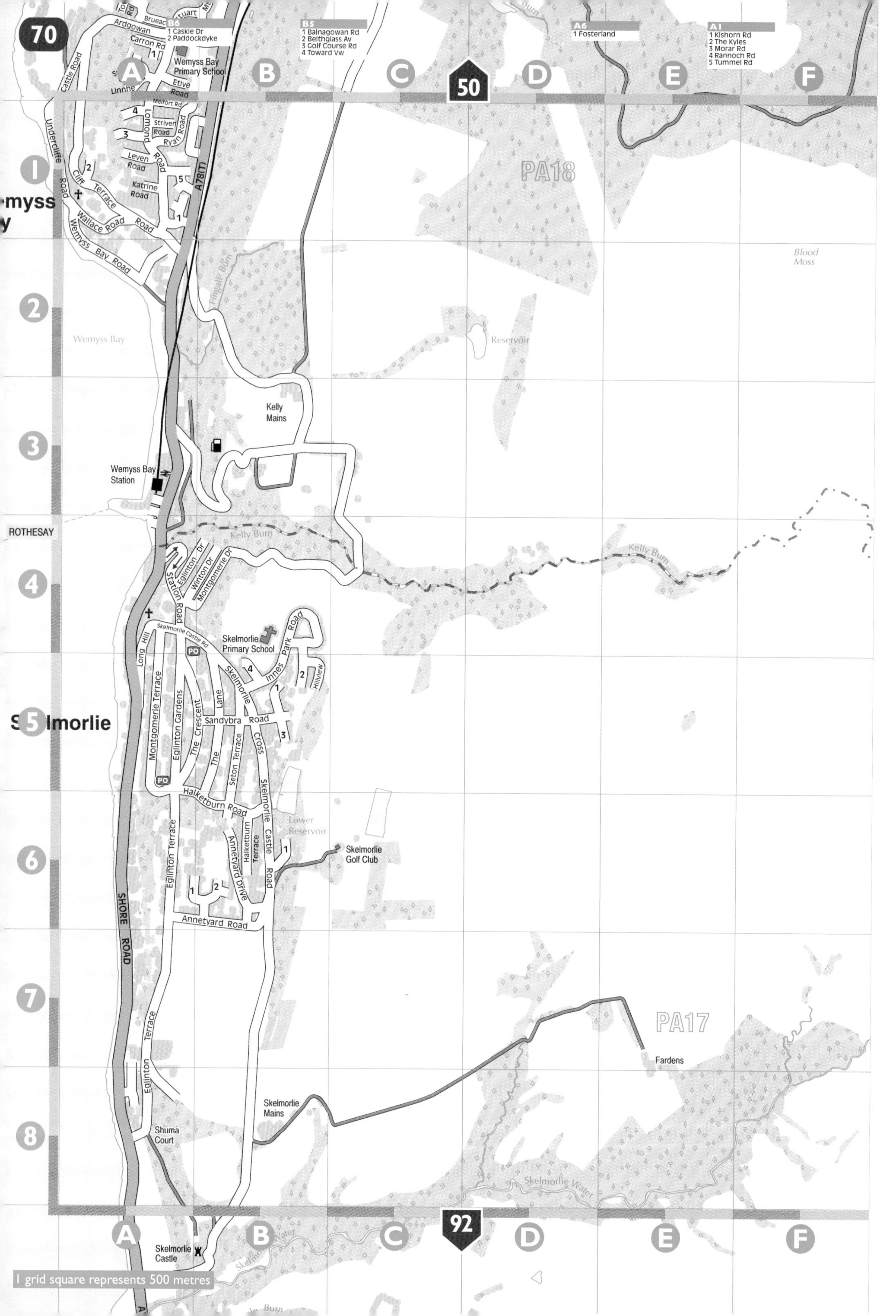
B6
1 Caskie Dr
2 Paddockdyke
B5
1 Balnagowan Rd
2 Beithglass Av
3 Golf Course Rd
4 Toward Vw
A6
1 Fosterland
A1
1 Kishorn Rd
2 The Kyles
3 Morar Rd
4 Rannoch Rd
5 Tummel Rd
A
B
C
50
D
E
F
Ardgowan
Carron Rd
Castle Road
Wemyss Bay Primary School
Linnhe
Etive Road
Melfort Rd
Striven Road
Lomond Road
Ryan Road
Leven Road
Katrine Road
Undercliffe Road
Cliff Terrace
Wallace Road
Wemyss Bay Road
A78(T)
PA18
Blood Moss
Fingall Burn
Wemyss Bay
Reservoir
Kelly Mains
Wemyss Bay Station
ROTHESAY
Kelly Burn
Eglinton Dr
Winton Dr
Montgomerie Dr
Station Road
Skelmorlie Castle Rd
Skelmorlie Primary School
Innes Park Road
Hillview
Long Hill
Skelmorlie
Sandybra Road
Montgomerie Terrace
Eglinton Gardens
The Crescent
The Lane
Seton Terrace
Cross
Halketburn Road
Skelmorlie Castle Road
Lower Reservoir
Skelmorlie Golf Club
Eglinton Terrace
Annetyard Drive
Halketburn Terrace
Annetyard Road
SHORE ROAD
PA17
Fardens
Skelmorlie Mains
Shuma Court
Skelmorlie Water
92
Skelmorlie Castle
1 grid square represents 500 metres

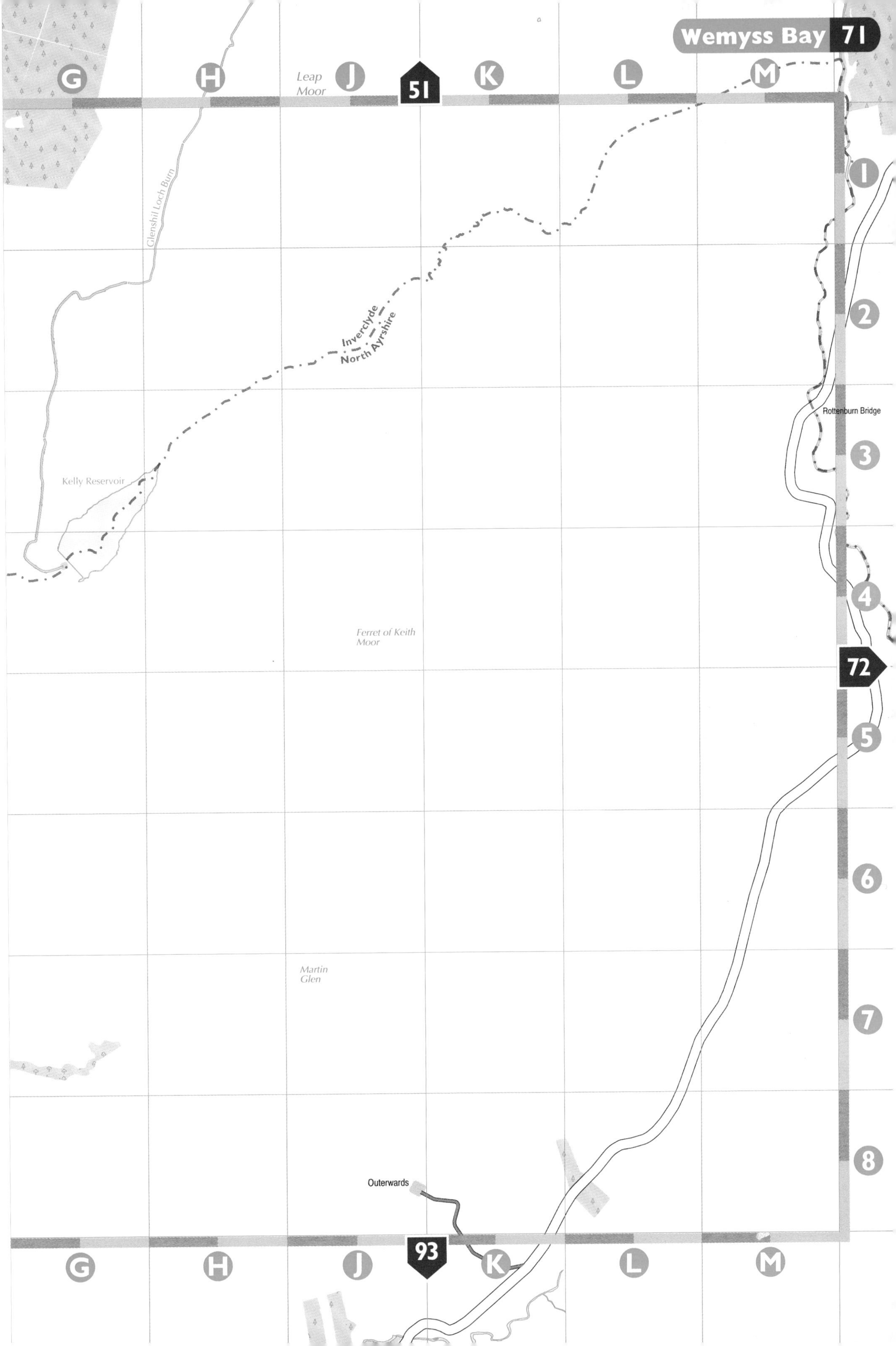
Leap Moor
51
Glenshil Loch Burn
Inverclyde
North Ayrshire
Rottenburn Bridge
Kelly Reservoir
Ferret of Keith Moor
72
Martin Glen
Outerwards
93
G
H
J
K
L
M
1
2
3
4
5
6
7
8

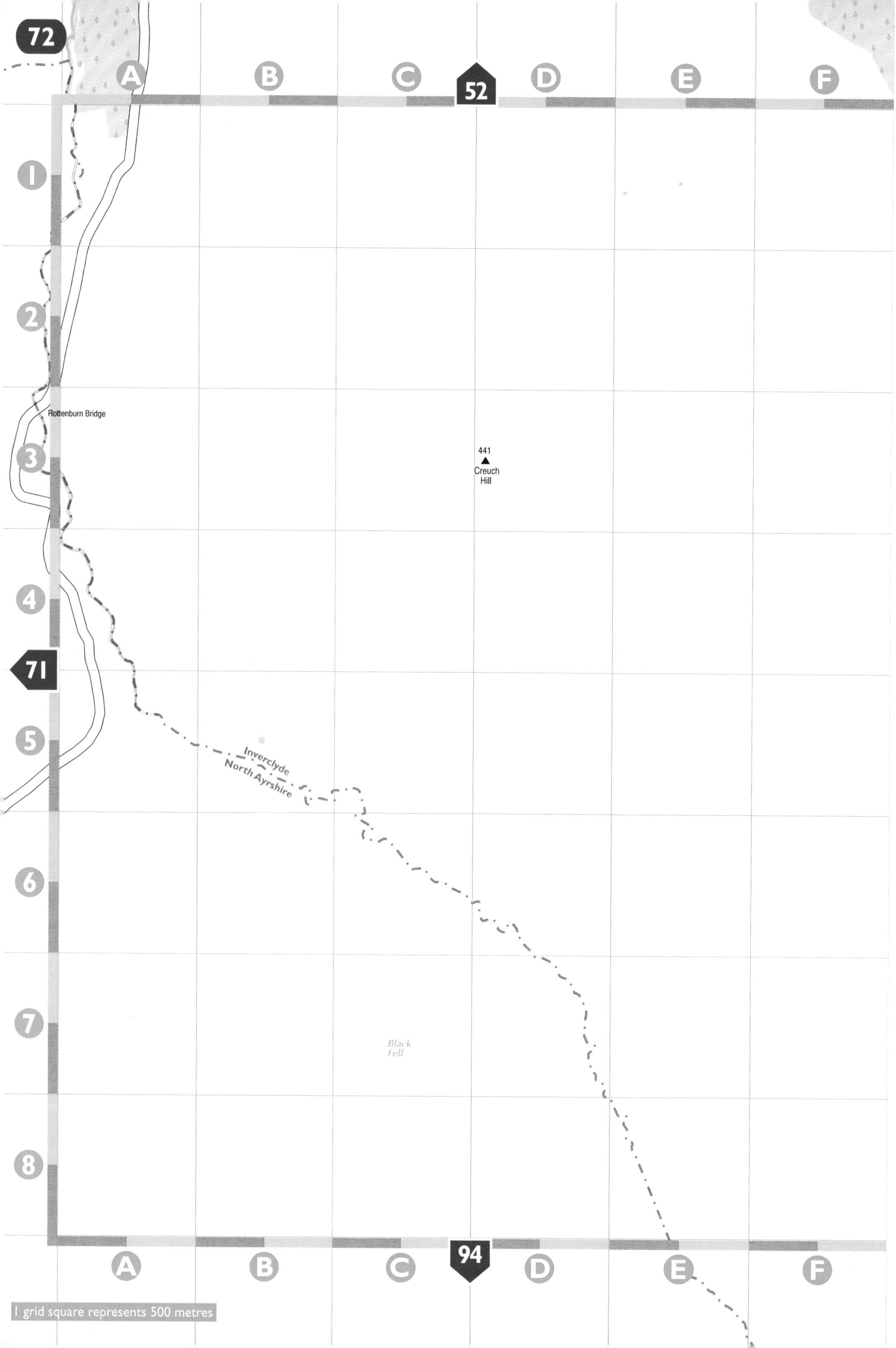
72
A
B
C
52
D
E
F
1
2
Rottenburn Bridge
3
441
Creuch
Hill
4
71
5
Inverclyde
North Ayrshire
6
7
Black
Fell
8
A
B
C
94
D
E
F
1 grid square represents 500 metres

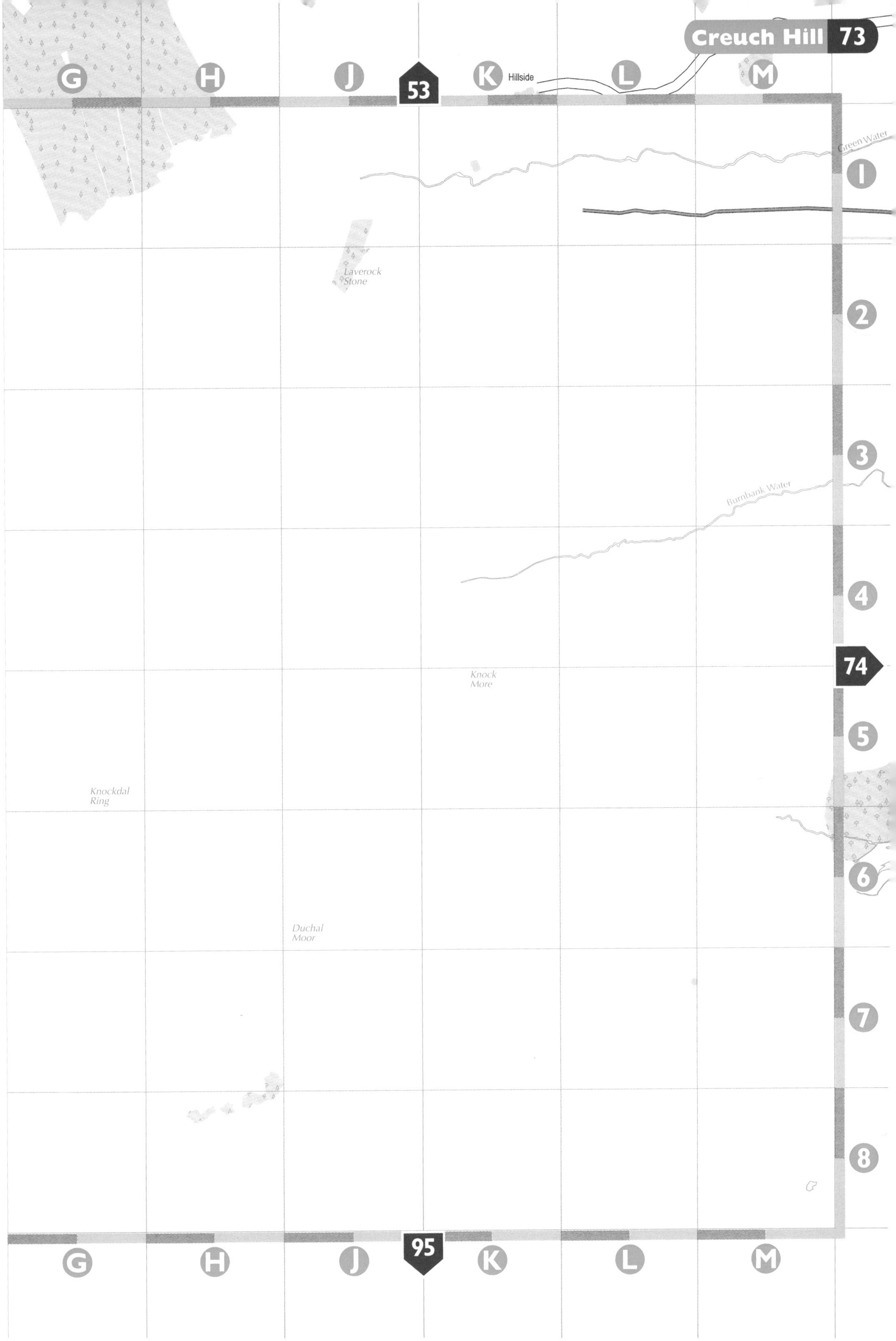
G
H
J
53
K
Hillside
L
M
Green Water
1
Laverock Stone
2
3
Burnbank Water
4
74
Knock More
5
Knockdal Ring
6
Duchal Moor
7
8
G
H
J
95
K
L
M

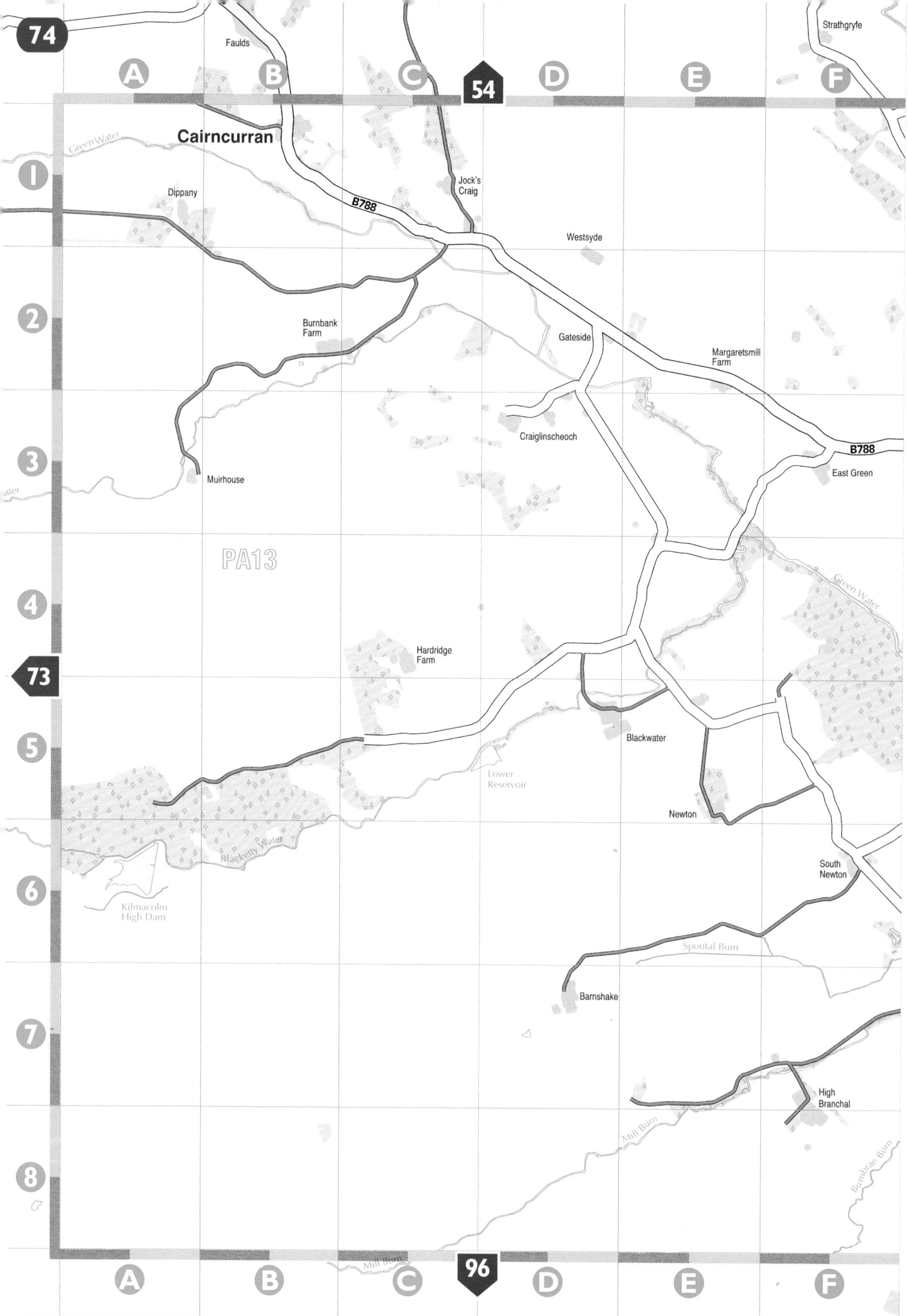
74
Faulds
Strathgryfe
A
B
C
54
D
E
F
Cairncurran
Green Water
1
Dippany
Jock's Craig
B788
Westsyde
2
Burnbank Farm
Gateside
Margaretsmill Farm
Craiglinscheoch
B788
3
Muirhouse
East Green
PA13
4
Green Water
Hardridge Farm
73
5
Blackwater
Lower Reservoir
Newton
Blacketty Water
6
South Newton
Kilmacolm High Dam
Spoutal Burn
Barnshake
7
High Branchal
Mill Burn
8
Burnbrae Burn
Mill Burn
96
A
B
C
D
E
F

1 grid square represents 500 metres

H1
1 Westfield Dr
J1
1 Carruth Dr
2 Orchard Gv
3 Park Rd
J2
1 Balmore Ct
2 Kenmore Rd
3 Rannoch Rd
4 Roslin Ct
GLASGOW ROAD
55
76
97
KILMACOLM
Netherwood
Slates
Mill Dam
Balrossie School
Balrossie Drive
Knockbuckle Road
Milburn Dr
Florence Drive
Hazelmere Road
Pacemuir Road
Broomknowe
Castlehill Crs
Castlehill Road
Whitelea Road
Primary School
Park Road
ROAD
B786
Police Station
St Columbas School
Gryffe
Duchal Road
Kilmacolm Primary School
Glenclune Court
Churchill
Myreton Avenue
Belmont
LOCHWINNOCH
Gryfe Water
Milton
New Surgery
Glencairn
Rowantreehill Road
Gowkhouse Road
Glenmosston Road
Glen Moss
Porterfield Road
BRIDGE OF WEIR ROAD
Kilallan Road
Houston Road
Gryffe Road
North Denniston
A761
Knapps Loch
B788
Lawpark
Duchal House
Craigends Dennistoun
Killochries
Duchal Mains
Hattrick Farm
Trout Farm
Burnbank
Glenmill
Craigends Avenue
Craigends Place
Church Road
Love Avenue
Hope Avenue
Elise Hospital
Quarriers Village
Carsemeadow School
Faith Avenue
Peace Avenue
North Branchal
Craigbet Place
Craigbet Avenue
Hospital
South Branchal
Carruth Burn
Carruth House
Gibblaston
Gotter Water
L7
1 Craigbet Crs
2 Hope Av
3 Torr Av
4 Torr La
L1
1 Barclaven Rd
2 Lodge Crs
K2
1 Beauly Crs
2 Porterfield Rd
K1
1 Gillburn Rd
2 Glebe Rd
3 Lyle Rd
4 Whitelea Crs

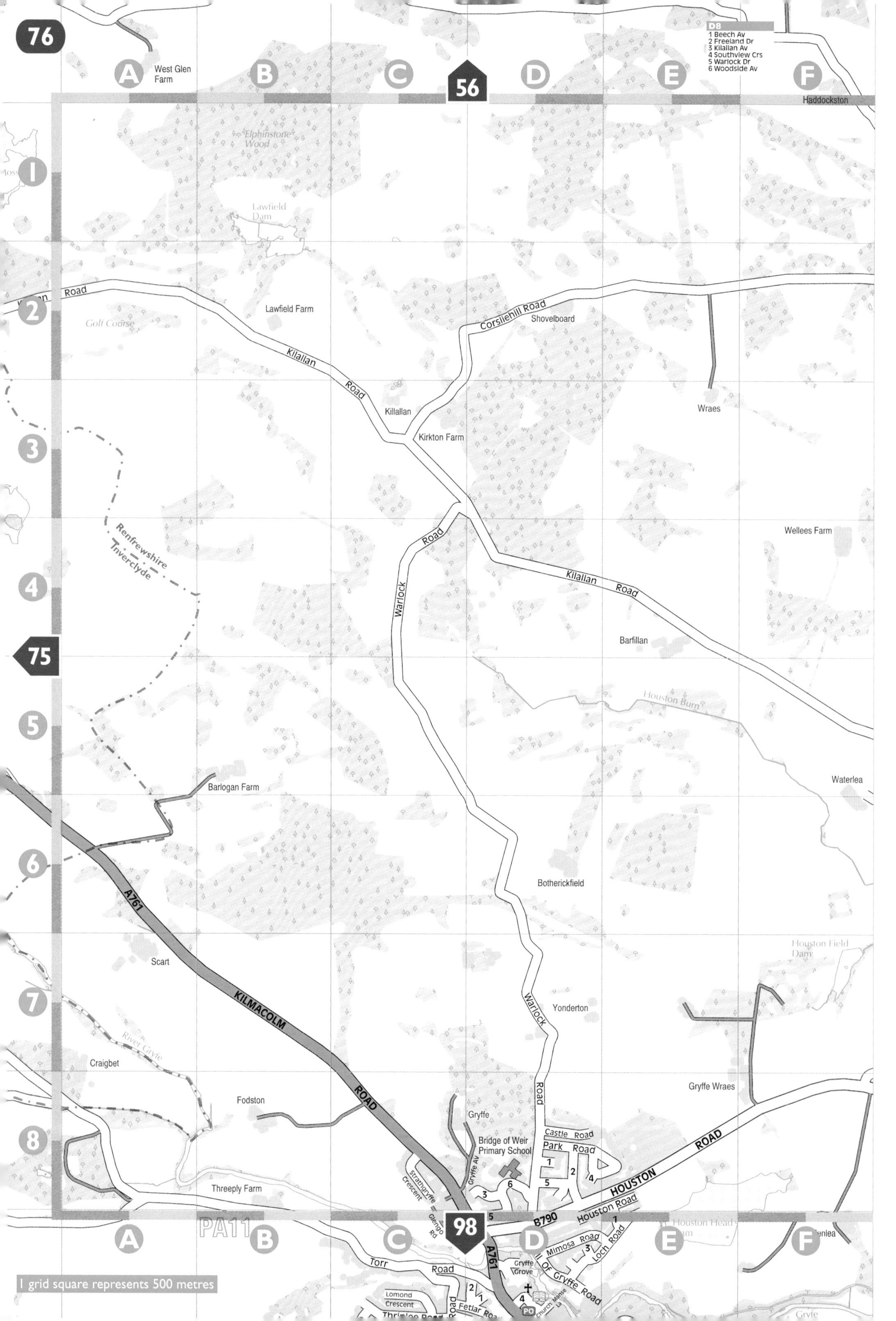
D8
1 Beech Av
2 Freeland Dr
3 Kilallan Av
4 Southview Crs
5 Warlock Dr
6 Woodside Av
56
Haddockston
West Glen Farm
Elphinstone Wood
Lawfield Dam
Lawfield Farm
Golf Course
Road
Kilallan Road
Corsliehill Road
Shovelboard
Killallan
Kirkton Farm
Wraes
Warlock Road
Renfrewshire
Inverclyde
Kilallan Road
Wellees Farm
Barfillan
Houston Burn
75
Barlogan Farm
Waterlea
Botherickfield
A761
Scart
Houston Field Dam
KILMACOLM ROAD
Warlock Road
Yonderton
River Gryfe
Craigbet
Fodston
Gryffe Wraes
Gryffe
Bridge of Weir Primary School
Castle Road
Park Road
Gryffe Av
Strathgryffe Crescent
HOUSTON ROAD
Threeply Farm
PA11
B790
Houston Road
Glengo Rd
98
Houston Head Dam
Mimosa Road
Loch Road
Torr Road
A761
Gryffe Grove
Mill of Gryffe Road
Lomond Crescent
Fetlar Road
Church
Monse La
PO
Gryfe
1 grid square represents 500 metres

G7
1 Glenartney
H6
1 Cricketfield La
2 Old Schoolhouse La
H7
1 Four Windings
2 Houston Rd
3 Manse Crs
Meiklefield
East Glenshi
57
G
H
J
K
L
M
B789
Towncroft
Reilly Road
Barochan
BAROCHAN ROAD
Corsliehill Road
Corsliehill
Reilly Farm
Road
Turningshaw
Corsliehill Road
B789
Stabilee
Barochan House
Chapel Farm
Barochan Moss
PA6
Cleaves Farm
Turningshaw Farm
78
BAROCHAN ROAD
Chapel Road
Kilallan Road
B789
Chapel Road
Turningshaw Road
Loanhead
HOUSTON ROAD
Kilmacolm Road
Houston Surgery
Houston House
North Mains
MAIN STREET
North St
Kirk Road
Burnlea Crs
Fleming Road
Bogstonhill Rd
South St
Kingslea Rd
B790
South Mains
Craigends Road
River Gryfe
Houstonfield Qd
South Street
Houston
B789
Road
HOUSTON ROAD
Houston Rd
Glebe Gdns
Hagart Rd
Manse Crs
Spiers Rd
St Fillans Dr
S Mound
Old Bridge Of Weir Rd
Primary School
Cemetery
Neuk Crs
Neuk Av
Crossways
Craigholme
Woodside
Argryfe
Birchgrove
Brackendene
Broomfield
Ardgryfe Crs
The Mdw
The Beeches
Riverside
Gryffe High School
B790 BRIDGE OF WEIR ROAD
Houston Rd
Houston Primary School
HOUSTON ROAD
Leepburn Av
Crosslee
Back O Hill
Houston R
Craigends
Whirlie Rd
Hewett Crs
Murchison Rd
Dunlin Crs
Crawford Road
Magnus Road
Gryfebank Crs
Gryfebank Avenue
Locher Av
Locher Wy
Auchans
Earlsgate
Crosslea Gdns
Brierie-Hill Rd
Hutton Av
Crosslee Pk
Beatrice
99
L8
1 Gryfebank Cl
2 Gryfebank Wy
3 Gryfewood Crs
4 Gryfewood Wy
5 Locher Crs
L8
1 Crosslee Crs
H8
1 Brierie Av
2 Dunnet Dr
3 Strawberry Field Rd
Goldenlee Vw
Brierie La
Brierie Hill
Whirlie Rd
Brierie-Hill Road
Piper Av
Bream Pl
Alwyn Av
Cormorant Av
Magnus Road
Claymore Dr
Berl Av
Hillside
Auchans Road
River Gryfe
B789
1
2
3
4
5
6
7
8

Junction 30
58
A
B
C
D
E
F
1
2
3
4
5
6
7
8
77
100
A8
M8
Dargavel Road
Linburn
Hotel
Lomond
Lubnaig
Millfield View
Millfield Wynd
Old
Barrangary
Craigmuir
Southbar
Dargavel House
GREENOCK ROAD
Nether Southbar
North Commonside
South Crooks
East Fulwood
B790
HOUSTON ROAD
Netherfield
Selvieland
OUSTON ROAD
Moss Road
Fulwood
River Gryfe
Birkenhead
Knowes
Auchans Road
Moss Cottage
Blackstoun
Auchans
Road
Candrens
Linwood
1 grid square represents 500 metres

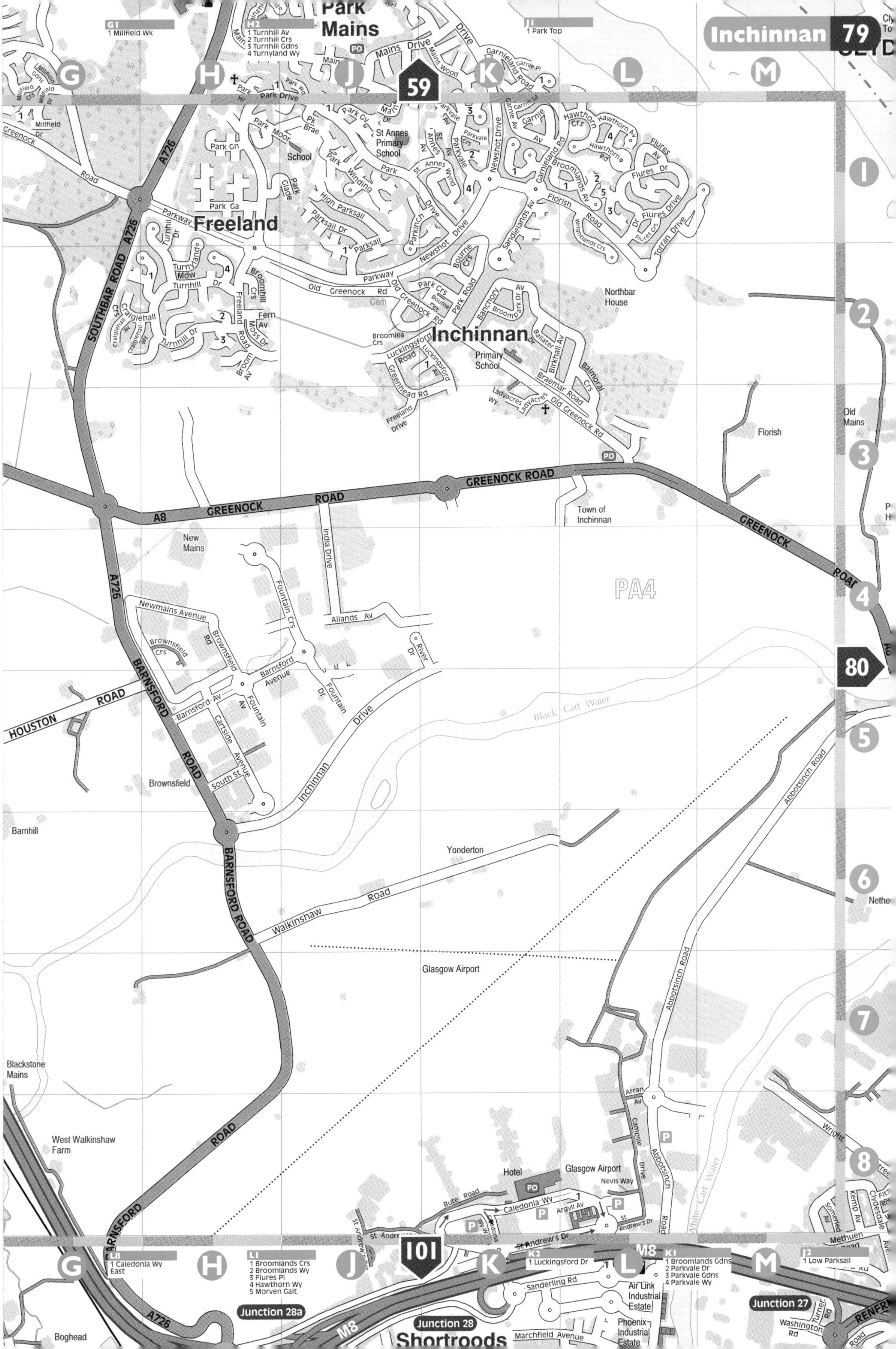
G1
1 Millfield Wk
H2
1 Turnhill Av
2 Turnhill Crs
3 Turnhill Gdns
4 Turnyland Wy
J1
1 Park Top
Park
Mains
Mains Drive
Garnieland Road
Park Drive
59
St Annes
Primary
School
School
Park Gn
Park Ga
Freeland
Parkway
Greenock
Road
Southbar Road
A726
Turnhill Dr
Craigiehall
Broomhill Crs
Freeland Road
Fern Av
Moss Dr
Broom Av
Old Greenock Rd
Cem
Broomlea Crs
Luckingsford Road
Greenhead Rd
Freeland Drive
Inchinnan
Primary
School
Park Road
Newshot Drive
High Parksail
Parksail Dr
Parksail
Parkinch Drive
Bourne Crs
Banchory Av
Broompark Dr
Birkhall Av
Balmoral Crs
Braemar Road
Ladyacres
Ladyacres Wy
Old Greenock Rd
Florish Road
Sandielands Av
Broomlands Av
Hawthorn Crs
Hawthorn Av
Flures Av
Flures Dr
Flures Drive
Torran Drive
Northbar
House
Old
Mains
Florish
A8
GREENOCK ROAD
Town of
Inchinnan
New
Mains
India Drive
Allands Av
Fountain Crs
Fountain Dr
PA4
River Dr
Newmains Avenue
Brownsfield Crs
Brownsfield Rd
Barnsford Avenue
Barnsford Av
Fountain Av
Cartside Avenue
South St
Brownsfield
BARNSFORD ROAD
HOUSTON ROAD
Inchinnan Drive
Black Cart Water
80
Barnhill
Yonderton
Walkinshaw Road
Glasgow Airport
Abbotsinch Road
Blackstone
Mains
West Walkinshaw
Farm
Arran Av
Campsie Drive
Hotel
Glasgow Airport
Nevis Way
Bute Road
Caledonia Wy
Argyll Av
St Andrew's Dr
White Cart Water
Kemp Av
Clydesdale Av
Methuen Road
Wright Street
Nethe
G
H
J
K
L
M
101
L8
1 Caledonia Wy
East
L1
1 Broomlands Crs
2 Broomlands Wy
3 Flures Pl
4 Hawthorn Wy
5 Morven Gait
K2
1 Luckingsford Dr
K1
1 Broomlands Gdns
2 Parkvale Dr
3 Parkvale Gdns
4 Parkvale Wy
J2
1 Low Parksail
M8
Junction 28a
Junction 28
Junction 27
Sanderling Rd
Air Link
Industrial
Estate
Phoenix
Industrial
Estate
Marchfield Avenue
Shortroods
Boghead
Washington Rd
Turner Rd

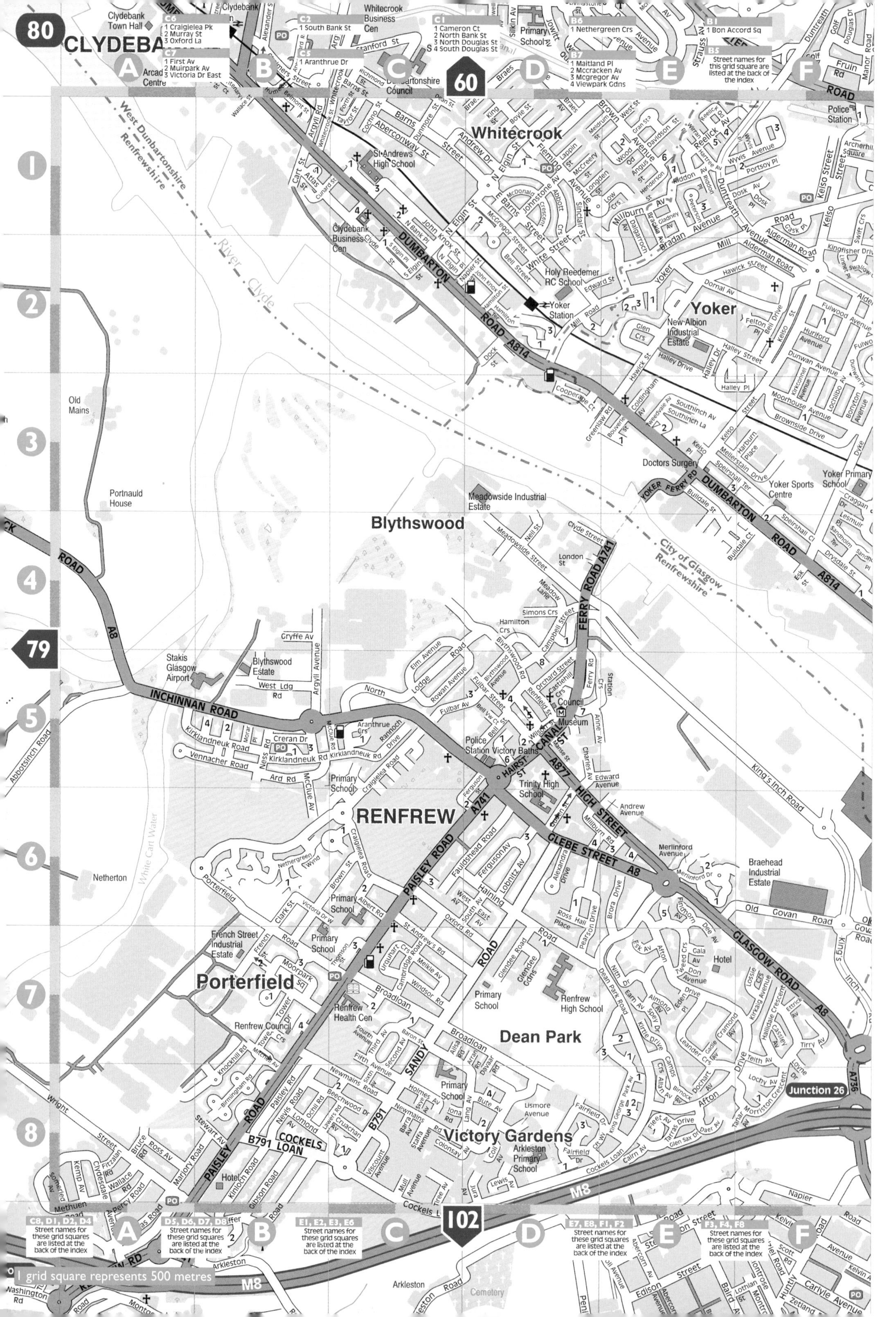
80
CLYDEBANK
Clydebank Town Hall
C6
1 Craigielea Pk
2 Murray St
3 Oxford La
C7
1 First Av
2 Muirpark Av
3 Victoria Dr East
C2
1 South Bank St
C5
1 Aranthrue Dr
C1
1 Cameron Ct
2 North Bank St
3 North Douglas St
4 South Douglas St
B6
1 Nethergreen Crs
B7
1 Maitland Pl
2 Mccracken Av
3 Mcgregor Av
4 Viewpark Gdns
B1
1 Bon Accord Sq
B5
Street names for this grid square are listed at the back of the index
60
Whitecrook
St Andrews High School
Clydebank Business Cen
Clydebank Council
DUMBARTON ROAD A814
River Clyde
West Dunbartonshire
Renfrewshire
Holy Redeemer RC School
Yoker Station
Yoker
New Albion Industrial Estate
Police Station
Doctors Surgery
Yoker Primary School
Yoker Sports Centre
City of Glasgow
Renfrewshire
Old Mains
Portnauld House
Meadowside Industrial Estate
Blythswood
FERRY ROAD A741
79
Stakis Glasgow Airport
Blythswood Estate
INCHINNAN ROAD
A8
RENFREW
Police Station
Victory Baths
Council
Museum
Trinity High School
HAIRST ST
CANAL ST
A877
HIGH STREET
GLEBE STREET A8
PAISLEY ROAD A741
Netherton
White Cart Water
French Street Industrial Estate
Porterfield
Renfrew Council
Renfrew Health Cen
Primary School
Renfrew High School
Dean Park
Braehead Industrial Estate
Hotel
GLASGOW ROAD A8
King's Inch Road
Junction 26
A736
Victory Gardens
Arkleston Primary School
B791 COCKELS LOAN
M8
102
C8, D1, D2, D4
Street names for these grid squares are listed at the back of the index
D5, D6, D7, D8
Street names for these grid squares are listed at the back of the index
E1, E2, E3, E6
Street names for these grid squares are listed at the back of the index
E7, E8, F1, F2
Street names for these grid squares are listed at the back of the index
F3, F4, F8
Street names for these grid squares are listed at the back of the index
Arkleston
Cemetery
1 grid square represents 500 metres
A
B
C
D
E
F
1
2
3
4
5
6
7
8

Numbered streets
The names of all numbered streets on this page are listed at the back of the index
61
82
103
G
H
J
K
L
M
1
2
3
4
5
6
7
8
Knightswood
Temple
Anniesland
Scotstoun
Jordanhill
Broomhill
Whiteinch
Shieldhall
Linthouse
G13
G14
GREAT WESTERN ROAD
A82
A739
A814
A8
DUMBARTON ROAD
VICTORIA PK DRIVE S
BEARSDEN ROAD
CROW RD
HOLMFAULD RD
RENFREW ROAD
Golf Course
Anniesland Industrial Estate
University of Glasgow
Munro Business Centre
Glasgow City Council
Anniesland Station
G H K Rugby Football Club
High School of Glasgow
University of Strathclyde
Jordanhill College School
Scotstounhill Station
Garscadden Station
Blawarthill Hospital
Jordanhill Station
St Thomas Aquinas RC Secondary School
Victoria Park
Whiteinch Indoor Bowling Stadium
Braehead Shopping Centre
River Clyde
Junction 25a
Renfrewshire
City of Glasgow
Southern General Hospital
St Anthonys School

Numbered streets
The names of all numbered streets on this page are listed at the back of the index
A
B
C
D
E
F
62
81
104
1
2
3
4
5
6
7
8
Maryhill
Kelvindale
Kelvinside
Dowanhill
Partick
Yorkhill
G20
G12
G11
MARYHILL ROAD
A81
GREAT WESTERN ROAD
A82
GT WESTERN RD
BYRES RD
B808
BEITH STREET
POINTHOUSE ROAD
BILSLAND DRIVE
Lambhill Cemetery
Forth & Clyde Canal
River Kelvin
Dawsholm Park
University of Glasgow
Glasgow Caledonian University
Gartnavel General Hospital
Gartnavel Royal Hospital
Glasgow Nuffield Hospital
Western Infirmary
Kelvin Hall
Museum of Transport
Glasgow Art Gallery & Museum
Hunterian Museum
Maryhill Station
Summerston Station
Gilshochill Station
Hyndland Station
Partick Station
Kelvinhall Stn
Hillhead Stn
Kelvinbridge Stn
Maryhill Football Club
Maryhill Health Centre
Wyndford Recreation Centre
Hillhead Rugby Club
West of Scotland Cricket Club
Castlebank Industrial Est
Dalsholm Industrial Estate
1 grid square represents 500 metres

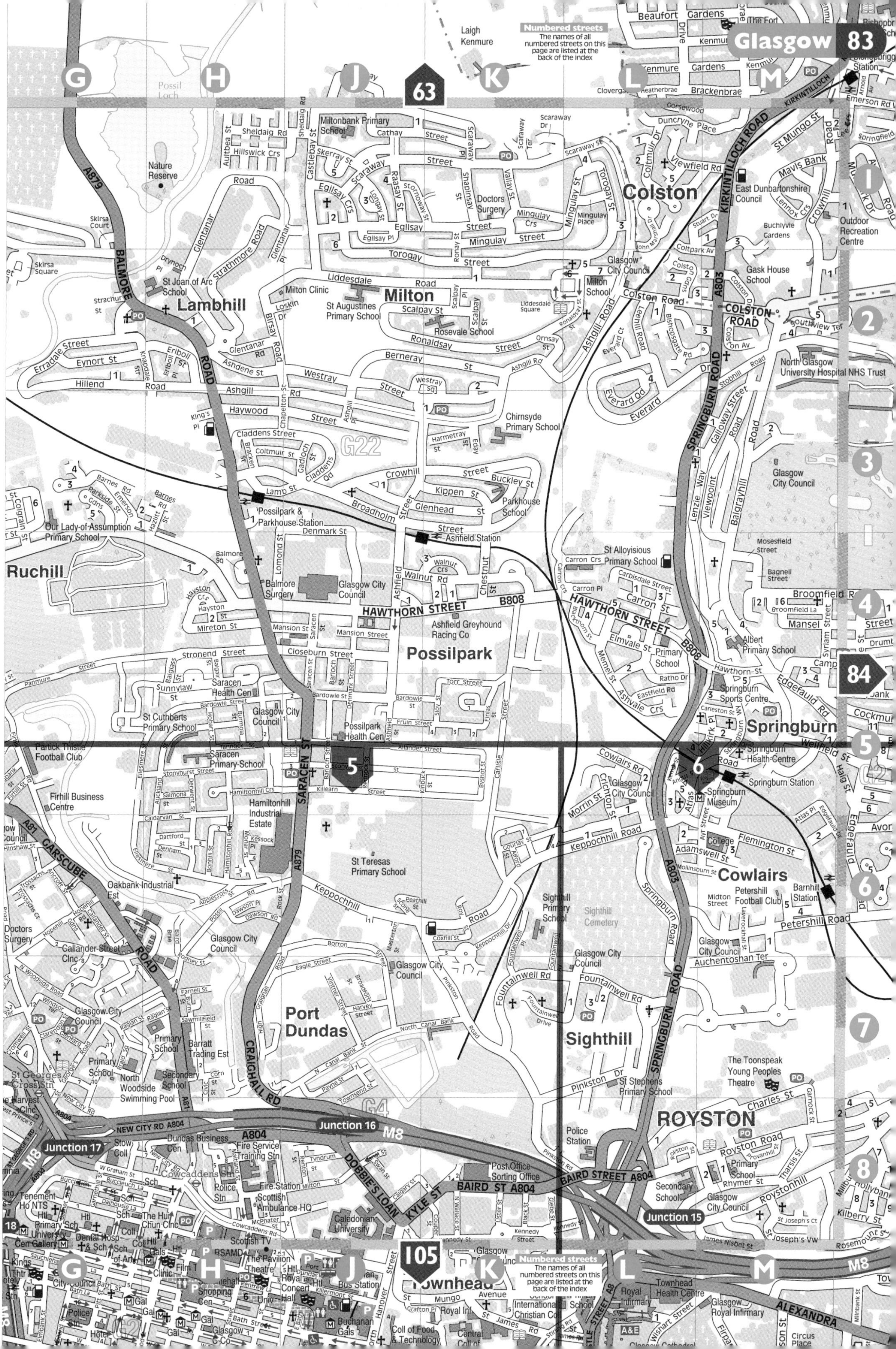
Numbered streets
The names of all numbered streets on this page are listed at the back of the index
63
Colston
Milton
Lambhill
Ruchill
Possilpark
Springburn
Cowlairs
Port Dundas
Sighthill
ROYSTON
Townhead
East Dunbartonshire Council
North Glasgow University Hospital NHS Trust
Ashfield Greyhound Racing Co
Partick Thistle Football Club
Firhill Business Centre
Hamiltonhill Industrial Estate
Oakbank Industrial Est
St Teresas Primary School
Sighthill Cemetery
Petershill Football Club
The Toonspeak Young Peoples Theatre
Junction 15
Junction 16
Junction 17
M8
84
105
Numbered streets
The names of all numbered streets on this page are listed at the back of the index

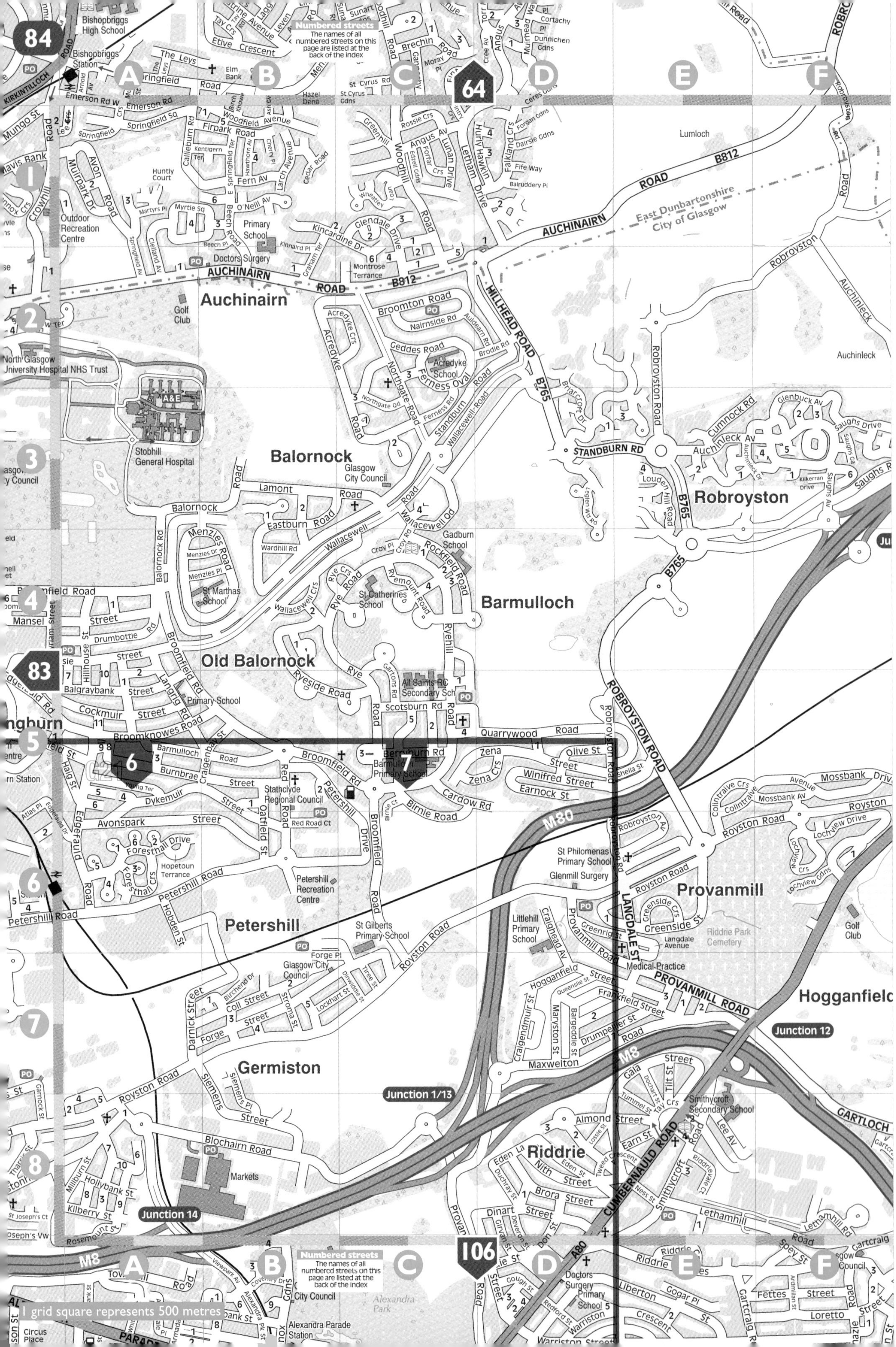

84
64
83
106
A
B
C
D
E
F
1
2
3
4
5
6
7
8
Numbered streets
The names of all numbered streets on this page are listed at the back of the index
1 grid square represents 500 metres
Bishopbriggs High School
Bishopbriggs Station
Kirkintilloch Road
Emerson Rd W
Emerson Rd
Springfield Road
The Leys
Elm Bank
Hazel Dene
St Cyrus Rd
St Cyrus Gdns
Brechin Road
Moray Pl
Angus Av
Cortachy Pl
Dunnichen Gdns
Ceres Gdns
Lumloch
Woodfield Avenue
Firpark Road
Kentigern Ter
Fern Av
Larch Avenue
Cedar Road
Huntly Court
Woodhill Road
Lunan Drive
Letham Drive
Falkland Crs
Forgan Gdns
Dairsie Gdns
Fife Way
Bairuddery Pl
B812
Road
East Dunbartonshire
City of Glasgow
Auchinairn Road
Robroyston Road
Outdoor Recreation Centre
Muirpark Dr
Avon Road
Myrtle Sq
O'Neill Av
Beech Road
Primary School
Doctors Surgery
Kincardine Dr
Glendale Drive
Montrose Terrace
Auchinairn
Golf Club
Broomton Road
Nairnside Rd
Auldearn Rd
Brodie Rd
Acredyke Crs
Acredyke Road
Geddes Road
Acredyke School
Ferness Oval
Northgate Road
Northgate Qd
Ferness Rd
Hillhead Road
B765
Briarcroft Dr
Standburn Road
Standburn Rd
Wallacewell Road
Auchinleck
Robroyston Road
Cumnock Rd
Glenbuck Av
Saughs Drive
Auchinleck Av
Kilkerran Drive
Saughs Av
Saughs Rd
Louden Hill Road
Robroyston
North Glasgow University Hospital NHS Trust
A&E
Stobhill General Hospital
Balornock
Glasgow City Council
Lamont Road
Balornock Road
Eastburn Road
Wardhill Rd
Menzies Road
Menzies Dr
Menzies Pl
St Marthas School
Wallacewell Qd
Croy Pl
Rockfield Road
Gadburn School
Rye Road
Rye Crs
Ryemount Road
St Catherines School
Barmulloch
Wallacewell Crs
Ryehill
Broomfield Road
Mansel Street
Drumbottie Rd
Old Balornock
Ryeside Road
Gartons Rd
All Saints RC Secondary Sch
Hillhouse St
Balgraybank Street
Langtrig Rd
Broomfield Rd
Primary School
Cockmuir Street
Broomknowes Road
Scotsburn Rd
Quarrywood Road
Barmulloch Road
Burnbrae Street
Craigendbank St
Bernburn Rd
Barmulloch Primary School
Zena St
Zena Crs
Olive St
Winifred Street
Earnock St
Sheila St
Cardow Rd
Birnie Road
Birnie Ct
Red Road
Stathclyde Regional Council
Red Road Ct
Petershill Drive
Haig St
Young Ter
Dykemuir Street
Avonspark Street
Oatfield St
Foresthall Drive
Foresthall Crs
Hopetoun Terrace
Eggefauld Road
Petershill Road
Petershill Recreation Centre
Hobden St
Petershill
St Gilberts Primary School
Royston Road
M80
Robroyston Av
St Philomenas Primary School
Glenmill Surgery
Royston Road
Provanmill
Greenside Crs
Greenside St
Langdale Avenue
Langdale St
Riddrie Park Cemetery
Golf Club
Mossbank Drive
Mossbank Av
Colintraive Crs
Colintraive Avenue
Lochview Drive
Lochview Crs
Lochview Gdns
Littlehill Primary School
Craighead Av
Provanmill Road
Medical Practice
Hogganfield Street
Frankfield Street
Provanmill Road
Hogganfield
Junction 12
Forge Pl
Glasgow City Council
Birchend Dr
Coll Street
Forge Street
Stroma St
Lockhart St
Dinwiddie St
Tiree St
Darnick Street
Germiston
Craigendmuir St
Maryston St
Bargeddie St
Drumpellier St
Maxwelton
M8
Junction 1/13
Siemens Street
Siemens Pl
Blochairn Road
Markets
Junction 14
Royston Road
Millburn St
Hollybank St
Kilberry St
Rosemount St
Gala
Tilt St
Tummel St
Tay Crs
Smithycroft Secondary School
Lee Av
Gartloch
Almond Street
Earn St
Riddrie
Eden St
Nith Street
Brora Street
Dinart Street
Cumbernauld Road
Smithycroft
Riddrievale Ct
Lethamhill
Lethamhill Rd
Provan Road
Ness St
A80
Riddrie Knowes
Liberton
Gogar Pl
Crescent
Gartcraig
Fettes Street
Loretto Street
Glasgow City Council
Doctors Surgery
Primary School
Redford St
Warriston Street
Viewpark Av
Alexandra Park
Alexandra Parade Station
City Council
Circus Place
Parade
Town Mill Road
St Joseph's Ct
St Joseph's Vw
Garnock St
Mungo St
Crowhill
Springfield Sq
Springfield Ct

G8
1 Caprington St
2 Claypotts Pl
3 Claypotts Rd
4 Gartcraig Rd
5 Milncroft Pl

H4
1 Fifth Av

H5
1 Craigbarnet Crs
2 Loudon Rd
3 Rowallan Ter

H6
1 Cardrona St

H7, H8
Street names for these grid squares are listed at the back of the index

L7
1 Clonbeith St
2 Craigievar St
3 Craigneil St

L4
1 Resipol Rd

L5
1 Craigendmuir Rd
2 Mossview Rd

L3
1 Mount Harriet Av

K7
1 Craiglockhart St
2 Horsburgh St
3 Tillycairn Dr

K8
1 Craiglockhart St
2 Kincardine Sq
3 Redcastle Sq

K3
1 Blenheim Av
2 Church Av

K5
1 Campsie Vw

J4
1 Bailaig Crs
2 Comrie Rd

J7
1 Cambus Pl
2 Camsbusmore Pl
3 Mossvcastle Rd
4 Mossvale Rd

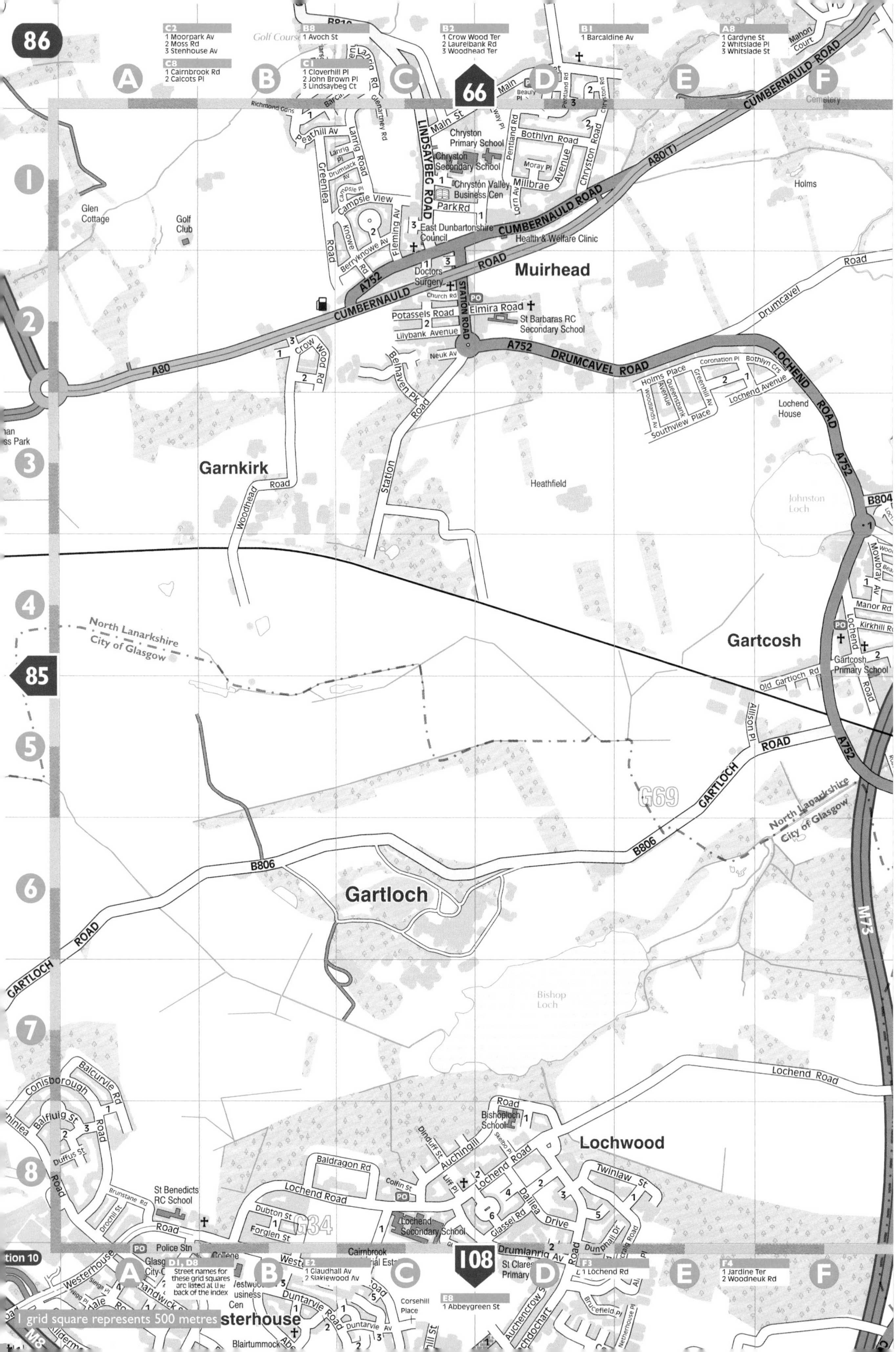
C2
1 Moorpark Av
2 Moss Rd
3 Stenhouse Av
C8
1 Cairnbrook Rd
2 Calcots Pl
B8
1 Avoch St
C1
1 Cloverhill Pl
2 John Brown Pl
3 Lindsaybeg Ct
B2
1 Crow Wood Ter
2 Laurelbank Rd
3 Woodhead Ter
B1
1 Barcaldine Av
A8
1 Gardyne St
2 Whitslade Pl
3 Whitslade St
66
85
108
Golf Course
A
B
C
D
E
F
1
2
3
4
5
6
7
8
Glen Cottage
Golf Club
Chryston Primary School
Chryston Secondary School
Chryston Valley Business Cen
East Dunbartonshire Council
Health & Welfare Clinic
Doctors Surgery
St Barbaras RC Secondary School
Muirhead
Holms
Lochend House
Johnston Loch
Heathfield
Garnkirk
Gartcosh
Gartcosh Primary School
North Lanarkshire
City of Glasgow
G69
Gartloch
Bishop Loch
Lochwood
Bishoploch School
Lochend Secondary School
St Benedicts RC School
G34
Police Stn
Cairnbrook Industrial Est
St Clares Primary
CUMBERNAULD ROAD
A80(T)
A80
A752
LINDSAYBEG ROAD
STATION ROAD
DRUMCAVEL ROAD
LOCHEND ROAD
GARTLOCH ROAD
B806
B804
M73
Drumcavel Road
Woodhead Road
Station Road
Lochend Road
Elmira Road
Potassels Road
Lilybank Avenue
Bothlyn Road
Millbrae
Campsie View
Holms Place
Southview Place
Lochend Avenue
Old Gartloch Rd
Allison Pl
Manor Rd
Kirkhill Rd
Baldragon Rd
Twinlaw St
Dalilea Drive
Drumlanrig Av
Auchingill
Conisborough
Balcurvie Rd
Balfluig St
Duffus St
Forglen St
Dubton St
Colfin St
Westerhouse
Duntarvie Road
Corsehill Place
D1, D8
Street names for these grid squares are listed at the back of the index
E2
1 Glaudhall Av
2 Slakiewood Av
E8
1 Abbeygreen St
F3
1 Lochend Rd
F4
1 Jardine Ter
2 Woodneuk Rd
1 grid square represents 500 metres

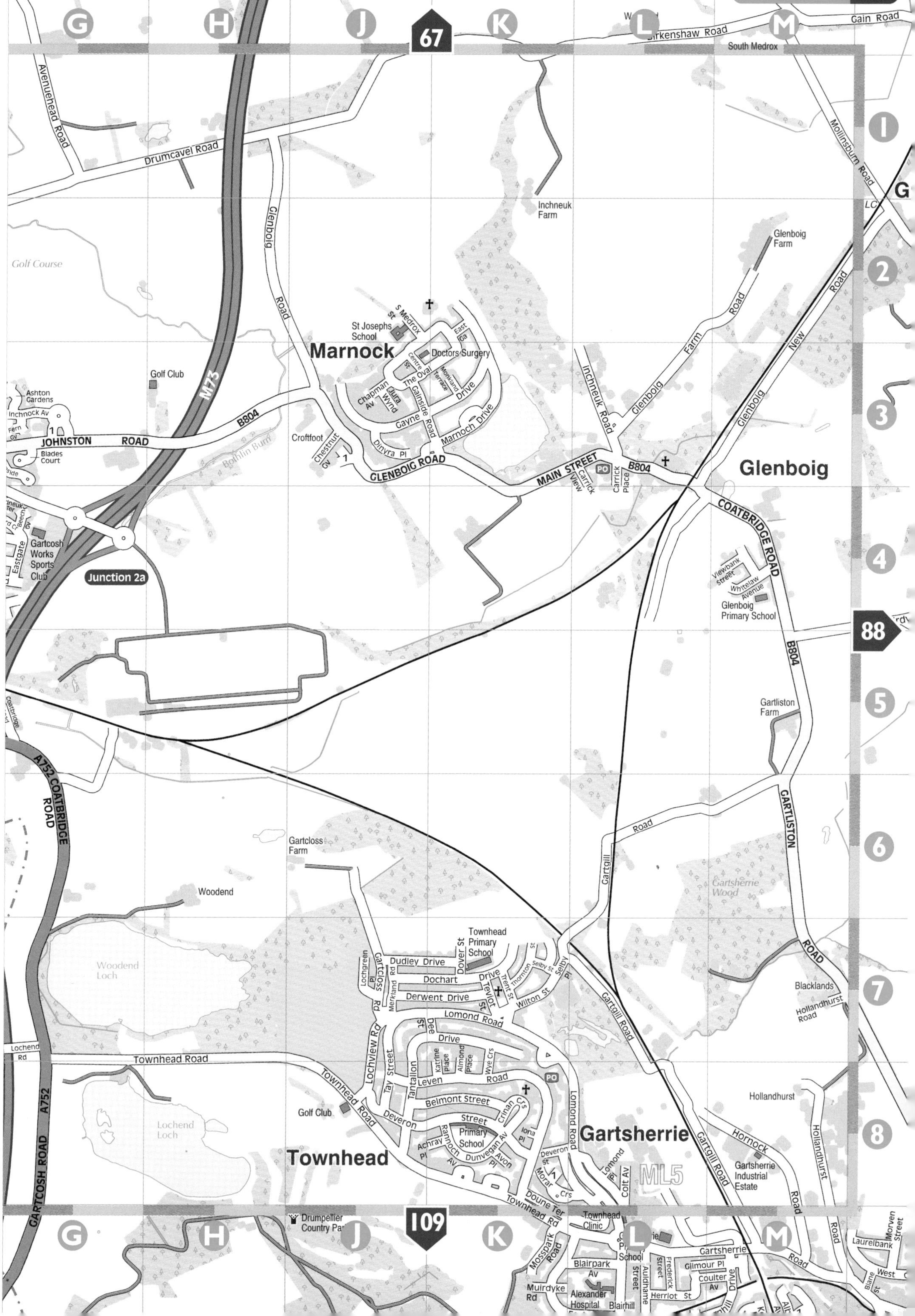
G3 1 Croftfoot Pl
J3 1 Glenburn Gdns
K8 1 Carron Pl
Leckethill
67
Birkenshaw Road
Gain Road
South Medrox
Avenuehead Road
Drumcavel Road
M73
Molinsburn Road
Inchneuk Farm
Glenboig Farm
Golf Course
Glenboig Road
St Josephs School
S Medrox St
East Ga
Marnock
Doctors Surgery
Centre St
The Oval
Monkland Terrace
Chapman Av
Jura Wynd
Gainside Road
Drive
Gayne
Marnoch Drive
Golf Club
Ashton Gardens
Inchnock Av
Fern Gv
B804
JOHNSTON ROAD
Blades Court
Croftfoot
Chestnut Gv
Dinyra Pl
GLENBOIG ROAD
Bothlin Burn
MAIN STREET
Carrick View
Carrick Place
B804
Inchneuk Road
Glenboig Farm Road
New Road
Glenboig
Glenboig
COATBRIDGE ROAD
Gartcosh Works Sports Club
Eastgate
Junction 2a
Viewbank Street
Whitelaw Avenue
Glenboig Primary School
88
B804
Coatbridge Road
Gartliston Farm
A752 COATBRIDGE ROAD
GARTLISTON ROAD
Road
Gartgill
Gartcloss Farm
Gartsherrie Wood
Woodend
Woodend Loch
Townhead Primary School
Dudley Drive
Dover St
Lochgreen Pl
Gartcloss Rd
Merkland Rd
Dochart Drive
Derwent Drive
Teviot St
Trent St
Thornton St
Selby St
Selby Pl
Wilton St
Blacklands
Hollandhurst Road
Lomond Road
Dee Drive
Lochview Rd
Katrine Place
Almond Place
Wye Crs
Lochend Rd
Townhead Road
Tay Street
Tantallon Leven Road
Gartgill Road
Belmont Street
Crinan Crs
Hollandhurst
Golf Club
Townhead Road
Deveron Street
Primary School
Iona Pl
Lomond Road
Gartsherrie
Lochend Loch
A752
Achray Pl
Rannoch Av
Dunvegan Av
Avon Pl
Deveron St
Lomond Pl
Colt Av
ML5
Gartgill Road
Hornock Road
Gartsherrie Industrial Estate
Hollandhurst Road
GARTCOSH ROAD
Morar Crs
Doune Ter
Townhead Rd
Drumpellier Country Park
109
Townhead Clinic
Mossspark Road
School
Gartsherrie Road
Morven Street
Laurelbank
Blairpark Av
Street
Auldhame Street
Frederick Street
Gilmour Pl
Coulter Av
Drive
West
Blane St
Muirdyke Rd
Alexander Hospital
Blairhill
Herriot St

F8
1 Beechbank Av
2 Commonhead La
3 Katrine Crs
4 Laidon Rd
5 Tayside
F7
1 Craigmochan Av
2 Dykehead Crs
3 Raebog Crs
4 Stalneybraes Pl
5 Strathmungo Crs
F5
1 Hawkwood Rd
F4
1 Banchory Av
2 Strathyre Gdns
Gain
Gain Road
Cleddans
B802
68
A
B
C
D
E
F
1
2
3
4
5
6
7
8
Cullochrig
Gaindykehead
Gartmillan
Greenfoot
LC
Mollinsburn Road
Yetts Hole Road
CONDORRAT
Haggmuir Farm
Mollinsburn Road
Brackenhirst Road
Brackenhirst
ROAD
87
Muirdyke Road
Burnlip Road
Palace
Ryden Mains
B802
Cemetery
New Monkland Primary School
RAEBOG
Crathie
Rochsoles
Glenmavis
Quarryside Street
Kirkstyle Place
Macarthur Avenue
Glenview
Glenwell Street
COATBRIDGE
GLENMAVIS
ROAD
Braidenhill Farm
Cromlet
Yetts Hole Road
Golf Club
Golfhill Primary School
Lochearn Crs
Burnfoot
Thrashb
Dykehead Road
B803
Kipps Farm
Kippsbyre
Hollandhurst Road
ROAD
B804
COLTSWOOD ROAD
WAVERLEY ST
Northburn Rd
Burnside Road
Greenside Street
Chassels St
Gilchrist St
Reid St
Alston Av
Primary School
Laurelbank
Morven Street
Place
Cameron St
110
Mosside
St Andrews RC Primary School
Ballochney St
Whinhall Road
Arran Dr
Leaend Road
Moss Side
Wester Mavisbank Avenue
Whinhall
Park Street
Mavisbank Street
Mitchell St
John Smith Ct
Mavisbank Sch
COMMONHEAD ST
COMMONSIDE ST
Hazelbank Wk
Garden Sq Wk
1 grid square represents 500 metres

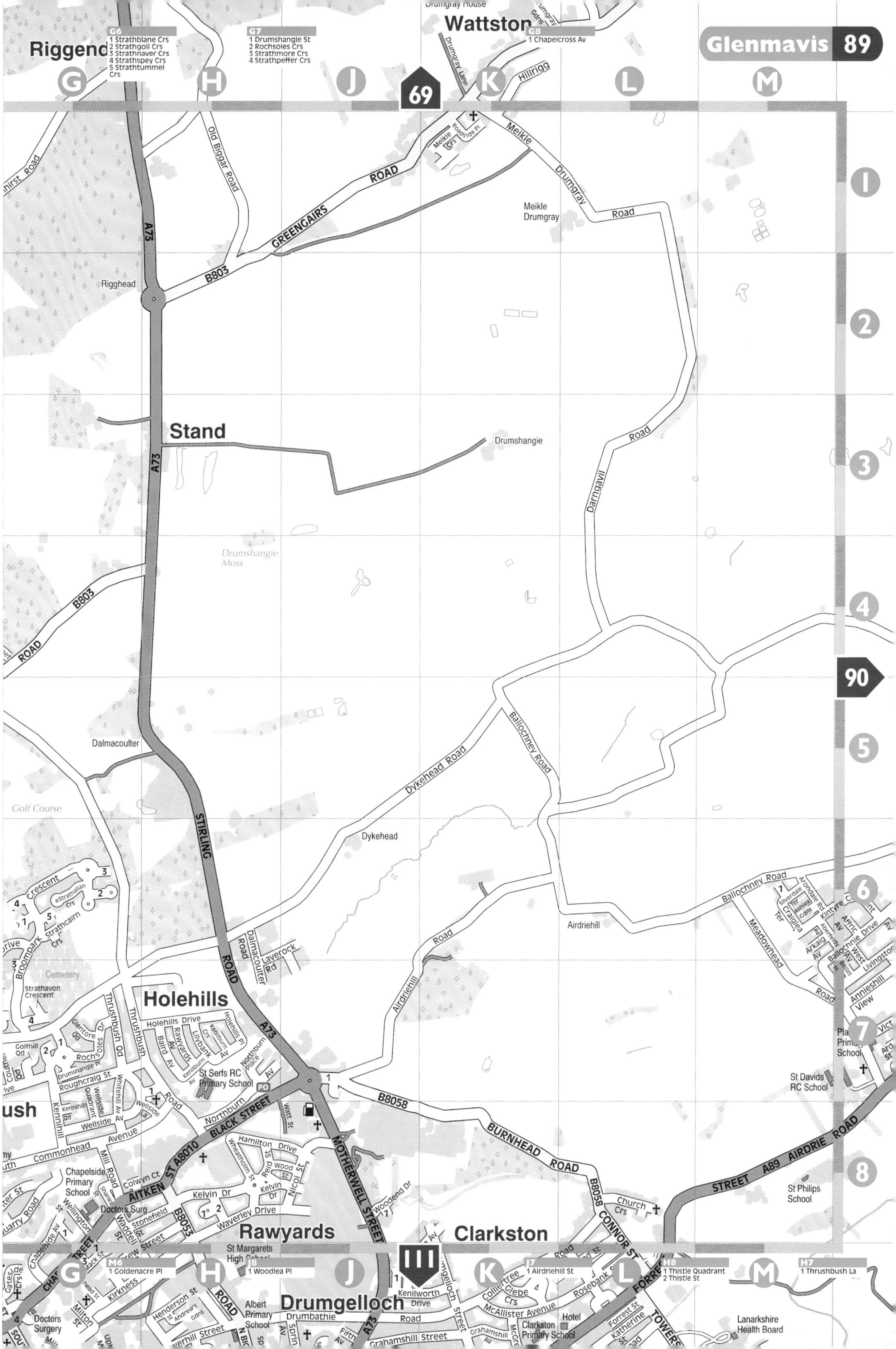

Drumgray House
Wattston
Riggend
G6
1 Strathblane Crs
2 Strathgoil Crs
3 Strathnaver Crs
4 Strathspey Crs
5 Strathtummel Crs
G7
1 Drumshangie St
2 Rochsoles Crs
3 Strathmore Crs
4 Strathpeffer Crs
G8
1 Chapelcross Av
G
H
J
69
K
L
M
Drumgray Lane
Hillrigg
Meikle Crs
Roadside Pl
Meikle
Drumgray
Road
Old Biggar Road
GREENGAIRS
ROAD
A73
B803
Rigghead
Meikle Drumgray
1
2
3
4
5
6
7
8
90
Stand
Drumshangie
Darngavil
Road
Drumshangie Moss
B803
ROAD
Ballochney Road
Dykehead Road
Dalmacoulter
Golf Course
STIRLING
ROAD
Dykehead
Ballochney Road
Airdriehill
Road
Airdriehill
Meadowhead
Road
Crescent
Strathallan Crs
Strathcairn Crs
Broompark
Cemetery
Strathavon Crescent
Dalmacoulter Road
Laverock Rd
Holehills
Holehills Drive
Holehills Pl
Thrushbush Qd
Thrushbush
Rawyards Av
Baird Av
Lilybank Av
Kenilburn Crs
Kenilburn Av
Northburn Place
Northburn Av
St Serfs RC Primary School
PO
Glentore Qd
Soles Dr
Golfhill Qd
Rochsoles Crs
Drumshangie Pl
Roughcraig St
Whitehill Av
Quadrant Av
Wellside Av
Wellside Qd
Wellside La
Road
Kennihill
Kenniihill Qd
Wellside Av
Avenue
Commonhead
Northburn
BLACK STREET
AITKEN ST A8010
Watt St
B8058
BURNHEAD
ROAD
MOTHERWELL STREET
Hamilton Drive
Wheatholm St
Reid St
Wood St
Nicol St
Kelvin Dr
Woodend Dr
Chapelside Primary School
Mill Road
Colwyn Ct
Doctors Surg
Stonefield St
Waddell St
Kelvin Dr
Waverley Drive
B8053
Rawyards
Clarkston
B8058
CONNOR ST
Church Crs
STREET
A89
AIRDRIE
ROAD
St Philips School
St Davids RC School
Plains Primary School
Silverdale Ter
Arondale Rd
Ashlea Gdns
Craiglea Ter
Kintyre Cr
Affric Av
Ballochnie Drive
Livingstone
Annieshill View
Arkaig Av
Aberfeldy Av
St Margarets High School
M6
1 Goldenacre Pl
J8
1 Woodlea Pl
111
J7
1 Airdriehill St
H8
1 Thistle Quadrant
2 Thistle St
H7
1 Thrushbush La
Chapelside Av
Kirkness St
Henderson St
St Andrew's Gdns
ROAD
Albert Primary School
Drumgelloch
Drumbathie Road
Kenilworth Drive
Colliertree Crs
Glebe Crs
McAllister Avenue
Hotel
Clarkston Primary School
Rosebank
Forrest St
Katherine St
TOWERS
Grahamshill Street
Doctors Surgery
Milton St
Lanarkshire Health Board

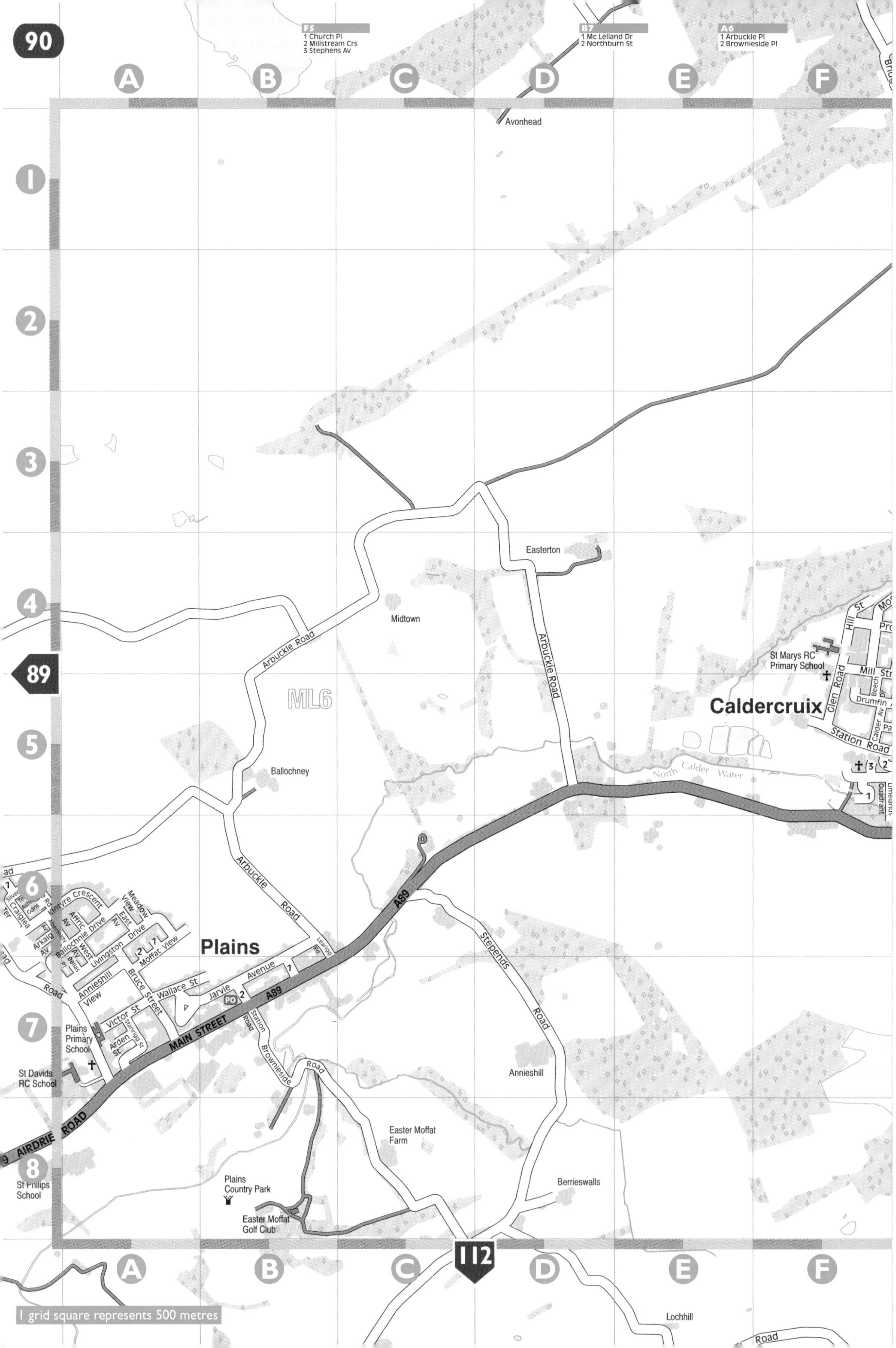
F5
1 Church Pl
2 Millstream Crs
3 Stephens Av
B7
1 Mc Lelland Dr
2 Northburn St
A6
1 Arbuckle Pl
2 Brownieside Pl
A
B
C
D
E
F
1
2
3
4
5
6
7
8
89
112
Avonhead
Easterton
Midtown
Arbuckle Road
ML6
Ballochney
St Marys RC
Primary School
Caldercruix
Hill St
Mill St
Glen Road
Drumfin
Station Road
North Calder Water
Quadrant
Plains
Kintyre Crescent
Meadow View
Affric
Ballochnie Drive
East
West
Livingston
Drive
Moffat View
Arkaig
Annieshill View
Bruce Street
Wallace St
Victor St
Arden St
Jarvie
Avenue
PO
MAIN STREET
A89
Learigg Rd
Station Road
Brownieside Road
Stepends Road
Plains Primary School
St Davids RC School
AIRDRIE ROAD
St Philips School
Annieshill
Easter Moffat Farm
Plains Country Park
Easter Moffat Golf Club
Berrieswalls
Lochhill
Road
1 grid square represents 500 metres

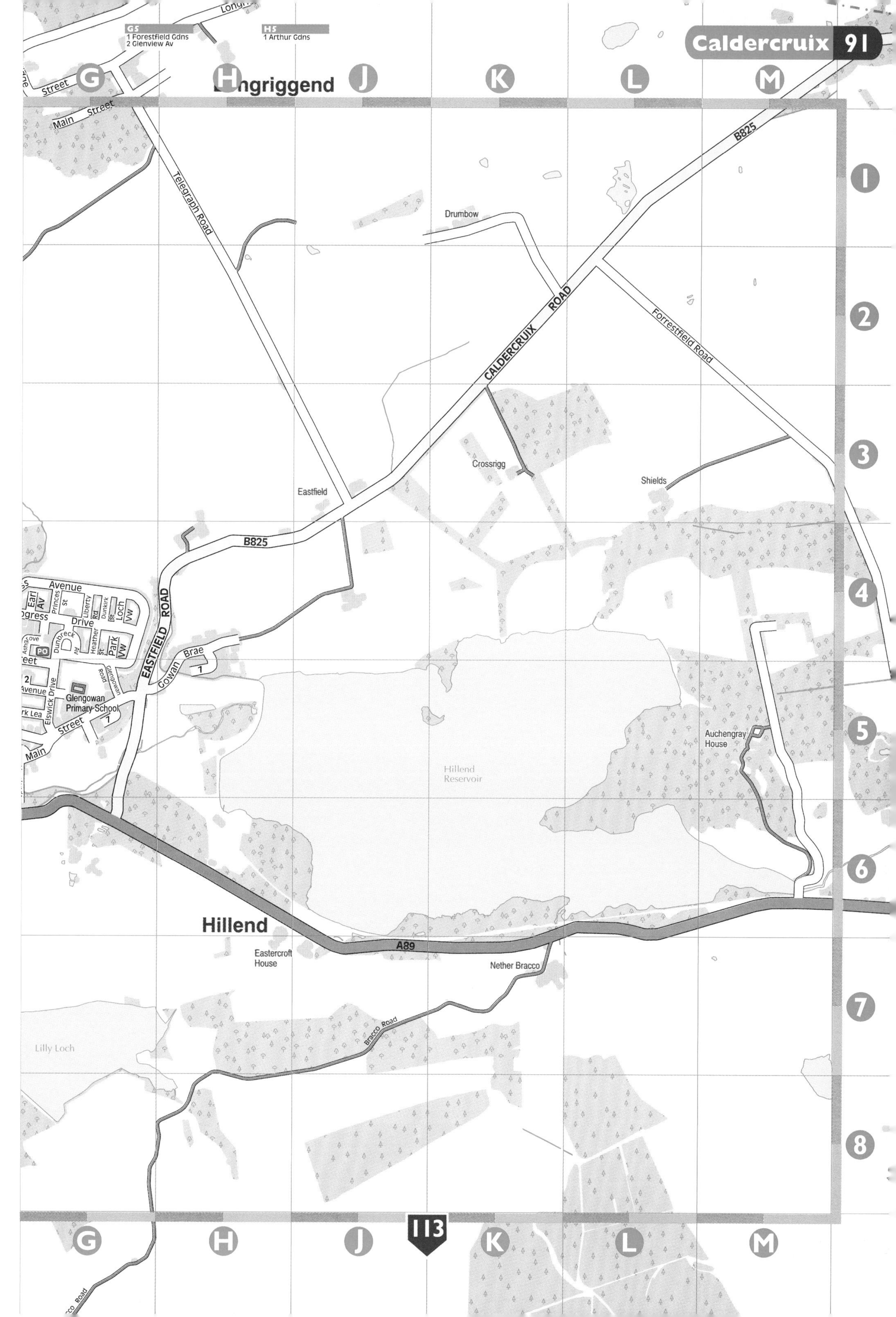
G5
1 Forestfield Gdns
2 Glenview Av
H5
1 Arthur Gdns
Longriggend
G
H
J
K
L
M
Main Street
Street
Telegraph Road
B825
Drumbow
CALDERCRUIX ROAD
Forrestfield Road
Crossrigg
Shields
Eastfield
EASTFIELD ROAD
Avenue
Earl Av
Princes St
Liberty Rd
Dunkirk St
Loch Vw
Drive
Dunbreck Av
Heather St
Park Vw
PO
Gowan Brae
Glengowan Road
Glengowan Primary School
Elswick Drive
Main Street
Hillend Reservoir
Auchengray House
Hillend
A89
Eastercroft House
Nether Bracco
Bracco Road
Lilly Loch
1
2
3
4
5
6
7
8
113

Skelmorlie Mains
Shuma Court
70
Skelmorlie Water
Skelmorlie Castle
Meigle Burn
A78(T)
Barr
Meigle
Meigle Bay
Thirdpart
Ashcraig
Dykes
Auchengarth
Millrig
Auchengarth Bridge
Blackhouse Moor
Blackhouse Burn
Home Farm
Constablewood
Knock Castle
Whittlieburn
Knock Farm
Craigton
Middleton Reservoir
Brisbane Mains
Middleton
Quarter
115
Routen Burn
Noddsdale
A
B
C
D
E
F
1
2
3
4
5
6
7
8

1 grid square represents 500 metres

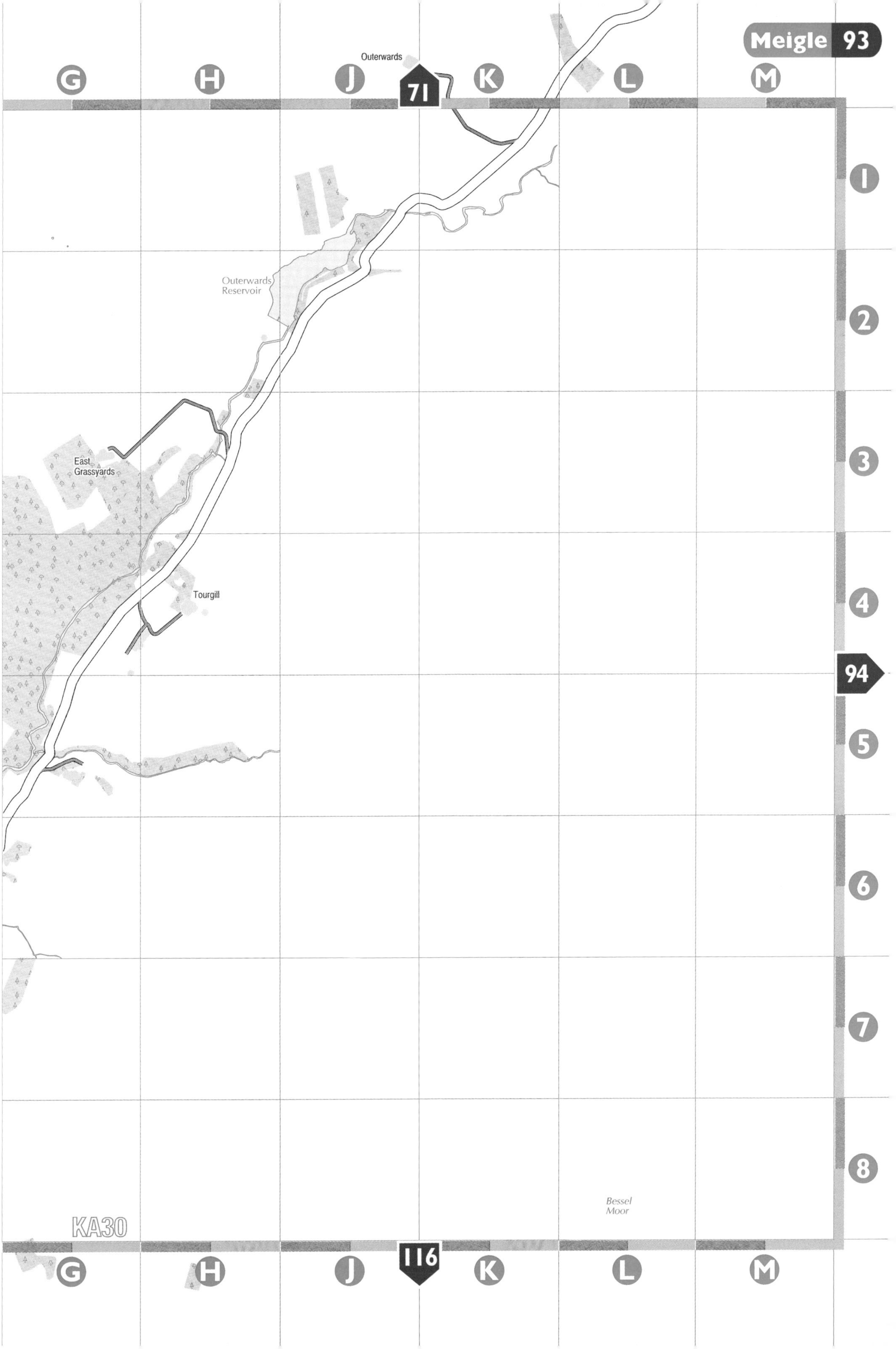
G
H
J
K
L
M
71
Outerwards
Outerwards Reservoir
East Grassyards
Tourgill
94
1
2
3
4
5
6
7
8
Bessel Moor
KA30
116

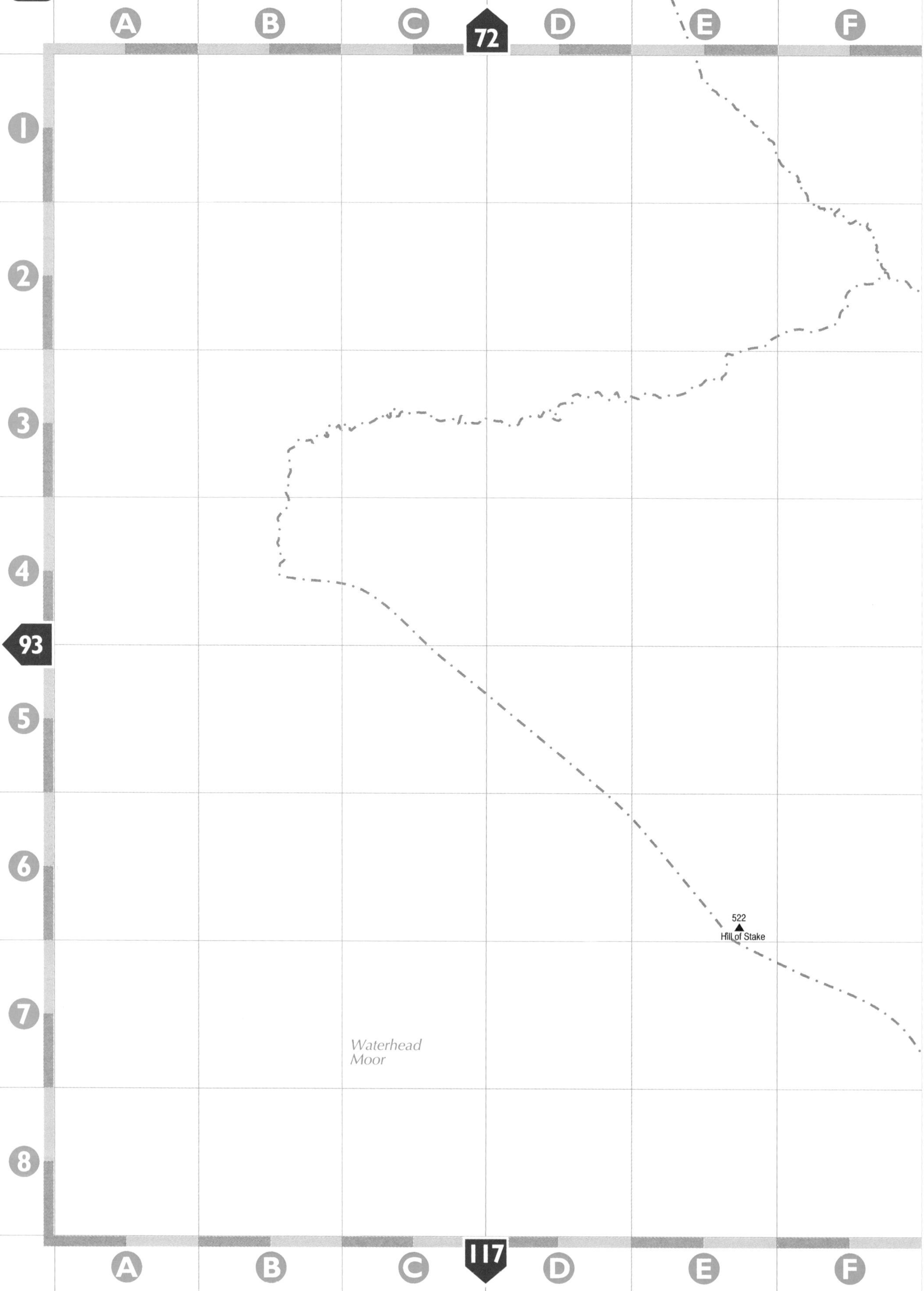
A
B
C
72
D
E
F
1
2
3
4
93
5
6
7
8
522
Hill of Stake
Waterhead
Moor
117

1 grid square represents 500 metres

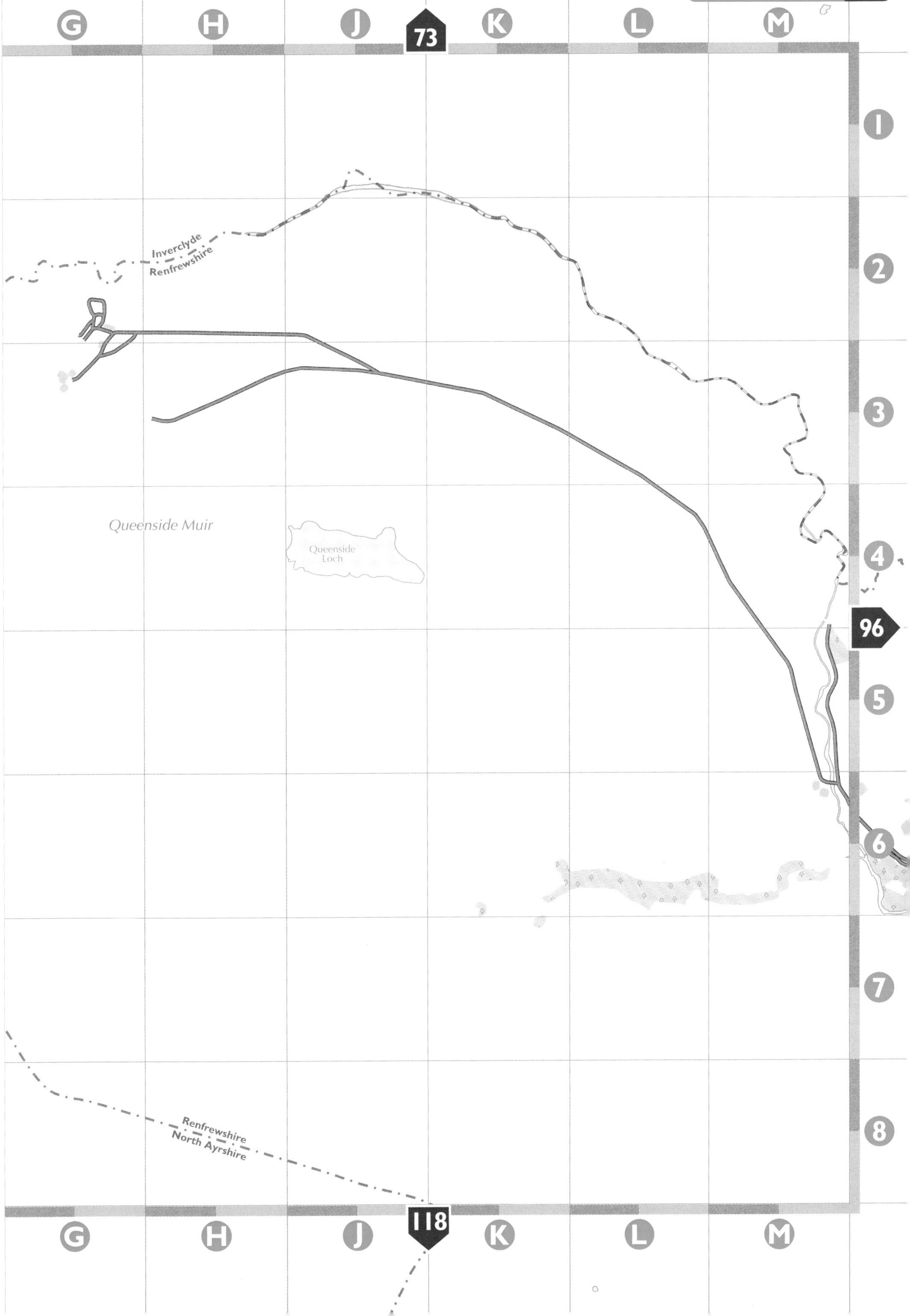
G
H
J
73
K
L
M
1
2
3
4
96
5
6
7
8
Inverclyde
Renfrewshire
Queenside Muir
Queenside Loch
Renfrewshire
North Ayrshire
118

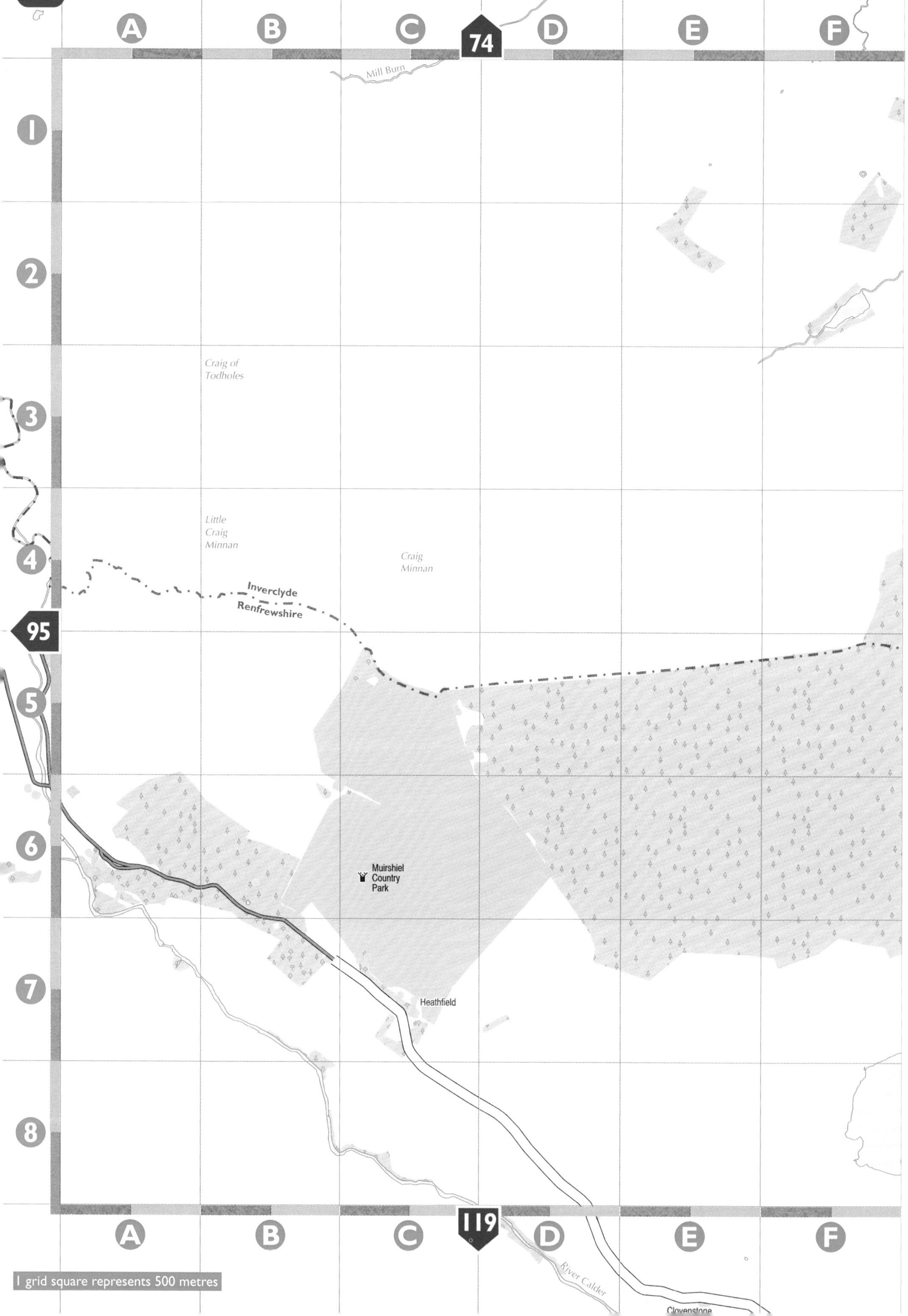
A
B
C
74
D
E
F
Mill Burn
1
2
Craig of Todholes
3
Little Craig Minnan
Craig Minnan
4
Inverclyde
Renfrewshire
95
5
6
Muirshiel Country Park
7
Heathfield
8
119
River Calder
Clovenstone
1 grid square represents 500 metres

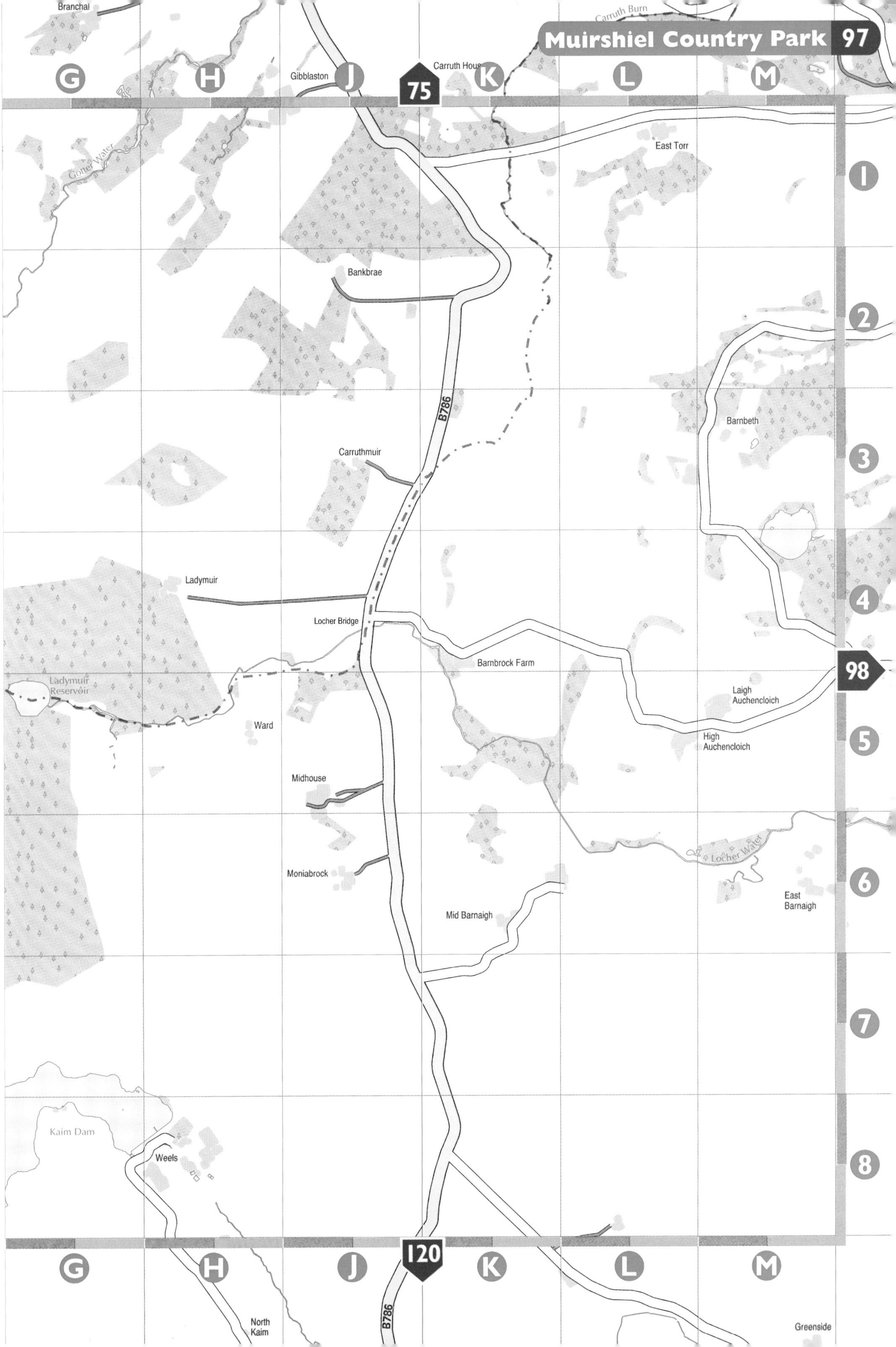

Branchal
Carruth Burn
Gibblaston
75
Carruth Hous
East Torr
Gotter Water
Bankbrae
B786
Carruthmuir
Barnbeth
Ladymuir
Locher Bridge
Barnbrock Farm
98
Ladymuir Reservoir
Laigh Auchencloich
High Auchencloich
Ward
Midhouse
Moniabrock
Locher Water
Mid Barnaigh
East Barnaigh
Kaim Dam
Weels
120
B786
North Kaim
Greenside
G
H
J
K
L
M
1
2
3
4
5
6
7
8

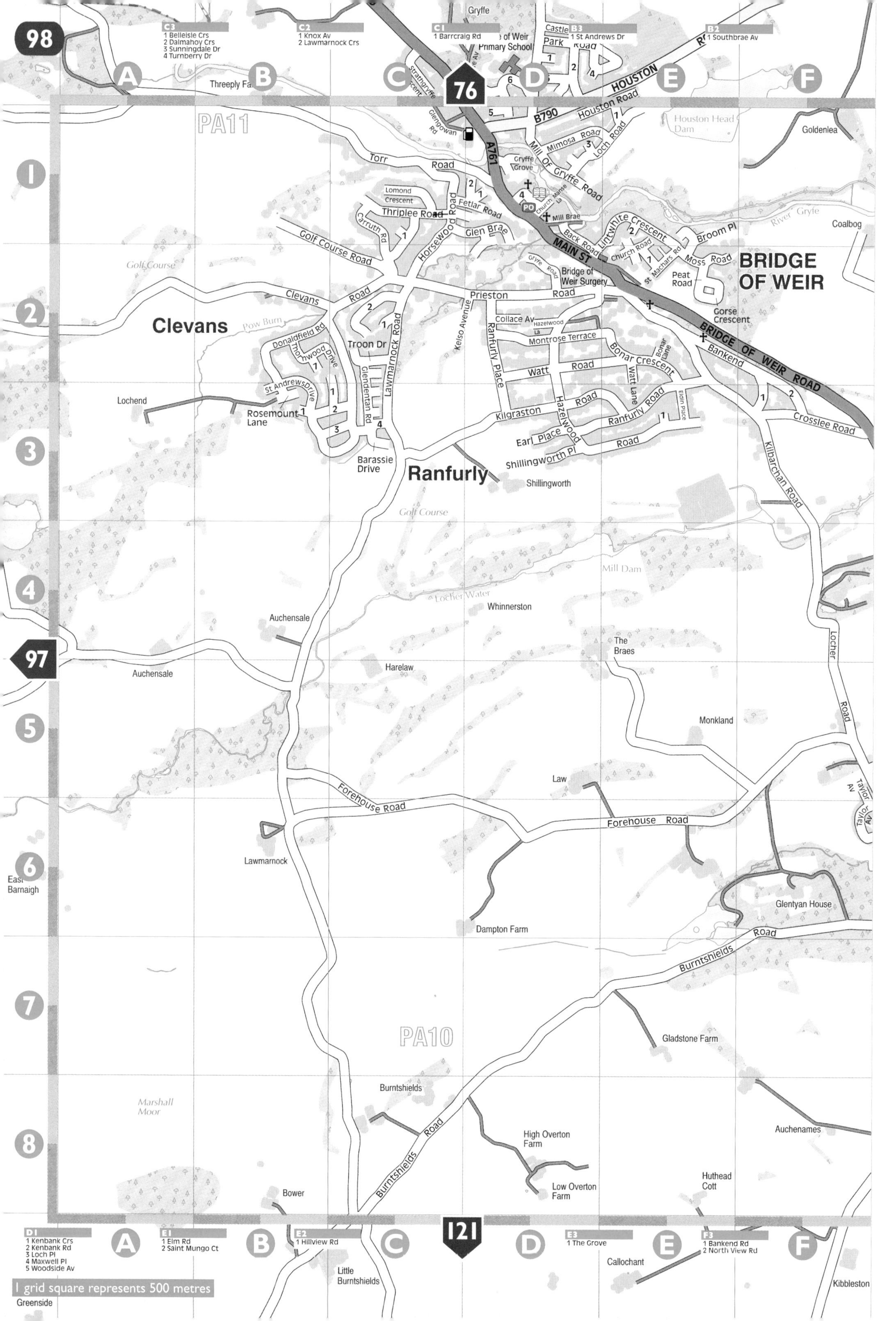
98
C3
1 Belleisle Crs
2 Dalmahoy Crs
3 Sunningdale Dr
4 Turnberry Dr
C2
1 Knox Av
2 Lawmarnock Crs
C1
1 Barrcraig Rd
B3
1 St Andrews Dr
B2
1 Southbrae Av
Gryffe
Bridge of Weir Primary School
Castle
Park Road
Threeply Farm
76
HOUSTON
Houston Road
B790
PA11
Glengowan Rd
Strathgryffe Crescent
Houston Head Dam
Goldenlea
Torr
Road
A761
Mimosa Road
Loch Road
Mill Of Gryffe Road
Gryffe Grove
Lomond Crescent
Thriplee Road
Fetlar Road
Horsewood Road
Carruth Rd
Glen Brae
Golf Course Road
Church La
Manse La
Mill Brae
River Gryfe
Coalbog
Lintwhite Crescent
Broom Pl
Back Road
MAIN ST
Church Road
St Machars Rd
Moss Road
Peat Road
BRIDGE OF WEIR
Golf Course
Gryfe Road
Bridge of Weir Surgery
Clevans
Road
Prieston
Road
Gorse Crescent
Clevans
Pow Burn
Troon Dr
Lawmarnock Road
Kelso Avenue
Ranfurly Place
Collace Av
Hazelwood La
Montrose Terrace
Bonar Crescent
Bonar Lane
BRIDGE OF WEIR ROAD
Bankend
Donaldfield Rd
Thornwood Drive
Glendentan Rd
Watt Road
Watt Lane
St Andrews Drive
Lochend
Rosemount Lane
Kilgraston Road
Hazelwood Road
Ranfurly Road
Eldin Place
Crosslee Road
Earl Place
Road
Barassie Drive
Ranfurly
Shillingworth Pl
Shillingworth
Kilbarchan Road
Golf Course
Mill Dam
Locher Water
Whinnerston
Auchensale
97
The Braes
Harelaw
Auchensale
Locher Road
Monkland
Law
Taylor Av
Forehouse Road
Forehouse Road
Lawmarnock
East Barnaigh
Glentyan House
Dampton Farm
Road
Burntshields
Gladstone Farm
PA10
Burntshields
Marshall Moor
High Overton Farm
Auchenames
Burntshields Road
Huthead Cott
Low Overton Farm
Bower
121
D1
1 Kenbank Crs
2 Kenbank Rd
3 Loch Pl
4 Maxwell Pl
5 Woodside Av
E1
1 Elm Rd
2 Saint Mungo Ct
E2
1 Hillview Rd
E3
1 The Grove
F3
1 Bankend Rd
2 North View Rd
Callochant
Little Burntshields
Kibbleston
1 grid square represents 500 metres
Greenside

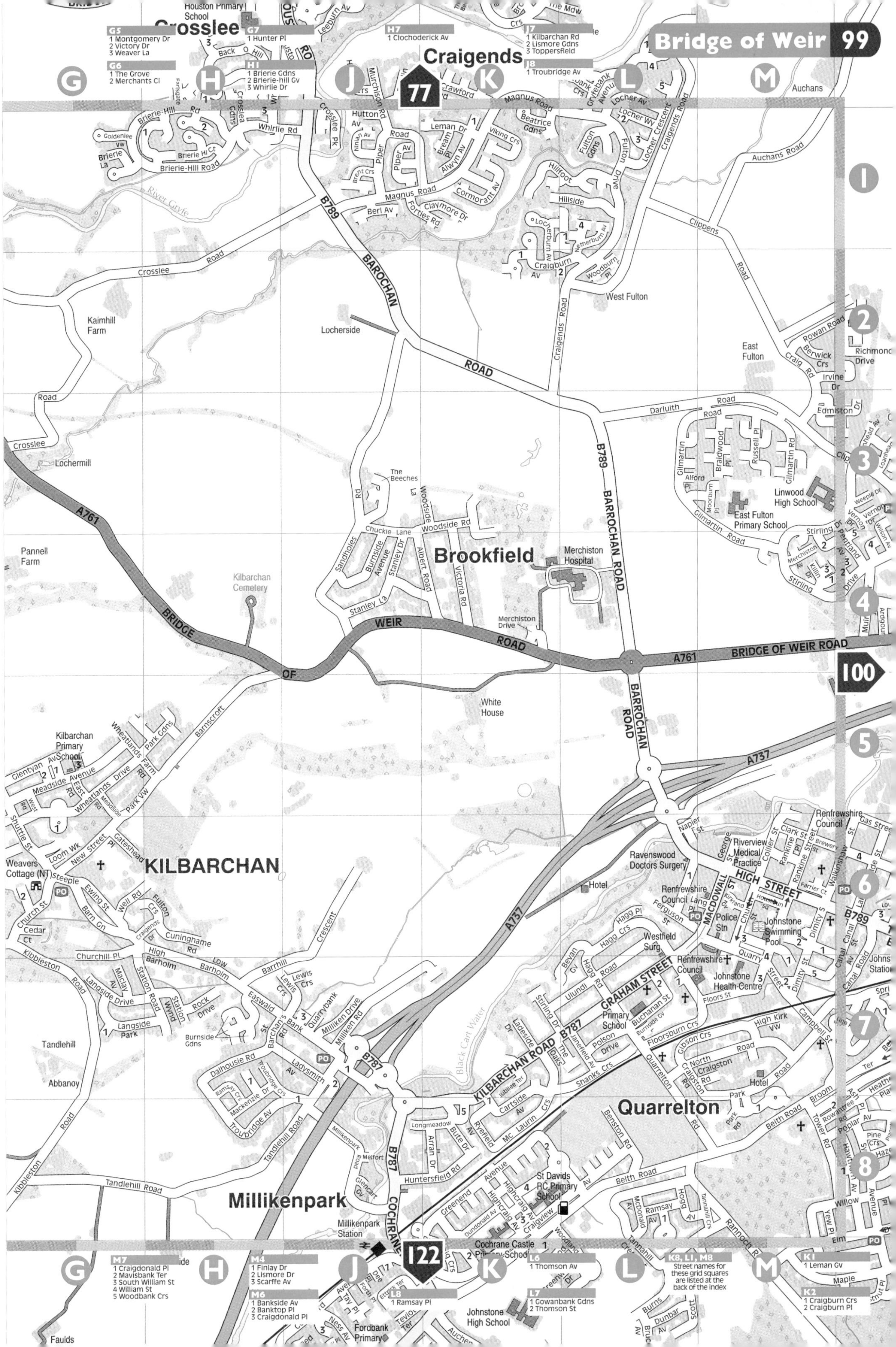
G5
1 Montgomery Dr
2 Victory Dr
3 Weaver La
G6
1 The Grove
2 Merchants Cl
G7
1 Hunter Pl
H1
1 Brierie Gdns
2 Brierie-hill Gv
3 Whirlie Dr
H7
1 Clochoderick Av
J7
1 Kilbarchan Rd
2 Lismore Gdns
3 Toppersfield
J8
1 Troubridge Av
Crosslee
Craigends
77
Houston Primary School
Brierie-Hill Rd
Whirlie Rd
Brierie-Hill Road
River Gryfe
Crosslee Road
Kaimhill Farm
Locherside
B789
BARROCHAN ROAD
Magnus Road
Cormorant Av
Claymore Dr
Hillside
Craigburn Av
West Fulton
Craigends Road
Auchans
Auchans Road
Clippens Road
East Fulton
Rowan Road
Berwick Crs
Richmond Drive
Irvine Dr
Edmiston Dr
Darluith Road
Gilmartin Rd
Braidwood Pl
Russell Pl
Linwood High School
East Fulton Primary School
Gilmartin Road
Stirling Dr
Pentland Av
Pannell Farm
Lochermill
A761
BRIDGE OF WEIR ROAD
Kilbarchan Cemetery
The Beeches
Chuckie Lane
Woodside Rd
Brookfield
Merchiston Hospital
Sandholes
Burnside Avenue
Stanley Dr
Albert Road
Victoria Rd
Stanley La
Merchiston Drive
100
White House
A737
Barnscroft
Kilbarchan Primary School
Wheatlands Farm
Park Gdns
Meadside Avenue
Wheatlands Drive
Park Vw
Weavers Cottage (NT)
Steeple St
New Street
Gateshead Pl
KILBARCHAN
Ewing St
Well Rd
Fulton Crs
Church St
Cedar Ct
Barn Gn
Cuninghame Rd
Churchill Pl
High Barholm
Low Barholm
Kibbleston Road
Langside Drive
Station Road
Rock Drive
Tandlehill
Abbanoy
Barrhill Crescent
Lewis Crs
Quarrybank
Milliken Drive
Burnside Gdns
Dalhousie Rd
Ladysmith Av
Troubridge Av
Tandlehill Road
Millikenpark
Millikenpark Station
Melfort
B787
COCHRANE
Longmeadow
Arran Dr
Huntersfield Rd
KILBARCHAN ROAD
Cartside Av
Mc Laurin Crs
Ryefield Av
St Davids RC Primary School
Highcraig Av
Craigview
122
Cochrane Castle Primary School
Ravenswood Doctors Surgery
Hotel
Napier St
Renfrewshire Council
Riverview Medical Practice
HIGH STREET
MACDOWALL ST
Police Stn
Johnstone Swimming Pool
Westfield Surg
Renfrewshire Council
Johnstone Health Centre
GRAHAM STREET
Primary School
Buchanan St
Floorsburn Crs
Black Cart Water
Ladeside Dr
Polson Drive
Shanks Crs
Quarrelton Rd
Craigston Rd
Quarrelton
Beith Road
Benston Rd
Ramsay Av
Tannahill Crs
Rannoch Rd
Campbell St
High Kirk Vw
Johnstone Station
Canal Road
Walkinshaw St
B789
Broom
Tower Rd
Poplar Av
Willow Av
Elm
Faulds
Fordbank Primary
Johnstone High School
M7
1 Craigdonald Pl
2 Mavisbank Ter
3 South William St
4 William St
5 Woodbank Crs
M4
1 Finlay Dr
2 Lismore Dr
3 Scarffe Av
M6
1 Bankside Av
2 Banktop Pl
3 Craigdonald Pl
L8
1 Ramsay Pl
L6
1 Thomson Av
L7
1 Gowanbank Gdns
2 Thomson St
K8, L1, M8
Street names for these grid squares are listed at the back of the index
K1
1 Leman Gv
K2
1 Craigburn Crs
2 Craigburn Pl

B7 1 Woodend Pl
B8 1 Sandringham Dr
B3 1 Blackstoun Av 2 Brydson Pl 3 Cochrane Sq 4 South Dr
A8 1 Tower Pl
A4, A6, A7, B4 Street names for these grid squares are listed at the back of the index
A3 1 Montclair Pl 2 Montrose Pl 3 Woodford Pl

78

99

123

C3 1 Greenhill Dr
C6 1 Castle Rd 2 Cherrywood Rd
C7 1 Beech Av 2 Willow Av
C8 1 Newlands Gdns
D7 1 Waverley Gdns
F4 1 Whites Bridge Av
F5 1 Baronscourt Dr 2 Howe St 3 Whites Bridge Av
F8 1 Cryffe Crs 2 Lauren Wy

1 grid square represents 500 metres

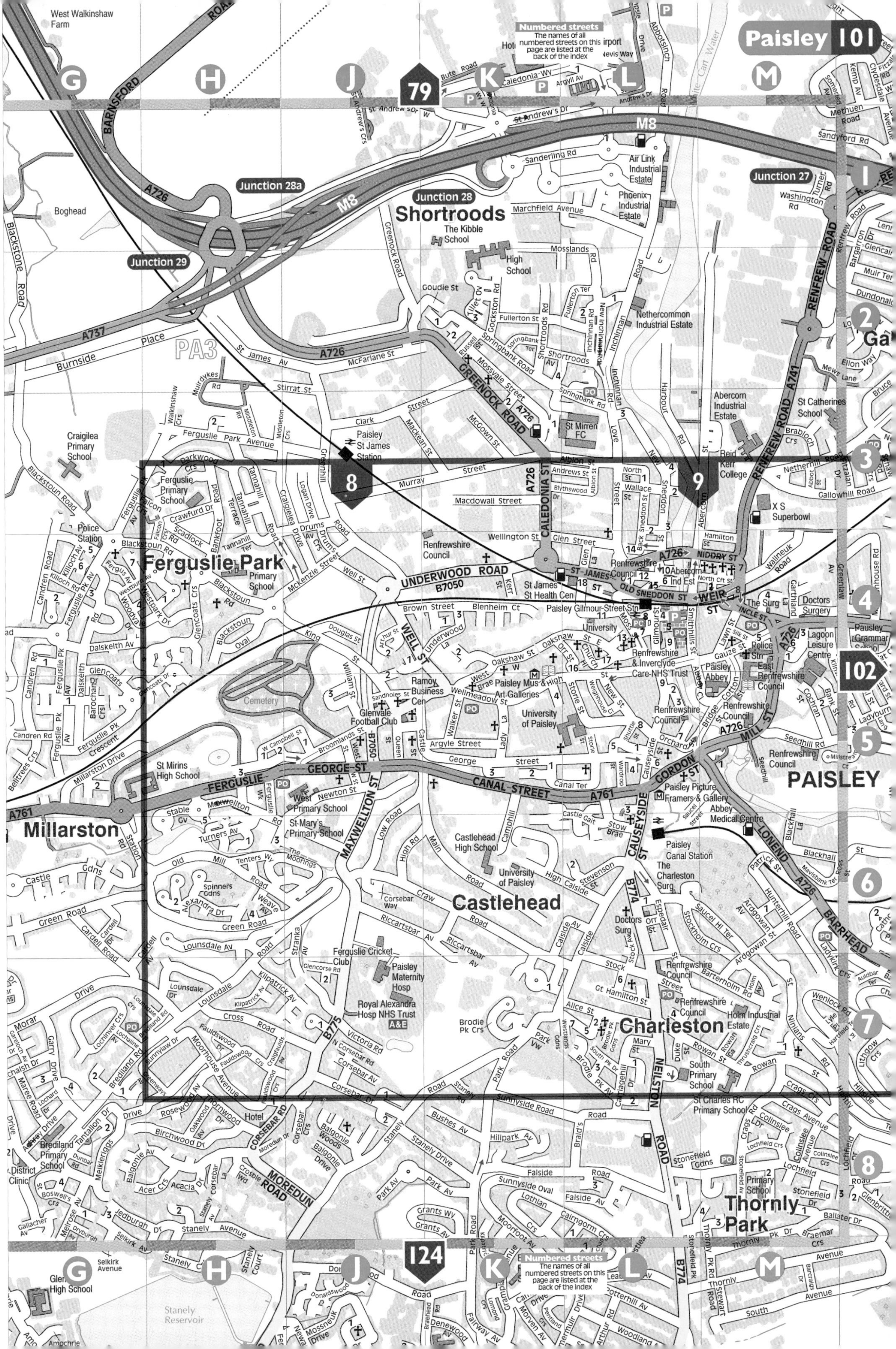
Numbered streets
The names of all numbered streets on this page are listed at the back of the index
West Walkinshaw Farm
Barnsford Road
Junction 28a
Junction 28
Junction 29
Junction 27
M8
A726
A737
A741
A761
B7050
B774
B775
Shortroods
The Kibble School
High School
Air Link Industrial Estate
Phoenix Industrial Estate
Nethercommon Industrial Estate
Abercorn Industrial Estate
St Catherines School
Boghead
Blackstone Road
Burnside Place
PA3
Craigilea Primary School
Paisley St James Station
St Mirren FC
Reid Kerr College
XS Superbowl
Ferguslie Primary School
Police Station
Ferguslie Park
Primary School
Renfrewshire Council
Underwood Road
St James St Health Cen
Paisley Gilmour Street Stn
University
Renfrewshire & Inverclyde Care NHS Trust
Paisley Abbey
Police Stn
East Renfrewshire Council
Lagoon Leisure Centre
Paisley Grammar School
Doctors Surgery
Cemetery
Ramoy Business Cen
Paisley Mus & High Art Galleries
University of Paisley
Glenvale Football Club
St Mirins High School
Millarston
George Street
Canal Street
Causeyside St
Gordon St
Paisley Picture Framers & Gallery
Abbey Medical Centre
PAISLEY
West Primary School
St Mary's Primary School
Maxwellton St
Castlehead High School
University of Paisley
Paisley Canal Station
The Charleston Surg
Castlehead
Spinners Gdns
Doctors Surg
Ferguslie Cricket Club
Paisley Maternity Hosp
Royal Alexandra Hosp NHS Trust
A&E
Charleston
Holm Industrial Estate
South Primary School
St Charles RC Primary School
Neilston Road
Brediland Primary School
District Clinic
Moredun Road
Corsebar Road
Hotel
Thornly Park
Primary School
Glen High School
Stanely Reservoir
Barrhead Road
Lonend
Mill St
Renfrew Road
79
8
9
102
124
G
H
J
K
L
M
1
2
3
4
5
6
7
8

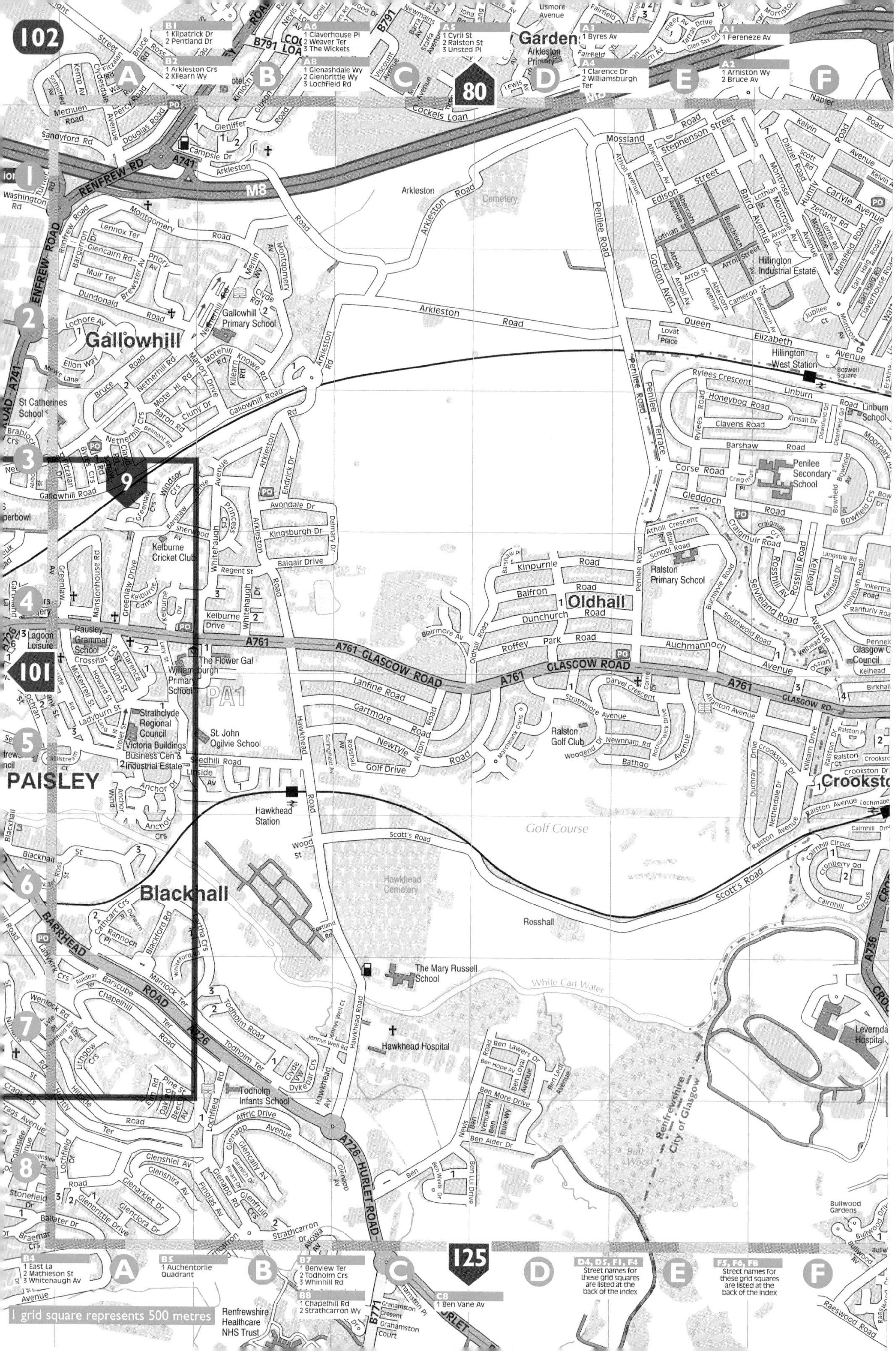
B1
1 Kilpatrick Dr
2 Pentland Dr
B2
1 Arkleston Crs
2 Kilearn Wy
A6
1 Claverhouse Pl
2 Weaver Ter
3 The Wickets
A8
1 Glenashdale Wy
2 Glenbrittle Wy
3 Lochfield Rd
A5
1 Cyril St
2 Ralston St
3 Unsted Pl
A3
1 Byres Av
A4
1 Clarence Dr
2 Williamsburgh Ter
A1
1 Fereneze Av
A2
1 Arniston Wy
2 Bruce Av
80
M8
Gallowhill
Gallowhill Primary School
Arkleston
Cemetery
Hillington Industrial Estate
Hillington West Station
Penilee Secondary School
Ralston Primary School
Oldhall
Kelburne Cricket Club
Paisley Grammar School
The Flower Gal
Williamsburgh Primary School
PA1
Strathclyde Regional Council
Victoria Buildings Business Cen & Industrial Estate
St. John Ogilvie School
PAISLEY
101
Hawkhead Station
Golf Course
Hawkhead Cemetery
Rosshall
Blackhall
Ralston Golf Club
Crookston
The Mary Russell School
White Cart Water
Hawkhead Hospital
Todholm Infants School
Renfrewshire
City of Glasgow
Bull Wood
Leverndale Hospital
Bullwood Gardens
125
B4
1 East La
2 Mathieson St
3 Whitehaugh Av
B5
1 Auchentorlie Quadrant
B7
1 Benview Ter
2 Todholm Crs
3 Whinhill Rd
B8
1 Chapelhill Rd
2 Strathcarron Wy
C8
1 Ben Vane Av
D4, D5, F1, F4
Street names for these grid squares are listed at the back of the index
F5, F6, F8
Street names for these grid squares are listed at the back of the index
1 grid square represents 500 metres
Renfrewshire Healthcare NHS Trust

Numbered streets
The names of all numbered streets on this page are listed at the back of the index
81
126
104
Junction
Junction 25
Junction
G
H
J
K
L
M
1
2
3
4
5
6
7
8
Shieldhall
Drumoyne
Craigton
Hillington
Cardonald
Mosspark
Corkerhill
Pollok
Linthouse
River Clyde
G51
G52
Southern General Hospital NHS Trust
A&E
M8
ROAD A8
SHIELDHALL ROAD A8
HILLINGTON RD
SANDWOOD RD A736
CROOKSTON RD
PAISLEY ROAD WEST A761
BERRYKNOWES RD
MEIKLEWOOD RD
HOLMFAULDHEAD RD
A739
Govan Road
Renfrew Road
Govan Rd
Renfrewshire
City of Glasgow
Fifty Pitches Place
Hillington East Station
Cardonald Station
Mosspark Station
Corkerhill Station
Crookston Station
Cemetery
Bellahouston Park
White Cart Water
Golf Course
Elder Park Primary School
Govan Health Centre
Langlands School
Govan High Secondary School
Greenfield Street School
Elderpark Clinic
St Anthonys School
Hillstrust Primary School
Drumoyne Primary School
Drumoyne Industrial Est
Glasgow City Council
Benburb Football Club
Police Stn
Hillington Primary School
Doctors Surg
Sandwood School
Westfield Health Clinic
Cardonald Clinic
Primary School
Bonnyholm Primary School
Ross Hall Hospital
Mcgill Primary School
Nethercraigs Sports Centre
Howford School
Crookston Castle (NT)
St Monicas School
Braidcraft Medical Centre
Leithland Road Primary School
St Marnocks Primary School
Lochinch Playing Fields & Sports Club
Police Station
Glasgow City

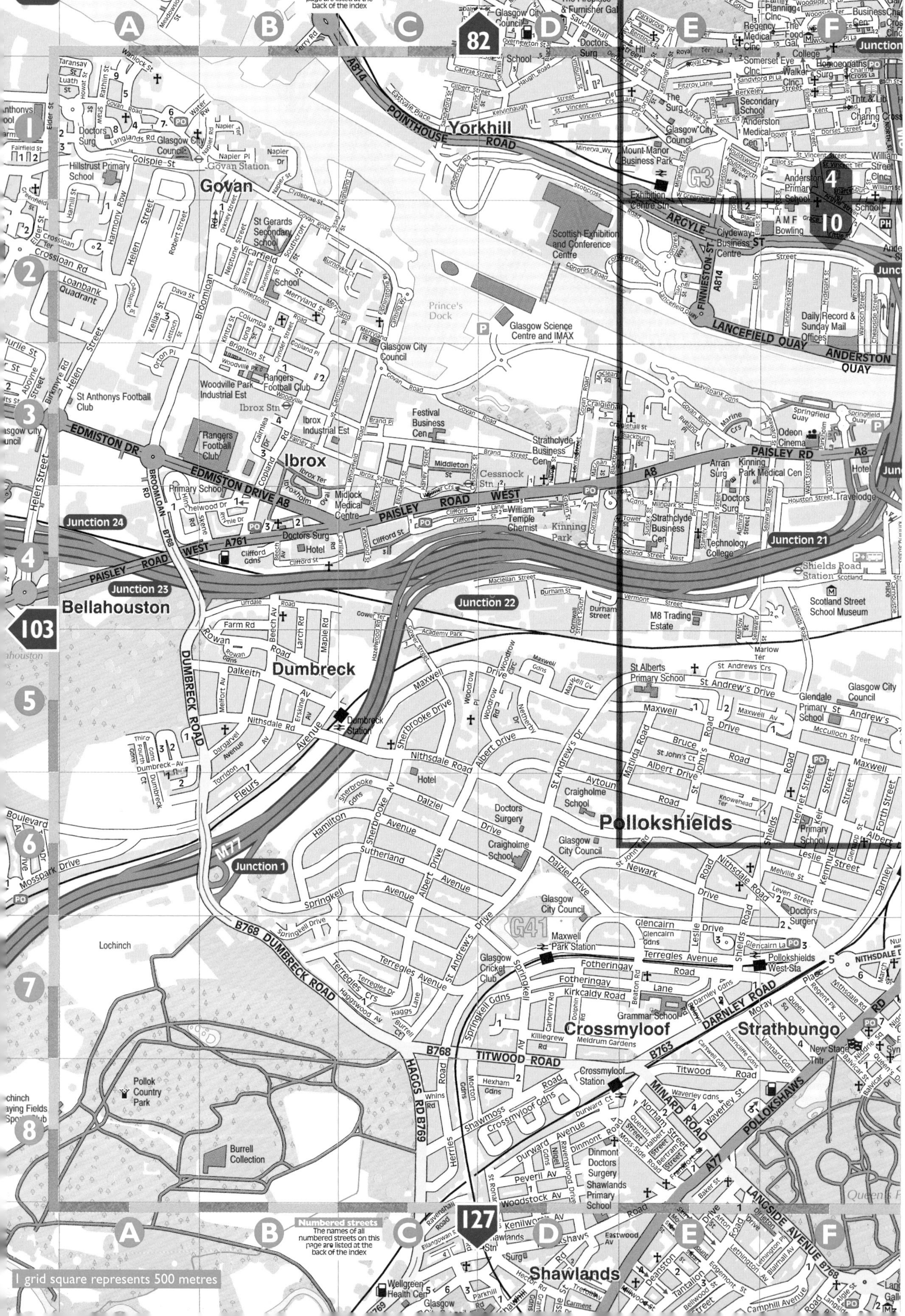
Numbered streets
The names of all numbered streets on this page are listed at the back of the index
82
127
103
4
10
A
B
C
D
E
F
1
2
3
4
5
6
7
8
Govan
Yorkhill
Ibrox
Bellahouston
Dumbreck
Pollokshields
Crossmyloof
Strathbungo
Shawlands
Pollokshaws
Lochinch
Pollok Country Park
Burrell Collection
Prince's Dock
Scottish Exhibition and Conference Centre
Glasgow Science Centre and IMAX
Rangers Football Club
Govan Station
Ibrox Stn
Cessnock Stn
Kinning Park
Dumbreck Station
Maxwell Park Station
Pollokshields West Sta
Crossmyloof Station
Exhibition Centre Stn
Shields Road Station
Scotland Street School Museum
Museum of Transport
Kelvin Hall
Art Gallery & Museum
Castlebank Industrial Est
Mount Manor Business Park
Clydeway Business Centre
M8 Trading Estate
Woodville Park Industrial Est
Ibrox Industrial Est
Festival Business Cen
Strathclyde Business Cen
Daily Record & Sunday Mail Offices
Pointhouse Road
Argyle St
Lancefield Quay
Anderston Quay
Finnieston St
Paisley Road West
Paisley Rd
Edmiston Drive
Dumbreck Road
Broomloan Rd
Haggs Rd
Titwood Road
Darnley Road
Minard Road
Langside Avenue
Nithsdale Road
Maxwell Drive
Albert Drive
St Andrew's Drive
Terregles Avenue
Springkell Avenue
Sherbrooke Avenue
Mosspark Drive
Helen Street
Junction 1
Junction 21
Junction 22
Junction 23
Junction 24
M77
A8
A761
A814
B768
B763
A77
G3
G41
1 grid square represents 500 metres

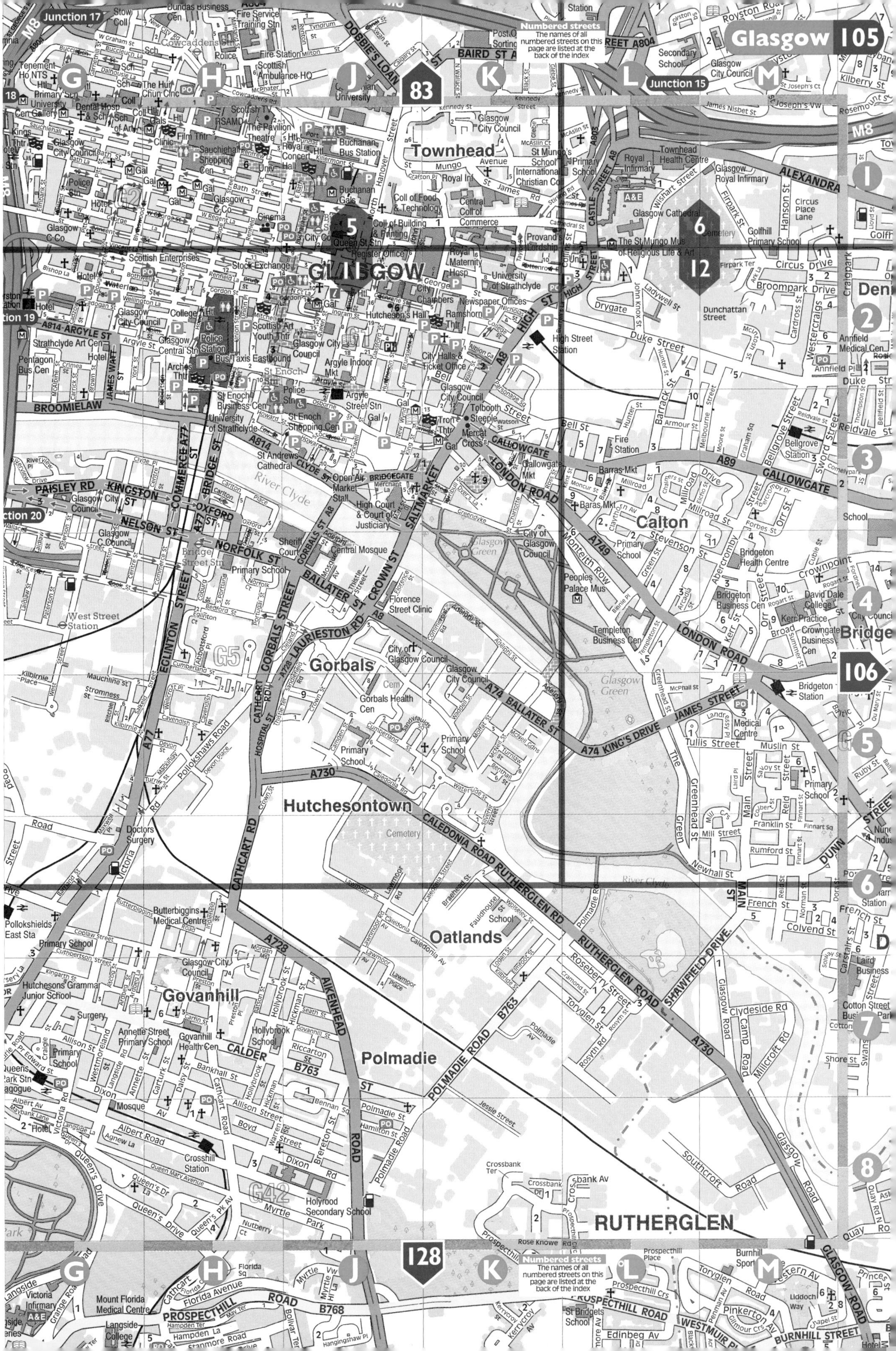
Numbered streets
The names of all numbered streets on this page are listed at the back of the index
Junction 17
Junction 15
Junction 19
Junction 20
83
128
106
G
H
J
K
L
M
1
2
3
4
5
6
7
8
Townhead
GLASGOW
Calton
Gorbals
Hutchesontown
Oatlands
Govanhill
Polmadie
RUTHERGLEN
M8
ALEXANDRA
Cowcaddens Stn
Glasgow Royal Infirmary
Glasgow Cathedral
The St Mungo Mus of Religious Life & Art
Provand's Lordship
Royal Infirmary
High Street Station
Queen St Stn
Buchanan Bus Station
Central Stn
Argyle Street Stn
St Enoch Stn
Bridge Street Stn
West Street Station
Bellgrove Station
Bridgeton Station
Pollokshields East Sta
Crosshill Station
Glasgow Green
River Clyde
Peoples Palace Mus
Central Mosque
University of Strathclyde
Strathclyde Art Cen
Tolbooth Steeple
Mercat Cross
Barras Mkt
Tron Thtr
City Halls & Ticket Office
BROOMIELAW
PAISLEY RD
KINGSTON ST
NELSON ST
NORFOLK ST
BALLATER ST
GORBALS STREET
CROWN ST
LAURIESTON RD
EGLINTON STREET
POLLOKSHAWS ROAD
CATHCART RD
CALEDONIA ROAD
RUTHERGLEN RD
RUTHERGLEN ROAD
SHAWFIELD DRIVE
KING'S DRIVE
JAMES STREET
LONDON ROAD
GALLOWGATE
DUKE STREET
HIGH ST
SALTMARKET
CASTLE STREET
DOBBIE'S LOAN
BAIRD ST
POLMADIE ROAD
AIKENHEAD ROAD
CALDER ST
PROSPECTHILL ROAD
Florida Avenue
Queen's Drive
Victoria Rd
Albert Road
Glasgow Road
Southcroft Road
BURNHILL STREET
GLASGOW ROAD
Holyrood Secondary School
Hutchesons Grammar Junior School
Mount Florida Medical Centre
Victoria Infirmary
Langside College

Numbered streets
The names of all numbered streets on this page are listed at the back of the index
Junction 14
84
105
129
M8
Blochairn Road
Markets
Riddrie
Golf Club
Alexandra Park
Glasgow City Council
Alexandra Parade Station
Alexandra Parade
Cumbernauld Road
Kennyhill School
Dennistoun
Whitehill Swimming Pool
Whitehill School
Duke Street Station
Duke Street
The Flower Gallery
Annfield Medical Cen
Glenpark Industrial Estate
Bellgrove Station
Haghill
Haghill School
Carntyne
Edinburgh Road
A8
A80
Riddrie Knowes
Liberton
Morningside
Warriston Street
Doctors Surgery
Primary School
Carntyne Road
Carntyne Station
Myreside Street
Shettleston Road
A89
G31
Biggar Street
Millerston St
Gallowgate
Virgin Cinema
Parkhead Hosp
Greater Glasgow Hlth Board
Celtic Football Club
Cemetery
Doctors Surgery
St Michaels Primary School
St Annes Primary School
Crownpoint Road
Fielden Street
Bridgeton
Law Street
Dalserf St
Westmuir St
Tollcross Rd
Parkhead
The Gal
Westmuir Medical Centre
The Surgery
Quarrybrae St
St Marks Primary School
Tollcross Park
Shettleston Day Hospital
Wellshot Primary School
A74
London Road
London Road Primary School
Barrowfield School
Dalmarnock Primary School
G40
Nuneaton Industrial Estate
Dunn Street
Belvidere Hospital
City of Glasgow
South Lanarkshire
Tollcross Park Gardens
Tollcross Road
Braidfauld
Cemetery
Dalmarnock Station
Dalmarnock
Dalmarnock Road
Laird Business Park
Cotton Street Business Park
Springfield Primary School
Strathclyde Street
Downiebrae Road
Dalmarnock Trading Estate
Duchess Industrial Estate
River Clyde
Drumhead Road
Drumhead Place
Rutherglen Station
Farmeloan Road
Farmeloan Industrial Estate
Cambuslang Road
Glasgow Road
A749
A724
B768
Main
1 grid square represents 500 metres

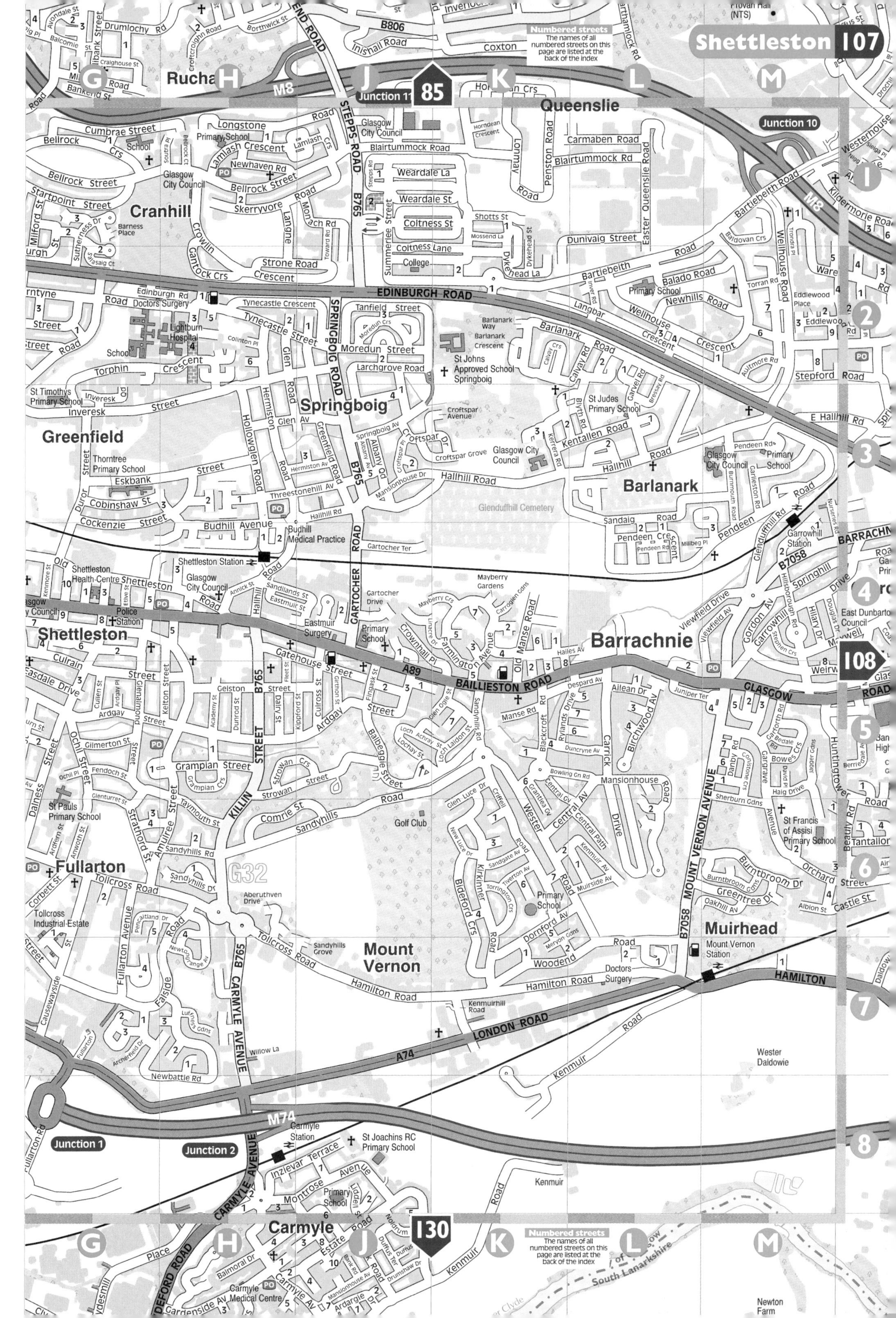
Numbered streets
The names of all numbered streets on this page are listed at the back of the index
Ruchazie
Queenslie
Junction 11
85
Junction 10
M8
B806
Cranhill
Springboig
Greenfield
Barlanark
Shettleston
Barrachnie
Fullarton
Mount Vernon
Muirhead
Carmyle
EDINBURGH ROAD
STEPPS ROAD
SPRINGBOIG ROAD
CARTOCHER ROAD
BAILLIESTON ROAD
A89
B765
B7058
KILLIN STREET
CARMYLE AVENUE
MOUNT VERNON AVENUE
LONDON ROAD
A74
HAMILTON ROAD
M74
Junction 1
Junction 2
G32
108
130
Glasgow City Council
Lightburn Hospital
St Johns Approved School Springboig
Glendufhill Cemetery
Shettleston Station
Garrowhill Station
Mount Vernon Station
Carmyle Station
Golf Club
Tollcross Industrial Estate
St Joachims RC Primary School
East Dunbartonshire Council
South Lanarkshire
Wester Daldowie
Kenmuir
Newton Farm
Provan Hall (NTS)

B4
1 Buchanan St
2 Hathersage Gdns
3 Queensby Av
4 Thornbridge Av
B1
1 Boyndie St
2 Duntarvie Dr
3 Duntarvie Pl
B3, B5, C1, C2
Street names for these grid squares are listed at the back of the index
A2, A4, A5, A6
Street names for these grid squares are listed at the back of the index
A1
1 Arnisdale Pl
2 Bogbain Rd
3 Dalcharn Pl
4 Grudie St
5 Struie St
6 Swordale Pl
Lochwood
86
Junction 10
Easterhouse
Westwood Business Cen
College
Police Stn
Glasgow City Council
Blairtummock Primary School
Cairnbrook Industrial Estate
Corsehill Place
St Clares Primary School
Drumlanrig Av
Commonhead Road
Heatheryknowe Road
Cuilhill Road
Denmiline Street
M8
Junction 9
Springhill Parkway
Springhill Drive South
Rogerfield Road
Denmilne Rd
Netherhouse Road
Netherhouse
M73
Easterhouse Station
Swinton
Garrowhill Station
Garrowhill
Garrowhill Primary School
Edinburgh Road
Coatbridge Road
Glasgow and Edinburgh Road
Junction 8/2
Crosshill
A752
A89
A8
107
East Dunbartonshire Council
Main Street
Bannerman High School
Cluny Gardens
Baillieston
Baillieston Health Centre
Baillieston Football Club
St Francis of Assisi Primary School
Baillieston Station
Ellismuir Farm
City of Glasgow
South Lanarkshire
North Calder Water
Woodhead Farm
Newlands Farm
Broomhouse
Hamilton Road
Glasgow Zoo
Boghall Road
Roundknowe Road
Golf Club
M74
A74
Junction 3
Birkenshaw
Aitkenhead Primary School
B7001
131
B6
1 Caledonia Dr
B7
1 Calderpark Crs
2 Lockhart Pl
3 North Calder Gv
4 Rosebank Gdns
B8
1 Baillieston Rd
C3, C4, C5
Street names for these grid squares are listed at the back of the index
D1, D3, D4, D5
Street names for these grid squares are listed at the back of the index
E8, F4, F8
Street names for these grid squares are listed at the back of the index
1 grid square represents 500 metres

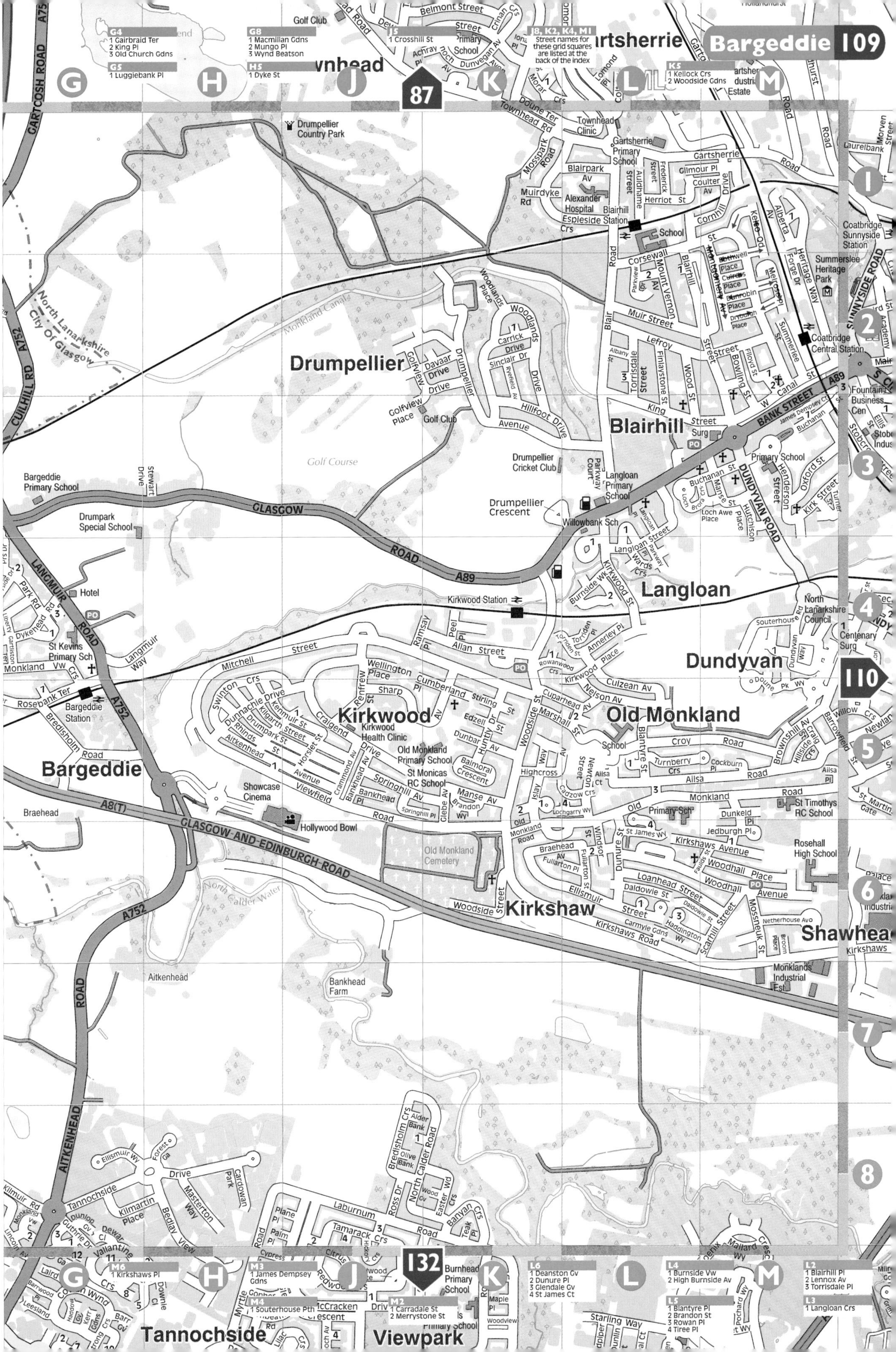
Drumpellier
Drumpellier Country Park
Blairhill
Langloan
Dundyvan
Kirkwood
Old Monkland
Bargeddie
Kirkshaw
Shawhead
Tannochside
Viewpark
Gartsherrie
Aitkenhead
Bankhead Farm
Braehead
Golf Course
Monkland Canal
North Calder Water
Old Monkland Cemetery
Kirkwood Station
Bargeddie Station
Blairhill Station
Coatbridge Central Station
Coatbridge Sunnyside Station
Summerlee Heritage Park
Showcase Cinema
Hollywood Bowl
Monklands Industrial Est
North Lanarkshire Council
North Lanarkshire
City Of Glasgow
GLASGOW ROAD
A89
BANK STREET
DUNDYVAN ROAD
LANGMUIR ROAD
A752
GARTCOSH ROAD
CUILHILL RD
AITKENHEAD ROAD
GLASGOW AND EDINBURGH ROAD
A8(T)
87
110
132
G
H
J
K
L
M
1
2
3
4
5
6
7
8

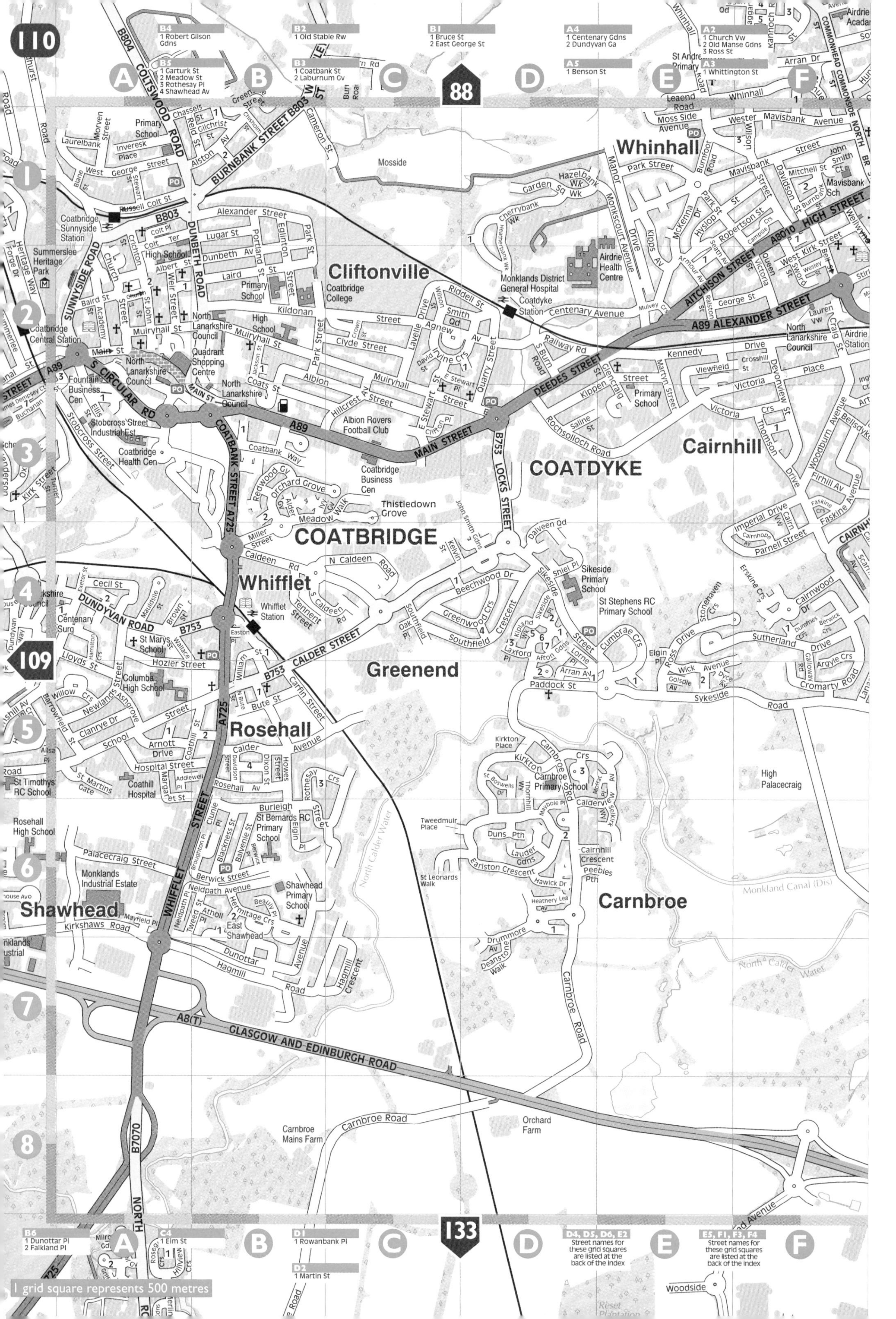
B4
1 Robert Gilson Gdns
B5
1 Garturk St
2 Meadow St
3 Rothesay Pl
4 Shawhead Av
B2
1 Old Stable Rw
B3
1 Coatbank St
2 Laburnum Gv
B1
1 Bruce St
2 East George St
A4
1 Centenary Gdns
2 Dundyvan Ga
A5
1 Benson St
A2
1 Church Vw
2 Old Manse Gdns
3 Ross St
A3
1 Whittington St
88
109
133
B6
1 Dunottar Pl
2 Falkland Pl
C4
1 Elm St
D1
1 Rowanbank Pl
D2
1 Martin St
D4, D5, D6, E2
Street names for these grid squares are listed at the back of the index
E5, F1, F3, F4
Street names for these grid squares are listed at the back of the index
Whinhall
Cliftonville
COATBRIDGE
COATDYKE
Cairnhill
Whifflet
Greenend
Rosehall
Shawhead
Carnbroe
Mosside
High Palacecraig
Orchard Farm
Carnbroe Mains Farm
Woodside
Coatbridge Sunnyside Station
Coatbridge Central Station
Coatdyke Station
Whifflet Station
Airdrie Station
Summerlee Heritage Park
Coatbridge College
Monklands District General Hospital
Airdrie Health Centre
Albion Rovers Football Club
Coatbridge Business Cen
Coatbridge Health Cen
Quadrant Shopping Centre
North Lanarkshire Council
Stobcross Street Industrial Est
Fountain Business Cen
Thistledown Grove
Sikeside Primary School
St Stephens RC Primary School
Carnbroe Primary School
St Bernards RC Primary School
Shawhead Primary School
Columba High School
Coathill Hospital
St Timothys RC School
Rosehall High School
Monklands Industrial Estate
Mavisbank Sch
A89 ALEXANDER STREET
A8010 HIGH STREET
AITCHISON STREET
DEEDES STREET
MAIN STREET
B753 LOCKS STREET
COATBANK STREET A725
WHIFFLET STREET
A725
B7070 NORTH ROAD
S CIRCULAR RD
DUNDYVAN ROAD
CALDER STREET
SUNNYSIDE ROAD
DUNBETH ROAD
COLTSWOOD ROAD
BURNBANK STREET B803
A8(T) GLASGOW AND EDINBURGH ROAD
Carnbroe Road
Sykeside Road
Centenary Avenue
Monkland Canal (Dis)
North Calder Water
1 grid square represents 500 metres

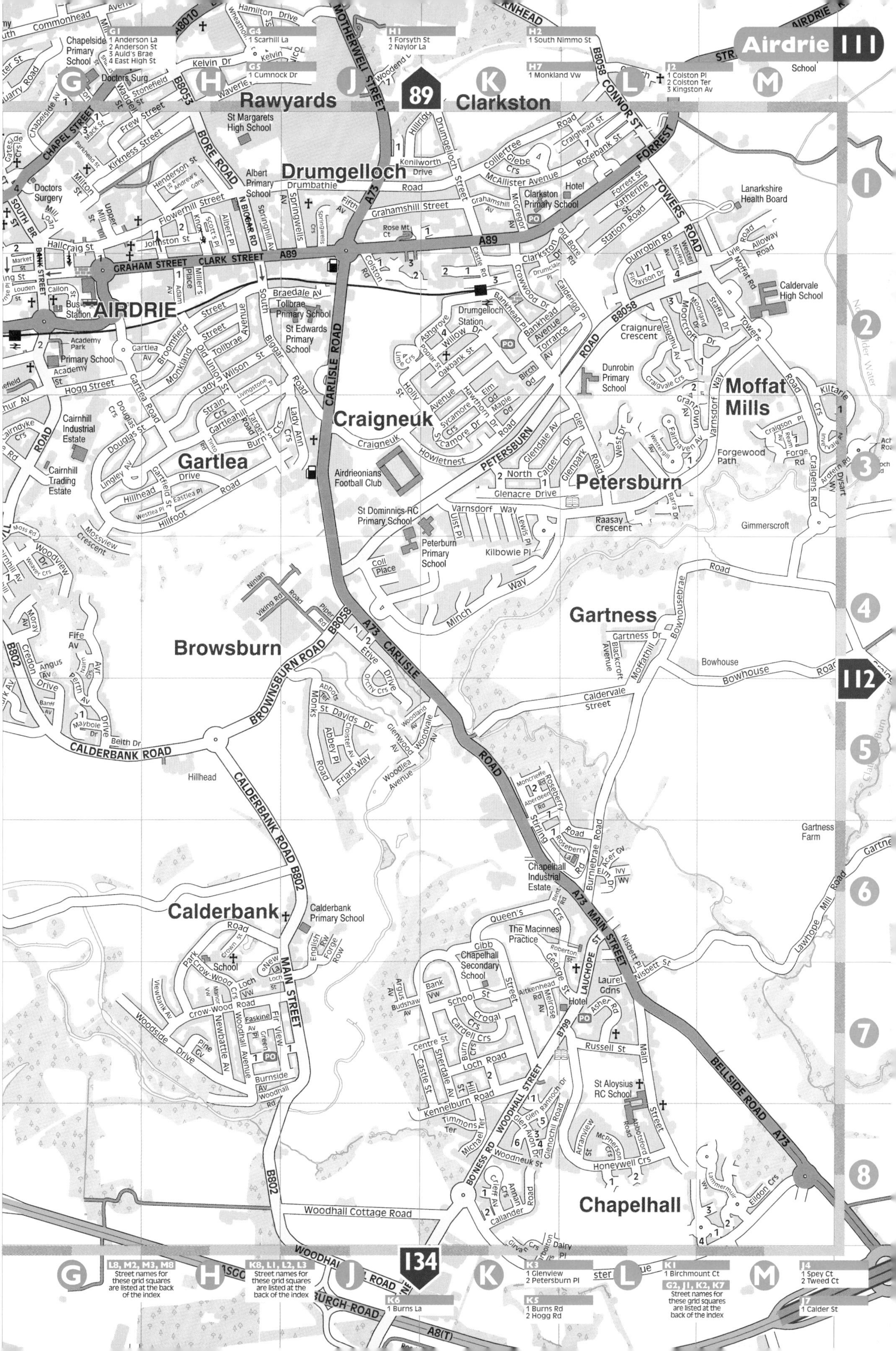
G1
1 Anderson La
2 Anderson St
3 Auld's Brae
4 East High St
G4
1 Scarhill La
G5
1 Cumnock Dr
H1
1 Forsyth St
2 Naylor La
H2
1 South Nimmo St
H7
1 Monkland Vw
J2
1 Colston Pl
2 Colston Ter
3 Kingston Av
89
Rawyards
Clarkston
Drumgelloch
AIRDRIE
Craigneuk
Gartlea
Moffat Mills
Petersburn
Gartness
Browsburn
Calderbank
Chapelhall
112
Chapelside Primary School
St Margarets High School
Albert Primary School
Clarkston Primary School
Lanarkshire Health Board
Caldervale High School
Tollbrae Primary School
St Edwards Primary School
Drumgelloch Station
Dunrobin Primary School
Airdrieonians Football Club
St Dominics RC Primary School
Peterburn Primary School
Calderbank Primary School
Chapelhall Secondary School
St Aloysius RC School
Cairnhill Industrial Estate
Cairnhill Trading Estate
Chapelhall Industrial Estate
The Macinnes Practice
Bus Station
Doctors Surgery
Hillhead
Bowhouse
Gimmerscroft
Gartness Farm
Forgewood Path
Craignure Crescent
Raasay Crescent
CARLISLE ROAD
MOTHERWELL STREET
GRAHAM STREET
CLARK STREET
TOWERS ROAD
CONNOR ST
PETERSBURN ROAD
BROWNSBURN ROAD
CALDERBANK ROAD
MAIN STREET
BELLSIDE ROAD
WOODHALL STREET
Woodhall Cottage Road
Bowhouse Road
Caldervale Street
Lawhope Mill Road
134
G
H
J
K
L
M
1
2
3
4
5
6
7
8
L8, M2, M3, M8
Street names for these grid squares are listed at the back of the index
K8, L1, L2, L3
Street names for these grid squares are listed at the back of the index
K3
1 Glenview
2 Petersburn Pl
K1
1 Birchmount Ct
G2, J1, K2, K7
Street names for these grid squares are listed at the back of the index
J4
1 Spey Ct
2 Tweed Ct
K6
1 Burns La
K5
1 Burns Rd
2 Hogg Rd
J7
1 Calder St

AIRDRIE
112
90
111
135
School
Plains Country Park
Easter Moffat Golf Club
Farm
Berrieswalls
A3
1 Burnwood Dr
A
B
C
D
E
F
1
2
3
4
5
6
7
8
Lochhill
Duntilland Road
Caldervale High School
North Calder Water
Wester Bracco
Stepends Road
Lady Bell's Moss
Kiltarie Crs
Road
Kiltarie Farm
Achnasheen Road
Balloch Road
Ardfern Rd
Dysart Wy
Forge
Roughrigg Road
Roughrigg Reservoir
Craigens Road
Easter Dunsyston
Dunsiston Road
Clattering Burn
Craigends
Roughrigg Road
Gartness Farm
Gartness Road
Lawhope Mill Road
Turdees
Craigens Road
Blackridge Farm
Wester Dunsyston
Langside
Bothwellshields Road
Bothwellshields
M8
Craigens Road
Budshaw
Shotts Burn
Peatpots
Edinburgh Road
Sandyford
M8
Glasgow and
B7066
North Linrigg
Junction 6

1 grid square represents 500 metres

G7
1 Lorne Gdns
H7
1 Bertram Dr
2 David St
3 Gibson St
4 Margaret Av
J7
1 Carvale Av
91
136
Bracco Road
283
Torrance
Mountcow
Duntilland Road
Duntilland Farm
Shottsburn
M8
Bogfoot Road
School Rd
HIRST ROAD
Kirk of Shotts
Manse Road
Muirhall Terrace
Reid Street
Crossart St
Bogfoot Rd
PO
B7066
Springfield Road
Blackcroft Terrace
Stonehill
Muirhead Gdns
Kirkview Av
Duntilland Av
Carnsdale Av
Carvale Avenue
Salsburgh
Glebe Farm
Newmill and Canthill Road
Westfield
Pappe
Sho

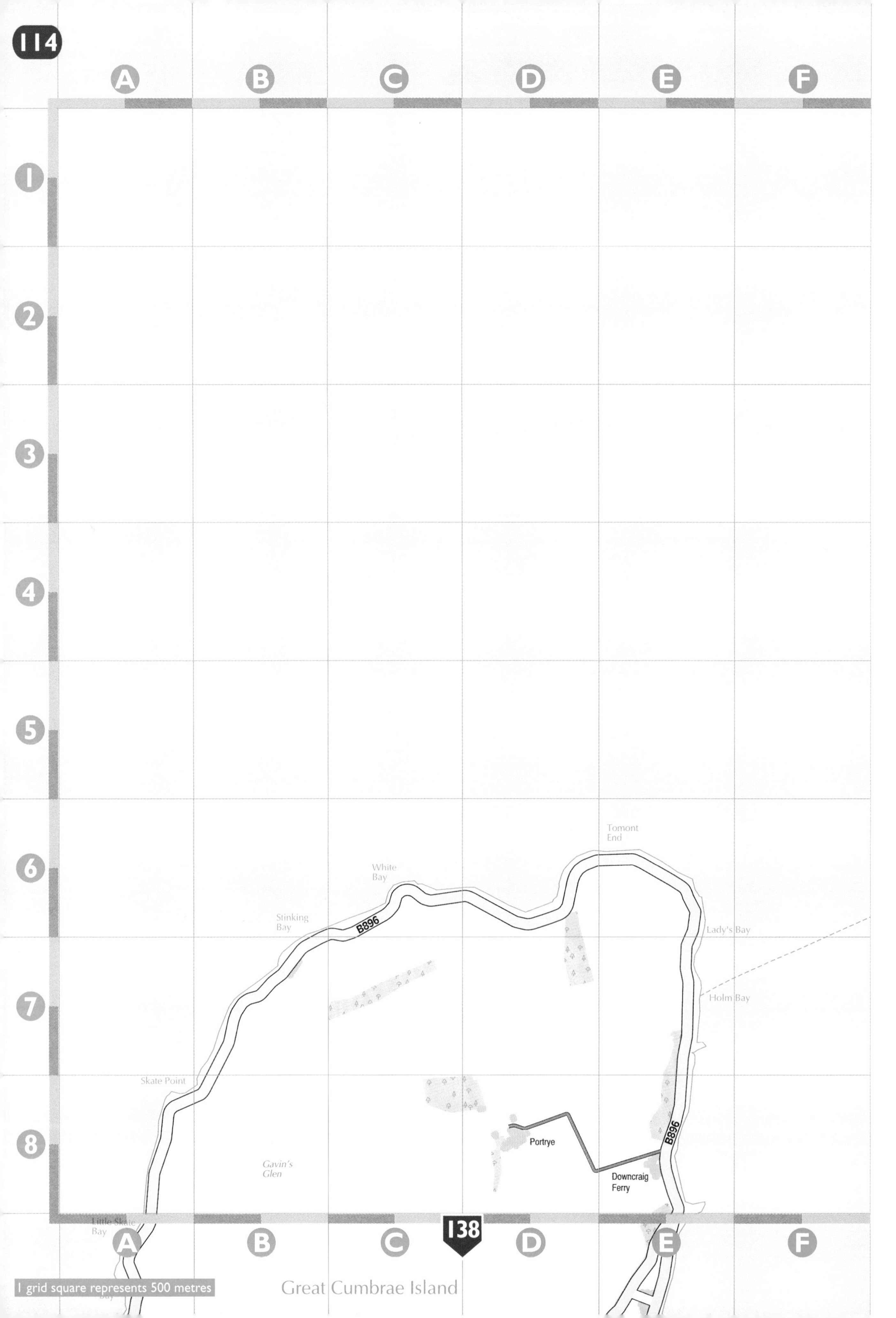
Tomont End
White Bay
Stinking Bay
B896
Lady's Bay
Holm Bay
Skate Point
Portrye
B896
Gavin's Glen
Downcraig Ferry
Little Skate Bay
138
1 grid square represents 500 metres
Great Cumbrae Island

H3
1 Boathouse Av
2 Boathouse Rd
3 Buchanan St
4 Newhaven Gv
5 Northfield Pk
6 Woodbank Gdns
J4
1 Brisbane Crs
J5
1 Cochrane Pl East
2 Gallowgate La
Brisbane Mains
J6
Street names for this grid square are listed at the back of the index
Middleton
G
H
J
92
K
L
M
Routen Burn
Noddsdale
Routenburn
A78(T)
Routenburn Road
Road
Holmwood Court
Bank-Head
GREENOCK ROAD
Danfield Avenue
Water
Kilburn
Glen
Harplaw
Underbank
Hollywood
Avenue
Raillies Rd
Raillies Av
Glen
Glen Gv
Netherhall
Routenburn Golf Club
Kilburn Farm
Netherpark Crs
Kelvin Walk
Kelvin Gardens
Brisbane
Glen Place
Chapelton Wy
Windsor Gardens
Inverclyde Vw
Noddleburn Road
Chapelton Dr
Barr Crs
Douglas Place
Laverock Dr
Burnside Wy
Douglas Street
Rankin
Drive
Aubery Crs
Spalding Dr
Moorburn Road
Hutton Pk
Crs
Brisbane Street
Brisbane Road
Burnside Road
Alexander Avenue
Sinclair Drive
Sinclair Ter
Mansefield Crs
Beachway
Glenburn Crs
Queens Av
Brisbane Primary School
Glenacre Drive
Largs Bay
Haco Street
Lindsay Crs
Holehouse Court
Greeto Falls Av
Braeside Av
Meadowbank Rd
Holehouse
Kelvin Street
GREENOCK ROAD
George Street
N Middleton Drive
Royal Av
Holehouse Road
Arran Vw
Seamore St
PO
Nelson Street
John Clark St
Moorburne Road
Middleton Dr
Auchenmaid Dr
Primary School
Linn Avenue
The Roundel
Eastern Avenue
Phillips Av
Mt Stuart Rd
Kyles View
GALLOWGATE ST
Court St
Boyd St
Allanpark St
Wilson St
School St
Vikingar
Harper Crs
Kelburn Primary School
Woodcroft Av
Flatt Road
Gateside St
Aitken St
Bellesdale Avenue
Flatt
MAIN ST
Fort St
New St
Silverdale Gdns
The Surgery
Frazer St
Waterside Street
BATH STREET
Church St
Crawford St
Largs Station
Union St
Stakehill
Gogo St
Gogo St
Viking Way
Stakehill
Gogoside Road
Burnlea Rd
Kelburn Ct
Lovat St
Gogoside Rd
Whinhill Av
Castlehill Dr
Halkshill Dr
Scott Dr
Scott Crs
LARGS
MACKERSTON PL
CHARLES STREET
Scott
Blackdales Av
Cunningham Dr
Hamilton Dr
Silverae Ct
Castle Hill Fort
Broomfield Pl
Largs Sailing Club
Blythswood Crs
Bankhouse Av
Castle Bay
John Street
IRVINE
Hill Street
Cunninghall
Broomfield Crs
Cathcart Rd
May Street
Hayle Gdns
Springfields Gardens
Duffield Dr
Acre Av
Warrenpark Road
Anthony Road
Warren Pk
Mews
Cemetery
ROAD
DALRY
ROAD
Walkerston Av
Seabank Av
Bowencraig
Largs Golf Club
Haylie Reservoir
Rockland Pl
A760
L5
1 Paton Quadrant
G
H
K8
1 Hutcheson Dr
2 Trigoni Ct
3 Walkerston Av
J
139
K
K6
1 East Castle Av
2 Greenhill
3 Millburn Gdns
4 Park Vw
5 Stakehill
L
K5
1 Scotlaw Dr
M
J7
1 Broomfield
K7
1 Bankhouse Crs
2 Haylie Neuk
116
1
2
3
4
5
6
7
8

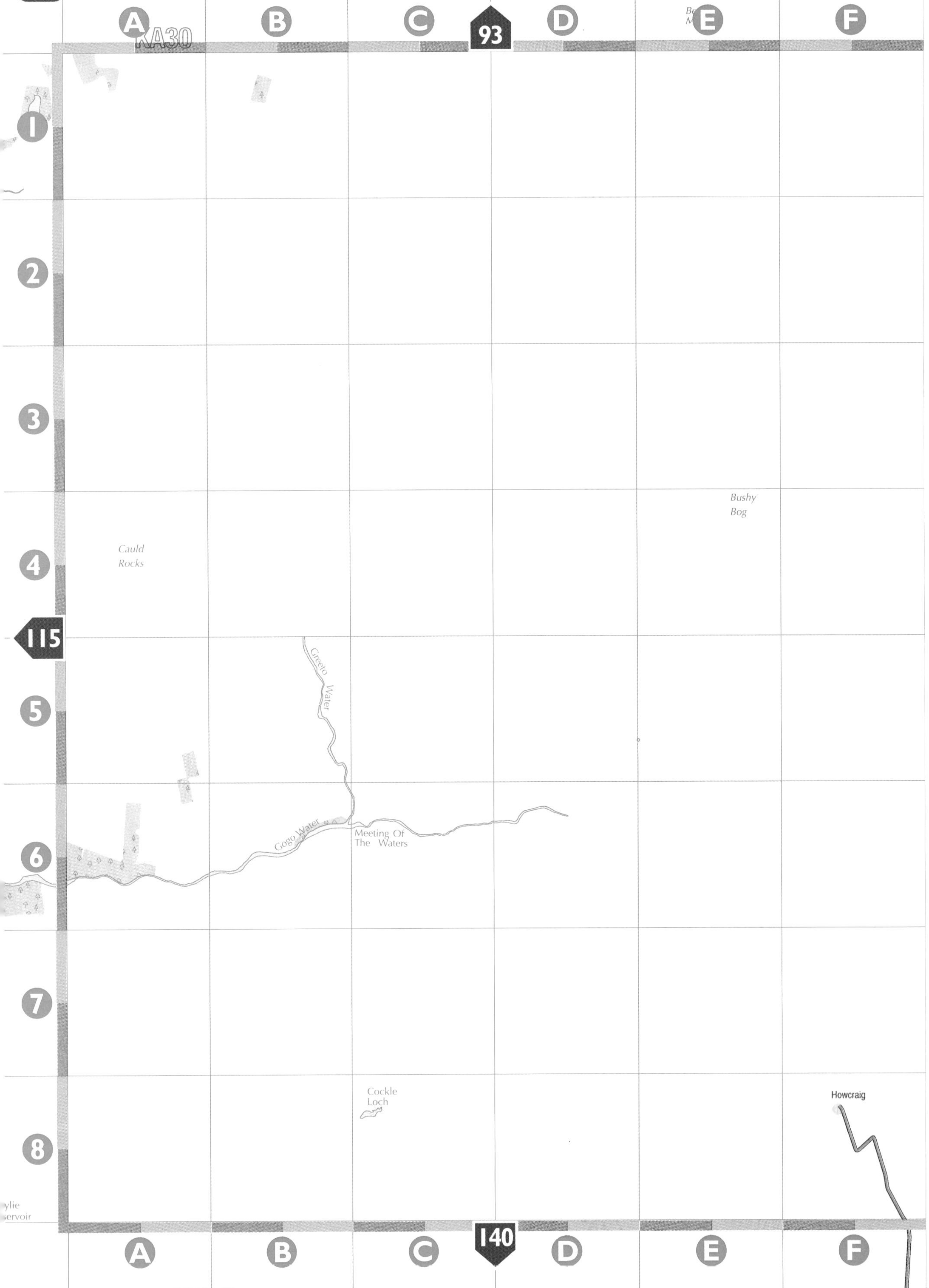
A
B
C
D
E
F
KA30
93
1
2
3
4
5
6
7
8
115
140
Cauld Rocks
Bushy Bog
Greeto Water
Gogo Water
Meeting Of The Waters
Cockle Loch
Howcraig

1 grid square represents 500 metres

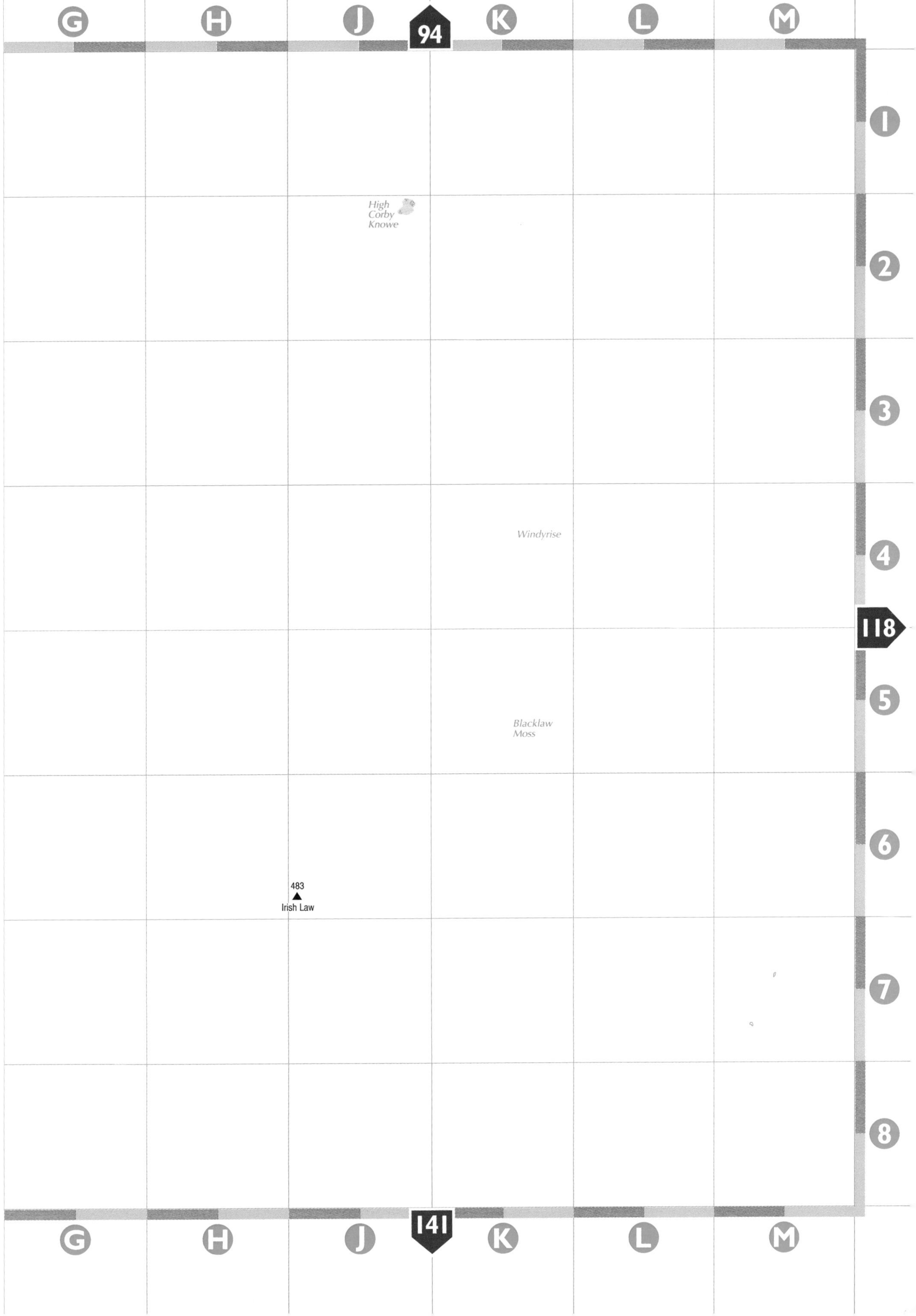
G
H
J
94
K
L
M
1
High Corby Knowe
2
3
Windyrise
4
118
5
Blacklaw Moss
6
483
Irish Law
7
8
G
H
J
141
K
L
M

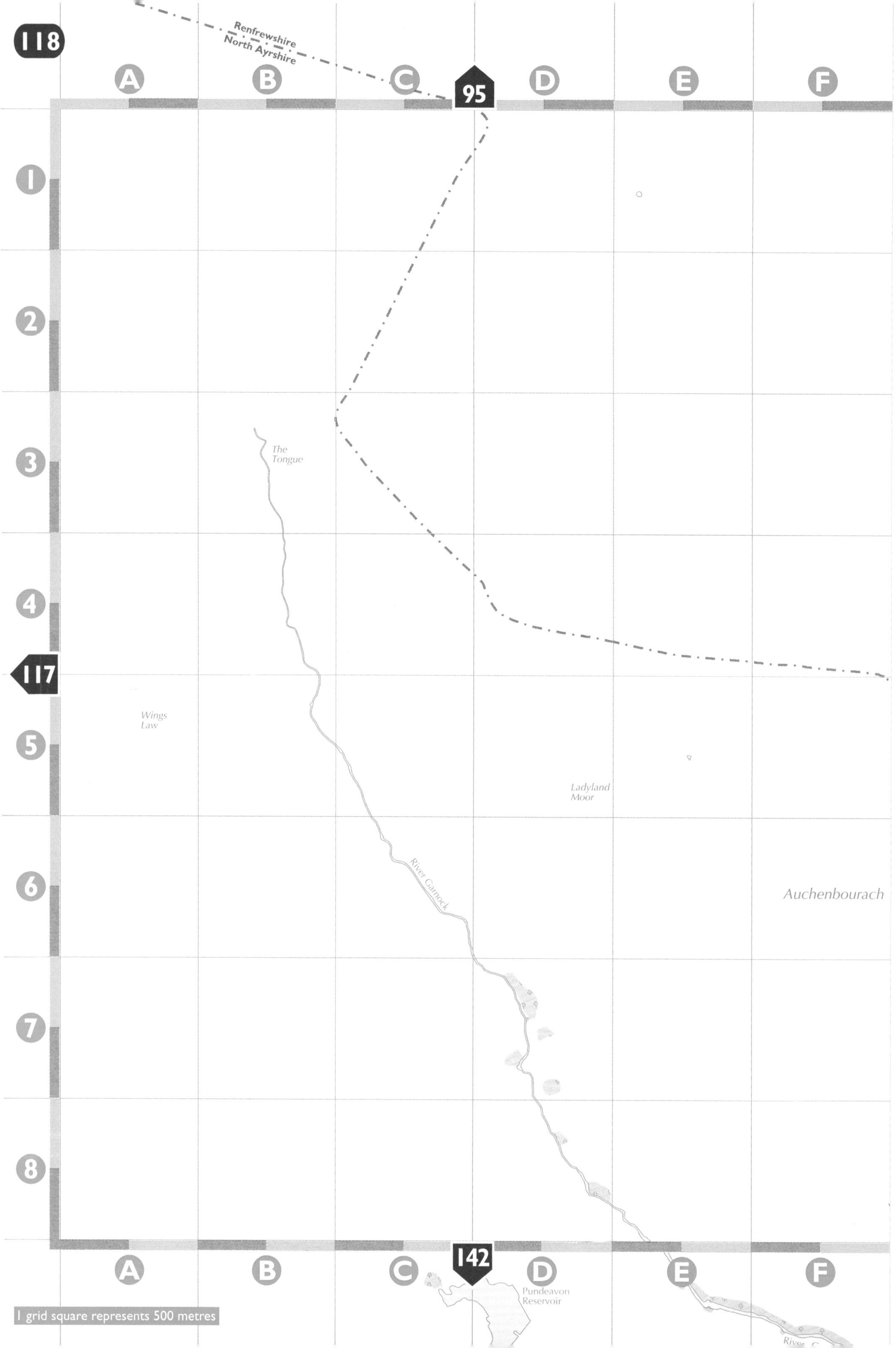
Renfrewshire
North Ayrshire
95
117
142
The Tongue
Wings Law
Ladyland Moor
Auchenbourach
River Garnock
Pundeavon Reservoir

1 grid square represents 500 metres

G
H
J
96
K
L
M
River Calder
Clovenstone
Tandlemuir
1
2
3
4
5
6
7
8
PA12
Muirfauldhouse
120
The Ward
Carpel Burn
Renfrewshire
North Ayrshire
Curling Pond
Gillsyard
Fairhills
Glenlora
Corsefield Road
Cockston
Maich Water
Easthills
Gavilmoss
Westhills
143
Lora Burn
Ladyland
Rashlieyett
Auchenhain
Plantilly

C7 1 John Gregor Pl 2 Johnstone Dr
C6 1 Calderpark St 2 Crookhill Dr 3 Crookhill Gdns
B7 1 Viewfield Av
B6 1 Garpel Wy

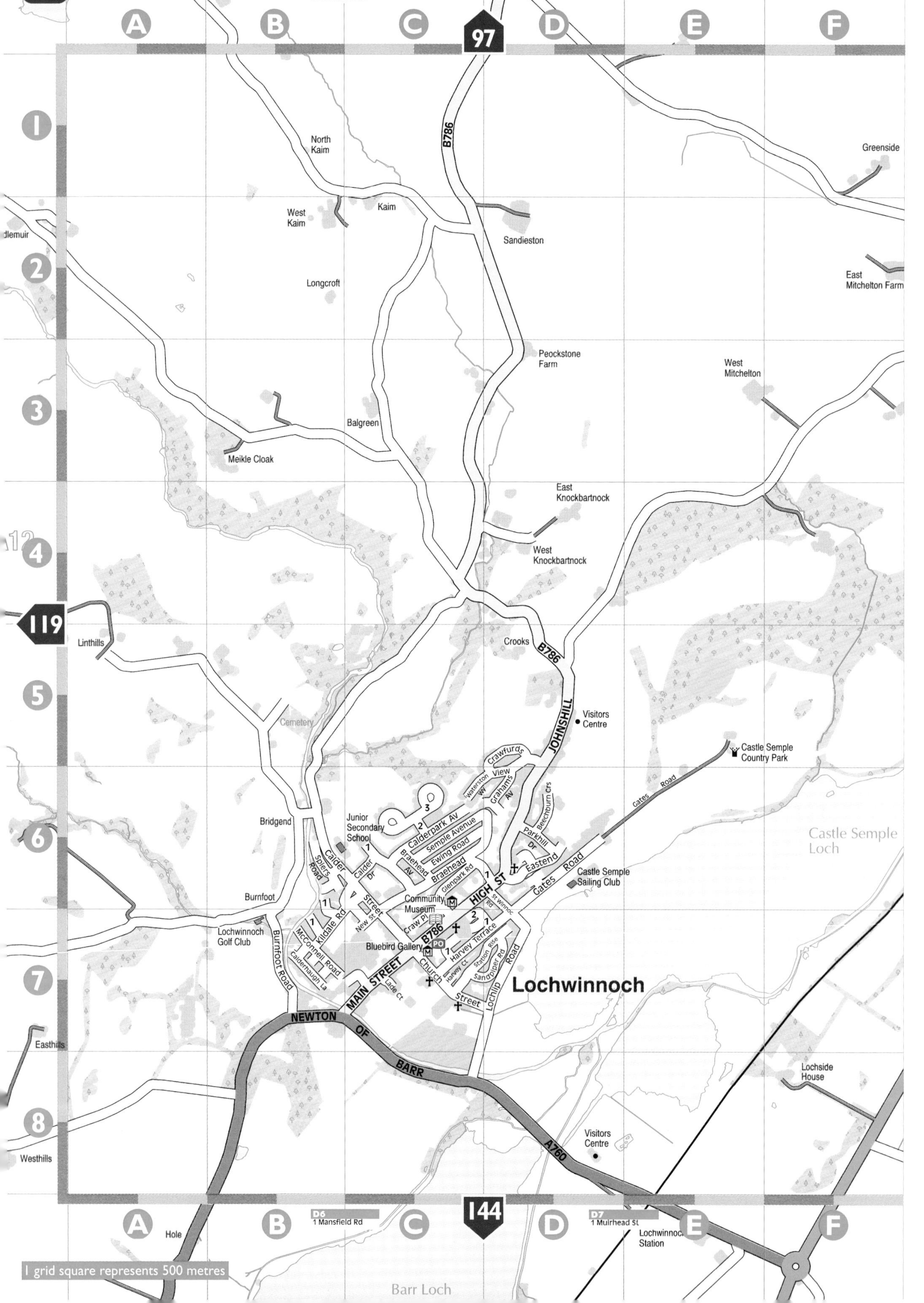

D6 1 Mansfield Rd
D7 1 Muirhead St

1 grid square represents 500 metres

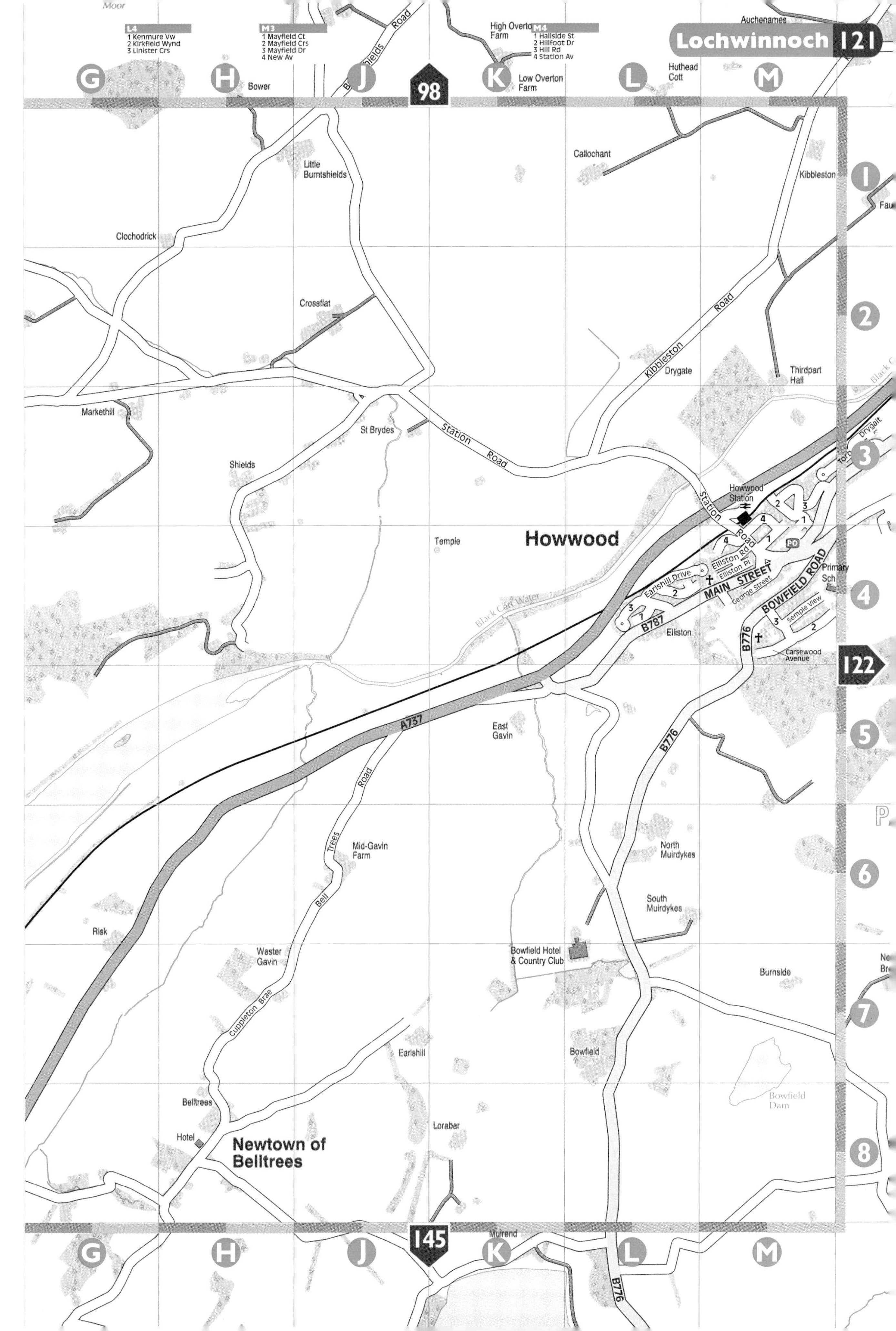
L4
1 Kenmure Vw
2 Kirkfield Wynd
3 Linister Crs
M3
1 Mayfield Ct
2 Mayfield Crs
3 Mayfield Dr
4 New Av
M4
1 Hallside St
2 Hillfoot Dr
3 Hill Rd
4 Station Av
Moor
Auchenames
High Overton Farm
Low Overton Farm
Huthead Cott
Bower
98
G
H
J
K
L
M
Callochant
Kibbleston
Little Burntshields
Clochodrick
Crossflat
Kibbleston Road
Drygate
Thirdpart Hall
Black Cart Water
Markethill
St Brydes
Station Road
Shields
Howwood Station
Howwood
Temple
PO
Primary Sch
Elliston Rd
Elliston Pl
Earlshill Drive
MAIN STREET
George Street
BOWFIELD ROAD
Semple View
B787
Elliston
B776
Carsewood Avenue
122
A737
East Gavin
Bell Trees Road
Mid-Gavin Farm
North Muirdykes
South Muirdykes
Risk
Wester Gavin
Bowfield Hotel & Country Club
Burnside
Cuppleton Brae
Earlshill
Bowfield
Bowfield Dam
Belltrees
Lorabar
Hotel
Newtown of Belltrees
145
Muirend
1
2
3
4
5
6
7
8

D2
1 Gladstone Av
2 Nightingale Pl
3 Swift Pl
D1
1 Charnwood Av
2 Craigbog Av
C3
1 Fulmar Pl
C1
1 Clyde Pl
2 Craigview Av
3 Don Pl
Millikenpark
Millikenpark Station
99
COCHRANEMILL RD
B787
Huntersfield Rd
Arran Dr
Melfort
Glencart Gv
Greenend
Avenue
Highcraig Av
St Davids RC Primary School
Craigview
Belth Road
Ramsay Av
Hogg Av
Tannahill Crs
Rannoch Road
Cartside
Kibbleston
Cochrane Castle Primary School
Blackwood Ter
Woodlands Crs
Greenwood Dr
Tannahill Crescent
Burns Drive
Scott Av
Dunbar Av
Bruce Av
Larch Pl
Johnstone High School
Faulds
Corseford Avenue
Dee Pl
Forth Pl
Tay Pl
Ettrick Ter
Teviot Ter
Tweed Pl
Ness Av
Spey Pl
Annan Pl
Fordbank Primary School
Auchengreoch Av
Auchengreoch Rd
Churchill Avenue
Palmerston Rd
Spateston Rd
Walpole Pl
Hallhill Rd
Finch Pl
Thrush Pl
Heron Pl
Falcon Rd
Kestrel Place
Tern Pl
Wren Pl
Golf Course
St Cuthberts RC School
St Anthonys RC Primary School
Swan Pl
Plover Pl
Martlet Dr
Curlew Pl
Linnet Av
Spateston
Spateston Road
Sanderling Pl
Sheldrake Pl
BEITH ROAD
A737
Black Cart Water
Thirdpart Hall
Meikle Corseford
Midton Road
Drygait
Torbracken
B787
Midton Road
Hallhill
Auchengreoch Road
Primary Sch
PO
Tor Bracken
121
Mountop
High Burnside
Skiff Wood
PA9
North Castlewalls
Nether Broadfield
Whittliemuir Midton Loch
Mid Hartfield
Hartfield
146
B775
A B C D E F
1 2 3 4 5 6 7 8
1 grid square represents 500 metres

G1
1 Laburnum Pl
K2
1 Littlesdale Av
L2
1 Hazelwood Av
2 Ravenswood Av
Hazel Avenue
Sycamore Avenue
Hawthorn Av
Willow
Alder Pl
Auchenlodment Primary School
Aspen Pl
Walnut Crs
Castle Av
Windsor Crs
Balmoral Road
Dunvegan Avenue
Glamis Av
Duart Dr
Dunrobin Av
Glenpatrick Road
100
Leitchland Farm
Glenpatrick
Leitchland Road
Mackie's Mill Road
Teviot Av
Esk Drive
Bredilland Rd
Beauly Dr
Avenue
Locksley Rd
Ivanhoe Road
Kenilworth Av
Heriot Primary School
Jarvie Wy
Woodstock Av
Foxbar
Bothwell Pl
Heriot Avenue
Mannering Rd
Marmion Rd
Montrose Road
Waverley Rd
Amochrie Road
Mogarth Avenue
Oliphant Crs
Spencer Drive
Bemersyde Rd
Breck Av
Elliot Av
Crosbie Drive
Roxburgh Rd
Abbotsford Crescent
Talisman Rd
Bredilland Road
Durrockstock Road
Durrockstock Crs
Roaden Av
Roaden Rd
Foxbar Rd
Hollows Avenue
Hollows Crescent
Foxbar Dr
Foxbar Crs
Rowanlea Av
Rosedale Av
Gallacher Av
Maple
Chestnut Pl
Acacia Pl
Juniper Place
Holly Pl
PO
Rannoch Road
Craigenfeoch
Robertson Park
CLENIFFER ROAD
B775
Craigmuir
Sergeant Law Road
124
Bent
Sergeantlaw
Renfrewshire
East Renfrewshire
Thornliemuir
Brownside
Lapwing Lodge
Caplaw
Caplaw Rd
Caplaw Dam
Mossneuk Farm
Shilford Road
Greenfieldmuir
Threepgrass Wood
Middleton
147
M1
1 Dinmont Av
2 Rotherwood Av
Sergeant Law Road
Fauldhead
Old Patrick Water
G
H
J
K
L
M
1
2
3
4
5
6
7
8

124
101
123
148
C3
1 Craigendon Ov
2 Craigendon Rd
3 Langcraigs Ter
C2
1 Browside Av
2 Glenfield Rd
3 Limecraigs Av
4 Redhurst Crs
5 Redhurst La
6 Redhurst Wy
C1
1 Craigiebar Dr
2 Langcraigs Ct
3 Rockwell Av
B2
1 Braeview Gdns
2 Limeview Crs
3 Limeview Wy
D3
1 Glenfield Crs
2 Glenfield Gdns
3 Glenfield Gv
E1
1 Lammermuir Ct
Thornly Park
Gleniffer High School
Stanely Reservoir
Glenburn
Gleniffer Road
B775
B774
Caplethill
Robertsons Sports Centre
Primary School
Bushes Primary School
Glenburn Clinic
Renfrew Council
PA2
Gleniffer Braes Country Park
Braemount
Procession Rd
Paisley Golf Club
Braehead Road
Brownside
Brownside Braes
Glen Park
Glenburn Reservoir
Harelaw Reservoir
Renfrewshire
East Renfrewshire
Thornliemuir
Woodneuk
West Arthurlie
Capellie Fm
Killoch Water
Killoch
Fereneze Road
Gateside Road
Wraes View
Donnies Brae
Lochlibo Road
A736
Nether Kirton
Foreside
1 grid square represents 500 metres

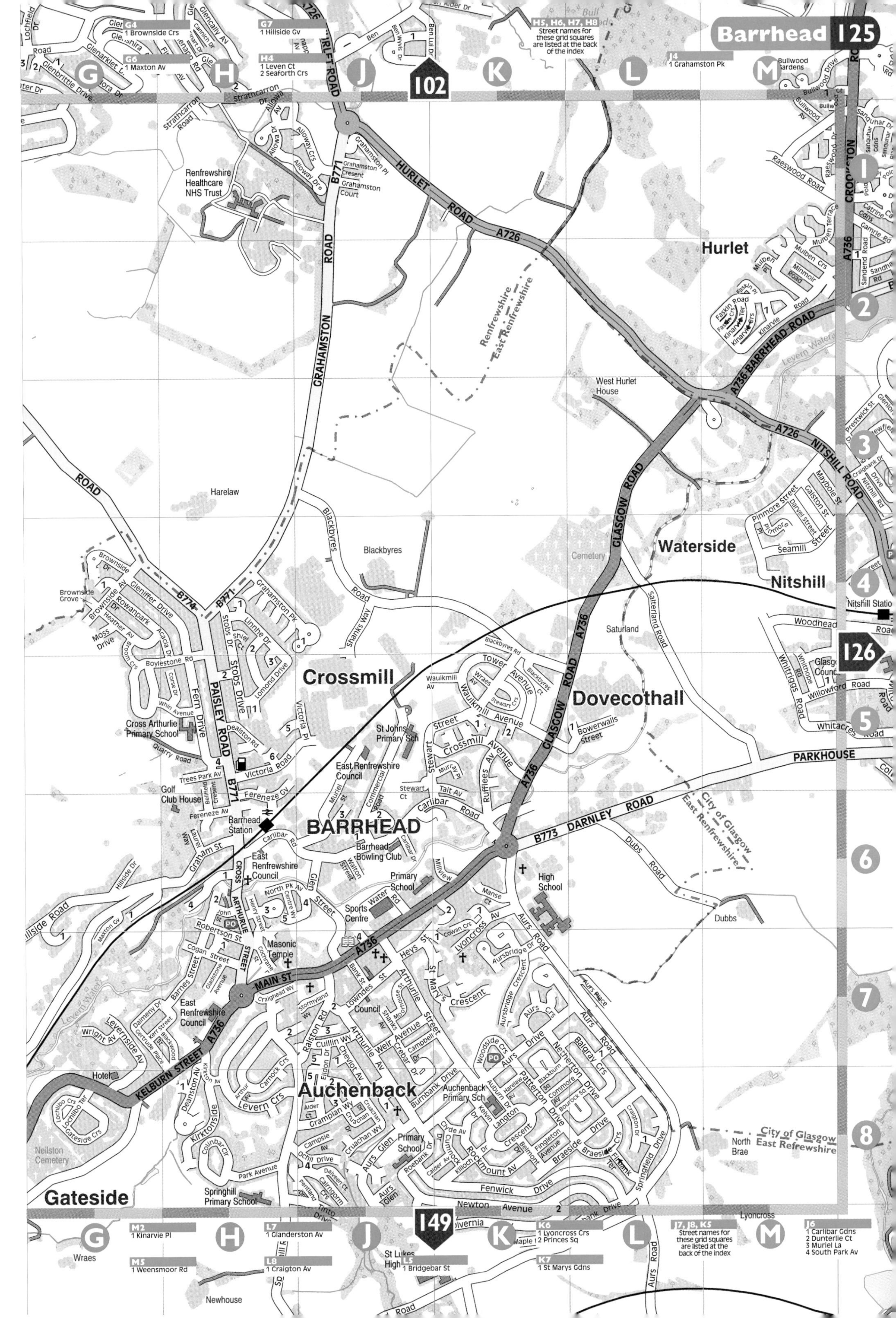
G4 1 Brownside Crs
G6 1 Maxton Av
G7 1 Hillside Gv
H4 1 Leven Ct 2 Seaforth Crs
H5, H6, H7, H8 Street names for these grid squares are listed at the back of the index
J4 1 Grahamston Pk
102
Bullwood Gardens
Renfrewshire Healthcare NHS Trust
GRAHAMSTON ROAD
B771
HURLET ROAD
A726
Hurlet
Renfrewshire
East Renfrewshire
A736 BARRHEAD ROAD
West Hurlet House
NITSHILL ROAD
CROOKSTON
Harelaw
Blackbyres
Blackbyres Road
Cemetery
GLASGOW ROAD
Waterside
Nitshill
Nitshill Station
Saturland
Crossmill
Dovecothall
126
PAISLEY ROAD
Cross Arthurlie Primary School
St Johns Primary Sch
East Renfrewshire Council
PARKHOUSE
Golf Club House
Barrhead Station
BARRHEAD
Barrhead Bowling Club
B773 DARNLEY ROAD
City of Glasgow
East Renfrewshire
High School
Primary School
Sports Centre
Masonic Temple
MAIN ST
Dubbs
Council
East Renfrewshire Council
KELBURN STREET
Hotel
Auchenback
Auchenback Primary Sch
Primary School
Neilston Cemetery
Springhill Primary School
Gateside
North Brae
149
M2 1 Kinarvie Pl
M5 1 Weensmoor Rd
L7 1 Glanderston Av
L8 1 Craigton Av
L5 1 Bridgebar St
K6 1 Lyoncross Crs 2 Princes Sq
K7 1 St Marys Gdns
J7, J8, K5 Street names for these grid squares are listed at the back of the index
J6 1 Carlibar Gdns 2 Dunterlie Ct 3 Muriel La 4 South Park Av
Wraes
St Lukes High
Newhouse
Lyoncross

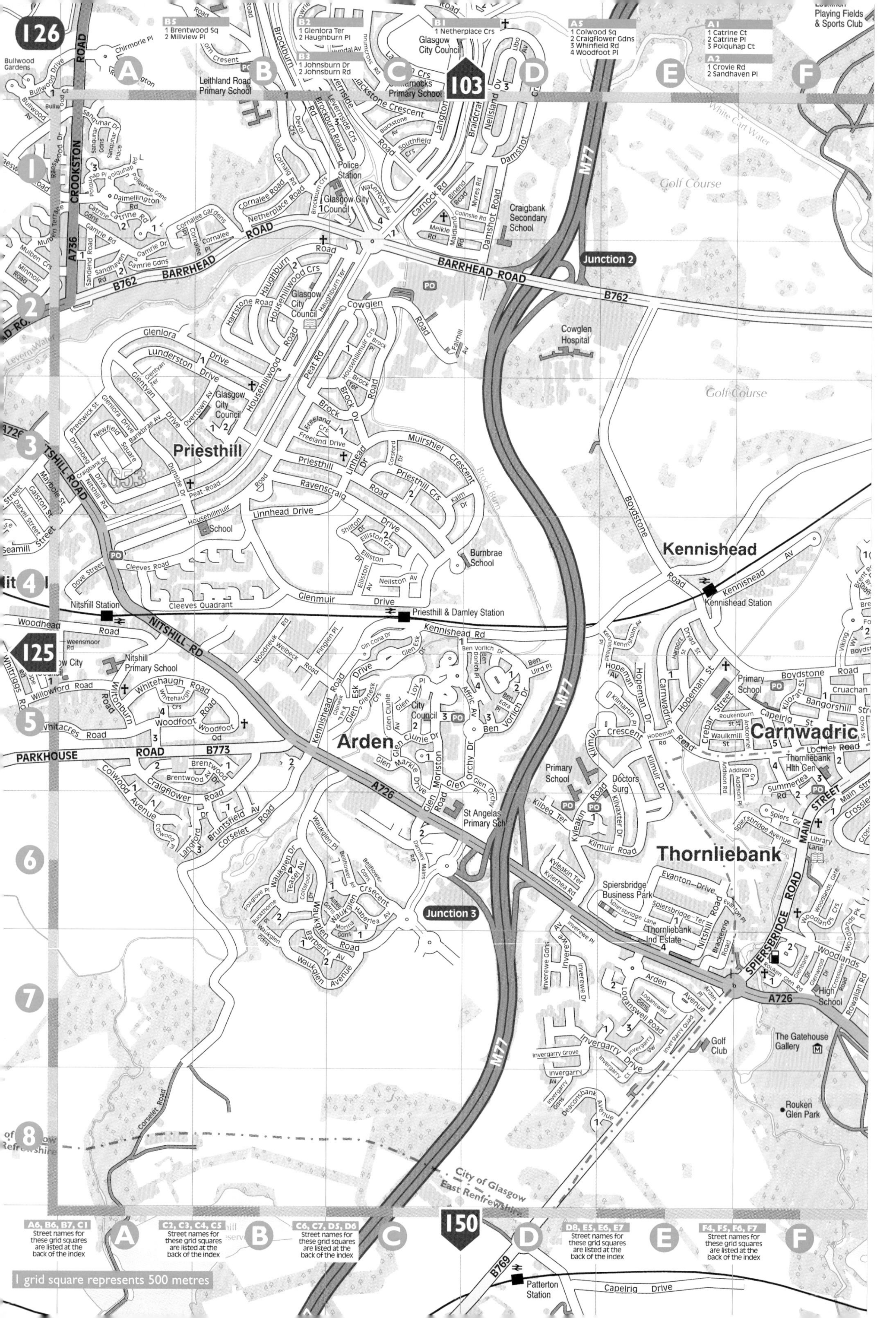
B5
1 Brentwood Sq
2 Millview Pl
B2
1 Glenlora Ter
2 Haughburn Pl
B3
1 Johnsburn Dr
2 Johnsburn Rd
B1
1 Netherplace Crs
A5
1 Colwood Sq
2 Craigflower Gdns
3 Whinfield Rd
4 Woodfoot Pl
A1
1 Catrine Ct
2 Catrine Pl
3 Polquhap Ct
A2
1 Crovie Rd
2 Sandhaven Pl
Playing Fields
& Sports Club
Bullwood Gardens
Leithland Road Primary School
Carnwarnocks Primary School
Glasgow City Council
103
Police Station
Craigbank Secondary School
Golf Course
White Cart Water
Junction 2
BARRHEAD ROAD
B762
CROOKSTON ROAD
A736
Cowglen Hospital
Levern Water
Priesthill
Glasgow City Council
Burnbrae School
Kennishead
Kennishead Station
Nitshill Station
Priesthill & Damley Station
125
NITSHILL RD
Nitshill Primary School
PARKHOUSE ROAD
B773
Arden
A726
St Angelas Primary Sch
Junction 3
M77
Carnwadric
Thornliebank
Spiersbridge Business Park
Thornliebank Ind Estate
SPIERSBRIDGE ROAD
MAIN STREET
Primary School
Doctors Surg
The Gatehouse Gallery
Golf Club
Rouken Glen Park
High School
City of Glasgow
East Renfrewshire
150
A6, B6, B7, C1
Street names for these grid squares are listed at the back of the index
C2, C3, C4, C5
Street names for these grid squares are listed at the back of the index
C6, C7, D5, D6
Street names for these grid squares are listed at the back of the index
D8, E5, E6, E7
Street names for these grid squares are listed at the back of the index
F4, F5, F6, F7
Street names for these grid squares are listed at the back of the index
Patterton Station
B769
Capelrig Drive
1 grid square represents 500 metres

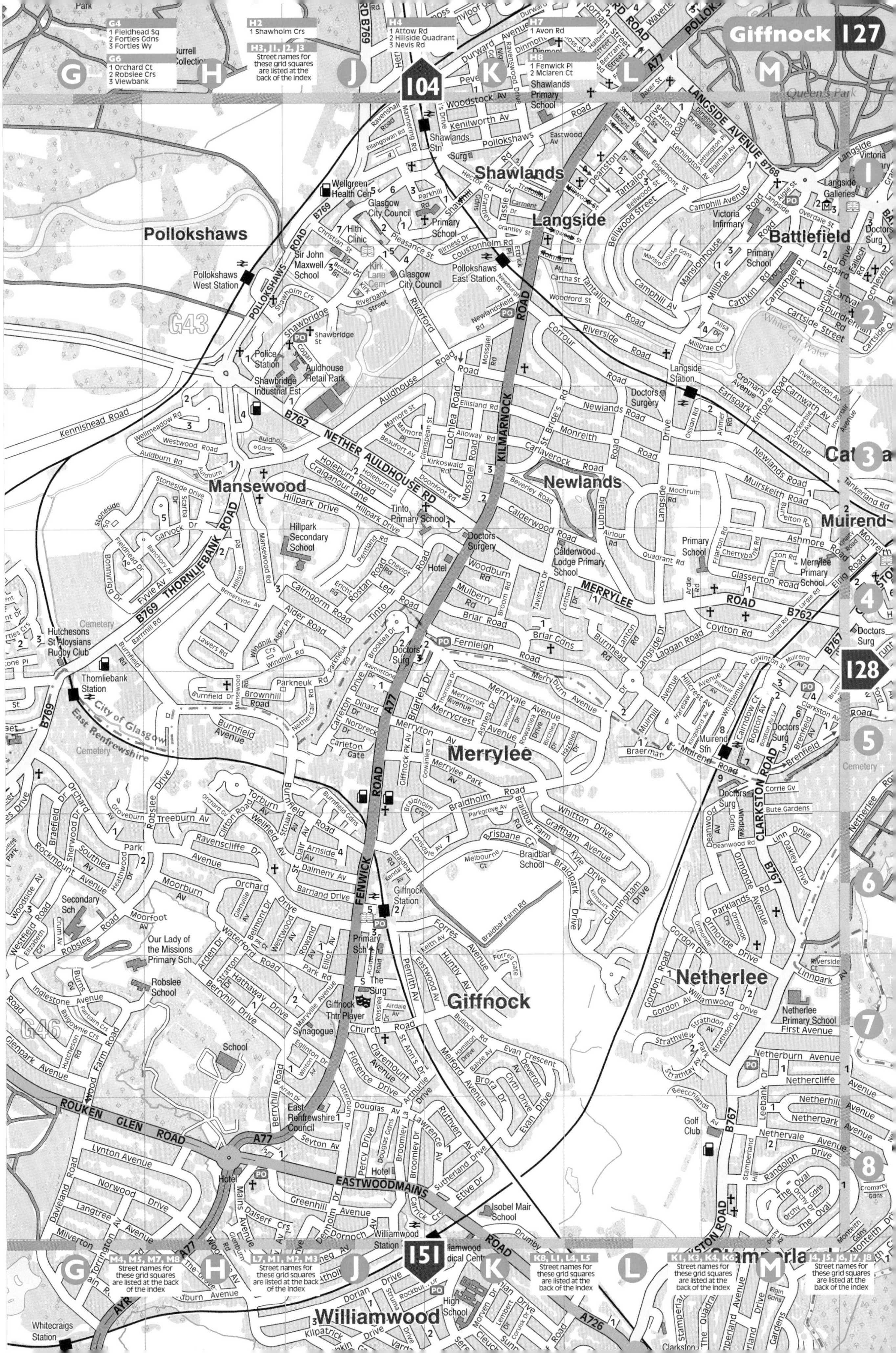
G4
1 Fieldhead Sq
2 Forties Gdns
3 Forties Wy
G6
1 Orchard Ct
2 Robslee Crs
3 Viewbank
H2
1 Shawholm Crs
H3, J1, J2, J3
Street names for these grid squares are listed at the back of the index
H4
1 Attow Rd
2 Hillside Quadrant
3 Nevis Rd
H7
1 Avon Rd
H8
1 Fenwick Pl
2 Mclaren Ct
M4, M5, M7, M8
Street names for these grid squares are listed at the back of the index
L7, M1, M2, M3
Street names for these grid squares are listed at the back of the index
K8, L1, L4, L5
Street names for these grid squares are listed at the back of the index
K1, K3, K4, K6
Street names for these grid squares are listed at the back of the index
J4, J5, J6, J7, J8
Street names for these grid squares are listed at the back of the index
104
128
151
G
H
J
K
L
M
1
2
3
4
5
6
7
8
Pollokshaws
Shawlands
Langside
Battlefield
Mansewood
Newlands
Muirend
Merrylee
Giffnock
Netherlee
Williamwood
Pollokshaws West Station
Pollokshaws East Station
Shawlands Stn
Langside Station
Thornliebank Station
Giffnock Station
Muirend Stn
Whitecraigs Station
Williamwood Station
G43
G46
KILMARNOCK ROAD
FENWICK ROAD
ROUKEN GLEN ROAD
EASTWOODMAINS ROAD
NETHER AULDHOUSE RD
THORNLIEBANK ROAD
POLLOKSHAWS ROAD
MERRYLEE ROAD
CLARKSTON ROAD
LANGSIDE AVENUE
City of Glasgow
East Renfrewshire

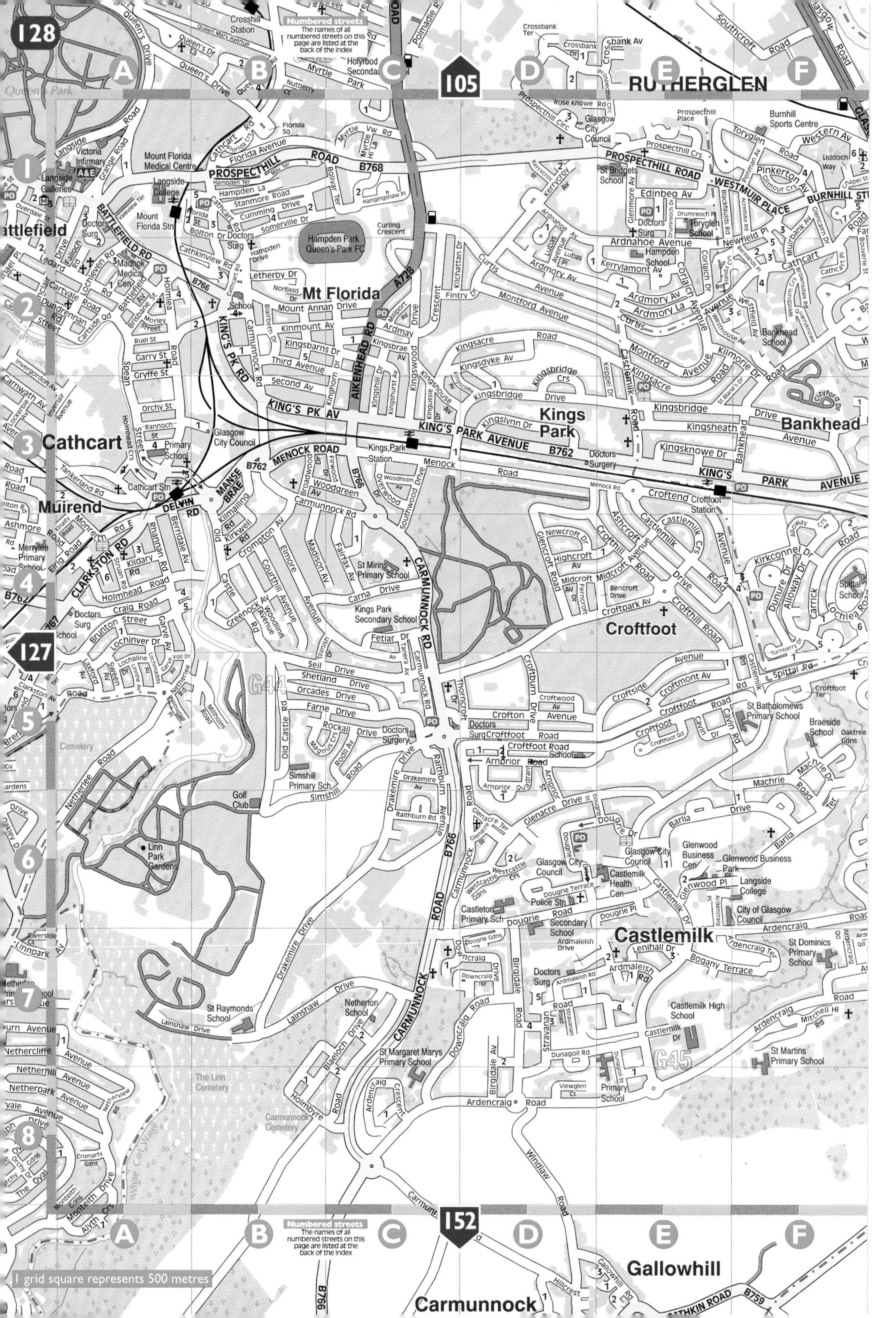
128
105
127
152
Numbered streets
The names of all numbered streets on this page are listed at the back of the index
A
B
C
D
E
F
1
2
3
4
5
6
7
8
RUTHERGLEN
Queen's Park
Crosshill Station
Queen's Drive
Queen Mary Avenue
Myrtle Park
Holyrood Secondary
Polmadie Rd
Crossbank Ter
Crossbank Dr
Southcroft Road
Prospecthill Circ
Rose Knowe Rd
Glasgow City Council
Prospecthill Place
Burnhill Sports Centre
Victoria Infirmary
A&E
Langside
Langside Galleries
Mount Florida Medical Centre
PROSPECTHILL ROAD
B768
Langside College
Florida Avenue
Hampden Ter
Hampden La
Stanmore Road
Cumming Drive
Somerville Dr
Bolivar Ter
Hangingshaw Pl
Mount Florida Stn
Doctors Surg
Hampden Park Queen's Park FC
Curling Crescent
Battlefield
BATTLEFIELD RD
Madhok Medical Cen
Cathkinview Rd
Letherby Dr
Mt Florida
Mount Annan Drive
Kinmount Av
Kingsbarns Dr
Third Avenue
Second Av
AIKENHEAD RD
A728
Ardmay
Kingsbrae Av
Prospecthill Crs
PROSPECTHILL ROAD
St Bridgets School
WESTMUIR PLACE
BURNHILL ST
Torygien Road
Pinkerton Av
Western Av
Edinbeg Av
Doctors Surg
Torygien School
Ardnahoe Avenue
Hampden School
Kerrylamont Av
Ardmory Av
Ardmory La
Curtis Avenue
Montford Avenue
Kilmorie Dr
Bankhead School
Cathcart
Kingsacre Road
Kingsdyke Av
Kingsbridge Crs
Kingsbridge Drive
Kings Park
Kingsheath Avenue
Bankhead
Kingsknowe Dr
KING'S PARK AVENUE
B762
Kingslynn Dr
Doctors Surgery
Menock Road
KING'S PK AV
KING'S PK RD
Kings Park Station
Holmlea Road
Brisbane St
Morley Street
Ruel St
Garry St
Gryffe St
Orchy St
Rannoch St
Primary School
Glasgow City Council
Cathcart
Muirend
Cathcart Stn
DELVIN RD
MANSE BRAE
MENOCK ROAD
B762
Broadwood Dr
Woodgreen Av
Carmunnock Rd
Southwood Drive
Croftend Av
Croftfoot Station
Newcroft Dr
Highcroft Av
Midcroft Av
Bencroft Drive
Croftpark Av
Croftfoot
Croftfoot Rd
Castlemilk Drive
Crofthill Road
Kirkconnel Dr
Alloway Dr
Dunure Dr
Carrick
Spittal School
CLARKSTON RD
Merrylee Primary School
Holmhead Road
Craig Road
Brunton Street
Lochinver Dr
Doctors Surg
Crompton Av
Courthill Avenue
Elmore Avenue
Madison Av
Fairfax Av
St Mirins Primary School
CARMUNNOCK RD
Carna Drive
Kings Park Secondary School
Fetlar Dr
Seil Drive
Shetland Drive
Orcades Drive
Farne Drive
Rockall Drive
Doctors Surgery
Simshill Primary Sch
Simshill Road
Old Castle Rd
G44
Cemetery
Netherlee Road
Millholm Road
Golf Club
Linn Park Gardens
Croftburn Drive
Croftwood Av
Crofton Avenue
Croftside Av
Croftmont Av
Spittal Rd
Croftfoot Ter
St Batholomews Primary School
Braeside School
Oaktree Gdns
Machrie Road
Machrie Dr
Barlia Drive
Croftfoot Road
Croftfoot Road School
Arnprior Road
Arnprior Quadrant
Glenacre Drive
Dougrie Dr
Glasgow City Council
Glenwood Business Cen
Glenwood Business Park
Castlemilk Health Cen
Langside College
Glenwood Pl
Police Stn
Dougrie Terrace
Castleton Primary Sch
Dougrie Road
Secondary School
City of Glasgow Council
Ardencraig Rd
Castlemilk
Lenihall Dr
Bogany Terrace
St Dominics Primary School
Ardmaleish Drive
Ardmaleish Rd
Drakemire Drive
Drakemire Av
Raithburn Avenue
Raithburn Rd
B766
CARMUNNOCK ROAD
Downcraig Road
Birgidale Road
Stravanan Road
Dunagoil Rd
Castlemilk High School
Castlemilk Dr
G45
Mitchell Hl
St Martins Primary School
Primary School
Viewglen Ct
Ardencraig Road
St Raymonds School
Lainshaw Drive
Netherton School
Blaeloch Drive
St Margaret Marys Primary School
Ardencraig Crescent
Holmbyre Road
Carmunnock Cemetery
The Linn Cemetery
White Cart Water
Nethercliffe Avenue
Netherhill Avenue
Netherpark Avenue
Netherview Rd
Riverside Ct
Linnpark
Cromarty Gdns
Monteith Drive
Alyth Crs
Windlaw Road
Gallowhill
Carmunnock
B759
1 grid square represents 500 metres

Numbered streets
The names of all numbered streets on this page are listed at the back of the index
106
G
H
J
K
L
M
Trading Estate
Industrial Estate
Rutherglen Station
Victoria Street
Farmeloan Industrial Estate
Farm Castle Industrial Estate
Clyde Industrial Estate
George Gray Street
CAMBUSLANG ROAD
A724
Cunninghame Rd
Ballochmill Rd
FARMELOAN ROAD
A749
MAIN STREET
B768
King St
Queen St
Mill St
Hotel
South Lanarkshire Council
Spectrum Business Centre
Reid Street
High School
Rutherglen Swimming Pool
Doctors Surg
School
John Hillhouse Industrial Estate
Richmond Pl
Hamilton Road
Woodside Avenue
Eastfield
County Avenue
Burn Ter
Bogleshole Road
Cambuslang Road
City of Glasgow
South Lanarkshire
Clydesmill
Trinity High School
Stonelaw High School
Rutherglen Health Centre
STONELAW ROAD
Dryburgh Avenue
Jedburgh Av
Melrose Av
Dunard Rd
Parkhill Drive
Johnstone Drive
Overtoun Drive
G73
Stonelaw Drive
Limeside Avenue
Rosslyn Av
Calderwood Rd
Dunbar Avenue
Ettrick Crs
Richmond Drive
Berwick Drive
Coldstream Road
Bullionslaw Drive
Colville Dr
Glenside Drive
Bothwell Street
Salvia St
Cambuslang Rangers FC
Cambuslang Station
MAIN STREET
Ardoch Medical Centre
The Surg
Quarry Pl
Whyte Av
Central Avenue
Prospect Avenue
Wellshot Drive
Hamilton Dr
High Crosshill
Victoria Rd
Rodger Drive
Crosshill Dr
Buchanan Drive
Calderwood Primary School
Greystone Avenue
The Gallery at Home Creations
St Ronans Dr
Underwood Rd
Cleveden Dr
Craigwell Av
DUKE'S ROAD
B762
Glenburn Avenue
Eastfield Avenue
Milton Av
Buchanan Drive
Richmond Dr
Kingsburn Dr
MILL STREET
A730
Rutherglen Cemetery
Albany Dr
Viewpark Drive
Albert Dr
Blairtum Dr
Highburgh Dr
Burnside Station
Drumsargard Road
Hawthorn Walk
York Dr
Kent Dr
Brownside Road
West Coats Road
BLAIRBETH ROAD
EAST KILBRIDE ROAD
A749
Burnside
Burnside Primary School
Stirling Dr
Douglas Av
Peveril Av
Bradda Avenue
Cambuslang Rugby Club
Langlea Rd
Stewarton Drive
West Coats Primary School
Douglas Dr
130
Kirkriggs School
St Marks RC Primary School
Rowantree Av
Golf Rd
Elm Rd
Crawford Rd
Upper Bourtree Drive
Langlea Avenue
Langlea Gv
Grenville Drive
W Coats Rd
St Anthonys RC School
Loch Primary School
Lochaber Dr
Cathkin High School
Whitlawburn Road
Holmhills Dr
Holmhills Grove
Fernhill Road
Tormusk Drive
Scarrel Dr
Ballantay Road
Woodend Road
Burnside Road
Beech Av
Lochbrae Drive
Tynwald Av
Kincath Av
St Stephens Av
Fennsbank Av
Cathkin By-Pass
Clifton Ter
Whitlawburn Shopping Centre
Western Road
Albany Ter
Arkle Ter
Buchan Terrace
Greenlees Gdns
Castlefern Road
Neilvaig Drive
Fernhill Road
Galloway Dr
Kirkmuir Dr
Craignure Rd
Fernbrae Avenue
Tormusk Primary School
Cathkin Primary School
Glentarbert Rd
Skye Road
Tobermory Road
Trossachs Road
Menteith Drive
Inchmurrin Dr
B759
GREENLEES ROAD
Golf Course
CATHKIN ROAD
South Lanarkshire
City of Glasgow
E KILBRIDE ROAD
Easthills Farm
GLASGOW
Glasgow Road
Cairnmuir Road
153
South Cathkin Farm
Muir
I
2
3
4
5
6
7
8

Junction 1
Junction 2
M74
107
154
129
A
B
C
D
E
F
1
2
3
4
5
6
7
8
Carmyle
St Joachins RC Primary School
Primary School
Carmyle Medical Centre
Clydeford Road
Carmyle Avenue
A763
Bridge Street
Clydesmill Place
Clydesmill Road
Clydesmill Drive
Clydesmill Grove
Gardenside Av
Gardenside Crs
Balmoral Dr
Estate Road
Park Road
Mansionhouse Av
Ardargie Dr
Noldrum Av
Duffus Ter
Duffus Pl
Drumshaw Dr
Kenmuir Road
River Road
River Clyde
City of Glasgow
South Lanarkshire
Newton Farm
Newton Farm Rd
Newton Farm Road
Light Burn
Newton Avenue
Westburn
Westburn Road
Westburn Farm Road
Mill Road
Lockhart Avenue
Mitchell Av
Henderson Av
McIver St
Dunlop St
Westburn Rd
Northbank Avenue
Newton
St Charles RC School
Newton Station
Newton Station Rd
Golf Club
Kincaid Gdns
Morriston Pk Dr
Aiton Primary School
Monkcastle Drive
Mansion St
Allison Drive
South Lanarkshire Council
Cambuslang Station
Main Street
Doctors Surg
The Surg
Birch Dr
Elm Drive
Fir Pl
Queen's Av
King's Crs
Westburn Cemetery
Old Mill Rd
Glencairn Gardens
Annick St
Dunlain St
Wiston St
Hallside Av
Alder Gate
Ash Wynd
Hallside
Village Road
Cedar Ct
Beech Crs
Birch Pl
Bowling Gn Vw
Busheyhill St
Tabernacle St
Hamilton Drive
Calder Dr
Cadzow Dr
Brownside Road
Douglas Gate
Kirkhill Station
Greenlees Road
B759
Primary School
Cambuslang Clinic
Vicars Wk
Borgie Crescent
Croft Road
Cadoc St
Meek Pl
Vicarland Rd
Robert Templeton Dr
Cairns Av
Cambuslang College
A724
Hamilton Road
Howieshill Rd
Macarthur Wynd
Mac Callum Drive
Cambuslang Recreation Centre
Graham Av
Medwin St
Gateside Avenue
Overton Road
Overton St
Clyde Place
Hallside Primary School
Hallside Road
Elm Wy
Elder Crs
Hallside Bvd
Sycamore Way
Lilac Wynd
Spruce Dr
Redwood Crs
Pine Av
Oak Wynd
Magnolia Dr
Maple Crs
Mulberry Wynd
South Lanarkshire Council
Flemington Industrial Est
New Rd
Lightburn Rd
Claude Av
Hutchinson Pl
Letterickhills Crs
Gilbertfield Road
Castle Chimmins Av
Castle Chimmins Road
Quarry Av
Deans Av
Dechmont Pl
Craigallian Avenue
Wellside Dr
Doctors Surg
Douglas Drive
Mansefield Av
Holmhill Av
Burncleuch Av
Kirkburn Av
Whitefield Avenue
Cambuslang Avory Club
CAMBUSLANG
Braeside Pl
Huntly Dr
Cairns Rd
Kinloch Av
Woodland Road
Janebank Av
Hamilton Crs
Langcroft Dr
Rosebank Drive
Cairnswell Avenue
Lilybank Avenue
Ivybank Avenue
School
Primary School
Flemington
Auld Kirk Rd
Holmhills Grove
Holmhills Dr
Greenlees Pk
Kirkhill Gdns
Kirkhill Ter
Kirkhill Avenue
Tanzieknowe Road
Kirkhill Gdns
E Greenlees Crs
Greenlees Av
East Greenlees Drive
East Greenlees Road
G72
Golf Course
Turnlaw Road
Flemington Farm
Glasgow Road
Dechmont

B6
1 Tanzieknowe Av
2 Tanzieknowe Dr
3 Tanzieknowe Pl

B4
1 Glebe Pl
2 Hamilton Rd
3 Howieshill Av
4 Johnson Dr
5 Kirkton Rd
6 Lochinver Gv
7 School Av

A4
1 Tabernacle La

A6
1 Kirkhill Gv

A2
1 Church Vw
2 Newpark Crs
3 Thomson Gv

A3, B1, B5, C1
Street names for these grid squares are listed at the back of the index

C3
1 Rowan Pl
2 Valley Vw

C4
1 Andrew Sillars Av
2 Hugh Murray Dr
3 Macfarlane Crs

C5
1 Cairnswell Pl
2 Fernbank Av
3 Oak Dr

C6
1 Trinity Dr

D3
1 Lockhart Dr
2 Northbank St
3 Westburn Av

D5, D6, E3, E4
Street names for these grid squares are listed at the back of the index

E5, E6, F5, F6
Street names for these grid squares are listed at the back of the index

1 grid square represents 500 metres

H7
1 Kyleakin Dr
2 Sanquhar Gdns
J6
1 Helmsdale Av
J7
1 Balmoral Gdns
2 Montrose Gdns
J8, K8, L1, L3
Street names for these grid squares are listed at the back of the index
K1
1 Dunvegan Pl
K2
1 Burnpark Av
2 Clydeford Dr
K7
1 Lintlaw
108
Junction 4/1
M74
Maryville
Cemetery
River Clyde
Greyfriars Road
GLASGOW ROAD
NEW EDINBURGH ROAD
A721
HOLMBRAE ROAD A752
OLD EDINBURGH ROAD
Birkenshaw
Kylepark
BLANTYRE FARM ROAD
B758
Uddington Station
Grammar School
MAIN STREET
B7071
UDDINGSTON
BELLSHILL ROAD
Uddingston Cricket & Sports Club
Bothwell Castle
BOTHWELL ROAD
Westburn Road
Calder Road
Dalton
GLASGOW ROAD A724
Castle Avenue
David Livingston Centre
Bothwell Primary School
Low Blantyre
Stonefield
South Lanarkshire Council
132
155
M3, M4, M7
Street names for these grid squares are listed at the back of the index
M2
1 Holm Av
2 Holmbrae Av
3 Prospect Av
4 Winton Gdns
M1
1 Morven Gdns
2 Seventh Av
3 Thorniewood Rd
L7
1 Lytham Mdw
2 Muirfield Mdw
L8
1 Knightswood Ter
2 Toward Ct
3 Village Gdns
L4
1 Easter Ms
L5
1 Regents Ga
L2
1 Alderside Gdns
2 Burnacre Gdns
3 Crawford Crs
4 Greenholm Av

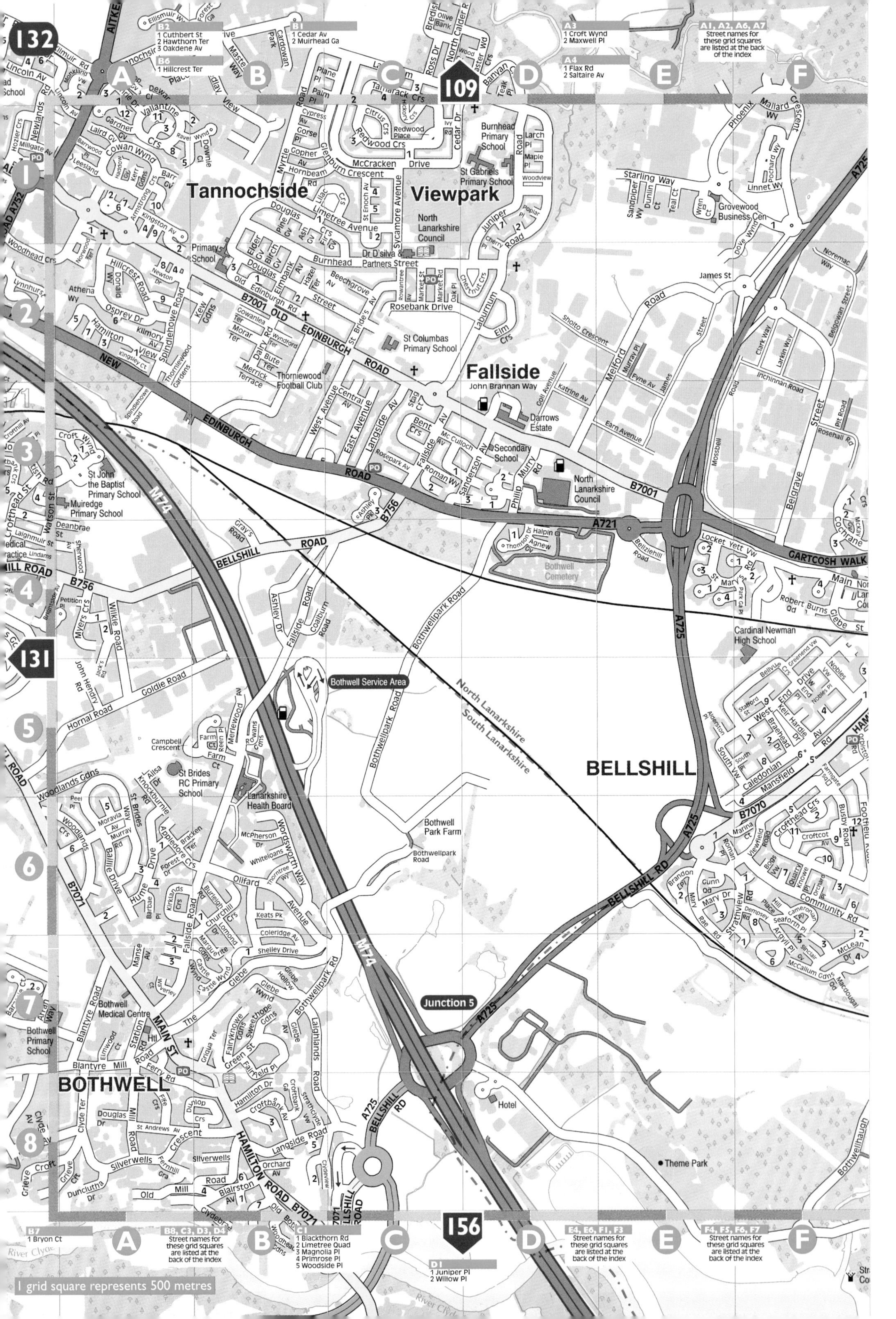
132
109
131
156
B2
1 Cuthbert St
2 Hawthorn Ter
3 Oakdene Av
B6
1 Hillcrest Ter
B1
1 Cedar Av
2 Muirhead Ga
A3
1 Croft Wynd
2 Maxwell Pl
A4
1 Flax Rd
2 Saltaire Av
A1, A2, A6, A7
Street names for these grid squares are listed at the back of the index
Tannochside
Viewpark
Fallside
BELLSHILL
BOTHWELL
Burnhead Primary School
St Gabriels Primary School
North Lanarkshire Council
Dr D'silva & Partners
St Columbas Primary School
Thorniewood Football Club
John Brannan Way
Darrows Estate
Secondary School
Grovewood Business Cen
Cardinal Newman High School
Bothwell Cemetery
St John the Baptist Primary School
Muiredge Primary School
Bothwell Service Area
North Lanarkshire
South Lanarkshire
St Brides RC Primary School
Lanarkshire Health Board
Bothwell Park Farm
Bothwell Medical Centre
Bothwell Primary School
Junction 5
Hotel
Theme Park
Edinburgh Road
Old Edinburgh Road
New Edinburgh Road
Bellshill Road
Hamilton Road B7071
Gartcosh Walk
Main St
B7001
A721
A725
M74
B756
B7070
B7071
River Clyde
B7
1 Bryon Ct
B8, C3, D3, D4
Street names for these grid squares are listed at the back of the index
C1
1 Blackthorn Rd
2 Limetree Quad
3 Magnolia Pl
4 Primrose Pl
5 Woodside Pl
D1
1 Juniper Pl
2 Willow Pl
E4, E6, F1, F3
Street names for these grid squares are listed at the back of the index
F4, F5, F6, F7
Street names for these grid squares are listed at the back of the index
1 grid square represents 500 metres

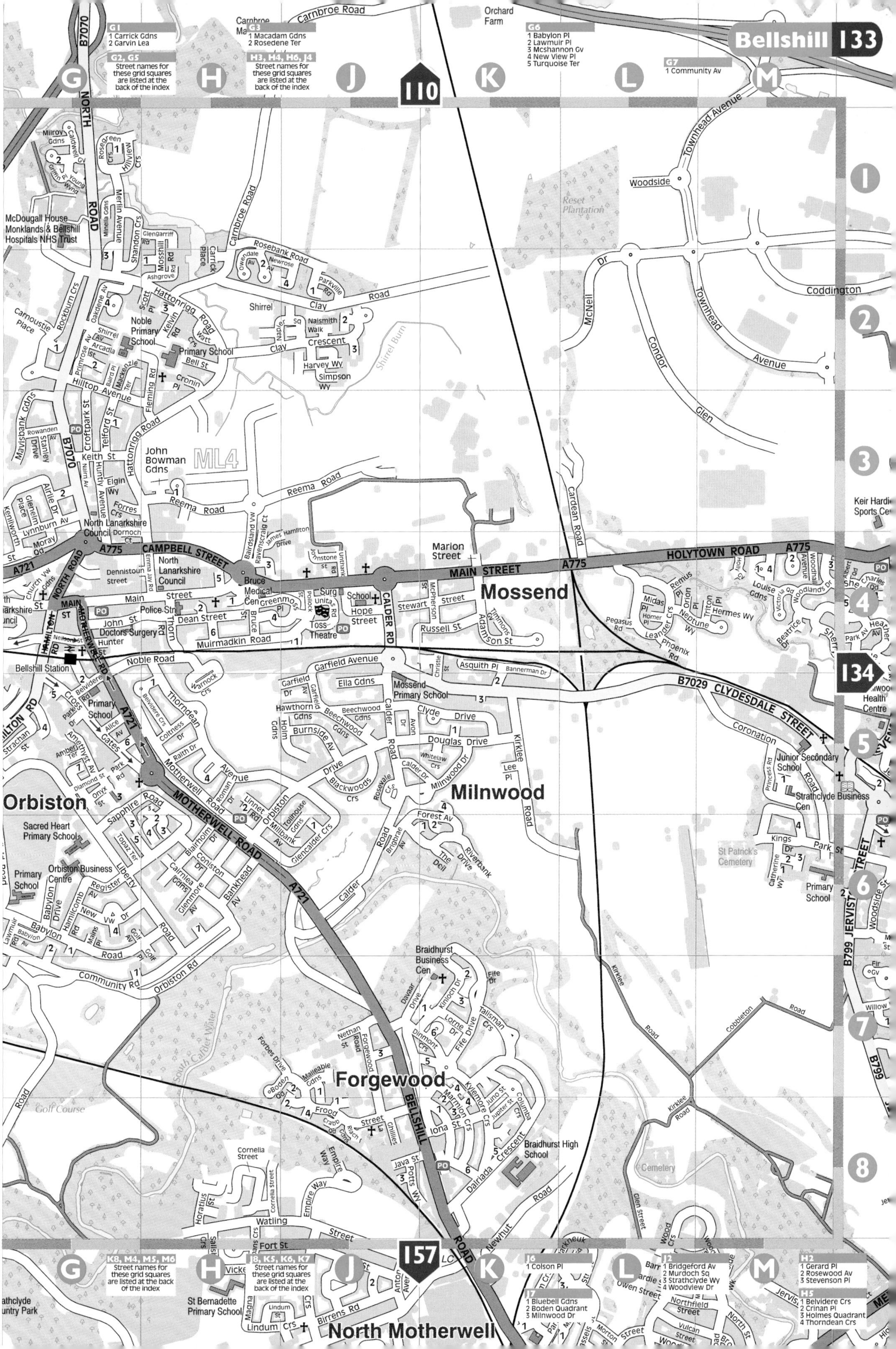
G1
1 Carrick Gdns
2 Garvin Lea
G2, G5
Street names for these grid squares are listed at the back of the index
G3
1 Macadam Gdns
2 Rosedene Ter
H3, H4, H6, J4
Street names for these grid squares are listed at the back of the index
G6
1 Babylon Pl
2 Lawmuir Pl
3 Mcshannon Gv
4 New View Pl
5 Turquoise Ter
G7
1 Community Av
110
134
157
K8, M4, M5, M6
Street names for these grid squares are listed at the back of the index
J8, K5, K6, K7
Street names for these grid squares are listed at the back of the index
J6
1 Colson Pl
J7
1 Bluebell Gdns
2 Boden Quadrant
3 Milnwood Dr
J2
1 Bridgeford Av
2 Murdoch Sq
3 Strathclyde Wy
4 Woodview Dr
H2
1 Gerard Pl
2 Rosewood Av
3 Stevenson Pl
H5
1 Belvidere Crs
2 Crinan Pl
3 Holmes Quadrant
4 Thorndean Crs
Orchard Farm
Carnbroe Road
Reset Plantation
Townhead Avenue
Woodside
Coddington
Condor Glen
McNeil Dr
McDougall House Monklands & Bellshill Hospitals NHS Trust
North Road
B7070
Shirrel
Noble Primary School
Primary School
Rosebank Road
Hattonrigg Road
Clay Road
Crescent
Shirrel Burn
Hilltop Avenue
John Bowman Gdns
ML4
Reema Road
Cardean Road
Keir Hardie Sports Centre
A775 Campbell Street
Main Street
Holytown Road
Marion Street
North Lanarkshire Council
Bruce Medical Cen
Mossend
Calder Rd
Hope Street
Toss Theatre
Muirmadkin Road
Bellshill Station
Noble Road
Garfield Avenue
Mossend Primary School
B7029 Clydesdale Street
Coronation Road
Junior Secondary School
Strathclyde Business Cen
St Patrick's Cemetery
Orbiston
Sacred Heart Primary School
Orbiston Business Centre
Primary School
Motherwell Road
A721
Milnwood
Kirklee Road
B799 Jervis Street
Braidhurst Business Cen
Forgewood
Bellshill Road
Braidhurst High School
Cemetery
Golf Course
South Calder Water
Community Rd
Orbiston Rd
Watling Street
Cornelia Street
Empire Way
St Bernadette Primary School
Strathclyde Country Park
North Motherwell
Newhut Road
Cobbleton Road
Health Centre

B5
1 Cherry Pl

B6
1 Klondike Ct
2 Silver Firs
3 Wrangholm Crs

A8
1 Coalhall Av
2 Jerviston Ct

B4
1 Cherry Pl

A5
1 Beauly Pl
2 Stevenston Ct
3 Thistle Gdns

A1
1 Woodhall

A4, A6, A7
Street names for these grid squares are listed at the back of the index

B7
1 Wallace Rd

B8
1 Byresknowe La
2 Coalhall Av
3 Eastend Av
4 Motherwell Rd

C6
1 Magnolia Gdns
2 Sycamore Pl

C7
1 Inveraray Gdns
2 Marian Dr
3 Newarthill Rd

C8
1 Cleland Rd
2 Colville Ct

D5
1 Braehead Qd
2 Brannock Pl
3 Legbrannock Crs

D6
1 Bernadette St
2 Dorain Rd

D7
1 Canon Ct
2 Dickens Gv

E5, E8, F4, F5
Street names for these grid squares are listed at the back of the index

1 grid square represents 500 metres

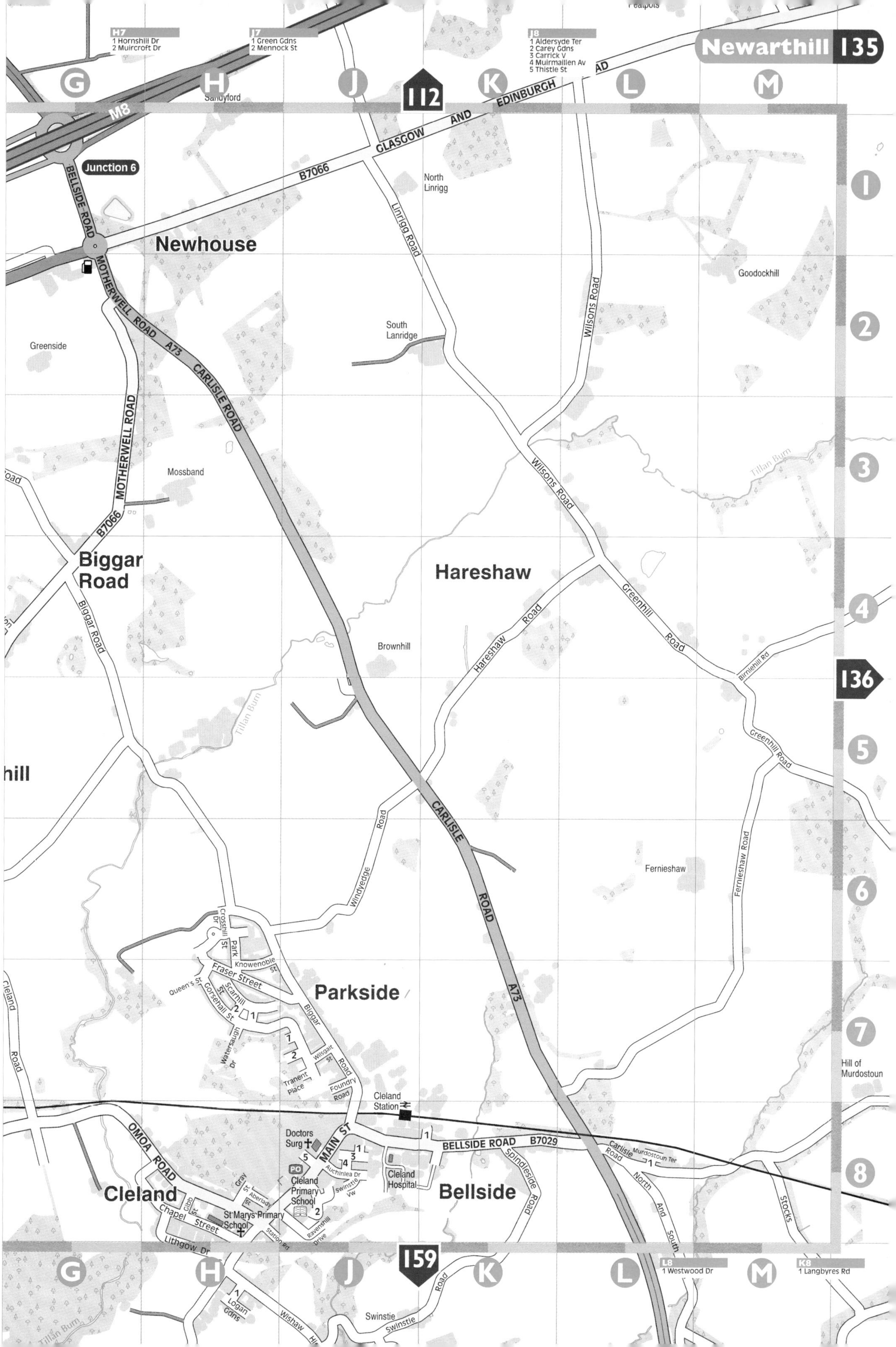
H7
1 Hornshill Dr
2 Muircroft Dr
J7
1 Green Gdns
2 Mennock St
J8
1 Aldersyde Ter
2 Carey Gdns
3 Carrick V
4 Muirmailien Av
5 Thistle St
112
136
159
L8
1 Westwood Dr
K8
1 Langbyres Rd
G
H
J
K
L
M
1
2
3
4
5
6
7
8
M8
Junction 6
Sandyford
GLASGOW AND EDINBURGH ROAD
B7066
BELLSIDE ROAD
Newhouse
North Linrigg
Linrigg Road
South Lanridge
Wilsons Road
Goodockhill
Greenside
MOTHERWELL ROAD
A73
CARLISLE ROAD
Mossband
Tillan Burn
Biggar Road
Hareshaw
Hareshaw Road
Greenhill Road
Birniehill Rd
Brownhill
hill
Windyedge Road
CARLISLE ROAD
A73
Fernieshaw
Fernieshaw Road
Crosshill Dr
Park St
Knowenoble St
Fraser Street
Queen's St
Corsehall St
Scarhill St
Parkside
Biggar Road
Watersaugh Dr
Wilsgait St
Tranent Place
Foundry Road
Cleland Station
Hill of Murdostoun
Cleland Road
OMOA ROAD
Doctors Surg
MAIN ST
PO
Cleland Primary School
Auchinlea Dr
Swinstie Vw
Cleland Hospital
BELLSIDE ROAD
B7029
Spindleside Road
Carlisle Road
Murdostoun Ter
North And South
Stocks
Cleland
Gray St
Aberlady St
Gibb St
Chapel Street
St Marys Primary School
Station Rd
Ravenshill Drive
Bellside
Lithgow Dr
Logan Gdns
Wishaw
Swinstie
Swinstie Road
Tillan Burn

A
B
C
D
E
F
113
1
2
3
4
5
6
7
8
135
160
Manse Road
Westfield
Roughdike
Muiredge and Jersy Road
Jersay
Birniehill Road
Road
Jersy
and
Muiredge
Penty
Hill of Murdostoun
Shawstonfoot Road
Foulburn Road
Hartwood Station
Ashgrove
Home Farm Rd
Newmill Gdns
Canthill
Hartwood Hospital
Hartwood Road
Castlerigg
Mill Road
Allan
Stocks Road
Calder Rd
Coltness
1 grid square represents 500 metres

K3
1 Alexander Rd
2 Graystonelee Rd

K4
1 Bertram Pl
2 Park Rd

L3
1 Ardgowan Pl
2 Cluanie Av
3 Kames Rd
4 Mossband La
5 Rannoch Pl
6 Rimmon Crs
7 Starryshaw Rd

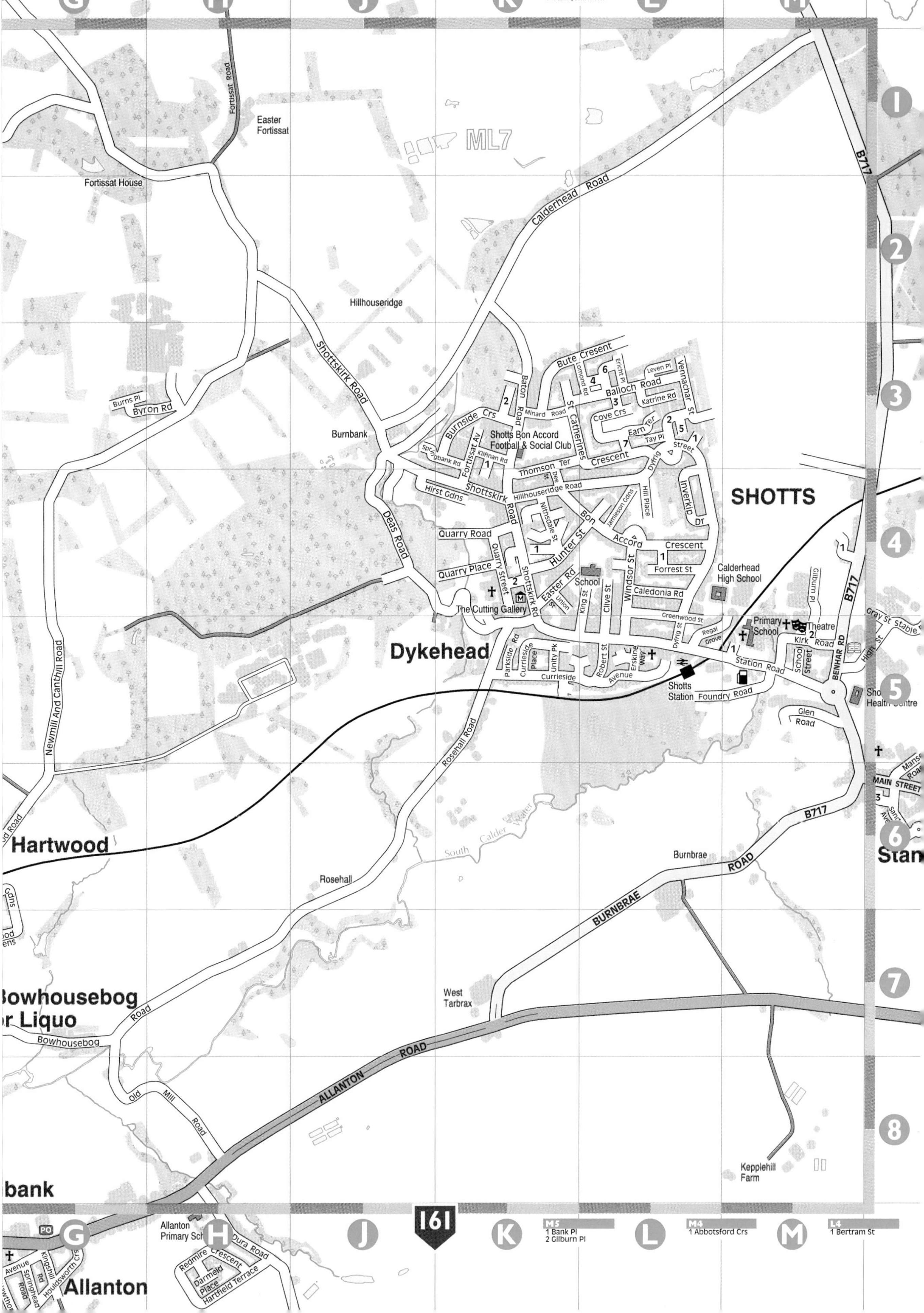
G
H
J
K
L
M
ML7
Fortissat Road
Easter Fortissat
Fortissat House
Calderhead Road
Hillhouseridge
Shottskirk Road
Burns Pl
Byron Rd
Burnbank
Baton Road
Bute Cresent
Lomond Rd
Ericht Pl
Leven Pl
Vennachar St
Balloch Road
Katrine Rd
Minard Road
St Catherines Crescent
Cove Crs
Earn Ter
Tay Pl
Street
Burnside Crs
Shotts Bon Accord Football & Social Club
Springbank Rd
Fortissat Av
Kilfinan Rd
Thomson Ter
Dyfrig
Hirst Gdns
Shottskirk Road
Hillhouseridge Road
Dee St
Inverkip Dr
SHOTTS
Deas Road
Quarry Road
Nithsdale St
Jamieson Gdns
Hill Place
Bon Accord Crescent
Hunter St
Quarry Place
Quarry Street
Windsor St
Forrest St
Calderhead High School
Easter Rd
School
Union St
King St
Clive St
Caledonia Rd
The Cutting Gallery
Shottskirk Rd
Greenwood St
Dyfrig St
Regal Grove
Primary School
Theatre
Kirk Road
School Street
Gilburn Pl
BENHAR RD
B717
Gray St
Stable
High St
Dykehead
Parkside Rd
Curriesiide Place
Unity Pk
Robert St
Erskine Way
Avenue
Curriesiide
Station Road
Shotts Station
Foundry Road
Health Centre
Glen Road
Newmill And Canthill Road
Rosehall Road
MAIN STREET
Manse Road
Hartwood
South Calder Water
Rosehall
Burnbrae
ROAD
BURNBRAE
Bowhousebog
Road
West Tarbrax
Bowhousebog
Old Mill Road
ALLANTON ROAD
Kepplehill Farm
bank
161
PO
Allanton Primary School
Dura Road
Redmire Crescent
Darmeid Place
Hartfield Terrace
Avenue
Kingshill Rd
Springhead Road
Houldsworth Crs
Allanton
1
2
3
4
5
6
7
8

M5
1 Bank Pl
2 Gilburn Pl

M4
1 Abbotsford Crs

L4
1 Bertram St

C6
1 Provost's Loan
B6
1 Craig St
2 Mountstuart St
3 Woodlands St
A7
1 Church Hill St
2 Quayhead
3 Ritchie St
114
162
Portrye
Downcraig Ferry
Gavin's Glen
Little Skate Bay
Bell Bay
Great Cumbrae Island
B896
B899
Figgatoch
Fairhaven
Stinking Goat
Ballochmartin
Minnemoor
Ballochmartin Bay
Glaid Stone
Wee Minnemoor
Sheriff's Common
KA28
Gawk Stone
Clashfarland Point
Craigengour
Upper Cumbrae Reservoir
Lower Cumbrae Resrvoir
Ballikillet
Lady Margaret Hospital
Golf Course
Butter Lump
Breakough
Millport
The College & Cathedral College
Craig-en-Ros Road
Cumbrae Primary School
Lady Margaret Hospital
College Street
Copeland Crs
Cumbrae Dr
Balloch Crs
Kames St
Hastie Av
FERRY ROAD
Ninian Brae
Marine Pde
Ninian St
Doctors Surgery
Barend St
KELBURN STREET
KAMES BAY
Museum of The Cumbraes
George St
Bute Terrace
Clifton St
Howard Street
GUILDFORD ST
North Ayrshire Council
GLASGOW STREET
CARDIFF ST
STUART ST
Miller St
Clyde St
Crichton St
Newtown Bay
Kames Bay
The Lion
Museum & Aquarium
The Eileans
Marine Station
Keppel Pier
MARINE PARADE
Millport Bay
Farland Bight
Farland Point
Luckie's Bight
A
B
C
D
E
F
1
2
3
4
5
6
7
8

1 grid square represents 500 metres

K5
1 Bay St
2 Marine Ct
K7
1 Fairlieburne Gdns
2 Kaim Vw
3 Lilybank La
4 Montgomerie Crs
K8
1 Montgomerie Av
115
140
163
G
H
J
K
L
M
1
2
3
4
5
6
7
8
Cemetery
Largs Golf Club
Haylie Reservoir
A760
A78(T)
Rockland Park
Walkerston Av
Seabank Av
Warren Pk
Bowencraig
Mews
Firpark Plantation
Kelburn Bridge
Kelburn Country Centre
Baillie Rd
Kelburn Avenue
Keppenburn Avenue
Pier Road
Bay Street
Jetty Rd
PO
Castle Pk Gdns
Fife Av
Fife Pl
Castle Walk
Bourtrees
Fairlie
School Brae
Kelburn Ter
The Cswy
Highfield Terrace
Castle Park Drive
MAIN ROAD
Glen Rd
Burnfoot Rd
Fairlie Burn
Fairlie Glen
Station Rd
Fairlie Station
KA29
Montgomerie Drive
Southannan Rd
Miller Av
Semple Crs
Southannan

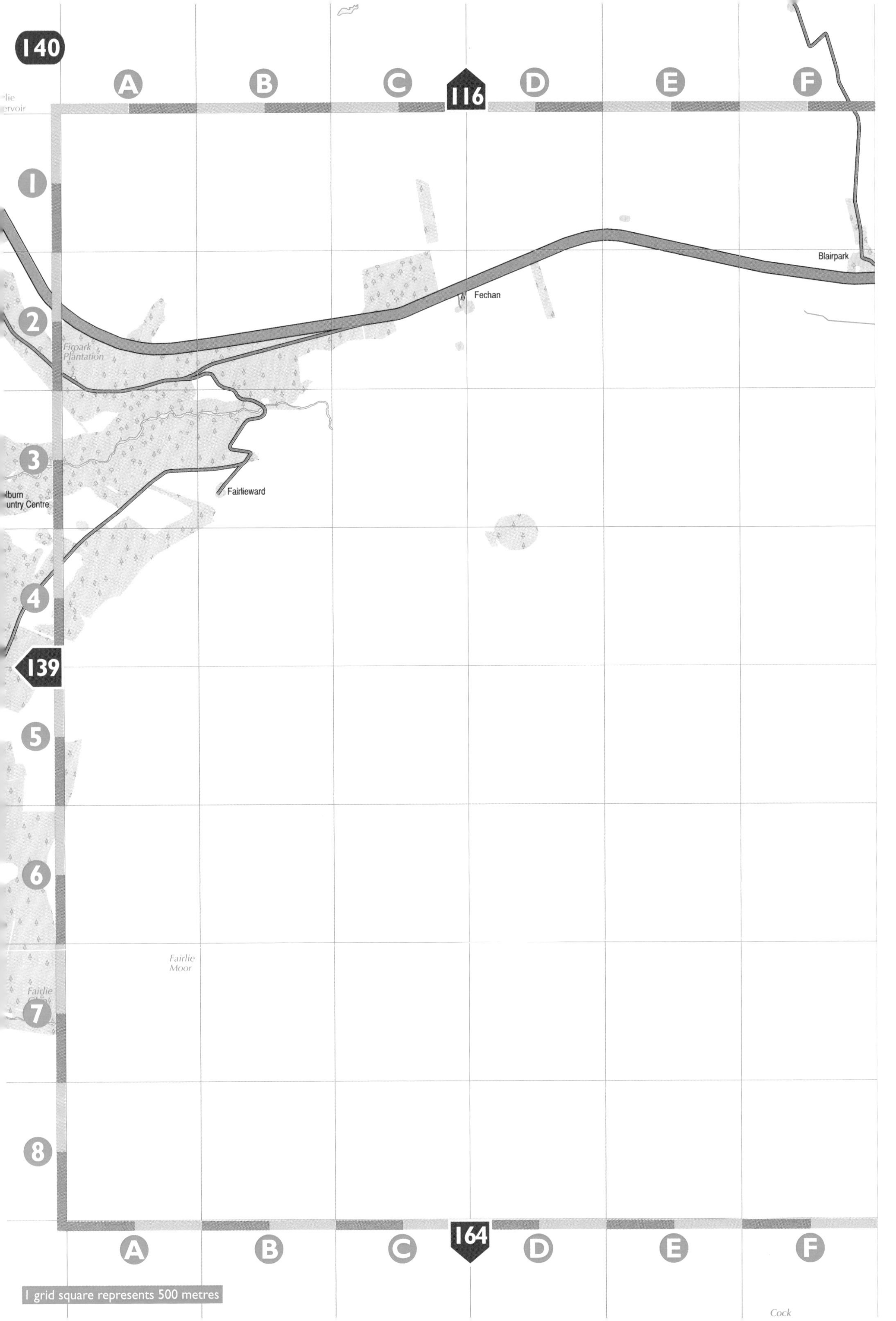
A
B
C
116
D
E
F
1
2
3
4
139
5
6
7
8
Blairpark
Fechan
Firpark Plantation
Fairlieward
Fairlie Moor
Fairlie
A
B
C
164
D
E
F
Cock

1 grid square represents 500 metres

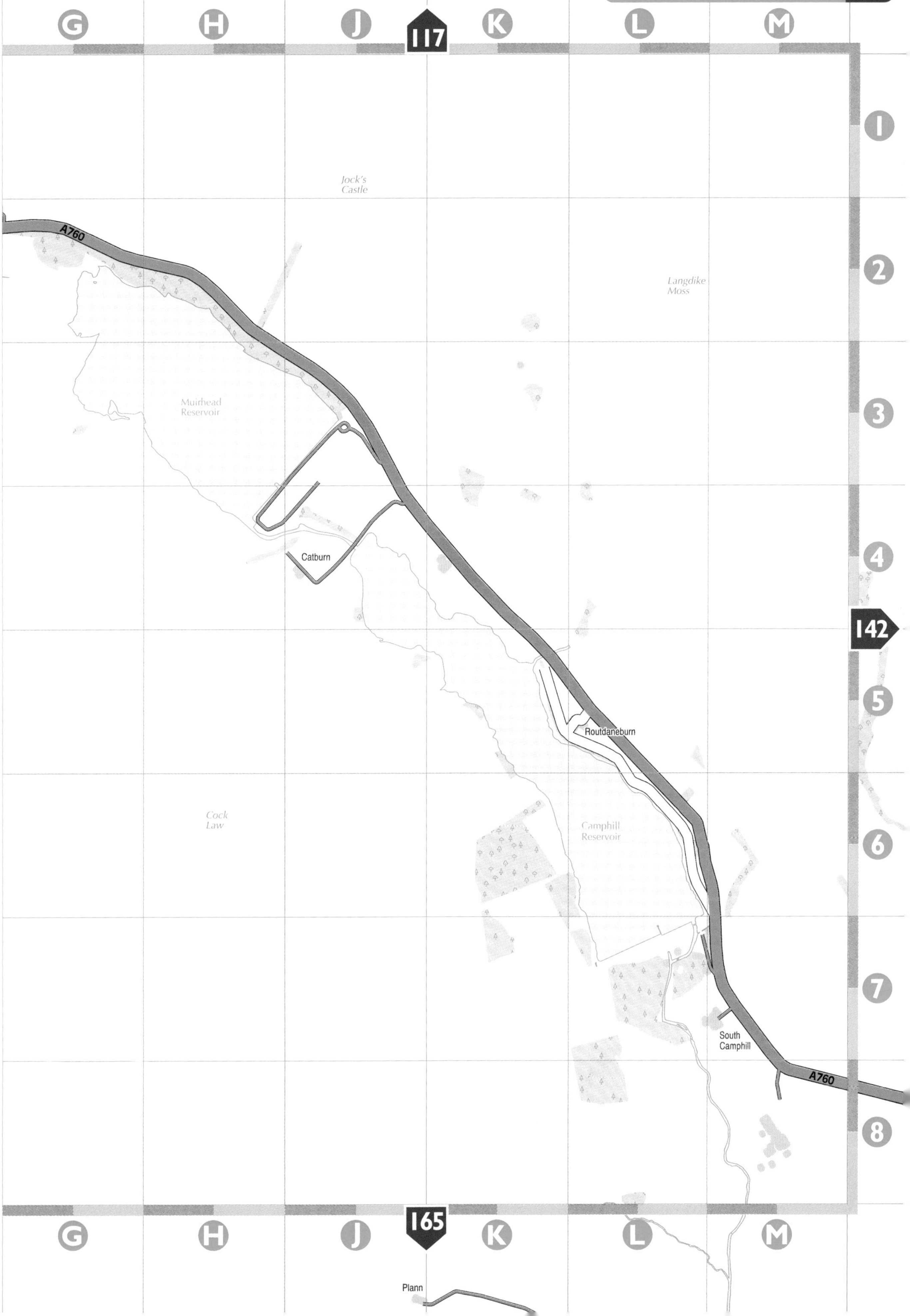
G
H
J
117
K
L
M
1
2
3
4
142
5
6
7
8
165
Jock's Castle
A760
Langdike Moss
Muirhead Reservoir
Catburn
Routdaneburn
Cock Law
Camphill Reservoir
South Camphill
Plann

F8
1 Alex Fleming Av

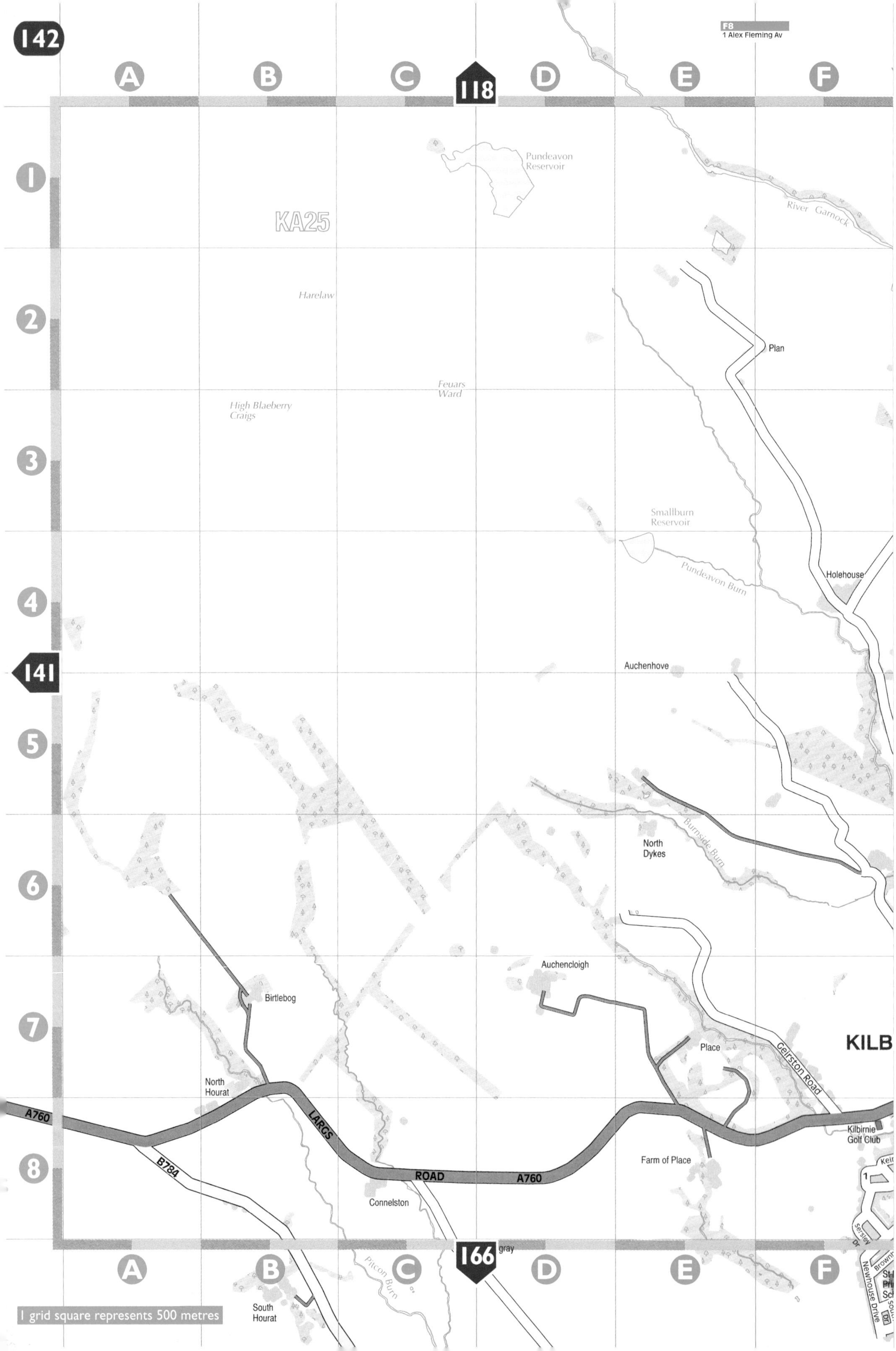
118
141
166
A
B
C
D
E
F
1
2
3
4
5
6
7
8
Pundeavon Reservoir
KA25
River Garnock
Harelaw
Plan
Feuars Ward
High Blaeberry Craigs
Smallburn Reservoir
Holehouse
Pundeavon Burn
Auchenhove
North Dykes
Burnside Burn
Auchencloigh
Birtlebog
Place
KILB
Geirston Road
North Hourat
A760
LARGS
ROAD
A760
B784
Kilbirnie Golf Club
Farm of Place
Connelston
Pitcon Burn
South Hourat
gray
Newhouse Drive

1 grid square represents 500 metres

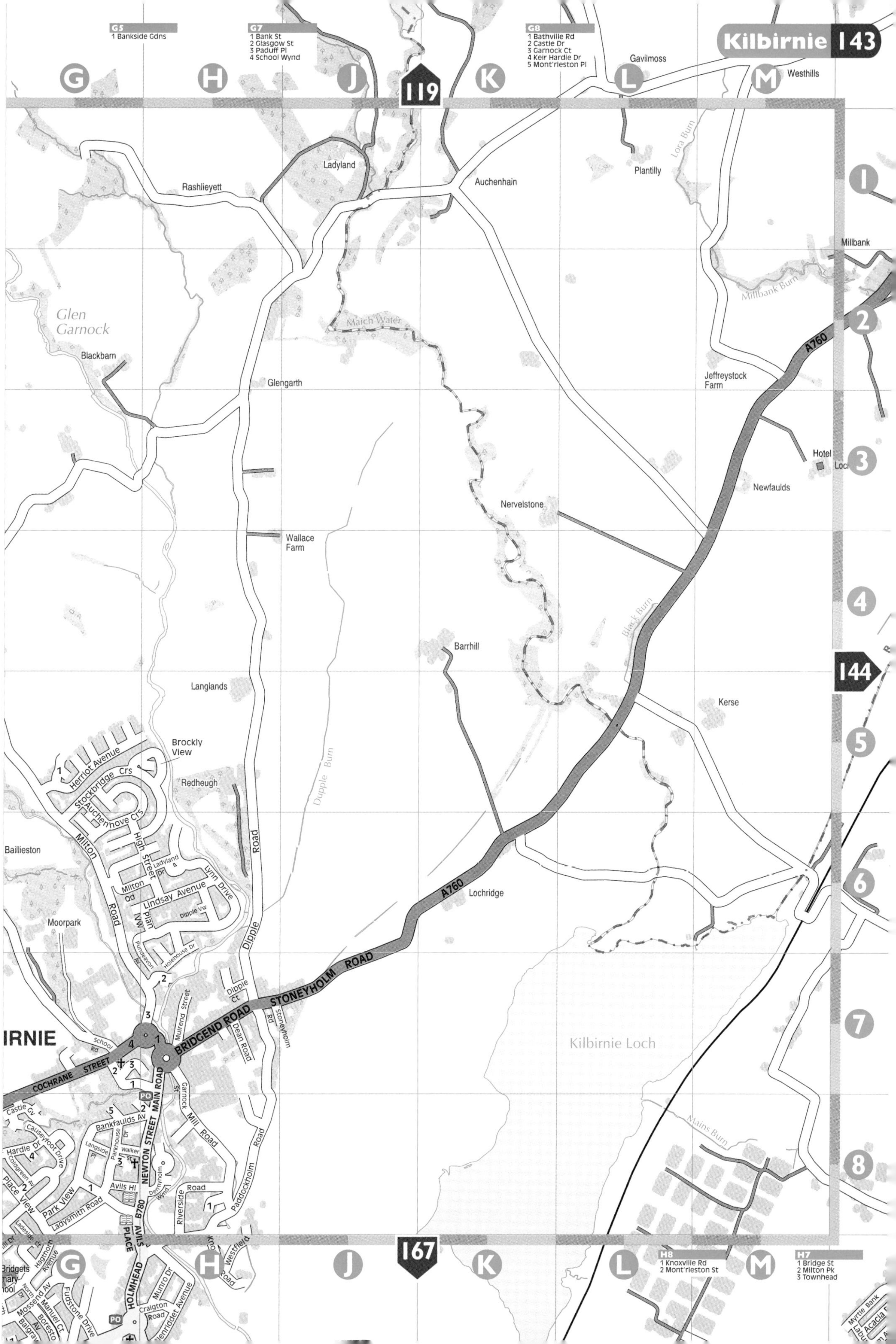
G5
1 Bankside Gdns
G7
1 Bank St
2 Glasgow St
3 Paduff Pl
4 School Wynd
G8
1 Bathville Rd
2 Castle Dr
3 Garnock Ct
4 Keir Hardie Dr
5 Mont'rieston Pl
119
144
167
H8
1 Knoxville Rd
2 Mont'rieston St
H7
1 Bridge St
2 Milton Pk
3 Townhead
Gavilmoss
Westhills
Ladyland
Rashlieyett
Auchenhain
Plantilly
Lora Burn
Millbank
Millbank Burn
Glen Garnock
Blackbarn
Maich Water
Glengarth
Jeffreystock Farm
A760
Hotel
Newfaulds
Nervelstone
Wallace Farm
Black Burn
Barrhill
Langlands
Kerse
Brockly View
Redheugh
Herriot Avenue
Stockbridge Crs
Auchenhove Crs
Dipple Burn
Dipple Road
Baillieston
Milton Road
High Street
Ladyland Dr
Lynn Drive
Lindsay Avenue
Milton Qd
Plan
Dipple Vw
Lochridge
Moorpark
Holehouse Dr
Dipple Ct
STONEYHOLM ROAD
BRIDGEND ROAD
Mulrend Street
Dean Road
Stoneyholm Rd
Kilbirnie Loch
School Rd
COCHRANE STREET
Garnock St
Mill Road
Castle Gv
Causeyfoot Drive
Bankfaulds Av
Langside Pl
Parkhouse Dr
Walker St
NEWTON STREET
MAIN ROAD
Hardie Dr
Place View
Park View
Ladysmith Road
Avils Hl
Dennyholm Wynd
Riverside Road
Paddockholm Road
Mains Burn
B780
AVILS PLACE
HOLMHEAD
Westfield
Hagthorn Avenue
Mossend Av
Manuel Ct
Boreston
Fudstone Drive
Munro Dr
Craigton Road
Glenriddet Avenue
Myrtle Bank
Acacia

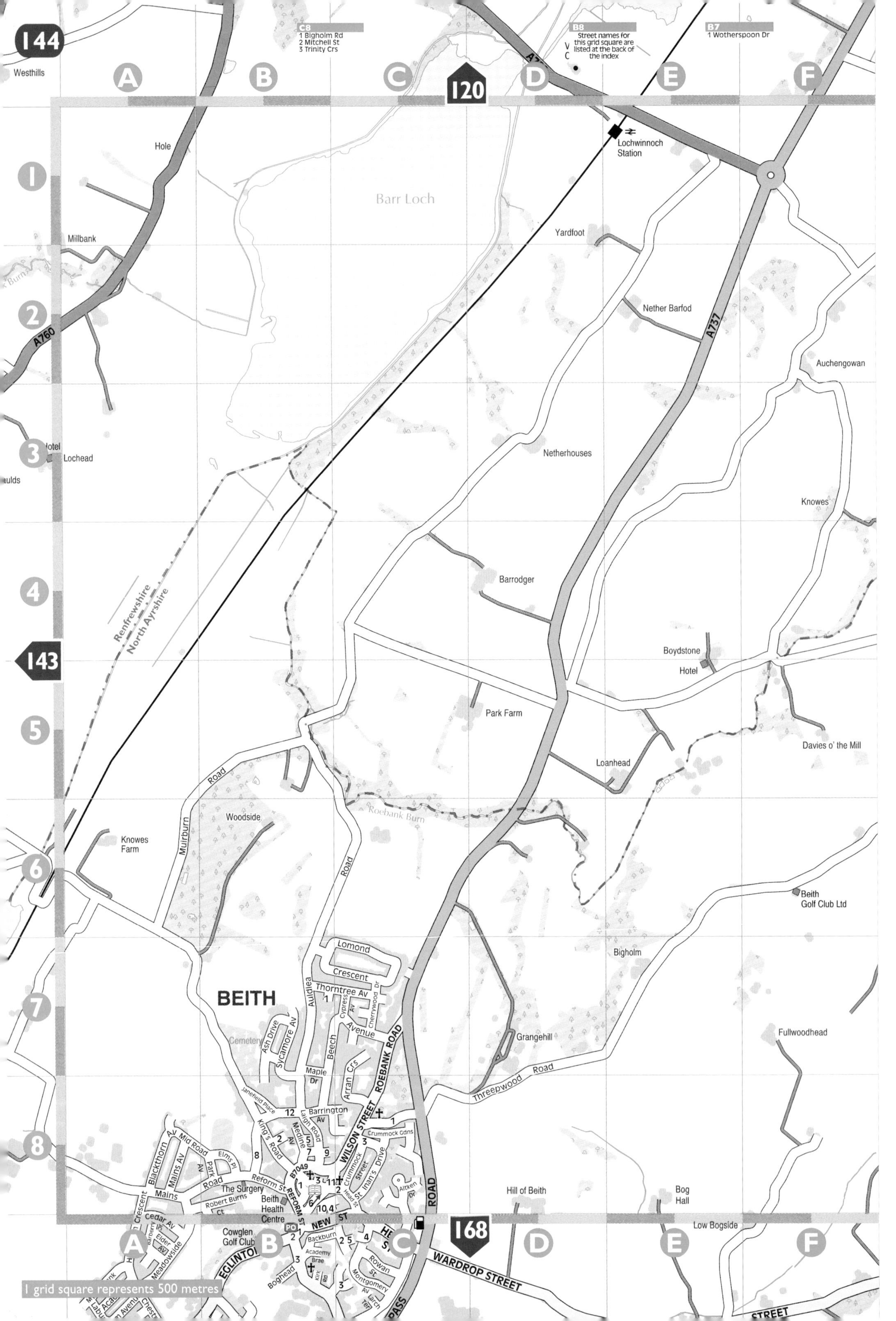

144
120
143
168
C8
1 Bigholm Rd
2 Mitchell St
3 Trinity Crs
B8
Street names for this grid square are listed at the back of the index
B7
1 Wotherspoon Dr
A
B
C
D
E
F
1
2
3
4
5
6
7
8
Westhills
Hole
Millbank
Lochead
Hotel
Lochwinnoch Station
Barr Loch
Yardfoot
Nether Barfod
A737
A760
Auchengowan
Netherhouses
Knowes
Barrodger
Boydstone
Hotel
Park Farm
Davies o' the Mill
Loanhead
Renfrewshire
North Ayrshire
Roebank Burn
Woodside
Knowes Farm
Muirburn Road
Road
Beith Golf Club Ltd
Bigholm
BEITH
Lomond
Crescent
Thorntree Av
Auldlea
Cypress Av
Cherrywood Dr
Avenue
Sycamore Av
Ash Drive
Cemetery
Beech
Maple Dr
Arran Crs
ROEBANK ROAD
Grangehill
Fullwoodhead
Threepwood Road
Janefield Place
Barrington Av
Laigh Road
Medine
WILSON STREET
Crummock Gdns
Crummock Street
St Inan's Drive
Aitken Dr
King's Road
Mid Road
Blackthorn Av
Mains Av
Park Road
Elms Pl
Reform St
B7049
The Surgery
Robert Burns Ct
Mains
Crescent
Beith Health Centre
REFORM ST
NEW ST
Heath St
ROAD
Hill of Beith
Bog Hall
Low Bogside
Cedar Av
Elder Av
Meadowside
Cowglen Golf Club
EGLINTON
PO
Backburn
Academy Brae
Boghead
Kirk Rd
Rowan St
Montgomery Av
Larch Ter
WARDROP STREET
STREET
1 grid square represents 500 metres

Hotel
Newtown of Belltrees
Lorabar
G
H
J
121
K
L
M
Muirend
B776
1
Auchengrange
Wateryett
Renfrewshire
North Ayrshire
2
Reivoch
Barcraigs Reservoir
Burnthills
Windyhill
3
4
Brownmuir Plantation
Burdiehouse
146
Threepwood
Kirkleegreen Rest
5
B776
Lowhouse
Rocking Stone
Cuffhill Resevoir
6
High Bogside
7
Hoodsyard
Mill Dam
Cuff Farm
8
Shutterflat
Lyonshield
169
Overton
B777
Over Hessilhead
B777

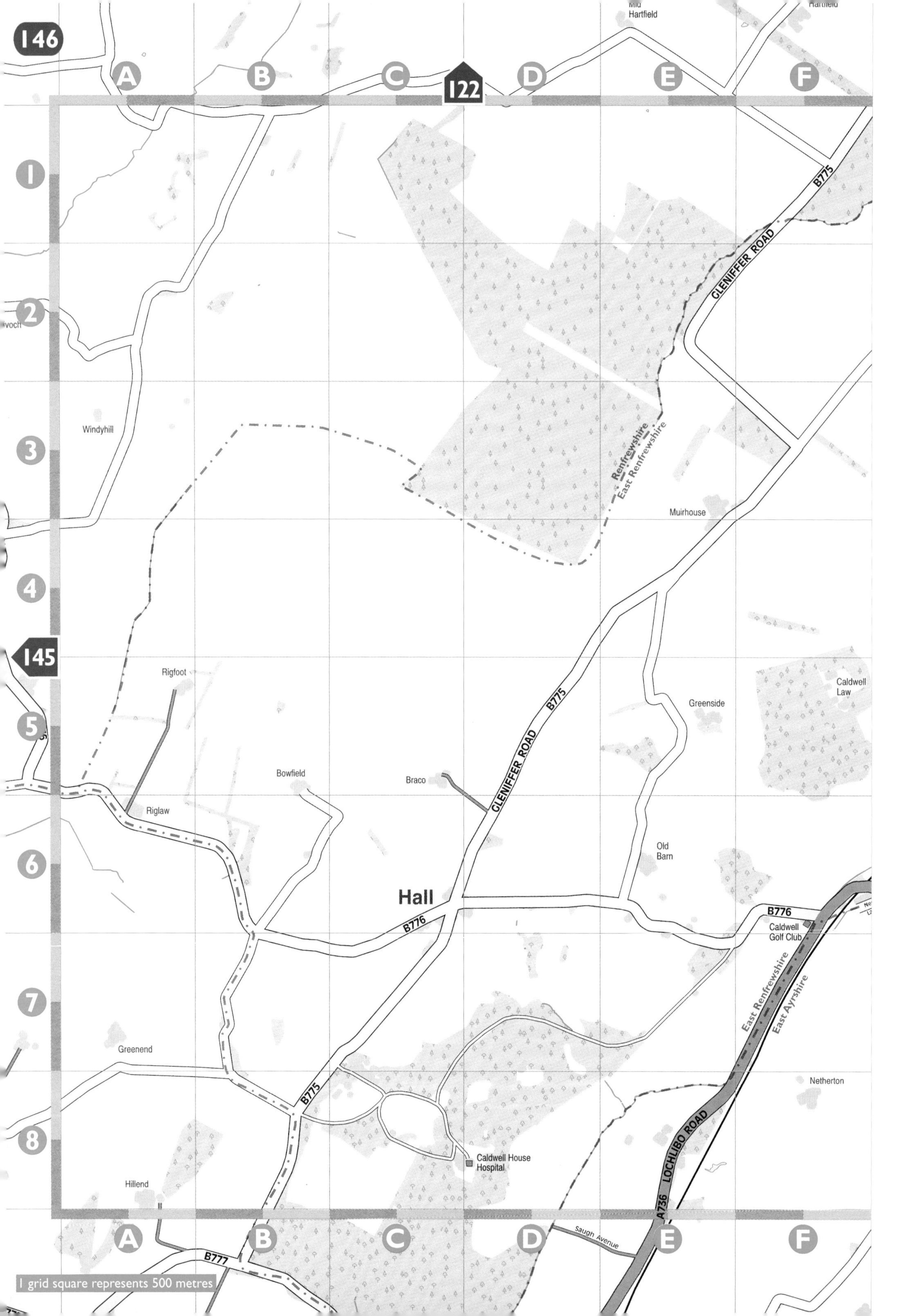

Mid Hartfield
Hartfield
122
145
A
B
C
D
E
F
1
2
3
4
5
6
7
8
Windyhill
Renfrewshire
East Renfrewshire
GLENIFFER ROAD
B775
Muirhouse
Rigfoot
Bowfield
Braco
Rigglaw
Greenside
Caldwell Law
Old Barn
Hall
B776
Caldwell Golf Club
Greenend
Netherton
LOCHLIBO ROAD
A736
East Ayrshire
Caldwell House Hospital
Hillend
B777
Saugh Avenue

1 grid square represents 500 metres

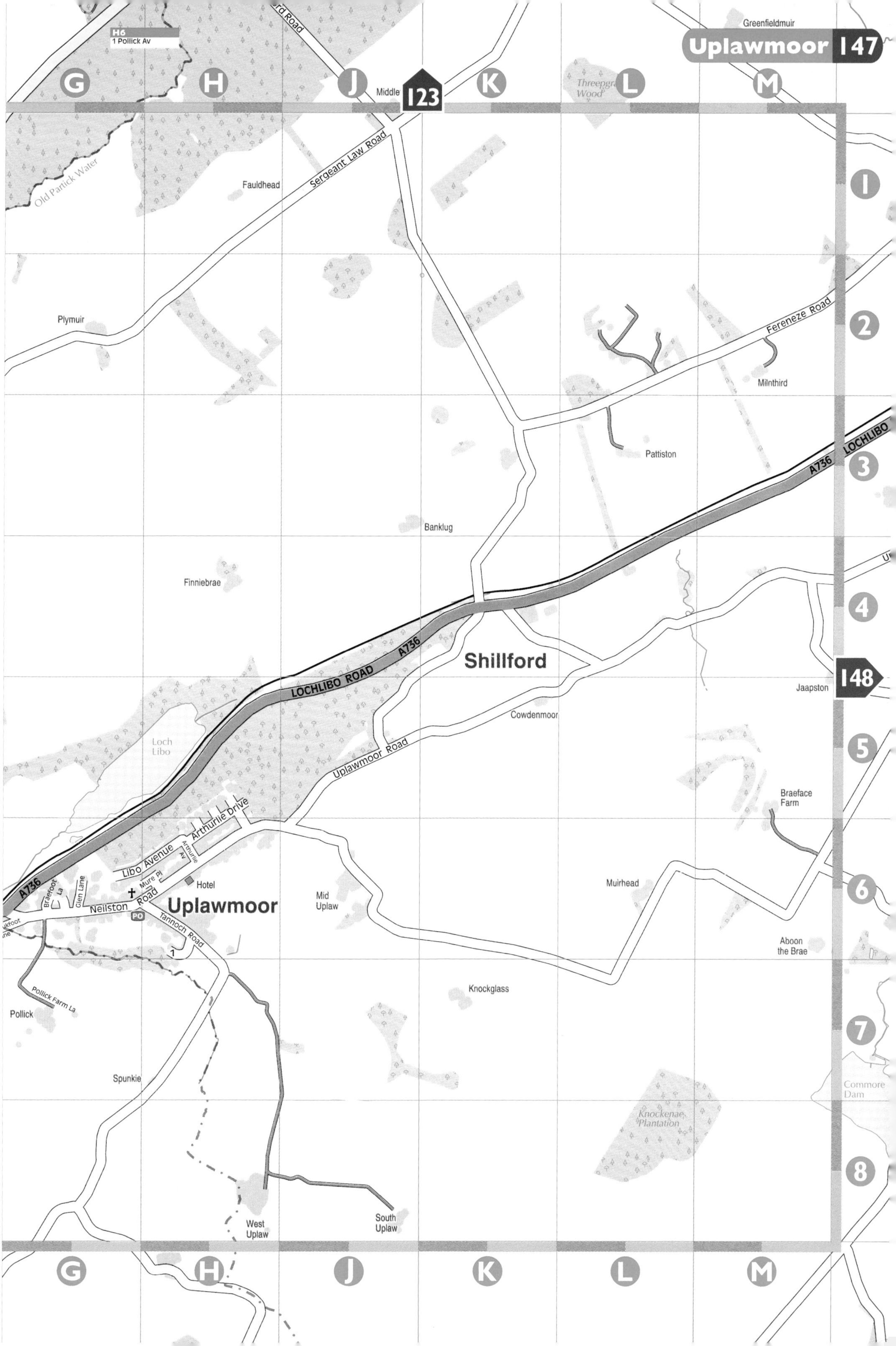
H6
1 Pollick Av
Greenfieldmuir
G
H
J
K
L
M
123
Middle
Threepgr Wood
Sergeant Law Road
Old Patrick Water
Fauldhead
Plymuir
Fereneze Road
Milnthird
Pattiston
A736 LOCHLIBO
Banklug
Finniebrae
Shillford
LOCHLIBO ROAD
A736
Jaapston
148
Cowdenmoor
Loch Libo
Uplawmoor Road
Braeface Farm
Arthurlie Drive
Libo Avenue
Arthurlie Av
Mure Pl
Hotel
Braefoot La
Glen Lane
Neilston Road
Uplawmoor
PO
Tannoch Road
Mid Uplaw
Muirhead
Aboon the Brae
Knockglass
Pollick Farm La
Pollick
Spunkie
Commore Dam
Knockenae Plantation
West Uplaw
South Uplaw
1
2
3
4
5
6
7
8

D2
1 Braehead Qd
2 Broadlie Ct
3 Chapel Pl
4 Dundonald Pl
5 Hillside Crs
6 Kirkstyle Crs
7 Low Broadlie Rd
8 Robertson Crs
C4
1 Glen Isla Av
C3
1 Glen Lyon Rd
2 Glen Mark Rd
3 Glen Muir Rd
4 The Grove
5 Molendinar Ter
6 Orr Ter
C2
1 Alexander Ter
2 Holehouse Ter
3 Millview Mdw
124
147
A
B
C
D
E
F
1
2
3
4
5
6
7
8
Gateside Road
Wraes View
Killoch
Fereneze Road
Donnies Brae
Nether Kirton
A736
LOCHLIBO ROAD
Station Brae
Foreside
Broadlie Road
Holehouse Brae
Crofthead Industrial Estate
G78
Gleniffer View
Barr Av
Manse Road
Neilston Road
Hartfield Crs
McDonald Pl
Springfield Road
Broadlie Rd
Primary School
Neilston Swimming Pool
Kirktonfield Road
Madras Place
Glen Avenue
Duncarnock Av
Duncarnock Cresent
Neilston Primary School
Hillside Road
Bank St
Lea Av
Braehead Av
Main St
PO
High St
Station Rd
Millview Ter
Mafeking Ter
Holehouse
Neilston Station
NEILSTON
Lintmill Ter
Wellpark Ter
Brig O'Lea Ter
Double Hedges Road
Harelaw Avenue
Maclellan Rd
Neilston House
Kirkton Road
Levern Water
Glenlivet Rd
Glenorrin Wy
Glen Creran Crs
Glen Doll Rd
Glen Gairn Crs
Glen Tarbert Dr
Glen Roy Dr
Kingston Av
Craig Road
Dyke
Glen Shee Av
Gln Finlet Road
Glen Falloch Crs
Uplawmoor Road
Crumyards
Kirkton Dam
Kilburn
Kingston Road
Craig of Neilston
Braeface Farm
Muirhead
Neilstonside
Snypes Dam
Snypes
Walton
Aboon the Brae
Drumler Craigs
Commore
Commore Dam
Harelaw
West Walton
High Walton
D3
1 Craighall Qd
2 Loanfoot Av
3 Luckiesfauld
D4
1 Glen Rinnes Dr
E1
1 Kirkhill Crs
E2
1 Kirkstyle La
1 grid square represents 500 metres

G
H
J
K
L
M
1
2
3
4
5
6
7
8
Gateside
Neilston Cemetery
1 Hawthorn Dr
2 Larchwood Ter
Springhill Primary School
Primary School
125
150
Newton Avenue
Divernia Way
Oakbank Drive
Maple Dr
Fenwick Drive
Lyoncross
Wraes
Newhouse
Springhill Road
St Lukes High School
Springfield Road
Springhill
Netherton
Aurs Road
Balgray Reservoir
Balgraystone
Balgraystone Road
Mains of Balgray
Waterside
Whitecraigs Rugby Club
Glanderston Mains
Glanderston Road
Glanderston Dam
Fingalton Road
Duncarnock Farm
B769
Netherplace
Netherplace Road
Burnside
DODSIDE ROAD
Cumnock House Farm
Caldcoats
Walton Dam
Burn Brock
Craigton Road
Craigton
Faulds Farm
Walton Burn
Middleton
Pilmuir
Langton Farm
A77
East Renfrewshire

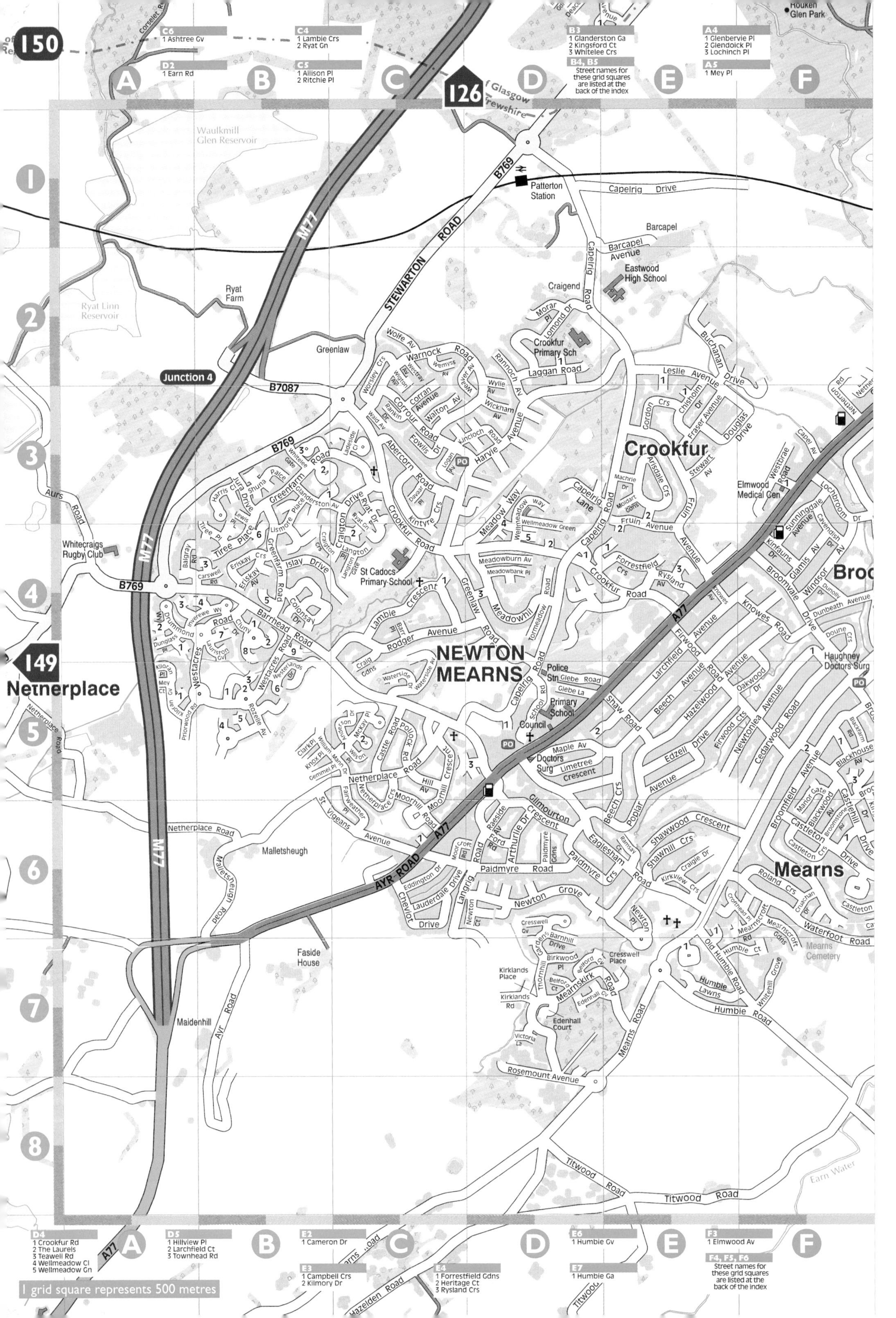

C6
1 Ashtree Gv

D2
1 Earn Rd

C4
1 Lambie Crs
2 Ryat Gn

C5
1 Allison Pl
2 Ritchie Pl

B3
1 Glanderston Ga
2 Kingsford Ct
3 Whitelee Crs

B4, B5
Street names for these grid squares are listed at the back of the index

A4
1 Glenbervie Pl
2 Glendoick Pl
3 Lochinch Pl

A5
1 Mey Pl

D4
1 Crookfur Rd
2 The Laurels
3 Teawell Rd
4 Wellmeadow Cl
5 Wellmeadow Gn

D5
1 Hillview Pl
2 Larchfield Ct
3 Townhead Rd

E2
1 Cameron Dr

E3
1 Campbell Crs
2 Kilmory Dr

E4
1 Forrestfield Gdns
2 Heritage Ct
3 Rysland Crs

E6
1 Humbie Gv

E7
1 Humbie Ga

F3
1 Elmwood Av

F4, F5, F6
Street names for these grid squares are listed at the back of the index

1 grid square represents 500 metres

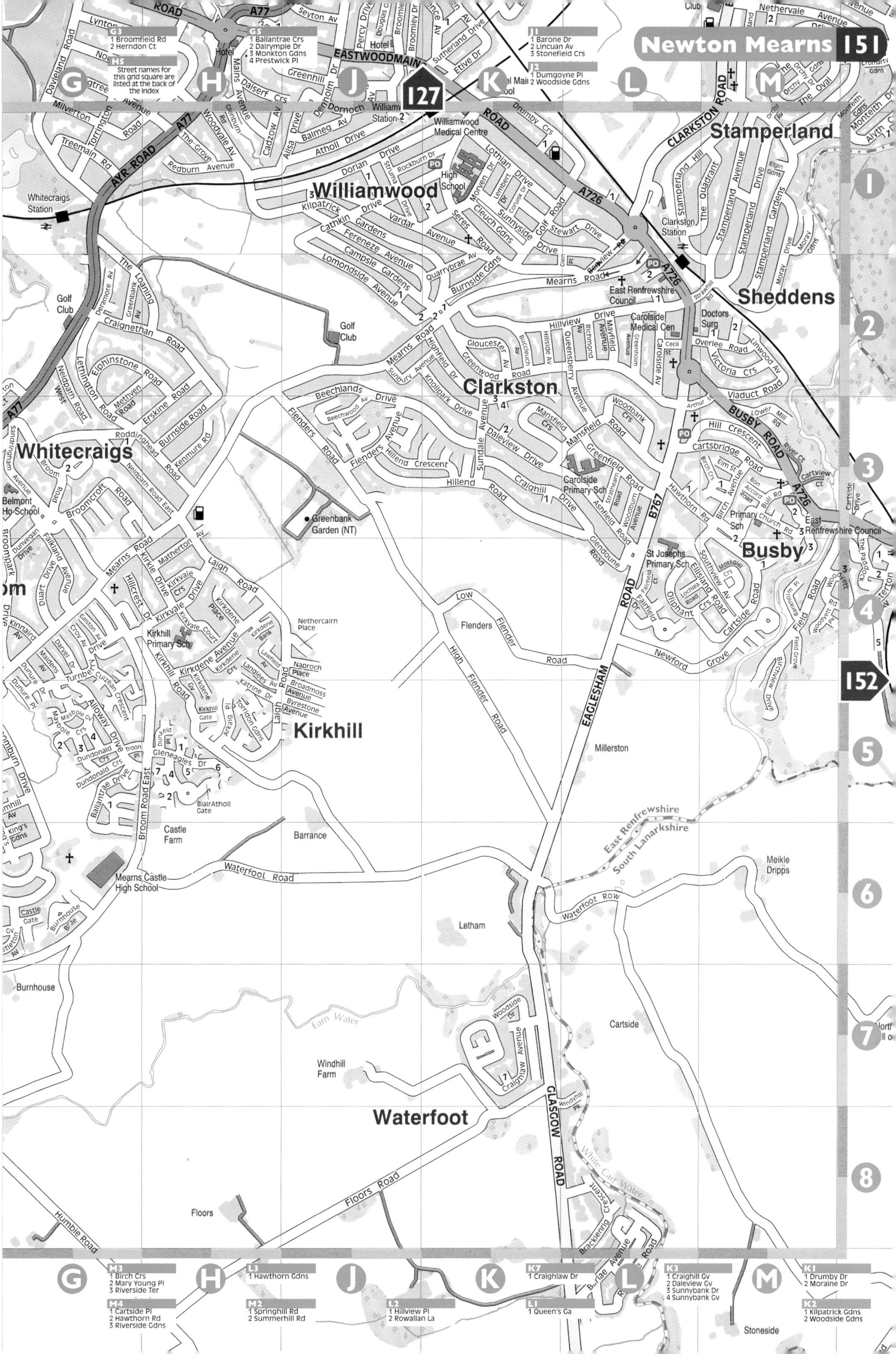
G3
1 Broomfield Rd
2 Herndon Ct
H5
Street names for this grid square are listed at the back of the index
G5
1 Ballantrae Crs
2 Dalrymple Dr
3 Monkton Gdns
4 Prestwick Pl
J1
1 Barone Dr
2 Lincuan Av
3 Stonefield Crs
J2
1 Dumgoyne Pl
2 Woodside Gdns
127
Stamperland
Whitecraigs Station
Williamwood
Williamwood Medical Centre
High School
Clarkston Station
Sheddens
Golf Club
East Renfrewshire Council
Carolside Medical Cen
Doctors Surg
Clarkston
Whitecraigs
Belmont Ho School
Carolside Primary Sch
Greenbank Garden (NT)
St Josephs Primary Sch
Busby
East Renfrewshire Council
Nethercairn Place
Flenders
Kirkhill Primary Sch
Kirkhill
152
Millerston
Castle Farm
Barrance
Mearns Castle High School
East Renfrewshire
South Lanarkshire
Meikle Dripps
Letham
Burnhouse
Earn Water
Cartside
Windhill Farm
Waterfoot
White Cart Water
Floors
Stoneside
AYR ROAD
EASTWOODMAINS ROAD
CLARKSTON ROAD
BUSBY ROAD
EAGLESHAM ROAD
GLASGOW ROAD
Waterfoot Road
Floors Road
Humbie Road
M3
1 Birch Crs
2 Mary Young Pl
3 Riverside Ter
M4
1 Cartside Pl
2 Hawthorn Rd
3 Riverside Gdns
L3
1 Hawthorn Gdns
M2
1 Springhill Rd
2 Summerhill Rd
L2
1 Hillview Pl
2 Rowallan La
K7
1 Craighlaw Dr
L1
1 Queen's Ga
K3
1 Craighill Gv
2 Daleview Gv
3 Sunnybank Dr
4 Sunnybank Gv
K1
1 Drumby Dr
2 Moraine Dr
K2
1 Kilpatrick Gdns
2 Woodside Gdns

152
128
151
170
C6 1 Park Pl
B6 1 Bishops Pk
A4 1 Glenville Ga 2 Glenville Ter 3 Hunthill Pl 4 Silvan Pl 5 Westerton La
A1 1 Alyth Gdns
D1 1 Old Playfield Rd 2 Waterside Rd
E1 1 Fair Oaks 2 High Beeches 3 The Willows
F5 1 Castlehill Gn 2 Ministers Pk
Gallowhill
Carmunnock
CATHKIN ROAD
B759
B766
Carmunnock Road
Windlaw Road
Ardencraig Road
Carmunnock Cemetery
Pedmyre
Pedmyre La
BUSBY ROAD
Carnbooth School
Carmunnock Primary Sch
Picketlaw Farm
Waterside Gdns
Kittochside Road
Parklea Farm
City of Glasgow
South Lanarkshire
CARMUNNOCK ROAD
CARMUNNOCK BY-PASS
Kittoch Water
East Renfrewshire Council
Busby Station
The Crescent
Westerton Av
South Road
Station Road
Easterton Av
Kippen Drive
Lister Gardens
A726
Waterside Road
Waterbank Road
Waterside
Agricultural Museum
Glen Road
Bushbyside Farm
East Renfrewshire
South Lanarkshire
EAST KILBRIDE ROAD A726
Westerfield Road
Cemetery
Peel Road
Stewartfield Way
Philipshill Road
Philipshill Gate
Braehead Road
Braehead
Thorntonhall
Thorntonhall Station
Osborne Crs
Wellknowe Rd
Wellknowe Pl
Park Drive
Thornton Rd
Thorn Av
Ravenscourt
Bishops Gate
Wellknowe Av
Gilmour Avenue
North Hill of Dripps
South Hill of Dripps
Thornton
Thornton Road
Barbana Road
Redwood Drive
Redwood Crescent
Redwood Place
Redwood Dr
Peel Park
Peel Park Place
Linwood
Burley Pl
South Lanarkshire Council
Hairmyres Station
EAGLESHAM RD
Hairmyres & Stonehouse Hospitals N H S Trust
A&E
Redwood Av
Peel Road
Bogton
Hayhill Road
Hayhill
Strathmore
Strathnaver Gardens
Strathdearn Gv
Hairmyres
1 grid square represents 500 metres

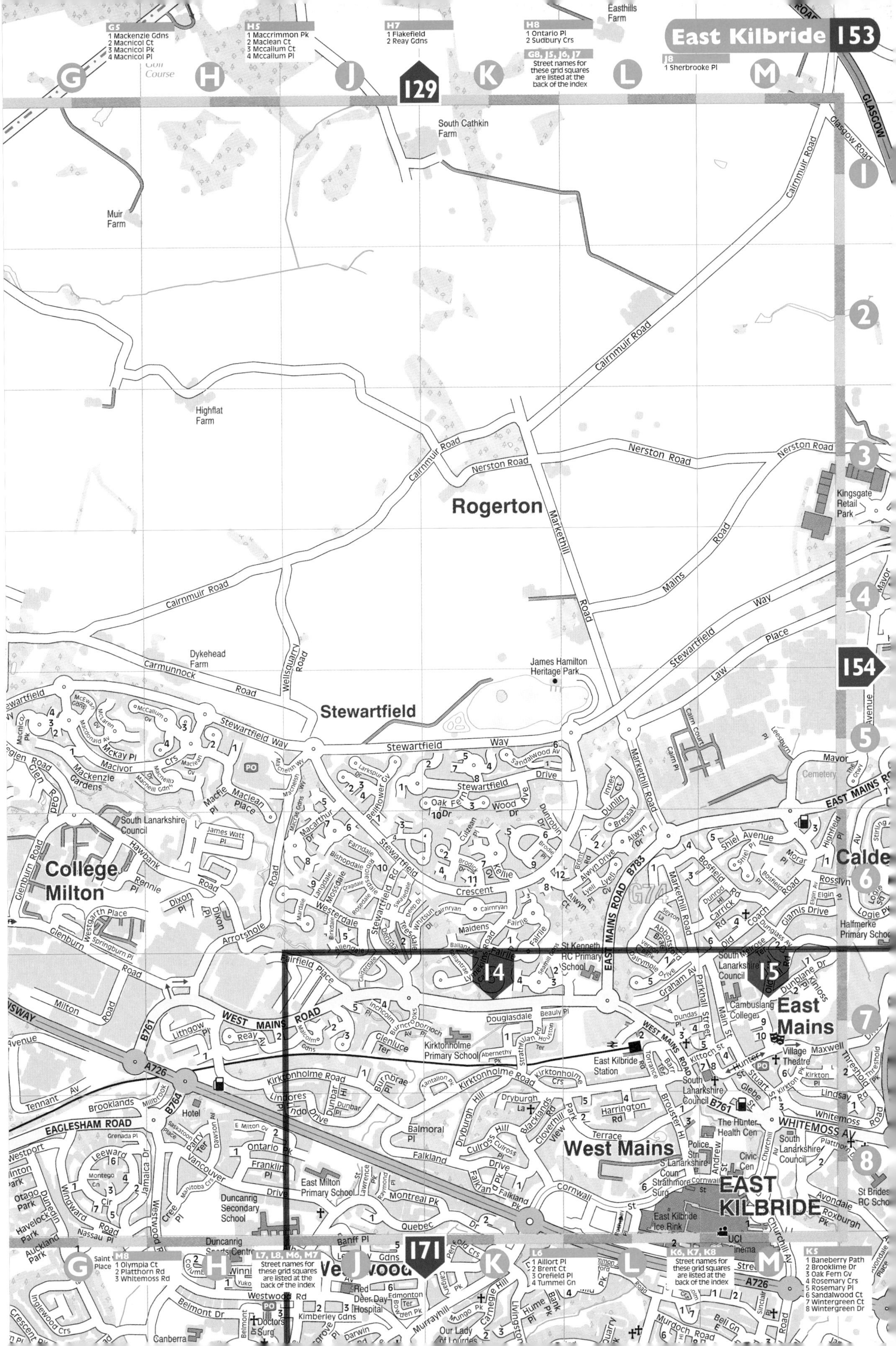
G5
1 Mackenzie Gdns
2 Macnicol Ct
3 Macnicol Pk
4 Macnicol Pl
H5
1 Maccrimmon Pk
2 Maclean Ct
3 Mccallum Ct
4 Mccallum Pl
H7
1 Flakefield
2 Reay Gdns
H8
1 Ontario Pl
2 Sudbury Crs
G8, J5, J6, J7
Street names for these grid squares are listed at the back of the index
J8
1 Sherbrooke Pl
Easthills Farm
129
South Cathkin Farm
Muir Farm
Highflat Farm
Cairnmuir Road
Nerston Road
Rogerton
Markethill Road
Mains Road
Stewartfield Way
Law Place
Kingsgate Retail Park
154
Dykehead Farm
Carmunnock Road
Wellsquarry Road
James Hamilton Heritage Park
Stewartfield
College Milton
South Lanarkshire Council
West Mains Road
East Mains Road
East Mains
West Mains
EAST KILBRIDE
East Kilbride Station
Kirktonholme Primary School
East Milton Primary School
Duncanrig Secondary School
Cambuslang College
Village Theatre
Eaglesham Road
A726
B761
B764
B783
14
15
171
M8
1 Olympia Ct
2 Platthorn Rd
3 Whitemoss Rd
L7, L8, M6, M7
Street names for these grid squares are listed at the back of the index
L6
1 Aillort Pl
2 Brent Ct
3 Orefield Pl
4 Tummel Gn
K6, K7, K8
Street names for these grid squares are listed at the back of the index
K5
1 Baneberry Path
2 Brooklime Dr
3 Oak Fern Gv
4 Rosemary Crs
5 Rosemary Pl
6 Sandalwood Ct
7 Wintergreen Ct
8 Wintergreen Dr

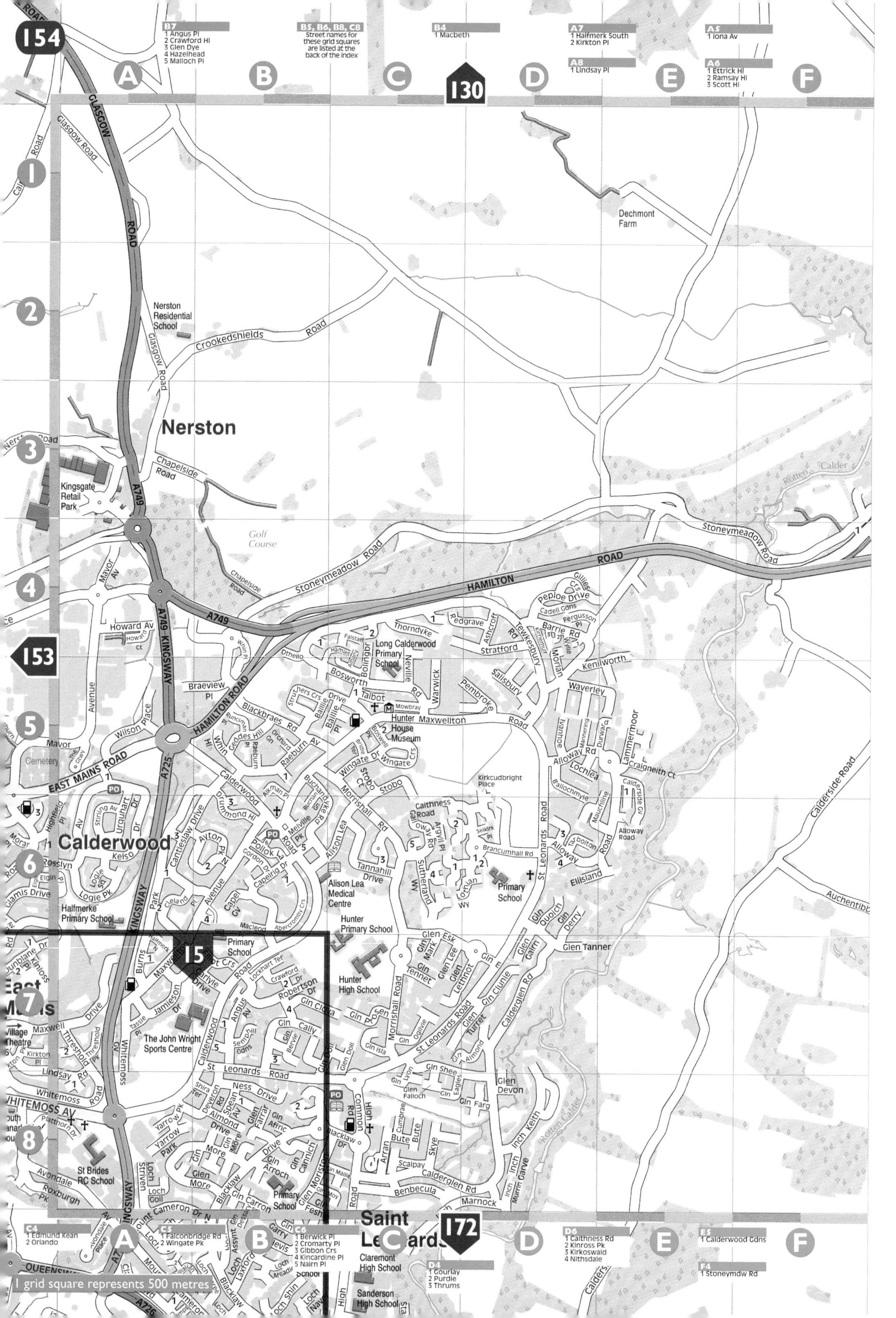

154
B7
1 Angus Pl
2 Crawford Hl
3 Glen Dye
4 Hazelhead
5 Malloch Pl
B5, B6, B8, C8
Street names for these grid squares are listed at the back of the index
B4
1 Macbeth
A7
1 Halfmerk South
2 Kirkton Pl
A8
1 Lindsay Pl
A5
1 Iona Av
A6
1 Ettrick Hl
2 Ramsay Hl
3 Scott Hl
A
B
C
130
D
E
F
1
2
3
4
5
6
7
8
153
GLASGOW ROAD
Glasgow Road
Dechmont Farm
Nerston Residential School
Crookedshields Road
Glasgow Road
Nerston
Chapelside Road
Kingsgate Retail Park
A749
Golf Course
Chapelside Road
Stoneymeadow Road
HAMILTON ROAD
A749
A749 KINGSWAY
Calder
Rotten
Stoneymeadow Road
Mavor Av
Howard Av
Howard Ct
Braeview Pl
Avenue
Wilson Place
HAMILTON ROAD
A725
Mavor
Cemetery
EAST MAINS ROAD
Long Calderwood Primary School
Thorndyke
Redgrave
Ashcroft Rd
Stratford
Tewkesbury
Peploe Drive
Cadell Gdns
Fergusson Pl
Barrie Rd
Morlan
Kenilworth
Waverley
Salisbury
Pembroke Road
Warwick
Bosworth
Talbot
Hunter House Museum
Maxwellton
Blackbraes Rd
Geddes Hill
Raeburn Av
Wingate Dr
Wingate Crs
Stobo Ct
Stobo
Morrishall Rd
Alison Lea
Calderwood
Drummond Hl
Buchanan Dr
Melville Pk
Pollok Pl
Capelrig Dr
Gordon Dr
Alison Lea Medical Centre
Tannahill Drive
Caithness Road
Argyll Pl
Sutherland Wy
Lothian Wy
Selkirk Pl
Brancumhall Rd
Primary School
St Leonards Road
Kirkcudbright Place
Ivanhoe
Alloway Rd
Lochlea
Ballochmyle
Mauchline
Lammermoor
Craigneith Ct
Calderside Gv
Alloway Road
Tarbolton
Alloway
Ellisland
Calderside Road
Auchentibb
Calderwood
Kelso
Rosslyn
Logie Sq
Logie Pk
Elgin
Glamis Drive
Halfmerke Primary School
Stirling Av
Urquhart Dr
Highfield Pl
Ayton Pk
Cantieslaw Drive
Cleland Pl
Avenue
Capel Gv
Macleod
Abercromby Crs
Hunter Primary School
Glen Esk
Glen Mark
Glen Lee
Glen Tennet
Glen Lethnot
Glen Quoich
Glen Derry
Glen Tanner
Glen Clunie
Calderglen Rd
Glen Cairn
Glen E
15
Primary School
Elliot Crs
Carlyle Drive
Lockhart Ter
Crawford Dr
Robertson Dr
Hunter High School
Morrishall Road
St Leonards Road
Glen Turret
Glen Almond
East Mains
Village Theatre
Maxwell Drive
Threshold
Threshold Pk
Kirkton Pl
Lindsay Rd
Whitemoss Road
WHITEMOSS AV
Burns
Maxwellton
Jamieson Dr
Tassie
Whitemoss Gv
The John Wright Sports Centre
Calderwood
Angus Av
Glen Clova
Glen Cally
Glen Bervie
Glen Isla
Glen Ogilvie
Glen Doll
Glen Prosen
St Leonards Road
Ness Drive
Glen Shee
Glen Falloch
Glen Farg
Glen Devon
Yarrow Pk
Yarrow Park
Almond Drive
Glen More
Glen Affric
Glen Arroch
Glen Cannich
Glen Moriston
Common Rd
High
Blacklaw Dr
Arran
Bute
Skye
Scalpay
Calderglen Rd
Benbecula
Marnock
Inch Keith
Inch Garve
Inch Murrin
Rotten Calder
Strathaven Pl
Plathorn Dr
St Brides RC School
Avondale
Roxburgh Pk
Strriven
Loch Goil
Blacklaw
Glen Carron
Primary School
Kingsway
Mount Cameron Dr N
Saint Leonards
172
Claremont High School
Sanderson High School
Queensway
A726
C4
1 Edmund Kean
2 Orlando
C5
1 Falconbridge Rd
2 Wingate Pk
C6
1 Berwick Pl
2 Cromarty Pl
3 Gibbon Crs
4 Kincardine Pl
5 Nairn Pl
D4
1 Gourlay
2 Purdie
3 Thrums
D6
1 Caithness Rd
2 Kinross Pk
3 Kirkoswald
4 Nithsdale
E5
1 Calderwood Gdns
F4
1 Stoneymdw Rd
1 grid square represents 500 metres

H2
1 Watson Pl

H3
1 Craigmuir Gdns

J1, J2
Street names for these grid squares are listed at the back of the index

J3
1 Barry Gdns

K1, K2, K3, K4
Street names for these grid squares are listed at the back of the index

131

173

M2
1 Auchinraith Rd

M4, M5, M6, M7
Street names for these grid squares are listed at the back of the index

L7
1 Aqua Ct
2 Boreland Dr
3 Mennock Ct

L8
1 Coylton Crs

L6
1 Bradshaw Crs
2 Hillhead Ter
3 Townhill Ter

L4
1 Fifth Rd
2 Seventh Rd
3 Warwick Gv

L5
1 Buckingham Ct

K8
1 Cumnock Dr

L2
1 Devlin Ct
2 Hawthorn Pl
3 Herbertson St
4 Rosendale Wy

K5
1 International Av

K7
1 Lendalfoot Gdns
2 Mauchline Ct
3 Maybole Gdns

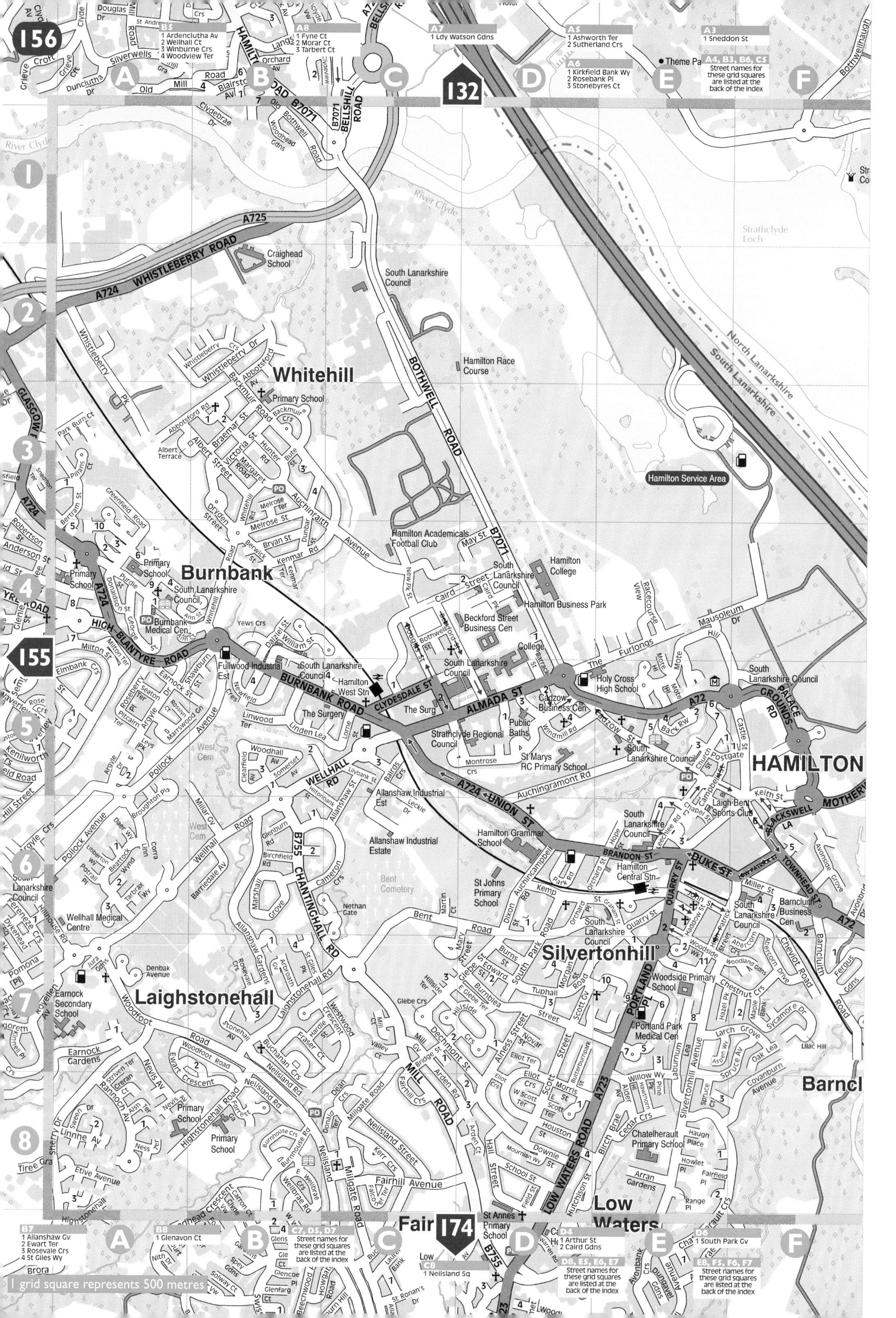
156
132
155
174
B5
1 Ardenclutha Av
2 Wellhall Ct
3 Winburne Crs
4 Woodview Ter
A8
1 Fyne Ct
2 Morar Ct
3 Tarbert Ct
A7
1 Ldy Watson Gdns
A5
1 Ashworth Ter
2 Sutherland Crs
A6
1 Kirkfield Bank Wy
2 Rosebank Pl
3 Stonebyres Ct
A3
1 Sneddon St
A4, B3, B6, C5
Street names for these grid squares are listed at the back of the index
Theme Pa
River Clyde
Strathclyde Loch
A725
A724 WHISTLEBERRY ROAD
Craighead School
South Lanarkshire Council
Hamilton Race Course
North Lanarkshire
South Lanarkshire
Hamilton Service Area
Whitehill
Primary School
BOTHWELL ROAD
B7071
Hamilton Academicals Football Club
Hamilton College
Hamilton Business Park
Beckford Street Business Cen
Burnbank
South Lanarkshire Council
Burnbank Medical Cen
HIGH BLANTYRE ROAD
Fullwood Industrial Est
BURNBANK ROAD
Hamilton West Stn
CLYDESDALE ST
ALMADA ST
Holy Cross High School
Cadzow Business Cen
Public Baths
Strathclyde Regional Council
St Marys RC Primary School
HAMILTON
PALACE GROUNDS RD
A72
A724 UNION ST
Allanshaw Industrial Est
Allanshaw Industrial Estate
Hamilton Grammar School
BRANDON ST
DUKE ST
Hamilton Central Stn
Laigh Bent Sports Club
St Johns Primary School
Bent Cemetery
West Cem
B755 CHANTINGHALL RD
Wellhall Medical Centre
Earnock Secondary School
Laighstonehall
Silvertonhill
Woodside Primary School
Portland Park Medical Cen
Barnclu Business Cen
Barncl
A723 LOW WATERS ROAD
Chatelherault Primary School
Low Waters
Primary School
MILL ROAD
Neilsland Rd
Fair
St Annes Primary School
B7
1 Allanshaw Gv
2 Ewart Ter
3 Rosevale Crs
4 St Giles Wy
B8
1 Glenavon Ct
C7, D5, D7
Street names for these grid squares are listed at the back of the index
C8
1 Neilsland Sq
D4
1 Arthur St
2 Caird Gdns
D8, E5, E6, E7
Street names for these grid squares are listed at the back of the index
D6
1 South Park Gv
E8, F5, F6, F7
Street names for these grid squares are listed at the back of the index
1 grid square represents 500 metres

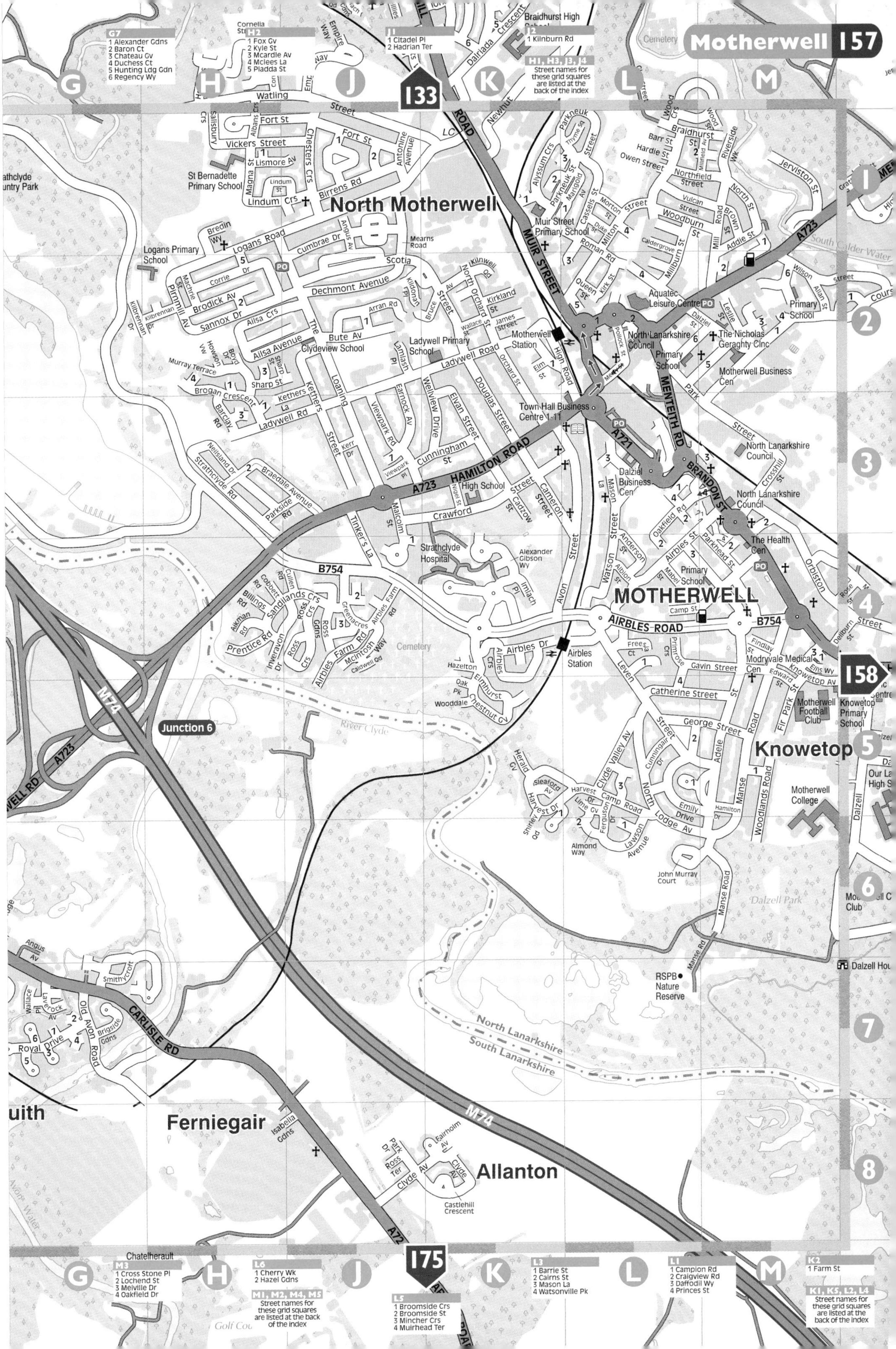
G7
1 Alexander Gdns
2 Baron Ct
3 Chateau Gv
4 Duchess Ct
5 Hunting Ldg Gdn
6 Regency Wy
H2
1 Fox Gv
2 Kyle St
3 Mcardle Av
4 Mclees La
5 Pladda St
J1
1 Citadel Pl
2 Hadrian Ter
J2
1 Kilnburn Rd
H1, H3, J3, J4
Street names for these grid squares are listed at the back of the index
133
175
158
North Motherwell
MOTHERWELL
Knowetop
Ferniegair
Allanton
Junction 6
M74
A723
A721
B754
HAMILTON ROAD
MUIR STREET
AIRBLES ROAD
MENTEITH RD
BRANDON ST
CARLISLE RD
North Lanarkshire
South Lanarkshire
River Clyde
Dalzell Park
RSPB Nature Reserve
Motherwell Station
Airbles Station
Strathclyde Hospital
Motherwell College
Motherwell Football Club
M3
1 Cross Stone Pl
2 Lochend St
3 Melville St
4 Oakfield Dr
L6
1 Cherry Wk
2 Hazel Gdns
M1, M2, M4, M5
Street names for these grid squares are listed at the back of the index
L5
1 Broomside Crs
2 Broomside St
3 Mincher Crs
4 Muirhead Ter
L3
1 Barrie St
2 Cairns St
3 Mason La
4 Watsonville Pk
L1
1 Campion Rd
2 Craigview Rd
3 Daffodil Wy
4 Princes St
K2
1 Farm St
K1, K5, L2, L4
Street names for these grid squares are listed at the back of the index

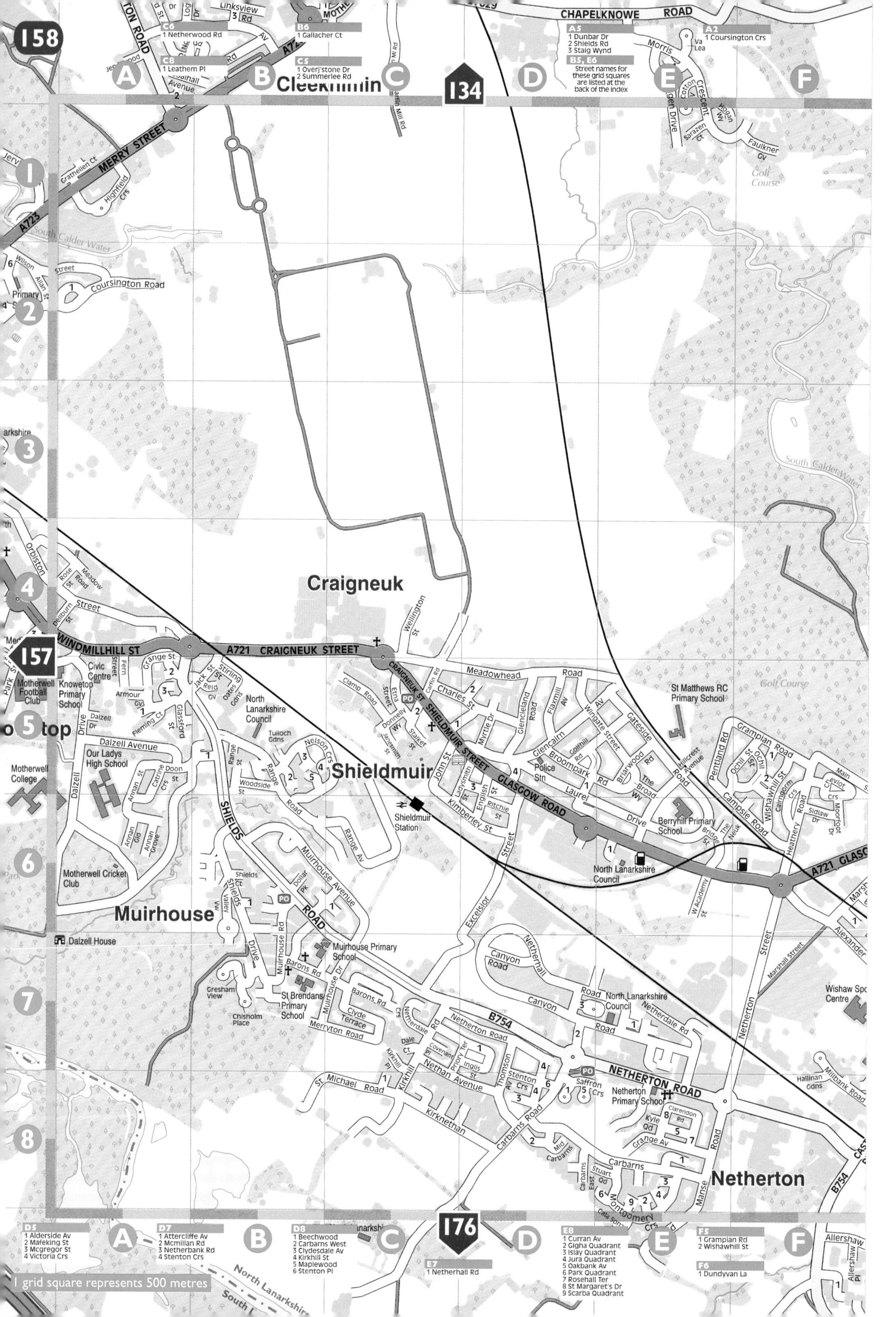

158
134
157
176
C6 1 Netherwood Rd
C8 1 Leathem Pl
B6 1 Gallacher Ct
C5 1 Overj'stone Dr 2 Summerlee Rd
A5 1 Dunbar Dr 2 Shields Rd 3 Staig Wynd
B5, E6 Street names for these grid squares are listed at the back of the index
A2 1 Coursington Crs
CHAPELKNOWE ROAD
Cleekhimin
MERRY STREET
A723
South Calder Water
Coursington Road
Golf Course
Craigneuk
A721 CRAIGNEUK STREET
WINDMILLHILL ST
Meadowhead Road
SHIELDMUIR STREET
GLASGOW ROAD
Shieldmuir
Shieldmuir Station
North Lanarkshire Council
St Matthews RC Primary School
Berryhill Primary School
Police Stn
Motherwell Football Club
Knowetop Primary School
Civic Centre
Our Ladys High School
Motherwell College
Motherwell Cricket Club
Muirhouse
Dalzell House
SHIELDS ROAD
Muirhouse Avenue
Muirhouse Primary School
St Brendans Primary School
Merryton Road
Netherton Road
B754
NETHERTON ROAD
Netherton Primary School
Netherton
Wishaw Sports Centre
A721 GLASGOW
D5 1 Alderside Av 2 Mafeking St 3 Mcgregor St 4 Victoria Crs
D7 1 Attercliffe Av 2 Mcmillan Rd 3 Netherbank Rd 4 Stenton Crs
D8 1 Beechwood 2 Carbarns West 3 Clydesdale Av 4 Kirkhill St 5 Maplewood 6 Stenton Pl
E7 1 Netherhall Rd
E8 1 Curran Av 2 Gigha Quadrant 3 Islay Quadrant 4 Jura Quadrant 5 Oakbank Av 6 Park Quadrant 7 Rosehall Ter 8 St Margaret's Dr 9 Scarba Quadrant
F5 1 Grampian Rd 2 Wishawhill St
F6 1 Dundyvan La
1 grid square represents 500 metres

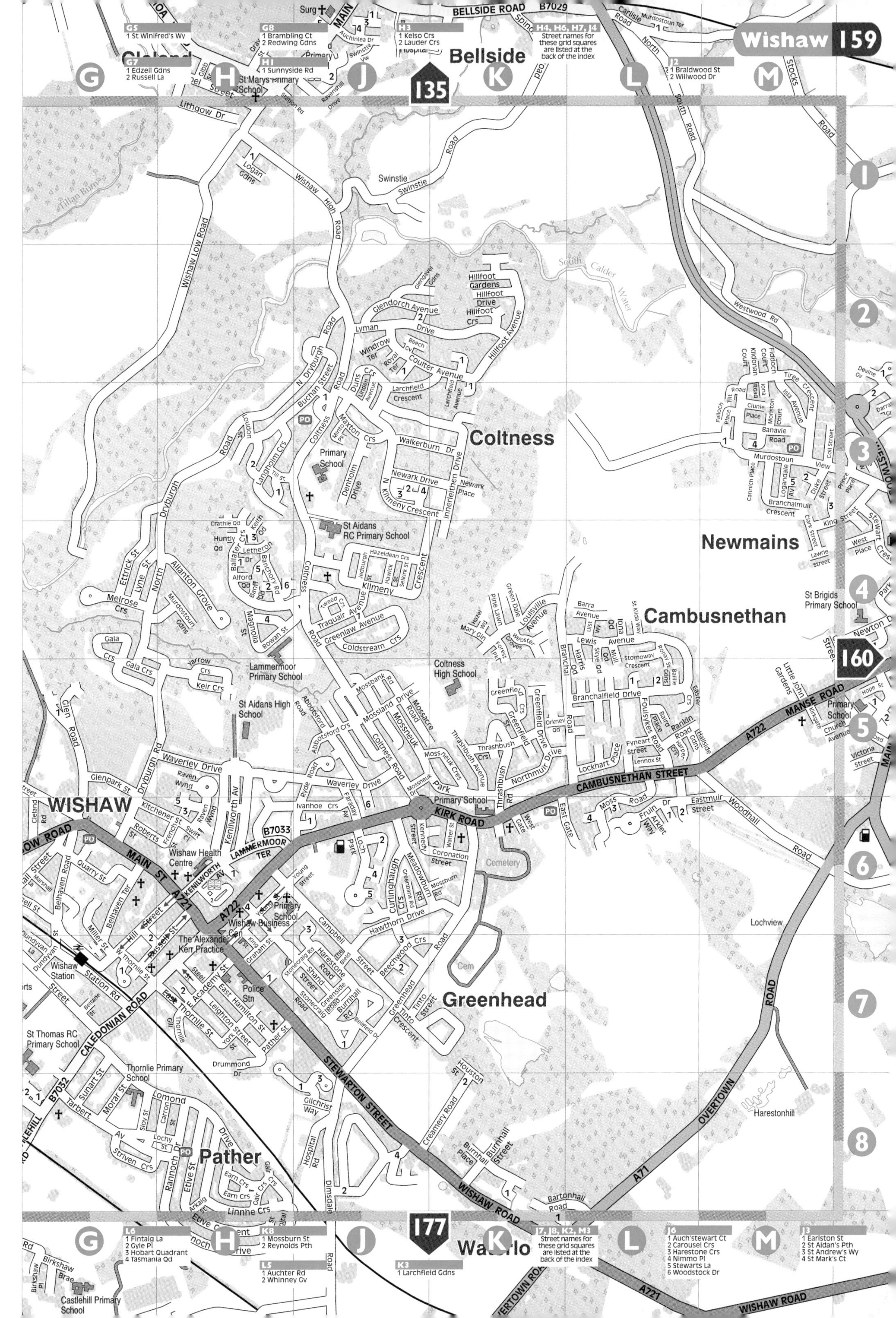
G5 1 St Winifred's Wy
G7 1 Edzell Gdns 2 Russell La
G8 1 Brambling Ct 2 Redwing Gdns
H1 1 Sunnyside Rd
H3 1 Kelso Crs 2 Lauder Crs
H4, H6, H7, J4 Street names for these grid squares are listed at the back of the index
J2 1 Braidwood St 2 Willwood Dr
135
Bellside
BELLSIDE ROAD B7029
Coltness
Newmains
Cambusnethan
WISHAW
Greenhead
Pather
Swinstie
Lochview
Harestonhill
South Calder Water
St Aidans RC Primary School
Coltness High School
Lammermoor Primary School
St Aidans High School
St Brigids Primary School
Wishaw Health Centre
Wishaw Station
Wishaw Business Cen
The Alexander Kerr Practice
Police Stn
St Thomas RC Primary School
Thornlie Primary School
Castlehill Primary School
Cemetery
CAMBUSNETHAN STREET
MANSE ROAD
KIRK ROAD
MAIN ST
STEWARTON STREET
WISHAW ROAD
CALEDONIAN ROAD
OVERTOWN ROAD
Wishaw Low Road
Wishaw High Road
Dryburgh Road
Coltness Road
Waverley Drive
Kilmeny Crescent
Hillfoot Avenue
Branchalfield Drive
A721
A722
A71
B7033
B7032
160
177
G6 1 Fintaig La 2 Cyle Pl 3 Hobart Quadrant 4 Tasmania Qd
K8 1 Mossburn St 2 Reynolds Pth
L5 1 Auchter Rd 2 Whinney Gv
K3 1 Larchfield Gdns
J7, J8, K2, M3 Street names for these grid squares are listed at the back of the index
J6 1 Auch'stewart Ct 2 Carousel Crs 3 Harestone Crs 4 Nimmo Pl 5 Stewarts La 6 Woodstock Dr
J3 1 Earlston St 2 St Aidan's Pth 3 St Andrew's Wy 4 St Mark's Ct
Waterloo

A5
1 Brown St
2 Parkview Crs
A4
1 Tollpark Crs
A3
1 Bailliesmuir Pl
2 Mccarrison Rd
3 Robert Wynd
A2
1 Aitken Cl
A
B
C
136
D
E
F
Allan
Castlerigg Pl
Stocks Road
Mill
Calder Rd
1
Coltness
Place
Allanbank Street
Wilso
Allanton Road
Mill Road
1
2
3
4
5
6
7
8
Murdostoun Castle
Devine Gv
Murray Crs
McMahon Drive
Darragh Gn
Tiree Crescent
Isla Avenue
Calder Av
Kilmichael Avenue
Coll Street
Castle Vw
View
Logandale Av
Duke Street
Prince Place
Inchalmuir Crescent
King Street
Clark Street
Stewart Crescent
West Place
Lawrie Street
Westwood Road
Northwood Dr
Eastwood Drive
Abernethyn Road
Bonds Drive
Woodside Crescent
Firtree Road
Firtree Place
Alcath Road
Bonkle
Bonkle Road
Meadowfield Place
Church Road
Cairney Pl
Brownhill View
Hawthorn Avenue
Mavisbank Street
Auchter Av
Braedale Crs
Muirhouse Avenue
Crindledyke Crescent
Bonkle Gdns
Crindledyke
A71
A73
Cathburn
St Brigids Primary School
Park Dr
Newton Drive
Manse Road Medical Centre
Blairlie
Little John Gardens
159
PO
Manse Road
Lanarkshire Health Board
Hope St
Primary School
Church Avenue
School Road
Victoria Street
Main Street
Morningside Road
Cathburn Road
Mill Road
Morningside Primary School
School Road
Torbush
Morningside
Morningside Road
Watsonfoot
Watsonmids
ML2
Main Street
Chapel Road
Chapel
Watsonhead
B4
1 Goddard Pl
2 Young Pl
C3
1 Lynnwood Rd
178
C4
1 Braedale Pl
F1
1 Auchterburn Rd
Bogside
Hyndshaw
1 grid square represents 500 metres

137
G
H
J
K
L
M
Kepplehill Farm
bank
A71
PO
Allanton Primary School
Dura Road
Redmire Crescent
Darmeid Place
Hartfield Terrace
Avenue
Springhead Road
Kingshill Rd
Houldsworth Crs
Allanton
Hartfield
Netherhall
Dura Road
Kirkhall
Daviesdykes
Dura
Brow
Dura Road
Auchterhead Farm
Summerside
Auchter Water
North Lanarkshire
South Lanarkshire
Kingshill Plantation
1
2
3
4
5
6
7
8
179

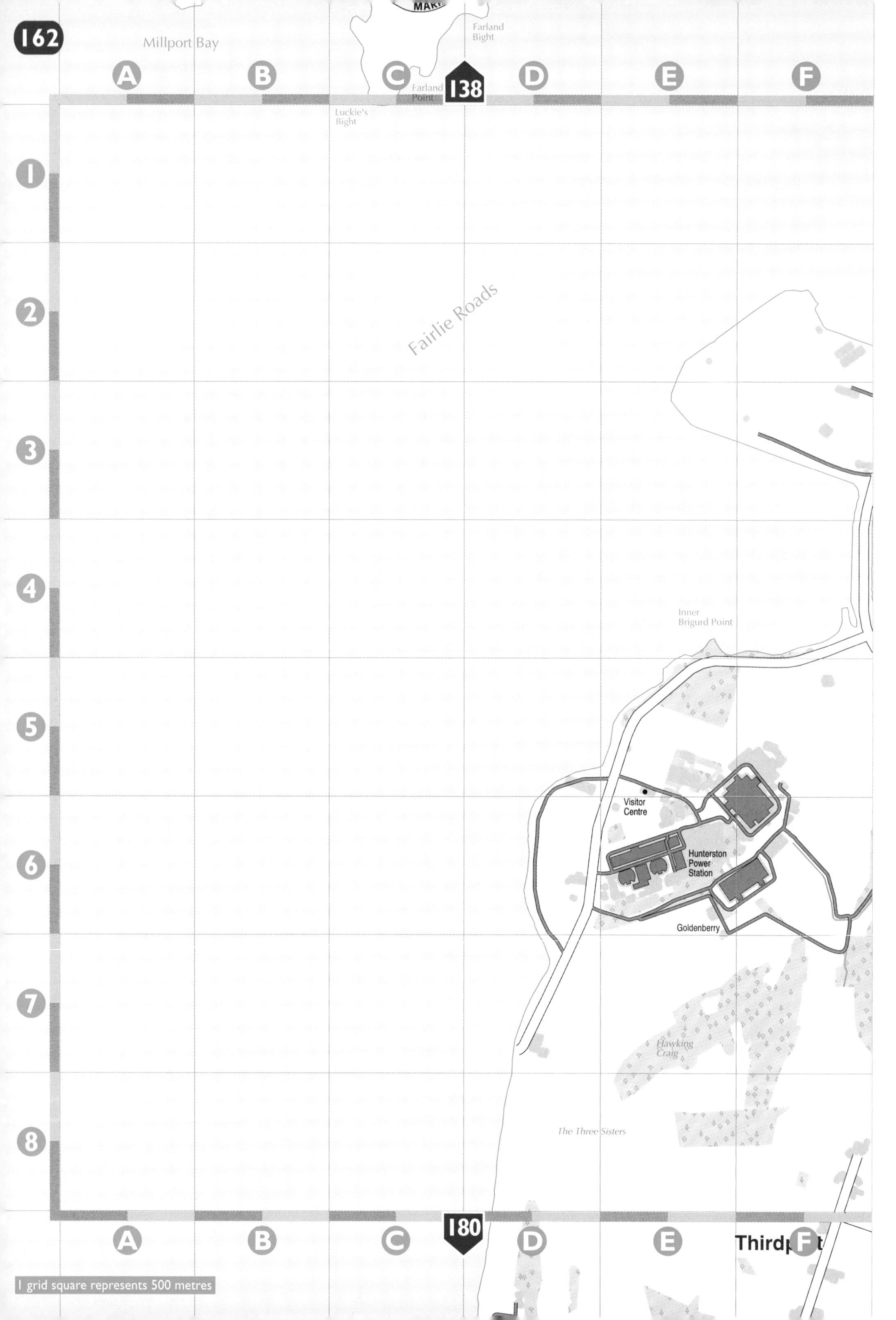
Millport Bay
Farland Bight
Farland Point
138
Luckie's Bight
Fairlie Roads
Inner Brigurd Point
Visitor Centre
Hunterston Power Station
Goldenberry
Hawking Craig
The Three Sisters
180
Thirdp
A
B
C
D
E
F
1
2
3
4
5
6
7
8
1 grid square represents 500 metres

G
H
J
K
L
M
139
181
164
1
2
3
4
5
6
7
8
Miller Av
Semple Crs
Southannan
Southannan Mains
Glenside
LC
The Glen
Glen Burn
Largs Avenue
Largs Av
Biglies Fm
Hunterston House
Hunterston Castle
A78(T)
Burn Gill
Campbelton
North Kilrusken
South Kilrusken
Dykes Plantation
Crosbie Reservoir
Millstonford
Bushglen
Avenue
Stairlie

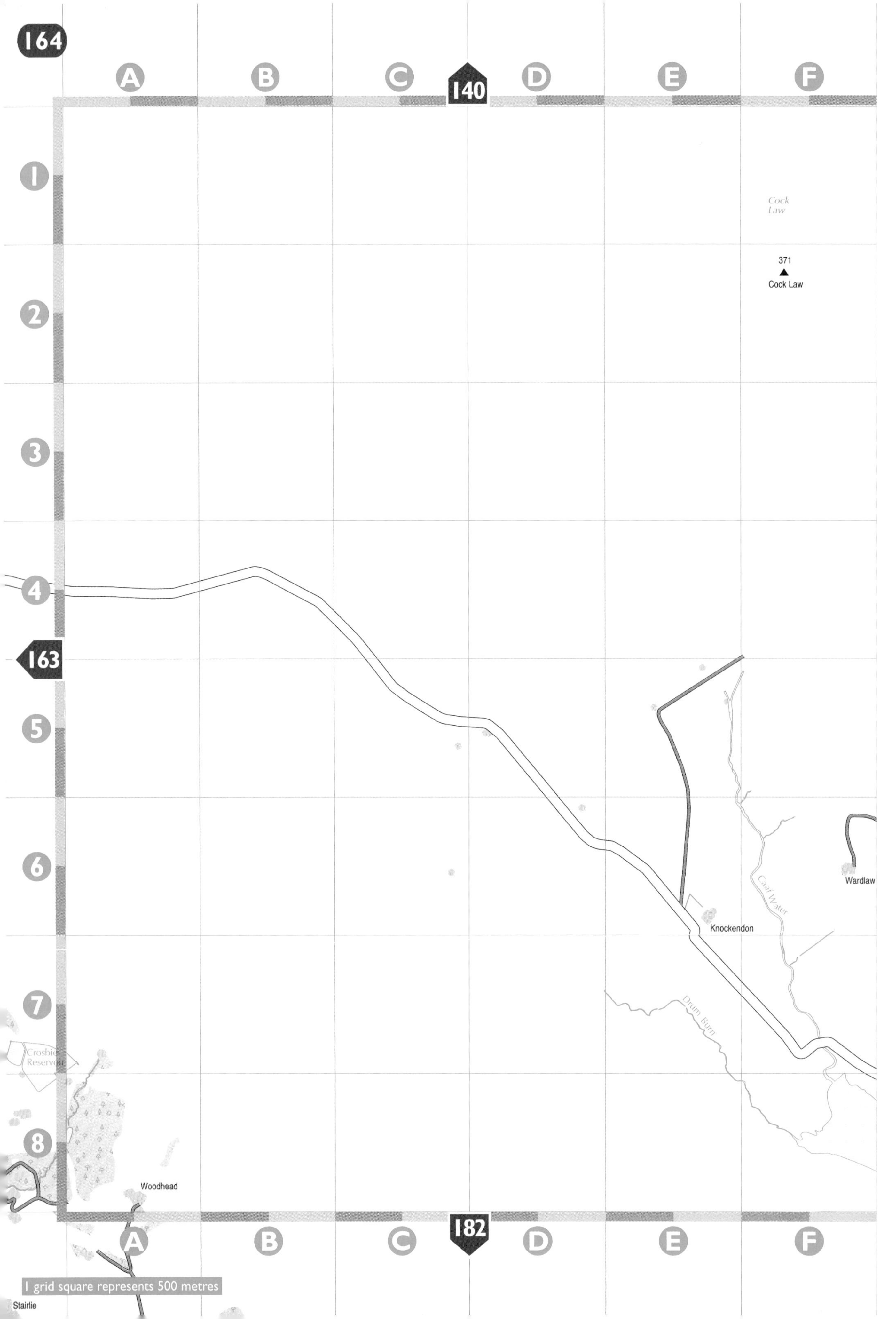
A
B
C
140
D
E
F
1
2
3
4
163
5
6
7
8
Cock Law
371
Cock Law
Wardlaw
Caaf Water
Knockendon
Drum Burn
Crosbie Reservoir
Woodhead
182
Stairlie

1 grid square represents 500 metres

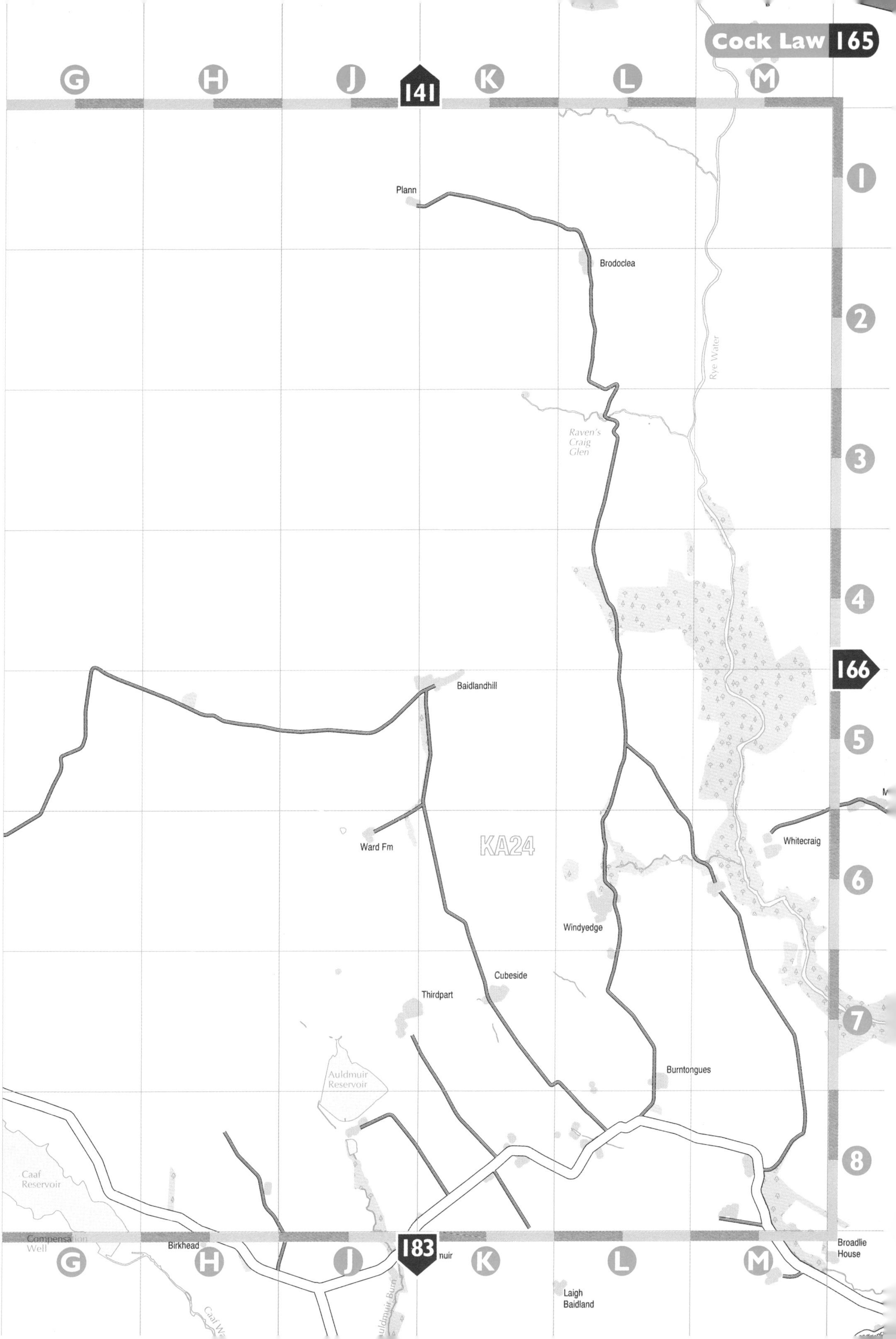
G
H
J
141
K
L
M
1
2
3
4
166
5
6
7
8
Plann
Brodoclea
Rye Water
Raven's
Craig
Glen
Baidlandhill
Ward Fm
KA24
Whitecraig
Windyedge
Cubeside
Thirdpart
Auldmuir
Reservoir
Burntongues
Caaf
Reservoir
Compensation
Well
Birkhead
183
Broadlie
House
Laigh
Baidland

B784
ROAD
A760
Golf Club
Farm of Place
C8
1 Ryeside Pl
Connel
142
A
B
C
D
E
F
Balgray
Pitcon Burn
South
Hourat
Newhouse Drive
Boag
Boagside
Farm
1
2
3
4
5
6
7
8
Swinlees
Mains
Thornyside
Burn
Langside
Tennox
Dykes
B780
Mossend
165
Newside
Gowanlea
Meiklemyre
Whitecraig
Lintseedridge
Farm
Hawhill
Pitcon
Mains
Mains Burn
Hindog
River Garnock
Kersland
Pitcon
Highfield
Ryefield
House
Drakemyre
Netherlee
Crs
Braehead Pl
184
Broadlie
House
Templand Rd
NORTH
BRAEHEAD
STREET
B780
BEITH ROAD
A737
St Palladius
Terrace
Nater
DALRY
Cemetery
1 grid square represents 500 metres

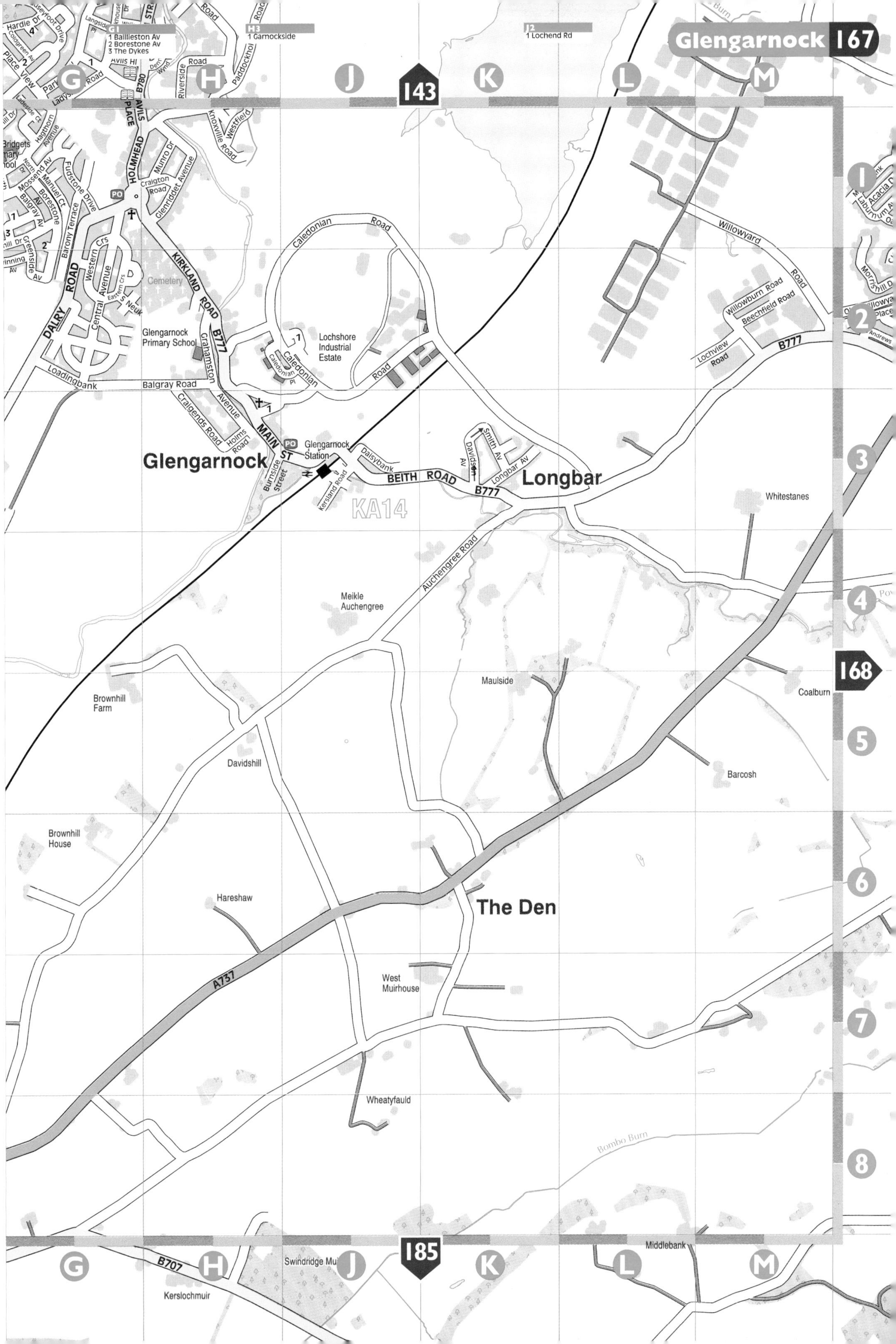
G1
1 Baillieston Av
2 Borestone Av
3 The Dykes
H3
1 Garnockside
J2
1 Lochend Rd
143
185
168
G
H
J
K
L
M
1
2
3
4
5
6
7
8
Glengarnock
Longbar
The Den
KA14
Cemetery
Glengarnock Primary School
Lochshore Industrial Estate
Glengarnock Station
Caledonian Road
Caledonian Pl
KIRKLAND ROAD
B777
B780
HOLMHEAD
AVILS PLACE
MAIN ST
BEITH ROAD
DALRY ROAD
Balgray Road
Loadingbank
Grahamston Avenue
Craigends Road
Holms Road
Burnside Street
Kersland Road
Daisybank
Davidson Av
Smith Av
Longbar Av
Knoxville Road
Westfield
Riverside Road
Paddockhol
Munro Dr
Craigton Road
Glenriddet Avenue
Fudstone Drive
Barony Terrace
Western Crs
Central Avenue
Eastern Crs
Neuk
Haghorn Avenue
Mossend Av
North Manuel Ct
Borestone
Balgray Av
Greenside Av
Ladeside Ct
Hardie Dr
Willowyard Road
Willowburn Road
Beechfield Road
Lochview Road
Auchengree Road
Meikle Auchengree
Whitestanes
Maulside
Coalburn
Brownhill Farm
Davidshill
Barcosh
Brownhill House
Hareshaw
West Muirhouse
Wheatyfauld
A737
Bombo Burn
B707
Kerslochmuir
Middlebank
PO
Acacia
Laburnum
Morrishill Dr
Willowyard Place
Andrews

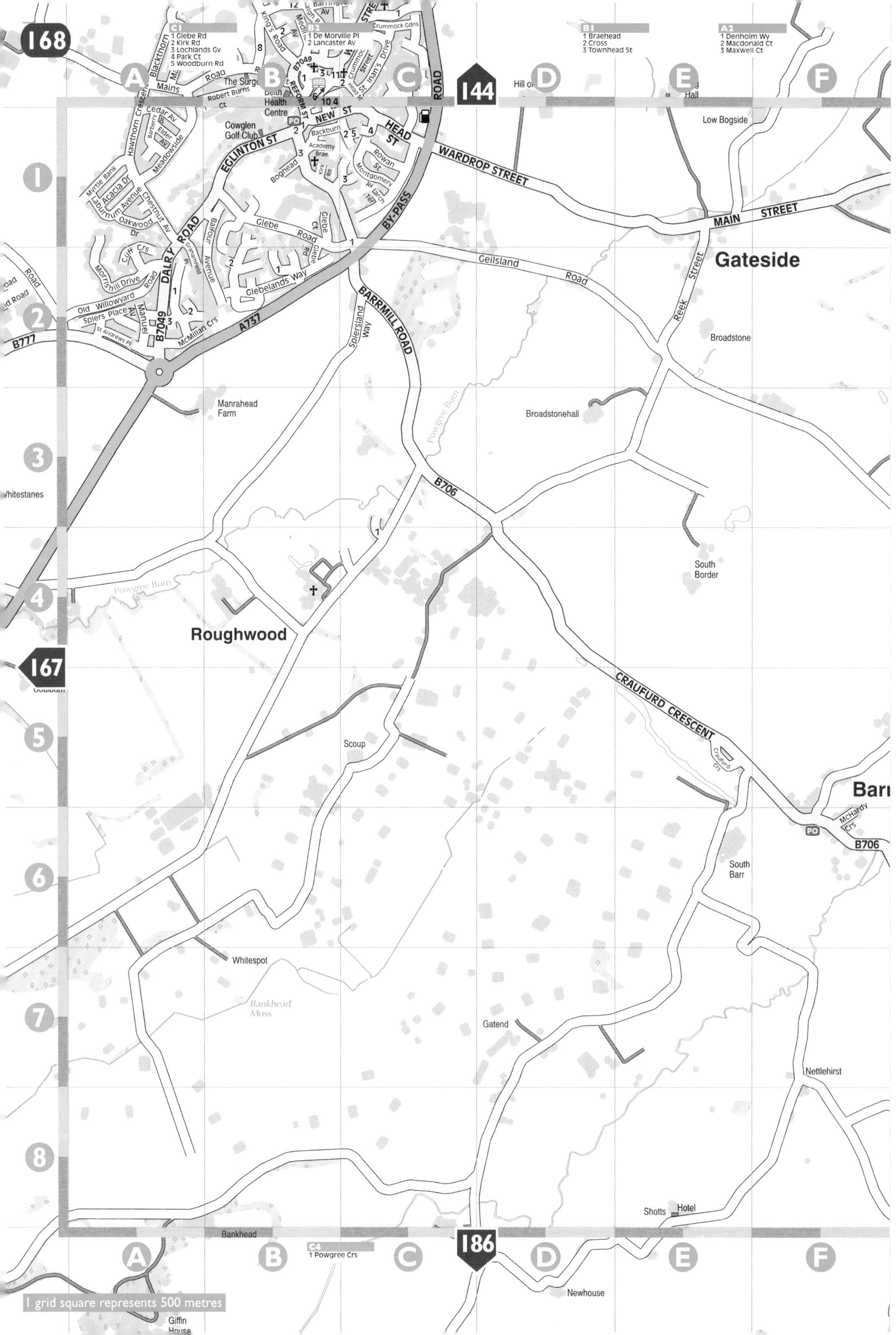
168
C1
1 Glebe Rd
2 Kirk Rd
3 Lochlands Gv
4 Park Ct
5 Woodburn Rd
B2
1 De Morville Pl
2 Lancaster Av
B1
1 Braehead
2 Cross
3 Townhead St
A2
1 Denholm Wy
2 Macdonald Ct
3 Maxwell Ct
144
Hill of
Hall
Low Bogside
Cowglen Golf Club
Health Centre
The Surgery
Robert Burns Ct
Mains Road
Blackthorn
Hawthorn Crescent
Cedar Av
Barberry
Elder Av
Meadowside
Myrtle Bank
Acacia Dr
Laburnum Avenue
Chestnut Av
Oakwood Dr
Cuff Crs
Morrishill Drive
Old Willowyard Road
Spiers Place
St Andrews Pl
Manuel Av
McMillan Crs
DALRY ROAD
Granamfield Pl
Balfour Avenue
Glebe Road
Glebe Ct
Glebe Rd
Clebelands Way
EGLINTON ST
REFORM ST
NEW ST
HEAD ST
Backburn
Academy Brae
Boghead
Kirk Rd
Rowan St
Montgomery Av
Larch Ter
Crummock Street
Crummock Gdns
St Inan's Drive
King's Road
BY-PASS ROAD
WARDROP STREET
MAIN STREET
Gateside
Geilsland Road
Reek Street
Broadstone
Broadstonehall
B7049
B777
A737
BARRMILL ROAD
Spiersland Way
Manrahead Farm
Powgree Burn
B706
Whitestanes
Roughwood
South Border
167
CRAUFURD CRESCENT
Craufurd Crs
Scoup
Barr
McHardy Crs
B706
South Barr
Whitespot
Bankhead Moss
Gatend
Nettlehirst
Shotts
Hotel
Bankhead
186
C4
1 Powgree Crs
Newhouse
Giffin House
A B C D E F
1 2 3 4 5 6 7 8
1 grid square represents 500 metres

G
H
J
145
K
L
M
Shutt
Lyonshield
Overton
B777
Over
Hessilhead
B777
Blaelochhead
Blae
Loch
Dusk Water
Hessilhead
Gatehead Farm
KA15
Tandleview
Middleton
Balgray Road
Highgate
Highgate
rmill
DUNLOP ROAD
Brownhills
A736
Gree
Greenhills
Nether
Gree
Lugton Water
BARRMILL
ROAD
Foreside
Burnhouse
North Ayrshire
East Ayrshire
Oldhall
South
Nettlehirst
187
Nether
Oldhall
B706
Oldhall
Murray Farm
1
2
3
4
5
6
7
8

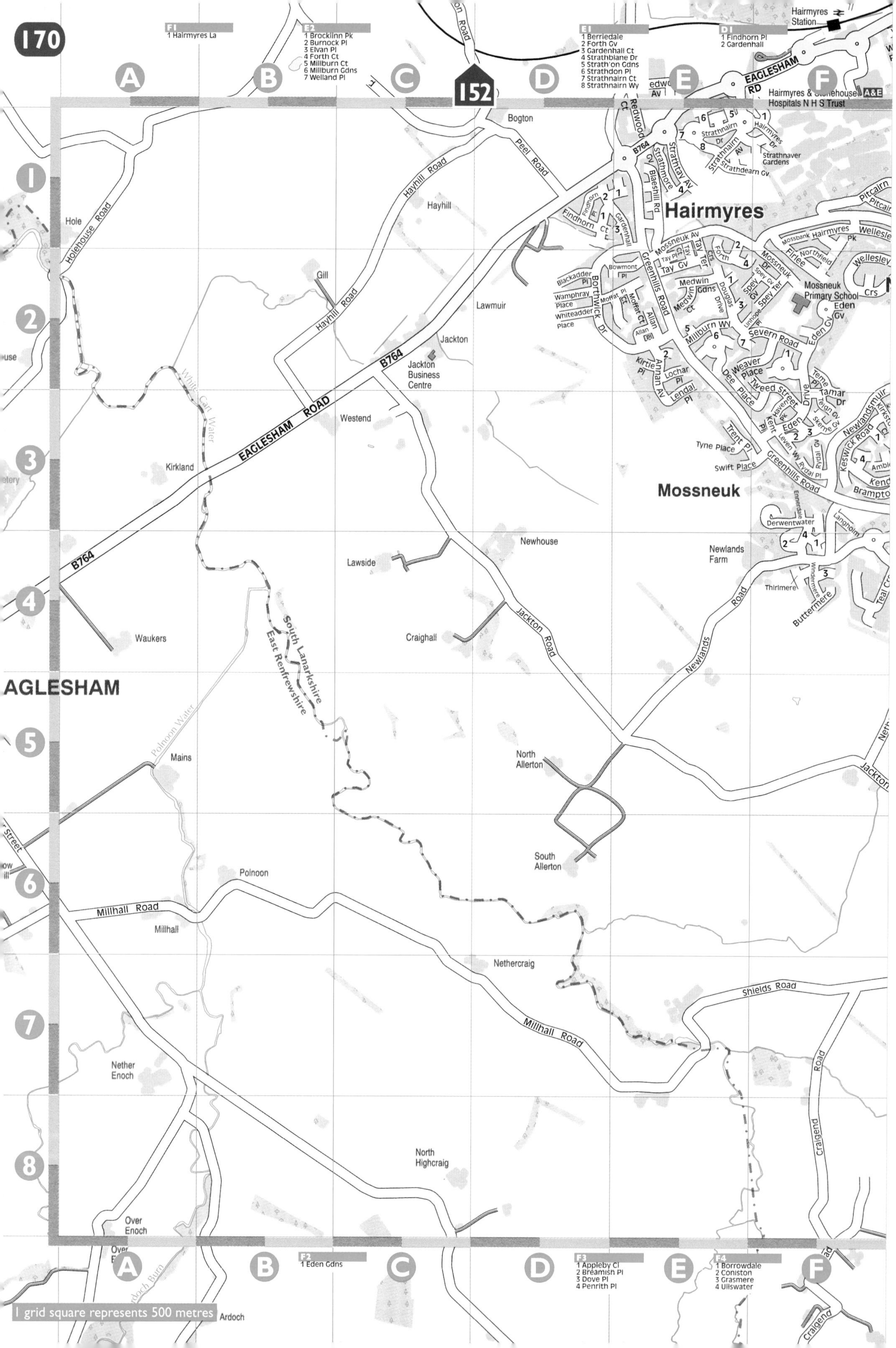
F1
1 Hairmyres La
E2
1 Brocklinn Pk
2 Burnock Pl
3 Elvan Pl
4 Forth Ct
5 Millburn Ct
6 Millburn Gdns
7 Welland Pl
E1
1 Berriedale
2 Forth Gv
3 Gardenhall Ct
4 Strathblane Dr
5 Strath'on Gdns
6 Strathdon Pl
7 Strathnairn Ct
8 Strathnairn Wy
D1
1 Findhorn Pl
2 Gardenhall
Hairmyres Station
152
A
B
C
D
E
F
1
2
3
4
5
6
7
8
EAGLESHAM RD
Hairmyres & Stonehouse Hospitals N H S Trust
A&E
Bogton
Peel Road
Hayhill Road
Hayhill
Hole
Holehouse Road
Gill
Lawmuir
Jackton
Jackton Business Centre
B764
EAGLESHAM ROAD
Westend
Kirkland
White Cart Water
Hairmyres
Mossneuk Av
Greenhills Road
Mossneuk Primary School
Severn Road
Weaver Place
Tweed Street
Dee Place
Lochar Pl
Lendal Pl
Trent Pl
Tyne Place
Swift Place
Greenhills Road
Mossneuk
Derwentwater
Newlands Farm
Thirlmere
Buttermere
Newlands Road
Newhouse
Lawside
Craighall
Jackton Road
Waukers
AGLESHAM
South Lanarkshire
East Renfrewshire
Polnoon Water
Mains
North Allerton
South Allerton
Polnoon
Millhall Road
Millhall
Nethercraig
Shields Road
Craigend Road
Nether Enoch
North Highcraig
Over Enoch
Ardoch
F2
1 Eden Gdns
F3
1 Appleby Cl
2 Breamish Pl
3 Dove Pl
4 Penrith Pl
F4
1 Borrowdale
2 Coniston
3 Grasmere
4 Ullswater
1 grid square represents 500 metres

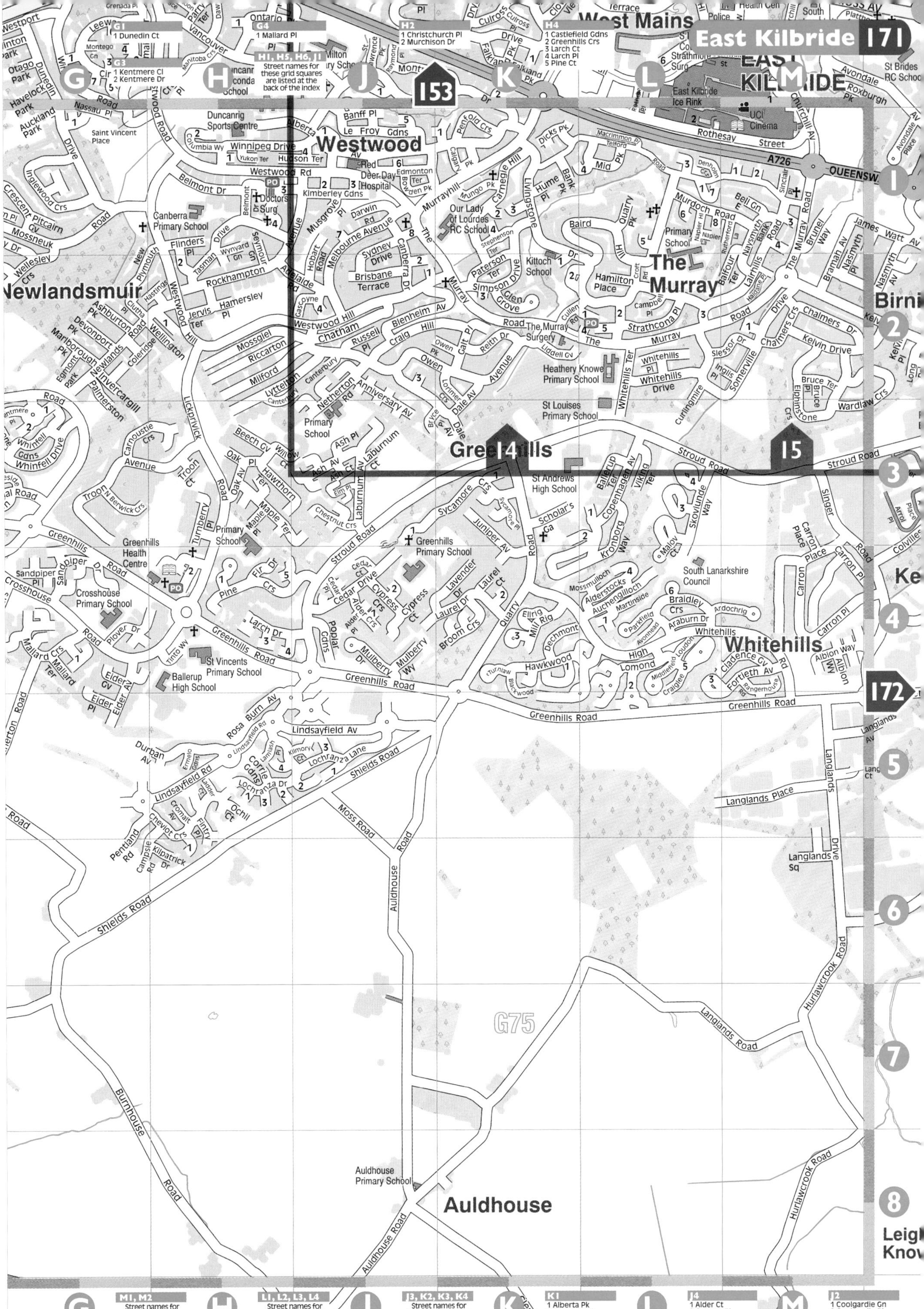

M1, M2
Street names for these grid squares are listed at the back of the index

L1, L2, L3, L4
Street names for these grid squares are listed at the back of the index

J3, K2, K3, K4
Street names for these grid squares are listed at the back of the index

K1
1 Alberta Pk
2 Carnegie Pl
3 Headhouse Ct
4 Stephenson Pl

J4
1 Alder Ct
2 Cypress Pl

J5
1 Bennan Pl
2 Merkland Wy
3 Penrioch Dr

J2
1 Coolgardie Gn
2 Coolgardie Pl
3 Macintosh Pl
4 Onslow

172
154
171
15
A
B
C
D
E
F
1
2
3
4
5
6
7
8
B2 1 Mt Cameron Dr S
B1 1 Loch Torridon 2 Mt Cameron Dr N
A2 1 The Boardwalk
A1 1 Nelson Ter 2 Tullialian Pl
St Brides RC School
Saint Leonards
Claremont High School
Sanderson High School
St Hilarys RC Primary School
Mount Cameron Primary School
Newhousemill
Newhousemill Road
Calderside Road
Birniehill
Edge Farm
Calderglen Country Park
East Kilbride Sports Club
Golf Course
Pro Lane Bowl
South Lanarkshire Council
Kelvin
STRATHAVEN ROAD
A726
A725
Rotten Burn
Crutherland Farm
Hotel
Calder Water
Hurlawcrook Farm
Greenhills Road
Quarry Farm
Leigh Knoweglass
1 grid square represents 500 metres

155
174
G
H
J
K
L
M
1
2
3
4
5
6
7
8
Newhousemill Road
Muttonhole Rd
Wellbrae Reservoir
Highstonehall Road
Highstonehall Rd
Brora Crs
Meikle Earnock Road
Muttonhole Road
Earnockmuir Farm
Kilwinning Crs
Torranyard Ter
A726

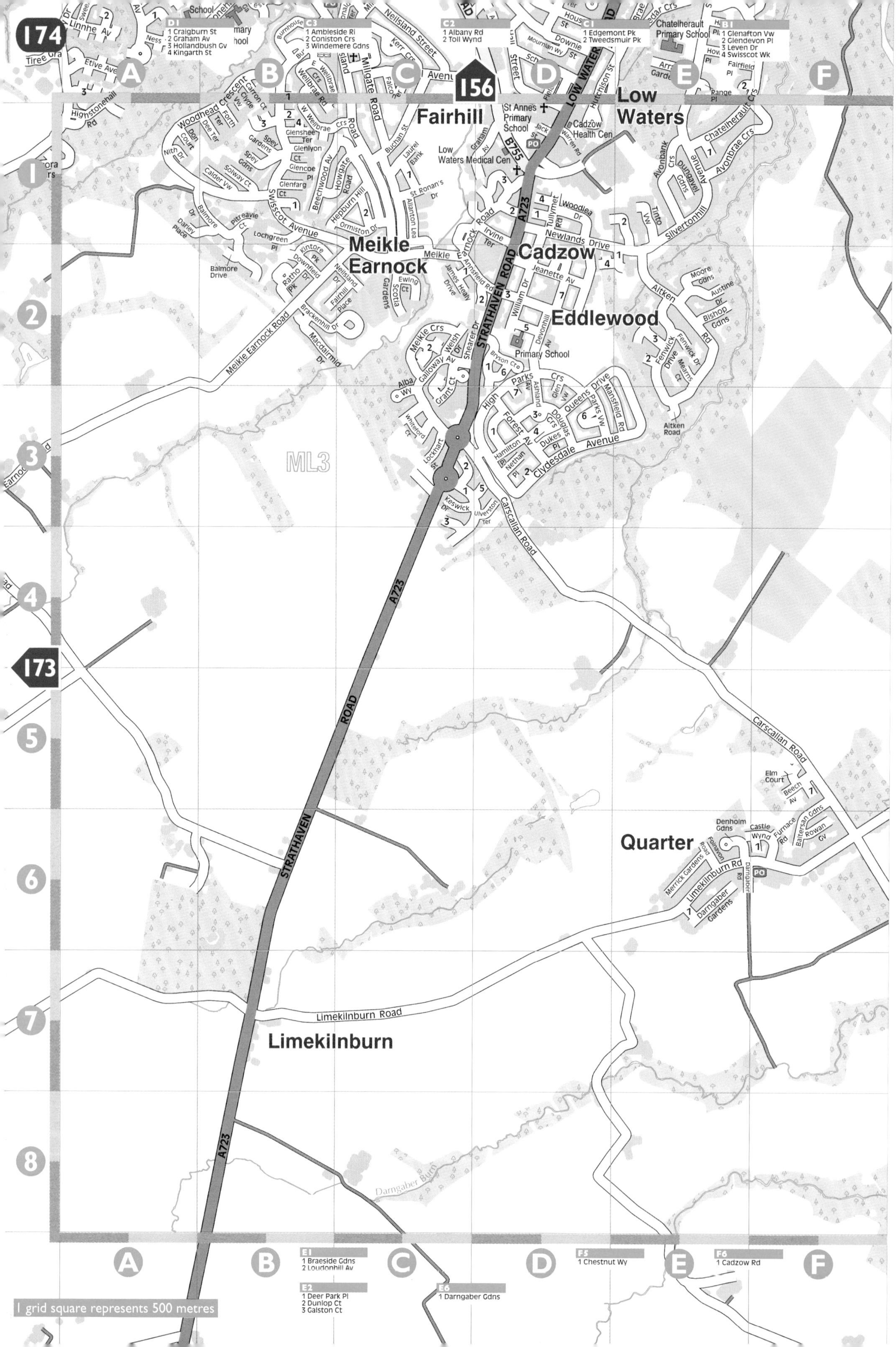
D1
1 Craigburn St
2 Graham Av
3 Hollandbush Gv
4 Kingarth St
C3
1 Ambleside Ri
2 Coniston Crs
3 Windemere Gdns
C2
1 Albany Rd
2 Toil Wynd
C1
1 Edgemont Pk
2 Tweedsmuir Pk
B1
1 Glenafton Vw
2 Glendevon Pl
3 Leven Dr
4 Swisscot Wk
156
173
Fairhill
Low Waters
Meikle Earnock
Cadzow
Eddlewood
Quarter
Limekilnburn
ML3
Chatelherault Primary School
St Annes Primary School
Cadzow Health Cen
Low Waters Medical Cen
Primary School
Low Water Road
Strathaven Road
A723
B755
Meikle Earnock Road
Swisscot Avenue
Woodhead Crescent
Milligate Road
Neilsland Street
Newlands Drive
Clydesdale Avenue
Queens Drive
Mansfield Rd
Carscallan Road
Limekilnburn Road
Limekilnburn Rd
Darngaber Burn
Darngaber Gardens
Merrick Gardens
Denholm Gdns
Castle Wynd
Furnace Rd
Baltersan Gdns
Rowan Gv
Elm Court
Beech Av
Aitken Road
Chatelherault Crs
Avonbrae Crs
Silvertonhill Avenue
Balmore Drive
Darley Place
Lochgreen Pl
Highstonehall Rd
Tiree Gra
Etive Ave
Linnhe Av
E1
1 Braeside Gdns
2 Loudonhill Av
E2
1 Deer Park Pl
2 Dunlop Ct
3 Galston Ct
E6
1 Darngaber Gdns
F5
1 Chestnut Wy
F6
1 Cadzow Rd
1 grid square represents 500 metres

L7
1 Braehead Av
M4
1 Lammermuir Wynd
2 Linnhe Ct
M5
1 High Avon St
2 Sunnyside St
Allanton
Castlehill Crescent
157
176
Chatelherault Visitor Centre
Golf Course
Chatelherault Country Park
Avon Water
CARLISLE ROAD
A72
LANARK ROAD
Merryton Road
B7078
HAMILTON RD
Pentland Crs
Fairholm St
Beaton St
GLENVIEW
LONDON STREET
South Lanarkshire Council
Ian Kenny Gallery
Strathclyde Regional Council
Empire Thtr
Sunnyside Road
Wee Sunnyside Road
Carscallan Road
Broomelton Road
Millheugh Road
Millheugh
Avonbank Rd
Watson Street
Avon Street
Raploch St
Macneil
Croft Rd
Croft Pl
Cherryhill View
Broomhill Vw
Primary School
LARKHALL
Larkhall Leisure Centre & Baths
Robert Smillie Memorial Primary School
Whinnie Knowe
Ferndale
Plotcock Road
M6
1 Mossblown St
2 Tarbolton Pth
3 Tribboch St

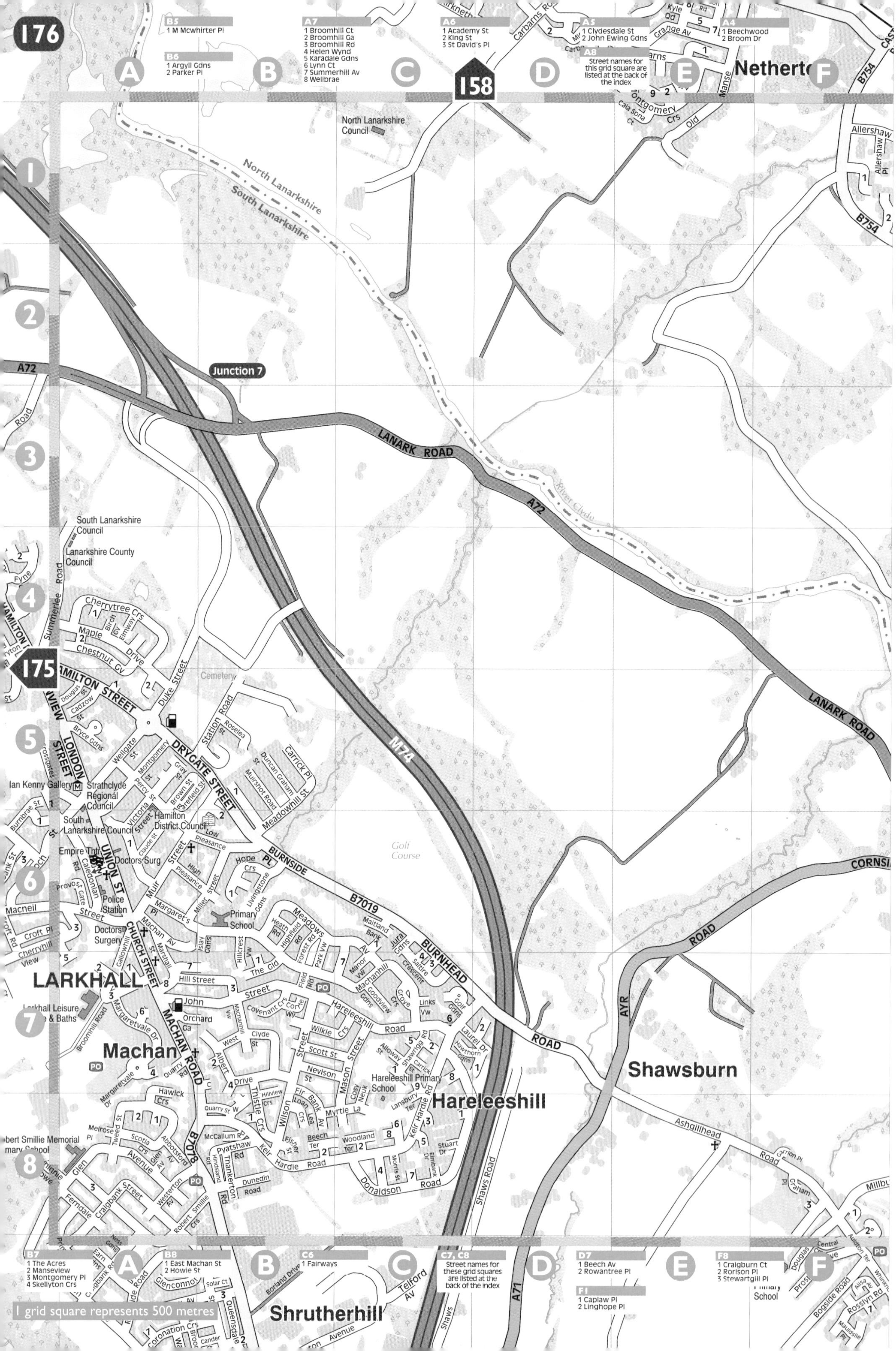
B5
1 M Mcwhirter Pl
B6
1 Argyll Gdns
2 Parker Pl
A7
1 Broomhill Ct
2 Broomhill Ga
3 Broomhill Rd
4 Helen Wynd
5 Karadale Gdns
6 Lynn Ct
7 Summerhill Av
8 Wellbrae
A6
1 Academy St
2 King St
3 St David's Pl
A5
1 Clydesdale St
2 John Ewing Gdns
A8
Street names for this grid square are listed at the back of the index
A4
1 Beechwood
2 Broom Dr
158
Netherton
B754
North Lanarkshire Council
North Lanarkshire
South Lanarkshire
A72
Junction 7
LANARK ROAD
River Clyde
South Lanarkshire Council
Lanarkshire County Council
175
Cemetery
M74
Golf Course
Strathclyde Regional Council
South Lanarkshire Council
Hamilton District Council
Empire Thtr
Doctors Surg
Police Station
Primary School
Doctors Surgery
B7019
BURNSIDE
BURNHEAD
CORNSILLOCH
AYR ROAD
LARKHALL
Larkhall Leisure Centre & Baths
Machan
MACHAN ROAD
Hareleeshill
Hareleeshill Primary School
Shawsburn
Shaws Road
Ashgillhead Road
B7078
A71
B7
1 The Acres
2 Manseview
3 Montgomery Pl
4 Skellyton Crs
B8
1 East Machan St
2 Howie St
C6
1 Fairways
C7, C8
Street names for these grid squares are listed at the back of the index
D7
1 Beech Av
2 Rowantree Pl
F1
1 Caplaw Pl
2 Linghope Pl
F8
1 Craigburn Ct
2 Rorison Pl
3 Stewartgill Pl
Shrutherhill
1 grid square represents 500 metres

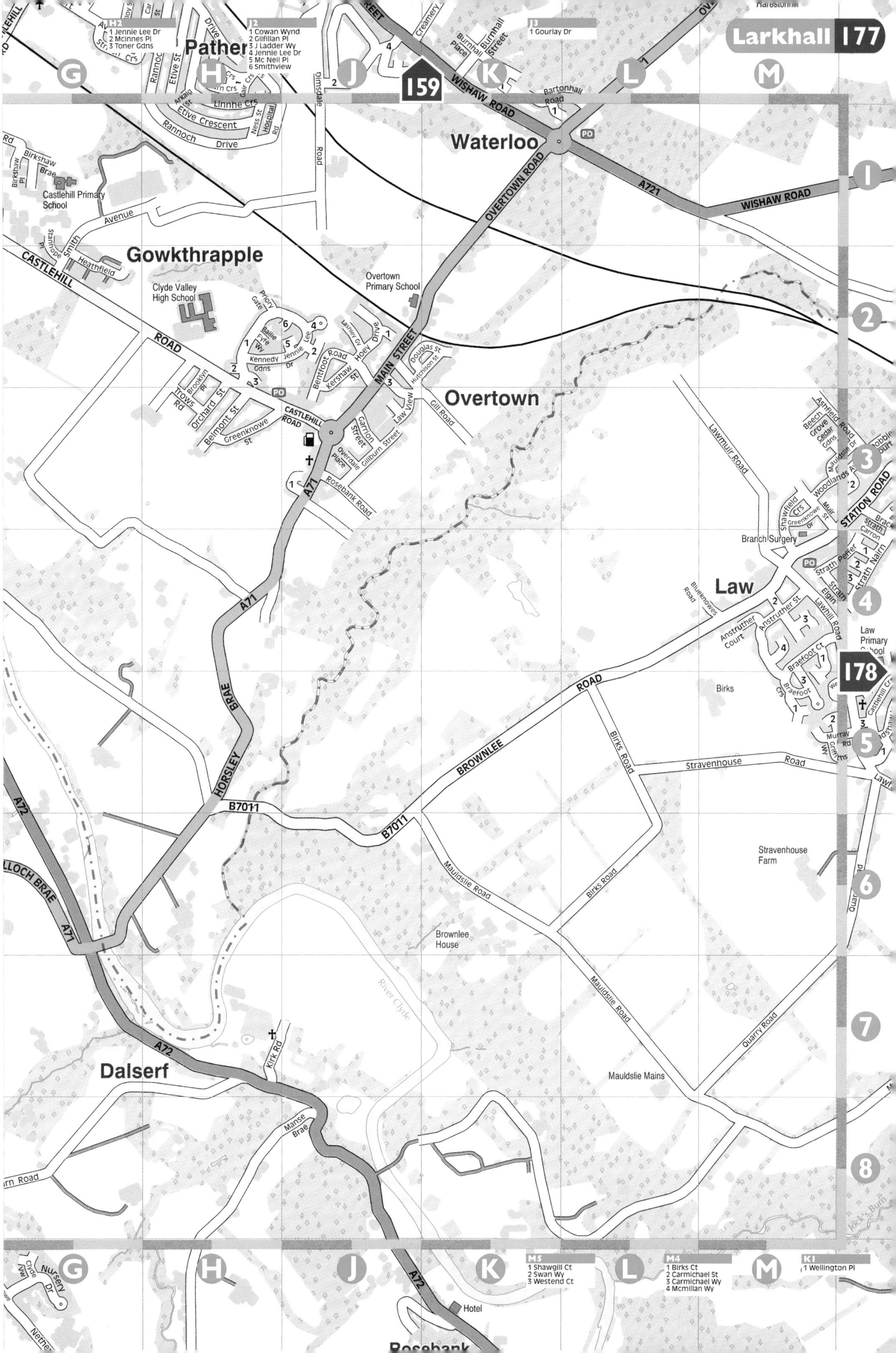
H2
1 Jennie Lee Dr
2 McInnes Pl
3 Toner Gdns
J2
1 Cowan Wynd
2 Gilfillan Pl
3 J Ladder Wy
4 Jennie Lee Dr
5 Mc Neil Pl
6 Smithview
J3
1 Gourlay Dr
159
178
G
H
J
K
L
M
1
2
3
4
5
6
7
8
Waterloo
Gowkthrapple
Overtown
Law
Dalserf
Rosebank
Birkshaw Brae
Birkshaw Pl
Castlehill Primary School
Avenue
Smith
Stanhope Pl
Heathfield
CASTLEHILL ROAD
Clyde Valley High School
Rannoch Drive
Etive Crescent
Linnhe Crs
Arkaig St
Ness St
Hospital Rd
Gair Crs
Etive St
Dimsdale Road
Creamery
Burnhall Place
Burnhall Street
WISHAW ROAD
Bartonhall Road
PO
A721
OVERTOWN ROAD
Overtown Primary School
Priory Gate
Baillie Fyfe Wy
Kennedy Gdns
Jennie Lee Dr
Lashley Gv
Hoey Drive
Bentfoot Road
Kershaw St
MAIN STREET
Douglas St
Hutchison St
Brooklyn Pl
Trows Rd
Orchard St
Belmont St
Greenknowe St
CASTLEHILL ROAD
Garrion Street
Law View
Gillburn Street
Gill Road
Overdale Place
Rosebank Road
A71
HORSLEY BRAE
B7011
BROWNLEE ROAD
A72
A71
Lawmuir Road
Ashfield Road
Beech Grove
Cedar Gdns
Mauldslie Dr
Woodlands Av
STATION ROAD
Shawfield Crs
Greenknowe Dr
Muir St
Branch Surgery
Strath Peffer
Strath Nairn
Strath Carron
Strath Elgin
Lawhill Road
Blueknowes Road
Anstruther Court
Anstruther St
Law Primary School
Braefoot Ct
Braefoot Crs
Birks
Castlehill Cres
Murray Rd
Griffiths Wy
Birks Road
Stravenhouse Road
Stravenhouse Farm
Mauldslie Road
Birks Road
Brownlee House
River Clyde
Mauldslie Road
Quarry Road
Mauldslie Mains
Kirk Rd
Manse Brae
Burn Road
Jock's Burn
Nursery Dr
Clyde Vw
Hotel
M5
1 Shawgill Ct
2 Swan Wy
3 Westend Ct
M4
1 Birks Ct
2 Carmichael St
3 Carmichael Wy
4 Mcmillan Wy
K1
1 Wellington Pl

E5
1 Craignethan Rd
2 Threave Ct
D7
1 Gillbank Av
2 Gowanside Pl
3 Moss-side Av
4 Westerhouse Ct
A5
1 Kingshill Vw
2 Manse Ct
3 Waterlands Pl
A4
1 Strath Dearn
2 Strath Halladale
3 Strath Naver
A3
1 Buchanan Dr
2 Galbraith Crs
160
177
188
Hyndshaw Road
Bogside
Hyndshaw
Lanarkshire Health Board
Blood Transfusion Service
Wildmanbridge
Gillhead
WILDMAN ROAD
Garrion Burn
Waterlands
Waterlands Road
A73
Castlehill Road
Belstane Place
Station Place
Station Row
STATION ROAD
B7011
Dobbies Court
Patterson Drive
Brackenhill Rd
Brackenhill
Law Primary School
Blackhill View
Castlehill Crs
Hyndshaw View
Murray Rd
Law Hill
East Law
Lawhill Road
Whiteshaw Road
Quarry Road
AIRDRIE ROAD
Heather Row
Bothwell Road
STEWART STREET
Gasworks Road
Lawhill Road
Mauldslie Road
Hallcraig
Golf Club
Golf Course
Jock's Burn
CARLUKE
Carluke Station
South Lanarkshire Council
Police Station
Carluke Health Cen
Kirkton Primary School
CLAMIS AVENUE
CHAPEL ST
School
St Athan Primary
KIRKTON STREET
LANARK ROAD
Shieldhill Rd
Under Shieldhill
E6
Street names for this grid square are listed at the back of the index
E7
1 Melville Pl
2 Nursery Pk
3 School La
E8
1 Chestnut Gv
2 Fleming Ct
3 Kenilworth Ct
4 Kirkton Ct
F6
1 Park Circ
F7
1 Cairnhill Ct
2 Chapel St
3 Lockhart St
4 Market Pl
5 Needle Gn
6 Newlands Ter
7 Stewart Pl
8 Windsor Ct
9 Windsor Qd
F8
1 Arnum Pl
2 Burnbank Braes
3 Hamilton St
4 Old Bridgend
1 grid square represents 500 metres

G6
1 Stonedyke Crs
2 Waterlands Gdns
G7
1 High Mill Rd
2 King's Crs
G8
1 Brookbank Ter
2 Hillfoot Ter
3 Strathlachlan Av
North Lanarkshire
South Lanarkshire
161
Gair Reservoirs
King's Law
Bowridge
Gair
Bogside
Gair Road
Thorn
Under Thorn
Thornhome
Moss-side
Stonedyke Road
Carluke Primary School
Deeside Drive
Braemar Crs
Gair Crescent
Belstane
Hillhead
Moorside Street
Hope Street
Woodend Road
Queen's Crescent
Cairneymount Road
Stanistone Rd
Miller Street
Carluke High School
West Quarter
Yieldshields
YIELDSHIELDS ROAD
Equestrian Centre
Croftfoot
ML8
A721
KILNCADZOW ROAD
Blenheim Rd
Ramillies Court
Malplaquet Ct
Corunna Court
Glenafeoch
Parkandarroch Crescent
Road
Kelso Dr
Ramage Road
Caneluk Avenue
Charles Crescent
Wilton Road
Angus Road
Glencoe Rd
Crawforddyke Primary School
Forest Kirk
High Meadow
Birkfield Loan
Hillhouse Gate
Hayward Av
Northflat Pl
Roadmeetings Hospital
189
Burnhead Farm
Cemetery
Goremire Road
Kilmory Road
Eldersiea Road
Lanark Road
Glencoe Road
Wilton
Carradale
Roadmeetings
J8
1 Goremire Rd
2 High Meadow
3 Meadow Ct
H8
1 Cameronian Dr
2 Mandora Ct
3 Muirlee Rd
4 Oudenarde Ct

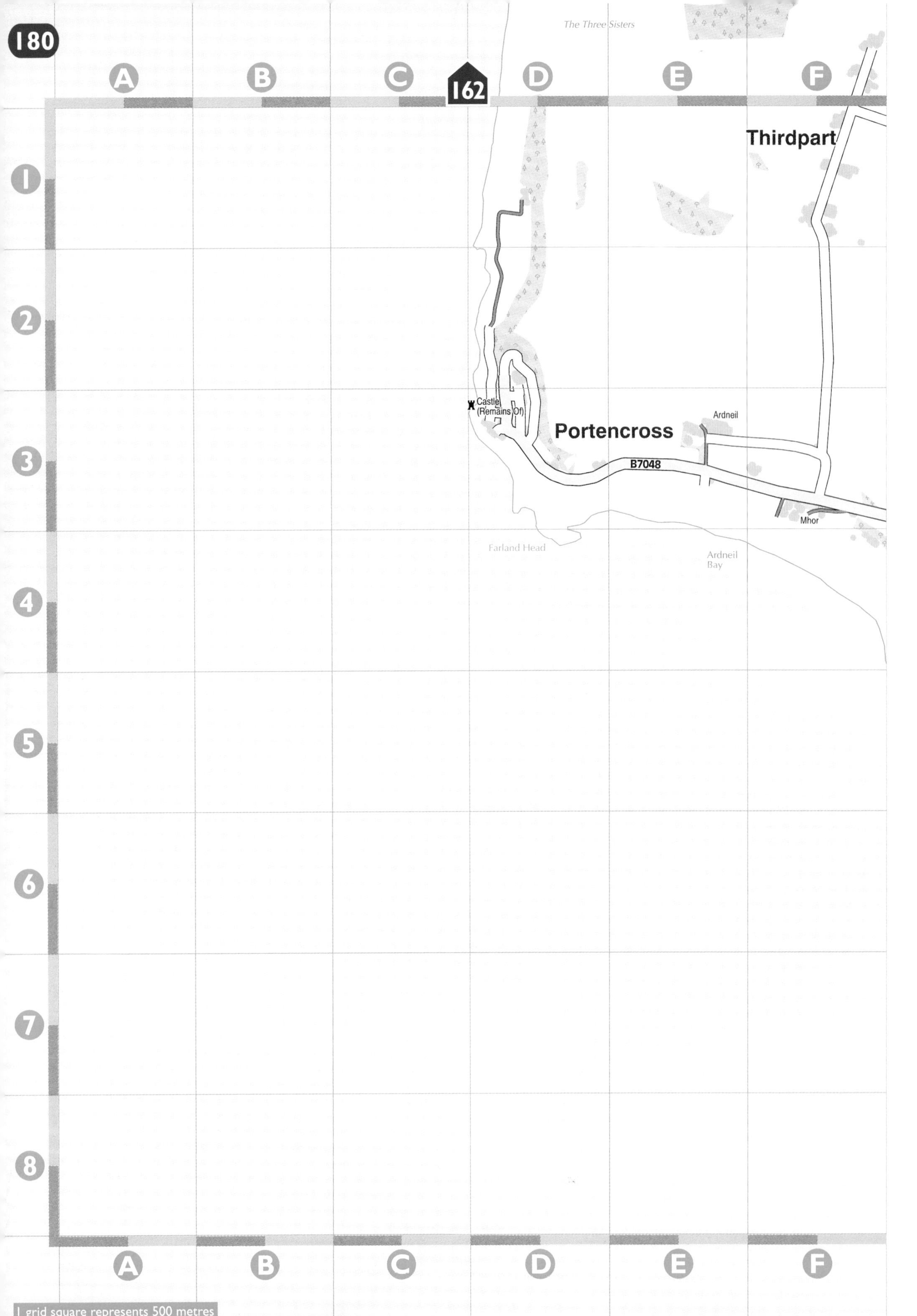
The Three Sisters
162
A
B
C
D
E
F
Thirdpart
1
2
3
4
5
6
7
8
Castle (Remains Of)
Portencross
Ardneil
B7048
Mhor
Farland Head
Ardneil Bay

1 grid square represents 500 metres

J4
1 Arthur Ct
2 Happyhills
3 Headrigg
J5
1 South Rd
K3
1 Drummilling Av
2 Drummilling Dr
163
190
182
G
H
J
K
L
M
1
2
3
4
5
6
7
8
Millstonford
Bushglen
Stairlie
Crosbie Burn
The Avenue
Carlung Farm
KA23
Carlung House
A78(T)
B782
Drummilling
Kilbride Burn
Lawoodhead
B781
Woodside
Cemetery
Underhill
Faulds Farm
Yonderfield
Blackshaw Dr
Avondale Rd
Drummilling Rd
Castle View
GATESIDE STREET
West Kilbride Station
St Bride's Road
CUBRIESHAW ST
HUNTERSTON RD
B7048
PORTENCROSS ROAD
Primary School
The Surgery
Corse St
Wellbank Gdns
Law Brae
Farmfield Ter
MAIN STREET
Halfway St
Arthur St
Glen Rd
Barony Glebe
Glenside Crs
Glenside Grove
Corsehill Dr
Jacks View
Well St
RITCHIE ST
The Gal
Orchard Street
Headrigg Rd
Overton Crs
Overton Dr
Overton Dr
Weston Ter
North Rd
Alton Street
MEADOWFOOT ROAD
Nethermiln Road
Castle Dr
Lawfield Av
Tarbert Av
Craufurd Av
Simson Avenue
Lawhill
Meadowfoot
Wildcat Rd
Summerlea Road
SNOWDON TERRACE
YERTON BRAE
B781
Merlewood Rd
Alknut Road
Bowfield Road
Bellard Rd
Goldenberry Av
Kirkton Av
B7047
Ardrossan High Road
Cubrieshaw Hall
West Kilbride Golf Club
Fullerton Drive
Maimhor Rd
SNOWDON TER
Caldwell Road
Hillside
Cumbrae Pl
Farlands Vw
Faith Road
WEST KILBRIDE
Kilruskin Drive
Woodside
Pantonville Road
Carlung Pl
Ardneil Av
Yonderton
Hyndman Rd
Sandy Ct
Sandy Road
ARDROSSAN ROAD
Glenbride Road
Chapelton La
SEAMILL
Gourock Water
Meadowhead
CHAPELTON ROAD
B7047
Chapelton
Kirkland Glen
South Inch
Glenhead
L5
1 Simson Av
L4
1 Highthorne Crs
K5
1 Crosbie Dr
2 Cubrieshaw Dr
3 Yonderton Pl
K4
1 Manse Rd
2 Meadowside
3 St Bride's Dr
4 Stairlie Crs

182
164
181
191
A
B
C
D
E
F
1
2
3
4
5
6
7
8
oodhead
Stairlie
B781
Blackshaw Farm
Ballees Farm
Gill
Munnoch Burn
Faulds Farm
Knockewart
Haupland Muir
Busbie Muir
erton
Gourock Water
B780
Coalhill
Busbie Muir Reservoir
Hauplands
Meikle Busbie
1 grid square represents 500 metres

Caaf Reservoir
Compensation Well
Birkhead
Auldmuir
Broadlie House
Laigh Baidland
Caaf Water
Auldmuir Burn
Greenhirst
Blackstone
Mosside
Giffordland
B780
Holms of Caaf
Dykehead
Munnoch
B781
Holmbyre
Munnoch Resrvoir
Tower
Caddell Burn
Bankhead
Meikle Ittington
Caddell
Yonderhouses
Girthill
Darleith
Muirlaught Farm
Kilwinning
Abbey Ruins
High Smith
165
184
192
G
H
J
K
L
M
1
2
3
4
5
6
7
8

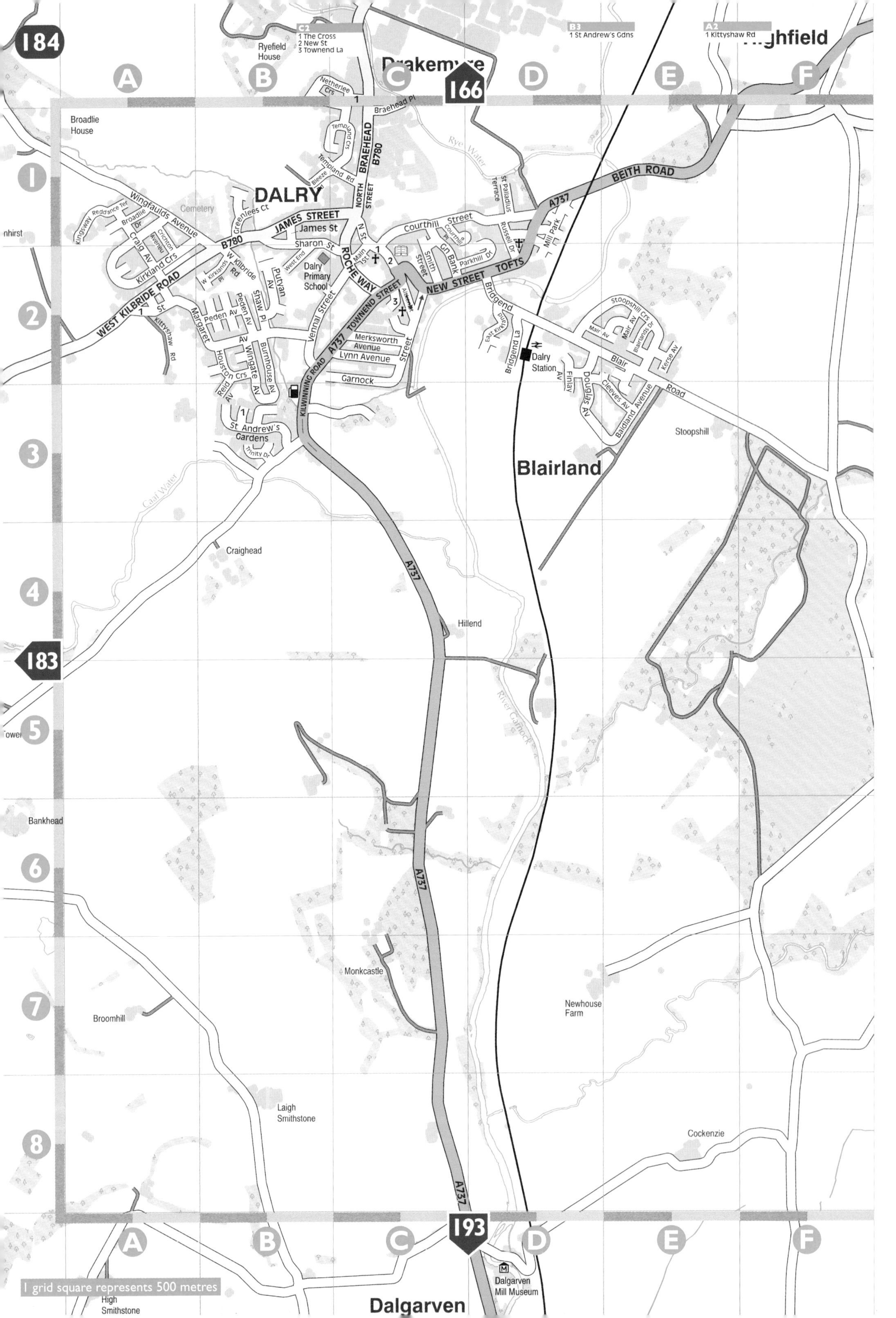
C2
1 The Cross
2 New St
3 Townend La
B3
1 St Andrew's Gdns
A2
1 Kittyshaw Rd
Ryefield House
Drakemyre
Highfield
166
A
B
C
D
E
F
Broadlie House
DALRY
Cemetery
Wingfaulds Avenue
JAMES STREET
James St
BRAEHEAD
B780
NORTH STREET
Braehead Pl
Netherlee Crs
Templand Crs
Templand Rd
Bleeze Rd
Rye Water
St Palladius Terrace
BEITH ROAD
A737
Courthill Street
Courthill Pl
Russell Dr
Mill Park
Sharon St
Greenlees Ct
Kingsway
Reddance Ter
Broadlie Dr
Craig Av
Crichton Avenue
Kirkland Crs
WEST KILBRIDE ROAD
W Kilbride Rd
W Kirklands Pl
West End
Dalry Primary School
ROCHE WAY
Main St
N St
Smith Street
Gn Bank
Parkhill Dr
NEW STREET
TOFTS
TOWNEND STREET
KILWINNING ROAD
Putyan Av
Shaw Pl
Peden Av
Margaret Av
Kittyshaw Rd
Vennal Street
Merksworth Avenue
Lynn Avenue
Garnock
Street
Houston Crs
Wingate Av
Burnhouse Av
Reid Av
St Andrew's Gardens
Trinity Dr
Bridgend
Bridgend La
East Kirkland
Dalry Station
Stoopshill Crs
Mair Av
Blairlands Dr
Kerse Av
Blair Road
Finlay Av
Douglas Av
Cleeves Av
Baidland Avenue
Stoopshill
Blairland
nhirst
Caaf Water
Craighead
Hillend
River Garnock
183
Tower
Bankhead
Monkcastle
Broomhill
Newhouse Farm
Laigh Smithstone
Cockenzie
193
Dalgarven Mill Museum
Dalgarven
High Smithstone
1
2
3
4
5
6
7
8
1 grid square represents 500 metres

Bombo Burn
G
H
J
167
K
L
M
B707
Swindridge Muir
Kerslochmuir
Middlebank
Bowertrapping
Knollhead
Lambridden
Farm
Pencot
B707
Templandmuir
Farm
Cleeves
Foxcover
Plantation
South
Auchenmade
Dusk Water
186
North
Lissens
Blair
Mill
South
Lissens
Lissens
Moss
Auchenskeith
Darmule
Jameston
High
Gooseloan
Benthead
194
Laigh
Gooseloan
Lylestone
B778
1
2
3
4
5
6
7
8

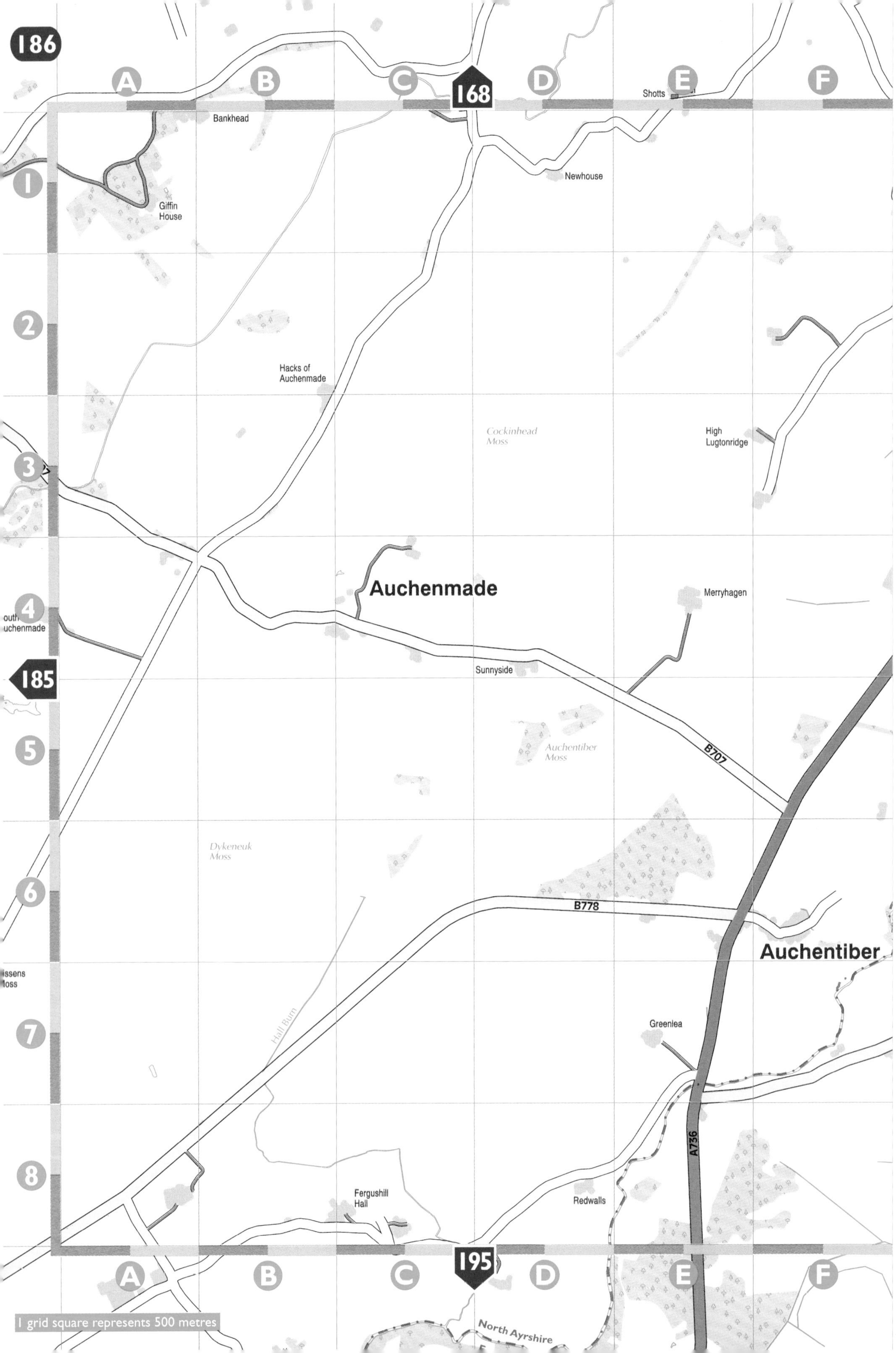
A
B
C
168
D
E
F
Shotts
Bankhead
Newhouse
1
Giffin House
2
Hacks of Auchenmade
Cockinhead Moss
High Lugtonridge
3
Auchenmade
Merryhagen
4
outh uchenmade
185
Sunnyside
B707
Auchentiber Moss
5
Dykeneuk Moss
6
B778
Auchentiber
issens loss
7
Hall Burn
Greenlea
A736
8
Fergushill Hall
Redwalls
195
North Ayrshire
1 grid square represents 500 metres

Burnhouse
Foreside
North Ayrshire
East Ayrshire
G
H
J
169
K
L
M
South Nettlehirst
Nether Oldhall
B706
Oldhall Murray Farm
A736
East Lugtonridge
Lugtonridge
Borland
1
2
3
4
5
6
7
8
Loanhead
Low Borland
ROAD
Deepstone
Sidehead
LOCHLIBO
North Ayrshire
East Ayrshire
Glazert Burn
Thorn Farm
Ravenslie
Netherhill
Cauldhame Farm
Brae
Gunshill
Bowhouse Farm
Kirkwood
B778
Wardlaw
Law
Bloakhillhead
South Kilbride Farm
196
Bloak Moss
Irvinehill
Gillmill

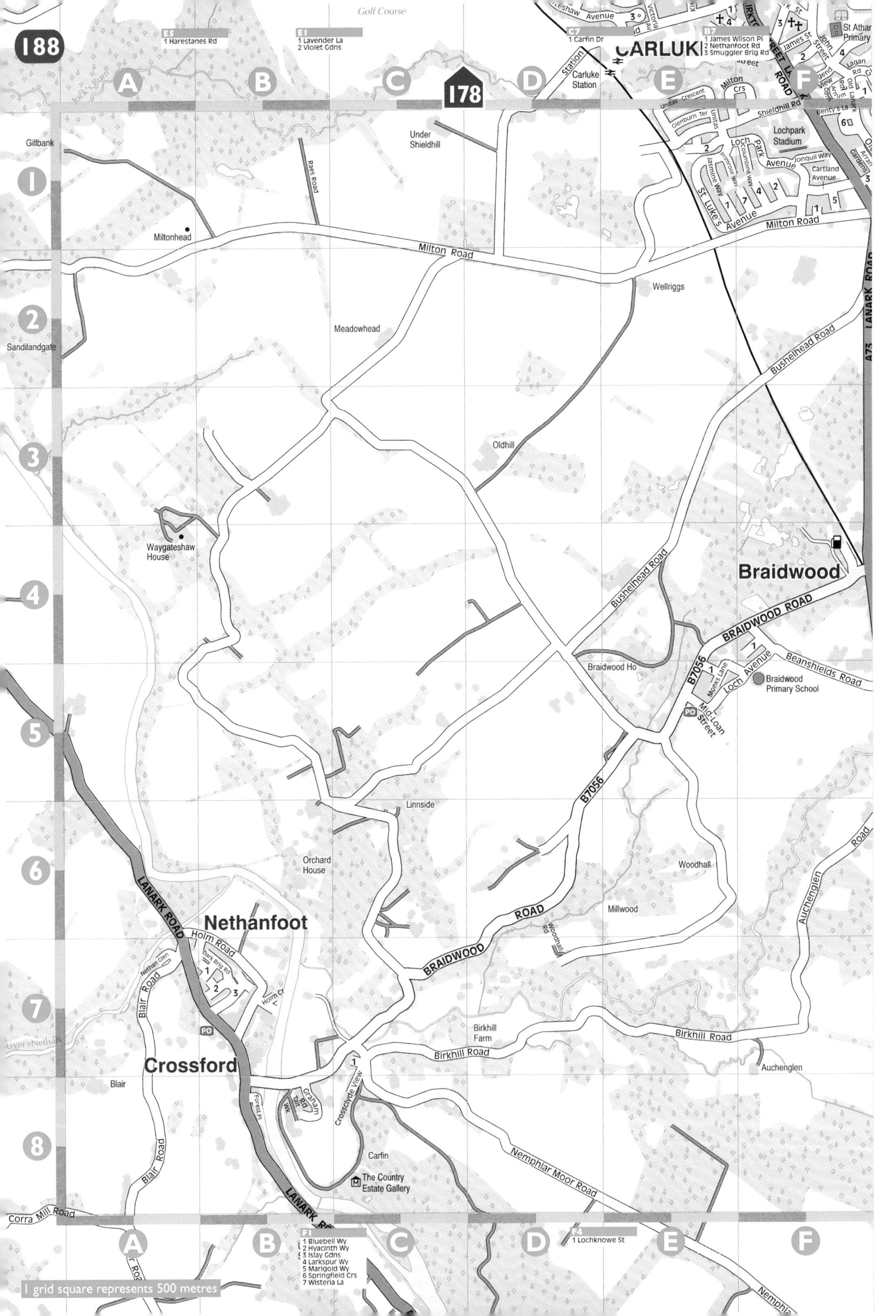
Golf Course
E5
1 Harestanes Rd
E1
1 Lavender La
2 Violet Gdns
C7
1 Carfin Dr
B7
1 James Wilson Pl
2 Nethanfoot Rd
3 Smuggler Brig Rd
CARLUKE
Carluke Station
St Athan Primary
178
A
B
C
D
E
F
1
2
3
4
5
6
7
8
Gillbank
Under Shieldhill
Raes Road
Shieldhill Rd
Unitas Crescent
Glenburn Ter
Milton Crs
Lochpark Stadium
Loch Park Avenue
Jonquil Way
Cartland Avenue
Jasmine Way
Primrose Way
Columbine Way
St Luke's Avenue
Milton Road
Miltonhead
Wellriggs
Sandilandgate
Meadowhead
Bushelhead Road
A73 LANARK ROAD
Oldhill
Waygateshaw House
Braidwood
BRAIDWOOD ROAD
Braidwood Ho
B7056
Monks Lane
Loch Avenue
Beanshields Road
Braidwood Primary School
Mid-Loan Street
PO
Linnside
Orchard House
Woodhall
Millwood
Woodhall Rd
Auchenglen Road
LANARK ROAD
Nethanfoot
Holm Road
Dark Brig Rd
Holm Cr
Nethan Glen
Blair Road
River Nethan
Birkhill Farm
Birkhill Road
Auchenglen
Crossford
Blair
Forest Pl
Graham Rd
Tait Wk
Crossclyde View
Carfin
The Country Estate Gallery
Nemphlar Moor Road
Corra Mill Road
F1
1 Bluebell Wy
2 Hyacinth Wy
3 Islay Gdns
4 Larkspur Wy
5 Marigold Wy
6 Springfield Crs
7 Wisteria La
F4
1 Lochknowe St

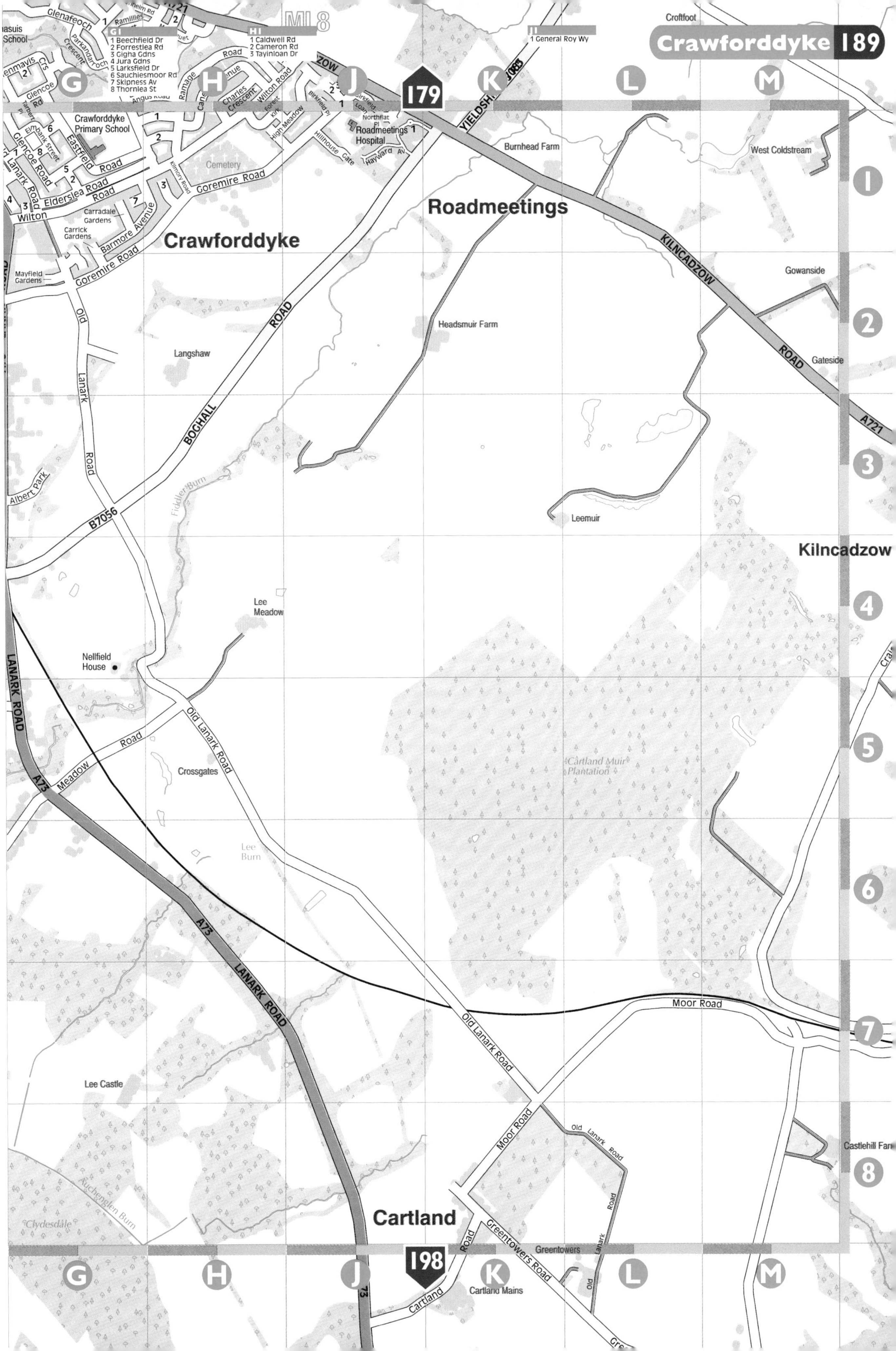
G1
1 Beechfield Dr
2 Forrestlea Rd
3 Gigha Gdns
4 Jura Gdns
5 Larksfield Dr
6 Sauchiesmoor Rd
7 Skipness Av
8 Thornlea St
H1
1 Caldwell Rd
2 Cameron Rd
3 Tayinloan Dr
J1
1 General Roy Wy
ML8
179
198
Croftfoot
Crawforddyke Primary School
Roadmeetings Hospital
Cemetery
Burnhead Farm
West Coldstream
Roadmeetings
Crawforddyke
Goremire Road
Eldersiea Road
Wilton
Carradale Gardens
Carrick Gardens
Barmore Avenue
Mayfield Gardens
Old Lanark Road
Langshaw
BOGHALL ROAD
B7056
Headsmuir Farm
KILNCADZOW ROAD
A721
Gowanside
Gateside
Albert Park
Fiddler Burn
Leemuir
Kilncadzow
Lee Meadow
Nellfield House
LANARK ROAD
A73
Meadow Road
Crossgates
Cartland Muir Plantation
Lee Burn
Moor Road
Lee Castle
Moor Road
Castlehill Farm
Auchenglen Burn
Clydesdale
Cartland
Greentowers
Greentowers Road
Cartland Mains
Cartland Road

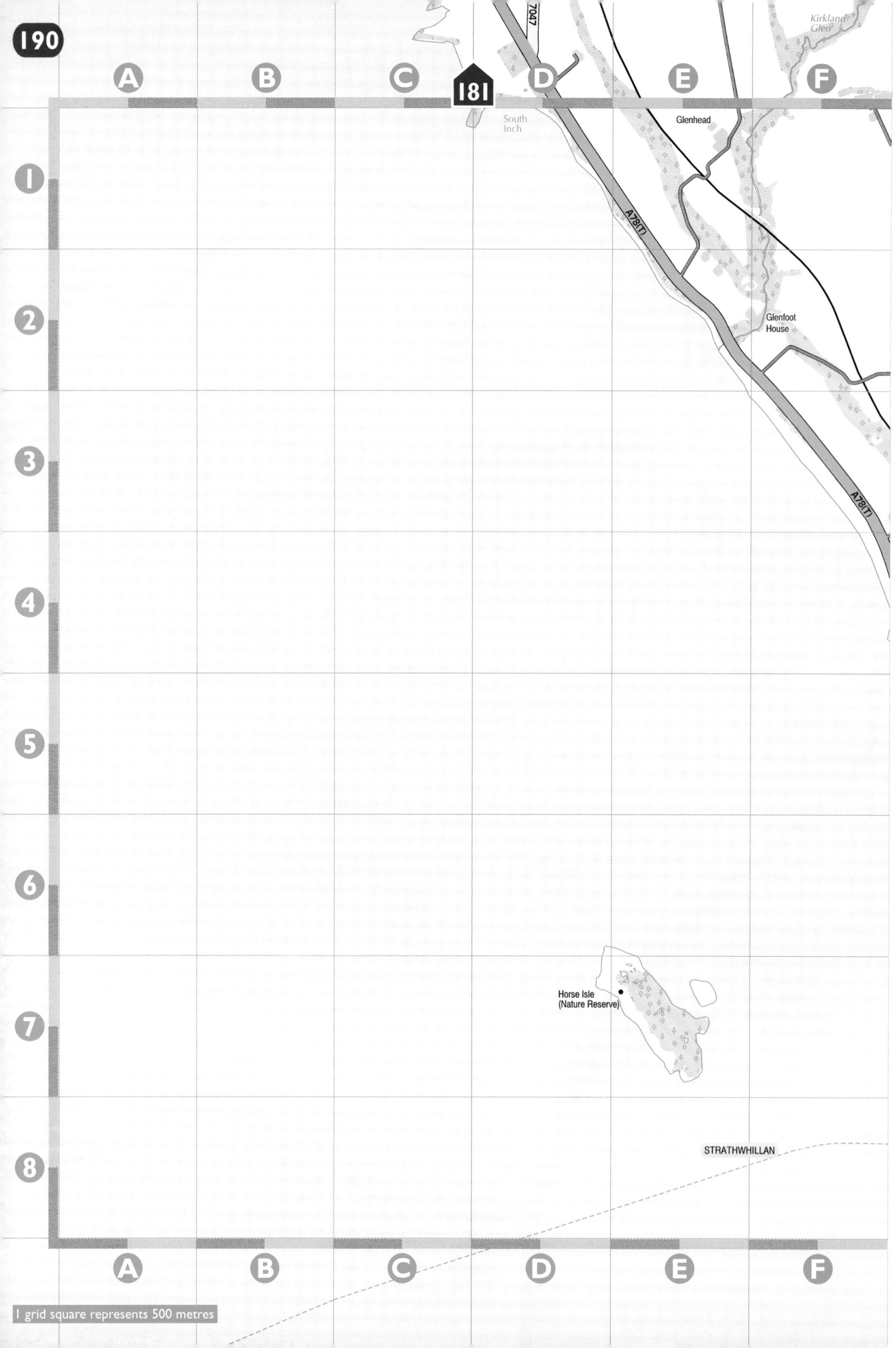
181
South Inch
Glenhead
Kirkland Glen
A78(T)
7047
Glenfoot House
Horse Isle (Nature Reserve)
STRATHWHILLAN
A B C D E F
1 2 3 4 5 6 7 8
1 grid square represents 500 metres

H8
1 Bute Pl
2 Dock Rd
3 Harbour Pl
4 Princes Pl

J5, J6, J7
Street names for these grid squares are listed at the back of the index

J8
1 Arran La
2 Arran Pl
3 Barr St
4 Church Pl
5 Currie Ct
6 Hill St
7 Pavilion Pl

182
192
200
KA22
ARDROSSAN
High Boydstone
Rashley
Boydstone Farm
Meikle Busbie
Craigspark
Mill Glen Reservoir
Rowanside Burn
Sorbie
Mill Farm
Montfode
Whitlees
B780
DALRY ROAD
EGLINTON ROAD
A78(T)
PARKHOUSE ROAD
GLASGOW STREET
HARBOUR STREET
SOUTH CRS ROAD
A738
SORBIE ROAD
S BEACH ROAD
HIGH ROAD
Stanley Road
North Crescent Road
Montgomerie Pier Road
Seafield School
Stanley Primary School
James Mcfarlane School
Winton Primary School
Dykesmains Primary School
Harbour Industrial Estate
Hill Street Industrial Est
Ardrossan Harbour Station
Ferry Terminal
Ardrossan Town Station
Ardrossan South Beach Station
South Beach Practice
Ardrossan Rugby Football Club
Cemetery
Swanley Burn
North Bay
Dock Road

M7
1 Kildonan Pl
2 Sanda Pl

M8
1 St Medan's Pl

L8
1 Stanley Pl

L5
1 Knock'voch Gdn

K8
1 Kilmeny Ter

K6
1 Broadway
2 Centenary Pl
3 Central Av
4 Mcdowall Pl

K5
1 Clyde Pl
2 St Ninian's Dr

192
Darleith
C8
1 Loccard Rd
2 Mayfield Crs
3 Mayfield Rd
A8
1 Duguid Dr
2 St Lawrence Pl
A7
1 Abbotsford Pl
2 Clark Pl
3 Jean Armour Pl
4 Keir Hardie Pl
5 Lochranza Pl
6 Mckinnon Pl
7 New England Rd
A6
1 Ellisland Pl
183
Abbey Ruins
Meikle Laught
Little Laught
Auld Clay Road
Lochwood
Knockrivoch
Diddup
KA21
Stevenston or Ashgrove Loch
191
Lochcraigs
Ardeer Golf Club
Corsankell
Sharphill
Middlepart
Hillhead
Greenhead
Kerelaw Road
Hillhead Road
Cambuskeith Road
Kerelaw School
Middlepart
Mayfield Primary School
Primrose Place
School
Stevenston Burn
Quarrel Burn
Haycocks Primary Sch
Hawkhill
Mayfield
Kerelaw
Hawkhill Cemetery
St Johns Primary School
Hawkhill Drive
Middlepart Crescent
Sinclair Street
GLENCAIRN STREET
HIGH ROAD
A78(T)
GLENCAIRN ST
TOWNHEAD ST
MAIN ST
KILWINNING ROAD
Kilwinning Road
Dubbs Road
Ardeer Mains
201
D8
1 Afton Rd
2 Burnside Pl
E6
1 Hawthorn Dr
E7
1 Ardchoille Dr
2 Ashgrove Av
3 Clements Pl
4 Kerelaw Av
5 Maxwell Pl
6 Oakland Dr
E8
1 Burn's Pl
2 Lumsden Pl
F7
1 Landsborough Pl
2 St Stephen's Pl
Auchenharvie
STEVENSTON
Glencairn Primary School
KA20
1 grid square represents 500 metres

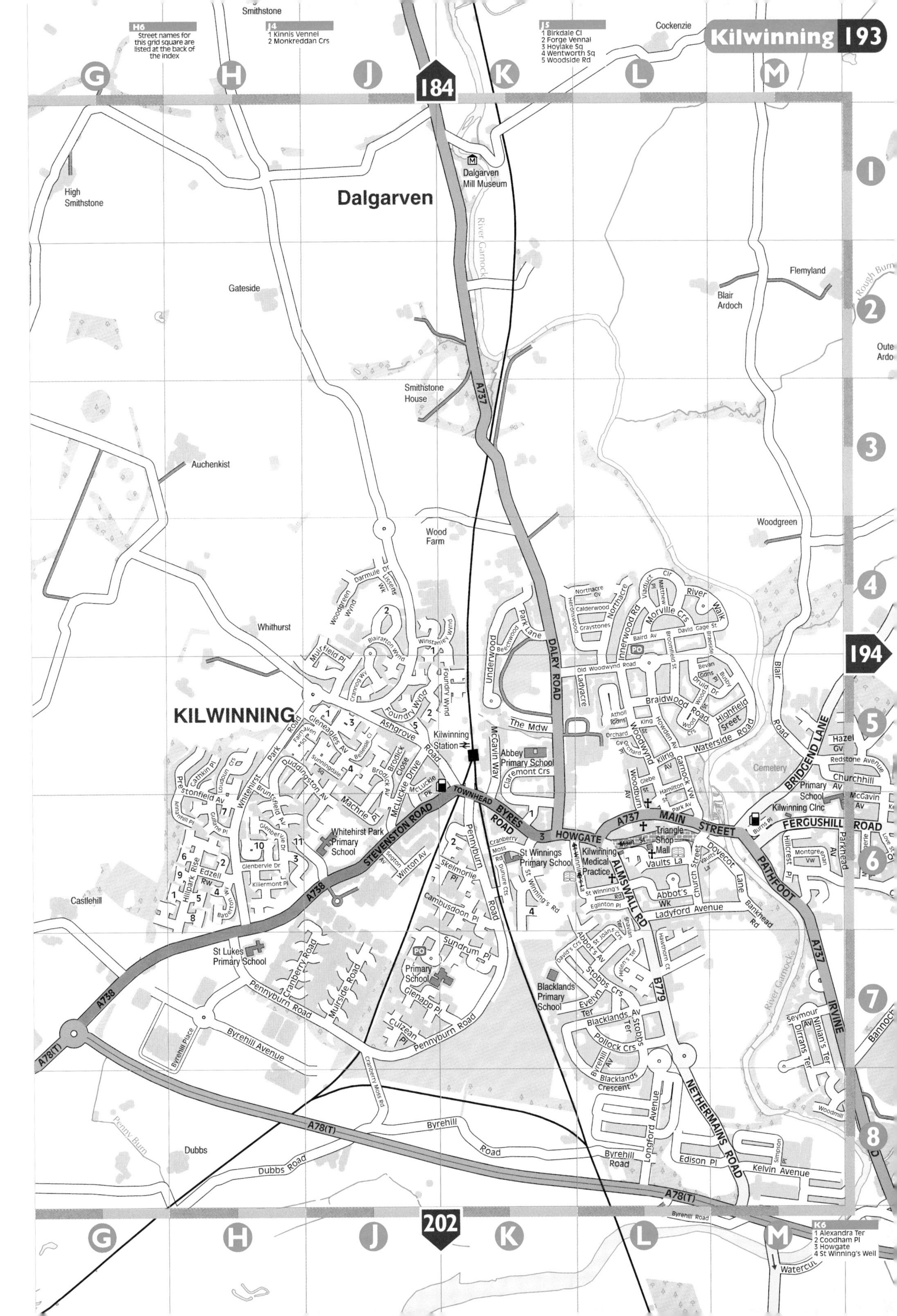
H6
Street names for this grid square are listed at the back of the index
J4
1 Kinnis Vennel
2 Monkreddan Crs
J5
1 Birkdale Cl
2 Forge Vennal
3 Hoylake Sq
4 Wentworth Sq
5 Woodside Rd
K6
1 Alexandra Ter
2 Coodham Pl
3 Howgate
4 St Winning's Well
184
194
202
Smithstone
Cockenzie
High Smithstone
Dalgarven
Dalgarven Mill Museum
River Garnock
Gateside
Blair Ardoch
Flemyland
Rough Burn
Smithstone House
Auchenkist
Wood Farm
Woodgreen
Whithurst
KILWINNING
Kilwinning Station
Castlehill
Dubbs
Penny Burn
Cemetery
A737
A738
A78(T)
B779
DALRY ROAD
STEVENSTON ROAD
TOWNHEAD
BYRES ROAD
HOWGATE
MAIN STREET
ALMSWALL RD
NETHERMAINS ROAD
PATHFOOT
IRVINE
BRIDGEND LANE
FERGUSHILL ROAD
Whitehirst Park Primary School
St Lukes Primary School
Abbey Primary School
St Winnings Primary School
Blacklands Primary School
Kilwinning Medical Practice
Triangle Shop Mall
Kilwinning Clnc
Primary School
Byrehill Avenue
Pennyburn Road
Byrehill Road
Dubbs Road
Kelvin Avenue
Edison Pl
Longford Avenue
Ladyford Avenue
Waterside Road
River Walk
Morville Crs
Braidwood Road
Vaults La
Abbot's Wk
Stobbs Crs
Blacklands Crescent
Pollock Crs
Cranberry Road
Muirside Road
Glenapp Pl
Culzean Pl
Sundrum Pl
Cambusdoon Pl
Skelmorlie Pl
Pennyburn Road
Winton Av
Ashgrove
Foundry Wynd
Gleneagles Av
Duddingston Av
Machrie Pl
McLuckie Drive
Brodick Close
Prestonfield Av
Whitehirst Park Road
Edzell Rw
Hillpark Rise
Glenbervie Dr
Killermont Pl
The Mdw
McGavin Way
Claremont Crs
Underwood
Park Lane
Ladyacre
Old Woodwynd Road
Innerwood Rd
Northacre
Calderwood
Graystones
Baird Av
David Gage St
Highfield Street
Woodwynd
Garnock Vw
Kilrig Av
Church Street
Dovecot Lane
Bankhead Rd
Seymour Av
Dirrans Ter
Ninian's Ter
Hazel Gv
Redstone Avenue
Churchhill Av
McGavin Av
Parkhead Av
Hillcrest Pl
Montgreenan Vw
Blair Road
Bannoch
Simpson Pl
Watercut
Outer Ardoch
Muirfield Pl
Darmule Dr
Lissens Wk
Woodgreen Wynd
Blairafton Wynd
Winstanley Wynd

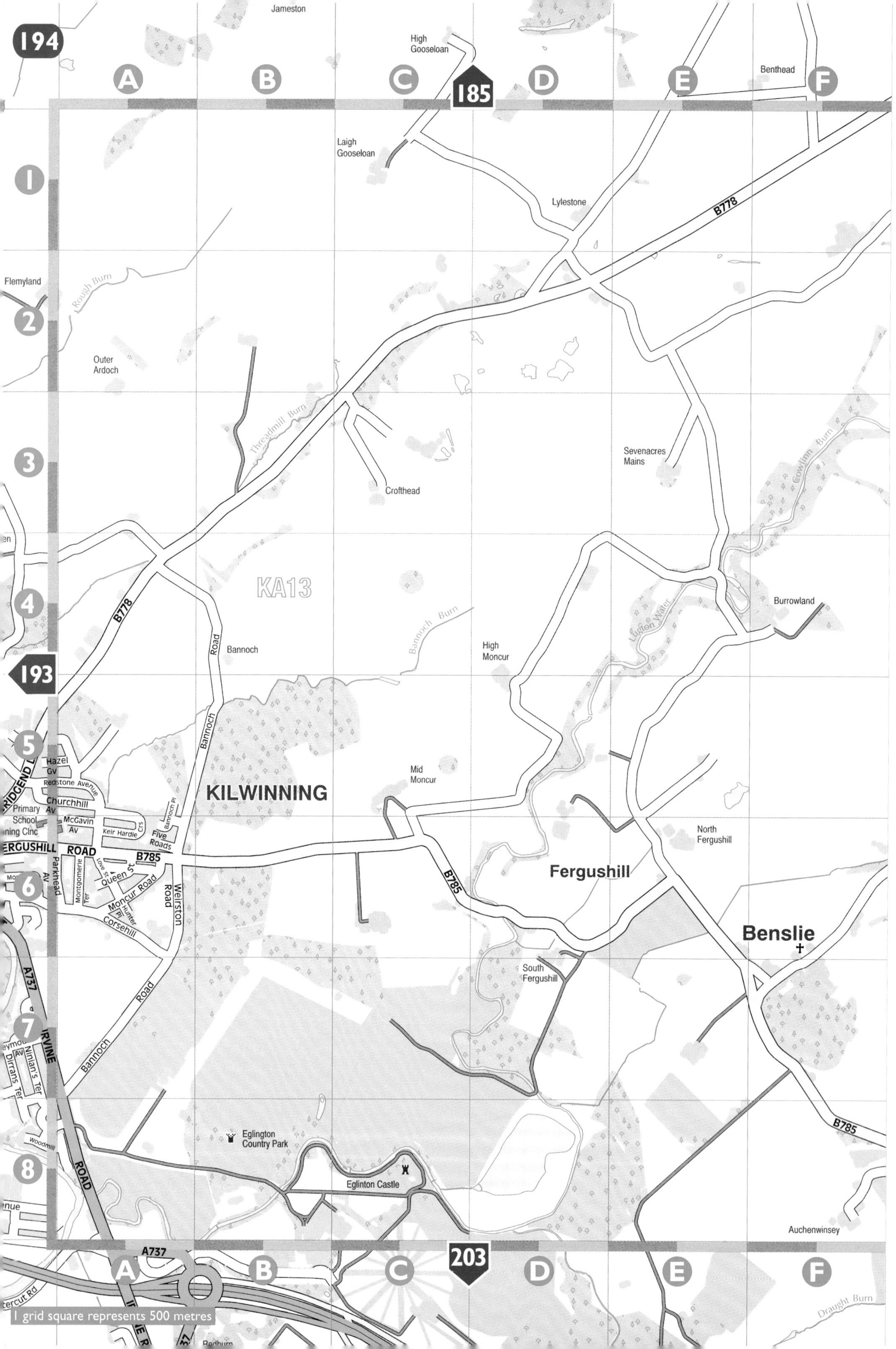
194
185
193
203
A
B
C
D
E
F
1
2
3
4
5
6
7
8
Jameston
High Gooseloan
Benthead
Laigh Gooseloan
Lylestone
B778
Flemyland
Rough Burn
Outer Ardoch
Threadmill Burn
Sevenacres Mains
Crofthead
Cowlinn Burn
KA13
Burrowland
Lugton Water
Bannoch Burn
Bannoch
Road
High Moncur
Bannoch
Mid Moncur
KILWINNING
Hazel Gv
Redstone Avenue
Churchhill Av
Primary School
McGavin Av
Keir Hardie Crs
Bannoch Pl
Five Roads
ERGUSHILL ROAD
B785
Parkhead Av
Montgomerie Ter
Love St
Queen St
Moncur Road
Hunter Pl
Corsehill
Weirston Road
B785
North Fergushill
Fergushill
Benslie
South Fergushill
A737
IRVINE
Ninian's Ter
Dirrans Ter
Bannoch Road
Woodmill
ROAD
Eglington Country Park
Eglinton Castle
B785
Auchenwinsey
A737
Draught Burn
Redburn
1 grid square represents 500 metres

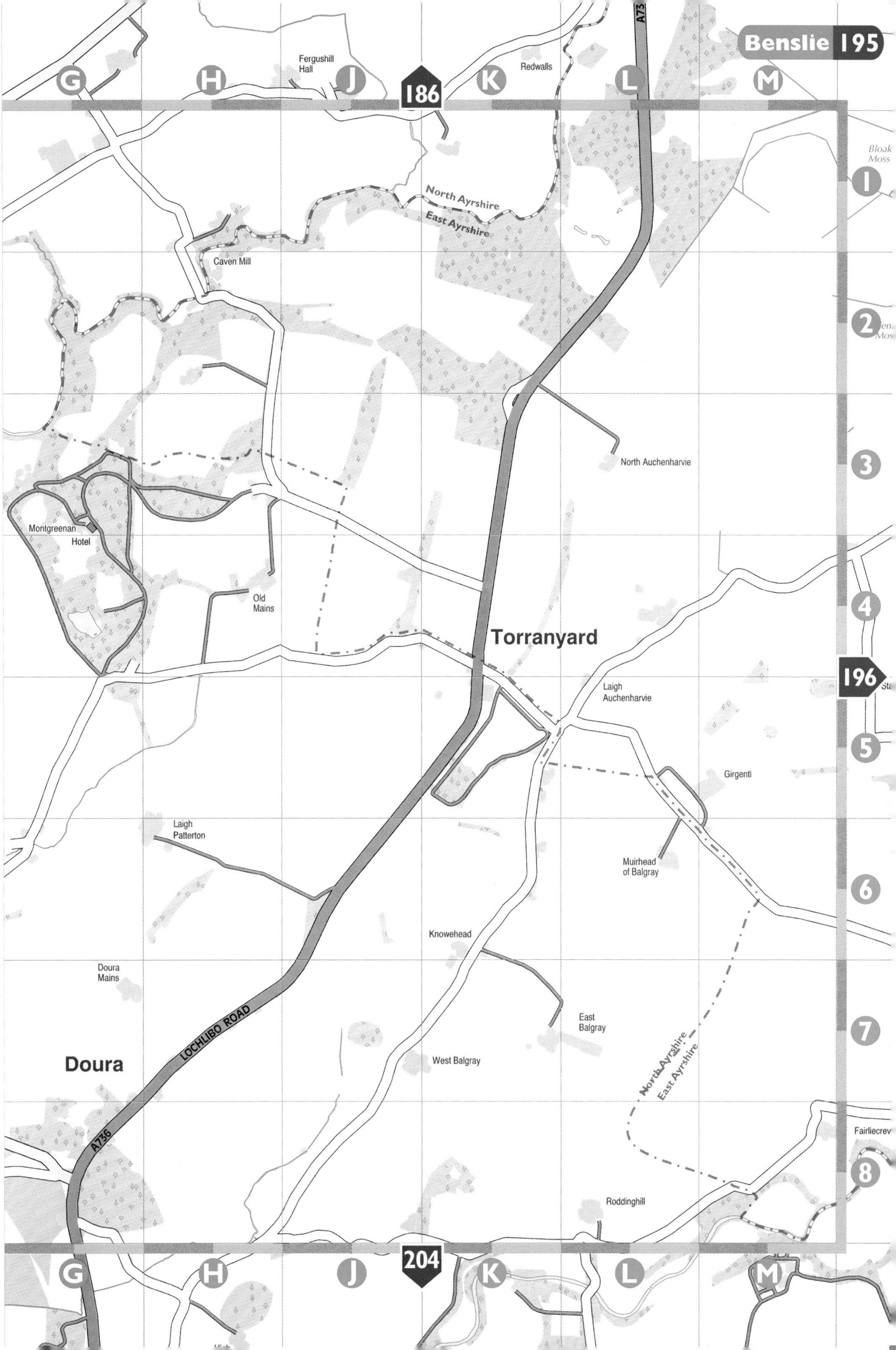
G
H
J
186
K
L
M
Fergushill Hall
Redwalls
A73
Bloak Moss
North Ayrshire
East Ayrshire
Caven Mill
North Auchenharvie
Montgreenan Hotel
Old Mains
Torranyard
196
Laigh Auchenharvie
Girgenti
Laigh Patterton
Muirhead of Balgray
Knowehead
Doura Mains
East Balgray
LOCHLIBO ROAD
West Balgray
Doura
North Ayrshire
East Ayrshire
A736
Fairliecrev
Roddinghill
1
2
3
4
5
6
7
8
204

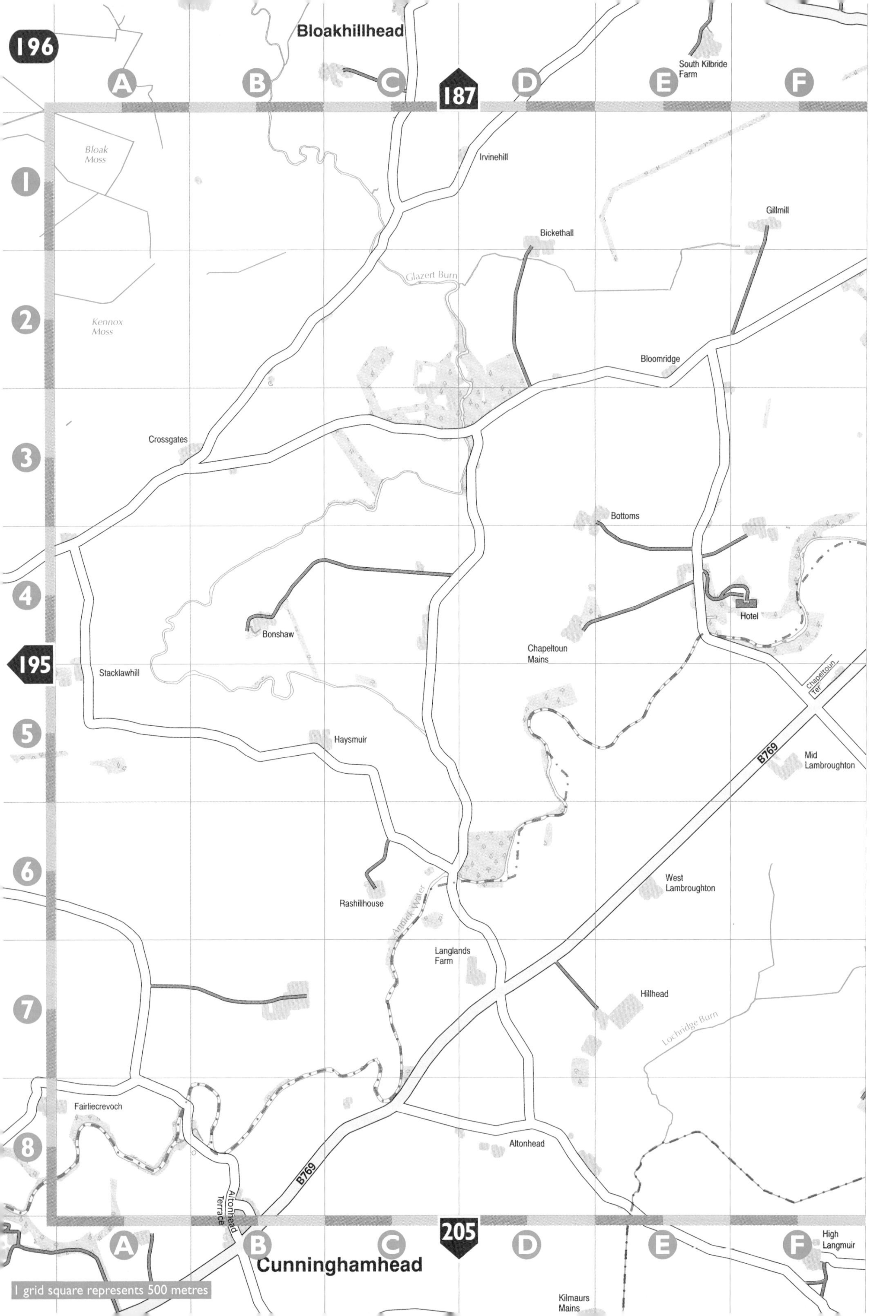
196
187
195
205
Bloakhillhead
South Kilbride Farm
Bloak Moss
Irvinehill
Gillmill
Bickethall
Glazert Burn
Kennox Moss
Bloomridge
Crossgates
Bottoms
Hotel
Bonshaw
Chapeltoun Mains
Stacklawhill
Chapeltoun Ter
Haysmuir
B769
Mid Lambroughton
West Lambroughton
Rashillhouse
Annick Water
Langlands Farm
Hillhead
Lochridge Burn
Fairliecrevoch
Altonhead
Altonhead Terrace
High Langmuir
Cunninghamhead
Kilmaurs Mains
1 grid square represents 500 metres

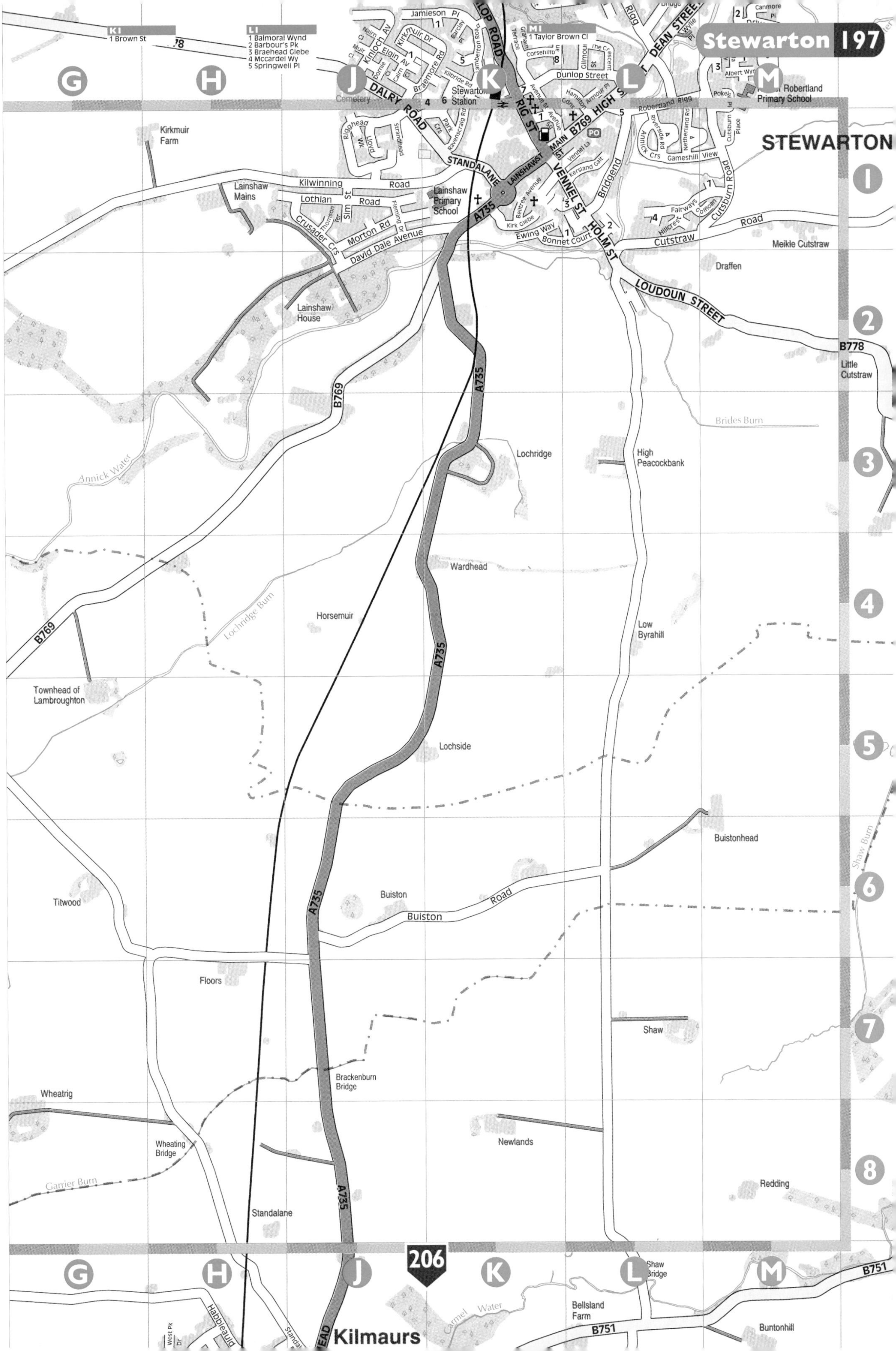
K1
1 Brown St
L1
1 Balmoral Wynd
2 Barbour's Pk
3 Braehead Glebe
4 Mccardel Wy
5 Springwell Pl
M1
1 Taylor Brown Cl
STEWARTON
Kirkmuir Farm
Lainshaw Mains
Kilwinning Road
Lothian Road
Lainshaw Primary School
Stewarton Station
Robertland Primary School
Dunlop Street
DALRY ROAD
STANDALANE
LAINSHAWS T
MAIN ST
VENNEL ST
HIGH ST
HOLM ST
Bridgend
Robertland Rigg
Gameshill View
Cutsburn Road
Cutstraw Road
Meikle Cutstraw
Draffen
LOUDOUN STREET
B778
Little Cutstraw
Morton Rd
David Dale Avenue
Crusader Crs
Lainshaw House
Ewing Way
Bonnet Court
B769
A735
Brides Burn
Lochridge
High Peacockbank
Annick Water
Wardhead
Horsemuir
Lochridge Burn
Low Byrahill
Townhead of Lambroughton
Lochside
Buistonhead
Shaw Burn
Titwood
Buiston
Buiston Road
Floors
Shaw
Brackenburn Bridge
Wheatrig
Wheating Bridge
Newlands
Garrier Burn
Redding
Standalane
206
Shaw Bridge
Bellsland Farm
Carmel Water
B751
Buntonhill
Kilmaurs
G
H
J
K
L
M
1
2
3
4
5
6
7
8

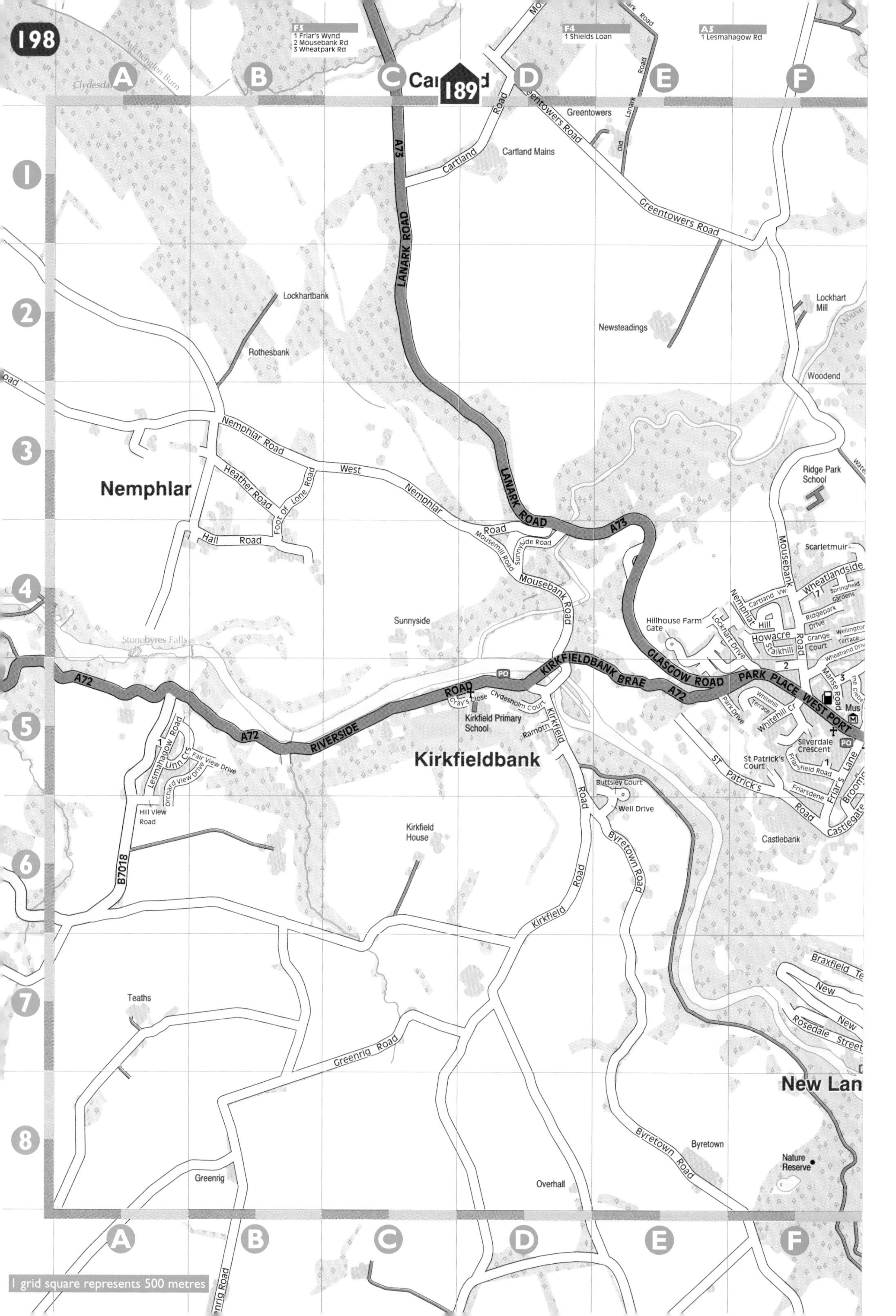
F5
1 Friar's Wynd
2 Mousebank Rd
3 Wheatpark Rd
F4
1 Shields Loan
A5
1 Lesmahagow Rd
189
Greentowers
Greentowers Road
Cartland Mains
Cartland Road
Lanark Road
Old Lanark Road
LANARK ROAD
A73
Lockhartbank
Rothesbank
Newsteadings
Lockhart Mill
Woodend
Nemphlar Road
West Nemphlar Road
Heather Road
Foot of Lone Road
Hall Road
Nemphlar
Ridge Park School
Scarletmuir
Wheatlandside
Mousebank
Sunnyside Road
Mousemill Road
Mousebank Road
Sunnyside
Hillhouse Farm Gate
Stonebyres Falls
A72
KIRKFIELDBANK BRAE
GLASGOW ROAD
PARK PLACE WEST PORT
RIVERSIDE ROAD
Kirkfield Primary School
Clydesholm Court
Ramoth
Kirkfield Road
Kirkfieldbank
Lesmahagow Road
Linn Crs
Fair View Drive
Orchard View Drive
Hill View Road
B7018
Buttsley Court
Well Drive
Byretown Road
Kirkfield House
Castlebank
St Patrick's Road
St Patrick's Court
Silverdale Crescent
Friarsfield Road
Friarsdene
Friar's Lane
Castlegate
Mus
PO
Braxfield Te
Rosedale Street
New Lan
Teaths
Greenrig Road
Greenrig
Overhall
Byretown
Nature Reserve
1 grid square represents 500 metres

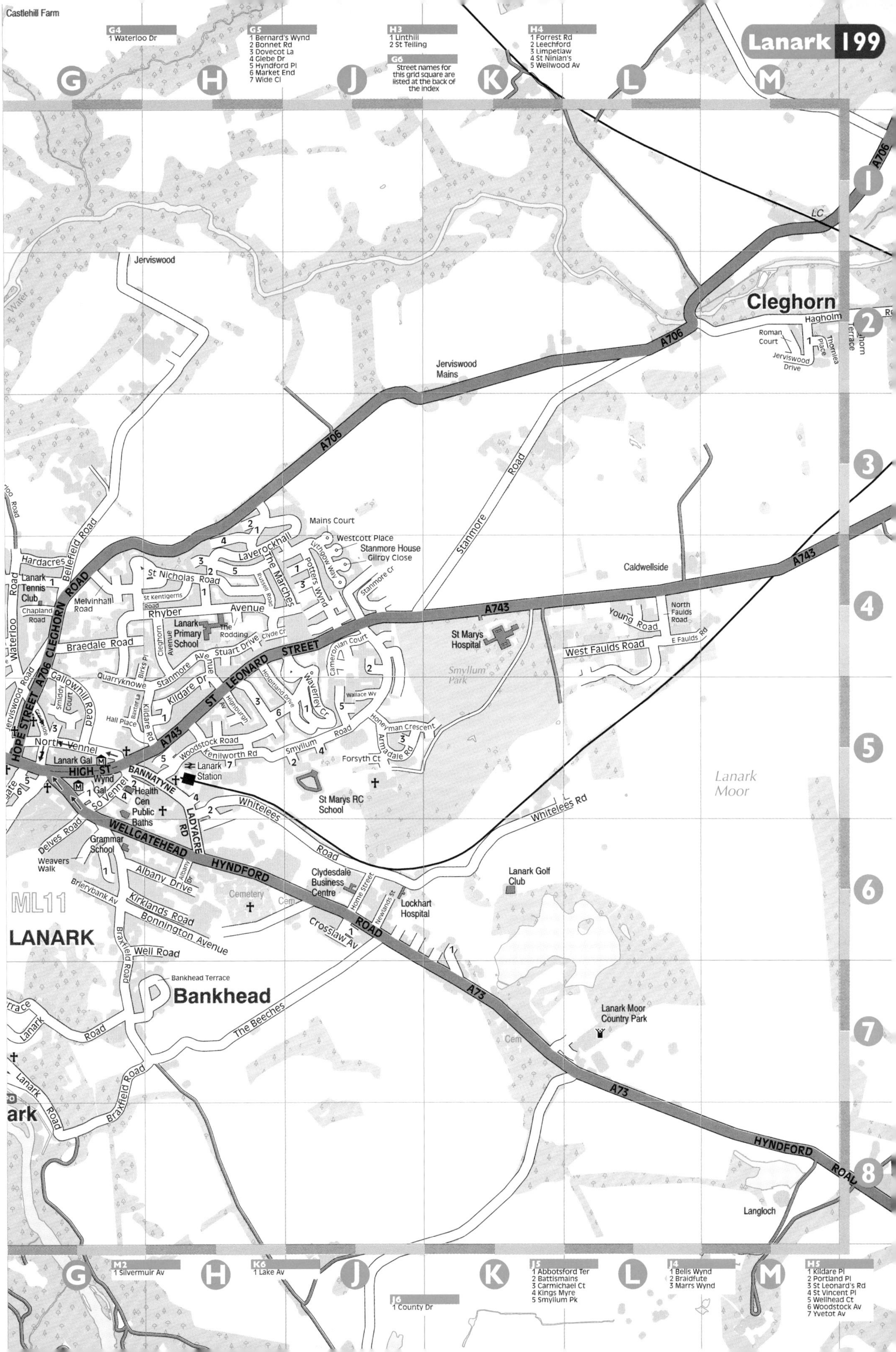
G4
1 Waterloo Dr
G5
1 Bernard's Wynd
2 Bonnet Rd
3 Dovecot La
4 Glebe Dr
5 Hyndford Pl
6 Market End
7 Wide Cl
H3
1 Linthill
2 St Telling
G6
Street names for this grid square are listed at the back of the index
H4
1 Forrest Rd
2 Leechford
3 Limpetlaw
4 St Ninian's
5 Wellwood Av
Castlehill Farm
Jerviswood
Cleghorn
Jerviswood Mains
Mains Court
Westcott Place
Stanmore House
Gilroy Close
Caldwellside
St Marys Hospital
Smyllum Park
Lanark Moor
Lanark Golf Club
Clydesdale Business Centre
Lockhart Hospital
Lanark Station
St Marys RC School
Lanark Primary School
Grammar School
Health Cen
Public Baths
Cemetery
ML11
LANARK
Bankhead
Bankhead Terrace
Lanark Moor Country Park
Langloch
A706
A743
A73
HYNDFORD ROAD
ST LEONARD STREET
HIGH ST
WELLGATEHEAD
M2
1 Silvermuir Av
K6
1 Lake Av
J6
1 County Dr
J5
1 Abbotsford Ter
2 Battismains
3 Carmichael Ct
4 Kings Myre
5 Smyllum Pk
J4
1 Bells Wynd
2 Braidfute
3 Marrs Wynd
H5
1 Kildare Pl
2 Portland Pl
3 St Leonard's Rd
4 St Vincent Pl
5 Wellhead Ct
6 Woodstock Av
7 Yvetot Av

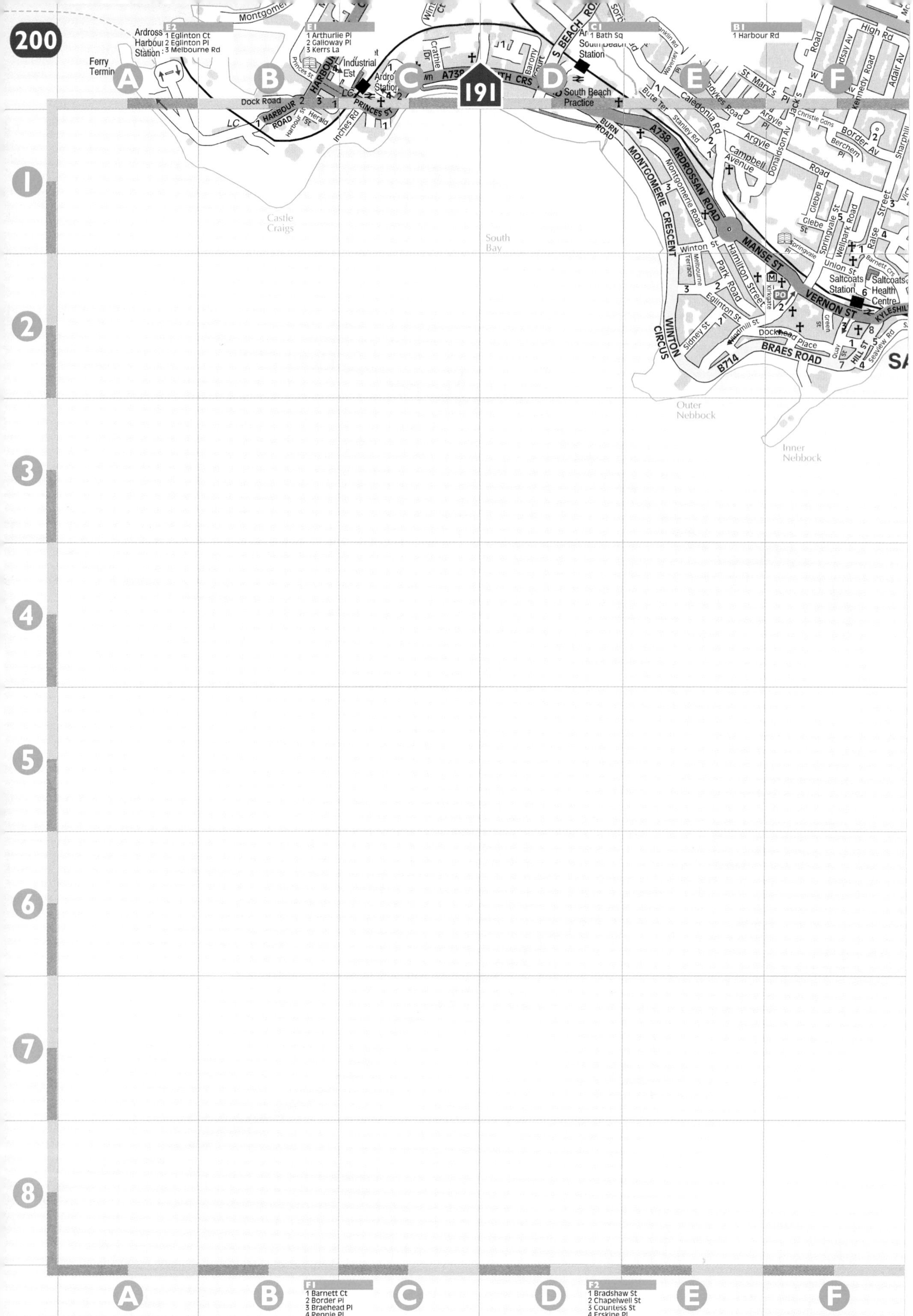
E2
1 Eglinton Ct
2 Eglinton Pl
3 Melbourne Rd
E1
1 Arthurlie Pl
2 Galloway Pl
3 Kerrs La
C1
1 Bath Sq
B1
1 Harbour Rd
191
Ardrossan Harbour Station
Ferry Terminal
Dock Road
HARBOUR ROAD
Harbour St
Herald St
PRINCES ST
Princes St
Inches Rd
Industrial Est
Ardrossan South Beach Station
Ardrossan Station
Crathie Dr
Barony Court
S BEACH ROAD
South Beach Practice
A738
BURN ROAD
MONTGOMERIE CRESCENT
Montgomerie Road
ARDROSSAN ROAD
MANSE ST
VERNON ST
Castle Craigs
South Bay
Bute Ter
Caledonia Rd
Stanley Rd
Campbell Avenue
Argyle
Donaldson Av
Jack's Rd
St Mary's Pl
Christie Gdns
Border Av
Berchem Pl
Kennedy Road
Adair Av
High Rd
Glebe Pl
Glebe St
Springvale St
Springvale Pl
Wellpark Road
Raise Street
Union St
Barnett Cres
Saltcoats Station
Saltcoats Health Centre
Winton St
Melbourne Terrace
Park Road
Hamilton Street
Kirkgate
Eglinton St
Sidney St
Windmill St
Dockhead Place
BRAES ROAD
B714
WINTON CIRCUS
Green St
Quay St
HILL ST
Seaview Rd
Outer Nebbock
Inner Nebbock
A
B
C
D
E
F
1
2
3
4
5
6
7
8

F1
1 Barnett Ct
2 Border Pl
3 Braehead Pl
4 Rennie Pl
5 Wellpark La

F2
1 Bradshaw St
2 Chapelwell St
3 Countess St
4 Erskine Pl
5 Findlay's Brae
6 Glencairn St
7 Harbour St
8 Nineyard St

1 grid square represents 500 metres

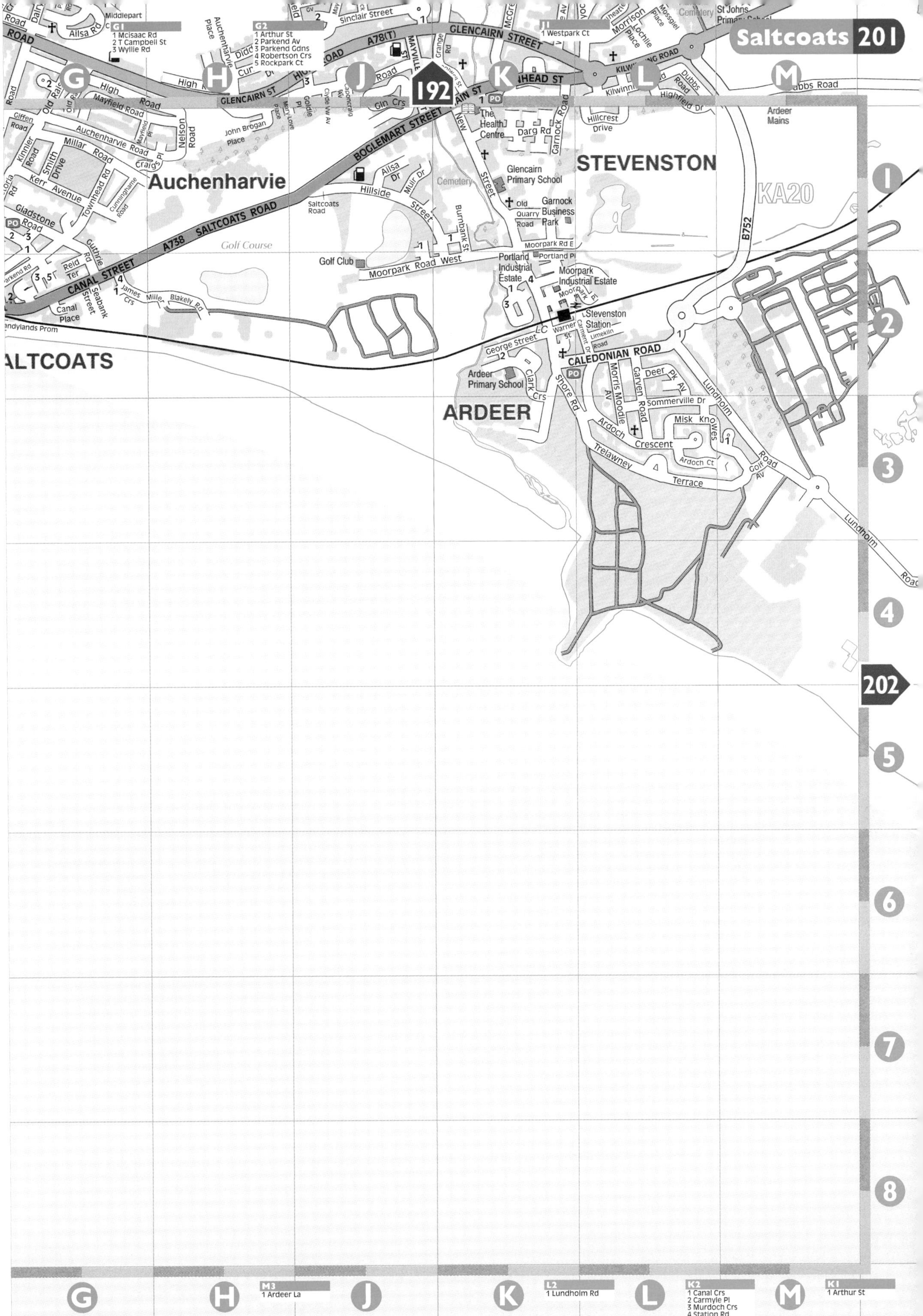
G1
1 Mcisaac Rd
2 T Campbell St
3 Wyllie Rd
G2
1 Arthur St
2 Parkend Av
3 Parkend Gdns
4 Robertson Crs
5 Rockpark Ct
J1
1 Westpark Ct
Auchenharvie
STEVENSTON
ARDEER
SALTCOATS
KA20
Golf Course
Golf Club
Glencairn Primary School
Ardeer Primary School
The Health Centre
Garnock Business Park
Portland Industrial Estate
Moorpark Industrial Estate
Stevenston Station
Cemetery
Ardeer Mains
GLENCAIRN STREET
BOGLEMART STREET
SALTCOATS ROAD
CANAL STREET
CALEDONIAN ROAD
A78(T)
A738
B752
192
202

M3
1 Ardeer La

L2
1 Lundholm Rd

K2
1 Canal Crs
2 Carmyle Pl
3 Murdoch Crs
4 Station Rd

K1
1 Arthur St

Penny Burn
Dubbs
bbs Road
Dubbs Road
A78(T)
Byrehill
Road
Byrehill
Road
Longford Ave
ERMAINS ROAD
Edison Pl
Simpson Pl
Kelv enue
Woodmill
193
A78(T)
Byrehill Road
Watercut Rd
Dykehead
B779
Ravenspa
Hospital
Lundholm
Road
Golf
Club
201
River Garnock
Stevenston Site
The Big Idea
Harbour
Beach
Drive
Magr
Beac
Park
Beach
Park
A
B
C
D
E
F
1
2
3
4
5
6
7
8
1 grid square represents 500 metres

G8 1 Bimson Pl 2 Bimson Rw 3 Linthouse Vennel
H5 1 Burnside Pl 2 Williamfield Gv 3 Williamfield Pk
H7 1 Church St
J5 1 Meadow Av
J6 1 Murchland Wy
J7 1 Carters Pl
Eglinton Country Park
194
Auchenwinsey
Draught Burn
A737
IRVINE RD
Redburn Industrial Estate
B7080
A78(T)
A736
CAIRNMOUNT ROAD
Rannoch Place
Ayrshire Central Hospital
Ravenspark Golf Club
Kidsneuk
HILL INTERCHANGE
LONG DRIVE
Littlestane
Smithstone Wy
Girdle Toll
KILWINNING ROAD
SANDY ROAD
Hunter Dr
Dickson Drive
Livingstone Terrace
Seaton Terrace
Paterson Crs
Paterson Avenue
Martin Av
Cemetery
Red Burn
Stanecastle Dr
Glenlyon Grove
Bank Street
204
KA12
Burnside Clinic
Alexander Place
Primary School
Stanecastle
B769
MIDDLETON
Haysholm School
St Marks Primary School
MANSON ROAD
Crompton Way
MARRESS ROAD
Woodlands Avenue
Woodlands Primary School
BANK STREET
Kilmarnock College
IRVINE
Berry Drive
Arkwright Way
River Irvine
Irvine Sports Club
FULLARTON STREET
HIGH ST
TOWNHEAD
Glebe Primary School
Broomlands Busway
Irvine Stn
Riverway Retail Park
Scottish Maritime Mus
Loudoun Montgomery Primary School
B7081
ANNICK ROAD
AYR ROAD
A71
Fullarton
Mackintosh Place
CORSEHILL MT RD
208
M6 1 Cheviot Head 2 Corserine Bank
L7 1 Adams Wk
M5 1 Stanecastle Rd
K8 1 Mcgibney Dr
K6 1 Mossgiel Dr 2 Thornhouse Av
K7 1 Beech Av
L5 1 Cedar Rd 2 Eastwood Av 3 Rowan Ter
J8 1 Greenbank Ct

A7
1 Kilpatrick Pl
2 Lewis Rl
3 Lewis Wynd
4 St Kilda Pl
A6
1 Kilsyth Crs
2 Pentland Pl
A5
1 Blaven Head
A3
1 Bowmore Ct
2 Cardow Crs
195
High Armsheugh
Sourlie
A736
Springbank Gdns
Holehouse
Braehead
Middleton
Overton Farm
Lawthorn
Perceton
Cardow Crescent
Ardmore Court
Littlestane Road
Perceton Mains
Gateside
Girdle Toll
West Bowhouse Garden
East Bowhouse Head
Stanecastle School
Newhouse Way
Fortacre Place
B769
Ramstane Place
Cairngorm Court
Annick Primary Sch
203
MIDDLETON ROAD
Lawer Place
Warwickdale
Whitewisp Court
Drummuir
Fencedyke Way
Fencedyke Primary School
St John Ogilvie Primary School
Bourtreehill Health Cen
Moorfoot
Broomlands
Bourtreehill
Primary School
Hillshaw Green
Springside Primary School
Towerlands Road
Broomlands Busway
Pladda Av
Gigha Ter
KA11
MAIN ROAD
B7081
MAIN STREET
St Kilda Bank
Broomlands Primary School
Cemetery
Dreghorn Primary School
Dreghorn
Overtoun Road
Caprington Burn
Annick Water
Greenwood Academy
CORSEHILL MT ROAD
LONG DRIVE
B7080
Annick Drive
TOWNFOOT
DUNDONALD
Corsehill
209
B2
1 Ormiston Pl
B3
1 Strathmore Pk
B6
1 Bencleuch Pl
B8
1 Broomlands Rd
2 Macrobert Av
C7
1 Glenleith Pl
2 Hopetoun Bank
3 Lowther Bank
4 Sidlaw Foot
B7
1 Garelet Pl
2 Shalloch Pl
Corsehill Mount Road
A71
1 grid square represents 500 metres

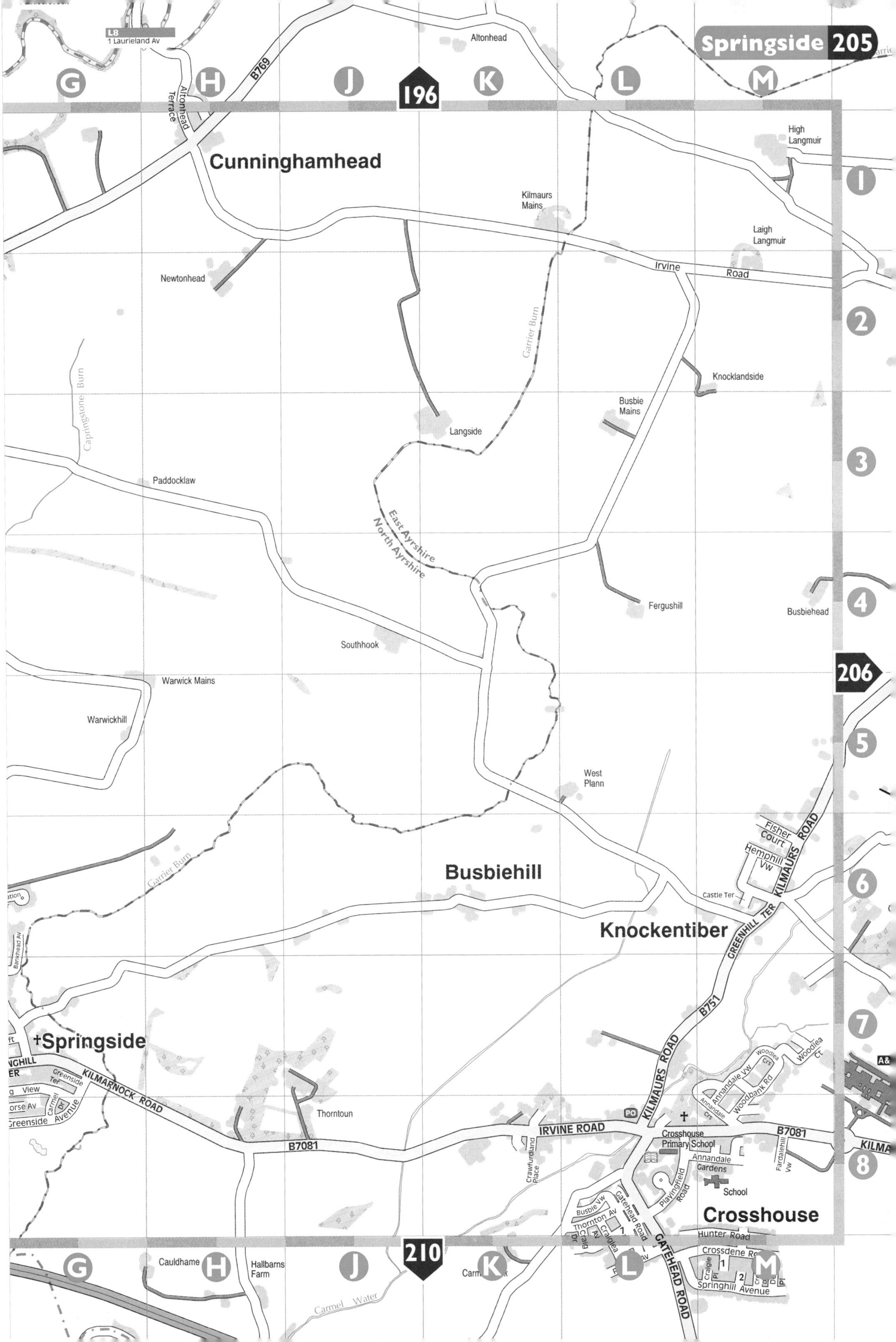
L8
1 Laurieland Av
Altonhead
Altonhead Terrace
B769
196
G
H
J
K
L
M
Cunninghamhead
High Langmuir
Kilmaurs Mains
Laigh Langmuir
Newtonhead
Irvine Road
Garrier Burn
Knocklandside
Busbie Mains
Caprington Burn
Langside
Paddocklaw
East Ayrshire
North Ayrshire
Fergushill
Busbiehead
Southhook
Warwick Mains
Warwickhill
206
West Plann
Fisher Court
Hemphill Vw
KILMAURS ROAD
Busbiehill
Castle Ter
GREENHILL TER
Knockentiber
Bankhead Av
B751
Woodlea Ct
Woodlea Crs
Springside
Greenside Ter
KILMARNOCK ROAD
View
Avenue
Greenside
Annandale Vw
Woodbank Rd
KILMAURS ROAD
Annandale Crs
Thorntoun
IRVINE ROAD
PO
B7081
Crosshouse Primary School
B7081
Fardalehill Vw
Crawfurdland Place
Annandale Gardens
Playingfield Road
School
Busbie Vw
Thornton Av
Gatehead Road
Crosshouse
Hunter Road
Craiglea Av
Crossdene Rd
Springhill Avenue
GATEHEAD ROAD
210
Cauldhame
Hallbarns Farm
Carmel Water
1
2
3
4
5
6
7
8

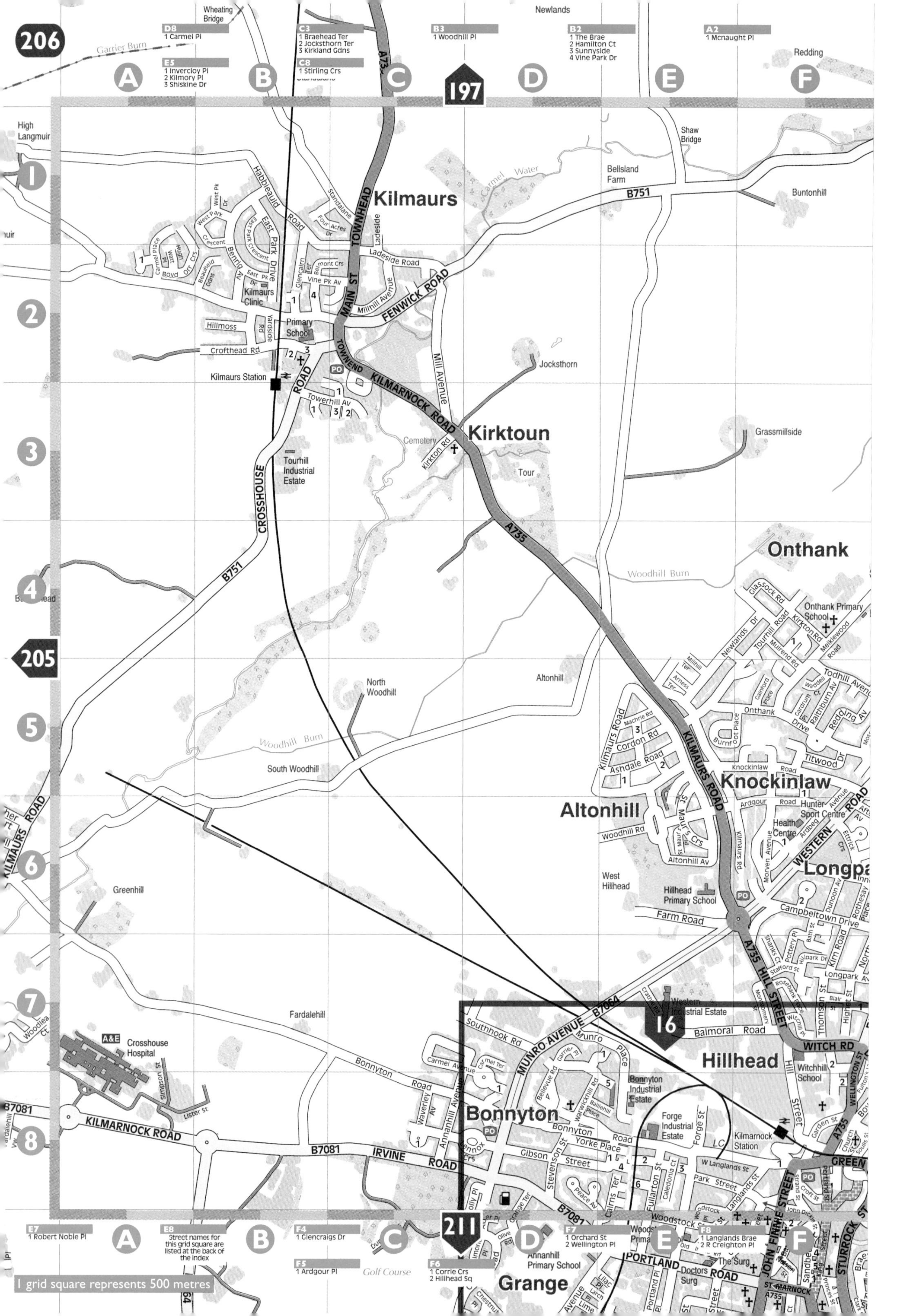

E7 1 Robert Noble Pl
E8 Street names for this grid square are listed at the back of the index
F4 1 Glencraigs Dr
F5 1 Ardgour Pl
F6 1 Corrie Crs 2 Hillhead Sq
F7 1 Orchard St 2 Wellington Pl
F8 1 Langlands Brae 2 R Creighton Pl

1 grid square represents 500 metres

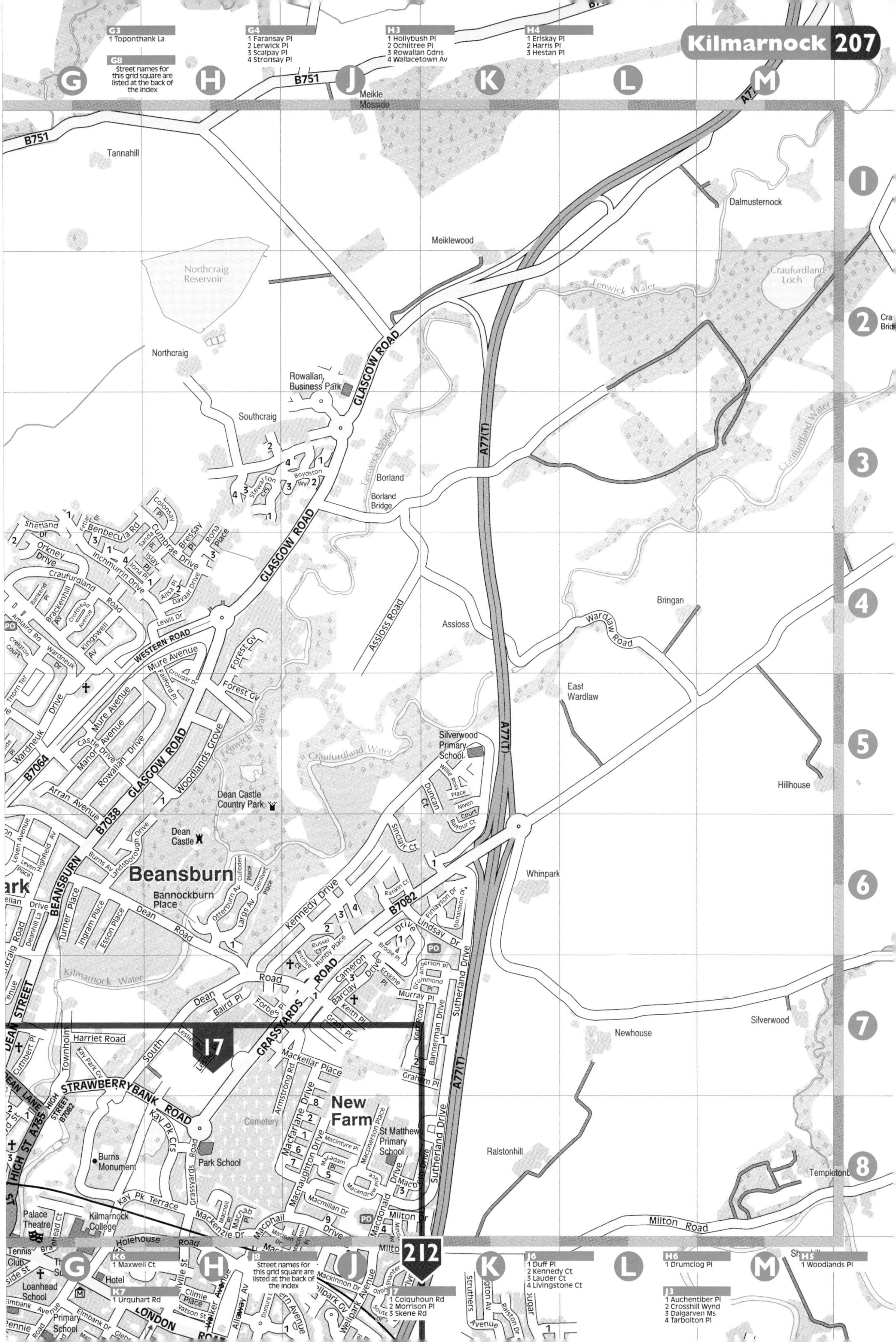
G3
1 Toponthank La
G8
Street names for this grid square are listed at the back of the index
G4
1 Faransay Pl
2 Lerwick Pl
3 Scalpay Pl
4 Stronsay Pl
H3
1 Hollybush Pl
2 Ochiltree Pl
3 Rowallan Gdns
4 Wallacetown Av
H4
1 Eriskay Pl
2 Harris Pl
3 Hestan Pl
B751
Meikle Mosside
Tannahill
Dalmusternock
Meiklewood
Northcraig Reservoir
Craufurdland Loch
Fenwick Water
Northcraig
GLASGOW ROAD
Rowallan Business Park
Southcraig
Craufurdland Water
A77(T)
Borland
Borland Bridge
Boydston Wy
Stewarton Crs
Shetland Dr
Benbecula Rd
Orkney Drive
Inchmurrin Drive
Cumbrae Drive
Bressay Pl
Rona Place
Colonsay Pl
Craufurdland Road
Lewis Dr
Davaar Drive
Ailsa Pl
Islay Pl
Iona Pl
Bankend Pl
Brackenhill Av
Crofthead Avenue
Kingswell Av
Amlaird Rd
Creighton Court
Wardneuk Dr
WESTERN ROAD
Bringan
Assloss
Assloss Road
Wardlaw Road
Mure Avenue
Crougar Dr
Fairlie Pl
Forest Gv
East Wardlaw
Thorn Ter
Wardneuk Drive
B7064
Castle Drive
Manor Drive
Rowallan Drive
GLASGOW ROAD
Woodlands Grove
Arran Avenue
B7038
Silverwood Primary School
Willie Ross Place
Duncan Ct
Niven Court
Balfour Ct
Hillhouse
Dean Castle Country Park
Dean Castle
Sinclair Ct
Leven Avenue
Highfield Av
Landsborough Drive
Burns Av
Beansburn
Whinpark
BEANSBURN
Bannockburn Place
Culloden Place
Glenlivet Place
Otterburn Av
Largs Av
Kennedy Drive
Rankin Ct
B7082
Finlayson Dr
Donaldson Dr
Lindsay Dr
Turner Place
Ingram Place
Esson Place
Dean Road
Deanhill La
Russel Ct
Ritchie Ct
Huntly Place
Brodie Pl
Kilmarnock Water
Road
Cameron Drive
Erskine Pl
Anderson Pl
Drummond Pl
Sutherland Drive
Murray Pl
Barclay Dr
Keith Pl
Grant Pl
Baird Pl
Forbes Pl
Dean Road
GRASSYARDS ROAD
Kerr Road
Bannerman Drive
DEAN STREET
Harriet Road
Leslie Rd
Cuthbert Pl
Townholm
South
I7
Mackellar Place
Graham Pl
Silverwood
Newhouse
Armstrong Rd
A77(T)
Kay Park Gv
STRAWBERRYBANK ROAD
DEAN LANE
HIGH STREET B7082
New Farm
Cemetery
Macfarlane Drive
Macpherson Place
St Matthews Primary School
Kay Pk Crs
Macintyre Pl
Macnaughton Drive
Burns Monument
Park School
Grassyards Road
Macadam Pl
Sutherland Drive
Ralstonhill
HIGH ST A735
Templeton
Kay Pk Terrace
Mackenzie Dr
Macmillan Dr
Macbeth Drive
Macdonald Drive
Milton Dr
Milton Road
Palace Theatre
Kilmarnock College
Holehouse Road
Macphail Dr
Tennis Club
Loanhead School
Hotel
Primary School
Elmbank Dr
LONDON ROAD
212
K6
1 Maxwell Ct
K7
1 Urquhart Rd
I8
Street names for this grid square are listed at the back of the index
J6
1 Duff Pl
2 Kennedy Ct
3 Lauder Ct
4 Livingstone Ct
H6
1 Drumclog Pl
H5
1 Woodlands Pl
J3
1 Auchentiber Pl
2 Crosshill Wynd
3 Dalgarven Ms
4 Tarbolton Pl
J7
1 Colquhoun Rd
2 Morrison Pl
3 Skene Rd
Mackinnon Dr
Wellpark Gv
Struthers Avenue
Clumie Place
Watson St
Walker Avenue
Alloway Av

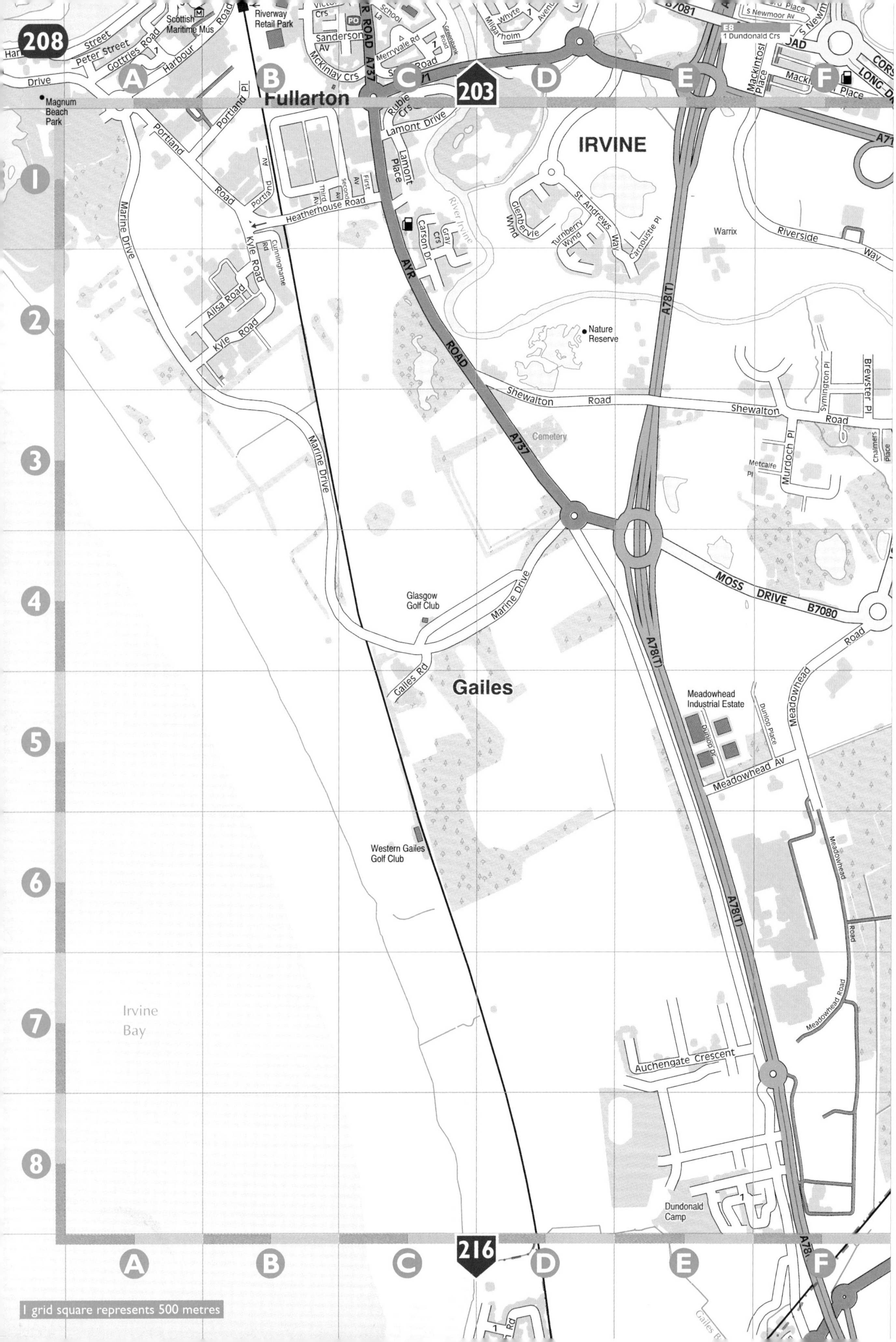
Fullarton
IRVINE
Gailes
Irvine Bay
Riverway Retail Park
Scottish Maritime Mus
Magnum Beach Park
Harbour Road
Peter Street
Gottries Road
Portland Pl
Portland Road
Portland Av
Heatherhouse Road
Kyle Road
Cunninghame Rd
Ailsa Road
Marine Drive
Sanderson Av
McKinlay Crs
Merryvale Rd
School La
Whyte Avenue
Milgarholm
Greenbank Road
Rubie Crs
Lamont Drive
Lamont Place
Third Av
Second Av
First Av
Carson Dr
Gray Crs
River Irvine
AYR ROAD A737
Glenbervie Wynd
Turnberry Wynd
St Andrews Way
Carnoustie Pl
Nature Reserve
Warrix
Riverside Way
A78(T)
A71
B7081
S Newmoor Av
1 Dundonald Crs
Mackintosh Place
Shewalton Road
Symington Pl
Brewster Pl
Cemetery
Metcalfe Pl
Murdoch Pl
Chalmers Place
MOSS DRIVE B7080
Meadowhead Road
Glasgow Golf Club
Gailes Rd
Meadowhead Industrial Estate
Dunlop Dr
Dunlop Place
Meadowhead Av
Western Gailes Golf Club
Auchengate Crescent
Dundonald Camp
203
216
A B C D E F
1 2 3 4 5 6 7 8
1 grid square represents 500 metres

Dreghorn
Dreghorn Primary School
Cemetery
Greer Academy
1 Corsehill Pk
Annick Water
Annick Drive
Dalmailing Av
Dunlop Crescent
Townfoot
Brae
Dundonald Road
Milton Rd
Milton Cres
Holms Avenue
Riverside Rd
Marble Av
Sharpe Av
Campbell Place
Corsehill Mt Road B7081
Coll Gdns
Monach Gdns
Corsehill Mount Road
Lismore Drive
The Glebe
Maid Morville Av
Corsehill
A71
B730
Newhouse
Steadman Place
Long Drive
North East
Nether Craig
Holms
River Irvine
Shewalton Road
Griers Walk
Dreghorn Road
Station Row
Main Street
Drybridge
Girtridge
Shewalton
Ploughland
Kilnford
Harperland
Dundonald Burn
Shewalton Moss
North Ayrshire
South Ayrshire
Palmer Mount
A759
Castleview
Auchans Dr
Cochrane Avenue
Guilliland Av
Newfield Dr
Dundonald Health Cen
Kilnford Drive
Old Auchans Vw
Coats Pl
Kilnford Crs
Wilson Pl
Parkthorn Vw
Vernon Pl
Yett
Winehouse
Drybridge Road
Fullarton Avenue
Primary School
Kilmarnock Road
Earl Dr
Dundonald Medical Practice
Dundonald Castle
Wallace Av
Bruce Av
Warly Drive
Warly Place
Dundonald
B750
Tarbolton Road
Laurieston
Merkland Loch
Hill House
G H J K L M
1 2 3 4 5 6 7 8
204
210
217

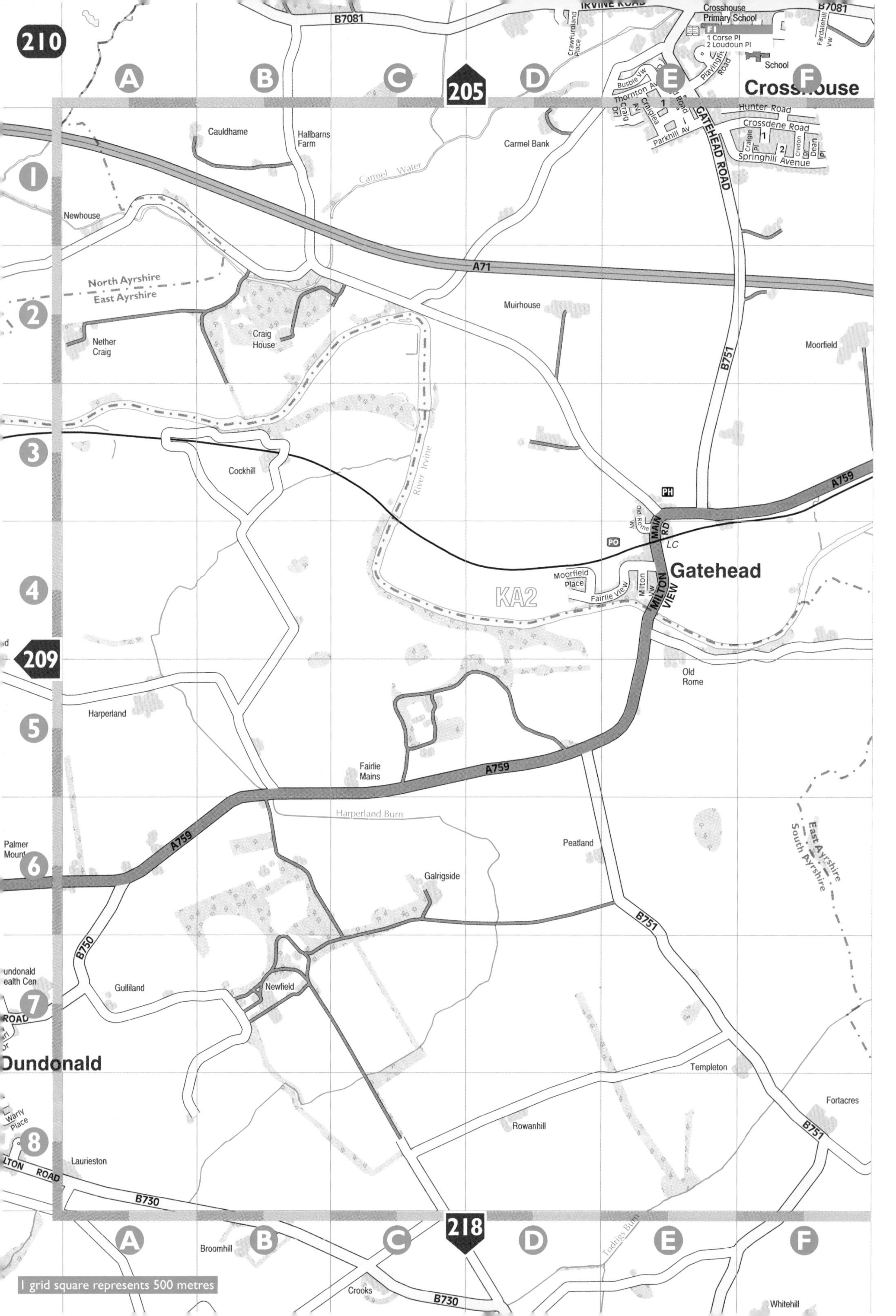
205
209
218
A B C D E F
1 2 3 4 5 6 7 8
Crosshouse
Crosshouse Primary School
1 Corse Pl
2 Loudoun Pl
School
B7081
IRVINE ROAD
Crawfurdland Place
Fardalehill Vw
Playingfield Road
Busbie Vw
Thornton Av
Craig Dr
Craig Av
Craiglea
Parkhill Av
GATEHEAD ROAD
Hunter Road
Crossdene Road
Craigie Pl
Credon Dr
Dean Pl
Springhill Avenue
Cauldhame
Hallbarns Farm
Carmel Bank
Carmel Water
Newhouse
A71
North Ayrshire
East Ayrshire
Muirhouse
Nether Craig
Craig House
Moorfield
B751
A759
Cockhill
River Irvine
PH
PO
Old Rome Vw
MAIN RD
LC
Gatehead
Moorfield Place
Fairlie View
Milton Vw
MILTON VIEW
KA2
Old Rome
Harperland
Fairlie Mains
Harperland Burn
Palmer Mount
Peatland
Galrigside
East Ayrshire
South Ayrshire
B750
Dundonald Health Cen
Gulliland
Newfield
ROAD
Dundonald
Templeton
Fortacres
Rowanhill
Warly Place
Laurieston
MILTON ROAD
B730
Broomhill
Todrigs Burn
Crooks
Whitehill
1 grid square represents 500 metres

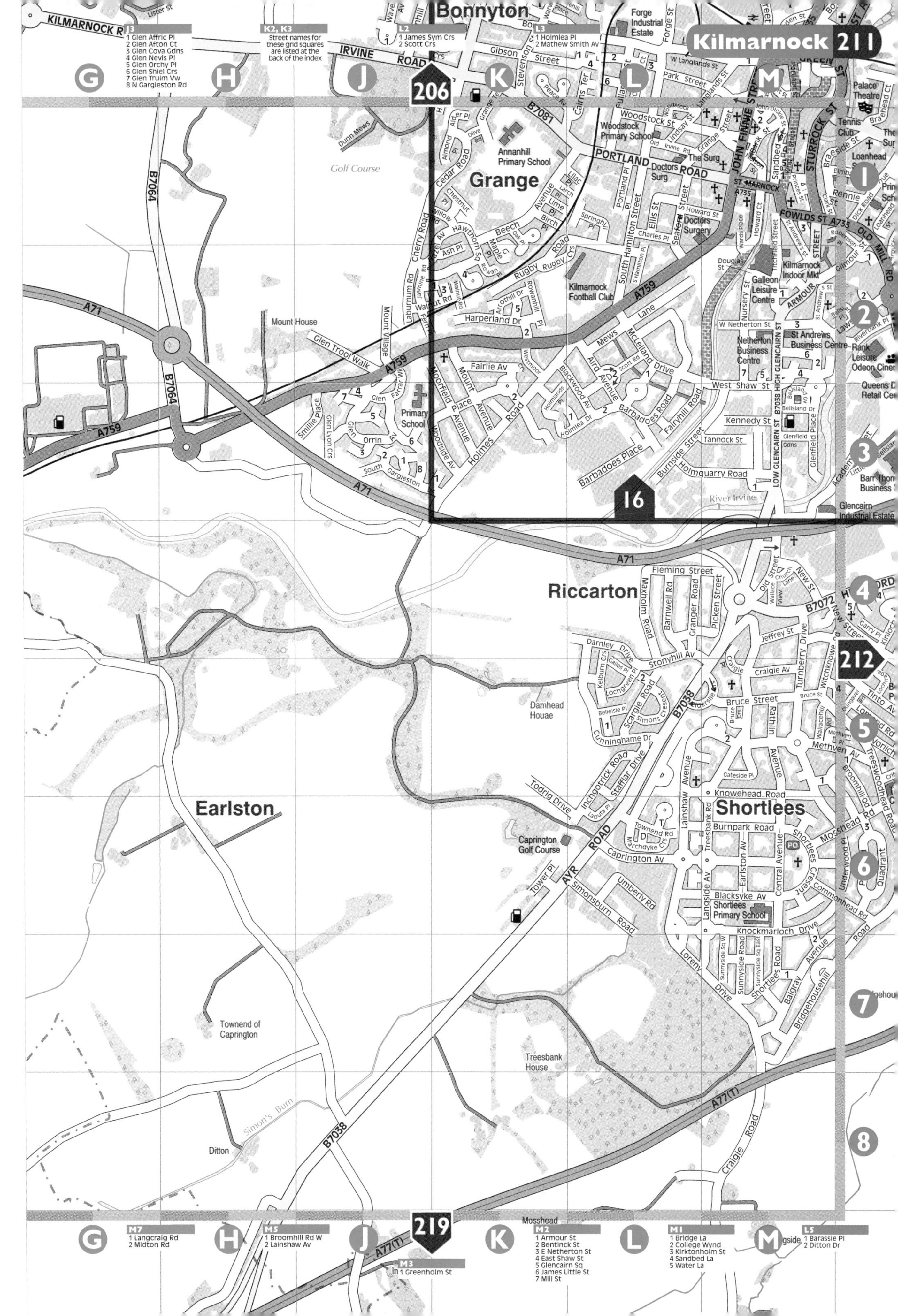
J3
1 Glen Affric Pl
2 Glen Afton Ct
3 Glen Cova Gdns
4 Glen Nevis Pl
5 Glen Orchy Pl
6 Glen Shiel Crs
7 Glen Truim Vw
8 N Gargieston Rd
K2, K3
Street names for these grid squares are listed at the back of the index
L2
1 James Sym Crs
2 Scott Crs
L3
1 Holmlea Pl
2 Mathew Smith Av
206
Bonnyton
Forge Industrial Estate
Grange
Annanhill Primary School
Golf Course
Woodstock Primary School
Kilmarnock Football Club
Galleon Leisure Centre
Kilmarnock Indoor Mkt
Netherton Business Centre
St Andrews Business Centre
Palace Theatre
Mount House
Primary School
16
River Irvine
Glencairn Industrial Estate
Riccarton
212
Damhead Houae
Earlston
Caprington Golf Course
Shortlees
Shortlees Primary School
Townend of Caprington
Treesbank House
Ditton
A71
A759
B7064
B7038
A77(T)
219
M7
1 Langcraig Rd
2 Midton Rd
M5
1 Broomhill Rd W
2 Lainshaw Av
M3
1 Greenholm St
M2
1 Armour St
2 Bentinck St
3 E Netherton St
4 East Shaw St
5 Glencairn Sq
6 James Little St
7 Mill St
M1
1 Bridge La
2 College Wynd
3 Kirktonholm St
4 Sandbed La
5 Water La
L5
1 Barassie Pl
2 Ditton Dr

212
207
211
17
KILMARNOCK
Crookedholm
Bellfield
A
B
C
D
E
F
1
2
3
4
5
6
7
8
B1
1 Middlemass Dr
B4
1 Ardle Av
2 Eden Pl
A5, A6
Street names for these grid squares are listed at the back of the index
A4
1 Annick Pl
2 Beauly Crs
3 Clyde Pl
4 Forth Pl
5 Katrine Ct
6 Tweed Crs
A1
1 Mitchell Ct
A2
1 Richardland Pl
2 Shawbank Pl
3 Waulkmill Pl
B5
1 Cruachan Pl
2 Princess Ct
3 Solway Pl
C1
1 Greenan Rd
2 Mackendrick Pl
3 Wellpark Ct
D1
1 Silverwood Rd
D2
1 Seright Crs
E3
1 Academy Ct
2 Wallace Ct
F2
1 Holyoake Ct
2 Marchmont Ct
St Matthews Primary School
Park School
Palace Theatre
Kilmarnock College
Tennis Club
The Surgery
Hotel
Loanhead School
Primary School
Kilmarnock Indoor Mkt
St Andrews Business Centre
Riverbank Business Centre
Rank Leisure
Odeon Cinema
Queens Drive Retail Centre
Queens Drive Retail Park
Barr Thomson Business Park
Glencairn Industrial Estate
Kirkstyle Primary School
Struthers
Kaimshill
Riccarton Cemetery
Kirklandside Hospital
Bellfield Primary School
Treeswoodhead Clinic
West Mosside
Bridgehouse Farm
Crossbush
Inchbean
Midton of Balgray
Braehead
Haining Mains
Barleith
Shawhill
Ralstonhill
Temple
The Surgery
Primary Sch
River Irvine
Cessnock Water
Milton Road
Milton Rd
Holehouse Road
Wilson Avenue
London Road
B7073
Old Mill Rd
A735
Welbeck St
Queen's Drive
A71
A77(T)
A76(T)
Riccarton Road
Main Road
Mauchline Road
Hurlford Road
B7072
Fowlds St
Armour St
Mackinlay Place
New Mill Road
Samson Avenue
Walker Avenue
Alloway Av
Linfern Avenue
Wellpark Avenue
Macgregor Dr
Macphail Drive
Cotter Drive
Ellisland Dr
Bunting Place
Finch Pl
Sparrow Gdns
Melville St
Climie Place
Watson St
Glebe Road
Glebe Av
Elmbank Avenue
Elmbank Dr
Rennie St
Dick Road
Braeside St
Braehead Ct
Robertson Pl
Gilmour St
Lawson St
Riverbank Pl
Bellsland Dr
Glenfield
Academy Street
Bellsland Road
Little Bellsland Road
Carron Av
Nith Place
Carron
Annan Rd
Strathy Place
Cessock Pl
Earn Pl
Teith Pl
Deveron Road
Kinloch Road
Garnock Rd
Spey Av
Avon Pl
Broom Pl
Ken Rd
Haining Avenue
Calder Pl
Croe Pl
Esk Road
Doon Pl
Dee Av
Merrick Road
Tinto Avenue
Lomond Rd
Vorlich Pl
Loudoun Avenue
Cromdale Rd
Treeswoodhead Road
Broomhill Rd
Methven Av
Mosshead Rd
Pentland Rd
Lammermuir Rd
Ochil Pl
Cairngorm Rd
Leadhills Rd
Cullin Pl
Kinnoull Rd
Sidlaw Pl
Grampian
Underwood Pl
Peatland Quadrant
Commonhead Rd
Central Avenue
Balgray Avenue
Wellington Av
Struthers Avenue
Ralston Dr
Seright Square
Grougar Road
Meadowside
Ralstonyards
Road
Portland Brae
Furnace Ct
Ried Court
Station Drive
Bellfield Avenue
Bellfield Ct
Maxwell Gdns
Walden Rd
Kersland Cresent
Roxburgh Rd
Morris Crs
Blair Crs
Blair Rd
Blair Avenue
Barnweill Drive
Leven Dr
Lomond Av
Cessnock Road
Sherwood Rd
Lifnock Avenue
Cessnock Avenue
Craigie Road
Drumleyhill Dr
Salisbury
Kermuir
Mackinnon Dr
Macmillan Dr
Macdonald Drive
Macpherson Drive
Sutherland Drive
Grassyards Road
Langside
Burn
Treeswoodhead Road
1 grid square represents 500 metres

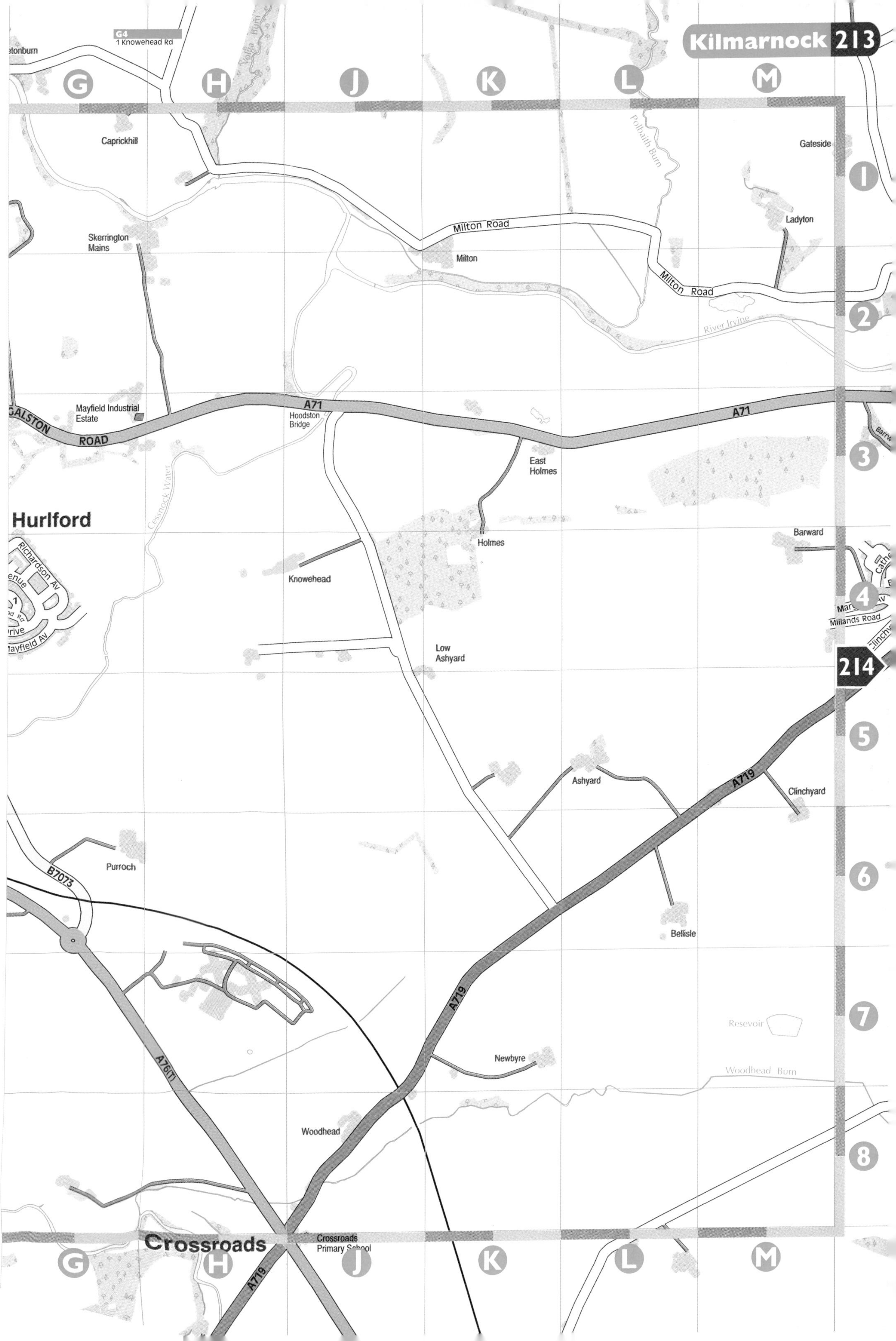
G4
1 Knowehead Rd
etonburn
G
H
J
K
L
M
Volga Burn
Caprickhill
Polbaith Burn
Gateside
1
Skerrington
Mains
Milton Road
Milton
Ladyton
Milton Road
2
River Irvine
Mayfield Industrial
Estate
GALSTON
ROAD
A71
Hoodston
Bridge
A71
3
East
Holmes
Cessnock Water
Hurlford
Richardson Av
enue
Mayfield Av
rive
Holmes
Barward
Knowehead
4
Millands Road
Low
Ashyard
214
5
A719
Ashyard
Clinchyard
Purroch
B7073
6
Bellisle
A719
7
Resevoir
A76(T)
Newbyre
Woodhead Burn
Woodhead
8
Crossroads
Crossroads
Primary School
A719
G
H
J
K
L
M

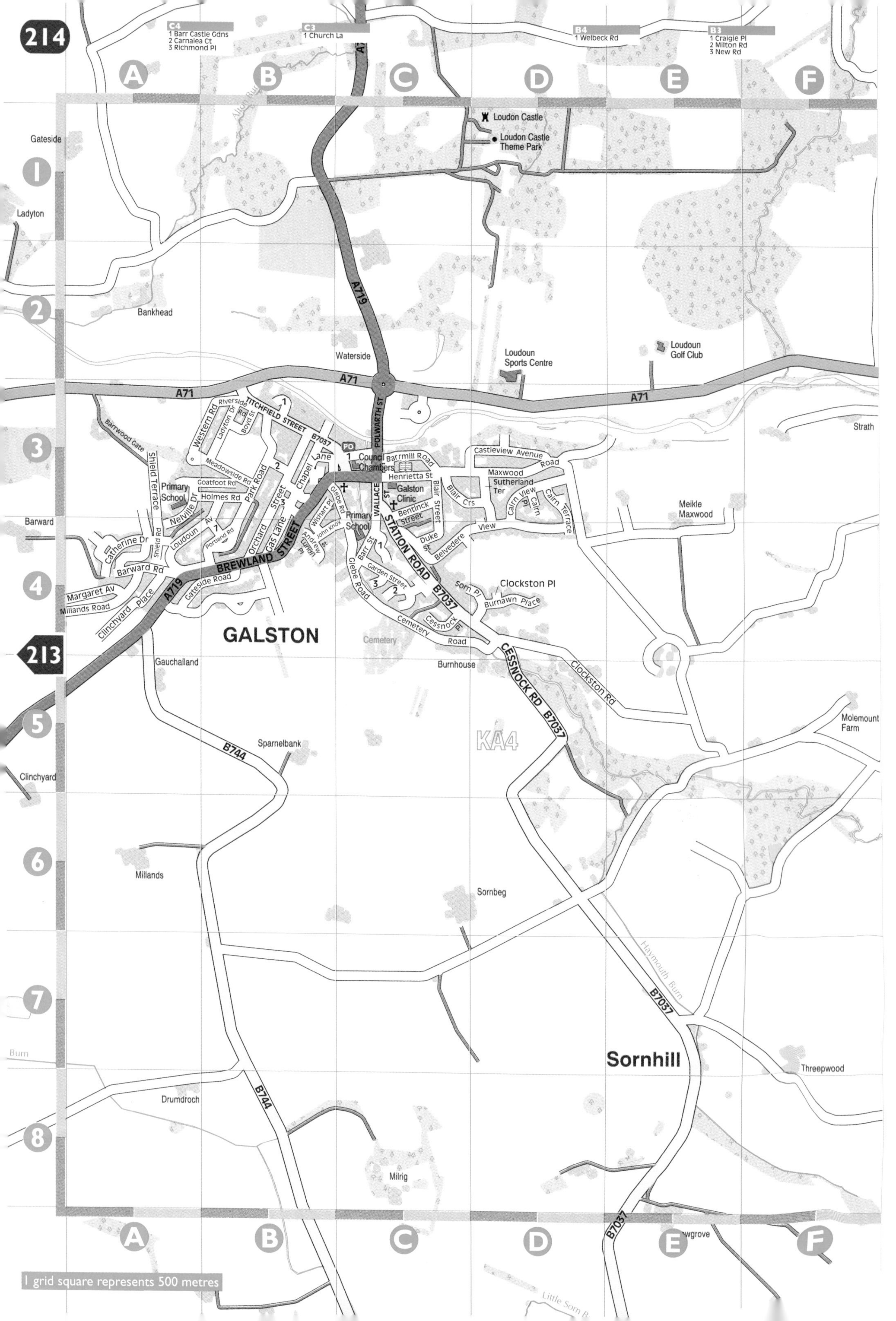
C4
1 Barr Castle Gdns
2 Carnalea Ct
3 Richmond Pl
C3
1 Church La
B4
1 Welbeck Rd
B3
1 Craigie Pl
2 Milton Rd
3 New Rd
Gateside
Ladyton
Bankhead
Loudon Castle
Loudon Castle Theme Park
Waterside
Loudoun Sports Centre
Loudoun Golf Club
A71
A719
Strath
Barward
Meikle Maxwood
GALSTON
Cemetery
Burnhouse
Gauchalland
Clockston Pl
Clockston Rd
KA4
Molemount Farm
Sparnelbank
B744
Clinchyard
Millands
Sornbeg
Haymouth Burn
B7037
Sornhill
Threepwood
Drumdroch
Milrig
Burn
Little Sorn
213
1 grid square represents 500 metres

G2
1 Fraser Ct
H3
1 Strath Crs
J2
1 Baldie's Brae
2 Covenanters Ct
3 Hillside Pl
4 Regents Ct
5 Shields Rd
G
H
J
K
L
M
1
2
3
4
5
6
7
8
Clearmount
Woodhead
NEWMILNS
KA16
Cemetery
Dry Ski Slope
Dalwhatswood Road
Huggin Craig Burn
Huggin Craig Rd
Borebrae Crs
Clearmount Av
Mair St
Darnleyhill Walk
Loudoun Crs
Borebrae
Kilnholm St
Drygatehead
High Street
King St
Campbell Street
Campbell Court
Isles Burn
Foulpapple Road
Alstonpapple
DARVEL ROAD
A71
ISLES STREET
MAIN STREET
KILNHOLM STREET
Greenside
Greenhead
Union St
Mill Crs
Mill Road
Ladeside
Brown's Road
PO
Nelson Street
Brown Street
Riverbank St
Queen's Crs
Doctors Surgery
The Clinic
Gilfoot
Girvan Crescent
LOUDOUN ROAD
Newmilns Primary School
Loudoun Road West
Macleod St
Irvine Rd
Lawrie St
Muire Pl
Stoneygate Rd
Strathholm Terrace
Greenholm
Mount Pleasant
High Dalloy
Windyhill
Windyhill Road
Stonyhall
Parkerston
Lanfine Home Farm
Gullyhill
Bonnieton
Downie's Burn
Middle Third
Molmontend
Hillhouse
Middlefield
Waterfalls
Burn Anne
Newfield
L2
1 Burn Rd
2 Weavers Pl
3 West Campbell St
K2
1 Bridgend
2 Castle St
3 Craigview Rd
4 Drygate St
5 East Church Ct
6 East Strd
7 King's Crs
8 West Church St

F1
1 Struthers Pl

E2
1 College Pk
2 Corrie Pl
3 Fairhaven
4 Hillocks Pl
5 Lang Rd
6 North Neuk
7 Steeples Vw

D6
1 Cessnock Rd

D2
1 Kilkerran Dr

D1
1 Rosemount Dr

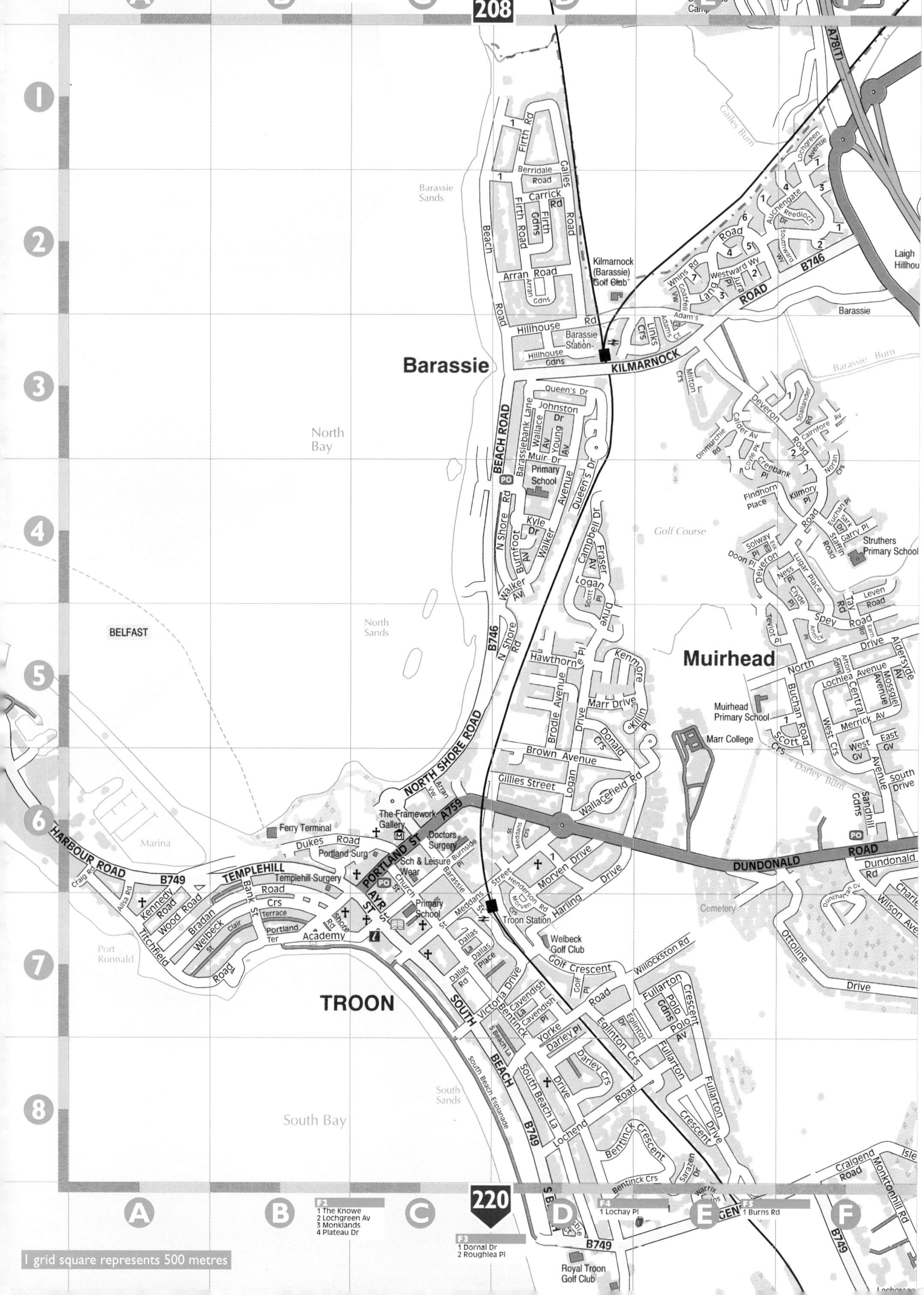

F2
1 The Knowe
2 Lochgreen Av
3 Monklands
4 Plateau Dr

F3
1 Dornal Dr
2 Roughlea Pl

F4
1 Lochay Pl

F5
1 Burns Rd

1 grid square represents 500 metres

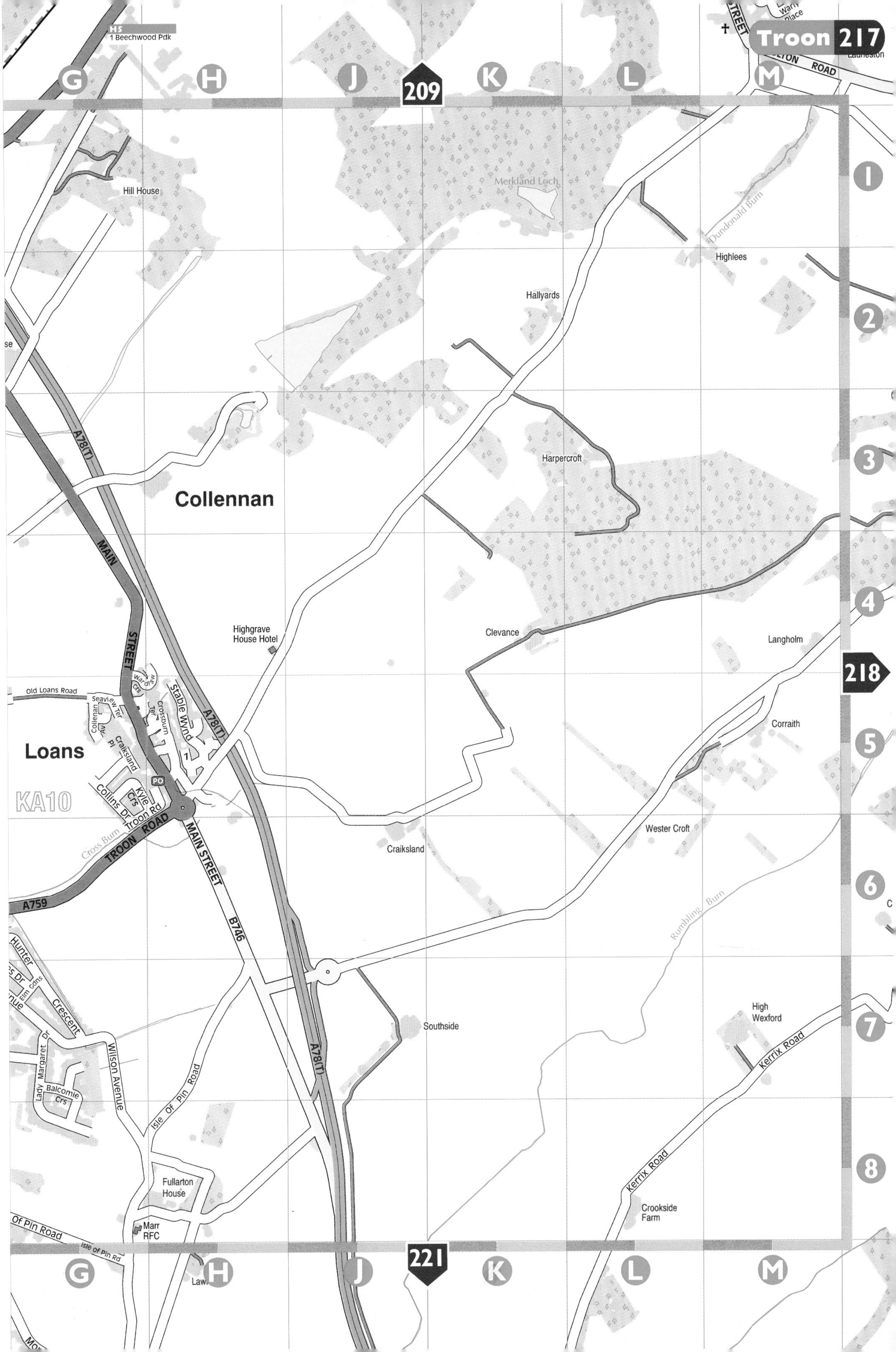
H5
1 Beechwood Pdk
G
H
J
209
K
L
M
1
2
3
4
218
5
6
7
8
221
Hill House
Merkland Loch
Dundonald Burn
Highlees
Hallyards
Harpercroft
Collennan
A78(T)
MAIN
STREET
Highgrave
House Hotel
Clevance
Langholm
Corraith
Old Loans Road
Seaview Ter
Wardlaw Crs
Stable Wynd
Crossburn Ter
Collenan Av
Craiksland Pl
Loans
KA10
PO
Collins Dr
Kyle Crs
Troon Rd
TROON ROAD
Cross Burn
MAIN STREET
Craiksland
Wester Croft
A759
B746
Rumbling Burn
Hunter
Elm Gdns
Crescent
Southside
High
Wexford
Kerrix Road
Lady Margaret Dr
Balcomie Crs
Wilson Avenue
Isle Of Pin Road
Fullarton
House
Marr
RFC
Of Pin Road
Isle of Pin Rd
Crookside
Farm

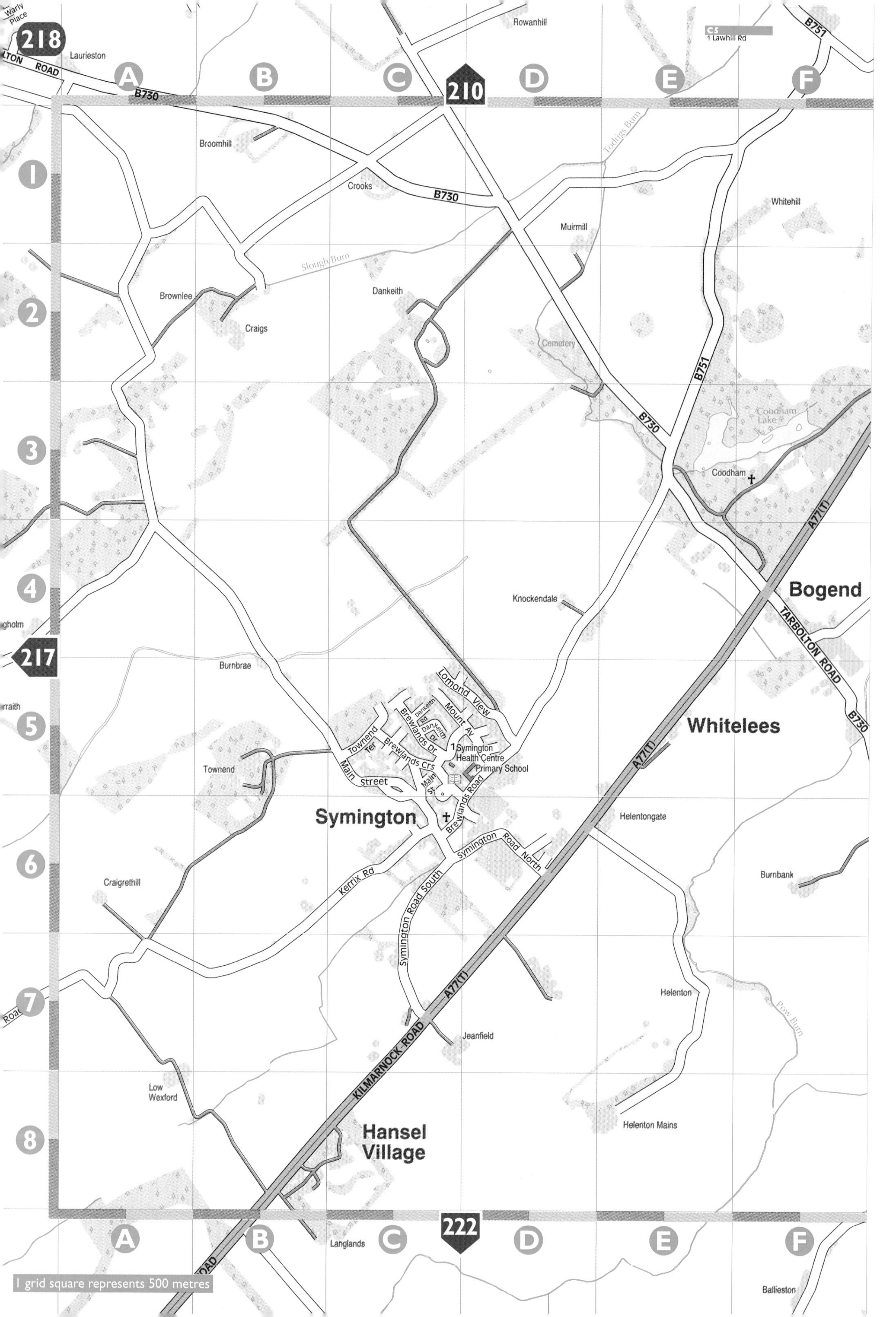

218
210
217
222
A
B
C
D
E
F
1
2
3
4
5
6
7
8
Laurieston
B730
Rowanhill
1 Lawhill Rd
B751
Broomhill
Crooks
Todrigs Burn
Whitehill
Muirmill
Slough Burn
Brownlee
Craigs
Dankeith
Cemetery
Coodham Lake
Coodham
Knockendale
Bogend
Tarbolton Road
A77(T)
Burnbrae
Whitelees
Lomond View
Mount Av
Dankeith Rd
Dankeith Dr
Brewlands Dr
Brewlands Crs
Townend Ter
Townend
Main Street
Main St
Symington Health Centre
Primary School
Brewlands Road
Symington
Helentongate
Symington Road North
Symington Road South
Kerrix Rd
Craigrethill
Burnbank
Helenton
Pow Burn
Jeanfield
Kilmarnock Road
Low Wexford
Hansel Village
Helenton Mains
Langlands
Balliestoun
1 grid square represents 500 metres

211
223
G
H
J
K
L
M
1
2
3
4
5
6
7
8
Ditton
Simon's Bu
B7038
A77(T)
Mosshead
Langside
Inchgotrick
Spittalhill
Gateside
Braeside
Stafflar
Harelaw
Howcommon
East Ayrshire
South Ayrshire
Muirhouse
Stonecalsey
Craigie
Langcraig
Main Street
Pow Burn
High
Langside
Catcraig
Laigh
Langside
B730
Plewlands
Caldrongill
Heughmill
A719
Barnweil
Midton
Underhills
Kirkhill

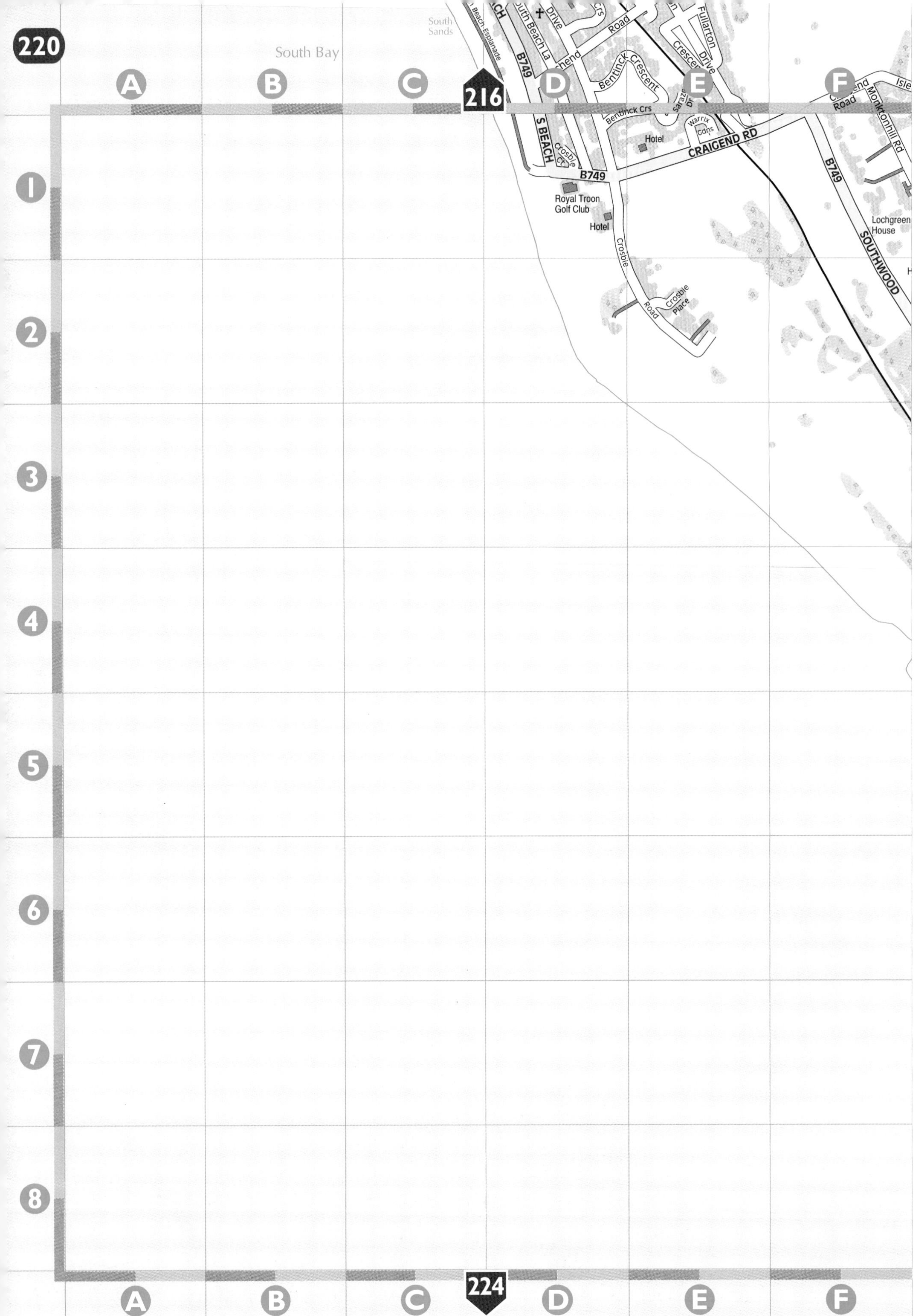
South Bay
South Sands
216
224
A
B
C
D
E
F
1
2
3
4
5
6
7
8
S Beach Esplanade
South Beach La
Drive
Road
Bentinck Crescent
Fullarton Drive
Crescent
Bentinck Crs
Sarazen Dr
Warrix Gdns
B749
S BEACH
Crosbie Ct
Hotel
CRAIGEND RD
Craigend Road
Monktonhill Rd
Royal Troon Golf Club
Crosbie Road
Crosbie Place
Lochgreen House
SOUTHWOOD

1 grid square represents 500 metres

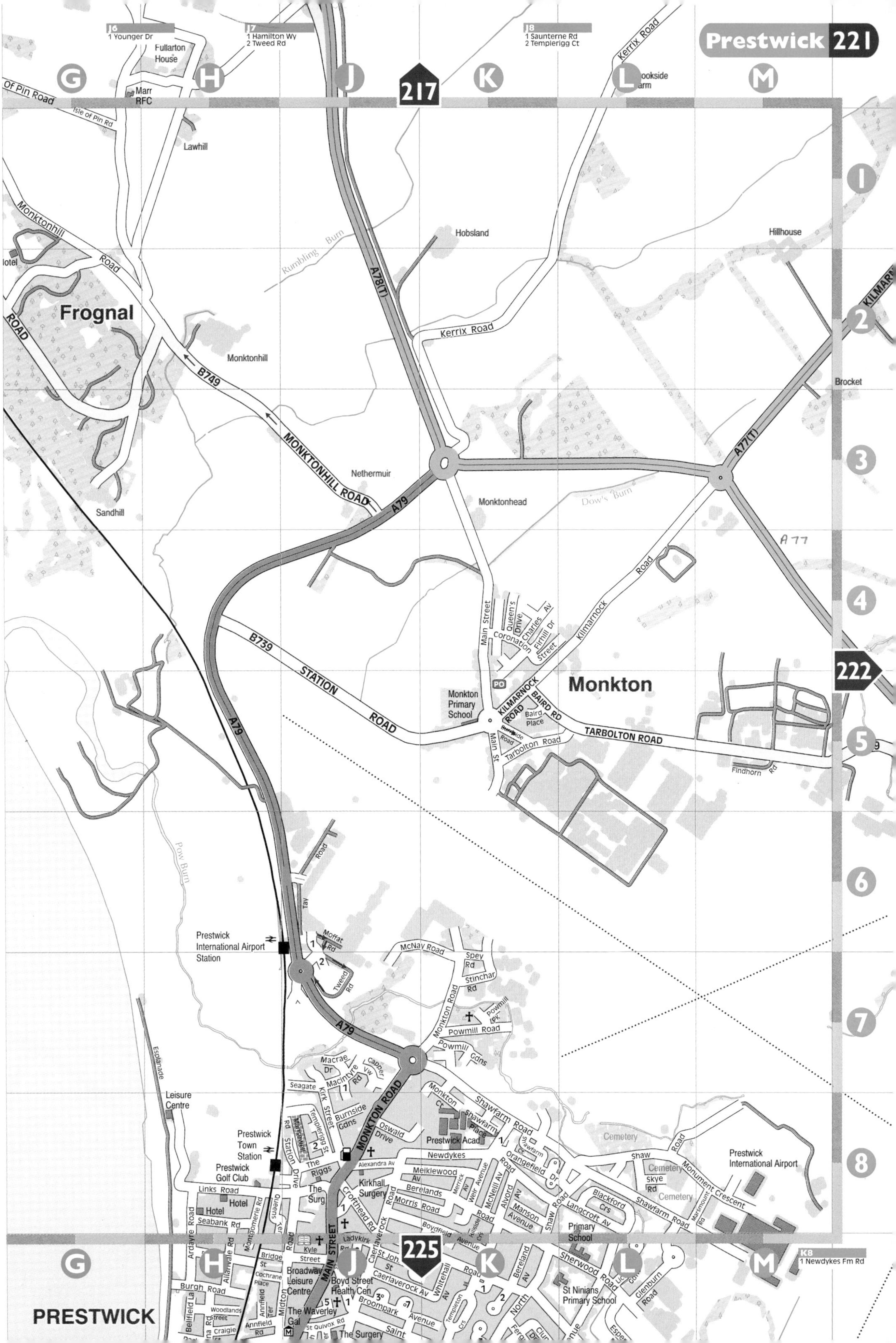
J6
1 Younger Dr
J7
1 Hamilton Wy
2 Tweed Rd
J8
1 Saunterne Rd
2 Templerigg Ct
G
H
J
217
K
L
M
Fullarton House
Marr RFC
Isle of Pin Road
Isle of Pin Rd
Lawhill
Kerrix Road
Brookside Farm
I
Monktonhill Road
Hotel
Frognal
ROAD
Rumbling Burn
Hobsland
Hillhouse
A78(T)
Kerrix Road
2
KILMARNOCK
Monktonhill
B749
Brocket
MONKTONHILL ROAD
A77(T)
3
Nethermuir
A79
Monktonhead
Dow's Burn
Sandhill
A77
Road
4
Main Street
Queen's Drive
Charles Av
Coronation Street
Firhill Dr
Kilmarnock
B739
STATION
ROAD
PO
Monkton
222
Monkton Primary School
KILMARNOCK ROAD
BAIRD RD
Baird Place
TARBOLTON ROAD
Burnside Road
Main St
Tarbolton Road
5
Findhorn Rd
A79
Pow Burn
Road
6
Tay
Prestwick International Airport Station
Moffat Rd
1
2
Tweed Rd
McNay Road
Spey Rd
Stinchar Rd
Monkton Road
Powmill Pk
Powmill Road
Powmill Gdns
7
A79
Esplanade
Macrae Dr
Macintyre Rd
Capper Vw
Seagate
Kirk Street
1
MONKTON ROAD
Monkton Ct
Shawfarm Place
Shawfarm Road
Leisure Centre
Templerigg St
Burnside Gdns
Oswald Drive
Prestwick Acad
Cemetery
Prestwick Town Station
Station Drive
Marchfield Rd
2
Alexandra Av
Newdykes
Orangefield Dr
Shaw
Road
Prestwick International Airport
8
Prestwick Golf Club
The Riggs
Meiklewood Av
Weir Avenue
McNeill Av
Cemetery
Skye Rd
Monument Crescent
Links Road
The Surg
Kirkhall Surgery
Berelands
Merrick Av
Alvord Av
Blackford Crs
Langcroft Av
Cemetery
Hotel
Hotel
Montgomerie Rd
Queens Ter
Crofthead Rd
Morris Road
Manson Avenue
Shaw Road
Shawfarm Road
Marsmount
Ardayre Road
Seabank Rd
Caerlaverock
Boydfield Avenue
Hillside Crs
Primary School
Allanvale Rd
Road
Kyle
MAIN STREET
Ladykirk Rd
225
Bridge St
Street
St John St
G
H
J
K
L
M
K8
1 Newdykes Fm Rd
Cochrane Place
Broadway Leisure Centre
Boyd Street Health Cen
Caerlaverock Av
Whitehall Av
Road
Bereland Av
Sherwood Road
Glenburn Road
Burgh Road
Annfield Ter
Midton
Broompark
Avenue
North
St Ninians Primary School
PRESTWICK
Bellfield La
Woodlands Street
Annfield Rd
Craigie
The Waverley
Gal
St Quivox Rd
The Surgery
Saint
Templeton Crs

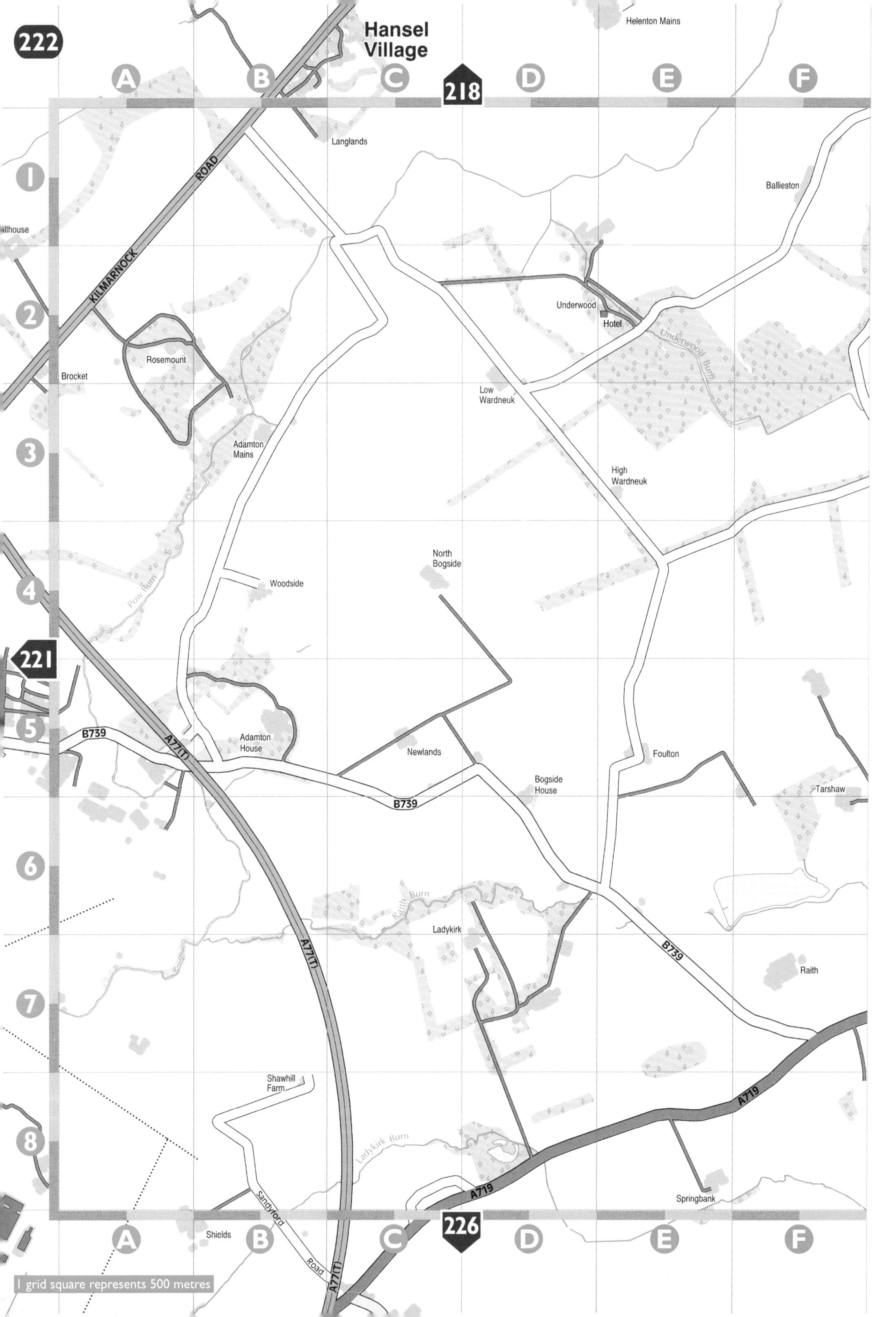
Hansel Village
Helenton Mains
218
A
B
C
D
E
F
Langlands
KILMARNOCK ROAD
Ballieston
illhouse
Underwood
Hotel
Underwood Burn
Rosemount
Brocket
Low Wardneuk
Adamton Mains
High Wardneuk
North Bogside
Woodside
Pow Burn
221
B739
A77(T)
Adamton House
Newlands
Foulton
Bogside House
Tarshaw
Raith Burn
Ladykirk
Raith
Shawhill Farm
A719
Ladykirk Burn
Springbank
Sandyford Road
Shields
226
1
2
3
4
5
6
7
8
1 grid square represents 500 metres

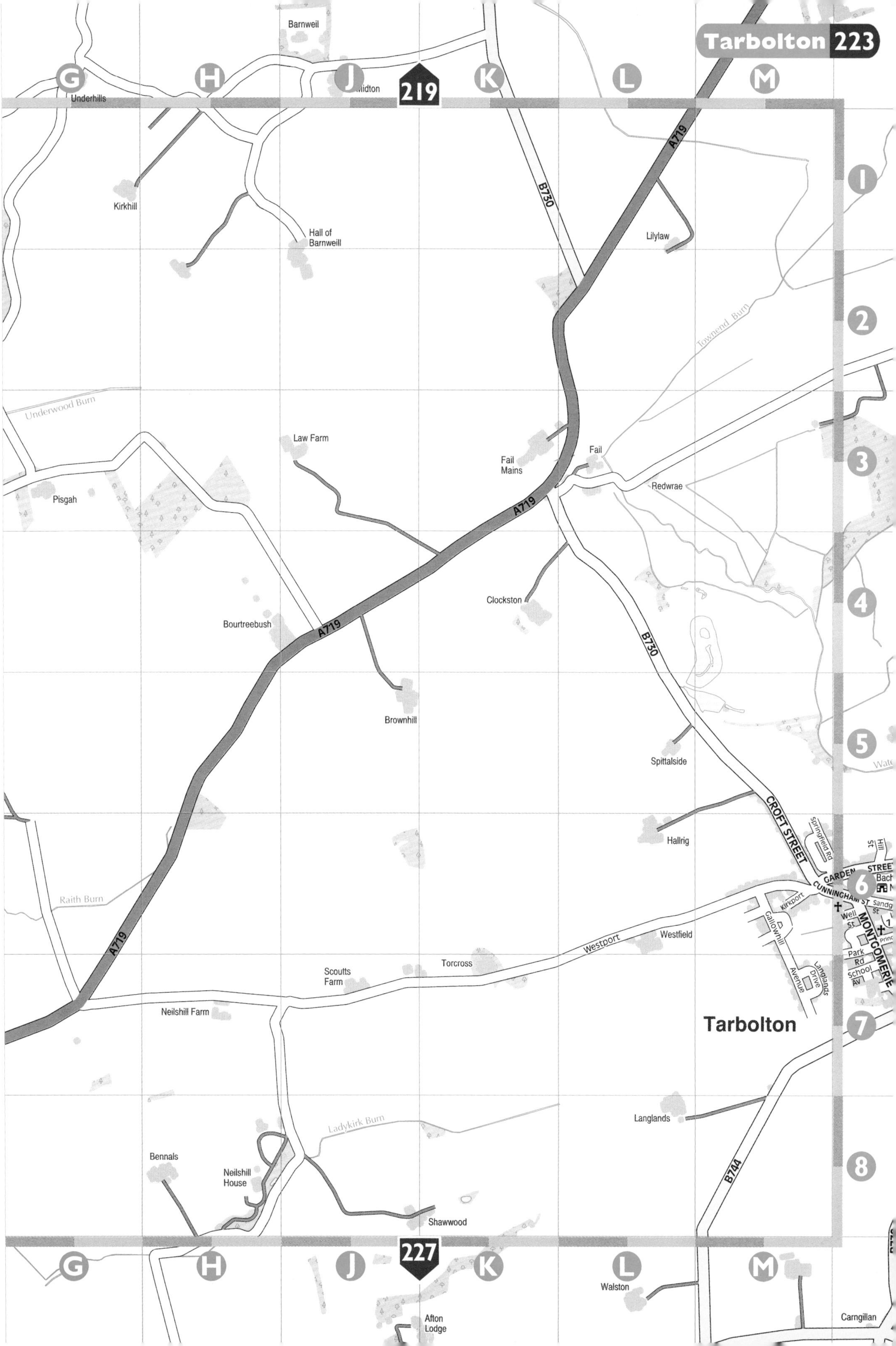
Barnweil
Underhills
G
H
J
K
L
M
219
227
I
2
3
4
5
6
7
8
Kirkhill
Hall of Barnweill
B730
A719
Lilylaw
Townend Burn
Underwood Burn
Law Farm
Fail
Fail Mains
Redwrae
Pisgah
Clockston
Bourtreebush
Brownhill
Spittalside
CROFT STREET
Springfield Rd
Hallrig
Hill St
GARDEN STREET
CUNNINGHAM ST
Kirkport
Well St
MONTGOMERIE
Gallowhill
Park Rd
School Av
Langlands Drive
Avenue
Raith Burn
Westport
Westfield
Scoutts Farm
Torcross
Neilshill Farm
Tarbolton
Langlands
Ladykirk Burn
Bennals
Neilshill House
B744
Shawwood
Walston
Afton Lodge
Carngillan

F8
1 Academy St
2 Cathcart St
3 St John St

F7
1 Halls Vennal
2 Saltfield La

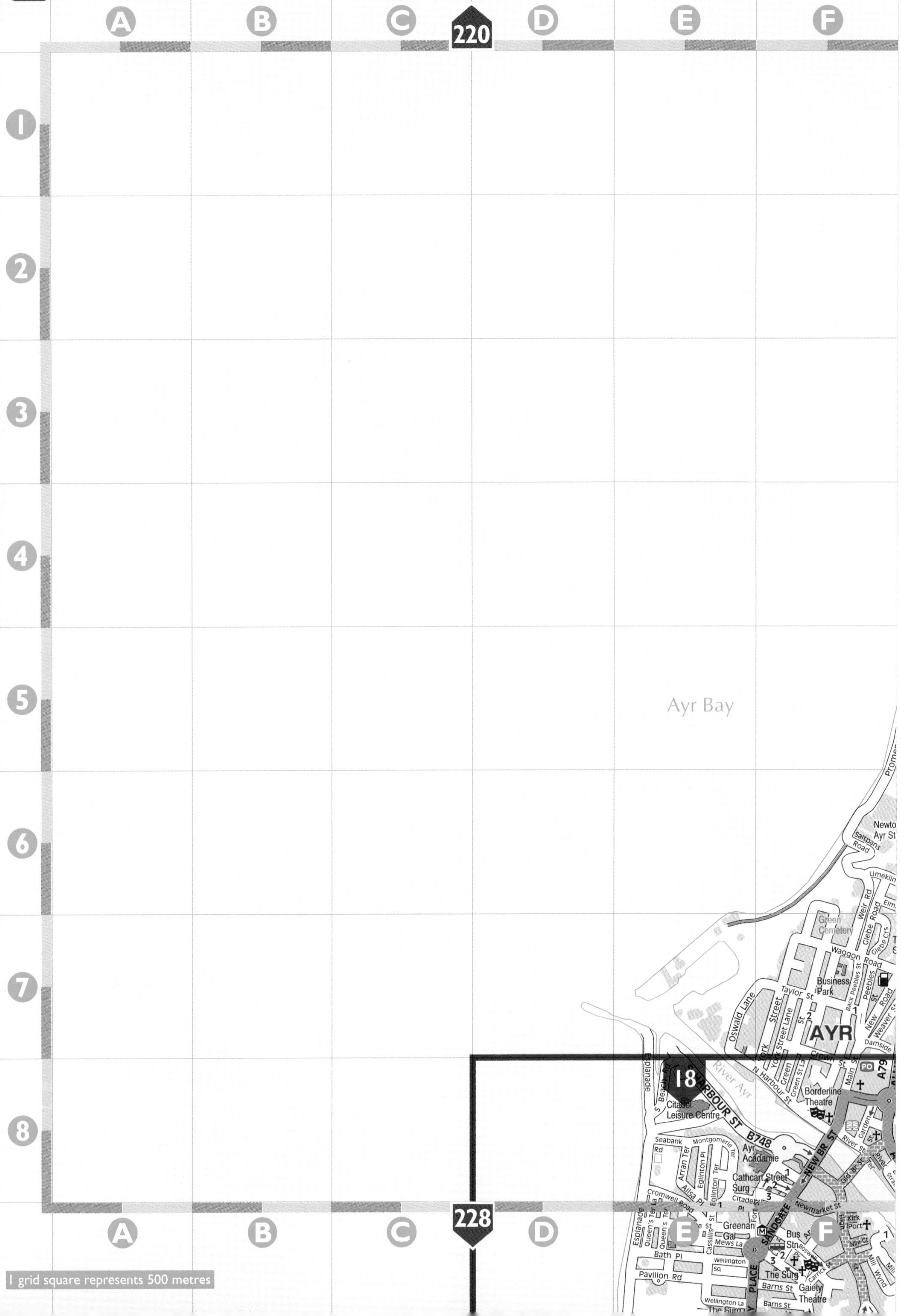

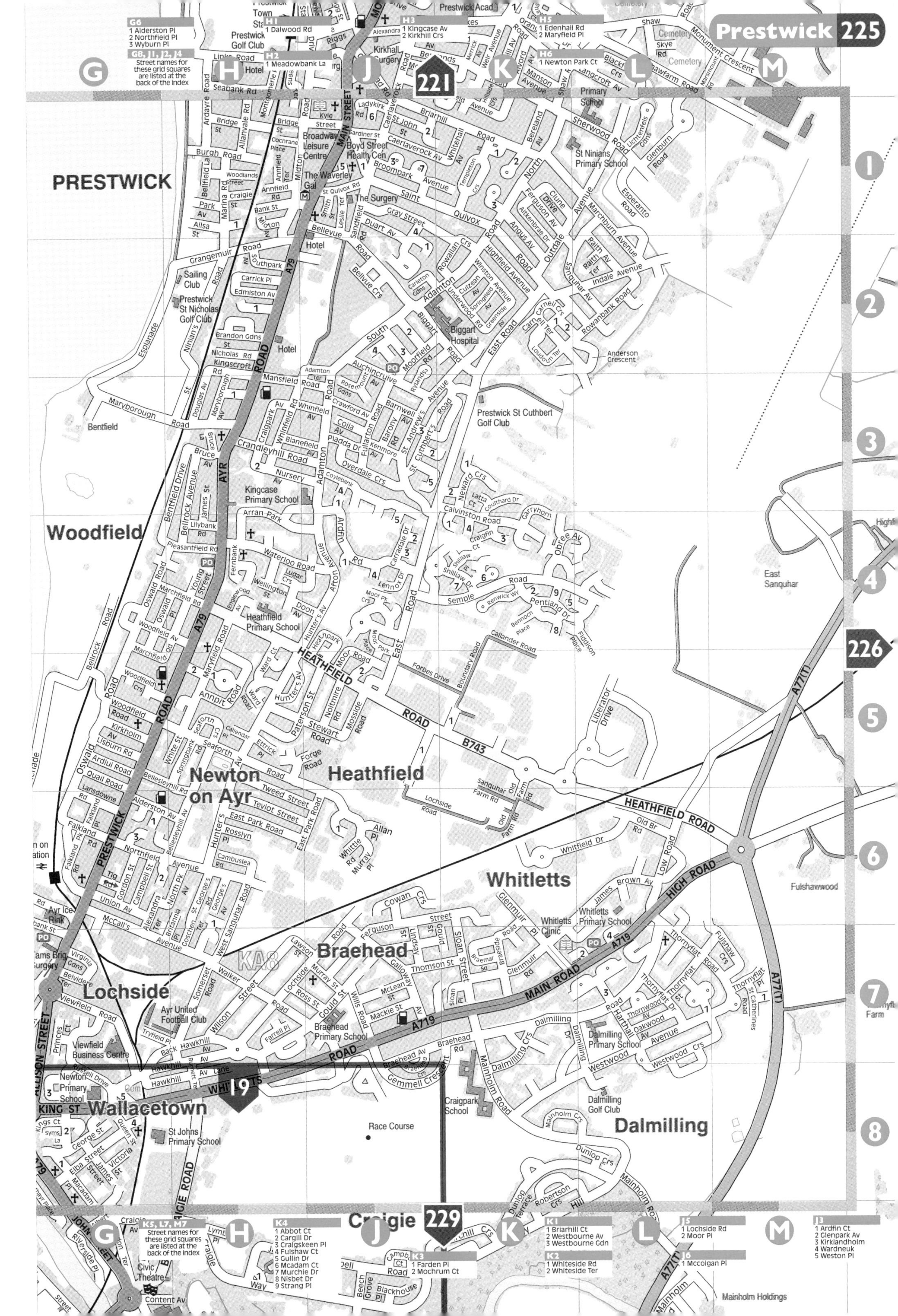
G6
1 Alderston Pl
2 Northfield Pl
3 Wyburn Pl
G8, J1, J2, J4
Street names for these grid squares are listed at the back of the index
H1
1 Dalwood Rd
H2
1 Meadowbank La
H3
1 Kingcase Av
2 Kirkhill Crs
H5
1 Edenhall Rd
2 Maryfield Pl
H6
1 Newton Park Ct
221
226
229
19
PRESTWICK
Woodfield
Newton on Ayr
Heathfield
Whitletts
Braehead
Lochside
Wallacetown
Dalmilling
Craigie
KA8
Prestwick Golf Club
Prestwick St Nicholas Golf Club
Prestwick St Cuthbert Golf Club
Sailing Club
Biggart Hospital
St Ninians Primary School
Kingcase Primary School
Heathfield Primary School
Whitletts Primary School
Whitletts Clinic
Braehead Primary School
Dalmilling Primary School
Dalmilling Golf Club
Newton Primary School
St Johns Primary School
Craigpark School
Ayr United Football Club
Viewfield Business Centre
Ayr Ice Rink
Race Course
Broadway Leisure Centre
Boyd Street Health Cen
The Surgery
Bentfield
East Sanquhar
Fulshawwood
Anderson Crescent
Mainholm Holdings
Civic Theatre
MAIN STREET
AYR ROAD
PRESTWICK ROAD
HEATHFIELD ROAD
HIGH ROAD
MAIN ROAD
A79
A719
A77(T)
B743
K5, L7, M7
Street names for these grid squares are listed at the back of the index
K4
1 Abbot Ct
2 Cargill Dr
3 Craigskeen Pl
4 Fulshaw Ct
5 Gullin Dr
6 Mcadam Ct
7 Murchie Dr
8 Nisbet Dr
9 Strang Pl
K3
1 Farden Pl
2 Mochrum Ct
K1
1 Briarhill Ct
2 Westbourne Av
3 Westbourne Gdn
K2
1 Whiteside Rd
2 Whiteside Ter
J5
1 Lochside Rd
2 Moor Pl
J6
1 Mccolgan Pl
J3
1 Ardfin Ct
2 Glenpark Av
3 Kirklandholm
4 Wardneuk
5 Weston Pl

A
B
C
D
E
F
1
2
3
4
5
6
7
8
222
225
230
F3
1 Raggithill Av
Ladykirk Burn
Springbank
Shields
Sandyford Road
A77(T)
19
Sandyford
Clune
Bogend
Raggithill
B742
Mossblown Farm
Arcon Av
Hillpark
SANDYFORD ROAD
Barwheys
Kirklandholm Farm
Highfield
Kevoc Cotts
B7035
St Quivox
B743
B744
River Ayr
Auchincruive Agricultural College
lshawwood
Oswald's Bridge
Thornyflat Farm
Laigland Holdings
Auchincruive Holdings
Tarholm
Bloomsbank Farm
Barclaugh
1 grid square represents 500 metres

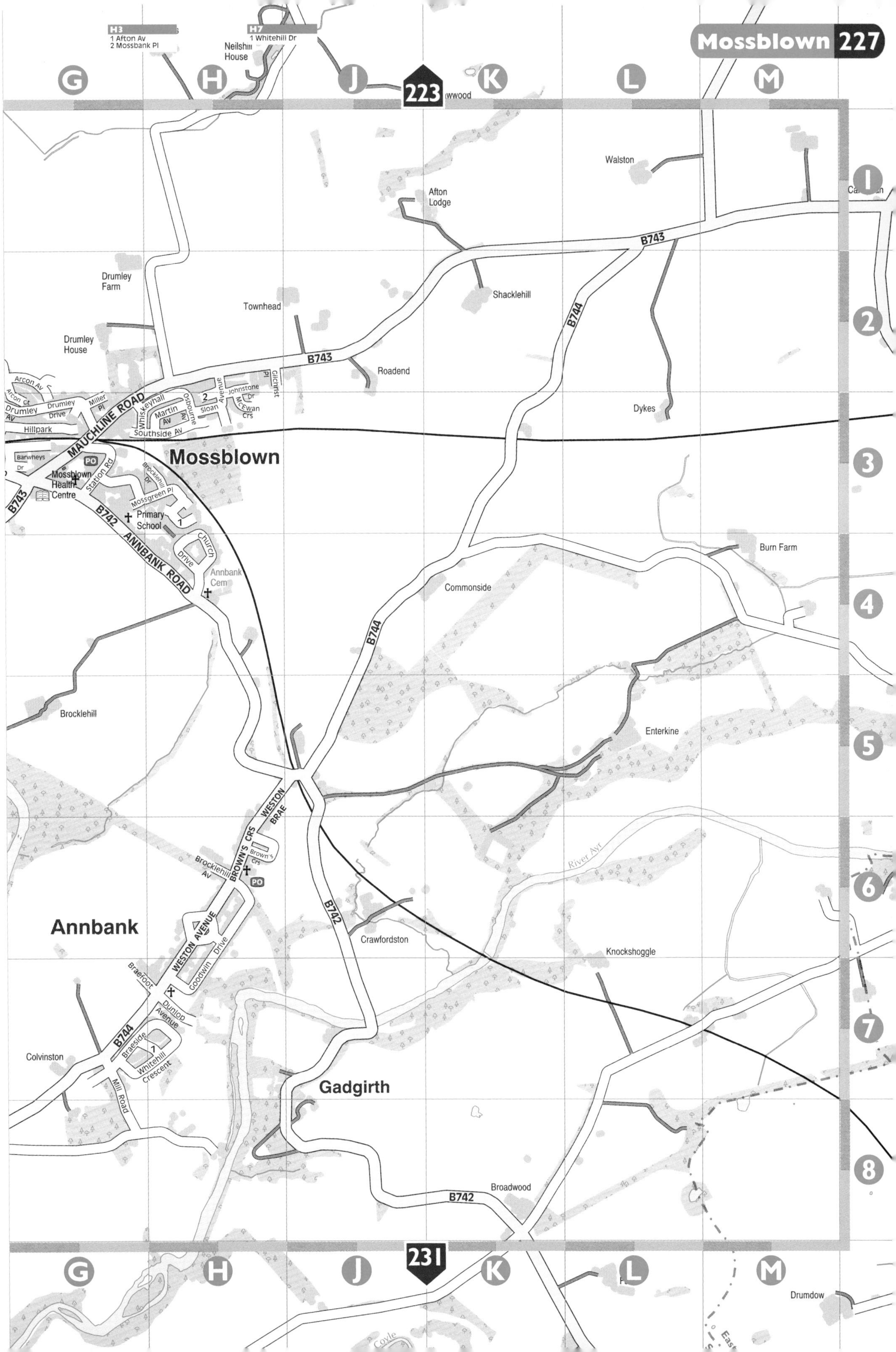
H3
1 Afton Av
2 Mossbank Pl
H7
1 Whitehill Dr
Neilshill House
223
231
Walston
Afton Lodge
B743
Drumley Farm
Townhead
Shacklehill
B744
Drumley House
Roadend
Dykes
Arcon Av
Arcon Ct
Drumley Drive
Drumley Av
Miller Pl
Mauchline Road
Whiskeyhall
Martin Av
Osbourne Av
Sloan
Avenue
Johnstone Dr
McEwan Crs
Gilchrist Pl
Southside Av
Hillpark
Barwheys Dr
Mossblown
Mossblown Health Centre
PO
Station Rd
Brocklehill Dr
Mossgreen Pl
Primary School
B742
Annbank Road
Church Drive
Annbank Cem
Burn Farm
Commonside
Brocklehill
Enterkine
Weston Brae
Brown's Crs
Brocklehill Av
River Ayr
Annbank
Weston Avenue
Goodwin Drive
Crawfordston
Knockshoggle
Braefoot
Dunlop Avenue
Braeside
Whitehill Crescent
Colvinston
Mill Road
Gadgirth
Broadwood
Drumdow
Coyle

E8
1 Burns' Wicket

E2
1 Craigwell Pl
2 Fairfield Rd

E1
1 Bruce Crs
2 C Street La

B6
1 Greenan Gv

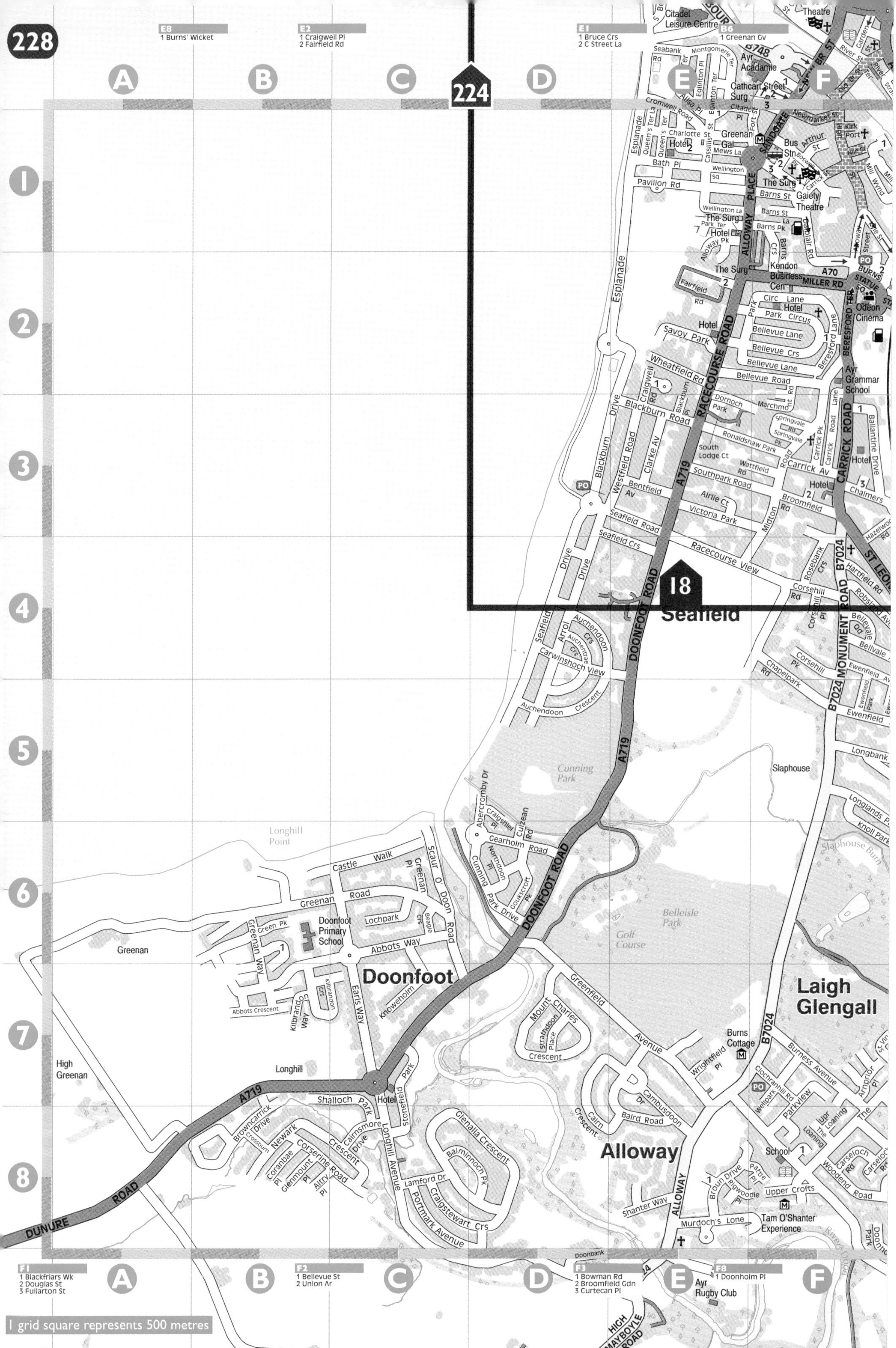

F1
1 Blackfriars Wk
2 Douglas St
3 Fullarton St

F2
1 Bellevue St
2 Union Ar

F3
1 Bowman Rd
2 Broomfield Gdn
3 Curtecan Pl

F8
1 Doonholm Pl

1 grid square represents 500 metres

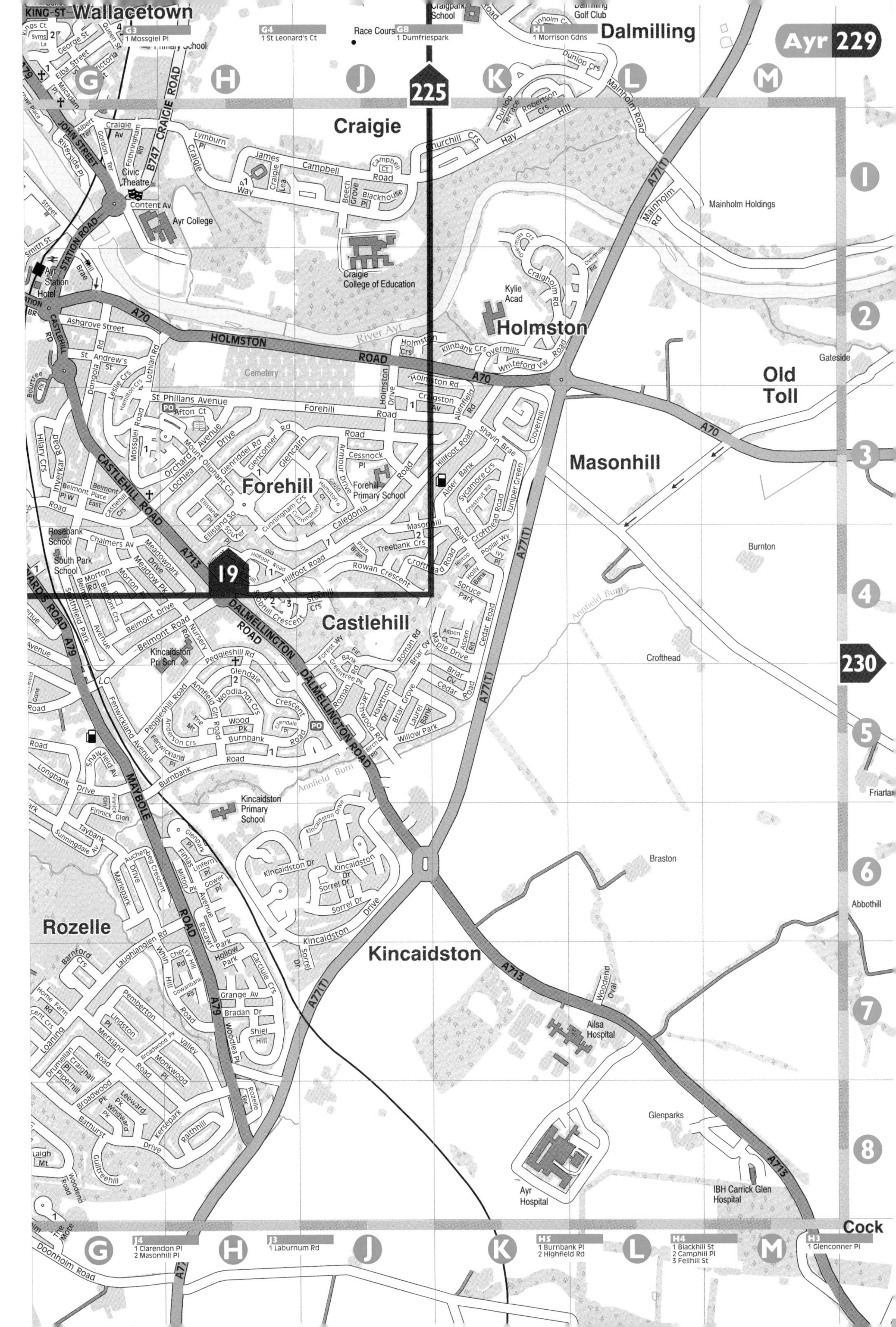
Wallacetown
Dalmilling
Dalmilling Golf Club
Craigpark School
Race Course
G3 1 Mossgiel Pl
G4 1 St Leonard's Ct
G8 1 Dumfriespark
H1 1 Morrison Gdns
225
Craigie
Churchill Crs
Hay Hill
Dunlop Terrace
Robertson Crs
Dunlop Crs
Mainholm Road
Mainholm Rd
Mainholm Holdings
Lymburn Pl
Craigie Av
Gordon Ter
Fothringham Rd
B747 CRAIGIE ROAD
JOHN STREET
Albert Ter
Riverside Pl
Civic Theatre
Content Av
Ayr College
James Campbell Road
Campbell Ct
Craigie Way
Craigie Lea
Beech Grove
Blackhouse Pl
Craigie College of Education
STATION ROAD
Smith St
Ayr Station
Mill Brae
Hotel
River Ayr
Overmills Crs
Overmills Rd
Craigholm Rd
Kylie Acad
Holmston
A70
HOLMSTON ROAD
Ashgrove Street
CASTLEHILL RD
St Andrew's St
Dongola Rd
Lothian Rd
Cemetery
Holmston Crs
Kilnbank Crs
Overmills
Whiteford Vw
Holmston Rd
Holmston Drive
Craigston Av
Allenfield Rd
Gateside
Old Toll
Bourtree Pk
Leslie Crs
Hamilton Crs
St Phillans Avenue
Afton Ct
Forehill Road
Mossgiel Road
Mount Oliphant Crs
Orchard Av
Lochlea
Drive
Glenriddel Rd
Glenconner Rd
Glencairn
Road
Armour Drive
Cessnock Pl
Shavin Brae
Cloverhill
Hillfoot Road
Alder Bank
Sycamore Crs
Juniper Green
Chestnut Rd
Crofthead Road
Masonhill
Hilary Crs
Inverkar Road
Belmont Place
Belmont Pl W
Belmont East
Castlehill Crs
CASTLEHILL ROAD
Forehill
Forehill Primary School
Gavin Hamilton Ct
Cunningham Crs
Cunningham Pl
Ellisland Pl
Ellisland Sq
Souter Pl
Caledonia
Masonhill
Treebank Crs
Poplar Wy
Ivy Pl
Holly Bank
Hilltop Pl
Rosebank School
Chalmers Av
Meadowpark Drive
Meadow Pk
South Park School
Morton Rd
Morton Av
A713
19
Old Hillfoot Road
Hillfoot Road
Pine Brae
Rowan Crescent
Crofthead Road
Spruce Park
Burnton
Annfield Burn
A77(T)
Belmont Crs
Belmont Avenue
Smithfield Park
Belmont Drive
Belmont Road
Nursery Rd
DALMELLINGTON ROAD
Stobhill Crescent
Stobhill Crs
Castlehill
Roman Rd
Aspen Ct
Aspen Rd
Maple Drive
Cedar Road
Briar Gv
Forest Wy
Fir Bank
Greentree Pk
230
Crofthead
A79
Kincaidston Pri Sch
Peggieshill Rd
Glendale
Woodlands Crs
Crescent
Roman Rd
Larchwood Rd
Hawthorn Dr
Briar Grove
Laurel Bank
Willow Park
Briar Gv
Cedar Road
Fenwickland Avenue
Peggieshill Road
Anderson Crs
Annfield Gln Road
The Mt
Wood Pk
Burnbank
Glendale Pl
Road
DALMELLINGTON ROAD
Birch Rd
Fenwickland Pl
Burnbank Road
Shawfield Av
Longbank Drive
Finnick Glen
Taybank
Sunningdale Av
MAYBOLE
Kincaidston Primary School
Kincaidston Drive
Kincaidston Dr
Sorrel Dr
Friarland
Braston
Abbothill
Auchendoon Drive
Marlepark
Glenpark Pl
Finlas
Linfern Pl
Milton Pk
Gower Pl
Avenue
Recawr Pl
Rozelle
Laughlanglen Rd
Barnford Crs
Cherry Hill Rd
Hollow Park
Whin Hill
Gowanbank Rd
Carcluie Crs
Kincaidston
Sorrel Dr
ROAD
A79
Woodend Oval
A713
Home Farm Rd
Pemberton
Lindston
Merkland Road
Grange Av
Bradan Dr
Shiel Hill
Woodlea Pl
Valley
Ailsa Hospital
Loaning
Drumellan Pl
Craighall
Pipehill
Broadwood Pk
Monkwood Pl
Leeward
Windward
Kersepark
Drive
Raithhill
Rozelle Ter
Bathurst
Glenparks
Laigh Mt
Gulltreehill
Woodend Road
Ayr Hospital
IBH Carrick Glen Hospital
A713
Cock
The Mote
Doonholm Road
J4 1 Clarendon Pl 2 Masonhill Pl
J3 1 Laburnum Rd
H5 1 Burnbank Pl 2 Highfield Rd
H4 1 Blackhill St 2 Camphill Pl 3 Fellhill St
H3 1 Glenconner Pl

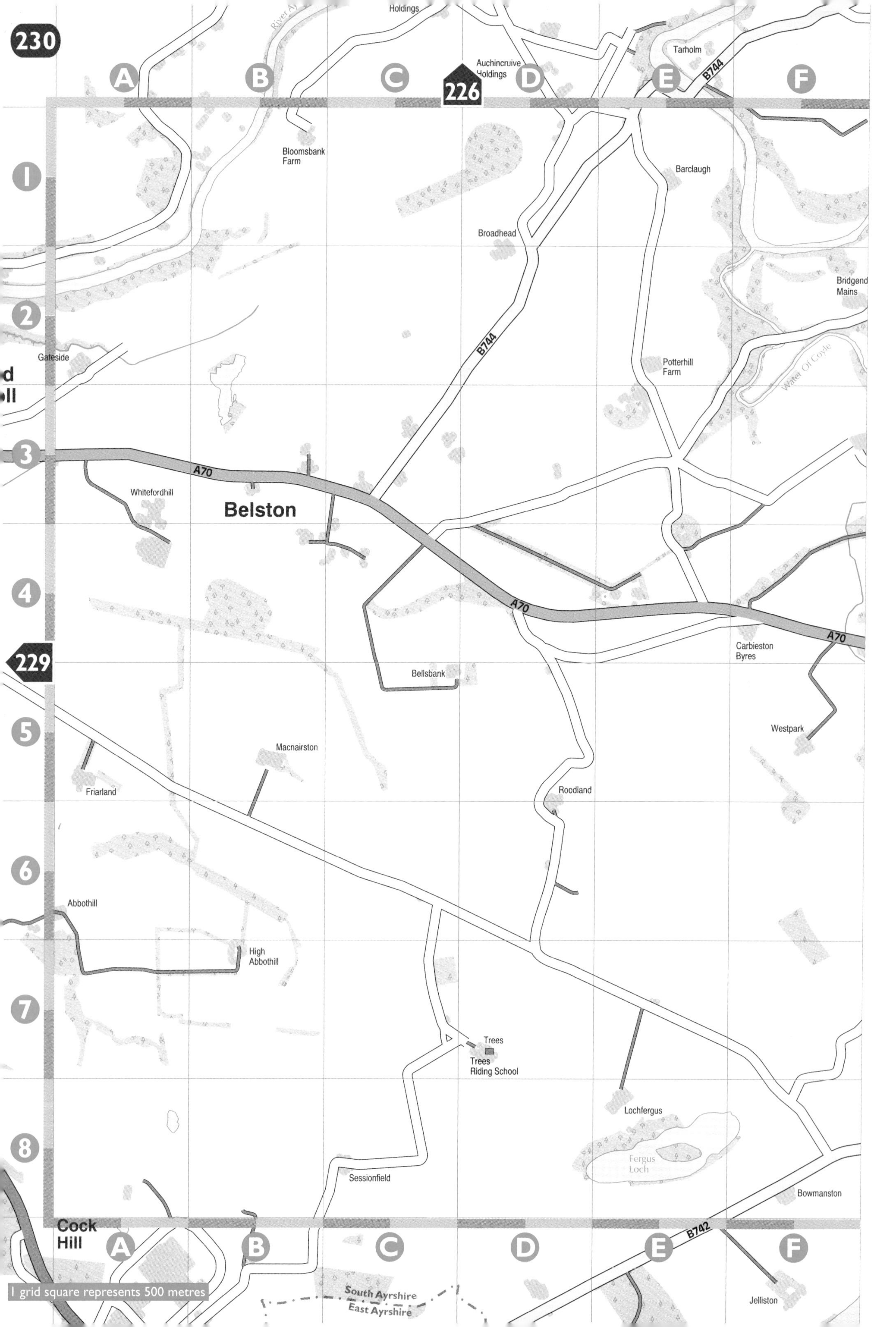
Holdings
Auchincruive Holdings
226
Tarholm
B744
A
B
C
D
E
F
Bloomsbank Farm
Barclaugh
Broadhead
Bridgend Mains
B744
Gateside
Potterhill Farm
Water Of Coyle
A70
Whitefordhill
Belston
A70
A70
Carbieston Byres
229
Bellsbank
Westpark
Macnairston
Friarland
Roodland
Abbothill
High Abbothill
Trees
Trees Riding School
Lochfergus
Fergus Loch
Sessionfield
Bowmanston
Cock Hill
B742
Jelliston
South Ayrshire
East Ayrshire
1
2
3
4
5
6
7
8

1 grid square represents 500 metres

G5
1 Laighpark Ct
2 Laighpark Vw

H4
1 Drumcoyle Dr

H5
Street names for this grid square are listed at the back of the index

227
B742
Broadwood
G
H
J
K
L
M
1
2
3
4
5
6
7
8
Raithhill Farm
Drumdow
East Ayrshire
South Ayrshire
Water Of Coyle
The Cushats
Ness Waterfall
Castle Drive
Barquhey
Bridgend
Sundrum Mains
Barclaugh
Meadowhead
Lochend Loch
Lochend
Woodhead Road
Kyle Crs
Carrick Vw
Sundrum Pk
Gallowhill Qd
Barclaugh Dr
A70
Thorn Av
Broadwood
The Beeches
Ashgrove
Hillhead
Joppa
Laighpark Rd
Laighpark
Fergus Wy
Garvine
Martnaham Dr
Hole Road
Road
Lorne Ter
Carbieston Av
Corsehill Av
Craigview
Manse Road
Cemetery
Coylton Primary School
Coylton Health Clinic
Highpark Rd
Dalrymple Vw
Springs Pk
Coylton
Highpark
Hole
Low Coylton
Auld Byres
Holebogs
Raithhill
Bogside
Bow Burn

L5
1 Duchray Pl

H6
1 Coats Pl
2 Douglas Brown Pl
3 Drumsuy Ct
4 Hamilton Pl

Abronhill 49 L6
Airdrie 111 G2
Alexandria 25 J4
Allanbank 136 F8
Allanton 157 K8
Allanton 161 G1
Alloway 228 D8
Altonhill 206 D6
Annathill 67 L7
Annbank 227 G6
Anniesland 81 K3
Ardeer 201 K3
Arden 126 C5
Ardoch 35 L3
Ardrossan 191 H7
Ashton 31 J2
Auchenback 125 J8
Auchenharvie 201 H1
Auchenmade 186 C4
Auchentibber 155 G7
Auchentiber 186 F6
Auchinairn 84 B2
Auchinloch 65 K7
Auchinraith 155 M2
Auchinreoch 46 B3
Auchinstarry 47 L3
Auldhouse 171 K8
Ayr 18 B4
Baillieston 108 B5
Balgrochan 29 J7
Balloch 48 B7
Balmore 63 L1
Balornock 84 B3
Bankhead 128 F3
Bankhead 199 H7
Barassie 216 C3
Bardowie 63 H2
Bardrainney 54 F2
Bargarran 58 F6
Bargeddie 109 G5
Barlanark 107 L3
Barmulloch 84 D4
Barncluith 156 F8
Barrachnie 107 L4
Barrhead 125 J6
Barrmill 168 F5
Battlefield 127 M1
Beansburn 207 G6
Bearsden 61 H4
Beith 144 B7
Bellahouston 104 A4
Bellfield 212 B5
Bellshill 132 D5
Bellside 135 K8
Bellsmyre 37 H2
Belston 230 B3
Benslie 194 E6
Biggar Road 135 G4
Birdston 45 J6
Birkenshaw 108 E8
Birniehill 15 J7
Bishopbriggs 64 B7
Bishopton 57 M6
Blackhall 9 M7
Blairhill 109 L3
Blairland 184 D3
Blairlinn 69 G4
Blairskaith 43 J6
Blanefield 27 G6
Blantyre 155 J2
Bloakhillhead 187 H8
Blythswood 80 C4
Bogend 218 F4
Bogside 178 C1
Bonkle 160 C3
Bonnyton 16 A1
Borland 187 M2
Bothwell 131 M8
Bourtreehill 204 D7
Bow Farm 32 B4
Bowhousebog or Liquo 136 F7
Bowling 58 E1
Brackenhirst 88 D3
Braehead 152 D6
Braehead 225 J7
Braeside 31 K6
Braidfauld 106 E6
Braidwood 188 F4
Branchton 31 M6
Bridgend 3 J7
Bridgend 66 D7
Bridge of Weir 98 F2
Bridgeton 12 E6
Broadfield 54 F1
Broadwood 67 K1
Brookfield 99 K4
Broom 150 F4
Broomhill 81 M6
Broomhouse 108 A7
Broomlands 204 A7
Browsburn 111 H4
Brucehill 36 C6
Buchley 63 J4
Burnbank 156 A4
Burnfoot 88 E7
Burnhouse 169 K8
Burnside 129 J4
Busbiehill 205 K6
Busby 151 M4
Cadder 64 B4
Cadzow 174 D2
Cairncurran 74 A1
Cairnhill 110 E3
Calderbank 111 H6
Caldercruix 90 E5
Calderwood 153 M6
Calton 12 B4
Cambuslang 130 A5
Cambusnethan 159 L4
Carbrain 49 H8
Cardonald 103 H4
Cardross 35 H1
Carfin 134 B7
Carluke 178 E8
Carmunnock 152 C1
Carmyle 130 B1
Carnbroe 110 E6
Carntyne 106 E2
Carnwadric 126 F5
Cartland 189 J8
Cartsdyke 3 H7
Castlehead 8 E7
Castlehill 36 B4
Castlehill 229 J4
Castlemilk 128 E7
Cathcart 127 M3
Central 2 C5
Chapelhall 111 L8
Charleston 9 H9
Chryston 66 C7
Clachan of Campsie 29 G6
Clarkston 89 K8
Clarkston 151 K2
Cleekhimin 134 B8
Cleghorn 199 M2
Cleland 135 G8
Clevans 98 A2
Cliftonville 110 C2
Clydebank 60 A8
Coatbridge 110 B4
Coatdyke 110 D3
College Milton 153 G6
Collennan 217 H3
Colston 83 L1
Coltness 159 K3
Condorrat 68 B2
Corkerhill 103 L7
Cowlairs 6 C1
Coylton 231 J6
Craigend 58 F8
Craigend 85 J6
Craigendoran 23 H2
Craigends 77 K8
Craigie 19 L3
Craigie 219 M4
Craigneuk 111 J3
Craigneuk 158 B4
Craigton 103 L4
Cranhill 107 G1
Crawforddyke 189 H1
Criagendmuir 85 L5
Crindledyke 160 B4
Croftfoot 128 E4
Crookedholm 212 E2
Crookfur 150 E3
Crookston 102 F5
Crossford 188 A7
Crosshill 108 D4
Crosshouse 205 M8
Crosslee 77 H8
Crossmill 125 J5
Crossmyloof 104 D7
Croy 47 M5
Cumbernauld 48 F8
Cumbernauld Village 49 J4
Cunninghamhead 205 H1
Dalgarven 193 J1
Dalmarnock 106 A6
Dalmilling 225 L8
Dalmuir 59 L5
Dalry 184 B1
Dalserf 177 G7
Dalshannon 68 A4
Dalton 131 G7
Dean Park 80 D7
Dennistoun 12 D1
Dennystown 36 E5
The Den 167 K6
Devol 54 D1
Doonfoot 228 C7
Doura 195 G7
Dovecothall 125 L5
Dowanhill 82 C6
Drakemyre 166 C8
Dreghorn 204 D8
Drumchapel 61 G7
Drumgelloch 111 H1
Drumpellier 109 J2
Drumry 60 C7
Drybridge 209 K4
Dullatur 48 C3
Dumbarton 37 G6
Dumbreck 104 B5
Dundonald 209 M7
Dundyvan 109 L4
Duntocher 59 M3
Dykehead 137 J5
Earlston 211 H6
Earnock 155 M8
Easterhouse 108 A1
Eastfield 48 C7
Eastfield 129 K2
East Kilbride 15 H5
East Mains 15 H1
Eddlewood 174 D2
Elderslie 100 C7
Erskine 59 G8
Faifley 60 C2
Fairhill 174 C1
Fairlie 139 L6
Fallside 132 D2
Fergushill 194 D6
Ferguslie Park 101 G4
Ferniegair 157 H8
Flemington 130 C6
Fluchter 43 H8
Forehill 19 K8
Forgewood 133 J7
Foxbar 123 M1
Freeland 79 H1
Frognal 221 G2
Fullarton 107 G6
Fullarton 203 H8
Gadgirth 227 J7
Gailes 208 C5
Gallowhill 102 A2
Gallowhill 152 E1
Galston 214 B4
Garnkirk 86 B3
Garrowhill 108 A4
Gartcosh 86 E4
Garthamlock 85 K7
Gartlea 111 H3
Gartloch 86 C6
Gartness 111 L4
Gartsherrie 87 L8
Gatehead 210 E4
Gateside 125 G8
Gateside 168 E2
Geilston 24 B8
Germiston 7 G5
Gibshill 33 L7
Giffnock 127 K7
Girdle Toll 204 A4
Glasgow 11 K1
Glenboig 87 L2
Glenburn 124 C1
Glengarnock 167 H3
Glenmavis 88 F5
Gorbals 11 J6
Gourock 31 L2
Govan 104 B1
Govanhill 105 H7
Gowkthrapple 177 G2
Grange 16 B4
Greenend 110 C5
Greenfaulds 68 F2
Greenfield 107 G3
Greenfoot 88 A1
Greengairs 69 M7
Greenhead 159 K7
Greenhills 14 B9
Greenholm 215 J3
Greenock 2 E3
Greenock West 32 C2
Haghill 13 L1
Hairmyres 170 E1
Hall 146 C6
Hallside 130 E4
Hamilton 156 F5
Hansel Village 218 C8
Hardgate 60 D3
Hareleeshill 176 C8
Hareshaw 135 K4
Harestanes 45 M7
Hartwood 137 G6
Haughhead 29 G6
Hayston 45 G8
Heathfield 225 J5
Helensburgh 20 B8
High Blawtyre 155 G4
High Crosshill 129 H3
Highfield 166 F8
High Gallowhill 65 G3
Hillend 91 H6
Hillhead 231 L5
Hillington 103 G3
Hogganfield 84 F7
Holehills 89 H7
Holehouse 148 C3
Holmston 229 K2
Holytown 134 A3
Houston 77 H7
Howwood 121 K4
Hurlet 125 M2
Hurlford 213 G3
Hutchesontown 11 K8
Ibrox 104 B3
Inchinnan 79 K2
Inverkip 50 E4
Irvine 203 G6
Jamestown 25 M2
Johnstone 100 A7
Joppa 231 G5
Jordanhill 81 K4
Kelburn 35 G8
Kelvin 172 A4
Kelvindale 82 C3
Kelvinside 82 A4
Kennishead 126 E4
Kilbarchan 99 G6
Kilbirnie 142 F7
Kilbowie 60 C5
Kildrum 49 H6
Kilmacolm 75 M1
Kilmarnock 17 H7
Kilmaurs 206 C1
Kilncadzow 189 M4
Kilnford 209 K5
Kilwinning 183 K8
Kilwinning 193 H5
Kincaidston 229 J7
Kings Park 128 D3
Kirkfieldbank 198 C5
Kirkhill 151 J5
Kirkintilloch 46 A8
Kirk of Shotts 113 K7
Kirkshaw 109 K6
Kirktonhill 36 E7
Kirktoun 206 D3
Kirkwood 109 J5
Knightswood 81 J2
Knockentiber 205 L6
Knockinlaw 206 E5
Knowetop 157 M5
Kylepark 131 K2
Ladyburn 33 M6
Laigh Glengall 228 F7
Laighstonehall 156 A7
Lambhill 83 H2
Lanark 199 G6
Langbank 56 A2
Langloan 109 L4
Langside 127 K1
Largs 115 L6
Larkfield 31 K5
Larkhall 175 M7
Law 177 M4
Law Hill 178 A5
Lawthorn 204 A3
Leigh Knoweglass 172 A8
Lennoxtown 44 E1
Lenzie 65 K4
Lenziemill 68 F1
Levan 30 E4
Lilybank 33 M8
Limekilnburn 174 B7
Linwood 100 B3
Loans 217 G5
Lochside 225 G7
Lochwinnoch 120 D7
Lochwood 86 D8
Longbar 167 K3
Longpark 206 F6
Low Blantyre 131 L8
Low Coylton 231 L6
Low Waters 156 E8
Luggiebank 69 H3
Machan 176 A7
Mansewood 127 H3
Marnock 87 J3
Maryhill 82 B2
Masonhill 19 M8
Meadowfoot 181 L5
Mearns 150 F6
Meigle 92 B2
Meikle Earnock 174 C2
Merrylee 127 K5
Mid Auchinleck 54 D2
Midton 31 K3
Millarston 101 G6
Millersneuk 65 M5
Millerston 85 G5
Millheugh 175 K7
Millikenpark 99 H8
Millport 138 A6
Milngavie 41 K8
Milnwood 133 K5
Milton 37 M8
Milton 75 J3
Milton 83 J2
Milton of Campsie 45 K4
Moffat Mills 111 M2
Mollinsburn 67 K5
Monkton 221 L5
Moodiesburn 66 E6
Morningside 160 C6
Mossblown 227 H3
Mossend 133 K4
Mossneuk 170 E3
Mosspark 103 L6
Motherwell 157 L4
Mountblow 59 J5
Mount Florida 128 B2
Mount Vernon 107 J7
Mugdock 42 C3
Muirend 127 M3
Muirhead 86 D2
Muirhead 107 M6
Muirhead 216 E5
Muirhouse 158 A6
The Murray 14 E7
Neilston 148 E3
Nemphlar 198 A3
Nerston 154 A3
Nethanfoot 188 B6
Nether Kirton 148 F1
Netherlee 127 L7
Netherplace 149 M5
Netherton 27 H5
Netherton 158 E8
Newarthill 134 F5
New Farm 17 M2
Newhouse 135 H1
Newhousemill 172 D1
New Lanark 198 F8
Newlands 127 K3
Newlandsmuir 170 F2
Newmains 159 M4
Newmilns 215 J1
New Stevenston 134 B5
Newton 130 F3
Newton Mearns 150 C4
Newton on Ayr 225 H5
Newtown of Belltrees 121 H8
Nitshill 125 M4
North Motherwell 157 J1
Oatlands 105 K6
Old Balornock 6 F1
Oldhall 102 D4
Old Kilpatrick 58 F3
Old Monkland 109 L5
Old Toll 229 M2
Onthank 206 F4
Orbiston 132 F5
Overton 32 C7
Overtown 177 K3
Oxgang 65 M2
Paisley 9 J5
Park Farm 55 H2
Parkhall 59 M4
Parkhead 13 L7
Parkhill 55 K1
Parklea 35 J8
Park Mains 59 J8
Parkside 135 J7
Partick 82 A7
Pather 159 H8
Peel Park 152 F7
Perceton 204 C3
Petersburn 111 L3
Pilmuir 149 L8
Plains 90 B6
Pollok 103 H7
Pollokshaws 127 H1
Pollokshields 104 D6
Polmadie 105 J7
Port Dundas 5 J5
Portencross 180 D3
Porterfield 80 B7
Port Glasgow 34 E7
Possil Park 83 J4
Prestwick 225 G1
Priesthill 126 A3
Provanmill 84 E6
Quarrelton 99 L8
Quarriers Village 75 K7
Quarter 174 E6
Queenslie 107 K1
Queenzieburn 46 F1
Radnor Park 60 A5
Ranfurly 98 C3
Rashielee 59 G7
Ravenscraig 32 B6
Rawyards 89 H8
Renfrew 80 C6
Renton 25 K8
Riccarton 211 K4
Riggend 69 G8
Roadmeetings 189 K1
Robroyston 84 E3
Rogerton 153 K3
Rosebank 66 A1
Rosehall 110 B5
Rossland 58 C7
Roughwood 168 A4
Royston 6 A6
Rozelle 229 G6
Ruchazie 85 H8
Ruchill 83 G4
Rutherglen 105 L8
Rutherglen 128 A1
Saint Leonards 172 C1
St Quivox 226 B4
Salsburgh 113 J8
Saltcoats 200 F2
Scotstoun 81 H4
Seafar 48 E8
Seafield 228 E4
Seamill 181 J7
Shawhead 109 M6
Shawlands 127 K1
Shawsburn 176 E7
Sheddens 151 M2
Sheildmuir 158 C5
Shettleston 107 G4
Shewalton 209 G4
Shieldhall 103 K1
Shillford 147 K4
Shortlees 211 M6
Shortroods 101 J1
Shotts 137 M4
Sighthill 6 A5
Silverton 37 H5
Silvertonhill 156 D7
Solsgirth 46 B8
Sornhill 214 E7
Sourlie 204 A2
Spango 31 K7
Springboig 107 J3
Springburn 83 M5
Springhill 149 J2
Springside 205 G7
Stamperland 151 M1
Stand 89 H3
Stanecastle 203 M5
Stepps 85 J4
Stevenston 201 L1
Stevenston Site 202 B5
Stewartheld 153 J4
Stewarton 197 M1
Stonefield 155 M1
Strathblane 27 J6
Strathbungo 104 E7
Strone 3 M9
Strone Farm 2 E9
Summerston 62 F8
Swinton 108 C3
Symington 218 B6
Tannochside 132 A1
Tarbolton 223 M7
Temple 81 L2
Thirdpart 180 E1
Thornliebank 126 E6
Thornly Park 101 M8
Thorntonhall 152 A6
Thrashbush 88 F8
Torbush 160 B6
Torrance 44 B8
Torranyard 195 K4
Townend 37 G3
Townhead 5 L8
Townhead 87 J8
Troon 216 B7
Twechar 46 E6
Uddingston 131 L4
Udston 155 M5
Uplawmoor 147 H6
Upper Dalguhurn 25 J7
Victory Gardens 80 C8
Viewpark 132 C1
Wallacetown 19 G1
Wardpark 49 J2
Waterfoot 151 J8
Waterloo 177 K1
Waterside 66 C2
Waterside 125 L4
Wattston 69 K8
West Arthurlie 124 F7
Westburn 130 E3
West Drumoyne 103 L2
Wester Auchinloch 65 K8
Westfield 67 M3
West Kilbride 181 K5
West Mains 14 D3
West Porton 58 A5
Westwood 14 A5
Whifflet 110 B4
Whinhall 110 E1
Whitecraigs 151 G3
Whitecrook 80 D1
Whitehill 156 B2
Whitehills 171 M4
Whiteinch 81 L7
Whitelees 218 E5
Whitletts 225 K6
Wildmanbridge 178 A2
Williamwood 151 J1
Wishaw 159 G6
Woodfield 225 G4
Woodhall 54 F1
Yett 134 C6
Yieldshields 179 L7
Yoker 80 E2
Yorkhill 104 C1

USING THE STREET INDEX

Street names are listed alphabetically. Each street name is followed by its postal town or area locality, the Postcode District, the page number, and the reference to the square in which the name is found.

Example: **Abbeygreen St** *ESTRH* G34.............. **86** E8 [1]

Some entries are followed by a number in a blue box. This number indicates the location of the street within the referenced grid square. The full street name is listed at the side of the map page.

GENERAL ABBREVIATIONS

ACC	ACCESS
ALY	ALLEY
AP	APPROACH
AR	ARCADE
ASS	ASSOCIATION
AV	AVENUE
BCH	BEACH
BLDS	BUILDINGS
BND	BEND
BNK	BANK
BR	BRIDGE
BRK	BROOK
BTM	BOTTOM
BUS	BUSINESS
BVD	BOULEVARD
BY	BYPASS
CATH	CATHEDRAL
CEM	CEMETERY
CEN	CENTRE
CFT	CROFT
CH	CHURCH
CHA	CHASE
CHYD	CHURCHYARD
CIR	CIRCLE
CIRC	CIRCUS
CL	CLOSE
CLFS	CLIFFS
CMP	CAMP
CNR	CORNER
CO	COUNTY
COLL	COLLEGE
COM	COMMON
COMM	COMMISSION
CON	CONVENT
COT	COTTAGE
COTS	COTTAGES
CP	CAPE
CPS	COPSE
CR	CREEK
CREM	CREMATORIUM
CRS	CRESCENT
CSWY	CAUSEWAY
CT	COURT
CTRL	CENTRAL
CTS	COURTS
CTYD	COURTYARD
CUTT	CUTTINGS
CV	COVE
CYN	CANYON
DEPT	DEPARTMENT
DL	DALE
DM	DAM
DR	DRIVE
DRO	DROVE
DRY	DRIVEWAY
DWGS	DWELLINGS
E	EAST
EMB	EMBANKMENT
EMBY	EMBASSY
ESP	ESPLANADE
EST	ESTATE
EX	EXCHANGE
EXPY	EXPRESSWAY
EXT	EXTENSION
F/O	FLYOVER
FC	FOOTBALL CLUB
FK	FORK
FLD	FIELD
FLDS	FIELDS
FLS	FALLS
FLS	FLATS
FM	FARM
FT	FORT
FWY	FREEWAY
FY	FERRY
GA	GATE
GAL	GALLERY
GDN	GARDEN
GDNS	GARDENS
GLD	GLADE
GLN	GLEN
GN	GREEN
GND	GROUND
GRA	GRANGE
GRG	GARAGE
GT	GREAT
GTWY	GATEWAY
GV	GROVE
HGR	HIGHER
HL	HILL
HLS	HILLS
HO	HOUSE
HOL	HOLLOW
HOSP	HOSPITAL
HRB	HARBOUR
HTH	HEATH
HTS	HEIGHTS
HVN	HAVEN
HWY	HIGHWAY
IMP	IMPERIAL
IN	INLET
IND EST	INDUSTRIAL ESTATE
INF	INFIRMARY
INFO	INFORMATION
INT	INTERCHANGE
IS	ISLAND
JCT	JUNCTION
JTY	JETTY
KG	KING
KNL	KNOLL
L	LAKE
LA	LANE
LDG	LODGE
LGT	LIGHT
LK	LOCK
LKS	LAKES
LNDG	LANDING
LTL	LITTLE
LWR	LOWER
MAG	MAGISTRATE
MAN	MANSIONS
MD	MEAD
MDW	MEADOWS
MEM	MEMORIAL
MKT	MARKET
MKTS	MARKETS
ML	MALL
ML	MILL
MNR	MANOR
MS	MEWS
MSN	MISSION
MT	MOUNT
MTN	MOUNTAIN
MTS	MOUNTAINS
MUS	MUSEUM
MWY	MOTORWAY
N	NORTH
NE	NORTH EAST
NW	NORTH WEST
O/P	OVERPASS
OFF	OFFICE
ORCH	ORCHARD
OV	OVAL
PAL	PALACE
PAS	PASSAGE
PAV	PAVILION
PDE	PARADE
PH	PUBLIC HOUSE
PK	PARK
PKWY	PARKWAY
PL	PLACE
PLN	PLAIN
PLNS	PLAINS
PLZ	PLAZA
POL	POLICE STATION
PR	PRINCE
PREC	PRECINCT
PREP	PREPARATORY
PRIM	PRIMARY
PROM	PROMENADE
PRS	PRINCESS
PRT	PORT
PT	POINT
PTH	PATH
PZ	PIAZZA
QD	QUADRANT
QU	QUEEN
QY	QUAY
R	RIVER
RBT	ROUNDABOUT
RD	ROAD
RDG	RIDGE
REP	REPUBLIC
RES	RESERVOIR
RFC	RUGBY FOOTBALL CLUB
RI	RISE
RP	RAMP
RW	ROW
S	SOUTH
SCH	SCHOOL
SE	SOUTH EAST
SER	SERVICE AREA
SH	SHORE
SHOP	SHOPPING
SKWY	SKYWAY
SMT	SUMMIT
SOC	SOCIETY
SP	SPUR
SPR	SPRING
SQ	SQUARE
ST	STREET
STN	STATION
STR	STREAM
STRD	STRAND
SW	SOUTH WEST
TDG	TRADING
TER	TERRACE
THWY	THROUGHWAY
TNL	TUNNEL
TOLL	TOLLWAY
TPK	TURNPIKE
TR	TRACK
TRL	TRAIL
TWR	TOWER
U/P	UNDERPASS
UNI	UNIVERSITY
UPR	UPPER
V	VALE
VA	VALLEY
VIAD	VIADUCT
VIL	VILLA
VIS	VISTA
VLG	VILLAGE
VLS	VILLAS
VW	VIEW
W	WEST
WD	WOOD
WHF	WHARF
WK	WALK
WKS	WALKS
WLS	WELLS
WY	WAY
YD	YARD
YHA	YOUTH HOSTEL

POSTCODE TOWNS AND AREA ABBREVIATIONS

AIRDRIE	Airdrie
ALEX/LLW	Alexandria/Loch Lomond west
ARD	Ardrossan
AYR	Ayr
AYRS	Ayr south
BAIL/MDB/MHD	Baillieston/Moodiesburn/Muirhead
BALLOCH	Balloch
BEITH	Beith
BLSH	Bellshill
BLTYR/CAMB	Blantyre/Cambuslang
BNYBR/BNK	Bonnybridge/Banknock
BRHD/NEIL	Barrhead/Neilston
BRWEIR	Bridge of Weir
BSDN	Bearsden
BSHPBGS	Bishopbriggs
BSHPTN	Bishopton
CAR/SHTL	Carmyle/Shettleston
CARD/HILL/MSPK	Cardonald/Hillington/Mosspark
CARLUKE	Carluke
CGLE	Central Glasgow east
CGLW	Central Glasgow west
CLYDBK	Clydebank
CMPF/LLE	Campsie Fells/Loch Lomond east
COWCAD	Cowcaddens
CRG/CRSL/HOU	Craigends/Crosslee/Houston
CRH/DND	Crosshouse/Dundonald
CRMNK/CLK/EAG	Carmunnock/Clarkston/Eaglesham
CSMK	Castlemilk
CTBR	Coatbridge
CUMB	Cumbernauld
DALRY	Dalry
DEN/PKHD	Dennistoun/Parkhead
DMBTN	Dumbarton
DMNK/BRGTN	Dalmarnock/Bridgeton
DRUM	Drumchapel
EKILN	East Kilbride north
EKILS	East Kilbride south
ERSK	Erskine
ESTRH	Easterhouse
FAIRLIE	Fairlie
FLK	Falkirk
GBLS	Gorbals
GIF/THBK	Giffnock/Thornliebank
GLGNK	Glengarnock
GLSTN	Galston
GOV/IBX	Govan/Ibrox
GRK	Gourock
GRNK	Greenock
GRNKW/INVK	Greenock West/Inverkip
GTCI	Great Cumbrae Island
GVH/MTFL	Govanhill/Mount Florida
HBR/GL	Helensburgh/Gare Loch
HMLTN	Hamilton
HWWD	Howwood
IRV	Irvine
IRVSE	Irvine south & east
JNSTN	Johnstone
KBRN	Kilbirnie
KKNTL	Kirkintilloch
KLBCH	Kilbarchan
KLMCLM	Kilmacolm
KLMNK	Kilmarnock
KLMNKN/STW	Kilmarnock north/Stewarton
KLWNG	Kilwinning
KNTSWD	Knightswood
KSYTH	Kilsyth
KVD/HLHD	Kelvindale/Hillhead
KVGV	Kelvingrove
LARGS	Largs
LNK/LMHG	Lanark/Lesmahagow
LNPK/KPK	Linn Park/King's Park
LOCHW	Lochwinnoch
LRKH	Larkhall
MAUCH/CAT	Mauchline/Catrine
MLNGV	Milngavie
MRYH/FIRH	Maryhill/Firhill
MTHW	Motherwell
NMLNS	Newmilns
NMRNS	Newton Mearns
OLDK	Old Kilpatrick
PGL	Port Glasgow
PLK/PH/NH	Pollock/Priesthill/Nitshill
PLKSD/SHW	Pollockshields/Shawlands
PLKSW/MSWD	Pollockshaws/Mansewood
PPK/MIL	Possil Park/Milton
PSLY	Paisley
PSLYN/LNWD	Paisley north/Linwood
PSLYS	Paisley south
PSTWK	Prestwick
PTCK	Partick
RAYR/DAL	Rural Ayr/Dalmellington
RNFRW	Renfrew
RUTH	Rutherglen
SALT	Saltcoats
SCOT	Scotstoun
SHOTTS	Shotts
SKLM	Skelmorlie
SMSTN	Summerston
SPRGB/BLRNK	Springburn/Balornock
STPS/GTHM/RID	Stepps/Garthamlock/Riddrie
STRHV	Strathaven
SVSTN	Stevenston
TROON	Troon
UD/BTH/TAN	Uddingston/Bothwell/Tannochside
WISHAW	Wishaw
WKIL	West Kilbride
WMYSB	Wemyss Bay

Index - streets

A

Abbey Cl *PSLY* PA1 **9** J4
Abbeycraig Rd *ESTRH* G34 **108** E1
Abbey Dr *SCOT* G14 **81** L5
Abbeygreen St *ESTRH* G34 **86** E8 [1]
Abbeyhill St *CAR/SHTL* G32 **106** E2
Abbeylands Rd *CLYDBK* G81 **60** C3
Abbey Pl *AIRDRIE* ML6 **111** J5
Abbey Rd *JNSTN* PA5 **100** B7
Abbot Ct *PSTWK* KA9 **225** K4 [1]
Abbot's Av *KLWNG* KA13 **193** L7
Abbots Crs *AYRS* KA7 **228** B7
Abbotsford *BSHPBGS* G64 **64** C7 [1]
Abbotsford Av *HMLTN* ML3 **156** B2
LRKH ML9 **176** A8
RUTH G73 **129** H2
Abbotsford Brae *EKILN* G74 **153** L6
Abbotsford Ct *CUMB* G67 **68** F2 [1]
Abbotsford Crs *HMLTN* ML3 **156** B3 [1]
PSLYS PA2 **123** K2
SHOTTS ML7 **137** M4 [1]
WISHAW ML2 **159** J5
Abbotsford La *BLSH* ML4 **132** F3 [1]
Abbotsford Pl *CUMB* G67 **68** F2
GBLS G5 **11** G7 [1]
SALT KA21 **192** A7 [1]
Abbotsford Rd *AIRDRIE* ML6 **111** L8
BSDN G61 **61** J3
CLYDBK G81 **60** B8
CUMB G67 **68** F2
HMLTN ML3 **156** A3
WISHAW ML2 **159** J5
Abbotsford Ter
LNK/LMHG ML11 **199** J5 [1]
Abbotshall Av *DRUM* G15 **60** E6
Abbotsinch Rd
PSLYN/LNWD PA3 **79** L7
Abbots Ter *AIRDRIE* ML6 **111** J5
Abbot St *GRNKW/INVK* PA16 **32** C6 [1]
PLKSD/SHW G41 **104** E8 [1]
PSLYN/LNWD PA3 **9** K1 [1]
Abbot's Wk *KLWNG* KA13 **193** L6
Abbots Wy *AYRS* KA7 **228** C6
Abbott Crs *CLYDBK* G81 **80** D1
Aberconway St *CLYDBK* G81 **80** C1
Abercorn Av
CARD/HILL/MSPK G52 **102** E1
Abercorn Crs *HMLTN* ML3 **156** F7
Abercorn Dr *HMLTN* ML3 **156** F6
Abercorn Pl *SMSTN* G23 **62** E8
Abercorn Rd *NMRNS* G77 **150** C3
Abercorn St *CLYDBK* G81 **60** E2 [1]
PSLYN/LNWD PA3 **9** J2
Abercrombie Crs
BAIL/MDB/MHD G69 **108** F4
Abercrombie Dr *BSDN* G61 **61** H1
Abercromby Crs *EKILN* G74 **154** B6
HBR/GL G84 **20** F6
Abercromby Dr *AYRS* KA7 **228** D6
DMNK/BRGTN G40 **12** C4
Abercromby Pl *EKILN* G74 **154** B6 [1]
Abercromby Pl West
HBR/GL G84 **20** D6 [1]
Abercromby St
DMNK/BRGTN G40 **12** B6 [1]
Abercromby St East
HBR/GL G84 **20** E6
Aberdalgie Rd *ESTRH* G34 **108** B1
Aberdeen Rd *AIRDRIE* ML6 **111** K5
Aberdour St *DEN/PKHD* G31 **13** J1
Aberfeldy Av *AIRDRIE* ML6 **89** M6
Aberfeldy St *DEN/PKHD* G31 **13** J1
Aberfoyle Rd *GRNK* PA15 **33** H7 [1]
Aberfoyle St *DEN/PKHD* G31 **13** J1
Aberlady Rd *GOV/IBX* G51 **103** L2
Aberlady St *MTHW* ML1 **135** H8
Aberlour Pl *IRVSE* KA11 **203** M3
Abernethy Dr
PSLYN/LNWD PA3 **100** A4
Abernethyn Rd *WISHAW* ML2 **160** A3
Abernethy Pk *EKILN* G74 **14** C2
Abernethy Pl *NMRNS* G77 **151** H5 [1]
Abernethy St *DEN/PKHD* G31 **13** J3
Aberuthven Dr *CAR/SHTL* G32 **107** H6
Abiegail Pl *BLTYR/CAMB* G72 **131** K8 [1]
Aboukir St *GOV/IBX* G51 **103** L1
Aboyne Dr *PSLYS* PA2 **101** M8 [1]
Aboyne St *GOV/IBX* G51 **103** M3
Acacia Dr *BEITH* KA15 **168** A1
BRHD/NEIL G78 **125** G4
PSLYS PA2 **101** H8
Acacia Pl *JNSTN* PA5 **123** G1
Academy Brae *BEITH* KA15 **168** B1
Academy Ct *KLMNK* KA1 **212** E3 [1]
Academy Gdns *IRV* KA12 **203** H5
Academy Pk *AIRDRIE* ML6 **111** G2
PLKSD/SHW G41 **104** C5
Academy Rd *GIF/THBK* G46 **127** J7
IRV KA12 **203** H6
Academy St *AIRDRIE* ML6 **111** G2
AYRS KA7 **18** E2
CAR/SHTL G32 **107** H5
CTBR ML5 **110** A2
KLMNK KA1 **16** F9
LRKH ML9 **176** A6 [1]
TROON KA10 **216** B7
Academy Ter *BLSH* ML4 **133** H4 [1]
Acer Crs *PSLYS* PA2 **101** G8
Acer Gv *AIRDRIE* ML6 **111** L6
Achamore Crs *DRUM* G15 **60** E5 [1]
Achamore Dr *DRUM* G15 **60** E5 [2]
Achamore Rd *DRUM* G15 **60** E5
Acherhill Gdns *KNTSWD* G13 **81** G1
Achnasheen Rd *AIRDRIE* ML6 **112** A3
Achray Av *ALEX/LLW* G83 **25** K3 [1]
Achray Dr *PSLYS* PA2 **101** G8
Achray Pl *CTBR* ML5 **87** J8
MLNGV G62 **41** K6
Achray Rd *CUMB* G67 **68** B3
Acorn Ct *DMNK/BRGTN* G40 **12** D7
Acorn St *DMNK/BRGTN* G40 **12** D7
Acre Av *LARGS* KA30 **115** K7
Acre Dr *MRYH/FIRH* G20 **62** B8
Acredyke Crs *SPRGB/BLRNK* G21 **84** B2
Acredyke Pl
SPRGB/BLRNK G21 **84** C3 [1]
Acredyke Rd *RUTH* G73 **128** F1
SPRGB/BLRNK G21 **84** B2
Acre Rd *MRYH/FIRH* G20 **62** B8
The Acres *LRKH* ML9 **176** B7 [1]
Acre Valley Rd *BSHPBGS* G64 **44** B7
Adair Av *SALT* KA21 **191** M8
Adam Av *AIRDRIE* ML6 **111** H2
Adams Av *SALT* KA21 **191** M8
Adams Ct *TROON* KA10 **216** E3
Adams Court La *CGLE* G1 **11** H3
Adam's Ga *TROON* KA10 **216** E3
Adamsliedrive *KKNTL* G66 **65** G1
Adamson St *BLSH* ML4 **133** K4
Adams Pl *KSYTH* G65 **47** K1 [1]
Adam St *GRK* PA19 **31** M2 [1]
GRNK PA15 **3** H8
Adams Wk *IRV* KA12 **203** L7 [1]
Adamswell St *SPRGB/BLRNK* G21 **6** C2
Adamswell Ter
BAIL/MDB/MHD G69 **67** G7 [1]
Adamton Rd North *PSTWK* KA9 **225** J2
Adamton Rd South *PSTWK* KA9 **225** J3
Adamton Ter *PSTWK* KA9 **225** J2
Addie St *MTHW* ML1 **157** M1
Addiewell Pl *CTBR* ML5 **110** A5
Addiewell St *CAR/SHTL* G32 **107** G2 [1]
Addison Gv *GIF/THBK* G46 **126** E5
Addison Pl *GIF/THBK* G46 **126** F5
Addison Rd *GIF/THBK* G46 **126** E5
KVD/HLHD G12 **82** D5
Adelaide Ct *CLYDBK* G81 **59** K4 [1]
Adelaide Rd *EKILS* G75 **171** H2
Adelaide St *GRK* PA19 **31** L1 [1]
HBR/GL G84 **20** E8 [1]
Adele St *MTHW* ML1 **157** M5
Adelphi St *GBLS* G5 **11** M6
Admiral St *PLKSD/SHW* G41 **10** B5
Admiralty Gv *OLDK* G60 **59** H4
Admiralty Pl *OLDK* G60 **59** H4 [1]
Advie Pl *GVH/MTFL* G42 **128** B1 [1]
Affric Av *AIRDRIE* ML6 **90** A6
GIF/THBK G46 **126** C5
Affric Dr *PSLYS* PA2 **102** B8
Afton Av *KLMNKN/STW* KA3 **206** F6
PSTWK KA9 **225** J4
RAYR/DAL KA6 **227** H3 [1]
Afton Ct *AYRS* KA7 **19** J7
Afton Crs *BSDN* G61 **62** B6
Afton Dr *RNFRW* PA4 **80** E7
Afton Gdns *BLTYR/CAMB* G72 **155** H3
CTBR ML5 **110** D4
TROON KA10 **216** F5
Afton Pl *ARD* KA22 **191** K5
Afton Rd *CUMB* G67 **49** H6
SVSTN KA20 **192** D8 [1]
Afton St *LRKH* ML9 **176** C7 [1]
PLKSD/SHW G41 **127** L1
Afton Vw *KKNTL* G66 **45** M8
Agamemnon St *CLYDBK* G81 **59** M7
Agnew Av *CTBR* ML5 **110** C2
Agnew Gv *UD/BTH/TAN* G71 **132** D4
Agnew La *GVH/MTFL* G42 **105** G8
Aikenhead Rd *GVH/MTFL* G42 **105** J7
LNPK/KPK G44 **128** C3
Aikman Pl *EKILN* G74 **154** B6
Aikman Rd *MTHW* ML1 **157** H4
Aiknut Rd *WKIL* KA23 **181** J5
Ailean Dr *CAR/SHTL* G32 **107** L5
Ailean Gdns *CAR/SHTL* G32 **107** L5 [1]
Aileymill Gdns
GRNKW/INVK PA16 **31** L6

Aillort Pl EKILN G74 153 L6
Ailort Av LNPK/KPK G44 128 A4
Ailsa Av MTHW ML1 157 H2
Ailsa Ct CTBR ML5 109 L5
HMLTN ML3 155 K8
Ailsa Crs MTHW ML1 157 H2
Ailsa Dr CLYDBK G81 60 B3
GIF/THBK G46 151 J1
GVH/MTFL G42 127 M2
KKNTL G66 45 M7
PSLYS PA2 124 D2
RUTH G73 128 F4
SVSTN KA20 201 J1
UD/BTH/TAN G71 132 A5
Ailsa Gdns ARD KA22 191 K6
Ailsa Pl KLMNKN/STW KA3 207 H4
AYRS KA7 18 C2
CTBR ML5 109 M5
Ailsa Rd BSHPBGS G64 64 B7
CTBR ML5 109 L5
GRK PA19 31 J3
IRV KA12 208 B2
RNFRW PA4 80 C7
SALT KA21 192 A8
TROON KA10 216 A7
Ailsa St PSTWK KA9 225 H1
Ainslie Rd
CARD/HILL/MSPK G52 103 H2
CUMB G67 49 J6
Airbles Crs MTHW ML1 157 K4
Airbles Dr MTHW ML1 157 K4
Airbles Farm Rd MTHW ML1 157 J4
Airbles Rd MTHW ML1 157 J4
Airbles St MTHW ML1 157 L4
Airdale Av GIF/THBK G46 127 J7
Aird Av KLMNK KA1 16 C7
Airdriehill Rd AIRDRIE ML6 89 J7
Airdriehill St AIRDRIE ML6 89 J7
Airdrie Rd AIRDRIE ML6 89 M8
CARLUKE ML8 178 E4
CUMB G67 67 L5
CUMB G67 68 A2
KSYTH G65 47 K1
Airgold Dr DRUM G15 60 F5
Airlie Av BSDN G61 61 L2
Airlie Ct AYRS KA7 18 D8
Airlie Dr BLSH ML4 133 G3
Airlie Gdns RUTH G73 129 K5
Airlie La KVD/HLHD G12 82 B6
Airlie Rd BAIL/MDB/MHD G69 108 A6
Airlie St KVD/HLHD G12 82 B6
Airlour Rd PLKSW/MSWD G43 127 L4
Airth Dr CARD/HILL/MSPK G52 103 M6
Airth La
CARD/HILL/MSPK G52 103 M6
Airthrey Av SCOT G14 81 L5
Airthrey La SCOT G14 81 L5
Airth Wy BALLOCH G68 67 L1
Aitchison Ct AIRDRIE ML6 110 F1
Aitchison St AIRDRIE ML6 110 E2
Aitkenbar Cir DMBTN G82 37 H4
Aitkenbar Dr DMBTN G82 37 H3
Aitkenbrae Dr PSTWK KA9 225 K1
Aitken Cl WISHAW ML2 160 A2
Aitken Dr BEITH KA15 144 C8
Aitkenhead Av CTBR ML5 109 H5
Aitkenhead Rd AIRDRIE ML6 111 K7
UD/BTH/TAN G71 109 G8
Aitken La ALEX/LLW G83 25 L2
Aitken Pl ARD KA22 191 J6
Aitken Rd HMLTN ML3 174 E2
Aitken St AIRDRIE ML6 89 G8
DALRY KA24 184 C2
DEN/PKHD G31 13 H2
LARGS KA30 115 J6
Alasdair Ct BRHD/NEIL G78 125 J7
Albans Crs MTHW ML1 157 H1
Albany EKILN G74 154 C5
Albany Av CAR/SHTL G32 107 J3
Albany Dr LNK/LMHG ML11 199 G6
RUTH G73 129 H3
Albany Qd CAR/SHTL G32 107 J3
Albany Rd HMLTN ML3 174 C2
Albany St CTBR ML5 109 L2
DMNK/BRGTN G40 12 E8
Albany Ter BLTYR/CAMB G72 129 L6
Alba Wy HMLTN ML3 174 C3
Alberta Av CTBR ML5 109 M1
EKILS G75 14 A5
Alberta Pk EKILS G75 14 B5
Albert Av GVH/MTFL G42 104 F8
Albert Dr BSDN G61 62 B6
HBR/GL G84 20 E7
LRKH ML9 176 B7
RUTH G73 129 H4
Albert Pk CARLUKE ML8 189 G3
Albert Pl AIRDRIE ML6 111 H1
Albert Qd MTHW ML1 134 A4
Albert Rd CLYDBK G81 59 M6
GRK PA19 31 G3
GRK PA19 31 K2
GVH/MTFL G42 105 G8
JNSTN PA5 99 J4
KKNTL G66 65 J6
RNFRW PA4 80 C6
Albert St ALEX/LLW G83 25 L5
CTBR ML5 110 A2
HBR/GL G84 20 E7
HMLTN ML3 156 B3
MTHW ML1 157 M2
Albert Ter AYR KA8 19 G3
HMLTN ML3 156 A3
Albion Ga CGLE G1 11 L2
Albion St BAIL/MDB/MHD G69 107 M6
CGLE G1 11 L2
CTBR ML5 110 B2
MTHW ML1 157 L4
PSLYN/LNWD PA3 9 G1
Albion Wy EKILS G75 171 M4
Alcaig Rd CARD/HILL/MSPK G52 103 L7
Alcath Rd WISHAW ML2 160 B3
Alder Av HMLTN ML3 156 E8
KKNTL G66 65 H4
Alder Bank AYRS KA7 229 K3
UD/BTH/TAN G71 109 J8
Alderbank Rd PGL PA14 34 A8
Alderbrae Rd PGL PA14 34 A8
Alder Ct BRHD/NEIL G78 125 J8
EKILS G75 171 J4
Alder Crs EKILS G75 171 J4
Alder Ga BLTYR/CAMB G72 130 E4
Alder Gn IRVSE KA11 204 A5
Alder Gv CTBR ML5 110 B3
Alderman Pl KNTSWD G13 81 J3
Alderman Rd KNTSWD G13 80 F2
Alder Pl EKILS G75 171 J4
JNSTN PA5 100 A8
KLMNK KA1 16 A4
PLKSW/MSWD G43 127 H4
Alder Rd CLYDBK G81 59 M4
CUMB G67 49 K7
DMBTN G82 36 E5
KKNTL G66 45 H4
PLKSW/MSWD G43 127 J4
Alderside Av WISHAW ML2 158 D5
Alderside Gdns
UD/BTH/TAN G71 131 L2
Alderstocks EKILS G75 171 L4
Alderston Av AYR KA8 225 G6
Alderston Pl AYR KA8 225 G6
BLSH ML4 132 E5
Aldersyde Av TROON KA10 216 F5
Aldersyde Pl
BLTYR/CAMB G72 131 J8
Aldersyde Ter MTHW ML1 135 J8
Alderwood Rd PGL PA14 34 B8
Aldrin Rd HBR/GL G84 23 H1
Alexander Av KSYTH G65 46 E5
LARGS KA30 115 L4
SVSTN KA20 192 E7
UD/BTH/TAN G71 132 C3
Alexander Balfour Gdns
HMLTN ML3 156 D8
Alexander Crs GBLS G5 11 H7
Alexander Fleming Av
KBRN KA25 142 F8
Alexander Gdns HMLTN ML3 157 G7
Alexander Gibson Wy
MTHW ML1 157 K4
Alexander Pl IRV KA12 203 H5
KKNTL G66 66 B2
Alexander Rd SHOTTS ML7 137 K3
Alexander St AIRDRIE ML6 110 E2
ALEX/LLW G83 25 L4
CLYDBK G81 60 B8
CTBR ML5 110 B1
DMBTN G82 36 D1
DMBTN G82 37 G5
WISHAW ML2 158 F6
Alexander Ter
BRHD/NEIL G78 148 C2
Alexandra Av PSTWK KA9 221 J8
STPS/GTHM/RID G33 85 K3
Alexandra Ct DEN/PKHD G31 7 G9
Alexandra Dr PSLY PA1 8 A7
RNFRW PA4 80 D6
Alexandra Gdns KKNTL G66 65 J5
Alexandra Pde DEN/PKHD G31 6 C8
Alexandra Pk KKNTL G66 65 J5
Alexandra Park St
DEN/PKHD G31 7 G8
Alexandra Rd KKNTL G66 65 J5
Alexandra St KKNTL G66 65 J1
Alexandra Ter AYR KA8 225 G7
KLWNG KA13 193 K6
Alexandria Qd MTHW ML1 134 A4
Alford Av KKNTL G66 65 H1
Alford Pl IRV KA12 203 L4
PSLYN/LNWD PA3 99 L3
Alford Qd WISHAW ML2 159 H4
Alford St SPRGB/BLRNK G21 5 M2
Algie St PLKSD/SHW G41 127 M1
Algoma Pl EKILS G75 171 H1
Alice Av BLSH ML4 133 G5
Alice St PSLYS PA2 9 G8
Aline Ct BRHD/NEIL G78 125 H5
Alison Ct GRNKW/INVK PA16 50 E4
Alison Lea EKILN G74 154 C6
Allan Av CARLUKE ML8 178 E6
RNFRW PA4 80 E8
Allanbank St SHOTTS ML7 160 F1
Allan Ct EKILS G75 170 E2
Allan Crs ALEX/LLW G83 25 K6
DMBTN G82 37 H3
Allandale Av MTHW ML1 134 F4
Allander Av MLNGV G62 63 G2
Allander Dr BSHPBGS G64 64 A1
Allander Gdns BSHPBGS G64 63 M5
Allander Rd MLNGV G62 42 A7
Allander St PPK/MIL G22 5 J1
Allands Av RNFRW PA4 79 J4
Allanfauld Rd CUMB G67 48 F7
Allan Glen Gdns BSHPBGS G64 64 B5
Allanpark St LARGS KA30 115 J6
Allan Pl AYR KA8 225 J6
DMBTN G82 37 G5
DMNK/BRGTN G40 106 B6
EKILS G75 170 E2
Allanshaw Gdns HMLTN ML3 156 B6
Allanshaw Gv HMLTN ML3 156 B7
Allanshaw St HMLTN ML3 156 C6
Allan Sq IRV KA12 203 L7
Allan St CTBR ML5 109 K4
DMNK/BRGTN G40 106 B7
MTHW ML1 157 M2
Allanton Av PSLY PA1 102 E5
Allanton Dr
CARD/HILL/MSPK G52 103 H4
Allanton Gv WISHAW ML2 159 H4
Allanton Lea HMLTN ML3 174 C1
Allanton Pl HMLTN ML3 156 E8
Allanton Rd SHOTTS ML7 137 J8
WISHAW ML2 160 E1
Allanvale Rd PSTWK KA9 225 H1
Allbany Crs BLSH ML4 133 M4
Allendale EKILN G74 153 J6
Allender Rd BSDN G61 61 K6
Allenfield Rd AYRS KA7 229 K3
Allen Wy RNFRW PA4 80 D8
Allerdyce Dr DRUM G15 60 F8
Allershaw Pl WISHAW ML2 176 F1
Allershaw Rd WISHAW ML2 176 F1
Allerton Gdns CAR/SHTL G32 107 M5
Alleysbank Rd RUTH G73 106 A8
Allison Av ERSK PA8 58 F7
Allison Dr BLTYR/CAMB G72 130 A3
Allison Pl BAIL/MDB/MHD G69 86 E5
NMRNS G77 150 C5
Allison St AYR KA8 19 G1
GVH/MTFL G42 105 G7
Allnach Pl ESTRH G34 108 E1
Alloway AYRS KA7 228 E8
Alloway Av KLMNKN/STW KA3 17 K5
PSLYS PA2 125 H1
Alloway Ct KKNTL G66 46 A7
Alloway Crs PSLYS PA2 125 J1
RUTH G73 128 F4
Alloway Dr CLYDBK G81 60 C6
KKNTL G66 46 A7
NMRNS G77 151 G5
PSLYS PA2 125 H1
RUTH G73 128 F4
Alloway Gdns HMLTN ML3 155 K8
KKNTL G66 46 A7
Alloway Gv KKNTL G66 45 M7
Alloway Pk AYRS KA7 18 D5
Alloway Pl ARD KA22 191 J5
AYRS KA7 18 D4
Alloway Place La AYRS KA7 18 D5
Alloway Rd AIRDRIE ML6 111 M1
EKILN G74 154 D6
PLKSW/MSWD G43 127 K3
Alloway St AYRS KA7 18 F5
LRKH ML9 176 C7
Alloway Ter KKNTL G66 45 M7
Almada La HMLTN ML3 156 D5
Almada St HMLTN ML3 156 D5
Alma St DEN/PKHD G31 13 G5
Almond Av RNFRW PA4 80 E7
Almond Crs PSLYS PA2 100 F7
Almond Dr BSHPTN PA7 58 B7
EKILN G74 15 L3
KKNTL G66 65 H4
Almond Pl CTBR ML5 87 K8
KLMNK KA1 16 A4
Almond Rd BSDN G61 61 J7
CUMB G67 49 M4
STPS/GTHM/RID G33 85 J4
Almond St STPS/GTHM/RID G33 7 M6
Almond V UD/BTH/TAN G71 132 A2
Almond Wy MTHW ML1 157 L6
Almswall Rd KLWNG KA13 193 L6
Alness Crs
CARD/HILL/MSPK G52 103 K6
Alness St HMLTN ML3 156 D7
Alness Ter HMLTN ML3 156 D7
Alpine Gv UD/BTH/TAN G71 131 M2
Alsatian Av CLYDBK G81 60 D7
Alsh Ter HMLTN ML3 156 A8
Alston Av CTBR ML5 110 B1
Alston Gdns BSDN G61 61 H1
Alstonpapple NMLNS KA16 215 L2
Altnacreag Gdns
BAIL/MDB/MHD G69 67 G5
Altonhead Ter
KLMNKN/STW KA3 196 B8
Altonhill Av KLMNKN/STW KA3 206 E6
Alton Rd PSLY PA1 102 C5
Alton St WKIL KA23 181 J4
Altpatrick Gdns JNSTN PA5 100 B6
Altry Pl AYRS KA7 228 B8
Altyre St CAR/SHTL G32 106 F6
Aluclutha Av DMBTN G82 37 H6
Alva Gdns
CARD/HILL/MSPK G52 103 L7
Alva Ga CARD/HILL/MSPK G52 103 L6
Alva Pl KKNTL G66 65 L5
Alva Ter GRK PA19 32 A2
Alvord Av PSTWK KA9 221 K8
Alwyn Av CRG/CRSL/HOU PA6 99 K1
Alwyn Ct EKILN G74 153 L6
Alwyn Dr EKILN G74 153 L6
Alyssum Crs MTHW ML1 157 K1
Alyth Crs CRMNK/CLK/EAG G76 152 A1
Alyth Gdns
CARD/HILL/MSPK G52 103 L6
CRMNK/CLK/EAG G76 152 A1
Amber Ter BLSH ML4 133 G5
Ambleside EKILS G75 170 F3
Ambleside Ri HMLTN ML3 174 C3
Amethyst Av BLSH ML4 133 G5
Amisfield St MRYH/FIRH G20 82 E4
Amlaird Rd KLMNKN/STW KA3 207 G4
Amochrie Dr PSLYS PA2 124 A1
Amochrie Gln PSLYS PA2 124 A1
Amochrie Rd PSLYS PA2 123 M1
Amochrie Wy PSLYS PA2 100 F8
Amulree Pl CAR/SHTL G32 107 G5
Amulree St CAR/SHTL G32 107 G6
Ancaster Dr KNTSWD G13 81 M3
Ancaster La KNTSWD G13 81 M3
Anchor Av PSLY PA1 9 L5
Anchor Crs PSLY PA1 9 M6
Anchor Dr PSLY PA1 9 M5
Anchor La CGLE G1 11 J1
Anchor Wynd PSLY PA1 9 M6
Ancroft St MRYH/FIRH G20 4 E2
Andersen Ct EKILS G75 171 L3
Anderside EKILS G75 171 L4
Anderson Ct BLSH ML4 133 H4
Anderson Crs AYRS KA7 229 H5
KSYTH G65 46 E1
PSTWK KA9 225 L2
Anderson Dr IRV KA12 203 K4
NMRNS G77 150 C5
RNFRW PA4 80 D5
SALT KA21 191 M7
Anderson La AIRDRIE ML6 111 G1
Anderson Pl KLMNKN/STW KA3 207 K7
Anderson Rd BSHPTN PA7 58 A5
Anderson St AIRDRIE ML6 111 G1
HMLTN ML3 155 M4
MTHW ML1 157 L4
PGL PA14 34 B7
PTCK G11 82 B7
Anderson Ter ARD KA22 191 J7
Anderson Quay KVGV G3 10 D3
Andrew Av KKNTL G66 65 K6
RNFRW PA4 80 E6
Andrew Dr CLYDBK G81 80 C1
Andrew Lundi Pl GLSTN KA4 214 B4
Andrew Pl CARLUKE ML8 178 E6
Andrew Sillars Av
BLTYR/CAMB G72 130 C4
Andrews St PSLYN/LNWD PA3 8 F1
Andrew St EKILN G74 15 G4
Anford Pl BLTYR/CAMB G72 155 L3
Angela Wy UD/BTH/TAN G71 131 M3
Angle Ga SCOT G14 81 K5
Angus Av AIRDRIE ML6 111 G4
BSHPBGS G64 64 D8
CARD/HILL/MSPK G52 103 J6
EKILN G74 15 L2
HMLTN ML3 157 G6
MTHW ML1 157 J1
PSTWK KA9 225 K1
Angus Gdns UD/BTH/TAN G71 131 M1
Angus Ov
CARD/HILL/MSPK G52 103 H5
Angus Pl
CARD/HILL/MSPK G52 103 H5
EKILN G74 15 L2
Angus Rd CARLUKE ML8 179 G8
GRNKW/INVK PA16 31 K5
PGL PA14 34 C8
Angus St ALEX/LLW G83 25 M5
CLYDBK G81 80 E1
SPRGB/BLRNK G21 6 B1
Annan Av EKILS G75 170 E2
Annan Crs AIRDRIE ML6 111 K8
Annandale Crs CRH/DND KA2 205 M8
Annandale Gdns CRH/DND KA2 205 L8
Annandale St GVH/MTFL G42 105 H6
Annandale Vw CRH/DND KA2 205 M8
Annandale Wy IRVSE KA11 204 A4
Annan Dr BSDN G61 61 J6
PSLYS PA2 100 E7
RUTH G73 129 K2
Annan Gld MTHW ML1 158 A6
Annan Gv MTHW ML1 158 A6
Annanhill Av KLMNK KA1 206 C8
Annanhill Pk KLWNG KA13 193 H6
Annan Pl JNSTN PA5 122 C1
Annan Rd KLMNK KA1 212 A4
Annan St GVH/MTFL G42 128 A1
MTHW ML1 158 A6
Annathill Gdns CTBR ML5 67 M7
Annbank Pl DEN/PKHD G31 12 D3
Annbank Rd RAYR/DAL KA6 227 G4
Annbank St DEN/PKHD G31 12 D3
LRKH ML9 175 M6
Ann Ct HMLTN ML3 156 A4
Anne Av RNFRW PA4 80 D5
Anne Crs KKNTL G66 65 K6
Annerley Pl CTBR ML5 109 L4
Annes Ct DMNK/BRGTN G40 12 B7
Annette St GVH/MTFL G42 105 G7
Annetyard Dr SKLM PA17 70 B6
Annetyard Rd SKLM PA17 70 A6
Annfield Gdns
BLTYR/CAMB G72 131 J8
Annfield Glen Rd AYRS KA7 229 H5
Annfield Pl DEN/PKHD G31 12 D2
Annfield Rd PSTWK KA9 225 H1
Annfield Ter PSTWK KA9 225 H1
Annick Crs KLMNKN/STW KA3 197 L1
Annick Dr DRUM G15 61 J6
IRVSE KA11 204 B8
Annick Pl KLMNK KA1 212 A4
TROON KA10 216 F5
Annick Rd IRVSE KA11 203 L8
Annick St BLTYR/CAMB G72 130 D4
CAR/SHTL G32 107 H4
Anniesdale Av
STPS/GTHM/RID G33 85 K3
Annieshill Vw AIRDRIE ML6 90 A7
Anniesland Crs SCOT G14 81 G4
Anniesland Rd KNTSWD G13 81 J3
SCOT G14 81 G4
Annieston KSYTH G65 46 F5
Anniversary Av EKILS G75 14 A8
Annpit Rd AYR KA8 225 H5
Annsfield Rd HMLTN ML3 174 C2
Ann St GRNK PA15 2 B6
HMLTN ML3 156 A4
JNSTN PA5 100 A6
Ansdell Av BLTYR/CAMB G72 155 J2
Anson St DMNK/BRGTN G40 12 C7
Anstruther Ct CARLUKE ML8 177 M4
Anstruther St CAR/SHTL G32 106 F5
CARLUKE ML8 177 M4
Antermony Rd KKNTL G66 45 K4
Anthony Rd LARGS KA30 115 K8
Anthony St CGLW G2 10 E1
Antigua St GRNK PA15 2 E6
Antigua Wy EKILS G75 153 G8
Anton Crs KSYTH G65 47 L1
Antonine KKNTL G66 46 B7
Antonine Av MTHW ML1 157 J1
Antonine Gdns CLYDBK G81 60 A3
Antonine Rd BSDN G61 61 H3
Anwoth St CAR/SHTL G32 107 G6
Appin Crs DEN/PKHD G31 13 H1
Appin Rd DEN/PKHD G31 13 H1
Appin Ter HMLTN ML3 155 L5
RUTH G73 129 K5
Appin Wy AIRDRIE ML6 88 E5
Appleby Cl EKILS G75 170 F3
Appleby St PPK/MIL G22 5 G2
Applecross Gdns
BAIL/MDB/MHD G69 66 F6
Applecross Qd WISHAW ML2 159 H4
Applecross Rd KKNTL G66 46 B8
Applecross St MRYH/FIRH G20 5 G3
Appledore Crs
UD/BTH/TAN G71 132 A6
Apsley La PTCK G11 82 A7
Apsley St PTCK G11 82 A7
Aqua Av HMLTN ML3 155 L7
Aqua Ct HMLTN ML3 155 L7
Aquila Wy CARLUKE ML8 178 D7
Araburn Dr EKILS G75 171 L4
Aranthrue Crs RNFRW PA4 80 C5
Aranthrue Dr RNFRW PA4 80 C5
Aray St MRYH/FIRH G20 82 D3
Arbroath Av
CARD/HILL/MSPK G52 103 H5
Arbroath Gv HMLTN ML3 156 B7
Arbuckle Pl AIRDRIE ML6 90 A6
Arbuckle Rd AIRDRIE ML6 90 B4
Arbuckle St KLMNK KA1 17 G5
Arcadia St BLSH ML4 133 G2
DMNK/BRGTN G40 12 B6
Arcan Crs DRUM G15 61 H7
Archerfield Av
CAR/SHTL G32 107 G7
Archerfield Crs
CAR/SHTL G32 107 G7
Archerfield Dr CAR/SHTL G32 107 G7
Archerfield Gv
CAR/SHTL G32 107 G7
Archerhill Av KNTSWD G13 81 G1
Archerhill Crs KNTSWD G13 81 H1
Archerhill Rd KNTSWD G13 81 G1
Archerhill Sq KNTSWD G13 80 F1
Archerhill Ter KNTSWD G13 81 G1
Archibald Ter KKNTL G66 45 H3
Archiebald Pl BLSH ML4 133 K5
Arcon Av RAYR/DAL KA6 226 F3
Arcon Ct RAYR/DAL KA6 227 G2
Ardargie Dr CAR/SHTL G32 130 C1
Ardargie Gv CAR/SHTL G32 130 C1
Ardargie Pl CAR/SHTL G32 130 C1
Ardayre Rd PSTWK KA9 225 H1
Ardbeg Av BSHPBGS G64 64 C8
KLMNKN/STW KA3 206 F6
RUTH G73 129 L6
Ardbeg Ct IRVSE KA11 203 M3
Ardbeg La GVH/MTFL G42 105 G7
Ardbeg Rd GRNK PA15 33 J7
Ardbeg St GVH/MTFL G42 105 G7
Ardchoille Dr SVSTN KA20 192 E7
Ardchoille La SVSTN KA20 192 E7
Ardconnel St GIF/THBK G46 126 F5
Ardeer La SVSTN KA20 201 M3
Arden Av GIF/THBK G46 126 E7
Ardencaple Dr HBR/GL G84 20 A7
Ardencaple Qd HBR/GL G84 20 A7
Ardenclutha Av HMLTN ML3 156 B5
Ardenclutha Dr PGL PA14 34 B8
Arden Ct HMLTN ML3 156 D8
Ardencraig Crs CSMK G45 128 C8
Ardencraig Dr CSMK G45 128 F7
Ardencraig La CSMK G45 128 C8
Ardencraig Pl CSMK G45 128 E6
Ardencraig Qd CSMK G45 128 F7
Ardencraig Rd CSMK G45 128 D8
Ardencraig St CSMK G45 129 G6
Ardencraig Ter CSMK G45 128 E7
Arden Dr GIF/THBK G46 127 H7
Ardenlea UD/BTH/TAN G71 131 M2
Ardenlea St
DMNK/BRGTN G40 106 B6
Arden Pl GIF/THBK G46 126 E7
Arden Rd GRNK PA15 33 K8
HMLTN ML3 156 C7
Arden St AIRDRIE ML6 90 A7
Arden Ter HMLTN ML3 156 C7
HMLTN ML3 156 D8
Ardery St PTCK G11 82 A7
Ardessie St SMSTN G23 62 D8
Ardfern Rd AIRDRIE ML6 111 M3
Ardfern St CAR/SHTL G32 107 G6
Ardfin Ct PSTWK KA9 225 J3
Ardfin Rd PSTWK KA9 225 J4
Ardgay Pl CAR/SHTL G32 107 G5
Ardgay St CAR/SHTL G32 107 G5
Ardgay Wy RUTH G73 129 H6
Ardgoil Dr BALLOCH G68 48 A8
Ardgour Dr PSLYN/LNWD PA3 100 A4
Ardgour Pl
KLMNKN/STW KA3 206 F5
Ardgour Rd KLMNKN/STW KA3 206 F6
Ardgowan Av PSLYS PA2 9 J7
Ardgowan Crs
GRNKW/INVK PA16 50 D5
Ardgowan Dr UD/BTH/TAN G71 131 M1
Ardgowan Pl SHOTTS ML7 137 L3
Ardgowan Rd WMYSB PA18 50 A8
Ardgowan St GRNK PA15 33 M7
GRNKW/INVK PA16 32 D3
PSLYS PA2 9 J8
Ardgryfe Crs
CRG/CRSL/HOU PA6 77 K8
Ardholm St CAR/SHTL G32 107 G4
Ardhu Pl DRUM G15 61 G6
Ardlaw St GOV/IBX G51 103 M3
Ardle Av KLMNK KA1 212 B4
Ardle Rd PLKSW/MSWD G43 127 L4
Ardlui Rd AYR KA8 225 G5
Ardlui St CAR/SHTL G32 106 F5
Ardmaleish Crs CSMK G45 128 E7
Ardmaleish Dr CSMK G45 128 D7
Ardmaleish Rd CSMK G45 128 D7
Ardmaleish St CSMK G45 128 D7
Ardmaleish Ter CSMK G45 128 E7
Ardmay Crs LNPK/KPK G44 128 C2
Ardmillan St
STPS/GTHM/RID G33 106 F1
Ardmore Ct IRVSE KA11 204 A3
Ardmore Pl GRNK PA15 2 A7
Ardmore Rd GRNK PA15 33 J8
PGL PA14 34 D8
Ardmory Av GVH/MTFL G42 128 D2
Ardmory La RUTH G73 128 E2
Ardmory Pl GVH/MTFL G42 128 E2
Ardnahoe Av GVH/MTFL G42 128 D1
Ardnahoe Pl GVH/MTFL G42 128 D1
Ardneil Av WKIL KA23 181 J6
Ardneil Rd GOV/IBX G51 103 M3
Ardnish St GOV/IBX G51 103 L2
Ardoch Ct SVSTN KA20 201 L3
Ardoch Crs DMBTN G82 36 D5
SVSTN KA20 201 L3
Ardoch Gv BLTYR/CAMB G72 129 M3
Ardochrig EKILS G75 171 L4
Ardoch Rd BSDN G61 62 B4
Ardoch St PPK/MIL G22 83 H5
Ardo Gdns GOV/IBX G51 104 A4
Ardressie Pl MRYH/FIRH G20 82 D4
Ard Rd RNFRW PA4 80 B5
Ardrossan High Rd WKIL KA23 181 K5
Ardrossan Rd SALT KA21 200 E1
WKIL KA23 181 J6
Ardshiel Rd GOV/IBX G51 103 L2
Ardsloy Pl SCOT G14 81 G5
Ard St CAR/SHTL G32 107 G5
Ardtoe Crs STPS/GTHM/RID G33 85 L4
Ardtoe Pl STPS/GTHM/RID G33 85 L4
Arduthie Rd GOV/IBX G51 103 L2

Ardwell Rd
CARD/HILL/MSPK G52 103 L6
Argus Av AIRDRIE ML6 111 J7
Argyle Crs AIRDRIE ML6 110 F5
HMLTN ML3 155 M6
Argyle Dr HMLTN ML3 156 A5
Argyle Gdns KKNTL G66 44 E2
Argyle Pl SALT KA21 200 E1
Argyle Rd BSDN G61 61 L2
GRK PA19 31 M3
SALT KA21 200 E1
Argyle St CGLE G1 11 J2
CGLW G2 11 G2
GRNK PA15 2 C3
KVGV G3 4 C9
KVGV G3 82 D8
PSLY PA1 8 E5
Argyle St East HBR/GL G84 20 E8
Argyle St West HBR/GL G84 20 C7
Argyll Av DMBTN G82 37 J5
PSLYN/LNWD PA3 79 K8
RNFRW PA4 80 B5
Argyll Gdns LRKH ML9 176 B6
Argyll Pl BLSH ML4 132 F6
DMBTN G82 37 J5
EKILN G74 154 C6
KSYTH G65 47 L1
Argyll Rd CLYDBK G81 80 B1
Argyll St ALEX/LLW G83 25 K3
Arisaig Dr BSDN G61 62 B6
CARD/HILL/MSPK G52 103 K6
Arisaig Pl CARD/HILL/MSPK G52 103 L6
Arisdale Crs NMRNS G77 150 E3
Arkaig Av AIRDRIE ML6 89 M6
Arkaig Pl NMRNS G77 151 H5
Arkaig St WISHAW ML2 177 H1
Ark La DEN/PKHD G31 12 C1
Arkleston Crs
PSLYN/LNWD PA3 102 B2
Arkleston Rd PSLY PA1 102 B3
PSLYN/LNWD PA3 102 A1
Arkle Ter BLTYR/CAMB G72 129 L6
Arklet Rd GOV/IBX G51 103 L3
Arklet Wy WISHAW ML2 159 L6
Arkwrights Wy PSLY PA1 8 B6
Arkwright Wy IRVSE KA11 203 M6
Arlington St KVGV G3 4 D6
Armadale Pl DEN/PKHD G31 6 F8
GRNK PA15 2 D5
Armadale Rd LNK/LMHG ML11 199 J5
Armadale St DEN/PKHD G31 6 F9
Armour Av AIRDRIE ML6 110 E2
Armour Ct BLTYR/CAMB G72 155 H3
KKNTL G66 46 A8
Armour Dr AYRS KA7 19 L7
KKNTL G66 46 A8
Armour Gv MTHW ML1 158 A5
Armour Pl ARD KA22 191 J5
JNSTN PA5 100 A6
Armour St COWCAD G4 12 B3
JNSTN PA5 100 A6
KLMNK KA1 16 F6
Armstrong Crs
UD/BTH/TAN G71 132 A1
Armstrong Gv EKILS G75 14 D7
Armstrong Rd HBR/GL G84 23 G1
KLMNKN/STW KA3 17 L1
Arness Ter KLMNKN/STW KA3 206 E5
Arngask Rd GOV/IBX G51 103 M1
Arnhall Pl
CARD/HILL/MSPK G52 103 L6
Arnhem St BLTYR/CAMB G72 130 D4
Arnholm Pl
CARD/HILL/MSPK G52 103 L6
Arnisdale Pl ESTRH G34 108 A1
Arnisdale Rd ESTRH G34 108 A1
Arnisdale Wy RUTH G73 129 H6
Arniston St CAR/SHTL G32 106 F2
Arniston Wy
PSLYN/LNWD PA3 102 A2
Arnold Av BSHPBGS G64 64 A8
Arnol Pl
STPS/GTHM/RID G33 107 M2
Arnott Dr CTBR ML5 110 A5
Arnott Qd MTHW ML1 133 J8
Arnott Wy BLTYR/CAMB G72 130 A3
Arnprior Crs CSMK G45 128 D6
Arnprior Pl AYRS KA7 228 F7
Arnprior Qd CSMK G45 128 D5
Arnprior Rd CSMK G45 128 D5
Arnprior St CSMK G45 128 D5
Arnside Av GIF/THBK G46 127 J6
Arnum Gdns CARLUKE ML8 178 F8
Arnum Pl CARLUKE ML8 178 F8
Arnwood Dr KVD/HLHD G12 82 A4
Arondale Rd AIRDRIE ML6 89 M6
Aron Ter BLTYR/CAMB G72 129 M6
Aros Dr CARD/HILL/MSPK G52 103 K7
Arran EKILN G74 154 C8
Arran Av CTBR ML5 110 D5
DMBTN G82 36 D4
KLMNKN/STW KA3 207 G5
PGL PA14 55 H2
PSLYN/LNWD PA3 79 L8
Arran Crs BEITH KA15 144 C8
Arran Dr AIRDRIE ML6 88 F4
AIRDRIE ML6 88 F8
CARD/HILL/MSPK G52 103 M6
CUMB G67 68 D1
GIF/THBK G46 127 H7
JNSTN PA5 99 K8
KKNTL G66 45 L8
PSLYS PA2 124 E2
Arran Gdns CARLUKE ML8 188 F1
HMLTN ML3 155 E8
TROON KA10 216 D2
Arran La ARD KA22 191 J8
Arran Pk PSTWK KA9 225 H4
Arran Pl ARD KA22 191 J8
CLYDBK G81 60 C7
CTBR ML5 110 D5
IRV KA12 203 H4
PSLYN/LNWD PA3 100 A3
SALT KA21 192 A7
Arran Rd GRK PA19 31 K3
MTHW ML1 157 J2
RNFRW PA4 80 D7
TROON KA10 216 D2
Arran Ter AYRS KA7 18 D2
RUTH G73 128 F4
Arran Vw KSYTH G65 47 K1
LARGS KA30 115 L5
TROON KA10 216 C6
Arranview St AIRDRIE ML6 111 L8
Arran Wy UD/BTH/TAN G71 131 M7
Arrochar Ct SMSTN G23 82 D1
Arrochar Dr SMSTN G23 62 D8
Arrochar St MRYH/FIRH G20 82 D1
SMSTN G23 62 D8
Arrol Dr AYRS KA7 228 D4
Arrol Pl EKILS G75 172 A3
Arrol St CARD/HILL/MSPK G52 102 E2
Arrothill Dr KLMNK KA1 16 B6
Arrotshole Rd EKILN G74 153 H6
Arrowsmith Av KNTSWD G13 81 K1
Arthur Av AIRDRIE ML6 110 F3
BRHD/NEIL G78 125 H8
Arthur Ct WKIL KA23 181 J4
Arthur Gdns AIRDRIE ML6 91 H5
Arthurlie Av BRHD/NEIL G78 125 J7
BRHD/NEIL G78 147 H6
Arthurlie Dr BRHD/NEIL G78 147 H6
GIF/THBK G46 127 J8
NMRNS G77 150 D6
Arthurlie Pl SALT KA21 200 E1
Arthurlie St BRHD/NEIL G78 125 H7
GOV/IBX G51 103 M2
Arthur Rd PSLYS PA2 124 E1
Arthurston Rd ALEX/LLW G83 25 M2
Arthurston Ter
RAYR/DAL KA6 231 H5
Arthur St ALEX/LLW G83 25 L5
AYRS KA7 18 E3
CRMNK/CLK/EAG G76 151 L3
GRNK PA15 3 G6
HMLTN ML3 156 D4
KVGV G3 82 D8
PSLY PA1 8 D3
SALT KA21 201 G2
SVSTN KA20 201 K1
WKIL KA23 181 J4
Arundel Dr BSHPBGS G64 64 B5
GVH/MTFL G42 128 A2
Ascaig Crs
CARD/HILL/MSPK G52 103 L7
Ascog Pl WMYSB PA18 50 A8
Ascog Rd BSDN G61 61 M7
Ascog St GVH/MTFL G42 105 G7
Ascot Av KVD/HLHD G12 81 M3
Ash Av EKILS G75 14 A9
Ashburn Gdns GRK PA19 31 J2
MLNGV G62 41 L8
Ashburn Ga GRK PA19 31 J2
Ashburn Rd MLNGV G62 41 L7
Ashburton La KVD/HLHD G12 82 B3
Ashburton Pk EKILS G75 171 G2
Ashburton Rd KVD/HLHD G12 82 A3
Ashby Crs KNTSWD G13 61 L8
Ash Ct EKILS G75 171 J3
Ashcroft EKILN G74 154 D4
Ashcroft Av KKNTL G66 44 E2
Ashcroft Dr LNPK/KPK G44 128 E3
Ashdale Av SALT KA21 191 M7
Ashdale Dr
CARD/HILL/MSPK G52 103 L6
Ashdale Rd KLMNKN/STW KA3 206 E5
Ashdene St PPK/MIL G22 83 H2
Ash Dr BEITH KA15 144 B7
Asher Rd AIRDRIE ML6 111 L7
Ashfield BSHPBGS G64 64 A6
Ashfield Rd CARLUKE ML8 177 M3
CRMNK/CLK/EAG G76 151 L3
MLNGV G62 42 A8
Ashfield St PPK/MIL G22 83 J5
Ashgillhead Rd LRKH ML9 176 E8
Ashgill Pl PPK/MIL G22 83 J3
Ashgill Rd PPK/MIL G22 83 H3
Ash Gv BSHPBGS G64 84 B1
KKNTL G66 65 H4
UD/BTH/TAN G71 132 B1
Ashgrove AIRDRIE ML6 91 G4
AIRDRIE ML6 111 K2
CTBR ML5 110 A5
IRV KA12 203 J4
RAYR/DAL KA6 231 H5
SHOTTS ML7 136 F6
Ashgrove Av GRK PA19 31 J2
SVSTN KA20 192 E7
Ashgrove La PGL PA14 34 D8
Ashgrove Rd ARD KA22 191 J5
BLSH ML4 133 H2
KLWNG KA13 193 J5
Ashgrove St AYRS KA7 19 G6
DMNK/BRGTN G40 106 A7
Ashiestiel Pl CUMB G67 68 E2
Ashkirk Dr
CARD/HILL/MSPK G52 103 L6
Ashland Av HMLTN ML3 174 D2
Ashlea Dr GIF/THBK G46 127 K5
Ashlea Gdns AIRDRIE ML6 89 M6
Ashley Dr UD/BTH/TAN G71 132 B4
Ashley La KVGV G3 4 D6
Ashley Pk UD/BTH/TAN G71 132 C3
Ashley Pl BLTYR/CAMB G72 155 J1
Ashley Ri ALEX/LLW G83 25 M8
Ashley St KVGV G3 4 D6
Ashmore Rd
PLKSW/MSWD G43 127 M4
Ash Pl JNSTN PA5 100 A7
KLMNK KA1 16 A6
Ash Rd BAIL/MDB/MHD G69 108 A6
CLYDBK G81 60 A4
CUMB G67 49 K4
DMBTN G82 36 F5
Ashton Dr HBR/GL G84 23 G1
Ashton Gdns
BAIL/MDB/MHD G69 87 G3
Ashton Gn EKILN G74 14 F1
Ashton La KVD/HLHD G12 82 D7
Ashton La North
KVD/HLHD G12 82 D7
Ashton Pl GRK PA19 31 J2
Ashton Rd GRK PA19 31 J2
KVD/HLHD G12 82 D7
RUTH G73 106 A8
Ashton St MTHW ML1 133 K7
Ashton Vw DMBTN G82 36 B5
Ashtree Ct OLDK G60 59 G3
Ashtree Gv NMRNS G77 150 C6
Ashtree Rd
PLKSW/MSWD G43 127 J2
Ashvale Crs SPRGB/BLRNK G21 83 L5
Ashworth Ter HMLTN ML3 156 A5
Ash Wynd BLTYR/CAMB G72 130 E5
Aspen Ct AYRS KA7 229 K4
Aspen Dr SPRGB/BLRNK G21 6 E2
Aspen Pl BLTYR/CAMB G72 130 E4
JNSTN PA5 100 A8
Aspen Rd AYRS KA7 229 K4
Aspen Wy HMLTN ML3 156 E7
Asquith Pl BLSH ML4 133 K4
Assloss Rd KLMNKN/STW KA3 207 J4
Aster Dr CSMK G45 129 G7
Aster Gdns MTHW ML1 157 L4
PLK/PH/NH G53 126 C6
Athelstane Dr CUMB G67 68 D2
Athelstane Rd KNTSWD G13 81 J2
Athena Wy UD/BTH/TAN G71 132 A2
Athole Gdns KVD/HLHD G12 82 C6
Athole La KVD/HLHD G12 82 C6
Athole St HBR/GL G84 20 F8
Athole Ter GRNKW/INVK PA16 31 K6
Atholl Av BSHPBGS G64 44 B8
CARD/HILL/MSPK G52 102 E2
Atholl Crs PSLY PA1 102 E4
Atholl Dr BALLOCH G68 47 M8
GIF/THBK G46 151 J1
Atholl Gdns BSDN G61 61 L2
BSHPBGS G64 63 M6
KLWNG KA13 193 L5
RUTH G73 129 L5
Atholl Pl CTBR ML5 110 B6
PSLYN/LNWD PA3 100 A3
Atholl St HMLTN ML3 156 B3
Atholl Ter UD/BTH/TAN G71 108 F8
Atlas Pl SPRGB/BLRNK G21 6 D2
Atlas Rd SPRGB/BLRNK G21 6 B1
Atlas St CLYDBK G81 80 B1
Atlin Dr MTHW ML1 134 B6
Attercliffe Av WISHAW ML2 158 D7
Attlee Av CLYDBK G81 60 D8
Attow Rd PLKSW/MSWD G43 127 H4
Aubery Crs LARGS KA30 115 J4
Auburn Dr BRHD/NEIL G78 125 K8
Auchans Dr CRH/DND KA2 209 L7
Auchanshangan Dr SALT KA21 191 L6
Auchans Rd CRG/CRSL/HOU PA6 99 M1
Auchenbeg Crs AYRS KA7 229 G6
Auchenbothie Gdns
KLMCLM PA13 55 H7
Auchenbothie Rd PGL PA14 54 F3
Auchencrow St ESTRH G34 108 D1
Auchencruive MLNGV G62 62 C1
Auchendarroch St GRNK PA15 3 K7
Auchendavie Rd KKNTL G66 46 B7
Auchendoon Crs AYRS KA7 228 D5
Auchendores Av PGL PA14 55 G2
Auchenfoil La PGL PA14 54 C1
Auchenfoil Rd GRNK PA15 33 L8
KLMCLM PA13 53 M3
PGL PA14 54 C1
Auchengarth Br SKLM PA17 92 B4
Auchengate TROON KA10 216 E2
Auchengate Crs IRVSE KA11 208 E7
Auchengeich Rd
BAIL/MDB/MHD G69 66 D5
Auchengilloch EKILS G75 171 L4
Auchenglen Rd CARLUKE ML8 188 F6
Auchengree Rd GLGNK KA14 167 K4
Auchengreoch Av JNSTN PA5 122 D1
Auchengreoch Rd JNSTN PA5 122 D1
Auchenharvie Pl SVSTN KA20 192 B8
Auchenharvie Rd SALT KA21 201 G1
Auchenhove Crs KBRN KA25 143 G5
Auchenhowie Rd MLNGV G62 62 C1
Auchenkilns Rd CUMB G67 68 D3
Auchenleck La PGL PA14 54 E2
Auchenleck Rd PGL PA14 54 E2
Auchenlodment Rd JNSTN PA5 100 B7
Auchenmaid Dr LARGS KA30 115 K5
Auchenreoch Av DMBTN G82 37 H3
Auchenstewart Ct
WISHAW ML2 159 J6
Auchentibber Rd
BLTYR/CAMB G72 154 F6
Auchentiber Pl
KLMNKN/STW KA3 207 J3
Auchentorlie Qd PSLY PA1 102 B5
Auchentorlie St PTCK G11 81 M7
Auchentoshan Av CLYDBK G81 59 M3
Auchentoshan Ter
SPRGB/BLRNK G21 6 B4
Auchentrae Crs AYRS KA7 228 D4
Auchinairn Rd BSHPBGS G64 84 D1
SPRGB/BLRNK G21 84 C2
Auchinbee Farm Rd
BALLOCH G68 48 B5
Auchinbee Wy BALLOCH G68 48 B6
Auchincampbell Rd
HMLTN ML3 156 D6
Auchincruive Av PSTWK KA9 225 J2
Auchineden Ct BSDN G61 61 J2
Auchingill Pl ESTRH G34 86 D8
Auchingill Rd ESTRH G34 86 C8
Auchingramont Rd
HMLTN ML3 156 D6
Auchinlea Dr MTHW ML1 135 J8
Auchinlea Rd ESTRH G34 85 M8
Auchinleck Av
STPS/GTHM/RID G33 84 E3
Auchinleck Crs
STPS/GTHM/RID G33 84 E3
Auchinleck Dr
STPS/GTHM/RID G33 84 E3
Auchinleck Gdns
STPS/GTHM/RID G33 84 E3
Auchinleck Rd CLYDBK G81 60 B3
STPS/GTHM/RID G33 84 F2
Auchinleck Ter CLYDBK G81 60 B2
Auchinloch Rd KKNTL G66 65 K5
Auchinloch St SPRGB/BLRNK G21 6 D3
Auchinraith Av HMLTN ML3 156 B3
Auchinraith Rd
BLTYR/CAMB G72 155 M2
Auchinraith Ter
BLTYR/CAMB G72 155 L3
Auchinvole Crs KSYTH G65 47 H1
Auchmannoch Av PSLY PA1 102 E4
Auchmead Rd
GRNKW/INVK PA16 31 L6
Auchmountain Rd GRNK PA15 3 J8
Auchnacraig Rd CLYDBK G81 60 C2
Auchneagh Av
GRNKW/INVK PA16 32 B5
Auchneagh Crs
GRNKW/INVK PA16 32 A5
Auchneagh Farm Rd
GRNKW/INVK PA16 32 B4
Auchneagh Rd
GRNKW/INVK PA16 32 B5
Auchter Av WISHAW ML2 160 C4
Auchterburn Rd SHOTTS ML7 160 F1
Auchter Rd WISHAW ML2 159 L5
Auckland Pk EKILS G75 171 G1
Auckland Pl CLYDBK G81 59 K5
Auckland St PPK/MIL G22 5 G2
Auldbar Rd
CARD/HILL/MSPK G52 103 M6
Auldbar Ter PSLYS PA2 9 L8
Auldburn Pl PLKSW/MSWD G43 127 H3
Auldburn Rd
PLKSW/MSWD G43 127 G3
Auld Clay Rd SALT KA21 192 E2
Auldearn Rd SPRGB/BLRNK G21 84 C2
Auldgirth Rd
CARD/HILL/MSPK G52 103 M6
Auldhame St CTBR ML5 109 L1
Auldhouse Av
PLKSW/MSWD G43 127 H3
Auldhouse Gdns
PLKSW/MSWD G43 127 H3
Auldhouse Rd EKILS G75 171 J8
PLKSW/MSWD G43 127 J3
Auldhouse Ter
PLKSW/MSWD G43 127 K3
Auld Kirk Rd BLTYR/CAMB G72 130 C6
Auldlea Rd BEITH KA15 144 B7
Auldmurroch Dr MLNGV G62 41 K7
The Auld Rd CUMB G67 49 G5
Auld's Brae AIRDRIE ML6 111 G1
Auld St CLYDBK G81 59 L6
Auldton Ter LRKH ML9 176 F8
Aultbea St PPK/MIL G22 83 H1
Aultmore Rd
STPS/GTHM/RID G33 107 M2
Aursbridge Crs BRHD/NEIL G78 125 K7
Aursbridge Dr BRHD/NEIL G78 125 K7
Aurs Crs BRHD/NEIL G78 125 K7
Aurs Dr BRHD/NEIL G78 125 K8
Aurs Gln BRHD/NEIL G78 125 J8
Aurs Pl BRHD/NEIL G78 125 L7
Aurs Rd BRHD/NEIL G78 125 K6
NMRNS G77 150 A4
Austen La KNTSWD G13 81 L4
Austen Rd KNTSWD G13 81 L4
Austine Dr HMLTN ML3 174 E2
Avenel Rd KNTSWD G13 61 L8
Avenue End Rd
STPS/GTHM/RID G33 85 H5
Avenuehead Rd
BAIL/MDB/MHD G69 87 G1
Avenuepark St MRYH/FIRH G20 82 E5
Avenue Sq KLMNKN/STW KA3 197 K1
Avenue St DMNK/BRGTN G40 12 E6
RUTH G73 106 B8
The Avenue WKIL KA23 181 L1
Aviemore Gdns BSDN G61 62 A4
Aviemore Rd
CARD/HILL/MSPK G52 103 L7
Avils Hl KBRN KA25 143 G8
Avils Pl KBRN KA25 143 G8
Avoch St ESTRH G34 86 B8
Avon Av BSDN G61 62 B5
CARLUKE ML8 178 D7
Avonbank Crs HMLTN ML3 174 E1
Avonbank Rd LRKH ML9 175 L7
RUTH G73 128 F2
Avonbrae Crs HMLTN ML3 174 E1
Avonbridge Dr HMLTN ML3 156 F6
Avondale Av EKILN G74 15 H4
Avondale Dr PSLY PA1 102 B3
Avondale Pl EKILN G74 15 J5
Avondale Rd WKIL KA23 181 J3
Avondale St
STPS/GTHM/RID G33 85 G8
Avon Dr BLSH ML4 133 J5
PSLYN/LNWD PA3 100 B3
Avonhead EKILS G75 171 L4
Avonhead Av CUMB G67 68 C2
Avonhead Gdns CUMB G67 68 C2
Avonhead Rd CUMB G67 68 C2
Avonmouth Pl
GRNKW/INVK PA16 31 M4
Avon Pl CTBR ML5 87 K8
KLMNK KA1 212 B4
Avon Rd BSHPBGS G64 84 A1
GIF/THBK G46 127 H7
Avonside Gv HMLTN ML3 156 F6
Avonspark St SPRGB/BLRNK G21 6 F2
Avon St HMLTN ML3 156 E6
LRKH ML9 175 M6
MTHW ML1 157 K4
Aylmer Rd PLKSW/MSWD G43 127 M3
Ayr Dr AIRDRIE ML6 111 G4
Ayr Rd IRV KA12 203 J8
KLMNK KA1 211 K6
LRKH ML9 176 E7
NMRNS G77 150 C6
PSTWK KA9 225 H3
Ayr St SPRGB/BLRNK G21 6 B2
TROON KA10 216 C7
Ayr Ter GRNKW/INVK PA16 31 L6
Ayton Pk North EKILN G74 154 B6
Ayton Pk South EKILN G74 154 B6
Aytoun Dr ERSK PA8 58 F6
Aytoun Rd PLKSD/SHW G41 104 D6

B

Baberton Wy KLWNG KA13 193 H6
Babylon Av BLSH ML4 133 G6
Babylon Dr BLSH ML4 133 G6
Babylon Pl BLSH ML4 133 G6
Babylon Rd BLSH ML4 133 G6
Backbrae St KSYTH G65 47 K1
Backburn BEITH KA15 168 B1
Back Cswy DEN/PKHD G31 13 M5
Back Hawkhill Av AYR KA8 225 G7
Backmuir Crs HMLTN ML3 156 B3
Backmuir Pl HMLTN ML3 156 B3
Backmuir Rd DRUM G15 61 H5
HMLTN ML3 156 B2
Back O' Barns HMLTN ML3 156 E5
Back O'barns HMLTN ML3 156 F5
Back O Dykes Rd KKNTL G66 66 B2
Back O Hl CRG/CRSL/HOU PA6 77 H8
Back O' Hill Rd BSHPBGS G64 43 L7
Back Peebles St AYR KA8 224 F7
Back Rd BRWEIR PA11 98 D1
Back Rw HMLTN ML3 156 E5
Back Sneddon St PSLY PA1 9 G2
PSLYN/LNWD PA3 9 H2
Back St DMBTN G82 25 K8
Badenheath Pl BALLOCH G68 67 K4
Badenoch Road. KKNTL G66 46 B8
Bagnell St SPRGB/BLRNK G21 83 M4
Bahamas Wy EKILS G75 153 G8
Baidland Av DALRY KA24 184 E3
Bailie Dr BSDN G61 61 K2
Bailie Fyfe Wy WISHAW ML2 177 H2
Baillie Dr EKILN G74 154 B5
UD/BTH/TAN G71 132 A6
Baillie Gdns WISHAW ML2 159 L5
Baillie Pl EKILN G74 154 C5
Baillie Rd FAIRLIE KA29 139 L4
Baillies La AIRDRIE ML6 111 G2
Bailliesmuir Pl WISHAW ML2 160 A3
Baillieston Av KBRN KA25 167 G1
Baillieston Rd CAR/SHTL G32 107 L5
UD/BTH/TAN G71 108 B8
Baillie Wynd
UD/BTH/TAN G71 132 A2
Bain Crs HBR/GL G84 20 E6
Bainfield Rd DMBTN G82 35 H2
Bainsford St CAR/SHTL G32 106 F3
Bain St DMNK/BRGTN G40 12 A4
Bain Wy ALEX/LLW G83 25 L3
Baird Av AIRDRIE ML6 89 H7
CARD/HILL/MSPK G52 102 E1
HBR/GL G84 20 B7
KLWNG KA13 193 L4
Baird Brae MRYH/FIRH G20 5 G3
Baird Crs ALEX/LLW G83 25 J2
CUMB G67 68 B2
Baird Dr BSDN G61 61 K4
ERSK PA8 58 F6
Baird Hl EKILS G75 14 D6
Baird Pl BLSH ML4 133 G2
KLMNKN/STW KA3 207 H7
PSTWK KA9 221 K5
WISHAW ML2 159 L5
Baird Rd AYRS KA7 228 E8
PSTWK KA9 221 K5
Bairds Crs HMLTN ML3 156 C5
Bairdsland Vw BLSH ML4 133 H4
Baird St COWCAD G4 5 L7
CTBR ML5 110 A2
Baker St GRNK PA15 2 F6
PLKSD/SHW G41 104 E8
Bakewell Rd
BAIL/MDB/MHD G69 108 A4
Balaclava St KVGV G3 10 E2
Balado Rd STPS/GTHM/RID G33 107 L2
Balbeggie St CAR/SHTL G32 107 J5
Balbeg St GOV/IBX G51 103 L3
Balblair Rd
CARD/HILL/MSPK G52 103 M7
Balcarres Av KVD/HLHD G12 82 C4
Balcomie Crs TROON KA10 217 G7
Balcomie St
STPS/GTHM/RID G33 85 G8
Balcurvie Rd ESTRH G34 86 A7
Baldernock Rd MLNGV G62 42 D7
Baldie's Brae NMLNS KA16 215 J2
Baldinnie Rd ESTRH G34 108 B1
Baldorran Crs BALLOCH G68 48 B6
Baldovan Crs
STPS/GTHM/RID G33 107 M1
Baldovie Rd
CARD/HILL/MSPK G52 103 J6
Baldragon Rd ESTRH G34 86 B8
Baldric Rd KNTSWD G13 81 J3
Baldwin Av KNTSWD G13 61 K8
Balerno Dr
CARD/HILL/MSPK G52 103 L6
Balfleurs St MLNGV G62 42 B7
Balfluig St ESTRH G34 85 M8
Balfour Av BEITH KA15 168 B2
Balfour Ct KLMNKN/STW KA3 207 K6
Balfour St MRYH/FIRH G20 82 D3
PGL PA14 34 B7
Balfour Ter EKILS G75 15 G7
Balfron Crs HMLTN ML3 155 M6
Balfron Rd GOV/IBX G51 103 L2
GRNK PA15 33 J8
PSLY PA1 102 D4
Balgair Dr PSLY PA1 102 B4
Balgair St PPK/MIL G22 83 H4
Balgair Ter CAR/SHTL G32 107 H4
Balglass St PPK/MIL G22 83 H5
Balgonie Av PSLYS PA2 101 G8
Balgonie Dr PSLYS PA2 101 J8
Balgonie Rd
CARD/HILL/MSPK G52 103 L5
Balgonie Woods PSLYS PA2 101 J8
Balgownie Crs GIF/THBK G46 127 G7
Balgray Av KBRN KA25 167 G1
KLMNK KA1 211 M7
Balgraybank St
SPRGB/BLRNK G21 84 A5
Balgray Crs BRHD/NEIL G78 125 L7
Balgray Rd BEITH KA15 169 G5
GLGNK KA14 167 H2
NMRNS G77 150 A4
Balgraystone Rd NMRNS G77 149 K4
Balgray Wy IRVSE KA11 204 A3
Balintore St CAR/SHTL G32 107 G4
Baliol La KVGV G3 4 D7

Balliol St KVGV G3 4 D6
Baljaffray Rd BSDN G61 61 G2
Ballachalairy Yett
CMPF/LLE G63 26 D5
Ballagan Pl MLNGV G62 41 K7
Ballaig Av BSDN G61 61 K4
Ballaig Crs
STPS/GTHM/RID G33 85 J4
Ballantay Qd CSMK G45 129 G6
Ballantay Rd CSMK G45 129 G6
Ballantay Ter CSMK G45 129 G6
Ballantine Av
CARD/HILL/MSPK G52 103 G2
Ballantine Dr AYRS KA7 18 F7
Ballantrae EKILN G74 153 K6
Ballantrae Crs NMRNS G77 151 G5
Ballantrae Dr NMRNS G77 151 G5
Ballantrae Rd
BLTYR/CAMB G72 155 L4
Ballater Crs WISHAW ML2 159 H4
Ballater Dr BSDN G61 61 M7
PSLYS PA2 101 M8
RNFRW PA4 79 K2
Ballater Pl GBLS G5 11 L7
Ballater St GBLS G5 11 J5
Ballayne Dr BAIL/MDB/MHD G69 67 G6
Ballerup Ter EKILS G75 171 L3
Ballewan Crs CMPF/LLE G63 27 G5
Ballindalloch Dr DEN/PKHD G31 7 G9
Ballindalloch La DEN/PKHD G31 6 F9
Balloch Crs GTCI KA28 138 C6
Balloch Gdns
CARD/HILL/MSPK G52 103 M6
Balloch Loop Rd BALLOCH G68 48 C7
Ballochmill Rd
BLTYR/CAMB G72 129 K1
Ballochmyle EKILN G74 154 D5
Ballochney Rd AIRDRIE ML6 89 K5
Ballochney St AIRDRIE ML6 88 E7
Ballochnie Dr AIRDRIE ML6 89 M7
Balloch Rd AIRDRIE ML6 112 A3
ALEX/LLW G83 25 K1
GRNK PA15 33 H7
SHOTTS ML7 137 L3
Balloch Vw CUMB G67 48 F7
Ballogie Rd LNPK/KPK G44 128 B2
Ballot Rd IRV KA12 203 J7
Balmartin Rd SMSTN G23 62 D8
Balmedie ERSK PA8 59 G7
Balmeg Av GIF/THBK G46 151 J1
Balminnoch Pk AYRS KA7 228 C8
Balmoral Av AIRDRIE ML6 88 F4
Balmoral Crs CTBR ML5 109 K5
RNFRW PA4 79 L2
Balmoral Dr BLTYR/CAMB G72 129 L4
BSDN G61 62 A7
CAR/SHTL G32 130 B1
Balmoral Gdns
BLTYR/CAMB G72 131 J7
UD/BTH/TAN G71 108 F8
Balmoral Pl EKILN G74 14 B3
GRK PA19 30 E4
Balmoral Rd JNSTN PA5 123 H1
KLMNKN/STW KA3 16 D1
Balmoral St SCOT G14 81 H6
Balmoral Wynd
KLMNKN/STW KA3 197 L1
Balmore Ct KLMCLM PA13 75 J2
Balmore Dr HMLTN ML3 174 A1
Balmore Pl PPK/MIL G22 83 H3
Balmore Rd BSHPBGS G64 63 L2
GRNK PA15 33 H8
MLNGV G62 62 F4
SMSTN G23 83 G2
Balmore Sq MRYH/FIRH G20 83 H4
Balmuildy Rd BSHPBGS G64 63 H5
BSHPBGS G64 63 L4
Balnagowan Rd SKLM PA17 70 B5
Balornock Rd
SPRGB/BLRNK G21 84 A4
Balrossie Dr KLMCLM PA13 75 G2
Balruddery Pl BSHPBGS G64 84 D1
Balshagray Av SCOT G14 81 M6
Balshagray Crs PTCK G11 81 L7
Balshagray Dr PTCK G11 81 M6
Balshagray La PTCK G11 81 M6
Balshagray Pl PTCK G11 81 M6
Baltersan Gdns HMLTN ML3 174 F6
Baltic Ct DMNK/BRGTN G40 106 A6
Baltic La DMNK/BRGTN G40 12 F9
Baltic Pl DMNK/BRGTN G40 12 D7
Baltic St DMNK/BRGTN G40 12 F9
DMNK/BRGTN G40 106 B6
Balure St DEN/PKHD G31 13 K2
Balvaird Crs RUTH G73 129 G2
Balvaird Dr RUTH G73 129 G2
Balvenie St CTBR ML5 110 B6
Balveny St STPS/GTHM/RID G33 85 K7
Balvicar Dr GVH/MTFL G42 104 F8
Balvicar St GVH/MTFL G42 104 F7
Balvie Av DRUM G15 61 G8
GIF/THBK G46 127 K7
Balvie Crs MLNGV G62 41 M7
Balvie Rd MLNGV G62 41 M7
Banavie Rd PTCK G11 82 B6
WISHAW ML2 159 M3
Banchory Av AIRDRIE ML6 88 F4
PLKSW/MSWD G43 127 H4
RNFRW PA4 79 K2
Banchory Crs BSDN G61 62 A7
Banchory Rd WISHAW ML2 159 H4
Baneberry Pth EKILN G74 153 K5
Banff Av AIRDRIE ML6 111 G5
Banff Pl EKILS G75 14 A5
GRNKW/INVK PA16 31 K4
Banff Qd WISHAW ML2 159 H4
Banff Rd GRNKW/INVK PA16 31 J5
Banff St STPS/GTHM/RID G33 85 H7
Bangorshill St GIF/THBK G46 126 F5
Bank Av MLNGV G62 42 A6
Bankbrae Av PLK/PH/NH G53 126 A3
Bank Ct IRV KA12 203 L5
Bankend BRWEIR PA11 98 E2
Bankend Pl KLMNKN/STW KA3 207 G4
Bankend Rd BRWEIR PA11 98 F3
DMBTN G82 36 F5
Bankend St
STPS/GTHM/RID G33 85 G8
Bankfaulds Av KBRN KA25 143 G8
Bankfield Dr HMLTN ML3 174 D2
Bankfoot Dr
CARD/HILL/MSPK G52 103 H4
Bankfoot Pl NMRNS G77 151 H5
Bankfoot Rd
CARD/HILL/MSPK G52 103 H5
PSLYN/LNWD PA3 8 B2
Bankglen Rd DRUM G15 61 H5
Bankhall St GVH/MTFL G42 105 H7
Bankhead Av AIRDRIE ML6 111 K2
BLSH ML4 133 H6
CTBR ML5 109 J5
IRVSE KA11 205 G7
KNTSWD G13 81 G3
Bankhead Dr RUTH G73 129 G2
Bankhead Pl AIRDRIE ML6 111 K2
CTBR ML5 109 J5
Bankhead Rd
CRMNK/CLK/EAG G76 152 D2
KKNTL G66 66 B2
KLWNG KA13 193 M6
RUTH G73 128 F2
Bankhead Ter LNK/LMHG ML11 199 H7
Bankholm Pl
CRMNK/CLK/EAG G76 151 M4
Bankhouse Av LARGS KA30 115 K7
Bankhouse Crs LARGS KA30 115 K7
Banknock St CAR/SHTL G32 106 E3
Bank Pk EKILS G75 14 D5
Bank Pl IRV KA12 203 L5
SHOTTS ML7 137 M5
Bank Rd CAR/SHTL G32 130 C1
Bankside Av JNSTN PA5 99 M6
Bankside Gdns KBRN KA25 143 G5
Banks Rd KKNTL G66 45 L8
Bank St AIRDRIE ML6 111 G1
ALEX/LLW G83 25 L5
BLTYR/CAMB G72 130 A3
BRHD/NEIL G78 125 J7
BRHD/NEIL G78 148 D2
CTBR ML5 109 M3
GRNK PA15 2 D6
IRV KA12 203 J7
KBRN KA25 143 G7
KLMNK KA1 16 E4
KVD/HLHD G12 4 A4
PSLY PA1 9 K4
PSTWK KA9 225 H1
TROON KA10 216 B6
Banktop Pl JNSTN PA5 99 M6
Bank Vw AIRDRIE ML6 111 K7
Bankview Dr KKNTL G66 65 G1
Bannachra Crs ALEX/LLW G83 25 J2
Bannachra Dr HBR/GL G84 20 B7
Bannatyne Av DEN/PKHD G31 13 H1
Bannatyne St LNK/LMHG ML11 199 G5
Bannercross Av
BAIL/MDB/MHD G69 108 A4
Bannercross Dr
BAIL/MDB/MHD G69 108 A3
Bannercross Gdns
BAIL/MDB/MHD G69 108 A4
Banner Dr KNTSWD G13 61 J8
Bannerman Dr BLSH ML4 133 K4
KLMNKN/STW KA3 207 K7
Bannerman Pl CLYDBK G81 60 B7
Banner Rd BSDN G61 61 K7
Bannoch Pl KLWNG KA13 194 A6
Bannoch Rd KLWNG KA13 194 B5
Bannockburn Dr LRKH ML9 176 C8
Bannockburn Pl
KLMNKN/STW KA3 207 H6
MTHW ML1 134 A7
Bannockburn St
GRNKW/INVK PA16 32 C6
Bantaskin St MRYH/FIRH G20 82 C2
Banton Pl STPS/GTHM/RID G33 108 A2
Banyan Crs UD/BTH/TAN G71 109 K8
Barassie EKILN G74 153 K6
Barassiebank La TROON KA10 216 D4
Barassie Ct UD/BTH/TAN G71 131 M7
Barassie Dr BRWEIR PA11 98 C3
Barassie Pl KLMNK KA1 211 L5
Barassie St TROON KA10 216 C6
Barbadoes Pl KLMNK KA1 16 C9
Barbadoes Rd KLMNK KA1 16 D8
Barbados Gn EKILS G75 153 G8
Barbae Pl UD/BTH/TAN G71 132 A6
Barbana Rd EKILN G74 152 E7
Barbegs Crs KSYTH G65 47 M5
Barberry Av PLK/PH/NH G53 126 B7
Barberry Dr BEITH KA15 168 A1
Barberry Gdns
PLK/PH/NH G53 126 B7
Barberry Pl PLK/PH/NH G53 126 B7
Barbeth Gdns CUMB G67 68 B4
Barbeth Pl CUMB G67 68 A3
Barbeth Rd CUMB G67 68 A3
Barbeth Wy CUMB G67 68 A3
Barbour's Pk
KLMNKN/STW KA3 197 L1
Barbreck Rd GVH/MTFL G42 104 F7
Barcaldine Av
BAIL/MDB/MHD G69 86 B1
Barcapel Av NMRNS G77 150 E2
Barclaugh Dr RAYR/DAL KA6 231 G5
Barclaven Rd KLMCLM PA13 75 L1
Barclay Av JNSTN PA5 100 B7
Barclay Ct OLDK G60 59 H3
Barclay Dr HBR/GL G84 20 C6
KLMNKN/STW KA3 207 J7
Barclay Gdns IRVSE KA11 204 D3
Barclay Rd MTHW ML1 157 H3
Barclay St SPRGB/BLRNK G21 83 M4
Barcraigs Dr PSLYS PA2 124 F1
Bard Av KNTSWD G13 81 H1
Bardowie St PPK/MIL G22 83 J5
Bardrain Av JNSTN PA5 100 C7
Bardrainney Av PGL PA14 54 F2
Bardrain Rd PSLYS PA2 124 C2
Bardrill Dr BSHPBGS G64 63 L8
Bardykes Rd BLTYR/CAMB G72 155 J1
Barefield St LRKH ML9 176 A5
Barend St GTCI KA28 138 B6
Barfillan Dr
CARD/HILL/MSPK G52 103 L4
Bargaran Rd PLK/PH/NH G53 103 H6
Bargarran Rd ERSK PA8 58 F7
Bargarron Dr PSLYN/LNWD PA3 102 A2
Bargeddie St
STPS/GTHM/RID G33 7 M4
Bar Hill Pl KSYTH G65 47 H1
Barhill Rd ERSK PA8 59 G6
Barholm Sq
STPS/GTHM/RID G33 85 K8
Barke Rd CUMB G67 49 G6
Barkly Ter EKILS G75 14 A6
Barlanark Av CAR/SHTL G32 107 J3
Barlanark Crs CAR/SHTL G32 107 K2
Barlanark Pl
STPS/GTHM/RID G33 107 L2
Barlanark Rd
STPS/GTHM/RID G33 107 K2
Barlanark Wy CAR/SHTL G32 107 K2
Barlandfauld St KSYTH G65 47 K1
Barlia Dr CSMK G45 128 E6
Barlia St CSMK G45 128 E6
Barlia Ter CSMK G45 128 F6
Barloan Crs DMBTN G82 37 G4
Barloan Pl DMBTN G82 37 G4
Barloch Av MLNGV G62 42 A7
Barloch Rd MLNGV G62 42 B8
Barloch St PPK/MIL G22 83 J5
Barlogan Av
CARD/HILL/MSPK G52 103 L4
Barlogan Qd
CARD/HILL/MSPK G52 103 L4
Barmore Av CARLUKE ML8 189 G1
Barmouth Av
GRNKW/INVK PA16 31 M4
Barmulloch Rd
SPRGB/BLRNK G21 6 F1
Barnbeth Rd PLK/PH/NH G53 103 H7
Barncluith Rd HMLTN ML3 156 F6
Barnes Rd MRYH/FIRH G20 83 G3
Barness Pl
STPS/GTHM/RID G33 107 G1
Barnes St BRHD/NEIL G78 125 H7
Barnett Ct SALT KA21 200 F1
Barnett Crs SALT KA21 200 F2
Barnflat St RUTH G73 106 B8
Barnford Crs AYRS KA7 229 G7
Barngore Dr RAYR/DAL KA6 231 H5
Barn Gn KLBCH PA10 99 G6
Barnhill Dr HMLTN ML3 155 K7
NMRNS G77 150 D6
SPRGB/BLRNK G21 6 F2
Barnhill Rd DMBTN G82 37 K6
Barnhill St GRNK PA15 3 J7
Barnkirk Av DRUM G15 61 G6
Barns Crs AYRS KA7 18 E4
Barnscroft KLBCH PA10 99 H5
Barnsford Av RNFRW PA4 79 H5
Barnsford Rd RNFRW PA4 79 H6
Barns Pk AYRS KA7 18 E4
Barns St AYRS KA7 18 E4
CLYDBK G81 60 C8
Barns Street La AYRS KA7 18 E4
Barns Ter AYRS KA7 18 E5
Barns Terrace La AYRS KA7 18 E5
Barnton St CAR/SHTL G32 106 E2
Barnweill Dr KLMNK KA1 212 E4
Barnweil Rd KLMNK KA1 211 L4
Barnwell Av PSTWK KA9 225 J3
Barnwell Ter GOV/IBX G51 103 L2
Barochan Crs
PSLYN/LNWD PA3 101 G5
Barochan Rd
CRG/CRSL/HOU PA6 57 H8
CRG/CRSL/HOU PA6 77 H5
CRG/CRSL/HOU PA6 99 J2
PLK/PH/NH G53 103 H6
Baronald Dr KVD/HLHD G12 82 B3
Baronald Ga KVD/HLHD G12 82 B3
Baronald St RUTH G73 106 B8
Baron Ct HMLTN ML3 157 G7
Barone Dr
CRMNK/CLK/EAG G76 151 J1
Baronhall Dr BLTYR/CAMB G72 155 J1
Baronhill CUMB G67 49 G4
Baron Rd PSLYN/LNWD PA3 102 A3
Baronscourt Dr PSLY PA1 100 F5
Baronscourt Gdns
PSLYN/LNWD PA3 100 F5
Baronscourt Rd JNSTN PA5 100 F6
Barons Ga UD/BTH/TAN G71 131 L5
Barons Rd MTHW ML1 158 C7
Baron St RNFRW PA4 80 C7
Barony Ct ARD KA22 191 K8
Barony Dr BAIL/MDB/MHD G69 108 B3
Barony Gdns
BAIL/MDB/MHD G69 108 B4
Barony Glebe WKIL KA23 181 K4
Barony Pl BALLOCH G68 47 L8
Barony Rd PSTWK KA9 225 J3
Barony Ter KBRN KA25 167 G2
Barony Wynd
BAIL/MDB/MHD G69 108 B3
Barra Av RNFRW PA4 80 C8
WISHAW ML2 159 L4
Barrachnie Ct
BAIL/MDB/MHD G69 107 M4
Barrachnie Crs
BAIL/MDB/MHD G69 107 M4
Barrachnie Rd
BAIL/MDB/MHD G69 108 A4
Barrack St COWCAD G4 12 B3
HMLTN ML3 156 D4
Barra Crs IRVSE KA11 204 C7
Barra Dr AIRDRIE ML6 111 L3
Barra Gdns OLDK G60 59 J4
Barra La IRVSE KA11 204 C7
Barra Pl IRVSE KA11 204 C7
Barra Rd OLDK G60 59 J4
Barraston Rd BSHPBGS G64 44 A6
Barra St MRYH/FIRH G20 82 C1
Barr Av BRHD/NEIL G78 148 E1
Barra Wynd IRVSE KA11 204 C7
Barr Castle Gdns GLSTN KA4 214 C4
Barrcraig Rd BRWEIR PA11 98 C1
Barr Crs CLYDBK G81 60 B4
LARGS KA30 115 J4
Barr Gv UD/BTH/TAN G71 132 A1
Barrhead Rd NMRNS G77 150 B4
PLK/PH/NH G53 125 M2
PSLYS PA2 9 M8
Barrhill Court. KKNTL G66 66 A1
Barrhill Crs KLBCH PA10 99 H7
Barrhill Rd GRK PA19 31 K2
KKNTL G66 66 A1
Barriedale Av HMLTN ML3 156 B6
Barrie Qd CLYDBK G81 60 A5
Barrie Rd CARD/HILL/MSPK G52 103 G2
EKILN G74 154 D4
Barrie St MTHW ML1 157 L3
Barrie Ter ARD KA22 191 K7
Barrington Av BEITH KA15 144 B8
Barrington Dr KVGV G3 4 C5
Barrisdale Rd MRYH/FIRH G20 82 D2
WISHAW ML2 159 M3
Barrisdale Wy RUTH G73 129 H5
Barrland Dr GIF/THBK G46 127 J6
Barrland St PLKSD/SHW G41 105 G6
Barrmill Rd BEITH KA15 168 C2
BEITH KA15 169 H7
GLSTN KA4 214 C3
PLKSW/MSWD G43 127 G4
Barrochan Rd
CRG/CRSL/HOU PA6 99 L3
JNSTN PA5 99 L5
Barrowfield St CTBR ML5 109 M5
DMNK/BRGTN G40 12 F6
Barrpath KSYTH G65 47 M2
Barr Pl NMRNS G77 150 C4
PSLY PA1 8 F5
Barrs Brae KLMCLM PA13 55 K8
PGL PA14 34 C8
Barrs Brae La PGL PA14 34 C8
Barrs Ct DMBTN G82 24 A8
Barrs Crs DMBTN G82 35 G1
Barrs Rd DMBTN G82 35 G1
Barrs Ter DMBTN G82 35 G1
Barr St ARD KA22 191 J8
GLSTN KA4 214 C4
MRYH/FIRH G20 4 F3
MTHW ML1 157 L1
Barr Ter EKILN G74 14 F2
Barrwood Gdns GLSTN KA4 214 A3
Barrwood Pl UD/BTH/TAN G71 132 A1
Barrwood St
STPS/GTHM/RID G33 84 E7
Barry Gdns BLTYR/CAMB G72 155 J3
Barscube Av PGL PA14 54 E2
Barscube Ter PSLYS PA2 9 M8
Barshaw Dr PSLY PA1 9 M1
Barshaw Pl PSLY PA1 102 D4
Barshaw Rd
CARD/HILL/MSPK G52 102 E3
Barskiven Rd PSLYN/LNWD PA3 100 F5
Barterholm Rd PSLYS PA2 9 H8
Bartholomew St
DMNK/BRGTN G40 12 E9
Bartiebeith Rd
STPS/GTHM/RID G33 107 K2
Bartonhall Rd WISHAW ML2 159 K8
Barty's Rd BLSH ML4 133 J4
Barward Rd GLSTN KA4 214 A4
Barwheys Dr RAYR/DAL KA6 227 G3
Barwood Hl DMBTN G82 37 H3
Bassett Av KNTSWD G13 81 H1
Bassett Crs KNTSWD G13 81 H1
Bathgate St DEN/PKHD G31 12 F3
Bathgo Av PSLY PA1 102 E5
Bath La CGLW G2 4 E8
Bath Pl AYRS KA7 18 C3
Bath Sq ARD KA22 200 C1
Bath St CGLW G2 4 D8
GRK PA19 31 L1
KLMNKN/STW KA3 206 F7
LARGS KA30 115 J6
Bathurst Dr AYRS KA7 229 G8
Bathville Rd KBRN KA25 143 C8
Baton Rd SHOTTS ML7 137 K3
Batson St GVH/MTFL G42 105 H7
Battery Park Dr
GRNKW/INVK PA16 32 B1
Battismains LNK/LMHG ML11 199 J5
Battlefield Av GVH/MTFL G42 128 A2
Battlefield Gdns
GVH/MTFL G42 128 A2
Battlefield Rd GVH/MTFL G42 128 A1
Bavelaw St STPS/GTHM/RID G33 85 K7
Bawhirley Rd GRNK PA15 3 H8
Baxter La ALEX/LLW G83 25 L2
LNK/LMHG ML11 199 G5
Baxter St GRNK PA15 3 L8
Bayfield Av DRUM G15 61 G6
Bayfield Ter DRUM G15 61 G6
Bay St FAIRLIE KA29 139 K5
PGL PA14 34 C8
Bay View Rd GRK PA19 31 M2
Beach Dr IRV KA12 202 F8
Beach Rd TROON KA10 216 C2
Beachway LARGS KA30 115 J5
Beaconsfield Rd KVD/HLHD G12 82 B4
Beagle Crs AYRS KA7 228 C6
Beansburn KLMNKN/STW KA3 207 G6
Beanshields Rd CARLUKE ML8 188 F4
Beard Crs BAIL/MDB/MHD G69 86 F4
Beardmore Pl CLYDBK G81 59 L6
Beardmore St CLYDBK G81 59 K6
Beardmore Wy CLYDBK G81 59 L7
Bearford Dr
CARD/HILL/MSPK G52 103 H4
Bearhope St GRNK PA15 2 C4
Bearsden Rd BSDN G61 81 M1
Beatock Pl GRNKW/INVK PA16 50 D5
Beaton Rd ALEX/LLW G83 25 L1
PLKSD/SHW G41 104 E7
Beaton St LRKH ML9 175 M5
Beaton Ter IRV KA12 203 J4
Beatrice Dr MTHW ML1 133 M4
Beatrice Gdns
CRG/CRSL/HOU PA6 99 K1
Beattock St DEN/PKHD G31 13 M6
Beattock Wynd HMLTN ML3 156 A6
Beatty Pl HBR/GL G84 21 G7
Beatty St CLYDBK G81 59 L6
Beaufield Gdns
KLMNKN/STW KA3 206 B2
Beaufort Av PLKSW/MSWD G43 127 J3
Beaufort Dr KKNTL G66 65 H1
Beaufort Gdns BSHPBGS G64 63 L8
Beauly Crs KLMCLM PA13 75 K2
KLMNK KA1 212 A4
Beauly Dr PSLYS PA2 100 E8
Beauly Pl BAIL/MDB/MHD G69 86 D1
CTBR ML5 110 B6
EKILN G74 14 D1
MRYH/FIRH G20 82 D3
MTHW ML1 134 A5
Beauly Rd BAIL/MDB/MHD G69 108 A6
Beaumont Ga PTCK G11 82 C7
Beckford St HMLTN ML3 156 C4
Bedale Rd BAIL/MDB/MHD G69 107 M5
Bedcow Vw KKNTL G66 65 M2
Bedford Av CLYDBK G81 60 D7
Bedford La GBLS G5 11 H6
GRNKW/INVK PA16 32 D2
Bedford St GBLS G5 11 G6
GRNKW/INVK PA16 32 D2
Bedlay Ct
BAIL/MDB/MHD G69 67 G6
Bedlay Pl CTBR ML5 67 M8
Bedlay Vw UD/BTH/TAN G71 109 H8
Beech Av BAIL/MDB/MHD G69 108 A4
BEITH KA15 144 B7
BLTYR/CAMB G72 129 M3
BRWEIR PA11 76 D8
BSDN G61 62 A2
GOV/IBX G51 104 B4
HMLTN ML3 174 F5
IRV KA12 203 K7
JNSTN PA5 100 C7
KLMNK KA1 16 B5
LRKH ML9 176 D7
MTHW ML1 134 B6
NMRNS G77 150 E5
PLKSD/SHW G41 104 B5
PSLYS PA2 102 A8
RUTH G73 129 J5
Beechbank Av AIRDRIE ML6 88 F8
Beechburn Crs LOCHW PA12 120 D6
Beech Crs BLTYR/CAMB G72 130 E5
MTHW ML1 134 C2
NMRNS G77 150 E6
Beech Dr AIRDRIE ML6 90 F5
CLYDBK G81 60 A4
Beeches Av CLYDBK G81 59 M3
Beeches Rd CLYDBK G81 59 M3
The Beeches
CRG/CRSL/HOU PA6 77 K8
JNSTN PA5 99 J3
LNK/LMHG ML11 199 H7
RAYR/DAL KA6 231 H5
Beechfield Dr CARLUKE ML8 189 G1
Beechfield Rd BEITH KA15 167 M2
Beech Gdns
BAIL/MDB/MHD G69 108 A4
Beech Gv AYR KA8 19 L4
BAIL/MDB/MHD G69 87 G4
CARLUKE ML8 177 M3
EKILS G75 171 H3
WISHAW ML2 159 J2
Beechgrove Av
UD/BTH/TAN G71 132 C2
Beechgrove Pl HBR/GL G84 23 G1
Beechgrove Qd MTHW ML1 134 A4
Beechgrove St
DMNK/BRGTN G40 106 B7
Beechlands Av LNPK/KPK G44 127 L7
Beechlands Dr
CRMNK/CLK/EAG G76 151 J3
Beechmount Rd KKNTL G66 65 J5
Beech Pl BLTYR/CAMB G72 155 L2
BSHPBGS G64 84 B1
GRK PA19 31 J3
Beech Rd BSHPBGS G64 84 B1
JNSTN PA5 99 K8
KKNTL G66 65 J3
MTHW ML1 134 C2
Beech Ter LRKH ML9 176 B8
Beechtree Ter KKNTL G66 45 J4
Beechwood KLWNG KA13 193 K4
LRKH ML9 176 A4
WISHAW ML2 158 D8
Beechwood Av
CRMNK/CLK/EAG G76 151 J3
HMLTN ML3 174 B1
PGL PA14 56 C2
RUTH G73 129 J3
Beechwood Ct BSDN G61 61 M6
CUMB G67 68 F1
Beechwood Crs WISHAW ML2 159 J7
Beechwood Dr CTBR ML5 110 C4
PTCK G11 81 M5
RNFRW PA4 80 B8
Beechwood Gdns BLSH ML4 133 J5
Beechwood Gv
BRHD/NEIL G78 125 J8
Beechwood La BSDN G61 61 M6
Beechwood Paddock
TROON KA10 217 H5
Beechwood Pl PTCK G11 81 M5
Beechwood Rd CUMB G67 48 F8
Beechworth Dr MTHW ML1 134 D7
Beecroft Pl BLTYR/CAMB G72 131 L8
Beggs Ter ARD KA22 191 K6
Beil Dr KNTSWD G13 80 F2
Beith Dr AIRDRIE ML6 111 G5
Beithglass Av SKLM PA17 70 B5
Beith Rd DALRY KA24 184 E1
GLGNK KA14 167 K3
GRNK PA15 2 B9
HWWD PA9 122 B3
JNSTN PA5 100 A7
Beith St PTCK G11 82 A8
Belford Ct NMRNS G77 150 D7
Belford Gv NMRNS G77 150 D7
Belgrave La KVD/HLHD G12 4 A3
Belgrave St BLSH ML4 132 F3
Belhaven Pk
BAIL/MDB/MHD G69 86 C2
Belhaven Rd HMLTN ML3 155 L6
WISHAW ML2 159 G6
Belhaven St PGL PA14 34 B7
Belhaven Ter KVD/HLHD G12 82 C5
WISHAW ML2 159 G6
Belhaven Terrace La
KVD/HLHD G12 82 C5

Belhaven Ter West
KVD/HLHD G12 82 C5
Belhaven Terrace West La
KVD/HLHD G12 82 C5
Bellahouston Dr
CARD/HILL/MSPK G52 103 L6
Bellairs Pl BLTYR/CAMB G72 131 J8
Bellard Rd WKIL KA23 181 J5
Bellas Pl AIRDRIE ML6 90 A7
Bell Crs IRV KA12 203 K4
Bell Dr BLTYR/CAMB G72 155 J5
Belleaire Dr
GRNKW/INVK PA16 32 C2
Bellefield Rd LNK/LMHG ML11 199 G4
Belleisle Av UD/BTH/TAN G71 131 L3
Belleisle Cl KLWNG KA13 193 J5
Belleisle Ct BALLOCH G68 48 E5
Belleisle Crs BRWEIR PA11 98 C3
Belleisle Dr BALLOCH G68 48 E5
Belleisle Gdns BALLOCH G68 48 E5
Belleisle Gv BALLOCH G68 48 E5
Belleisle Pl GRK PA19 31 G3
KLMNK KA1 211 L5
Belleisle St GVH/MTFL G42 105 H8
Bellesdale Av LARGS KA30 115 L6
Bellesleyhill Av AYR KA8 225 H6
Bellesleyhill Rd AYR KA8 225 G5
Bellevale Qd AYRS KA7 228 F4
Bellevue Av KKNTL G66 65 H1
Bellevue Crs AYRS KA7 18 D6
Bellevue La AYRS KA7 18 E6
Bellevue Rd AYRS KA7 18 D6
KKNTL G66 65 H1
KLMNK KA1 16 B2
PSTWK KA9 225 J1
Bellevue St AYRS KA7 18 F6
Bellfield Av KLMNK KA1 212 D3
Bellfield Ct KLMNK KA1 212 D3
Bellfield Crs BRHD/NEIL G78 125 H6
Bellfield Dr WISHAW ML2 159 J7
Bellfield La PSTWK KA9 225 H1
Bellfield Rd KKNTL G66 65 H1
Bellfield St DEN/PKHD G31 12 E3
Bellflower Av PLK/PH/NH G53 126 C6
Bellflower Ct EKILN G74 153 J6
Bellflower Gdns
PLK/PH/NH G53 126 C6
Bellflower Gv EKILN G74 153 J6
Bellflower Pl
PLK/PH/NH G53 126 C6
Bell Gn East EKILS G75 15 G6
Bell Gn West EKILS G75 14 F5
Bellgrove St DEN/PKHD G31 12 D3
Bellman's Cl BEITH KA15 144 B8
LARGS KA30 115 J6
Bellrock Av PSTWK KA9 225 H4
Bellrock Ct
STPS/GTHM/RID G33 107 H1
Bellrock Crs
STPS/GTHM/RID G33 107 G1
Bellrock Rd AYR KA8 225 G5
Bellrock St
STPS/GTHM/RID G33 107 G1
Bellscroft Av RUTH G73 128 F2
Bellsdyke Rd AIRDRIE ML6 110 F3
Bellshaugh Gdns KVD/HLHD G12 82 C4
Bellshaugh La KVD/HLHD G12 82 C4
Bellshaugh Pl KVD/HLHD G12 82 C4
Bellshaugh Rd KVD/HLHD G12 82 C4
Bellshill Rd BLSH ML4 132 E6
MTHW ML1 133 J7
UD/BTH/TAN G71 131 M4
UD/BTH/TAN G71 132 C8
UD/BTH/TAN G71 156 C1
Bellside Rd AIRDRIE ML6 111 M8
MTHW ML1 135 G1
MTHW ML1 135 K8
Bellsland Dr KLMNK KA1 16 F8
Bellsland Pl KLMNK KA1 16 F7
Bellsmyre Av DMBTN G82 37 G3
Bell St AIRDRIE ML6 110 F2
BLSH ML4 133 H2
CGLE G1 11 L2
CLYDBK G81 80 D2
COWCAD G4 12 A3
GRNK PA15 33 L7
RNFRW PA4 80 D5
WISHAW ML2 158 F6
Bells Wynd LNK/LMHG ML11 199 J4
Belltree Av KLMNKN/STW KA3 197 K1
Belltrees Crs PSLYN/LNWD PA3 101 G5
Bell Trees Rd HWWD PA9 121 J6
Bellvale Av AYRS KA7 228 F4
Bell View Ct RNFRW PA4 80 D5
Bellvue Crs BLSH ML4 132 F5
PSTWK KA9 225 J2
Bellwood St PLKSD/SHW G41 127 L1
Bellziehill Rd BLSH ML4 132 E4
Belmont Av AYRS KA7 19 G8
Belmont Crs AYRS KA7 19 H9
KLMNKN/STW KA3 206 B2
KVD/HLHD G12 4 B3
Belmont Dr AYRS KA7 229 G4
BRHD/NEIL G78 125 K8
EKILS G75 171 H1
GIF/THBK G46 127 H6
RUTH G73 129 H2
Belmont La KVD/HLHD G12 4 B3
Belmont Pl East AYRS KA7 19 G8
Belmont Pl West AYRS KA7 19 G8
Belmont Rd AYRS KA7 229 G4
BLTYR/CAMB G72 129 L6
KLMCLM PA13 75 J2
PSLYN/LNWD PA3 102 A3
Belmont St CLYDBK G81 60 B8
CTBR ML5 87 J8
KVD/HLHD G12 4 B3
WISHAW ML2 177 H3
Belses Dr CARD/HILL/MSPK G52 103 J4
Belses Gdns
CARD/HILL/MSPK G52 103 J4
Belstane Pk CARLUKE ML8 178 F6
Belstane Pl UD/BTH/TAN G71 132 A6
Belstane Rd CARLUKE ML8 179 G6
CUMB G67 68 F4
Belsyde Av DRUM G15 61 G7
Beltane St KVGV G3 4 D8
WISHAW ML2 159 G7
Beltrees Av PLK/PH/NH G53 103 G8
Beltrees Crs PLK/PH/NH G53 103 G7
Beltrees Rd PLK/PH/NH G53 103 G8
Belvedere Vw GLSTN KA4 214 C4
Belvidere Crs BLSH ML4 133 H5
BSHPBGS G64 64 A7
Belvidere Rd BLSH ML4 133 G5
Belvidere Ter AYR KA8 225 G7
Belville Av GRNK PA15 3 H7
Belville St GRNK PA15 3 H7
Belvoir Pl BLTYR/CAMB G72 155 K1
Bemersyde BSHPBGS G64 64 C7
Bemersyde Av
PLKSW/MSWD G43 127 H4
Bemersyde Pl LRKH ML9 176 A8
Bemersyde Rd PSLYS PA2 123 K1
Ben Alder Dr PSLYS PA2 102 D8
Benalder St PTCK G11 82 C7
Benbain Pl IRVSE KA11 204 A3
Benbecula EKILN G74 154 C8
Benbecula Rd
KLMNKN/STW KA3 207 G3
Ben Bouie Dr HBR/GL G84 21 G8
Benbow Rd CLYDBK G81 59 M7
Bencleuch Pl IRVSE KA11 204 B6
Bencloich Crs KKNTL G66 29 L8
Bencloich Rd KKNTL G66 44 E1
Benclutha PGL PA14 34 E8
Bencroft Dr LNPK/KPK G44 128 E4
Ben Donich Pl GIF/THBK G46 126 D4
Ben Edra Pl GIF/THBK G46 126 D5
Benford Av MTHW ML1 134 D5
Benford Knowe MTHW ML1 134 D5
Bengairn St DEN/PKHD G31 13 K2
Bengal Pl PLKSW/MSWD G43 127 J2
Bengal St PLKSW/MSWD G43 127 J2
Ben Garrisdale Pl
GIF/THBK G46 126 D5
Benhar Pl
STPS/GTHM/RID G33 106 F2
Benhar Rd SHOTTS ML7 137 M5
Benholm St CAR/SHTL G32 106 F6
Ben Hope Av PSLYS PA2 102 D7
Ben Laga Pl GIF/THBK G46 126 D5
Ben Lawers Dr BALLOCH G68 48 B7
PSLYS PA2 102 D7
Ben Ledi Av PSLYS PA2 102 D7
Ben Ledi Crs BALLOCH G68 48 B7
Ben Loyal Av PSLYS PA2 102 D7
Ben Lui Dr PSLYS PA2 102 D8
Ben Lui Pl BALLOCH G68 48 B7
GIF/THBK G46 126 D5
Ben Macdui Gdns
GIF/THBK G46 126 D5
Benmore PSTWK KA9 225 J4
Ben More Dr BALLOCH G68 48 A7
PSLYS PA2 102 D7
Bennan Pl EKILS G75 171 J5
Bennan Sq GVH/MTFL G42 105 J7
Ben Nevis Rd PSLYS PA2 102 C8
Ben Nevis Wy BALLOCH G68 48 B7
Bennoch Pl PSTWK KA9 225 K4
Benrig Av KLMNKN/STW KA3 206 B2
Bensley Av IRVSE KA11 203 M4
Bensley Ri IRVSE KA11 203 M5
Benson St CTBR ML5 110 A5
Benston Rd JNSTN PA5 99 L8
Bent Crs UD/BTH/TAN G71 132 C3
Bentfield Av AYRS KA7 18 C8
Bentfield Dr PSTWK KA9 225 H4
Bentfoot Rd WISHAW ML2 177 J3
Benthall St GBLS G5 11 L8
Bentinck Crs TROON KA10 216 D8
Bentinck Dr TROON KA10 216 D7
Bentinck St GLSTN KA4 214 C3
GRNKW/INVK PA16 32 D1
KLMNK KA1 16 F7
KVGV G3 4 A7
Bent Rd AIRDRIE ML6 111 K6
HMLTN ML3 156 C6
Bents Rd BAIL/MDB/MHD G69 108 B4
Benty's La CARLUKE ML8 188 F1
Ben Uird Pl GIF/THBK G46 126 D5
Ben Vane Av PSLYS PA2 102 C8
Ben Venue Rd BALLOCH G68 48 A7
Benview Av PGL PA14 54 E1
Benview Rd
CRMNK/CLK/EAG G76 151 L2
PGL PA14 54 E1
Benview St MRYH/FIRH G20 82 F5
Benview Ter PSLYS PA2 102 B7
Ben Vorlich Dr GIF/THBK G46 126 D5
Benvue Rd KKNTL G66 44 E2
Ben Wyvis Dr PSLYS PA2 102 C8
Berchem Pl SALT KA21 200 F1
Bereland Av PSTWK KA9 225 K1
Berelands Crs RUTH G73 128 E2
Berelands Pl RUTH G73 128 F2
Berelands Rd PSTWK KA9 221 J8
Beresford Av SCOT G14 81 L5
Beresford Gv IRV KA12 203 L4
Beresford La AYRS KA7 18 F6
Beresford Ter AYRS KA7 18 F6
Berkeley St KVGV G3 4 B8
Berkeley Terrace La KVGV G3 4 C8
Berkley Dr BLTYR/CAMB G72 131 J8
Berl Av CRG/CRSL/HOU PA6 99 J1
Bernadette Crs MTHW ML1 134 D7
Bernadette St MTHW ML1 134 D6
Bernard St DMNK/BRGTN G40 12 F7
Bernard's Wynd
LNK/LMHG ML11 199 G5
Bernard Ter DMNK/BRGTN G40 12 E7
Berneray St PPK/MIL G22 83 J2
Berridale Av LNPK/KPK G44 128 A4
Berridale Rd TROON KA10 216 D2
Berriedale EKILS G75 170 E1
Berriedale Av
BAIL/MDB/MHD G69 108 A5
Berriedale Qd WISHAW ML2 159 H4
Berryburn Rd SPRGB/BLRNK G21 7 J1
Berry Dr IRV KA12 203 L6
Berryhill Av IRVSE KA11 204 B4
Berryhill Dr GIF/THBK G46 127 H7
Berryhill Rd CUMB G67 48 E8
GIF/THBK G46 127 H8
Berryknowe Av
BAIL/MDB/MHD G69 86 C2
Berryknowes Av
CARD/HILL/MSPK G52 103 J4
Berryknowes La
CARD/HILL/MSPK G52 103 J4
Berryknowes Rd
CARD/HILL/MSPK G52 103 J4
GOV/IBX G51 103 K3
Berryyards Rd GRNK PA15 2 C7
Bertram Dr SHOTTS ML7 113 H7
Bertram Pl SHOTTS ML7 137 K4
Bertram St HMLTN ML3 156 A4
LRKH ML9 176 C8
PLKSD/SHW G41 104 E8
SHOTTS ML7 137 L4
Bervie St GOV/IBX G51 103 M3
Berwick Crs AIRDRIE ML6 110 F4
PSLYN/LNWD PA3 99 M2
Berwick Dr
CARD/HILL/MSPK G52 103 H5
RUTH G73 129 K2
Berwick Pl CTBR ML5 110 B6
EKILN G74 154 C6
GRNKW/INVK PA16 31 K5
Berwick Rd
GRNKW/INVK PA16 31 J5
PGL PA14 34 C8
Berwick St CTBR ML5 110 B6
HMLTN ML3 156 B4
Bessemer Dr EKILS G75 172 A4
Betula Dr CLYDBK G81 60 A4
Bevan Ct ARD KA22 191 H5
Bevan Gdns KLWNG KA13 193 L5
Bevan Gv JNSTN PA5 99 L7
Beveridge Ter BLSH ML4 133 K5
Beverley Rd PLKSW/MSWD G43 127 K3
Bevin Av CLYDBK G81 60 D8
Bideford Crs CAR/SHTL G32 107 K6
The Bield WISHAW ML2 159 J7
Biggar Rd MTHW ML1 134 F3
Biggar St DEN/PKHD G31 13 H4
Biggart Rd PSTWK KA9 225 J2
Bigholm Rd BEITH KA15 144 C8
Bigton St STPS/GTHM/RID G33 85 H7
Bilby Ter IRV KA12 203 J4
Billings Rd MTHW ML1 157 H4
Bilsland Ct MRYH/FIRH G20 83 H4
Bilsland Dr MRYH/FIRH G20 82 F4
Bilsland Pl DMBTN G82 25 K8
Bimson Pl IRV KA12 203 G8
Bimson Rw IRV KA12 203 G8
Binend Rd PLK/PH/NH G53 126 C1
Binniehill Rd BALLOCH G68 48 D7
Binnie La GRK PA19 31 L2
Binnie Pl DMNK/BRGTN G40 12 A6
Binnie St GRK PA19 31 K1
Binns Rd STPS/GTHM/RID G33 85 J7
Birch Av CRMNK/CLK/EAG G76 151 M3
Birch Brae HMLTN ML3 156 E8
Birch Crs
CRMNK/CLK/EAG G76 151 M3
JNSTN PA5 100 A8
Birch Dr BLTYR/CAMB G72 130 C3
KKNTL G66 65 K4
Birchend Dr SPRGB/BLRNK G21 7 G4
Birchend Pl SPRGB/BLRNK G21 7 G4
Birchfield Dr SCOT G14 81 H5
Birchfield Rd HMLTN ML3 156 B6
Birchgrove CRG/CRSL/HOU PA6 77 K7
Birch Gv LRKH ML9 176 A4
UD/BTH/TAN G71 132 B2
Birch Knowe BSHPBGS G64 84 B1
Birchlea Dr GIF/THBK G46 127 K5
Birchmount Ct AIRDRIE ML6 111 K1
Birch Pl BLTYR/CAMB G72 130 F5
BLTYR/CAMB G72 155 K1
KLMNK KA1 16 B5
Birch Qd AIRDRIE ML6 111 K2
Birch Rd AYRS KA7 229 J5
CLYDBK G81 60 A5
CUMB G67 49 L6
DMBTN G82 36 F5
Birch St GBLS G5 11 L9
MTHW ML1 134 B4
Birch Ter ARD KA22 191 J6
Birch Vw BSDN G61 62 A4
Birchview Dr
CRMNK/CLK/EAG G76 151 M4
Birchwood Av CAR/SHTL G32 107 L5
Birchwood Dr PSLYS PA2 101 H8
Birchwood Pl CAR/SHTL G32 107 L5
Birdsfield Dr BLTYR/CAMB G72 155 K3
Birdsfield St BLTYR/CAMB G72 155 M3
Birdston Rd KKNTL G66 45 J5
SPRGB/BLRNK G21 84 C3
Birgidale Av CSMK G45 128 D8
Birgidale Rd CSMK G45 128 D7
Birgidale Ter CSMK G45 128 D7
Birkdale EKILN G74 153 J6
Birkdale Cl KLWNG KA13 193 J5
Birkdale Ct
UD/BTH/TAN G71 131 M7
Birkdale Crs BALLOCH G68 48 F3
Birkenburn Rd CUMB G67 49 M3
Birken Rd KKNTL G66 65 L5
Birkenshaw Rd CTBR ML5 67 L8
Birkenshaw St DEN/PKHD G31 13 H1
Birkfield Loan CARLUKE ML8 179 J8
Birkfield Pl CARLUKE ML8 179 J8
Birkhall Av
CARD/HILL/MSPK G52 102 F5
RNFRW PA4 79 K2
Birkhall Dr BSDN G61 61 M7
Birkhill Av BSHPBGS G64 64 B7
Birkhill Gdns BSHPBGS G64 64 B7
Birkhill Rd CARLUKE ML8 188 C7
HMLTN ML3 174 D2
Birkmyre Av PGL PA14 34 A7
Birkmyre Rd GOV/IBX G51 103 M3
Birkscairn Wy IRVSE KA11 204 C7
Birks Ct CARLUKE ML8 177 M4
Birkshaw Brae WISHAW ML2 177 G1
Birkshaw Pl WISHAW ML2 177 G1
Birks Hl IRVSE KA11 204 A5
Birks Pl LNK/LMHG ML11 199 G5
Birks Rd CARLUKE ML8 177 L6
Birkwood Pl NMRNS G77 150 D7
Birkwood St
DMNK/BRGTN G40 106 B7
Birmingham Rd RNFRW PA4 80 B8
Birnam Av BSHPBGS G64 64 B7
Birnam Crs BSDN G61 62 B4
Birnam Pl HMLTN ML3 155 L6
NMRNS G77 151 H5
Birnam Rd DEN/PKHD G31 13 M9
Birness Dr PLKSW/MSWD G43 127 K2
Birnie Ct SPRGB/BLRNK G21 7 J1
Birniehill Rd MTHW ML1 135 M5
Birnie Rd SPRGB/BLRNK G21 7 K1
Birnock Av RNFRW PA4 80 E8
Birrell Rd MLNGV G62 41 M6
Birrens Rd MTHW ML1 157 J1
Birsay Rd PPK/MIL G22 83 H2
Bishopdale EKILN G74 153 J6
Bishop Gdns BSHPBGS G64 63 L7
HMLTN ML3 174 E2
Bishop La KVGV G3 10 E1
Bishopmill Pl
SPRGB/BLRNK G21 84 C5
Bishops Ga EKILN G74 152 C6
Bishopsgate Rd
SPRGB/BLRNK G21 83 L2
Bishops Pk EKILN G74 152 B6
Bissett Crs CLYDBK G81 59 L3
Blackadder Pl EKILS G75 170 D2
Blackbog Rd CUMB G67 68 F7
Blackbraes Rd EKILN G74 154 B5
Blackburn Crs DMBTN G82 36 D5
KKNTL G66 66 A1
Blackburn Dr AYRS KA7 18 B8
Blackburn Pl AYRS KA7 18 C7
Blackburn Rd AYRS KA7 18 C7
Blackburn Sq BRHD/NEIL G78 125 K8
Blackburn St GOV/IBX G51 10 A4
Blackbyres Ct BRHD/NEIL G78 125 K5
Blackbyres Rd BRHD/NEIL G78 125 J3
Blackcraig Av DRUM G15 61 G6
Blackcroft Av AIRDRIE ML6 111 L4
Blackcroft Gdns
CAR/SHTL G32 107 K5
Blackcroft Rd CAR/SHTL G32 107 K5
Blackcroft Ter SHOTTS ML7 113 H7
Blackdales Av LARGS KA30 115 K7
Blackdyke Rd KKNTL G66 65 L1
Blackfarm Rd NMRNS G77 150 F5
Blackfaulds Rd RUTH G73 128 E1
Blackford Crs PSTWK KA9 221 L8
Blackford Rd PSLYS PA2 9 M7
Blackfriars St CGLE G1 11 L2
Blackfriars Wk AYRS KA7 18 F3
Blackhall La PSLY PA1 9 K6
Blackhall St PSLY PA1 9 K6
Blackhill Dr HBR/GL G84 20 D5
Blackhill Pl STPS/GTHM/RID G33 7 M5
Blackhill Rd SMSTN G23 62 F7
Blackhill St AYRS KA7 19 K9
Blackhill Vw CARLUKE ML8 178 A4
Blackhouse Av NMRNS G77 150 F5
Blackhouse Gdns
NMRNS G77 150 F5
Blackhouse Pl AYR KA8 19 M4
Blackhouse Rd NMRNS G77 150 F5
Blackie St KVGV G3 104 D1
Blacklands Av KLWNG KA13 193 L7
Blacklands Crs KLWNG KA13 193 L8
Blacklands Pl KKNTL G66 65 M5
Blacklands Rd EKILN G74 14 D3
Blacklaw Dr EKILN G74 15 L4
Blacklaw La PSLYN/LNWD PA3 9 H2
Blackmoor Pl MTHW ML1 134 A6
Blackmoss Dr BLSH ML4 132 F5
Blackness St CTBR ML5 110 B6
Blackshaw Dr WKIL KA23 181 K3
Blackstone Av PLK/PH/NH G53 126 C1
Blackstone Crs PLK/PH/NH G53 103 J8
Blackstone Rd
PSLYN/LNWD PA3 101 G1
Blackstoun Av
PSLYN/LNWD PA3 100 B3
Blackstoun Ov PSLYN/LNWD PA3 8 B3
Blackstoun Rd PSLYN/LNWD PA3 8 B2
Black St AIRDRIE ML6 89 H8
COWCAD G4 5 M7
Blackswell La HMLTN ML3 156 F6
Blacksyke Av KLMNK KA1 211 M6
Blackthorn Av BEITH KA15 144 A8
KKNTL G66 65 G4
Blackthorn Gv KKNTL G66 65 H4
Blackthorn Rd CUMB G67 49 L5
UD/BTH/TAN G71 132 C1
Blackthorn St PPK/MIL G22 83 L4
Blackwood EKILS G75 171 K4
Blackwood Av KLMNK KA1 16 B7
NMRNS G77 150 F6
PSLYN/LNWD PA3 100 A4
Blackwood Gdns MTHW ML1 133 J8
Blackwood Rd BALLOCH G68 47 L8
MLNGV G62 41 M6
Blackwoods Crs BLSH ML4 133 J5
Blackwood St BRHD/NEIL G78 125 G7
KNTSWD G13 81 L2
Blackwood Ter JNSTN PA5 122 D1
Bladda La PSLY PA1 9 J5
Blades Ct BAIL/MDB/MHD G69 87 G3
Bladnoch Dr DRUM G15 61 J7
Blaeloch Av CSMK G45 128 C8
Blaeloch Dr CSMK G45 128 C8
Blaeloch Ter CSMK G45 128 B8
Blaeshill Rd EKILS G75 170 E1
Blairafton Wynd KLWNG KA13 193 J4
Blairatholl Av PTCK G11 82 A6
Blairatholl Crs NMRNS G77 151 H5
Blair Atholl Dr LRKH ML9 176 C8
Blairatholl Gdns PTCK G11 82 A6
Blair Atholl Ga NMRNS G77 151 H5
Blair Av KLMNK KA1 212 E3
Blairbeth Dr LNPK/KPK G44 128 B2
Blairbeth Rd RUTH G73 129 H4
Blairbeth Ter RUTH G73 129 J4
Blair Crs
BAIL/MDB/MHD G69 108 A6
GLSTN KA4 214 C3
KLMNK KA1 212 E3
Blairdardie Rd DRUM G15 61 H8
Blairdenan Av
BAIL/MDB/MHD G69 66 F6
Blairdenon Dr BALLOCH G68 48 C6
Blairdenon Wy IRVSE KA11 204 B7
Blair Dr KKNTL G66 45 H4
Blair Gdns BSHPBGS G64 44 B8
GRK PA19 30 F4
NMRNS G77 150 B4
Blairgowrie Rd
CARD/HILL/MSPK G52 103 J5
Blairhall Av PLKSD/SHW G41 127 M1
Blairhill Av KKNTL G66 66 A3
Blairhill Pl CTBR ML5 109 L2
Blairhill St CTBR ML5 109 M2
Blairholm Dr BLSH ML4 133 H6
Blairlands Dr DALRY KA24 184 E2
Blairlinn Rd CUMB G67 68 F3
Blair Linn Vw CUMB G67 69 G3
Blairlogie St
STPS/GTHM/RID G33 85 H8
Blairmore Av PSLY PA1 102 C4
Blairmore Crs GRNK PA15 3 J9
Blairmore Rd GRNK PA15 33 H7
Blairpark Av CTBR ML5 109 L1
Blair Pth MTHW ML1 157 M4
Blair Rd CARLUKE ML8 188 A8
CTBR ML5 109 L2
DALRY KA24 184 E2
KLMNK KA1 212 E3
KLWNG KA13 193 M5
PSLY PA1 102 E3
Blairston Av UD/BTH/TAN G71 132 B8
Blairston Gdns
UD/BTH/TAN G71 132 B8
Blair St CAR/SHTL G32 106 F4
GLSTN KA4 214 C3
KLMNKN/STW KA3 206 F7
Blairtum Dr RUTH G73 129 H4
Blairtummock Rd
STPS/GTHM/RID G33 107 K1
Blakely Rd SALT KA21 201 H2
Blake Rd CUMB G67 49 G7
Blane Av CMPF/LLE G63 27 G5
Blane Crs CMPF/LLE G63 27 G5
Blane Dr MLNGV G62 42 B6
Blanefield Av PSTWK KA9 225 H3
Blane Pl CMPF/LLE G63 27 G5
Blane St CTBR ML5 110 A1
Blaneview STPS/GTHM/RID G33 85 K5
Blantyre Crs CLYDBK G81 59 L2
Blantyre Dr BSHPTN PA7 58 A5
Blantyre Farm Rd
BLTYR/CAMB G72 131 J7
UD/BTH/TAN G71 131 J3
Blantyre Gdns BALLOCH G68 47 L8
Blantyre Mill Rd
UD/BTH/TAN G71 132 A7
Blantyre Pl CTBR ML5 109 L5
Blantyre Rd UD/BTH/TAN G71 132 A7
Blantyre St CTBR ML5 109 L5
KVGV G3 82 D8
Blaven Ct
BAIL/MDB/MHD G69 108 C5
Blaven Head IRVSE KA11 204 A5
Blawarthill St SCOT G14 80 F4
Bleachfield MLNGV G62 41 M6
Bleasdale Ct CLYDBK G81 60 B7
Bleeze Rd DALRY KA24 184 B1
Blenheim Av EKILS G75 14 B8
STPS/GTHM/RID G33 85 K3
Blenheim Ct PSLY PA1 8 E3
Blenheim Rd CARLUKE ML8 179 G8
Blochairn Rd SPRGB/BLRNK G21 6 F6
Bluebell Gdns CSMK G45 129 G7
MTHW ML1 133 J7
Bluebell Wy AIRDRIE ML6 88 F7
CARLUKE ML8 188 F1
KKNTL G66 44 F2
Blueknowes Rd CARLUKE ML8 177 L4
Bluevale St DEN/PKHD G31 12 F3
Blythe Pl
STPS/GTHM/RID G33 107 K3
Blyth Rd STPS/GTHM/RID G33 107 L3
Blythswood Av RNFRW PA4 80 D5
Blythswood Crs LARGS KA30 115 K7
Blythswood Dr PSLYN/LNWD PA3 8 F1
Blythswood Rd RNFRW PA4 80 D4
Blythswood Sq CGLW G2 4 F9
Blythswood St CGLW G2 5 G9
Boathouse Av LARGS KA30 115 H3
Boathouse Rd LARGS KA30 115 H3
Boclair Av BSDN G61 61 M5
Boclair Crs BSDN G61 62 A5
BSHPBGS G64 64 A8
Boclair Rd BSDN G61 62 A4
BSHPBGS G64 64 A7
Boclair St KNTSWD G13 81 L1
Bodden Sq MTHW ML1 134 E2
Boden Qd MTHW ML1 133 J7
Boden St DMNK/BRGTN G40 12 F8
Bodmin Gdns
BAIL/MDB/MHD G69 66 F6
Bogany Ter CSMK G45 128 E7
Bogbain Rd ESTRH G34 108 A1
Bogfoot Rd SHOTTS ML7 113 G6
Boggknowe UD/BTH/TAN G71 131 K1
Boghall Rd CARLUKE ML8 189 H3
UD/BTH/TAN G71 108 A6
Boghall St STPS/GTHM/RID G33 85 H8
Boghead BEITH KA15 168 B1
Boghead Av DMBTN G82 37 H5
Boghead Rd DMBTN G82 37 G5
KKNTL G66 65 G4
SPRGB/BLRNK G21 84 A5
Bogiewood Rd PGL PA14 34 B8
Boglemart St SVSTN KA20 201 J1
Bogleshole Rd
BLTYR/CAMB G72 129 L2
Boglestone Av PGL PA14 54 E1
Bogle St GRNK PA15 2 E5
Bogmoor Pl GOV/IBX G51 81 J8
Bogmoor Rd GOV/IBX G51 103 J1
Bogside Rd KSYTH G65 47 K2
PGL PA14 54 F1
STPS/GTHM/RID G33 85 G4
Bogside St DMNK/BRGTN G40 13 H8
Bogstonhill Rd
CRG/CRSL/HOU PA6 77 H6
Bogston La GRNK PA15 33 M7
Bogs Vw BLSH ML4 132 F6
Bogton Av LNPK/KPK G44 127 M5

Bogton Avenue La
LNPK/KPK G44 127 M5
Boleyn Rd PLKSD/SHW G41 104 E7
Bolingbroke EKILN G74 154 C5
Bolivar Ter GVH/MTFL G42 128 C1
Bolton Dr GVH/MTFL G42 128 A1
Bolton Ter KKNTL G66 44 E1
Bon Accord Crs SHOTTS ML7 137 K4
Bon Accord Rd
CRMNK/CLK/EAG G76 151 M3
Bon Accord Sq CLYDBK G81 80 B1
Bonar Crs BRWEIR PA11 98 E2
Bonar La BRWEIR PA11 98 E2
Bonar Law Av HBR/GL G84 20 B7
Bonawe St MRYH/FIRH G20 4 D2
Bonds Dr WISHAW ML2 160 B3
Bo'ness Rd AIRDRIE ML6 134 C1
MTHW ML1 134 B3
Boness St DMNK/BRGTN G40 13 H8
Bonhill Rd DMBTN G82 37 C5
Bonhill St PPK/MIL G22 5 G2
Bonkle Gdns WISHAW ML2 160 B4
Bonkle Rd WISHAW ML2 160 B4
Bonnar St DMNK/BRGTN G40 106 A6
Bonnaughton Rd BSDN G61 61 H3
Bonnet Ct KLMNKN/STW KA3 197 K1
Bonnet Rd LNK/LMHG ML11 199 G5
Bonnington Av
LNK/LMHG ML11 199 G6
Bonnyholm Av PLK/PH/NH G53 103 G6
Bonnyrigg Dr
PLKSW/MSWD G43 127 G4
Bonnyton Pl IRVSE KA11 204 A4
Bonnyton Rd KLMNK KA1 16 A2
Bontine Av DMBTN G82 36 D5
Bonyton Av KNTSWD G13 80 F3
Boon Dr DRUM G15 61 H7
Boquhanran Rd CLYDBK G81 60 A6
Borden La KNTSWD G13 81 L4
Borden Rd KNTSWD G13 81 L4
Border Av SALT KA21 200 F1
Border Pl SALT KA21 200 F1
Border St GRNK PA15 3 J8
Border Wy KKNTL G66 65 L1
Borebrae NMLNS KA16 215 J2
Borebrae Crs NMLNS KA16 215 J2
Boreland Dr HMLTN ML3 155 L7
KNTSWD G13 81 H2
Boreland Pl KNTSWD G13 81 H3
Bore Rd AIRDRIE ML6 111 H1
Borestone Av KBRN KA25 167 G1
Borgie Crs BLTYR/CAMB G72 130 A4
Borland Br KLMNKN/STW KA3 207 J3
Borland Rd BSDN G61 62 A6
Borron St COWCAD G4 5 J3
Borrowdale EKILS G75 170 F4
Borthwick Dr EKILS G75 170 D2
Borthwick St
STPS/GTHM/RID G33 85 H8
Bosfield Cnr EKILN G74 153 M6
Bosfield Pl EKILN G74 153 M6
Bosfield Rd EKILN G74 153 L6
Boston Dr HBR/GL G84 20 F6
Boswell Ct PLKSD/SHW G41 127 M2
Boswell Dr BLTYR/CAMB G72 155 K2
Boswell Pk AYRS KA7 18 E3
EKILN G74 154 C5
Boswell Sq
CARD/HILL/MSPK G52 102 F2
Bosworth Rd EKILN G74 154 C5
Botanic Crs MRYH/FIRH G20 82 D5
Bothlin Dr STPS/GTHM/RID G33 85 K3
Bothlyn Av KKNTL G66 65 L2
Bothlyn Crs BAIL/MDB/MHD G69 86 E2
Bothlyn Rd BAIL/MDB/MHD G69 86 D1
Bothwellhaugh Qd
BLSH ML4 132 F6
Bothwellhaugh Rd BLSH ML4 132 F8
Bothwell La CGLW G2 10 F1
KVD/HLHD G12 4 B4
Bothwellpark Pl
UD/BTH/TAN G71 132 D3
Bothwellpark Rd
UD/BTH/TAN G71 132 C5
Bothwell Pl CTBR ML5 109 M2
PSLYS PA2 123 L1
Bothwell Rd CARLUKE ML8 178 E5
HMLTN ML3 156 C2
UD/BTH/TAN G71 131 M5
Bothwellshields Rd MTHW ML1 112 D7
Bothwell St BLTYR/CAMB G72 129 L3
CGLW G2 10 F1
HMLTN ML3 156 C4
The Boulevard KKNTL G66 29 G8
Boundary Rd AYR KA8 225 K5
PSTWK KA9 225 K5
Bourne Ct RNFRW PA4 79 K2
Bourne Crs RNFRW PA4 79 K2
Bournemouth Rd
GRNKW/INVK PA16 31 L4
Bourne St HMLTN ML3 156 F6
Bourock Sq BRHD/NEIL G78 125 K8
Bourtree Pk AYRS KA7 19 G7
Bourtree Rd HMLTN ML3 155 L8
Bouverie St PGL PA14 34 C8
RUTH G73 128 F1
SCOT G14 80 E3
Bowden Dr
CARD/HILL/MSPK G52 103 H3
Bowden Pk EKILS G75 14 B6
Bowencraig LARGS KA30 115 K8
Bower St KVD/HLHD G12 4 A3
Bowerwalls St BRHD/NEIL G78 125 L5
Bowes Crs BAIL/MDB/MHD G69 107 M5
Bowfield Av
CARD/HILL/MSPK G52 102 F3
Bowfield Crs
CARD/HILL/MSPK G52 102 F3
Bowfield Dr
CARD/HILL/MSPK G52 102 F3
Bowfield Pl
CARD/HILL/MSPK G52 102 F3
Bowfield Rd HWWD PA9 121 M4
WKIL KA23 181 J5
Bowhousebog Rd SHOTTS ML7 137 G7
Bowhousebrae Rd
AIRDRIE ML6 111 L4
Bowhouse Ri IRVSE KA11 204 B4
Bowhouse Rd AIRDRIE ML6 111 M5
Bowie Rd ALEX/LLW G83 25 L3
Bowie St DMBTN G82 36 E6
Bowling Green La SCOT G14 81 K6
Bowling Green Rd
BAIL/MDB/MHD G69 86 D1
CAR/SHTL G32 107 K5
LNPK/KPK G44 128 A4
SCOT G14 81 K6
Bowling Green St BLSH ML4 133 H4
Bowling Green Vw
BLTYR/CAMB G72 130 F5
Bowling St CTBR ML5 109 M2
Bowman Rd AYRS KA7 18 F7
Bowman St GVH/MTFL G42 105 G7
Bowmont Pl EKILS G75 170 D2
Bowmont Ter KVD/HLHD G12 82 C6
Bowmore Ct IRVSE KA11 204 A3
Bowmore Gdns RUTH G73 129 L6
UD/BTH/TAN G71 131 L1
Bowmore Rd
CARD/HILL/MSPK G52 103 L4
Bowmount Gdns
KVD/HLHD G12 82 C6
Bow Rd GRNKW/INVK PA16 32 B5
Bowyer Vennel BLSH ML4 132 F3
Boyd Ct KLMNKN/STW KA3 17 G2
Boyd Dr MTHW ML1 157 H2
Boydfield Av PSTWK KA9 221 K8
Boyd Orr Crs KLMNKN/STW KA3 206 A2
Boyd Orr Rd SALT KA21 192 A7
Boydstone Pl GIF/THBK G46 126 F4
Boydstone Rd GIF/THBK G46 126 F5
PLKSW/MSWD G43 126 E3
Boydston Rd ARD KA22 191 J5
Boydston Wy
KLMNKN/STW KA3 207 J3
Boyd St GLSTN KA4 214 B3
GVH/MTFL G42 105 H8
KLMNKN/STW KA3 16 F2
LARGS KA30 115 J5
PSTWK KA9 225 J1
Boylestone Rd BRHD/NEIL G78 125 G5
Boyle St CLYDBK G81 80 D1
Boyndie St ESTRH G34 108 B1
Brabloch Crs PSLYN/LNWD PA3 101 M3
Bracadale Dr
BAIL/MDB/MHD G69 108 D5
Bracadale Gdns
BAIL/MDB/MHD G69 108 D5
Bracadale Gv
BAIL/MDB/MHD G69 108 C5
Bracadale Rd
BAIL/MDB/MHD G69 108 C5
Bracco Rd AIRDRIE ML6 113 G1
Brachelston St
GRNKW/INVK PA16 32 D5
Brackenbrae Av BSHPBGS G64 63 L7
Brackenbrae Rd BSHPBGS G64 63 M8
Brackenburn Br
KLMNKN/STW KA3 197 J7
Brackendene
CRG/CRSL/HOU PA6 77 K8
Brackenhill Av
KLMNKN/STW KA3 207 G4
Brackenhill Dr HMLTN ML3 174 B2
Brackenhill Rd CARLUKE ML8 178 A3
Brackenhirst Rd AIRDRIE ML6 88 D3
Brackenhurst St DMBTN G82 37 J3
Brackenknowe Rd AIRDRIE ML6 69 K6
Brackenrig Rd GIF/THBK G46 126 E7
Bracken Rd PGL PA14 55 G1
Bracken St MTHW ML1 134 A6
PPK/MIL G22 83 H3
Bracken Ter UD/BTH/TAN G71 132 A6
Brackla Av KNTSWD G13 80 E1
Bradan Av KNTSWD G13 80 E2
Bradan Dr AYRS KA7 229 H7
Bradan Rd TROON KA10 216 A7
Bradda Av RUTH G73 129 J5
Bradfield Av KVD/HLHD G12 82 C4
Bradshaw Crs HMLTN ML3 155 L6
Bradshaw St SALT KA21 200 F2
Brady Crs BAIL/MDB/MHD G69 67 G6
Braedale Av AIRDRIE ML6 111 H2
MTHW ML1 157 H3
Braedale Crs WISHAW ML2 160 B4
Braedale Pl WISHAW ML2 160 C4
Braedale Rd LNK/LMHG ML11 199 G4
Braeface Rd CUMB G67 48 E7
Braefield Dr GIF/THBK G46 127 G6
Braefoot IRV KA12 203 M4
RAYR/DAL KA6 227 G7
Braefoot Av MLNGV G62 62 A1
Braefoot Ct CARLUKE ML8 177 M5
Braefoot Crs CARLUKE ML8 177 M5
PSLYS PA2 124 F1
Braefoot La BRHD/NEIL G78 147 G6
Braehead BEITH KA15 168 B1
BLTYR/CAMB G72 155 K3
DALRY KA24 184 C1
LOCHW PA12 120 C6
Braehead Av BRHD/NEIL G78 148 D2
CLYDBK G81 60 A2
CTBR ML5 109 K6
LOCHW PA12 120 C6
LRKH ML9 175 L7
MLNGV G62 41 M8
Braehead Ct KLMNKN/STW KA3 17 G4
Braehead Crs CLYDBK G81 60 A2
Braehead Dr BLSH ML4 132 F5
Braehead Glebe
KLMNKN/STW KA3 197 L1
Braehead Pl BLSH ML4 132 F5
DALRY KA24 184 C1
SALT KA21 200 F1
Braehead Qd
BRHD/NEIL G78 148 D2
MTHW ML1 134 D5
Braehead Rd AYR KA8 225 J7
CLYDBK G81 60 A2
CUMB G67 49 H6
EKILN G74 152 C6
PGL PA14 54 E1
PSLYS PA2 124 D1
Braehead St KKNTL G66 45 J8
Braehead Ter
KLMNKN/STW KA3 206 C3
Braemar Av CLYDBK G81 59 M5
Braemar Ct GIF/THBK G46 127 L5
Braemar Crs BSDN G61 61 M7
CARLUKE ML8 179 G6
PSLYS PA2 101 M8
Braemar Dr JNSTN PA5 100 B8
Braemar Rd RNFRW PA4 79 K2
RUTH G73 129 K6
Braemar Sq AYR KA8 225 K7
Braemar St GVH/MTFL G42 127 M2
HMLTN ML3 156 B3
Braemar Vw CLYDBK G81 59 M4
Braemore Gdns PPK/MIL G22 83 K5
Braemount Av PSLYS PA2 124 C3
Braes Av CLYDBK G81 60 D8
Braesburn Pl CUMB G67 49 M3
Braesburn Rd CUMB G67 49 M3
Braeside IRV KA12 203 M4
KLWNG KA13 193 L4
RAYR/DAL KA6 227 G7
Braeside Av
BAIL/MDB/MHD G69 66 F7
LARGS KA30 115 L5
MLNGV G62 62 A1
RUTH G73 129 J2
Braeside Crs
BAIL/MDB/MHD G69 108 F4
BRHD/NEIL G78 125 L8
Braeside Dr BRHD/NEIL G78 125 K8
DMBTN G82 37 H4
Braeside Gdns HMLTN ML3 174 E1
Braeside Pl BLTYR/CAMB G72 130 B5
Braeside Rd AYR KA8 225 K7
GRNKW/INVK PA16 31 K6
MTHW ML1 134 D5
Braeside St KLMNK KA1 17 G4
MRYH/FIRH G20 4 D2
Braes O' Yetts KKNTL G66 66 A1
Braes Rd SALT KA21 200 E2
The Brae KLMNKN/STW KA3 206 B2
Brae Vw GRNKW/INVK PA16 32 C4
Braeview Av PSLYS PA2 124 B2
Braeview Dr PSLYS PA2 124 B2
Braeview Gdns PSLYS PA2 124 B2
Braeview Pl EKILN G74 154 A5
Braeview Rd PSLYS PA2 124 B2
Braidbar Farm Rd
GIF/THBK G46 127 K6
Braidbar Rd GIF/THBK G46 127 J6
Braid Ct KLWNG KA13 193 H6
Braidcraft Pl
PLK/PH/NH G53 126 C1
Braidcraft Rd PLK/PH/NH G53 126 D1
Braidcraft Ter
PLK/PH/NH G53 103 K8
Braidfauld Gdns CAR/SHTL G32 106 F6
Braidfauld Pl CAR/SHTL G32 106 F7
Braidfauld St CAR/SHTL G32 106 F7
Braidfield Gv CLYDBK G81 60 B4
Braidfield Rd CLYDBK G81 60 C4
Braidfute LNK/LMHG ML11 199 J4
Braidholm Crs GIF/THBK G46 127 J5
Braidholm Rd GIF/THBK G46 127 K5
Braidhurst St MTHW ML1 157 L1
Braidley Crs EKILS G75 171 L4
Braidpark Dr GIF/THBK G46 127 K6
Braid Sq COWCAD G4 4 F5
Braid's Rd PSLYS PA2 101 L8
Braid St COWCAD G4 4 F5
Braidwood Pl PSLYN/LNWD PA3 99 M3
Braidwood Rd CARLUKE ML8 188 C7
KLWNG KA13 193 L5
Braidwood St WISHAW ML2 159 J2
Bramah Av EKILS G75 15 H7
Bramblehedge Pth
ALEX/LLW G83 25 M2
Brambling Ct WISHAW ML2 159 G8
Bramley Pl AIRDRIE ML6 111 L3
KKNTL G66 65 L5
Brampton EKILS G75 170 F3
Branchalfield Dr WISHAW ML2 159 L5
Branchalmuir Crs WISHAW ML2 159 M3
Branchal Rd WISHAW ML2 159 K4
Branchock Av
BLTYR/CAMB G72 130 D5
Branchton Rd
GRNKW/INVK PA16 31 M6
Brancumhall Rd EKILN G74 154 D6
Brandon Dr BSDN G61 61 L2
Brandon Gdns
BLTYR/CAMB G72 129 L4
PSTWK KA9 225 H2
Brandon Pl BLSH ML4 132 E6
Brandon St CTBR ML5 109 L5
DEN/PKHD G31 12 D3
HMLTN ML3 156 E6
MTHW ML1 157 L3
Brandon Wy CTBR ML5 109 K5
Brand Pl GOV/IBX G51 104 C3
Brand St GOV/IBX G51 104 D3
Brankholm Brae HMLTN ML3 155 K5
Brannock Av MTHW ML1 134 D5
Brannock Pl MTHW ML1 134 D5
Brannock Rd MTHW ML1 134 D6
Brassey St MRYH/FIRH G20 82 E3
Braxfield Rd LNK/LMHG ML11 199 G8
Braxfield Ter LNK/LMHG ML11 198 F7
Breadalbane Crs MTHW ML1 133 K8
Breadalbane Gdns RUTH G73 129 K5
Breadalbane St KVGV G3 4 C9
Breadie Dr MLNGV G62 61 M1
Breamish Pl EKILS G75 170 F3
Bream Pl CRG/CRSL/HOU PA6 99 K1
Brechin Rd BSHPBGS G64 64 C8
Brechin St KVGV G3 4 B8
Breck Av PSLYS PA2 123 K2
Brediland Rd PSLYN/LNWD PA3 100 A3
PSLYS PA2 100 F8
Bredin Wy MTHW ML1 157 H1
Bredisholm Crs
UD/BTH/TAN G71 109 J8
Bredisholm Dr
BAIL/MDB/MHD G69 108 C5
Bredisholm Rd
BAIL/MDB/MHD G69 108 C5
Bredisholm Ter
BAIL/MDB/MHD G69 108 C5
Brenfield Av LNPK/KPK G44 127 M5
Brenfield Dr LNPK/KPK G44 127 M5
Brenfield Rd LNPK/KPK G44 127 M5
Brent Ct EKILN G74 153 L6
Brent Crs CRG/CRSL/HOU PA6 99 J1
Brent Dr GIF/THBK G46 126 F4
Brent Gdns GIF/THBK G46 126 F4
Brent Rd EKILN G74 153 L6
GIF/THBK G46 126 F4
Brent Wy GIF/THBK G46 126 F4
Brentwood Av PLK/PH/NH G53 126 A5
Brentwood Dr PLK/PH/NH G53 126 A5
Brentwood Sq
PLK/PH/NH G53 126 B5
Brereton St GVH/MTFL G42 105 J8
Bressay EKILN G74 153 L6
Bressay Pl KLMNKN/STW KA3 207 H4
Bressay Rd
STPS/GTHM/RID G33 107 L3
Breval Crs CLYDBK G81 60 A2
Brewery Rd KLMNK KA1 16 F7
Brewery St JNSTN PA5 99 M6
Brewlands Crs KLMNK KA1 218 C5
Brewlands Dr KLMNK KA1 218 C5
Brewlands Rd KLMNK KA1 218 C6
Brewland St GLSTN KA4 214 B4
Brewster Av PSLYN/LNWD PA3 102 A2
Brewster Pl IRVSE KA11 208 F2
Briar Bank KKNTL G66 45 H4
Briarcroft Dr
STPS/GTHM/RID G33 84 D2
Briarcroft Pl
STPS/GTHM/RID G33 84 E3
Briarcroft Rd
STPS/GTHM/RID G33 84 D3
Briar Dr CLYDBK G81 60 B5
Briar Gdns PLKSW/MSWD G43 127 K4
Briar Gv AYRS KA7 229 J5
PLKSW/MSWD G43 127 K4
Briarhill Ct PSTWK KA9 225 K1
Briarhill Rd PSTWK KA9 225 J1
Briarhill St PSTWK KA9 225 J1
Briarlea Dr GIF/THBK G46 127 J5
Briar Neuk BSHPBGS G64 84 B1
Briar Pl GRK PA19 31 K3
Briar Rd KKNTL G66 65 M1
PLKSW/MSWD G43 127 K4
Briar Wk KKNTL G66 66 A1
Briarwell La MLNGV G62 42 B8
Briarwell Rd MLNGV G62 42 B8
Briarwood Ct CAR/SHTL G32 107 L7
Briarwood Rd WISHAW ML2 158 E5
Brick La PSLYN/LNWD PA3 9 J2
Bridgebar St BRHD/NEIL G78 125 L5
Bridgeburn Dr
BAIL/MDB/MHD G69 66 E7
Bridgeford Av BLSH ML4 133 J2
Bridgegait MLNGV G62 62 C1
Bridgegate CGLE G1 11 K4
IRV KA12 203 J7
Bridgehousehill Rd KLMNK KA1 211 M7
Bridgend DALRY KA24 184 D2
KLMNKN/STW KA3 197 L1
NMLNS KA16 215 K2
Bridgend Av PGL PA14 54 E1
Bridgend Crs
BAIL/MDB/MHD G69 66 E7
Bridgend La DALRY KA24 184 D2
KLWNG KA13 193 M5
Bridgend Pl
BAIL/MDB/MHD G69 66 E7
Bridgend Rd GRNK PA15 3 K9
KBRN KA25 143 H7
Bridgend Vw CARLUKE ML8 178 F8
Bridge of Weir Rd
CRG/CRSL/HOU PA6 77 G8
JNSTN PA5 99 H4
KLMCLM PA13 75 L3
PSLYN/LNWD PA3 100 B4
Bridgepark ARD KA22 191 K8
Bridge Rd PGL PA14 54 E1
Bridge St ALEX/LLW G83 25 L5
BLTYR/CAMB G72 130 A3
CLYDBK G81 59 L6
DMBTN G82 36 E6
GBLS G5 11 H4
HMLTN ML3 156 C7
KBRN KA25 143 H7
PSLY PA1 9 H5
PSLYN/LNWD PA3 100 C3
PSTWK KA9 225 H1
WISHAW ML2 158 E6
Bridgeway Ct KKNTL G66 65 M2
Bridgeway Rd KKNTL G66 65 M2
Bridgeway Ter KKNTL G66 65 M2
Bridie Ter EKILN G74 154 C5
Brierie Av CRG/CRSL/HOU PA6 77 H8
Brierie Gdns
CRG/CRSL/HOU PA6 99 H1
Brierie Hill Ct
CRG/CRSL/HOU PA6 99 H1
Brierie-Hill Gv
CRG/CRSL/HOU PA6 99 H1
Brierie-Hill Rd
CRG/CRSL/HOU PA6 99 G1
Brierie La CRG/CRSL/HOU PA6 99 G1
Brierybank Av LNK/LMHG ML11 199 G6
Brigbrae Av BLSH ML4 133 J6
Brigham Pl SMSTN G23 82 E1
Brighton Pl GOV/IBX G51 104 B3
Brighton St GOV/IBX G51 104 B3
Brightside Av PGL PA14 55 G1
UD/BTH/TAN G71 131 M4
Brig O'lea Ter BRHD/NEIL G78 148 C3
Brigside Gdns HMLTN ML3 157 G7
Brisbane Ct GIF/THBK G46 127 K6
Brisbane Crs LARGS KA30 115 J4
Brisbane Glen Rd LARGS KA30 115 K3
Brisbane Rd BSHPTN PA7 58 B6
LARGS KA30 115 K4
Brisbane St CLYDBK G81 59 K5
GRNKW/INVK PA16 32 D3
LARGS KA30 115 J4
LNPK/KPK G44 128 A2
Brisbane Ter EKILS G75 14 A7
Britannia Pl AYR KA8 225 H7
Broadfield Av PGL PA14 55 G1
Broadford St COWCAD G4 5 K4
Broadholm St PPK/MIL G22 83 J3
Broadleys Av BSHPBGS G64 63 M7
Broadlie Ct BRHD/NEIL G78 148 D2
Broadlie Dr DALRY KA24 184 A1
KNTSWD G13 81 G3
Broadlie Rd BRHD/NEIL G78 148 C2
Broadloan RNFRW PA4 80 C7
Broadmoss Av NMRNS G77 151 J5
Broad Sq BLTYR/CAMB G72 155 J1
Broadstone Av PGL PA14 34 A8
Broad St DMNK/BRGTN G40 12 D6
Broadway ARD KA22 191 K6
The Broad Wy WISHAW ML2 158 E5
Broadwood RAYR/DAL KA6 231 H5
Broadwood Dr LNPK/KPK G44 128 B3
Broadwood Pk AYRS KA7 229 G8
Brockburn Crs PLK/PH/NH G53 126 B1
Brockburn Rd PLK/PH/NH G53 103 H8
Brockburn Ter
PLK/PH/NH G53 126 C1
Brocklehill Av RAYR/DAL KA6 227 H6
Brocklehill Dr RAYR/DAL KA6 227 G3
Brocklinn Pk EKILS G75 170 E2
Brockly Vw KBRN KA25 143 H5
Brock Ov PLK/PH/NH G53 126 C3
Brock Pl PLK/PH/NH G53 126 C2
Brock Rd PLK/PH/NH G53 126 B3
Brock Ter PLK/PH/NH G53 126 C3
Brockville St CAR/SHTL G32 106 F3
Brodick Av KLWNG KA13 193 J5
MTHW ML1 157 H2
Brodick Cl KLWNG KA13 193 J5
Brodick Dr EKILN G74 153 K6
GRK PA19 30 F4
HBR/GL G84 20 F6
Brodick St SPRGB/BLRNK G21 6 E6
Brodie Av TROON KA10 216 D5
Brodie Park Av PSLYS PA2 9 G9
Brodie Park Crs PSLYS PA2 8 E8
Brodie Park Gdns PSLYS PA2 9 G9
Brodie Pl EKILN G74 153 K6
KLMNKN/STW KA3 207 J6
Brodie Rd SPRGB/BLRNK G21 84 D2
Brogan Crs MTHW ML1 157 H2
Bron Wy CUMB G67 49 G8
Brookbank Ter CARLUKE ML8 179 G8
Brookfield Rd PGL PA14 54 F1
Brooklands ALEX/LLW G83 25 K3
EKILN G74 153 G8
Brooklands Av
UD/BTH/TAN G71 131 L2
Brooklea Dr GIF/THBK G46 127 J4
PLKSW/MSWD G43 127 J4
Brooklime Dr EKILN G74 153 K5
Brooklime Gdns EKILN G74 153 J5
Brooklyn Pl WISHAW ML2 177 H3
Brookside St DMNK/BRGTN G40 12 E6
Brook St CLYDBK G81 59 M5
DMNK/BRGTN G40 12 D5
Broom Av ERSK PA8 79 H2
Broomberry Dr GRK PA19 31 L2
Broomburn Dr NMRNS G77 150 F5
Broom Crs BRHD/NEIL G78 125 G4
EKILS G75 171 K4
Broomcroft Rd NMRNS G77 151 G3
Broom Dr CLYDBK G81 60 A5
LRKH ML9 176 A4
Broomelton Rd HMLTN ML3 175 K8
Broomfield CRG/CRSL/HOU PA6 77 K8
LARGS KA30 115 J7
Broomfield Av
BLTYR/CAMB G72 129 K2
NMRNS G77 150 F6
Broomfield Crs LARGS KA30 115 J7
Broomfield Gdn AYRS KA7 18 E8
Broomfield La
SPRGB/BLRNK G21 83 M4
Broomfield Pl LARGS KA30 115 J7
SPRGB/BLRNK G21 83 M4
Broomfield Rd AYRS KA7 18 E8
NMRNS G77 151 G3
SPRGB/BLRNK G21 83 M4
Broomfield St AIRDRIE ML6 111 H2
KLWNG KA13 193 L4
Broomfield Ter
UD/BTH/TAN G71 108 F8
Broomfield Wk KKNTL G66 65 K1
Broom Gdns KKNTL G66 65 H3
Broomgate LNK/LMHG ML11 198 F6
Broomhill Av CAR/SHTL G32 130 B1
NMRNS G77 150 F5
PTCK G11 81 M7
Broomhill Ct LRKH ML9 176 A7
Broomhill Crs BLSH ML4 132 F6
ERSK PA8 79 H2
Broomhill Dr DMBTN G82 37 H4
PTCK G11 81 M6
RUTH G73 129 H4
Broomhill Farm Ms KKNTL G66 45 L8
Broomhill Gdns NMRNS G77 150 F5
PTCK G11 81 M6
Broomhill Ga LRKH ML9 176 A7
Broomhill La PTCK G11 81 M6
Broomhill Pl PTCK G11 81 M7
Broomhill Qd KLMNK KA1 212 A5
Broomhill Rd LRKH ML9 176 A7
Broomhill Rd East
KLMNK KA1 212 A5
Broomhill Rd West
KLMNK KA1 211 M5
Broomhill St GRNK PA15 2 B6
Broomhill Ter PTCK G11 81 M7
Broomhill Vw LRKH ML9 175 L7
Broomieknowe Dr
RUTH G73 129 H3
Broomieknowe Gdns
RUTH G73 129 G3
Broomieknowe Rd RUTH G73 129 H3
Broomielaw KVGV G3 10 E3
Broomknoll St AIRDRIE ML6 111 G2
Broomknowe BALLOCH G68 48 D6
Broomknowe Rd KLMCLM PA13 75 J1
Broomknowes Av KKNTL G66 65 L5
Broomknowes Rd
SPRGB/BLRNK G21 84 A5
Broomlands Av ERSK PA8 79 K1
Broomlands Busway
IRVSE KA11 203 M7
Broomlands Crs ERSK PA8 79 L1

Broomlands Dr IRV KA12 203 J7
Broomlands Gdns ERSK PA8 79 K1
Broomlands Rd CUMB G67 69 G1
IRVSE KA11 204 B8
Broomlands St PSLY PA1 8 C5
Broomlands Wy ERSK PA8 79 L1
Broomlea Crs RNFRW PA4 79 J2
Broomlee Rd CUMB G67 68 F3
Broomley Crs ALEX/LLW G83 25 J2
ALEX/LLW G83 25 K2
Broomley Dr GIF/THBK G46 127 J8
Broomley La GIF/THBK G46 127 J8
Broomloan Rd GOV/IBX G51 104 A3
Broompark Av
BLTYR/CAMB G72 155 J3
PSTWK KA9 225 J1
Broompark Circ DEN/PKHD G31 6 D9
Broompark Crs AIRDRIE ML6 89 G7
PSTWK KA9 225 J1
Broompark Dr DEN/PKHD G31 12 C1
NMRNS G77 150 F3
RNFRW PA4 79 K2
Broompark La DEN/PKHD G31 12 D1
Broompark Rd
BLTYR/CAMB G72 155 J2
WISHAW ML2 158 D5
Broompark St DEN/PKHD G31 12 D1
Broom Pl BRWEIR PA11 98 E1
CTBR ML5 109 M6
KLMNK KA1 212 B4
MTHW ML1 134 C5
Broom Rd CUMB G67 49 K4
NMRNS G77 151 G3
PLKSW/MSWD G43 127 K4
WMYSB PA18 50 A8
Broom Rd East NMRNS G77 151 H6
Broomside Crs MTHW ML1 157 L5
Broomside St MTHW ML1 157 L5
Broomstone Av NMRNS G77 150 F6
Broom Ter JNSTN PA5 99 M8
Broomton Rd
SPRGB/BLRNK G21 84 C2
Broomvale Dr NMRNS G77 150 F4
Broomward Dr JNSTN PA5 100 B6
Brora Crs HMLTN ML3 173 M1
Brora Dr BSDN G61 62 B5
GIF/THBK G46 127 K7
RNFRW PA4 80 E6
Brora Gdns BSHPBGS G64 64 B8
Brora Rd BSHPBGS G64 64 B8
Brora St STPS/GTHM/RID G33 7 L7
Brougham St GRNKW/INVK PA16 32 E2
Broughton EKILS G75 171 L4
Broughton Dr SMSTN G23 82 E1
Broughton Gdns SMSTN G23 62 F8
Broughton Pl CTBR ML5 110 B6
HMLTN ML3 156 A6
Broughton Rd SMSTN G23 62 E8
Broun Dr AYRS KA7 228 E8
Brouster Hl EKILN G74 14 F3
Brouster Pl EKILN G74 14 F3
Brown Av CLYDBK G81 80 D1
DMBTN G82 37 J5
TROON KA10 216 D6
Browncarrick Dr AYRS KA7 228 B8
Brownhill Dr KBRN KA25 166 F1
Brownhill Rd GIF/THBK G46 127 H5
Brownhill Vw WISHAW ML2 160 D3
Brownieside Pl AIRDRIE ML6 90 A6
Brownieside Rd AIRDRIE ML6 90 B7
Brownlee Rd CARLUKE ML8 177 K5
WISHAW ML2 177 H5
Brownlie St GVH/MTFL G42 128 B1
Brown Pl BLTYR/CAMB G72 130 A3
Brown Rd CUMB G67 48 F7
Brownsburn Rd AIRDRIE ML6 111 H5
Brown's Crs RAYR/DAL KA6 227 H6
Brownsdale Rd RUTH G73 128 F2
Brownsfield Crs RNFRW PA4 79 H4
Brownsfield Rd RNFRW PA4 79 H4
Brownshill Av CTBR ML5 109 M5
Brownside Av
BLTYR/CAMB G72 129 L4
BRHD/NEIL G78 125 G4
Brownside Crs
BRHD/NEIL G78 125 G4
Brownside Dr BRHD/NEIL G78 125 G4
KNTSWD G13 80 F3
Brownside Gv BRHD/NEIL G78 125 G4
Brownside Rd RUTH G73 129 K4
Brown's La PSLY PA1 9 G5
Brown's Rd NMLNS KA16 215 K2
Brown St CARLUKE ML8 178 F6
CTBR ML5 110 A4
GRNK PA15 3 L8
KLMNKN/STW KA3 197 K1
KVGV G3 10 A8
LRKH ML9 176 A5
MTHW ML1 157 M1
NMLNS KA16 215 J2
PGL PA14 34 B7
PSLY PA1 8 D3
RNFRW PA4 80 C6
WISHAW ML2 160 A5
Brown Wk IRV KA12 203 J4
Browside Av PSLYS PA2 124 C2
Bruce Av CRH/DND KA2 209 M7
JNSTN PA5 122 E1
MTHW ML1 157 K2
PSLYN/LNWD PA3 102 A2
PSTWK KA9 225 H3
Bruce Crs AYRS KA7 18 D3
KLMNK KA1 211 M5
Brucefield Pl ESTRH G34 108 D1
Brucehill Rd DMBTN G82 36 C5
Bruce La PSTWK KA9 225 H3
Bruce Pl EKILS G75 15 H8
Bruce Rd BSHPTN PA7 58 A6
MTHW ML1 134 B7
PLKSD/SHW G41 10 A8
PSLYN/LNWD PA3 102 A3
RNFRW PA4 80 A8
Bruce St AIRDRIE ML6 90 A7
BLSH ML4 133 H4
CLYDBK G81 60 B8
CTBR ML5 110 B1
DMBTN G82 37 G7
GRNK PA15 2 B4
KLMNK KA1 211 M5
PGL PA14 34 D8
Bruce Ter BLTYR/CAMB G72 131 L8
EKILS G75 15 H8
IRV KA12 203 K4
Brueacre Rd WMYSB PA18 50 A8
Brunel Wy EKILS G75 15 H6
Brunstane Rd ESTRH G34 86 A8
Brunswick La CGLE G1 11 K2
Brunswick St CGLE G1 11 K2
Brunton St LNPK/KPK G44 128 A4
Brunton Ter LNPK/KPK G44 127 M5
Bruntsfield Av KLWNG KA13 193 H5
PLK/PH/NH G53 126 B6
Bruntsfield Gdns
PLK/PH/NH G53 126 B6
Bryan St HMLTN ML3 156 B4
Bryce Gdns LRKH ML9 176 A5
Bryce Pl EKILS G75 14 B9
Brydson Pl PSLYN/LNWD PA3 100 B3
Brymner St GRNK PA15 2 E4
Bryon Ct UD/BTH/TAN G71 132 B7
Bryson Ct HMLTN ML3 174 D2
Bryson St CLYDBK G81 60 E2
Buccleuch Av
CARD/HILL/MSPK G52 102 E1
CRMNK/CLK/EAG G76 151 K2
Buccleuch Dr BSDN G61 61 L2
Buccleuch La KVGV G3 4 F7
Buccleuch St KVGV G3 4 E7
Buccleugh St GRNK PA15 2 C4
Buchanan Av BSHPTN PA7 58 B5
Buchanan Crs HMLTN ML3 156 B7
SPRGB/BLRNK G21 84 C2
Buchanan Dr BLTYR/CAMB G72 129 L3
BSDN G61 62 A5
BSHPBGS G64 84 C1
CARLUKE ML8 178 A3
KKNTL G66 65 K5
NMRNS G77 150 E2
RUTH G73 129 H3
Buchanan Gv
BAIL/MDB/MHD G69 108 B4
Buchanan Pl BSHPBGS G64 44 B8
Buchanan Rd HBR/GL G84 21 C8
Buchanan St AIRDRIE ML6 111 G2
BAIL/MDB/MHD G69 108 B4
CGLE G1 11 H2
CTBR ML5 109 M3
DMBTN G82 37 G7
GRNKW/INVK PA16 32 B5
JNSTN PA5 99 L7
LARGS KA30 115 H3
MLNGV G62 42 B7
Buchandyke Rd EKILN G74 154 B5
Buchan Gn EKILN G74 154 B6
Buchan Rd MTHW ML1 134 A7
TROON KA10 216 F5
Buchan St HMLTN ML3 174 C1
WISHAW ML2 159 J3
Buchan Ter BLTYR/CAMB G72 129 L6
Buchlyvie Gdns BSHPBGS G64 83 M1
Buchlyvie Pth ESTRH G34 108 B2
Buchlyvie Rd PSLY PA1 102 E4
Buchlyvie St ESTRH G34 108 B2
Buckingham Ct HMLTN ML3 155 L5
Buckingham Dr
CAR/SHTL G32 107 H8
RUTH G73 129 K2
Buckingham St
KVD/HLHD G12 82 D6
Buckingham Ter KVD/HLHD G12 82 D6
Bucklaw Gdns
CARD/HILL/MSPK G52 103 J5
Bucklaw Pl
CARD/HILL/MSPK G52 103 J5
Bucklaw Ter
CARD/HILL/MSPK G52 103 J5
Buckley St PPK/MIL G22 83 K3
Bucksburn Rd
SPRGB/BLRNK G21 84 C5
Buckthorne Pl PLK/PH/NH G53 126 B6
Buddon St DMNK/BRGTN G40 13 J8
Budhill Av CAR/SHTL G32 107 H4
Budshaw Av AIRDRIE ML6 111 J7
Buiston Rd KLMNKN/STW KA3 197 J6
Bulldale Ct SCOT G14 80 F3
Bulldale St SCOT G14 80 E3
Bullionslaw Dr RUTH G73 129 K3
Bulloch Rd GIF/THBK G46 127 K7
Bull Rd CRMNK/CLK/EAG G76 151 M3
Bullwood Av PLK/PH/NH G53 102 F8
Bullwood Ct PLK/PH/NH G53 125 M1
Bullwood Dr PLK/PH/NH G53 102 F8
Bullwood Gdns
PLK/PH/NH G53 102 F8
Bullwood Pl PLK/PH/NH G53 102 F8
Bunbury Ter EKILS G75 14 A6
Bunessan St
CARD/HILL/MSPK G52 103 M4
Bunhouse Rd KVGV G3 82 C8
Bunting Pl KLMNK KA1 17 L7
Burghead Dr GOV/IBX G51 103 L1
Burghead Pl GOV/IBX G51 103 L1
Burgher St DEN/PKHD G31 13 K7
Burgh Hall La PTCK G11 82 B7
Burgh Hall St PTCK G11 82 B7
Burgh La KVD/HLHD G12 82 D6
Burgh Rd PSTWK KA9 225 H1
Burgh Wk GRK PA19 31 L1
Burgoyne Dr RAYR/DAL KA6 231 H5
Burleigh Rd UD/BTH/TAN G71 132 B6
Burleigh St CTBR ML5 110 B6
GOV/IBX G51 104 A1
Burley Pl EKILN G74 152 F7
Burlington Av KVD/HLHD G12 82 B3
Burmola St PPK/MIL G22 83 H5
Burnacre Gdns
UD/BTH/TAN G71 131 L2
Burnawn Pl GLSTN KA4 214 D4
Burnbank Braes
CARLUKE ML8 178 F8
Burnbank Centre
HMLTN ML3 156 A4
Burnbank Dr BRHD/NEIL G78 125 J8
Burnbank Gdns MRYH/FIRTH G20 4 D4
Burnbank Pl AYRS KA7 229 H5
MRYH/FIRH G20 4 D4
Burnbank Qd AIRDRIE ML6 110 F1
Burnbank Rd AYRS KA7 229 H5
HMLTN ML3 156 B5
Burnbank St AIRDRIE ML6 110 F1
CTBR ML5 110 B1
SVSTN KA20 201 K1
Burnbank Ter COWCAD G4 4 D5
Burnblea St HMLTN ML3 156 D7
Burnbrae CLYDBK G81 60 A3
KSYTH G65 46 F5
Burnbrae Av
BAIL/MDB/MHD G69 67 G7
BSDN G61 62 A2
Burnbrae Crs IRVSE KA11 204 C4
Burnbrae Dr IRVSE KA11 204 C4
PSLYN/LNWD PA3 100 D5
RUTH G73 129 K4
Burnbrae Pl EKILN G74 14 B2
Burnbrae Rd
BAIL/MDB/MHD G69 66 B6
BLTYR/CAMB G72 155 J2
JNSTN PA5 100 B5
KKNTL G66 65 M7
KKNTL G66 66 B2
SHOTTS ML7 137 L7
Burnbrae St CLYDBK G81 60 D1
LRKH ML9 175 M6
SPRGB/BLRNK G21 6 F1
Burncleuch Av
BLTYR/CAMB G72 130 A5
Burn Crs AIRDRIE ML6 111 K7
MTHW ML1 134 A5
Burncrooks Av BSDN G61 61 K2
EKILN G74 14 B2
Burndale La KLMCLM PA13 75 K1
Burndyke Ct GOV/IBX G51 104 B2
Burndyke Sq GOV/IBX G51 104 C2
Burness Av AYRS KA7 228 F7
Burnet Rose Ct EKILN G74 153 J5
Burnet Rose Gdns EKILN G74 153 J5
Burnet Rose Pl EKILN G74 153 J5
Burnett Rd
STPS/GTHM/RID G33 107 L2
Burnett Ter AYR KA8 225 H7
Burnfield Av GIF/THBK G46 127 H5
Burnfield Dr GIF/THBK G46 127 H5
Burnfield Gdns GIF/THBK G46 127 J5
Burnfield Rd GIF/THBK G46 127 G4
Burnfoot DMBTN G82 35 H2
Burnfoot Av TROON KA10 216 D4
Burnfoot Crs PSLYS PA2 124 C2
RUTH G73 129 K4
Burnfoot Dr
CARD/HILL/MSPK G52 103 H4
Burnfoot La ARD KA22 191 H5
Burnfoot Pl KLMNKN/STW KA3 206 E5
Burnfoot Rd AIRDRIE ML6 110 E1
FAIRLIE KA29 139 K7
LOCHW PA12 120 B7
Burngreen KSYTH G65 47 L1
Burnhall Pl WISHAW ML2 159 K8
Burnhall Rd WISHAW ML2 159 J7
Burnhall St WISHAW ML2 159 K8
Burnham Rd SCOT G14 81 G5
Burnhaven ERSK PA8 59 G7
Burnhead La PGL PA14 54 C1
Burnhead Rd AIRDRIE ML6 89 K8
BALLOCH G68 48 C7
LRKH ML9 176 C6
PGL PA14 54 C1
PLKSW/MSWD G43 127 L4
Burnhead St GRNK PA15 3 H9
UD/BTH/TAN G71 132 B2
Burnhill Qd RUTH G73 128 F1
Burnhill St RUTH G73 128 F1
Burnhouse Av BALLOCH G68 48 B7
DALRY KA24 184 B2
Burnhouse Brae NMRNS G77 151 G6
Burnhouse Crs HMLTN ML3 156 B8
Burnhouse Rd EKILS G75 171 G7
HMLTN ML3 156 B8
Burnhouse St MRYH/FIRH G20 82 D3
Burniebrae AIRDRIE ML6 110 F1
Burniebrae Rd AIRDRIE ML6 111 L6
Burnlea Crs CRG/CRSL/HOU PA6 77 G7
Burnlea Pl SVSTN KA20 192 E7
Burnlea Rd LARGS KA30 115 J6
Burnlip Rd CTBR ML5 88 A5
Burnmouth Pl BSDN G61 62 A4
Burnmouth Rd
STPS/GTHM/RID G33 107 M3
Burnock Pl EKILS G75 170 E2
Burnpark Av
UD/BTH/TAN G71 131 K2
Burnpark Rd KLMNK KA1 211 M6
Burn Pl BLTYR/CAMB G72 129 L2
Burn Rd ARD KA22 200 D1
CARLUKE ML8 178 E6
NMLNS KA16 215 L2
Burns Av BSHPTN PA7 58 B6
KLMNKN/STW KA3 207 G6
SALT KA21 191 M6
Burns Ct KKNTL G66 46 A8
Burn's Crs AIRDRIE ML6 111 H3
IRVSE KA11 203 M4
Burns Dr JNSTN PA5 122 E1
KKNTL G66 46 A7
Burns Gdns BLTYR/CAMB G72 131 J8
Burns Gv GIF/THBK G46 127 G7
Burnside BSDN G61 61 J2
Burnside Av AIRDRIE ML6 111 H7
BLSH ML4 133 J5
BRHD/NEIL G78 125 H5
JNSTN PA5 99 J4
KKNTL G66 65 H2
PGL PA14 54 F1
Burnside Ct BSDN G61 61 J3
RUTH G73 129 J4
Burnside Crs ALEX/LLW G83 25 M2
BLTYR/CAMB G72 155 M3
CLYDBK G81 60 B2
SHOTTS ML7 137 K3
Burnside Gdns
CRMNK/CLK/EAG G76 151 K2
KLBCH PA10 99 H7
PSTWK KA9 221 J8
Burnside Ga RUTH G73 129 J4
Burnside Gv JNSTN PA5 99 L7
Burnside La HMLTN ML3 156 E7
Burnside Pl DMBTN G82 37 H7
IRV KA12 203 H5
LRKH ML9 176 B6
PSLYN/LNWD PA3 101 G2
SVSTN KA20 192 D8
TROON KA10 216 C6
Burnside Qd MTHW ML1 134 A4
Burnside Rd CTBR ML5 88 C8
GIF/THBK G46 151 H3
GRK PA19 31 M3
JNSTN PA5 100 C8
LARGS KA30 115 K4
MTHW ML1 134 D5
PSTWK KA9 221 K5
RUTH G73 129 J4
Burnside St GLGNK KA14 167 H3
KLMNK KA1 16 D9
MTHW ML1 158 B5
Burnside Vw CTBR ML5 109 L4
Burnside Wk CTBR ML5 109 L4
Burnside Wy LARGS KA30 115 L4
Burns La AIRDRIE ML6 111 K6
Burns Pk EKILN G74 15 K1
Burns Pl KLWNG KA13 193 M6
SHOTTS ML7 137 G3
SVSTN KA20 192 E8
Burns Rd AIRDRIE ML6 111 K5
CUMB G67 49 G6
GRNKW/INVK PA16 31 K5
KKNTL G66 45 M8
TROON KA10 216 F5
Burns Sq ARD KA22 191 J5
GRNKW/INVK PA16 31 K5
Burns Statue Sq AYRS KA7 18 F5
Burns St ALEX/LLW G83 25 L1
CLYDBK G81 59 L6
COWCAD G4 5 G4
DMBTN G82 25 L7
HMLTN ML3 156 D7
IRV KA12 203 H6
Burns Ter ARD KA22 191 J5
Burn St ALEX/LLW G83 25 M5
Burn Street La ALEX/LLW G83 25 M5
Burns' Wicket AYRS KA7 228 E8
Burntbroom Dr
BAIL/MDB/MHD G69 107 M6
Burntbroom Gdns
CAR/SHTL G32 107 M6
Burntbroom Rd
UD/BTH/TAN G71 107 M7
Burntbroom St
STPS/GTHM/RID G33 107 K1
Burn Ter BLTYR/CAMB G72 129 L2
Burntshields Rd KLBCH PA10 98 C8
Burn Vw CUMB G67 49 J6
Burnwood Dr AIRDRIE ML6 112 A3
Burra Gdns BSHPBGS G64 64 D7
Burrell Ct PLKSD/SHW G41 104 C7
Burrell's La COWCAD G4 12 A1
Burrelton Rd
PLKSW/MSWD G43 127 M3
Burton La GVH/MTFL G42 105 G8
Busbiehill Pl KLMNK KA1 16 B2
Busbie Vw CRH/DND KA2 205 L8
Busby Pl KLWNG KA13 193 M5
Busby Rd BLSH ML4 132 F6
CRMNK/CLK/EAG G76 151 M3
CRMNK/CLK/EAG G76 152 D2
Bush Crs WISHAW ML2 159 J7
Bushelhead Rd CARLUKE ML8 188 E4
Bushes Av PSLYS PA2 101 K8
Busheyhill St BLTYR/CAMB G72 130 A4
Bute EKILN G74 154 C8
Bute Av MTHW ML1 157 J2
PGL PA14 55 H1
RNFRW PA4 80 D8
Bute Crs BSDN G61 61 M7
OLDK G60 59 J4
PSLYS PA2 124 D2
SHOTTS ML7 137 K3
Bute Dr JNSTN PA5 99 K8
OLDK G60 59 J4
Bute Gdns KVD/HLHD G12 82 D7
LNPK/KPK G44 127 M6
OLDK G60 59 J3
Bute La KVD/HLHD G12 82 D7
Bute Pl ARD KA22 191 H8
Bute Rd KKNTL G66 66 B1
PSLYN/LNWD PA3 79 K8
Bute St CTBR ML5 110 B5
GRK PA19 31 K3
HMLTN ML3 156 B3
Bute Ter RUTH G73 129 G4
SALT KA21 191 L8
UD/BTH/TAN G71 132 B2
Butt Av HBR/GL G84 20 E6
Butterbiggins Rd
GVH/MTFL G42 105 G6
Butterburnpark St HMLTN ML3 156 D8
Butterfield Pl GVH/MTFL G42 105 G6
Buttermere EKILS G75 170 F4
Buttsley Ct LNK/LMHG ML11 198 E5
Byars Rd KKNTL G66 65 H1
By-pass Rd BEITH KA15 168 C1
Byrebush Rd PLK/PH/NH G53 103 J8
Byrehill Av KLWNG KA13 193 H7
KLWNG KA13 193 L8
Byrehill Rd KLWNG KA13 193 J8
KLWNG KA13 202 E1
Byres Av PSLYN/LNWD PA3 9 L1
Byres Crs PSLYN/LNWD PA3 102 A3
Byresknowe La MTHW ML1 134 B8
Byres Rd JNSTN PA5 100 D7
KLWNG KA13 193 K6
KVD/HLHD G12 82 D7
MTHW ML1 134 E5
Byrestone Av NMRNS G77 151 J5
Byretown Rd LNK/LMHG ML11 198 E6
Byron Rd SHOTTS ML7 137 G3
Byron St CLYDBK G81 60 A5
PTCK G11 81 M7
Byshot St PPK/MIL G22 5 L1

C

Cable Depot Rd CLYDBK G81 59 M8
Cables Dr ALEX/LLW G83 25 M4
Cadder Ct BSHPBGS G64 64 B4
Cadder Pl MRYH/FIRH G20 82 E2
Cadder Rd BSHPBGS G64 64 A3
MRYH/FIRH G20 82 E2
Cadder Wy BSHPBGS G64 64 B4
Caddlehill St GRNKW/INVK PA16 32 D4
Cadell Gdns EKILN G74 154 D4
Cadger's Sheuch KSYTH G65 48 A1
Cadoc St BLTYR/CAMB G72 130 B4
Cadogan St CGLW G2 10 F1
Cadzow Av GIF/THBK G46 151 H1
Cadzow Crs CTBR ML5 109 K5
Cadzow Dr BLTYR/CAMB G72 130 A4
Cadzow Gn EKILN G74 14 D2
Cadzow Pk HMLTN ML3 156 E5
Cadzow Rd HMLTN ML3 174 F6
Cadzow St CGLW G2 10 E2
HMLTN ML3 156 D5
LRKH ML9 176 A5
MTHW ML1 157 K3
Caerlaverock Av PSTWK KA9 225 J1
Caerlaverock Rd PSTWK KA9 225 J1
Caird Av GRNKW/INVK PA16 32 C2
Caird Dr PTCK G11 82 B7
Caird Gdns HMLTN ML3 156 D4
Caird Pk HMLTN ML3 156 D4
Caird St HMLTN ML3 156 C4
Cairn Av RNFRW PA4 80 E8
Cairnban St GOV/IBX G51 103 K3
Cairnbrook Rd ESTRH G34 86 C8
Cairn Ct EKILN G74 153 L5
Cairn Crs AYRS KA7 228 D8
Cairncurran Ct GRNK PA15 2 A7
Cairndhu Av HBR/GL G84 20 A7
Cairndhu Gdns HBR/GL G84 20 A7
Cairndow Av LNPK/KPK G44 127 M5
Cairndow Avenue La
LNPK/KPK G44 127 M5
Cairndow Ct LNPK/KPK G44 127 M5
Cairn Dr PSLYN/LNWD PA3 100 B3
Cairndyke Crs AIRDRIE ML6 111 G3
Cairneymount Rd
CARLUKE ML8 178 F7
Cairney Pl WISHAW ML2 160 D3
Cairnfore Av TROON KA10 216 F3
Cairngorm Ct IRVSE KA11 204 B4
Cairngorm Crs BRHD/NEIL G78 125 J8
BSDN G61 61 H3
PSLYS PA2 101 K8
WISHAW ML2 158 F6
Cairngorm Gdns BALLOCH G68 48 A8
Cairngorm Rd KLMNK KA1 212 A6
PLKSW/MSWD G43 127 J4
Cairnhill Av AIRDRIE ML6 110 F4
Cairnhill Circ
CARD/HILL/MSPK G52 102 F6
Cairnhill Ct CARLUKE ML8 178 F7
Cairnhill Crs CTBR ML5 110 D6
Cairnhill Dr
CARD/HILL/MSPK G52 102 F6
Cairnhill Pl
CARD/HILL/MSPK G52 102 F6
Cairnhill Rd AIRDRIE ML6 110 F4
BSDN G61 61 M8
Cairnhope Av AIRDRIE ML6 110 F4
Cairnlea Dr GOV/IBX G51 104 B3
Cairnlea Gdns BLSH ML4 133 H6
Cairnlea Rd MLNGV G62 41 L8
Cairnmount Rd IRVSE KA11 203 M2
Cairnmuir Rd EKILN G74 153 H4
Cairnoch Hl BALLOCH G68 48 C7
Cairn Pl EKILN G74 153 L5
GLSTN KA4 214 D3
Cairnryan EKILN G74 153 K6
Cairns Av BLTYR/CAMB G72 130 B4
Cairns Dr MLNGV G62 42 A7
Cairnsmore Dr AYRS KA7 228 C8
BSDN G61 61 H2
Cairnsmore Rd DRUM G15 60 F7
Cairnsmore Wy IRVSE KA11 204 B7
Cairns Rd BLTYR/CAMB G72 130 B5
BSHPTN PA7 58 A5
Cairns St MTHW ML1 157 L3
Cairns Ter KLMNK KA1 16 C4
Cairn St SPRGB/BLRNK G21 83 M3
Cairnswell Av BLTYR/CAMB G72 130 C5
Cairnswell Pl
BLTYR/CAMB G72 130 C5
Cairn Ter GLSTN KA4 214 D3
Cairntoul Ct BALLOCH G68 48 B7
Cairntoul Dr KNTSWD G13 81 G3
Cairntoul Pl SCOT G14 81 G4
Cairn Vw AIRDRIE ML6 110 F3
GLSTN KA4 214 D3
KKNTL G66 66 A2
Cairnview Rd KKNTL G66 45 H4
Cairnwood Dr AIRDRIE ML6 110 F4
Caithness Rd EKILN G74 154 D6
GRNKW/INVK PA16 31 J5
Caithness St BLTYR/CAMB G72 155 J3
MRYH/FIRH G20 82 F5
Cala Sona Ct WISHAW ML2 176 E1
Calcots Pl ESTRH G34 86 C8
Caldarvan St PPK/MIL G22 5 G2
Caldeen Rd CTBR ML5 110 B4
Calder Av AIRDRIE ML6 90 F5
BRHD/NEIL G78 125 J8
CTBR ML5 110 B5
TROON KA10 216 E3
WISHAW ML2 160 A3
Calderbank Rd AIRDRIE ML6 111 G5
Calderbank Ter MTHW ML1 157 M1
Calderbank Vw
BAIL/MDB/MHD G69 108 B6
Calderbraes Av
UD/BTH/TAN G71 131 L1
Caldercruix Rd AIRDRIE ML6 91 K2
Caldercuilt Rd MRYH/FIRH G20 62 C8
Calder Dr BLSH ML4 133 J5
BLTYR/CAMB G72 130 A4
LOCHW PA12 120 C6
Calder Ga BSHPBGS G64 63 M5

Calderglen Av
BLTYR/CAMB G72 131 J6
Calderglen Rd EKILN G74 154 C8
Caldergrove MTHW ML1 157 L1
Calderhaugh La LOCHW PA12 120 B7
Calderhead Rd SHOTTS ML7 137 K2
Calderigg Pl AIRDRIE ML6 111 K2
Calderpark Av LOCHW PA12 120 C6
UD/BTH/TAN G71 108 B7
Calderpark Crs
UD/BTH/TAN G71 108 B7
Calderpark St LOCHW PA12 120 C6
Calder Pl
BAIL/MDB/MHD G69 108 B5
KLMNK KA1 212 A4
Calder Rd BLSH ML4 133 J5
PSLYN/LNWD PA3 101 G4
SHOTTS ML7 160 F1
UD/BTH/TAN G71 131 J4
Calderside Gv EKILN G74 154 E5
Calderside Rd EKILN G74 172 D1
Calder St AIRDRIE ML6 111 J7
BLTYR/CAMB G72 155 K1
CTBR ML5 110 B5
GVH/MTFL G42 105 H7
LOCHW PA12 120 B6
Caldervale St AIRDRIE ML6 111 L5
Calder Vw HMLTN ML3 174 B1
MTHW ML1 157 M2
Calderview Av CTBR ML5 110 D6
Calderwood KLWNG KA13 193 L4
Calderwood Av
BAIL/MDB/MHD G69 108 A6
Calderwood Dr
BAIL/MDB/MHD G69 108 A6
BLTYR/CAMB G72 155 K3
Calderwood Gdns
BAIL/MDB/MHD G69 108 A6
EKILN G74 154 E5
Calderwood Rd EKILN G74 15 L3
PLKSW/MSWD G43 127 K3
RUTH G73 129 J2
Caldon Rd IRV KA12 203 K5
Caldwell Av KNTSWD G13 81 G3
PSLYN/LNWD PA3 100 A4
Caldwell Gv BLSH ML4 133 G1
Caldwell Qd MTHW ML1 157 J4
Caldwell Rd CARLUKE ML8 189 H1
WKIL KA23 181 J5
Caledonia Av GBLS G5 105 J6
RUTH G73 129 H1
Caledonia Ct KLMNK KA1 16 D3
PSLYN/LNWD PA3 101 K3
Caledonia Crs ARD KA22 191 J7
GRK PA19 31 M2
Caledonia Dr
BAIL/MDB/MHD G69 108 B6
MTHW ML1 134 E5
Caledonian Av BLSH ML4 132 F5
Caledonian Ct EKILN G74 14 F5
Caledonian Crs KVD/HLHD G12 4 B4
Caledonian Pl GLGNK KA14 167 H2
Caledonian Rd GLGNK KA14 167 J2
LRKH ML9 176 A6
SVSTN KA20 201 K2
WISHAW ML2 159 G7
Caledonia Rd ARD KA22 191 J7
AYRS KA7 19 K8
BEITH KA15 144 B8
GBLS G5 11 H7
SALT KA21 191 L8
SHOTTS ML7 137 L4
UD/BTH/TAN G71 108 A6
Caledonia St CLYDBK G81 59 L7
GBLS G5 105 K6
PGL PA14 34 D8
PSLYN/LNWD PA3 8 F1
Caledonia Ter DMBTN G82 36 C6
Caledonia Wy PSLYN/LNWD PA3 79 K8
Caledonia Wy East
PSLYN/LNWD PA3 79 L8
Caledonia Wy West
PSLYN/LNWD PA3 79 K8
Caledon La KVD/HLHD G12 82 C7
Caledon St KVD/HLHD G12 82 C6
Calfhill Rd PLK/PH/NH G53 103 H6
Calfmuir Rd KKNTL G66 66 A3
Calgary Pk EKILS G75 14 C5
Calgary St COWCAD G4 5 K7
Callaghan Wynd
BLTYR/CAMB G72 131 H8
Callander Ct BALLOCH G68 48 F5
Callander Rd AIRDRIE ML6 111 K8
BALLOCH G68 48 F5
PSTWK KA9 225 K4
Callander St MRYH/FIRH G20 4 F3
Callendar Pl AYR KA8 225 H5
Callieburn Rd BSHPBGS G64 84 A1
Callon St AIRDRIE ML6 111 G2
Cally Av DRUM G15 61 G6
Calside PSLYS PA2 9 G7
Calside Av PSLYS PA2 8 F7
Calvay Crs STPS/GTHM/RID G33 107 K2
Calvay Rd STPS/GTHM/RID G33 107 K2
Calvinston Rd PSTWK KA9 225 K3
Cambourne Rd
BAIL/MDB/MHD G69 66 F6
Cambridge Av CLYDBK G81 60 C7
GRK PA19 32 A3
Cambridge Rd
GRNKW/INVK PA16 31 K5
RNFRW PA4 80 C7
Cambridge St CGLW G2 5 G8
Camburn St CAR/SHTL G32 106 F4
Cambusdoon Dr AYRS KA7 228 E7
Cambusdoon Pl KLWNG KA13 193 J6
Cambusdoon Rd
STPS/GTHM/RID G33 85 J7
Cambuskeith Rd SVSTN KA20 192 E7
Cambuskenneth Gdns
CAR/SHTL G32 107 K4
Cambuslang Rd
BLTYR/CAMB G72 129 L1
CAR/SHTL G32 129 M1
RUTH G73 106 C8
Cambuslea Rd AYR KA8 225 H6
Cambusnethan St
WISHAW ML2 159 L5
Cambus Pl
STPS/GTHM/RID G33 85 J7
Camden St GBLS G5 11 J8
Camelon Crs BLTYR/CAMB G72 155 K2
Camelon St CAR/SHTL G32 106 F3
Cameron Av BSHPTN PA7 58 B6
Cameron Ct CLYDBK G81 80 C1
Cameron Crs
CRMNK/CLK/EAG G76 152 E2
HMLTN ML3 156 B6
Cameron Dr ALEX/LLW G83 25 K2
BSDN G61 62 A6
KLMNKN/STW KA3 207 J7
NMRNS G77 150 E2
UD/BTH/TAN G71 132 A1
Cameronian Ct
LNK/LMHG ML11 199 J4
Cameronian Dr
CARLUKE ML8 179 H8
Cameronian Pl BLSH ML4 132 F6
Cameron Rd AIRDRIE ML6 69 J7
CARLUKE ML8 189 H1
Cameron Sq CLYDBK G81 60 C3
Cameron St
CARD/HILL/MSPK G52 102 E2
CTBR ML5 110 B1
MTHW ML1 157 K3
Cameron Wy
BLTYR/CAMB G72 155 K1
Camlachie St DEN/PKHD G31 13 G5
DMNK/BRGTN G40 12 F4
Campbell Av BSHPTN PA7 58 B5
DMBTN G82 37 J5
MLNGV G62 42 A8
SALT KA21 200 E1
SVSTN KA20 192 D7
Campbell Ct AYR KA8 19 M3
GRNKW/INVK PA16 32 E2
NMLNS KA16 215 L2
Campbell Crs ALEX/LLW G83 25 K2
NMRNS G77 150 E3
UD/BTH/TAN G71 132 A5
Campbell Dr BRHD/NEIL G78 125 J7
BSDN G61 61 K4
DMBTN G82 37 J5
HBR/GL G84 23 G2
TROON KA10 216 D4
Campbell Pl BSHPBGS G64 44 B8
EKILS G75 14 E7
IRVSE KA11 209 G1
Campbell St ALEX/LLW G83 25 M5
AYR KA8 225 G6
BLSH ML4 133 H4
GRNKW/INVK PA16 32 D3
HBR/GL G84 20 C7
HMLTN ML3 156 E6
JNSTN PA5 99 M7
MRYH/FIRH G20 82 D2
NMLNS KA16 215 L2
RNFRW PA4 80 D5
WISHAW ML2 159 J6
Campbell Ter DMBTN G82 37 J5
Campbeltown Dr
KLMNKN/STW KA3 206 F6
Camperdown Ct HBR/GL G84 21 G7
Camphill PSLYS PA2 8 F6
Camphill Av KKNTL G66 65 J1
PLKSD/SHW G41 127 M1
Camphill Crs BSHPTN PA7 58 C6
Camphill Dr KBRN KA25 166 F2
Camphill Gdns BSHPTN PA7 58 C6
Camphill Pl AYRS KA7 229 H4
Campion Rd MTHW ML1 157 L1
Camp Rd BAIL/MDB/MHD G69 108 B4
MTHW ML1 157 L5
RUTH G73 105 M7
Camps Crs RNFRW PA4 80 E7
Campsie Av BRHD/NEIL G78 125 J8
IRVSE KA11 204 B6
Campsie Ct LRKH ML9 175 L4
Campsie Crs AIRDRIE ML6 110 F1
Campsie Dene Rd
CMPF/LLE G63 27 G5
Campsie Dr BSDN G61 61 K2
MLNGV G62 42 B7
PSLYN/LNWD PA3 79 L8
PSLYS PA2 124 D1
Campsie Gdns
CRMNK/CLK/EAG G76 151 J1
Campsie Pl BAIL/MDB/MHD G69 86 C1
Campsie Rd BSHPBGS G64 44 D7
EKILS G75 171 G6
KKNTL G66 45 G3
KLMNK KA1 212 A6
PGL PA14 55 G3
WISHAW ML2 158 E5
Campsie St SPRGB/BLRNK G21 83 M4
Campsie Vw
BAIL/MDB/MHD G69 86 C1
BAIL/MDB/MHD G69 108 F4
BLTYR/CAMB G72 130 E6
CUMB G67 48 F8
HMLTN ML3 155 M7
KKNTL G66 65 G1
STPS/GTHM/RID G33 85 K5
UD/BTH/TAN G71 132 A1
Campsie View Dr CMPF/LLE G63 27 H5
Campsie Wy IRVSE KA11 204 A7
Campston Pl
STPS/GTHM/RID G33 85 H8
Camp St MTHW ML1 157 L4
Camsail Av HBR/GL G84 20 B7
Camsbusmore Pl
STPS/GTHM/RID G33 85 J7
Camsdale Av SHOTTS ML7 113 H7
Camstradden Dr East BSDN G61 61 J5
Camstradden Dr West
BSDN G61 61 J5
Camus Pl DRUM G15 60 F5
Canal Av JNSTN PA5 100 A7
Canal Crs SVSTN KA20 201 K2
Canal La KKNTL G66 45 K8
Canal Pl SALT KA21 201 G2
Canal Rd JNSTN PA5 100 A7
Canal St COWCAD G4 5 K6
JNSTN PA5 100 A6
JNSTN PA5 100 D6
KKNTL G66 45 K8
PSLY PA1 8 E5
RNFRW PA4 80 D5
SALT KA21 201 G2
Canal Ter PSLY PA1 8 F5
Canberra Av CLYDBK G81 59 K5
Canberra Dr EKILS G75 14 B6
Cander Rigg BSHPBGS G64 64 A5
Candleriggs CGLE G1 11 L3
Candren Rd PSLYN/LNWD PA3 100 D3
PSLYN/LNWD PA3 101 G5
Candren Wy
PSLYN/LNWD PA3 101 G4
Caneluk Av CARLUKE ML8 179 H8
Canmore Crs GRNKW/INVK PA16 32 A5
Canmore Pl DEN/PKHD G31 13 L8
Canmore St DEN/PKHD G31 13 L8
Cannerton Crs KKNTL G66 45 H4
Cannerton Pk KKNTL G66 45 H5
Cannich Dr PSLYS PA2 102 B8
Cannich Pl WISHAW ML2 159 M3
Canniesburn Rd BSDN G61 61 J7
Canonbie St ESTRH G34 86 D8
Canon Ct MTHW ML1 134 D7
Canterbury EKILS G75 171 H2
Canthill Gdns SHOTTS ML7 136 F6
Cantieslaw Dr EKILN G74 154 A6
Canting Wy GOV/IBX G51 104 C2
Canyon Rd WISHAW ML2 158 D7
Capel Av NMRNS G77 150 F3
Capel Gv EKILN G74 154 B6
Capel Pl IRVSE KA11 204 B7
Capelrig Dr EKILN G74 154 B6
NMRNS G77 150 E1
Capelrig La NMRNS G77 150 D3
Capelrig Rd NMRNS G77 150 D1
Capelrig St GIF/THBK G46 126 F5
Caplaw Pl WISHAW ML2 176 F1
Caplaw Rd BRHD/NEIL G78 123 J7
PSLYS PA2 124 C3
Caplethill Rd PSLYS PA2 124 F3
Caponcraig Av SVSTN KA20 192 C8
Capper Vw PSTWK KA9 221 J7
Caprington Av KLMNK KA1 211 L6
Caprington St
STPS/GTHM/RID G33 85 G8
Captain St GRNK PA15 2 B5
Cara Dr GOV/IBX G51 103 L1
Carbarns WISHAW ML2 158 E8
Carbarns East WISHAW ML2 158 D8
Carbarns Rd WISHAW ML2 158 D8
Carbarns West WISHAW ML2 158 D8
Carberry Rd PLKSD/SHW G41 104 D7
Carbeth Rd MLNGV G62 41 M8
Carbeth St PPK/MIL G22 83 H5
Carbieston Av RAYR/DAL KA6 231 L5
Carbisdale St PPK/MIL G22 83 L4
Carbost St SMSTN G23 62 D8
Carbrook St PSLY PA1 8 C4
SPRGB/BLRNK G21 6 E7
Carcluie Crs AYRS KA7 229 H7
Cardarrach St
SPRGB/BLRNK G21 84 A5
Cardean Rd BLSH ML4 133 L3
Cardell Av PSLYS PA2 101 G7
Cardell Crs AIRDRIE ML6 111 K7
Cardell Dr PSLYS PA2 101 G6
Cardell Rd PSLYS PA2 101 G6
Cardonald Dr
CARD/HILL/MSPK G52 103 G5
Cardonald Gdns
CARD/HILL/MSPK G52 103 H5
Cardonald Place Rd
CARD/HILL/MSPK G52 103 H5
Cardowan Dr BALLOCH G68 47 K8
STPS/GTHM/RID G33 85 K4
Cardowan Pk UD/BTH/TAN G71 109 H8
Cardowan Rd CAR/SHTL G32 106 F3
STPS/GTHM/RID G33 85 L3
Cardow Crs IRVSE KA11 204 A3
Cardow Rd SPRGB/BLRNK G21 7 K1
Cardrona St
STPS/GTHM/RID G33 85 H6
Cardross Av PGL PA14 54 E1
Cardross Crs GRNK PA15 33 J7
Cardross Pl GRNK PA15 33 J7
Cardross Rd DMBTN G82 23 L8
DMBTN G82 25 H7
DMBTN G82 36 B5
HBR/GL G84 22 F1
Cardross St DEN/PKHD G31 12 D2
Cardwell Rd GRK PA19 31 M2
Cardwell St PLKSD/SHW G41 10 F8
Cardyke St SPRGB/BLRNK G21 6 F1
Careston Pl BSHPBGS G64 64 D8
Carey Gdns MTHW ML1 135 J8
Carey Rd SALT KA21 191 M6
Carfin Dr CARLUKE ML8 188 C7
Carfin Mill Rd MTHW ML1 134 C8
Carfin Rd MTHW ML1 134 D7
WISHAW ML2 158 C5
Carfin St CTBR ML5 110 B5
GVH/MTFL G42 105 H7
MTHW ML1 134 A6
Carfrae St KVGV G3 10 A1
Cargill Dr PSTWK KA9 225 K4
Cargill Sq BSHPBGS G64 84 B1
Carham Dr
CARD/HILL/MSPK G52 103 J4
Carillon Rd GOV/IBX G51 104 C4
Carisbrooke Crs
BSHPBGS G64 64 B5
Carlaverock Rd
PLKSW/MSWD G43 127 K3
Carleith Av CLYDBK G81 59 M3
Carleith Qd GOV/IBX G51 103 K2
Carleith Ter CLYDBK G81 59 M3
Carleston St SPRGB/BLRNK G21 83 M5
Carleton Ct GIF/THBK G46 127 J5
Carleton Dr GIF/THBK G46 127 J5
Carleton Gdns PSTWK KA9 225 J2
Carleton Ga GIF/THBK G46 127 J5
Carlibar Av KNTSWD G13 80 F3
Carlibar Dr BRHD/NEIL G78 125 J6
Carlibar Gdns
BRHD/NEIL G78 125 J6
Carlibar Rd BRHD/NEIL G78 125 H6
Carlile Pl PSLYN/LNWD PA3 9 H1
Carlisle Rd AIRDRIE ML6 111 J4
HMLTN ML3 157 G7
LRKH ML9 175 L3
MTHW ML1 135 H2
Carlisle St SPRGB/BLRNK G21 5 M1
Carlowrie Av BLTYR/CAMB G72 131 J7
Carlton Ct GBLS G5 11 G4
Carlton Pl GBLS G5 11 H4
Carlung Pl WKIL KA23 181 J6
Carlyle Av
CARD/HILL/MSPK G52 102 F1
Carlyle Dr EKILN G74 15 L1
Carmaben Rd
STPS/GTHM/RID G33 107 K1
Carman Rd DMBTN G82 25 K8
DMBTN G82 35 J1
Carmel Av KLMNK KA1 206 C7
Carmel Dr IRVSE KA11 205 G8
Carmel Pl KLMNK KA1 16 A2
KLMNKN/STW KA3 206 A2
Carmel Ter KLMNK KA1 16 A1
Carment Dr PLKSD/SHW G41 127 K1
SVSTN KA20 201 L2
Carmen Vw DMBTN G82 37 G3
Carmichael Ct
LNK/LMHG ML11 199 J5
Carmichael Pl GVH/MTFL G42 127 M2
Carmichael St CARLUKE ML8 177 M4
GOV/IBX G51 104 B3
GRNKW/INVK PA16 32 D3
Carmichael Wy
CARLUKE ML8 177 M4
Carmunnock By-Pass
CRMNK/CLK/EAG G76 152 C3
CSMK G45 152 B1
Carmunnock Rd
CRMNK/CLK/EAG G76 152 B3
CSMK G45 128 C8
EKILN G74 153 J6
LNPK/KPK G44 128 B2
Carmyle Av CAR/SHTL G32 107 H8
CAR/SHTL G32 130 B1
Carmyle Gdns CTBR ML5 109 L6
Carmyle Pl SVSTN KA20 201 K2
Carna Dr LNPK/KPK G44 128 C4
Carnalea Ct GLSTN KA4 214 C4
Carnarvon St KVGV G3 4 D6
Carnbroe Rd BLSH ML4 133 H1
CTBR ML5 110 D7
Carneddans Rd MLNGV G62 41 J5
Carnegie Hl EKILS G75 14 C6
Carnegie Pl EKILS G75 14 C6
Carnegie Rd
CARD/HILL/MSPK G52 103 G2
Carnell Crs PSTWK KA9 225 K2
Carnell Dr RAYR/DAL KA6 231 H5
Carnell Ter PSTWK KA9 225 K2
Carnoch St SMSTN G23 62 D8
Carnock Crs BRHD/NEIL G78 125 H8
Carnock Rd PLK/PH/NH G53 126 C1
Carnock St GRNK PA15 2 F6
Carnoustie Av GRK PA19 31 G3
Carnoustie Ct KLWNG KA13 193 H6
UD/BTH/TAN G71 131 M7
Carnoustie Crs BSHPBGS G64 64 C8
EKILS G75 171 G3
Carnoustie Pl BLSH ML4 133 G2
GBLS G5 10 D6
IRVSE KA11 208 E2
Carnoustie Wy BALLOCH G68 48 F3
Carntynehall Rd
CAR/SHTL G32 106 F2
Carntyne Pl CAR/SHTL G32 13 M2
Carntyne Rd CAR/SHTL G32 107 H2
DEN/PKHD G31 13 K3
Carnwadric Rd GIF/THBK G46 126 E5
Carnwath Av
PLKSW/MSWD G43 127 M3
Carnwath Rd CARLUKE ML8 178 F8
Caroline St DEN/PKHD G31 106 E4
Carolside Av
CRMNK/CLK/EAG G76 151 L2
Carolside Dr DRUM G15 61 H6
Carousel Crs WISHAW ML2 159 J6
Carradale Crs BALLOCH G68 67 M1
Carradale Dr PSTWK KA9 225 J4
Carradale Gdns CARLUKE ML8 189 G1
Carradale Pl PSLYN/LNWD PA3 100 A3
Carradale St CTBR ML5 109 M2
Carranbuie Rd CARLUKE ML8 178 F6
Carrbridge Dr
MRYH/FIRH G20 82 D3
Carresbrook Av KKNTL G66 66 A3
Carriagehill Av PSLYS PA2 9 G9
Carriagehill Dr PSLYS PA2 101 L8
Carrickarden Rd BSDN G61 61 M6
Carrick Av AYRS KA7 18 E7
SALT KA21 192 A6
Carrick Ct KKNTL G66 46 A7
Carrick Crs GIF/THBK G46 127 J8
Carrick Dr CAR/SHTL G32 107 L5
CTBR ML5 109 K2
IRV KA12 203 H4
RUTH G73 129 G4
Carrick Gdns AYRS KA7 18 F8
BLSH ML4 133 G1
BLTYR/CAMB G72 155 K3
CARLUKE ML8 189 G1
HMLTN ML3 155 L7
Carrick Gv CAR/SHTL G32 107 L5
Carrick Pk AYRS KA7 18 E7
Carrick Pl ARD KA22 191 J6
BLSH ML4 133 H1
CTBR ML5 87 L4
CTBR ML5 109 K2
LRKH ML9 176 B5
PSTWK KA9 225 H2
Carrick Rd AYRS KA7 18 F7
BSHPBGS G64 64 C8
BSHPTN PA7 58 B7
CUMB G67 49 G5
EKILN G74 153 M6
RUTH G73 128 F4
TROON KA10 216 D2
Carrick Road La AYRS KA7 18 F7
Carrickstone Rd BALLOCH G68 48 E5
Carrickstone Vw
BALLOCH G68 48 F4
Carrick St AYRS KA7 18 E4
KVGV G3 10 F3
LRKH ML9 176 C7
Carrick Ter DMBTN G82 36 B5
GRNKW/INVK PA16 31 K6
Carrick V MTHW ML1 135 J8
Carrick Vw CTBR ML5 87 L3
RAYR/DAL KA6 231 H4
Carrington St COWCAD G4 4 D5
Carrochan Crs ALEX/LLW G83 25 M1
Carrochan Rd ALEX/LLW G83 25 L1
Carroglen Gdns CAR/SHTL G32 107 K4
Carroglen Gv CAR/SHTL G32 107 K4
Carroll Crs MTHW ML1 134 C7
Carron Av KLMNK KA1 212 B4
Carron Ct HMLTN ML3 156 B8
Carron Crs BSDN G61 61 J6
BSHPBGS G64 64 B8
KKNTL G66 65 L5
SPRGB/BLRNK G21 83 K4
Carron Dr BSHPTN PA7 58 C7
Carron Pl CTBR ML5 87 K8
EKILS G75 171 M3
IRV KA12 203 J3
PPK/MIL G22 83 L4
Carron Rd WMYSB PA18 50 A8
Carron St PPK/MIL G22 83 L4
WISHAW ML2 159 H8
Carrour Gdns BSHPBGS G64 63 M7
Carruth Dr KLMCLM PA13 75 J1
Carruth Rd BRWEIR PA11 98 C1
Carsaig Dr
CARD/HILL/MSPK G52 103 L4
Carscallan Rd HMLTN ML3 174 D3
Carsegreen Av PSLYS PA2 124 B3
Carseloch Rd AYRS KA7 228 F8
Carseview Dr BSDN G61 62 A3
Carsewood Av HWWD PA9 121 M4
Carson Dr IRV KA12 208 C1
Carson Rd ALEX/LLW G83 25 L1
Carstairs St DMNK/BRGTN G40 106 A7
Carswell Gdns PLKSD/SHW G41 104 E7
Carswell Rd NMRNS G77 150 B4
Cartcraigs Rd
PLKSW/MSWD G43 127 H3
Carters Pl IRV KA12 203 J7
Cartha St PLKSW/MSWD G43 127 K2
Cartland Av CARLUKE ML8 188 F1
Cartland Rd LNK/LMHG ML11 198 C1
Cartland Vw LNK/LMHG ML11 198 F4
Cart La PSLYN/LNWD PA3 9 H1
Cartsbridge Rd
CRMNK/CLK/EAG G76 151 L3
Cartsburn St GRNK PA15 2 F7
Cartsdyke Av GRNK PA15 3 J5
Cartside Av JNSTN PA5 99 K8
RNFRW PA4 79 H5
Cartside Dr
CRMNK/CLK/EAG G76 152 A3
Cartside Pl
CRMNK/CLK/EAG G76 151 M4
Cartside Qd PLKSW/MSWD G43 128 A2
Cartside Rd
CRMNK/CLK/EAG G76 151 M4
Cartside St GVH/MTFL G42 127 M2
Cart St CLYDBK G81 80 B1
Cartvale La PSLYN/LNWD PA3 101 L3
Cartvale Rd GVH/MTFL G42 127 M2
Cartview Ct
CRMNK/CLK/EAG G76 151 M3
Carvale Av SHOTTS ML7 113 J7
Carwinshoch Vw AYRS KA7 228 D4
Carwood St GRNK PA15 3 K7
Caskie Dr BLTYR/CAMB G72 131 L8
SKLM PA17 70 B6
Cassels Gv MTHW ML1 133 J8
Cassels St CARLUKE ML8 178 F7
MTHW ML1 157 L1
Cassillis St AYRS KA7 18 D3
Cassiltoun Gdns CSMK G45 128 D7
Cassley Av RNFRW PA4 80 F7
Castburn Rd CUMB G67 49 M3
Castle Av HBR/GL G84 20 A7
JNSTN PA5 100 B8
MTHW ML1 134 B3
SVSTN KA20 192 E6
UD/BTH/TAN G71 131 L6
Castlebank Ct KNTSWD G13 81 L3
Castlebank Crs PTCK G11 82 A8
Castlebank Gdns KNTSWD G13 81 L3
Castlebank St PTCK G11 81 M8
Castlebank Vls KNTSWD G13 81 L3
Castlebay Dr PPK/MIL G22 63 J8
Castlebay Pl PPK/MIL G22 83 J1
Castlebay St PPK/MIL G22 83 J1
Castlebrae DMBTN G82 36 C4
Castlecary Rd CUMB G67 49 K2
Castle Chimmins Av
BLTYR/CAMB G72 130 D5
Castle Chimmins Rd
BLTYR/CAMB G72 130 D6
Castle Ct CUMB G67 49 M1
KKNTL G66 65 K1
Castle Crs BSHPTN PA7 58 B7
Castlecroft Gdns
UD/BTH/TAN G71 131 M4
Castle Dr KBRN KA25 143 G8
KLMNKN/STW KA3 207 G5
MTHW ML1 134 B3
RAYR/DAL KA6 231 H3
WKIL KA23 181 K4
Castlefern Rd RUTH G73 129 G6
Castlefield Gdns EKILS G75 171 H4
Castle Gait PSLY PA1 9 G6
Castle Gdns
BAIL/MDB/MHD G69 66 F7
PSLYS PA2 101 G6
Castlegate LNK/LMHG ML11 198 F6
Castle Ga NMRNS G77 151 G6
UD/BTH/TAN G71 131 L4
Castleglen Rd EKILN G74 152 F5
Castlegreen Crs DMBTN G82 37 H7
Castlegreen St DMBTN G82 37 G7
Castle Gv KBRN KA25 143 G8
Castlehill Av PGL PA14 55 G1
Castlehill Crs AIRDRIE ML6 111 M8
AYRS KA7 19 H8
CARLUKE ML8 178 A5
HMLTN ML3 157 K8

KLMCLM PA13 55 H8 1
RNFRW PA4 80 D5
Castlehill Dr LARGS KA30 115 K6
NMRNS G77 150 F5
Castlehill Gdns HMLTN ML3 156 F7 1
Castlehill Gn EKILN G74 152 F5 1
Castlehill Qd DMBTN G82 36 C4 1
Castlehill Rd AYRS KA7 19 H7
BSDN G61 61 H3
CARLUKE ML8 178 E4
DMBTN G82 36 C4
KLMCLM PA13 75 J1
WISHAW ML2 158 F8
Castle Keep Gdns IRVSE KA11 203 M5
Castlelaw Gdns
CAR/SHTL G32 107 H3 1
Castlelaw St CAR/SHTL G32 107 H3 2
Castle Mains Rd MLNGV G62 41 K7
Castlemilk Crs LNPK/KPK G44 128 E4
Castlemilk Dr CSMK G45 128 E6
Castlemilk Rd LNPK/KPK G44 128 E2
RUTH G73 128 F4 3
Castlemount Av NMRNS G77 150 F6 1
Castle Park Dr FAIRLIE KA29 139 L6
Castle Park Gdns FAIRLIE KA29 139 L6
Castle Qd AIRDRIE ML6 111 K2 1
Castle Rd AIRDRIE ML6 111 K1
ARD KA22 191 K6
BRWEIR PA11 76 D8
DMBTN G82 37 G8
GRNK PA15 3 J9
JNSTN PA5 100 C6 1
NMRNS G77 150 C5
PGL PA14 34 D8
WMYSB PA18 50 A8
Castle St AIRDRIE ML6 111 J7
BAIL/MDB/MHD G69 107 M6
CLYDBK G81 59 L6
COWCAD G4 6 B7
DMBTN G82 36 F6
HMLTN ML3 156 F5
IRV KA12 203 H6
NMLNS KA16 215 K2 2
PSLY PA1 8 D4
PTCK G11 82 C8
RUTH G73 129 G1 1
Castle Ter CRH/DND KA2 205 M6
Castleton Av NMRNS G77 150 F6
SPRGB/BLRNK G21 83 L2 1
Castleton Crs NMRNS G77 150 F6
Castleton Dr NMRNS G77 150 F6
Castleton Gv NMRNS G77 150 F6
Castleview BALLOCH G68 49 L1
CRH/DND KA2 209 L6
KKNTL G66 28 F6
Castle Vw KKNTL G66 29 G8
WISHAW ML2 160 A3
WKIL KA23 181 K3
Castleview Av GLSTN KA4 214 D3
PSLYS PA2 124 A2
Castleview Dr PSLYS PA2 124 A2
Castle Wk AYRS KA7 228 C6
FAIRLIE KA29 139 L6
Castle Wy CUMB G67 49 J6
Castle Wynd HMLTN ML3 174 E6
UD/BTH/TAN G71 132 B7
Catacol Av SALT KA21 191 M7
Cathay St PPK/MIL G22 83 J1
Cathburn Rd WISHAW ML2 160 C5
Cathcart Crs PSLYS PA2 9 L7
Cathcart Pl RUTH G73 128 F2
Cathcart Rd GBLS G5 11 H7
GVH/MTFL G42 105 H7 1
GVH/MTFL G42 128 B2 2
LARGS KA30 115 K7
LNPK/KPK G44 128 B2
RUTH G73 128 F2 3
Cathcart Sq GRNK PA15 2 E4 1
Cathcart St AYRS KA7 18 E2
GRNK PA15 2 E4
Cathedral Sq COWCAD G4 12 A1 1
Cathedral St CGLE G1 5 K9
Catherine Dr GLSTN KA4 214 A4
Catherine St MTHW ML1 157 L5
Catherine Wy MTHW ML1 133 M6
Cathkin Av BLTYR/CAMB G72 129 L3
RUTH G73 129 J2 1
Cathkin By-Pass RUTH G73 129 K6
Cathkin Crs BALLOCH G68 48 E4
Cathkin Dr
CRMNK/CLK/EAG G76 151 J1
Cathkin Pl BLTYR/CAMB G72 129 L3 1
KLWNG KA13 193 H5
Cathkin Rd
CRMNK/CLK/EAG G76 152 E1
GVH/MTFL G42 127 M2
UD/BTH/TAN G71 108 E8 1
Cathkinview Pl
GVH/MTFL G42 128 B2 3
Cathkinview Rd GVH/MTFL G42 128 A2
Catrine EKILN G74 14 C1
Catrine Ct PLK/PH/NH G53 126 A1 1
Catrine Crs MTHW ML1 158 A5
Catrine Gdns PLK/PH/NH G53 126 A1
Catrine Pl PLK/PH/NH G53 126 A1 2
Catrine Rd PLK/PH/NH G53 126 A1
Catrine St LRKH ML9 176 C7 2
Cauldstream Pl MLNGV G62 41 L8 2
Causewayside Crs
CAR/SHTL G32 107 G6 1
Causewayside St
CAR/SHTL G32 107 G7
The Causeway FAIRLIE KA29 139 K6
Causeyfoot Dr KBRN KA25 143 G8
Causeyside St PSLY PA1 9 H4 1
PSLYS PA2 9 H6
Cavendish Dr NMRNS G77 150 F3
Cavendish La TROON KA10 216 D7
Cavendish Pl GBLS G5 11 G7
TROON KA10 216 D7
Cavendish St GBLS G5 11 G7
Cavin Dr CSMK G45 128 E5
Cavin Rd CSMK G45 128 E5
Cawder Ct BALLOCH G68 48 D4 1
Cawder Pl BALLOCH G68 48 E4
Cawder Rd BALLOCH G68 48 E4
Cawder Vw BALLOCH G68 48 E4 1
Cawder Wy BALLOCH G68 48 E4
Cawdor Crs BSHPTN PA7 58 B7
GRNKW/INVK PA16 32 A5 1
Cawdor Pl GRNKW/INVK PA16 32 A5 2
Cawdor Wy EKILN G74 153 K6 2
Cayton Gdns
BAIL/MDB/MHD G69 107 M5 2
Cecil St CRMNK/CLK/EAG G76 151 L2
CTBR ML5 110 A4
KVD/HLHD G12 82 D6
Cedar Av BEITH KA15 168 A1
CLYDBK G81 59 K5
JNSTN PA5 122 F1
UD/BTH/TAN G71 132 B1 1
Cedar Ct BLTYR/CAMB G72 130 E5
EKILS G75 171 J4
KLBCH PA10 99 G6
MRYH/FIRH G20 4 F4
Cedar Crs GRNK PA15 33 L7
HMLTN ML3 156 E8
Cedar Dr EKILS G75 171 J4
KKNTL G66 45 J4
KKNTL G66 65 J4
UD/BTH/TAN G71 132 D1
Cedar Gdns CARLUKE ML8 177 M3
MTHW ML1 134 C5
RUTH G73 129 J6
Cedar Gv DMBTN G82 35 H2
Cedar La MTHW ML1 134 B4
Cedar Pl BLTYR/CAMB G72 131 J8 5
EKILS G75 171 J4
GRK PA19 31 K3 2
Cedar Rd AYRS KA7 229 K5
BSHPBGS G64 84 B1
CUMB G67 49 K6
IRV KA12 203 K5 1
KLMNK KA1 16 A5
Cedar St MRYH/FIRH G20 4 F4
Cedarwood Av NMRNS G77 150 F4 1
Cedarwood Rd NMRNS G77 150 F5
Cedric Pl KNTSWD G13 81 K2 1
Cedric Rd KNTSWD G13 81 K2
Celtic St MRYH/FIRH G20 82 C2
Cemetery Rd BLTYR/CAMB G72 155 J3
CARD/HILL/MSPK G52 103 L5 1
GLSTN KA4 214 C4
Centenary Av AIRDRIE ML6 110 D2
Centenary Ct CLYDBK G81 60 B8
Centenary Gdns CTBR ML5 110 A4 1
HMLTN ML3 156 E7 2
Centenary Pl ARD KA22 191 K6 2
Centenary Qd MTHW ML1 134 A4 4
Central Av ARD KA22 191 K6 3
BLTYR/CAMB G72 129 M3
BLTYR/CAMB G72 155 L4
CAR/SHTL G32 107 K6
KBRN KA25 167 G2
KLMNK KA1 211 M6
MTHW ML1 133 M4 2
MTHW ML1 134 A7
PTCK G11 81 M7 4
TROON KA10 216 F5
UD/BTH/TAN G71 132 C3
Central Gv CAR/SHTL G32 107 K5
Central Pth CAR/SHTL G32 107 L6
Central Qd ARD KA22 191 J6 2
Central Rd PSLY PA1 9 H3 1
Central Wy CUMB G67 48 F7
PSLY PA1 9 H3
Centre St AIRDRIE ML6 111 J7
CTBR ML5 87 J3
GBLS G5 11 G4
Centre Wy BRHD/NEIL G78 125 H6
Ceres Gdns BSHPBGS G64 64 D8
Cessnock Av KLMNK KA1 212 F4
Cessnock Dr KLMNK KA1 212 F3
Cessnock Pl AYRS KA7 19 L8
GLSTN KA4 214 C4
Cessnock Rd GLSTN KA4 214 D4
KLMNK KA1 212 F3
STPS/GTHM/RID G33 85 G4
TROON KA10 216 D6 1
Cessnock St GOV/IBX G51 104 C4
Cessock Pl KLMNK KA1 212 B4
Chalmers Av AYRS KA7 19 G9
Chalmers Crs EKILS G75 15 G8
Chalmers Dr EKILS G75 15 H7
Chalmers Ga DMNK/BRGTN G40 12 B4
Chalmers Rd AYRS KA7 19 G8
Chalmers St CLYDBK G81 60 B8
DMNK/BRGTN G40 12 B4
GRK PA19 31 M2 3
Chamberlain La KNTSWD G13 81 L4 4
Chamberlain Rd KNTSWD G13 81 L3 4
Chancellor St PTCK G11 82 B7 4
Chantinghall Rd HMLTN ML3 156 B6
Chantinghall Ter HMLTN ML3 156 B6 2
Chapelacre Gv HBR/GL G84 20 E6
Chapel Ct RUTH G73 128 F1 2
Chapel Crs HMLTN ML3 174 D3 1
Chapelcross Av AIRDRIE ML6 89 G8 1
Chapelhill Mt ARD KA22 191 J4
Chapelhill Rd PSLYS PA2 9 M8
PSLYS PA2 102 B8 1
Chapelknowe Rd MTHW ML1 134 D8
Chapel La GLSTN KA4 214 B3
Chapelpark Rd AYRS KA7 228 F4
Chapel Pl BRHD/NEIL G78 148 D2 3
Chapel Rd CLYDBK G81 60 A3
CRG/CRSL/HOU PA6 77 H6
WISHAW ML2 160 B8
Chapelside Av AIRDRIE ML6 111 G1
Chapelside Rd EKILN G74 154 A3
Chapel St AIRDRIE ML6 111 G1
CARLUKE ML8 178 F7 2
GRK PA19 31 M2 4
GRNK PA15 2 F5
HMLTN ML3 156 E6
KKNTL G66 44 D1
MRYH/FIRH G20 82 E4
MTHW ML1 135 H8
RUTH G73 128 F1
Chapelton Av BSDN G61 61 M5
DMBTN G82 37 G4
Chapelton Dr LARGS KA30 115 K3
Chapelton Gdns BSDN G61 61 M5
DMBTN G82 37 G4
Chapelton La WKIL KA23 181 J6
Chapelton Rd CUMB G67 68 D3
WKIL KA23 181 K7
Chapelton St PGL PA14 34 A7 1
PPK/MIL G22 83 J3
Chapelton Wy LARGS KA30 115 K3
Chapeltoun Ter
KLMNKN/STW KA3 196 F5
Chapelwell St SALT KA21 200 F2 2
Chapland Rd LNK/LMHG ML11 199 G4
Chaplet Av KNTSWD G13 81 J1
Chapman Av CTBR ML5 87 J3
Chapmans Ter KLMNK KA1 17 J6
Chapman St GVH/MTFL G42 105 G7 2
Chappell St BRHD/NEIL G78 125 H6 1
Charing Cross La KVGV G3 4 D8 1
Charles Av PSTWK KA9 221 K4
RNFRW PA4 80 D5
Charles Crs CARLUKE ML8 179 H8
KKNTL G66 65 K6
Charles Dr TROON KA10 216 F6
Charleson Rw KSYTH G65 47 M6
Charles Pl GRNK PA15 2 C3 1
KLMNK KA1 16 D5
Charles Qd MTHW ML1 134 A4
Charles St KLMNK KA1 16 D5
LARGS KA30 115 J7
SPRGB/BLRNK G21 6 C6
WISHAW ML2 158 C5
Charlotte Av BSHPBGS G64 64 B1
Charlotte Pl PSLYS PA2 9 G8 1
Charlotte St AYRS KA7 18 C3
CGLE G1 11 M4
DMBTN G82 36 D5
HBR/GL G84 20 E7
Charlotte Street La AYRS KA7 18 C3
Charnwood Av JNSTN PA5 122 D1 1
Chassels St CTBR ML5 110 A1
Chateau Gv HMLTN ML3 157 G7 3
Chatelherault Av
BLTYR/CAMB G72 129 L4 3
Chatelherault Crs HMLTN ML3 174 E1
Chatham EKILS G75 14 A8
Chatton St SMSTN G23 62 D8
Cheapside St KVGV G3 10 D2
Chelmsford Dr KVD/HLHD G12 82 B4
Cherry Bank KKNTL G66 65 H4 3
Cherrybank Rd
PLKSW/MSWD G43 127 M4
Cherrybank Wk CTBR ML5 110 D1
Cherry Crs CLYDBK G81 60 A5
Cherry Gdns IRV KA12 203 L4
Cherry Hill Rd AYRS KA7 229 H7
Cherryhill Vw LRKH ML9 175 M7
Cherry Pl BSHPBGS G64 84 B1
JNSTN PA5 100 A8
KKNTL G66 45 H4
MTHW ML1 134 B4 1
MTHW ML1 134 B5 1
UD/BTH/TAN G71 132 D1
Cherry Rd KLMNK KA1 211 J2
Cherrytree Crs LRKH ML9 176 A4
Cherrytree Dr
BLTYR/CAMB G72 130 E5 1
Cherry Wk MTHW ML1 157 L6 1
Cherrywood Dr BEITH KA15 144 C7
Cherrywood Rd JNSTN PA5 100 C6 2
Chesterfield Av KVD/HLHD G12 82 A4
Chester Rd GRNKW/INVK PA16 31 L5
Chesters Crs MTHW ML1 157 J1
Chesters Pl RUTH G73 129 G2 4
Chesters Rd BSDN G61 61 J5
Chester St CAR/SHTL G32 107 G4 3
Chestnut Av BEITH KA15 168 A1
BSHPTN PA7 57 M4
CUMB G67 49 L4
Chestnut Ct CUMB G67 49 L4 1
KKNTL G66 45 H4
Chestnut Crs EKILS G75 171 J3
HMLTN ML3 156 E7
UD/BTH/TAN G71 132 C2
Chestnut Dr CLYDBK G81 60 A4
KKNTL G66 65 H3 1
Chestnut Gv BLTYR/CAMB G72 155 J1
CARLUKE ML8 178 E8 1
CTBR ML5 87 J3
LRKH ML9 176 A4
MTHW ML1 157 K5
RAYR/DAL KA6 231 H5 5
Chestnut La MLNGV G62 41 L8
Chestnut Pl CUMB G67 49 L4 2
JNSTN PA5 123 G1
KLMNK KA1 16 A5
Chestnut Rd AYRS KA7 229 K3
Chestnut St PPK/MIL G22 83 K4
Chestnut Wy HMLTN ML3 174 F5 1
Cheviot Av BRHD/NEIL G78 125 J7
Cheviot Crs EKILS G75 171 G5
WISHAW ML2 158 F6
Cheviot Dr NMRNS G77 150 C6
Cheviot Head IRVSE KA11 203 M6 1
Cheviot Pl KLMNK KA1 212 A6 1
Cheviot Rd HMLTN ML3 156 F7
LRKH ML9 176 C7 3
PLKSW/MSWD G43 127 J4
PSLYS PA2 101 L8 1
Cheviot St BLTYR/CAMB G72 155 J2
Cheviot Wy IRVSE KA11 204 A6
Chillin Pl LRKH ML9 176 C7 4
Chirmorie Pl PLK/PH/NH G53 103 G8
Chirnside Pl
CARD/HILL/MSPK G52 103 G3
Chirnside Rd
CARD/HILL/MSPK G52 103 G3
Chisholm Av BSHPTN PA7 58 C6
Chisholm Dr NMRNS G77 150 E3
Chisholm Pl MTHW ML1 158 B7
Chisholm St CTBR ML5 110 B1
Chisolm St CGLE G1 11 L3 1
Chrighton Gn
UD/BTH/TAN G71 132 A1 3
Chriss Av HMLTN ML3 174 D2 3
Christchurch Pl EKILS G75 171 H2 1
Christian St PLKSW/MSWD G43 127 J1
Christie Gdns SALT KA21 200 F1
Christie La PSLY PA1 9 H2
Christie St BLSH ML4 133 K5
PSLY PA1 9 K3
Christopher St SPRGB/BLRNK G21 6 E6
Chromars Pl GRNK PA15 2 A7
Chryston Rd
BAIL/MDB/MHD G69 86 D1
KKNTL G66 66 C3
Chuckie La JNSTN PA5 99 J3
Church Av DMBTN G82 35 G1
RUTH G73 129 J4 3
STPS/GTHM/RID G33 85 K3 2
WISHAW ML2 159 M5
Church Ct DMBTN G82 36 F6 1
Church Crs AIRDRIE ML6 89 L8
Church Dr RAYR/DAL KA6 227 H4
Church Hl PSLY PA1 9 G3
Church Hill St GTCI KA28 138 A7 1
Churchill Av EKILN G74 15 G3
JNSTN PA5 122 C1
KLWNG KA13 193 M5
Churchill Crs AYR KA8 19 M3
UD/BTH/TAN G71 132 B6
Churchill Dr ARD KA22 191 J5
BSHPTN PA7 58 B6
PTCK G11 82 A6
Churchill Pl KLBCH PA10 99 G7
Churchill Rd KLMCLM PA13 75 J2
Churchill Sq HBR/GL G84 21 G7 2
Church La CTBR ML5 110 A2
GLSTN KA4 214 C3 1
KLMNK KA1 211 M4
Church Manse La BRWEIR PA11 98 D1
Church Pl AIRDRIE ML6 90 F5 1
ARD KA22 191 J8 4
Church Rd BAIL/MDB/MHD G69 86 C2
BRWEIR PA11 75 L6
BRWEIR PA11 98 E2
CRMNK/CLK/EAG G76 151 M3
GIF/THBK G46 127 J7
WISHAW ML2 160 D3
Church St ALEX/LLW G83 25 L5
BAIL/MDB/MHD G69 108 C5
BLTYR/CAMB G72 155 L2
CLYDBK G81 60 A6
CTBR ML5 110 A2
DMBTN G82 36 F5 1
GRK PA19 31 L1 3
HMLTN ML3 156 E5
IRV KA12 203 H7 1
JNSTN PA5 99 M6
KLBCH PA10 99 G6
KLMNKN/STW KA3 16 F3
KLWNG KA13 193 L6
KSYTH G65 47 K1
LARGS KA30 115 J6
LOCHW PA12 120 C7
LRKH ML9 176 A6
MTHW ML1 134 F5 1
PGL PA14 34 C7
PTCK G11 82 C8
TROON KA10 216 C6
UD/BTH/TAN G71 131 L4
Church Vw BLTYR/CAMB G72 130 A2 1
CTBR ML5 110 A2 1
Church View Gdns BLSH ML4 133 G4
Circus Dr DEN/PKHD G31 12 D1
Circus Pl DEN/PKHD G31 12 D1
Circus Place La DEN/PKHD G31 6 D9
Citadel Pl AYRS KA7 18 D2
MTHW ML1 157 J1 1
Citizen La CGLE G1 11 J1
Citrus Crs UD/BTH/TAN G71 132 C1
Cityford Dr RUTH G73 128 F3
Civic St COWCAD G4 5 G6
Civic Wy KKNTL G66 65 J2
Clachan Dr GOV/IBX G51 103 L1 3
The Clachan WISHAW ML2 159 H6 1
Claddens Pl KKNTL G66 65 M5 1
Claddens Qd PPK/MIL G22 83 J3
Claddens St PPK/MIL G22 83 H3
Cladence Gv EKILS G75 171 M4
Claire St WISHAW ML2 159 M4
Clairinch Gdns RNFRW PA4 80 C8 1
Clairmont Gdns KVGV G3 4 C7
Clair Rd BSHPBGS G64 64 D8
Clamp Rd WISHAW ML2 158 C5
Clamps Gv EKILN G74 15 K6
Clamps Ter EKILN G74 15 L6
Clamps Wd EKILS G75 15 K6
Clanrye Dr CTBR ML5 110 A5
Clapperhow Rd MTHW ML1 134 A8
Claremont Av KKNTL G66 45 H8
Claremont Crs KLWNG KA13 193 K5
Claremont Dr MLNGV G62 42 A7
Claremont Gdns MLNGV G62 42 A8 2
Claremont Pas KVGV G3 4 C7 1
Claremont Pl KVGV G3 4 C7 2
Claremont St KVGV G3 4 B8
Claremont Ter KVGV G3 4 B7
Claremount Av GIF/THBK G46 127 J7
Claremount Terrace La KVGV G3 4 B7
Clarence Dr PSLY PA1 9 M4
PTCK G11 82 A6
Clarence Gdns PTCK G11 82 A6
Clarence La PTCK G11 82 B6 1
Clarence St CLYDBK G81 60 C7
GRNKW/INVK PA16 2 C1
PSLY PA1 9 L3
Clarendon Pl AYRS KA7 19 L9 1
COWCAD G4 4 E5
Clarendon Rd WISHAW ML2 158 E8
Clarendon St MRYH/FIRH G20 4 E5
Clare St SPRGB/BLRNK G21 6 E6
Clarinda Crs KKNTL G66 46 A7
Clarinda Pl MTHW ML1 134 C6
Clarion Crs KNTSWD G13 81 G1
Clarion Rd KNTSWD G13 81 G2
Clark Crs SVSTN KA20 201 K2
Clark Dr IRV KA12 203 K7
Clarke Av AYRS KA7 18 C8
Clark Pl NMRNS G77 150 B5
SALT KA21 192 A7 2
Clarkston Av LNPK/KPK G44 127 M5
Clarkston Dr AIRDRIE ML6 111 K2
Clarkston Rd
CRMNK/CLK/EAG G76 151 L1
LNPK/KPK G44 127 M4
Clark St AIRDRIE ML6 111 H2
CLYDBK G81 59 M5
JNSTN PA5 99 M6
KLMNK KA1 16 F5
PSLYN/LNWD PA3 101 J3
RNFRW PA4 80 B6
WISHAW ML2 159 M3
Clarkwell Rd HMLTN ML3 155 L6
Clarkwell Ter HMLTN ML3 155 M6
Clathic Av BSDN G61 62 A6
Claude Av BLTYR/CAMB G72 130 E6
Claude St LRKH ML9 176 A6
Claud Rd PSLYN/LNWD PA3 102 A3
Clavens Rd
CARD/HILL/MSPK G52 102 E3
Claverhouse Pl PSLYS PA2 9 M7
Claverhouse Rd
CARD/HILL/MSPK G52 102 F2
Clavering St East PSLY PA1 8 D3
Clavering St West PSLY PA1 8 D4
Clay Crs BLSH ML4 133 H2
Clayhouse Rd
STPS/GTHM/RID G33 85 L5
Claymore Dr
CRG/CRSL/HOU PA6 99 K1
Claypotts Pl
STPS/GTHM/RID G33 85 G8 2
Claypotts Rd
STPS/GTHM/RID G33 85 G8 3
Clay Rd BLSH ML4 133 J2
Clayslaps Rd KVGV G3 82 D8 2
Clayslaps Vw KLMNK KA1 212 B5
Claythorn Av DMNK/BRGTN G40 12 A5
Claythorn Circ
DMNK/BRGTN G40 12 A5
Claythorn Pk DMNK/BRGTN G40 12 A5
Claythorn Ter DMNK/BRGTN G40 12 B4
Clayton Av IRV KA12 203 J5
Clayton Ter DEN/PKHD G31 12 D1
Clearfield Av HMLTN ML3 156 B5
Clearmount Av NMLNS KA16 215 J2
Cleddans Crs CLYDBK G81 60 C3
Cleddans Rd CLYDBK G81 60 C4
KKNTL G66 45 L8 2
Cleddans Vw AIRDRIE ML6 88 E5
Cleddens Ct BSHPBGS G64 64 A8 1
Cleeves Av DALRY KA24 184 D3
Cleeves Qd PLK/PH/NH G53 126 A4
Cleeves Rd PLK/PH/NH G53 126 A4
Cleghorn Av LNK/LMHG ML11 199 H4
Cleghorn Rd LNK/LMHG ML11 199 G4
Cleghorn St PPK/MIL G22 5 G2
Cleish Av BSDN G61 61 J1
Cleland La GBLS G5 11 H6
Cleland Pl EKILN G74 154 A6
Cleland Rd MTHW ML1 134 C8 1
WISHAW ML2 159 G6
Cleland St GBLS G5 11 J6
Clelland Av BSHPBGS G64 84 A1
Clem Attlee Gdns LRKH ML9 176 B7
Clements Pl SVSTN KA20 192 E7 3
Clerwood St CAR/SHTL G32 13 M3
Cleuch Gdns
CRMNK/CLK/EAG G76 151 K1
Clevans Rd BRWEIR PA11 98 B2
Cleveden Crs KVD/HLHD G12 82 B4
Cleveden Crescent La
KVD/HLHD G12 82 B4
Cleveden Dr KVD/HLHD G12 82 B4
RUTH G73 129 J3
Cleveden Drive La
KVD/HLHD G12 82 C5
Cleveden Gdns KVD/HLHD G12 82 C4
Cleveden La KVD/HLHD G12 82 B3 2
Cleveden Pl KVD/HLHD G12 82 B3
Cleveden Rd KVD/HLHD G12 82 B3
Cleveland La CGLW G2 4 D8
Cleveland St KVGV G3 4 D8
Clifford Gdns GOV/IBX G51 104 B4
Clifford La GOV/IBX G51 104 D4 1
Clifford Pl GOV/IBX G51 104 D4 2
Clifford St GOV/IBX G51 104 B4
Cliff Rd KVGV G3 4 C6
Cliff Terrace Rd WMYSB PA18 70 A1
Clifton Pl CTBR ML5 110 C3
KVGV G3 4 B8
Clifton Rd GIF/THBK G46 127 H6
Clifton St GTCI KA28 138 A6
KVGV G3 4 B7
Clifton Ter BLTYR/CAMB G72 129 L6
Climie Pl KLMNKN/STW KA3 17 J4
Clincarthill Rd RUTH G73 129 G2 5
RUTH G73 129 H2 2
Clincart Rd GVH/MTFL G42 128 B1 3
Clinchyard Pl GLSTN KA4 214 A4
Clippens Rd CRG/CRSL/HOU PA6 99 L1
PSLYN/LNWD PA3 100 A4
Clive St SHOTTS ML7 137 L4
Cloak Rd PGL PA14 55 H4
Cloan Av DRUM G15 61 H7
Cloan Crs BSHPBGS G64 64 B5
Clober Farm La MLNGV G62 41 L6 1
Cloberfield MLNGV G62 41 M5
Cloberfield Gdns MLNGV G62 41 M6 2
Cloberhill Rd KNTSWD G13 61 J8
Clober Rd MLNGV G62 42 A7
Clochbar Av MLNGV G62 41 M6 3
Clochbar Gdns MLNGV G62 41 M7
Cloch Brae GRK PA19 31 G3
Clochoderick Av KLBCH PA10 99 H7 1
Clochranhill Rd AYRS KA7 228 F7
Cloch Rd GRK PA19 30 F3
Cloch St STPS/GTHM/RID G33 107 G1 1
Clockerhill Pl MTHW ML1 134 E5 2
Clockston Pl GLSTN KA4 214 D4
Clockston Rd GLSTN KA4 214 D5
Cloister Av AIRDRIE ML6 111 J5
Clonbeith St
STPS/GTHM/RID G33 85 L7 1
Closeburn St PPK/MIL G22 83 J4
Cloth St BRHD/NEIL G78 125 J7 2
Clouden Rd CUMB G67 49 H7
Cloudhowe Ter
BLTYR/CAMB G72 131 J8 6
Clouston La MRYH/FIRH G20 4 A1
Clouston St MRYH/FIRH G20 82 D5
Clova Pl UD/BTH/TAN G71 131 M3
Clova St GIF/THBK G46 126 F5
Clove Mill Wynd LRKH ML9 175 L7
Cloverbank St SPRGB/BLRNK G21 6 F6
Clovergate BSHPBGS G64 63 L8
Cloverhill AYRS KA7 229 K3

Cloverhill Pl
BAIL/MDB/MHD G69 ... 86 C1 1
Cloverhill Ter EKILN G74 ... 14 E3
Cloverhill Vw EKILN G74 ... 14 D3
Clover Leaf Pth ALEX/LLW G83 ... 25 L5
Cluanie Av SHOTTS ML7 ... 137 L3 2
Clune Brae PGL PA14 ... 34 E8
Clune Dr PSTWK KA9 ... 225 K1
Clune Park St PGL PA14 ... 34 E8 1
Clunie Pl CTBR ML5 ... 110 B6
WISHAW ML2 ... 159 M3
Clunie Rd
CARD/HILL/MSPK G52 ... 103 L5
Cluny Av BSDN G61 ... 62 A7
CLYDBK G81 ... 60 C2 1
Cluny Dr BSDN G61 ... 62 A7
NMRNS G77 ... 150 B4
PSLYN/LNWD PA3 ... 102 A3
Cluny Gdns
BAIL/MDB/MHD G69 ... 108 A5
SCOT G14 ... 81 L5
Clutha Pl EKILS G75 ... 171 G2
Clutha St GOV/IBX G51 ... 104 D3 1
Clyde Av BRHD/NEIL G78 ... 125 K8
BSHPBGS G64 ... 64 B1
HMLTN ML3 ... 157 J8
UD/BTH/TAN G71 ... 131 M8
Clydebrae Dr UD/BTH/TAN G71 ... 156 B1
Clydebrae St GOV/IBX G51 ... 104 B1
Clyde Crs LNK/LMHG ML11 ... 199 H4
Clyde Dr BLSH ML4 ... 133 J5
Clydeford Dr CAR/SHTL G32 ... 106 E6
UD/BTH/TAN G71 ... 131 K2 2
Clydeford Rd BLTYR/CAMB G72 ... 130 B3
CAR/SHTL G32 ... 130 A1
Clydeholm Rd SCOT G14 ... 81 K7 1
Clydeholm Ter CLYDBK G81 ... 80 D2 1
Clydeneuk Dr UD/BTH/TAN G71 ... 131 K2
Clyde Pl ARD KA22 ... 191 K5 1
BLTYR/CAMB G72 ... 130 D5
GBLS G5 ... 10 F3
JNSTN PA5 ... 122 C1 1
KLMNK KA1 ... 212 A4 3
MTHW ML1 ... 134 A5
TROON KA10 ... 216 F4
Clyde Rd GRK PA19 ... 31 M3
PSLYN/LNWD PA3 ... 102 B2
Clydesdale Av HMLTN ML3 ... 174 D3
PSLYN/LNWD PA3 ... 80 A8
WISHAW ML2 ... 158 D8 3
Clydesdale Pl HMLTN ML3 ... 174 D3 2
Clydesdale St BLSH ML4 ... 133 M5
HMLTN ML3 ... 156 C5
LRKH ML9 ... 176 A5 1
Clydesholm Ct LNK/LMHG ML11 ... 198 D5
Clydeshore Rd DMBTN G82 ... 36 E7
Clydeside Rd RUTH G73 ... 105 M7
Clydesmill Dr CAR/SHTL G32 ... 130 A2
Clydesmill Gv CAR/SHTL G32 ... 130 A2
Clydesmill Pl CAR/SHTL G32 ... 130 A1
Clydesmill Rd CAR/SHTL G32 ... 130 A1
Clyde St CARLUKE ML8 ... 178 E7
CGLE G1 ... 11 H3
CLYDBK G81 ... 80 C2
CTBR ML5 ... 110 C2
RNFRW PA4 ... 80 D4
Clyde St East HBR/GL G84 ... 22 E1
Clyde Ter ARD KA22 ... 191 K5
MTHW ML1 ... 158 C7
UD/BTH/TAN G71 ... 132 A8
Clydevale UD/BTH/TAN G71 ... 132 B8 2
Clyde Valley Av MTHW ML1 ... 157 L5
Clyde Vw HMLTN ML3 ... 156 B8
PSLYS PA2 ... 102 B7
Clydeview DMBTN G82 ... 36 E7
UD/BTH/TAN G71 ... 132 B8
Clyde View Av SVSTN KA20 ... 192 C8
Clyde View Ct OLDK G60 ... 58 C1 1
Clydeview Rd GRNK PA15 ... 3 G9
PGL PA14 ... 54 E1
Clydeview Ter CAR/SHTL G32 ... 130 C1 3
Clyde Wynd GRNK PA15 ... 2 A7
GRNK PA15 ... 32 D6 1
Clynder Rd GRNK PA15 ... 33 J7
Clynder St GOV/IBX G51 ... 104 B3
Clyth Dr GIF/THBK G46 ... 127 K7
Coach Cl KSYTH G65 ... 48 A1
Coach Pl KSYTH G65 ... 47 L2
Coach Rd KSYTH G65 ... 47 M2
Coalburn Rd UD/BTH/TAN G71 ... 132 B4
Coalburn St AIRDRIE ML6 ... 69 M7
Coalhall Av MTHW ML1 ... 134 A8 1
MTHW ML1 ... 134 B8 2
Coalhill St DEN/PKHD G31 ... 13 H5
Coatbank St CTBR ML5 ... 110 B3 1
Coatbank Wy CTBR ML5 ... 110 B3
Coatbridge Rd AIRDRIE ML6 ... 88 D6
BAIL/MDB/MHD G69 ... 86 F5
BAIL/MDB/MHD G69 ... 108 C4
CTBR ML5 ... 87 M4
Coathill St CTBR ML5 ... 110 A5
Coats Crs BAIL/MDB/MHD G69 ... 108 A4
Coats Dr PSLYS PA2 ... 8 A7
Coatshill Av BLTYR/CAMB G72 ... 131 J8
Coats Pl CRH/DND KA2 ... 209 L7
RAYR/DAL KA6 ... 231 H6 1
Coats St CTBR ML5 ... 110 B2
Cobbett Rd MTHW ML1 ... 157 H4
Cobbleton Rd MTHW ML1 ... 133 M7
Cobham St GRNK PA15 ... 33 L7
Cobington Pl
STPS/GTHM/RID G33 ... 85 H8 1
Cobinshaw St CAR/SHTL G32 ... 107 G3
Coburg St GBLS G5 ... 11 G5
Cochno Rd CLYDBK G81 ... 60 A1
Cochno St CLYDBK G81 ... 80 C1
Cochrane Av CRH/DND KA2 ... 209 L7
Cochranemill Rd JNSTN PA5 ... 99 J8
Cochrane Pl HBR/GL G84 ... 21 G7 3
PSTWK KA9 ... 225 H1
Cochrane Pl East
LARGS KA30 ... 115 J5 1
Cochrane Sq
PSLYN/LNWD PA3 ... 100 B3 1
Cochrane St BLSH ML4 ... 132 F3
BRHD/NEIL G78 ... 125 H7
CGLE G1 ... 11 K1
IRV KA12 ... 203 G7
KBRN KA25 ... 143 G7
Cochran St PSLY PA1 ... 9 K4
Cockburn Pl CTBR ML5 ... 109 M5
Cockels Loan RNFRW PA4 ... 80 B8
Cockenzie St CAR/SHTL G32 ... 107 G4
Cockhill Wy
UD/BTH/TAN G71 ... 132 D3 2
Cockmuir St SPRGB/BLRNK G21 ... 84 A5
Coddington Crs BLSH ML4 ... 133 M2
Cogan Pl BRHD/NEIL G78 ... 125 H7 1
Cogan Rd PLKSW/MSWD G43 ... 127 J3 1
Cogan St BRHD/NEIL G78 ... 125 H7
PLKSW/MSWD G43 ... 127 J2
Coila Av PSTWK KA9 ... 225 J3
Colbert St DMNK/BRGTN G40 ... 12 C9
Colbreggan Ct CLYDBK G81 ... 60 C3 1
Colbreggan Gdns CLYDBK G81 ... 60 C3
Colchester Dr KVD/HLHD G12 ... 82 A3
Coldgreen Av KBRN KA25 ... 143 G8
Coldingham Av SCOT G14 ... 80 E3
Coldstream Crs WISHAW ML2 ... 159 J4
Coldstream Dr PSLYS PA2 ... 101 G8 1
RUTH G73 ... 129 K3
Coldstream Pl COWCAD G4 ... 5 K3
Coldstream Rd CLYDBK G81 ... 60 B8
Coldstream St
BLTYR/CAMB G72 ... 155 K2 1
Colebrooke Pl KVD/HLHD G12 ... 4 B3
Colebrooke St
BLTYR/CAMB G72 ... 130 A3 3
KVD/HLHD G12 ... 4 B3
Colebrooke Ter KVD/HLHD G12 ... 4 B3
Coleburn St IRVSE KA11 ... 203 M3
Coleridge EKILS G75 ... 171 G2
Coleridge Av UD/BTH/TAN G71 ... 132 B7
Colfin St ESTRH G34 ... 86 C8
Colgrain St MRYH/FIRH G20 ... 83 G3
Colgrave Crs CAR/SHTL G32 ... 106 F6 2
Colinbar Cir BRHD/NEIL G78 ... 125 H8
Colinslee Av PSLYS PA2 ... 101 M8
Colinslee Crs PSLYS PA2 ... 101 M8
Colinslee Dr PSLYS PA2 ... 101 M8
Colinslie Rd PLK/PH/NH G53 ... 126 C1
Colinton Pl CAR/SHTL G32 ... 107 H2
Colintraive Av
STPS/GTHM/RID G33 ... 84 E6
Colintraive Crs
STPS/GTHM/RID G33 ... 84 E6
Coll EKILN G74 ... 172 C2
Collace Av BRWEIR PA11 ... 98 D2
Colla Gdns BSHPBGS G64 ... 64 D7
Coll Av PGL PA14 ... 55 H2
RNFRW PA4 ... 80 D8
College La CGLE G1 ... 11 M2
College Pk IRVSE KA11 ... 216 E2 2
College St CGLE G1 ... 11 L2
DMBTN G82 ... 36 F5 2
GTCI KA28 ... 138 A6
College Wynd KLMNK KA1 ... 16 E4
Collenan Av TROON KA10 ... 217 G5
Collessie Dr
STPS/GTHM/RID G33 ... 85 J7
Coll Gdns IRVSE KA11 ... 209 G1
Collier St JNSTN PA5 ... 99 M6
Colliertree Rd AIRDRIE ML6 ... 111 K1
Collina St MRYH/FIRH G20 ... 82 C3
Collingwood Pl HBR/GL G84 ... 21 G7 2
Collins Dr TROON KA10 ... 217 G5
Collins Rd HBR/GL G84 ... 23 G1
Collins St CLYDBK G81 ... 60 C3
COWCAD G4 ... 12 A1
Coll Pl AIRDRIE ML6 ... 111 J4
SPRGB/BLRNK G21 ... 7 H4
Coll St SPRGB/BLRNK G21 ... 7 G4
WISHAW ML2 ... 159 M3
Collylinn Rd BSDN G61 ... 61 L5
Colmonell Av KNTSWD G13 ... 80 F2 1
Colonsay EKILN G74 ... 15 M8
Colonsay Av PGL PA14 ... 55 H2
RNFRW PA4 ... 80 C8
Colonsay Dr NMRNS G77 ... 150 B4
Colonsay Pl KLMNKN/STW KA3 ... 207 H3
Colonsay Rd
CARD/HILL/MSPK G52 ... 103 L4 3
PSLYS PA2 ... 124 D2
Colquhoun DMBTN G82 ... 37 H4
Colquhoun Av
CARD/HILL/MSPK G52 ... 103 G2
Colquhoun Dr ALEX/LLW G83 ... 25 L2
BSDN G61 ... 61 K4
Colquhoun Rd DMBTN G82 ... 37 L8
KLMNKN/STW KA3 ... 207 J7 1
Colquhoun Sq HBR/GL G84 ... 20 C8 1
Colquhoun St DMBTN G82 ... 37 G5
HBR/GL G84 ... 20 D7
Colson Pl BLSH ML4 ... 133 J6 1
Colston Av SPRGB/BLRNK G21 ... 83 M2
Colston Dr BSHPBGS G64 ... 83 M2
Colston Gdns BSHPBGS G64 ... 83 L2
Colston Pth
SPRGB/BLRNK G21 ... 83 L2 2
Colston Pl AIRDRIE ML6 ... 111 J2 1
SPRGB/BLRNK G21 ... 83 L2 1
Colston Rd AIRDRIE ML6 ... 111 J2
PPK/MIL G22 ... 83 L2
SPRGB/BLRNK G21 ... 83 M2
Colston Ter AIRDRIE ML6 ... 111 J2 2
Colt Av CTBR ML5 ... 87 L8
Coltmuir Crs BSHPBGS G64 ... 83 L1 1
Coltmuir Dr PPK/MIL G22 ... 83 L1
Coltmuir Gdns PPK/MIL G22 ... 83 L1 2
Coltmuir St PPK/MIL G22 ... 83 H3
Coltness Av SHOTTS ML7 ... 160 F1
Coltness Dr BLSH ML4 ... 133 H5
Coltness La
STPS/GTHM/RID G33 ... 107 J2
Coltness Rd WISHAW ML2 ... 159 J5
Coltness St
STPS/GTHM/RID G33 ... 107 J1
Coltpark Av BSHPBGS G64 ... 83 L1
Coltpark La BSHPBGS G64 ... 83 M1 1
Colt Pl CTBR ML5 ... 110 A1
Coltsfoot Dr PLK/PH/NH G53 ... 126 B6
Coltswood Rd CTBR ML5 ... 88 A8
Colt Ter CTBR ML5 ... 110 A2
Columba Crs MTHW ML1 ... 133 K7
Columba Pth
BLTYR/CAMB G72 ... 155 J1 2
Columba St GOV/IBX G51 ... 104 B2
GRNKW/INVK PA16 ... 32 D5
HBR/GL G84 ... 20 D7 1
Columbia Pl EKILS G75 ... 171 H1 2
Columbia Wy EKILS G75 ... 171 H1
Columbine Wy CARLUKE ML8 ... 188 F1
Colvend Dr RUTH G73 ... 129 H6 2
Colvend St DMNK/BRGTN G40 ... 105 M6
Colville Ct MTHW ML1 ... 134 C8 2
Colville Dr RUTH G73 ... 129 K3
Colvilles Pl EKILS G75 ... 15 L9
Colvilles Rd EKILS G75 ... 172 A4
Colwood Av PLK/PH/NH G53 ... 126 A5
Colwood Gdns
PLK/PH/NH G53 ... 126 A6 1
Colwood Pl PLK/PH/NH G53 ... 126 A6
Colwood Sq PLK/PH/NH G53 ... 126 A5 1
Colwyn Ct AIRDRIE ML6 ... 89 G8
Colzium Vw KSYTH G65 ... 47 L1
Combe Qd BLSH ML4 ... 132 E6 2
Comedie Rd
STPS/GTHM/RID G33 ... 85 L5
Comely Bank HMLTN ML3 ... 155 M6
Comelybank La DMBTN G82 ... 36 D5 2
Comelybank Rd DMBTN G82 ... 36 D5 3
Comelypark St DEN/PKHD G31 ... 12 D4
Commerce St GBLS G5 ... 11 G5
Commercial Rd BRHD/NEIL G78 ... 125 J6
GBLS G5 ... 11 K7
Commoncraig Pl
GRNKW/INVK PA16 ... 50 C5
Common Gn HMLTN ML3 ... 156 E5 3
Commonhead Av AIRDRIE ML6 ... 88 F8
Commonhead La
AIRDRIE ML6 ... 88 F8 2
Commonhead Rd ESTRH G34 ... 108 D1
KLMNK KA1 ... 211 M6
Commonhead St AIRDRIE ML6 ... 88 F8
Commonside St AIRDRIE ML6 ... 88 F8
Commore Av BRHD/NEIL G78 ... 125 K8
Commore Dr KNTSWD G13 ... 81 G2
Community Av BLSH ML4 ... 133 G7 1
Community Pl BLSH ML4 ... 133 H6 1
Community Rd BLSH ML4 ... 132 F6
Comrie Crs HMLTN ML3 ... 155 K6
Comrie Rd
STPS/GTHM/RID G33 ... 85 J4 2
Comrie St CAR/SHTL G32 ... 107 H6
Cona St GIF/THBK G46 ... 126 E5 1
Condor Gln BLSH ML4 ... 133 L2
Condorrat Ring Rd CUMB G67 ... 68 B1
Condorrat Rd AIRDRIE ML6 ... 88 D2
CUMB G67 ... 68 B4
Congress Rd KVGV G3 ... 104 D2
Congress Wy KVGV G3 ... 10 A1
Conifer Pl KKNTL G66 ... 65 H3
Conisborough Rd ESTRH G34 ... 85 M7
Coniston EKILS G75 ... 170 F4 2
Coniston Crs HMLTN ML3 ... 174 C3 2
Coniston Dr BLSH ML4 ... 133 H6
Conistone Crs
BAIL/MDB/MHD G69 ... 107 M5
Connal St DMNK/BRGTN G40 ... 106 B6 3
Connell Crs MLNGV G62 ... 42 C8
Conniston St CAR/SHTL G32 ... 106 E2 2
Connor Rd BRHD/NEIL G78 ... 125 H6 2
Connor St AIRDRIE ML6 ... 89 L8
Conon Av BSDN G61 ... 61 K6
Conservation Pl
WISHAW ML2 ... 159 J8 1
Consett La
STPS/GTHM/RID G33 ... 107 J1 1
Constarry Rd BALLOCH G68 ... 48 A6
KSYTH G65 ... 47 L4
Container Wy GRNK PA15 ... 2 D2
Content Av AYR KA8 ... 19 H4
Content St AYR KA8 ... 19 G2
Contin Pl MRYH/FIRH G20 ... 82 D4
Coodham Pl KLWNG KA13 ... 193 K6 2
Cook Rd ALEX/LLW G83 ... 25 M1
Cook St GBLS G5 ... 10 F5
Coolgardie Pl EKILS G75 ... 14 B7
Cooperage Ct KNTSWD G13 ... 80 D3
Co-operative Ter JNSTN PA5 ... 100 A6 1
Cooper Av CARLUKE ML8 ... 178 E6 1
Copeland Crs GTCI KA28 ... 138 B6
Copenhagen Av EKILS G75 ... 171 L3
Copland Pl GOV/IBX G51 ... 104 B3
Copland Qd GOV/IBX G51 ... 104 B3 2
Copland Rd GOV/IBX G51 ... 104 B4
Coplaw St GVH/MTFL G42 ... 105 G6
Copperfield La
UD/BTH/TAN G71 ... 132 A2 2
Coralmount Gdns KKNTL G66 ... 65 L2 1
Coranbae Pl AYRS KA7 ... 228 B8
Corbett Ct CAR/SHTL G32 ... 106 F6 1
Corbett St CAR/SHTL G32 ... 107 G6
Corbie Pl MLNGV G62 ... 41 K7
Cordale Av DMBTN G82 ... 25 K7
Cordiner St LNPK/KPK G44 ... 128 B2 1
Cordon Rd KLMNKN/STW KA3 ... 206 E5
Corkerhill Gdns
CARD/HILL/MSPK G52 ... 103 L5 2
Corkerhill Pl
CARD/HILL/MSPK G52 ... 103 K7
Corkerhill Rd
CARD/HILL/MSPK G52 ... 103 K6
Corlaich Av GVH/MTFL G42 ... 128 E2
Corlaich Dr RUTH G73 ... 128 E2
Corlic St GRNK PA15 ... 3 H9
Cormack Av BSHPBGS G64 ... 44 C8
Cormorant Av
CRG/CRSL/HOU PA6 ... 99 K1
Cornaig Rd PLK/PH/NH G53 ... 126 B1
Cornalee Gdns PLK/PH/NH G53 ... 126 A1
Cornalee Pl PLK/PH/NH G53 ... 126 B2
Cornalee Rd PLK/PH/NH G53 ... 126 B1
Cornelian Ter BLSH ML4 ... 133 G5 1
Cornelia St MTHW ML1 ... 133 H8
Cornhaddock St GRNK PA15 ... 32 D5
Cornhill Dr CTBR ML5 ... 109 L1
Cornhill St SPRGB/BLRNK G21 ... 84 A4 1
Cornock Crs CLYDBK G81 ... 60 B6 1
Cornock St CLYDBK G81 ... 60 B6
Cornsilloch Brae LRKH ML9 ... 176 F6
Corn St COWCAD G4 ... 5 G5
Cornwall Av RUTH G73 ... 129 K4 2
Cornwall St EKILN G74 ... 14 E4
GOV/IBX G51 ... 104 D4
Cornwall St South
PLKSD/SHW G41 ... 104 D5
Coronation Pl
BAIL/MDB/MHD G69 ... 86 E2
Coronation Rd MTHW ML1 ... 133 M5
Coronation St PSTWK KA9 ... 221 K4
WISHAW ML2 ... 159 K6
Coronation Wy BSDN G61 ... 61 M7
Corpach Pl ESTRH G34 ... 86 D8 3
Corra Linn HMLTN ML3 ... 156 A6
Corran Av NMRNS G77 ... 150 C3
Corran St STPS/GTHM/RID G33 ... 106 F1
Correen Gdns BSDN G61 ... 61 H2
Corrie Ct HMLTN ML3 ... 155 M7
Corrie Crs KLMNKN/STW KA3 ... 206 F6 1
SALT KA21 ... 191 M7
Corrie Dr MTHW ML1 ... 157 H2
PSLY PA1 ... 102 E5
Corrie Gdns EKILS G75 ... 171 H5
Corrie Gv LNPK/KPK G44 ... 127 M5
Corrie Pl HBR/GL G84 ... 20 F6 3
KKNTL G66 ... 65 L5
TROON KA10 ... 216 E2 2
Corrie Vw BALLOCH G68 ... 67 M1 1
Corrie Wy LRKH ML9 ... 176 B7
Corrour Rd NMRNS G77 ... 150 C3
PLKSW/MSWD G43 ... 127 K2
Corsankell Wynd SALT KA21 ... 191 L6
Corse Av IRVSE KA11 ... 204 F8
Corsebar Av PSLYS PA2 ... 8 C9
Corsebar Crs PSLYS PA2 ... 101 J8
Corsebar Dr PSLYS PA2 ... 8 C9
Corsebar La PSLYS PA2 ... 101 H8
Corsebar Rd PSLYS PA2 ... 101 H8
Corsebar Wy PSLYS PA2 ... 8 D6 1
Corse Dr BRHD/NEIL G78 ... 125 H5
Corsefield Rd LOCHW PA12 ... 119 L7
Corseford Av JNSTN PA5 ... 122 C1
Corsehill KLWNG KA13 ... 194 A6
Corsehill Av RAYR/DAL KA6 ... 231 L5
Corsehill Dr WKIL KA23 ... 181 J4
Corsehill Mount Rd IRVSE KA11 ... 203 M8
Corsehill Pk AYRS KA7 ... 228 F4
IRVSE KA11 ... 209 K1 1
Corsehill Pl AYRS KA7 ... 228 F4
ESTRH G34 ... 108 C1
Corsehill Rd AYRS KA7 ... 18 E9
Corsehill St ESTRH G34 ... 108 C1
Corselet Rd PLK/PH/NH G53 ... 126 A8
Corse Pl CRH/DND KA2 ... 210 F1 1
Corserine Bank IRVSE KA11 ... 203 M6 2
Corserine Rd AYRS KA7 ... 228 B8
Corse Rd CARD/HILL/MSPK G52 ... 102 E3
Corse St WKIL KA23 ... 181 J4
Corsewall Av CAR/SHTL G32 ... 107 L6 1
Corsewall St CTBR ML5 ... 109 L2
Corsford Dr PLK/PH/NH G53 ... 126 C3
Corsliehill Rd
CRG/CRSL/HOU PA6 ... 76 D2
Corsock Av HMLTN ML3 ... 155 L7
Corsock St DEN/PKHD G31 ... 13 J1
Corston St STPS/GTHM/RID G33 ... 7 L9
Cortachy Pl BSHPBGS G64 ... 64 D8
Coruisk Dr
CRMNK/CLK/EAG G76 ... 151 K1
Corunna Ct CARLUKE ML8 ... 179 H8
Corunna St KVGV G3 ... 4 A8
Coshneuk Rd
STPS/GTHM/RID G33 ... 85 H4
Cosy Neuk LRKH ML9 ... 176 C8
Cottar St MRYH/FIRH G20 ... 82 E2
Cotter Dr KLMNKN/STW KA3 ... 17 M5
Cotton Av PSLYN/LNWD PA3 ... 100 B4 1
Cotton St DMNK/BRGTN G40 ... 105 M7
PSLY PA1 ... 9 J4
Cotton V MTHW ML1 ... 134 E8
Coulin Gdns PPK/MIL G22 ... 83 K5 2
Coulport Pl HBR/GL G84 ... 20 B7
Coulter Av CTBR ML5 ... 109 L1
WISHAW ML2 ... 159 L2
Coulthard Dr PSTWK KA9 ... 225 K3
Countess St SALT KA21 ... 200 F2 3
County Av BLTYR/CAMB G72 ... 129 K2
County Dr LNK/LMHG ML11 ... 199 J6 1
County Pl PSLY PA1 ... 9 H3
County Sq PSLY PA1 ... 9 H3
Couper St COWCAD G4 ... 5 L7
Coursington Crs MTHW ML1 ... 158 A2 1
Coursington Gdns
MTHW ML1 ... 157 M2 3
Coursington Pl MTHW ML1 ... 157 M2 4
Coursington Rd MTHW ML1 ... 157 M2 2
Courthill BSDN G61 ... 61 K3
Courthill Av LNPK/KPK G44 ... 128 B4
Courthill Crs KSYTH G65 ... 47 L1
Courthill Pl DALRY KA24 ... 184 C1
Courthill St DALRY KA24 ... 184 C1
Courtrai Av HBR/GL G84 ... 20 B7
Court Rd PGL PA14 ... 34 C8
Court St LARGS KA30 ... 115 J5
Coustonholm Rd
PLKSW/MSWD G43 ... 127 K2
Couther Qd AIRDRIE ML6 ... 89 G7
Covanburn Av HMLTN ML3 ... 156 F8
Cove Crs SHOTTS ML7 ... 137 L5
Covenant Crs LRKH ML9 ... 176 B7
Covenanters Ct NMLNS KA16 ... 215 J2 2
Covenant Pl WISHAW ML2 ... 158 C7
Coventry Dr DEN/PKHD G31 ... 7 G8
Cove Pl HBR/GL G84 ... 20 B7 3
Cove Rd GRK PA19 ... 31 M2
Cowal Crs GRK PA19 ... 31 H3
KKNTL G66 ... 46 B8
Cowal Dr PSLYN/LNWD PA3 ... 100 A4
Cowal St MRYH/FIRH G20 ... 82 C2
Cowal Vw GRK PA19 ... 31 H3
Cowan Crs AYR KA8 ... 225 J6
BRHD/NEIL G78 ... 125 K7
Cowan La KVD/HLHD G12 ... 4 B4
Cowan Rd BALLOCH G68 ... 48 B7
Cowan St KVD/HLHD G12 ... 4 A4
Cowan Wilson Av
BLTYR/CAMB G72 ... 155 K1
Cowan Wynd UD/BTH/TAN G71 ... 132 A1
WISHAW ML2 ... 177 J2 1
Cowcaddens Rd COWCAD G4 ... 5 G7
Cowcaddens St CGLW G2 ... 5 H8
Cowdenhill Circ KNTSWD G13 ... 81 K1
Cowdenhill Pl KNTSWD G13 ... 81 K1 1
Cowdenhill Rd KNTSWD G13 ... 81 J1
Cowden St GOV/IBX G51 ... 103 K2 1
Cowdray Crs RNFRW PA4 ... 80 D6 1
Cowgate KKNTL G66 ... 65 J1 1
Cowglen Rd PLK/PH/NH G53 ... 126 C2
Cowlairs Rd SPRGB/BLRNK G21 ... 6 A1
Coxdale Av KKNTL G66 ... 65 H1
Coxhill St COWCAD G4 ... 5 L3
Coxton Pl STPS/GTHM/RID G33 ... 85 K8
Coylebank PSTWK KA9 ... 225 J3
Coyle Pk TROON KA10 ... 216 E4
Coylton Crs HMLTN ML3 ... 155 L8 1
Coylton Rd PLKSW/MSWD G43 ... 127 M4
Crabb Qd MTHW ML1 ... 133 J8
Cragdale EKILN G74 ... 153 J6
Craggan Dr KNTSWD G13 ... 80 F3
Crags Av PSLYS PA2 ... 101 M8
Crags Crs PSLYS PA2 ... 9 K9
Crags Rd PSLYS PA2 ... 101 M8
Cragwell Pk
CRMNK/CLK/EAG G76 ... 152 E2
Craigallian Av
BLTYR/CAMB G72 ... 130 D6
MLNGV G62 ... 42 A5
Craiganour La
PLKSW/MSWD G43 ... 127 J3
Craigard Pl RUTH G73 ... 129 K6
Craigash Qd MLNGV G62 ... 41 L7
Craigash Rd MLNGV G62 ... 41 L7
Craig Av ALEX/LLW G83 ... 25 J2 3
DALRY KA24 ... 184 A1
Craigbank Dr PLK/PH/NH G53 ... 126 A3
Craigbank St LRKH ML9 ... 176 A8
Craigbarnet Av BSHPBGS G64 ... 64 A1 1
Craigbarnet Crs
STPS/GTHM/RID G33 ... 85 H5 1
Craigbarnet Rd MLNGV G62 ... 41 K7
Craigbet Av BRWEIR PA11 ... 75 L7
Craigbet Crs BRWEIR PA11 ... 75 L7 1
Craigbet Pl BRWEIR PA11 ... 75 L7
Craigbo Av SMSTN G23 ... 62 D8 3
Craigbog Av JNSTN PA5 ... 122 D1 2
Craigbo Rd SMSTN G23 ... 62 D8
Craigbo St SMSTN G23 ... 62 D8 3
Craigburn Av
CRG/CRSL/HOU PA6 ... 99 K2
Craigburn Ct LRKH ML9 ... 176 F8 1
Craigburn Crs
CRG/CRSL/HOU PA6 ... 99 K2 1
Craigburn Pl
CRG/CRSL/HOU PA6 ... 99 K2 2
Craigburn St HMLTN ML3 ... 174 D1 1
Craigdene Dr SVSTN KA20 ... 192 E8
Craigdhu Av AIRDRIE ML6 ... 111 L2
MLNGV G62 ... 41 M8
Craigdhu Rd MLNGV G62 ... 41 M8
MLNGV G62 ... 42 A8 1
Craigdonald Pl JNSTN PA5 ... 99 M6 1
JNSTN PA5 ... 99 M7 1
Craig Dr CRH/DND KA2 ... 205 L8
Craigellan Rd
PLKSW/MSWD G43 ... 127 K3 2
Craigelvan Av CUMB G67 ... 67 M3
Craigelvan Ct CUMB G67 ... 67 M3 1
Craigelvan Dr CUMB G67 ... 67 M3 2
Craigelvan Gdns CUMB G67 ... 67 M3 3
Craigelvan Gv CUMB G67 ... 67 M3 4
Craigelvan Pl CUMB G67 ... 67 M3
Craigelvan Vw CUMB G67 ... 67 M3 5
Craigenbay Crs KKNTL G66 ... 65 L4
Craigenbay Rd KKNTL G66 ... 65 K5
Craigenbay St SPRGB/BLRNK G21 ... 7 G1
Craigend Crs MLNGV G62 ... 41 M7
Craigend Dr CTBR ML5 ... 109 J5
Craigend Dr West MLNGV G62 ... 41 L7
Craigendmuir Rd
STPS/GTHM/RID G33 ... 85 L5 1
Craigendmuir St
STPS/GTHM/RID G33 ... 7 L5
Craigendon Ov PSLYS PA2 ... 124 C3 1
Craigendon Rd PSLYS PA2 ... 124 C3 2
Craigendoran Av HBR/GL G84 ... 22 F1
Craigend Pl KNTSWD G13 ... 81 L3 3
Craigend Rd CUMB G67 ... 67 M4 1
EKILS G75 ... 170 F8
TROON KA10 ... 216 F8
Craigends Av BRWEIR PA11 ... 75 L6
Craigends Dr KLBCH PA10 ... 99 G6
Craigends Pl BRWEIR PA11 ... 75 L6
Craigends Rd
CRG/CRSL/HOU PA6 ... 77 L7
GLGNK KA14 ... 167 H3
Craigend St KNTSWD G13 ... 81 L3 3
Craigend Vw CUMB G67 ... 67 M4
Craigenfeoch Av JNSTN PA5 ... 99 K8 2
Craigenlay Av CMPF/LLE G63 ... 27 J5
Craig-en-ros Rd GTCI KA28 ... 138 B6
Craigens Rd AIRDRIE ML6 ... 112 A4
Craigfaulds Av PSLYS PA2 ... 8 B9
Craigfell Ct HMLTN ML3 ... 155 L7
Craigfern Dr CMPF/LLE G63 ... 27 J5
Craigfin Ct PSTWK KA9 ... 225 K4
Craigflower Gdns
PLK/PH/NH G53 ... 126 A5 2
Craigflower Rd
PLK/PH/NH G53 ... 126 A5
Craig Gdns NMRNS G77 ... 150 C5
Craighalbert Rd BALLOCH G68 ... 48 C6
Craighalbert Wy BALLOCH G68 ... 48 C5
Craighall Pl AYRS KA7 ... 229 G7
Craighall Qd BRHD/NEIL G78 ... 148 D3 1
Craighall Rd COWCAD G4 ... 5 H5
Craighaw St CLYDBK G81 ... 60 D1
Craighead Av
STPS/GTHM/RID G33 ... 7 M3
Craighead Dr MLNGV G62 ... 41 K7
Craighead Rd BSHPTN PA7 ... 58 B7
KKNTL G66 ... 45 J3
Craighead St AIRDRIE ML6 ... 111 L1
Craighead Wy BRHD/NEIL G78 ... 125 H7
Craig Hl EKILS G75 ... 14 B8
Craighill Dr
CRMNK/CLK/EAG G76 ... 151 K3
Craighill Gv
CRMNK/CLK/EAG G76 ... 151 K3 1
Craighirst Dr CLYDBK G81 ... 60 A2

Craighirst Rd MLNGV G62 41 K7
Craighlaw Av
CRMNK/CLK/EAG G76 151 K7
Craighlaw Dr
CRMNK/CLK/EAG G76 151 K7
Craigholme CRG/CRSL/HOU PA6 77 K7
Craigholm Rd AYRS KA7 229 K2
Craighouse St
STPS/GTHM/RID G33 85 G8
Craighton Gdns KKNTL G66 44 F1
Craighurst Rd MLNGV G62 41 K7
Craigie Av AYR KA8 19 H3
KLMNK KA1 211 M5
Craigiebar Dr PSLYS PA2 124 C1
Craigieburn Gdns
MRYH/FIRH G20 82 B1
Craigieburn Rd CUMB G67 48 F8
Craigie Dr NMRNS G77 150 E6
Craigiehall Av ERSK PA8 79 G2
Craigiehall Crs ERSK PA8 79 G2
Craigiehall Pl GOV/IBX G51 104 D3
Craigiehall St GOV/IBX G51 104 D3
Craigiehall Wy ERSK PA8 79 G2
Craigieknowes St GRNK PA15 3 K8
Craigie Lea AYR KA8 19 K4
Craigielea Crs MLNGV G62 41 L7
Craigielea Dr PSLYN/LNWD PA3 8 C1
Craigielea Pk RNFRW PA4 80 C6
Craigielea Rd CLYDBK G81 59 M2
RNFRW PA4 80 C6
Craigielea St DEN/PKHD G31 12 F1
Craigielinn Av PSLYS PA2 124 B3
Craigie Pk KKNTL G66 65 L4
Craigie Pl CRH/DND KA2 210 F1
GLSTN KA4 214 B3
KLMNK KA1 211 M4
Craigie Rd AYR KA8 19 J3
KLMNK KA1 211 M8
KLMNK KA1 212 F4
Craigie St GVH/MTFL G42 105 G7
PSTWK KA9 225 H1
Craigievar Pl NMRNS G77 150 B4
Craigievar St
STPS/GTHM/RID G33 85 L7
Craigie Wy AYR KA8 19 J3
Craiglea Av CRH/DND KA2 205 L8
Craiglea Pl AIRDRIE ML6 111 J1
Craiglea Ter AIRDRIE ML6 89 M6
Craiglee EKILS G75 171 L5
Craigleith St CAR/SHTL G32 106 E3
Craiglinn Park Rd BALLOCH G68 48 A8
Craiglockhart St
STPS/GTHM/RID G33 85 K7
STPS/GTHM/RID G33 85 K8
Craiglomond Gdns
ALEX/LLW G83 25 K1
Craiglynn Gdns
ALEX/LLW G83 25 M1
Craigmaddie Gdns
BSHPBGS G64 64 A1
Craigmaddie Rd MLNGV G62 42 F4
Craigmaddie Terrace La
KVGV G3 4 A7
Craigmarloch Av BSHPBGS G64 64 B1
Craigmarloch Vw
CMPF/LLE G63 27 H5
Craigmillar Av MLNGV G62 42 B7
Craigmillar Rd
GVH/MTFL G42 128 A2
Craigmochan Av AIRDRIE ML6 88 F7
Craigmont Dr MRYH/FIRH G20 82 E4
Craigmont St MRYH/FIRH G20 82 E3
Craigmore Rd BSDN G61 61 H2
Craigmore St DEN/PKHD G31 13 J3
Craigmount Av PSLYS PA2 124 C3
Craigmuir Crs
CARD/HILL/MSPK G52 102 F3
Craigmuir Gdns
BLTYR/CAMB G72 155 H3
Craigmuir Pl
CARD/HILL/MSPK G52 102 E3
Craigmuir Rd BLTYR/CAMB G72 155 H3
CARD/HILL/MSPK G52 102 E3
Craigmuschat Rd GRK PA19 31 L2
Craignaw Pl IRVSE KA11 204 B6
Craigneil Dr PSTWK KA9 225 J2
Craigneil St
STPS/GTHM/RID G33 85 L7
Craigneith Ct EKILN G74 154 E5
Craignethan Rd
CARLUKE ML8 178 E5
GIF/THBK G46 151 G2
Craigneuk Av AIRDRIE ML6 111 J3
Craigneuk St MTHW ML1 158 B4
WISHAW ML2 158 C5
Craignure Crs AIRDRIE ML6 111 L2
Craignure Rd RUTH G73 129 H6
Craigpark DEN/PKHD G31 12 E1
Craigpark Av PSTWK KA9 225 H3
Craigpark Dr DEN/PKHD G31 12 E1
Craigpark St CLYDBK G81 60 D2
Craigpark Wy
UD/BTH/TAN G71 132 A2
Craig Pl NMRNS G77 150 B4
Craig Rd BRHD/NEIL G78 148 D3
LNPK/KPK G44 128 A4
PSLYN/LNWD PA3 99 M2
TROON KA10 216 A6
Craigs Av CLYDBK G81 60 C2
Craigsheen Av
CRMNK/CLK/EAG G76 152 D2
Craigshiel Pl AYRS KA7 228 D5
Craigside Ct BALLOCH G68 67 M2
Craigside Rd BALLOCH G68 67 M2
Craigskeen Pl PSTWK KA9 225 K4
Craigson Pl AIRDRIE ML6 111 M3
Craigspark ARD KA22 191 J5
Craigs Pl SALT KA21 201 G1
Craigstewart Crs AYRS KA7 228 C8
The Craigs GRNKW/INVK PA16 32 C2
Craigston Av AYRS KA7 19 M7
Craigstone Vw KSYTH G65 47 M1
Craigston Rd JNSTN PA5 99 L7
Craig St AIRDRIE ML6 110 F2
BLTYR/CAMB G72 155 L2
CTBR ML5 109 M5
GTCI KA28 138 B6
Craigton Av BRHD/NEIL G78 125 L8
MLNGV G62 41 M7
Craigton Crs NMRNS G77 150 B4
Craigton Dr BRHD/NEIL G78 125 L8
GOV/IBX G51 103 L3
NMRNS G77 150 C4
Craigton Gdns MLNGV G62 41 M6
Craigton Pl BLTYR/CAMB G72 131 K8
GOV/IBX G51 103 L3
Craigton Rd GOV/IBX G51 103 M2
KBRN KA25 167 H1
MLNGV G62 41 L6
NMRNS G77 149 H6
Craigton St CLYDBK G81 60 D1
Craigvale Crs AIRDRIE ML6 111 L2
Craigvicar Gdns
CAR/SHTL G32 107 K5
Craig Vw IRVSE KA11 204 F7
Craigview RAYR/DAL KA6 231 L5
Craigview Av JNSTN PA5 122 C1
Craigview Rd MTHW ML1 157 L1
NMLNS KA16 215 K2
Craigview Ter JNSTN PA5 99 K8
Craigwell Rd AYRS KA7 18 C7
Craigwell Av RUTH G73 129 K3
Craigwell Pl TROON KA10 217 G5
Craigwell St DEN/PKHD G31 13 M6
Crammond Av CTBR ML5 109 J5
Cramond Av RNFRW PA4 80 E7
Cramond Pl IRVSE KA11 203 M7
Cramond St GBLS G5 105 K7
Cramond Ter CAR/SHTL G32 107 H4
Cramond Wy IRVSE KA11 203 M7
Cranberry Moss Rd
KLWNG KA13 193 K6
Cranberry Rd KLWNG KA13 193 H7
Cranborne Rd KVD/HLHD G12 82 A4
Cranbrooke Dr MRYH/FIRH G20 82 D2
Crandleyhill Rd PSTWK KA9 225 H3
Crannog Rd DMBTN G82 37 L8
Crannog Wy KLWNG KA13 193 J5
Cranston St KVGV G3 10 C1
Cranworth La KVD/HLHD G12 82 D6
Cranworth St KVD/HLHD G12 82 D6
Crarae Av BSDN G61 61 L7
Crarea Pl NMRNS G77 150 B4
Crathes Ct LNPK/KPK G44 127 L5
Crathie Dr AIRDRIE ML6 88 F5
ARD KA22 191 J8
PTCK G11 82 A7
Crathie Pl NMRNS G77 151 H5
Crathie Qd WISHAW ML2 159 H4
Crathie Rd KLMNKN/STW KA3 206 E7
Craufurd Av WKIL KA23 181 L5
Craufurd Crs BEITH KA15 168 D5
Craufurdland Rd
KLMNKN/STW KA3 207 G4
Craven Gv IRV KA12 203 L4
Crawberry Rd GRNK PA15 2 F9
Crawford Av KKNTL G66 65 L6
PSTWK KA9 225 J3
Crawford Crs
BLTYR/CAMB G72 131 K8
UD/BTH/TAN G71 131 L2
Crawford Dr DRUM G15 61 G8
EKILN G74 15 M1
HBR/GL G84 20 E6
Crawford Gdns MTHW ML1 157 J4
Crawford Hl EKILN G74 15 M1
Crawford Rd
CRG/CRSL/HOU PA6 77 K8
MLNGV G62 41 M5
Crawford St HMLTN ML3 156 A4
LARGS KA30 115 J6
MTHW ML1 157 K3
PGL PA14 34 C7
PTCK G11 82 A7
PTCK G11 82 A8
Crawfurd Av RUTH G73 129 H4
Crawfurd Dr PSLYN/LNWD PA3 8 A1
Crawfurd Gdns RUTH G73 129 J5
Crawfurdland Pl CRH/DND KA2 205 K8
Crawfurd Rd RUTH G73 129 H5
Crawfurd St GRNKW/INVK PA16 2 C1
Crawfurds Vw LOCHW PA12 120 D6
Crawhin Gdns
GRNKW/INVK PA16 32 D6
Craw Pl LOCHW PA12 120 C7
Crawriggs Av KKNTL G66 65 K3
Craw Rd PSLYS PA2 8 D6
Creamery Rd WISHAW ML2 159 J8
Crebar Dr BRHD/NEIL G78 125 J7
Crebar St GIF/THBK G46 126 E5
Credon Dr AIRDRIE ML6 111 G4
CRH/DND KA2 210 F1
Cree Av BSHPBGS G64 64 D8
Creebank Pl TROON KA10 216 E3
Cree Gdns CAR/SHTL G32 106 F4
Cree Pl EKILS G75 153 H8
Creighton Gv EKILN G74 14 F3
Creigton Ct KLMNKN/STW KA3 207 G4
Creran Ct HMLTN ML3 156 A8
PSTWK KA9 225 J4
Creran Dr RNFRW PA4 80 B5
Crescent Rd SCOT G14 81 H4
Crescent St GRNK PA15 3 G6
The Crescent CLYDBK G81 59 L6
CRMNK/CLK/EAG G76 152 A4
SKLM PA17 70 B5
Cresswell Gv NMRNS G77 150 D6
Cresswell La KVD/HLHD G12 82 D6
Cresswell Pl NMRNS G77 150 E7
Cresswell St KVD/HLHD G12 82 D6
Cressy St GOV/IBX G51 103 L1
Crest Av KNTSWD G13 81 H1
Crestlea Av PSLYS PA2 124 E1
Creveul Ct ALEX/LLW G83 25 L4
Crichton Av DALRY KA24 184 A1
Crichton St CTBR ML5 110 A1
SPRGB/BLRNK G21 6 A1
Cricketfield La
CRG/CRSL/HOU PA6 77 H6
Crieff Av AIRDRIE ML6 111 K8
Criffell Gdns CAR/SHTL G32 107 K6
Criffell Rd CAR/SHTL G32 107 K5
Criffel Pl KLMNK KA1 212 A5
Crighton Wynd
UD/BTH/TAN G71 132 D4
Crimea St CGLW G2 10 E2
Crinan Crs CTBR ML5 87 K8
Crinan Gdns BSHPBGS G64 64 C8
Crinan Pl ARD KA22 191 J4
BLSH ML4 133 H5
Crinan St DEN/PKHD G31 7 G8
Crindledyke Crs WISHAW ML2 160 A3
Cripps Av CLYDBK G81 60 D8
Crisswell Cl GRNKW/INVK PA16 31 J7
Crocus Gv IRV KA12 203 J6
Croe Pl KLMNK KA1 212 A5
Croftbank Av UD/BTH/TAN G71 132 B8
Croftbank Crs
UD/BTH/TAN G71 131 M3
UD/BTH/TAN G71 132 B8
Croftbank Ga UD/BTH/TAN G71 132 B8
Croftbank St SPRGB/BLRNK G21 6 D1
SPRGB/BLRNK G21 83 M5
Croftburn Dr LNPK/KPK G44 128 D5
Croftcot Av BLSH ML4 132 F6
Croftcroighn Rd
STPS/GTHM/RID G33 85 H8
Croftend Av LNPK/KPK G44 128 E3
Croftend La RUTH G73 128 F4
Croftfoot Crs CSMK G45 129 G5
Croftfoot Dr CSMK G45 128 F5
Croftfoot Pl
BAIL/MDB/MHD G69 87 G3
Croftfoot Qd CSMK G45 128 E5
Croftfoot Rd CSMK G45 128 D5
LNPK/KPK G44 128 D5
Croftfoot St CSMK G45 129 G5
Croftfoot Ter CSMK G45 128 F5
Crofthead Av
KLMNKN/STW KA3 207 G4
Crofthead Crs BLSH ML4 132 F6
Crofthead Dr KKNTL G66 29 J8
Crofthead Pl BLSH ML4 132 F6
NMRNS G77 150 E6
Crofthead Rd AYRS KA7 19 M9
KLMNKN/STW KA3 206 B2
PSTWK KA9 221 J8
Crofthead St UD/BTH/TAN G71 131 M3
Crofthill Av UD/BTH/TAN G71 131 M3
Crofthill Rd LNPK/KPK G44 128 E5
Crofthouse Dr
LNPK/KPK G44 128 E5
Croftmont Av LNPK/KPK G44 128 E5
Croftmoraig Av
BAIL/MDB/MHD G69 67 G5
Crofton Av LNPK/KPK G44 128 D5
Croftpark Av LNPK/KPK G44 128 E4
Croftpark Crs BLTYR/CAMB G72 155 L3
Croftpark Rd CLYDBK G81 60 B2
Croftpark St BLSH ML4 133 G3
Croft Pl LRKH ML9 175 M6
Croft Rd BLTYR/CAMB G72 130 B4
EKILS G75 14 E7
LRKH ML9 175 M6
Croftside Av LNPK/KPK G44 128 E5
Croftspar Av CAR/SHTL G32 107 K3
Croftspar Dr CAR/SHTL G32 107 J3
Croftspar Gv CAR/SHTL G32 107 K3
Croftspar Pl CAR/SHTL G32 107 J3
Croft St ALEX/LLW G83 25 M6
KLMNK KA1 16 F3
MAUCH/CAT KA5 223 M5
Croft Ter IRVSE KA11 204 F7
Croft Wy RNFRW PA4 80 D8
Croftwood Av LNPK/KPK G44 128 D5
Croftwood Rd HMLTN ML3 156 D8
Croft Wynd
UD/BTH/TAN G71 132 A3
Crogal Crs AIRDRIE ML6 111 K7
Cromalt Av EKILS G75 171 H5
Cromalt Crs BSDN G61 61 J1
Cromarty Av BSHPBGS G64 64 D7
PLKSW/MSWD G43 127 M2
Cromarty Crs BSDN G61 61 M2
Cromarty Gdns
CRMNK/CLK/EAG G76 128 A8
Cromarty Pl
BAIL/MDB/MHD G69 66 D8
EKILN G74 154 C6
Cromarty Rd AIRDRIE ML6 110 F5
Crombie Gdns
BAIL/MDB/MHD G69 107 M6
Cromdale Rd KLMNK KA1 212 A5
PGL PA14 54 F3
Cromdale St GOV/IBX G51 103 L3
Cromdale Wy MTHW ML1 134 A7
Cromer St MRYH/FIRH G20 82 F4
Crompton Av LNPK/KPK G44 128 B4
Crompton Wy IRV KA12 203 L5
Cromwell La COWCAD G4 4 E5
Cromwell Rd AYRS KA7 18 C2
Cromwell St COWCAD G4 4 E5
Crona Dr HMLTN ML3 155 L5
Cronberry Qd
CARD/HILL/MSPK G52 102 F6
Cronberry Ter
CARD/HILL/MSPK G52 102 F6
Cronin Pl BLSH ML4 133 H2
Cronulla Pl KSYTH G65 47 M1
Crookedshields Rd EKILN G74 154 B2
Crookfur Rd NMRNS G77 150 D4
Crookhill Dr LOCHW PA12 120 C6
Crookhill Gdns LOCHW PA12 120 C6
Crookston Av
CARD/HILL/MSPK G52 103 G5
Crookston Ct
CARD/HILL/MSPK G52 103 G5
Crookston Dr
CARD/HILL/MSPK G52 102 F5
PSLY PA1 102 F5
Crookston Gdns
CARD/HILL/MSPK G52 102 F5
Crookston Gv
CARD/HILL/MSPK G52 103 G5
Crookston Pl
CARD/HILL/MSPK G52 102 F5
Crookston Qd
CARD/HILL/MSPK G52 102 F5
Crookston Rd
CARD/HILL/MSPK G52 102 F6
PLK/PH/NH G53 102 F7
Crookston Ter
CARD/HILL/MSPK G52 103 G5
Crosbie Ct TROON KA10 220 D1
Crosbie Dr PSLYS PA2 123 L2
WKIL KA23 181 K5
Crosbie La MRYH/FIRH G20 82 C1
Crosbie Pl TROON KA10 220 E2
Crosbie Rd TROON KA10 220 D1
Crosbie St MRYH/FIRH G20 82 C1
Crosbie Wd PSLYS PA2 101 H8
Cross BEITH KA15 168 B1
Crossan Dr KKNTL G66 29 G8
Cross Arthurlie Stree
BRHD/NEIL G78 125 H6
Crossbank Av GVH/MTFL G42 105 L8
Crossbank Dr GVH/MTFL G42 105 K8
Crossbank Rd
GVH/MTFL G42 105 K8
Crossbank Ter GVH/MTFL G42 105 K8
Crossburn AYRS KA7 228 B8
Crossburn Av MLNGV G62 41 M8
Crossburn Ter TROON KA10 217 H5
Crossclyde Vw CARLUKE ML8 188 C8
Crossdene Rd CRH/DND KA2 210 F1
Crossdykes KKNTL G66 66 A2
Crossflat Crs PSLY PA1 9 L3
Crossford Dr SMSTN G23 62 E8
Cross Gates BLSH ML4 133 G5
Crossgates St LRKH ML9 175 M5
Crosshill Av GVH/MTFL G42 105 H8
KKNTL G66 65 K3
Crosshill Dr MTHW ML1 135 H6
RUTH G73 129 H3
Crosshill Pl PGL PA14 54 F2
Crosshill Rd BSHPBGS G64 64 C4
KKNTL G66 65 J6
PGL PA14 54 E2
Crosshill St AIRDRIE ML6 110 F2
CTBR ML5 109 J5
KKNTL G66 29 K8
MTHW ML1 157 M3
Crosshill Wynd
KLMNKN/STW KA3 207 J3
Crosshouse Rd EKILS G75 170 F4
KKNTL G66 29 G5
KLMNKN/STW KA3 206 B4
Crosslaw Av LNK/LMHG ML11 199 J6
Crosslea Gdns
CRG/CRSL/HOU PA6 77 H8
Crosslee Crs
CRG/CRSL/HOU PA6 77 J8
Crosslee Pk CRG/CRSL/HOU PA6 77 J8
Crosslee Rd BRWEIR PA11 99 G2
JNSTN PA5 98 F3
Crosslees Dr GIF/THBK G46 126 F6
Crosslees Pk GIF/THBK G46 126 F6
Crosslees Rd GIF/THBK G46 126 F7
Crosslee St
CARD/HILL/MSPK G52 103 K4
Crosslet Ct DMBTN G82 37 H6
Crosslet Pl DMBTN G82 37 H6
Crosslet Rd DMBTN G82 37 G6
Crossloan Rd GOV/IBX G51 103 M2
Crossloan Ter GOV/IBX G51 103 M2
Crossmill Av BRHD/NEIL G78 125 K5
Crosspoint Dr SMSTN G23 62 E8
Cross Rd PSLYS PA2 8 B8
Cross Stone Pl MTHW ML1 157 M3
Cross St CAR/SHTL G32 107 J8
PSLY PA1 8 D4
The Cross DALRY KA24 184 C2
Crosstobs Rd PLK/PH/NH G53 103 G8
Crossveggate MLNGV G62 42 B8
Crossview Av
BAIL/MDB/MHD G69 108 D4
Crossview Pl
BAIL/MDB/MHD G69 108 D4
Crossways CRG/CRSL/HOU PA6 77 K7
Crovie Rd PLK/PH/NH G53 126 A2
Crow Av MTHW ML1 134 B4
Crowflats Rd
UD/BTH/TAN G71 131 L3
Crowflat Vw
UD/BTH/TAN G71 109 J8
Crowhill Crs AIRDRIE ML6 88 F7
Crowhill Rd BSHPBGS G64 83 M1
Crowhill St PPK/MIL G22 83 J3
Crow La KNTSWD G13 81 M4
Crowlin Crs
STPS/GTHM/RID G33 107 H1
Crown Av CLYDBK G81 60 A6
Crown Circ KVD/HLHD G12 82 C6
Crown Gdns KVD/HLHD G12 82 C6
Crownhall Pl CAR/SHTL G32 107 J4
Crownhall Rd CAR/SHTL G32 107 J4
Crownpoint Rd
DMNK/BRGTN G40 12 F5
Crown Rd North
KVD/HLHD G12 82 C6
Crown Rd South KVD/HLHD G12 82 C6
Crown St AIRDRIE ML6 111 H6
AYR KA8 224 F7
BAIL/MDB/MHD G69 107 M6
CTBR ML5 110 C2
GBLS G5 11 J7
GRNK PA15 2 D4
Crown Ter KVD/HLHD G12 82 B6
Crow Rd CMPF/LLE G63 29 K2
KKNTL G66 29 H5
KNTSWD G13 81 M2
PTCK G11 82 A6
Crow-Wood Crs AIRDRIE ML6 111 H7
Crowwood Dr AIRDRIE ML6 111 K2
Crow-Wood Rd AIRDRIE ML6 111 H7
Crow Wood Rd
BAIL/MDB/MHD G69 86 B2
Crow Wood Ter
BAIL/MDB/MHD G69 86 B2
Croy EKILN G74 153 K6
Croy Av NMRNS G77 151 G4
Croy Pl SPRGB/BLRNK G21 84 C4
Croy Rd CTBR ML5 109 L5
SPRGB/BLRNK G21 84 C4
Cruachan Av PSLYS PA2 124 E1
RNFRW PA4 80 C8
Cruachan Dr BRHD/NEIL G78 125 J8
NMRNS G77 150 F6
Cruachan Pl KLMNK KA1 212 B5
Cruachan Rd BSDN G61 61 H2
RUTH G73 129 K6
Cruachan St GIF/THBK G46 126 F5
Cruachan Wy BRHD/NEIL G78 125 J8
Cruden St GOV/IBX G51 103 M3
Crum Av GIF/THBK G46 127 G6
Crummock Gdns BEITH KA15 144 C8
Crummock St BEITH KA15 144 C8
Crusader Av KNTSWD G13 61 K8
Crusader Crs KLMNKN/STW KA3 197 J1
Cubie St DMNK/BRGTN G40 12 D5
Cubrieshaw Dr WKIL KA23 181 K5
Cubrieshaw St WKIL KA23 181 K3
Cuckoo Wy MTHW ML1 134 B4
Cuff Crs BEITH KA15 168 A2
Cuilhill Rd BAIL/MDB/MHD G69 109 G3
CTBR ML5 108 F1
Cuillin Pl IRVSE KA11 204 A5
KLMNK KA1 212 A6
Cuillins Av PGL PA14 54 F3
The Cuillins BAIL/MDB/MHD G69 67 G5
UD/BTH/TAN G71 108 E8
Cuillin Wy BRHD/NEIL G78 125 J7
Cuilmuir Ter KSYTH G65 47 M4
Cuilmuir Vw KSYTH G65 47 L4
Cuilt Pl CMPF/LLE G63 27 G5
Cuilts Rd CMPF/LLE G63 26 A5
Culbin Dr KNTSWD G13 80 F1
Cullen La EKILS G75 14 D7
Cullen Pl UD/BTH/TAN G71 132 A1
Cullen Rd EKILS G75 14 D7
MTHW ML1 157 J4
Cullen St ALEX/LLW G83 25 J2
CAR/SHTL G32 107 G5
Cullins Rd RUTH G73 129 K6
Cullion Wy MTHW ML1 134 F4
Cullochrig Rd AIRDRIE ML6 68 E7
Culloch Rd BSDN G61 61 J1
Culloden Pl KLMNKN/STW KA3 207 H6
Culloden St DEN/PKHD G31 7 G8
Culrain Gdns CAR/SHTL G32 107 G4
Culrain St CAR/SHTL G32 107 G4
Culross Hl EKILN G74 14 C3
Culross Pl CTBR ML5 109 M2
EKILN G74 14 C3
Culross St CAR/SHTL G32 107 J5
Culross Wy
BAIL/MDB/MHD G69 67 G6
Cult Rd KKNTL G66 65 L5
Cults St GOV/IBX G51 103 M3
Culvain Av BSDN G61 61 H2
Culzean AIRDRIE ML6 88 F4
Culzean Av CTBR ML5 109 L5
PSTWK KA9 225 K2
Culzean Crs
BAIL/MDB/MHD G69 108 A5
KLMNKN/STW KA3 17 K4
NMRNS G77 151 G4
Culzean Dr CAR/SHTL G32 107 K5
GRK PA19 30 F4
MTHW ML1 134 C6
Culzean Pl EKILN G74 153 K6
KLWNG KA13 193 J7
Culzean Rd AYRS KA7 228 D6
Cumberland Av HBR/GL G84 20 A6
Cumberland Pl CTBR ML5 109 J5
GBLS G5 11 K8
Cumberland Rd
GRNKW/INVK PA16 31 L5
Cumberland St GBLS G5 11 J7
Cumbernauld Rd
BAIL/MDB/MHD G69 67 G7
BAIL/MDB/MHD G69 86 D1
CUMB G67 67 K5
DEN/PKHD G31 13 G2
DMNK/BRGTN G40 12 E8
STPS/GTHM/RID G33 7 L9
Cumbrae EKILN G74 154 C8
Cumbrae Av PGL PA14 55 H2
Cumbrae Ct CLYDBK G81 60 B7
Cumbrae Crs CTBR ML5 110 E4
Cumbrae Crs North
DMBTN G82 36 C4
Cumbrae Crs South DMBTN G82 36 B4
Cumbrae Dr GTCI KA28 138 C6
KLMNKN/STW KA3 207 H3
MTHW ML1 157 J2
Cumbrae Pl AIRDRIE ML6 110 E5
GRK PA19 31 K3
WKIL KA23 181 J5
Cumbrae Rd PSLYS PA2 124 E2
RNFRW PA4 80 D8
SALT KA21 191 M7
Cumbrae St
STPS/GTHM/RID G33 107 G1
Cumlodden Dr MRYH/FIRH G20 82 C2
Cumming Dr GVH/MTFL G42 128 B1
Cumnock Dr AIRDRIE ML6 111 G5
BRHD/NEIL G78 125 K8
HMLTN ML3 155 K8
Cumnock Rd
STPS/GTHM/RID G33 84 E3
Cumroch Rd KKNTL G66 29 J8
Cunard St CLYDBK G81 80 B1
Cuninghame Dr SVSTN KA20 192 B8
Cuninghame Rd ARD KA22 191 J6
KLBCH PA10 99 H6
Cunningair Dr MTHW ML1 157 L5
Cunningham Crs AYRS KA7 19 K8
Cunningham Dr GIF/THBK G46 127 L6
LARGS KA30 115 K7
Cunninghame Dr KLMNK KA1 211 L5
Cunninghame Rd EKILN G74 14 E2
IRV KA12 208 B1
PSTWK KA9 225 J2
RUTH G73 129 J1
SALT KA21 201 G1
Cunningham Pl AYRS KA7 19 K8
Cunningham Rd
CARD/HILL/MSPK G52 102 F1
Cunningham St
MAUCH/CAT KA5 223 M6
MTHW ML1 157 J3
Cunning Park Dr AYRS KA7 228 D6
Cupar Dr GRNKW/INVK PA16 31 M6
Cuparhead Av CTBR ML5 109 K5
Cuppleton Brae HWWD PA9 121 H7
Curfew Rd KNTSWD G13 61 K8
Curle St SCOT G14 81 K7
Curlew Crs GRNKW/INVK PA16 32 B5

Curlew La GRNKW/INVK PA16 32 B5
Curlew Pl JNSTN PA5 122 C2
Curling Crs GVH/MTFL G42 128 C1
Curlinghall LARGS KA30 115 J7
Curlinghaugh Crs WISHAW ML2 159 J6
Curlingmire EKILS G75 14 F9
Curran Av WISHAW ML2 158 E8
Currie Ct ARD KA22 191 J8
Currieside Av SHOTTS ML7 137 K5
Currieside Pl SHOTTS ML7 137 K5
Currie St MRYH/FIRH G20 82 E3
Curtecan Pl AYRS KA7 18 F8
Curtis Av LNPK/KPK G44 128 D2
Curzon St MRYH/FIRH G20 82 E3
Customhouse Pl GRNK PA15 2 F4
Cuthbert Pl KLMNKN/STW KA3 17 G1
Cuthbertson St
PLKSD/SHW G41 105 G6
Cuthbert St
UD/BTH/TAN G71 132 B2
Cuthelton Dr DEN/PKHD G31 106 E5
Cuthelton St DEN/PKHD G31 13 M8
Cuthelton Ter DEN/PKHD G31 13 M8
Cutsburn Pl KLMNKN/STW KA3 197 M1
Cutsburn Rd KLMNKN/STW KA3 197 M1
Cutstraw Rd KLMNKN/STW KA3 197 L1
Cypress Av BEITH KA15 144 C7
BLTYR/CAMB G72 155 J1
UD/BTH/TAN G71 132 B1
Cypress Ct EKILS G75 171 J4
HMLTN ML3 156 E7
KKNTL G66 65 H3
Cypress Crs EKILS G75 171 J4
Cypress Gdns IRV KA12 203 L4
Cypress Pl EKILS G75 171 J4
Cypress St PPK/MIL G22 83 K4
Cyprus Av JNSTN PA5 100 B7
Cyril St PSLY PA1 9 M4

D

Daer Av RNFRW PA4 80 E8
Daer Wy HMLTN ML3 156 A6
Daff Av GRNKW/INVK PA16 50 D4
Daffodil Wy MTHW ML1 157 L1
Dairsie Gdns BSHPBGS G64 84 D1
Dairsie St LNPK/KPK G44 127 M5
Daisybank GLGNK KA14 167 J3
Daisy St GVH/MTFL G42 105 H7
Dalbeth Rd CAR/SHTL G32 106 F7
Dalblair Rd AYRS KA7 18 E4
Dalcharn Pl ESTRH G34 108 A1
Dalcraig Crs BLTYR/CAMB G72 131 J8
Dalcross St PTCK G11 82 C7
Dalcruin Gdns
BAIL/MDB/MHD G69 67 G5
Daldowie Av CAR/SHTL G32 107 K6
Daldowie Rd UD/BTH/TAN G71 108 A7
Daldowie St CTBR ML5 109 L6
Dale Av EKILS G75 14 B8
Dale Ct WISHAW ML2 158 C7
Dale Crs IRV KA12 203 K5
Dale Dr MTHW ML1 134 A5
Dale St DMNK/BRGTN G40 12 D8
Daleview Av KVD/HLHD G12 82 B3
Daleview Dr
CRMNK/CLK/EAG G76 151 K3
Daleview Gv
CRMNK/CLK/EAG G76 151 K3
Dale Wy RUTH G73 129 G5
Dalfoil Ct PSLY PA1 102 F5
Dalgarroch Av KNTSWD G13 80 E1
Dalgarven Ms
KLMNKN/STW KA3 207 J3
Dalgleish Av CLYDBK G81 59 M3
Dalgraig Crs BLTYR/CAMB G72 131 J7
Dalhousie Gdns BSHPBGS G64 63 M7
Dalhousie La KVGV G3 4 F7
Dalhousie Rd KLBCH PA10 99 H7
Dalhousie St CGLW G2 4 F8
COWCAD G4 5 G7
Dalilea Dr ESTRH G34 86 D8
Dalilea Pl ESTRH G34 86 D8
Dalintober St GBLS G5 10 E4
Dalkeith Av BSHPBGS G64 64 B6
PLKSD/SHW G41 104 B5
Dalkeith Rd BSHPBGS G64 64 B5
Dallas La TROON KA10 216 C7
Dallas Pl TROON KA10 216 C7
Dallas Rd TROON KA10 216 C7
Dalmacoulter Rd AIRDRIE ML6 89 H6
Dalmahoy Crs BRWEIR PA11 98 C3
Dalmahoy St CAR/SHTL G32 106 E2
Dalmahoy Wy KLWNG KA13 193 H6
Dalmailing Av IRVSE KA11 204 B8
Dalmally St GRNK PA15 33 M7
MRYH/FIRH G20 4 D2
Dalmarnock Rd
DMNK/BRGTN G40 12 D8
Dalmary Dr PSLY PA1 102 B3
Dalmellington Ct HMLTN ML3 155 K8
Dalmellington Dr EKILN G74 14 D1
Dalmellington Rd AYRS KA7 229 J5
PLK/PH/NH G53 126 A1
Dalmeny Av GIF/THBK G46 127 J6
Dalmeny Dr BRHD/NEIL G78 125 G7
Dalmeny Rd HMLTN ML3 156 D7
Dalmeny St GBLS G5 105 L7
Dalmilling Crs AYR KA8 225 K8
Dalmilling Dr AYR KA8 225 K7
Dalmilling Rd AYR KA8 225 K7
Dalmoak Rd GRNK PA15 33 J8
Dalmonach Rd ALEX/LLW G83 25 M5
Dalmore Crs HBR/GL G84 20 A6
Dalmore Pl IRVSE KA11 203 M3
Dalmore Wy IRVSE KA11 203 M3
Dalnair Pl MLNGV G62 41 K8
Dalnair St KVGV G3 82 C8
Dalness St CAR/SHTL G32 107 G6
Dalnottar Av OLDK G60 59 H3
Dalnottar Dr OLDK G60 59 H4
Dalnottar Gdns OLDK G60 59 H4
Dalnottar Hill Rd OLDK G60 59 H4
Dalreoch Av
BAIL/MDB/MHD G69 108 C4
Dalreoch Ct DMBTN G82 36 D5
Dalriada Crs MTHW ML1 133 K8
Dalriada Dr BSHPBGS G64 44 C8
Dalriada Rd GRNKW/INVK PA16 31 K7
Dalriada St DMNK/BRGTN G40 13 J7
Dalry Gdns HMLTN ML3 155 K7
Dalrymple Ct IRV KA12 203 L6
Dalrymple Dr EKILN G74 14 F1
IRV KA12 203 K7
NMRNS G77 151 G5
Dalrymple St GRNK PA15 2 D3
Dalrymple Vw RAYR/DAL KA6 231 H6
Dalry Pl AIRDRIE ML6 134 D1
Dalry Rd ARD KA22 191 J5
BEITH KA15 168 A2
KBRN KA25 167 G2
KLWNG KA13 193 K4
LARGS KA30 115 L8
SALT KA21 192 A8
UD/BTH/TAN G71 132 B2
Dalry St CAR/SHTL G32 107 H5
Dalserf Crs GIF/THBK G46 127 H8
Dalserf St DEN/PKHD G31 13 G6
Dalsetter Av DRUM G15 60 F7
Dalsetter Pl DRUM G15 61 G7
Dalshannon Pl CUMB G67 68 B2
Dalshannon Rd CUMB G67 68 B2
Dalshannon Vw CUMB G67 68 B2
Dalsholm Rd MRYH/FIRH G20 82 B2
Dalskeith Av PSLYN/LNWD PA3 101 G4
Dalskeith Crs
PSLYN/LNWD PA3 101 G4
Dalskeith Rd PSLYN/LNWD PA3 101 G5
Dalswinton Pth ESTRH G34 108 D1
Dalswinton St ESTRH G34 108 C1
Dalton Av CLYDBK G81 60 E8
Dalton Hl HMLTN ML3 155 K7
Dalton St DEN/PKHD G31 106 E4
Dalvait Gdns ALEX/LLW G83 25 L1
Dalvait Rd ALEX/LLW G83 25 L1
Dalveen Ct BRHD/NEIL G78 125 J8
Dalveen Dr UD/BTH/TAN G71 131 L1
Dalveen Qd CTBR ML5 110 D4
Dalveen St CAR/SHTL G32 106 F4
Dalveen Wy RUTH G73 129 J6
Dalwhatswood Rd
NMLNS KA16 215 L1
Dalwhinnie Av
BLTYR/CAMB G72 131 J7
Dalwood Rd PSTWK KA9 225 H1
Daly Gdns BLTYR/CAMB G72 131 K8
Dalzell Av MTHW ML1 158 A5
Dalzell Dr MTHW ML1 158 A6
Dalziel Dr PLKSD/SHW G41 104 C6
Dalziel Rd
CARD/HILL/MSPK G52 102 F1
Dalziel St HMLTN ML3 156 B4
MTHW ML1 157 L2
Damhead Rd KLMNK KA1 211 L6
Damshot Crs PLK/PH/NH G53 126 D1
Damshot Rd PLK/PH/NH G53 126 D2
Damside AYR KA8 224 F7
Danby Rd BAIL/MDB/MHD G69 107 M5
Danefield Av LARGS KA30 115 H2
Danes Av SCOT G14 81 J5
Danes Crs SCOT G14 81 H4
Danes La North SCOT G14 81 J5
Danes La South SCOT G14 81 J5
Daniel Mclaughlin Pl
KKNTL G66 45 L8
Dankeith Dr KLMNK KA1 218 C5
Dankeith Rd KLMNK KA1 218 C5
Dargarvel Av PLKSD/SHW G41 104 B5
Dargavel Av BSHPTN PA7 58 B7
Dargavel Rd ERSK PA8 58 D8
Darg Rd SVSTN KA20 201 K1
Dark Brig Rd CARLUKE ML8 188 B7
Darkwood Ct PSLYN/LNWD PA3 8 A1
Darkwood Crs PSLYN/LNWD PA3 8 A1
Darleith Rd ALEX/LLW G83 25 L3
DMBTN G82 24 A8
Darleith St CAR/SHTL G32 106 F4
Darley Crs TROON KA10 216 D8
Darley Pl HMLTN ML3 174 A1
TROON KA10 216 D8
Darley Rd BALLOCH G68 48 E4
Darluith Rd PSLYN/LNWD PA3 99 L3
Darmeid Pl SHOTTS ML7 161 H1
Darmule Dr KLWNG KA13 193 J4
Darnaway Av
STPS/GTHM/RID G33 85 K7
Darnaway Dr
STPS/GTHM/RID G33 85 K7
Darnaway St
STPS/GTHM/RID G33 85 K7
Darndaff Rd GRNK PA15 2 F8
Darngaber Gdns HMLTN ML3 174 E6
Darngaber Rd HMLTN ML3 174 E6
Darngavil Rd AIRDRIE ML6 89 L3
Darnick St SPRGB/BLRNK G21 6 F3
Darnley Crs BSHPBGS G64 63 M6
Darnley Dr KLMNK KA1 211 L4
Darnley Gdns PLKSD/SHW G41 104 E7
Darnleyhill Wk NMLNS KA16 215 J2
Darnley Mains Rd
PLK/PH/NH G53 126 C6
Darnley Pl PLKSD/SHW G41 104 E7
Darnley Rd BRHD/NEIL G78 125 L6
PLKSD/SHW G41 104 E7
Darnley St PLKSD/SHW G41 104 F6
Darnshaw Cl IRVSE KA11 204 C4
Darragh Gn WISHAW ML2 160 A3
Darroch Av GRK PA19 31 L2
Darroch Dr ERSK PA8 58 F6
GRK PA19 31 L2
Darroch Wy CUMB G67 49 G6
Dartford St PPK/MIL G22 5 G2
Dartmouth Av
GRNKW/INVK PA16 31 L4
Darvel Crs PSLY PA1 102 D5
Darvel Dr NMRNS G77 151 G4
Darvel Rd NMLNS KA16 215 M2
Darvel St PLK/PH/NH G53 125 M3
Darwin Pl CLYDBK G81 59 K6
Darwin Rd EKILS G75 14 A6
Davaar EKILN G74 154 C8
Davaar Dr CTBR ML5 109 K2
KLMNKN/STW KA3 207 H4
MTHW ML1 133 J7
PSLYS PA2 124 E2
Davaar Pl NMRNS G77 150 C3
Davaar Rd GRNKW/INVK PA16 31 J6
RNFRW PA4 80 D8
SALT KA21 191 M7
Davaar St DMNK/BRGTN G40 13 H7
Dava St GOV/IBX G51 104 A2
Daventry Dr KVD/HLHD G12 82 A4
Davey St GRNKW/INVK PA16 32 B4
David Dale Av
KLMNKN/STW KA3 197 J2
David Gage St KLWNG KA13 193 L4
David Gray Dr KKNTL G66 46 A8
David Orr St KLMNK KA1 16 C3
David Pl BAIL/MDB/MHD G69 107 M5
David's Crs KLWNG KA13 193 K7
Davidson Av GLGNK KA14 167 K3
Davidson Crs KSYTH G65 46 E6
Davidson Dr GRK PA19 31 L2
Davidson Pl CAR/SHTL G32 107 J3
Davidson Qd CLYDBK G81 59 L2
Davidson Rd ALEX/LLW G83 25 M2
Davidson St AIRDRIE ML6 110 F1
CLYDBK G81 80 E1
CTBR ML5 110 B5
DMNK/BRGTN G40 106 A7
David St CTBR ML5 110 C2
DMNK/BRGTN G40 12 F5
SHOTTS ML7 113 H7
Davieland Rd GIF/THBK G46 127 G8
Davie's Acre EKILN G74 152 F5
Davies Dr ALEX/LLW G83 25 L3
Davies Qd MTHW ML1 133 K7
Davington Dr HMLTN ML3 155 K7
Daviot St GOV/IBX G51 103 K3
Dawson Av EKILS G75 153 H8
Dawson Pl COWCAD G4 5 H3
Dawson Rd COWCAD G4 5 H3
Deaconsbank Av GIF/THBK G46 126 D8
Deaconsbank Crs
GIF/THBK G46 126 D8
Deacons Rd KSYTH G65 47 K1
Dealston Rd BRHD/NEIL G78 125 H5
Deanbrae St
UD/BTH/TAN G71 131 M3
Dean Crs BAIL/MDB/MHD G69 66 D8
HMLTN ML3 156 C8
Deanfield Qd
CARD/HILL/MSPK G52 102 F3
Deanfield Quadrant
CARD/HILL/MSPK G52 102 F3
Deanhill La KLMNKN/STW KA3 207 G6
Dean La KLMNKN/STW KA3 17 G1
Dean Park Av
UD/BTH/TAN G71 132 A7
Dean Park Dr
BLTYR/CAMB G72 130 D5
Dean Park Rd RNFRW PA4 80 D7
Dean Pl CRH/DND KA2 210 F1
Dean Rd KBRN KA25 143 H7
KLMNKN/STW KA3 207 G6
Deans Av BLTYR/CAMB G72 130 D6
Deanside Rd
CARD/HILL/MSPK G52 103 G1
Deanston Av BRHD/NEIL G78 125 H8
Deanston Dr PLKSD/SHW G41 127 L1
Deanstone Pl CTBR ML5 110 D6
Deanstone Wk CTBR ML5 110 D7
Deanston Gv CTBR ML5 109 L6
Deanston Pk
BRHD/NEIL G78 125 H8
Dean St BLSH ML4 133 H4
CLYDBK G81 60 C8
KLMNKN/STW KA3 17 G1
Deanwood Av GIF/THBK G46 127 M6
Deanwood Rd GIF/THBK G46 127 M6
Deas Rd SHOTTS ML7 137 J4
Dechmont EKILS G75 171 K4
Dechmont Av
BLTYR/CAMB G72 130 D6
MTHW ML1 157 J2
Dechmont Gdns
BLTYR/CAMB G72 131 J8
Dechmont Pl BLTYR/CAMB G72 130 D6
Dechmont Rd
UD/BTH/TAN G71 108 E8
Dechmont St DEN/PKHD G31 13 K7
HMLTN ML3 156 C7
Dechmont Vw BLSH ML4 132 F6
UD/BTH/TAN G71 132 A2
Dee Av KLMNK KA1 212 B5
PSLYS PA2 100 F7
RNFRW PA4 80 E6
Deedes St AIRDRIE ML6 110 D3
Dee Dr PSLYS PA2 100 F8
Deep Dl EKILN G74 153 J6
Deepdene Rd
BAIL/MDB/MHD G69 66 F7
BSDN G61 61 K6
Dee Pl EKILS G75 170 E2
JNSTN PA5 122 C1
Deerdykes Ct North
BALLOCH G68 67 L3
Deerdykes Ct South
BALLOCH G68 67 L4
Deerdykes Pl BALLOCH G68 67 L3
Deerdykes Rd BALLOCH G68 67 K4
Deerdykes Vw BALLOCH G68 67 K4
Deer Park Av SVSTN KA20 201 L2
Deer Park Ct HMLTN ML3 174 D2
Deer Park Pl HMLTN ML3 174 E2
Deeside Dr CARLUKE ML8 179 G6
Dee St CTBR ML5 87 J7
GRNKW/INVK PA16 32 B4
SHOTTS ML7 137 K4
STPS/GTHM/RID G33 7 L8
Dee Ter HMLTN ML3 174 B1
Delfie Dr GRNKW/INVK PA16 32 B5
Delhi Av CLYDBK G81 59 J5
Dellburn St MTHW ML1 157 M4
Dellingburn St GRNK PA15 2 E6
The Dell BLSH ML4 133 K6
Delny Pl STPS/GTHM/RID G33 107 L2
Delves Rd LNK/LMHG ML11 199 G6
Delvin Rd LNPK/KPK G44 128 A3
De Morville Pl BEITH KA15 168 B2
Dempsey Rd BLSH ML4 132 F6
Dempster St GRNK PA15 2 A5
Denbak Av HMLTN ML3 156 A7
Denbeck St CAR/SHTL G32 106 F4
Denbrae St CAR/SHTL G32 106 F4
Denewood Av PSLYS PA2 124 D1
Denham St PPK/MIL G22 5 G2
Denholm Crs EKILS G75 14 F5
Denholm Dr GIF/THBK G46 151 J1
WISHAW ML2 159 J3
Denholm Gdns
GRNKW/INVK PA16 32 C4
HMLTN ML3 174 E6
Denholm Gn EKILS G75 15 G5
Denholm St GRNKW/INVK PA16 32 D3
Denholm Ter GRNKW/INVK PA16 32 D4
HMLTN ML3 155 L6
Denholm Wy BEITH KA15 168 A2
Denmark St PPK/MIL G22 83 J5
Denmilne Rd
BAIL/MDB/MHD G69 108 D2
Denmilne St ESTRH G34 108 C2
Dennistoun Crs HBR/GL G84 22 F2
Dennistoun Rd PGL PA14 56 B2
Dennistoun St BLSH ML4 133 G4
Dennyholm Wynd KBRN KA25 143 H8
Dennystoun Forge DMBTN G82 36 E5
Dentdale EKILN G74 153 J6
Deramore Av GIF/THBK G46 151 G2
Derby St KVGV G3 4 A8
Derby Terrace La KVGV G3 82 D8
Derrywood Rd KKNTL G66 45 J3
Derwent Dr CTBR ML5 87 J7
Derwent St PPK/MIL G22 5 G1
Derwentwater EKILS G75 170 F3
Despard Av CAR/SHTL G32 107 K5
Despard Gdns CAR/SHTL G32 107 L5
Deveron Av GIF/THBK G46 127 K7
Deveron Crs HMLTN ML3 155 K5
Deveron Rd BSDN G61 61 J7
EKILN G74 15 L3
KLMNK KA1 212 A4
MTHW ML1 134 B3
TROON KA10 216 E3
Deveron St CTBR ML5 87 J8
STPS/GTHM/RID G33 7 L7
Devilla Ct PSTWK KA9 225 J4
Devine Gv WISHAW ML2 160 A2
Devlin Ct BLTYR/CAMB G72 155 L2
Devlin Gv BLTYR/CAMB G72 155 L2
Devol Av PGL PA14 34 A8
Devol Crs PLK/PH/NH G53 126 B1
Devol Rd PGL PA14 54 C4
Devondale Av
BLTYR/CAMB G72 131 J8
Devon Dr BSHPTN PA7 58 C6
Devon Gdns BSHPBGS G64 63 M6
CARLUKE ML8 178 E7
Devonhill Av HMLTN ML3 174 D2
Devon Pl GVH/MTFL G42 11 G8
Devonport Pk EKILS G75 171 G2
Devon Rd GRNKW/INVK PA16 31 K5
Devonshire Gardens La
KVD/HLHD G12 82 B5
Devonshire Ter KVD/HLHD G12 82 B5
Devonshire Terrace La
KVD/HLHD G12 82 B5
Devon St GBLS G5 11 G8
Devonview Pl AIRDRIE ML6 110 F3
Devonview St AIRDRIE ML6 110 F2
Devon Wk BALLOCH G68 67 L1
Devon Wy MTHW ML1 157 H3
De Walden Ter
KLMNKN/STW KA3 17 H3
Dewar Cl UD/BTH/TAN G71 109 G8
Dhuhill Dr East HBR/GL G84 20 E5
Diamond St BLSH ML4 133 G5
Diana Av KNTSWD G13 81 H1
Diana Qd MTHW ML1 134 A4
Diana Vernon Ct HBR/GL G84 22 F1
Dick Crs IRV KA12 203 K4
Dickens Av CLYDBK G81 59 M5
Dick Rd KLMNK KA1 17 G5
Dickson Dr IRV KA12 203 J4
Dickson St LRKH ML9 176 C8
Dicks Pk EKILS G75 14 D5
Dick St MRYH/FIRH G20 4 D3
Dick Ter IRV KA12 203 K4
Diddup Dr SVSTN KA20 192 B8
Differ Av KSYTH G65 46 F7
Dillichip Cl ALEX/LLW G83 25 M7
Dillichip Gdns ALEX/LLW G83 25 M6
Dillichip Loan ALEX/LLW G83 25 L6
Dilwara Av SCOT G14 81 L7
Dimity St JNSTN PA5 99 M7
Dimsdale Crs WISHAW ML2 159 J8
Dimsdale Rd WISHAW ML2 159 J8
Dinard Dr GIF/THBK G46 127 J5
Dinart St STPS/GTHM/RID G33 7 L7
Dinduff St ESTRH G34 86 C8
Dingwall Dr
GRNKW/INVK PA16 31 M6
Dinmont Av PSLYS PA2 123 M1
Dinmont Crs MTHW ML1 133 J7
Dinmont Rd PLKSD/SHW G41 104 D8
Dinmurchie Rd TROON KA10 216 E4
Dinwiddie St SPRGB/BLRNK G21 7 J4
Dinyra Pl CTBR ML5 87 J3
Dippin Pl SALT KA21 191 M7
Dipple Ct KBRN KA25 143 H7
Dipple Pl DRUM G15 61 H7
Dipple Rd KBRN KA25 143 H6
Dipple Vw KBRN KA25 143 H6
Dirleton Dr PLKSD/SHW G41 127 L1
PSLYS PA2 101 G8
Dirleton Ga BSDN G61 61 K6
Dirrans Ter KLWNG KA13 193 M7
Ditton Dr KLMNK KA1 211 L5
Divernia Wy BRHD/NEIL G78 149 K1
Divert Rd GRK PA19 31 J3
Dixon Av DMBTN G82 36 E6
GVH/MTFL G42 105 G7
Dixon Dr DMBTN G82 36 D7
Dixon Pl EKILN G74 153 H6
Dixon Rd GVH/MTFL G42 105 J8
HBR/GL G84 20 E6
Dixon St CGLE G1 11 H3
CTBR ML5 110 B5
HMLTN ML3 156 D6
PSLY PA1 9 K4
Dickens Gv MTHW ML1 134 D7
Dobbies Ct CARLUKE ML8 178 A3
Dobbie's Loan CGLW G2 5 K6
COWCAD G4 5 K7
Dobbie's Loan Pl COWCAD G4 5 L8
Dochart Av RNFRW PA4 80 E8
Dochart Dr CTBR ML5 87 J7
Dochart St STPS/GTHM/RID G33 84 E7
Dock Breast GRNK PA15 2 F4
Dockhead Pl SALT KA21 200 E2
Dock Rd ARD KA22 191 H8
Dock St CLYDBK G81 80 D2
Dodhill Pl KNTSWD G13 81 H3
Dodside Gdns CAR/SHTL G32 107 J5
Dodside Pl CAR/SHTL G32 107 J5
Dodside St CAR/SHTL G32 107 J5
Dolan St BAIL/MDB/MHD G69 108 B4
Dollar Pk MTHW ML1 158 B6
Dollar Ter MRYH/FIRH G20 82 C1
Dolphin Rd PLKSD/SHW G41 104 D7
Dominica Gn EKILS G75 153 G8
Donald Crs TROON KA10 216 D5
Donaldfield Rd BRWEIR PA11 98 B2
Donaldson Av KSYTH G65 47 K2
SALT KA21 200 F1
SVSTN KA20 192 E7
Donaldson Crs KKNTL G66 65 J2
Donaldson Dr IRV KA12 203 K5
KLMNKN/STW KA3 207 K6
RNFRW PA4 80 D6
Donaldson Gn
UD/BTH/TAN G71 132 A1
Donaldson Rd LRKH ML9 176 C8
Donaldson St HMLTN ML3 156 A4
KKNTL G66 65 J2
Donaldswood Pk PSLYS PA2 124 C1
Donaldswood Rd PSLYS PA2 124 C1
Donald Ter HMLTN ML3 156 C8
Donald Wy UD/BTH/TAN G71 132 A2
Don Av RNFRW PA4 80 E7
Doncaster St MRYH/FIRH G20 4 E2
Don Ct HMLTN ML3 174 A1
Don Dr PSLYS PA2 100 F8
Dongola Rd AYRS KA7 19 G7
Donnelly Wy WISHAW ML2 158 C5
Donnies Brae BRHD/NEIL G78 124 F8
Don Pl JNSTN PA5 122 C1
Don St GRNKW/INVK PA16 32 C4
STPS/GTHM/RID G33 7 L8
Doon Av PSTWK KA9 225 H4
Doon Crs BSDN G61 61 K6
Doonfoot Gdns EKILN G74 14 D1
Doonfoot Rd AYRS KA7 228 D6
PLKSW/MSWD G43 127 J3
Doonholm Pk AYRS KA7 228 F8
Doonholm Pl AYRS KA7 228 F8
Doon Pl KKNTL G66 45 M7
KLMNK KA1 212 B5
SALT KA21 192 A6
TROON KA10 216 E4
Doon Rd KKNTL G66 45 M8
Doon Side CUMB G67 49 H7
Doon St CLYDBK G81 60 C6
LRKH ML9 176 C7
MTHW ML1 158 A5
Doon Wy KKNTL G66 46 A8
Dorain Rd MTHW ML1 134 D6
Dora St DMNK/BRGTN G40 106 A6
Dorchester Av KVD/HLHD G12 82 A3
Dorchester Ct KVD/HLHD G12 82 A3
Dorchester Pl KVD/HLHD G12 82 A4
Dorian Dr CRMNK/CLK/EAG G76 151 J1
Dorlin Rd STPS/GTHM/RID G33 85 L4
Dormanside Ct
PLK/PH/NH G53 103 H6
Dormanside Ga
PLK/PH/NH G53 103 H6
Dormanside Gv
PLK/PH/NH G53 103 H6
Dormanside Rd
PLK/PH/NH G53 103 H6
Dornal Av KNTSWD G13 80 E2
Dornal Dr TROON KA10 216 F3
Dornford Av CAR/SHTL G32 107 K7
Dornford Rd CAR/SHTL G32 107 K7
Dornie Dr CAR/SHTL G32 130 B1
Dornoch Av GIF/THBK G46 127 J8
Dornoch Ct BLSH ML4 133 G4
KLWNG KA13 193 H6
Dornoch Pk AYRS KA7 18 D7
Dornoch Pl
BAIL/MDB/MHD G69 66 D8
EKILN G74 14 C2
Dornoch Rd BSDN G61 61 K7
MTHW ML1 134 B4
Dornoch St DMNK/BRGTN G40 12 C5
Dornoch Wy AIRDRIE ML6 110 F4
BALLOCH G68 49 G4
Dorset Rd GRNKW/INVK PA16 31 L5
Dorset St KVGV G3 4 C9
Dosk Av KNTSWD G13 80 E1
Dosk Pl KNTSWD G13 80 F1
Double Hedges Rd
BRHD/NEIL G78 148 D3
Dougalston Av MLNGV G62 42 B8
Dougalston Crs MLNGV G62 42 B8
Dougalston Gdns North
MLNGV G62 42 B8
Dougalston Gdns South
MLNGV G62 42 B8
Dougalston Rd SMSTN G23 62 E8
Douglas Av CAR/SHTL G32 107 H8
DALRY KA24 184 D2
GIF/THBK G46 127 J8
JNSTN PA5 100 B7
KKNTL G66 65 K4
PGL PA14 56 C2
PSTWK KA9 225 H3
RUTH G73 129 J4
Douglas Brown Pl
RAYR/DAL KA6 231 H6
Douglas Crs AIRDRIE ML6 111 G3
ERSK PA8 58 F6
HMLTN ML3 174 D3
UD/BTH/TAN G71 132 B1
Douglasdale EKILN G74 14 C1
Douglas Dr
BAIL/MDB/MHD G69 107 M4

BLSH ML4 133 K5
BLTYR/CAMB G72 129 M5
DRUM G15 60 F8
EKILS G75 170 E2
HBR/GL G84 20 D5
NMRNS G77 150 E3
UD/BTH/TAN G71 132 A8
Douglas Dr East HBR/GL G84 20 E6
Douglas Gdns BSDN G61 61 M5
GIF/THBK G46 127 J8
UD/BTH/TAN G71 131 M4
Douglas Ga BLTYR/CAMB G72 130 A4
Douglas La AYRS KA7 18 E3 1
CGLW G2 4 F9 2
Douglas Muir Dr MLNGV G62 41 J6
Douglas Muir Gdns
MLNGV G62 41 J6 1
Douglas Muir Pl MLNGV G62 41 J6
Douglas Muir Rd CLYDBK G81 60 D2
MLNGV G62 41 K7
Douglas Park Crs BSDN G61 62 A3
Douglas Park La HMLTN ML3 156 C5 1
Douglas Pl BSDN G61 61 L4 1
HMLTN ML3 174 D3 3
KKNTL G66 65 K4
LARGS KA30 115 J4
Douglas Rd DMBTN G82 37 H6
RAYR/DAL KA6 231 H5 1
RNFRW PA4 102 A1
Douglas St AIRDRIE ML6 111 G3
AYRS KA7 18 E3
BLTYR/CAMB G72 155 J3
CARLUKE ML8 178 E7
CGLW G2 4 F8
HMLTN ML3 156 C5 2
KLMNK KA1 16 E6
LARGS KA30 115 J4
LRKH ML9 176 A5
MTHW ML1 157 K2
PSLY PA1 8 D3
UD/BTH/TAN G71 132 B2
WISHAW ML2 177 J2
Douglas Ter PLKSD/SHW G41 104 F7 2
Dougliehill Pl PGL PA14 54 C1
Dougliehill Rd PGL PA14 54 C1
Dougliehill Ter PGL PA14 54 C1
Dougray Pl BRHD/NEIL G78 125 J7 1
Dougrie Dr CSMK G45 128 D6
Dougrie Pl CSMK G45 128 E6
Dougrie Rd CSMK G45 128 D6
Dougrie St CSMK G45 128 D6
Dougrie Ter CSMK G45 128 D6
Dougrie Gdns CSMK G45 128 D7
Doune Crs AIRDRIE ML6 111 K8 1
BSHPBGS G64 64 B5
NMRNS G77 150 F4
Doune Gdns GRK PA19 30 F4
MRYH/FIRH G20 4 B2
Doune Gardens La
MRYH/FIRH G20 4 B2
Doune Park Wy CTBR ML5 109 M5
Doune Qd MRYH/FIRH G20 4 B2
Doune Ter CTBR ML5 87 K8
Doura Dr IRVSE KA11 203 M4
Dovecot PLKSW/MSWD G43 127 J1 1
Dovecote Vw KKNTL G66 65 M2
Dovecot La KLWNG KA13 193 L6
LNK/LMHG ML11 199 G5 1
Doveholm DMBTN G82 37 G4 1
Doveholm Av DMBTN G82 37 H4
Dove Pl EKILS G75 170 F3 1
Dover St CTBR ML5 87 K7
KVGV G3 4 C9
Dove St PLK/PH/NH G53 126 A4
Dove Wynd BLSH ML4 132 F2
Dowanfield Rd CUMB G67 48 D8
Dowanhill St PTCK G11 82 C7
Dowan Rd MLNGV G62 42 F7
Dowanside La KVD/HLHD G12 82 C6 1
Dowanside Rd KVD/HLHD G12 82 C6
Downcraig Dr CSMK G45 128 C7
Downcraig Gv CSMK G45 128 C7 1
Downcraig Rd CSMK G45 128 C7
Downcraig Ter CSMK G45 128 D7
Downfield Dr HMLTN ML3 174 B2
Downfield Gdns
UD/BTH/TAN G71 131 M7
Downfield St CAR/SHTL G32 106 E6
Downhill St KVD/HLHD G12 82 C6
Downiebrae Rd RUTH G73 106 B7
Downie Cl UD/BTH/TAN G71 132 B1
Downie St HMLTN ML3 156 D8
Downs St SPRGB/BLRNK G21 83 M4 1
Dowrie Crs PLK/PH/NH G53 103 H8
Draffen St MTHW ML1 157 M2 1
Drakemire Av CSMK G45 128 C5
Drakemire Dr CSMK G45 128 B7
Drake St DMNK/BRGTN G40 12 B5
Dreghorn Rd IRVSE KA11 209 K3
Dreghorn St DEN/PKHD G31 13 J2
Dresling Rd GRNK PA15 2 A7
Drimnin Rd STPS/GTHM/RID G33 85 M4
Drive Rd GOV/IBX G51 103 L1
Drochil St ESTRH G34 86 A8
Drove Hl BALLOCH G68 48 B6
Druid Dr KLWNG KA13 193 L5
Drumadoon Dr HBR/GL G84 20 F7
Drumbathie Rd AIRDRIE ML6 111 J1
Drumbeg Dr PLK/PH/NH G53 126 A3
Drumbeg Ter MLNGV G62 41 K7
Drumbottie Rd
SPRGB/BLRNK G21 84 A4
Drumbreck Pl KKNTL G66 65 L5
Drumby Crs
CRMNK/CLK/EAG G76 127 K8
Drumby Dr
CRMNK/CLK/EAG G76 151 K1 1
Drumcarn Dr MLNGV G62 41 M8
Drumcavel Rd
BAIL/MDB/MHD G69 86 D2
Drumchapel Gdns DRUM G15 61 G7 2
Drumchapel Pl DRUM G15 61 H7
Drumchapel Rd DRUM G15 61 H7
Drumclair Pl AIRDRIE ML6 111 K2
Drumclog Av MLNGV G62 42 A5
Drumclog Gdns
STPS/GTHM/RID G33 84 F3 1
Drumclog Pl
KLMNKN/STW KA3 207 H6 1
Drumcoyle Dr
RAYR/DAL KA6 231 H4 1
Drumcross Rd BSHPTN PA7 58 D6
PLK/PH/NH G53 103 J8
Drumduff EKILS G75 171 K4 1
Drumellan Rd AYRS KA7 229 G7
Drumfin Av AIRDRIE ML6 90 F5
Drumfork Ct HBR/GL G84 22 F1 2
Drumfork Rd HBR/GL G84 23 G1
Drumfrochar Pl GRNK PA15 2 C7
Drumfrochar Rd GRNK PA15 2 B6
GRNKW/INVK PA16 32 D6
Drumgelloch St AIRDRIE ML6 111 K1
Drumglass Vw KSYTH G65 47 M5 1
Drumgray Gdns AIRDRIE ML6 69 K8
Drumgray La AIRDRIE ML6 69 K8
Drumhead Pl CAR/SHTL G32 106 F8
Drumhead Rd CAR/SHTL G32 106 F8
Drumhill KKNTL G66 46 B7
Drumilaw Rd RUTH G73 129 G4
Drumilaw Wy RUTH G73 129 G4 1
Drumillan Hl GRNKW/INVK PA16 31 J7
Drumkinnon Rd
ALEX/LLW G83 25 K1 2
Drumlaken Av
MRYH/FIRH G20 62 C8 1
Drumlaken Ct
MRYH/FIRH G20 62 C8 2
Drumlaken St MRYH/FIRH G20 62 C8
Drumlanrig Av ESTRH G34 108 D1
Drumlanrig Pl ESTRH G34 108 D1 1
Drumley Av RAYR/DAL KA6 227 G3
Drumley Dr RAYR/DAL KA6 227 G3
Drumleyhill Dr KLMNK KA1 212 F4
Drumlin Dr MLNGV G62 61 M1
Drumloch Gdns EKILS G75 171 L4 3
Drumlochy Rd
STPS/GTHM/RID G33 85 G8
Drum Mains Pk BALLOCH G68 67 J1
Drummilling Av WKIL KA23 181 K3 1
Drummilling Dr WKIL KA23 181 K3 2
Drummilling Rd WKIL KA23 181 K3
Drummond Av RUTH G73 128 F1 3
Drummond Crs AYR KA8 225 L7 1
Drummond Dr PSLY PA1 102 D5 1
WISHAW ML2 159 H7
Drummond Hl EKILN G74 154 B6
Drummond Pl EKILN G74 154 B6 3
KLMNKN/STW KA3 207 J7
Drummond St
GRNKW/INVK PA16 32 C5
Drummond Wy NMRNS G77 150 A4
Drummore Av CTBR ML5 110 D7
Drummore Rd DRUM G15 61 G4
Drumnessie Ct BALLOCH G68 67 M1 2
Drumnessie Rd BALLOCH G68 67 M2
Drumnessie Vw
BALLOCH G68 67 M1 3
Drumore Av AIRDRIE ML6 111 K8 2
Drumover Dr DEN/PKHD G31 106 E5
Drumoyne Av GOV/IBX G51 103 L2 2
Drumoyne Circ GOV/IBX G51 103 L3
Drumoyne Dr GOV/IBX G51 103 L2
Drumoyne Pl GOV/IBX G51 103 L3 3
Drumoyne Qd GOV/IBX G51 103 L3 3
Drumoyne Rd GOV/IBX G51 103 L2
Drumoyne Sq GOV/IBX G51 103 L2 3
Drumpark St CTBR ML5 109 H5
GIF/THBK G46 126 F5 1
Drumpellier Av
BAIL/MDB/MHD G69 108 B6
CTBR ML5 109 K2
CUMB G67 68 C2
Drumpellier Ct CUMB G67 68 C2 1
Drumpellier Crs CTBR ML5 109 K3
Drumpellier Gdns CUMB G67 68 C2 2
Drumpellier Gv CUMB G67 68 C2 3
Drumpellier Pl
BAIL/MDB/MHD G69 108 B5 2
CUMB G67 68 C2 4
Drumpellier Rd
BAIL/MDB/MHD G69 108 A6
Drumpellier St
STPS/GTHM/RID G33 7 M5
Drumreoch Dr GVH/MTFL G42 128 E2
Drumreoch Pl GVH/MTFL G42 128 E1
Drumry Rd CLYDBK G81 60 C6
Drumry Rd East DRUM G15 60 F7
Drumsack Av
BAIL/MDB/MHD G69 86 B1
Drumsargard Rd RUTH G73 129 K4
Drums Av PSLYN/LNWD PA3 8 C2
Drums Crs PSLYN/LNWD PA3 8 C1
Drumshangie Pl AIRDRIE ML6 89 G7
Drumshangie St AIRDRIE ML6 89 G7 1
Drumshantie Rd GRK PA19 31 L2 1
Drumshaw Dr CAR/SHTL G32 130 C1
Drums Rd PLK/PH/NH G53 103 G6
Drums Ter GRNKW/INVK PA16 32 B1 2
Drumsuy Ct RAYR/DAL KA6 231 H6 3
Drumtrocher St KSYTH G65 47 K1 1
Drury St CGLW G2 11 H1
Dryad St GIF/THBK G46 126 E4
Drybridge Rd CRH/DND KA2 209 L7
Dryburgh Av PSLYS PA2 101 G8
RUTH G73 129 H2
Dryburgh Gdns MRYH/FIRH G20 4 C2
Dryburgh Hl EKILN G74 14 C3
Dryburgh La EKILN G74 14 D3
Dryburgh Pl CTBR ML5 109 M2
Dryburgh Rd BSDN G61 61 J3 2
WISHAW ML2 159 G5
Dryburgh St HMLTN ML3 156 B3 1
Dryburgh Wk
BAIL/MDB/MHD G69 67 G6 2
Dryburn Av
CARD/HILL/MSPK G52 103 G4
Dryden St HMLTN ML3 156 B3
Drygait HWWD PA9 122 A3
Drygate COWCAD G4 12 A1
Drygatehead NMLNS KA16 215 K1
Drygate St LRKH ML9 176 A5
NMLNS KA16 215 K2 1
Drygrange Rd
STPS/GTHM/RID G33 85 J7
Drymen Pl KKNTL G66 65 K6
Drymen Rd BSDN G61 61 L4
Drymen St
CARD/HILL/MSPK G52 103 L4
Drynoch Pl PPK/MIL G22 83 H2
Drysdale St SCOT G14 80 F4
Duart Av PSTWK KA9 225 J1
Duart Crs PSTWK KA9 225 J1 1
Duart Dr EKILN G74 153 K6 1
JNSTN PA5 100 B8
NMRNS G77 151 G4
Duart St MRYH/FIRH G20 82 C1
Dubbs Rd PGL PA14 54 D1
SVSTN KA20 192 E8
Dubs Rd BRHD/NEIL G78 125 L6
Dubton St ESTRH G34 86 B8
Duchall Pl SCOT G14 81 H5 1
Duchal Rd KLMCLM PA13 75 K1
Duchal St PGL PA14 54 D1
Duchess Ct HMLTN ML3 157 G7 1
Duchess Dr HBR/GL G84 20 B5
Duchess Palace RUTH G73 129 J1
Duchess Pk HBR/GL G84 20 B6
Duchess Rd RUTH G73 106 C8
Duchray Dr PSLY PA1 102 F5
Duchray La STPS/GTHM/RID G33 7 L7
Duchray Pl RAYR/DAL KA6 231 L5 1
Duchray St STPS/GTHM/RID G33 7 L7
Duddingston Av KLWNG KA13 193 H5
Dudhope St
STPS/GTHM/RID G33 85 K7
Dudley Dr CTBR ML5 87 J7
KVD/HLHD G12 82 A6
Dudley La KVD/HLHD G12 82 A6
Duffield Dr LARGS KA30 115 K7
Duff Pl KLMNKN/STW KA3 207 J6 1
SALT KA21 192 A7
Duff St GRNK PA15 2 E4
Duffus Pl CAR/SHTL G32 130 C1
Duffus St ESTRH G34 85 M8
Duffus Ter CAR/SHTL G32 130 C1
Duguid Dr SALT KA21 192 A8 1
Duich Gdns SMSTN G23 62 E8
Duisdale Rd CAR/SHTL G32 130 C1 1
Dukes Ga UD/BTH/TAN G71 131 L5
Dukes Pl HMLTN ML3 174 D3
Dukes Rd BAIL/MDB/MHD G69 108 F4
RUTH G73 129 K4
TROON KA10 216 B6
Duke St COWCAD G4 12 A2
DEN/PKHD G31 13 J3
GLSTN KA4 214 C4
HMLTN ML3 156 E6
LRKH ML9 176 A5
MTHW ML1 157 L1
PSLYS PA2 9 H9
WISHAW ML2 159 M3
Dulnain St BLTYR/CAMB G72 130 D4
Dulsie Rd SPRGB/BLRNK G21 84 C3 1
Dumbarton Rd CLYDBK G81 59 K5
OLDK G60 58 C1
PTCK G11 81 M7
SCOT G14 80 E3
Dumbreck Av
CARD/HILL/MSPK G52 104 A6
Dumbreck Ct PLKSD/SHW G41 104 A6
Dumbreck Pth
PLKSD/SHW G41 104 A6 1
Dumbreck Pl
PLKSD/SHW G41 104 A6 2
Dumbreck Rd PLKSD/SHW G41 104 B7
Dumbreck Sq
PLKSD/SHW G41 104 A5 1
Dumbrock Crs CMPF/LLE G63 27 J6 1
Dumbrock Dr CMPF/LLE G63 27 H6 1
Dumbrock Rd CMPF/LLE G63 27 H6
MLNGV G62 41 K7
Dumbuck Crs DMBTN G82 37 J7
Dumbuck Gdns DMBTN G82 37 H7 1
Dumbuck Rd DMBTN G82 37 G4
Dumbuie Av DMBTN G82 37 H5
Dumfries Crs AIRDRIE ML6 110 F4
Dumfriespark RAYR/DAL KA6 229 G8 1
Dumgoyne Av MLNGV G62 41 M8
Dumgoyne Dr BSDN G61 61 K2
Dumgoyne Pl
CRMNK/CLK/EAG G76 151 J2 1
Dumgoyne Rd KLMNK KA1 212 A6 2
Dunagoil Rd CSMK G45 128 D7
Dunagoil St CSMK G45 128 E7
Dunagoil Ter CSMK G45 128 E8 1
Dunalastair Dr
STPS/GTHM/RID G33 85 H4
Dunan Pl
STPS/GTHM/RID G33 107 L2 1
Dunard Rd RUTH G73 129 H2
Dunard St MRYH/FIRH G20 4 D1
Dunaskin St PTCK G11 82 C8
Dunavon Pl CTBR ML5 110 D5 2
Dunbar Av CTBR ML5 109 K5
JNSTN PA5 122 E1
RUTH G73 129 J2
Dunbar Dr MTHW ML1 158 A5 1
Dunbar Hl EKILN G74 14 A3
Dunbar La MTHW ML1 134 A7
Dunbar Pl EKILN G74 14 A3
Dunbar Rd PSLYS PA2 101 G8
Dunbar St HMLTN ML3 156 B4
Dunbeath Av NMRNS G77 150 F4
Dunbeith Pl MRYH/FIRH G20 82 D4 1
Dunbeth Av CTBR ML5 110 B2
Dunbeth Rd CTBR ML5 110 A1
Dunblane Dr EKILN G74 15 H1
Dunblane Pl EKILN G74 15 H1
Dunblane St CGLW G2 5 H7
COWCAD G4 5 H6
Dunbrach Rd BALLOCH G68 48 B6
Dunbreck Av AIRDRIE ML6 91 G4
Dunbritton Rd DMBTN G82 37 J6
Duncan Av SCOT G14 81 J6
Duncan Ct KLMNKN/STW KA3 207 K5
MTHW ML1 133 K8 1
Duncan Dr IRV KA12 203 K7
Duncan Graham St LRKH ML9 176 B5
Duncan La North SCOT G14 81 J5 1
Duncan La South SCOT G14 81 J5 2
Duncan Mcintosh Rd
BALLOCH G68 49 H2
Duncan Rd HBR/GL G84 20 E6
PGL PA14 34 B8 3
Duncansby Rd
STPS/GTHM/RID G33 107 K3 2
Duncan St CLYDBK G81 60 B6 2
GRNK PA15 2 B5
Duncarnock Av BRHD/NEIL G78 148 E2
Duncarnock Crs
BRHD/NEIL G78 148 E2
Dunchattan Gv TROON KA10 216 F7
Dunchattan Pl DEN/PKHD G31 12 C3
Dunchattan St DEN/PKHD G31 12 C1
Dunchurch Rd PSLY PA1 102 D4
Dunclutha Dr UD/BTH/TAN G71 132 A8
Dunclutha St
DMNK/BRGTN G40 106 B7
Duncolm Pl MLNGV G62 41 K7
Duncombe Av CLYDBK G81 60 B2
Duncombe St MRYH/FIRH G20 82 D2
Duncraig Crs JNSTN PA5 122 C1
Duncrub Dr BSHPBGS G64 63 L8
Duncruin St MRYH/FIRH G20 82 C2
Duncruin Ter MRYH/FIRH G20 82 D2
Duncryne Av CAR/SHTL G32 107 K5
Duncryne Gdns
CAR/SHTL G32 107 L5 3
Duncryne Pl BSHPBGS G64 83 L1
Duncryne Rd ALEX/LLW G83 25 L3 2
CAR/SHTL G32 107 K5 1
Dundaff Hl BALLOCH G68 48 C7 2
Dundas Av BSHPBGS G64 64 B1
Dundashill COWCAD G4 5 H5
Dundas Pl EKILN G74 14 F1
Dundas St CGLE G1 5 J9
Dundee Dr
CARD/HILL/MSPK G52 103 H6
Dundonald Av JNSTN PA5 99 K8 1
Dundonald Crs IRVSE KA11 208 E8 1
NMRNS G77 151 G5
Dundonald Dr HMLTN ML3 174 D2 3
Dundonald Pl
BRHD/NEIL G78 148 D2 1
Dundonald Rd IRVSE KA11 204 C8
KLMNK KA1 211 J2
KVD/HLHD G12 82 C5
PSLYN/LNWD PA3 102 A2
TROON KA10 216 F6
Dundonald St
BLTYR/CAMB G72 155 J1
Dundrennan Rd GVH/MTFL G42 127 M2
Dundyvan Ga CTBR ML5 110 A4 2
Dundyvan La WISHAW ML2 158 F6 1
Dundyvan Rd CTBR ML5 110 A4
Dundyvan St WISHAW ML2 159 G7
Dundyvan Wy CTBR ML5 109 M4
Dunearn Pl PSLYS PA2 9 L7
Dunearn St COWCAD G4 4 D5
Dunedin Ct EKILS G75 171 G1 1
Dunedin Dr EKILS G75 153 G8
Dunedin Rd LRKH ML9 176 B8
Dunellan Av
BAIL/MDB/MHD G69 67 G7 2
Dunellan Crs
BAIL/MDB/MHD G69 67 G7
Dunellan Dr CLYDBK G81 60 B2
Dunellan Gdns
BAIL/MDB/MHD G69 67 G7
Dunellan Rd MLNGV G62 41 J7
Dunellan St
CARD/HILL/MSPK G52 103 L4
Dungavel Gdns HMLTN ML3 174 E1
Dungavel Rd KLMNK KA1 212 A5
Dungeonhill Rd ESTRH G34 108 D1
Dunglass Av EKILN G74 153 M6
SCOT G14 81 J5 3
Dunglass La SCOT G14 81 J5 1
Dunglass La North SCOT G14 81 J5 3
Dunglass La South SCOT G14 81 J5 3
Dunglass Pl MLNGV G62 41 L6
NMRNS G77 150 A4
Dunglass Rd BSHPTN PA7 58 C7
Dunglass Sq EKILN G74 153 M6 2
Dunglass Vw CMPF/LLE G63 27 K5
Dungoil Av BALLOCH G68 48 B6 1
Dungoil Rd KKNTL G66 65 L5 1
Dungourney Dr
GRNKW/INVK PA16 32 C2 3
Dungoyne St MRYH/FIRH G20 82 C1 2
Dunira St CAR/SHTL G32 106 F6
Dunivaig St
STPS/GTHM/RID G33 107 K1
Dunkeld Av RUTH G73 129 H2
Dunkeld Dr BSDN G61 62 B5
Dunkeld Pl CTBR ML5 109 M5
HMLTN ML3 155 K5
NMRNS G77 151 H5
Dunkeld St DEN/PKHD G31 13 K7
Dunkenny Rd DRUM G15 60 F5
Dunkirk St AIRDRIE ML6 91 G4
Dunlin EKILN G74 153 L6
Dunlin Ct BLSH ML4 132 E1
Dunlin Crs CRG/CRSL/HOU PA6 77 J8
Dunlop Av RAYR/DAL KA6 227 H7
Dunlop Ct HMLTN ML3 174 E2 2
Dunlop Crs AYR KA8 225 K8
IRVSE KA11 204 B8
UD/BTH/TAN G71 132 A8
Dunlop Gv UD/BTH/TAN G71 109 G8
Dunlop Pl MLNGV G62 41 M6 1
Dunlop Rd BEITH KA15 169 G6
Dunlop St BLTYR/CAMB G72 130 E3
CGLE G1 11 J4
GRNKW/INVK PA16 32 C6
KLMNK KA1 16 E3 1
PSLYN/LNWD PA3 100 C3
RNFRW PA4 80 D5 2
Dunlop Ter AYR KA8 229 K1
Dunmore Dr MLNGV G62 62 C1
Dunmore St CLYDBK G81 80 C1
Dunnachie Dr CTBR ML5 109 H5
Dunnet Av AIRDRIE ML6 88 F4
Dunnet Dr
CRG/CRSL/HOU PA6 77 H8 2
Dunnett Av KLMNK KA1 17 J6
Dunnichen Gdns BSHPBGS G64 64 D8
Dunnikier Wk BALLOCH G68 47 L8 3
Dunning St DEN/PKHD G31 13 M8 1
Dunn Ms KLMNK KA1 211 J1
Dunnottar Ct EKILN G74 153 J6 3
Dunnottar Crs EKILN G74 153 J6 4
Dunnottar St BSHPBGS G64 64 D7
STPS/GTHM/RID G33 85 H7
Dunn St CLYDBK G81 59 L6
CLYDBK G81 59 M3
DMNK/BRGTN G40 12 D9
GRNK PA15 2 A6
PSLY PA1 9 L3
Dunns Wood Rd CUMB G67 49 K3
Dunolly Dr NMRNS G77 150 F4
Dunolly St SPRGB/BLRNK G21 6 E6
Dunoon Av KLMNKN/STW KA3 206 F6
Dunottar Av CTBR ML5 110 B7
Dunottar Pl CTBR ML5 110 B6 1
Dunphail Dr ESTRH G34 108 D1
Dunphail Rd ESTRH G34 108 D1
Dunragit St DEN/PKHD G31 13 J2
Dunrobin Av JNSTN PA5 100 B8
Dunrobin Ct EKILN G74 153 K6 5
Dunrobin Crs EKILN G74 153 K6 6
Dunrobin Dr EKILN G74 153 K5
GRK PA19 31 G3 1
Dunrobin Pl CTBR ML5 109 M2
Dunrobin Rd AIRDRIE ML6 111 L2
Dunrobin St DEN/PKHD G31 13 H4
Dunrod Hl EKILN G74 153 M6
Dunrod Rd GRNKW/INVK PA16 51 G2
Dunrod St CAR/SHTL G32 107 H5
Dunscore Brae HMLTN ML3 155 L7
Duns Crs WISHAW ML2 159 J3
Dunside Dr PLK/PH/NH G53 126 A3
Dunsiston Rd AIRDRIE ML6 112 B5
Dunskaith Pl ESTRH G34 108 D2
Dunskaith St ESTRH G34 108 D1
Dunsmore Rd BSHPTN PA7 58 A5
Dunsmuir St GOV/IBX G51 104 B2
Duns Pth CTBR ML5 110 D6
Dunswin Av CLYDBK G81 59 L6
Dunsyre Pl SMSTN G23 62 E8 1
Dunsyre St
STPS/GTHM/RID G33 106 E1 1
Duntarvie Av ESTRH G34 108 C1
Duntarvie Cl ESTRH G34 108 C1 1
Duntarvie Crs ESTRH G34 108 C1 2
Duntarvie Dr ESTRH G34 108 B1 2
Duntarvie Gdns ESTRH G34 108 C1 3
Duntarvie Pl ESTRH G34 108 B1 3
Duntarvie Quadrant
ESTRH G34 108 C1 4
Duntarvie Rd ESTRH G34 108 B1
Dunterlie Av KNTSWD G13 81 G3
Dunterlie Ct BRHD/NEIL G78 125 J6 2
Duntiblae Rd KKNTL G66 66 A2
Duntiglennan Rd CLYDBK G81 60 A3 1
Duntilland Av SHOTTS ML7 113 H7
Duntilland Rd AIRDRIE ML6 112 E1
Duntocher Rd BSDN G61 61 K3 1
CLYDBK G81 60 A4 1
Duntreath Av DRUM G15 60 F7
KNTSWD G13 80 E1
Duntreath Dr DRUM G15 60 F8
Duntreath Gdns DRUM G15 60 F7
Duntreath Gv DRUM G15 60 F8 1
Duntreath Ter KSYTH G65 47 K1 4
Duntroon St DEN/PKHD G31 7 G8
Dunure Cts KLWNG KA13 193 K6
Dunure Dr HMLTN ML3 155 K7
KLMNKN/STW KA3 17 K5
NMRNS G77 151 G4
RUTH G73 128 F4
Dunure Pl CTBR ML5 109 L6 2
NMRNS G77 151 G5
Dunure St CTBR ML5 109 L6
MRYH/FIRH G20 82 D2
Dunvegan AIRDRIE ML6 88 E5
Dunvegan Av CTBR ML5 87 K8
GRK PA19 30 F4
JNSTN PA5 100 B8
Dunvegan Dr BSHPBGS G64 64 A5
NMRNS G77 151 G4
Dunvegan Pl EKILN G74 153 K6 7
IRV KA12 203 J4
UD/BTH/TAN G71 131 K1 1
Dunvegan Qd RNFRW PA4 80 B5 1
Dunwan Av KNTSWD G13 80 F2
Dunwan Pl KNTSWD G13 80 F2
Dura Rd SHOTTS ML7 161 H1
Durban Av CLYDBK G81 59 K5
EKILS G75 171 G5
Durham Rd
GRNKW/INVK PA16 31 L4 1
Durham St PLKSD/SHW G41 104 D4
Durisdeer Dr HMLTN ML3 155 L8
Durness Av BSDN G61 62 B4
Duror St CAR/SHTL G32 107 G3
Durris Gdns CAR/SHTL G32 107 K6 5
Durrockstock Crs PSLYS PA2 123 M2
Durrockstock Rd PSLYS PA2 123 M2
Durward EKILN G74 154 E5
Durward Av PLKSD/SHW G41 104 D8
Durward Ct PLKSD/SHW G41 104 D8
Durward Crs PSLYS PA2 100 F8
Duthie Rd GRK PA19 32 A3
Duthil St GOV/IBX G51 103 K3
Dyce Av AIRDRIE ML6 110 E5
Dyce La PTCK G11 82 A7
Dyer's La CGLE G1 11 L4
Dyers' Wynd PSLY PA1 9 H3
Dyfrig St BLTYR/CAMB G72 155 J1 1
SHOTTS ML7 137 L5
Dykebar Av KNTSWD G13 81 G3
Dykebar Crs PSLYS PA2 102 B7
Dykehead Crs AIRDRIE ML6 88 F7 2
Dykehead La
STPS/GTHM/RID G33 107 K2
Dykehead Rd AIRDRIE ML6 88 F7
BAIL/MDB/MHD G69 108 F4
BALLOCH G68 48 C3
Dykehead Sq HMLTN ML3 155 M6
Dykehead St
STPS/GTHM/RID G33 107 K2
Dykemuir Pl SPRGB/BLRNK G21 7 G1
Dykemuir Qd
SPRGB/BLRNK G21 6 E1 1
Dykemuir St SPRGB/BLRNK G21 6 F1
Dykeneuk Rd PGL PA14 54 D2
Dyke Rd KNTSWD G13 81 G1
Dykesfield Pl SALT KA21 191 L7

Dykesmains Rd SALT KA21 191 L7
Dykes Pl SALT KA21 191 M7
The Dykes KBRN KA25 167 G1
Dyke St BAIL/MDB/MHD G69 108 C4
CTBR ML5 109 H5
Dysart Ct BALLOCH G68 47 L8
Dysart Wy AIRDRIE ML6 112 A3

E

Eagle Crs BSDN G61 61 H3
Eaglesham Ct GOV/IBX G51 10 A4
Eaglesham Pl GOV/IBX G51 10 A4
Eaglesham Rd
CRMNK/CLK/EAG G76 151 L5
EKILS G75 152 E8
NMRNS G77 150 D6
Eagle St COWCAD G4 5 J4
Earl Av AIRDRIE ML6 91 G4
Earlbank Av SCOT G14 81 J5
Earlbank La North SCOT G14 81 J5
Earlbank La South SCOT G14 81 J5
Earl Dr CRH/DND KA2 209 M7
Earl Haig Rd
CARD/HILL/MSPK G52 102 F2
Earl La SCOT G14 81 J6
Earl Pl BRWEIR PA11 98 D3
SCOT G14 81 J5
Earlsburn Rd KKNTL G66 65 L5
Earlscourt
BAIL/MDB/MHD G69 66 F8
Earlsgate CRG/CRSL/HOU PA6 77 H8
Earl's Ga UD/BTH/TAN G71 131 L6
Earl's Hl BALLOCH G68 48 B6
Earlshill Dr HWWD PA9 121 L4
Earlspark Av
PLKSW/MSWD G43 127 M3
Earlston Av KLMNK KA1 211 M6
Earlston Crs CTBR ML5 110 D6
Earlston St WISHAW ML2 159 J3
Earl St SCOT G14 81 H5
Earls Wy AYRS KA7 228 C7
Earn Av BSDN G61 62 B5
RNFRW PA4 80 E7
Earn Crs WISHAW ML2 159 H8
Earnhill Rd GRK PA19 31 J5
Earnock Av MTHW ML1 157 J2
Earnock Gdns HMLTN ML3 156 A7
Earnock Rd HMLTN ML3 155 K7
Earnock St HMLTN ML3 156 A5
STPS/GTHM/RID G33 7 L1
Earn Pl KLMNK KA1 212 B4
Earn Rd NMRNS G77 150 D2
TROON KA10 216 F5
Earnside St CAR/SHTL G32 107 H4
Earn St STPS/GTHM/RID G33 84 E8
Earn Ter SHOTTS ML7 137 L3
Easdale EKILN G74 15 L7
Easdale Dr CAR/SHTL G32 106 F5
Easdale Pl NMRNS G77 150 B4
Easdale Ri HMLTN ML3 155 L6
East Academy St WISHAW ML2 159 H7
East Av AIRDRIE ML6 90 A6
BLTYR/CAMB G72 155 K4
CARLUKE ML8 178 D7
MTHW ML1 134 A7
RNFRW PA4 80 D6
UD/BTH/TAN G71 132 C3
Eastbank Dr CAR/SHTL G32 107 J4
East Barmoss Av PGL PA14 54 F2
East Barns St CLYDBK G81 80 D1
East Bath La CGLE G1 5 J9
East Blackhall St GRNK PA15 2 F6
East Bowhouse Head
IRVSE KA11 204 B4
East Bowhouse Wy IRVSE KA11 204 B4
East Breast GRNK PA15 2 E4
East Buchanan St PSLY PA1 9 J3
Eastburn Crs
SPRGB/BLRNK G21 84 B3
Eastburn Rd SPRGB/BLRNK G21 84 B4
East Burnside St KSYTH G65 47 K1
East Campbell St COWCAD G4 12 A3
East Castle Av LARGS KA30 115 K6
East Church Ct NMLNS KA16 215 K2
Eastcote Av SCOT G14 81 L5
East Crawford St GRNK PA15 3 K7
Eastcroft RUTH G73 129 H1
Eastcroft Ter SPRGB/BLRNK G21 6 E1
East Dean St BLSH ML4 133 H4
Eastend LOCHW PA12 120 D6
Eastend Av MTHW ML1 134 B8
Easter Craigs DEN/PKHD G31 7 H9
Easter Crs WISHAW ML2 159 L5
Easter Garngaber Rd KKNTL G66 65 L4
Easterhill Pl CAR/SHTL G32 106 F6
Easterhill Rd HBR/GL G84 20 E6
Easterhill St CAR/SHTL G32 106 F6
Easterhouse Pl ESTRH G34 108 C1
Easterhouse Qd ESTRH G34 108 C2
Easterhouse Rd
BAIL/MDB/MHD G69 108 B4
ESTRH G34 108 C2
Eastermains KKNTL G66 46 B7
Easter Ms UD/BTH/TAN G71 131 L4
Eastern Av LARGS KA30 115 L6
Eastern Crs KBRN KA25 167 G2
Easter Queenslie Rd
STPS/GTHM/RID G33 107 L1
Easter Rd CRMNK/CLK/EAG G76 152 A4
SHOTTS ML7 137 K4
Easterton Av
CRMNK/CLK/EAG G76 152 A4
Easter Wood Crs
UD/BTH/TAN G71 109 K8
East Faulds Rd
LNK/LMHG ML11 199 L4
Eastfield Av BLTYR/CAMB G72 129 L4
Eastfield Crs DMBTN G82 37 H7
Eastfield Pl DMBTN G82 37 H7
Eastfield Rd AIRDRIE ML6 91 G5
BALLOCH G68 48 B6
CARLUKE ML8 189 G1
FLK FK1 91 M1
SPRGB/BLRNK G21 83 L5
Eastfield Ter BLSH ML4 133 K5
Eastgate BAIL/MDB/MHD G69 87 G4
East Ga CTBR ML5 87 K2
WISHAW ML2 159 K6
East George St CTBR ML5 110 B1
East Glebe Ter HMLTN ML3 156 D7
East Greenlees Av
BLTYR/CAMB G72 130 C6
East Greenlees Crs
BLTYR/CAMB G72 130 B6
East Greenlees Dr
BLTYR/CAMB G72 130 C6
East Greenlees Rd
BLTYR/CAMB G72 130 A6
East Gv TROON KA10 216 F5
East Hallhill Rd
BAIL/MDB/MHD G69 107 M3
Easthall Pl
STPS/GTHM/RID G33 107 M2
East Hamilton St GRNK PA15 3 K6
WISHAW ML2 159 H7
East High St AIRDRIE ML6 111 G1
KKNTL G66 45 J8
East Kilbride Rd
BLTYR/CAMB G72 129 M8
CRMNK/CLK/EAG G76 152 D5
RUTH G73 129 J4
East Kirkland DALRY KA24 184 D2
East La PSLY PA1 102 B4
Eastlea Pl AIRDRIE ML6 111 H3
East Lennox Dr HBR/GL G84 20 E6
East Machan St LRKH ML9 176 B8
East Mains Rd EKILN G74 153 M5
East Milton Gv EKILS G75 153 H8
East Montrose St HBR/GL G84 20 E7
Eastmuir St CAR/SHTL G32 107 H4
WISHAW ML2 159 L6
East Netherton St KLMNK KA1 16 F7
Easton Pl CTBR ML5 110 B4
East Park Crs
KLMNKN/STW KA3 206 B1
East Park Dr KLMNKN/STW KA3 206 B2
East Park Rd AYR KA8 225 H6
East Rd IRV KA12 203 J7
KLBCH PA10 99 G5
MTHW ML1 134 A5
PSTWK KA9 225 J5
East Rossdhu Dr HBR/GL G84 20 E6
East Scott Ter HMLTN ML3 156 D8
East Shaw St GRNK PA15 2 C4
KLMNK KA1 16 F8
Eastside KKNTL G66 45 K8
East Springfield Ter
BSHPBGS G64 84 B1
East Stewart Pl CTBR ML5 110 C2
East Stewart St CTBR ML5 110 C3
GRNK PA15 3 G6
East Strd NMLNS KA16 215 K2
East St GRNK PA15 33 M7
East Thomson St CLYDBK G81 60 B6
East Thornlie St WISHAW ML2 159 H7
Eastvale Pl KVGV G3 104 C1
East Wellbrae Crs HMLTN ML3 156 B8
East Wellington St
DEN/PKHD G31 13 L5
East William St GRNK PA15 3 J7
Eastwood Av GIF/THBK G46 127 J7
IRV KA12 203 K5
PLKSD/SHW G41 127 K1
Eastwood Crs GIF/THBK G46 126 F5
Eastwood Dr WISHAW ML2 160 A4
Eastwood La HBR/GL G84 22 F1
Eastwoodmains Rd
GIF/THBK G46 127 J8
Eastwood Rd
BAIL/MDB/MHD G69 66 F7
East Woodside Av PGL PA14 54 F3
Eastwood Vw
BLTYR/CAMB G72 130 E3
Easwald Bank KLBCH PA10 99 H7
Ebroch Dr KSYTH G65 47 L1
Ebroch Pk KSYTH G65 47 L1
Eccles St PPK/MIL G22 83 L4
Eckford St CAR/SHTL G32 107 G5
Eday St PPK/MIL G22 83 K3
Edderton Pl
STPS/GTHM/RID G33 108 A2
Eddington Dr NMRNS G77 150 C6
Eddlewood Ct
STPS/GTHM/RID G33 108 A2
Eddlewood Pth
STPS/GTHM/RID G33 107 M2
Eddlewood Pl
STPS/GTHM/RID G33 107 M2
Eddlewood Rd
STPS/GTHM/RID G33 107 M2
Eden Ct KLWNG KA13 193 H6
Eden Dr EKILS G75 170 F3
Eden Gdns EKILS G75 170 F2
Eden Gv EKILS G75 170 F2
Edenhall Ct NMRNS G77 150 D7
Edenhall Gv NMRNS G77 150 D7
Edenhall Rd AYR KA8 225 H5
Edenkill Pl CMPF/LLE G63 27 J6
Eden La STPS/GTHM/RID G33 7 L6
Eden Pk UD/BTH/TAN G71 131 M7
Eden Pl KLMNK KA1 212 B4
RNFRW PA4 80 E7
Edenside BALLOCH G68 49 H2
Eden St STPS/GTHM/RID G33 7 M6
Edenwood St
DEN/PKHD G31 106 E4
Edgam Dr
CARD/HILL/MSPK G52 103 J4
Edgefauld Av SPRGB/BLRNK G21 6 D2
Edgefauld Dr SPRGB/BLRNK G21 6 D1
Edgefauld Pl
SPRGB/BLRNK G21 83 M4
Edgefauld Rd
SPRGB/BLRNK G21 83 M5
Edgehill La PTCK G11 82 A5
Edgehill Rd BSDN G61 61 L3
PTCK G11 81 M5
Edgemont Pk HMLTN ML3 174 C1
Edgemont St PLKSD/SHW G41 127 L1
Edinbeg Av GVH/MTFL G42 128 E1
Edinbeg Pl GVH/MTFL G42 128 E1
Edinburgh Dr GRK PA19 30 E4
Edinburgh Rd CAR/SHTL G32 107 G2
MTHW ML1 134 D3
STPS/GTHM/RID G33 106 E2
Edington Gdns
BAIL/MDB/MHD G69 66 F6
Edington St COWCAD G4 5 G5
Edison Pl KLWNG KA13 193 L8
Edison St CARD/HILL/MSPK G52 102 E1
Edmiston Av PSTWK KA9 225 H2
Edmiston Dr GOV/IBX G51 104 A3
PSLYN/LNWD PA3 99 M3
Edmonstone Dr KSYTH G65 47 K2
Edmonton Ter EKILS G75 14 B5
Edmund Kean EKILN G74 154 C4
Edrom Ct CAR/SHTL G32 106 F4
Edrom St CAR/SHTL G32 106 F5
Edward Av RNFRW PA4 80 D5
Edward Dr HBR/GL G84 20 C6
Edward St BAIL/MDB/MHD G69 108 F4
CLYDBK G81 80 D2
HMLTN ML3 156 D7
MTHW ML1 157 M4
Edwin St GOV/IBX G51 104 D4
Edzell Ct SCOT G14 81 K7
Edzell Dr JNSTN PA5 100 D7
NMRNS G77 150 E5
Edzell Gdns BSHPBGS G64 84 C1
WISHAW ML2 159 G7
Edzell Pl SCOT G14 81 K6
Edzell Rw KLWNG KA13 193 H6
Edzell St CTBR ML5 109 K5
SCOT G14 81 K7
Egidia Av GIF/THBK G46 127 J7
Egilsay Crs PPK/MIL G22 83 J1
Egilsay Pl PPK/MIL G22 83 J1
Egilsay St PPK/MIL G22 83 J1
Egilsay Ter PPK/MIL G22 83 J1
Eglinton Ct GBLS G5 11 G6
SALT KA21 200 E2
Eglinton Crs TROON KA10 216 D7
Eglinton Dr GIF/THBK G46 127 J7
SKLM PA17 70 A4
TROON KA10 216 D7
Eglinton Gdns SKLM PA17 70 A5
Eglinton Pl AYRS KA7 18 D2
KLWNG KA13 193 L6
SALT KA21 200 E2
Eglinton Rd ARD KA22 191 H5
Eglinton Sq ARD KA22 191 J6
Eglinton St BEITH KA15 168 B1
CTBR ML5 110 B1
GBLS G5 11 G8
IRV KA12 203 J6
SALT KA21 200 E2
Eglinton Ter AYRS KA7 18 D2
SKLM PA17 70 A8
Egmont Pk EKILS G75 171 G2
Eider Av EKILS G75 171 G5
Eider Gv EKILS G75 171 G4
Eider Pl EKILS G75 171 G5
Eighth St UD/BTH/TAN G71 108 E8
Eildon Crs AIRDRIE ML6 111 M8
Eildon Dr BRHD/NEIL G78 125 J8
Eildon Rd KKNTL G66 65 M1
Eileen Gdns BSHPBGS G64 64 B7
Elba St AYR KA8 19 G2
Elcho St DMNK/BRGTN G40 12 C4
Elder Av BEITH KA15 168 A1
Elderbank BSDN G61 61 L6
Elder Crs BLTYR/CAMB G72 130 E5
Elder Gv UD/BTH/TAN G71 132 B2
Elderpark Gdns
GOV/IBX G51 103 M2
Elderpark Gv GOV/IBX G51 103 M2
Elderpark St GOV/IBX G51 103 M2
Eldersiea Rd CARLUKE ML8 189 G1
Elderslie Crs KLMNK KA1 211 L5
Elderslie St KVGV G3 4 C8
Elder St GOV/IBX G51 103 M2
Eldin Pl BRWEIR PA11 98 E3
JNSTN PA5 100 B7
Eldon Gdns BSHPBGS G64 63 L8
Eldon Pl GRNKW/INVK PA16 32 C1
Eldon St GRNKW/INVK PA16 32 C1
KVGV G3 4 B5
Elgin Av EKILN G74 153 M6
Elgin Gdns
CRMNK/CLK/EAG G76 151 M1
Elgin Pl AIRDRIE ML6 110 E4
CTBR ML5 110 B6
EKILN G74 153 M6
Elgin Rd BSDN G61 61 M2
Elgin Ter HMLTN ML3 155 L5
Elgin Wy BLSH ML4 133 G3
Elibank St STPS/GTHM/RID G33 85 G8
Elie St PTCK G11 82 C7
Eliot Crs HMLTN ML3 156 D8
Eliot Ter HMLTN ML3 156 D7
Elizabeth Av KKNTL G66 45 H3
Elizabeth Crs GIF/THBK G46 127 G7
Elizabeth Qd MTHW ML1 133 M4
Elizabeth St GOV/IBX G51 104 C4
Elizabeth Wynd HMLTN ML3 174 D2
Ella Gdns BLSH ML4 133 J5
Ellangowan Rd MLNGV G62 42 A8
PLKSD/SHW G41 127 J1
Ellergreen Rd BSDN G61 61 L5
Ellerslie St JNSTN PA5 100 A6
Ellesmere St PPK/MIL G22 4 F1
Elliot Av GIF/THBK G46 127 J7
PSLYS PA2 123 L2
Elliot Ct MTHW ML1 133 K8
Elliot Crs EKILN G74 15 L1
Elliot Dr GIF/THBK G46 127 J6
Elliot Pl KVGV G3 10 B1
Elliot St KVGV G3 10 B2
Ellisland EKILN G74 154 D6
KKNTL G66 46 B7
Ellisland Av CLYDBK G81 60 C6
Ellisland Crs CSMK G45 128 F4
Ellisland Dr BLTYR/CAMB G72 155 H3
KKNTL G66 46 A7
KLMNKN/STW KA3 17 M5
Ellisland Pl AYRS KA7 19 J8
SALT KA21 192 A6
Ellisland Rd
CRMNK/CLK/EAG G76 151 L4
CUMB G67 49 H7
PLKSW/MSWD G43 127 K3
Ellisland Sq AYRS KA7 19 J8
Ellismuir Farm Rd
BAIL/MDB/MHD G69 108 D5
Ellismuir Pl
BAIL/MDB/MHD G69 108 C5
Ellismuir Rd
BAIL/MDB/MHD G69 108 C5
Ellismuir St CTBR ML5 109 L6
Ellismuir Wy UD/BTH/TAN G71 109 G8
Ellis St CTBR ML5 110 A3
KLMNK KA1 16 D5
Elliston Av PLK/PH/NH G53 126 C4
Elliston Crs PLK/PH/NH G53 126 C4
Elliston Dr PLK/PH/NH G53 126 C4
Elliston Pl HWWD PA9 121 M4
Elliston Rd HWWD PA9 121 M4
Ellis Wy MTHW ML1 157 M4
Ellon Dr PSLYN/LNWD PA3 100 A4
Ellon Wy PSLYN/LNWD PA3 102 A2
Ellrig EKILS G75 171 K4
Elm Av KKNTL G66 65 J3
RNFRW PA4 80 C5
Elm Bank BSHPBGS G64 84 B1
KKNTL G66 65 K1
Elmbank Av KLMNK KA1 17 G4
UD/BTH/TAN G71 132 B2
Elmbank Crs CGLW G2 4 E8
HMLTN ML3 156 A5
Elmbank Dr ALEX/LLW G83 25 M4
KLMNK KA1 17 G4
LRKH ML9 176 C8
Elmbank Rd PGL PA14 56 C2
Elmbank St AYR KA8 224 F6
BLSH ML4 133 G5
CARLUKE ML8 189 G1
CGLW G2 4 E9
Elmbank Street La KVGV G3 4 E9
Elmbank Ter IRV KA12 203 K5
Elm Ct HMLTN ML3 174 F5
Elm Crs UD/BTH/TAN G71 132 D2
Elm Dr AIRDRIE ML6 111 L6
BLTYR/CAMB G72 130 C4
CUMB G67 49 M5
JNSTN PA5 122 F1
Elmfoot St GBLS G5 105 K7
Elm Gdns BSDN G61 61 L3
TROON KA10 217 G7
Elm Gv PGL PA14 56 C2
Elmhurst MTHW ML1 157 K5
Elmira Rd BAIL/MDB/MHD G69 86 C2
Elmore Av LNPK/KPK G44 128 B4
Elm Pl EKILS G75 171 J3
Elm Qd AIRDRIE ML6 111 K3
Elm Rd BRWEIR PA11 98 E1
CLYDBK G81 60 A4
DMBTN G82 36 F5
MTHW ML1 134 A7
PSLYS PA2 102 A8
RUTH G73 129 H5
Elmslie Ct BAIL/MDB/MHD G69 108 C5
Elms Pl BEITH KA15 144 B8
SVSTN KA20 192 E7
Elm St BLTYR/CAMB G72 155 L2
CRMNK/CLK/EAG G76 151 M3
CTBR ML5 110 C4
KKNTL G66 44 E1
MTHW ML1 157 K2
SCOT G14 81 K6
Elm Ter GRK PA19 31 L3
Elmvale Rw PPK/MIL G22 83 L4
Elmvale St PPK/MIL G22 83 L4
Elm View Ct BLSH ML4 133 K5
Elm Wk BSDN G61 61 L3
Elm Wy BLTYR/CAMB G72 130 E5
Elmway LRKH ML9 176 A4
Elmwood Av NMRNS G77 150 F3
PTCK G11 81 M5
Elmwood Ct UD/BTH/TAN G71 132 A7
Elmwood La PTCK G11 81 M5
Elphinstone Crs EKILS G75 15 H9
Elphinstone Pl GOV/IBX G51 104 C2
Elphinstone Rd GIF/THBK G46 151 G2
Elphin St SMSTN G23 62 D8
Elrig Rd LNPK/KPK G44 127 M4
Elspeth Gdns BSHPBGS G64 64 C7
Elswick Dr AIRDRIE ML6 91 G5
Eltham St PPK/MIL G22 5 G2
Elvan Pl EKILS G75 170 E2
Elvan St CAR/SHTL G32 106 F4
MTHW ML1 157 K3
Embo Dr KNTSWD G13 81 H3
Emerald Ter BLSH ML4 133 G5
Emerson Rd BSHPBGS G64 84 A1
Emerson Rd West BSHPBGS G64 64 A8
Emerson St MRYH/FIRH G20 83 G3
Emily Dr MTHW ML1 157 L5
Emma Jay Rd BLSH ML4 133 H4
Empire Wy MTHW ML1 133 J8
Empress Ct GRNK PA15 3 G6
Empress Dr HBR/GL G84 20 A6
Endfield Av KVD/HLHD G12 82 B3
Endrick Bank BSHPBGS G64 64 A5
Endrick Dr BSDN G61 61 M5
PSLY PA1 102 B3
Endrick Rd GRNK PA15 33 H8
Endrick St SPRGB/BLRNK G21 5 M2
Endrick Wy ALEX/LLW G83 25 K3
Engels St ALEX/LLW G83 25 L2
Englewood Av AYR KA8 225 H4
English Rw AIRDRIE ML6 111 J6
English St WISHAW ML2 158 D6
Ennerdale EKILS G75 170 F3
Ennisfree Rd BLTYR/CAMB G72 155 K1
Ensay St PPK/MIL G22 83 K2
Enterkin St CAR/SHTL G32 106 F5
Eriboll Pl PPK/MIL G22 83 H2
Eriboll St PPK/MIL G22 83 H2
Ericht Pl SHOTTS ML7 137 L3
Ericht Rd PLKSW/MSWD G43 127 J4
Eriska Av SCOT G14 81 G4
Eriskay Av HMLTN ML3 155 M7
NMRNS G77 150 B4
PGL PA14 55 H2
Eriskay Crs NMRNS G77 150 B4
Eriskay Dr OLDK G60 59 J3
Eriskay Pl KLMNKN/STW KA3 207 H4
Ermelo Gdns EKILS G75 171 H5
Erradale St PPK/MIL G22 83 G2
Errogie St ESTRH G34 108 B1
Erskine Av PLKSD/SHW G41 104 B5
Erskine Br ERSK PA8 59 G4
Erskine Crs AIRDRIE ML6 110 F4
Erskinefauld Rd
PSLYN/LNWD PA3 100 B3
Erskine Ferry Rd OLDK G60 59 G4
Erskine Pl KLMNKN/STW KA3 207 J7
SALT KA21 200 F2
Erskine Rd GIF/THBK G46 151 H3
Erskine Sq
CARD/HILL/MSPK G52 102 F2
Erskine Wy SHOTTS ML7 137 L5
Ervie St ESTRH G34 108 C2
Escart Rd CARLUKE ML8 178 F6
Esdaile Ct MTHW ML1 134 A6
Esk Av RNFRW PA4 80 E7
Eskbank St CAR/SHTL G32 107 G3
Esk Dl EKILN G74 153 J6
Eskdale Dr RUTH G73 129 K2
Eskdale Rd BSDN G61 61 K7
Eskdale St GVH/MTFL G42 105 H8
Esk Dr PSLYS PA2 100 E8
Esk Rd KLMNK KA1 212 B5
TROON KA10 216 E4
Esk St SCOT G14 80 F4
Esmond St KVGV G3 82 C8
Espedair St PSLYS PA2 9 H6
Esperanto Rd PSTWK KA9 225 L1
Espieside Crs CTBR ML5 109 L1
Esplanade AYRS KA7 18 C1
GRNKW/INVK PA16 32 C1
PSTWK KA9 221 H7
PSTWK KA9 225 G2
Essenside Av DRUM G15 61 J7
Essex Dr SCOT G14 81 L5
Essex La SCOT G14 81 L6
Essex Rd GRNKW/INVK PA16 31 L5
Esslemont Av SCOT G14 81 H5
Esson Pl KLMNKN/STW KA3 207 G6
Estate Qd CAR/SHTL G32 130 C1
Estate Rd CAR/SHTL G32 130 C1
Etive Av BSDN G61 62 B5
HMLTN ML3 156 A8
Etive Ct CLYDBK G81 60 C4
CUMB G67 68 B3
Etive Crs BSHPBGS G64 64 B8
CUMB G67 68 B3
WISHAW ML2 177 H1
Etive Dr AIRDRIE ML6 111 J4
BSHPTN PA7 58 C7
CUMB G67 68 B3
GIF/THBK G46 127 K8
Etive Pl CUMB G67 68 C3
IRV KA12 203 K4
Etive Rd WMYSB PA18 50 A8
Etive St CAR/SHTL G32 107 G4
WISHAW ML2 159 H8
Etna St WISHAW ML2 158 C5
Eton La KVD/HLHD G12 4 A4
Ettrick Av BLSH ML4 133 G2
RNFRW PA4 80 F7
Ettrick Crs KLMNKN/STW KA3 206 F6
RUTH G73 129 J2
Ettrick Dr BSDN G61 61 J2
BSHPTN PA7 58 C7
Ettrick Hl EKILN G74 154 A6
Ettrick Pl AYR KA8 225 H5
PLKSW/MSWD G43 127 K2
Ettrick St WISHAW ML2 159 G4
Ettrick Ter JNSTN PA5 122 C1
Euchan Pl TROON KA10 216 F4
Evan Crs GIF/THBK G46 127 K7
Evan Dr GIF/THBK G46 127 K8
Evanton Dr GIF/THBK G46 126 E6
Evanton Pl GIF/THBK G46 126 E6
Evelyn Ter KLWNG KA13 193 L7
Everard Ct SPRGB/BLRNK G21 83 L2
Everard Dr SPRGB/BLRNK G21 83 L3
Everard Pl SPRGB/BLRNK G21 83 L2
Everard Qd SPRGB/BLRNK G21 83 L2
Eversley St CAR/SHTL G32 107 G6
Everton Rd PLK/PH/NH G53 103 J7
Ewart Crs HMLTN ML3 156 A7
Ewart Ter HMLTN ML3 156 B7
Ewenfield Av AYRS KA7 228 F4
Ewenfield Gdns AYRS KA7 228 F5
Ewenfield Pk AYRS KA7 228 F5
Ewenfield Rd AYRS KA7 228 F5
Ewing Ct HMLTN ML3 174 C2
Ewing Pl DEN/PKHD G31 13 K6
Ewing Rd LOCHW PA12 120 C6
Ewing St KLBCH PA10 99 G6
RUTH G73 129 G2
Ewing Wk MLNGV G62 42 C8
Ewing Wy KLMNKN/STW KA3 197 K1
Excelsior St WISHAW ML2 158 D6
Exeter Dr PTCK G11 82 A7
Exeter St CTBR ML5 110 A4
Exmouth Pl
GRNKW/INVK PA16 31 L4
Eynort St PPK/MIL G22 83 G2
Eyrepoint Ct
STPS/GTHM/RID G33 107 G1

F

Factory Rd MTHW ML1 157 L4
Fagan Ct BLTYR/CAMB G72 131 L8
Faifley Rd CLYDBK G81 60 C2
Failford Pl KLMNKN/STW KA3 207 H4
Fairbairn Crs GIF/THBK G46 127 G7
Fairburn St CAR/SHTL G32 106 F5
Fairfax Av LNPK/KPK G44 128 C4
Fairfield Ct
CRMNK/CLK/EAG G76 151 L4
Fairfield Dr
CRMNK/CLK/EAG G76 151 L4
RNFRW PA4 80 D8
Fairfield Gdns GOV/IBX G51 103 M1
Fairfield Pl EKILN G74 153 H7
GOV/IBX G51 103 M1
HMLTN ML3 156 E8
UD/BTH/TAN G71 132 B7
Fairfield Rd AYRS KA7 18 D5
Fairfield St GOV/IBX G51 103 M1

Fairford Dr CUMB G67 68 D3
Fairhaven TROON KA10 216 E2
Fairhaven Av AIRDRIE ML6 111 L3
Fairhaven Rd SMSTN G23 82 D1
Fairhaven Sq KLWNG KA13 193 H5
Fairhill Av HMLTN ML3 156 C8
PLK/PH/NH G53 126 C2
Fairhill Crs HMLTN ML3 156 C8
Fairhill Pl HMLTN ML3 174 B2
Fairholm Av HMLTN ML3 157 K8
Fairholm St CAR/SHTL G32 106 F5
LRKH ML9 175 M5
Fairley St GOV/IBX G51 104 B3
Fairlie EKILN G74 14 D1
Fairlie Av KLMNK KA1 16 A7
Fairlieburne Gdns
FAIRLIE KA29 139 K7
Fairlie Dr IRVSE KA11 204 B3
Fairlie Park Dr PTCK G11 82 A7
Fairlie Vw CRH/DND KA2 210 D4
Fair Oaks
CRMNK/CLK/EAG G76 152 E1
Fairrie St GRNK PA15 3 L8
Fair View Dr LNK/LMHG ML11 198 B5
Fairway BSDN G61 61 H4
Fair Wy DMBTN G82 35 G1
Fairway Av PSLYS PA2 124 D1
Fairways KLMNKN/STW KA3 197 L1
LRKH ML9 176 C6
Fairways Vw CLYDBK G81 60 D3
Fairweather Pl NMRNS G77 150 C5
Fairyhill Pl KLMNK KA1 16 D8
Fairyhill Rd KLMNK KA1 16 D8
Fairyknowe Gdns
UD/BTH/TAN G71 132 B7
Faith Av BRWEIR PA11 75 L7
Falconbridge Rd EKILN G74 154 C5
Falcon Crs GRNKW/INVK PA16 32 A3
PSLYN/LNWD PA3 8 A2
Falconer St PGL PA14 34 C7
Falconer Ter HMLTN ML3 156 C8
Falcon Rd JNSTN PA5 122 D2
Falcon Ter MRYH/FIRH G20 82 C1
Falcon Terrace La
MRYH/FIRH G20 82 C1
Falfield St GBLS G5 10 F7
Falkland Av NMRNS G77 151 G3
Falkland Crs BSHPBGS G64 84 D1
Falklandcrs BSHPBGS G64 64 D8
Falkland Dr EKILN G74 14 C3
Falkland La KVD/HLHD G12 82 B6
Falkland Pk EKILN G74 14 D4
Falkland Park Rd AYR KA8 225 G6
Falkland Pl AYR KA8 225 G6
CTBR ML5 110 B6
EKILN G74 14 D4
Falkland Rd AYR KA8 225 G6
Falkland St KVD/HLHD G12 82 B6
Falloch Pl WISHAW ML2 159 M3
Falloch Rd BSDN G61 61 J7
GVH/MTFL G42 128 A2
MLNGV G62 41 L6
Fallside Av UD/BTH/TAN G71 132 C3
Fallside Rd UD/BTH/TAN G71 132 A7
UD/BTH/TAN G71 132 B4
Falmouth Dr GRNKW/INVK PA16 31 M4
Falside Av PSLYS PA2 101 L8
Falside Rd CAR/SHTL G32 107 G7
PSLYS PA2 101 K8
Falstaff EKILN G74 154 C4
Fancy Farm Pl
GRNKW/INVK PA16 31 M5
Fancy Farm Rd
GRNKW/INVK PA16 31 M5
Faraday Av WISHAW ML2 159 J5
Faransay Pl
KLMNKN/STW KA3 207 G4
Fara St SMSTN G23 82 F1
Fardalehill Vw CRH/DND KA2 205 M8
Farden Pl PSTWK KA9 225 K3
Farie St RUTH G73 128 F1
Farlands Vw WKIL KA23 181 J5
Farm Ct UD/BTH/TAN G71 132 B5
Farm Crs MTHW ML1 134 F5
Farmeloan Rd RUTH G73 129 H1
Farmfield Ter WKIL KA23 181 K4
Farmgate Sq BLSH ML4 132 F5
Farmington Av
CAR/SHTL G32 107 K5
Farmington Gdns
CAR/SHTL G32 107 K4
Farmington Gv
CAR/SHTL G32 107 K4
Farm La BLSH ML4 132 F6
Farm Pk KKNTL G66 65 K5
Farm Rd BLTYR/CAMB G72 131 K8
CLYDBK G81 59 K6
CLYDBK G81 60 A2
HMLTN ML3 155 M5
KLMNKN/STW KA3 206 E6
PGL PA14 54 E2
PLKSD/SHW G41 104 B4
Farm St MTHW ML1 157 K2
Farm Ter HMLTN ML3 155 M5
Farndale EKILN G74 153 J6
Farne Dr LNPK/KPK G44 128 B5
Farnell St COWCAD G4 5 G4
Farquhar Rd PGL PA14 33 M7
Farrell Pl AYR KA8 225 H7
Farrier Ct JNSTN PA5 99 M6
Faskally Av BSHPBGS G64 63 L6
Faskin Crs PLK/PH/NH G53 125 M2
Faskine Av AIRDRIE ML6 110 F4
AIRDRIE ML6 111 H7
Faskine Crs AIRDRIE ML6 110 F3
Faskin Pl PLK/PH/NH G53 125 M2
Faskin Rd PLK/PH/NH G53 125 M2
Fasque Pl DRUM G15 60 E5
Fauldhouse St GBLS G5 105 K6
Faulds BAIL/MDB/MHD G69 108 C4
Faulds Gdns
BAIL/MDB/MHD G69 108 C4
Fauldshead Rd RNFRW PA4 80 C6
Fauldspark Crs
BAIL/MDB/MHD G69 108 C3
Faulds Park Rd GRK PA19 30 E4
Faulds St CTBR ML5 109 L6
Fauldswood Crs PSLYS PA2 8 B9
Fauldswood Dr PSLYS PA2 8 A9
Faulkner Gv MTHW ML1 158 F1
Fearnan Pl GRNKW/INVK PA16 32 A5
Fearnmore Rd MRYH/FIRH G20 82 D2
Fearnoch PSTWK KA9 225 J4
Fellhill St AYRS KA7 229 H4
The Fells KKNTL G66 44 E1
Fellsview Av KKNTL G66 45 M8
Felton Pl KNTSWD G13 80 F2
Fencedyke Wy IRVSE KA11 204 A6
Fendoch St CAR/SHTL G32 107 G5
Fenella St CAR/SHTL G32 107 H4
Fennsbank Av RUTH G73 129 K6
Fenwick Dr BRHD/NEIL G78 125 K8
HMLTN ML3 174 E2
RNFRW PA4 80 E6
Fenwickland Av AYRS KA7 229 G5
Fenwickland Pl AYRS KA7 229 G5
Fenwick Pl GIF/THBK G46 127 H8
Fenwick Rd GIF/THBK G46 127 J6
KLMNKN/STW KA3 206 C2
Ferclay St CLYDBK G81 60 D2
Fereneze Av BRHD/NEIL G78 125 H6
CRMNK/CLK/EAG G76 151 J1
RNFRW PA4 102 A1
Fereneze Crs HMLTN ML3 155 M6
KNTSWD G13 80 F2
Fereneze Dr PSLYS PA2 124 B1
Fereneze Gv BRHD/NEIL G78 125 H6
Fereneze Rd BRHD/NEIL G78 147 M2
Fergus Av PSLYN/LNWD PA3 101 G4
Fergus Dr GRNKW/INVK PA16 32 A5
MRYH/FIRH G20 4 B1
PSLYN/LNWD PA3 101 G4
Fergus Gdns HMLTN ML3 156 F7
Fergushill Rd KLWNG KA13 193 M6
Fergus La MRYH/FIRH G20 4 C1
Ferguslie PSLY PA1 8 A5
Ferguslie Park Av
PSLYN/LNWD PA3 101 G5
Ferguslie Park Crs
PSLYN/LNWD PA3 101 G5
Ferguslie Wk PSLY PA1 8 B5
Ferguson Av MLNGV G62 42 A8
PSTWK KA9 225 K1
RNFRW PA4 80 D6
Ferguson Dr MTHW ML1 157 L6
Ferguson St AYR KA8 225 J7
JNSTN PA5 99 L6
RNFRW PA4 80 D6
Fergus Pl GRNKW/INVK PA16 32 A5
Fergus Rd GRNKW/INVK PA16 32 A5
Fergusson Pl EKILN G74 154 D4
Fergusson Rd CUMB G67 48 F7
Ferguston Rd BSDN G61 61 M5
Fergus Wy RAYR/DAL KA6 231 G5
Fernan St CAR/SHTL G32 106 F4
Fern Av BSHPBGS G64 84 B1
ERSK PA8 79 H2
KKNTL G66 65 J5
Fernbank PSTWK KA9 225 H4
Fernbank Av
BLTYR/CAMB G72 130 C5
Fernbank St PPK/MIL G22 83 L4
Fernbrae Av RUTH G73 129 H7
Fernbrae Wy RUTH G73 129 H6
Ferncroft Dr LNPK/KPK G44 128 D4
Ferndale LRKH ML9 176 A8
Ferndale Ct SMSTN G23 82 D1
Ferndale Dr MRYH/FIRH G20 82 C1
Ferndale Gdns SMSTN G23 82 D1
Ferndale Pl SMSTN G23 82 D1
Fern Dr BRHD/NEIL G78 125 H5
Ferness Ov SPRGB/BLRNK G21 84 C2
Ferness Pl SPRGB/BLRNK G21 84 C2
Ferness Rd SPRGB/BLRNK G21 84 C3
Fern Gv BAIL/MDB/MHD G69 66 F8
Ferngrove Av KVD/HLHD G12 82 B3
Fernhill Gra UD/BTH/TAN G71 132 A8
Fernhill Rd RUTH G73 129 G5
Ferniegair Av HBR/GL G84 20 A7
Fernie Gdns MRYH/FIRH G20 82 E2
Ferniesshaw Rd MTHW ML1 135 M6
Fern La KNTSWD G13 81 M4
Fernlea BSDN G61 61 L6
Fernleigh Rd
PLKSW/MSWD G43 127 K4
Fern Pl KLMNK KA1 211 J2
Fernslea Av BLTYR/CAMB G72 155 J1
Fern St MTHW ML1 158 A5
Ferryden St SCOT G14 81 L7
Ferry Loan ALEX/LLW G83 25 L4
Ferry Rd BSHPTN PA7 58 A5
DMBTN G82 35 H3
GTCI KA28 138 C6
KVGV G3 82 C8
RNFRW PA4 80 D5
UD/BTH/TAN G71 131 L3
UD/BTH/TAN G71 132 A7
Fersit St PLKSW/MSWD G43 127 J3
Fetlar Dr KLMNKN/STW KA3 207 G3
LNPK/KPK G44 128 C4
Fetlar Rd BRWEIR PA11 98 C1
Fettercairn Av DRUM G15 60 E5
Fettes St STPS/GTHM/RID G33 106 F1
Fiddison Pl PSTWK KA9 225 L4
Fiddoch Ct WISHAW ML2 159 M2
Fidra St STPS/GTHM/RID G33 106 F1
Fielden Pl DMNK/BRGTN G40 12 F6
Fielden St DMNK/BRGTN G40 12 F6
Field Gv CRMNK/CLK/EAG G76 151 M4
Fieldhead Dr
PLKSW/MSWD G43 127 G4
Fieldhead Sq
PLKSW/MSWD G43 127 G4
Field Rd CLYDBK G81 60 D1
CRMNK/CLK/EAG G76 151 M4
LRKH ML9 176 B7
Fields La CRG/CRSL/HOU PA6 77 H6
Field St HMLTN ML3 156 D8
Fife Av AIRDRIE ML6 111 G4
CARD/HILL/MSPK G52 103 L5
FAIRLIE KA29 139 L5
Fife Crs UD/BTH/TAN G71 132 A8
Fife Dr GRNKW/INVK PA16 31 K4
MTHW ML1 133 K7
Fife Pl FAIRLIE KA29 139 L6
Fife Rd GRNKW/INVK PA16 31 L6
Fife Wy BSHPBGS G64 84 D1
Fifth Av AIRDRIE ML6 111 J1
KVD/HLHD G12 81 M4
RNFRW PA4 80 C7
STPS/GTHM/RID G33 85 H4
Fifth Rd BLTYR/CAMB G72 155 L4
Fifty Pitches Pl GOV/IBX G51 103 J2
Fifty Pitches Rd GOV/IBX G51 103 H3
Finart Dr PSLYS PA2 102 B8
Finaven Gdns BSDN G61 61 H1
Finch Dr KNTSWD G13 80 F1
Finch Pl JNSTN PA5 122 D2
KLMNKN/STW KA3 17 L6
Finch Rd GRNKW/INVK PA16 32 B4
Findhorn Av PSLYS PA2 100 F8
RNFRW PA4 80 E6
Findhorn Ct EKILS G75 170 D1
Findhorn Pl EKILS G75 170 D1
TROON KA10 216 E4
Findhorn Rd PSTWK KA9 221 M5
Findhorn St STPS/GTHM/RID G33 7 L8
Findlay's Brae SALT KA21 200 F2
Findlay St KSYTH G65 47 K1
MTHW ML1 157 M4
Findochty St
STPS/GTHM/RID G33 85 L8
Fingal La MRYH/FIRH G20 82 C2
Fingal St MRYH/FIRH G20 82 D2
Fingalton Rd NMRNS G77 149 L4
Fingask St CAR/SHTL G32 107 J5
Finglas Av PSLYS PA2 102 B8
Finglen Pl PLK/PH/NH G53 126 B5
Fingleton Av BRHD/NEIL G78 125 K8
Finhaven St CAR/SHTL G32 106 E6
Finlarig St ESTRH G34 108 C2
Finlas Av AYRS KA7 229 H6
Finlas St PPK/MIL G22 83 K5
Finlay Av DALRY KA24 184 D2
Finlay Dr DEN/PKHD G31 12 F2
PSLYN/LNWD PA3 99 M4
Finlay Ri MLNGV G62 62 C1
Finlayson Dr AIRDRIE ML6 111 L2
KLMNKN/STW KA3 207 K6
Finlayson Qd AIRDRIE ML6 111 L2
Finlaystone Pl KLMCLM PA13 55 K7
Finlaystone Rd KLMCLM PA13 55 K7
PGL PA14 55 G2
Finlaystone St CTBR ML5 109 L2
Finnart Crs GRK PA19 31 J3
Finnart Rd GRNKW/INVK PA16 32 D3
Finnart Sq DMNK/BRGTN G40 12 D9
Finnart St DMNK/BRGTN G40 12 D9
GRNKW/INVK PA16 32 C2
Finneston St GRNK PA15 3 H7
Finnick Gln AYRS KA7 229 G6
Finnieston Sq KVGV G3 4 B9
Finnieston St KVGV G3 10 B2
Finnie Ter GRK PA19 31 K3
IRVSE KA11 204 F7
Finnie Wynd MTHW ML1 158 B5
Finnockbog Dr
GRNKW/INVK PA16 50 D5
Finnockbog Rd
GRNKW/INVK PA16 50 D5
Finsbay St GOV/IBX G51 103 K3
Fintaig La WISHAW ML2 159 L6
Fintrie Ter HMLTN ML3 155 L5
Fintry Av PSLYS PA2 124 E1
Fintry Crs BRHD/NEIL G78 125 J8
BSHPBGS G64 64 C8
Fintry Dr LNPK/KPK G44 128 C2
Fintry Gdns BSDN G61 61 J1
Fintry Pl EKILS G75 171 H5
IRVSE KA11 204 A7
Fintry Rd GRNK PA15 33 H8
Fir Bank AYRS KA7 229 J4
Firbank Av BSHPBGS G64 64 B1
Fir Bank Av LRKH ML9 176 B7
Firbank Ter BRHD/NEIL G78 125 L8
Firdon Crs DRUM G15 61 G8
Fir Dr EKILS G75 171 H4
Fir Gv MTHW ML1 134 A7
UD/BTH/TAN G71 132 C2
Firhill Av AIRDRIE ML6 110 F3
Firhill Dr PSTWK KA9 221 K4
Firhill Rd MRYH/FIRH G20 83 G5
Firhill St MRYH/FIRH G20 4 E1
Firlee EKILS G75 170 F2
Firpark Rd BSHPBGS G64 84 B1
Firpark St DEN/PKHD G31 6 C9
Fir Park St MTHW ML1 157 M5
Firpark Ter DEN/PKHD G31 12 C1
Fir Pl BAIL/MDB/MHD G69 108 A6
BLTYR/CAMB G72 130 C4
JNSTN PA5 100 A7
First Av ALEX/LLW G83 25 M4
BSDN G61 62 A6
DMBTN G82 37 J7
IRV KA12 208 C1
KKNTL G66 65 K8
LNPK/KPK G44 127 M7
RNFRW PA4 80 C7
STPS/GTHM/RID G33 85 H4
UD/BTH/TAN G71 131 L1
First Gdns PLKSD/SHW G41 104 A5
Fir St GRNK PA15 33 L7
First Rd BLTYR/CAMB G72 155 L4
First St UD/BTH/TAN G71 131 M1
First Ter CLYDBK G81 60 A6
Fir Ter GRK PA19 31 K3
Firth Crs GRK PA19 31 H3
Firth Gdns TROON KA10 216 D2
Firth Rd IRVSE KA11 216 D1
Firth View Ter ARD KA22 191 K5
Firthview Ter DMBTN G82 36 C6
Firtree Pl WISHAW ML2 160 B3
Firtree Rd WISHAW ML2 160 B3
Fir Vw AIRDRIE ML6 111 H7
Firwood Cts NMRNS G77 150 E5
Firwood Dr LNPK/KPK G44 128 C3
Firwood Rd NMRNS G77 150 E4
Fischer Gdns PSLYN/LNWD PA3 100 F4
Fisher Av KSYTH G65 47 K1
PSLYN/LNWD PA3 100 F5
Fisher Ct CRH/DND KA2 205 M6
Fisher Crs CLYDBK G81 60 B4
Fisher Dr PSLYN/LNWD PA3 100 F5
Fisher Pl HBR/GL G84 21 G7
Fisher St LRKH ML9 176 B8
Fisher Wy PSLYN/LNWD PA3 100 F5
Fisherwood Rd ALEX/LLW G83 25 L1
Fishescoates Av RUTH G73 129 J5
RUTH G73 129 K4
Fishescoates Gdns
RUTH G73 129 K4
Fitzalan Rd PSLYN/LNWD PA3 80 A8
Fitzroy La KVGV G3 4 A8
Five Roads KLWNG KA13 194 A6
Flakefield EKILN G74 153 H7
Flanders St CLYDBK G81 60 C2
Flatterton Rd
GRNKW/INVK PA16 31 J7
Flatt Rd LARGS KA30 115 K6
Flaxfield Gv MTHW ML1 133 K7
Flaxmill Av WISHAW ML2 158 D5
Flax Rd UD/BTH/TAN G71 132 A4
Fleck Av SALT KA21 192 A7
Fleet Av RNFRW PA4 80 E8
Fleet St CAR/SHTL G32 107 H5
Fleming Av BAIL/MDB/MHD G69 86 C2
CLYDBK G81 80 D1
Fleming Ct CARLUKE ML8 178 E8
HMLTN ML3 155 L5
MTHW ML1 158 A5
Fleming Crs SALT KA21 192 A6
Fleming Dr KLMNKN/STW KA3 197 J1
Fleming Pl EKILS G75 14 D5
Fleming Rd BLSH ML4 133 H3
BSHPTN PA7 58 B6
CRG/CRSL/HOU PA6 77 G7
CUMB G67 48 F7
Fleming St DEN/PKHD G31 13 H3
KLMNK KA1 211 L4
PSLYN/LNWD PA3 101 L2
Fleming Ter IRV KA12 203 H4
Flemington St SPRGB/BLRNK G21 6 C2
Fleming Wy HMLTN ML3 155 K5
Flenders Av
CRMNK/CLK/EAG G76 151 J3
Flenders Rd
CRMNK/CLK/EAG G76 151 J3
Fletcher Av GRK PA19 31 L3
Fleurs Av PLKSD/SHW G41 104 B6
Fleurs Rd PLKSD/SHW G41 104 B5
Flinders Pl EKILS G75 171 H1
Flint Mill La GRNK PA15 3 G9
Flloyd St CTBR ML5 109 M2
Floorsburn Crs JNSTN PA5 99 L7
Floors Rd CRMNK/CLK/EAG G76 151 J8
Floors St JNSTN PA5 99 M7
Flora Gdns BSHPBGS G64 64 C7
Florence Dr GIF/THBK G46 127 J7
KLMCLM PA13 75 H1
Florence Gdns RUTH G73 129 J5
Florence St GBLS G5 11 K6
GRNKW/INVK PA16 32 B5
Florida Av GVH/MTFL G42 128 B1
Florida Crs GVH/MTFL G42 128 B1
Florida Dr GVH/MTFL G42 128 A1
Florida Gdns
BAIL/MDB/MHD G69 108 A4
Florida Sq GVH/MTFL G42 128 B1
Florida St GVH/MTFL G42 128 A1
Florish Rd ERSK PA8 79 K1
Flowerdale Pl
PLK/PH/NH G53 126 B6
Flowerhill St AIRDRIE ML6 111 H1
Fluchter Rd MLNGV G62 43 G8
Flures Av ERSK PA8 79 L1
Flures Crs RNFRW PA4 79 L1
Flures Dr ERSK PA8 79 L1
RNFRW PA4 79 L1
Flures Pl ERSK PA8 79 L1
Fochabers Dr
CARD/HILL/MSPK G52 103 J3
Fogo Pl MRYH/FIRH G20 82 D3
Foinavon Rd HMLTN ML3 174 E6
Footfield Rd BLSH ML4 132 F6
Foot of Lone Rd
LNK/LMHG ML11 198 B4
Forbes Dr DMNK/BRGTN G40 12 C5
MTHW ML1 133 H7
PSTWK KA9 225 J5
Forbes Pl KLMNKN/STW KA3 207 H7
PSLY PA1 9 H4
Forbes St DMNK/BRGTN G40 12 C4
Ford Av IRVSE KA11 204 D8
Forde Crs SVSTN KA20 192 F7
Fordneuk St DMNK/BRGTN G40 12 E5
Fordoun St ESTRH G34 108 D1
Ford Rd KVD/HLHD G12 82 D5
NMRNS G77 150 D6
Fordyce St PTCK G11 82 B7
Forehill Rd AYRS KA7 19 K7
Forehouse Rd KLBCH PA10 98 C5
Fore Rw HMLTN ML3 156 E5
Forest Av BLSH ML4 133 J6
HMLTN ML3 174 D3
Forest Dr UD/BTH/TAN G71 132 A6
Forestfield Gdns AIRDRIE ML6 91 G5
Forest Gdns KKNTL G66 65 G5
Forest Ga UD/BTH/TAN G71 109 H8
Forest Gv KLMNKN/STW KA3 207 H5
Foresthall Crs SPRGB/BLRNK G21 6 E2
Foresthall Dr SPRGB/BLRNK G21 6 E2
Forest Kirk CARLUKE ML8 189 H1
Forest La HMLTN ML3 174 D3
Forest Pk WISHAW ML2 159 K4
Forest Pl CARLUKE ML8 188 B8
KKNTL G66 65 G5
PSLYS PA2 9 G9
Fore St PGL PA14 34 C7
SCOT G14 81 J6
Forest Rd CUMB G67 49 M4
LRKH ML9 176 B7
Forest Vw CUMB G67 49 J6
Forest Wy AYRS KA7 229 J4
Forfar Av
CARD/HILL/MSPK G52 103 H5
Forfar Crs BSHPBGS G64 84 C1
Forfar Rd GRNKW/INVK PA16 31 M6
Forgan Gdns BSHPBGS G64 84 D1
Forge Dr CTBR ML5 109 M2
Forge Pl SPRGB/BLRNK G21 7 H3
Forge Rd AIRDRIE ML6 111 M3
AYR KA8 225 H5
Forge Rw AIRDRIE ML6 111 J6
Forge St KLMNK KA1 16 D3
SPRGB/BLRNK G21 7 G5
Forge Vennal KLWNG KA13 193 J5
Forgewood Pth AIRDRIE ML6 111 M3
Forgewood Rd MTHW ML1 133 J7
Forglen St ESTRH G34 86 B8
Formby Dr SMSTN G23 82 D1
Forres Av GIF/THBK G46 127 K6
Forres Crs BLSH ML4 133 G3
Forres Ga GIF/THBK G46 127 K7
Forres Qd WISHAW ML2 159 H4
Forres St BLTYR/CAMB G72 155 J3
SMSTN G23 62 E8
Forrest Dr BSDN G61 41 H8
Forrester Ct BSHPBGS G64 83 M1
Forrestfield Crs NMRNS G77 150 E4
Forrestfield Gdns
NMRNS G77 150 E4
Forrestfield Rd AIRDRIE ML6 91 L2
Forrestfield St SPRGB/BLRNK G21 6 E7
Forrest Ga HMLTN ML3 156 B8
Forrestlea Rd CARLUKE ML8 189 G1
Forrest Rd LNK/LMHG ML11 199 H4
Forrest St AIRDRIE ML6 111 L1
BLTYR/CAMB G72 155 M2
DMNK/BRGTN G40 12 E5
SHOTTS ML7 137 L4
Forsyth Ct LNK/LMHG ML11 199 J5
Forsyth Gv
GRNKW/INVK PA16 32 D3
Forsyth St AIRDRIE ML6 111 H1
GRNKW/INVK PA16 32 D3
Fortacre Pl IRVSE KA11 204 B4
Forteviot Av
BAIL/MDB/MHD G69 108 C3
BAIL/MDB/MHD G69 108 C4
Forteviot Pl
BAIL/MDB/MHD G69 108 C4
Forth Av PSLYS PA2 100 E8
Forth Ct EKILS G75 170 E2
Forth Crs EKILS G75 170 E1
Forth Gv EKILS G75 170 E1
Forth Pl JNSTN PA5 122 C1
KLMNK KA1 212 A4
Forth Rd BLTYR/CAMB G72 155 L4
BSDN G61 61 K7
BSHPBGS G64 64 B1
Forth St CLYDBK G81 80 C1
GRNKW/INVK PA16 32 B4
Forth Ter HMLTN ML3 174 B1
Forties Ct GIF/THBK G46 126 F4
Forties Crs GIF/THBK G46 126 F4
Forties Gdns GIF/THBK G46 127 G4
Forties Rd CRG/CRSL/HOU PA6 99 J1
Forties Wy GIF/THBK G46 127 G4
Fortieth Av EKILS G75 171 M4
Fortingall Av KVD/HLHD G12 82 C3
Fortingall Pl KVD/HLHD G12 82 C3
Fortingall Rd BLTYR/CAMB G72 155 M4
Fortissat Av SHOTTS ML7 137 K4
Fortissat Rd SHOTTS ML7 137 H1
Fortisset Rd SHOTTS ML7 137 H1
Fort Matilda Pl
GRNKW/INVK PA16 32 B2
Fortrose St PTCK G11 82 B7
Fort St AYRS KA7 18 E3
LARGS KA30 115 J6
MTHW ML1 157 H1
Fossil Gv KKNTL G66 46 A8
Fosterland SKLM PA17 70 A6
Foswell Pl DRUM G15 60 F4
Fotheringay La
PLKSD/SHW G41 104 D7
Fotheringay Rd
PLKSD/SHW G41 104 D7
Fothringham Rd AYR KA8 19 H3
Foulburn Rd MTHW ML1 136 C7
Foulis La KNTSWD G13 81 M3
Foulis St KNTSWD G13 81 M3
Foulpapple Rd NMLNS KA16 215 M1
Foulsykes Rd WISHAW ML2 159 L5
Foundry La BRHD/NEIL G78 125 J7
Foundry Rd MTHW ML1 135 J7
SHOTTS ML7 137 L5
Foundry Wynd KLWNG KA13 193 J5
Fountain Av RNFRW PA4 79 H5
Fountain Crs RNFRW PA4 79 H4
Fountain Dr RNFRW PA4 79 J5
Fountainwell Av COWCAD G4 5 M4
Fountainwell Dr COWCAD G4 5 M4
Fountainwell Pl COWCAD G4 5 M4
Fountainwell Rd COWCAD G4 5 M4
Fountainwell Sq COWCAD G4 6 A4
Fountainwell Ter
SPRGB/BLRNK G21 6 A4
Four Acres Dr
KLMNKN/STW KA3 206 B1
Fourth Av DMBTN G82 37 J6
KKNTL G66 65 K8
RNFRW PA4 80 C7
STPS/GTHM/RID G33 85 H4
Fourth Gdns PLKSD/SHW G41 104 A5
Fourth St UD/BTH/TAN G71 108 F8
Four Windings
CRG/CRSL/HOU PA6 77 H7
Fowlds St KLMNK KA1 16 F5
Fowler Pl EKILS G75 15 J9
Fowlis Dr NMRNS G77 150 C3
Foxbar Crs PSLYS PA2 123 L2
Foxbar Dr KNTSWD G13 81 H3
PSLYS PA2 123 L2
Foxbar Rd PSLYS PA2 123 L2
Foxes Gv KKNTL G66 65 L4
Foxglove Pl PLK/PH/NH G53 126 B6
Fox Gv MTHW ML1 157 H2
Foxhills Pl SMSTN G23 62 E8
Foxley St CAR/SHTL G32 107 J8
Fox St CGLE G1 11 H3
GRNKW/INVK PA16 32 D2
Foyers Ter SPRGB/BLRNK G21 6 E1
Francis St GBLS G5 10 F7
Frankfield Rd
STPS/GTHM/RID G33 85 L4
Frankfield St
STPS/GTHM/RID G33 7 M4
Frankfort St PLKSD/SHW G41 104 E8
Franklin Pl EKILS G75 153 H8
Franklin Rd SALT KA21 191 L8

Franklin St DMNK/BRGTN G40 ...... 12 C9
Fraser Av BSHPTN PA7 ...... 58 A5
DMBTN G82 ...... 37 J5
JNSTN PA5 ...... 100 A7
NMRNS G77 ...... 150 E3
RUTH G73 ...... 129 J2
TROON KA10 ...... 216 D4
Fraser Ct HMLTN ML3 ...... 156 B7
NMLNS KA16 ...... 215 G2 1
Fraser Gdns KKNTL G66 ...... 65 H1
Fraser St BLTYR/CAMB G72 ...... 129 L3
MTHW ML1 ...... 135 H7
Frazer Av HBR/GL G84 ...... 20 A6
Frazer St DMNK/BRGTN G40 ...... 13 G6
LARGS KA30 ...... 115 J6
Frederick St CTBR ML5 ...... 109 L1
Freeland Ct PLK/PH/NH G53 ...... 126 C3 1
Freeland Crs PLK/PH/NH G53 ...... 126 B3
Freeland Dr BRWEIR PA11 ...... 76 D8 2
ERSK PA8 ...... 79 J3
PLK/PH/NH G53 ...... 126 B3
Freeland Pl KKNTL G66 ...... 65 K1
Freeland Rd ERSK PA8 ...... 79 H2
Freelands Crs OLDK G60 ...... 59 H4
Freelands Rd OLDK G60 ...... 59 J5
Freesia Ct MTHW ML1 ...... 157 L4
French St CLYDBK G81 ...... 59 L6
DMNK/BRGTN G40 ...... 105 M6
RNFRW PA4 ...... 80 B7
WISHAW ML2 ...... 159 H6
Freuchie St ESTRH G34 ...... 108 B2
Frew St AIRDRIE ML6 ...... 111 G1
Frew Ter IRV KA12 ...... 203 J4
Friar Av BSHPBGS G64 ...... 64 B5
Friarscourt Av KNTSWD G13 ...... 61 K8
Friarscourt Rd
BAIL/MDB/MHD G69 ...... 66 B8
Friars Cft IRV KA12 ...... 203 H7
KKNTL G66 ...... 65 L1
Friarsdene LNK/LMHG ML11 ...... 198 F5
Friarsfield Rd LNK/LMHG ML11 ...... 198 F5
Friar's La LNK/LMHG ML11 ...... 198 F6
Friars Pl KNTSWD G13 ...... 81 K1 2
Friars Wy AIRDRIE ML6 ...... 111 J5
Friar's Wynd
LNK/LMHG ML11 ...... 198 F5 1
Friarton Rd PLKSW/MSWD G43 ...... 127 M4
Frobisher Pl HBR/GL G84 ...... 21 G7 5
Frood St MTHW ML1 ...... 133 J8
Fruin Av NMRNS G77 ...... 150 E3
Fruin Dr WISHAW ML2 ...... 159 L6
Fruin Ri HMLTN ML3 ...... 155 L7
Fruin Rd DRUM G15 ...... 60 F8
Fruin St PPK/MIL G22 ...... 83 J5
Fudstone Dr KBRN KA25 ...... 167 G1
Fulbar Av RNFRW PA4 ...... 80 C5
Fulbar Ct RNFRW PA4 ...... 80 D5 3
Fulbar Crs PSLYS PA2 ...... 100 F7
Fulbar Gdns PSLYS PA2 ...... 100 F7
Fulbar La RNFRW PA4 ...... 80 D5 2
Fulbar Rd GOV/IBX G51 ...... 103 J2
PSLYS PA2 ...... 100 F7
Fulbar St RNFRW PA4 ...... 80 D5
Fullarton Av CAR/SHTL G32 ...... 107 G7
CRH/DND KA2 ...... 209 M7
Fullarton Crs TROON KA10 ...... 216 E7
Fullarton Dr TROON KA10 ...... 216 E8
Fullarton La CAR/SHTL G32 ...... 107 G7
Fullarton Pl CTBR ML5 ...... 109 K6
Fullarton Rd BALLOCH G68 ...... 48 E4
CAR/SHTL G32 ...... 107 G8
PSTWK KA9 ...... 225 J3
Fullarton St AYRS KA7 ...... 18 E3
CTBR ML5 ...... 109 L6
IRV KA12 ...... 203 H7
KLMNK KA1 ...... 16 C4
Fullers Ga CLYDBK G81 ...... 60 C2
Fullerton Dr WKIL KA23 ...... 181 H5
Fullerton La GRNK PA15 ...... 33 L6
Fullerton Sq ARD KA22 ...... 191 J7 2
Fullerton St PSLYN/LNWD PA3 ...... 101 K2
Fullerton Ter PSLYN/LNWD PA3 ...... 101 L2
Fulmar Pk EKILN G74 ...... 153 K6 3
Fulmar Pl JNSTN PA5 ...... 122 C3 1
Fulshaw Ct PSTWK KA9 ...... 225 K4 2
Fulshaw Crs AYR KA8 ...... 225 M7
Fulton Crs KLBCH PA10 ...... 99 H6
Fulton Dr CRG/CRSL/HOU PA6 ...... 99 L1
Fulton Gdns CRG/CRSL/HOU PA6 ...... 99 L1
Fulton Rd MLNGV G62 ...... 42 B8 2
Fulton's La KLMNKN/STW KA3 ...... 16 F2
Fulton St KNTSWD G13 ...... 81 L2
Fulwood Av KNTSWD G13 ...... 80 F2
PSLYN/LNWD PA3 ...... 100 B3
Fulwood Pl KNTSWD G13 ...... 80 F2
The Furlongs HMLTN ML3 ...... 156 D5
Furnace Ct KLMNK KA1 ...... 212 D3
Furnace Rd HMLTN ML3 ...... 174 F6
Fyfe Shore Rd PGL PA14 ...... 34 E8
Fyffe Park Rd PGL PA14 ...... 34 E8
Fyneart St WISHAW ML2 ...... 159 L5
Fyne Ct HMLTN ML3 ...... 156 A8 1
Fyne Crs LRKH ML9 ...... 175 M4
Fynloch Pl CLYDBK G81 ...... 59 L2
Fyvie Av PLKSW/MSWD G43 ...... 127 G4
Fyvie Crs AIRDRIE ML6 ...... 111 L2 2

G

Gabriel St GRNK PA15 ...... 3 G9
Gadgirth Ct RAYR/DAL KA6 ...... 231 H5 2
Gadie Av RNFRW PA4 ...... 80 E7
Gadie St STPS/GTHM/RID G33 ...... 7 L8
Gadloch Av KKNTL G66 ...... 65 K7
Gadloch St PPK/MIL G22 ...... 83 J3
Gadloch Vw KKNTL G66 ...... 65 K7
Gadsburn Ct
SPRGB/BLRNK G21 ...... 84 C3 4
Gadshill St SPRGB/BLRNK G21 ...... 6 C6
Gael St GRNKW/INVK PA16 ...... 32 C5
Gailes Pk UD/BTH/TAN G71 ...... 131 M7
Gailes Pl KLMNK KA1 ...... 211 L5
Gailes Rd BALLOCH G68 ...... 48 F4
IRVSE KA11 ...... 208 C5
Gailes St DMNK/BRGTN G40 ...... 13 H8
Gain & Shankburn Rd
AIRDRIE ML6 ...... 68 D7
Gainburn Ct CUMB G67 ...... 67 M3 2
Gainburn Crs CUMB G67 ...... 67 M4
Gainburn Gdns CUMB G67 ...... 67 M4
Gainburn Pl CUMB G67 ...... 67 M3 3
Gainford Pl KLMNKN/STW KA3 ...... 206 F5
Gain Rd CTBR ML5 ...... 67 M8
Gainside Rd CTBR ML5 ...... 87 J3
Gairbraid Av MRYH/FIRH G20 ...... 82 C3
Gairbraid Ct MRYH/FIRH G20 ...... 82 C3 2
Gairbraid Pl MRYH/FIRH G20 ...... 82 D3 3
Gairbraid Ter
BAIL/MDB/MHD G69 ...... 109 G4 1
Gair Crs CARLUKE ML8 ...... 179 G6
WISHAW ML2 ...... 159 H8
Gair Rd CARLUKE ML8 ...... 179 H4
Gaitskell Av ALEX/LLW G83 ...... 25 K2
Gala Av RNFRW PA4 ...... 80 E7
Gala Crs WISHAW ML2 ...... 159 G5
Gala St STPS/GTHM/RID G33 ...... 7 M6
Galbraith Crs CARLUKE ML8 ...... 178 A3 2
Galbraith Dr GOV/IBX G51 ...... 103 L1 1
MLNGV G62 ...... 61 M1
Galdenoch St
STPS/GTHM/RID G33 ...... 85 H7
Gallacher Av PSLYS PA2 ...... 101 G8
Gallacher Ct MTHW ML1 ...... 158 B6 1
Gallacher Crs ALEX/LLW G83 ...... 25 M1
Gallahill Av PGL PA14 ...... 55 G2
Gallan Av SMSTN G23 ...... 62 E8
Galloway Av AYR KA8 ...... 225 J7
HMLTN ML3 ...... 174 C2
Galloway Dr RUTH G73 ...... 129 H6
Galloway Pl SALT KA21 ...... 200 E1 2
Galloway Rd AIRDRIE ML6 ...... 110 F4
EKILN G74 ...... 154 C6
Galloway St SPRGB/BLRNK G21 ...... 83 M3
Gallowflat St RUTH G73 ...... 129 H1 2
Gallowgate CGLE G1 ...... 11 M3
COWCAD G4 ...... 12 A4
DEN/PKHD G31 ...... 13 H5
DMNK/BRGTN G40 ...... 12 D4
Gallowgate La LARGS KA30 ...... 115 J5 2
Gallowgate St LARGS KA30 ...... 115 J6
Gallowhill LRKH ML9 ...... 176 A7
Gallowhill Av KKNTL G66 ...... 65 J3
MAUCH/CAT KA5 ...... 223 M6
Gallowhill Qd RAYR/DAL KA6 ...... 231 H5
Gallowhill Rd
CRMNK/CLK/EAG G76 ...... 152 E1
KKNTL G66 ...... 65 J3
LNK/LMHG ML11 ...... 199 G4
PSLYN/LNWD PA3 ...... 9 K1
Galrigside Rd KLMNK KA1 ...... 16 B7 1
Galston Av NMRNS G77 ...... 151 G4
Galston Ct HMLTN ML3 ...... 174 E2 3
Galston Rd KLMNK KA1 ...... 212 F3
KLMNK KA1 ...... 213 J3
Galston St PLK/PH/NH G53 ...... 125 M3
Galt Av IRV KA12 ...... 203 K6
Galt Pl EKILS G75 ...... 14 C8
Galt St GRNK PA15 ...... 3 J7
Gameshill Vw
KLMNKN/STW KA3 ...... 197 L1
Gamrie Dr PLK/PH/NH G53 ...... 126 A2
Gamrie Gdns PLK/PH/NH G53 ...... 126 A2
Gamrie Rd PLK/PH/NH G53 ...... 126 A1
Gannochy Dr BSHPBGS G64 ...... 64 C8
Gantock Crs
STPS/GTHM/RID G33 ...... 107 H2
Ganton Ct KLWNG KA13 ...... 193 H6 3
Gardenhall EKILS G75 ...... 170 D1 2
Gardenhall Ct EKILS G75 ...... 170 E1 3
Gardenside BLSH ML4 ...... 133 G5 4
Gardenside Av CAR/SHTL G32 ...... 130 B1
UD/BTH/TAN G71 ...... 131 L3
Gardenside Crs CAR/SHTL G32 ...... 130 B1
Gardenside Pl CAR/SHTL G32 ...... 130 B1 2
Gardenside Rd HMLTN ML3 ...... 156 D7 3
Gardenside St
UD/BTH/TAN G71 ...... 131 L3
Garden Square Wk
AIRDRIE ML6 ...... 110 D1
Garden St AYR KA8 ...... 18 F2
GLSTN KA4 ...... 214 C4
KLMNKN/STW KA3 ...... 16 F2
MAUCH/CAT KA5 ...... 223 M6
Gardiner St PSTWK KA9 ...... 225 J1
Gardner Gv UD/BTH/TAN G71 ...... 132 A1
Gardner St PTCK G11 ...... 82 B7
Gardrum Pl KLMNKN/STW KA3 ...... 206 F5
Gardyne St ESTRH G34 ...... 86 A8 1
Garelet Pl IRVSE KA11 ...... 204 B7 1
Gareloch Av AIRDRIE ML6 ...... 88 F7
PSLYS PA2 ...... 101 G7
Gareloch La PGL PA14 ...... 54 D1
Gareloch Rd GRNK PA15 ...... 2 F8
PGL PA14 ...... 54 D1
Garfield Av BLSH ML4 ...... 133 J5
Garfield Dr BLSH ML4 ...... 133 J5
Garfield St DEN/PKHD G31 ...... 12 E3
Garforth Rd
BAIL/MDB/MHD G69 ...... 107 M5
Gargrave Av
BAIL/MDB/MHD G69 ...... 107 M5
Garion Dr KNTSWD G13 ...... 81 H4 2
Garlieston Rd
STPS/GTHM/RID G33 ...... 107 M3
Garmouth Ct GOV/IBX G51 ...... 104 A1 2
Garmouth Gdns
GOV/IBX G51 ...... 104 A1 3
Garmouth St GOV/IBX G51 ...... 103 M1
Garnethill St KVGV G3 ...... 4 F7
Garnet St CGLW G2 ...... 4 E8
Garngaber Av KKNTL G66 ...... 65 K4
Garngaber Ct KKNTL G66 ...... 65 L4 1
Garnhall Farm Rd BALLOCH G68 ...... 49 L1
Garnie Av ERSK PA8 ...... 79 K1
Garnieland Rd ERSK PA8 ...... 59 K8
Garnie La ERSK PA8 ...... 79 K1
Garnie Ov ERSK PA8 ...... 59 K8 1
Garnie Pl ERSK PA8 ...... 59 K8
Garnkirk La STPS/GTHM/RID G33 ...... 85 L4
Garnock Ct KBRN KA25 ...... 143 G8 3
Garnock Pk EKILN G74 ...... 15 L3
Garnock Rd KLMNK KA1 ...... 212 A4
SVSTN KA20 ...... 201 K1
Garnockside GLGNK KA14 ...... 167 H3 1
Garnock St DALRY KA24 ...... 184 C2
KBRN KA25 ...... 143 H7
SPRGB/BLRNK G21 ...... 6 D5
Garnock Vw KLWNG KA13 ...... 193 L5
Garpel Wy LOCHW PA12 ...... 120 B6 1
Garrawy Rd HBR/GL G84 ...... 20 F8
Garrell Pl KSYTH G65 ...... 47 J1
Garrell Rd KSYTH G65 ...... 47 J1
Garrell Wy CUMB G67 ...... 48 E7
KSYTH G65 ...... 47 J1
Garrier Pl KLMNK KA1 ...... 16 B1
Garrier Rd IRVSE KA11 ...... 204 F7
Garrioch Crs MRYH/FIRH G20 ...... 82 D4 3
Garrioch Dr MRYH/FIRH G20 ...... 82 D4
Garrioch Ga MRYH/FIRH G20 ...... 82 D4 2
Garriochmill Rd MRYH/FIRH G20 ...... 82 D5
Garrioch Qd MRYH/FIRH G20 ...... 82 D4
Garrioch Rd MRYH/FIRH G20 ...... 82 D5
Garrion Pl LRKH ML9 ...... 176 F8
Garrion St WISHAW ML2 ...... 177 J3
Garrowhill Dr
BAIL/MDB/MHD G69 ...... 107 M4
Garry Av BSDN G61 ...... 62 A7
Garry Dr PSLYS PA2 ...... 101 G7
Garryhorn PSTWK KA9 ...... 225 K4
Garry Pl KLMNK KA1 ...... 212 A4
TROON KA10 ...... 216 F4
Garry St LNPK/KPK G44 ...... 128 A2
Garscadden Rd DRUM G15 ...... 60 F7
Garscadden Rd South
DRUM G15 ...... 80 F1 1
KNTSWD G13 ...... 81 G1
Garscube Rd COWCAD G4 ...... 5 G7
Garshake Av DMBTN G82 ...... 37 J4
Garshake Rd DMBTN G82 ...... 37 J5
Gartartan Rd PSLY PA1 ...... 102 F4 1
Gartcarron Hl BALLOCH G68 ...... 48 C6
Gartcloss Rd CTBR ML5 ...... 87 J7
Gartconnell Dr BSDN G61 ...... 61 L3
Gartconnell Gdns BSDN G61 ...... 61 L3 1
Gartconnell Rd BSDN G61 ...... 61 L4 2
Gartconner Av KKNTL G66 ...... 66 B1
Gartcosh Rd
BAIL/MDB/MHD G69 ...... 108 F3
CTBR ML5 ...... 109 G1
Gartcosh Wk BLSH ML4 ...... 132 F4
Gartcraig Pl
STPS/GTHM/RID G33 ...... 84 F8
Gartcraig Rd
STPS/GTHM/RID G33 ...... 85 G8 2
Gartferry Av
BAIL/MDB/MHD G69 ...... 66 F7
Gartferry Rd
BAIL/MDB/MHD G69 ...... 66 E6
Gartferry St
SPRGB/BLRNK G21 ...... 84 A5 2
Gartfield St AIRDRIE ML6 ...... 111 H3
Gartgill Rd CTBR ML5 ...... 87 L6
Garthamlock Rd
STPS/GTHM/RID G33 ...... 85 L8
Garthland Dr ARD KA22 ...... 191 J5 3
DEN/PKHD G31 ...... 12 F2
Garthland La PSLY PA1 ...... 9 K2
Garth St CGLE G1 ...... 11 K2
Gartlea Av AIRDRIE ML6 ...... 111 G2
Gartleahill AIRDRIE ML6 ...... 111 H3
Gartlea Rd AIRDRIE ML6 ...... 111 G2
Gartliston Rd CTBR ML5 ...... 87 M6
Gartliston Ter
BAIL/MDB/MHD G69 ...... 109 G4
Gartloch Rd
BAIL/MDB/MHD G69 ...... 85 M7
BAIL/MDB/MHD G69 ...... 86 E5
STPS/GTHM/RID G33 ...... 84 F8
Gartly St LNPK/KPK G44 ...... 127 M5 3
Gartmore Gdns
UD/BTH/TAN G71 ...... 131 L1 2
Gartmore Rd PSLY PA1 ...... 102 C5
Gartmore Ter BLTYR/CAMB G72 ...... 129 L6
Gartness Dr AIRDRIE ML6 ...... 111 L4
Gartness Rd AIRDRIE ML6 ...... 112 A6
Gartocher Dr CAR/SHTL G32 ...... 107 J4
Gartocher Rd CAR/SHTL G32 ...... 107 J4
Gartocher Ter CAR/SHTL G32 ...... 107 J4
Gartons Rd SPRGB/BLRNK G21 ...... 84 C4
Gartsherrie Rd CTBR ML5 ...... 109 L1
Gartshore Crs KSYTH G65 ...... 46 F7
Gartshore Gdns BALLOCH G68 ...... 47 L8 3
Gartshore Rd BALLOCH G68 ...... 67 H3
Garturk St CTBR ML5 ...... 110 B5 1
GVH/MTFL G42 ...... 105 H7
Garvald St DMNK/BRGTN G40 ...... 106 B6
GRNK PA15 ...... 3 J7
Garve Av LNPK/KPK G44 ...... 128 A5
Garvel Crs
STPS/GTHM/RID G33 ...... 107 L3 1
Garvel Dr GRNK PA15 ...... 32 D6
Garvel Pl MLNGV G62 ...... 41 K7 3
Garvel Rd MLNGV G62 ...... 41 K7
STPS/GTHM/RID G33 ...... 107 L3
Garven Rd SVSTN KA20 ...... 201 L2
Garvie Av GRK PA19 ...... 31 M3
Garvine Rd RAYR/DAL KA6 ...... 231 H5
Garvin Lea BLSH ML4 ...... 133 G1 2
Garvock Dr GRNKW/INVK PA16 ...... 32 D6
PLKSW/MSWD G43 ...... 127 H4
Garwhitter Dr MLNGV G62 ...... 42 B7 2
Gascoyne EKILS G75 ...... 14 A7
Gask Pl KNTSWD G13 ...... 80 F1
Gas La GLSTN KA4 ...... 214 B4
Gas St JNSTN PA5 ...... 100 A6
Gasworks Rd CARLUKE ML8 ...... 178 C6
Gatehead Rd CRH/DND KA2 ...... 205 L8
Gatehouse St CAR/SHTL G32 ...... 107 H4
Gateshead Pl KLBCH PA10 ...... 99 G6
Gateside IRVSE KA11 ...... 204 A3
Gateside Av BLTYR/CAMB G72 ...... 130 D4
GRNKW/INVK PA16 ...... 32 B5
KSYTH G65 ...... 47 H1
Gateside Crs AIRDRIE ML6 ...... 111 G1
BRHD/NEIL G78 ...... 125 G8
Gateside Gdns
GRNKW/INVK PA16 ...... 32 B5 4
Gateside Pk KSYTH G65 ...... 47 H1
Gateside Pl KLMNK KA1 ...... 211 M5
Gateside Rd BRHD/NEIL G78 ...... 124 F8
GLSTN KA4 ...... 214 A4
WISHAW ML2 ...... 158 E5
Gateside St DEN/PKHD G31 ...... 13 G3
HMLTN ML3 ...... 156 E6 2
LARGS KA30 ...... 115 J6
WKIL KA23 ...... 181 K3
Gates Rd LOCHW PA12 ...... 120 E6
The Gateway EKILN G74 ...... 154 A5
Gauldry Av
CARD/HILL/MSPK G52 ...... 103 J6
Gauze St PSLY PA1 ...... 9 H3
Gavell Rd KSYTH G65 ...... 46 F2
Gavinburn Gdns OLDK G60 ...... 59 G2 2
Gavinburn Pl OLDK G60 ...... 59 G2
Gavin Hamilton Ct AYRS KA7 ...... 19 L8 1
Gavin's Mill Rd MLNGV G62 ...... 42 A8 3
Gavins Rd CLYDBK G81 ...... 60 B4
Gavin St MTHW ML1 ...... 157 L4
Gavinton St LNPK/KPK G44 ...... 127 M4
Gayne Dr CTBR ML5 ...... 87 J3
Gean Ct CUMB G67 ...... 49 M5
Gearholm Rd AYRS KA7 ...... 228 D6
Geary St SMSTN G23 ...... 62 D8
Geddes Hl EKILN G74 ...... 154 B5
Geddes Rd SPRGB/BLRNK G21 ...... 84 C2
Geelong Gdns KKNTL G66 ...... 29 K8
Geils Av DMBTN G82 ...... 37 J7
Geilsland Rd BEITH KA15 ...... 168 D2
Geils Qd DMBTN G82 ...... 37 J7
Geilston Pk DMBTN G82 ...... 35 G2
Geirston Rd KBRN KA25 ...... 142 F7
Gelston St CAR/SHTL G32 ...... 107 H5
Gemmell Crs AYR KA8 ...... 19 M1
Gemmel Pl NMRNS G77 ...... 150 B5
General Roy Wy
CARLUKE ML8 ...... 189 J1 1
Gentle Rw CLYDBK G81 ...... 59 M3
George Av CLYDBK G81 ...... 60 C6 3
George Crs CLYDBK G81 ...... 60 C6 1
George Gray St RUTH G73 ...... 129 J1
George La PSLY PA1 ...... 9 H5
George Mann Ter RUTH G73 ...... 129 G5 3
George Pl PSLY PA1 ...... 9 G5
George Reith Av KVD/HLHD G12 ...... 81 M4
George Rd GRK PA19 ...... 31 L3
George's Av AYR KA8 ...... 225 H6
George Sq CGLE G1 ...... 11 J1
George St AIRDRIE ML6 ...... 110 E2
AIRDRIE ML6 ...... 111 K6
ALEX/LLW G83 ...... 25 M6
AYR KA8 ...... 19 G2
BAIL/MDB/MHD G69 ...... 108 B5
BRHD/NEIL G78 ...... 125 H6 3
CGLE G1 ...... 11 L1
GTCI KA28 ...... 138 B6
HBR/GL G84 ...... 20 E8
HMLTN ML3 ...... 156 A4
HWWD PA9 ...... 121 M4
JNSTN PA5 ...... 99 M6
LARGS KA30 ...... 115 K5
MTHW ML1 ...... 134 A5
MTHW ML1 ...... 157 L5
PSLY PA1 ...... 8 E5
SVSTN KA20 ...... 201 K2
George Street La
ALEX/LLW G83 ...... 25 M6 2
George Ter IRV KA12 ...... 203 J6
Gerard Pl BLSH ML4 ...... 133 H2 1
Gertrude Pl BRHD/NEIL G78 ...... 125 G7
Ghillies La MTHW ML1 ...... 133 J8
Gibbon Crs EKILN G74 ...... 154 C6 3
Gibb St AIRDRIE ML6 ...... 111 K6
MTHW ML1 ...... 135 H8
Gibshill Rd GRNK PA15 ...... 33 L7
Gibson Av DMBTN G82 ...... 37 H5
Gibson Crs JNSTN PA5 ...... 99 L7
Gibson La KLMCLM PA13 ...... 55 K8
Gibson Qd MTHW ML1 ...... 133 J8 1
Gibson Rd RNFRW PA4 ...... 102 B1
Gibson St DMBTN G82 ...... 37 G5
DMNK/BRGTN G40 ...... 12 A4
GRNK PA15 ...... 33 L7
KLMNK KA1 ...... 16 A3
KVD/HLHD G12 ...... 4 A4
SHOTTS ML7 ...... 113 H7 3
Giffen Rd SALT KA21 ...... 201 G1
Giffnock Park Av GIF/THBK G46 ...... 127 J5
Gifford Dr
CARD/HILL/MSPK G52 ...... 103 G4
Gifford Wynd JNSTN PA5 ...... 100 F7
Gigha Crs IRVSE KA11 ...... 204 B7
Gigha Gdns CARLUKE ML8 ...... 189 G1 3
Gigha La IRVSE KA11 ...... 204 B7
Gigha Pl IRVSE KA11 ...... 204 B7
Gigha Qd WISHAW ML2 ...... 158 E8 2
Gigha Ter IRVSE KA11 ...... 204 B7
Gigha Wynd IRVSE KA11 ...... 204 B7
Gilbertfield Pl
STPS/GTHM/RID G33 ...... 85 H7 2
Gilbertfield Rd
BLTYR/CAMB G72 ...... 130 D6
Gilbertfield St
STPS/GTHM/RID G33 ...... 85 H7
Gilbert St KVGV G3 ...... 104 C1
Gilburn Pl SHOTTS ML7 ...... 137 M5 2
Gilchrist St CTBR ML5 ...... 110 B1
Gilchrist Wy WISHAW ML2 ...... 159 J8
Gilchrist Pl RAYR/DAL KA6 ...... 227 H2
Gilderdale EKILN G74 ...... 14 B1
Gilfillan Av SALT KA21 ...... 192 A7
Gilfillan Pl WISHAW ML2 ...... 177 J2 2
Gilfoot NMLNS KA16 ...... 215 G2
Gilhill St MRYH/FIRH G20 ...... 82 D2
Gillbank Av CARLUKE ML8 ...... 178 D7 1
Gillburn Rd KLMCLM PA13 ...... 75 K1 1
Gillburn St WISHAW ML2 ...... 177 J3
Gillespie Dr HBR/GL G84 ...... 20 D5
Gillies Crs EKILN G74 ...... 154 D4
Gillies La BAIL/MDB/MHD G69 ...... 108 C5
Gillies St TROON KA10 ...... 216 D6
Gill Rd WISHAW ML2 ...... 177 K3
Gilmartin Rd PSLYN/LNWD PA3 ...... 99 L3
Gilmerton St CAR/SHTL G32 ...... 107 G5
Gilmour Av CLYDBK G81 ...... 60 B4
EKILN G74 ...... 152 B7
Gilmour Crs RUTH G73 ...... 128 F1
Gilmour Dr HMLTN ML3 ...... 155 M7
Gilmour Pl BLSH ML4 ...... 132 F4 1
CTBR ML5 ...... 109 L1
GBLS G5 ...... 11 K8
Gilmour St ALEX/LLW G83 ...... 25 K4
CLYDBK G81 ...... 60 C5
GRNK PA15 ...... 3 K8
KLMNK KA1 ...... 17 G6
PSLY PA1 ...... 9 H3
Gilmourton Crs NMRNS G77 ...... 150 D5
Gilroy Cl LNK/LMHG ML11 ...... 199 J4
Gimmerscroft Crs
AIRDRIE ML6 ...... 111 M3 1
Girdle Ct IRV KA12 ...... 203 M4
Girthon St CAR/SHTL G32 ...... 107 J5
Girvan Crs AIRDRIE ML6 ...... 111 K8
NMLNS KA16 ...... 215 G2
Girvan St STPS/GTHM/RID G33 ...... 7 L7
The Glade LRKH ML9 ...... 176 B7
Gladney Av KNTSWD G13 ...... 80 E1
Gladsmuir Rd
CARD/HILL/MSPK G52 ...... 103 G3
Gladstone Av BRHD/NEIL G78 ...... 125 H7
JNSTN PA5 ...... 122 D2 1
Gladstone Ct HMLTN ML3 ...... 156 A4 3
Gladstone Rd SALT KA21 ...... 201 G1
Gladstone St BLSH ML4 ...... 133 H4 3
CLYDBK G81 ...... 59 M7 1
COWCAD G4 ...... 4 E5
Glaive Rd KNTSWD G13 ...... 61 K8
Glamis Av CARLUKE ML8 ...... 178 F7
JNSTN PA5 ...... 100 B8
NMRNS G77 ...... 150 F4
Glamis Ct MTHW ML1 ...... 134 C6
Glamis Dr EKILN G74 ...... 153 M6
GRNKW/INVK PA16 ...... 32 A4
Glamis Pl GRNKW/INVK PA16 ...... 32 A4 1
Glamis Rd DEN/PKHD G31 ...... 13 L7
Glanderston Av
BRHD/NEIL G78 ...... 125 L7 1
NMRNS G77 ...... 150 B3
Glanderston Ct KNTSWD G13 ...... 81 G2 1
Glanderston Dr KNTSWD G13 ...... 81 G2 1
Glanderston Ga NMRNS G77 ...... 150 B3 1
Glanderston Rd NMRNS G77 ...... 149 J4
Glasgow & Edinburgh Rd
BAIL/MDB/MHD G69 ...... 108 C4
MTHW ML1 ...... 134 E1
Glasgow Br KKNTL G66 ...... 64 F2
Glasgow La ARD KA22 ...... 191 J7
Glasgow Rd
BAIL/MDB/MHD G69 ...... 107 M5
BALLOCH G68 ...... 68 B1
BLTYR/CAMB G72 ...... 130 A8
BLTYR/CAMB G72 ...... 155 L2
BRHD/NEIL G78 ...... 125 K5
CLYDBK G81 ...... 60 C3
CMPF/LLE G63 ...... 27 G5
CRMNK/CLK/EAG G76 ...... 151 K7
CTBR ML5 ...... 109 H3
CUMB G67 ...... 49 H5
DMBTN G82 ...... 36 E6
EKILN G74 ...... 154 A2
HMLTN ML3 ...... 156 A4
KKNTL G66 ...... 65 G1
KLMNKN/STW KA3 ...... 207 G5
KSYTH G65 ...... 46 F2
LNK/LMHG ML11 ...... 198 E4
MLNGV G62 ...... 62 B1
PGL PA14 ...... 34 F8
PLK/PH/NH G53 ...... 125 L4
PSLY PA1 ...... 9 J3
RNFRW PA4 ...... 80 E7
RUTH G73 ...... 105 M7
UD/BTH/TAN G71 ...... 108 C8
WISHAW ML2 ...... 158 D5
Glasgow St ARD KA22 ...... 191 J8
GTCI KA28 ...... 138 A7
HBR/GL G84 ...... 20 C7
KBRN KA25 ...... 143 G7 2
KVD/HLHD G12 ...... 4 A3
Glasgow Vennel IRV KA12 ...... 203 J7
Glassel Rd ESTRH G34 ...... 86 D8
Glasserton Pl
PLKSW/MSWD G43 ...... 127 M4 1
Glasserton Rd
PLKSW/MSWD G43 ...... 127 M4
Glassford St CGLE G1 ...... 11 K2
MTHW ML1 ...... 158 A5
Glassock Rd KLMNKN/STW KA3 ...... 206 F4
Glaudhall Av
BAIL/MDB/MHD G69 ...... 86 E2 1
Glazert Dr KKNTL G66 ...... 29 G8
Glazert Meadow KKNTL G66 ...... 44 E2
Glazert Park Dr KKNTL G66 ...... 44 E2
Glazert Pl KKNTL G66 ...... 45 H4
Glebe Av CRMNK/CLK/EAG G76 ...... 152 D2
CTBR ML5 ...... 109 K6
KLMNK KA1 ...... 17 H5
UD/BTH/TAN G71 ...... 132 B7
Glebe Ct BEITH KA15 ...... 168 B1
COWCAD G4 ...... 5 M8
Glebe Crs AIRDRIE ML6 ...... 111 K1
AYR KA8 ...... 224 F7
EKILN G74 ...... 15 G3
HMLTN ML3 ...... 156 C7
Glebe Dr LNK/LMHG ML11 ...... 199 G5 1
Glebe Gdns ALEX/LLW G83 ...... 25 L5
CRG/CRSL/HOU PA6 ...... 77 H7
Glebe Hollow UD/BTH/TAN G71 ...... 132 B7
Glebelands Wy BEITH KA15 ...... 168 B2
Glebe La NMRNS G77 ...... 150 D5
Glebe Pk DMBTN G82 ...... 37 H4
Glebe Pl BLTYR/CAMB G72 ...... 130 B4 1
RUTH G73 ...... 128 F1 2
SALT KA21 ...... 200 F1
Glebe Rd AYR KA8 ...... 224 F7
BEITH KA15 ...... 168 C1 1
GLSTN KA4 ...... 214 B3
GRNKW/INVK PA16 ...... 50 E4 1
KLMCLM PA13 ...... 75 K1 1
KLMNK KA1 ...... 17 H6
NMRNS G77 ...... 150 D5
Glebe St BLSH ML4 ...... 132 F4
COWCAD G4 ...... 5 M7
EKILN G74 ...... 15 G3
HMLTN ML3 ...... 156 D7
KLWNG KA13 ...... 193 L5
RNFRW PA4 ...... 80 D6
SALT KA21 ...... 200 F1

SVSTN KA20 192 C8
The Glebe IRVSE KA11 204 C8
LNK/LMHG ML11 198 F5
UD/BTH/TAN G71 132 A7
Glebe Wynd UD/BTH/TAN G71 132 B7
Gleddoch Rd
CARD/HILL/MSPK G52 102 E3
Gledstane Rd BSHPTN PA7 58 B7
Glenacre Crs UD/BTH/TAN G71 131 L1
Glenacre Dr AIRDRIE ML6 111 K3
CSMK G45 128 D6
LARGS KA30 115 K5
Glenacre Rd CUMB G67 68 F1
Glenacre St CSMK G45 128 D6
Glenacre Ter CSMK G45 128 D6
Glenafeoch Rd CARLUKE ML8 179 G8
Glen Affric EKILN G74 15 M3
Glen Affric Dr AIRDRIE ML6 111 K8 3
Glen Affric Pl CRH/DND KA2 211 J3 1
Glen Affric Wy AIRDRIE ML6 111 K8 4
Glen Afton Ct CRH/DND KA2 211 J3 2
Glenafton Vw HMLTN ML3 174 B1 1
Glen Alby Pl GIF/THBK G46 126 C5 1
Glenalla Crs AYRS KA7 228 C8
Glenallan Ter MTHW ML1 133 K8 4
Glen Almond EKILN G74 154 C7
Glenalmond St CAR/SHTL G32 107 G5
Glenapp Av PSLYS PA2 102 B8
Glenapp Pl KLWNG KA13 193 J7
Glenapp Qd KLMNK KA1 17 K6
Glenapp Rd PSLYS PA2 102 B8
Glenapp St PLKSD/SHW G41 104 F6
Glenarklet Dr PSLYS PA2 102 A8
Glen Arroch EKILN G74 15 L4
Glenartney
CRG/CRSL/HOU PA6 77 G7 1
Glenartney Rd
BAIL/MDB/MHD G69 66 C8
Glenashdale Wy PSLYS PA2 102 A8 1
Glen Av BAIL/MDB/MHD G69 66 F7
BRHD/NEIL G78 148 E2
CAR/SHTL G32 107 H3
GRK PA19 31 M3
LARGS KA30 115 K3
LRKH ML9 176 A8
PGL PA14 34 B7
Glenavon Ct HMLTN ML3 156 B8 1
Glen Avon Dr AIRDRIE ML6 111 K8
Glenavon Rd MRYH/FIRH G20 82 D2
Glenbank Av KKNTL G66 65 K5
Glenbank Dr GIF/THBK G46 126 F7
Glenbank Rd KKNTL G66 65 K5
Glenbarr St SPRGB/BLRNK G21 6 B6
Glen Bervie EKILN G74 15 M2
Glenbervie Dr KLWNG KA13 193 H6
Glenbervie Pl GRK PA19 31 H3 1
NMRNS G77 150 A4 1
SMSTN G23 62 D8 8
Glenbervie Wynd IRVSE KA11 208 D1
Glenboig Farm Rd CTBR ML5 87 L3
Glenboig New Rd CTBR ML5 87 M3
Glenboig Rd CTBR ML5 87 H2
Glen Brae BRWEIR PA11 98 D1
Glenbrae La GRNK PA15 3 G9 1
Glenbrae Rd GRNK PA15 3 G9
PGL PA14 54 D2
Glenbride Rd WKIL KA23 181 J6
Glenbrittle Dr PSLYS PA2 102 A8
Glenbrittle Wy PSLYS PA2 102 A8 2
Glenbuck Av
STPS/GTHM/RID G33 84 F3
Glenbuck Dr
STPS/GTHM/RID G33 84 F3 2
Glenburn Av
BAIL/MDB/MHD G69 66 F7
BAIL/MDB/MHD G69 108 C4
BLTYR/CAMB G72 129 K4
MTHW ML1 134 C5
Glenburn Crs KKNTL G66 45 J4
LARGS KA30 115 J5
PSLYS PA2 124 D2
UD/BTH/TAN G71 132 B1
Glenburn Gdns BSHPBGS G64 63 M7
CTBR ML5 87 J3 1
Glenburnie Pl
STPS/GTHM/RID G33 107 M2 4
Glenburn La KLMCLM PA13 55 K8 1
MRYH/FIRH G20 82 E2
Glenburn Rd BSDN G61 61 K4
EKILN G74 153 G6
GIF/THBK G46 127 H8
HMLTN ML3 156 B6
KLMCLM PA13 55 K8 2
PSLYS PA2 124 B1
PSTWK KA9 225 L1
Glenburn St MRYH/FIRH G20 82 E2
PGL PA14 34 A7 2
Glenburn Ter CARLUKE ML8 188 E1
MTHW ML1 134 B8
Glenburn Wy EKILN G74 152 F6
Glencairn Av WISHAW ML2 158 D5
Glencairn Ct RUTH G73 128 F1 5
Glencairn Dr
BAIL/MDB/MHD G69 66 E7
PLKSD/SHW G41 104 E7
RUTH G73 128 F1
Glencairn Gdns
BLTYR/CAMB G72 130 D4
PLKSD/SHW G41 104 E7
Glencairn La PLKSD/SHW G41 104 E7
Glencairn Rd AYRS KA7 19 K8
CUMB G67 49 J7
DMBTN G82 36 C6
GRNKW/INVK PA16 31 L6
KLMCLM PA13 75 L1
PGL PA14 56 C2 3
PSLYN/LNWD PA3 102 A2
Glencairn Sq KLMNK KA1 16 F8 1
Glencairn St MTHW ML1 157 L4 3
SALT KA21 200 F2 6
SVSTN KA20 192 D8
Glencairn Ter
KLMNKN/STW KA3 206 B2
Glencalder Crs BLSH ML4 133 J6
Glen Cally EKILN G74 15 M2
Glencally Av PSLYS PA2 102 B8
Glen Cannich EKILN G74 15 M4
Glen Carron EKILN G74 15 L4
Glencart Gv KLBCH PA10 99 J8
Glencleland Rd WISHAW ML2 158 D5
Glenclora Dr PSLYS PA2 102 A8
Glen Clova EKILN G74 15 M1
Glen Clova Dr BALLOCH G68 48 C5 1
Glencloy St MRYH/FIRH G20 82 C2 2
Glenclune Ct KLMCLM PA13 75 J2
Glen Clunie EKILN G74 154 D7
Glen Clunie Av GIF/THBK G46 126 C5
Glen Clunie Dr GIF/THBK G46 126 C5
Glen Clunie Pl GIF/THBK G46 126 C5 2
Glencoats Crs PSLYN/LNWD PA3 8 A3
Glencoats Dr PSLYN/LNWD PA3 101 G4
Glencoe Dr MTHW ML1 134 A4
Glencoe Pl HMLTN ML3 174 B1
KNTSWD G13 81 L2
Glencoe Rd CARLUKE ML8 179 G8
RUTH G73 129 K6 1
Glencoe St KNTSWD G13 81 M2
Glen Cona Dr GIF/THBK G46 126 C4
Glenconner Pl AYRS KA7 19 K8 1
Glenconner Rd AYRS KA7 19 K8
Glencorse Rd PSLYS PA2 8 C8
Glencorse St
STPS/GTHM/RID G33 106 E2
Glen Cova Gdns
CRH/DND KA2 211 J3 3
Glencraigs Dr
KLMNKN/STW KA3 206 F4 1
Glencraig St AIRDRIE ML6 110 E2
Glen Creran Crs
BRHD/NEIL G78 148 C3
Glen Crs GRNKW/INVK PA16 50 E4
KNTSWD G13 80 E2
SVSTN KA20 192 C8
Glencroft Av UD/BTH/TAN G71 131 L1
Glencroft Rd LNPK/KPK G44 128 D4
Glencryan Rd CUMB G67 49 H8
Glendale Av AIRDRIE ML6 111 K3
Glendale Crs AYRS KA7 229 H5
BSHPBGS G64 84 C1 2
Glendale Dr BSHPBGS G64 84 C1
Glendale Gv CTBR ML5 109 L6 3
Glendale Pl AYRS KA7 229 H5
DEN/PKHD G31 13 G3
SPRGB/BLRNK G21 84 C2 4
Glendale St DEN/PKHD G31 13 G3
Glendaruel Av BSDN G61 62 B5
Glendaruel Rd
CRMNK/CLK/EAG G76 129 L7
Glendarvel Gdns PPK/MIL G22 83 K5 3
Glendee Gdns RNFRW PA4 80 D7
Glendee Rd RNFRW PA4 80 D7
Glendentan Rd BRWEIR PA11 98 C2
Glen Derry EKILN G74 154 D6
Glen Dessary EKILN G74 15 L5
Glen Devon EKILN G74 154 D8
Glendevon Pl CLYDBK G81 59 M6
HMLTN ML3 174 B1 2
Glendevon Sq
STPS/GTHM/RID G33 85 H7 3
Glendinning Rd KNTSWD G13 61 L8
Glendoick Pl NMRNS G77 150 A4 2
Glen Doll EKILN G74 15 M3
Glen Doll Rd BRHD/NEIL G78 148 B3
Glendorch Av WISHAW ML2 159 J2
Glendore St SCOT G14 81 L7 2
Glen Douglas Dr BALLOCH G68 48 C5
Glen Douglas Rd
GRNKW/INVK PA16 32 C6
Glendoune Rd
CRMNK/CLK/EAG G76 151 L4
Glen Dr HBR/GL G84 20 D5
MTHW ML1 134 B4
Glenduffhill Rd
BAIL/MDB/MHD G69 107 M4
Glen Dye EKILN G74 15 M2
Glen Eagles EKILN G74 154 C8
Gleneagles Av BALLOCH G68 49 G4
KLWNG KA13 193 J5
Gleneagles Dr GRK PA19 31 G3
NMRNS G77 151 H5
Gleneagles Gdns BSHPBGS G64 63 M6
Gleneagles Ga NMRNS G77 151 H5 6
Gleneagles La North SCOT G14 81 J5
Gleneagles La South SCOT G14 81 J6
Gleneagles Pk
UD/BTH/TAN G71 131 M7 3
Glenelg Crs KKNTL G66 46 A8
Glenelg Qd ESTRH G34 86 D8 5
Glenelm Pl BLSH ML4 133 G3
Glen Esk EKILN G74 154 D7
Glenesk Crs GIF/THBK G46 126 C5
Glen Esk Dr GIF/THBK G46 126 C5
Glenesk Pl GIF/THBK G46 126 C5
Glen Etive Pl
CRMNK/CLK/EAG G76 129 L7 1
Glen Falloch EKILN G74 154 C8
Glen Falloch Crs
BRHD/NEIL G78 148 C4
Glen Farg EKILN G74 154 C8
Glenfarg Ct HMLTN ML3 174 B1
Glenfarg Crs BSDN G61 62 B5
Glenfarg Rd RUTH G73 129 H5
Glenfarg St MRYH/FIRH G20 4 E5
Glenfarm Rd MTHW ML1 134 E5
Glen Farrar EKILN G74 15 L3
Glen Farrar Wk CRH/DND KA2 211 J3
Glen Feshie EKILN G74 15 M4
Glenfield Av PSLYS PA2 124 E3
Glenfield Crs PSLYS PA2 124 D3 1
Glenfield Gdns KLMNK KA1 16 F8
PSLYS PA2 124 D3 2
Glenfield Gv PSLYS PA2 124 D3 3
Glenfield Pl KLMNK KA1 16 F9
Glenfield Rd EKILS G75 15 K9
PSLYS PA2 124 C2 2
Glenfinlas St HBR/GL G84 20 E8 3
Glen Finlet Rd BRHD/NEIL G78 148 B4
Glenfinnan Dr BSDN G61 62 B6
MRYH/FIRH G20 82 D3
Glenfinnan Pl
MRYH/FIRH G20 82 D3 5
Glenfinnan Rd MRYH/FIRH G20 82 D4
Glenfruin Crs PSLYS PA2 102 B8
Glen Fruin Dr LRKH ML9 176 C8 3
Glen Fruin Pl AIRDRIE ML6 111 K7 1
Glenfruin Rd BLTYR/CAMB G72 155 J2
Glen Fruin Rd
GRNKW/INVK PA16 32 D6 3
Glen Fyne Rd BALLOCH G68 48 B5
Glen Gairn EKILN G74 154 D7
Glen Gairn Crs BRHD/NEIL G78 148 C3
Glen Gdns JNSTN PA5 100 C6
Glengarriff Rd BLSH ML4 133 H1
Glen Garry EKILN G74 15 M5
Glengarry Dr
CARD/HILL/MSPK G52 103 J4 2
Glengavel Crs
STPS/GTHM/RID G33 84 F3 3
Glengavel Gdns WISHAW ML2 159 J2
Glengowan Rd AIRDRIE ML6 91 G5
BRWEIR PA11 98 C1
Glen Gv EKILS G75 14 C7
LARGS KA30 115 K3
Glengyre St ESTRH G34 108 C1
Glenhead Crs CLYDBK G81 60 A2
PPK/MIL G22 83 J3 1
Glenhead Rd CLYDBK G81 60 A4
KKNTL G66 65 J5
Glenhead St PPK/MIL G22 83 J3
Glenholme Av PSLYS PA2 101 H8 1
Glenhove Rd CUMB G67 49 G7
Glenhuntly Rd PGL PA14 34 B8
Glenhuntly Ter PGL PA14 34 B8
Gleniffer Av KNTSWD G13 81 G3
Gleniffer Crs JNSTN PA5 100 C8
Gleniffer Dr BRHD/NEIL G78 125 G4
Gleniffer Rd BRHD/NEIL G78 146 B8
BRHD/NEIL G78 146 D6
PSLYS PA2 123 H7
PSLYS PA2 123 L4
RNFRW PA4 102 B1
Gleniffer Vw BRHD/NEIL G78 148 D1
Gleninver Rd GRNKW/INVK PA16 31 M5
Glen Isla EKILN G74 154 C7
Glenisla Av BAIL/MDB/MHD G69 67 G5
Glen Isla Av BRHD/NEIL G78 148 C4 1
Glenisla St DEN/PKHD G31 13 M9
Glen Kinglas Av
GRNKW/INVK PA16 32 D7 1
Glen Kinglas Rd
GRNKW/INVK PA16 32 C7
Glenkirk Dr DRUM G15 61 H7
Glen La BRHD/NEIL G78 147 G6
PSLYN/LNWD PA3 9 G2
Glen Lee EKILN G74 154 C7
Glenlee St HMLTN ML3 155 M4
Glenleith Pl IRVSE KA11 204 C7 1
Glen Lethnot EKILN G74 154 C7
Glen Livet Pl GIF/THBK G46 126 C5 3
Glenlivet Pl KLMNKN/STW KA3 207 H6
Glenlivet Rd BRHD/NEIL G78 148 C3
Glen Lochay Gdns BALLOCH G68 48 B5
Glenlora Dr PLK/PH/NH G53 126 A3
Glenlora Ter PLK/PH/NH G53 126 B2 1
Glen Loy Pl GIF/THBK G46 126 C5
Glen Luce Dr CAR/SHTL G32 107 K6
Glenluce Gdns
BAIL/MDB/MHD G69 67 G6
Glenluce Ter EKILN G74 14 B2
Glenluggie Rd KKNTL G66 66 A2 1
Glenlui Av RUTH G73 129 H4 1
Glen Luss Gdns BALLOCH G68 48 B5
Glen Luss Pl CTBR ML5 110 D4 1
Glen Luss Rd
GRNKW/INVK PA16 32 C7 1
Glen Lyon EKILN G74 154 C8
Glen Lyon Ct BALLOCH G68 48 B5 2
Glenlyon Ct HMLTN ML3 174 B1
Glen Lyon Crs CRH/DND KA2 211 J3
Glenlyon Gv IRV KA12 203 M4
Glenlyon Pl RUTH G73 129 J6
Glen Lyon Rd
BRHD/NEIL G78 148 C3 1
Glenmalloch Pl JNSTN PA5 100 C6
Glenmanor Av
BAIL/MDB/MHD G69 66 E6
Glen Mark EKILN G74 154 C7
Glen Markie Dr GIF/THBK G46 126 C5
Glen Mark Rd
BRHD/NEIL G78 148 C3 2
Glenmavis Crs CARLUKE ML8 178 F8
Glenmavis Rd AIRDRIE ML6 88 E6
Glenmavis St COWCAD G4 5 H7
Glen More EKILN G74 15 L4
Glenmore Av ALEX/LLW G83 25 K3
BLSH ML4 133 H6
GVH/MTFL G42 128 E1
Glenmore Rd MTHW ML1 134 C5
Glen Moriston EKILN G74 15 M4
Glen Moriston Rd BALLOCH G68 48 B5
GIF/THBK G46 126 C4 1
Glenmoss Av ERSK PA8 58 F8
Glenmosston Rd KLMCLM PA13 75 L1
Glenmount Pl AYRS KA7 228 B8
Glen Moy EKILN G74 15 M4
Glenmuir Dr PLK/PH/NH G53 126 B4
Glenmuir Pl AYR KA8 225 K6
Glenmuir Rd AYR KA8 225 K7
Glen Muir Rd BRHD/NEIL G78 148 C3 3
Glen Nevis EKILN G74 15 M5
Glen Nevis Pl CRH/DND KA2 211 J3 4
RUTH G73 129 J7
Glenochil Rd AIRDRIE ML6 111 K8
Glen Ogilvie EKILN G74 154 C7
Glen Ogle St CAR/SHTL G32 107 J5
Glenoran Rd HBR/GL G84 20 A5
Glenorchard Rd BSHPBGS G64 43 K6
Glen Orchy Ct BALLOCH G68 48 B4
Glen Orchy Dr BALLOCH G68 48 B5
GIF/THBK G46 126 C5
Glen Orchy Pl AIRDRIE ML6 111 K8 5
BALLOCH G68 48 B4
CRH/DND KA2 211 J3 5
GIF/THBK G46 126 D5
Glen Orrin Av CRH/DND KA2 211 J3
Glenorrin Wy BRHD/NEIL G78 148 C3
Glenpark AIRDRIE ML6 111 L3
Glenpark Av GIF/THBK G46 126 F7
PSTWK KA9 225 J3 2
Glenpark Dr PGL PA14 34 A7
Glenpark Gdns
BLTYR/CAMB G72 129 L2 2
Glenpark Pl AYRS KA7 229 H6
Glenpark Rd DEN/PKHD G31 13 G4
LOCHW PA12 120 C6
Glenpark St DEN/PKHD G31 13 G3
WISHAW ML2 159 G5
Glenpark Ter
BLTYR/CAMB G72 129 L2 3
Glenpath DMBTN G82 37 J6
Glenpatrick Rd JNSTN PA5 100 C8
Glen Pl CRMNK/CLK/EAG G76 151 L2
LARGS KA30 115 K3
Glen Prosen EKILN G74 154 C7
Glen Quoich EKILN G74 154 D6
Glenraith Rd
STPS/GTHM/RID G33 85 H6
Glen Rannoch Dr AIRDRIE ML6 111 K8
Glenriddet Av KBRN KA25 167 H1
Glen Rinnes Dr
BRHD/NEIL G78 148 D4 1
Glen Rd AIRDRIE ML6 90 F5
AIRDRIE ML6 111 L3
BSHPTN PA7 58 A5
CAR/SHTL G32 107 H2
EKILN G74 152 F5
FAIRLIE KA29 139 K7
KKNTL G66 29 G7
MTHW ML1 134 D2
OLDK G60 59 H3
SHOTTS ML7 137 M5
WISHAW ML2 159 G5
WKIL KA23 181 K4
Glen Rosa Gdns BALLOCH G68 48 B5
Glen Roy Dr BRHD/NEIL G78 148 C3
Glen Sannox Dr BALLOCH G68 48 B5
Glen Sannox Vw BALLOCH G68 48 B5
Glen Sannox Wy BALLOCH G68 48 C5
Glen Sax Dr RNFRW PA4 80 E8
Glen Shee EKILN G74 154 C7
Glen Shee Av BRHD/NEIL G78 148 C3
Glen Shee Crs AIRDRIE ML6 111 K8 6
Glenshee St DEN/PKHD G31 13 M8
Glenshee Ter HMLTN ML3 174 B1
Glenshiel Av PSLYS PA2 102 A8
Glen Shiel Crs KLMNK KA1 211 J3 3
Glenshira Av PSLYS PA2 102 A8
Glen Shirva Rd KSYTH G65 46 F5
Glenside Av PLK/PH/NH G53 103 H7
Glenside Crs WKIL KA23 181 K4
Glenside Dr BLTYR/CAMB G72 129 K3
Glenside Gv WKIL KA23 181 K4
Glenside Rd DMBTN G82 37 J3
PGL PA14 54 D2
Glenspean Pl CTBR ML5 110 D4 2
Glenspean St
PLKSW/MSWD G43 127 K3
Glen St BLTYR/CAMB G72 130 D5 3
BRHD/NEIL G78 125 J6
GRNKW/INVK PA16 32 D2 2
MTHW ML1 133 L8
MTHW ML1 134 D5
PSLYN/LNWD PA3 9 G2
Glentanar Dr
BAIL/MDB/MHD G69 67 G7 3
Glentanar Pl PPK/MIL G22 83 H2
Glentanar Rd PPK/MIL G22 83 H2
Glen Tanner EKILN G74 154 D7
Glen Tarbert Dr BRHD/NEIL G78 148 C3
Glentarbert Rd RUTH G73 129 K6
Glen Tennet EKILN G74 154 C7
Glentore Qd AIRDRIE ML6 89 G7
Glentrool Gdns
BAIL/MDB/MHD G69 67 G6 4
PPK/MIL G22 83 K5 4
Glen Trool Wk CRH/DND KA2 211 J2
Glen Truim Vw CRH/DND KA2 211 J3 7
Glen Turret EKILN G74 154 D7
Glenturret St CAR/SHTL G32 107 G5
Glentyan Av KLBCH PA10 99 G5
Glentyan Dr PLK/PH/NH G53 126 A2
Glentyan Ter PLK/PH/NH G53 126 A3
Glen Urquhart EKILN G74 15 M3
Glen Vw CUMB G67 49 J6
DMBTN G82 25 K7 1
HMLTN ML3 174 D3
Glenview AIRDRIE ML6 111 K3 1
LRKH ML9 175 M5
Glenview Av AIRDRIE ML6 91 G5 2
Glenview Crs
BAIL/MDB/MHD G69 66 F6
Glenview Pl
BLTYR/CAMB G72 131 K8 3
Glenview St AIRDRIE ML6 88 E5
Glenville Av GIF/THBK G46 127 H6
Glenville Ga
CRMNK/CLK/EAG G76 152 A4 1
Glenville Ter
CRMNK/CLK/EAG G76 152 A4 2
Glenward Av KKNTL G66 44 E1
Glenwell St AIRDRIE ML6 88 E6
Glenwood Av AIRDRIE ML6 111 J5
Glenwood Ct KKNTL G66 65 G4 1
Glenwood Dr GIF/THBK G46 126 F7
Glenwood Gdns KKNTL G66 65 G4
Glenwood Pth CSMK G45 128 E6 2
Glenwood Pl CSMK G45 128 E6
KKNTL G66 65 G4
Glenwood Rd KKNTL G66 65 G4
Glorat Av KKNTL G66 44 E1
Gloucester Av
CRMNK/CLK/EAG G76 151 K2
RUTH G73 129 K4 3
Gloucester St GBLS G5 10 D5
Goatfell Vw TROON KA10 216 E2
Goatfoot Rd GLSTN KA4 214 A3
Gockston Rd PSLYN/LNWD PA3 101 K2
Goddard Pl WISHAW ML2 160 B4 1
Gogar Pl STPS/GTHM/RID G33 106 E1
Gogar St
STPS/GTHM/RID G33 106 E1 2
Gogoside Dr LARGS KA30 115 K6
Gogoside Rd LARGS KA30 115 K6
Gogo St LARGS KA30 115 J6
Goldberry Av SCOT G14 81 H4
Goldenacre Pl AIRDRIE ML6 89 M6 1
Goldenberry Av WKIL KA23 181 J5
Goldenlee Vw
CRG/CRSL/HOU PA6 99 G1
Goldie Pl SVSTN KA20 192 C8
Goldie Rd UD/BTH/TAN G71 132 A5
Golf Av BLSH ML4 133 G6
SVSTN KA20 201 M3
Golf Course Rd BRWEIR PA11 98 B1
BSHPBGS G64 63 K1
SKLM PA17 70 B5 3
Golf Crs TROON KA10 216 D7
Golf Dr DRUM G15 60 F8
PGL PA14 54 D1
PSLY PA1 102 C5
Golffields Rd IRV KA12 203 K8
Golf Gdns LRKH ML9 176 C7
Golfhill Dr ALEX/LLW G83 25 M4
DEN/PKHD G31 6 E9
HBR/GL G84 20 F7
Golfhill Qd AIRDRIE ML6 89 G7
Golfhill Rd WISHAW ML2 158 D5
Golfloan KLMNKN/STW KA3 197 L1
Golf Pl BLSH ML4 133 H6
GRNKW/INVK PA16 32 C2 4
IRV KA12 203 H4
TROON KA10 216 D7
Golf Rd BSHPTN PA7 58 A4
CRMNK/CLK/EAG G76 151 K1
GRK PA19 31 J3
RUTH G73 129 H5
Golfview BSDN G61 61 H4
Golf Vw CLYDBK G81 59 M5
Golfview Dr CTBR ML5 109 J2
Golfview Pl CTBR ML5 109 J3
Golspie Av AIRDRIE ML6 110 E5
Golspie St GOV/IBX G51 104 A1
Goodview Gdns LRKH ML9 176 C7
Goodwin Dr RAYR/DAL KA6 227 H7
Goosedubbs CGLE G1 11 K4
Gooseholm Crs DMBTN G82 37 G4
Gooseholm Rd DMBTN G82 37 G4
Gopher Av UD/BTH/TAN G71 132 B1
Gorbals St GBLS G5 11 J5
Gordon Av BAIL/MDB/MHD G69 107 M4
BSHPTN PA7 58 A5
CARD/HILL/MSPK G52 102 E2
LNPK/KPK G44 127 L7
Gordon Crs NMRNS G77 150 E3
Gordon Dr EKILN G74 154 B6
GIF/THBK G46 127 L6
Gordon La CGLE G1 11 H1 1
Gordon Pl BLSH ML4 132 F7 1
Gordon Rd HMLTN ML3 155 M5
LNPK/KPK G44 127 L7
Gordon St AYR KA8 225 G6
CGLE G1 11 H1
CGLW G2 11 G1
GRNK PA15 2 A6
PSLY PA1 9 H5
Gordon Ter AYR KA8 19 H3
BLTYR/CAMB G72 131 J7
HMLTN ML3 155 M6
Gorebridge St CAR/SHTL G32 106 E2 5
Goremire Rd CARLUKE ML8 179 J8 1
Gorget Av KNTSWD G13 61 J8
Gorget Pl KNTSWD G13 61 J8
Gorget Qd DRUM G15 61 H8
Gorse Crs BRWEIR PA11 98 E2
Gorsehall St MTHW ML1 135 H7
Gorse Pl UD/BTH/TAN G71 132 B1
Gorsewood BSHPBGS G64 63 L8
Gorstan Pl MRYH/FIRH G20 82 C4
Gorstan St SMSTN G23 82 D1
Goschen Ter AYR KA8 225 H7
Gosford La SCOT G14 81 G5 1
Gottries Rd IRV KA12 203 G8
Goudie St PSLYN/LNWD PA3 101 K2
Gough St STPS/GTHM/RID G33 7 L8
Goukscroft Pk AYRS KA7 228 D6
Gould St AYR KA8 225 J7
Gourlay EKILN G74 154 D4 1
Gourlay Dr WISHAW ML2 177 J3 1
Gourlay St SPRGB/BLRNK G21 5 M2
Gourock St GBLS G5 10 F8 1
Govan Dr ALEX/LLW G83 25 K3 4
Govanhill St GVH/MTFL G42 105 H7 2
Govan Rd GOV/IBX G51 81 K8
Gowanbank Gdns JNSTN PA5 99 L7 1
Gowanbank Rd AYRS KA7 229 H7
Gowan Brae AIRDRIE ML6 91 H5
Gowanlea Av DRUM G15 61 G8
Gowanlea Dr GIF/THBK G46 127 K5
Gowanlea Ter
UD/BTH/TAN G71 132 B2
Gowanside Pl CARLUKE ML8 178 D7 2
Gower Pl AYRS KA7 229 H6
Gower St PLKSD/SHW G41 104 C4
Gower Ter PLKSD/SHW G41 104 C4
Gowkhall Av MTHW ML1 134 F6
Gowkhouse Rd KLMCLM PA13 75 L1
Goyle Av DRUM G15 61 J6
Grace Av BAIL/MDB/MHD G69 108 F4
Grace St KVGV G3 10 C1
Graeme Ct MTHW ML1 133 K7 4
Graffham Av GIF/THBK G46 127 K6
Grafton Pl CGLE G1 5 K9
Graham Av BLTYR/CAMB G72 130 D5
CLYDBK G81 60 B6
EKILN G74 14 F1
HMLTN ML3 174 D1 2
Graham Crs DMBTN G82 35 H2
Grahamfield Pl BEITH KA15 168 A1
Graham Pl HBR/GL G84 21 G7 7
KLMNKN/STW KA3 17 M1
LRKH ML9 176 F8
Graham Rd CARLUKE ML8 188 B8
DMBTN G82 36 D5
Grahams Av LOCHW PA12 120 D6
Grahamsdyke Rd KKNTL G66 45 L8
Grahamshill Av AIRDRIE ML6 111 K1
Grahamshill St AIRDRIE ML6 111 J1
Graham Sq DMNK/BRGTN G40 12 C4
Grahamston Av GLGNK KA14 167 H3
Grahamston Ct PSLYS PA2 125 J1
Grahamston Crs PSLYS PA2 125 J1
Grahamston Pk
BRHD/NEIL G78 125 J4 1
Grahamston Pl PSLYS PA2 125 J1
Grahamston Rd PSLYS PA2 125 J3
Graham St AIRDRIE ML6 111 G2
BRHD/NEIL G78 125 H6
GRNKW/INVK PA16 32 C4 2
HMLTN ML3 156 E6
JNSTN PA5 99 L7

MTHW ML1 134 A4
WISHAW ML2 159 H7
Graham Ter BSHPBGS G64 84 B2
Graignestock Pl
DMNK/BRGTN G40 12 B6
Graignestock St
DMNK/BRGTN G40 12 B5
Graigside Pl BALLOCH G68 67 M2
Grainger Rd BSHPBGS G64 64 D8
Grampian Av PSLYS PA2 124 D1
Grampian Ct IRVSE KA11 204 B5
Grampian Crs AIRDRIE ML6 111 M8
CAR/SHTL G32 107 H5
Grampian Pl CAR/SHTL G32 107 H5
Grampian Rd KLMNK KA1 212 A6
PGL PA14 55 G3
WISHAW ML2 158 F5
Grampian St CAR/SHTL G32 107 H5
Grampian Wy BALLOCH G68 48 A7
BRHD/NEIL G78 125 J8
BSDN G61 61 J1
BSDN G61 61 K2
Granby La KVD/HLHD G12 82 D7
Grandtuly Dr KVD/HLHD G12 82 C3
Grange Av AYRS KA7 229 H7
MLNGV G62 42 B7
WISHAW ML2 158 E8
Grange Ct LNK/LMHG ML11 198 F4
Grange Gdns
UD/BTH/TAN G71 132 B8
Grangemuir Rd PSTWK KA9 225 H2
Grangeneuk Gdns
BALLOCH G68 48 C8
Grange Pl ALEX/LLW G83 25 L4
Grange Rd BSDN G61 61 M4
GVH/MTFL G42 128 A1
SVSTN KA20 192 D8
Granger Rd ALEX/LLW G83 25 M1
KLMNK KA1 211 L4
Grange St KLMNK KA1 16 D4
MTHW ML1 158 A5
Grange Ter KLMNK KA1 16 A4
Gran St CLYDBK G81 80 E1
Grant Ct HMLTN ML3 174 C3
Grant Crs DMBTN G82 25 K8
Grantholm Av MTHW ML1 134 B3
Grantlea Gv CAR/SHTL G32 107 K5
Grantlea Ter CAR/SHTL G32 107 K5
Grantley Gdns PLKSD/SHW G41 127 K1
Grantley St PLKSW/MSWD G43 127 K1
Grantoften Pth EKILS G75 171 L3
Granton St GBLS G5 105 L7
Grantown Av AIRDRIE ML6 111 L3
Grantown Gdns AIRDRIE ML6 88 F4
Grant Pl KLMNKN/STW KA3 207 J7
Grants Av PSLYS PA2 101 J8
Grant St GRNK PA15 3 J7
HBR/GL G84 20 D8
KVGV G3 4 D6
Grants Wy PSLYS PA2 101 J8
Granville St CLYDBK G81 60 B6
HBR/GL G84 20 F8
KVGV G3 4 D8
Grasmere EKILS G75 170 F4
Grasmere Ct HMLTN ML3 174 D3
Grassyards Rd
KLMNKN/STW KA3 17 J3
Grathellen Ct MTHW ML1 158 A1
Gray Crs IRV KA12 208 C1
Gray Dr BSDN G61 61 M6
Gray's Cl LNK/LMHG ML11 198 C5
Grayshill Rd BALLOCH G68 67 K2
Gray's Rd UD/BTH/TAN G71 132 B4
Graystonelee Rd
SHOTTS ML7 137 K3
Graystones KLWNG KA13 193 L4
Gray St ALEX/LLW G83 25 L4
GRNK PA15 3 H8
KKNTL G66 66 B2
KVGV G3 4 A7
LRKH ML9 176 A5
MTHW ML1 135 H8
PSTWK KA9 225 J1
Great Dovehill COWCAD G4 11 M3
Great George La KVD/HLHD G12 82 D7
Great Hamilton St PSLYS PA2 9 G8
Great Kelvin La KVD/HLHD G12 4 A4
Great Western Rd CLYDBK G81 60 C5
KNTSWD G13 81 J1
KVD/HLHD G12 82 B4
OLDK G60 58 B1
Great Western Ter
KVD/HLHD G12 82 C5
Great Western Terrace La
KVD/HLHD G12 82 C5
Green LARGS KA30 115 J6
Greenacres ARD KA22 191 L6
MTHW ML1 157 J4
Greenan Av LNPK/KPK G44 128 E2
Greenan Gv AYRS KA7 228 B6
Greenan Pl AYRS KA7 228 C6
Greenan Rd AYRS KA7 228 B6
KLMNKN/STW KA3 17 L5
Greenan Wy AYRS KA7 228 B6
Green Av IRV KA12 203 J5
Green Bank DALRY KA24 184 C2
Greenbank Av GIF/THBK G46 151 G2
Greenbank Ct IRV KA12 203 J8
Greenbank Dr PSLYS PA2 124 D2
Green Bank Rd BALLOCH G68 48 C7
Greenbank Rd IRV KA12 203 J8
WISHAW ML2 159 J6
Greenbank Ter CARLUKE ML8 178 F7
Green Dl WISHAW ML2 159 K4
Greendyke St CGLE G1 11 L4
Greenend Av JNSTN PA5 99 K8
Greenend Pl CAR/SHTL G32 107 J2
Greenend Vw BLSH ML4 132 F5
Greenfarm Rd NMRNS G77 150 B3
Green Farm Rd
PSLYN/LNWD PA3 100 B3
Greenfaulds Crs CUMB G67 69 G1
Greenfaulds Rd CUMB G67 68 D2
Greenfield Av AYRS KA7 228 D7
Greenfield Crs WISHAW ML2 159 K5
Greenfield Dr IRV KA12 203 K7
WISHAW ML2 159 K5
Greenfield Qd MTHW ML1 134 F5
Greenfield Rd CAR/SHTL G32 107 J3
CARLUKE ML8 178 F6
CRMNK/CLK/EAG G76 151 L3
HMLTN ML3 156 A3
Greenfield St GOV/IBX G51 103 M1
WISHAW ML2 159 K5
Greengairs Av GOV/IBX G51 103 K2
Greengairs Rd AIRDRIE ML6 69 L7
Green Gdns MTHW ML1 135 J7
Greenhall Pl BLTYR/CAMB G72 155 J3
Greenhead NMLNS KA16 215 K2
Greenhead Av SVSTN KA20 192 E7
Greenhead Rd BSDN G61 61 M5
DMBTN G82 37 J6
RNFRW PA4 79 J2
WISHAW ML2 159 J7
Greenhead St
DMNK/BRGTN G40 12 B6
Greenhill BSHPBGS G64 84 C1
LARGS KA30 115 K6
Greenhill Av
BAIL/MDB/MHD G69 86 E2
GIF/THBK G46 127 J8
Greenhill Ct IRVSE KA11 204 B3
RUTH G73 129 G1
Greenhill Crs JNSTN PA5 100 D7
PSLYN/LNWD PA3 100 B4
Greenhill Dr
PSLYN/LNWD PA3 100 C3
Greenhill Rd MTHW ML1 135 M5
PSLYN/LNWD PA3 101 J3
RUTH G73 129 G2
Greenhills Crs EKILS G75 171 H4
Greenhills Rd EKILS G75 171 G3
Greenhill St RUTH G73 129 G2
Greenhill Ter CRH/DND KA2 205 M7
Greenholm Av
CRMNK/CLK/EAG G76 151 L2
UD/BTH/TAN G71 131 L2
Greenholme St
LNPK/KPK G44 128 B3
Greenholm St KLMNK KA1 16 E9
Greenknowe Dr CARLUKE ML8 177 M3
Greenknowe Rd
PLKSW/MSWD G43 127 H3
Greenknowe St WISHAW ML2 177 H3
Greenlaw Av PSLY PA1 9 L2
WISHAW ML2 159 J4
Greenlaw Crs PSLY PA1 9 M1
Greenlaw Dr PSLY PA1 9 M3
Greenlaw Rd NMRNS G77 150 C4
SCOT G14 80 D3
Greenlea Rd
BAIL/MDB/MHD G69 86 B1
Greenlea St KNTSWD G13 81 L3
Greenlees Ct DALRY KA24 184 B1
Greenlees Gdns
BLTYR/CAMB G72 129 M6
Greenlees Gv CTBR ML5 110 D4
Greenlees Pk BLTYR/CAMB G72 130 A6
Greenlees Rd BLTYR/CAMB G72 129 M7
BLTYR/CAMB G72 130 A4
Greenloan Av GOV/IBX G51 103 K1
Greenmoss Pl BLSH ML4 133 H4
Greenmount PPK/MIL G22 83 G2
Greenock Av LNPK/KPK G44 128 B4
Greenock Rd BSHPTN PA7 57 H3
GRNK PA15 33 L6
LARGS KA30 115 G2
PGL PA14 34 E8
PSLYN/LNWD PA3 101 K2
RNFRW PA4 79 H3
Green Pk AYRS KA7 228 B6
Green Pl AIRDRIE ML6 111 H7
Greenrig UD/BTH/TAN G71 131 M3
Greenrigg Rd CUMB G67 49 H8
Greenrigg St
UD/BTH/TAN G71 131 M3
Greenrig St STPS/GTHM/RID G33 7 M3
Green Rd PSLYS PA2 101 G6
Greens Av KKNTL G66 65 J2
Greens Crs KKNTL G66 65 J2
Greenshields Rd
BAIL/MDB/MHD G69 108 B4
Greenside NMLNS KA16 215 K2
Greenside Av IRVSE KA11 204 F8
KBRN KA25 167 G1
PSTWK KA9 225 K2
Greenside Crs
STPS/GTHM/RID G33 84 E6
Greenside La LNK/LMHG ML11 199 G5
Greenside Pl BSDN G61 61 J1
Greenside Rd CLYDBK G81 60 B2
MTHW ML1 134 C2
WISHAW ML2 159 J7
Greenside St CTBR ML5 88 B8
MTHW ML1 134 F5
STPS/GTHM/RID G33 84 E6
Greenside Ter IRVSE KA11 205 G7
Greenside Wy IRVSE KA11 204 A5
Greens Rd CUMB G67 68 F3
Green St AYR KA8 18 E1
CLYDBK G81 60 A6
DMNK/BRGTN G40 12 B5
KLMNK KA1 16 F3
SALT KA21 200 F2
UD/BTH/TAN G71 132 B7
Green Street La AYR KA8 18 E1
The Green DMNK/BRGTN G40 12 B7
Greentowers Rd
LNK/LMHG ML11 189 K8
Greentree Dr
BAIL/MDB/MHD G69 107 M6
Greentree Pk AYRS KA7 229 J4
Greenview St
PLKSW/MSWD G43 127 J1
Greenways Av PSLYS PA2 101 G7
Greenways Ct PSLYS PA2 101 G7
Greenwood Av
BLTYR/CAMB G72 130 E3
Greenwood Crs CTBR ML5 110 C4
Greenwood Dr BSDN G61 62 A5
JNSTN PA5 122 D1
Greenwood Qd CLYDBK G81 60 D8
Greenwood Rd
CRMNK/CLK/EAG G76 151 K2
IRVSE KA11 204 C8
Greenwood St SHOTTS ML7 137 L5
Greer Qd CLYDBK G81 60 B5
Greeto Falls Av LARGS KA30 115 L5
Grenada Pl EKILS G75 153 G8
Grenadier Gdns MTHW ML1 157 K5
Grenville Dr BLTYR/CAMB G72 129 M5
Grenville Rd GRK PA19 31 M3
Gresham Vw MTHW ML1 158 B7
Greta Meek La KKNTL G66 45 J3
Gretna St DMNK/BRGTN G40 13 H8
Greyfriars Rd UD/BTH/TAN G71 131 J1
Greyfriars St CAR/SHTL G32 106 F2
Greystone Av RUTH G73 129 J3
Greywood St KNTSWD G13 81 L2
Grier Pl LRKH ML9 175 M7
Grierson La
STPS/GTHM/RID G33 7 L9
Grierson St STPS/GTHM/RID G33 7 L9
Griers Wk IRVSE KA11 209 K3
Grieve Cft UD/BTH/TAN G71 131 M8
Grieve Rd CUMB G67 49 G6
GRNKW/INVK PA16 32 B4
Griffen Av PSLYN/LNWD PA3 100 E4
Griffin Pl BLSH ML4 133 G1
Griffiths Wy CARLUKE ML8 177 M5
Griqua Ter UD/BTH/TAN G71 132 B7
Grogarry Rd DRUM G15 61 G5
Grossart St SHOTTS ML7 113 G7
Grosvenor Crs KVD/HLHD G12 82 D6
Grosvenor Crescent La
KVD/HLHD G12 82 D6
Grosvenor La KVD/HLHD G12 82 D6
Grosvenor Rd GRNK PA15 3 L8
Grosvenor Ter KVD/HLHD G12 82 D6
Grougar Dr KLMNKN/STW KA3 207 H4
Grougar Rd KLMNKN/STW KA3 212 D1
Groveburn Av GIF/THBK G46 127 G5
Grove Crs LRKH ML9 176 C7
Grove Pk KKNTL G66 65 K5
Grovepark Ct MRYH/FIRH G20 4 F4
Grove Park Gdns MRYH/FIRH G20 4 E4
Grovepark St MRYH/FIRH G20 4 E3
The Groves
SPRGB/BLRNK G21 84 C2
The Grove BRHD/NEIL G78 148 C3
BRWEIR PA11 98 E3
BSHPTN PA7 58 A6
GIF/THBK G46 151 H1
KLBCH PA10 99 G6
Grudie St ESTRH G34 108 A1
Gryfebank Av
CRG/CRSL/HOU PA6 77 L8
Gryfebank Cl
CRG/CRSL/HOU PA6 77 L8
Gryfebank Crs
CRG/CRSL/HOU PA6 77 K8
Gryfebank Wy
CRG/CRSL/HOU PA6 77 L8
Gryfe Rd BRWEIR PA11 98 D2
PGL PA14 54 E2
Gryfe St GRNK PA15 3 H9
Gryfewood Crs
CRG/CRSL/HOU PA6 77 L8
Gryfewood Wy
CRG/CRSL/HOU PA6 77 L8
Gryffe Av BRWEIR PA11 76 D8
RNFRW PA4 80 B4
Gryffe Crs PSLYS PA2 100 F8
Gryffe Gv BRWEIR PA11 98 D1
Gryffe Rd KLMCLM PA13 75 K2
Gryffe St LNPK/KPK G44 128 A3
Guildford St GTCI KA28 138 A7
STPS/GTHM/RID G33 85 J8
Guiltreehill AYRS KA7 229 G8
Gullane Crs BALLOCH G68 48 F3
Gullane Pl KLWNG KA13 193 H6
Gullane St PTCK G11 82 B8
Gulliland Av CRH/DND KA2 209 M7
Gullin Dr PSTWK KA9 225 K4
Gunn Qd BLSH ML4 132 E6
Guthrie Dr UD/BTH/TAN G71 109 G8
Guthrie Pl BSHPBGS G64 64 C1
EKILN G74 15 H1
Guthrie Rd SALT KA21 201 G1
Guthrie St HMLTN ML3 156 D5
MRYH/FIRH G20 82 D3
Guy Mannering Rd HBR/GL G84 22 F1
Gyle Pl WISHAW ML2 159 L6

H

Habbieauld Rd
KLMNKN/STW KA3 206 B1
Haberlea Av PLK/PH/NH G53 126 C6
Haberlea Gdns
PLK/PH/NH G53 126 C7
Haco St LARGS KA30 115 K5
Haddington Gdns IRVSE KA11 204 B3
Haddington Wy CTBR ML5 109 L6
Haddow Gv UD/BTH/TAN G71 132 A1
Haddow St HMLTN ML3 156 E6
Hadrian Ter MTHW ML1 157 J1
Hagart Rd CRG/CRSL/HOU PA6 77 H7
Hagen Dr MTHW ML1 134 E8
Hagg Crs JNSTN PA5 99 L6
Hagg Pl JNSTN PA5 99 L6
Hagg Rd JNSTN PA5 99 L7
Haggs La PLKSD/SHW G41 104 C7
Haggs Rd PLKSD/SHW G41 104 C8
Haggswood Av
PLKSD/SHW G41 104 C7
Haghill Rd DEN/PKHD G31 13 J3
Hagholm Rd LNK/LMHG ML11 199 M2
Hagmill Crs CTBR ML5 110 C7
Hagmill Rd CTBR ML5 110 B7
Hagthorn Av KBRN KA25 167 G1
Haig Dr BAIL/MDB/MHD G69 107 M5
Haig St GRNK PA15 2 C2
SPRGB/BLRNK G21 6 E1
Hailes Av CAR/SHTL G32 107 K4
Haining Av KLMNK KA1 212 A5
Haining Rd RNFRW PA4 80 D6
The Haining RNFRW PA4 80 D7
Hairmyres Dr EKILS G75 170 F1
Hairmyres La EKILS G75 170 F1
Hairmyres Pk EKILS G75 170 F1
Hairmyres St GVH/MTFL G42 105 J7
Hairst St RNFRW PA4 80 D5
Halbeath Av DRUM G15 60 F6
Halbert St PLKSD/SHW G41 104 E8
Haldane La SCOT G14 81 K6
Haldane Pl EKILS G75 15 G7
Haldane St SCOT G14 81 K6
Halfmerk North EKILN G74 15 K1
Halfmerk South EKILN G74 15 K1
Halfway St WKIL KA23 181 J4
Halgreen Av DRUM G15 60 E6
Halketburn Rd SKLM PA17 70 A6
Halketburn Ter SKLM PA17 70 B6
Halkett Crs ALEX/LLW G83 25 L2
Halkshill Dr LARGS KA30 115 L6
Hallbrae St
STPS/GTHM/RID G33 84 E7
Hallcraig St AIRDRIE ML6 111 G1
Halley Dr KNTSWD G13 80 E2
Halley Pl KNTSWD G13 80 E3
Halley St KNTSWD G13 80 E2
Hallforest St
STPS/GTHM/RID G33 85 H7
Hallgraig Pl CARLUKE ML8 178 D7
Hallhill Crs
STPS/GTHM/RID G33 107 L3
Hallhill Rd BAIL/MDB/MHD G69 108 A3
CAR/SHTL G32 107 K3
JNSTN PA5 122 C2
Halliburton Crs ESTRH G34 107 M2
Halliburton Ter ESTRH G34 108 A2
Hallidale Crs RNFRW PA4 80 F7
Hallinan Gdns WISHAW ML2 158 F8
Hall Pl LNK/LMHG ML11 199 G5
Hall Rd LNK/LMHG ML11 198 B4
Hallrule Dr
CARD/HILL/MSPK G52 103 J4
Hallside Av BLTYR/CAMB G72 130 E4
Hallside Bvd BLTYR/CAMB G72 130 F6
Hallside Crs
BLTYR/CAMB G72 130 E4
Hallside Dr BLTYR/CAMB G72 130 E4
Hallside Gdns WISHAW ML2 159 L5
Hallside Pl GBLS G5 11 K8
Hallside Rd BLTYR/CAMB G72 130 E5
Hallside St HWWD PA9 121 M4
Hall St ALEX/LLW G83 25 M5
CLYDBK G81 60 B8
DMBTN G82 36 D1
HMLTN ML3 156 D8
MTHW ML1 134 A5
Halls Vennal AYR KA8 224 F7
Hallydown Dr KNTSWD G13 81 J4
Halpin Cl UD/BTH/TAN G71 132 D4
Halton Gdns
BAIL/MDB/MHD G69 107 M5
Hamersley Pl EKILS G75 171 H2
Hamilcomb Rd BLSH ML4 133 G6
Hamill Dr KSYTH G65 47 M1
Hamilton Av PLKSD/SHW G41 104 B6
Hamilton Ct
KLMNKN/STW KA3 206 B2
Hamilton Crs AYRS KA7 19 H7
BLTYR/CAMB G72 130 C5
BSDN G61 61 L2
BSHPTN PA7 57 M6
CTBR ML5 110 A4
RNFRW PA4 80 D4
SVSTN KA20 192 F7
Hamilton Dr AIRDRIE ML6 89 H8
BLTYR/CAMB G72 130 A4
BLTYR/CAMB G72 155 H4
ERSK PA8 58 F6
GIF/THBK G46 127 K7
KVD/HLHD G12 4 A2
LARGS KA30 115 K6
MTHW ML1 157 M5
UD/BTH/TAN G71 132 B8
Hamiltonhill Crs PPK/MIL G22 5 H1
Hamiltonhill Rd PPK/MIL G22 5 H2
Hamilton Park Av KVD/HLHD G12 4 B2
Hamilton Pl EKILS G75 14 E7
HMLTN ML3 174 D3
MTHW ML1 134 B5
RAYR/DAL KA6 231 H6
Hamilton Rd BLSH ML4 132 F5
BLTYR/CAMB G72 130 B4
BLTYR/CAMB G72 155 G3
CAR/SHTL G32 107 J7
EKILN G74 154 B5
LRKH ML9 175 M4
MTHW ML1 157 K3
RUTH G73 129 H2
UD/BTH/TAN G71 107 M7
UD/BTH/TAN G71 132 B8
Hamilton St CARLUKE ML8 178 F8
CLYDBK G81 80 D2
GVH/MTFL G42 105 J8
KLWNG KA13 193 L6
LRKH ML9 175 M5
PSLYN/LNWD PA3 9 J2
SALT KA21 200 E1
Hamilton Ter CLYDBK G81 80 D2
Hamilton Vw UD/BTH/TAN G71 132 A2
Hamilton Wy PSTWK KA9 221 J7
Hamlet EKILN G74 154 C4
Hampden Dr LNPK/KPK G44 128 B2
Hampden La GVH/MTFL G42 128 B1
Hampden Ter GVH/MTFL G42 128 B1
Hangingshaw Pl
GVH/MTFL G42 128 C1
Hanover Cl GVH/MTFL G42 128 A1
Hanover Ct CGLE G1 5 K9
Hanover St CGLE G1 11 J1
HBR/GL G84 22 E1
Hanson St DEN/PKHD G31 12 D1
Hapland Av PLK/PH/NH G53 103 J7
Hapland Rd PLK/PH/NH G53 103 J7
Happyhills WKIL KA23 181 J4
Harbour La PSLY PA1 9 H2
Harbour Pl ARD KA22 191 H8
Harbour Rd ARD KA22 200 B1
IRV KA12 203 G8
PSLYN/LNWD PA3 101 L2
Harbour St ARD KA22 191 H8
IRV KA12 202 F8
SALT KA21 200 F2
Harburn Pl SCOT G14 80 F3
SMSTN G23 62 E7
Harcourt Dr DEN/PKHD G31 7 G8
Hardacres LNK/LMHG ML11 199 G4
Hardgate Dr GOV/IBX G51 103 J1
Hardgate Gdns GOV/IBX G51 103 J2
Hardgate Pl GOV/IBX G51 103 J1
Hardgate Rd GOV/IBX G51 103 J1
Hardie Av RUTH G73 129 J1
Hardie St ALEX/LLW G83 25 K2
BLTYR/CAMB G72 155 K2
HMLTN ML3 156 B7
MTHW ML1 157 L1
Hardmuir Gdns KKNTL G66 45 L8
Hardridge Av
CARD/HILL/MSPK G52 103 L7
Hardridge Pl
CARD/HILL/MSPK G52 103 L7
Hardridge Rd
CARD/HILL/MSPK G52 103 K7
Hardy Hl HBR/GL G84 21 G7
Harefield Dr SCOT G14 81 H4
Harelaw Av BRHD/NEIL G78 125 K8
BRHD/NEIL G78 148 D3
LNPK/KPK G44 127 L5
PGL PA14 54 D1
Harelaw Crs PSLYS PA2 124 C2
Hareleeshill Rd LRKH ML9 176 C7
Hareshaw Rd MTHW ML1 135 K4
Harestanes Gdns KKNTL G66 46 A8
Harestanes Rd CARLUKE ML8 188 E5
Harestone Crs WISHAW ML2 159 J6
Harestone Rd WISHAW ML2 159 J7
Harhill St GOV/IBX G51 104 A2
Harkins Av BLTYR/CAMB G72 155 J2
Harkness Av KKNTL G66 45 H4
Harland St SCOT G14 81 J6
Harley St GOV/IBX G51 104 C4
Harling Dr TROON KA10 216 D7
Harmetray St PPK/MIL G22 83 K3
Harmony Pl GOV/IBX G51 104 A2
Harmony Rw GOV/IBX G51 104 A1
Harmony Sq GOV/IBX G51 104 A2
Harmsworth St PTCK G11 81 L7
Harper Crs LARGS KA30 115 K5
WISHAW ML2 159 L5
Harperland Dr KLMNK KA1 16 A7
Harport St GIF/THBK G46 126 E5
Harriet Pl PLKSW/MSWD G43 127 H3
Harriet Rd KLMNKN/STW KA3 17 G1
Harriet St RUTH G73 129 G1
Harrington Rd EKILN G74 14 E3
Harris Cl NMRNS G77 150 B3
Harris Crs OLDK G60 59 H4
Harris Dr OLDK G60 59 H4
Harris Gdns OLDK G60 59 J4
Harrison Dr GOV/IBX G51 104 B3
Harrison Pl DMBTN G82 25 K7
Harris Pl KLMNKN/STW KA3 207 H4
Harris Qd WISHAW ML2 159 L4
Harris Rd OLDK G60 59 H4
PGL PA14 55 H2
SMSTN G23 62 D8
Harrow Ct DRUM G15 60 F6
Harrow Pl DRUM G15 60 F6
Hartfield Ct DMBTN G82 37 G5
Hartfield Crs BRHD/NEIL G78 148 E2
Hartfield Rd AYRS KA7 18 F9
Hartfield Ter PSLYS PA2 9 K9
SHOTTS ML7 161 H1
Harthall AYR KA8 225 L7
Hartlaw Crs
CARD/HILL/MSPK G52 103 G3
Hartree Av KNTSWD G13 80 E1
Hartstone Rd PLK/PH/NH G53 126 B2
Hart St CLYDBK G81 60 D2
DEN/PKHD G31 106 E4
PSLYN/LNWD PA3 100 B4
Hartwood Gdns SHOTTS ML7 136 F7
Hartwood Rd SHOTTS ML7 136 F8
Harvest Dr MTHW ML1 157 K5
Harvey Ct LOCHW PA12 120 C7
Harvey St ARD KA22 191 J6
COWCAD G4 5 J4
Harvey Ter LOCHW PA12 120 C7
Harvey Wy BLSH ML4 133 J2
Harvie Av NMRNS G77 150 D3
Harvie St GOV/IBX G51 104 D3
Harwood Gdns
BAIL/MDB/MHD G69 67 G6
Harwood St CAR/SHTL G32 106 E2
Hastie Av GTCI KA28 138 B6
Hastie St KVGV G3 82 D8
Hastings EKILS G75 171 G2
Hatfield Dr KVD/HLHD G12 81 M4
Hathaway Dr GIF/THBK G46 127 H7
Hathaway La MRYH/FIRH G20 82 E4
Hathaway St MRYH/FIRH G20 82 E4
Hathersage Av
BAIL/MDB/MHD G69 108 B4
Hathersage Dr
BAIL/MDB/MHD G69 108 B4
Hathersage Gdns
BAIL/MDB/MHD G69 108 B4
Hatton Gdns
CARD/HILL/MSPK G52 103 G5
Hatton Pl MTHW ML1 134 C7
Hattonrigg Rd BLSH ML4 133 H2
Hatton Ter MTHW ML1 134 C7
Haughburn Pl
PLK/PH/NH G53 126 B2
Haughburn Rd PLK/PH/NH G53 126 B2
Haughburn Ter
PLK/PH/NH G53 126 B2
Haugh Pl HMLTN ML3 156 E8
Haugh Rd KSYTH G65 47 J1
KVGV G3 104 D1
Haughton Av KSYTH G65 47 L1
Haughview Rd MTHW ML1 157 H3
Haupland Rd ARD KA22 191 H4
Havelock La PTCK G11 82 C7
Havelock Pk EKILS G75 153 G8
Havelock Pl HBR/GL G84 20 F7
Havelock St HBR/GL G84 20 E7
PTCK G11 82 C7
Haven Pk EKILS G75 170 F3
Havoc Rd DMBTN G82 36 B6
Hawbank Rd EKILN G74 153 G6
Hawick Av PSLYS PA2 101 H8
Hawick Ct GRNK PA15 3 G7

Hawick Crs LRKH ML9 176 A7
Hawick Dr CTBR ML5 110 D6
Hawick St KNTSWD G13 80 E2
WISHAW ML2 159 J4
Hawkhead Av PSLYS PA2 102 B8
Hawkhead Rd PSLY PA1 102 B5
PSLYS PA2 102 C7
Hawkhill Av AYR KA8 19 H1
Hawkhill Avenue La AYR KA8 19 H1
Hawkhill Dr SVSTN KA20 192 F8
Hawkhill Pl SVSTN KA20 192 E7
Hawkwood EKILS G75 171 K4
Hawkwood Rd AIRDRIE ML6 88 F5 1
Hawthorn Av BSDN G61 62 A2
BSHPBGS G64 84 B1
DMBTN G82 36 B4
ERSK PA8 79 L1
JNSTN PA5 100 A8
KKNTL G66 65 J4
PSTWK KA9 225 J2 3
WISHAW ML2 160 C3
Hawthorn Ct KLWNG KA13 193 L7
Hawthorn Crs BEITH KA15 168 A1
ERSK PA8 79 L1
Hawthornden Gdns
SMSTN G23 62 E7 1
Hawthorn Dr AIRDRIE ML6 111 K2
AYRS KA7 229 J5
BRHD/NEIL G78 149 K1 1
CTBR ML5 110 D4 1
MTHW ML1 134 B6
SVSTN KA20 192 E6 1
WISHAW ML2 159 J7
Hawthorne Pl GRK PA19 31 H3 2
TROON KA10 216 D5
Hawthorn Gdns BLSH ML4 133 H5
CRMNK/CLK/EAG G76 151 L3 1
LRKH ML9 176 C7
PSTWK KA9 225 J2 1
Hawthorn Hl HMLTN ML3 156 E8
Hawthornhill Rd DMBTN G82 36 B4
Hawthorn Pl
BLTYR/CAMB G72 155 L2 2
SHOTTS ML7 160 F1
Hawthorn Qd PPK/MIL G22 83 J4 1
Hawthorn Rd
CRMNK/CLK/EAG G76 151 M4 2
CUMB G67 49 M5
ERSK PA8 79 L1
Hawthorn Sq KLMNK KA1 16 A5
Hawthorn St BSHPBGS G64 44 C8
CLYDBK G81 60 A5
PPK/MIL G22 83 J4
SPRGB/BLRNK G21 83 M4
Hawthorn Ter EKILS G75 171 H3
UD/BTH/TAN G71 132 B2 1
Hawthorn Wk
BLTYR/CAMB G72 129 K4
Hawthorn Wy ERSK PA8 79 L1 1
Hay Av BSHPTN PA7 58 C6
Hayburn Crs PTCK G11 82 A6
Hayburn Ga PTCK G11 82 B7
Hayburn La KVD/HLHD G12 82 A6
PTCK G11 82 A6
Hayburn St PTCK G11 82 B8
Hay Dr JNSTN PA5 100 B6
Hayes Gv ALEX/LLW G83 25 L3 3
Hayfield St GBLS G5 11 L7
Hay Hl AYR KA8 229 K1
Hayhill Rd EKILN G74 170 B2
Hayle Gdns BAIL/MDB/MHD G69 66 F6
Haylie Gdns LARGS KA30 115 K7
Haylie Neuk LARGS KA30 115 K7 2
Haymarket St CAR/SHTL G32 106 F2
Hayocks Rd SVSTN KA20 192 E8
Haystack Pl KKNTL G66 65 K5 1
Hayston Crs MRYH/FIRH G20 83 H4
Hayston Rd BALLOCH G68 48 E5
KKNTL G66 65 G1
Hayston St MRYH/FIRH G20 83 H4
Hay St GRNK PA15 2 D6
Haywood St PPK/MIL G22 83 H3
Hazel Av ARD KA22 191 J5 1
BSDN G61 62 A2
DMBTN G82 36 A4
JNSTN PA5 100 A8
KKNTL G66 65 K3
KLMNK KA1 16 A6
LNPK/KPK G44 127 M5 3
Hazel Bank KKNTL G66 45 H5
Hazelbank Wk AIRDRIE ML6 110 D1
Hazeldean Crs WISHAW ML2 159 J4
Hazel Dene BSHPBGS G64 64 B8
Hazel Gdns MTHW ML1 157 L6 2
Hazel Gv KKNTL G66 65 K3
KLWNG KA13 193 M5
Hazelhead EKILN G74 15 M1
Hazellea Dr GIF/THBK G46 127 L5
Hazelmere Rd KLMCLM PA13 75 H1
Hazel Pk HMLTN ML3 156 E7
Hazel Rd CUMB G67 49 K6
Hazel Ter GRK PA19 31 J3 2
UD/BTH/TAN G71 132 B2
Hazelton MTHW ML1 157 K4
Hazel Wd WISHAW ML2 159 K4
Hazelwood Av NMRNS G77 150 E5
PSLYS PA2 123 L2 1
Hazelwood Dr
BLTYR/CAMB G72 155 J1
Hazelwood Gdns RUTH G73 129 J5 2
Hazelwood La BRWEIR PA11 98 D2
Hazelwood Rd AYRS KA7 18 F9
BRWEIR PA11 98 D3
PLKSD/SHW G41 104 C5
Hazlitt Gdns MRYH/FIRH G20 83 G3 1
Hazlitt Pl MRYH/FIRH G20 83 G3 2
Hazlitt St MRYH/FIRH G20 83 H4
Headhouse Ct EKILS G75 14 C6
Headrigg WKIL KA23 181 J4 3
Headrigg Rd WKIL KA23 181 J4
Headsmuir Av CARLUKE ML8 178 D7
Head St BEITH KA15 144 C8
Heath Av BSHPBGS G64 84 B1 3
KKNTL G66 65 J5
Heathcliffe Av
BLTYR/CAMB G72 131 J8
Heathcot Av DRUM G15 60 E7
Heathcot Pl DRUM G15 60 D7 1
Heather Av ALEX/LLW G83 25 L3
BRHD/NEIL G78 125 G4
BSDN G61 61 K1
CLYDBK G81 60 A2
MTHW ML1 134 A4
Heatherbank Wk CTBR ML5 110 D1
Heatherbrae BSHPBGS G64 63 L8
Heather Dr KKNTL G66 65 G5
Heathergardens KKNTL G66 65 G5
Heatherhouse Rd IRV KA12 208 B1
Heather Pl JNSTN PA5 100 A7
KLMNK KA1 16 A6
Heather Rd LNK/LMHG ML11 198 B3
Heather Rw CARLUKE ML8 178 E5
Heatherstane Bank IRVSE KA11 204 B7
Heatherstane Wy IRVSE KA11 204 C7
Heather St AIRDRIE ML6 91 G4
Heather Vw KKNTL G66 29 L8 1
Heathery Knowe EKILS G75 14 E7
Heatheryknowe Rd
BAIL/MDB/MHD G69 108 E1
Heathery Lea Av CTBR ML5 110 D6
Heathery Rd WISHAW ML2 158 F6
Heathfield WISHAW ML2 177 G2
Heathfield Av
BAIL/MDB/MHD G69 67 G7
Heathfield Dr MLNGV G62 42 B6
Heathfield Rd AYR KA8 225 H5
Heathfield St
STPS/GTHM/RID G33 107 J1 2
Heathpark AYR KA8 225 J4
Heath Rd LRKH ML9 176 B6
Heathside Rd GIF/THBK G46 127 K6 1
Heathwood Dr GIF/THBK G46 127 G6
Hecla Av DRUM G15 60 F6
Hecla Pl DRUM G15 60 F6
Hecla Sq DRUM G15 60 F6
Hector Rd PLKSD/SHW G41 127 K1
Heggies Av PGL PA14 55 G1
Helensburgh Dr KNTSWD G13 81 K3
Helenslea BLTYR/CAMB G72 130 E5 2
Helenslea Pl BLSH ML4 132 F5 1
Helenslee Ct DMBTN G82 36 D6 1
Helenslee Crs DMBTN G82 36 D6
Helenslee Rd DMBTN G82 36 D6
PGL PA14 56 C2 4
Helen's Ter KLWNG KA13 193 L7
Helen St CARD/HILL/MSPK G52 103 M5
GOV/IBX G51 104 A3
Helenvale Ct DEN/PKHD G31 13 L6
Helenvale St DEN/PKHD G31 13 K7
Helen Wy ALEX/LLW G83 25 M7 1
Helen Wynd LRKH ML9 176 A7 1
Helmsdale Av
BLTYR/CAMB G72 131 J6 1
Helmsdale Dr PSLYS PA2 100 F7
Hemlock St KNTSWD G13 81 M2
Hemmingen Ct
CARLUKE ML8 178 E6 2
Hemphill Vw CRH/DND KA2 205 M6
Henderland Dr BSDN G61 61 L7
Henderland Rd BSDN G61 61 L7 1
Henderson Av
BLTYR/CAMB G72 130 D3
Henderson Rd TROON KA10 216 D6
Henderson St AIRDRIE ML6 111 H1
CTBR ML5 109 M3
KNTSWD G13 80 E1
MRYH/FIRH G20 4 C3
PSLY PA1 8 E3
Henderson Ter GRK PA19 31 L3 2
Henrietta St GLSTN KA4 214 C3
SCOT G14 81 J6 1
Henry Bell St HBR/GL G84 20 E8
Henry St BRHD/NEIL G78 125 H6
Hepburn Hl HMLTN ML3 174 B1
Hepburn Rd
CARD/HILL/MSPK G52 103 G2
Hepburn Wy IRVSE KA11 204 B2
Herald Av KNTSWD G13 61 K8
Herald Gv MTHW ML1 157 K5
Herald St ARD KA22 200 B1
Herbert Rd MRYH/FIRH G20 4 C3
Herbertson Crs IRV KA12 203 K5
Herbertson Gv
BLTYR/CAMB G72 131 H8
Herbertson St
BLTYR/CAMB G72 155 L2 3
Herbert St MRYH/FIRH G20 4 D3
Heriot Av PSLYS PA2 123 M1
Heriot Crs BSHPBGS G64 64 A6
Heriot Rd KKNTL G66 65 J6
Heritage Ct NMRNS G77 150 E4 2
Heritage Wy CTBR ML5 109 M1
Herma St SMSTN G23 82 E1
Hermes Wy BLSH ML4 133 M4
Hermiston Av CAR/SHTL G32 107 H3
Hermiston Pl CAR/SHTL G32 107 J3 1
Hermiston Rd CAR/SHTL G32 107 H3
Hermitage Av KNTSWD G13 81 J2
Hermitage Crs CTBR ML5 110 B6
Herndon Ct NMRNS G77 151 G3 2
Heron Ct CLYDBK G81 60 B4
Heron Pl JNSTN PA5 122 D2
Heron Rd GRNKW/INVK PA16 32 A5
Heronswood KLWNG KA13 193 K4
Herriet St PLKSD/SHW G41 10 C9
Herriot Av KBRN KA25 143 G5
Herriot St CTBR ML5 109 L1
Herschell St KNTSWD G13 81 M3 1
Hertford Av KVD/HLHD G12 82 B3 1
Hestan Pl KLMNKN/STW KA3 207 H4 1
Hewett Crs CRG/CRSL/HOU PA6 77 J8
Hexham Gdns PLKSD/SHW G41 104 D8
Heys St BRHD/NEIL G78 125 J7
Hibernia St
GRNKW/INVK PA16 32 D5 1
Hickman St GVH/MTFL G42 105 H8
Hickman Ter GVH/MTFL G42 105 J7 1
Hickory Crs UD/BTH/TAN G71 109 J8
Hickory St PPK/MIL G22 83 L4 1
High Avon St LRKH ML9 175 M5 1
High Barholm KLBCH PA10 99 H6
High Barrwood Rd KSYTH G65 47 M1
High Beeches
CRMNK/CLK/EAG G76 152 E1 2
High Blantyre Rd
BLTYR/CAMB G72 155 M4
HMLTN ML3 156 A4
Highburgh Av LNK/LMHG ML11 199 H5
Highburgh Dr RUTH G73 129 H4
Highburgh Rd KVD/HLHD G12 82 C7
High Burnside Av CTBR ML5 109 L4 2
High Calside PSLYS PA2 8 F6
High Carnegie Rd PGL PA14 54 F1
High Common Rd EKILN G74 15 M7
EKILN G74 154 C8
Highcraig Av JNSTN PA5 99 K8
High Craigends KSYTH G65 47 L1
Highcroft Av LNPK/KPK G44 128 E4 1
Highcross Av CTBR ML5 109 K5
Highet Gdns IRV KA12 203 H5
Highfield Av KLMNKN/STW KA3 207 G6
PSLYS PA2 124 C2
PSTWK KA9 225 K2
Highfield Ct KKNTL G66 65 M1 1
Highfield Crs MTHW ML1 158 A1
PSLYS PA2 124 D2
Highfield Dr
CRMNK/CLK/EAG G76 151 K2
KVD/HLHD G12 82 B3
RUTH G73 129 J6
SVSTN KA20 192 E8
Highfield Pl EKILN G74 153 M6
KVD/HLHD G12 82 B3 3
Highfield Rd AYRS KA7 229 H5 1
KKNTL G66 45 L8
LRKH ML9 176 B6
Highfield St KLWNG KA13 193 M5
Highfield Ter FAIRLIE KA29 139 L6
High Flender Rd
CRMNK/CLK/EAG G76 151 K4
High Glencairn St KLMNK KA1 16 F8
High Craighall Rd COWCAD G4 5 H5
Highholm Av PGL PA14 34 B8
Highholm St PGL PA14 34 B7
High Kirk Vw JNSTN PA5 99 M7
Highland Av BLTYR/CAMB G72 155 J1
Highland La GOV/IBX G51 104 C2
High Mains Av DMBTN G82 37 J6
High Meadow CARLUKE ML8 179 J8 2
High Mill Rd CARLUKE ML8 179 G7 1
Highpark Rd RAYR/DAL KA6 231 H6
High Parksail ERSK PA8 79 J1
High Parks Crs HMLTN ML3 174 D3
High Patrick St HMLTN ML3 156 E7
High Pleasance LRKH ML9 176 A6
High Rd AYR KA8 225 L6
MTHW ML1 157 K2
PSLYS PA2 8 D6
SALT KA21 191 M8
SVSTN KA20 192 B8
Highstonehall Rd HMLTN ML3 156 A8
High St AIRDRIE ML6 110 F1
AYRS KA7 18 F3
BRHD/NEIL G78 148 E2
COWCAD G4 11 M2
DMBTN G82 36 E6
GRNK PA15 2 D4
IRV KA12 203 J7
JNSTN PA5 99 M6
KBRN KA25 143 G6
KLMCLM PA13 55 K8
KLMNKN/STW KA3 17 G2
KLMNKN/STW KA3 197 L1
LNK/LMHG ML11 199 G5
LOCHW PA12 120 C6
MTHW ML1 134 E5
NMLNS KA16 215 K2
PSLY PA1 8 F4
RNFRW PA4 80 D6
RUTH G73 129 G1 2
SHOTTS ML7 137 M5
Highthorne Crs WKIL KA23 181 L4 1
High Whitehills Rd EKILS G75 171 L4
Hilary Crs AYRS KA7 19 G7
Hilary Dr BAIL/MDB/MHD G69 107 M4
Hillary Av RUTH G73 129 K3 1
Hill Av NMRNS G77 150 C5
Hillbank St ALEX/LLW G83 25 M5
Hill Crs CRMNK/CLK/EAG G76 151 M3
Hillcrest BAIL/MDB/MHD G69 86 D1 2
CRMNK/CLK/EAG G76 152 D1
KLMNKN/STW KA3 197 L1
Hillcrest Av CAR/SHTL G32 130 B1 1
CLYDBK G81 60 A2
CTBR ML5 110 C3
CUMB G67 68 F1 1
LNPK/KPK G44 127 L5
PSLYS PA2 124 B3
WISHAW ML2 158 E5
Hillcrest Dr NMRNS G77 151 G4
SVSTN KA20 201 L1
Hillcrest Pl KLWNG KA13 193 M6
Hillcrest Rd BSDN G61 61 M5
CAR/SHTL G32 130 C1 1
KSYTH G65 46 E1
UD/BTH/TAN G71 132 A2
Hillcrest St MLNGV G62 42 B7 3
Hillcrest Ter
UD/BTH/TAN G71 132 B6 1
Hillcrest Vw LRKH ML9 176 B7
Hillcroft Ter BSHPBGS G64 83 M1 1
Hillend Crs CLYDBK G81 59 M2
CRMNK/CLK/EAG G76 151 J3
Hillend Dr GRNK PA15 3 J8
Hillend Pl GRNK PA15 3 J8
Hillend Rd
CRMNK/CLK/EAG G76 151 K3
PPK/MIL G22 83 G2
RUTH G73 129 H5
Hillfoot CRG/CRSL/HOU PA6 99 K1
DMBTN G82 25 K7
Hillfoot Av DMBTN G82 37 J5
RUTH G73 129 G2 1
WISHAW ML2 159 K2
Hillfoot Crs AYRS KA7 19 J9
WISHAW ML2 159 J6
Hillfoot Dr BSDN G61 61 M4
CTBR ML5 109 K3
HWWD PA9 121 M4 2
WISHAW ML2 159 K2
Hillfoot Gdns UD/BTH/TAN G71 131 L1
WISHAW ML2 159 K2
Hillfoot Rd AIRDRIE ML6 111 H3
AYRS KA7 19 K9
Hillfoot St DEN/PKHD G31 12 E2
Hillfoot Ter CARLUKE ML8 179 G8 2
Hillhead Av BAIL/MDB/MHD G69 66 F7
CARLUKE ML8 179 G7
MTHW ML1 134 A7
RUTH G73 129 H5
Hillhead Crs HMLTN ML3 155 L6
MTHW ML1 134 A7 1
Hillhead Dr AIRDRIE ML6 111 G3
MTHW ML1 134 A8
Hillhead Pl RUTH G73 129 H5 2
Hillhead Rd KKNTL G66 45 K8
SPRGB/BLRNK G21 84 D2
SVSTN KA20 192 E6
Hillhead Sq
KLMNKN/STW KA3 206 F6 2
Hillhead St KVD/HLHD G12 82 D7 3
MLNGV G62 42 A7
Hillhead Ter HMLTN ML3 155 L6 2
Hillhouse Crs HMLTN ML3 155 M6
Hillhouse Farm Ga
LNK/LMHG ML11 198 E4
Hillhouse Gdns TROON KA10 216 D3
Hillhouse Ga CARLUKE ML8 189 J1
Hillhouseridge Rd SHOTTS ML7 137 K4
Hillhouse Rd BLTYR/CAMB G72 155 K5
HMLTN ML3 155 M6
TROON KA10 216 D3
Hillhouse St SPRGB/BLRNK G21 84 A5
Hillhouse Ter HMLTN ML3 155 M6 1
Hillington Gdns
CARD/HILL/MSPK G52 103 J5
Hillington Park Circ
CARD/HILL/MSPK G52 103 J4 3
Hillington Qd
CARD/HILL/MSPK G52 103 G4
Hillington Rd
CARD/HILL/MSPK G52 103 G1 1
Hillington Rd South
CARD/HILL/MSPK G52 103 G3
Hillington Ter
CARD/HILL/MSPK G52 103 G4
Hill Int IRV KA12 203 L3
Hillkirk Pl SPRGB/BLRNK G21 6 C1
Hillkirk St SPRGB/BLRNK G21 83 M5 1
Hill La ARD KA22 191 J7
Hillmoss KLMNKN/STW KA3 206 B2
Hillneuk Av BSDN G61 61 M4
Hillneuk Dr BSDN G61 62 A4
Hillocks Pl TROON KA10 216 E2 1
Hillpark RAYR/DAL KA6 226 F3
Hillpark Av PSLYS PA2 101 K8
Hillpark Dr KLMNKN/STW KA3 206 F7
PLKSW/MSWD G43 127 H3
Hillpark Ri KLWNG KA13 193 H6
Hill Pl ARD KA22 191 J8
BLSH ML4 132 F6
MTHW ML1 134 C7
SHOTTS ML7 137 L4
Hillrigg AIRDRIE ML6 69 K8
Hillrigg Av AIRDRIE ML6 111 J1
Hill Rd CUMB G67 48 E7
GRNKW/INVK PA16 50 D5 1
HWWD PA9 121 M4 3
Hillsborough Rd
BAIL/MDB/MHD G69 107 M4
Hillshaw Gn IRVSE KA11 204 C7
Hillside CRG/CRSL/HOU PA6 99 K1
KSYTH G65 47 M4
WKIL KA23 181 J5
Hillside Av ALEX/LLW G83 25 K6
BSDN G61 61 M4
CRMNK/CLK/EAG G76 151 K2
KLMCLM PA13 55 K8
Hillside Ct GIF/THBK G46 126 F6 1
Hillside Crs BRHD/NEIL G78 148 D2 3
CTBR ML5 109 M5
HMLTN ML3 156 D7
MTHW ML1 134 D6
PSTWK KA9 225 K1
Hillside Dr BRHD/NEIL G78 125 G6
BSDN G61 62 A4
BSHPBGS G64 64 A7
PGL PA14 34 B8
Hillside Gardens La PTCK G11 82 B6 2
Hillside Gv BRHD/NEIL G78 125 G7 1
Hillside La HMLTN ML3 156 C7 2
Hillside Pk CLYDBK G81 60 B3
Hillside Pl MTHW ML1 134 D6
NMLNS KA16 215 J2 3
Hillside Qd
PLKSW/MSWD G43 127 H4 2
Hillside Rd BRHD/NEIL G78 124 F7
BRHD/NEIL G78 148 D2
DMBTN G82 24 B8
GRK PA19 31 K2 1
GRNK PA15 3 H9
PLKSW/MSWD G43 127 H4
PSLYS PA2 9 L9
Hillside St SVSTN KA20 201 J1
Hillside Ter HMLTN ML3 156 C7
KKNTL G66 45 H4
Hill St AIRDRIE ML6 90 F4
AIRDRIE ML6 111 K7
ALEX/LLW G83 25 K4 1
ARD KA22 191 J8 3
DMBTN G82 36 D6
GRNK PA15 2 E6
HMLTN ML3 155 M6
IRV KA12 203 J7
KLMNKN/STW KA3 16 E1
KVGV G3 4 F7
LARGS KA30 115 K7
LRKH ML9 176 A7
SALT KA21 200 F2
WISHAW ML2 159 G7
Hillswick Crs PPK/MIL G22 83 H1
Hill Ter MTHW ML1 134 C7
Hilltop Av BLSH ML4 133 G2
Hilltop Crs GRK PA19 31 M3
Hilltop Pl AYRS KA7 229 K4
Hilltop Rd BAIL/MDB/MHD G69 66 F7
GRNKW/INVK PA16 31 L3
Hill Vw DMBTN G82 37 M8
EKILS G75 14 E6
Hillview AIRDRIE ML6 69 M7
SKLM PA17 70 B5
Hillview Av KKNTL G66 44 E1
KSYTH G65 47 K2
Hillview Crs BLSH ML4 133 G1
LRKH ML9 176 B8
UD/BTH/TAN G71 131 L1
Hillview Dr BLTYR/CAMB G72 131 K7
CRMNK/CLK/EAG G76 151 K2
HBR/GL G84 20 D5
Hillview Gdns
SPRGB/BLRNK G21 84 D1 1
Hillview Pl
CRMNK/CLK/EAG G76 151 L2 1
NMRNS G77 150 D5 1
Hillview Rd BRWEIR PA11 98 E2 1
JNSTN PA5 100 C7
Hill View Rd LNK/LMHG ML11 198 A6
Hillview St CAR/SHTL G32 106 F4
Hiltonbank St HMLTN ML3 156 B5
Hilton Gdns KNTSWD G13 81 M2
Hilton Pk BSHPBGS G64 63 M6
Hilton Rd BSHPBGS G64 63 M6
MLNGV G62 41 L7
Hilton Ter BLTYR/CAMB G72 129 L6 2
BSHPBGS G64 63 M6
KNTSWD G13 81 L2
Hindsland Rd LRKH ML9 176 B8
Hinshaw St MRYH/FIRH G20 4 E2
Hinshelwood Dr GOV/IBX G51 104 A4
Hinshelwood Pl
GOV/IBX G51 104 B4 1
Hirst Gdns SHOTTS ML7 137 J4
Hirst Rd SHOTTS ML7 113 K7
Hobart Crs CLYDBK G81 59 K4
Hobart Qd WISHAW ML2 159 L6 3
Hobart Rd EKILS G75 14 A6
Hobart St PPK/MIL G22 83 H5
Hobden St SPRGB/BLRNK G21 6 F3
Hoddam Av CSMK G45 128 F6
Hoddam Ter CSMK G45 129 G6
Hoey Dr WISHAW ML2 177 J2
Hogan Wy MTHW ML1 134 E8
Hogarth Av CAR/SHTL G32 13 L1
SALT KA21 191 L7
Hogarth Ct ALEX/LLW G83 25 L3 3
Hogarth Gdns CAR/SHTL G32 13 L1
Hogganfield St
STPS/GTHM/RID G33 7 L4
Hogg Av JNSTN PA5 99 L8
Hogg Rd AIRDRIE ML6 111 K5 2
Hogg St AIRDRIE ML6 111 G2
Holeburn La
PLKSW/MSWD G43 127 J3
Holeburn Rd
PLKSW/MSWD G43 127 J3
Hole Farm Rd
GRNKW/INVK PA16 32 C6
Holehills Dr AIRDRIE ML6 89 H7
Holehills Pl AIRDRIE ML6 89 H7
Holehouse Brae
BRHD/NEIL G78 148 C2
Holehouse Ct LARGS KA30 115 L5
Holehouse Dr KBRN KA25 143 H7
KNTSWD G13 81 G3
Holehouse Rd
KLMNKN/STW KA3 17 K4
LARGS KA30 115 L5
Holehouse Ter
BRHD/NEIL G78 148 C2 2
Hole Rd RAYR/DAL KA6 231 H6
Hollandbush Gv HMLTN ML3 174 D1 3
Hollandhurst Rd CTBR ML5 87 M7
Holland St CGLW G2 4 E9
Hollinwell Rd SMSTN G23 82 D1
Hollowglen Rd CAR/SHTL G32 107 H3
Hollow Pk AYRS KA7 229 H7
Hollows Av PSLYS PA2 123 M2
Hollows Crs PSLYS PA2 123 M2
Holly Bank AYRS KA7 229 K4
Hollybank Pl
BLTYR/CAMB G72 130 B5 1
Hollybank St SPRGB/BLRNK G21 6 E7
Hollybrook St GVH/MTFL G42 105 H8
Hollybush Av PSLYS PA2 124 B3
Hollybush Pl
KLMNKN/STW KA3 207 H3 1
Hollybush Rd
CARD/HILL/MSPK G52 102 F4
Holly Dr DMBTN G82 36 B4
SPRGB/BLRNK G21 6 E3
Holly Gv BLSH ML4 133 M4
Hollymount BSDN G61 61 M7
Holly Pl JNSTN PA5 123 G1
KLMNK KA1 16 A4
Holly St AIRDRIE ML6 111 J2
CLYDBK G81 60 A5
Hollywood LARGS KA30 115 H2
Holm Av PSLYS PA2 9 J8
UD/BTH/TAN G71 131 M2 1
Holmbank Av
PLKSW/MSWD G43 127 K2
Holmbrae Av
UD/BTH/TAN G71 131 M2 2
Holmbrae Rd UD/BTH/TAN G71 131 M2
Holmbyre Rd CSMK G45 128 B8
Holmbyre Ter CSMK G45 128 C7 2
Holm Crest CARLUKE ML8 188 B7
Holmes Av RNFRW PA4 80 C8
Holmes Crs KLMNK KA1 16 B8
Holmes Farm Rd KLMNK KA1 16 B8
Holmes Qd BLSH ML4 133 H5 3
Holmes Rd GLSTN KA4 214 B3
KLMNK KA1 16 B8
Holmfauldhead Dr
GOV/IBX G51 103 L1
Holmfauldhead Pl GOV/IBX G51 81 L8
Holmfauld Rd GOV/IBX G51 103 L1 5
Holm Gdns BLSH ML4 133 J5
Holmhead KBRN KA25 167 G1
Holmhead Crs LNPK/KPK G44 128 A3
Holmhead Pl LNPK/KPK G44 128 A3 1
Holmhead Rd LNPK/KPK G44 128 A4
Holmhill Av BLTYR/CAMB G72 130 A5
Holmhills Dr BLTYR/CAMB G72 129 M6
Holmhills Gdns
BLTYR/CAMB G72 129 M5
Holmhills Gv BLTYR/CAMB G72 129 M5
Holmhills Pl
BLTYR/CAMB G72 129 M5 1
Holmhills Rd BLTYR/CAMB G72 129 M6

Holmhills Ter BLTYR/CAMB G72 129 M5
Holmlands Pl KLMNK KA1 16 B8
Holm La EKILN G74 14 E2
Holmlea Dr KLMNK KA1 16 C8
Holmlea Pl KLMNK KA1 16 B8
Holmlea Rd GVH/MTFL G42 128 A2
Holm Pl PSLYN/LNWD PA3 100 B2
Holmquarry Rd KLMNK KA1 16 D9
Holm Rd CARLUKE ML8 188 A6
Holms Av IRVSE KA11 204 D8
Holms Crs ERSK PA8 58 F7
Holmscroft Av GRNK PA15 2 A5
Holmscroft St GRNK PA15 2 A4
Holms Pl BAIL/MDB/MHD G69 86 E2
Holms Rd GLGNK KA14 167 H3
Holmston Crs AYRS KA7 19 M6
Holmston Dr AYRS KA7 19 M7
Holmston Rd AYRS KA7 19 H6
AYRS KA7 19 M6
Holm St CARLUKE ML8 178 E7
CGLW G2 11 G2
KLMNKN/STW KA3 197 L1
MTHW ML1 134 A6
Holmswood Av
BLTYR/CAMB G72 155 K1
Holmwood Av
UD/BTH/TAN G71 131 M2
Holmwood Ct LARGS KA30 115 H2
Holmwood Gdns
UD/BTH/TAN G71 131 M3
Holyknowe Crs KKNTL G66 44 E1
Holyknowe Rd KKNTL G66 44 E2
Holyoake Ct KLMNK KA1 212 F2
Holyrood Crs MRYH/FIRH G20 4 D4
Holyrood Qd MRYH/FIRH G20 4 C4
Holyrood St HMLTN ML3 156 A4
Holytown Rd BLSH ML4 133 L4
Holywell St DEN/PKHD G31 13 H5
Home Farm Rd AYRS KA7 229 G7
SHOTTS ML7 136 F6
Homer Pl BLSH ML4 133 L4
Homeston Av
UD/BTH/TAN G71 132 A6
Home St LNK/LMHG ML11 199 J6
Honeybank Crs CARLUKE ML8 178 F6
Honeybog Rd
CARD/HILL/MSPK G52 102 E3
Honeyman Crs
LNK/LMHG ML11 199 J5
Honeysuckle La
ALEX/LLW G83 25 M2
Honeywell Crs AIRDRIE ML6 111 L8
Hood St CLYDBK G81 60 C7
GRNK PA15 2 C2
Hope Av BRWEIR PA11 75 L7
Hope Crs LRKH ML9 176 B6
Hopefield Av KVD/HLHD G12 82 C4
Hopehill Gdns MRYH/FIRH G20 4 E3
Hopehill Rd MRYH/FIRH G20 4 E3
Hopeman ERSK PA8 59 G6
Hopeman Av GIF/THBK G46 126 E5
Hopeman Dr GIF/THBK G46 126 E5
Hopeman Rd GIF/THBK G46 126 E5
Hopeman St GIF/THBK G46 126 E5
Hope St BLSH ML4 133 J4
CARLUKE ML8 179 G7
CGLW G2 11 H1
GRNK PA15 2 D6
HBR/GL G84 22 F1
HMLTN ML3 156 E6
LNK/LMHG ML11 199 G5
MTHW ML1 157 L2
WISHAW ML2 160 A5
Hopetoun Bank IRVSE KA11 204 C7
Hopetoun Pl SMSTN G23 62 E8
Hopetoun Ter SPRGB/BLRNK G21 6 F2
Horatius St MTHW ML1 133 H8
Hornal Rd UD/BTH/TAN G71 132 A5
Hornbeam Dr CLYDBK G81 59 M5
Hornbeam Rd CUMB G67 49 M4
UD/BTH/TAN G71 132 B1
Horndean Crs
STPS/GTHM/RID G33 85 K8
Horne St PPK/MIL G22 83 L4
Hornock Rd CTBR ML5 87 M8
Hornshill Dr MTHW ML1 135 H7
Hornshill Farm Rd
STPS/GTHM/RID G33 85 L3
Hornshill St SPRGB/BLRNK G21 6 E1
Horsburgh St
STPS/GTHM/RID G33 85 K7
Horse Shoe Rd BSDN G61 61 L5
Horsewood Rd BRWEIR PA11 98 C2
Horslethill Rd KVD/HLHD G12 82 C5
Horslet St CTBR ML5 109 J5
Horsley Brae WISHAW ML2 177 H5
Horton Pl HBR/GL G84 21 G6
Hospital Rd WISHAW ML2 159 J8
Hospital St CTBR ML5 110 A5
GBLS G5 11 H8
Hospitland Dr LNK/LMHG ML11 199 H4
Hotspur St MRYH/FIRH G20 82 E5
Houldsworth Crs SHOTTS ML7 161 G1
Houldsworth La KVGV G3 4 B9
Houldsworth St KVGV G3 4 B9
Househillmuir Crs
PLK/PH/NH G53 126 C3
Househillmuir Pl
PLK/PH/NH G53 126 C2
Househillmuir Rd
PLK/PH/NH G53 126 A4
Househillwood Crs
PLK/PH/NH G53 126 B2
Househillwood Rd
PLK/PH/NH G53 126 B3
Housel Av KNTSWD G13 81 H3
Houston Crs DALRY KA24 184 B2
Houstonfield Qd
CRG/CRSL/HOU PA6 77 G7
Houston Pl GBLS G5 10 C4
JNSTN PA5 100 C7
Houston Rd BRWEIR PA11 98 D1
CRG/CRSL/HOU PA6 77 H7
KLMCLM PA13 75 L2
RNFRW PA4 79 G5
Houston St GRNKW/INVK PA16 2 B1
HMLTN ML3 156 D8
PLKSD/SHW G41 10 C5
RNFRW PA4 80 D5
WISHAW ML2 159 K7
Houston Ter EKILN G74 14 D2
Houstoun Sq JNSTN PA5 99 M6
Howacre LNK/LMHG ML11 198 F4
Howard Av EKILN G74 154 A4
Howard Ct EKILN G74 154 A4
Howard Park Dr KLMNK KA1 16 D7
Howard St CGLE G1 11 J3
GTCI KA28 138 A7
KLMNK KA1 16 D5
LRKH ML9 176 C8
PSLY PA1 9 L3
Howat Crs IRV KA12 203 L6
Howatshaws Rd DMBTN G82 37 H3
Howat St GOV/IBX G51 104 A1
Howden Av KLWNG KA13 193 L5
MTHW ML1 134 D1
Howden Dr
PSLYN/LNWD PA3 100 A4
Howden Pl MTHW ML1 134 A4
Howe Gdns
UD/BTH/TAN G71 132 A2
Howe Rd KSYTH G65 47 K2
Howes St CTBR ML5 110 B5
Howe St PSLY PA1 100 F5
Howford Rd
CARD/HILL/MSPK G52 103 H5
Howgate KLWNG KA13 193 K6
Howgate Av DRUM G15 60 F6
Howgate Rd HMLTN ML3 174 C1
Howieshill Av
BLTYR/CAMB G72 130 B4
Howieshill Rd
BLTYR/CAMB G72 130 B5
Howie St LRKH ML9 176 B8
Howletnest Rd AIRDRIE ML6 111 J3
Howlet Pl HMLTN ML3 156 E8
Howson Lea MTHW ML1 158 B5
Howson Vw MTHW ML1 157 H2
Howth Dr KNTSWD G13 81 M1
Howth Ter KNTSWD G13 81 M1
Hoylake Pk UD/BTH/TAN G71 131 M7
Hoylake Pl SMSTN G23 62 E8
Hoylake Sq KLWNG KA13 193 J5
Hozier Crs UD/BTH/TAN G71 131 M1
Hozier St CARLUKE ML8 178 F7
CTBR ML5 110 A5
Hudson Ter EKILS G75 171 H1
Hudson Wy EKILS G75 14 A5
Huggin Craig Rd NMLNS KA16 215 J1
Hughenden Dr
KVD/HLHD G12 82 B5
Hughenden Gdns
KVD/HLHD G12 82 A5
Hughenden La
KVD/HLHD G12 82 B5
Hughenden Rd
KVD/HLHD G12 82 B5
Hugh Murray Dr
BLTYR/CAMB G72 130 C4
Hugh Watt Pl
KLMNKN/STW KA3 206 A2
Hugo St MRYH/FIRH G20 82 F4
Hulks Rd AIRDRIE ML6 69 H6
Humbie Ct NMRNS G77 150 E7
Humbie Ga NMRNS G77 150 E7
Humbie Gv NMRNS G77 150 E6
Humbie Lawns NMRNS G77 150 E7
Humbie Rd NMRNS G77 150 E7
Hume Dr UD/BTH/TAN G71 131 L2
Hume Pl EKILS G75 14 D6
Hume Rd CUMB G67 49 G6
Hume St CLYDBK G81 60 B8
Hunter Av ARD KA22 191 K7
Hunter Crs TROON KA10 217 G6
Hunter Dr IRV KA12 203 H3
Hunterfield Dr
BLTYR/CAMB G72 129 L4
Hunterhill Av PSLYS PA2 9 J7
Hunterhill Rd PSLYS PA2 9 J6
Hunter Pl KLBCH PA10 99 G7
KLWNG KA13 194 A6
MLNGV G62 41 L8
Hunter Rd CRH/DND KA2 210 F1
HMLTN ML3 156 B3
MLNGV G62 41 L8
RUTH G73 106 C8
Hunter's Av AYR KA8 225 J4
DMBTN G82 37 J6
Huntersfield Rd JNSTN PA5 99 J8
Hunters Hill Ct
SPRGB/BLRNK G21 83 M3
Huntershill Rd BSHPBGS G64 84 A1
Huntershill St
SPRGB/BLRNK G21 83 L3
Huntershill Wy BSHPBGS G64 83 M2
Hunters Pl GRNK PA15 2 D3
Hunterston Rd WKIL KA23 181 J3
Hunter St AIRDRIE ML6 88 F8
BLSH ML4 133 G4
COWCAD G4 12 A3
EKILN G74 15 G2
PSLY PA1 9 G3
PSTWK KA9 225 J1
SHOTTS ML7 137 K4
Hunt Hl BALLOCH G68 47 J8
Hunthill La BLTYR/CAMB G72 155 H3
Hunthill Pl
CRMNK/CLK/EAG G76 152 A4
Hunthill Rd BLTYR/CAMB G72 155 H3
Huntingdon Rd COWCAD G4 6 A5
Huntingdon Sq
SPRGB/BLRNK G21 6 A4
Hunting Lodge Gdns
HMLTN ML3 157 G7
Huntingtower Rd
BAIL/MDB/MHD G69 107 M5
Huntley Gdns KVD/HLHD G12 82 D6
Huntly Av BLSH ML4 133 G3
GIF/THBK G46 127 K6
Huntly Ct BSHPBGS G64 84 A1
Huntly Dr BLTYR/CAMB G72 130 B5
BSDN G61 61 L2
CTBR ML5 109 K5
GRNKW/INVK PA16 31 M6
Huntly Pl KLMNKN/STW KA3 207 J7
PGL PA14 34 B7
Huntly Qd WISHAW ML2 159 H4
Huntly Rd
CARD/HILL/MSPK G52 102 F1
KVD/HLHD G12 82 C6
Huntly Ter PGL PA14 34 B7
PSLYS PA2 9 K9
Hurlawcrook Rd EKILS G75 171 M8
Hurlet Rd PSLYS PA2 102 C8
Hurlford Av KNTSWD G13 80 F2
Hurlford Rd KLMNK KA1 212 A4
Hurly Hawkin BSHPBGS G64 84 D1
Hutcheson Dr LARGS KA30 115 K8
Hutcheson Rd GIF/THBK G46 127 G7
Hutcheson St CGLE G1 11 K3
Hutchinson Pl
BLTYR/CAMB G72 130 E6
Hutchison Dr BSDN G61 62 A7
Hutchison Pl CTBR ML5 109 M3
Hutchison St HMLTN ML3 156 D8
WISHAW ML2 177 J2
Hutton KVD/HLHD G12 82 A3
Hutton Av CRG/CRSL/HOU PA6 99 J1
Hutton Dr GOV/IBX G51 103 L1
Hutton Park Crs LARGS KA30 115 J4
Huxley St MRYH/FIRH G20 82 F3
Hyacinth Wy CARLUKE ML8 188 F1
Hydepark St KVGV G3 10 C2
Hyndal Av PLK/PH/NH G53 103 J8
Hyndford Pl
LNK/LMHG ML11 199 G5
Hyndford Rd LNK/LMHG ML11 199 H6
LNK/LMHG ML11 199 M8
Hyndland Av PTCK G11 82 B7
Hyndland Rd KVD/HLHD G12 82 C6
Hyndland St PTCK G11 82 C7
Hyndlee Dr
CARD/HILL/MSPK G52 103 J4
Hyndman Rd WKIL KA23 181 J6
Hyndshaw Rd CARLUKE ML8 178 F6
WISHAW ML2 178 C1
Hyndshaw Vw CARLUKE ML8 178 A5
Hyslop Pl CLYDBK G81 60 A6
Hyslop Rd SVSTN KA20 192 E7
Hyslop St AIRDRIE ML6 110 E1

I

Iain Dr BSDN G61 61 J3
Iain Rd BSDN G61 61 J3
Ian Smith Ct CLYDBK G81 80 D1
Ibroxholm Ov GOV/IBX G51 104 B3
Ibroxholm Pl GOV/IBX G51 104 B4
Ibrox St GOV/IBX G51 104 C3
Ibrox Ter GOV/IBX G51 104 B3
Ida Qd BLSH ML4 132 F4
Iddesleigh Av MLNGV G62 42 A7
Ilay Av BSDN G61 82 A1
Ilay Ct BSDN G61 82 A1
Ilay Rd BSDN G61 82 A1
Imlach Pl MTHW ML1 157 K4
Imperial Dr AIRDRIE ML6 110 F4
Inchbrae Rd
CARD/HILL/MSPK G52 103 J5
Inchcolm Pl EKILN G74 14 B1
Inches Rd ARD KA22 200 B1
Inchfad Dr DRUM G15 60 E6
Inchfad Pl DRUM G15 60 E6
Inch Garve EKILN G74 154 D8
Inchgotrick Rd KLMNK KA1 211 L6
Inchgreen St GRNK PA15 33 M7
Inchholm La PTCK G11 81 L7
Inchholm St PTCK G11 81 L7
Inchinnan Dr RNFRW PA4 79 J5
Inchinnan Rd PSLYN/LNWD PA3 101 L2
RNFRW PA4 80 A5
Inch Keith EKILN G74 154 D8
Inchkeith Pl CAR/SHTL G32 107 H2
Inchlaggan Pl DRUM G15 60 E5
Inchlee St SCOT G14 81 L7
Inch Marnock EKILN G74 172 C1
Inch Murrin EKILN G74 154 D8
Inchmurrin Av KKNTL G66 66 B1
Inchmurrin Dr
CRMNK/CLK/EAG G76 129 K7
KLMNKN/STW KA3 207 G4
Inchmurrin Gdns
CRMNK/CLK/EAG G76 129 K7
Inchmurrin Pl
CRMNK/CLK/EAG G76 129 K7
Inchneuk Rd CTBR ML5 87 L3
Inchnock Av
BAIL/MDB/MHD G69 87 G3
Inchoch St STPS/GTHM/RID G33 85 L7
Incholm Gdns
BAIL/MDB/MHD G69 67 G6
Inchrory Pl DRUM G15 60 E5
Inchwood Ct BALLOCH G68 68 A2
Inchwood Pl BALLOCH G68 67 M2
Inchwood Rd BALLOCH G68 67 M2
Incle St PSLY PA1 9 J3
Indale Av PSTWK KA9 225 L2
India Dr RNFRW PA4 79 J4
India St ALEX/LLW G83 25 L4
CGLW G2 4 E8
Industry St KKNTL G66 65 K2
Inga St MRYH/FIRH G20 82 E2
Ingerbreck Av RUTH G73 129 K4
Ingleby Dr DEN/PKHD G31 12 F1
Inglefield Ct AIRDRIE ML6 110 F2
Inglefield St GVH/MTFL G42 105 H7
Ingleneuk Av
STPS/GTHM/RID G33 85 H4
Inglestone Av GIF/THBK G46 127 G7
Ingleston St GRNK PA15 2 F7
Inglewood Crs EKILS G75 171 G1
Inglis Pl EKILS G75 14 F8
Inglis St DEN/PKHD G31 12 F3
WISHAW ML2 158 D7
Ingliston Dr BSHPTN PA7 57 M6
Ingram Pl KLMNKN/STW KA3 207 G6
Ingram St CGLE G1 11 L2
Inishail Rd STPS/GTHM/RID G33 85 J8
Inkerman Pl KLMNK KA1 16 C3
Inkerman Rd
CARD/HILL/MSPK G52 102 F4
Innellan Dr KLMNKN/STW KA3 206 F6
Innellan Rd WMYSB PA18 50 A8
Innerleithen Dr WISHAW ML2 159 K3
Innermanse Qd MTHW ML1 134 F4
Innerwick Dr
CARD/HILL/MSPK G52 103 H4
Innerwood Rd KLWNG KA13 193 L5
Innes Ct EKILN G74 153 L5
Innes Park Rd SKLM PA17 70 B5
International Av
BLTYR/CAMB G72 155 K5
Inveraray Gdns MTHW ML1 134 C7
Inverary Dr BSHPBGS G64 64 B5
Inveravon Dr MTHW ML1 157 H4
Invercanny Dr DRUM G15 61 G5
Invercanny Pl DRUM G15 61 G5
Invercargill EKILS G75 171 G2
Invercloy Ct EKILS G75 171 H5
Invercloy Pl
KLMNKN/STW KA3 206 E5
Inverclyde Gdns RUTH G73 129 K6
Inverclyde Vw LARGS KA30 115 K3
Inveresk Pl CTBR ML5 110 A1
Inveresk Qd CAR/SHTL G32 107 G3
Inveresk St CAR/SHTL G32 107 G3
Inverewe Av GIF/THBK G46 126 D7
Inverewe Dr GIF/THBK G46 126 D7
Inverewe Gdns GIF/THBK G46 126 D7
Inverewe Pl GIF/THBK G46 126 D6
Inverewe Wy NMRNS G77 150 A4
Invergarry Av GIF/THBK G46 126 D8
Invergarry Ct GIF/THBK G46 126 E7
Invergarry Dr GIF/THBK G46 126 D7
Invergarry Gdns GIF/THBK G46 126 D8
Invergarry Gv GIF/THBK G46 126 D7
Invergarry Pl GIF/THBK G46 126 E7
Invergarry Quad GIF/THBK G46 126 E7
Invergarry Vw GIF/THBK G46 126 E7
Inverglas Av RNFRW PA4 80 F8
Invergordon Av
PLKSW/MSWD G43 127 M2
Invergyle Dr
CARD/HILL/MSPK G52 103 H4
Inverkar Dr PSLYS PA2 101 G7
Inverkar Rd AYRS KA7 19 G8
Inverkip Dr SHOTTS ML7 137 L4
Inverkip Rd GRNKW/INVK PA16 31 L6
Inverkip St GRNK PA15 2 B4
Inverlair Av PLKSW/MSWD G43 127 M3
Inverleith St CAR/SHTL G32 13 L3
Inverleven Pl IRVSE KA11 203 M2
Inverlochy St
STPS/GTHM/RID G33 85 K8
Inverness St GOV/IBX G51 103 K3
Inveroran Dr BSDN G61 62 B5
Inver Rd STPS/GTHM/RID G33 107 L2
Invershiel Rd SMSTN G23 62 D8
Invershin Dr MRYH/FIRH G20 82 D4
Inverurie St SPRGB/BLRNK G21 5 M2
Invervale Av AIRDRIE ML6 111 M3
Inzievar Ter CAR/SHTL G32 107 H8
Iona Av EKILN G74 154 A5
Iona Crs GRK PA19 31 J3
OLDK G60 59 J4
Iona Dr PSLYS PA2 124 D2
Iona Gdns OLDK G60 59 J4
Iona Pl CTBR ML5 87 K8
KLMNKN/STW KA3 207 G4
Iona Qd WISHAW ML2 159 L4
Iona Rdg HMLTN ML3 155 L8
Iona Rd PGL PA14 55 G2
RNFRW PA4 80 C8
RUTH G73 129 L6
WISHAW ML2 159 M3
Iona St GOV/IBX G51 104 B2
GRNKW/INVK PA16 32 C5
MTHW ML1 157 H2
Iona Wy KKNTL G66 66 A1
STPS/GTHM/RID G33 85 L5
Iona Wynd ALEX/LLW G83 25 M8
Iris Av CSMK G45 129 G6
Irongray St DEN/PKHD G31 13 K1
Irvine Crs CTBR ML5 110 C2
Irvine Dr PSLYN/LNWD PA3 99 M2
Irvine Gdns KKNTL G66 45 H4
Irvine Mains Crs IRV KA12 203 J5
Irvine Rd CRH/DND KA2 205 K8
IRV KA12 203 G1
KLMNK KA1 206 C8
KLMNKN/STW KA3 205 L2
KLWNG KA13 193 M7
LARGS KA30 115 K7
NMLNS KA16 215 H2
Irvine St AIRDRIE ML6 88 F5
DMNK/BRGTN G40 13 G9
Irvine Ter HMLTN ML3 174 D1
Irving Av CLYDBK G81 60 B4
Irving Ct CLYDBK G81 60 B3
Irving Qd CLYDBK G81 60 B3
Irwin St GRNK PA15 33 L7
Isabella Gdns HMLTN ML3 157 H8
Isla Av WISHAW ML2 159 M3
Island Rd CUMB G67 68 D1
Island Vw ARD KA22 191 H5
Islay Av PGL PA14 55 H2
RUTH G73 129 L6
Islay Ct HMLTN ML3 155 M7
Islay Crs OLDK G60 59 J4
PSLYS PA2 124 D2
SALT KA21 191 M7
Islay Dr NMRNS G77 150 B4
OLDK G60 59 J4
Islay Gdns CARLUKE ML8 188 F1
LRKH ML9 176 B6
Islay Pl KLMNKN/STW KA3 207 H4
Islay Qd WISHAW ML2 158 E8
Islay Rd KKNTL G66 66 A1
Islay Wy CTBR ML5 109 K5
Isle of Pin Rd TROON KA10 216 F8
Isles St NMLNS KA16 215 L2
Ivanhoe EKILN G74 154 D5
Ivanhoe Ct CARLUKE ML8 178 D8
Ivanhoe Crs WISHAW ML2 159 J6
Ivanhoe Dr KKNTL G66 65 L1
SALT KA21 192 A8
Ivanhoe Rd CUMB G67 68 E1
KNTSWD G13 81 K1
PSLYS PA2 100 E8
Ivybank Av BLTYR/CAMB G72 130 C5
Ivybank Crs PGL PA14 34 A8
Ivybank Rd PGL PA14 34 B8
Ivy Crs GRK PA19 31 L3
Ivy Gv CTBR ML5 110 B3
Ivy Pl AYRS KA7 229 K4
BLTYR/CAMB G72 155 J1
MTHW ML1 134 A6
Ivy Rd UD/BTH/TAN G71 132 C1
Ivy Ter MTHW ML1 134 A4
Ivy Wy AIRDRIE ML6 111 L6

J

Jackson Pl CARLUKE ML8 178 E6
DMBTN G82 25 K7
Jackson St CTBR ML5 110 B2
Jack's Rd SALT KA21 200 F1
UD/BTH/TAN G71 132 A5
Jack St HMLTN ML3 174 D1
MTHW ML1 158 B5
Jacks Vw WKIL KA23 181 J4
Jackton Rd EKILS G75 170 D4
Jacobs Dr GRK PA19 31 K2
Jacob's Ladder Wy
WISHAW ML2 177 J2
Jagger Gdns
BAIL/MDB/MHD G69 107 M5
Jamaica Dr EKILS G75 153 H8
Jamaica La GRNK PA15 2 B2
Jamaica St CGLE G1 11 H3
GRNK PA15 2 B2
James Brown Av AYR KA8 225 L6
James Campbell Rd AYR KA8 19 K3
James Crs IRV KA12 203 H5
James Dempsey Ct CTBR ML5 109 M3
James Dempsey Gdns
CTBR ML5 109 M3
James Dunlop Gdns
BSHPBGS G64 84 B2
James Gray St
PLKSD/SHW G41 127 L1
James Hamilton Dr BLSH ML4 133 H4
James Healy Dr HMLTN ML3 174 C2
James Leeson Ct KKNTL G66 45 H3
James Little St KLMNK KA1 16 F7
James Miller Crescen
SALT KA21 201 G2
James Morrison St CGLE G1 11 L4
James Nisbet St
SPRGB/BLRNK G21 6 C8
James St ALEX/LLW G83 25 L4
AYR KA8 19 G2
BLSH ML4 132 E2
CARLUKE ML8 178 F8
DALRY KA24 184 B1
DMNK/BRGTN G40 12 B7
HBR/GL G84 20 D7
MTHW ML1 157 K2
PSTWK KA9 225 H4
James Sym Crs KLMNK KA1 16 C8
James Vw MTHW ML1 133 M6
James Watt Av EKILS G75 15 J6
James Watt Pl EKILN G74 153 H6
James Watt Rd MLNGV G62 41 M6
James Watt St KVGV G3 10 F2
James Watt Wy GRNK PA15 3 J5
James Wilson Pl
CARLUKE ML8 188 B7
Jamieson Ct CLYDBK G81 60 B2
GVH/MTFL G42 105 H7
Jamieson Dr EKILN G74 15 K2
Jamieson Gdns SHOTTS ML7 137 L4
Jamieson St GVH/MTFL G42 105 H7
Janebank Av BLTYR/CAMB G72 130 C5
Janefield Av JNSTN PA5 99 L7
Janefield Pl BEITH KA15 144 B8
BLTYR/CAMB G72 155 J3
KKNTL G66 29 K8
Janefield St DEN/PKHD G31 13 H5
DMNK/BRGTN G40 13 J7
Jane Rae Gdns CLYDBK G81 80 D1
Jane's Brae CUMB G67 68 F1
Janesmith St WISHAW ML2 158 C5
Janetta St CLYDBK G81 60 A6
Jardine St MRYH/FIRH G20 4 C3
Jardine Ter
BAIL/MDB/MHD G69 86 F4
Jarvie Av AIRDRIE ML6 90 B7
Jarvie Crs KSYTH G65 47 K2
Jarvie Wy PSLYS PA2 123 L1
Jasmine Pl CUMB G67 68 B2
Jasmine Rd KLMNK KA1 211 J2
Jasmine Wy CARLUKE ML8 188 E1
Java St MTHW ML1 133 J8
Jean Armour Dr CLYDBK G81 60 C6
Jean Armour Pl SALT KA21 192 A7
Jean Armour Ter
GRNKW/INVK PA16 31 K6
Jeanette Av HMLTN ML3 174 D2
Jeanie Deans Dr HBR/GL G84 23 G1
Jean Maclean Pl
BSHPBGS G64 64 B5
Jean St PGL PA14 34 B7
Jedburgh Av RUTH G73 129 H2
Jedburgh Dr PSLYS PA2 101 G8
Jedburgh Gdns
MRYH/FIRH G20 4 C2
Jedburgh Pl CTBR ML5 109 M6
EKILN G74 15 G1
Jedburgh St BLTYR/CAMB G72 155 K2
WISHAW ML2 159 J4
Jedworth Av DRUM G15 61 H6
Jedworth Rd DRUM G15 61 H6
Jeffrey St KLMNK KA1 211 M4
Jellicoe Pl HBR/GL G84 21 G7
Jellicoe St CLYDBK G81 59 L6
Jennie Lee Dr WISHAW ML2 177 H2
WISHAW ML2 177 J2
Jennys Well Ct PSLYS PA2 102 B7
Jennys Well Rd PSLYS PA2 102 B7
Jermond Dr IRV KA12 203 K5
Jervis Pl HBR/GL G84 21 G7
Jervis Ter EKILS G75 171 H2
Jerviston Ct MTHW ML1 134 A8
Jerviston Rd MTHW ML1 134 A8
STPS/GTHM/RID G33 85 J7

Jerviston St MTHW ML1 134 A5
MTHW ML1 157 M1
Jerviswood MTHW ML1 134 A8
Jerviswood Dr
LNK/LMHG ML11 199 M2
Jerviswood Rd
LNK/LMHG ML11 199 G5
Jetty Rd FAIRLIE KA29 139 K6
Joanna Ter BLTYR/CAMB G72 155 K1
Jocelyn Sq CGLE G1 11 K4
Jocksthorn Ter
KLMNKN/STW KA3 206 C3
John Bowman Gdns BLSH ML4 133 H3
John Brannan Wy
UD/BTH/TAN G71 132 D3
John Brogan Pl SVSTN KA20 201 H1
John Brown Pl
BAIL/MDB/MHD G69 86 C1
John Burnside Dr CLYDBK G81 60 C2
John Campbell St GRK PA19 31 M2
John Clark St LARGS KA30 115 K5
John Dickie St KLMNK KA1 16 E3
John Ewing Gdns LRKH ML9 176 A5
John Finnie St KLMNK KA1 16 E4
John Gregor Pl LOCHW PA12 120 C7
John Hendry Rd
UD/BTH/TAN G71 132 A5
John Knox St CLYDBK G81 80 D2
COWCAD G4 12 B1
GLSTN KA4 214 B4
John Lang St JNSTN PA5 100 A6
John Marshall Dr PPK/MIL G22 83 L1
John Murray Ct MTHW ML1 157 L6
Johnsburn Dr
PLK/PH/NH G53 126 B3
Johnsburn Rd
PLK/PH/NH G53 126 B3
Johnshaven St
PLKSW/MSWD G43 127 J2
Johnshill LOCHW PA12 120 D5
John Smith Ct AIRDRIE ML6 110 F1
John Smith Gdns CTBR ML5 110 C3
Johnson Ct HBR/GL G84 20 F8
Johnson Dr
BLTYR/CAMB G72 130 B4
Johnston Av KSYTH G65 47 K2
Johnston Dr TROON KA10 216 D3
Johnstone Av
CARD/HILL/MSPK G52 103 H2
CLYDBK G81 80 D1
Johnstone Dr LOCHW PA12 120 C7
RAYR/DAL KA6 227 H3
RUTH G73 129 G2
Johnstone Rd HMLTN ML3 156 E7
Johnstone St BLSH ML4 133 J4
Johnstone Ter KSYTH G65 46 F6
Johnston Rd
BAIL/MDB/MHD G69 86 F3
Johnston St AIRDRIE ML6 111 H1
GRNKW/INVK PA16 32 D2
PSLY PA1 9 H5
Johnston Ter
GRNKW/INVK PA16 32 D2
John St AYR KA8 19 G2
BLSH ML4 133 G4
BLTYR/CAMB G72 155 L2
BRHD/NEIL G78 125 H6
CARLUKE ML8 178 F8
CGLE G1 11 K2
DMBTN G82 36 D1
GRK PA19 31 L2
GRNK PA15 3 G7
HBR/GL G84 20 C8
HMLTN ML3 156 E6
KKNTL G66 45 K8
LARGS KA30 115 J7
LRKH ML9 176 A7
WISHAW ML2 158 C5
John Street La HBR/GL G84 20 C7
John Wilson St GRNK PA15 3 L8
John Wood St PGL PA14 34 C8
Jones Wynd MTHW ML1 134 E8
Jonquil Wy CARLUKE ML8 188 F1
Joppa RAYR/DAL KA6 231 H5
Joppa St
STPS/GTHM/RID G33 106 E2
Jordanhill Crs KNTSWD G13 81 K4
Jordanhill Dr KNTSWD G13 81 K4
Jordanhill La KNTSWD G13 81 L4
Jordan St SCOT G14 81 K7
Jordanvale Av SCOT G14 81 K7
Jowitt Av CLYDBK G81 60 D8
Jubilee Ct
CARD/HILL/MSPK G52 102 F2
Jubilee Gdns BSDN G61 61 L5
Jubilee Ter JNSTN PA5 99 K8
Julian Av KVD/HLHD G12 82 C5
Julian La KVD/HLHD G12 82 C5
Juniper Av EKILS G75 171 K3
Juniper Ct KKNTL G66 65 H4
Juniper Dr KKNTL G66 45 H5
Juniper Gn AYRS KA7 229 K3
Juniper Gv HMLTN ML3 156 F7
Juniper Pl CAR/SHTL G32 107 M5
JNSTN PA5 123 G1
UD/BTH/TAN G71 132 D1
Juniper Rd UD/BTH/TAN G71 132 D1
Juniper Ter CAR/SHTL G32 107 L5
Juno St MTHW ML1 133 K8
Juno Ter GRNKW/INVK PA16 31 K6
Jupiter St MTHW ML1 133 K8
Jupiter Ter GRNKW/INVK PA16 31 K6
Jura EKILN G74 15 M7
Jura Av RNFRW PA4 80 D8
Jura Dr BLTYR/CAMB G72 131 J6
NMRNS G77 150 B3
OLDK G60 59 J4
Jura Gdns CARLUKE ML8 189 G1
HMLTN ML3 156 A7
LRKH ML9 176 C6
Jura Pl TROON KA10 216 E2
Jura Qd WISHAW ML2 158 E8
Jura Rd OLDK G60 59 J4
PSLYS PA2 124 D2
Jura St CARD/HILL/MSPK G52 103 M4
GRNKW/INVK PA16 32 C5
Jura Wynd CTBR ML5 87 J3
Jutland Ct HBR/GL G84 20 A7

K

Kaim Dr PLK/PH/NH G53 126 C3
Kaim Vw FAIRLIE KA29 139 K7
Kames Bay GTCI KA28 138 C6
Kames Ct IRVSE KA11 204 B3
Kames Rd SHOTTS ML7 137 L3
Kames St GTCI KA28 138 B6
Kane St DMBTN G82 25 K7
Karadale Gdns LRKH ML9 176 A7
Katewell Av DRUM G15 60 E5
Katewell Pl DRUM G15 60 E5
Katherine Pl DMBTN G82 25 L7
Katherine St AIRDRIE ML6 111 L1
Kathleen Pk HBR/GL G84 20 A6
Katrine Av BSHPBGS G64 64 B8
Katrine Ct KLMNK KA1 212 A4
Katrine Crs AIRDRIE ML6 88 F8
Katrine Dr NMRNS G77 151 H5
PSLYS PA2 100 F7
Katrine Pl BLTYR/CAMB G72 130 A3
CTBR ML5 87 K8
IRV KA12 203 K3
Katrine Rd GRNK PA15 2 F8
SHOTTS ML7 137 L3
WMYSB PA18 70 A1
Kay Gdns MTHW ML1 157 H3
Kay Park Crs KLMNKN/STW KA3 17 J2
Kay Park Ter KLMNKN/STW KA3 17 H3
Kaystone Rd DRUM G15 61 G8
Kay St SPRGB/BLRNK G21 83 M5
Keal Av DRUM G15 61 H8
Keal Crs DRUM G15 81 G1
Keal Dr DRUM G15 81 G1
Keal Pl DRUM G15 81 G1
Kearn Av DRUM G15 61 H8
Kearn Pl DRUM G15 61 H8
Keats Pk UD/BTH/TAN G71 132 B6
Keil Crs DMBTN G82 36 D6
Keir Crs WISHAW ML2 159 H5
Keir Dr BSHPBGS G64 63 M7
Keir Hardie Av MTHW ML1 134 B4
Keir Hardie Crs KLWNG KA13 194 A6
Keir Hardie Dr ARD KA22 191 H5
BLSH ML4 132 F5
KBRN KA25 143 G8
KSYTH G65 47 K2
Keir Hardie Pl SALT KA21 192 A7
Keir Hardie Rd LRKH ML9 176 B8
SVSTN KA20 192 E8
Keir Hardie St GRNK PA15 33 L7
Keir's Wk BLTYR/CAMB G72 130 A3
Keith Av GIF/THBK G46 127 J6
Keith Ct PTCK G11 82 C7
Keith Pl KLMNKN/STW KA3 207 J7
Keith Qd WISHAW ML2 159 H4
Keith St BLSH ML4 133 G3
HMLTN ML3 156 F5
PTCK G11 82 C7
Kelbourne Crs BLSH ML4 132 F4
Kelbourne St MRYH/FIRH G20 82 E5
Kelburn Av FAIRLIE KA29 139 L5
Kelburn Br FAIRLIE KA29 139 L3
Kelburn Ct LARGS KA30 115 J6
Kelburn Crs KLMNK KA1 211 L5
Kelburne Dr PSLY PA1 102 B4
Kelburne Gdns
BAIL/MDB/MHD G69 108 A6
PSLY PA1 9 M2
Kelburne Ov PSLY PA1 9 M3
Kelburn St BRHD/NEIL G78 125 G8
GTCI KA28 138 B6
Kelburn Ter FAIRLIE KA29 139 K6
PGL PA14 34 F8
Kelhead Av
CARD/HILL/MSPK G52 102 F5
Kelhead Dr
CARD/HILL/MSPK G52 102 F4
Kelhead Pth
CARD/HILL/MSPK G52 102 F4
Kelhead Pl PSLY PA1 102 F4
Kellas St GOV/IBX G51 104 A2
Kellie Gv EKILN G74 153 K6
Kellock Crs CTBR ML5 109 K5
Kells Pl DRUM G15 60 E5
Kelly St GRNK PA15 2 B2
GRNKW/INVK PA16 32 D4
Kelso Av BRWEIR PA11 98 C2
PSLYS PA2 101 G8
RUTH G73 129 H2
Kelso Crs WISHAW ML2 159 H3
Kelso Dr CARLUKE ML8 179 H8
EKILN G74 154 A6
Kelso Gdns
BAIL/MDB/MHD G69 66 F6
Kelso Pl SCOT G14 80 E3
Kelso Qd CTBR ML5 109 M1
Kelso St KNTSWD G13 80 F1
SCOT G14 80 E3
Kelton St CAR/SHTL G32 107 H5
Kelvin Av CARD/HILL/MSPK G52 102 F1
KLWNG KA13 193 M8
Kelvin Ct KKNTL G66 45 J8
Kelvin Crs BSDN G61 61 M7
Kelvindale Gdns
MRYH/FIRH G20 82 C3
Kelvindale Pl MRYH/FIRH G20 82 D3
Kelvindale Rd KVD/HLHD G12 82 C4
Kelvin Dr AIRDRIE ML6 89 H8
BAIL/MDB/MHD G69 66 E7
BRHD/NEIL G78 125 K8
BSHPBGS G64 64 A7
EKILS G75 15 H8
KKNTL G66 65 G1
MRYH/FIRH G20 82 D5
Kelvin Gdns HMLTN ML3 155 L5
KSYTH G65 47 K2
LARGS KA30 115 J3
Kelvingrove St KVGV G3 4 A8
Kelvinhaugh Ga KVGV G3 104 D1
Kelvinhaugh Pl KVGV G3 104 D1
Kelvinhaugh St KVGV G3 104 D1
Kelvin Pk South EKILS G75 172 A5
Kelvin Pl EKILS G75 15 J8
Kelvin Rd BLSH ML4 133 H2
CUMB G67 69 G1
EKILS G75 15 H7
MLNGV G62 41 L6
UD/BTH/TAN G71 131 L2
Kelvin Rd North CUMB G67 69 G1
Kelvinside Av MRYH/FIRH G20 4 C1
MRYH/FIRH G20 82 E5
Kelvinside Dr MRYH/FIRH G20 4 C1
Kelvinside Gdns MRYH/FIRH G20 4 B1
Kelvinside Gdns East
MRYH/FIRH G20 4 C2
Kelvinside Gardens La
MRYH/FIRH G20 4 B1
Kelvinside Ter South
MRYH/FIRH G20 4 A2
Kelvinside Ter West
MRYH/FIRH G20 4 A2
Kelvin St CTBR ML5 110 C4
LARGS KA30 115 K5
Kelvinvale KKNTL G66 45 K8
Kelvin Vw BSHPBGS G64 64 C1
KSYTH G65 46 F7
Kelvin Wk LARGS KA30 115 J3
Kelvin Wy KKNTL G66 65 G1
KVGV G3 82 D8
Kemp Av PSLYN/LNWD PA3 80 A8
Kempock Pl GRK PA19 31 L1
Kempock St DMNK/BRGTN G40 13 J8
GRK PA19 31 L1
Kempsthorn Cresent
PLK/PH/NH G53 103 G8
Kempsthorn Rd
PLK/PH/NH G53 103 G8
Kemp St HMLTN ML3 156 D6
SPRGB/BLRNK G21 6 B1
Kenbank Crs BRWEIR PA11 98 D1
Kenbank Rd BRWEIR PA11 98 D1
Kendal Av GIF/THBK G46 127 J6
KVD/HLHD G12 82 A3
Kendal Dr KVD/HLHD G12 82 A3
Kendal Rd EKILS G75 170 F3
Kendoon Av DRUM G15 60 E6
Kenilburn Av AIRDRIE ML6 89 H7
Kenilburn Crs AIRDRIE ML6 89 H7
Kenilworth EKILN G74 154 D5
Kenilworth Av HBR/GL G84 23 G2
PLKSD/SHW G41 127 K1
PSLYS PA2 123 M1
WISHAW ML2 159 H6
Kenilworth Ct CARLUKE ML8 178 E8
Kenilworth Crs BLSH ML4 133 G3
BSDN G61 61 J3
GRNKW/INVK PA16 32 D6
HMLTN ML3 155 M5
Kenilworth Dr AIRDRIE ML6 111 J1
SALT KA21 192 A7
Kenilworth Rd KKNTL G66 65 L1
LNK/LMHG ML11 199 H5
Kenllworth Ct CUMB G67 68 E1
Kenmar Gdns
UD/BTH/TAN G71 131 L1
Kenmar Rd HMLTN ML3 156 B4
Kenmar Ter HMLTN ML3 156 B4
Kenmore TROON KA10 216 D5
Kenmore Av PSTWK KA9 225 J3
Kenmore Dr GRNKW/INVK PA16 32 A5
Kenmore Gdns BSDN G61 62 B4
Kenmore Pl GRNKW/INVK PA16 32 A5
Kenmore Rd CUMB G67 49 H7
KLMCLM PA13 75 J2
Kenmore St CAR/SHTL G32 107 G4
Kenmuiraid Pl BLSH ML4 132 F6
Kenmuir Av CAR/SHTL G32 107 L6
Kenmuirhill Rd CAR/SHTL G32 107 K7
Kenmuir Rd CAR/SHTL G32 130 D1
Kenmuir St CTBR ML5 109 H5
Kenmure Av BSHPBGS G64 63 L8
Kenmure Crs BSHPBGS G64 63 M8
Kenmure Dr BSHPBGS G64 63 M8
Kenmure Gdns BSHPBGS G64 63 L8
Kenmure La BSHPBGS G64 63 M8
Kenmure Rd GIF/THBK G46 151 H3
Kenmure St PLKSD/SHW G41 104 F6
Kenmure Vw HWWD PA9 121 L4
Kenmure Wy RUTH G73 129 H6
Kennedar Dr GOV/IBX G51 103 L1
Kennedy Ct
KLMNKN/STW KA3 207 J6
Kennedy Dr AIRDRIE ML6 110 E2
HBR/GL G84 20 D5
KLMNKN/STW KA3 207 J6
Kennedy Gdns WISHAW ML2 177 H2
Kennedy Rd SALT KA21 200 F1
TROON KA10 216 A7
Kennedy St COWCAD G4 5 M7
KLMNK KA1 16 E8
WISHAW ML2 159 J6
Kennelburn Rd AIRDRIE ML6 111 K8
Kenneth Rd MTHW ML1 157 J4
Kennihill AIRDRIE ML6 89 G8
Kennihill Qd AIRDRIE ML6 89 G8
Kennishead Av GIF/THBK G46 126 E4
Kennishead Pl GIF/THBK G46 126 E4
Kennishead Rd
GIF/THBK G46 126 F5
Kennisholm Av GIF/THBK G46 126 E4
Kennoway Dr PTCK G11 81 M7
Kennyhill Sq DEN/PKHD G31 7 H9
Ken Rd KLMNK KA1 212 A4
Kensington Dr GIF/THBK G46 127 K8
Kensington Ga
KVD/HLHD G12 82 C5
Kensington Gate La
KVD/HLHD G12 82 C5
Kensington Rd KVD/HLHD G12 82 C5
Kentallen Rd
STPS/GTHM/RID G33 107 K3
Kent Dr HBR/GL G84 21 G6
RUTH G73 129 K4
Kentigern Ter BSHPBGS G64 84 A1
Kentmere Cl EKILS G75 171 G3
Kentmere Dr EKILS G75 171 G3
Kentmere Pl EKILS G75 170 F3
Kent Pl EKILS G75 170 F3
Kent Rd KVGV G3 4 B8
Kent St CGLE G1 12 A4
Keppel Dr LNPK/KPK G44 128 E2
Keppenburn Av FAIRLIE KA29 139 L5
Keppochhill Dr COWCAD G4 5 L3
Keppochhill Rd COWCAD G4 5 K3
Keppoch St SPRGB/BLRNK G21 5 M2
Kerelaw Av SVSTN KA20 192 E7
Kerelaw Rd SVSTN KA20 192 D8
Kerfield Pl DRUM G15 60 E5
Kerr Av SALT KA21 201 G1
Kerr Crs HMLTN ML3 156 C8
Kerr Dr DMNK/BRGTN G40 12 C6
IRV KA12 203 K7
MTHW ML1 157 J3
Kerrera Pl
STPS/GTHM/RID G33 107 K3
Kerrera Rd
STPS/GTHM/RID G33 107 K3
Kerr Gdns UD/BTH/TAN G71 132 A1
Kerrix Rd PSTWK KA9 217 L8
Kerrmuir Av KLMNK KA1 212 F4
Ker Rd MLNGV G62 41 L6
Kerr Pl DMNK/BRGTN G40 12 C6
IRV KA12 203 K7
Kerrs La SALT KA21 200 E1
Kerr St BLTYR/CAMB G72 155 L1
BRHD/NEIL G78 125 G7
DMNK/BRGTN G40 12 C6
KKNTL G66 65 J1
PSLYN/LNWD PA3 8 F2
Kerrycroy Av GVH/MTFL G42 128 D1
Kerrycroy Pl GVH/MTFL G42 128 D1
Kerrycroy St GVH/MTFL G42 128 D1
Kerrydale St DMNK/BRGTN G40 13 H7
Kerrylamont Av
GVH/MTFL G42 128 D2
Kerry Pl DRUM G15 60 E6
Kerse Av DALRY KA24 184 E2
Kersepark AYRS KA7 229 G8
Kershaw St WISHAW ML2 177 J3
Kersland Crs KLMNK KA1 212 E3
Kersland Dr MLNGV G62 42 B7
Kersland Gait
KLMNKN/STW KA3 197 L1
Kersland La KVD/HLHD G12 82 D6
MLNGV G62 42 B7
Kersland Rd GLGNK KA14 167 J3
Kersland St KVD/HLHD G12 82 D6
Ker St GRNK PA15 2 C1
Kerswinning Av KBRN KA25 166 F2
Kessington Dr BSDN G61 62 A5
Kessington Rd BSDN G61 62 A6
Kessock Dr PPK/MIL G22 5 H2
Kessock Pl PPK/MIL G22 5 H2
Kestrel Ct CLYDBK G81 60 A4
Kestrel Crs GRNKW/INVK PA16 32 A4
Kestrel Pl GRNKW/INVK PA16 32 A4
JNSTN PA5 122 D2
Kestrel Rd KNTSWD G13 81 J3
Keswick Dr HMLTN ML3 174 C3
Keswick Rd EKILS G75 170 F3
Kethers La MTHW ML1 157 H3
Kethers St MTHW ML1 157 J2
Kevoc Cotts RAYR/DAL KA6 226 A4
Kew Gdns UD/BTH/TAN G71 132 B2
Kew La KVD/HLHD G12 82 D6
Kew Ter KVD/HLHD G12 82 D5
Keystone Av MLNGV G62 62 A1
Keystone Qd MLNGV G62 61 M1
Keystone Rd MLNGV G62 62 A1
Kibbleston Rd KLBCH PA10 99 G8
Kidsneuk IRV KA12 203 G3
Kidsneuk Gdns IRV KA12 203 G3
Kidston Dr HBR/GL G84 20 A7
Kierhill Rd BALLOCH G68 48 C7
Kilallan Av BRWEIR PA11 76 D8
Kilallan Rd CRG/CRSL/HOU PA6 75 M2
CRG/CRSL/HOU PA6 77 G5
Kilbarchan Rd JNSTN PA5 98 F3
JNSTN PA5 99 K8
KLBCH PA10 99 J7
Kilbarchan St GBLS G5 11 G6
Kilbeg Ter GIF/THBK G46 126 D6
Kilberry St SPRGB/BLRNK G21 6 E7
Kilbirnie St GBLS G5 10 F7
Kilblain St GRNK PA15 2 C3
Kilbowie Pl AIRDRIE ML6 111 K4
Kilbowie Rd CLYDBK G81 60 B8
CUMB G67 69 G1
Kilbrandon Crs AYRS KA7 228 B7
Kilbrandon Wy AYRS KA7 228 B7
Kilbrannan Av SALT KA21 191 M7
Kilbrannan Dr
GRNKW/INVK PA16 32 B6
Kilbreck Gdns BSDN G61 61 J1
Kilbrennan Dr MTHW ML1 157 G2
Kilbrennan Rd
PSLYN/LNWD PA3 100 B3
Kilbride Dr HBR/GL G84 20 E6
Kilbride St GBLS G5 105 K7
Kilbride Vw
UD/BTH/TAN G71 132 A2
Kilburn Gv BLTYR/CAMB G72 131 K8
Kilburn Pl KNTSWD G13 81 H3
Kilburn Water LARGS KA30 115 L2
Kilchattan Dr LNPK/KPK G44 128 C2
Kilchattan Pl WMYSB PA18 50 A7
Kilchoan Rd
STPS/GTHM/RID G33 85 J7
Kilcloy Av DRUM G15 61 G5
Kilcreggan Vw GRNK PA15 33 J7
Kildale Rd LOCHW PA12 120 B7
Kildale Wy RUTH G73 128 F1
Kildare Dr LNK/LMHG ML11 199 H5
Kildare Pl LNK/LMHG ML11 199 H5
Kildare Rd LNK/LMHG ML11 199 G5
Kildary Av LNPK/KPK G44 128 A4
Kildary Rd LNPK/KPK G44 128 A4
Kildermorie Rd ESTRH G34 107 M1
Kildonan Ct WISHAW ML2 159 M2
Kildonan Dr HBR/GL G84 20 F7
PTCK G11 82 A7
Kildonan Pl MTHW ML1 157 J2
SALT KA21 191 M7
Kildonan St CTBR ML5 110 B2
Kildrostan St
PLKSD/SHW G41 104 F7
Kildrummy Pl EKILN G74 153 K6
Kildrum Rd CUMB G67 49 J7
Kilearn Rd PSLYN/LNWD PA3 102 B2
Kilearn Wy PSLYN/LNWD PA3 102 B2
Kilfinan Rd SHOTTS ML7 137 K3
Kilfinan St PPK/MIL G22 83 H2
Kilgarth St CTBR ML5 109 H5
Kilgraston Rd BRWEIR PA11 98 D3
Kilkerran Ct NMRNS G77 150 B5
Kilkerran Dr
STPS/GTHM/RID G33 84 F3
TROON KA10 216 D2
Kilkerran Pk NMRNS G77 150 B5
Kilkerran Wy NMRNS G77 150 B5
Killearn Dr PSLY PA1 102 F5
Killearn Rd GRNK PA15 33 H7
Killearn St PPK/MIL G22 5 K1
Killermont Av BSDN G61 62 B7
Killermont Mdw
UD/BTH/TAN G71 131 L7
Killermont Pl KLWNG KA13 193 H6
Killermont Rd BSDN G61 61 M6
Killermont St CGLE G1 5 J8
Killermont Vw MRYH/FIRH G20 62 A7
Killiegrew Rd PLKSD/SHW G41 104 D7
Killin Dr PSLYN/LNWD PA3 99 M4
Killin Pl GRNKW/INVK PA16 32 A5
TROON KA10 216 D5
Killin St CAR/SHTL G32 107 H6
Killoch Av PSLYN/LNWD PA3 101 G4
Killoch Dr BRHD/NEIL G78 125 K8
KNTSWD G13 81 G2
Killoch La PSLYN/LNWD PA3 101 G4
Killoch Pl IRVSE KA11 203 M5
Killoch Rd PSLYN/LNWD PA3 101 G4
Killoch Wy IRVSE KA11 203 M5
PSLYN/LNWD PA3 101 G4
Kilmacolm Pl GRNK PA15 33 J8
Kilmacolm Rd BRWEIR PA11 76 B7
CRG/CRSL/HOU PA6 77 H6
GRNK PA15 3 H9
PGL PA14 54 F2
Kilmahew Av DMBTN G82 24 A8
Kilmahew Ct DMBTN G82 24 A8
Kilmahew Dr DMBTN G82 24 A8
Kilmahew Gv DMBTN G82 24 B8
Kilmahew St ARD KA22 191 J8
Kilmailing Rd LNPK/KPK G44 128 B4
Kilmair Pl MRYH/FIRH G20 82 D4
Kilmaluag Ter GIF/THBK G46 126 D6
Kilmany Dr CAR/SHTL G32 106 F4
Kilmany Gdns CAR/SHTL G32 106 F4
Kilmardinny Av BSDN G61 61 M3
Kilmardinny Crs BSDN G61 62 A3
Kilmardinny Dr BSDN G61 61 M3
Kilmardinny Ga BSDN G61 61 M4
Kilmardinny Gv BSDN G61 61 M3
Kilmarnock Rd CRH/DND KA2 206 A8
CRH/DND KA2 209 M7
IRVSE KA11 205 G7
KLMNK KA1 218 C8
KLMNKN/STW KA3 206 C2
PLKSW/MSWD G43 127 K3
PSTWK KA9 221 L4
TROON KA10 216 D3
Kilmartin Pl GIF/THBK G46 126 E5
UD/BTH/TAN G71 109 G8
Kilmaurs Dr GIF/THBK G46 127 L6
Kilmaurs Rd CRH/DND KA2 205 L8
KLMNKN/STW KA3 206 F6
Kilmaurs St GOV/IBX G51 103 M3
Kilmeny Crs WISHAW ML2 159 J4
Kilmeny Ter ARD KA22 191 K8
Kilmichael Av WISHAW ML2 160 A3
Kilmorie Dr RUTH G73 128 E2
Kilmory Av UD/BTH/TAN G71 132 A2
Kilmory Ct EKILS G75 171 H5
Kilmory Dr NMRNS G77 150 E3
Kilmory Gdns CARLUKE ML8 178 F6
Kilmory Pl KLMNKN/STW KA3 206 E5
TROON KA10 216 F4
Kilmory Rd CARLUKE ML8 189 H1
SALT KA21 191 M7
Kilmuir Crs GIF/THBK G46 126 D5
Kilmuir Dr GIF/THBK G46 126 E5
Kilmuir Rd GIF/THBK G46 126 D6
UD/BTH/TAN G71 108 F8
Kilmun Rd GRNK PA15 2 E8
Kilmun St MRYH/FIRH G20 82 D2
Kilnbank Crs AYRS KA7 229 K2
Kilnburn Rd MTHW ML1 157 J2
Kilncadzow Rd CARLUKE ML8 179 H8
Kilnford Crs CRH/DND KA2 209 K7
Kilnford Dr CRH/DND KA2 209 K7
Kilnholm St NMLNS KA16 215 J2
Kilnside Rd PSLY PA1 9 K3
Kilnwell Qd MTHW ML1 157 K2
Kiloran Gv NMRNS G77 150 A5
Kiloran Pl NMRNS G77 150 A5
Kiloran St GIF/THBK G46 126 F5
Kilpatrick Av PSLYS PA2 8 B8
Kilpatrick Crs PSLYS PA2 101 K8
Kilpatrick Dr BSDN G61 61 J1
EKILS G75 171 H6
ERSK PA8 59 H7
RNFRW PA4 102 B1
Kilpatrick Gdns
CRMNK/CLK/EAG G76 151 K2
Kilpatrick Pl IRVSE KA11 204 A7
Kilpatrick Vw DMBTN G82 37 H5
Kilpatrick Wy
UD/BTH/TAN G71 132 A1
Kilrig Av KLWNG KA13 193 L5
Kilruskin Dr WKIL KA23 181 J6
Kilsyth Crs IRVSE KA11 204 A6
Kilsyth Rd KKNTL G66 45 K8
KSYTH G65 46 E2
Kiltarie Crs AIRDRIE ML6 111 M3
Kiltearn Rd
STPS/GTHM/RID G33 107 M2
Kilvaxter Dr GIF/THBK G46 126 E6
Kilwinning Crs HMLTN ML3 155 L8
Kilwinning Rd DALRY KA24 184 B3
IRV KA12 203 H5
KLMNKN/STW KA3 197 J1
SVSTN KA20 192 E8
Kimberley Gdns EKILS G75 14 A6
Kimberley St CLYDBK G81 59 K4
WISHAW ML2 158 C6
Kinalty Rd PLKSW/MSWD G43 128 A4
Kinarvie Crs PLK/PH/NH G53 125 M2
Kinarvie Pl PLK/PH/NH G53 125 M2
Kinarvie Rd PLK/PH/NH G53 125 M2

Kinarvie Ter *PLK/PH/NH* G53 ...... 125 M2
Kinbuck St *PPK/MIL* G22 ...... 5 L1
Kincaid Dr *KKNTL* G66 ...... 29 J8
Kincaid Fld *KKNTL* G66 ...... 45 J4
Kincaid Gdns *BLTYR/CAMB* G72 .. 130 A5
Kincaidston Dr *AYRS* KA7 ...... 229 J7
Kincaid St *GRNKW/INVK* PA16 ... 32 B1
Kincaid Wy *KKNTL* G66 ...... 45 H4
Kincardine Dr *BSHPBGS* G64 ...... 84 B1
Kincardine Pl *EKILN* G74 ...... 154 C6
SPRGB/BLRNK G21 ...... 84 C2
Kincardine Sq
STPS/GTHM/RID G33 ...... 85 K8
Kincath Av *RUTH* G73 ...... 129 J6
Kinclaven Av *DRUM* G15 ...... 61 G6
Kincraig St *GOV/IBX* G51 ...... 103 K3
Kinellan Rd *BSDN* G61 ...... 61 M8
Kinellar Dr *SCOT* G14 ...... 81 G3
Kinfauns Dr *DRUM* G15 ...... 60 F6
DRUM G15 ...... 61 J6
NMRNS G77 ...... 150 F4
Kingarth La *GVH/MTFL* G42 ...... 105 G7
Kingarth St *HMLTN* ML3 ...... 174 D1
PLKSD/SHW G41 ...... 105 G7
Kingcase Av *PSTWK* KA9 ...... 225 H3
King Edward La *KNTSWD* G13 ... 81 L4
King Edward Rd
KNTSWD G13 ...... 81 M4
King Edward St *ALEX/LLW* G83 .. 25 L3
Kingfisher Dr *KNTSWD* G13 ...... 80 F2
King George Ct *RNFRW* PA4 ...... 80 E8
King George Gdns
RNFRW PA4 ...... 80 E7
King George Park Av
RNFRW PA4 ...... 80 E8
King George Pl *RNFRW* PA4 ...... 80 E8
King George Wy *RNFRW* PA4 ...... 80 E8
Kinghorn Dr *LNPK/KPK* G44 ...... 128 C3
Kinglas Rd *BSDN* G61 ...... 61 J7
King Pl *BAIL/MDB/MHD* G69 ...... 109 G4
Kingsacre Rd *LNPK/KPK* G44 ...... 128 C2
RUTH G73 ...... 128 E2
Kingsbarns Dr *LNPK/KPK* G44 ...... 128 B2
Kingsborough Gdns
KVD/HLHD G12 ...... 82 B5
Kingsborough Ga
KVD/HLHD G12 ...... 82 B6
Kingsborough La
KVD/HLHD G12 ...... 82 B6
Kingsborough La East
KVD/HLHD G12 ...... 82 B6
Kingsbrae Av *LNPK/KPK* G44 ...... 128 C2
Kingsbridge Crs *LNPK/KPK* G44 .. 128 D3
Kingsbridge Dr
LNPK/KPK G44 ...... 128 C3
RUTH G73 ...... 128 E3
Kingsburgh Dr *PSLY* PA1 ...... 102 B4
Kingsburn Dr *RUTH* G73 ...... 129 G3
Kingsburn Gv *RUTH* G73 ...... 129 G3
Kingscliffe Av *LNPK/KPK* G44 ...... 128 C2
Kings Ct *AYR* KA8 ...... 19 G1
BEITH KA15 ...... 144 B8
Kingscourt Av
LNPK/KPK G44 ...... 128 D3
King's Crs *BLTYR/CAMB* G72 ...... 130 B4
CARLUKE ML8 ...... 179 G7
HBR/GL G84 ...... 20 E8
JNSTN PA5 ...... 100 C6
NMLNS KA16 ...... 215 K2
Kingscroft Rd *PSTWK* KA9 ...... 225 H2
Kingsdale Av *LNPK/KPK* G44 ... 128 C2
King's Dr *BALLOCH* G68 ...... 48 F3
DMNK/BRGTN G40 ...... 12 A8
MTHW ML1 ...... 133 M6
NMRNS G77 ...... 150 F6
Kingsdyke Av *LNPK/KPK* G44 ...... 128 D2
Kingsford Av *LNPK/KPK* G44 ...... 127 L5
Kingsford Ct *NMRNS* G77 ...... 150 B3
King's Gdns *NMRNS* G77 ...... 151 G6
Kingsheath Av *RUTH* G73 ...... 128 E3
Kingshill Av *BALLOCH* G68 ...... 47 L8
Kingshill Dr *LNPK/KPK* G44 ...... 128 C3
Kingshill Rd *SHOTTS* ML7 ...... 161 G1
Kingshill Vw *CARLUKE* ML8 ...... 178 A5
Kingshouse Av *LNPK/KPK* G44 ...... 128 C2
Kingshurst Av *LNPK/KPK* G44 ...... 128 C3
King's Inch Rd *RNFRW* PA4 ...... 80 F5
Kingsknowe Dr *RUTH* G73 ...... 128 E3
Kingsland Dr
CARD/HILL/MSPK G52 ...... 103 H3
Kingslea Rd *CRG/CRSL/HOU* PA6 .. 77 H7
Kingsley Av *GVH/MTFL* G42 ...... 105 H8
Kingsley Ct *UD/BTH/TAN* G71 ...... 132 A2
Kingslynn Dr *LNPK/KPK* G44 ...... 128 D3
Kings Myre *LNK/LMHG* ML11 ...... 199 J5
Kings Pk *BSHPBGS* G64 ...... 44 C8
King's Park Av *LNPK/KPK* G44 ...... 128 B3
RUTH G73 ...... 128 E3
King's Park Rd *LNPK/KPK* G44 ...... 128 B2
King's Pl *PPK/MIL* G22 ...... 83 H3
King's Rd *BEITH* KA15 ...... 144 B8
JNSTN PA5 ...... 100 B7
Kingston Av *AIRDRIE* ML6 ...... 111 J2
BRHD/NEIL G78 ...... 148 D3
UD/BTH/TAN G71 ...... 132 A1
Kingston Gv *BSHPTN* PA7 ...... 58 B6
Kingston Pl *CLYDBK* G81 ...... 59 J5
Kingston Rd *BRHD/NEIL* G78 ...... 148 C4
BSHPTN PA7 ...... 58 C5
Kingston St *GBLS* G5 ...... 10 F4
King St *AYR* KA8 ...... 19 G1
CGLE G1 ...... 11 K4
CLYDBK G81 ...... 80 D1
CTBR ML5 ...... 109 L3
DMBTN G82 ...... 25 K8
GRK PA19 ...... 31 L2
GRNK PA15 ...... 2 D4
HMLTN ML3 ...... 155 M5
KLMNK KA1 ...... 16 F4
KLWNG KA13 ...... 193 L5
KSYTH G65 ...... 47 K1
LRKH ML9 ...... 176 A6
NMLNS KA16 ...... 215 K2
PGL PA14 ...... 34 C7
PSLY PA1 ...... 8 C3
RUTH G73 ...... 129 G1
SHOTTS ML7 ...... 137 L4
WISHAW ML2 ...... 159 H7
WISHAW ML2 ...... 159 M4
King St East *HBR/GL* G84 ...... 20 D8
King Street La *RUTH* G73 ...... 129 G1
King's Vw *BALLOCH* G68 ...... 48 F3
King's Wy *DMBTN* G82 ...... 36 C4
Kingsway *DALRY* KA24 ...... 184 A1
EKILN G74 ...... 15 K5
GRK PA19 ...... 31 K3
KKNTL G66 ...... 46 B7
SCOT G14 ...... 81 H4
Kingsway Ct *SCOT* G14 ...... 81 H4
Kingswell Av *KLMNKN/STW* KA3 .. 207 G4
Kingswood Dr *LNPK/KPK* G44 ...... 128 C3
Kingswood Rd *BSHPTN* PA7 ...... 57 M5
Kingussie Dr *LNPK/KPK* G44 ...... 128 C3
Kiniver Dr *DRUM* G15 ...... 61 G8
Kinkell Gdns *KKNTL* G66 ...... 46 B7
Kinloch Av *BLTYR/CAMB* G72 ...... 130 B5
PSLYN/LNWD PA3 ...... 100 A4
Kinloch Dr *MTHW* ML1 ...... 133 K7
Kinloch Rd *KLMNK* KA1 ...... 212 A4
NMRNS G77 ...... 150 C3
RNFRW PA4 ...... 80 B8
Kinloch St *DMNK/BRGTN* G40 ...... 13 J7
Kinloch Ter *GRNKW/INVK* PA16 ...... 31 L6
Kinloss Pl *EKILN* G74 ...... 15 H1
Kinmount Av *LNPK/KPK* G44 ...... 128 B2
Kinnaird Av *NMRNS* G77 ...... 151 G4
Kinnaird Crs *BSDN* G61 ...... 62 B4
Kinnaird Dr *PSLYN/LNWD* PA3 ...... 100 B3
Kinnaird Pl *BSHPBGS* G64 ...... 84 B1
Kinnear Rd *DMNK/BRGTN* G40 ...... 13 G9
Kinneil Pl *HMLTN* ML3 ...... 155 M7
Kinnell Av
CARD/HILL/MSPK G52 ...... 103 J6
Kinnell Crs
CARD/HILL/MSPK G52 ...... 103 J6
Kinnell Pl *CARD/HILL/MSPK* G52 .. 103 K6
Kinnier Rd *SALT* KA21 ...... 201 G1
Kinning St *GBLS* G5 ...... 10 D5
Kinnis Vennel *KLWNG* KA13 ...... 193 J4
Kinnoul La *KVD/HLHD* G12 ...... 82 C6
Kinnoull Pl *BLTYR/CAMB* G72 ...... 155 K2
Kinnoull Rd *KLMNK* KA1 ...... 212 A6
Kinpurnie Rd *PSLY* PA1 ...... 102 D4
Kinross Av
CARD/HILL/MSPK G52 ...... 103 H5
PGL PA14 ...... 34 C8
Kinross Pk *EKILN* G74 ...... 154 D6
Kinsail Dr
CARD/HILL/MSPK G52 ...... 102 F3
Kinstone Av *SCOT* G14 ...... 81 G4
Kintessack Pl *BSHPBGS* G64 ...... 64 D7
Kintillo Dr *KNTSWD* G13 ...... 81 H3
Kintore Pk *HMLTN* ML3 ...... 174 B2
Kintore Rd *PLKSW/MSWD* G43 ...... 127 M3
Kintra St *GOV/IBX* G51 ...... 104 B2
Kintyre Av *PSLYN/LNWD* PA3 ...... 100 A5
Kintyre Crs *AIRDRIE* ML6 ...... 89 M6
NMRNS G77 ...... 150 C3
Kintyre Gdns *KKNTL* G66 ...... 46 B7
Kintyre Rd *BLTYR/CAMB* G72 ...... 155 J1
Kintyre St *SPRGB/BLRNK* G21 ...... 6 E7
Kintyre Ter *GRNKW/INVK* PA16 ...... 31 K6
Kip Av *GRNKW/INVK* PA16 ...... 50 D5
Kipland Wk *CTBR* ML5 ...... 110 D4
Kippen Dr
CRMNK/CLK/EAG G76 ...... 152 B4
Kippen St *AIRDRIE* ML6 ...... 110 D3
PPK/MIL G22 ...... 83 K3
Kipperoch Rd *DMBTN* G82 ...... 36 A2
Kippford Pl *AIRDRIE* ML6 ...... 111 M8
Kippford St *CAR/SHTL* G32 ...... 107 J5
Kipps Av *AIRDRIE* ML6 ...... 110 E1
Kirkaig Av *RNFRW* PA4 ...... 80 F7
Kirkbean Av *RUTH* G73 ...... 129 G5
Kirkbriggs Gdns *RUTH* G73 ...... 129 H4
Kirkburn Av *BLTYR/CAMB* G72 ...... 130 A5
Kirkburn Dr *CMPF/LLE* G63 ...... 27 J6
Kirkburn Rd *CMPF/LLE* G63 ...... 27 J6
Kirkcaldy Rd *PLKSD/SHW* G41 ...... 104 D7
Kirkconnel Av *BALLOCH* G68 ...... 47 L8
KNTSWD G13 ...... 80 F3
Kirkconnel Dr *RUTH* G73 ...... 128 F4
Kirk Crs *OLDK* G60 ...... 59 G2
Kirkcudbright Pl *EKILN* G74 ...... 154 D5
Kirkdale Dr
CARD/HILL/MSPK G52 ...... 103 L5
Kirkdene Av *NMRNS* G77 ...... 151 H4
Kirkdene Bank *NMRNS* G77 ...... 151 H4
Kirkdene Crs *NMRNS* G77 ...... 151 H4
Kirkdene Gv *NMRNS* G77 ...... 151 H4
Kirkdene Pl *NMRNS* G77 ...... 151 H4
Kirkfieldbank Brae
LNK/LMHG ML11 ...... 198 D5
Kirkfield Bank Wy
HMLTN ML3 ...... 156 A6
Kirkfield Rd *LNK/LMHG* ML11 ...... 198 D6
UD/BTH/TAN G71 ...... 132 A6
Kirkfield Wynd *HWWD* PA9 ...... 121 L4
Kirkford Rd
BAIL/MDB/MHD G69 ...... 66 E7
Kirkgate *IRV* KA12 ...... 203 J7
SALT KA21 ...... 200 F1
WISHAW ML2 ...... 159 M5
Kirk Glebe *KLMNKN/STW* KA3 ...... 197 K1
Kirkhall Gdns *ARD* KA22 ...... 191 K7
Kirkhall Rd *MTHW* ML1 ...... 134 D5
Kirkhill Av *BLTYR/CAMB* G72 ...... 130 A6
Kirkhill Crs *BRHD/NEIL* G78 ...... 148 E1
PSTWK KA9 ...... 225 H3
Kirkhill Dr *MRYH/FIRH* G20 ...... 82 D4
Kirkhill Gdns *BLTYR/CAMB* G72 .. 130 A6
Kirkhill Ga *NMRNS* G77 ...... 151 H5
Kirkhill Gv *BLTYR/CAMB* G72 ...... 130 A6
Kirkhill Pl *MRYH/FIRH* G20 ...... 82 D4
WISHAW ML2 ...... 158 C7
Kirkhill Rd *BAIL/MDB/MHD* G69 ...... 86 F4
NMRNS G77 ...... 151 H4
UD/BTH/TAN G71 ...... 131 L1
WISHAW ML2 ...... 158 C8
Kirkhill St *WISHAW* ML2 ...... 158 D8
Kirkhill Ter *BLTYR/CAMB* G72 ...... 130 A6
Kirkholm Av *AYR* KA8 ...... 225 G5
Kirkhope Dr *DRUM* G15 ...... 61 H7
Kirkhouse Av *CMPF/LLE* G63 ...... 27 H5
Kirkhouse Crs *CMPF/LLE* G63 ...... 27 J5
Kirkhouse Rd *CMPF/LLE* G63 ...... 27 H5
Kirkinner Rd *CAR/SHTL* G32 ...... 107 K6
Kirkintilloch Rd *BSHPBGS* G64 ...... 83 M1
KKNTL G66 ...... 45 G7
KKNTL G66 ...... 65 K2
KKNTL G66 ...... 66 B1
Kirkland Av *CMPF/LLE* G63 ...... 27 J5
Kirkland Crs *DALRY* KA24 ...... 184 A2
Kirkland Gdns
KLMNKN/STW KA3 ...... 206 C3
Kirkland Gv *JNSTN* PA5 ...... 99 M6
Kirklandholm *PSTWK* KA9 ...... 225 J3
Kirkland La *ALEX/LLW* G83 ...... 25 M6
Kirklandneuk Rd *RNFRW* PA4 ...... 80 A5
Kirkland Rd *GLGNK* KA14 ...... 167 H2
Kirklands Crs *KSYTH* G65 ...... 47 K2
UD/BTH/TAN G71 ...... 132 A6
Kirklands Pl *NMRNS* G77 ...... 150 D7
Kirklands Rd *LNK/LMHG* ML11 ...... 199 G6
NMRNS G77 ...... 150 D7
Kirkland St *MRYH/FIRH* G20 ...... 4 D2
MTHW ML1 ...... 157 K2
Kirkland Ter *IRVSE* KA11 ...... 204 F7
Kirk La *BSDN* G61 ...... 61 L4
PLKSW/MSWD G43 ...... 127 J2
Kirklea Gdns
PSLYN/LNWD PA3 ...... 101 G4
Kirkle Dr *NMRNS* G77 ...... 151 G4
Kirklee Circ *KVD/HLHD* G12 ...... 82 C5
KVD/HLHD G12 ...... 82 D5
Kirklee Gdns *KVD/HLHD* G12 ...... 82 C5
Kirklee Gardens La
KVD/HLHD G12 ...... 82 C5
Kirklee Pl *KVD/HLHD* G12 ...... 82 D5
Kirklee Qd *KVD/HLHD* G12 ...... 82 D5
Kirklee Quadrant La
KVD/HLHD G12 ...... 82 D5
Kirklee Rd *BLSH* ML4 ...... 133 K5
KVD/HLHD G12 ...... 82 C5
MTHW ML1 ...... 133 L8
Kirklee Ter *KVD/HLHD* G12 ...... 82 C5
Kirklee Terrace La
KVD/HLHD G12 ...... 82 D5
Kirklee Terrace Rd
KVD/HLHD G12 ...... 82 C5
Kirkliston St *CAR/SHTL* G32 ...... 106 F3
Kirkmichael Av *PTCK* G11 ...... 82 A6
Kirkmichael Gdns *PTCK* G11 ...... 82 A6
Kirkmichael Rd *HBR/GL* G84 ...... 20 F8
Kirkmuir Dr *RUTH* G73 ...... 129 H6
Kirkness St *AIRDRIE* ML6 ...... 111 G1
Kirknethan *WISHAW* ML2 ...... 158 C8
Kirknewton St
CAR/SHTL G32 ...... 107 H3
Kirkoswald *EKILN* G74 ...... 154 D6
Kirkoswald Dr *CLYDBK* G81 ...... 60 D6
Kirkoswald Rd *MTHW* ML1 ...... 134 E5
PLKSW/MSWD G43 ...... 127 K3
Kirkpatrick Crs *ALEX/LLW* G83 ... 25 K2
Kirkpatrick St
DMNK/BRGTN G40 ...... 12 E7
Kirk Pl *BSDN* G61 ...... 61 L4
CUMB G67 ...... 68 A2
Kirk Port *AYRS* KA7 ...... 18 F3
Kirkport *MAUCH/CAT* KA5 ...... 223 M6
Kirkriggs Av *RUTH* G73 ...... 129 H4
Kirk Rd *BEITH* KA15 ...... 168 C1
BSDN G61 ...... 61 L4
CARLUKE ML8 ...... 178 E7
CRG/CRSL/HOU PA6 ...... 77 H6
CRMNK/CLK/EAG G76 ...... 152 D2
LRKH ML9 ...... 177 H7
MTHW ML1 ...... 134 D2
SHOTTS ML7 ...... 137 M5
WISHAW ML2 ...... 159 K6
Kirkshaws Av *CTBR* ML5 ...... 109 L6
Kirkshaws Pl *CTBR* ML5 ...... 109 M6
Kirkshaws Rd *CTBR* ML5 ...... 109 L6
Kirkstall Gdns *BSHPBGS* G64 ...... 64 B5
Kirkstone Cl *EKILS* G75 ...... 170 F3
Kirk St *CARLUKE* ML8 ...... 178 E7
CTBR ML5 ...... 109 M3
MLNGV G62 ...... 41 L7
MTHW ML1 ...... 157 L2
PSTWK KA9 ...... 221 J7
Kirkstyle Av *CARLUKE* ML8 ...... 178 E8
Kirkstyle Crs *AIRDRIE* ML6 ...... 88 F7
BRHD/NEIL G78 ...... 148 D2
Kirkstyle La *BRHD/NEIL* G78 ...... 148 E2
Kirkstyle Pl *AIRDRIE* ML6 ...... 88 D5
Kirksyde Av *KKNTL* G66 ...... 65 K2
Kirkton *ERSK* PA8 ...... 59 G6
Kirkton Av *BLTYR/CAMB* G72 ...... 155 J4
BRHD/NEIL G78 ...... 125 H7
CARLUKE ML8 ...... 178 E8
KNTSWD G13 ...... 81 G3
WKIL KA23 ...... 181 K5
Kirkton Ct *CARLUKE* ML8 ...... 178 E8
Kirkton Crs *CTBR* ML5 ...... 110 D5
DMBTN G82 ...... 24 A8
KKNTL G66 ...... 45 J4
KNTSWD G13 ...... 81 G3
Kirktonfield Rd *BRHD/NEIL* G78 .. 148 E2
Kirkton Ga *EKILN* G74 ...... 14 F2
Kirktonholme Crs *EKILN* G74 ...... 14 D2
Kirktonholme Rd *EKILN* G74 ...... 14 A2
EKILN G74 ...... 153 H7
Kirkton Pk *EKILN* G74 ...... 15 H2
Kirkton Pl *CTBR* ML5 ...... 110 D5
EKILN G74 ...... 15 H2
Kirkton Rd *BLTYR/CAMB* G72 ...... 130 B4
BRHD/NEIL G78 ...... 148 E3
DMBTN G82 ...... 35 G1
DMBTN G82 ...... 36 D7
KLMNKN/STW KA3 ...... 206 C3
KLMNKN/STW KA3 ...... 206 F4
Kirktonside *BRHD/NEIL* G78 ...... 125 H8
Kirkton St *CARLUKE* ML8 ...... 178 F8
Kirkton Ter *KKNTL* G66 ...... 28 F6
Kirkvale Ct *NMRNS* G77 ...... 151 H4
Kirkvale Crs *NMRNS* G77 ...... 151 H4
Kirkvale Dr *NMRNS* G77 ...... 151 H4
Kirk Vennel *IRV* KA12 ...... 203 J7
Kirk Vw *BEITH* KA15 ...... 144 B8
Kirkview *CUMB* G67 ...... 68 A3
Kirkview Av *SHOTTS* ML7 ...... 113 J7
Kirkview Ct *CUMB* G67 ...... 68 A3
Kirkview Crs *NMRNS* G77 ...... 150 E6
Kirkview Gdns
UD/BTH/TAN G71 ...... 131 L1
Kirkville Pl *DRUM* G15 ...... 61 H8
Kirkwall *CUMB* G67 ...... 49 H4
Kirkwall Av *BLTYR/CAMB* G72 ...... 131 J6
Kirkwall Rd *GRNKW/INVK* PA16 ...... 31 M6
Kirkwell Rd *LNPK/KPK* G44 ...... 128 B4
Kirkwood Av *CLYDBK* G81 ...... 60 E8
Kirkwood Pl *CTBR* ML5 ...... 109 L5
Kirkwood St *CTBR* ML5 ...... 109 L4
GOV/IBX G51 ...... 104 C4
RUTH G73 ...... 129 G1
Kirn Dr *GRK* PA19 ...... 31 J3
Kirn Rd *KLMNKN/STW* KA3 ...... 206 F7
Kirn St *MRYH/FIRH* G20 ...... 82 C1
Kirriemuir *EKILN* G74 ...... 154 D4
Kirriemuir Av
CARD/HILL/MSPK G52 ...... 103 J6
Kirriemuir Gdns *BSHPBGS* G64 ...... 64 C7
Kirriemuir Pl
CARD/HILL/MSPK G52 ...... 103 J5
Kirriemuir Rd *BSHPBGS* G64 ...... 64 C8
Kirstie Pl *ALEX/LLW* G83 ...... 25 M7
Kirtle Dr *RNFRW* PA4 ...... 80 E7
Kirtle Pl *EKILS* G75 ...... 170 E2
Kishorn Pl *STPS/GTHM/RID* G33 ...... 85 J8
Kishorn Rd *WMYSB* PA18 ...... 70 A1
Kitchener St *WISHAW* ML2 ...... 159 G6
Kittoch Pl *EKILN* G74 ...... 15 G2
Kittochside Rd
CRMNK/CLK/EAG G76 ...... 152 E2
Kittoch St *EKILN* G74 ...... 14 F2
Kittyshaw Rd *DALRY* KA24 ...... 184 A2
Klondike Ct *MTHW* ML1 ...... 134 B6
Knapdale St *PPK/MIL* G22 ...... 83 G2
Knightsbridge St *KNTSWD* G13 ...... 81 K3
Knightscliffe Av *KNTSWD* G13 ...... 81 K1
Knights Ga *UD/BTH/TAN* G71 ...... 131 L4
Knightswood Rd *KNTSWD* G13 ...... 81 K1
Knightswood Ter
BLTYR/CAMB G72 ...... 131 L8
Knivysbridge Pl *BLSH* ML4 ...... 132 F6
Knockbuckle Av
KLMCLM PA13 ...... 55 H8
Knockbuckle Rd *KLMCLM* PA13 ...... 75 H1
Knockburnie Rd
UD/BTH/TAN G71 ...... 132 A5
Knockhall St
STPS/GTHM/RID G33 ...... 85 K7
Knockhill Dr *LNPK/KPK* G44 ...... 128 B2
Knockhill Rd *RNFRW* PA4 ...... 80 B8
Knockinlaw Rd
KLMNKN/STW KA3 ...... 206 E5
Knockmarloch Dr *KLMNK* KA1 ...... 211 M6
Knocknair St *PGL* PA14 ...... 54 E1
Knockrivoch Gdns *ARD* KA22 ...... 191 L5
Knockrivoch Pl *ARD* KA22 ...... 191 L6
Knockrivoch Wynd *ARD* KA22 ...... 191 L5
Knockside Av *PSLYS* PA2 ...... 124 D2
Knoll Pk *AYRS* KA7 ...... 228 F6
Knollpark Dr
CRMNK/CLK/EAG G76 ...... 151 K2
Knowe Crs *MTHW* ML1 ...... 134 D5
Knowehead Dr
UD/BTH/TAN G71 ...... 131 L3
Knowehead Gdns
PLKSD/SHW G41 ...... 10 C9
UD/BTH/TAN G71 ...... 131 L3
Knowehead Rd *KKNTL* G66 ...... 28 F5
KLMNK KA1 ...... 211 M5
KLMNK KA1 ...... 212 F4
KLMNK KA1 ...... 213 G4
WISHAW ML2 ...... 159 J7
Knowehead Ter
PLKSD/SHW G41 ...... 10 B9
Knoweholm *AYRS* KA7 ...... 228 C7
Knowenoble St *MTHW* ML1 ...... 135 H7
Knowe Rd *BAIL/MDB/MHD* G69 ...... 86 C1
GRNK PA15 ...... 3 H6
PSLYN/LNWD PA3 ...... 102 B2
Knowes Av *NMRNS* G77 ...... 150 E4
Knowes Rd *NMRNS* G77 ...... 150 F4
Knowe St *MLNGV* G62 ...... 41 M7
Knowetap St *MRYH/FIRH* G20 ...... 82 E2
The Knowe *TROON* KA10 ...... 216 F2
Knowetop Av *MTHW* ML1 ...... 157 M4
Knowetop Crs *DMBTN* G82 ...... 36 C4
Knox Av *BRWEIR* PA11 ...... 98 C2
Knoxland Sq *DMBTN* G82 ...... 37 G6
Knox Pl *NMRNS* G77 ...... 150 B5
SALT KA21 ...... 192 A8
Knox St *AIRDRIE* ML6 ...... 111 H1
PSLY PA1 ...... 8 B4
Knoxville Rd *KBRN* KA25 ...... 143 H8
Kronborg Wy *EKILS* G75 ...... 171 L4
Kyleakin Dr
BLTYR/CAMB G72 ...... 131 H7
Kyleakin Rd *GIF/THBK* G46 ...... 126 D6
Kyleakin Ter *GIF/THBK* G46 ...... 126 D6
Kyle Av *IRVSE* KA11 ...... 204 F7
Kyle Crs *RAYR/DAL* KA6 ...... 231 H4
TROON KA10 ...... 217 G5
Kyle Dr *GIF/THBK* G46 ...... 127 L6
TROON KA10 ...... 216 D4
Kyle Gv *MTHW* ML1 ...... 134 A6
Kylemore Crs *MTHW* ML1 ...... 133 K7
MTHW ML1 ...... 133 K8
Kylemore Ter *GRNKW/INVK* PA16 .. 31 K6
Kylepark Av *UD/BTH/TAN* G71 ...... 131 K3
Kylepark Crs *UD/BTH/TAN* G71 ...... 131 K2
Kylepark Dr *UD/BTH/TAN* G71 ...... 131 K2
Kyle Qd *WISHAW* ML2 ...... 158 E8
Kylerhea Rd *GIF/THBK* G46 ...... 126 D6
Kyle Rd *CUMB* G67 ...... 49 H7
IRV KA12 ...... 208 B1
Kyleshill *SALT* KA21 ...... 200 F2
Kyle Sq *CSMK* G45 ...... 128 F4
The Kyles *WMYSB* PA18 ...... 70 A1
Kyle St *AYRS* KA7 ...... 18 F4
COWCAD G4 ...... 5 L7
MTHW ML1 ...... 157 H2
PSTWK KA9 ...... 225 J1
Kyles Vw *LARGS* KA30 ...... 115 L5
Kyle Ter *DMBTN* G82 ...... 36 B5

L

La Belle Allee *KVGV* G3 ...... 4 B7
La Belle Pl *KVGV* G3 ...... 4 B7
Laberge Gdns *MTHW* ML1 ...... 134 B6
Laburnum Av *BEITH* KA15 ...... 168 A1
EKILS G75 ...... 171 J3
Laburnum Ct *EKILS* G75 ...... 14 B9
Laburnum Crs *WISHAW* ML2 ...... 159 H4
Laburnum Dr *KKNTL* G66 ...... 45 H4
Laburnum Gdns *KKNTL* G66 ...... 65 H4
Laburnum Gv *CTBR* ML5 ...... 110 B3
Laburnum Lea *HMLTN* ML3 ...... 156 E8
Laburnum Pl *JNSTN* PA5 ...... 123 G1
Laburnum Rd *AYRS* KA7 ...... 19 M7
CUMB G67 ...... 49 K7
KLMNK KA1 ...... 211 J2
PLKSD/SHW G41 ...... 104 C5
UD/BTH/TAN G71 ...... 109 J8
Laburnum St *GRNK* PA15 ...... 33 M7
Lachlan Crs *ERSK* PA8 ...... 58 E8
Lacy St *PSLY* PA1 ...... 9 M3
Ladder Ct *EKILS* G75 ...... 171 H5
Lade Ct *LOCHW* PA12 ...... 120 C7
Ladeside *KLMNKN/STW* KA3 ...... 206 C2
NMLNS KA16 ...... 215 L2
Ladeside Cl *NMRNS* G77 ...... 150 C3
Ladeside Ct *KBRN* KA25 ...... 143 G8
Ladeside Dr *JNSTN* PA5 ...... 99 K7
Ladeside Rd *KLMNKN/STW* KA3 .. 206 C2
Lade St *LARGS* KA30 ...... 115 J6
Lade Ter *CARD/HILL/MSPK* G52 .. 103 G5
The Lade *ALEX/LLW* G83 ...... 25 M4
Ladhope Pl *KNTSWD* G13 ...... 80 E1
Ladyacre *KLWNG* KA13 ...... 193 L5
Ladyacre Rd *LNK/LMHG* ML11 ...... 199 H5
Ladyacres *RNFRW* PA4 ...... 79 K3
Ladyacres Wy *RNFRW* PA4 ...... 79 K3
Lady Ann Crs *AIRDRIE* ML6 ...... 111 J3
Lady Anne St *SCOT* G14 ...... 80 F4
Ladybank *BALLOCH* G68 ...... 48 F3
Ladybank Ct *EKILN* G74 ...... 14 F2
Ladybank Dr
CARD/HILL/MSPK G52 ...... 103 L5
Ladybank Gdns *EKILN* G74 ...... 14 F2
Ladybank Pl *EKILN* G74 ...... 14 F2
Ladyburn Ct *IRVSE* KA11 ...... 203 M3
Ladyburn St *GRNK* PA15 ...... 3 M9
PSLY PA1 ...... 9 L4
Ladyford Av *KLWNG* KA13 ...... 193 L6
Ladyhill Dr
BAIL/MDB/MHD G69 ...... 108 A5
Lady Isle Crs *UD/BTH/TAN* G71 ...... 131 L3
Lady Jane Ga *UD/BTH/TAN* G71 .. 131 L5
Ladykirk Crs
CARD/HILL/MSPK G52 ...... 103 H3
PSLYS PA2 ...... 9 K7
Ladykirk Dr
CARD/HILL/MSPK G52 ...... 103 H3
Ladykirk Rd *PSTWK* KA9 ...... 225 J1
Ladyland Dr *KBRN* KA25 ...... 143 H6
Lady La *PSLY* PA1 ...... 8 F5
Ladyloan Av *DRUM* G15 ...... 60 F5
Ladyloan Ct *DRUM* G15 ...... 60 E5
Ladyloan Gdns *DRUM* G15 ...... 60 F5
Lady Margaret Dr *TROON* KA10 .. 217 G7
Ladymuir Cir *ERSK* PA8 ...... 58 F8
Ladymuir Crs *PLK/PH/NH* G53 ...... 103 J7
Lady's Ga *ALEX/LLW* G83 ...... 25 M8
Ladysmith Av *KLBCH* PA10 ...... 99 J7
Ladysmith Rd *KBRN* KA25 ...... 143 G8
Ladysmith St *WISHAW* ML2 ...... 158 C6
Ladyton *ALEX/LLW* G83 ...... 25 M6
Ladyton Dr *GLSTN* KA4 ...... 214 B3
Lady Watson Gdns
HMLTN ML3 ...... 156 A7
Ladywell Rd *MTHW* ML1 ...... 157 H3
Ladywell St *COWCAD* G4 ...... 12 B1
Lady Wilson St *AIRDRIE* ML6 ...... 111 H2
Ladywood *MLNGV* G62 ...... 42 B7
Lagan Rd *CARLUKE* ML8 ...... 178 F8
Laggan Qd *AIRDRIE* ML6 ...... 88 E8
Laggan Rd *AIRDRIE* ML6 ...... 88 F8
BSHPBGS G64 ...... 64 B8
NMRNS G77 ...... 150 D2
PLKSW/MSWD G43 ...... 127 L4
Laggan Ter *RNFRW* PA4 ...... 80 B5
Laidlaw Av *MTHW* ML1 ...... 133 M6
Laidlaw Gdns
UD/BTH/TAN G71 ...... 108 F8
Laidlaw St *GBLS* G5 ...... 10 E6
Laidon Rd *AIRDRIE* ML6 ...... 88 F8
Laighcartside St *JNSTN* PA5 ...... 100 A6
Laigh Ct *BEITH* KA15 ...... 144 B8
Laighdykes Rd *SALT* KA21 ...... 191 L8
Laighland *PSTWK* KA9 ...... 225 J4
Laighlands Rd
UD/BTH/TAN G71 ...... 132 B7
Laigh Mt *AYRS* KA7 ...... 229 G8
Laighmuir St *UD/BTH/TAN* G71 .. 131 M4
Laighpark Av *BSHPTN* PA7 ...... 58 B6
Laighpark Ct *RAYR/DAL* KA6 ...... 231 G5
Laighpark Rd *RAYR/DAL* KA6 ...... 231 G5
Laighpark Vw
PSLYN/LNWD PA3 ...... 101 L2
RAYR/DAL KA6 ...... 231 G5
Laigh Rd *BEITH* KA15 ...... 144 B8
NMRNS G77 ...... 151 H4
Laighstonehall Rd *HMLTN* ML3 .. 156 B7
Laightoun Ct *CUMB* G67 ...... 68 A3
Laightoun Dr *CUMB* G67 ...... 68 A3
Laightoun Gdns *CUMB* G67 ...... 68 A3
Lainshaw Av *KLMNK* KA1 ...... 211 M5
Lainshaw Dr *CSMK* G45 ...... 128 B7
LNPK/KPK G44 ...... 128 A7
Lainshaw St *KLMNKN/STW* KA3 .. 197 K1
Laird Gv *UD/BTH/TAN* G71 ...... 132 A1
Laird Pl *DMNK/BRGTN* G40 ...... 12 C8
Lairds Ga *UD/BTH/TAN* G71 ...... 131 K4
Lairds Hl *CUMB* G67 ...... 48 E7
Laird's Hill Ct *KSYTH* G65 ...... 47 G1
Laird's Hill Pl *KSYTH* G65 ...... 47 G1
Laird St *CTBR* ML5 ...... 110 B2
GRNK PA15 ...... 2 D2
Laird Weir *ARD* KA22 ...... 191 K6
Lairg Dr *BLTYR/CAMB* G72 ...... 131 J7

Lairhills Rd EKILS G75 .... 14 F7
Lake Av LNK/LMHG ML11 .... 199 K6 1
Lamberton Dr
CARD/HILL/MSPK G52 .... 103 H3
Lamberton Gdns IRVSE KA11 .... 204 C4
Lambhill St PLKSD/SHW G41 .... 104 D4
Lambie Crs NMRNS G77 .... 150 C4 1
Lamb St HMLTN ML3 .... 156 E6 3
PPK/MIL G22 .... 83 H3
Lamerton Rd CUMB G67 .... 49 J7
Lamford Dr AYRS KA7 .... 228 C8
Lamington Rd
CARD/HILL/MSPK G52 .... 103 H5
Lamlash Crs
STPS/GTHM/RID G33 .... 107 H1
Lamlash Pl EKILS G75 .... 171 H5
HBR/GL G84 .... 20 F7 1
MTHW ML1 .... 157 J2
STPS/GTHM/RID G33 .... 107 H1 1
Lammermoor EKILN G74 .... 154 E5
Lammermoor Av
CARD/HILL/MSPK G52 .... 103 J6
Lammermoor Crs KKNTL G66 .... 65 M1
Lammermoor Dr CUMB G67 .... 68 E2
Lammermoor Rd KKNTL G66 .... 65 M2
Lammermoor Ter WISHAW ML2 .. 159 H6
Lammermuir Ct PSLYS PA2 .... 124 E1 1
Lammermuir Dr PSLYS PA2 .... 124 D1
Lammermuir Gdns BSDN G61 .... 61 J2
Lammermuir Rd KLMNK KA1 .... 212 A6
Lammermuir Wy AIRDRIE ML6 .... 111 M8
Lammermuir Wynd
LRKH ML9 .... 175 M4 1
Lamont Av BSHPTN PA7 .... 58 C6
Lamont Crs DMBTN G82 .... 25 K7
Lamont Dr IRV KA12 .... 208 C1
Lamont Pl IRV KA12 .... 208 C1
Lamont Rd SPRGB/BLRNK G21 .... 84 B3
Lanark Av AIRDRIE ML6 .... 110 F5
Lanark Rd CARLUKE ML8 .... 178 F8
LRKH ML9 .... 175 L2
LRKH ML9 .... 176 C3
Lancaster Av AIRDRIE ML6 .... 134 E1
BEITH KA15 .... 168 B2 1
Lancaster Crs KVD/HLHD G12 .... 82 C5
Lancaster Crescent La
KVD/HLHD G12 .... 82 C5 10
Lancaster Rd BSHPBGS G64 .... 64 B5
Lancefield Quay KVGV G3 .... 10 A2
Lancefield St KVGV G3 .... 10 C2
Landemer Dr RUTH G73 .... 128 F3
Landressy Pl DMNK/BRGTN G40 .. 12 B7
Landressy St DMNK/BRGTN G40 .. 12 C7
Landsborough Dr
KLMNKN/STW KA3 .... 207 G6
Landsborough Pl
SVSTN KA20 .... 192 F7 1
Landsdowne Gdns
HMLTN ML3 .... 156 F6 2
Landsdowne Rd LRKH ML9 .... 176 C7 2
The Lane BALLOCH G68 .... 48 D3
SKLM PA17 .... 70 B5
Lanfine Rd PSLY PA1 .... 102 C5
Lanfine Ter IRVSE KA11 .... 203 M3
Lanfine Wy IRVSE KA11 .... 203 M3
Langa St MRYH/FIRH G20 .... 82 E2
Lang Av BSHPTN PA7 .... 58 C6 2
RNFRW PA4 .... 80 D8
Langbank Dr KLMCLM PA13 .... 55 L8
Langbank Ri KLMCLM PA13 .... 55 L8
Langbar Crs
STPS/GTHM/RID G33 .... 107 M2 2
Langbyres Rd MTHW ML1 .... 135 K8 1
Langcraig Rd KLMNK KA1 .... 211 M7 1
Langcraigs Ct PSLYS PA2 .... 124 C1 2
Langcraigs Dr PSLYS PA2 .... 124 C3
Langcraigs Ter PSLYS PA2 .... 124 C3 3
Langcroft Av PSTWK KA9 .... 221 L8
Langcroft Dr BLTYR/CAMB G72 .. 130 C5
Langcroft Pl GOV/IBX G51 .... 103 J2 1
Langcroft Rd GOV/IBX G51 .... 103 K2
Langcroft Ter GOV/IBX G51 .... 103 K2 2
Langdale EKILN G74 .... 153 J6
Langdale Av
STPS/GTHM/RID G33 .... 84 E6
Langdales Av BALLOCH G68 .... 48 C7
Langdale St
STPS/GTHM/RID G33 .... 84 E6
Langfaulds Crs CLYDBK G81 .... 60 E3 1
Langford Dr PLK/PH/NH G53 .... 126 A6
Langford Pl PLK/PH/NH G53 ... 126 B6 3
Langhill Dr BALLOCH G68 .... 48 D6
Langholm EKILS G75 .... 170 F3
Langholm Crs WISHAW ML2 .... 159 H3
Langholm Dr PSLYN/LNWD PA3 .. 100 B4
Langhouse Av
GRNKW/INVK PA16 .... 50 E4
Langhouse Pl
GRNKW/INVK PA16 .... 50 E4 3
Langhouse Rd
GRNKW/INVK PA16 .... 50 E4
Langlands Av EKILS G75 .... 171 M5
GOV/IBX G51 .... 103 K2 3
Langlands Ct EKILS G75 .... 172 A5
GOV/IBX G51 .... 103 M2 3
Langlands Dr EKILS G75 .... 171 M5
GOV/IBX G51 .... 103 J1
MAUCH/CAT KA5 .... 223 M7
Langlands Pl EKILS G75 .... 171 M5
Langlands Rd EKILS G75 .... 171 L7
GOV/IBX G51 .... 103 K2
Langlands Sq EKILS G75 .... 171 M6
Langlands St KLMNK KA1 .... 16 E3
Langlands Ter DMBTN G82 .... 37 H3
Langlea Av BLTYR/CAMB G72 .... 129 K5
Langlea Ct BLTYR/CAMB G72 .... 129 L5
Langlea Dr BLTYR/CAMB G72 .... 129 L4
Langlea Gdns
BLTYR/CAMB G72 .... 129 L4 4
Langlea Gv BLTYR/CAMB G72 .... 129 L5
Langlea Rd BLTYR/CAMB G72 .... 129 L5
Langlees Av NMRNS G77 .... 151 H4
Langley Av KNTSWD G13 .... 81 H2
Langloan Crs CTBR ML5 .... 109 L3 1
Langloan Pl CTBR ML5 .... 109 L3
Langloan St CTBR ML5 .... 109 L4
Langmuir Av IRVSE KA11 .... 204 C4
KKNTL G66 .... 45 L8
Langmuirhead Rd KKNTL G66 .... 85 G1
Langmuir Rd
BAIL/MDB/MHD G69 .... 109 G4
KKNTL G66 .... 45 M8
Langmuir Wy CTBR ML5 .... 109 G4
Langness Rd
STPS/GTHM/RID G33 .... 107 H1
Langoreth Av HMLTN ML3 .... 155 M7
Lang Pl JNSTN PA5 .... 99 L6
Langrig Rd NMRNS G77 .... 150 C6
SPRGB/BLRNK G21 .... 84 A5
Lang Rd TROON KA10 .... 216 E2 5
Langshaw Crs CARLUKE ML8 .... 178 F7
Langshot St GOV/IBX G51 .... 104 D4 3
Langside Av KLMNK KA1 .... 211 M6
PLKSD/SHW G41 .... 104 E8
UD/BTH/TAN G71 .... 132 C3
Langside Ct
UD/BTH/TAN G71 .... 132 B8 3
Langside Dr KLBCH PA10 .... 99 G7
PLKSW/MSWD G43 .... 127 L5
Langside Gdns
GVH/MTFL G42 .... 128 A2 4
Langside La GVH/MTFL G42 .... 105 G8
Langside Pk KLBCH PA10 .... 99 G7
Langside Pl KBRN KA25 .... 143 G8
PLKSD/SHW G41 .... 127 M1
Langside Rd GVH/MTFL G42 .... 105 G7
UD/BTH/TAN G71 .... 132 B8
Langside St CLYDBK G81 .... 60 D3
Langside Ter PGL PA14 .... 54 D1
Langstile Rd
CARD/HILL/MSPK G52 .... 102 F4
Lang St PSLY PA1 .... 9 L4
Langton Crs BRHD/NEIL G78 .... 125 K8
PLK/PH/NH G53 .... 103 J8
Langton Gdns
BAIL/MDB/MHD G69 .... 107 M5 5
Langton Ga NMRNS G77 .... 150 C4
Langton Pl NMRNS G77 .... 150 C4
Langton Rd PLK/PH/NH G53 .... 126 C1
Langtree Av GIF/THBK G46 .... 127 G8
Lanrig Pl BAIL/MDB/MHD G69 .... 86 B1
Lanrig Rd BAIL/MDB/MHD G69 .... 66 C8
Lansbury Gdns
PSLYN/LNWD PA3 .... 101 K2 1
Lansbury St ALEX/LLW G83 .... 25 K1
GRNK PA15 .... 33 M7
Lansbury Ter LRKH ML9 .... 176 C8
Lansdowne Crs MRYH/FIRH G20 .... 4 C4
Lansdowne Crescent La
COWCAD G4 .... 4 C4
Lansdowne Dr BALLOCH G68 .... 48 F5
Lansdowne Rd AYR KA8 .... 225 G5
Lantana Gv MTHW ML1 .... 157 K1 1
Lanton Dr
CARD/HILL/MSPK G52 .... 103 H4
Lanton Rd PLKSW/MSWD G43 .... 127 L4
Lappin St CLYDBK G81 .... 80 D1
Laputa Pl KLMNK KA1 .... 211 L6
Larbert St CGLW G2 .... 5 H7
Larch Av BSHPBGS G64 .... 84 B1
KKNTL G66 .... 65 J4
Larch Ct BLTYR/CAMB G72 .... 155 J1
CUMB G67 .... 49 L5
EKILS G75 .... 171 H4 3
Larch Crs KKNTL G66 .... 65 J3
Larch Dr EKILS G75 .... 171 H4
The Larches
BAIL/MDB/MHD G69 .... 67 G5
Larchfield Av NMRNS G77 .... 150 E5
SCOT G14 .... 81 H5
WISHAW ML2 .... 159 K3
Larchfield Ct NMRNS G77 .... 150 D5 2
Larchfield Crs WISHAW ML2 .... 159 J3
Larchfield Dr RUTH G73 .... 129 J5
Larchfield Gdns
WISHAW ML2 .... 159 K3 1
Larchfield Gv WISHAW ML2 .... 159 K2 1
Larchfield Pl SCOT G14 .... 81 H5 2
Larchfield Rd BSDN G61 .... 61 M8
Larch Gv CUMB G67 .... 49 K5
HMLTN ML3 .... 156 E7
KKNTL G66 .... 45 H4
Larchgrove Av CAR/SHTL G32 .. 107 J3 4
Larchgrove Pl CAR/SHTL G32 .. 107 J2 2
Larchgrove Rd CAR/SHTL G32 .. 107 J2
Larch Pl EKILS G75 .... 171 H4 4
JNSTN PA5 .... 122 F1
KLMNK KA1 .... 16 B5
UD/BTH/TAN G71 .... 132 D1
Larch Rd CUMB G67 .... 49 K5
PLKSD/SHW G41 .... 104 B5
Larch Ter BEITH KA15 .... 168 C1
Larchwood Rd AYRS KA7 .... 229 J5
Larchwood Ter
BRHD/NEIL G78 .... 149 K1 2
Larghill La AYRS KA7 .... 19 K9
Largie Rd LNPK/KPK G44 .... 127 M4
Largo Pl GOV/IBX G51 .... 103 L2 2
Largs Av KLMNKN/STW KA3 .... 207 H6
WKIL KA23 .... 163 H5
Largs Rd KBRN KA25 .... 142 B8
Larkfield Ct BLTYR/CAMB G72 .... 155 J3
Larkfield Dr BLTYR/CAMB G72 .... 155 K3
Larkfield Gv
GRNKW/INVK PA16 .... 31 M5 2
Larkfield Rd GRK PA19 .... 31 L3 4
GRNKW/INVK PA16 .... 31 M4
KKNTL G66 .... 65 L4
Larkfield St GVH/MTFL G42 .... 105 H6 2
Larkin Gdns
PSLYN/LNWD PA3 .... 101 K2 2
Larksfield Dr CARLUKE ML8 .... 189 G1 5
Larkspur Dr EKILN G74 .... 153 J5
Larkspur Wy CARLUKE ML8 .... 188 F1 4
Lashley Gv WISHAW ML2 .... 177 J2
Lasswade St SCOT G14 .... 80 E3 1
Latherton Dr MRYH/FIRH G20 .. 82 D4 3
Latimer Gdns
CARD/HILL/MSPK G52 .... 103 G5 4
Latta Ct PSTWK KA9 .... 225 K3
Latta St DMBTN G82 .... 37 G5
Lauchope Rd MTHW ML1 .... 134 D2
Lauchope St AIRDRIE ML6 .... 111 L7
Lauder Ct KLMNKN/STW KA3 .... 207 J6 3
Lauder Crs WISHAW ML2 .... 159 H3 2
Lauderdale Dr NMRNS G77 .... 150 C6
Lauderdale Gdns PTCK G11 .... 82 B6
Lauderdale La KVD/HLHD G12 .... 82 B6
Lauder Dr PSLYN/LNWD PA3 .... 100 B4
RUTH G73 .... 129 K2 2
RUTH G73 .... 129 K3 2
Lauder Gdns BLTYR/CAMB G72 .. 131 J7
CTBR ML5 .... 110 D6
Lauder Gn EKILN G74 .... 154 B5 1
Lauder St GBLS G5 .... 10 F8 2
Laudervale Gdns
ALEX/LLW G83 .... 25 K1 3
Laughland Dr MTHW ML1 .... 134 D6
Laughlanglen Rd AYRS KA7 .... 229 G7
Laundry La STPS/GTHM/RID G33 .. 85 J4
Lauranne Pl BLSH ML4 .... 132 E4 1
Laurel Av CLYDBK G81 .... 59 K5
KKNTL G66 .... 65 K3
Laurel Bank AYRS KA7 .... 229 J5
Laurelbank CTBR ML5 .... 110 A1
Laurel Bank HMLTN ML3 .... 174 C1
Laurelbank Rd
BAIL/MDB/MHD G69 .... 86 B2 2
CAR/SHTL G32 .... 130 C1 7
Laurel Ct EKILS G75 .... 171 K4
Laurel Dr EKILS G75 .... 171 K4
LRKH ML9 .... 176 C7
WISHAW ML2 .... 158 D5
Laurel Gdns AIRDRIE ML6 .... 111 L7
UD/BTH/TAN G71 .... 131 M1
Laurel Gv AIRDRIE ML6 .... 69 M7
Laurel Park Gdns
KNTSWD G13 .... 81 J4 1
Laurel Pl EKILS G75 .... 171 K4 2
KLMNK KA1 .... 16 A6
PTCK G11 .... 82 A7
The Laurels NMRNS G77 .... 150 D4 2
Laurel St PTCK G11 .... 82 A7
Laurel Wy BRHD/NEIL G78 .... 125 H6
Laurence Dr BSDN G61 .... 61 K3
Lauren Vw AIRDRIE ML6 .... 110 F2
Lauren Wy PSLYS PA2 .... 100 F8 2
Laurieland Av CRH/DND KA2 .. 205 L8 1
Laurieston Rd GBLS G5 .... 11 H7
Laurieston Wy RUTH G73 .... 129 G5 1
Lauriston Gv NMRNS G77 .... 150 B4
Lavelle Dr CTBR ML5 .... 110 C2
Lavender Dr EKILS G75 .... 171 K4
Lavender La CARLUKE ML8 .... 188 E1 1
Laverock Av
GRNKW/INVK PA16 .... 32 D6 4
HMLTN ML3 .... 157 G7
Laverock Dr LARGS KA30 .... 115 K4
Laverockhall LNK/LMHG ML11 .... 199 H4
Laverockhall St
SPRGB/BLRNK G21 .... 6 C3
Laverock Rd AIRDRIE ML6 .... 89 H7
Laverock Ter
BAIL/MDB/MHD G69 .... 66 F8
Law Brae WKIL KA23 .... 181 K4
Law Dr MTHW ML1 .... 134 C5
Lawer Pl IRVSE KA11 .... 204 A5
Lawers Crs KLMNK KA1 .... 212 A5 2
Lawers Dr BSDN G61 .... 61 H2
Lawers Pl GRNKW/INVK PA16 .... 32 A5 7
Lawers Rd KLMNK KA1 .... 212 A5 3
PLKSW/MSWD G43 .... 127 H4
RNFRW PA4 .... 80 B8
Lawfield Av NMRNS G77 .... 151 H4
WKIL KA23 .... 181 K4
Lawhill Av CSMK G45 .... 128 D5 1
Lawhill Rd CARLUKE ML8 .... 177 M4
KLMNK KA1 .... 218 C5 1
Lawhope Mill Rd AIRDRIE ML6 .... 111 M6
Lawmarnock Crs
BRWEIR PA11 .... 98 C2 2
Lawmarnock Rd BRWEIR PA11 .... 98 C3
Lawmoor Av GBLS G5 .... 105 J6
Lawmoor Pl GBLS G5 .... 105 J7 4
Lawmoor St GBLS G5 .... 11 J9
Lawmuir Crs CLYDBK G81 .... 60 E2 3
Lawmuir Pl BLSH ML4 .... 133 G6 2
Lawmuir Rd BLSH ML4 .... 133 G6
WISHAW ML2 .... 177 M3
Lawnmoor Rd GBLS G5 .... 105 J6
Lawn Pk MLNGV G62 .... 42 C8
Lawn St PSLY PA1 .... 9 J3
Law Pl EKILN G74 .... 153 M5
Lawrence Av GIF/THBK G46 .... 127 J8
HBR/GL G84 .... 23 G2
Lawrence St PTCK G11 .... 82 C7
Lawrie St NMLNS KA16 .... 215 H2
PTCK G11 .... 82 B7
WISHAW ML2 .... 159 M4
Lawson Av MTHW ML1 .... 157 L6
Lawson Dr ARD KA22 .... 191 K5
Lawson St AYR KA8 .... 225 H7
KLMNK KA1 .... 17 G7
Law St DEN/PKHD G31 .... 12 F6
Lawthorn Rd IRVSE KA11 .... 204 B4
Law Vw WISHAW ML2 .... 177 J3
Laxford Av LNPK/KPK G44 .... 128 A5
Laxford Pl CTBR ML5 .... 110 D4
Laxford Rd ERSK PA8 .... 58 E8
Laxton Dr KKNTL G66 .... 65 L5
Lea Av BRHD/NEIL G78 .... 148 D2
Leabank Av PSLYS PA2 .... 124 E1
Leadburn Rd SPRGB/BLRNK G21 .... 7 J1
Leadburn St CAR/SHTL G32 .... 106 E2 2
Leader St STPS/GTHM/RID G33 .... 7 M6
Leadhills Rd KLMNK KA1 .... 212 A6
Leaend Rd AIRDRIE ML6 .... 88 E8
Leander Crs BLSH ML4 .... 133 L4
RNFRW PA4 .... 80 E7
Learigg Rd AIRDRIE ML6 .... 90 B6
Learmont Pl MLNGV G62 .... 41 M7
Leathem Pl WISHAW ML2 .... 158 C8 1
Leathen Pl ERSK PA8 .... 58 E8
Leckethill Av BALLOCH G68 .... 67 M2
Leckethill Ct BALLOCH G68 .... 67 M2 3
Leckethill Pl BALLOCH G68 .... 67 M2 4
Leckethill Vw BALLOCH G68 .... 67 M2 5
Leckie Dr HMLTN ML3 .... 156 C6
Leckie Pl ALEX/LLW G83 .... 25 L3
Leckie St PLKSW/MSWD G43 .... 127 J1 3
Ledaig St DEN/PKHD G31 .... 13 K1
Ledard Rd GVH/MTFL G42 .... 127 M2
Ledcameroch Crs BSDN G61 .... 61 K5
Ledcameroch Pk BSDN G61 .... 61 K5 1
Ledcameroch Rd BSDN G61 .... 61 K5
Ledgate KKNTL G66 .... 45 K8
Ledgowan Pl MRYH/FIRH G20 .... 82 D1
Ledi Dr BSDN G61 .... 61 H2
Ledi Rd PLKSW/MSWD G43 .... 127 J4
Ledmore Dr DRUM G15 .... 60 F5
Lednock Rd
CARD/HILL/MSPK G52 .... 103 G4
STPS/GTHM/RID G33 .... 85 J4
Lee Av STPS/GTHM/RID G33 .... 84 E8
Leebank Dr LNPK/KPK G44 .... 127 M8
Leeburn Av CRG/CRSL/HOU PA6 .. 77 J8
Leechford LNK/LMHG ML11 .... 199 H4 2
Leechlee Rd HMLTN ML3 .... 156 E6
Lee Crs BSHPBGS G64 .... 83 M1
Leefield Dr LNPK/KPK G44 .... 127 M7 1
Leehill Rd SPRGB/BLRNK G21 .... 83 L2
Lee Pl BLSH ML4 .... 133 K5
Leesburn Pl EKILN G74 .... 153 M5
Leesland UD/BTH/TAN G71 .... 132 A1
Leeward Cir EKILS G75 .... 153 G8
Leeward Pk AYRS KA7 .... 229 G8
Leewood Dr LNPK/KPK G44 .... 128 A7 1
Le Froy Gdns EKILS G75 .... 14 A5
Le Froy La EKILS G75 .... 14 B5
Lefroy St CTBR ML5 .... 109 L2
Legbrannock Av MTHW ML1 .... 134 D3
Legbrannock Crs MTHW ML1 .. 134 D5 1
Legbrannock Rd MTHW ML1 .... 134 E3
Leglen Wood Rd
STPS/GTHM/RID G33 .... 84 D3
Leicester Av KVD/HLHD G12 .... 82 B4
Leighton St MRYH/FIRH G20 .... 82 E3
WISHAW ML2 .... 159 H7
Leitchland Rd PSLYS PA2 .... 123 K1
Leitch St GRNK PA15 .... 3 M8
Leithland Av
PLK/PH/NH G53 .... 103 H8 1
Leithland Rd PLK/PH/NH G53 .... 103 H8
Leith St STPS/GTHM/RID G33 .... 7 M9
Leman Dr CRG/CRSL/HOU PA6 .... 99 K1
Leman Gv CRG/CRSL/HOU PA6 .. 99 K1 1
Lembert Dr
CRMNK/CLK/EAG G76 .... 151 K1
Lemmon St GRNKW/INVK PA16 .... 32 D6
Lendale La BSHPBGS G64 .... 64 A6
Lendalfoot Gdns HMLTN ML3 .. 155 K7 1
Lendal Pl EKILS G75 .... 170 E3
Lendel Pl GOV/IBX G51 .... 104 D3 2
Lenihall Dr CSMK G45 .... 128 E7
Lenihall Ter CSMK G45 .... 128 E7 3
Lennox Av BSHPTN PA7 .... 58 B6
CTBR ML5 .... 109 L2 2
MLNGV G62 .... 42 A8
SCOT G14 .... 81 J6
Lennox Crs BSHPBGS G64 .... 83 M1
KLMNK KA1 .... 206 C8
Lennox Dr BSDN G61 .... 61 M3 1
CLYDBK G81 .... 60 D2
PSTWK KA9 .... 225 J4
Lennox Gdns DMBTN G82 .... 36 A5
SCOT G14 .... 81 K5 1
Lennox La East SCOT G14 .... 81 K6
Lennox La West SCOT G14 .... 81 K5 5
Lennox Rd CUMB G67 .... 48 F7
DMBTN G82 .... 37 H6
DMBTN G82 .... 37 M8
KKNTL G66 .... 29 J8
Lennox St ALEX/LLW G83 .... 25 L4 7
DMBTN G82 .... 36 D1
DMBTN G82 .... 37 G6 2
MRYH/FIRH G20 .... 82 C2 3
WISHAW ML2 .... 159 L5
Lennox Ter PSLYN/LNWD PA3 .... 102 A1
Lentran St ESTRH G34 .... 108 D2
Lenwood Gdns
ALEX/LLW G83 .... 25 M6 4
Leny St MRYH/FIRH G20 .... 82 F5
Lenziemill Rd CUMB G67 .... 68 F2
Lenzie Rd KKNTL G66 .... 65 K2
KKNTL G66 .... 85 L1
STPS/GTHM/RID G33 .... 85 K2
Lenzie St SPRGB/BLRNK G21 .. 83 M4 3
Lenzie Wy SPRGB/BLRNK G21 .... 83 L3
Leperstone Av KLMCLM PA13 .... 55 K7
PGL PA14 .... 54 E2
Lerwick Pl KLMNKN/STW KA3 .. 207 G4 2
Lesley Pl SVSTN KA20 .... 192 E8
Lesley Qd BLSH ML4 .... 132 F7 2
Leslie Av BSHPTN PA7 .... 58 B6
NMRNS G77 .... 150 E2
Leslie Crs AYRS KA7 .... 19 H7
Leslie Pl KLMNKN/STW KA3 .... 17 J1
Leslie Rd KLMNKN/STW KA3 .... 17 J1
PLKSD/SHW G41 .... 104 D6
Leslie St MTHW ML1 .... 157 M2
PLKSD/SHW G41 .... 104 F6
Leslie Ter PSTWK KA9 .... 225 J1
Lesmahagow Rd
LNK/LMHG ML11 .... 198 A5 1
Lesmuir Dr SCOT G14 .... 81 G4
Lesmuir Pl SCOT G14 .... 80 F4
Letham Ct
PLKSW/MSWD G43 .... 127 L4 1
Letham Dr BSHPBGS G64 .... 84 C1
PLKSW/MSWD G43 .... 127 L4
Letham Gra BALLOCH G68 .... 48 F5
Lethamhill Pl
STPS/GTHM/RID G33 .... 84 E8 1
Lethamhill Rd
STPS/GTHM/RID G33 .... 84 F8
Letham Ov BSHPBGS G64 .... 84 D1 2
Lethbridge Pl EKILS G75 .... 14 B5 1
Letherby Dr LNPK/KPK G44 .... 128 B2
Letheron Dr WISHAW ML2 .... 159 H4
Lethington Av PLKSD/SHW G41 .. 127 L1
Lethington Pl PLKSD/SHW G41 .. 127 L1
Lethington Rd GIF/THBK G46 .... 151 G2
Letterfearn Rd SMSTN G23 .... 62 D7 1
Letterickhills Crs
BLTYR/CAMB G72 .... 130 E6
Lettoch St GOV/IBX G51 .... 104 A2
Levanne Gdns GRK PA19 .... 30 F3 1
Levanne Pl GRK PA19 .... 30 F3
Leven Av BSHPBGS G64 .... 64 B8
KLMNKN/STW KA3 .... 207 G6
Levenbank Gdns ALEX/LLW G83 .... 25 M2
Leven Ct BRHD/NEIL G78 .... 125 H4 1
KLMNK KA1 .... 212 F3
Levencroft Ms ALEX/LLW G83 .. 25 M5 2
Leven Dr BSDN G61 .... 61 M5
HMLTN ML3 .... 174 B1 1
KLMNK KA1 .... 212 F3
Levenford Ter DMBTN G82 .... 36 E6 3
Levenhowe Pl ALEX/LLW G83 .. 25 L2 4
Levenhowe Rd ALEX/LLW G83 .. 25 L2 5
Leven Pl ERSK PA8 .... 58 E8
GRNK PA15 .... 33 J8 1
IRV KA12 .... 203 K3
KLMNKN/STW KA3 .... 207 G6
SHOTTS ML7 .... 137 L3
Leven Qd AIRDRIE ML6 .... 88 F7
Leven Rd CTBR ML5 .... 87 J8
GRNK PA15 .... 33 H7
PGL PA14 .... 56 C2 1
TROON KA10 .... 216 F4
WMYSB PA18 .... 70 A1
Leven St ALEX/LLW G83 .... 25 L5
DMBTN G82 .... 36 D1
DMBTN G82 .... 37 G6
MTHW ML1 .... 157 L4
PLKSD/SHW G41 .... 104 F6
Leven Ter MTHW ML1 .... 134 C7
Leven Wy EKILS G75 .... 170 F3
Levern Crs BRHD/NEIL G78 .... 125 H8
Levern Gdns BRHD/NEIL G78 .. 125 H6 4
Levernside Av BRHD/NEIL G78 .... 125 G7
PLK/PH/NH G53 .... 126 C1 1
Levernside Crs PLK/PH/NH G53 .. 103 H8
Levernside Rd PLK/PH/NH G53 .. 103 H8
Lever Rd HBR/GL G84 .... 20 F6
Lewis Av RNFRW PA4 .... 80 D8
WISHAW ML2 .... 159 L4
Lewis Crs IRVSE KA11 .... 203 M7
KLBCH PA10 .... 99 J7
OLDK G60 .... 59 J4
Lewis Dr KLMNKN/STW KA3 .... 207 H4
OLDK G60 .... 59 H4
Lewis Gdns BSDN G61 .... 61 H3 1
OLDK G60 .... 59 J4
Lewis Gv OLDK G60 .... 59 J4
Lewis Pl AIRDRIE ML6 .... 111 K3
NMRNS G77 .... 150 B3
OLDK G60 .... 59 J4
Lewis Ri IRVSE KA11 .... 204 A7 1
Lewis Rd GRNKW/INVK PA16 .... 32 C5
PGL PA14 .... 55 H2 2
Lewis Ter IRVSE KA11 .... 204 A7
Lewiston Dr SMSTN G23 .... 62 D8 10
Lewiston Pl SMSTN G23 .... 62 D8 11
Lewiston Rd SMSTN G23 .... 62 D8 12
Lewis Wynd IRVSE KA11 .... 204 A7 3
Lexwell Av JNSTN PA5 .... 100 D6
Leyden Gdns MRYH/FIRH G20 .. 82 E4 2
Leyden St MRYH/FIRH G20 .... 82 E4
Leys Pk HMLTN ML3 .... 156 A5
The Leys BSHPBGS G64 .... 64 A8
Libberton Wy HMLTN ML3 .... 156 A6
Liberator Dr AYR KA8 .... 225 L5
Liberton St STPS/GTHM/RID G33 .... 7 M9
Liberty Av BAIL/MDB/MHD G69 .. 108 F4
Liberty Rd AIRDRIE ML6 .... 91 G4
BLSH ML4 .... 133 G6
Libo Av BRHD/NEIL G78 .... 147 G6
PLK/PH/NH G53 .... 103 K8
Libo Pl ERSK PA8 .... 58 E7
Library Gdns
BLTYR/CAMB G72 .... 129 M3 2
Library La GIF/THBK G46 .... 126 F6
Library Rd WISHAW ML2 .... 159 H6 1
Lichtenfels Gdns PSTWK KA9 .... 225 L1
Lickprivick Rd EKILS G75 .... 171 H2
Liddell Gv EKILS G75 .... 14 D8
Liddells Ct BSHPBGS G64 .... 84 A2 1
Liddell St CAR/SHTL G32 .... 107 J8
Liddel Rd CUMB G67 .... 48 E8
Liddesdale Pl PPK/MIL G22 .... 83 L2 5
Liddesdale Rd PPK/MIL G22 .... 83 J2
Liddesdale Sq PPK/MIL G22 .... 83 L2 6
Liddesdale Ter PPK/MIL G22 .... 83 L2 7
Liddoch Wy RUTH G73 .... 128 F1
Liff Gdns BSHPBGS G64 .... 84 D1 3
Liff Pl ESTRH G34 .... 86 C8
Lifnock Av KLMNK KA1 .... 212 F3
Lightburn Pl CAR/SHTL G32 .... 107 H2 3
Lightburn Rd BLTYR/CAMB G72 .. 130 D5
DEN/PKHD G31 .... 13 K4
Lilac Av CLYDBK G81 .... 59 K4
CUMB G67 .... 49 L4
Lilac Ct CUMB G67 .... 49 M4 2
Lilac Crs UD/BTH/TAN G71 .... 132 B1
Lilac Gdns BSHPBGS G64 .... 84 B1 4
Lilac Hl CUMB G67 .... 49 M4
HMLTN ML3 .... 156 F7
Lilac Pl CUMB G67 .... 49 M4
KLMNK KA1 .... 16 B4
Lilac Wynd BLTYR/CAMB G72 .... 130 F6
Lillyburn Pl DRUM G15 .... 60 E5
Lilybank Av AIRDRIE ML6 .... 89 H7
BAIL/MDB/MHD G69 .... 86 C2
BLTYR/CAMB G72 .... 130 B5
Lilybank Gdns KVD/HLHD G12 .... 82 D7
Lilybank Gardens La
KVD/HLHD G12 .... 82 D7 4
Lilybank La FAIRLIE KA29 .... 139 K7 3
KVD/HLHD G12 .... 82 D7 5
Lilybank Rd PGL PA14 .... 33 M7
PSTWK KA9 .... 225 H4
Lilybank St HMLTN ML3 .... 156 C5
Lilybank Ter KVD/HLHD G12 .... 82 D7 6
Lilybank Terrace La
KVD/HLHD G12 .... 82 D7 7
Lily St DMNK/BRGTN G40 .... 13 G9
Limecraigs Av PSLYS PA2 .... 124 C2 3
Limecraigs Crs PSLYS PA2 .... 124 C2
Limecraigs Rd PSLYS PA2 .... 124 C2
Lime Crs AIRDRIE ML6 .... 111 J2
CUMB G67 .... 49 L6
Lime Gv BLTYR/CAMB G72 .... 131 J8
KKNTL G66 .... 65 K4
MTHW ML1 .... 157 L5
Limegrove St BLSH ML4 .... 133 G2 2
Limekilnburn Rd HMLTN ML3 .... 174 B7
Limekiln Rd AYR KA8 .... 224 F6
SVSTN KA20 .... 201 L2
Limekilns Rd CUMB G67 .... 68 F3

Limekilns St *CLYDBK* G81 ... 60 D3
Limelands Qd *AIRDRIE* ML6 ... 90 F5
Lime Loan *MTHW* ML1 ... 134 B5
Lime Pl *KLMNK* KA1 ... 16 B5
Lime Rd *DMBTN* G82 ... 36 F5
Limeside Av *RUTH* G73 ... 129 J2
Limeside Gdns *RUTH* G73 ... 129 J2
Lime St *GRNK* PA15 ... 2 A6
SCOT G14 ... 81 K6
Limetree Av *UD/BTH/TAN* G71 ... 132 B1
Limetree Ct *HMLTN* ML3 ... 156 A4
Limetree Crs *NMRNS* G77 ... 150 D5
Limetree Dr *CLYDBK* G81 ... 60 A5
Limetree Qd
UD/BTH/TAN G71 ... 132 C1
Limetree Wk *KKNTL* G66 ... 45 H5
Limeview Av *PSLYS* PA2 ... 124 B2
Limeview Crs *PSLYS* PA2 ... 124 B2
Limeview Wy *PSLYS* PA2 ... 124 B2
Limonds Wynd *AYR* KA8 ... 19 G1
Limpetlaw *LNK/LMHG* ML11 ... 199 H4
Linacre Dr *CAR/SHTL* G32 ... 107 J4
Linacre Gdns *CAR/SHTL* G32 ... 107 K4
Linburn Pl
CARD/HILL/MSPK G52 ... 103 G3
Linburn Rd
CARD/HILL/MSPK G52 ... 102 F2
ERSK PA8 ... 58 E8
Lincoln Av *KNTSWD* G13 ... 81 H3
UD/BTH/TAN G71 ... 108 F8
Lincoln Rd *GRNKW/INVK* PA16 ... 31 K5
Lincuan Av *GIF/THBK* G46 ... 151 J1
Lindams *UD/BTH/TAN* G71 ... 131 M4
Linden Av *WISHAW* ML2 ... 159 J3
Linden Dr *CLYDBK* G81 ... 60 A3
Linden Lea *HMLTN* ML3 ... 156 B5
KKNTL G66 ... 45 H4
Linden Pl *KNTSWD* G13 ... 81 M2
Linden St *KNTSWD* G13 ... 81 M2
Lindon Aisle *LARGS* KA30 ... 115 J6
Lindon Ct *LARGS* KA30 ... 115 J6
Lindores Av *RUTH* G73 ... 129 H2
Lindores Dr *EKILN* G74 ... 153 H8
Lindores Pl *EKILN* G74 ... 14 A3
Lindores St *GVH/MTFL* G42 ... 128 B1
Lindrick Dr *SMSTN* G23 ... 62 D8
Lindsay Av *KBRN* KA25 ... 143 H6
SALT KA21 ... 191 M8
Lindsaybeg Ct
BAIL/MDB/MHD G69 ... 86 C1
Lindsaybeg Rd
BAIL/MDB/MHD G69 ... 86 C1
KKNTL G66 ... 65 L5
Lindsay Crs *LARGS* KA30 ... 115 K5
Lindsay Dr *KLMNKN/STW* KA3 ... 207 J6
KVD/HLHD G12 ... 82 B3
Lindsayfield Av *EKILS* G75 ... 171 J5
Lindsayfield Rd *EKILS* G75 ... 171 H5
Lindsay Gdns *ALEX/LLW* G83 ... 25 L3
Lindsay Gv *EKILN* G74 ... 15 H2
Lindsay Pl *EKILN* G74 ... 15 J3
KVD/HLHD G12 ... 82 B3
Lindsay Rd *EKILN* G74 ... 15 H3
Lindsay St *AYR* KA8 ... 225 J7
KLMNK KA1 ... 16 D4
Lindsay Ter *KKNTL* G66 ... 44 E1
Lindston Pl *AYRS* KA7 ... 229 G7
Lindum Crs *MTHW* ML1 ... 157 H1
Lindum St *MTHW* ML1 ... 157 H1
Linfern Av East *KLMNK* KA1 ... 17 L6
Linfern Av West *KLMNK* KA1 ... 17 L6
Linfern Pl *AYRS* KA7 ... 229 H6
Linfern Rd *KVD/HLHD* G12 ... 82 C6
Linghope Pl *WISHAW* ML2 ... 176 F1
Lingley Av *AIRDRIE* ML6 ... 111 G3
Linhead Dr *PLK/PH/NH* G53 ... 126 C3
Linhope Pl *EKILS* G75 ... 170 E2
Linister Crs *HWWD* PA9 ... 121 L4
Links Crs *TROON* KA10 ... 216 E3
Links Rd *CAR/SHTL* G32 ... 107 K6
LNPK/KPK G44 ... 128 B5
PSTWK KA9 ... 221 H8
SALT KA21 ... 191 M7
The Links *BALLOCH* G68 ... 49 H3
Links Vw *LRKH* ML9 ... 176 C7
Linksview Rd *MTHW* ML1 ... 134 B8
Linkwood Av *DRUM* G15 ... 60 F6
Linkwood Ct *IRVSE* KA11 ... 204 A3
Linkwood Crs *DRUM* G15 ... 61 G6
Linkwood Dr *DRUM* G15 ... 60 F6
Linkwood Gdns *DRUM* G15 ... 61 H6
Linkwood Pl *DRUM* G15 ... 60 F6
Linlithgow Gdns
CAR/SHTL G32 ... 107 K4
Linn Av *LARGS* KA30 ... 115 L6
Linnburn Ter *ARD* KA22 ... 191 H5
Linn Crs *LNK/LMHG* ML11 ... 198 A5
PSLYS PA2 ... 124 C2
Linn Dr *LNPK/KPK* G44 ... 127 M6
Linnet Av *JNSTN* PA5 ... 122 C2
Linnet Pl *KNTSWD* G13 ... 80 F2
Linnet Rd *BLSH* ML4 ... 133 H5
GRNKW/INVK PA16 ... 32 B5
Linnet Wy *BLSH* ML4 ... 132 F1
Linn Gdns *BALLOCH* G68 ... 47 M7
Linn Gln *KKNTL* G66 ... 44 F1
Linnhead Dr *PLK/PH/NH* G53 ... 126 B4
Linnhead Pl *SCOT* G14 ... 81 H5
Linnhe Av *BSHPBGS* G64 ... 64 B8
HMLTN ML3 ... 156 A8
LNPK/KPK G44 ... 128 A5
Linnhe Ct *LRKH* ML9 ... 175 M4
Linnhe Crs *WISHAW* ML2 ... 177 H1
Linnhe Dr *BRHD/NEIL* G78 ... 125 H4
Linnhe Pl *BLTYR/CAMB* G72 ... 131 J7
ERSK PA8 ... 58 E8
Linnhe Rd *WMYSB* PA18 ... 50 A8
Linnpark Av *LNPK/KPK* G44 ... 127 M7
Linn Park Gdns *JNSTN* PA5 ... 100 A7
Linn Rd *ARD* KA22 ... 191 J5
Linnwell Crs *PSLYS* PA2 ... 124 D2
Linrigg Rd *MTHW* ML1 ... 135 J1
Linthaugh Ter
PLK/PH/NH G53 ... 103 K8
Linthill *LNK/LMHG* ML11 ... 199 H3
Linthouse Buildings
GOV/IBX G51 ... 103 L1
Linthouse Rd *GOV/IBX* G51 ... 81 K8
Linthouse Vennel *IRV* KA12 ... 203 G8
Lintie Rd *MTHW* ML1 ... 134 C5
Lintlaw *BLTYR/CAMB* G72 ... 131 K7
Lintlaw Dr
CARD/HILL/MSPK G52 ... 103 H3
Lintmill Ter *BRHD/NEIL* G78 ... 148 C3
Linton St *STPS/GTHM/RID* G33 ... 106 E1
Lintwhite Crs *BRWEIR* PA11 ... 98 E2
Linwood Av
CRMNK/CLK/EAG G76 ... 151 M2
EKILN G74 ... 152 F7
Linwood Rd *PSLYN/LNWD* PA3 ... 100 D4
Linwood Ter *HMLTN* ML3 ... 156 B5
Lion Bank *KKNTL* G66 ... 45 J8
Lisburn Rd *AYR* KA8 ... 225 G5
Lismore *EKILN* G74 ... 172 C1
Lismore Av *MTHW* ML1 ... 157 H1
PGL PA14 ... 55 H2
RNFRW PA4 ... 80 D8
Lismore Dr *IRVSE* KA11 ... 209 H1
PSLYN/LNWD PA3 ... 99 M4
PSLYS PA2 ... 124 D2
Lismore Gdns *KLBCH* PA10 ... 99 J7
Lismore Hl *HMLTN* ML3 ... 155 K6
Lismore Pl
BAIL/MDB/MHD G69 ... 67 G6
NMRNS G77 ... 150 B4
Lismore Rd *KVD/HLHD* G12 ... 82 B4
Lissens Wk *KLWNG* KA13 ... 193 J4
Lister Gdns
CRMNK/CLK/EAG G76 ... 152 A4
Lister Pl *CARD/HILL/MSPK* G52 ... 103 G2
Lister Rd *CARD/HILL/MSPK* G52 ... 102 F2
Lister St *COWCAD* G4 ... 5 M7
CRH/DND KA2 ... 206 A8
Lithgow Av *PGL* PA14 ... 56 B2
Lithgow Crs *PSLYS* PA2 ... 9 L9
Lithgow Dr *MTHW* ML1 ... 135 H8
Lithgow Pl *EKILN* G74 ... 153 H7
Little Bellsland Rd *KLMNK* KA1 ... 16 F9
Little Dovehill *COWCAD* G4 ... 11 M3
Littlehill St *SPRGB/BLRNK* G21 ... 6 E1
Littleholm Pl *CLYDBK* G81 ... 59 L5
Little John Gdns *WISHAW* ML2 ... 159 M5
Littlemill Av *BALLOCH* G68 ... 47 L8
Littlemill La *OLDK* G60 ... 58 C1
Littlesdale Av *PSLYS* PA2 ... 123 K2
Littlestane Ri *IRVSE* KA11 ... 204 A3
Littlestane Rd *IRVSE* KA11 ... 203 M3
Littleston Gdns *ERSK* PA8 ... 58 F8
Little St *KVGV* G3 ... 10 C1
Littleton St *MRYH/FIRH* G20 ... 62 D8
Livingston Dr *AIRDRIE* ML6 ... 90 A7
Livingstone Av
CARD/HILL/MSPK G52 ... 103 G1
Livingstone Bvd
BLTYR/CAMB G72 ... 155 J4
Livingstone Ct
KLMNKN/STW KA3 ... 207 J6
Livingstone Crs
BLTYR/CAMB G72 ... 131 K8
EKILS G75 ... 14 D7
Livingstone Dr *EKILS* G75 ... 14 D5
Livingstone Gdns *LRKH* ML9 ... 176 B6
Livingstone Pl *AIRDRIE* ML6 ... 111 H3
Livingstone St *CLYDBK* G81 ... 60 D8
HMLTN ML3 ... 155 M5
Livingstone Ter *IRV* KA12 ... 203 K5
Lloyd Av *CAR/SHTL* G32 ... 107 G7
Lloyd Dr *MTHW* ML1 ... 134 A8
Lloyds St *CTBR* ML5 ... 110 A4
Lloyd St *DEN/PKHD* G31 ... 6 E9
MTHW ML1 ... 134 A8
RUTH G73 ... 106 B8
Lloyd Wk *KLMNKN/STW* KA3 ... 197 J1
Loach Av *IRV* KA12 ... 203 K8
Loadingbank *KBRN* KA25 ... 167 G2
Loanbank Pl *GOV/IBX* G51 ... 104 A2
Loanbank Qd *GOV/IBX* G51 ... 104 A2
Loancroft Av
BAIL/MDB/MHD G69 ... 108 C6
Loancroft Gdns
UD/BTH/TAN G71 ... 131 M4
Loancroft Ga *UD/BTH/TAN* G71 ... 131 L4
Loancroft Pl
BAIL/MDB/MHD G69 ... 108 B6
Loanfoot Av *BRHD/NEIL* G78 ... 148 D3
KLMNK KA1 ... 16 A3
KNTSWD G13 ... 81 G2
Loanfoot Rd
BLTYR/CAMB G72 ... 155 K4
Loanhead Av *MTHW* ML1 ... 134 D6
PSLYN/LNWD PA3 ... 100 A3
RNFRW PA4 ... 80 D6
Loanhead Crs *MTHW* ML1 ... 134 D6
Loanhead Rd *ARD* KA22 ... 191 K7
MTHW ML1 ... 134 C6
PSLYN/LNWD PA3 ... 100 A3
Loanhead St *CAR/SHTL* G32 ... 106 F2
CTBR ML5 ... 109 L6
Loaninghead Dr *DMBTN* G82 ... 37 H3
The Loaning *AYRS* KA7 ... 228 F8
GIF/THBK G46 ... 151 G2
MTHW ML1 ... 157 J2
Loan Lea Crs *LRKH* ML9 ... 176 B8
The Loan *MLNGV* G62 ... 41 J5
Lobnitz Av *RNFRW* PA4 ... 80 D6
Loccard Rd *SVSTN* KA20 ... 192 C8
Lochaber Dr *RUTH* G73 ... 129 K5
Lochaber Pl *EKILN* G74 ... 153 M6
Lochaber Rd *BSDN* G61 ... 62 B7
Loch Achray St *CAR/SHTL* G32 ... 107 J5
Lochaline Av *PSLYS* PA2 ... 101 G7
Lochaline Dr *LNPK/KPK* G44 ... 128 A5
Lochalsh Crs *KKNTL* G66 ... 45 J2
Lochalsh Dr *PSLYS* PA2 ... 100 F7
Lochalsh Pl *BLTYR/CAMB* G72 ... 131 H7
Lochar Crs *PLK/PH/NH* G53 ... 103 K7
Lochard Dr *PSLYS* PA2 ... 101 G8
Lochar Pl *EKILS* G75 ... 170 E2
Loch Assynt *EKILN* G74 ... 15 L5
Loch Av *CARLUKE* ML8 ... 188 E5
Loch Awe *EKILN* G74 ... 15 K5
Loch Awe Pl *CTBR* ML5 ... 109 M3
Lochay Pl *TROON* KA10 ... 216 F4
Lochay St *CAR/SHTL* G32 ... 107 J5
Lochbrae Dr *RUTH* G73 ... 129 K5
Lochbridge Rd *ESTRH* G34 ... 108 A2
Lochbroom Dr *NMRNS* G77 ... 150 F3
PSLYS PA2 ... 101 G7
Loch Brora Crs *CTBR* ML5 ... 109 L3
Lochbuie La *AIRDRIE* ML6 ... 88 E5
Lochburn Crs *MRYH/FIRH* G20 ... 82 E2
Lochburn Pas
MRYH/FIRH G20 ... 82 E2
Lochburn Rd *MRYH/FIRH* G20 ... 82 E2
Lochdochart Rd *ESTRH* G34 ... 108 D1
Loch Dr *HBR/GL* G84 ... 20 A7
Lochearn Crs *AIRDRIE* ML6 ... 88 F7
PSLYS PA2 ... 101 G7
Lochend Av
BAIL/MDB/MHD G69 ... 86 E3
Lochend Crs *BSDN* G61 ... 61 K6
Lochend Dr *BSDN* G61 ... 61 K6
Lochend Rd
BAIL/MDB/MHD G69 ... 86 F3
BSDN G61 ... 61 L6
ESTRH G34 ... 86 B8
GLGNK KA14 ... 167 J2
TROON KA10 ... 216 D8
Lochend St *MTHW* ML1 ... 157 M3
Locher Av *CRG/CRSL/HOU* PA6 ... 77 L8
Locher Br *KLMCLM* PA13 ... 97 J4
Locherburn Av
CRG/CRSL/HOU PA6 ... 99 K1
Locherburn Pl
CRG/CRSL/HOU PA6 ... 99 L1
Locher Crs
CRG/CRSL/HOU PA6 ... 77 L8
Locher Gait
CRG/CRSL/HOU PA6 ... 99 L1
Locher Gdns
CRG/CRSL/HOU PA6 ... 99 L1
Locher Rd *KLBCH* PA10 ... 98 F4
Locher Wy *CRG/CRSL/HOU* PA6 ... 99 L1
Lochfauld Rd *SMSTN* G23 ... 63 G7
Lochfield Crs *PSLYS* PA2 ... 101 M8
Lochfield Dr *PSLYS* PA2 ... 102 A8
Lochfield Rd *PSLYS* PA2 ... 102 A8
Lochgarry Wy *CTBR* ML5 ... 109 K5
Lochgilp St *MRYH/FIRH* G20 ... 82 C2
Loch Goil *EKILN* G74 ... 15 K4
Lochgoin Av *DRUM* G15 ... 60 E5
Lochgreen Av *TROON* KA10 ... 216 F2
Lochgreen Pl *CTBR* ML5 ... 87 J7
HMLTN ML3 ... 174 B1
KLMNK KA1 ... 211 L5
Lochgreen St
STPS/GTHM/RID G33 ... 7 M3
Lochhead Av *PSLYN/LNWD* PA3 ... 100 B4
Lochiel Dr *KKNTL* G66 ... 45 J3
Lochiel Rd *GIF/THBK* G46 ... 126 F5
Lochinch Pl *NMRNS* G77 ... 150 A4
Lochinvar Rd *CUMB* G67 ... 68 D2
Lochinver Crs *PSLYS* PA2 ... 101 G7
Lochinver Dr *LNPK/KPK* G44 ... 128 A4
Lochinver Gv
BLTYR/CAMB G72 ... 130 B4
Lochknowe St *CARLUKE* ML8 ... 188 F4
Loch Laidon St *CAR/SHTL* G32 ... 107 K5
Lochlands Gv *BEITH* KA15 ... 168 C1
Loch Laxford *EKILN* G74 ... 15 L6
Lochlea *EKILN* G74 ... 154 D5
Loch Lea *KKNTL* G66 ... 45 M7
Lochlea Av *CLYDBK* G81 ... 60 C6
TROON KA10 ... 216 F5
Lochlea Dr *AYRS* KA7 ... 19 J8
Lochlea Rd
CRMNK/CLK/EAG G76 ... 151 L4
CUMB G67 ... 49 H6
PLKSW/MSWD G43 ... 127 K3
RUTH G73 ... 128 F4
SALT KA21 ... 192 A6
Lochlea Wy *MTHW* ML1 ... 134 E5
Lochleven La *GVH/MTFL* G42 ... 128 A2
Lochleven Rd *GVH/MTFL* G42 ... 128 A2
Lochlibo Av *KNTSWD* G13 ... 80 F3
Lochlibo Ct *IRVSE* KA11 ... 204 A3
Lochlibo Crs *BRHD/NEIL* G78 ... 125 G8
Lochlibo Rd *BEITH* KA15 ... 169 L6
BEITH KA15 ... 187 G4
BRHD/NEIL G78 ... 147 G6
IRVSE KA11 ... 195 H7
IRVSE KA11 ... 204 A3
Lochlibo Ter *BRHD/NEIL* G78 ... 125 G8
Lochlie Pl *SVSTN* KA20 ... 192 E8
Lochlip Rd *LOCHW* PA12 ... 120 D7
Loch Long *EKILN* G74 ... 15 K5
Loch Loyal *EKILN* G74 ... 15 M6
Lochmaben Rd
CARD/HILL/MSPK G52 ... 102 F5
Lochmaddy Av *LNPK/KPK* G44 ... 128 A5
Loch Maree *EKILN* G74 ... 15 L5
Loch Meadie *EKILN* G74 ... 15 M5
Lochnagar Dr *BSDN* G61 ... 61 H2
Lochnagar Rd *KLMNK* KA1 ... 212 A5
Loch Naver *EKILN* G74 ... 15 M6
Lochore Av *PSLYN/LNWD* PA3 ... 102 A2
Lochpark *AYRS* KA7 ... 228 C6
Loch Pk *WISHAW* ML2 ... 159 J6
Loch Park Av *CARLUKE* ML8 ... 188 E1
Loch Park Pl *LRKH* ML9 ... 176 A8
Loch Pl *BRWEIR* PA11 ... 98 D1
Lochranza Dr *EKILS* G75 ... 171 H5
HBR/GL G84 ... 20 F7
Lochranza La *EKILS* G75 ... 171 J5
Lochranza Pl *SALT* KA21 ... 192 A7
Loch Rd *AIRDRIE* ML6 ... 111 K7
BRWEIR PA11 ... 98 D1
KKNTL G66 ... 65 L2
MLNGV G62 ... 42 B6
STPS/GTHM/RID G33 ... 85 K4
Loch Shin *EKILN* G74 ... 15 M6
Lochside *BAIL/MDB/MHD* G69 ... 86 F3
BSDN G61 ... 61 M6
Lochside Rd *AYR* KA8 ... 225 J5
Lochside St *PLKSD/SHW* G41 ... 104 E8
Loch St *AIRDRIE* ML6 ... 111 H7
Loch Striven *EKILN* G74 ... 15 K4
Loch Torridon *EKILN* G74 ... 15 L6
Loch Vw *AIRDRIE* ML6 ... 91 G4
AIRDRIE ML6 ... 111 H7
Lochview Av *GRK* PA19 ... 32 A2
Lochview Crs
STPS/GTHM/RID G33 ... 84 F6
Lochview Dr
STPS/GTHM/RID G33 ... 84 F6
Lochview Gdns
STPS/GTHM/RID G33 ... 84 F6
Lochview Pl
STPS/GTHM/RID G33 ... 84 F6
Lochview Rd *BEITH* KA15 ... 167 M2
BSDN G61 ... 61 L6
CTBR ML5 ... 87 J8
PGL PA14 ... 34 B8
Loch Voil St *CAR/SHTL* G32 ... 107 K5
Lochwinnoch Rd *KLMCLM* PA13 ... 75 H2
Lochwood Loan
BAIL/MDB/MHD G69 ... 67 G6
Lochwood St
STPS/GTHM/RID G33 ... 84 E7
Lochy Av *RNFRW* PA4 ... 80 F8
Lochy Pl *ERSK* PA8 ... 58 E7
Lochy St *WISHAW* ML2 ... 159 G8
Lockerbie Av
PLKSW/MSWD G43 ... 127 M3
Locket Yett Vw *BLSH* ML4 ... 132 E4
Lockhart Av *BLTYR/CAMB* G72 ... 130 D3
Lockhart Dr
BLTYR/CAMB G72 ... 130 D3
LNK/LMHG ML11 ... 198 E4
Lockhart Pl
UD/BTH/TAN G71 ... 108 B7
WISHAW ML2 ... 159 L5
Lockhart St *CARLUKE* ML8 ... 178 F7
HMLTN ML3 ... 174 C3
SPRGB/BLRNK G21 ... 7 H4
Lockhart Ter *EKILN* G74 ... 15 L1
Locksley Av *CUMB* G67 ... 68 E3
KNTSWD G13 ... 81 J1
Locksley Ct *CUMB* G67 ... 68 E3
Locksley Crs *CUMB* G67 ... 68 E3
Locksley Pl *CUMB* G67 ... 68 E3
Locksley Rd *CUMB* G67 ... 68 E3
PSLYS PA2 ... 100 F8
Locks St *CTBR* ML5 ... 110 D3
Lodge Crs *KLMCLM* PA13 ... 75 L1
Lodge Gdns *KLMCLM* PA13 ... 55 L8
Lodge Gv *KLMCLM* PA13 ... 55 L8
Lodge Pk *KLMCLM* PA13 ... 55 L8
Logan Av *NMRNS* G77 ... 150 C3
Logandale Av *WISHAW* ML2 ... 159 M3
Logan Dr *BALLOCH* G68 ... 48 D6
PSLYN/LNWD PA3 ... 8 C1
TROON KA10 ... 216 D6
Logan Gdns *MTHW* ML1 ... 159 H1
Loganlea Dr *MTHW* ML1 ... 134 A8
Logans Rd *MTHW* ML1 ... 157 H1
Logan St *BLTYR/CAMB* G72 ... 155 L2
GBLS G5 ... 105 K7
Loganswell Dr *GIF/THBK* G46 ... 126 E7
Loganswell Gdns *GIF/THBK* G46 ... 126 E7
Loganswell Pl *GIF/THBK* G46 ... 126 E7
Loganswell Rd *GIF/THBK* G46 ... 126 E7
Logie Pk *EKILN* G74 ... 154 A6
Logie Sq *EKILN* G74 ... 154 A6
Lomax St *STPS/GTHM/RID* G33 ... 7 L8
Lomond *EKILS* G75 ... 171 L4
Lomond Av *KLMNK* KA1 ... 212 F3
PGL PA14 ... 54 D1
RNFRW PA4 ... 80 B8
Lomond Ct *BRHD/NEIL* G78 ... 125 J7
CUMB G67 ... 68 C2
Lomond Crs *ALEX/LLW* G83 ... 25 K2
BEITH KA15 ... 144 B7
BRWEIR PA11 ... 98 C1
CUMB G67 ... 68 C2
PSLYS PA2 ... 124 D1
Lomond Dr *AIRDRIE* ML6 ... 88 E8
ALEX/LLW G83 ... 25 K2
BRHD/NEIL G78 ... 125 H5
BSHPBGS G64 ... 63 M6
CUMB G67 ... 68 B2
DMBTN G82 ... 37 H3
NMRNS G77 ... 150 D2
UD/BTH/TAN G71 ... 132 B6
WISHAW ML2 ... 159 G8
Lomond Gdns *JNSTN* PA5 ... 100 C7
Lomond Gv *CUMB* G67 ... 68 C2
Lomond Pl *CTBR* ML5 ... 87 L8
CUMB G67 ... 68 B2
ERSK PA8 ... 58 E8
IRV KA12 ... 203 K3
STPS/GTHM/RID G33 ... 85 K5
Lomond Rd *ALEX/LLW* G83 ... 25 K2
BSDN G61 ... 61 L7
CTBR ML5 ... 87 K7
GRNK PA15 ... 2 F8
KKNTL G66 ... 65 K4
KLMNK KA1 ... 212 A5
SHOTTS ML7 ... 137 K3
UD/BTH/TAN G71 ... 108 F8
WMYSB PA18 ... 70 A1
Lomondside Av
CRMNK/CLK/EAG G76 ... 151 J2
Lomond St *HBR/GL* G84 ... 20 E8
PPK/MIL G22 ... 83 H4
Lomond Vw *CUMB* G67 ... 68 C2
HMLTN ML3 ... 155 M7
KLMNK KA1 ... 218 C5
Lomond Wy *IRVSE* KA11 ... 204 A5
London Rd *CAR/SHTL* G32 ... 106 F7
DEN/PKHD G31 ... 13 L8
DMNK/BRGTN G40 ... 12 A4
KLMNKN/STW KA3 ... 17 H4
London St *LRKH* ML9 ... 176 A5
RNFRW PA4 ... 80 D4
Lonend *PSLY* PA1 ... 9 J6
Longay Pl *PPK/MIL* G22 ... 83 J1
Longay St *PPK/MIL* G22 ... 83 J1
Longbank Dr *AYRS* KA7 ... 229 G5
Longbank Rd *AYRS* KA7 ... 228 F5
Longbar Av *GLGNK* KA14 ... 167 K3
Long Crags Vw *DMBTN* G82 ... 37 J3
Longcraigs Av *ARD* KA22 ... 191 J4
Longden St *CLYDBK* G81 ... 80 D1
Long Dr *EKILS* G75 ... 15 J8
IRV KA12 ... 203 M3
IRVSE KA11 ... 203 M8
IRVSE KA11 ... 209 G3
Longfield Av *SALT* KA21 ... 191 L7
Longfield Pl *SALT* KA21 ... 191 L7
Longford Av *KLWNG* KA13 ... 193 L8
Longford St *STPS/GTHM/RID* G33 ... 7 M8
Long Hl *SKLM* PA17 ... 70 A5
Longhill Av *AYRS* KA7 ... 228 C8
Longlands Pk *AYRS* KA7 ... 228 F5
Longlee *BAIL/MDB/MHD* G69 ... 108 B5
Longmeadow *JNSTN* PA5 ... 99 J8
Longpark Av *KLMNKN/STW* KA3 ... 206 F7
Long Rw *BAIL/MDB/MHD* G69 ... 108 C3
Longrow Gdns *IRVSE* KA11 ... 203 M2
Longstone Rd
STPS/GTHM/RID G33 ... 107 H1
Longwill Ter *CUMB* G67 ... 49 H5
Lonmay Rd
STPS/GTHM/RID G33 ... 107 K1
Lonsdale Av *GIF/THBK* G46 ... 127 J6
Loom Wk *KLBCH* PA10 ... 99 G6
Lora Dr
CARD/HILL/MSPK G52 ... 103 L5
Loreny Dr *KLMNK* KA1 ... 211 L7
Loretto Pl
STPS/GTHM/RID G33 ... 106 F1
Loretto St *STPS/GTHM/RID* G33 ... 106 F1
Lorimer Crs *EKILS* G75 ... 14 C8
Lorn Av *BAIL/MDB/MHD* G69 ... 86 D1
Lorne Crs *BSHPBGS* G64 ... 64 D7
Lorne Dr *MTHW* ML1 ... 133 K7
PSLYN/LNWD PA3 ... 100 A4
Lorne Gdns *SHOTTS* ML7 ... 113 G7
Lorne Pl *CTBR* ML5 ... 110 D4
Lorne Rd *CARD/HILL/MSPK* G52 ... 102 F1
Lorne St *GOV/IBX* G51 ... 104 D3
HBR/GL G84 ... 20 D7
HMLTN ML3 ... 156 C5
Lorne Ter *BLTYR/CAMB* G72 ... 129 M6
RAYR/DAL KA6 ... 231 K5
Lorn Pl *KKNTL* G66 ... 46 C8
Lorraine Gdns
KVD/HLHD G12 ... 82 C5
Lorraine Gardens La
KVD/HLHD G12 ... 82 C5
Lorraine Rd *KVD/HLHD* G12 ... 82 C5
Lorraine Wy *ALEX/LLW* G83 ... 25 M8
Loskin Dr *PPK/MIL* G22 ... 83 H2
Lossie Crs *RNFRW* PA4 ... 80 F7
Lossie St *STPS/GTHM/RID* G33 ... 7 M6
Lothian Crs *PSLYS* PA2 ... 101 K8
Lothian Dr
CRMNK/CLK/EAG G76 ... 151 K1
Lothian Gdns *MRYH/FIRH* G20 ... 4 B2
Lothian Rd *AYRS* KA7 ... 19 H7
GRNKW/INVK PA16 ... 31 K5
KLMNKN/STW KA3 ... 197 J1
Lothian St
CARD/HILL/MSPK G52 ... 102 E1
Lothian Wy *EKILN* G74 ... 154 C6
Louden Hill Pl
STPS/GTHM/RID G33 ... 84 E3
Louden Hill Rd
STPS/GTHM/RID G33 ... 84 E3
Louden St *AIRDRIE* ML6 ... 111 G2
Loudon *EKILS* G75 ... 171 L4
Loudon Gdns *JNSTN* PA5 ... 100 A6
Loudonhill Av *HMLTN* ML3 ... 174 E1
Loudon Rd
STPS/GTHM/RID G33 ... 85 H5
Loudon St *WISHAW* ML2 ... 159 H3
Loudoun Av *GLSTN* KA4 ... 214 A4
KLMNK KA1 ... 212 A5
Loudoun Crs *KLWNG* KA13 ... 193 H5
NMLNS KA16 ... 215 J2
Loudoun Pl *CRH/DND* KA2 ... 210 F1
Loudoun Rd *NMLNS* KA16 ... 215 G2
Loudoun Rd West *NMLNS* KA16 ... 215 G2
Loudoun St *KLMNKN/STW* KA3 ... 197 L2
Loudoun Ter *PSTWK* KA9 ... 225 K2
Louise Gdns *BLSH* ML4 ... 133 M4
Louisville Av *WISHAW* ML2 ... 159 K4
Lounsdale Av *PSLYS* PA2 ... 8 A7
Lounsdale Crs *PSLYS* PA2 ... 101 G7
Lounsdale Dr *PSLYS* PA2 ... 8 A8
Lounsdale Pl *SCOT* G14 ... 81 H5
Lounsdale Rd *PSLYS* PA2 ... 8 A8
Lourdes Av
CARD/HILL/MSPK G52 ... 103 K5
Lovat Av *BSDN* G61 ... 61 L2
Lovat Dr *KKNTL* G66 ... 65 H1
Lovat Pl *CARD/HILL/MSPK* G52 ... 102 E2
RUTH G73 ... 129 K5
Lovat St *LARGS* KA30 ... 115 K6
Love Av *BRWEIR* PA11 ... 75 L7
Love St *KLWNG* KA13 ... 194 A6
PSLYN/LNWD PA3 ... 101 L3
Low Barholm *KLBCH* PA10 ... 99 H7
Low Broadlie Rd
BRHD/NEIL G78 ... 148 D2
Low Craigends *KSYTH* G65 ... 47 L1
Low Crs *CLYDBK* G81 ... 80 E1
Lower Auchingramont Rd
HMLTN ML3 ... 156 E5
Lower Bourtree Dr *RUTH* G73 ... 129 J5
Lower Bouverie St *PGL* PA14 ... 34 D8
Lower Millgate
UD/BTH/TAN G71 ... 131 M3
Lower Mill Rd
CRMNK/CLK/EAG G76 ... 151 M3
Lower Stoneymollan Rd
ALEX/LLW G83 ... 25 J1
Lower Sutherland Crs
HBR/GL G84 ... 20 B6
Low Flender Rd
CRMNK/CLK/EAG G76 ... 151 K4
Low Glencairn St *KLMNK* KA1 ... 16 F9
Low Green Rd *IRV* KA12 ... 203 H6
Lowndes St *BRHD/NEIL* G78 ... 125 J7
Low Parksail *ERSK* PA8 ... 79 J2
Low Patrick St *HMLTN* ML3 ... 156 F6
Low Pleasance *LRKH* ML9 ... 176 B6
Low Rd *AYR* KA8 ... 225 L6
PSLYS PA2 ... 8 D6
Lowther Av *BSDN* G61 ... 61 J2
Lowther Bank *IRVSE* KA11 ... 204 C7
Lowther Pl *KLMNK* KA1 ... 212 A5
Lowther Ter *KVD/HLHD* G12 ... 82 C5
Low Waters Rd *HMLTN* ML3 ... 174 D1
Loyal Av *ERSK* PA8 ... 58 F8
Loyal Gdns *BSDN* G61 ... 61 H1
Loyal Pl *ERSK* PA8 ... 58 F8
Loyne Dr *RNFRW* PA4 ... 80 F7

Luath St *GOV/IBX* G51 .... 104 A1
Lubas Av *GVH/MTFL* G42 .... 128 D2
Lubas Pl *GVH/MTFL* G42 .... 128 D2
Lubnaig Dr *ERSK* PA8 .... 58 E8
Lubnaig Gdns *BSDN* G61 .... 61 J2
Lubnaig Pl *AIRDRIE* ML6 .... 88 E7
Lubnaig Rd *PLKSW/MSWD* G43 .. 127 L4
Luce Av *KLMNK* KA1 .... 212 A4
Luckiesfauld *BRHD/NEIL* G78 .. 148 D3
Luckingsford Av *RNFRW* PA4 .... 79 K2
Luckingsford Dr *RNFRW* PA4 ..... 79 K2
Luckingsford Rd *RNFRW* PA4 .... 79 J2
Lucy Brae *UD/BTH/TAN* G71 .... 131 L1
Luffness Gdns *CAR/SHTL* G32 ...... 107 H7
Lugar Crs *PSTWK* KA9 .... 225 H4
Lugar Dr *CARD/HILL/MSPK* G52 .. 103 L5
Lugar Pl *LNPK/KPK* G44 .... 128 E4
TROON KA10 .... 216 F4
Lugar St *CTBR* ML5 .... 110 B1
Luggiebank Pl
BAIL/MDB/MHD G69 .... 109 G5
Luggiebank Rd *KKNTL* G66 .... 65 K1
Luggie Rd *CARLUKE* ML8 .... 178 D7
Luggie Vw *CUMB* G67 .... 68 A2
Luing Rd
CARD/HILL/MSPK G52 .... 103 L4
Luma Gdns *GOV/IBX* G51 .... 103 J2
Lumloch St
SPRGB/BLRNK G21 .... 84 A5
Lumsden La *KVGV* G3 .... 82 D8
Lumsden Pl *SVSTN* KA20 .... 192 E8
Lumsden St *KVGV* G3 .... 104 D1
Lunan Dr *BSHPBGS* G64 .... 84 C1
Lunan Pl *GOV/IBX* G51 .... 103 L2
Luncarty Pl *CAR/SHTL* G32 .... 107 G6
Luncarty St *CAR/SHTL* G32 .... 107 G6
Lunderston Dr *PLK/PH/NH* G53 .. 126 A2
Lundholm Rd *SVSTN* KA20 .... 201 L2
Lundie Gdns *BSHPBGS* G64 .... 84 D1
Lundie St *CAR/SHTL* G32 .... 106 E6
Lurg St *PGL* PA14 .... 54 D1
Luss Av *GRNK* PA15 .... 33 H8
Luss Brae *HMLTN* ML3 .... 155 L7
Lusset Gln *OLDK* G60 .... 59 H3
Lusset Rd *OLDK* G60 .... 59 H3
Lusshill Ter *UD/BTH/TAN* G71 ...... 108 B7
Luss Pl *GRNK* PA15 .... 33 J8
Luss Rd *ALEX/LLW* G83 .... 25 K2
GOV/IBX G51 .... 103 M2
HBR/GL G84 .... 21 G4
Lye Brae *CUMB* G67 .... 49 G7
Lyell Gv *EKILN* G74 .... 153 L6
Lyell Pl *EKILN* G74 .... 153 L6
Lyle Crs *BSHPTN* PA7 .... 57 M5
Lylefoot Crs
GRNKW/INVK PA16 .... 32 B1
Lylefoot Pl *GRNKW/INVK* PA16 ...... 32 B2
Lyle Gv *GRNKW/INVK* PA16 .... 32 B2
Lyle Pl *GRNKW/INVK* PA16 .... 32 A2
PSLYS PA2 .... 9 K9
Lyle Rd *AIRDRIE* ML6 .... 111 M2
GRNKW/INVK PA16 .... 32 A1
KLMCLM PA13 .... 75 K1
Lylesland Ct *PSLYS* PA2 .... 9 H8
Lyle Sq *MLNGV* G62 .... 41 L7
Lyle St *GRNK* PA15 .... 2 D5
Lyman Dr *WISHAW* ML2 .... 159 J2
Lymburn Pl *AYR* KA8 .... 19 J3
Lymburn St *KVGV* G3 .... 82 D8
Lymekilns Rd *EKILN* G74 .... 14 C1
Lyndale Pl *MRYH/FIRH* G20 .... 82 D1
Lyndale Rd *MRYH/FIRH* G20 .... 82 D1
Lyndhurst Gdns *MRYH/FIRH* G20 ..... 4 D2
Lyndhurst Gardens La
MRYH/FIRH G20 .... 4 B2
Lyne Cft *BSHPBGS* G64 .... 64 A5
Lynedoch Crs *KVGV* G3 .... 4 C6
Lynedoch Crescent La *KVGV* G3 ...... 4 C6
Lynedoch Pl *KVGV* G3 .... 4 C7
Lynedoch St *GRNK* PA15 .... 2 D6
KVGV G3 .... 4 C7
Lynedoch Ter *KVGV* G3 .... 4 C7
Lyne St *WISHAW* ML2 .... 159 G4
Lynmouth Pl
GRNKW/INVK PA16 .... 31 L4
Lynn Av *DALRY* KA24 .... 184 C2
Lynnburn Av *BLSH* ML4 .... 133 G4
Lynn Ct *LRKH* ML9 .... 176 A7
Lynn Dr *KBRN* KA25 .... 143 H6
MLNGV G62 .... 42 C7
Lynne Dr *SMSTN* G23 .... 62 E8
Lynnhurst *UD/BTH/TAN* G71 .... 131 M2
Lynnwood Rd *WISHAW* ML2 .... 160 C3
Lynton Av *GIF/THBK* G46 .... 127 G8
Lyoncross Av *BRHD/NEIL* G78 .... 125 K7
Lyoncross Crs
BRHD/NEIL G78 .... 125 K6
Lyoncross Rd *PLK/PH/NH* G53 .... 103 H7
Lyon Rd *ERSK* PA8 .... 58 E8
PSLYN/LNWD PA3 .... 100 B5
PSLYS PA2 .... 100 F8
Lysa Vale Pl *BLSH* ML4 .... 132 E4
Lytham Dr *SMSTN* G23 .... 62 E8
Lytham Mdw
UD/BTH/TAN G71 .... 131 L7
Lythgow Wy *LNK/LMHG* ML11 .... 199 J4
Lyttelton *EKILS* G75 .... 171 H2

M

Mabel St *MTHW* ML1 .... 157 L4
Macadam Gdns *BLSH* ML4 .... 133 G3
Macadam Pl *AYR* KA8 .... 19 G2
EKILS G75 .... 14 F6
KLMNKN/STW KA3 .... 17 L2
Macallan Pl *IRVSE* KA11 .... 203 M2
Macallister Pl
KLMNKN/STW KA3 .... 17 L2
Macalpine Pl *KLMNKN/STW* KA3 .... 17 L1
Macandrew Pl
KLMNKN/STW KA3 .... 17 M3
Macara Dr *IRV* KA12 .... 203 L6
Macarthur Av *AIRDRIE* ML6 .... 88 D6
Macarthur Ct *EKILN* G74 .... 153 J6
Macarthur Crs *EKILN* G74 .... 153 J5
Macarthur Dr *EKILN* G74 .... 153 J6
Macarthur Gdns *EKILN* G74 ...... 153 J6
Macarthur Wynd
BLTYR/CAMB G72 .... 130 C4
Macaulay Pl *HBR/GL* G84 .... 20 A7
Macauley Pl *KLMNKN/STW* KA3 .... 17 L2
Macbeth *EKILN* G74 .... 154 B4
Macbeth Dr *KLMNKN/STW* KA3 .... 17 M3
Macbeth Pl *DEN/PKHD* G31 .... 13 L7
Macbeth Rd *GRNKW/INVK* PA16 .... 32 A4
Macbeth St *DEN/PKHD* G31 .... 13 L8
Mac Callum Dr
BLTYR/CAMB G72 .... 130 C4
Maccrimmon Pk *EKILN* G74 ..... 153 H5
Macdairmid Dr *HMLTN* ML3 .... 174 B2
Macdonald Av *EKILN* G74 .... 153 G5
Macdonald Ct *BEITH* KA15 .... 168 A2
Macdonald Crs *KSYTH* G65 .... 46 F6
Macdonald Dr
KLMNKN/STW KA3 .... 17 M3
Macdonald Gv *BLSH* ML4 .... 132 F7
Macdonald Pl
KLMNKN/STW KA3 .... 17 M3
Macdonald St *MTHW* ML1 .... 157 M4
RUTH G73 .... 129 G2
Macdougall Pl
KLMNKN/STW KA3 .... 17 L3
Macdougall St *GRNK* PA15 .... 3 L7
PLKSW/MSWD G43 .... 127 J2
Macdougal Qd *BLSH* ML4 .... 132 F7
Macdowall St *JNSTN* PA5 .... 99 M6
PSLYN/LNWD PA3 .... 8 E1
Macduff Pl *DEN/PKHD* G31 .... 13 L8
Macduff St *DEN/PKHD* G31 .... 13 L8
Macedonian Gv *MTHW* ML1 .... 134 C5
Mace Rd *KNTSWD* G13 .... 61 J8
Macewan Pl *KLMNKN/STW* KA3 .... 17 L4
Macfarlane Crs
BLTYR/CAMB G72 .... 130 C4
Macfarlane Dr
KLMNKN/STW KA3 .... 17 L2
Macfarlane Rd *BSDN* G61 .... 61 M6
Macfie Pl *EKILN* G74 .... 153 H5
Macgregor Dr
KLMNKN/STW KA3 .... 17 K4
Machan Av *LRKH* ML9 .... 176 A6
Machanhill *LRKH* ML9 .... 176 C7
Machanhill Vw *LRKH* ML9 .... 176 B7
Machan Rd *LRKH* ML9 .... 176 A7
Machrie Dr *CSMK* G45 .... 128 F5
HBR/GL G84 .... 20 F6
NMRNS G77 .... 150 E3
Machrie Gn *EKILS* G75 .... 171 H5
Machrie Pl *KLWNG* KA13 .... 193 J6
Machrie Rd *CSMK* G45 .... 128 F5
KLMNKN/STW KA3 .... 206 E5
Machrie St *CSMK* G45 .... 128 F6
MTHW ML1 .... 157 H2
Macinnes Pl *KLMNKN/STW* KA3 .... 17 L2
Macintosh Pl *EKILS* G75 .... 14 B8
Macintyre Pl *KLMNKN/STW* KA3 .... 17 L2
Macintyre Rd *PSTWK* KA9 .... 221 J7
Macintyre St *KVGV* G3 .... 10 D1
Macivor Crs *EKILN* G74 .... 153 G5
Macivor Pl *KLMNKN/STW* KA3 .... 17 L3
Mackean St *PSLYN/LNWD* PA3 .... 101 J3
Mackeith St *DMNK/BRGTN* G40 .... 12 C7
Mackellar Pl *KLMNKN/STW* KA3 .... 17 L1
Mackenzie Dr *KLBCH* PA10 .... 99 H8
KLMNKN/STW KA3 .... 17 J3
Mackenzie Gdns *EKILN* G74 ...... 153 G5
Mackenzie St *GRNK* PA15 .... 3 L7
Mackenzie Ter *BLSH* ML4 .... 133 G2
Mackerston Pl *LARGS* KA30 .... 115 J6
Mackie Av *PGL* PA14 .... 34 A8
Mackie Pl *KLMNKN/STW* KA3 .... 17 L2
Mackie's Mill Rd *JNSTN* PA5 .... 123 K1
Mackie St *AYR* KA8 .... 225 J7
Mackinlay Pl *KLMNK* KA1 .... 17 H6
Mackinlay St *GBLS* G5 .... 11 G8
Mackinnon Dr
KLMNKN/STW KA3 .... 17 L4
Mackinnon Ter *IRV* KA12 .... 203 L5
Mackintosh Pl *IRVSE* KA11 .... 203 L8
Mack St *AIRDRIE* ML6 .... 111 G1
Maclachlan Pl *HBR/GL* G84 .... 20 E6
Maclachlan Rd *HBR/GL* G84 .... 20 E6
Maclaren Pl *KLMNKN/STW* KA3 .... 17 L4
Maclay Av *KLBCH* PA10 .... 99 G7
Maclean Ct *EKILN* G74 .... 153 H5
Maclean Dr *KLMNKN/STW* KA3 .... 17 K3
Maclean Gv *EKILN* G74 .... 153 H5
Maclean Pl *EKILN* G74 .... 153 H5
Maclean Sq *GOV/IBX* G51 .... 10 A3
Maclean St *CLYDBK* G81 .... 80 E1
GOV/IBX G51 .... 104 D3
Maclehose Rd *CUMB* G67 .... 49 J6
Maclellan Rd *BRHD/NEIL* G78 .... 148 D3
Macleod Crs *HBR/GL* G84 .... 20 B5
Macleod Dr *HBR/GL* G84 .... 20 C5
KLMNKN/STW KA3 .... 17 L4
Macleod Pl *EKILN* G74 .... 154 B6
Macleod St *COWCAD* G4 .... 12 A1
NMLNS KA16 .... 215 H2
Macmillan Dr *GRK* PA19 .... 31 K3
Macmillan Gdns
UD/BTH/TAN G71 .... 109 G8
Macmillan Pl *KLMNKN/STW* KA3 .... 17 L3
Macmillan St *LRKH* ML9 .... 175 M7
Macnab Pl *KLMNKN/STW* KA3 .... 17 K3
Macnaughton Dr
KLMNKN/STW KA3 .... 17 L3
Macneill Dr *EKILN* G74 .... 153 H5
Macneill Gdns *EKILN* G74 .... 153 G5
Macneil Pl *KLMNKN/STW* KA3 .... 17 K3
Macneil St *LRKH* ML9 .... 175 M6
Macneish Wy *EKILN* G74 .... 153 H5
Macnicol Ct *EKILN* G74 .... 153 C5
Macnicol Pk *EKILN* G74 .... 153 G5
Macnicol Pl *EKILN* G74 .... 153 G5
KLMNKN/STW KA3 .... 17 L3
Macphail Dr *KLMNKN/STW* KA3 ...... 17 K3
Macpherson Pk *EKILN* G74 ...... 153 J6
Macpherson Pl
KLMNKN/STW KA3 .... 17 M3
Macphie Rd *DMBTN* G82 .... 37 J4
Macrae Dr *PSTWK* KA9 .... 221 J7
Macrae Gdns *EKILN* G74 .... 153 J6
Macreadie Pl *IRVSE* KA11 .... 204 D3
Macrimmon Pl *EKILS* G75 .... 14 E5
Macrobert Av *IRVSE* KA11 .... 204 B8
Mactaggart Rd *CUMB* G67 .... 68 E1
Madeira La *GRNKW/INVK* PA16 ...... 32 D2
Madeira St *GRNKW/INVK* PA16 ...... 32 D2
Madison Av *LNPK/KPK* G44 .... 128 B4
Madras Pl *BRHD/NEIL* G78 .... 148 E2
Madras St *DMNK/BRGTN* G40 .... 12 C9
Mafeking St *GOV/IBX* G51 .... 104 B3
WISHAW ML2 .... 158 D5
Mafeking Ter *BRHD/NEIL* G78 .... 148 C2
Magna St *MTHW* ML1 .... 157 H1
Magnolia Dr *BLTYR/CAMB* G72 ...... 130 F6
Magnolia Gdns *MTHW* ML1 ...... 134 C6
Magnolia Pl
UD/BTH/TAN G71 .... 132 C1
Magnolia St *WISHAW* ML2 .... 159 H4
Magnus Crs *LNPK/KPK* G44 .... 128 B5
Magnus Rd *CRG/CRSL/HOU* PA6 ...... 99 J1
Magpie Crs *GRNKW/INVK* PA16 ...... 50 E4
Mahon Ct *BAIL/MDB/MHD* G69 ...... 66 F8
Maidens *EKILN* G74 .... 153 K6
Maidens Av *NMRNS* G77 .... 151 G4
Maidland Rd *PLK/PH/NH* G53 .... 126 C2
Maid Morville Av *IRVSE* KA11 .... 209 J1
Mailerbeg Gdns
BAIL/MDB/MHD G69 .... 66 F6
Mailing Av *BSHPBGS* G64 .... 64 B7
Maimhor Rd *WKIL* KA23 .... 181 H5
Mainhill Av
BAIL/MDB/MHD G69 .... 108 D4
Mainhill Dr
BAIL/MDB/MHD G69 .... 108 C4
Mainhill Pl *BAIL/MDB/MHD* G69 .. 108 C4
Mainhill Rd
BAIL/MDB/MHD G69 .... 108 F4
Mainholm Crs *AYR* KA8 .... 225 K8
Mainholm Rd *AYR* KA8 .... 225 K7
RAYR/DAL KA6 .... 229 L1
Main Rd *AYR* KA8 .... 225 L7
CRH/DND KA2 .... 210 E4
CUMB G67 .... 67 L5
DMBTN G82 .... 35 H1
FAIRLIE KA29 .... 139 K7
IRVSE KA11 .... 204 F7
JNSTN PA5 .... 100 C6
KBRN KA25 .... 143 H8
KLMNKN/STW KA3 .... 212 D2
PGL PA14 .... 56 B2
PGL PA14 .... 56 E3
PSLYS PA2 .... 8 E6
Mains Av *BEITH* KA15 .... 144 A8
GIF/THBK G46 .... 127 H8
HBR/GL G84 .... 20 A6
Mains Ct *LNK/LMHG* ML11 .... 199 J3
Mainscroft *ERSK* PA8 .... 59 J8
Mains Dr *ERSK* PA8 .... 59 J8
Mains Hl *ERSK* PA8 .... 59 H8
Mainshill Av *ERSK* PA8 .... 59 H8
Mainshill Gdns *ERSK* PA8 .... 59 H8
Mains Pl *BLSH* ML4 .... 133 G6
Mains River *ERSK* PA8 .... 59 J8
Mains Rd *BEITH* KA15 .... 144 A8
EKILN G74 .... 153 L4
Main St *AIRDRIE* ML6 .... 90 A7
AIRDRIE ML6 .... 91 G1
AIRDRIE ML6 .... 91 G5
AIRDRIE ML6 .... 111 J6
AIRDRIE ML6 .... 111 L6
ALEX/LLW G83 .... 25 L4
ALEX/LLW G83 .... 25 M5
AYR KA8 .... 18 F1
BAIL/MDB/MHD G69 .... 86 C1
BAIL/MDB/MHD G69 .... 108 C5
BEITH KA15 .... 144 B8
BEITH KA15 .... 168 E1
BLSH ML4 .... 132 F4
BLTYR/CAMB G72 .... 129 M3
BLTYR/CAMB G72 .... 155 J3
BRHD/NEIL G78 .... 125 H7
BRHD/NEIL G78 .... 148 D2
BRWEIR PA11 .... 98 D1
BSDN G61 .... 62 A2
BSHPBGS G64 .... 64 B1
CRG/CRSL/HOU PA6 .... 77 G6
CRH/DND KA2 .... 209 M8
CRMNK/CLK/EAG G76 .... 151 M3
CTBR ML5 .... 87 K4
CTBR ML5 .... 110 A3
CUMB G67 .... 49 H4
DALRY KA24 .... 184 C2
DMBTN G82 .... 25 K7
DMNK/BRGTN G40 .... 12 C9
EKILN G74 .... 15 G1
GIF/THBK G46 .... 126 F6
GLGNK KA14 .... 167 H3
GRNK PA15 .... 3 H6
GRNKW/INVK PA16 .... 50 D4
HWWD PA9 .... 121 M4
IRVSE KA11 .... 204 B8
IRVSE KA11 .... 209 K3
KKNTL G66 .... 44 D1
KLMNK KA1 .... 218 C5
KLMNKN/STW KA3 .... 197 K1
KLMNKN/STW KA3 .... 206 C2
KLWNG KA13 .... 193 L6
KSYTH G65 .... 46 F5
KSYTH G65 .... 47 K1
LARGS KA30 .... 115 J6
LOCHW PA12 .... 120 C7
MLNGV G62 .... 42 A8
MTHW ML1 .... 134 A4
MTHW ML1 .... 135 J8
NMLNS KA16 .... 215 J2
PSTWK KA9 .... 221 K5
PSTWK KA9 .... 225 J1
RUTH G73 .... 129 G1
SVSTN KA20 .... 201 K1
TROON KA10 .... 217 H6
UD/BTH/TAN G71 .... 131 L3
UD/BTH/TAN G71 .... 132 A7
WISHAW ML2 .... 159 G6
WISHAW ML2 .... 160 A5
WISHAW ML2 .... 177 J2
WKIL KA23 .... 181 J4
Mains Wd *ERSK* PA8 .... 59 K8
Mair Av *DALRY* KA24 .... 184 D2
Mair St *GOV/IBX* G51 .... 10 A4
NMLNS KA16 .... 215 J2
Maitland Bank *LRKH* ML9 .... 176 C6
Maitland Dr *BSHPBGS* G64 .... 44 B8
Maitland Pl *RNFRW* PA4 .... 80 B7
Maitland St *COWCAD* G4 .... 5 H6
HBR/GL G84 .... 20 D8
Malborough La North
PTCK G11 .... 81 M6
Malborough La South *PTCK* G11 .. 81 M6
Malcolm Gdns *EKILN* G74 .... 14 A2
Malcolm Pl *HBR/GL* G84 .... 20 F7
Malcolm St *MTHW* ML1 .... 157 J3
Malin Pl *STPS/GTHM/RID* G33 ...... 106 F1
Mallaig Pl *GOV/IBX* G51 .... 103 K2
Mallaig Rd *GOV/IBX* G51 .... 103 K2
PGL PA14 .... 54 F2
Mallard Crs *EKILS* G75 .... 171 G4
GRNKW/INVK PA16 .... 32 A3
Mallard Pl *EKILS* G75 .... 171 G4
Mallard Rd *CLYDBK* G81 .... 60 B4
Mallard Ter *EKILS* G75 .... 171 G4
Mallard Wy *BLSH* ML4 .... 109 M8
Malleable Gdns *MTHW* ML1 .... 133 J7
Malletsheugh Rd *NMRNS* G77 .... 150 B6
Malloch Crs *JNSTN* PA5 .... 100 B7
Malloch Pl *EKILN* G74 .... 15 L2
Malloch St *MRYH/FIRH* G20 .... 82 E4
Malov Ct *EKILS* G75 .... 171 L4
Malplaquet Ct *CARLUKE* ML8 .... 179 H8
Maltbarns St *MRYH/FIRH* G20 .... 4 E2
Mambeg Dr *GOV/IBX* G51 .... 103 L1
Mamore Pl *PLKSW/MSWD* G43 ...... 127 J3
Mamore St *PLKSW/MSWD* G43 ...... 127 J3
Manchester Dr *KVD/HLHD* G12 ...... 82 A3
Mandora Ct *CARLUKE* ML8 .... 179 H8
Manitoba Crs *EKILS* G75 .... 153 H8
Mannering *EKILN* G74 .... 154 D5
Mannering Ct
PLKSD/SHW G41 .... 127 J1
Mannering Rd *PLKSD/SHW* G41 .. 127 J1
PSLYS PA2 .... 123 L1
Mannofield *BSDN* G61 .... 61 K5
Manor Av *KLMNKN/STW* KA3 .... 207 G5
Manor Crs *GRK* PA19 .... 31 M2
Manor Dr *AIRDRIE* ML6 .... 110 E1
Manor Ga *NMRNS* G77 .... 150 F6
Manor Rd *BAIL/MDB/MHD* G69 .... 86 F4
DRUM G15 .... 60 F8
PSLYS PA2 .... 100 F8
SCOT G14 .... 81 L5
Manor Vw *AIRDRIE* ML6 .... 111 H7
LRKH ML9 .... 176 C7
Manor Wy *RUTH* G73 .... 129 J5
Manresa Pl *COWCAD* G4 .... 5 G5
Manse Av *BSDN* G61 .... 61 M4
CTBR ML5 .... 109 K5
UD/BTH/TAN G71 .... 132 A7
Manse Brae *LNPK/KPK* G44 .... 128 B3
LRKH ML9 .... 177 J8
Manse Ct *BRHD/NEIL* G78 .... 125 K6
CARLUKE ML8 .... 178 A5
KSYTH G65 .... 47 K2
LARGS KA30 .... 115 J6
Manse Crs
CRG/CRSL/HOU PA6 .... 77 H7
Mansefield Av
BLTYR/CAMB G72 .... 130 A5
Mansefield Crs *LARGS* KA30 .... 115 J4
OLDK G60 .... 59 G2
Manse Garden's
ALEX/LLW G83 .... 25 M1
Manse La *EKILN* G74 .... 153 M6
Mansel St *SPRGB/BLRNK* G21 .... 83 M4
Manse Pl *AIRDRIE* ML6 .... 110 F2
Manse Rd *BAIL/MDB/MHD* G69 ..... 108 E3
BRHD/NEIL G78 .... 148 D2
BSDN G61 .... 61 M4
CAR/SHTL G32 .... 107 K5
CRMNK/CLK/EAG G76 .... 152 D2
KSYTH G65 .... 47 K2
LNK/LMHG ML11 .... 198 F5
MTHW ML1 .... 157 M5
OLDK G60 .... 58 D1
RAYR/DAL KA6 .... 231 L5
SHOTTS ML7 .... 113 K7
WISHAW ML2 .... 159 M5
WKIL KA23 .... 181 K4
Manse St *CTBR* ML5 .... 109 M3
KLMNK KA1 .... 17 H5
RNFRW PA4 .... 80 D5
SALT KA21 .... 200 E1
Manseview *LRKH* ML9 .... 176 B7
Manse Vw *MTHW* ML1 .... 134 F5
Mansewell Rd *PSTWK* KA9 .... 221 J8
Mansewood Dr *DMBTN* G82 .... 37 H4
Mansewood Rd *GIF/THBK* G46 .... 127 H5
PLKSW/MSWD G43 .... 127 H4
Mansfield Crs
CRMNK/CLK/EAG G76 .... 151 K3
Mansfield Rd *BLSH* ML4 .... 132 F5
CARD/HILL/MSPK G52 .... 102 F2
CRMNK/CLK/EAG G76 .... 151 L3
HMLTN ML3 .... 174 D2
LOCHW PA12 .... 120 D6
PSTWK KA9 .... 225 H3
Mansfield St *PTCK* G11 .... 82 C7
Mansfield Wy *IRVSE* KA11 .... 204 A4
Mansion Av *PGL* PA14 .... 55 H1
Mansion Ct *BLTYR/CAMB* G72 . 130 A3
Mansionhouse Av
CAR/SHTL G32 .... 130 C1
Mansionhouse Dr
CAR/SHTL G32 .... 107 J3
Mansionhouse Gdns
PLKSD/SHW G41 .... 127 L2
Mansionhouse Gv
CAR/SHTL G32 .... 107 L6
Mansionhouse Rd
CAR/SHTL G32 .... 107 L5
PLKSD/SHW G41 .... 127 L2
PSLY PA1 .... 9 L3
Mansion St *BLTYR/CAMB* G72 .... 130 A3
PPK/MIL G22 .... 83 J4
Manson Av *PSTWK* KA9 .... 221 K8
Manson Pl *EKILS* G75 .... 172 A4
Manson Rd *IRV* KA12 .... 203 L5
Manuel Av *BEITH* KA15 .... 168 A2
Manuel Ct *KBRN* KA25 .... 167 G1
Maple Av *DMBTN* G82 .... 36 A4
KKNTL G66 .... 45 H4
NMRNS G77 .... 150 D5
Maple Bank *HMLTN* ML3 .... 156 F7
Maple Ct *CUMB* G67 .... 49 M4
Maple Crs *BLTYR/CAMB* G72 .... 130 F6
Maple Dr *AYRS* KA7 .... 229 K4
BEITH KA15 .... 144 B7
BRHD/NEIL G78 .... 149 K1
CLYDBK G81 .... 59 M4
JNSTN PA5 .... 122 F1
KKNTL G66 .... 65 G4
LRKH ML9 .... 176 A4
Maple Pl *EKILS* G75 .... 171 H3
KLMNK KA1 .... 16 A5
UD/BTH/TAN G71 .... 132 D1
Maple Qd *AIRDRIE* ML6 .... 111 K3
Maple Rd *CUMB* G67 .... 49 M4
GRNKW/INVK PA16 .... 32 B6
MTHW ML1 .... 134 B4
PLKSD/SHW G41 .... 104 B5
Maple Ter *EKILS* G75 .... 171 H3
Maplewood *WISHAW* ML2 .... 158 D8
Mar Av *BSHPTN* PA7 .... 58 B6
Marble Av *IRVSE* KA11 .... 209 K1
Marchbank Gdns *PSLY* PA1 .... 102 D5
Marchburn Av *PSTWK* KA9 .... 225 L1
Marchdyke Crs *KLMNK* KA1 .... 211 L6
The Marches *LNK/LMHG* ML11 .... 199 H4
Marchfield Av
PSLYN/LNWD PA3 .... 101 K1
Marchfield Qd *AYR* KA8 .... 225 G4
Marchfield Rd *AYR* KA8 .... 225 G4
Marchglen Pl *GOV/IBX* G51 ...... 103 K2
Marchmont Ct *KLMNK* KA1 .... 212 F2
Marchmont Gdns *BSHPBGS* G64 .. 63 M6
Marchmont Rd *AYRS* KA7 .... 18 E7
Marchmont Road La *AYRS* KA7 .... 18 D6
Marchmont Ter
KVD/HLHD G12 .... 82 C6
March St *PLKSD/SHW* G41 .... 104 F7
Mardale *EKILN* G74 .... 153 J6
Mar Dr *BSDN* G61 .... 61 M2
Maree Dr
CARD/HILL/MSPK G52 .... 103 L5
CUMB G67 .... 68 B2
Maree Gdns *BSHPBGS* G64 .... 64 B8
Maree Pl *IRV* KA12 .... 203 K2
Maree Rd *PSLYS* PA2 .... 101 G7
Marfield St *CAR/SHTL* G32 .... 106 E2
Mar Gdns *RUTH* G73 .... 129 K5
Margaret Av *GLSTN* KA4 .... 214 A4
SHOTTS ML7 .... 113 H7
Margaret Dr *ALEX/LLW* G83 .... 25 K4
Margaret Pl *BLSH* ML4 .... 132 E4
Margaret Rd *HMLTN* ML3 .... 156 B3
Margaret's Pl *LRKH* ML9 .... 176 A6
Margaret St *CTBR* ML5 .... 110 A5
GRK PA19 .... 31 M2
GRNKW/INVK PA16 .... 32 D2
Margaretvale Dr *LRKH* ML9 .... 176 A7
Marguerite Av *KKNTL* G66 .... 65 J3
Marguerite Gdns
UD/BTH/TAN G71 .... 132 B7
Marian Dr *MTHW* ML1 .... 134 C7
Marigold Av *MTHW* ML1 .... 157 L1
Marigold Wy *CARLUKE* ML8 .... 188 F1
Marina Ct *BLSH* ML4 .... 132 E6
Marina Rd *PSTWK* KA9 .... 225 H1
Marine Ct *FAIRLIE* KA29 .... 139 K5
Marine Crs *GOV/IBX* G51 .... 10 B4
Marine Dr *IRV* KA12 .... 208 A1
Marine Gdns *GOV/IBX* G51 .... 10 B4
Marine Pde *GTCI* KA28 .... 138 C6
Mariner Ct *CLYDBK* G81 .... 60 A7
Marion St *BLSH* ML4 .... 133 K4
Mariscat Rd *PLKSD/SHW* G41 .. 104 E7
Marjory Dr *PSLYN/LNWD* PA3 .... 102 A2
Marjory Rd *RNFRW* PA4 .... 80 A8
Market End *LNK/LMHG* ML11 .. 199 G5
Markethill Rd *EKILN* G74 .... 153 L5
Market Pl *CARLUKE* ML8 .... 178 F7
Market Rd *CARLUKE* ML8 .... 178 F7
KKNTL G66 .... 66 A2
UD/BTH/TAN G71 .... 132 C2
Market St *AIRDRIE* ML6 .... 111 G2
KSYTH G65 .... 47 K1
UD/BTH/TAN G71 .... 132 C2
Markinch Rd *PGL* PA14 .... 54 F3
Marlborough Av *PTCK* G11 .... 81 M6
Marlborough Pk *EKILS* G75 .... 171 G2
Marldon La *PTCK* G11 .... 81 M6
Marlepark *AYRS* KA7 .... 229 G6
Marley Wy *KKNTL* G66 .... 45 G3
Marlfield Gdns *BLSH* ML4 .... 133 G2
Marloch Av *PGL* PA14 .... 54 F3
Marlow St *PLKSD/SHW* G41 .... 10 B7
Marmion Av *HBR/GL* G84 .... 23 G2
Marmion Crs *MTHW* ML1 .... 133 K7
Marmion Dr *KKNTL* G66 .... 65 M1
Marmion Pl *CUMB* G67 .... 68 E2
Marmion Rd *CUMB* G67 .... 68 E2
PSLYS PA2 .... 123 L1
Marne St *DEN/PKHD* G31 .... 13 G1
Marnoch Dr *CTBR* ML5 .... 87 K3
Marnock Ter *PSLYS* PA2 .... 9 L8
Marr Dr *TROON* KA10 .... 216 D5
Marress Rd *IRV* KA12 .... 203 H6
Marrswood Gn *HMLTN* ML3 .... 156 A5
Marrs Wynd *LNK/LMHG* ML11 ...... 199 J4
Marrwood Av *KKNTL* G66 .... 66 B3
Marshall Gv *HMLTN* ML3 .... 156 B6
Marshall La *WISHAW* ML2 .... 159 G6
Marshall's La *PSLY* PA1 .... 9 H4
Marshall St *CTBR* ML5 .... 109 K5
LRKH ML9 .... 176 A6
WISHAW ML2 .... 158 F7
Marsmount Rd *PSTWK* KA9 .... 221 L8
Mars Rd *GRNKW/INVK* PA16 .... 31 J6
Martha St *CGLE* G1 .... 5 K9
Martin Av *IRV* KA12 .... 203 K4
RAYR/DAL KA6 .... 227 H3
Martin Ct *HMLTN* ML3 .... 156 C6
Martin Crs *BAIL/MDB/MHD* G69 .. 108 C4
Martin Pl *MTHW* ML1 .... 134 C6
Martinside *EKILS* G75 .... 171 L4
Martin Sq *SALT* KA21 .... 192 A7
Martin St *CTBR* ML5 .... 110 D2

DMNK/BRGTN G40 105 M6 2
Martlet Dr JNSTN PA5 122 C2
Martnaham Dr RAYR/DAL KA6 231 H5
Mart St CGLE G1 11 K4 2
Martyn St AIRDRIE ML6 110 E2
Martyrs Pl BSHPBGS G64 84 A1
Marwick St DEN/PKHD G31 13 H1
Maryborough Av PSTWK KA9 225 H3
Maryborough Rd PSTWK KA9 225 G3
Mary Dr BLSH ML4 132 E6
Maryfield Pl AYR KA8 225 H5 2
Maryfield Rd AYR KA8 225 H5
Mary Gln WISHAW ML2 159 K4
Maryhill Rd BSDN G61 62 A7
COWCAD G4 4 E6
MRYH/FIRH G20 4 D2
Maryknowe Rd MTHW ML1 134 C8
Maryland Dr
CARD/HILL/MSPK G52 103 L4
Maryland Gdns
CARD/HILL/MSPK G52 103 L4
Maryland Rd DMBTN G82 37 J3
Mary Love Pl SVSTN KA20 192 B8
Marypark Rd PGL PA14 56 B2
Mary Rae Rd BLSH ML4 132 E6
Maryston St STPS/GTHM/RID G33 7 M4
Mary St GRNKW/INVK PA16 32 C5 1
HMLTN ML3 156 D7
JNSTN PA5 100 A6
PGL PA14 34 A7 3
PSLYS PA2 9 H9
Maryville Av GIF/THBK G46 127 J7
Maryville Gdns GIF/THBK G46 127 J7 2
Maryville Vw UD/BTH/TAN G71 108 D8
Marywood Sq
PLKSD/SHW G41 104 F7 1
Mary Young Pl
CRMNK/CLK/EAG G76 151 M3 2
Masonfield Av BALLOCH G68 48 D7
Masonhill Pl AYRS KA7 19 M9 1
Mason La MTHW ML1 157 L3 3
Mason St LRKH ML9 176 C8
Masterton St COWCAD G4 5 K3
Masterton Wy
UD/BTH/TAN G71 109 H8
Matherton Av NMRNS G77 151 H4
Mathew Smith Av KLMNK KA1 16 C8
Mathie Crs GRK PA19 31 L3
Mathieson Rd RUTH G73 106 C8
Mathieson St PSLY PA1 102 B4 2
Matilda Rd PLKSD/SHW G41 10 A8
Matthew Mcwhirter Pl
LRKH ML9 176 B5 1
Matthew Pl KLWNG KA13 193 L4
Mauchline EKILN G74 154 D6
Mauchline Av KKNTL G66 46 A7
Mauchline Ct HMLTN ML3 155 K7 2
Mauchline Rd KLMNK KA1 212 F3
RAYR/DAL KA6 227 G3
Mauchline Ter
GRNKW/INVK PA16 31 L6 1
Maukinfauld Ct
DEN/PKHD G31 13 M9 1
Maukinfauld Rd CAR/SHTL G32 106 E6
Mauldslie Dr CARLUKE ML8 177 M3
Mauldslie Rd CARLUKE ML8 177 K6
Mauldslie St BLSH ML4 133 G5 5
CTBR ML5 110 A4
DMNK/BRGTN G40 13 G7
Maule Dr PTCK G11 82 A7
Mausoleum Dr HMLTN ML3 156 E4
Mavis Bank BSHPBGS G64 83 M1
Mavisbank Gdns BLSH ML4 133 G3
GOV/IBX G51 10 A3
Mavisbank Rd GOV/IBX G51 104 D3 3
Mavisbank St AIRDRIE ML6 110 E1
WISHAW ML2 160 C3
Mavisbank Ter JNSTN PA5 99 M7 2
PSLY PA1 9 K6
Mavis Rd GRNKW/INVK PA16 32 A4
Mavor Av EKILN G74 153 M5
Maxholm Rd KLMNK KA1 211 L4
Maxton Av BRHD/NEIL G78 125 G6 1
Maxton Crs WISHAW ML2 159 J3
Maxton Gv BRHD/NEIL G78 125 G7
Maxton Ter BLTYR/CAMB G72 129 M6
Maxwell Av
BAIL/MDB/MHD G69 108 A5
BSDN G61 61 L7
PLKSD/SHW G41 10 B8
Maxwell Ct BEITH KA15 168 A2 3
KLMNKN/STW KA3 207 K6 1
Maxwell Crs BLTYR/CAMB G72 155 K3
Maxwell Dr
BAIL/MDB/MHD G69 107 M4
EKILN G74 15 H2
ERSK PA8 58 F6
PLKSD/SHW G41 104 C5
Maxwell Gdns KLMNK KA1 212 E3
PLKSD/SHW G41 104 D5
Maxwell Gn IRVSE KA11 204 A5
Maxwell Gv PLKSD/SHW G41 104 D5
Maxwell La PLKSD/SHW G41 10 B8
Maxwell Ov PLKSD/SHW G41 10 C8
Maxwell Pl BRWEIR PA11 98 D1 1
PLKSD/SHW G41 10 F9
SVSTN KA20 192 E7 3
UD/BTH/TAN G71 132 A3 2
Maxwell Rd BSHPTN PA7 58 B6
PLKSD/SHW G41 10 C8
Maxwell St
BAIL/MDB/MHD G69 108 B5 4
CGLE G1 11 J3
CLYDBK G81 59 M5
PGL PA14 34 E8 2
PSLY PA1 9 H2
Maxwellton Av EKILN G74 15 K1
Maxwellton Pl EKILN G74 154 B6 1
Maxwellton Rd EKILN G74 154 C5
PGL PA14 54 F3 1
PSLY PA1 8 B6
Maxwellton St PSLY PA1 8 C6
Maxwelton Rd
STPS/GTHM/RID G33 7 L5
Maxwood Rd GLSTN KA4 214 D3
Maybank La GVH/MTFL G42 105 G8
Maybank St GVH/MTFL G42 105 G8 2
Mayberry Crs CAR/SHTL G32 107 J4
Mayberry Gdns CAR/SHTL G32 107 K4
Mayberry Gv CAR/SHTL G32 107 K4 7
Mayberry Pl BLTYR/CAMB G72 155 K1
Maybole Crs NMRNS G77 151 G5
Maybole Dr AIRDRIE ML6 111 G5
Maybole Gdns HMLTN ML3 155 K7 3
Maybole Gv NMRNS G77 151 G5
Maybole Pl CTBR ML5 110 D6
Maybole Rd AYRS KA7 229 G5
PGL PA14 54 F3
Maybole St PLK/PH/NH G53 125 M3
Mayfield Av
CRMNK/CLK/EAG G76 151 L2
KLMNK KA1 212 F4
Mayfield Ct HWWD PA9 121 M3 1
Mayfield Crs HWWD PA9 121 M3 2
SVSTN KA20 192 C8 2
Mayfield Dr HWWD PA9 121 M3 3
Mayfield Gdns CARLUKE ML8 189 G2
Mayfield Gv SVSTN KA20 192 C8
Mayfield Pl CTBR ML5 110 A6
SALT KA21 201 G1
Mayfield Rd HMLTN ML3 155 M5
SALT KA21 192 A8
SVSTN KA20 192 C8 3
Mayfield St MRYH/FIRH G20 82 F3
May Rd PSLYS PA2 124 E2
May St HMLTN ML3 156 D4
LARGS KA30 115 K7
May Ter GIF/THBK G46 127 J6 3
GVH/MTFL G42 128 B1
Mayville St SVSTN KA20 192 C8
Mcadam Ct PSTWK KA9 225 K4 3
Mc Alister Rd ALEX/LLW G83 25 L4 2
Mcallister Av AIRDRIE ML6 111 K1
Mcalpine St KVGV G3 10 E3
WISHAW ML2 159 H7 1
Mcardle Av MTHW ML1 157 H2 3
Mcarthur Pk KKNTL G66 65 J2 2
Mcarthur St
PLKSW/MSWD G43 127 J2 3
Mcaslin Ct COWCAD G4 5 M8
Mcaslin St COWCAD G4 6 A8
Mcauslan Pl HBR/GL G84 20 F7 2
Mccall's Av AYR KA8 225 G6
Mccallum Av RUTH G73 129 H1 3
Mccallum Ct EKILN G74 153 H5 3
Mccallum Crs GRK PA19 31 L2 2
Mccallum Gdns BLSH ML4 132 F7
Mccallum Gv EKILN G74 153 G5
Mccallum Pl EKILN G74 153 H5 1
Mccallum Rd LRKH ML9 176 B8
Mccardel Wy
KLMNKN/STW KA3 197 L1 4
Mccarrison Rd WISHAW ML2 160 A3 2
Mccash Pl KKNTL G66 65 J2
Mcclue Av RNFRW PA4 80 B5
Mcclue Rd RNFRW PA4 80 B5
Mccolgan Pl AYR KA8 225 J6 1
Mccoll Pl ALEX/LLW G83 25 J3 1
Mcconnell Rd LOCHW PA12 120 B7
Mccormack Gdns
MTHW ML1 134 E5 3
Mccracken Av RNFRW PA4 80 B7 2
Mccracken Dr
UD/BTH/TAN G71 132 C1
Mccreery St CLYDBK G81 80 D1
Mc Culloch Av
UD/BTH/TAN G71 132 C3
Mcculloch St PLKSD/SHW G41 10 C8
Mcdonald Av JNSTN PA5 99 L8
Mcdonald Crs CLYDBK G81 80 D1
Mcdonald Dr IRV KA12 203 K5
Mcdonald Pl BRHD/NEIL G78 148 E2
MTHW ML1 134 A4 3
Mcdowall Av ARD KA22 191 K7
Mcdowall Pl ARD KA22 191 K6 4
Mcewan Crs RAYR/DAL KA6 227 H3
Mcewan Dr HBR/GL G84 20 F6 4
Mcewan Gdns EKILN G74 153 G5
Mcfarlane St COWCAD G4 12 A4
PSLYN/LNWD PA3 101 J2
Mcgavin Av KLWNG KA13 194 A6
Mcgavin Wy KLWNG KA13 193 K5
Mc Ghee St CLYDBK G81 60 B6
Mcgibney Dr IRV KA12 203 K8 1
Mcgillivray Av SALT KA21 191 M8
Mcgowan Pl HMLTN ML3 156 A4 1
Mcgown St PSLYN/LNWD PA3 101 K3
Mcgregor Av AIRDRIE ML6 111 K1
RNFRW PA4 80 B7 3
SVSTN KA20 192 D8
Mcgregor Dr DMBTN G82 37 J5
Mcgregor Rd CUMB G67 48 E8
Mcgregor St CLYDBK G81 80 D1
GOV/IBX G51 103 M3
WISHAW ML2 158 D5 3
Mcgrigor Rd MLNGV G62 41 M6
Mchardy Crs BEITH KA15 168 F6
Mcinnes Ct WISHAW ML2 159 H7 2
Mcinnes Pl WISHAW ML2 177 H2 3
Mcintosh Qd BLSH ML4 132 F7 4
Mcintosh St DEN/PKHD G31 12 C2
Mcintosh Wy MTHW ML1 157 J4
Mcintyre Pl PSLYS PA2 9 G9
Mcintyre Ter
BLTYR/CAMB G72 130 A3 3
Mcisaac Rd SALT KA21 201 G1 1
Mciver St BLTYR/CAMB G72 130 D3
Mckay Crs JNSTN PA5 100 A7
Mckay Gv BLSH ML4 132 F3
Mckay Pl EKILN G74 153 G5
NMRNS G77 150 C5
Mckechnie St GOV/IBX G51 104 A1 3
Mckellar Av ARD KA22 191 K7
Mckenna Dr AIRDRIE ML6 110 E1
Mckenzie Av CLYDBK G81 60 B5
Mckenzie St PSLYN/LNWD PA3 8 C2
Mckerrell St PSLY PA1 9 L3
Mckillop Pl SALT KA21 191 L7
Mckinlay Crs IRV KA12 203 H8
Mckinnon Pl SALT KA21 192 A7 1
Mclaren Av RNFRW PA4 80 C8 2
Mclaren Ct GIF/THBK G46 127 H8 2
Mclaren Crs MRYH/FIRH G20 82 E2
Mclaren Gdns
MRYH/FIRH G20 82 E2 4
Mclaren Gv EKILN G74 153 G5
Mc Laurin Crs JNSTN PA5 99 K8
Mclean Dr BLSH ML4 132 F7
Mclean Pl PSLYN/LNWD PA3 101 K2 3
Mclean St AYR KA8 225 J7
Mclees La MTHW ML1 157 H2 1
Mc Lelland Dr AIRDRIE ML6 90 B7 1
Mclelland Dr KLMNK KA1 16 C7
Mclennan St GVH/MTFL G42 128 B1 3
Mcleod Rd DMBTN G82 37 J5
Mcleod St GRNK PA15 3 M8
Mcluckie Dr KLWNG KA13 193 J6
Mcluckie Pk KLWNG KA13 193 J5
Mcmahon Dr WISHAW ML2 160 A3
Mcmahon Gv BLSH ML4 133 H3 1
Mcmillan Crs BEITH KA15 168 A2
Mcmillan Dr ARD KA22 191 G5
Mcmillan Rd WISHAW ML2 158 D7 2
Mcmillan Wy CARLUKE ML8 177 M4 4
Mcnair St CAR/SHTL G32 107 G4 3
Mcnaught Pl
KLMNKN/STW KA3 206 A2 1
Mcnay Crs SALT KA21 191 M8
Mcnay Rd PSTWK KA9 221 J6
Mcneil Av CLYDBK G81 60 E8
Mcneil Dr BLSH ML4 133 L2
MTHW ML1 134 B2
Mcneil Gdns GBLS G5 11 M7
Mcneill Av PSTWK KA9 221 K8
Mc Neil Pl WISHAW ML2 177 J2 3
Mcneil St GBLS G5 11 M7
Mcphail Av MTHW ML1 134 F4
Mcphail St DMNK/BRGTN G40 12 B7
Mc Phail St GRNK PA15 3 L8
Mcphater St CGLW G2 5 H7
Mcpherson Crs AIRDRIE ML6 111 L8
Mcpherson Dr GRK PA19 31 K2 2
UD/BTH/TAN G71 132 B6
Mcpherson St BLSH ML4 133 K4
Mcshannon Gv BLSH ML4 133 G6 3
Meadow Av BLTYR/CAMB G72 155 K3
IRV KA12 203 J5 1
Meadowbank La PSTWK KA9 225 H2 1
Meadowbank Pl NMRNS G77 150 D4
Meadowbank Rd LARGS KA30 115 L5
Meadowbank St DMBTN G82 36 E5 2
DMBTN G82 36 F5 3
Meadowburn BSHPBGS G64 64 A5
Meadowburn Av KKNTL G66 65 L4
NMRNS G77 150 D4
Meadowburn Rd WISHAW ML2 159 J6
Meadow Ct CARLUKE ML8 179 J8 3
DMBTN G82 36 F4 1
Meadowfield Pl WISHAW ML2 160 C3
Meadowfoot Rd WKIL KA23 181 K4
Meadowhead Av IRVSE KA11 208 E5
Meadowhead Rd AIRDRIE ML6 89 M6
IRVSE KA11 208 F5
WISHAW ML2 158 D5
Meadowhill NMRNS G77 150 D4
Meadowhill St LRKH ML9 176 B6
Meadow La RNFRW PA4 80 D4
Meadow Pk AYRS KA7 19 H9
RAYR/DAL KA6 231 H5 3
Meadowpark Dr AYRS KA7 19 H9
Meadowpark St DEN/PKHD G31 7 G9
Meadow Rd CARLUKE ML8 189 G5
DMBTN G82 37 G5
MTHW ML1 158 A4
PTCK G11 82 A8
Meadows Av LRKH ML9 176 B6
Meadowside BEITH KA15 168 A1
HMLTN ML3 174 D3 3
KLMNKN/STW KA3 212 D1
WKIL KA23 181 K4 2
Meadowside Av JNSTN PA5 100 D7
Meadowside Gdns
AIRDRIE ML6 111 K2 2
Meadowside Pl AIRDRIE ML6 111 K2 3
Meadowside Rd GLSTN KA4 214 B3
KSYTH G65 46 E1
Meadowside St PTCK G11 82 A8
RNFRW PA4 80 D4
The Meadows
CRG/CRSL/HOU PA6 77 K8
KLWNG KA13 193 K5
Meadow St CTBR ML5 110 B5 2
Meadow Vw AIRDRIE ML6 90 A6
CUMB G67 49 J6
Meadow Wk CTBR ML5 110 B4
Meadow Wy NMRNS G77 150 D4
Meadowwell St
CAR/SHTL G32 107 H4 3
Meadside Av KLBCH PA10 99 G5
Meadside Rd KLBCH PA10 99 G5
Mealkirk St CLYDBK G81 60 C2 2
Mearns Ct HMLTN ML3 174 E2
Mearnscroft Gdns NMRNS G77 150 F6
Mearnscroft Rd NMRNS G77 150 F6
Mearnskirk Rd NMRNS G77 150 D7
Mearns Rd MTHW ML1 157 J1
NMRNS G77 150 E7
Mearns St GRNK PA15 2 C6
Medine Av BEITH KA15 144 B8
Medine Ct BEITH KA15 144 B8 7
Medlar Rd CUMB G67 49 K7
Medrox Gdns CUMB G67 67 M4
Medwin Ct EKILS G75 170 E2
Medwin Gdns EKILS G75 170 E2
Medwin St BLTYR/CAMB G72 130 D4
Medwyn St SCOT G14 81 K6
Meek Pl BLTYR/CAMB G72 130 B4
Meetinghouse La PSLY PA1 9 G3 3
Megan Ga DMNK/BRGTN G40 12 C7
Megan St DMNK/BRGTN G40 12 C7
Meikle Av RNFRW PA4 80 C7
Meikle Bin Brae KKNTL G66 44 E2
Meikle Crs AIRDRIE ML6 89 K1
HMLTN ML3 174 C2
Meikle Drumgray Rd
AIRDRIE ML6 89 K1
Meikle Earnock Rd HMLTN ML3 173 M3
Meiklehill Ct KKNTL G66 45 L8
Meiklehill Rd KKNTL G66 45 L8
Meiklerig Crs PLK/PH/NH G53 103 J7
Meikleriggs Dr PSLYS PA2 101 G8
Meikle Rd PLK/PH/NH G53 126 C1
Meiklewood Av PSTWK KA9 221 J8
Meiklewood Rd GOV/IBX G51 103 K3
KLMNKN/STW KA3 206 F4
Melbourne Av CLYDBK G81 59 K4
EKILS G75 14 A6
Melbourne Ct GIF/THBK G46 127 K6
Melbourne Gn EKILS G75 14 A6 1
Melbourne Rd SALT KA21 200 E2 3
Melbourne St DEN/PKHD G31 12 C3
Melbourne Ter SALT KA21 200 E2
Meldon Pl GOV/IBX G51 103 K2 3
Meldrum Gdns
PLKSD/SHW G41 104 D7
Meldrum Mains AIRDRIE ML6 88 E5
Meldrum St CLYDBK G81 80 D1
Melford Av GIF/THBK G46 127 K7
KKNTL G66 65 H1
Melford Rd BLSH ML4 132 E3
Melfort Av CLYDBK G81 60 C6
PLKSD/SHW G41 104 B5
Melfort Gdns KLBCH PA10 99 J8
Melfort Rd HMLTN ML3 155 L7
WMYSB PA18 70 A1
Mellerstain Dr SCOT G14 80 E3
Melness Pl GOV/IBX G51 103 K2 7
Melrose Av AIRDRIE ML6 111 K7
BAIL/MDB/MHD G69 108 F4 1
MTHW ML1 134 B3
PSLYN/LNWD PA3 100 B4
PSLYS PA2 101 G8
RUTH G73 129 H2
Melrose Crs WISHAW ML2 159 G4
Melrose Gdns MRYH/FIRH G20 4 C2
Melrose Pl BLTYR/CAMB G72 131 J8 3
CTBR ML5 109 M2
LRKH ML9 176 A8
Melrose Rd CUMB G67 68 E2
PGL PA14 54 F2
Melrose St COWCAD G4 4 D6
HMLTN ML3 156 B4
Melrose Ter EKILN G74 15 G1
HMLTN ML3 156 B3
Melvaig Pl MRYH/FIRH G20 82 D4 3
Melvick Pl GOV/IBX G51 103 K2 3
Melville Ct CGLE G1 11 K3 1
Melville Dr MTHW ML1 157 M3 3
Melville Gdns BSHPBGS G64 64 A7
Melville Pk EKILN G74 154 B6
Melville Pl CARLUKE ML8 178 E7 1
Melville St KLMNKN/STW KA3 17 J5
PLKSD/SHW G41 104 F6
Melvinhall Rd LNK/LMHG ML11 199 G4
Memel St PPK/MIL G22 83 L4
Memus Av
CARD/HILL/MSPK G52 103 J5
Mennock Ct HMLTN ML3 155 L7 3
Mennock Dr BSHPBGS G64 64 A5 2
Mennock St MTHW ML1 135 J7 2
Menock Rd LNPK/KPK G44 128 C3
Menteith Av BSHPBGS G64 64 B8
Menteith Dr RUTH G73 129 K7
Menteith Gdns BSDN G61 61 J1
Menteith Pl RUTH G73 129 K7
Menteith Rd MTHW ML1 157 L2 2
Menzies Dr SPRGB/BLRNK G21 84 A4
Menzies Pl SPRGB/BLRNK G21 84 A4
Menzies Rd SPRGB/BLRNK G21 84 A4
Merchant La CGLE G1 11 K4
Merchants Cl KLBCH PA10 99 G6 2
Merchiston Av PSLYN/LNWD PA3 99 M4
Merchiston Dr JNSTN PA5 99 K4
Merchiston St CAR/SHTL G32 106 E2
Merino Rd GRNK PA15 2 A7 1
Merkins Av DMBTN G82 37 H3
Merkland Dr KKNTL G66 46 A8
Merkland Pl KKNTL G66 45 M8
Merkland Rd AYRS KA7 229 G7
CTBR ML5 87 J7
Merkland St PTCK G11 82 B7 3
Merkland Wy EKILS G75 171 J5 2
Merksworth Av DALRY KA24 184 C2
Merlewood Av
UD/BTH/TAN G71 132 B5
Merlewood Rd WKIL KA23 181 H5
Merlin Av BLSH ML4 133 G1
GRNKW/INVK PA16 32 A3
Merlinford Av RNFRW PA4 80 E6 1
Merlinford Crs RNFRW PA4 80 E6 1
Merlinford Dr RNFRW PA4 80 E6 2
Merlinford Wy RNFRW PA4 80 E6 2
Merlin La GRNKW/INVK PA16 32 A4
Merlin Wy PSLYN/LNWD PA3 102 B2
Merrick Av PSTWK KA9 221 K8
TROON KA10 216 F5
Merrick Gdns BSDN G61 61 J2
GOV/IBX G51 104 B4 3
HMLTN ML3 174 E6
Merrick Rd KLMNK KA1 212 B5
Merrick Ter UD/BTH/TAN G71 132 B2
Merrick Wy RUTH G73 129 H6 3
Merryburn Av
PLKSW/MSWD G43 127 K5
Merrycrest Av GIF/THBK G46 127 K5
Merrycroft Av GIF/THBK G46 127 K5
Merryflats KSYTH G65 46 F5 1
Merryland Pl GOV/IBX G51 104 B2
Merryland St GOV/IBX G51 104 B2
Merrylee Av PGL PA14 54 D2
Merrylee Crs
PLKSW/MSWD G43 127 J4 2
Merrylee Pk GIF/THBK G46 127 J4 3
Merrylee Park Av
GIF/THBK G46 127 K5
Merrylee Rd PLKSW/MSWD G43 127 L4
Merrylees Rd BLTYR/CAMB G72 155 J2
Merrystone St CTBR ML5 109 M2 2
Merry St MTHW ML1 157 L2
Merryton Av DRUM G15 61 H6
GIF/THBK G46 127 J5
Merryton Pl DRUM G15 61 H6
Merryton Rd LRKH ML9 175 M3
MTHW ML1 158 B7
Merryton St LRKH ML9 175 M4
Merryvale Av
PLKSW/MSWD G43 127 K5
Merryvale Pl
PLKSW/MSWD G43 127 K4 2
Merryvale Rd IRV KA12 203 J8
Merton Dr CARD/HILL/MSPK G52 103 G4
Meryon Gdns CAR/SHTL G32 107 K7
Meryon Rd CAR/SHTL G32 107 K6 3
Methil Rd PGL PA14 54 F3
Methil St SCOT G14 81 J6
Methlan Pk DMBTN G82 36 D7
Methlick Av AIRDRIE ML6 110 E5 3
Methuen Rd PSLYN/LNWD PA3 101 M1
Methven Av BSDN G61 62 B4
KLMNK KA1 211 M5
Methven Pl EKILN G74 14 B2
KLMNK KA1 211 M5
Methven Rd GIF/THBK G46 151 G3
Methven St CLYDBK G81 59 M5
DEN/PKHD G31 13 M9
Metropole La CGLE G1 11 J4
Mews La AYRS KA7 18 D3
GRNKW/INVK PA16 32 C1
KLMNK KA1 16 C7
PSLYN/LNWD PA3 101 M2
Mey Ct NMRNS G77 150 A5
Mey Pl NMRNS G77 150 A5 1
Mharie Pl ALEX/LLW G83 25 M7
Michael Mcparland Dr
BSHPBGS G64 44 B8 1
Michael Ter AIRDRIE ML6 111 K8
Micklehouse Ov
BAIL/MDB/MHD G69 108 B3 2
Micklehouse Pl
BAIL/MDB/MHD G69 108 B3 3
Micklehouse Rd
BAIL/MDB/MHD G69 108 B3
Micklehouse Wynd
BAIL/MDB/MHD G69 108 B3 4
Midas Pl BLSH ML4 133 L4
Mid Av PGL PA14 54 F1
Mid Barrwood Rd KSYTH G65 47 M2
Mid Barwood Rd KSYTH G65 48 A1
Mid Carbarns WISHAW ML2 158 D8
Midcroft Av LNPK/KPK G44 128 D4
Middlefield EKILS G75 171 L4
Middlehouse Ct CARLUKE ML8 178 D7
Middlemass Dr
KLMNKN/STW KA3 17 J5
Middlemuir Rd KKNTL G66 65 K3
Middlepart SVSTN KA20 192 C7
Middlepart Crs SALT KA21 192 A7
Middlepenny Pl PGL PA14 56 B2 2
Middlepenny Rd PGL PA14 56 B2
Middlerigg Rd BALLOCH G68 48 D7
Middlesex Gdns
PLKSD/SHW G41 10 A5
Middlesex St PLKSD/SHW G41 10 A5
Middleton Crs
PSLYN/LNWD PA3 101 H3
Middleton Dr HBR/GL G84 22 F1
LARGS KA30 115 K5
MLNGV G62 42 B7
Middleton La HBR/GL G84 22 F1 3
Middleton Pk IRVSE KA11 204 A5
Middleton Rd IRVSE KA11 204 A5
PSLYN/LNWD PA3 100 C2
PSLYN/LNWD PA3 101 H3
Middleton St ALEX/LLW G83 25 K4 2
GOV/IBX G51 104 C3
Middle Ward St CLYDBK G81 60 D2 1
Mid Dykes Rd SALT KA21 191 L7
Midfaulds Av RNFRW PA4 80 E7 2
Midland St CGLE G1 11 G2
Midlem Dr
CARD/HILL/MSPK G52 103 J4
Midlem Ov
CARD/HILL/MSPK G52 103 J4 3
Mid-loan St CARLUKE ML8 188 E5
Midlock St GOV/IBX G51 104 C4
Midlothian Dr
PLKSD/SHW G41 104 D8 1
Mid Pk EKILS G75 14 E5
Mid Rd BEITH KA15 144 A8
CUMB G67 68 F3
Midton Av PSTWK KA9 225 H1
Midton Rd AYRS KA7 18 E9
HWWD PA9 122 A3
KLMNK KA1 211 M7 2
PSTWK KA9 225 J1
Midton St SPRGB/BLRNK G21 6 C3
Mid-wharf St COWCAD G4 5 K5
Migvie Pl MRYH/FIRH G20 82 C4
Milford EKILS G75 171 H2
Milford St STPS/GTHM/RID G33 107 G1
Milgarholm Av IRV KA12 203 K8
Millands Av BLTYR/CAMB G72 131 J8
Millands Rd GLSTN KA4 213 M4
Millarbank St SPRGB/BLRNK G21 6 B1
Millar Gv HMLTN ML3 156 B6
Millar Rd SALT KA21 201 G1
Millars Pl KKNTL G66 65 K5 2
Millarston Av PSLY PA1 101 G5 2
Millarston Dr PSLY PA1 101 G5
Millar St GRNK PA15 3 H9
PSLY PA1 9 K3
Mill Av KLMNKN/STW KA3 206 C2
Millbank Av BLSH ML4 133 H6
Millbank Rd PGL PA14 54 C1 1
WISHAW ML2 158 F7
Millbeg Crs
STPS/GTHM/RID G33 107 M4 3
Millbeg Pl STPS/GTHM/RID G33 107 L4
Mill Brae AYRS KA7 19 G5
BRWEIR PA11 98 D1
Millbrae Av BAIL/MDB/MHD G69 86 D1
Millbrae Crs GVH/MTFL G42 127 L2
KNTSWD G13 80 D2 2
Millbrae Gdns
PLKSD/SHW G41 127 M2 3
Millbrae Rd GVH/MTFL G42 127 M2 1
Millbrix Av SCOT G14 81 G4
Millbrook EKILN G74 153 G8
Millburn Av KNTSWD G13 80 E1
RNFRW PA4 80 D6 1
RUTH G73 129 G3
Millburn Ct EKILS G75 170 E2 2
Millburn Crs DMBTN G82 37 H6
Millburn Dr KLMCLM PA13 75 H1
RNFRW PA4 80 E6 1
Millburn Gdns EKILS G75 170 E2 3
LARGS KA30 115 K6 3
Millburn Rd ALEX/LLW G83 25 K6
DMBTN G82 37 H6
LRKH ML9 176 F8

PGL PA14 .... 54 C1 2
RNFRW PA4 .... 80 D6
Millburn St KKNTL G66 .... 44 D1
MTHW ML1 .... 157 L2
SPRGB/BLRNK G21 .... 6 E7
Millburn Ter IRVSE KA11 .... 204 A2
Millburn Wy EKILS G75 .... 170 E2
RNFRW PA4 .... 80 E6 4
Mill Ct HMLTN ML3 .... 156 C7
RUTH G73 .... 129 G1 5
Mill Crs BSHPBGS G64 .... 44 C8
DMNK/BRGTN G40 .... 12 C9
IRV KA12 .... 203 L7
NMLNS KA16 .... 215 L2
Millcroft Rd CUMB G67 .... 49 H8
CUMB G67 .... 68 E5
CUMB G67 .... 69 G5
RUTH G73 .... 105 M7
Milldam Rd CLYDBK G81 .... 60 C2
Miller Av FAIRLIE KA29 .... 139 K8
Miller Ct DMBTN G82 .... 37 H5
Millerfield Pl DMNK/BRGTN G40 .. 106 B6
Miller Field Pl HMLTN ML3 .... 156 F6 5
Millerfield Rd
DMNK/BRGTN G40 .... 106 B6
Miller Pl ARD KA22 .... 191 G5
RAYR/DAL KA6 .... 227 G3
Miller Rd ALEX/LLW G83 .... 25 M1
AYRS KA7 .... 18 E5
Millerslea Gdns HBR/GL G84 .... 20 F8 1
Millersneuk Av KKNTL G66 .... 65 K5
Millersneuk Ct KKNTL G66 .... 65 K5 5
Millersneuk Crs
STPS/GTHM/RID G33 .... 85 G4
Millersneuk Dr KKNTL G66 .... 65 K5
Millersneuk Rd KKNTL G66 .... 65 K5 1
Miller's Pl AIRDRIE ML6 .... 111 H2
Millerston St DEN/PKHD G31 .... 12 F4
Miller St BAIL/MDB/MHD G69 .... 108 B5
CARLUKE ML8 .... 179 G7
CGLE G1 .... 11 J2
CLYDBK G81 .... 60 B8
CTBR ML5 .... 110 B4
DMBTN G82 .... 37 H5
HMLTN ML3 .... 156 F6
JNSTN PA5 .... 100 B6
LRKH ML9 .... 176 A6
WISHAW ML2 .... 159 G6
Millfield Av ERSK PA8 .... 58 F8
MTHW ML1 .... 157 M1
Millfield Crs ERSK PA8 .... 59 G8
Millfield Dr ERSK PA8 .... 59 G8
RNFRW PA4 .... 79 G1
Millfield Gdns ERSK PA8 .... 59 G8
Millfield Hl ERSK PA8 .... 58 F8
Millfield Mdw ERSK PA8 .... 58 F8
Millfield Pl ERSK PA8 .... 58 F8 1
Millfield Vw ERSK PA8 .... 58 F8
Millfield Wk RNFRW PA4 .... 79 G1 1
Millfield Wynd ERSK PA8 .... 58 F8
Millford Dr PSLYN/LNWD PA3 .... 100 B4
Millgate Av UD/BTH/TAN G71 .... 131 M1
Millgate Ct UD/BTH/TAN G71 .... 131 M2
Millgate Rd HMLTN ML3 .... 156 C8
Millglen Rd ARD KA22 .... 191 K5
Mill Gv HMLTN ML3 .... 156 C7
Millhall Rd
CRMNK/CLK/EAG G76 .... 170 A6
Millheugh Brae LRKH ML9 .... 175 L7
Millheugh Pl BLTYR/CAMB G72 .... 155 J3
Millheugh Rd LRKH ML9 .... 175 L8
Millhill Av KLMNKN/STW KA3 .... 206 C2
Millhill Ter KLMNKN/STW KA3 .... 206 E4
Millholm Rd LNPK/KPK G44 .... 128 B5
Millhouse Crs MRYH/FIRH G20 .. 82 C2 1
Millhouse Dr MRYH/FIRH G20 .... 82 B2
Millhouse Rd GRNKW/INVK PA16 .. 50 E4
Millichen Rd SMSTN G23 .... 62 D5
Millig St HBR/GL G84 .... 20 C6
Milliken Dr KLBCH PA10 .... 99 J7
Milliken Park Rd KLBCH PA10 .... 99 J8
Milliken Rd KLBCH PA10 .... 99 J7
Mill Loan AIRDRIE ML6 .... 111 G1
Mill of Gryffe Rd BRWEIR PA11 .... 98 D1
Mill Pk DALRY KA24 .... 184 D2
Mill Pl PSLYN/LNWD PA3 .... 100 A3
Millport Av LNPK/KPK G44 .... 128 C2
Millport Rd PGL PA14 .... 54 F3
Mill Rig EKILS G75 .... 171 K4
Mill Ri KKNTL G66 .... 65 K5
Mill Rd AIRDRIE ML6 .... 69 G8
AIRDRIE ML6 .... 89 G8
BLTYR/CAMB G72 .... 130 D5
CARLUKE ML8 .... 178 E8
DMBTN G82 .... 24 A8
HMLTN ML3 .... 156 C7
IRV KA12 .... 203 K7
KBRN KA25 .... 143 H8
KNTSWD G13 .... 80 D2
KSYTH G65 .... 46 E2
MTHW ML1 .... 157 M1
NMLNS KA16 .... 215 L2
RAYR/DAL KA6 .... 227 G7
SHOTTS ML7 .... 160 F1
UD/BTH/TAN G71 .... 132 A8
WISHAW ML2 .... 160 C6
Millroad Dr DMNK/BRGTN G40 .... 12 B4
Millroad St DMNK/BRGTN G40 .... 12 A4
Millstream Ct PSLY PA1 .... 9 K5
Millstream Crs AIRDRIE ML6 .... 90 F5 2
Mill St AIRDRIE ML6 .... 90 F4
AYRS KA7 .... 19 G4
DMNK/BRGTN G40 .... 12 C9
GRNK PA15 .... 2 B6
KLMNK KA1 .... 16 E7
PSLY PA1 .... 9 J4
RUTH G73 .... 129 G1
Millview BRHD/NEIL G78 .... 125 K6
Millview Mdw
BRHD/NEIL G78 .... 148 C2 8
Millview Pl PLK/PH/NH G53 .... 126 B5 2
Millview Ter BRHD/NEIL G78 .... 148 C2
Mill Wy KKNTL G66 .... 66 A2
Millwood St PLKSD/SHW G41 .... 127 L1
Mill Wynd AYRS KA7 .... 18 F3
Milnbank St DEN/PKHD G31 .... 6 E9
Milncroft Pl
STPS/GTHM/RID G33 .... 85 G8 5
Milncroft Rd
STPS/GTHM/RID G33 .... 85 G8
Milndavie Crs CMPF/LLE G63 .... 27 J6
Milndavie Rd CMPF/LLE G63 .... 27 H7
Milner La KNTSWD G13 .... 81 L4 2
Milner Rd KNTSWD G13 .... 81 L4 3
Milngavie Rd BSDN G61 .... 61 M6
CMPF/LLE G63 .... 27 J7
Milnpark Gdns GOV/IBX G51 .... 104 D4
Milnpark St PLKSD/SHW G41 .... 10 A5
Milnwood Dr BLSH ML4 .... 133 K5
MTHW ML1 .... 133 J7 3
Milovaig Av SMSTN G23 .... 62 D8 13
Milovaig St SMSTN G23 .... 62 D8
Milrig Rd RUTH G73 .... 128 F2
Milroy Gdns BLSH ML4 .... 133 G1
Milton Av BLTYR/CAMB G72 .... 129 L4
KLMNKN/STW KA3 .... 17 M3
Milton Brae DMBTN G82 .... 37 K6
Milton Ct DMBTN G82 .... 37 M7
IRVSE KA11 .... 204 C8
Milton Crs CARLUKE ML8 .... 178 E8
IRVSE KA11 .... 204 C8
TROON KA10 .... 216 E3
Milton Douglas Rd CLYDBK G81 .... 60 A3
Milton Dr BSHPBGS G64 .... 83 M2 2
KLMNKN/STW KA3 .... 17 M3
Milton Gdns UD/BTH/TAN G71 .... 131 L1
Milton Hl DMBTN G82 .... 37 M8
Milton Mains Rd CLYDBK G81 .... 60 A4
Milton Pk AYRS KA7 .... 229 H6
KBRN KA25 .... 143 H7 2
RAYR/DAL KA6 .... 231 H5 3
Milton Qd KBRN KA25 .... 143 G6
Milton Rd EKILN G74 .... 153 G7
GLSTN KA4 .... 214 B3 2
IRVSE KA11 .... 204 C8
KBRN KA25 .... 143 G6
KKNTL G66 .... 44 E2
KKNTL G66 .... 45 J7
KLMNKN/STW KA3 .... 17 M4
KLMNKN/STW KA3 .... 207 L8
PGL PA14 .... 54 E3
Milton St AIRDRIE ML6 .... 111 G1
CARLUKE ML8 .... 178 E7
CGLW G2 .... 5 J7
HMLTN ML3 .... 156 A4
MTHW ML1 .... 157 L1
Milton Ter HMLTN ML3 .... 156 A4
Milton Vw CRH/DND KA2 .... 210 E4
Milverton Av BSDN G61 .... 61 J3
Milverton Rd GIF/THBK G46 .... 127 G8
Mimosa Rd BRWEIR PA11 .... 98 D1
Minard Rd PGL PA14 .... 54 E2
PLKSD/SHW G41 .... 104 E8
SHOTTS ML7 .... 137 K3
Minard Wy UD/BTH/TAN G71 .. 132 A2 8
Mincher Crs MTHW ML1 .... 157 L5 5
Minch Wy AIRDRIE ML6 .... 111 K4
Minella Gdns BLSH ML4 .... 133 G1
Minerva St KVGV G3 .... 4 A9
Minerva Ter GRNKW/INVK PA16 .... 31 K6
Minerva Wy KVGV G3 .... 104 D1
Mingarry La MRYH/FIRH G20 .... 4 A1
Mingarry St MRYH/FIRH G20 .... 4 A1
Mingulay Crs PPK/MIL G22 .... 83 K1
Mingulay Pl PPK/MIL G22 .... 83 L1
Mingulay St PPK/MIL G22 .... 83 K1
Ministers Pk EKILN G74 .... 152 F5 2
Minmoir Rd PLK/PH/NH G53 .... 125 M2
Minstrel Rd KNTSWD G13 .... 61 K8
Mintalto Av MTHW ML1 .... 134 A8
Minto Av RUTH G73 .... 129 K5 4
Minto Crs
CARD/HILL/MSPK G52 .... 103 M4
Minto Pk WISHAW ML2 .... 159 J3
Minto St CARD/HILL/MSPK G52 .... 103 M4
GRNKW/INVK PA16 .... 32 D5
Mireton St PPK/MIL G22 .... 83 H4
Mirren Dr CLYDBK G81 .... 59 M2
Mirren's Shore PGL PA14 .... 34 C7 3
Mirrlees Dr KVD/HLHD G12 .... 82 C5
Mirrlees La KVD/HLHD G12 .... 82 C5
Misk Knowes SVSTN KA20 .... 201 L3
Mitchell Av BLTYR/CAMB G72 .... 130 E3
RNFRW PA4 .... 80 B7
Mitchell Ct EKILN G74 .... 14 A2
Mitchell Dr DMBTN G82 .... 35 H3 1
MLNGV G62 .... 42 C8
RUTH G73 .... 129 H3 2
Mitchell Gv EKILN G74 .... 14 A1
Mitchell Hill Rd CSMK G45 .... 128 F7
Mitchell La CGLE G1 .... 11 H1
Mitchell Pl SALT KA21 .... 191 L8
Mitchell Rd CUMB G67 .... 48 F7
Mitchell St AIRDRIE ML6 .... 110 F1
BEITH KA15 .... 144 C8 2
CGLE G1 .... 11 H2
CTBR ML5 .... 109 H4
GRNK PA15 .... 33 M7
Mitchell Wy ALEX/LLW G83 .... 25 L4
Mitchison Rd CUMB G67 .... 49 G6
Mitre Ct PTCK G11 .... 81 M6
Mitre La SCOT G14 .... 81 L5 2
Mitre La West SCOT G14 .... 81 K5 3
Mitre Rd PTCK G11 .... 81 M5
SCOT G14 .... 81 L5
Moat Av KNTSWD G13 .... 81 J2
Mochrum Ct PSTWK KA9 .... 225 K3 2
Mochrum Rd
PLKSW/MSWD G43 .... 127 L3
Moffat Ct EKILS G75 .... 170 E2
Moffathill AIRDRIE ML6 .... 111 L5
Moffat Pl BLTYR/CAMB G72 .... 131 K8
CTBR ML5 .... 110 D5
EKILS G75 .... 170 D2
Moffat Rd AIRDRIE ML6 .... 111 M2
PSTWK KA9 .... 221 J6
Moffat St GBLS G5 .... 11 L7
GRNK PA15 .... 3 K8
Moffat Vw AIRDRIE ML6 .... 90 A7
Mogarth Av PSLYS PA2 .... 123 M1
Moidart Av RNFRW PA4 .... 80 B5 3
Moidart Ct BRHD/NEIL G78 .... 125 H5 3
Moidart Crs
CARD/HILL/MSPK G52 .... 103 M4 1
Moidart Gdns KKNTL G66 .... 46 B8
NMRNS G77 .... 150 E3
Moidart Pl
CARD/HILL/MSPK G52 .... 103 M4 2
Moidart Rd
CARD/HILL/MSPK G52 .... 103 L4
PGL PA14 .... 54 E2
Moir St CGLE G1 .... 11 M4
Molendinar St CGLE G1 .... 11 M3
Molendinar Ter
BRHD/NEIL G78 .... 148 C3 5
Mollinsburn Rd AIRDRIE ML6 .... 88 C3
CTBR ML5 .... 87 M1
CUMB G67 .... 67 L6
Mollinsburn St SPRGB/BLRNK G21 .. 6 B2
Mollins Ct BALLOCH G68 .... 67 K4 2
Mollins Rd BALLOCH G68 .... 47 H8
BALLOCH G68 .... 67 J4
Monach Gdns IRVSE KA11 .... 209 H1
Monach Rd PGL PA14 .... 55 G2 2
STPS/GTHM/RID G33 .... 107 J1
Monaebrook Pl HBR/GL G84 .... 22 F1 3
Monar Dr PPK/MIL G22 .... 5 H2
Monar St PPK/MIL G22 .... 5 H2
Monart Pl MRYH/FIRH G20 .... 82 F5
Moncrieff Av KKNTL G66 .... 65 K4
Moncrieffe Rd AIRDRIE ML6 .... 111 K5
Moncrieff St PSLY PA1 .... 9 G2
Moncur Rd KLWNG KA13 .... 194 A6
Moncur St DMNK/BRGTN G40 .... 12 A4
Moness Dr
CARD/HILL/MSPK G52 .... 103 L5
Money Gv MTHW ML1 .... 158 B5 4
Monifieth Av
CARD/HILL/MSPK G52 .... 103 K6
Monikie Gdns BSHPBGS G64 .... 64 D8 1
Monkcastle Dr
BLTYR/CAMB G72 .... 130 A3
Monkland Av KKNTL G66 .... 65 K3
Monklands TROON KA10 .... 216 F2 3
Monkland St AIRDRIE ML6 .... 111 H2
Monkland Ter CTBR ML5 .... 87 K3
Monkland Vw AIRDRIE ML6 .... 111 H7 1
UD/BTH/TAN G71 .... 109 G8
Monkland View Crs
BAIL/MDB/MHD G69 .... 109 G4
Monkreddan Crs
KLWNG KA13 .... 193 J4 2
Monksbridge Av KNTSWD G13 .. 81 K1 1
Monkscourt Av AIRDRIE ML6 .... 110 E1
Monkscroft Av PTCK G11 .... 82 A6 4
Monkscroft Ct PTCK G11 .... 82 A7 6
Monkscroft Gdns PTCK G11 .... 82 A7 7
Monks La CARLUKE ML8 .... 188 E5
Monks Rd AIRDRIE ML6 .... 111 J5
Monkton Ct PSTWK KA9 .... 221 K7
Monkton Dr DRUM G15 .... 61 H8
Monkton Gdns NMRNS G77 .... 151 G5 3
Monktonhill Rd PSTWK KA9 .... 221 J3
TROON KA10 .... 216 F8
Monkton Rd PSTWK KA9 .... 221 K7
Monkwood Pl AYRS KA7 .... 229 G7
Monmouth Av KVD/HLHD G12 .. 82 A4 1
Monreith Av BSDN G61 .... 61 K7
Monreith Rd
PLKSW/MSWD G43 .... 127 K3
Monreith Rd East
LNPK/KPK G44 .... 128 A4
Monroe Dr UD/BTH/TAN G71 .... 108 F8
Monroe Pl UD/BTH/TAN G71 .... 108 F8 6
Montague La KVD/HLHD G12 .... 82 B5
Montague St KVGV G3 .... 4 C5
Montalto Av MTHW ML1 .... 134 A8
Montclair Pl
PSLYN/LNWD PA3 .... 100 A3 1
Montego Gn EKILS G75 .... 153 G8
Monteith Dr
CRMNK/CLK/EAG G76 .... 152 A1
Monteith Gdns
CRMNK/CLK/EAG G76 .... 151 M1
Monteith Pl
DMNK/BRGTN G40 .... 12 A5 1
Monteith Rw CGLE G1 .... 11 M4
DMNK/BRGTN G40 .... 12 A5
Montfode Ct ARD KA22 .... 191 H5
Montfode Dr ARD KA22 .... 191 H5
Montford Av LNPK/KPK G44 .... 128 D2
RUTH G73 .... 128 E2
Montgomerie Av
FAIRLIE KA29 .... 139 K8 1
Montgomerie Crs
FAIRLIE KA29 .... 139 K7 4
SALT KA21 .... 200 E1
Montgomerie Dr
FAIRLIE KA29 .... 139 K7
SKLM PA17 .... 70 B4
Montgomerie Pier Rd
ARD KA22 .... 191 H8
Montgomerie Rd PSTWK KA9 .... 225 H1
SALT KA21 .... 200 E1
Montgomerieston Plac
KBRN KA25 .... 143 G8 5
Montgomerieston Stre
KBRN KA25 .... 143 H8 2
Montgomerie St ARD KA22 .... 191 H8
PGL PA14 .... 34 D8 2
Montgomerie Ter AYRS KA7 .... 18 D2
KLWNG KA13 .... 194 A6
SKLM PA17 .... 70 A4
Montgomery Av BEITH KA15 .... 168 C1
CTBR ML5 .... 109 M1
PSLYN/LNWD PA3 .... 102 B1
Montgomery Crs WISHAW ML2 .. 158 E8
Montgomery Dr
GIF/THBK G46 .... 127 J8 1
KLBCH PA10 .... 99 G5 1
Montgomery Pl EKILN G74 .... 15 G2 1
LRKH ML9 .... 176 B7 3
Montgomery Rd
PSLYN/LNWD PA3 .... 102 A1
Montgomery St
BLTYR/CAMB G72 .... 130 E4 4
DMNK/BRGTN G40 .... 12 E7
EKILN G74 .... 15 G2 2
IRV KA12 .... 203 G8
KLMNKN/STW KA3 .... 206 F7
LRKH ML9 .... 176 A5
Montgomery Ter KKNTL G66 .... 45 H4
Montgreenan Vw KLWNG KA13 .. 193 M6
Montraive St RUTH G73 .... 106 C8 2
Montrave St
CARD/HILL/MSPK G52 .... 103 K5
Montreal Pk EKILS G75 .... 14 B4
Montrose Av CAR/SHTL G32 .... 107 H8
CARD/HILL/MSPK G52 .... 102 F1
PGL PA14 .... 54 E2
Montrose Crs HMLTN ML3 .... 156 D5
Montrose Dr BSDN G61 .... 61 L2
Montrose Gdns
BLTYR/CAMB G72 .... 131 J7 2
MLNGV G62 .... 42 A6
Montrose Pl
PSLYN/LNWD PA3 .... 100 A3 2
Montrose Rd PSLYS PA2 .... 123 M1
Montrose St CGLE G1 .... 11 L2
CLYDBK G81 .... 60 B7
MTHW ML1 .... 133 K8 6
Montrose Ter BRWEIR PA11 .... 98 D2
SPRGB/BLRNK G21 .... 84 C2
Monument Crs PSTWK KA9 .... 221 L8
Monument Rd AYRS KA7 .... 228 F4
Monymusk Gdns BSHPBGS G64 .... 64 D7
Monymusk Pl CLYDBK G81 .... 60 E4
Moodiesburn St
STPS/GTHM/RID G33 .... 7 M5
Moorburn Av GIF/THBK G46 .... 127 H6
Moorburn Pl PSLYN/LNWD PA3 .... 99 M3
Moorburn Rd LARGS KA30 .... 115 K6
Moorcroft Dr AIRDRIE ML6 .... 111 L2
Moorcroft Rd NMRNS G77 .... 150 C6
Moore Dr BSDN G61 .... 61 M6
HBR/GL G84 .... 23 G2 1
Moore Gdns HMLTN ML3 .... 174 E2
Moore St DMNK/BRGTN G40 .... 12 C3
MTHW ML1 .... 134 A6
Moorfield Av KLMNK KA1 .... 16 A7
KLMNK KA1 .... 211 J2
PGL PA14 .... 54 D2
Moorfield Crs AIRDRIE ML6 .... 111 M2 1
Moorfield La GRK PA19 .... 31 J3 3
Moorfield Pl CRH/DND KA2 .... 210 D4
Moorfield Rd BLTYR/CAMB G72 .. 155 J3
GRK PA19 .... 31 J3
PSTWK KA9 .... 225 J2
Moorfoot Av GIF/THBK G46 .... 127 G6
PSLYS PA2 .... 101 K8
Moorfoot Dr GRK PA19 .... 31 J3
WISHAW ML2 .... 158 F6
Moorfoot Gdns EKILS G75 .... 171 H6 1
Moorfoot St CAR/SHTL G32 .... 106 E3
Moorfoot Wy BSDN G61 .... 61 J1
IRVSE KA11 .... 204 A6
Moorhill Crs NMRNS G77 .... 150 C6
Moorhill Rd NMRNS G77 .... 150 C5
Moorhouse Av KNTSWD G13 .... 80 F3
PSLYS PA2 .... 8 A9
Moorhouse St BRHD/NEIL G78 .... 125 J7
The Moorings PSLY PA1 .... 8 B6
Moorland Dr AIRDRIE ML6 .... 111 L2
Moorpark Av AIRDRIE ML6 .... 111 L2 3
BAIL/MDB/MHD G69 .... 86 C2 1
CARD/HILL/MSPK G52 .... 102 F3
Moor Park Crs PSTWK KA9 .... 225 J4
Moorpark Dr
CARD/HILL/MSPK G52 .... 103 G3
Moor Park Pl PSTWK KA9 .... 225 J4
Moorpark Pl SVSTN KA20 .... 201 K2
Moorpark Rd East SVSTN KA20 .... 201 K1
Moorpark Rd West SVSTN KA20 .. 201 J2
Moorpark Sq RNFRW PA4 .... 80 B7
Moor Pl AYR KA8 .... 225 J5 2
Moor Rd AYR KA8 .... 225 J5
CMPF/LLE G63 .... 27 J8
LNK/LMHG ML11 .... 189 K8
MLNGV G62 .... 42 B7
Moorside St CARLUKE ML8 .... 179 G7
Morag Av BLTYR/CAMB G72 .... 131 J8
Moraine Av DRUM G15 .... 61 G8
Moraine Circ DRUM G15 .... 61 G8
Moraine Dr
CRMNK/CLK/EAG G76 .... 151 K1 2
DRUM G15 .... 61 G8
Moraine Pl DRUM G15 .... 61 H8 2
Morar Av CLYDBK G81 .... 60 B5
Morar Ct CUMB G67 .... 68 B1
HMLTN ML3 .... 156 A8 2
Morar Crs AIRDRIE ML6 .... 88 E8
BSHPBGS G64 .... 63 M7
BSHPTN PA7 .... 58 C7
CLYDBK G81 .... 60 B5
CTBR ML5 .... 87 K8
Morar Dr BSDN G61 .... 62 B6
CLYDBK G81 .... 60 B5
CUMB G67 .... 68 B2
PSLYN/LNWD PA3 .... 100 A4
PSLYS PA2 .... 100 F7
RUTH G73 .... 129 H6
Morar Pl CLYDBK G81 .... 60 B5
EKILN G74 .... 153 M6
IRV KA12 .... 203 J2
NMRNS G77 .... 150 D2
RNFRW PA4 .... 80 B5
Morar Rd CARD/HILL/MSPK G52 .. 103 L4
CLYDBK G81 .... 60 B5
PGL PA14 .... 54 E2
WMYSB PA18 .... 70 A1 3
Morar St WISHAW ML2 .... 159 G8
Morar Ter RUTH G73 .... 129 K5 3
UD/BTH/TAN G71 .... 132 B2
Moravia Av UD/BTH/TAN G71 .... 132 A6
Moray Av AIRDRIE ML6 .... 111 G4
Moray Dr BSHPBGS G64 .... 44 B8
CRMNK/CLK/EAG G76 .... 151 M2
Moray Gdns BALLOCH G68 .... 48 F4 2
CRMNK/CLK/EAG G76 .... 151 M1
UD/BTH/TAN G71 .... 131 M1
Moray Ga UD/BTH/TAN G71 .... 131 M5
Moray Pl BAIL/MDB/MHD G69 .... 86 D1
BLTYR/CAMB G72 .... 155 J3
BSHPBGS G64 .... 64 C8
KKNTL G66 .... 46 A8
PLKSD/SHW G41 .... 104 E7
PSLYN/LNWD PA3 .... 100 A3
Moray Qd BLSH ML4 .... 133 G4
Moray Rd PGL PA14 .... 34 C8
Mordaunt St DMNK/BRGTN G40 .... 12 F9
Moredun Crs CAR/SHTL G32 .... 107 J2
Moredun Dr PSLYS PA2 .... 101 H8
Moredun Rd PSLYS PA2 .... 101 H8
Moredun St CAR/SHTL G32 .... 107 J2
Morefield Rd GOV/IBX G51 .... 103 K2
Morgan Ms GVH/MTFL G42 .... 105 H6
Morgan St HMLTN ML3 .... 156 D7
LRKH ML9 .... 175 M6
Morina Gdns PLK/PH/NH G53 .... 126 C6
Morion Rd KNTSWD G13 .... 81 K1
Moriston Ct WISHAW ML2 .... 159 M3
Morland EKILN G74 .... 154 D4
Morley St LNPK/KPK G44 .... 128 A2
Morna La SCOT G14 .... 81 L7 5
Morningside Rd WISHAW ML2 .... 160 C6
Morningside St
STPS/GTHM/RID G33 .... 7 L9
Morrin St SPRGB/BLRNK G21 .... 6 A2 1
Morris Crs BLTYR/CAMB G72 .... 155 K2
KLMNK KA1 .... 212 E3
MTHW ML1 .... 134 E8
Morrishall Rd EKILN G74 .... 154 C5
Morrishill Dr BEITH KA15 .... 168 A2
Morris La KLMNKN/STW KA3 .... 16 F2
Morris Moodie Av SVSTN KA20 .... 201 L2
Morrison Av SVSTN KA20 .... 192 E8
Morrison Ct SVSTN KA20 .... 192 E8
Morrison Dr KKNTL G66 .... 44 E2
Morrison Gdns AYR KA8 .... 19 K3
Morrison Pl KLMNKN/STW KA3 .... 17 M1
Morrison Qd CLYDBK G81 .... 60 E8
Morrison St CLYDBK G81 .... 59 M3
GBLS G5 .... 10 E4
Morris Rd PSTWK KA9 .... 221 J8
Morris St GRNK PA15 .... 3 K8
HMLTN ML3 .... 156 D8
LARGS KA30 .... 115 J6 3
LRKH ML9 .... 176 C8
Morriston Crs RNFRW PA4 .... 80 F8
Morriston Park Dr
BLTYR/CAMB G72 .... 130 A2
Morriston St BLTYR/CAMB G72 .. 130 A3
Morton Av AYRS KA7 .... 19 H9
Morton Gdns PLKSD/SHW G41 .... 104 C8
Morton Pl KLMNK KA1 .... 16 D4
Morton Rd AYRS KA7 .... 19 G9
KLMNKN/STW KA3 .... 197 J1
Morton St MTHW ML1 .... 157 L1
Morven Av BLTYR/CAMB G72 .... 131 J8
BSHPBGS G64 .... 64 C8
KLMNKN/STW KA3 .... 206 F6
PSLYS PA2 .... 124 D1
Morven Crs TROON KA10 .... 216 D7
Morven Dr
CRMNK/CLK/EAG G76 .... 151 K1
PSLYN/LNWD PA3 .... 100 A4
TROON KA10 .... 216 D6
Morven Gait ERSK PA8 .... 79 L1 5
Morven Gdns
UD/BTH/TAN G71 .... 131 M1 1
Morven Rd
BLTYR/CAMB G72 .... 129 M6
BSDN G61 .... 61 L3
Morven St
CARD/HILL/MSPK G52 .... 103 L4
CTBR ML5 .... 110 A1
Morville Crs KLWNG KA13 .... 193 L4
Mosesfield St SPRGB/BLRNK G21 .. 83 M4
Mosque Av GBLS G5 .... 11 J5
Mossacre Rd WISHAW ML2 .... 159 J5
Moss Av AIRDRIE ML6 .... 90 F4
PSLYN/LNWD PA3 .... 100 B3
Mossband La SHOTTS ML7 .... 137 L3 4
Mossbank BLTYR/CAMB G72 .... 155 K3 3
EKILS G75 .... 170 F1
Mossbank Av STPS/GTHM/RID G33 84 F5
Mossbank Crs MTHW ML1 .... 134 F6
Mossbank Dr STPS/GTHM/RID G33 84 F5
Mossbank Pl RAYR/DAL KA6 .... 227 H3 2
Mossbank Rd WISHAW ML2 .... 159 J5
Mossblown St LRKH ML9 .... 175 M6 1
Mossburn Rd WISHAW ML2 .... 159 K6
Mossburn St WISHAW ML2 .... 159 K8 1
Mosscastle Rd
STPS/GTHM/RID G33 .... 85 J7 3
Mossdale EKILN G74 .... 153 J6
Mossdale Gdns HMLTN ML3 .... 155 K7
Moss Dr BRHD/NEIL G78 .... 125 G4
ERSK PA8 .... 79 H2
IRVSE KA11 .... 208 E4
Mossend Av HBR/GL G84 .... 20 F8 2
KBRN KA25 .... 167 G1
Mossend La
STPS/GTHM/RID G33 .... 107 K1
Mossend St
STPS/GTHM/RID G33 .... 107 K2 2
Mossgiel EKILS G75 .... 171 H2
Mossgiel Av KLMNKN/STW KA3 .... 17 M5
RUTH G73 .... 129 G4
TROON KA10 .... 216 F5
Mossgiel Crs
CRMNK/CLK/EAG G76 .... 151 M4
Mossgiel Dr CLYDBK G81 .... 60 C6
IRV KA12 .... 203 K6 1
Mossgiel Gdns KKNTL G66 .... 45 M8
UD/BTH/TAN G71 .... 131 L1
Mossgiel Pl AYRS KA7 .... 19 H7 1
RUTH G73 .... 129 G4 2
SVSTN KA20 .... 192 E8
Mossgiel Rd ARD KA22 .... 191 K5
AYRS KA7 .... 19 H8
CUMB G67 .... 49 H6
PLKSW/MSWD G43 .... 127 K2
SALT KA21 .... 192 A6
Mossgiel Ter BLTYR/CAMB G72 .... 131 J7
Mossgreen Pl RAYR/DAL KA6 .... 227 G3
Mosshall Gv MTHW ML1 .... 134 F5
Mosshall Rd MTHW ML1 .... 134 D2
Mosshall St MTHW ML1 .... 134 F6
Mosshead Rd BSDN G61 .... 61 M2
KLMNK KA1 .... 211 M6
Moss Heights Av
CARD/HILL/MSPK G52 .... 103 K4
Mosshill Rd BLSH ML4 .... 133 H2
Mosside Pl KLMNKN/STW KA3 .... 206 F5
Mosside Rd AYR KA8 .... 225 J5
Moss Knowe CUMB G67 .... 49 H7
Mossland Dr WISHAW ML2 .... 159 J5
Mossland Rd
CARD/HILL/MSPK G52 .... 102 D1

Mosslands Rd
PSLYN/LNWD PA3 .... 101 K2
Mosslingal *EKILS* G75 .... 171 L4 5
Mossmulloch *EKILS* G75 .... 171 K4
Mossneuk Av *EKILS* G75 .... 170 E2
Mossneuk Crs *WISHAW* ML2 .... 159 J5
Mossneuk Dr *EKILS* G75 .... 170 F2
PSLYS PA2 .... 124 C1
WISHAW ML2 .... 159 J5
Mossneuk Pk *WISHAW* ML2 .... 159 J5
Mossneuk Rd *EKILS* G75 .... 171 G1
Mossneuk St *CTBR* ML5 .... 109 M6
Mosspark Av
CARD/HILL/MSPK G52 .... 103 M6
MLNGV G62 .... 42 A6
Mosspark Bvd
CARD/HILL/MSPK G52 .... 103 M6
Mosspark Dr
CARD/HILL/MSPK G52 .... 103 L7
Mosspark Ov
CARD/HILL/MSPK G52 .... 103 L6
Mosspark Rd *CTBR* ML5 .... 109 K1
MLNGV G62 .... 42 A6
Mosspark Sq
CARD/HILL/MSPK G52 .... 103 L6
Moss Rd *AIRDRIE* ML6 .... 111 G3
BAIL/MDB/MHD G69 .... 86 C2 2
BRWEIR PA11 .... 98 E2
CRG/CRSL/HOU PA6 .... 78 B6
CUMB G67 .... 49 L5
DMBTN G82 .... 23 J5
EKILS G75 .... 171 J5
GOV/IBX G51 .... 103 K1
KKNTL G66 .... 65 H3
KLMCLM PA13 .... 75 K1
PGL PA14 .... 54 F2
PSLYN/LNWD PA3 .... 100 C3
WISHAW ML2 .... 159 L6
Moss Side Av *AIRDRIE* ML6 .... 110 E1
Moss-Side Av *CARLUKE* ML8 .... 178 D7 5
Moss-Side Rd *PLKSD/SHW* G41 .... 104 E8
Moss St *PSLY* PA1 .... 9 G3
Mossvale La
PSLYN/LNWD PA3 .... 101 K3 2
Mossvale Rd
STPS/GTHM/RID G33 .... 85 H7 5
STPS/GTHM/RID G33 .... 85 J7 5
Mossvale Sq
STPS/GTHM/RID G33 .... 85 H7 6
Mossvale St *PSLYN/LNWD* PA3 .... 101 K2
Mossvale Ter
BAIL/MDB/MHD G69 .... 67 G6 5
Mossview Crs *AIRDRIE* ML6 .... 111 G3
Mossview La
CARD/HILL/MSPK G52 .... 103 J4 5
Mossview Qd
CARD/HILL/MSPK G52 .... 103 K4 1
Mossview Rd
STPS/GTHM/RID G33 .... 85 L5 2
Mosswell Rd *MLNGV* G62 .... 42 B6 2
Mossyde Av *PGL* PA14 .... 54 F2
Mossywood Ct *BALLOCH* G68 .... 67 M2 2
Mossywood Pl *BALLOCH* G68 .... 67 M2 7
Mossywood Rd *BALLOCH* G68 .... 67 L2
Mote Hl *HMLTN* ML3 .... 156 E5
Mote Hill Rd *PSLYN/LNWD* PA3 .... 102 A3
Motehill Rd *PSLYN/LNWD* PA3 .... 102 B2
Motherwell Rd *BLSH* ML4 .... 133 G5
HMLTN ML3 .... 156 F6
MTHW ML1 .... 134 B8 2
MTHW ML1 .... 135 G3
Motherwell St *AIRDRIE* ML6 .... 89 J8
Moulin Circ
CARD/HILL/MSPK G52 .... 103 H5 2
Moulin Pl *CARD/HILL/MSPK* G52 .. 103 G5
Moulin Rd
CARD/HILL/MSPK G52 .... 103 G5
Moulin Ter
CARD/HILL/MSPK G52 .... 103 G6
Mountainblue St
DMNK/BRGTN G40 .... 12 F5
Mount Annan Dr
LNPK/KPK G44 .... 128 B2
Mount Av *KLMNK* KA1 .... 16 A7
KLMNK KA1 .... 218 C5
Mountblow Rd *CLYDBK* G81 .... 59 K3
Mount Cameron Dr North
EKILN G74 .... 15 K5
Mount Cameron Dr South
EKILN G74 .... 15 K5
Mount Charles Crs *AYRS* KA7 .... 228 D7
Mountgarrie Rd *GOV/IBX* G51 .... 103 K2
Mount Harriet Av
STPS/GTHM/RID G33 .... 85 L3 1
Mount Harriet Dr
STPS/GTHM/RID G33 .... 85 K3
Mountherrick *EKILS* G75 .... 171 L4 5
Mount Lockhart
UD/BTH/TAN G71 .... 108 B7
Mount Oliphant Crs *AYRS* KA7 .... 19 J7
Mount Oliphant Pl *AYRS* KA7 .... 19 J7 1
Mount Pl *KLMNK* KA1 .... 16 A8
Mount Pleasant Crs *KKNTL* G66 .... 45 H3
Mount Pleasant Dr *OLDK* G60 .... 59 H2
Mount Pleasant St *GRNK* PA15 .... 2 A5
Mount Stewart St
CARLUKE ML8 .... 178 E7
Mount St *MRYH/FIRH* G20 .... 4 D2
Mount Stuart Rd *LARGS* KA30 .... 115 L5
Mountstuart St *GTCI* KA28 .... 138 B6 2
Mount Stuart St
PLKSD/SHW G41 .... 127 L1
The Mount *AYRS* KA7 .... 229 H5
Mount Vernon Av
CAR/SHTL G32 .... 107 L6
CTBR ML5 .... 109 L2
Mount Vw *IRVSE* KA11 .... 204 C8
Mount Village *KLMNK* KA1 .... 211 J2
Mournian Wy *HMLTN* ML3 .... 156 D8
Mousebank Rd
LNK/LMHG ML11 .... 198 F5 2
Mousemill Rd *LNK/LMHG* ML11 .. 198 D4
Mowbray *EKILN* G74 .... 154 C5
Mowbray Av
BAIL/MDB/MHD G69 .... 86 F4
Moyne Rd *PLK/PH/NH* G53 .... 103 G7
Moy St *PTCK* G11 .... 82 C7 7
Muckcroft Rd
BAIL/MDB/MHD G69 .... 66 B5
Mugdock Rd *MLNGV* G62 .... 42 A7
Muirbank Av *RUTH* G73 .... 128 F2
Muirbank Gdns *RUTH* G73 .... 128 F2 2
Muirbrae Rd *RUTH* G73 .... 129 H5
Muirbrae Wy *RUTH* G73 .... 129 H5 3
Muirburn Rd *BEITH* KA15 .... 144 A6
Muircroft Dr *MTHW* ML1 .... 135 H7 2
Muir Dr *IRV* KA12 .... 203 K6
SVSTN KA20 .... 201 J1
TROON KA10 .... 216 D3
Muirdrum Av
CARD/HILL/MSPK G52 .... 103 K6
Muirdyke Rd *CTBR* ML5 .... 88 A4
CTBR ML5 .... 109 K1
Muirdykes Av
CARD/HILL/MSPK G52 .... 103 G4 1
PGL PA14 .... 54 D2
Muirdykes Crs
PSLYN/LNWD PA3 .... 101 H3 2
Muirdykes Rd
CARD/HILL/MSPK G52 .... 103 G4
PSLYN/LNWD PA3 .... 101 H3
Muiredge And Jersy Rd
MTHW ML1 .... 136 B6
SHOTTS ML7 .... 136 C2
SHOTTS ML7 .... 136 F1
Muiredge Ct
UD/BTH/TAN G71 .... 131 M3 2
Muiredge Ter
BAIL/MDB/MHD G69 .... 108 B5 3
Muirend Av *LNPK/KPK* G44 .... 127 M4
Muirend Rd *DMBTN* G82 .... 35 G1
KLMNKN/STW KA3 .... 206 F4
LNPK/KPK G44 .... 127 L5
Muirend St *KBRN* KA25 .... 143 H7
Muirfield Ct *LNPK/KPK* G44 .... 127 M5 7
Muirfield Crs *SMSTN* G23 .... 62 E8
Muirfield Mdw
UD/BTH/TAN G71 .... 131 L7 2
Muirfield Pl *KLWNG* KA13 .... 193 J5
Muirfield Rd *BALLOCH* G68 .... 49 G4
Muirhall Ter *SHOTTS* ML7 .... 113 H7
Muirhead Dr *MTHW* ML1 .... 134 F5
PSLYN/LNWD PA3 .... 100 A4
Muirhead Gdns
BAIL/MDB/MHD G69 .... 108 C5 4
SHOTTS ML7 .... 113 H7
Muirhead Ga
UD/BTH/TAN G71 .... 132 B1 2
Muirhead Gv
BAIL/MDB/MHD G69 .... 108 C5 5
Muirhead Rd
BAIL/MDB/MHD G69 .... 108 B6
Muirhead St *LOCHW* PA12 .... 120 D7 1
Muirhead Ter *MTHW* ML1 .... 157 L5 1
Muirhead Wy *BSHPBGS* G64 .... 64 D8
Muirhill Av *LNPK/KPK* G44 .... 127 L5
Muirhill Crs *KNTSWD* G13 .... 80 F2
Muirhouse Av *MTHW* ML1 .... 158 B6
WISHAW ML2 .... 160 B3
Muirhouse Dr *MTHW* ML1 .... 158 C7
Muirhouse La *EKILS* G75 .... 15 G6 1
Muirhouse Pk *BSDN* G61 .... 61 K1 1
Muirhouse Rd *MTHW* ML1 .... 158 B7
Muirhouse St *PLKSD/SHW* G41 .. 10 F9 1
Muirkirk Dr *HMLTN* ML3 .... 155 K7
KNTSWD G13 .... 81 M2 2
Muirlee Rd *CARLUKE* ML8 .... 179 H8 3
Muirlees Crs *MLNGV* G62 .... 41 L7
Muirmadkin Rd *BLSH* ML4 .... 133 H4
Muirmaillen Av *MTHW* ML1 .... 135 J8 1
Muirpark Av *RNFRW* PA4 .... 80 C7 2
Muirpark Dr *BSHPBGS* G64 .... 84 A1
Muirpark Rd *BEITH* KA15 .... 144 B8 3
Muirpark St *PTCK* G11 .... 82 B7 2
Muirpark Ter *BSHPBGS* G64 .... 84 A1 2
Muir Rd *DMBTN* G82 .... 37 J3
Muirshiel Crs *PLK/PH/NH* G53 .... 126 C3
Muirshiel La *PGL* PA14 .... 54 D1 3
Muirshiel Rd *PGL* PA14 .... 54 D1
Muirshot Rd *LRKH* ML9 .... 176 B5
Muirside Av *CAR/SHTL* G32 .... 107 L6
KKNTL G66 .... 66 A1
Muirside Pl *WISHAW* ML2 .... 159 M3 2
Muirside Rd
BAIL/MDB/MHD G69 .... 108 B5
KLWNG KA13 .... 193 J7
Muirside St
BAIL/MDB/MHD G69 .... 108 B5
Muirskeith Crs
PLKSW/MSWD G43 .... 128 A3 2
Muirskeith Pl
PLKSW/MSWD G43 .... 127 M3 1
Muirskeith Rd
PLKSW/MSWD G43 .... 127 M3
Muir St *ALEX/LLW* G83 .... 25 K2
BLTYR/CAMB G72 .... 155 K3
BSHPBGS G64 .... 64 A8
CARLUKE ML8 .... 177 M3
CTBR ML5 .... 109 L2
HMLTN ML3 .... 156 E5
LRKH ML9 .... 176 A6
MTHW ML1 .... 157 K1
RNFRW PA4 .... 80 D5 6
Muir Ter *PSLYN/LNWD* PA3 .... 102 A2
Muirton Dr *BSHPBGS* G64 .... 63 M6
Muiryfauld Dr *CAR/SHTL* G32 .... 106 E5
Muiryhall St *CTBR* ML5 .... 110 B2
Muiryhall St East *CTBR* ML5 .... 110 C2
Mulben Crs *PLK/PH/NH* G53 .... 125 M2
Mulben Pl *PLK/PH/NH* G53 .... 125 M2
Mulben Ter *PLK/PH/NH* G53 .... 125 M2
Mulberry Dr *EKILS* G75 .... 171 J4
Mulberry Rd
PLKSW/MSWD G43 .... 127 K4
UD/BTH/TAN G71 .... 109 J8 2
Mulberry Wy *EKILS* G75 .... 171 J4
Mulberry Wynd
BLTYR/CAMB G72 .... 130 F6
Mulgrew Av *SVSTN* KA20 .... 192 A7
Mull *EKILN* G74 .... 172 C2
Mullardoch St *SMSTN* G23 .... 62 D8 14
Mull Av *PGL* PA14 .... 55 G2
PSLYS PA2 .... 124 E2
RNFRW PA4 .... 80 C8
Mull Crs *IRVSE* KA11 .... 204 A7
Mull Pl *IRVSE* KA11 .... 204 A7
Mull Qd *WISHAW* ML2 .... 159 L4
Mull St *SPRGB/BLRNK* G21 .... 7 G4
Mull Ter *IRVSE* KA11 .... 204 A6
Mulvey Crs *AIRDRIE* ML6 .... 110 E2
Mungo Pk *EKILS* G75 .... 14 C6
Mungo Pl *UD/BTH/TAN* G71 .... 109 G8 2
Munlochy Rd *GOV/IBX* G51 .... 103 K2
Munnoch Crs *ARD* KA22 .... 191 H5
Munro Av *KLMNK* KA1 .... 16 A3
Munro Ct *CLYDBK* G81 .... 59 M3
Munro Dr *KBRN* KA25 .... 167 H1
KKNTL G66 .... 45 H4
Munro Dr East *HBR/GL* G84 .... 20 E6
Munro Dr West *HBR/GL* G84 .... 20 D6
Munro La *KNTSWD* G13 .... 81 L4
Munro La East *KNTSWD* G13 .... 81 L4 1
Munro Pl *EKILN* G74 .... 154 B6 5
KLMNK KA1 .... 16 B1
KNTSWD G13 .... 81 L2
SALT KA21 .... 192 A7
Munro Rd *KNTSWD* G13 .... 81 L4
Munro St *ALEX/LLW* G83 .... 25 L4 10
GRNKW/INVK PA16 .... 32 A5
Murano St *MRYH/FIRH* G20 .... 82 F5
Murchie Dr *PSTWK* KA9 .... 225 K4 7
Murchison Dr *EKILS* G75 .... 171 H2 2
Murchison Rd
CRG/CRSL/HOU PA6 .... 77 J8
Murchland Wy *IRV* KA12 .... 203 J6 1
Murdieston St *GRNK* PA15 .... 32 D5
Murdoch Crs *SVSTN* KA20 .... 201 K2 3
Murdoch Dr *MLNGV* G62 .... 62 D1 1
Murdoch Pl *IRVSE* KA11 .... 208 F3
MTHW ML1 .... 133 M6 3
Murdoch Rd *EKILS* G75 .... 14 F6
Murdoch's Lone *AYRS* KA7 .... 228 E8
Murdoch Sq *BLSH* ML4 .... 133 J2 2
Murdostoun Gdns
WISHAW ML2 .... 159 H4
Murdostoun Ter *MTHW* ML1 .... 135 L8
Murdostoun Vw *WISHAW* ML2 .... 159 M3
Mure Av *KLMNKN/STW* KA3 .... 207 G5
Mure Pl *BRHD/NEIL* G78 .... 147 G6
NMLNS KA16 .... 215 H2
Murial Blue Ct *GRK* PA19 .... 31 M2 7
Muriel La *BRHD/NEIL* G78 .... 125 J6 3
Muriel St *BRHD/NEIL* G78 .... 125 J6
Murray Av *KSYTH* G65 .... 47 K1
SALT KA21 .... 191 L7
Murray Crs *WISHAW* ML2 .... 160 A2
Murrayfield Dr *BSDN* G61 .... 61 L8
Murrayfield St
CAR/SHTL G32 .... 106 E2 5
Murrayhill *EKILS* G75 .... 14 C5
Murray Pl *AYR* KA8 .... 225 J6
BLSH ML4 .... 132 E2
BRHD/NEIL G78 .... 125 K5
DMBTN G82 .... 37 J5
GRK PA19 .... 31 L3 5
KLMNKN/STW KA3 .... 207 J7
Murray Rd *CARLUKE* ML8 .... 177 M5
UD/BTH/TAN G71 .... 132 A6
The Murray Rd *EKILS* G75 .... 14 C7
Murray St *AYR* KA8 .... 225 J7
GRNKW/INVK PA16 .... 32 C4
PSLYN/LNWD PA3 .... 8 C1
RNFRW PA4 .... 80 C6 2
Murray Ter *MTHW* ML1 .... 157 H2
Murrin Av *BSHPBGS* G64 .... 64 D8 2
Murroch Av *DMBTN* G82 .... 37 H3
Murroes Rd *GOV/IBX* G51 .... 103 K2
Musgrove Pl *EKILS* G75 .... 14 A6
Muslin St *DMNK/BRGTN* G40 .... 12 C8
Muttonhole Rd *HMLTN* ML3 .... 173 H1
Mybster Pl *GOV/IBX* G51 .... 103 K2 5
Myers Crs *UD/BTH/TAN* G71 .... 132 A4
Myreside Pl *CAR/SHTL* G32 .... 13 M3 1
Myreside St *CAR/SHTL* G32 .... 106 E3
Myres Rd *PLK/PH/NH* G53 .... 126 D1
Myreton Av *KLMCLM* PA13 .... 75 J2
Myrie Gdns *BSHPBGS* G64 .... 64 B8
Myrtle Av *KKNTL* G66 .... 65 J4
Myrtle Bank *BEITH* KA15 .... 168 A1
Myrtle Dr *MTHW* ML1 .... 134 B4
WISHAW ML2 .... 158 D5
Myrtle Hill La *GVH/MTFL* G42 .... 128 C1
Myrtle La *LRKH* ML9 .... 176 B8
Myrtle Pk *GVH/MTFL* G42 .... 105 H8
Myrtle Pl *GVH/MTFL* G42 .... 128 C1 1
Myrtle Rd *CLYDBK* G81 .... 59 K5
UD/BTH/TAN G71 .... 132 B1
Myrtle Sq *BSHPBGS* G64 .... 84 A1
Myrtle St *BLTYR/CAMB* G72 .... 131 K8
Myrtle View Rd *GVH/MTFL* G42 .. 128 C1
Myrtle Wk *BLTYR/CAMB* G72 .... 129 M3
Myvot Av *CUMB* G67 .... 68 B3
Myvot Rd *CUMB* G67 .... 68 B3 1

N

Nairn Av *BLSH* ML4 .... 133 G3
BLTYR/CAMB G72 .... 131 J7
Nairn Ct *KLWNG* KA13 .... 193 H6 7
Nairn Crs *AIRDRIE* ML6 .... 111 G4
Nairn Dr *GRNKW/INVK* PA16 .... 31 K4 3
Nairn Pl *CLYDBK* G81 .... 59 M6
EKILN G74 .... 154 C6 5
Nairn Qd *WISHAW* ML2 .... 159 H4 5
Nairn Rd *GRNKW/INVK* PA16 .... 31 K5
Nairnside Rd *SPRGB/BLRNK* G21 .. 84 C2
Nairn St *BLTYR/CAMB* G72 .... 155 J3
CLYDBK G81 .... 59 M6
KVGV G3 .... 82 D8
LRKH ML9 .... 175 M7
Nairn Wy *BALLOCH* G68 .... 49 G4
Naismith St *CAR/SHTL* G32 .... 130 C1 5
Naismith Wk *BLSH* ML4 .... 133 J2
Nansen St *MRYH/FIRH* G20 .... 4 E3
Napier Av *DMBTN* G82 .... 35 H1
Napier Ct *BALLOCH* G68 .... 49 K1
DMBTN G82 .... 35 H1 1
OLDK G60 .... 59 J4
Napier Crs *DMBTN* G82 .... 36 D6
Napier Dr *GOV/IBX* G51 .... 104 B1
Napier Gdns *PSLYN/LNWD* PA3 .... 100 C3
Napier Hl *EKILS* G75 .... 14 F6
Napier La *EKILS* G75 .... 14 F6 1
Napier Pk *BALLOCH* G68 .... 49 J3
Napier Pl *BALLOCH* G68 .... 49 J1
GOV/IBX G51 .... 104 B1
OLDK G60 .... 59 J4 2
Napier Rd *BALLOCH* G68 .... 49 J2
CARD/HILL/MSPK G52 .... 80 F8
GOV/IBX G51 .... 104 B1
Napiershall La *COWCAD* G4 .... 4 D4
Napiershall Pl *MRYH/FIRH* G20 .... 4 D4
Napiershall St *COWCAD* G4 .... 4 D4
MRYH/FIRH G20 .... 4 D3
Napier Sq *BLSH* ML4 .... 133 J2
Napierston Rd *ALEX/LLW* G83 .... 25 M4
Napier St *CLYDBK* G81 .... 80 C2
GOV/IBX G51 .... 104 B1
JNSTN PA5 .... 99 L6
PSLYN/LNWD PA3 .... 100 C3
Napier Ter *GOV/IBX* G51 .... 104 B1
Napier Wy *BALLOCH* G68 .... 49 J2
Naproch Pl *NMRNS* G77 .... 151 J4
Naseby Av *PTCK* G11 .... 81 M6 5
Naseby La *PTCK* G11 .... 81 M6
Nasmyth Av *BSDN* G61 .... 61 H1
EKILS G75 .... 15 H7
Nasmyth Pl *EKILS* G75 .... 15 H7
Nasmyth Rd
CARD/HILL/MSPK G52 .... 103 G2 2
Nasmyth Rd North
CARD/HILL/MSPK G52 .... 103 G2
Nasmyth Rd South
CARD/HILL/MSPK G52 .... 103 G2
Nassau Pl *EKILS* G75 .... 153 G8
National Bank La *CGLE* G1 .... 11 H1 2
Navar Pl *PSLYS* PA2 .... 9 L9
Naver St *STPS/GTHM/RID* G33 .. 84 E8 2
Naylor La *AIRDRIE* ML6 .... 111 H1 2
Naysmyth Bank *EKILS* G75 .... 15 G6
Needle Gn *CARLUKE* ML8 .... 178 F7 5
Neidpath Av *CTBR* ML5 .... 110 A6
Neidpath Pl *CTBR* ML5 .... 110 A6
Neidpath Rd *CARLUKE* ML8 .... 178 E6 5
Neidpath Rd East *NMRNS* G77 .... 151 G3
Neidpath Rd West *NMRNS* G77 .. 151 G2
Neil Av *IRV* KA12 .... 203 K4
Neilsland Dr *HMLTN* ML3 .... 174 B2
MTHW ML1 .... 157 H3
Neilsland Ov *PLK/PH/NH* G53 .... 126 D1
Neilsland Rd *HMLTN* ML3 .... 156 B7
Neilsland Sq *HMLTN* ML3 .... 156 C8 1
PLK/PH/NH G53 .... 103 K8 5
Neilsland St *HMLTN* ML3 .... 156 C8
Neilson Ct *HMLTN* ML3 .... 156 E7 5
Neilson St *BLSH* ML4 .... 133 G4
Neilston Av *PLK/PH/NH* G53 .... 126 C4
Neilston Rd *BRHD/NEIL* G78 .... 147 G6
BRHD/NEIL G78 .... 148 E2
PSLYS PA2 .... 9 H8
Neil St *GRNKW/INVK* PA16 .... 32 A5
RNFRW PA4 .... 80 D4
Neilvaig Dr *RUTH* G73 .... 129 J6
Neistpoint Dr
STPS/GTHM/RID G33 .... 107 G2 2
Nelson Av *CTBR* ML5 .... 109 L5
Nelson Crs *MTHW* ML1 .... 158 B5
Nelson Mandela Pl *CGLW* G2 .... 5 J9 1
Nelson Pl *BAIL/MDB/MHD* G69 .... 108 B5
HBR/GL G84 .... 21 G7 10
Nelson Rd *GRK* PA19 .... 31 M3
SALT KA21 .... 201 H1
Nelson St *BAIL/MDB/MHD* G69 .... 108 B5
GBLS G5 .... 10 F4
GRNK PA15 .... 2 B3
KLMNK KA1 .... 16 E4
LARGS KA30 .... 115 J5
NMLNS KA16 .... 215 J2
Nelson Ter *EKILN* G74 .... 15 K6
Nelville Dr *GLSTN* KA4 .... 214 A4
Nemphlar Moor Rd
CARLUKE ML8 .... 188 D8
Nemphlat Hl *LNK/LMHG* ML11 .... 198 E4
Neptune St *GOV/IBX* G51 .... 104 B2
Neptune Wy *BLSH* ML4 .... 133 L4
Nerston Rd *EKILN* G74 .... 153 K3
Ness Av *JNSTN* PA5 .... 122 C1
Ness Dr *BLTYR/CAMB* G72 .... 131 L8
EKILN G74 .... 15 L3
Ness Gdns *BSHPBGS* G64 .... 64 B8 2
Ness Pl *TROON* KA10 .... 216 F4
Ness Rd *GRNKW/INVK* PA16 .... 32 C4 3
RNFRW PA4 .... 80 B5
Ness St *STPS/GTHM/RID* G33 .... 84 E8
WISHAW ML2 .... 177 H1
Ness Ter *HMLTN* ML3 .... 156 A8
Nethan Av *WISHAW* ML2 .... 158 C7
Nethanfoot Rd
CARLUKE ML8 .... 188 B7 2
Nethan Ga *HMLTN* ML3 .... 156 C6
Nethan Gln *CARLUKE* ML8 .... 188 A7
Nethan Pl *HMLTN* ML3 .... 174 D3
Nethan St *MTHW* ML1 .... 133 J7
Nether Auldhouse Rd
PLKSW/MSWD G43 .... 127 J3
Netherbank Rd *WISHAW* ML2 .. 158 D7 3
Netherbog Rd *DMBTN* G82 .... 37 H5
Netherburn Av
CRG/CRSL/HOU PA6 .... 99 L2
LNPK/KPK G44 .... 127 M7
Netherburn Gdns
CRG/CRSL/HOU PA6 .... 99 L1 2
Netherby Dr *PLKSD/SHW* G41 .... 104 D5
Nethercairn Pl *NMRNS* G77 .... 151 J4
Nethercairn Rd *GIF/THBK* G46 .... 127 J5
Nethercliffe Av *LNPK/KPK* G44 .... 127 M7
Nethercraigs Dr *PSLYS* PA2 .... 124 C1
Nethercraigs Rd *PSLYS* PA2 .... 124 B2
Nethercroy Rd *KSYTH* G65 .... 47 L4
Netherdale Crs *WISHAW* ML2 .... 158 C7
Netherdale Dr *PSLY* PA1 .... 102 F6
Netherdale Rd *WISHAW* ML2 .... 158 E7
Netherfield St *DEN/PKHD* G31 .. 13 J3 1
Nethergreen Crs *RNFRW* PA4 .... 80 B6 1
Nethergreen Rd *RNFRW* PA4 .... 80 B6 1
Nethergreen Wynd *RNFRW* PA4 .. 80 B6
Netherhall Rd *WISHAW* ML2 .... 158 E7 1
Netherhill Av *LNPK/KPK* G44 .... 127 M8
Netherhill Crs
PSLYN/LNWD PA3 .... 102 A3
Netherhill Rd
BAIL/MDB/MHD G69 .... 66 F8
PSLYN/LNWD PA3 .... 9 K1
Netherhouse Av *CTBR* ML5 .... 109 M6
KKNTL G66 .... 65 L5
Netherhouse Pl
BAIL/MDB/MHD G69 .... 108 E1
Netherhouse Rd
BAIL/MDB/MHD G69 .... 108 E2
Netherland Rd
KLMNKN/STW KA3 .... 197 L1
Netherlee Crs *DALRY* KA24 .... 166 B8
Netherlee Pl *LNPK/KPK* G44 .... 128 A5
Netherlee Rd *LNPK/KPK* G44 .... 128 A5
Nethermains Rd *KLWNG* KA13 .... 193 L8
MLNGV G62 .... 62 A1
Nethermiln Rd *WKIL* KA23 .... 181 K5
Netherpark Av *LNPK/KPK* G44 .... 127 M8
Netherpark Crs *LARGS* KA30 .... 115 J3
Netherplace Crs *NMRNS* G77 .... 150 C5
PLK/PH/NH G53 .... 126 B1 1
Netherplace Rd *NMRNS* G77 .... 149 M5
PLK/PH/NH G53 .... 126 B1
Netherton Av *PGL* PA14 .... 55 G2
Netherton Ct *NMRNS* G77 .... 150 F3
Netherton Dr *BRHD/NEIL* G78 .... 125 K7
Netherton Hl *KKNTL* G66 .... 29 G8
Netherton Ov *KKNTL* G66 .... 44 B1
Netherton Rd *EKILS* G75 .... 14 A9
EKILS G75 .... 170 F5
KNTSWD G13 .... 81 L1
NMRNS G77 .... 150 F3
WISHAW ML2 .... 158 C7
Netherton St *KNTSWD* G13 .... 81 M2 5
WISHAW ML2 .... 158 F7
Nethervale Av *LNPK/KPK* G44 .... 127 M8
Netherview Rd *LNPK/KPK* G44 .... 128 A8
Netherway *LNPK/KPK* G44 .... 127 M8 1
Netherwood Av *BALLOCH* G68 .. 68 A1 1
Netherwood Ct *BALLOCH* G68 .... 68 A1
Netherwood Gv *BALLOCH* G68 .... 68 A1
Netherwood Rd *BALLOCH* G68 .... 67 M1
MTHW ML1 .... 158 C6 1
Netherwood Wy *BALLOCH* G68 .. 68 A1
Neuk Av *BAIL/MDB/MHD* G69 .... 86 C2
CRG/CRSL/HOU PA6 .... 77 J8
Neuk Crs *CRG/CRSL/HOU* PA6 .... 77 J7
Neukfoot La *BRHD/NEIL* G78 .... 146 F6
The Neuk *WISHAW* ML2 .... 158 E6
Neville *EKILN* G74 .... 154 C4
Nevis Av *HMLTN* ML3 .... 156 A8
Nevis Ct *BRHD/NEIL* G78 .... 125 J8 5
Nevis Dr *BSHPBGS* G64 .... 44 B8
Nevison St *LRKH* ML9 .... 176 B7
Nevis Pl *KLMNK* KA1 .... 212 A5
Nevis Rd *BSDN* G61 .... 61 H2
PLKSW/MSWD G43 .... 127 H4 5
RNFRW PA4 .... 80 B8
Nevis Wy *IRVSE* KA11 .... 204 A5
PSLYN/LNWD PA3 .... 79 L8
Neward Crs *PSTWK* KA9 .... 225 K3
Newark Av *GRNKW/INVK* PA16 .. 32 C2 5
Newark Crs *AYRS* KA7 .... 228 B8
Newark Dr *PLKSD/SHW* G41 .... 104 E6
PSLYS PA2 .... 124 C1
WISHAW ML2 .... 159 J3
Newark Pl *PGL* PA14 .... 34 D8 5
WISHAW ML2 .... 159 K3
Newark St *GRNKW/INVK* PA16 .... 32 B1
Newarthill Rd *MTHW* ML1 .... 134 C7 5
New Ashtree St
WISHAW ML2 .... 158 E6 1
New Av *HWWD* PA9 .... 121 M3 1
Newbarns St *CARLUKE* ML8 .... 178 F6
Newbattle Av *AIRDRIE* ML6 .... 111 H7
Newbattle Ct *CAR/SHTL* G32 .... 107 H7 1
Newbattle Gdns
CAR/SHTL G32 .... 107 H7 2
Newbattle Pl *CAR/SHTL* G32 .... 107 H7 5
Newbattle Rd *CAR/SHTL* G32 .... 107 G8
Newbold Av
SPRGB/BLRNK G21 .... 83 M2 5
New Bridge St *AYRS* KA7 .... 18 E2
Newburgh St
PLKSW/MSWD G43 .... 127 K2
Newcastleton Dr *SMSTN* G23 .... 62 E8 5
New City Rd *COWCAD* G4 .... 4 F6
New Cordale Rd *DMBTN* G82 .... 25 K7
Newcraigs Drive
CRMNK/CLK/EAG G76 .... 152 D2
Newcroft Dr *LNPK/KPK* G44 .... 128 D4
New Dock La *GRNK* PA15 .... 2 F4 2
Newdyke Rd *KKNTL* G66 .... 65 L1
Newdykes Farm Rd
PSTWK KA9 .... 221 K8 1
Newdykes Rd *PSTWK* KA9 .... 221 K8
New Edinburgh Rd
UD/BTH/TAN G71 .... 131 L2
UD/BTH/TAN G71 .... 132 D3 5
New England Rd *SALT* KA21 .... 192 A7 2
Newfield Crs *HMLTN* ML3 .... 156 B5
Newfield Dr *CRH/DND* KA2 .... 209 M7
Newfield Pl *GIF/THBK* G46 .... 126 F7 1
IRVSE KA11 .... 204 A4
RUTH G73 .... 128 E2
Newfield Sq *PLK/PH/NH* G53 .... 126 A3
Newford Gv
CRMNK/CLK/EAG G76 .... 151 L4
Newhall St *DMNK/BRGTN* G40 .... 12 B9
Newhaven Gv *LARGS* KA30 .... 115 H3 1
Newhaven Rd
STPS/GTHM/RID G33 .... 107 H1
Newhaven St *CAR/SHTL* G32 .... 107 G2 5
Newhills Rd
STPS/GTHM/RID G33 .... 107 L2
Newhouse Dr *KBRN* KA25 .... 166 F1
Newhousemill Rd *EKILN* G74 .... 172 C2
Newhouse Wy *IRVSE* KA11 .... 204 A4
Newhut Rd *MTHW* ML1 .... 157 K1
New Inchinnan Rd
PSLYN/LNWD PA3 .... 101 L2
Newington St *CAR/SHTL* G32 .... 106 F3
New Kirk Rd *BSDN* G61 .... 61 L4
New Lairdsland Rd *KKNTL* G66 .... 65 K1
New Lanark Rd
LNK/LMHG ML11 .... 198 F7
Newlands Dr *HMLTN* ML3 .... 174 D1
KLMNKN/STW KA3 .... 206 E4

Newlandsfield Rd
PLKSW/MSWD G43 .... **127** K2
Newlands Gdns *JNSTN* PA5 ..... **100** C8 1
Newlandsmuir Rd *EKILS* G75 ...... **170** F3
Newlands Pl *EKILN* G74 .... **14** F4
Newlands Rd *EKILS* G75 .... **170** E5
PLKSW/MSWD G43 .... **127** L3
UD/BTH/TAN G71 .... **131** M1
Newlands St *CTBR* ML5 .... **110** A5
LNK/LMHG ML11 .... **199** J6
Newlands Ter *CARLUKE* ML8 .... **178** F7 5
New La *AIRDRIE* ML6 .... **111** H7
New Luce Dr *CAR/SHTL* G32 .... **107** K6
Newmains Av *RNFRW* PA4 .... **79** G4
Newmains Rd *RNFRW* PA4 .... **80** C8
Newmarket St *AYRS* KA7 .... **18** E3
Newmill & Canthill Rd
SHOTTS ML7 .... **113** M7
SHOTTS ML7 .... **137** G5
Newmill Gdns *SHOTTS* ML7 .... **136** F7
New Mill Rd *KLMNK* KA1 .... **17** H6
Newmill Rd
SPRGB/BLRNK G21 .... **84** C4 1
Newnham Rd *PSLY* PA1 .... **102** D5
Newpark Crs
BLTYR/CAMB G72 .... **130** A2 2
New Park St *HMLTN* ML3 .... **156** C4
New Plymouth *EKILS* G75 .... **171** G2
New Rd *AYR* KA8 .... **224** F7
BLTYR/CAMB G72 .... **130** E5
GLSTN KA4 .... **214** B3 5
Newrose Av *BLSH* ML4 .... **133** H2
Newshot Dr *ERSK* PA8 .... **79** K1
RNFRW PA4 .... **79** K2
New Sneddon St
PSLYN/LNWD PA3 .... **101** L3
Newstead Gdns *SMSTN* G23 ...... **62** F8 2
New Stevenston Rd
MTHW ML1 .... **134** B7
New St *BEITH* KA15 .... **168** B1
BLTYR/CAMB G72 .... **155** J2
CLYDBK G81 .... **60** A3
DALRY KA24 .... **184** C2 2
IRV KA12 .... **203** H7
KLBCH PA10 .... **99** G6
KLMNK KA1 .... **211** M4
LARGS KA30 .... **115** K6
LOCHW PA12 .... **120** C7
PSLY PA1 .... **9** H4
SVSTN KA20 .... **201** K1
Newton Av *BLTYR/CAMB* G72 ...... **130** D3
BRHD/NEIL G78 .... **149** K1
JNSTN PA5 .... **100** E6
Newton Brae *BLTYR/CAMB* G72 .. **130** F4
Newton Ct *NMRNS* G77 .... **150** D6
Newton Dr *JNSTN* PA5 .... **100** E6
UD/BTH/TAN G71 .... **132** A2
WISHAW ML2 .... **160** A4
Newton Farm Rd
BLTYR/CAMB G72 .... **130** F2
Newtongrange Av
CAR/SHTL G32 .... **107** H7
Newtongrange Gdns
CAR/SHTL G32 .... **107** H7 1
Newton Gv *NMRNS* G77 .... **150** D6
Newtonlea Av *NMRNS* G77 .... **150** E6
Newton of Barr *LOCHW* PA12 ...... **120** B7
Newton Park Ct *AYR* KA8 .... **225** H6 1
Newton Pl *KVGV* G3 .... **4** C7
NMRNS G77 .... **150** E6
Newton Rd *BSHPTN* PA7 .... **57** M6
KKNTL G66 .... **65** L5
Newton Station Rd
BLTYR/CAMB G72 .... **130** E4
Newton St *CTBR* ML5 .... **109** L5
GRNK PA15 .... **2** A4
GRNKW/INVK PA16 .... **32** D3
KBRN KA25 .... **143** H8
PSLY PA1 .... **8** C5
Newton Ter *PSLYS* PA2 .... **100** F6
Newton Terrace La *KVGV* G3 .... **4** C8
Newtown St *KSYTH* G65 .... **47** K1
Newtyle Pl *BSHPBGS* G64 .... **64** D8 1
Newtyle Rd *PSLY* PA1 .... **102** C5
New View Dr *BLSH* ML4 .... **133** G6
New View Pl *BLSH* ML4 .... **133** G6 1
New Wynd *CGLE* G1 .... **11** K3 2
Nicholas St *CGLE* G1 .... **11** M1
Nicholson St *GBLS* G5 .... **11** H4
Nicklaus Wy *MTHW* ML1 .... **134** E2
Nicol Dr *GRNKW/INVK* PA16 .... **32** B4
Nicolson Ct *STPS/GTHM/RID* G33 .. **85** K4
Nicolson St *GRNK* PA15 .... **2** B3
Nicol St *AIRDRIE* ML6 .... **89** J8
GRNKW/INVK PA16 .... **32** B5
Niddrie Rd *GVH/MTFL* G42 .... **104** F7
Niddrie Sq *GVH/MTFL* G42 .... **104** F8 1
Niddry St *PSLYN/LNWD* PA3 .... **9** H2
Nigel Gdns *PLKSD/SHW* G41 .... **104** D8
Nigel St *MTHW* ML1 .... **157** K3
Nigg Pl *ESTRH* G34 .... **108** A1
Nightingale Pl *JNSTN* PA5 .... **122** D2 2
Nile Ct *AYRS* KA7 .... **18** F3
Nile St *GRNK* PA15 .... **2** C6
Nimmo Dr *GOV/IBX* G51 .... **103** L2
Nimmo Pl *CARLUKE* ML8 .... **178** E6 2
WISHAW ML2 .... **159** J6 1
Nimmo St *GRNKW/INVK* PA16 .... **32** C5
Nineyard St *SALT* KA21 .... **200** F2 1
Ninian Av *CRG/CRSL/HOU* PA6 ...... **99** J1
Ninian Rd *AIRDRIE* ML6 .... **111** H4
Ninian's Ri *KKNTL* G66 .... **65** M2
Ninian's Ter *KLWNG* KA13 .... **193** M7
Ninian St *GTCI* KA28 .... **138** C6
Nisbet Dr *PSTWK* KA9 .... **225** K4 1
Nisbet St *DEN/PKHD* G31 .... **13** M6
Nisbett Pl *AIRDRIE* ML6 .... **111** L6
Nisbett St *AIRDRIE* ML6 .... **111** L6
Nith Av *PSLYS* PA2 .... **100** F8
Nith Dr *HMLTN* ML3 .... **174** A1
RNFRW PA4 .... **80** E7
Nith Pl *KLMNK* KA1 .... **17** H9
Nith Qd *MTHW* ML1 .... **134** C6
Nithsdale *EKILN* G74 .... **154** D6 1
Nithsdale Crs *BSDN* G61 .... **61** J3
Nithsdale Dr *PLKSD/SHW* G41 .... **104** F7
Nithsdale Pl *PLKSD/SHW* G41 .. **104** F6 2
Nithsdale Rd *ARD* KA22 .... **191** K4
PLKSD/SHW G41 .... **104** C5
PLKSD/SHW G41 .... **104** F7
PLKSD/SHW G41 .... **104** F7 5
Nithsdale St *PLKSD/SHW* G41 .. **104** F7 5
SHOTTS ML7 .... **137** K4
Nith St *STPS/GTHM/RID* G33 .... **7** L6
Nitshill Rd *GIF/THBK* G46 .... **126** E7 1
PLK/PH/NH G53 .... **125** M3
PLK/PH/NH G53 .... **126** C6 2
Niven Ct *KLMNKN/STW* KA3 .... **207** K5
Niven St *MRYH/FIRH* G20 .... **82** C3
Noble Rd *BLSH* ML4 .... **133** G4
Nobles Pl *BLSH* ML4 .... **132** F5
Nobleston *ALEX/LLW* G83 .... **25** M7
Nobles Vw *BLSH* ML4 .... **132** F5
Noddleburn Rd *LARGS* KA30 .... **115** J4
Noldrum Av *CAR/SHTL* G32 .... **130** C1
Noldrum Gdns
CAR/SHTL G32 .... **130** C1 2
Noltmire Rd *AYR* KA8 .... **225** J5
Noran Crs *TROON* KA10 .... **216** F4
Norbreck Dr *GIF/THBK* G46 .... **127** J5
Norby Rd *PTCK* G11 .... **81** M6 5
Norfield Dr *LNPK/KPK* G44 .... **128** B2
Norfolk Ct *GBLS* G5 .... **11** H5
Norfolk Crs *BSHPBGS* G64 .... **63** L6
Norfolk Rd *GRNKW/INVK* PA16 .... **31** L5
Norfolk St *GBLS* G5 .... **11** H5
Norham St *PLKSD/SHW* G41 .... **104** E8
Norman Crs *IRV* KA12 .... **203** H4
Norman St *DMNK/BRGTN* G40 .... **105** M6
Norse La North *SCOT* G14 .... **81** J5
Norse La South *SCOT* G14 .... **81** J5 9
Norse Pl *SCOT* G14 .... **81** J5 10
Norse Rd *SCOT* G14 .... **81** J5
Northacre *KLWNG* KA13 .... **193** L4
Northacre Gv *KLWNG* KA13 .... **193** L4
Northall Qd *MTHW* ML1 .... **134** A8
Northampton Dr *KVD/HLHD* G12 .. **82** B3
North And South Rd
MTHW ML1 .... **135** L8
North Av *BLTYR/CAMB* G72 ..... **129** M3 5
CARLUKE ML8 .... **178** D7
CLYDBK G81 .... **60** A7
MTHW ML1 .... **134** A7 5
Northbank Av
BLTYR/CAMB G72 .... **130** D3
North Bank Pl *CLYDBK* G81 .... **80** C1
Northbank Rd *KKNTL* G66 .... **65** J1
Northbank St
BLTYR/CAMB G72 .... **130** D3 2
North Bank St *CLYDBK* G81 .... **80** C1 2
North Barr Av *ERSK* PA8 .... **59** G6
North Berwick Av
BALLOCH G68 .... **48** F4 5
North Berwick Crs *EKILS* G75 .... **171** G3
North Biggar Rd *AIRDRIE* ML6 .... **111** H1
North Birbiston Rd *KKNTL* G66 .... **44** D1
Northbrae Pl *KNTSWD* G13 .... **81** H3 5
North Bridge St *AIRDRIE* ML6 .... **110** F1
North British Rd
UD/BTH/TAN G71 .... **131** M3
Northburn Av *AIRDRIE* ML6 .... **89** H8
Northburn Pl *AIRDRIE* ML6 .... **89** H7
Northburn Rd *CTBR* ML5 .... **88** C8
Northburn St *AIRDRIE* ML6 .... **90** B7 2
North Bute St *CTBR* ML5 .... **110** B5
North Caldeen Rd *CTBR* ML5 .... **110** C4
North Calder Dr *AIRDRIE* ML6 .... **111** K3
North Calder Gv
UD/BTH/TAN G71 .... **108** B7 5
North Calder Rd
UD/BTH/TAN G71 .... **109** J8
North Campbell Av *MLNGV* G62 .... **41** M8
North Canal Bank *COWCAD* G4 .... **5** K5
North Canal Bank St *COWCAD* G4 .. **5** J5
North Carbrain Rd *CUMB* G67 .... **49** G7
North Claremont La
MLNGV G62 .... **42** A7 2
North Claremont St *KVGV* G3 .... **4** B7
North Corsebar Rd *PSLYS* PA2 .... **8** C9
North Ct *CGLE* G1 .... **11** J1
North Court La *CGLE* G1 .... **11** J1
Northcraig Rd
KLMNKN/STW KA3 .... **206** F7
North Crescent Av *ARD* KA22 .... **191** H6
North Crescent Rd *ARD* KA22 .... **191** H6
Northcroft Rd
BAIL/MDB/MHD G69 .... **66** E7
North Croft St *PSLYN/LNWD* PA3 .... **9** H2
North Dean Park Av
UD/BTH/TAN G71 .... **132** A7 2
Northdoon Pl *AYRS* KA7 .... **228** D6
North Douglas St *CLYDBK* G81 .. **80** C1 5
North Dr *KBRN* KA25 .... **167** G1
PSLYN/LNWD PA3 .... **100** B3
TROON KA10 .... **216** F5
North Dryburgh Rd
WISHAW ML2 .... **159** J3
North Dumgoyne Av
MLNGV G62 .... **41** M7
North Elgin Pl *CLYDBK* G81 .... **80** C2
North Elgin St *CLYDBK* G81 .... **80** D1
North Erskine Pk *BSDN* G61 .... **61** K4
North Faulds Rd
LNK/LMHG ML11 .... **199** L4
Northfield *EKILS* G75 .... **170** F2
Northfield Av *AYR* KA8 .... **225** G6
PGL PA14 .... **54** F1
Northfield Dr *ALEX/LLW* G83 .... **25** M4
Northfield Pk *LARGS* KA30 .... **115** H3 5
Northfield Pl *AYR* KA8 .... **225** G6 2
Northfield Rd *ALEX/LLW* G83 .... **25** M5 5
Northfield St *MTHW* ML1 .... **157** L1
Northflat Pl *CARLUKE* ML8 .... **189** J1
North Frederick St *CGLE* G1 .... **5** K9 1
North Gardner St *PTCK* G11 .... **82** B7
North Gargieston Rd
KLMNK KA1 .... **211** J3 2
Northgate Qd
SPRGB/BLRNK G21 .... **84** C3
Northgate Rd
SPRGB/BLRNK G21 .... **84** C2
North Gower St
GOV/IBX G51 .... **104** C4 1
North Grange Rd *BSDN* G61 .... **61** L3
North Hamilton Pl
KLMNK KA1 .... **16** D3 1
North Hamilton St *KLMNK* KA1 .... **16** D4
North Hanover St *CGLE* G1 .... **5** K9
Northinch St *SCOT* G14 .... **81** K7
North Iverton Park Rd
JNSTN PA5 .... **100** A6
North Kilmeny Crs
WISHAW ML2 .... **159** J3
Northland Av *SCOT* G14 .... **81** J4 2
Northland Dr *SCOT* G14 .... **81** J5 11
Northland Gdns *SCOT* G14 .... **81** J4 5
Northland La *SCOT* G14 .... **81** J5
North La *PSLYN/LNWD* PA3 .... **100** C3
North Lodge Av *MTHW* ML1 .... **157** L5
North Lodge Rd *RNFRW* PA4 .... **80** C5
North Main St *ALEX/LLW* G83 .... **25** K3
North Middleton Driv
LARGS KA30 .... **115** K5
Northmuir Dr *WISHAW* ML2 .... **159** K5
Northmuir Rd *DRUM* G15 .... **61** H5
North Neuk *IRVSE* KA11 .... **216** E2 5
North Orchard St *MTHW* ML1 .... **157** K2
North Park Av *AYR* KA8 .... **225** H6
BRHD/NEIL G78 .... **125** H6
GIF/THBK G46 .... **126** F5 1
Northpark St *MRYH/FIRH* G20 .... **4** D1
North Portland St *CGLE* G1 .... **11** L1
North Rd *BALLOCH* G68 .... **68** A1
BLSH ML4 .... **110** A8
BLSH ML4 .... **133** G4
JNSTN PA5 .... **99** L7
PGL PA14 .... **54** E1
WKIL KA23 .... **181** J4
North Shore Rd *TROON* KA10 .... **216** D4
North St *ALEX/LLW* G83 .... **25** L4
CGLW G2 .... **4** D9
CRG/CRSL/HOU PA6 .... **77** H6
DALRY KA24 .... **184** C1
GRNKW/INVK PA16 .... **32** C1 2
MTHW ML1 .... **157** M1
PSLYN/LNWD PA3 .... **9** G1
Northumberland St
MRYH/FIRH G20 .... **82** E5 1
North Vennel *LNK/LMHG* ML11 .... **199** G5
North Vw *BSDN* G61 .... **61** K7
North View Rd *JNSTN* PA5 .... **98** F3 2
North Wallace St *COWCAD* G4 .... **5** L7
Northway *BLTYR/CAMB* G72 .... **131** J8
Northwood Dr *WISHAW* ML2 .... **160** A3
North Woodside Rd *COWCAD* G4 .... **4** C4
MRYH/FIRH G20 .... **4** D3
Norval St *PTCK* G11 .... **82** A7
Norwich Dr *KVD/HLHD* G12 .... **82** B4 5
Norwood Av *KKNTL* G66 .... **45** H8
Norwood Dr *GIF/THBK* G46 .... **127** G8
Norwood Pk *BSDN* G61 .... **61** M6
Norwood Ter *UD/BTH/TAN* G71 .. **132** A2
Nottingham Av
KVD/HLHD G12 .... **82** B3 5
Nottingham La
KVD/HLHD G12 .... **82** B3 2
Novar Dr *KVD/HLHD* G12 .... **82** A5
Novar Gdns *BSHPBGS* G64 .... **63** L8
Novar St *HMLTN* ML3 .... **156** D7
Nuneaton St *DMNK/BRGTN* G40 .... **12** F9
Nurseries Rd
BAIL/MDB/MHD G69 .... **107** M3
Nursery Av *BSHPTN* PA7 .... **58** E5
KLMNK KA1 .... **17** H6
PSTWK KA9 .... **225** H3
Nursery Ct *CARLUKE* ML8 .... **178** E6
Nursery Gv *KLMCLM* PA13 .... **55** J8
Nursery La *KLMCLM* PA13 .... **55** J8
PLKSD/SHW G41 .... **104** F7
Nursery Pk *CARLUKE* ML8 .... **178** E7 2
Nursery Pl *BLTYR/CAMB* G72 .... **155** K3
Nursery Rd *AYRS* KA7 .... **229** H4
Nursery St *HBR/GL* G84 .... **22** F1 7
KLMNK KA1 .... **16** E7
PLKSD/SHW G41 .... **105** G6 5
Nutberry Ct *GVH/MTFL* G42 .... **105** H8

O

Oak Av *BSDN* G61 .... **61** M2
EKILS G75 .... **171** H3
Oakbank Av *WISHAW* ML2 .... **158** E8 5
Oakbank Dr *BRHD/NEIL* G78 .... **149** L1
Oakbank Rd *PGL* PA14 .... **54** F1 2
Oakbank St *AIRDRIE* ML6 .... **111** K2
Oakburn Av *MLNGV* G62 .... **41** M8
Oakburn Crs *MLNGV* G62 .... **41** M8
Oak Crs *BAIL/MDB/MHD* G69 ... **108** A5 2
Oakdene Av *BLSH* ML4 .... **133** G2
UD/BTH/TAN G71 .... **132** B2 5
Oakdene Crs *MTHW* ML1 .... **134** C5
Oak Dr *BLTYR/CAMB* G72 .... **130** C5 2
KKNTL G66 .... **65** H4
Oak Fern Dr *EKILN* G74 .... **153** K5
Oak Fern Gv *EKILN* G74 .... **153** K5 5
Oakfield Av *KVD/HLHD* G12 .... **4** A3 1
Oakfield Dr *MTHW* ML1 .... **157** M3 1
Oakfield La *KVD/HLHD* G12 .... **4** A5
Oakfield Rd *MTHW* ML1 .... **157** L4
Oakhill Av *CAR/SHTL* G32 .... **107** M6
Oakland Dr *SVSTN* KA20 .... **192** E7 1
Oaklands Av *IRV* KA12 .... **203** J5
Oak Lea *HMLTN* ML3 .... **156** F7
Oaklea Crs *BLTYR/CAMB* G72 .... **155** J1 5
Oakleigh Dr
GRNKW/INVK PA16 .... **32** D1 2
Oakley Dr *LNPK/KPK* G44 .... **127** M6
Oakley Ter *DEN/PKHD* G31 .... **12** D2
Oak Pk *BSHPBGS* G64 .... **84** B1
MTHW ML1 .... **157** K5
Oak Pl *CTBR* ML5 .... **110** C4
EKILS G75 .... **171** H3
KLMNK KA1 .... **16** B5
UD/BTH/TAN G71 .... **132** C2
Oak Rd *ARD* KA22 .... **191** J5
CLYDBK G81 .... **59** M4
CUMB G67 .... **49** L5
PSLYS PA2 .... **102** A8
Oakshaw Brae *PSLY* PA1 .... **8** E3
Oakshawhead *PSLY* PA1 .... **8** E3
Oakshaw St East *PSLY* PA1 .... **8** F3
Oakshaw St West *PSLY* PA1 .... **8** F3
The Oaks *JNSTN* PA5 .... **99** K7
Oak St *KVGV* G3 .... **10** E1
Oaktree Gdns *CSMK* G45 .... **128** F5
DMBTN G82 .... **37** J7
Oakview Qd *BLSH* ML4 .... **132** F6 5
Oakwood Av *AYR* KA8 .... **225** L7
PSLYS PA2 .... **101** H8
Oakwood Dr *BEITH* KA15 .... **168** A1
CTBR ML5 .... **109** K4 1
NMRNS G77 .... **150** F5
Oak Wynd *BLTYR/CAMB* G72 .... **130** F6
Oates Gdns *MTHW* ML1 .... **158** B5
Oatfield St *SPRGB/BLRNK* G21 .... **7** G1
Oban Dr *MRYH/FIRH* G20 .... **4** B1
Oban La *MRYH/FIRH* G20 .... **4** B1
Obiston Gdns *CAR/SHTL* G32 ... **107** G4 5
Obree Av *PSTWK* KA9 .... **225** K4
Observatory Rd
KVD/HLHD G12 .... **82** D6 5
Ochil Ct *EKILS* G75 .... **171** H5
IRVSE KA11 .... **204** A4
Ochil Dr *BRHD/NEIL* G78 .... **125** J8
PSLYS PA2 .... **124** D1
Ochil Pl *CAR/SHTL* G32 .... **107** G5
KLMNK KA1 .... **212** B6
Ochil Rd *BSDN* G61 .... **61** H2
BSHPBGS G64 .... **64** C8
RNFRW PA4 .... **80** B8
Ochil St *CAR/SHTL* G32 .... **107** G5
WISHAW ML2 .... **158** F5
Ochiltree Av *KNTSWD* G13 .... **81** M2
Ochiltree Dr *HMLTN* ML3 .... **155** L8
Ochiltree Pl
KLMNKN/STW KA3 .... **207** H3 2
Ochil Vw *UD/BTH/TAN* G71 ...... **132** A1 7
Octavia Ter *GRNKW/INVK* PA16 .... **32** B1
Odense Ct *EKILS* G75 .... **171** L3 5
Ogilvie Pl *DEN/PKHD* G31 .... **13** M7 1
Ogilvie St *DEN/PKHD* G31 .... **13** M7
O'hare *ALEX/LLW* G83 .... **25** M5
Old Aisle Rd *KKNTL* G66 .... **65** M2
Old Auchans Vw *CRH/DND* KA2 .. **209** K7
Old Avon Rd *HMLTN* ML3 .... **157** G7
Old Biggar Rd *AIRDRIE* ML6 .... **89** H1
Old Bore Rd *AIRDRIE* ML6 .... **111** K1
Old Bothwell Rd
UD/BTH/TAN G71 .... **132** B8
Old Bridgend *CARLUKE* ML8 .... **178** F8 1
Old Bridge of Weir Rd
CRG/CRSL/HOU PA6 .... **77** G7
Old Bridge Rd *AYR* KA8 .... **225** L6
Old Bridge St *AYRS* KA7 .... **18** F2
Old Caley Rd *IRV* KA12 .... **203** J5
Old Castle Rd *LNPK/KPK* G44 .... **128** A3 5
Old Church Gdns
BAIL/MDB/MHD G69 .... **109** G4 5
Old Coach Rd *EKILN* G74 .... **153** M6
Old Dalmarnock Rd
DMNK/BRGTN G40 .... **12** E9 1
Old Dalnottar Rd *OLDK* G60 .... **59** H4
Old Dullatur Rd *BALLOCH* G68 .... **48** D3
Old Dumbarton Rd *KVGV* G3 .... **82** D8 5
Old Edinburgh Rd
UD/BTH/TAN G71 .... **132** B2
Old Farm Rd *AYR* KA8 .... **225** K6
Old Gartloch Rd
BAIL/MDB/MHD G69 .... **86** F5
Old Glasgow Rd *CUMB* G67 .... **49** G5
UD/BTH/TAN G71 .... **131** K1
Old Govan Rd *RNFRW* PA4 .... **80** F6
Old Greenock Rd *BSHPTN* PA7 .... **58** A6
ERSK PA8 .... **78** F1
ERSK PA8 .... **79** J2
PGL PA14 .... **55** L2
Oldhall Dr *KLMCLM* PA13 .... **55** K8
Oldhall Rd *PSLY* PA1 .... **102** D4
Old Hillfoot Rd *AYRS* KA7 .... **19** K9
Old Humbie Rd *NMRNS* G77 .... **150** E7
Old Inverkip Rd
GRNKW/INVK PA16 .... **32** C5
Old Irvine Rd *KLMNK* KA1 .... **16** D4
Old Lanark Rd *CARLUKE* ML8 .... **178** F8
CARLUKE ML8 .... **188** F1
LNK/LMHG ML11 .... **198** E1
Old Largs Rd *GRNK* PA15 .... **2** A9
GRNK PA15 .... **52** D4
Old Loans Rd *TROON* KA10 .... **217** G5
Old Luss Rd *ALEX/LLW* G83 .... **25** J1
HBR/GL G84 .... **22** F1
Old Manse Gdns *CTBR* ML5 .... **110** A2 2
Old Manse Rd *CAR/SHTL* G32 .... **107** K5
WISHAW ML2 .... **176** E1
Old Mill Rd *BLTYR/CAMB* G72 .... **130** D4
CLYDBK G81 .... **60** A3
EKILN G74 .... **15** G1
KLMNK KA1 .... **17** G5
PSLY PA1 .... **8** A6
SHOTTS ML7 .... **137** G8
UD/BTH/TAN G71 .... **131** M2
Old Mill Vw *KSYTH* G65 .... **47** M6
Old Monkland Rd *CTBR* ML5 .... **109** K6
Old Mugdock Rd *MLNGV* G62 .... **42** C2
Old Playfield Rd
CRMNK/CLK/EAG G76 .... **152** D1 1
Old Quarry Rd *BALLOCH* G68 .... **67** K4
SVSTN KA20 .... **201** K1
Old Raise Rd *SALT* KA21 .... **201** G1
Old Renfrew Rd *RNFRW* PA4 .... **81** G7
Old Rd *JNSTN* PA5 .... **100** C6
Old Rome Wy *CRH/DND* KA2 .... **210** E3
Old Rutherglen Rd *GBLS* G5 .... **11** J6 1
GBLS G5 .... **11** L8 1
Old Schoolhouse La
CRG/CRSL/HOU PA6 .... **77** H6 2
Old Shettleston Rd
CAR/SHTL G32 .... **107** G4
Old Sneddon St *PSLY* PA1 .... **9** G2
Old Stable Rw *CTBR* ML5 .... **110** B2 1
Old St *CLYDBK* G81 .... **59** M3
KLMNK KA1 .... **211** M4
Old Union St *AIRDRIE* ML6 .... **111** H2
Old Willowyard Rd *BEITH* KA15 .... **168** A2
Old Wishaw Rd *CARLUKE* ML8 .... **178** E6
Old Wood Rd
BAIL/MDB/MHD G69 .... **108** A6
Old Woodwynd Rd
KLWNG KA13 .... **193** L5
Old Wynd *CGLE* G1 .... **11** K3 5
Olifard Av *UD/BTH/TAN* G71 .... **132** B6
Oliphant Crs
CRMNK/CLK/EAG G76 .... **151** L4
PSLYS PA2 .... **123** L1
Oliphant Dr *KLMNKN/STW* KA3 ...... **17** M4
Olive Bank *UD/BTH/TAN* G71 .... **109** J8
Olive Rd *KLMNK* KA1 .... **16** A4
Olive St *STPS/GTHM/RID* G33 .... **7** M1
Olympia Ct *EKILN* G74 .... **15** G5
Olympia St *DMNK/BRGTN* G40 .... **12** C6
Omoa Rd *MTHW* ML1 .... **135** G8
O'Neill Av *BSHPBGS* G64 .... **84** B1
O'Neil Ter *ALEX/LLW* G83 .... **25** L5 5
Onslow *EKILS* G75 .... **14** A7
Onslow Dr *DEN/PKHD* G31 .... **12** F1
Onslow Rd *CLYDBK* G81 .... **60** C7
Onslow Sq *DEN/PKHD* G31 .... **12** E1
Ontario Pk *EKILS* G75 .... **153** H8
Ontario Pl *EKILS* G75 .... **153** H8 1
Onthank Dr *KLMNKN/STW* KA3 .... **206** F5
Onyx St *BLSH* ML4 .... **133** G5
Open Shore *GRNK* PA15 .... **2** F4 5
Oran Gdns *MRYH/FIRH* G20 .... **82** E4 5
Oran Ga *MRYH/FIRH* G20 .... **82** E4
Orangefield Dr *PSTWK* KA9 .... **221** K8
Orangefield La *GRNK* PA15 .... **2** A4 1
Oran Pl *MRYH/FIRH* G20 .... **82** E5 5
Oran St *MRYH/FIRH* G20 .... **82** E5
Orbiston Dr *BLSH* ML4 .... **133** H6
CLYDBK G81 .... **60** D2 2
Orbiston Pl *CLYDBK* G81 .... **60** D2 5
Orbiston Rd *BLSH* ML4 .... **132** F5
Orbiston Sq *BLSH* ML4 .... **132** F6 5
Orbiston St *MTHW* ML1 .... **157** M4
Orcades Dr *LNPK/KPK* G44 .... **128** B5
Orchard Av *AYRS* KA7 .... **19** J8
UD/BTH/TAN G71 .... **132** B8
Orchard Ct *CAR/SHTL* G32 .... **130** B1 5
GIF/THBK G46 .... **127** G6 1
Orchard Dr *BLTYR/CAMB* G72 .... **155** J1
GIF/THBK G46 .... **127** H6
RUTH G73 .... **128** F2 5
Orchard Fld *KKNTL* G66 .... **65** K5
Orchard Ga *LRKH* ML9 .... **176** A7
Orchard Gn *EKILN* G74 .... **154** B5
Orchard Gv *CTBR* ML5 .... **110** B3
GIF/THBK G46 .... **127** H5
KLMCLM PA13 .... **75** J1 2
KLWNG KA13 .... **193** L5
Orchard Pk *GIF/THBK* G46 .... **127** J6 5
Orchard Park Av *GIF/THBK* G46 .. **127** G5
Orchard Pl *AYRS* KA7 .... **19** J7 2
BLSH ML4 .... **132** F6
HMLTN ML3 .... **156** D6
KKNTL G66 .... **65** M2
KLWNG KA13 .... **193** L5
Orchard St
BAIL/MDB/MHD G69 .... **107** M6 5
CARLUKE ML8 .... **178** F8
GLSTN KA4 .... **214** B4
GRNK PA15 .... **3** G7
HMLTN ML3 .... **156** D6
KLMNKN/STW KA3 .... **16** F1
MTHW ML1 .... **157** K2
PSLY PA1 .... **9** H4
RNFRW PA4 .... **80** D5
WISHAW ML2 .... **177** H3
WKIL KA23 .... **181** J4
Orchardton Rd *BALLOCH* G68 .... **67** K2
Orchard View Dr
LNK/LMHG ML11 .... **198** A6
Orchy Av *CRMNK/CLK/EAG* G76 .. **151** M1
Orchy Ct *CLYDBK* G81 .... **60** C4
Orchy Crs *AIRDRIE* ML6 .... **111** J4
BSDN G61 .... **61** K8
PSLYS PA2 .... **100** F8
Orchy Dr *CRMNK/CLK/EAG* G76 .. **127** M8
Orchy Gdns
CRMNK/CLK/EAG G76 .... **127** M8
Orchy St *LNPK/KPK* G44 .... **128** A3
Orefield Pl *EKILN* G74 .... **153** L6 5
Oregon Pl *GBLS* G5 .... **11** K8 2
Orion Pl *BLSH* ML4 .... **133** L4
Orion Wy *BLTYR/CAMB* G72 .... **130** A3 7
CARLUKE ML8 .... **178** D7
Orkney Dr *KLMNKN/STW* KA3 .... **207** G4
Orkney Pl *GOV/IBX* G51 .... **104** B2 1
Orkney Qd *WISHAW* ML2 .... **159** K5
Orkney St *GOV/IBX* G51 .... **104** B2
Orlando *EKILN* G74 .... **154** C4 2
Orleans Av *SCOT* G14 .... **81** L6
Orleans La *SCOT* G14 .... **81** L6 2
Ormiston Av *SCOT* G14 .... **81** J5
Ormiston Dr *HMLTN* ML3 .... **174** C1
Ormiston La *SCOT* G14 .... **81** J5 12
Ormiston La North *SCOT* G14 .. **81** J5 13
Ormiston La South *SCOT* G14 .. **81** J5 14
Ormiston Pl *IRVSE* KA11 .... **204** B2 1
Ormonde Av *LNPK/KPK* G44 .... **127** M6
Ormonde Ct *LNPK/KPK* G44 .... **127** L6
Ormonde Crs *LNPK/KPK* G44 .... **127** M6
Ormonde Dr *LNPK/KPK* G44 .... **127** M6
Ornsay St *PPK/MIL* G22 .... **83** K2
Oronsay Av *PGL* PA14 .... **55** G3
Oronsay Crs *BSDN* G61 .... **62** B6
OLDK G60 .... **59** J3
Oronsay Gdns *OLDK* G60 .... **59** J3
Oronsay Pl *OLDK* G60 .... **59** J3
Orr Sq *PSLY* PA1 .... **9** G3
Orr St *DMNK/BRGTN* G40 .... **12** C6
PSLY PA1 .... **8** F3
PSLYS PA2 .... **9** H7
Orr Ter *BRHD/NEIL* G78 .... **148** C3 5
Orton Pl *GOV/IBX* G51 .... **104** A3
Osborne Crs *EKILN* G74 .... **152** B6
Osborne St *CGLE* G1 .... **11** J3
CLYDBK G81 .... **60** A6
Osbourne Av *RAYR/DAL* KA6 .... **227** H3
Osprey Dr *KLMNK* KA1 .... **17** L6
UD/BTH/TAN G71 .... **132** A2
Osprey Rd *GRNKW/INVK* PA16 .... **32** A5
Ossian Av *PSLY* PA1 .... **102** F4
Ossian Rd *PLKSW/MSWD* G43 .... **127** L3
Oswald Dr *PSTWK* KA9 .... **221** J8
Oswald La *AYR* KA8 .... **224** E7
Oswald Pl *AYR* KA8 .... **225** G4
Oswald Rd *AYR* KA8 .... **225** G5
Oswald's Br *RAYR/DAL* KA6 .... **226** D6

Oswald St *CGLE* G1 ... 11 G3
Oswald Wk *MLNGV* G62 ... 62 C1
Otago La *KVD/HLHD* G12 ... 4 B4
Otago La North *KVD/HLHD* G12 .. 4 B4
Otago Pk *EKILS* G75 ... 153 G8
Otago St *KVD/HLHD* G12 ... 4 B4
Othello *EKILN* G74 ... 154 B4
Ottawa Crs *CLYDBK* G81 ... 59 K5
Otterburn Av
KLMNKN/STW KA3 ... 207 H6
Otterburn Dr *GIF/THBK* G46 ... 127 J7
Otterswick Pl
STPS/GTHM/RID G33 ... 85 J7
Ottoline Dr *TROON* KA10 ... 216 F7
Oudenarde Ct *CARLUKE* ML8 ... 179 H8
Outdale Av *PSTWK* KA9 ... 225 K2
The Oval *CRMNK/CLK/EAG* G76 ... 127 M8
CTBR ML5 ... 87 J3
Overbrae Pl *DRUM* G15 ... 60 F4
Overburn Av *DMBTN* G82 ... 36 F5
Overburn Crs *DMBTN* G82 ... 36 F4
Overdale Av *GVH/MTFL* G42 ... 127 M1
Overdale Crs *PSTWK* KA9 ... 225 J3
Overdale Gdns
GVH/MTFL G42 ... 127 M1
Overdale Pl *WISHAW* ML2 ... 177 J3
Overdale St *GVH/MTFL* G42 ... 127 M1
Overjohnstone Dr
WISHAW ML2 ... 158 C5
Overlea Av *RUTH* G73 ... 129 K3
Overlee Rd
CRMNK/CLK/EAG G76 ... 151 L2
Overmills Crs *AYRS* KA7 ... 229 K2
Overmills Rd *AYRS* KA7 ... 229 L2
Overnewton Pl *KVGV* G3 ... 104 D1
Overnewton Sq *KVGV* G3 ... 104 D1
Overnewton St *KVGV* G3 ... 82 D8
Overton Crs *GRNK* PA15 ... 32 D6
JNSTN PA5 ... 100 B7
WKIL KA23 ... 181 J4
Overton Dr *WKIL* KA23 ... 181 H4
Overton Gdns *KLMCLM* PA13 ... 55 L8
Overton Gv *KLMCLM* PA13 ... 55 L8
Overton Rd *ALEX/LLW* G83 ... 25 K5
BLTYR/CAMB G72 ... 130 D5
JNSTN PA5 ... 100 A7
Overton St *ALEX/LLW* G83 ... 25 K5
BLTYR/CAMB G72 ... 130 D5
Overtoun Av *DMBTN* G82 ... 37 H7
Overtoun Dr *CLYDBK* G81 ... 59 M5
RUTH G73 ... 129 G2
Overtoun Rd *CLYDBK* G81 ... 59 M5
IRVSE KA11 ... 204 F6
Overtown Av *PLK/PH/NH* G53 ... 126 A3
Overtown Rd *WISHAW* ML2 ... 159 M8
Overtown St *DEN/PKHD* G31 ... 12 F6
Overwood Dr *DMBTN* G82 ... 37 H5
LNPK/KPK G44 ... 128 C3
Owen Av *EKILS* G75 ... 14 A8
Owendale Av *BLSH* ML4 ... 133 H2
Owen Pk *EKILS* G75 ... 14 C8
Owen St *MTHW* ML1 ... 157 L1
O'Wood Av *MTHW* ML1 ... 134 B3
Oxford Av *GRK* PA19 ... 32 A3
Oxford Dr *PSLYN/LNWD* PA3 ... 100 B3
Oxford La *GBLS* G5 ... 11 H5
RNFRW PA4 ... 80 C6
Oxford Rd *GRNKW/INVK* PA16 ... 31 K5
RNFRW PA4 ... 80 C6
Oxford St *CTBR* ML5 ... 109 M3
GBLS G5 ... 11 G4
KKNTL G66 ... 65 J1
Oxgang Pl *KKNTL* G66 ... 65 L2
Oxhill Pl *DMBTN* G82 ... 36 D6
Oxhill Rd *DMBTN* G82 ... 36 D6
Oxton Dr *CARD/HILL/MSPK* G52 .. 103 H4

P

Pacemuir Rd *KLMCLM* PA13 ... 75 J1
Paddockdyke *SKLM* PA17 ... 70 B6
Paddockholm Rd *KBRN* KA25 ... 143 H8
Paddock St *CTBR* ML5 ... 110 D5
The Paddock
CRMNK/CLK/EAG G76 ... 152 A4
Paduff Pl *KBRN* KA25 ... 143 G7
Paidmyre Crs *NMRNS* G77 ... 150 D6
Paidmyre Gdns *NMRNS* G77 ... 150 D6
Paidmyre Rd *NMRNS* G77 ... 150 D6
Paisley Rd *BRHD/NEIL* G78 ... 125 H5
GBLS G5 ... 10 D4
PLKSD/SHW G41 ... 10 C4
RNFRW PA4 ... 80 B8
Paisley Rd West
CARD/HILL/MSPK G52 ... 103 K5
GOV/IBX G51 ... 104 C4
Paisley St *ARD* KA22 ... 191 J7
Palacecraig St *CTBR* ML5 ... 110 A6
Palace Grounds Rd *HMLTN* ML3 .. 156 F5
Paladin Av *KNTSWD* G13 ... 81 H1
Palermo St *SPRGB/BLRNK* G21 ... 6 B1
Palladium Pl *SCOT* G14 ... 81 K6
Palmer Av *KNTSWD* G13 ... 61 K8
Palmerston *EKILS* G75 ... 171 G2
Palmerston Pl *JNSTN* PA5 ... 122 C2
KVGV G3 ... 104 D1
Palm Pl *UD/BTH/TAN* G71 ... 109 H8
Pandora Wy
UD/BTH/TAN G71 ... 132 A2
Pankhurst Pl *EKILN* G74 ... 15 G2
Panmure St *MRYH/FIRH* G20 ... 83 G5
Pantonville Rd *WKIL* KA23 ... 181 J6
Papermill Rd *GRNKW/INVK* PA16 .. 32 D7
Parkandarroch Crs
CARLUKE ML8 ... 179 G8
Park Av *BEITH* KA15 ... 144 B8
BRHD/NEIL G78 ... 125 H8
BSHPBGS G64 ... 64 A6
CARLUKE ML8 ... 178 F6
DMBTN G82 ... 37 H6
GRK PA19 ... 32 A2
JNSTN PA5 ... 100 C7
KKNTL G66 ... 65 J1
KLWNG KA13 ... 193 L6
KSYTH G65 ... 46 F5
KVGV G3 ... 4 C5
MLNGV G62 ... 42 A8
MTHW ML1 ... 134 A4
PSLYS PA2 ... 101 J8
PSTWK KA9 ... 225 H1
Park Bank *ERSK* PA8 ... 59 H8
Park Brae *ERSK* PA8 ... 79 J1
Parkbrae Gdns
MRYH/FIRH G20 ... 83 G3
Parkbrae Pl *MRYH/FIRH* G20 ... 83 G3
Parkburn Av *KKNTL* G66 ... 65 J3
Park Burn Ct *HMLTN* ML3 ... 156 A3
Park Circ *AYRS* KA7 ... 18 E5
CARLUKE ML8 ... 178 F6
KVGV G3 ... 4 B6
Park Circus La *AYRS* KA7 ... 18 E5
KVGV G3 ... 4 B6
Park Circus Pl *KVGV* G3 ... 4 C6
Park Ct *BEITH* KA15 ... 168 C1
BSHPBGS G64 ... 64 B6
GIF/THBK G46 ... 127 H6
Park Crs *BLTYR/CAMB* G72 ... 155 J3
BSDN G61 ... 61 J4
BSHPBGS G64 ... 44 C8
BSHPBGS G64 ... 64 A6
DMBTN G82 ... 36 F4
KLMNKN/STW KA3 ... 197 K1
RNFRW PA4 ... 79 J2
Park Dr *BLSH* ML4 ... 133 G5
EKILN G74 ... 152 C6
ERSK PA8 ... 79 J1
HMLTN ML3 ... 157 J8
LNK/LMHG ML11 ... 198 E5
RUTH G73 ... 129 G2
WISHAW ML2 ... 160 A4
Parkend Av *SALT* KA21 ... 201 G2
Parkend Gdns *SALT* KA21 ... 201 G2
Parkend Rd *SALT* KA21 ... 200 F2
Parker Pl *KSYTH* G65 ... 47 K1
LRKH ML9 ... 176 B6
Parkfield *EKILS* G75 ... 171 L4
Park Gdns *KLBCH* PA10 ... 99 H5
KVGV G3 ... 4 B7
Park Gardens La *KVGV* G3 ... 4 B7
Park Ga *ERSK* PA8 ... 79 H1
KVGV G3 ... 4 B6
Park Gate Pl *BLSH* ML4 ... 132 F4
Park Gld *ERSK* PA8 ... 79 J1
Park Gn *ERSK* PA8 ... 79 H1
Park Gv *DMBTN* G82 ... 35 H1
ERSK PA8 ... 79 J1
Parkgrove Av *GIF/THBK* G46 ... 127 K6
Parkgrove Ter *KVGV* G3 ... 4 A7
Parkgrove Terrace La *KVGV* G3 ... 4 A7
Parkhall Rd *CLYDBK* G81 ... 59 M5
Parkhall St *EKILN* G74 ... 14 F1
Parkhall Ter *CLYDBK* G81 ... 59 M4
Parkhead Av *KLWNG* KA13 ... 193 M6
Parkhead St *AIRDRIE* ML6 ... 111 G1
MTHW ML1 ... 157 M4
Park Hl *ERSK* PA8 ... 59 H8
Parkhill Av *CRH/DND* KA2 ... 210 E1
PGL PA14 ... 55 G1
Parkhill Dr *DALRY* KA24 ... 184 C2
LOCHW PA12 ... 120 D6
RUTH G73 ... 129 G2
Parkhill Rd *PLKSW/MSWD* G43 ... 127 J1
Parkholm La *GBLS* G5 ... 10 C4
Parkhouse Dr *KBRN* KA25 ... 143 G8
Parkhouse Rd *ARD* KA22 ... 191 K7
PLK/PH/NH G53 ... 125 M5
Parkhouse St *AYRS* KA7 ... 18 F6
Parkinch *ERSK* PA8 ... 79 J2
Parklands Rd *LNPK/KPK* G44 ... 127 M6
Park La *ARD* KA22 ... 191 J6
BLTYR/CAMB G72 ... 155 K1
CARLUKE ML8 ... 178 E8
DMNK/BRGTN G40 ... 12 D6
KLWNG KA13 ... 193 K4
KSYTH G65 ... 47 K1
Park Lea *AIRDRIE* ML6 ... 90 F5
Parklee Dr
CRMNK/CLK/EAG G76 ... 152 E2
Park Moor *ERSK* PA8 ... 79 H1
Parkneuk Rd *BLTYR/CAMB* G72 .. 155 G7
PLKSW/MSWD G43 ... 127 H5
Parkneuk St *MTHW* ML1 ... 157 K1
Park Pl *BLSH* ML4 ... 132 E6
CMPF/LLE G63 ... 27 G5
EKILN G74 ... 152 C6
IRV KA12 ... 203 H4
LNK/LMHG ML11 ... 198 F5
Park Qd *KVGV* G3 ... 4 B6
WISHAW ML2 ... 158 E8
Park Rd *AIRDRIE* ML6 ... 111 H7
ARD KA22 ... 191 J7
BAIL/MDB/MHD G69 ... 86 C1
BAIL/MDB/MHD G69 ... 108 F4
BAIL/MDB/MHD G69 ... 109 G4
BLSH ML4 ... 133 G5
BRWEIR PA11 ... 76 D8
BSHPBGS G64 ... 64 A7
CAR/SHTL G32 ... 130 C1
CLYDBK G81 ... 59 M6
GIF/THBK G46 ... 127 J7
GLSTN KA4 ... 214 B3
HMLTN ML3 ... 156 D6
JNSTN PA5 ... 99 M8
KLMCLM PA13 ... 75 J1
KVGV G3 ... 4 B5
MLNGV G62 ... 42 A8
MTHW ML1 ... 134 B7
PSLYS PA2 ... 124 D1
RNFRW PA4 ... 79 K2
SALT KA21 ... 200 E2
SHOTTS ML7 ... 137 K4
Parksail *ERSK* PA8 ... 79 J2
Parksail Dr *ERSK* PA8 ... 79 J1
Parkside *IRVSE* KA11 ... 204 A6
Parkside Gdns *MRYH/FIRH* G20 ... 83 G3
Parkside Pl *MRYH/FIRH* G20 ... 83 G3
Parkside Rd *MTHW* ML1 ... 157 H3
SHOTTS ML7 ... 137 K5
Park St *AIRDRIE* ML6 ... 110 E1
ALEX/LLW G83 ... 25 K4
CARLUKE ML8 ... 178 F8
CTBR ML5 ... 110 B2
DMBTN G82 ... 37 G6
KKNTL G66 ... 66 B2
KLMNK KA1 ... 16 D3
MTHW ML1 ... 133 M6
MTHW ML1 ... 135 H6
MTHW ML1 ... 157 L2
Park St South *KVGV* G3 ... 4 B6
Parks Vw *HMLTN* ML3 ... 174 D3
Park Ter *AYRS* KA7 ... 18 D4
DMBTN G82 ... 35 G1
EKILN G74 ... 14 E3
GRK PA19 ... 31 L2
KVGV G3 ... 4 B6
Park Terrace East La *KVGV* G3 ... 4 B6
Park Terrace La *KVGV* G3 ... 4 B6
Parkthorn Vw *CRH/DND* KA2 ... 209 L7
Park Top *ERSK* PA8 ... 79 J1
Parkvale Av *ERSK* PA8 ... 79 K1
Parkvale Crs *ERSK* PA8 ... 79 K1
Parkvale Dr *ERSK* PA8 ... 79 K1
Parkvale Gdns *ERSK* PA8 ... 79 K1
Parkvale Wy *ERSK* PA8 ... 79 K1
Parkview *AYRS* KA7 ... 228 F8
Park Vw *AIRDRIE* ML6 ... 91 G4
ARD KA22 ... 191 K7
KBRN KA25 ... 143 G8
KLBCH PA10 ... 99 G5
LARGS KA30 ... 115 K6
LRKH ML9 ... 176 B7
PSLYS PA2 ... 8 F9
Parkview Av *KKNTL* G66 ... 65 K2
Parkview Ct *KKNTL* G66 ... 65 K2
Parkview Crs *WISHAW* ML2 ... 160 A5
Parkview Dr *CTBR* ML5 ... 109 L2
STPS/GTHM/RID G33 ... 85 L3
Parkville Dr *BLTYR/CAMB* G72 ... 155 L3
Parkville Rd *BLSH* ML4 ... 133 J2
Park Wy *CUMB* G67 ... 49 H5
Parkway *ERSK* PA8 ... 79 H1
Parkway Ct *CTBR* ML5 ... 109 L3
Parkway Pl *CTBR* ML5 ... 109 L4
Park Winding *ERSK* PA8 ... 79 J1
Park Wd *ERSK* PA8 ... 59 J8
Parnell St *AIRDRIE* ML6 ... 110 F4
Parnie St *CGLE* G1 ... 11 L3
Parry Ter *EKILS* G75 ... 153 H8
Parsonage Rw *COWCAD* G4 ... 11 M2
Parsonage Sq *COWCAD* G4 ... 11 M2
Parterre *IRV* KA12 ... 203 J7
Partick Bridge St *PTCK* G11 ... 82 C8
Partickhill Av *PTCK* G11 ... 82 B7
Partickhill Rd *PTCK* G11 ... 82 B7
Partridge Rd
GRNKW/INVK PA16 ... 32 A3
Paterson Av *IRV* KA12 ... 203 K5
Paterson Crs *IRV* KA12 ... 203 K6
Paterson Dr *HBR/GL* G84 ... 20 B5
Paterson Pl *BSDN* G61 ... 61 J1
Paterson St *AYR* KA8 ... 225 H5
GBLS G5 ... 10 E6
MTHW ML1 ... 157 L2
Paterson Ter *EKILS* G75 ... 14 C7
Pather St *WISHAW* ML2 ... 159 H7
Pathfoot *KLWNG* KA13 ... 193 M6
Pathhead Gdns
STPS/GTHM/RID G33 ... 84 F3
Pathhead Rd
CRMNK/CLK/EAG G76 ... 152 D2
Patna Ct *HMLTN* ML3 ... 155 L8
Patna St *DMNK/BRGTN* G40 ... 13 G9
Paton Qd *LARGS* KA30 ... 115 L5
Paton St *DEN/PKHD* G31 ... 13 G2
GRNKW/INVK PA16 ... 32 C5
Patrick Av *SVSTN* KA20 ... 192 C8
Patrick St *GRNKW/INVK* PA16 ... 2 A3
PSLYS PA2 ... 9 J6
Patterson Dr *CARLUKE* ML8 ... 178 A3
Patterton Dr *BRHD/NEIL* G78 ... 125 K8
Pattison St *CLYDBK* G81 ... 59 L6
Pattle Pl *AYRS* KA7 ... 228 F8
Pavilion Pl *ARD* KA22 ... 191 J8
Pavilion Rd *AYRS* KA7 ... 18 C4
Payne St *COWCAD* G4 ... 5 J6
Peace Av *BRWEIR* PA11 ... 75 M7
KLMNK KA1 ... 16 B3
Peacock Av *PSLYS* PA2 ... 100 F7
Peacock Dr *HMLTN* ML3 ... 156 C5
PSLYS PA2 ... 100 F7
Pearce La *GOV/IBX* G51 ... 104 A1
Pearce St *GOV/IBX* G51 ... 104 A1
Pearl St *BLSH* ML4 ... 133 H6
Pearson Dr *RNFRW* PA4 ... 80 D7
Pearson Pl *PSLYN/LNWD* PA3 .. 100 B4
Peathill Av *BAIL/MDB/MHD* G69 .. 66 B8
Peathill St *PPK/MIL* G22 ... 5 K3
Peatland Qd *KLMNK* KA1 ... 212 A6
Peatland Rd *KLMNK* KA1 ... 212 A6
Peat Rd *BRWEIR* PA11 ... 98 E2
GRNKW/INVK PA16 ... 32 D6
PLK/PH/NH G53 ... 126 A3
Peden Av *DALRY* KA24 ... 184 B2
Pedmyre La
CRMNK/CLK/EAG G76 ... 152 C2
Peebles Dr *RUTH* G73 ... 129 K2
Peebles Pth *CTBR* ML5 ... 110 D6
Peebles St *AYR* KA8 ... 224 F7
Peel Glen Gdns *DRUM* G15 ... 61 G4
Peel Glen Rd *BSDN* G61 ... 61 G3
Peel La *PTCK* G11 ... 82 A7
Peel Park Pl *EKILN* G74 ... 152 F7
Peel Pl *CTBR* ML5 ... 109 K4
UD/BTH/TAN G71 ... 132 A6
Peel Rd *EKILN* G74 ... 152 C5
Peel St *DMBTN* G82 ... 35 H2
PTCK G11 ... 82 B7
Pegasus Av *CARLUKE* ML8 ... 178 E7
PSLYN/LNWD PA3 ... 100 D4
Pegasus Rd *BLSH* ML4 ... 133 L4
Peggieshill Rd *AYRS* KA7 ... 229 G5
Peile St *GRNKW/INVK* PA16 ... 32 C3
Pemberton Va *AYRS* KA7 ... 229 G7
Pembroke *EKILN* G74 ... 154 C5
Pembroke Rd
GRNKW/INVK PA16 ... 31 K5
Pembroke St *KVGV* G3 ... 4 C9
Pencaitland Dr *CAR/SHTL* G32 ... 107 G6
Pencaitland Gv
CAR/SHTL G32 ... 107 G6
Pencaitland Pl *SMSTN* G23 ... 62 E8
Pencil Vw *LARGS* KA30 ... 139 K1
Pendeen Crs
STPS/GTHM/RID G33 ... 107 L4
Pendeen Pl
STPS/GTHM/RID G33 ... 107 M3
Pendeen Rd
STPS/GTHM/RID G33 ... 107 M4
Pendicle Crs *BSDN* G61 ... 61 K6
Pendicle Rd *BSDN* G61 ... 61 K6
Penfold Crs *EKILS* G75 ... 14 C5
Penicuik St *CAR/SHTL* G32 ... 13 L3
Penilee Rd *PSLYN/LNWD* PA3 ... 102 D1
Penilee Ter
CARD/HILL/MSPK G52 ... 102 E2
Peninver Dr *GOV/IBX* G51 ... 103 K1
Penman Av *RUTH* G73 ... 128 F1
Pennan Pl *SCOT* G14 ... 81 G4
Penneld Rd
CARD/HILL/MSPK G52 ... 102 F4
Penniecroft Av *DMBTN* G82 ... 37 J4
Pennyburn Rd *KLWNG* KA13 ... 193 K6
Pennyfern Dr
GRNKW/INVK PA16 ... 32 B6
Pennyfern Rd
GRNKW/INVK PA16 ... 32 B6
Pennyroyal Ct *EKILN* G74 ... 153 K6
Pennyvenie Wy *IRVSE* KA11 ... 204 A4
Penrioch Dr *EKILS* G75 ... 171 J5
Penrith Av *GIF/THBK* G46 ... 127 J7
Penrith Dr *KVD/HLHD* G12 ... 82 A3
Penrith Pl *EKILS* G75 ... 170 F3
Penryn Gdns *CAR/SHTL* G32 ... 107 K6
Penston Rd
STPS/GTHM/RID G33 ... 107 K1
Pentland Av *PGL* PA14 ... 54 F3
PSLYN/LNWD PA3 ... 100 A3
Pentland Crs *LRKH* ML9 ... 175 M4
PSLYS PA2 ... 124 D1
Pentland Dr *BRHD/NEIL* G78 ... 125 J8
BSHPBGS G64 ... 64 D7
PSTWK KA9 ... 225 K4
RNFRW PA4 ... 102 B1
Pentland Pl *BSDN* G61 ... 61 H2
IRVSE KA11 ... 204 A6
Pentland Road.
BAIL/MDB/MHD G69 ... 66 D8
Pentland Rd
BAIL/MDB/MHD G69 ... 86 D1
EKILS G75 ... 171 G6
KLMNK KA1 ... 212 A6
PLKSW/MSWD G43 ... 127 J4
WISHAW ML2 ... 158 E5
Penzance Wy
BAIL/MDB/MHD G69 ... 66 F7
Peockland Gdns *JNSTN* PA5 ... 100 A6
Peockland Pl *JNSTN* PA5 ... 100 A6
Peploe Dr *EKILN* G74 ... 154 D4
Perchy Vw *WISHAW* ML2 ... 159 J8
Percy Dr *GIF/THBK* G46 ... 127 J8
Percy Rd *PSLYN/LNWD* PA3 ... 102 A1
Percy St *GOV/IBX* G51 ... 104 C4
LRKH ML9 ... 176 A5
Perran Gdns
BAIL/MDB/MHD G69 ... 66 E7
Perray Av *DMBTN* G82 ... 36 B4
Perrays Crs *DMBTN* G82 ... 36 A4
Perrays Dr *DMBTN* G82 ... 36 A4
Perrays Wy *DMBTN* G82 ... 36 A4
Perth Av *AIRDRIE* ML6 ... 111 G4
Perth Crs *CLYDBK* G81 ... 59 K4
Perth St *KVGV* G3 ... 10 D1
Peter D Stirling Rd *KKNTL* G66 .. 45 K8
Petersburn Pl *AIRDRIE* ML6 ... 111 K3
Petersburn Rd *AIRDRIE* ML6 ... 111 K3
Petershill Dr *SPRGB/BLRNK* G21 ... 7 H1
Petershill Pl *SPRGB/BLRNK* G21 ... 7 H1
Petershill Rd *SPRGB/BLRNK* G21 ... 6 C3
Peterson Dr *KNTSWD* G13 ... 80 E1
Peterson Gdns *KNTSWD* G13 ... 80 E1
Peter St *IRV* KA12 ... 203 G8
Petition Pl *UD/BTH/TAN* G71 ... 132 A4
Pettigrew St *CAR/SHTL* G32 ... 107 G4
Peveril Av *PLKSD/SHW* G41 ... 104 D8
RUTH G73 ... 129 J4
Philip Murry Rd
UD/BTH/TAN G71 ... 132 D3
Philipshill Ga *EKILN* G74 ... 152 E6
Philipshill Rd *EKILN* G74 ... 152 E6
Philip Sq *AYR* KA8 ... 19 G1
Phillips Av *LARGS* KA30 ... 115 L5
Phoenix Crs *BLSH* ML4 ... 132 F1
Phoenix Pl *JNSTN* PA5 ... 100 D6
MTHW ML1 ... 134 A6
Phoenix Rd *BLSH* ML4 ... 133 L4
Piccadilly St *KVGV* G3 ... 10 D2
Picken St *KLMNK* KA1 ... 211 M4
Pickerstonhill *MTHW* ML1 ... 134 E5
Picketlaw Dr
CRMNK/CLK/EAG G76 ... 152 D2
Picketlaw Farm Rd
CRMNK/CLK/EAG G76 ... 152 C2
Pier Rd *FAIRLIE* KA29 ... 139 K5
Piershill St *CAR/SHTL* G32 ... 106 F2
Piersland Pl *IRVSE* KA11 ... 204 A4
Pikeman Rd *KNTSWD* G13 ... 81 J2
Pillans Ct *HMLTN* ML3 ... 156 A3
Pilmuir Av *LNPK/KPK* G44 ... 127 M5
Pilrig St *CAR/SHTL* G32 ... 106 E2
Pilton Rd *DRUM* G15 ... 61 G6
Pine Av *BLTYR/CAMB* G72 ... 130 F6
Pine Brae *AYRS* KA7 ... 19 L9
Pine Cl *CUMB* G67 ... 49 L5
Pine Ct *CUMB* G67 ... 49 L5
EKILS G75 ... 171 H4
Pine Crs *CUMB* G67 ... 49 L5
EKILS G75 ... 171 H4
JNSTN PA5 ... 100 A8
Pine Gv *AIRDRIE* ML6 ... 111 H7
CUMB G67 ... 49 L5
UD/BTH/TAN G71 ... 132 B1
Pine Lawn *WISHAW* ML2 ... 159 K4
Pine Pk *HMLTN* ML3 ... 156 E8
Pine Pl *CUMB* G67 ... 49 L5
GBLS G5 ... 11 K7
Pine Rd *CLYDBK* G81 ... 59 K5
CUMB G67 ... 49 L5
DMBTN G82 ... 36 F5
KLMNK KA1 ... 16 A6
Pine St *AIRDRIE* ML6 ... 111 K2
GRNK PA15 ... 2 A6
KKNTL G66 ... 44 E1
PSLYS PA2 ... 9 M9
Pinewood Av *KKNTL* G66 ... 65 G4
Pinewood Ct *DMBTN* G82 ... 37 H4
KKNTL G66 ... 65 G4
Pinewood Pl *KKNTL* G66 ... 65 G4
Pinkerton Av *RUTH* G73 ... 128 F1
Pinkerton La *RNFRW* PA4 ... 80 D8
Pinkston Dr *COWCAD* G4 ... 6 A5
Pinkston Rd *COWCAD* G4 ... 5 L4
Pinmore Pl *PLK/PH/NH* G53 ... 125 M4
Pinmore St *PLK/PH/NH* G53 ... 125 M4
Pinwherry Dr
STPS/GTHM/RID G33 ... 84 F3
Pinwherry Pl
UD/BTH/TAN G71 ... 132 A6
Piper Av *CRG/CRSL/HOU* PA6 ... 99 J1
Piperhill *AYRS* KA7 ... 229 G7
Piper Rd *AIRDRIE* ML6 ... 111 J4
CRG/CRSL/HOU PA6 ... 99 J1
Pirnie Pl *KSYTH* G65 ... 47 K1
Pirnmill Av *EKILS* G75 ... 171 H5
MTHW ML1 ... 157 H2
Pirnmill Pl *HBR/GL* G84 ... 20 F7
Pirnmill Rd *SALT* KA21 ... 191 M7
Pitcairn Crs *EKILS* G75 ... 170 F1
Pitcairn Gv *EKILS* G75 ... 171 G1
Pitcairn Pl *EKILS* G75 ... 170 F1
Pitcairn St *DEN/PKHD* G31 ... 106 E5
Pitcairn Ter *HMLTN* ML3 ... 156 A5
Pitcaple Dr
PLKSW/MSWD G43 ... 127 H3
Pitlochry Dr
CARD/HILL/MSPK G52 ... 103 H5
LRKH ML9 ... 176 C8
Pitmedden Rd *BSHPBGS* G64 ... 64 D7
Pitmilly Rd *DRUM* G15 ... 61 J5
Pitreavie Ct *HMLTN* ML3 ... 174 B1
Pitreavie Pl
STPS/GTHM/RID G33 ... 85 J7
Pit Rd *BLSH* ML4 ... 132 F3
KKNTL G66 ... 66 B2
Pitt St *CGLW* G2 ... 4 F9
Place of Bonhill *ALEX/LLW* G83 ... 25 K6
Place Vw *KBRN* KA25 ... 142 F8
Pladda Av *IRVSE* KA11 ... 204 A7
PGL PA14 ... 55 H2
Pladda Ct *IRVSE* KA11 ... 204 B7
Pladda Crs *IRVSE* KA11 ... 204 A7
Pladda Dr *PSTWK* KA9 ... 225 J3
Pladda Rd *RNFRW* PA4 ... 80 D8
SALT KA21 ... 191 M7
Pladda St *MTHW* ML1 ... 157 H2
Pladda Ter *IRVSE* KA11 ... 204 B7
Pladda Wy *HBR/GL* G84 ... 20 F7
Pladda Wynd *IRVSE* KA11 ... 204 A7
Plaintrees Ct *PSLYS* PA2 ... 101 L8
Plane Pl *UD/BTH/TAN* G71 ... 109 H8
Planetree Pl *JNSTN* PA5 ... 100 A8
Planetree Rd *CLYDBK* G81 ... 60 A5
Plantation Av *MTHW* ML1 ... 134 B3
Plantation Park Gdns
GOV/IBX G51 ... 104 D4
Plantation Sq *GOV/IBX* G51 ... 10 A4
Plant St *DEN/PKHD* G31 ... 13 J3
Plan Vw *KBRN* KA25 ... 143 H6
Plateau Dr *TROON* KA10 ... 216 F2
Platthorn Dr *EKILN* G74 ... 15 J3
Platthorn Rd *EKILN* G74 ... 15 H4
Playfair St *DMNK/BRGTN* G40 ... 12 E9
Playingfield Rd *CRH/DND* KA2 ... 205 L8
Pleaknowe Crs
BAIL/MDB/MHD G69 ... 66 E7
Pleamuir Pl *BALLOCH* G68 ... 48 C7
Plean St *SCOT* G14 ... 81 G4
Pleasance St
PLKSW/MSWD G43 ... 127 J1
Pleasantfield Rd *PSTWK* KA9 ... 225 H4
Pleasantside Av *PGL* PA14 ... 55 G1
Plover Dr *EKILS* G75 ... 171 G4
Plover Pl *JNSTN* PA5 ... 122 C2
Plymouth Av *GRNKW/INVK* PA16 .. 31 L4
Pochard Wy *BLSH* ML4 ... 132 F1
Poet's Vw *KKNTL* G66 ... 65 M2
Poindfauld Ter *DMBTN* G82 ... 37 G5
Pointhouse Rd *KVGV* G3 ... 104 C1
Pollick Av *BRHD/NEIL* G78 ... 147 H6
Pollick Farm La *BRHD/NEIL* G78 .. 147 G7
Pollock Av *HMLTN* ML3 ... 156 A5
Pollock Crs *KLWNG* KA13 ... 193 L7
Pollock Rd *BSDN* G61 ... 62 A6
NMRNS G77 ... 150 C5
Pollock St *BLSH* ML4 ... 133 J4
MTHW ML1 ... 157 L2
Pollok Dr *BSHPBGS* G64 ... 63 L8
Pollok La *EKILN* G74 ... 154 B6
Pollok Pl *EKILN* G74 ... 154 B6
Pollokshaws Rd
PLKSD/SHW G41 ... 11 G8
PLKSW/MSWD G43 ... 127 H2
Pollokshields Sq
PLKSD/SHW G41 ... 104 E7
Polmadie Rd *GBLS* G5 ... 105 L6
GVH/MTFL G42 ... 105 K8
Polmadie St *GVH/MTFL* G42 ... 105 J8
Polnoon Av *KNTSWD* G13 ... 81 G3
Polo Av *TROON* KA10 ... 216 E7
Polo Gdns *TROON* KA10 ... 216 E7
Polquhap Ct *PLK/PH/NH* G53 .. 126 A1
Polquhap Gdns
PLK/PH/NH G53 ... 126 A1
Polquhap Pl *PLK/PH/NH* G53 ... 126 A1
Polquhap Rd *PLK/PH/NH* G53 ... 126 A1
Polson Dr *JNSTN* PA5 ... 99 L7
Polsons Crs *PSLYS* PA2 ... 8 F8
Polwarth La *KVD/HLHD* G12 ... 82 B6
Polwarth St *GLSTN* KA4 ... 214 C3
KVD/HLHD G12 ... 82 B6
Pomona Pl *HMLTN* ML3 ... 155 M7
Poplar Av *BSHPTN* PA7 ... 58 B7
JNSTN PA5 ... 100 A8
NMRNS G77 ... 150 E6
PTCK G11 ... 81 M5
Poplar Crs *BSHPTN* PA7 ... 58 B7
Poplar Dr *CLYDBK* G81 ... 59 M4
KKNTL G66 ... 45 J4
KKNTL G66 ... 65 G4

Poplar Gdns EKILS G75 171 J4
Poplar Pl BLTYR/CAMB G72 131 J8
GRK PA19 31 J3 4
MTHW ML1 134 B5
UD/BTH/TAN G71 132 D1
Poplar Rd DMBTN G82 36 F5
The Poplars BSDN G61 61 K1 2
Poplar St AIRDRIE ML6 111 J2
GRNK PA15 33 M7
Poplar Wy AYRS KA7 229 K4
BLTYR/CAMB G72 130 F6 1
Poplin St DMNK/BRGTN G40 12 D9
DMNK/BRGTN G40 105 M6 5
Porchester St
STPS/GTHM/RID G33 85 K7
Portal Rd KNTSWD G13 81 J1
Port Dundas Pl CGLW G2 5 J8
Port Dundas Rd COWCAD G4 5 H6
Portencross Rd WKIL KA23 181 J4
Porterfield Rd KLMCLM PA13 75 K2 2
RNFRW PA4 80 B6
Porter St GOV/IBX G51 104 C4 3
Porters Well UD/BTH/TAN G71 131 L4
Portessie ERSK PA8 59 G7
Port Glasgow Rd GRNK PA15 33 M6
PGL PA14 55 H5
Portland Av IRV KA12 208 B1
Portland Brae
KLMNKN/STW KA3 212 E2
Portland Pk HMLTN ML3 156 E7 6
Portland Pl HMLTN ML3 156 E7
IRV KA12 208 B1
KLMNK KA1 16 C5
LNK/LMHG ML11 199 H5 2
SVSTN KA20 201 K2
Portland Rd BALLOCH G68 48 F4
GLSTN KA4 214 B4
IRV KA12 208 A1
KLMNK KA1 16 C4
PSLYS PA2 102 B6
Portland Sq HMLTN ML3 156 E7 7
Portland St CTBR ML5 110 B1
KLMNK KA1 16 F3
KLMNKN/STW KA3 16 F3
TROON KA10 216 C6
Portland Ter TROON KA10 216 B7
Portman St PLKSD/SHW G41 10 B5
Portmark Av AYRS KA7 228 C8
Portmarnock Dr SMSTN G23 82 E1 3
Portpatrick Rd OLDK G60 58 F2
Portreath Rd
BAIL/MDB/MHD G69 66 F6
Portsmouth Dr
GRNKW/INVK PA16 31 L4 4
Portsoy Av KNTSWD G13 80 F1 2
Portsoy Pl KNTSWD G13 80 F1
Port St KVGV G3 10 C1
Portugal St GBLS G5 11 H6
Portwell HMLTN ML3 156 E5 6
Possil Rd COWCAD G4 5 G4
Postgate HMLTN ML3 156 E5
Potassels Rd
BAIL/MDB/MHD G69 86 C2
Potrail Pl HMLTN ML3 156 A6
Potter Cl CAR/SHTL G32 106 E6 2
Potter Gv CAR/SHTL G32 106 E6 3
Potterhill Av PSLYS PA2 124 E1
Potterhill Rd PLK/PH/NH G53 103 G7
Potter Pl CAR/SHTL G32 106 E6 4
Potter St CAR/SHTL G32 106 E6
Potters Wynd LNK/LMHG ML11 199 J4
Pottery Pl KLMNKN/STW KA3 206 F7
Pottery St GRNK PA15 33 L6
Potts Wy MTHW ML1 133 J8
Powbrone EKILS G75 171 L4 6
Powburn Crs UD/BTH/TAN G71 131 K2
Powfoot St DEN/PKHD G31 13 M6
Powforth Cl LRKH ML9 175 L6
Powgree Crs BEITH KA15 168 C4 1
Powmill Gdns PSTWK KA9 221 K7
Powmill Pk PSTWK KA9 221 K7
Powmill Rd PSTWK KA9 221 K7
Powrie St STPS/GTHM/RID G33 85 J6
Prentice La
UD/BTH/TAN G71 132 A1 8
Prentice Rd HMLTN ML3 157 H4
Prestonfield MLNGV G62 41 L8
Prestonfield Av KLWNG KA13 193 H5
Preston Pl GRK PA19 31 K2 3
GVH/MTFL G42 105 H7
Preston St GVH/MTFL G42 105 H7
Prestwick Ct BALLOCH G68 48 F5 1
Prestwick Pl NMRNS G77 151 G5 4
Prestwick Rd AYR KA8 225 G6
Prestwick St PLK/PH/NH G53 126 A3
Priestfield St BLTYR/CAMB G72 155 J3
Priesthill Av PLK/PH/NH G53 126 C3 2
Priesthill Crs PLK/PH/NH G53 126 C3
Priesthill Rd PLK/PH/NH G53 126 B3
Prieston Rd BRWEIR PA11 98 D2
Primrose Av BLSH ML4 133 C2
GRNKW/INVK PA16 50 E4
Primrose Crs GRNKW/INVK PA16 50 E4
MTHW ML1 157 L4
Primrose Pl CUMB G67 68 B2
GRNKW/INVK PA16 50 E4 4
SALT KA21 192 A7
UD/BTH/TAN G71 132 C1 4
Primrose St SCOT G14 81 J6
Primrose Wy CARLUKE ML8 188 E1
Prince Albert Rd KVD/HLHD G12 82 B6
Prince Edward St
GVH/MTFL G42 105 G7
Prince of Wales Gdns
MRYH/FIRH G20 82 C1
Prince Pl WISHAW ML2 160 A3
Princes Ct AYR KA8 225 G7
Prince's Gdns KVD/HLHD G12 82 B6
Princes Ga RUTH G73 129 G1 6
UD/BTH/TAN G71 131 L5
Princes Pk BSHPTN PA7 58 E5
Princes Pl ARD KA22 191 H8 4
KVD/HLHD G12 82 C6
Princess Ct KLMNK KA1 212 B5 2
Princess Crs PSLY PA1 102 B3
Princess Dr
BAIL/MDB/MHD G69 109 G4
Princes Sq BRHD/NEIL G78 125 K6 2
Princess Rd MTHW ML1 133 M5
Princes St AIRDRIE ML6 91 G4
ARD KA22 191 H8
GRNK PA15 2 B3
KLMNK KA1 16 F5
MTHW ML1 157 L1 4
PGL PA14 34 B7 4
RUTH G73 129 G1
Princes St East HBR/GL G84 20 D8
Prince's Ter KVD/HLHD G12 82 C6
Princes Terrace La
KVD/HLHD G12 82 C6 9
Priorwood Rd NMRNS G77 150 A5
Priory Av PSLYN/LNWD PA3 102 A2
Priory Dr UD/BTH/TAN G71 131 K2
Priory Ga WISHAW ML2 177 H2
Priory Pl BALLOCH G68 47 L8 6
KNTSWD G13 81 K2 2
Priory Rd KNTSWD G13 81 K2
Priory St BLTYR/CAMB G72 155 K2
Priory Ter WISHAW ML2 158 C7
Procession Rd PSLYS PA2 124 D3
Progress Dr AIRDRIE ML6 90 F4
Promenade AYR KA8 224 F6
Prosen St CAR/SHTL G32 106 E6
Prospect Av BLTYR/CAMB G72 129 M3
UD/BTH/TAN G71 131 M2 3
Prospect Ct BLTYR/CAMB G72 155 K4
Prospecthill Circ
GVH/MTFL G42 105 K8
Prospecthill Crs GVH/MTFL G42 128 E1
Prospecthill Dr
GVH/MTFL G42 128 C1 2
Prospecthill Pl GRNK PA15 2 A5
RUTH G73 128 E1
Prospecthill Rd GVH/MTFL G42 128 B1
SALT KA21 192 A8
Prospecthill Sq
GVH/MTFL G42 128 D1 3
Prospecthill St GRNK PA15 2 A6
Prospect Rd BALLOCH G68 48 C3
PLKSW/MSWD G43 127 K1 1
Provand Hall Crs
BAIL/MDB/MHD G69 108 B6
Provanhill St
SPRGB/BLRNK G21 6 C6
Provanmill Rd
STPS/GTHM/RID G33 7 M3
Provan Rd DEN/PKHD G31 7 K7
Provost Driver Ct RNFRW PA4 80 E7 3
Provost Ga LRKH ML9 175 M6
Provost's Loan GTCI KA28 138 C6 1
Pundeavon Av KBRN KA25 143 G6
Purdie EKILN G74 154 D4 2
Purdie St HMLTN ML3 156 A4
Purdon St PTCK G11 82 B7
Putyan Av DALRY KA24 184 B2
Pyatshaw Rd LRKH ML9 176 B8

Q

Quadrant Rd
PLKSW/MSWD G43 127 L4
The Quadrant
CRMNK/CLK/EAG G76 151 M1
Quail Rd AYR KA8 225 G5
Quarrelton Gv JNSTN PA5 99 M8 1
Quarrelton Rd JNSTN PA5 99 L7
Quarrier St GRNK PA15 3 M8
Quarry Av BLTYR/CAMB G72 130 D6
Quarrybank KLBCH PA10 99 J7
Quarrybrae Av
CRMNK/CLK/EAG G76 151 K2
Quarrybrae Gdns
UD/BTH/TAN G71 132 C3 2
Quarrybrae St DEN/PKHD G31 13 M6
DEN/PKHD G31 106 E4
Quarry Dr KKNTL G66 65 M1
KLMCLM PA13 55 K7
Quarry Knowe DMBTN G82 36 D4
Quarryknowe LNK/LMHG ML11 199 G5
RUTH G73 128 F2
Quarryknowe Gdns
DEN/PKHD G31 106 E4 2
Quarry Knowe Pl BLSH ML4 132 F6
Quarryknowe St CLYDBK G81 60 E2 4
DEN/PKHD G31 106 E4
Quarry La KKNTL G66 29 K8
Quarry Pk EKILS G75 14 E6
Quarry Pl BLTYR/CAMB G72 129 L3
DMBTN G82 36 D4
SHOTTS ML7 137 K4
Quarry Rd AIRDRIE ML6 88 F8
BRHD/NEIL G78 125 H5 4
CARLUKE ML8 177 M7
EKILS G75 171 K4
IRV KA12 203 J6
LRKH ML9 176 A7
PGL PA14 54 F2
PSLYS PA2 101 M8 2
SHOTTS ML7 137 K4
Quarryside St AIRDRIE ML6 88 D5
Quarry St CTBR ML5 110 D3
HMLTN ML3 156 E6
JNSTN PA5 99 M6
LRKH ML9 176 B8
MTHW ML1 134 A5
SHOTTS ML7 137 K4
WISHAW ML2 159 G6
Quarrywood Av
SPRGB/BLRNK G21 84 C5 4
Quarrywood Rd
SPRGB/BLRNK G21 84 D5
STPS/GTHM/RID G33 7 L1
Quayhead GTCI KA28 138 A7 2
Quay Pend DMBTN G82 36 E6 4
Quay Rd RUTH G73 129 G1
Quay Rd North RUTH G73 106 A8
Quay St DMBTN G82 36 F6 2
SALT KA21 200 F2
Quebec Dr EKILS G75 14 A4
Quebec Wynd
CAR/SHTL G32 130 C1 10
Queen Elizabeth Av
CARD/HILL/MSPK G52 102 E2
Queen Margaret Dr
KVD/HLHD G12 4 A2
Queen Margaret Rd
MRYH/FIRH G20 4 A1
Queen Mary Av CLYDBK G81 60 D7
GVH/MTFL G42 105 H8
Queen Mary St
DMNK/BRGTN G40 12 D8
Queen Rd IRV KA12 203 J4
Queen's Av BLTYR/CAMB G72 130 B3
LARGS KA30 115 K5
Queensbank Av
BAIL/MDB/MHD G69 86 E2
Queensberry Av BSDN G61 61 L2
CRMNK/CLK/EAG G76 151 L2
Queensborough Gdns
KVD/HLHD G12 82 A5
Queensby Av
BAIL/MDB/MHD G69 108 B4 3
Queensby Pl
BAIL/MDB/MHD G69 108 C3 2
Queensby Rd
BAIL/MDB/MHD G69 108 B3
Queen's Ct MLNGV G62 62 A1
Queen's Crs AIRDRIE ML6 111 K6
BAIL/MDB/MHD G69 108 F4
BLSH ML4 132 F5 6
CARLUKE ML8 179 G7
COWCAD G4 4 D5
MTHW ML1 133 M6 4
NMLNS KA16 215 H2
Queen's Dr ALEX/LLW G83 25 K6
ARD KA22 191 J6
BALLOCH G68 48 F3
BSHPTN PA7 58 C6
GVH/MTFL G42 104 F7
HMLTN ML3 174 D3
KLMNK KA1 17 G7
PSTWK KA9 221 K4
TROON KA10 216 D3
Queensferry St GBLS G5 105 L7 3
Queen's Gdns KVD/HLHD G12 82 C6
Queen's Ga
CRMNK/CLK/EAG G76 151 L1 1
Queenside Crs ERSK PA8 58 F8
Queensland Ct
CARD/HILL/MSPK G52 103 J3 1
Queensland Dr
CARD/HILL/MSPK G52 103 J3
Queensland Gdns
CARD/HILL/MSPK G52 103 J3
Queensland La East
CARD/HILL/MSPK G52 103 J3 2
Queensland La West
CARD/HILL/MSPK G52 103 J3 3
Queenslie St
STPS/GTHM/RID G33 7 M4
Queen's Park Av
GVH/MTFL G42 105 H8
Queen's Pl KVD/HLHD G12 82 C6
Queen's Qd AYR KA8 19 H1
Queen Sq PLKSD/SHW G41 104 F7
Queen's Rd JNSTN PA5 100 C7
Queen's St MTHW ML1 135 H7
Queen's Ter AYRS KA7 18 C3
PSTWK KA9 221 H8
Queen's Terrace La AYRS KA7 18 C3
Queen St ALEX/LLW G83 25 K5
AYR KA8 19 H1
CGLE G1 11 J2
HBR/GL G84 20 C6
HMLTN ML3 156 A4 7
KKNTL G66 65 J1 4
KLMNK KA1 16 F5
KLWNG KA13 194 A6
MTHW ML1 157 L2
PGL PA14 34 C7 4
PSLY PA1 8 D4
RNFRW PA4 80 D6
RUTH G73 129 G1
WISHAW ML2 159 M3 3
Queens Vw BSHPBGS G64 64 B1
Queens Wy ALEX/LLW G83 25 K5
Queensway EKILS G75 15 H5
GRK PA19 31 J3 5
Queen Victoria Dr SCOT G14 81 J5
Queen Victoria Ga SCOT G14 81 J4 4
Queen Victoria St AIRDRIE ML6 110 F2
Quendale Dr CAR/SHTL G32 106 F6
Quentin St PLKSD/SHW G41 104 E8
Quinton Gdns
BAIL/MDB/MHD G69 108 A4 4

R

Raasay Crs AIRDRIE ML6 111 L3
Raasay Dr PSLYS PA2 124 D2
Raasay Gdns NMRNS G77 150 B4 6
Raasay Pl PPK/MIL G22 83 J1 4
Raasay St PPK/MIL G22 83 J1
Racecourse Rd AYRS KA7 18 D7
Racecourse Vw HMLTN ML3 156 E4
Rachan St ESTRH G34 86 D8 6
Radnor St CLYDBK G81 60 A6 2
Raeberry St MRYH/FIRH G20 4 C3
Raebog Crs AIRDRIE ML6 88 F7 3
Raebog Rd AIRDRIE ML6 88 F5
Raeburn Av EKILN G74 154 B5
Raeburn Crs HMLTN ML3 155 L6
Raeburn Pl EKILN G74 154 B5
Raeside Av NMRNS G77 150 D6
Raes Rd CARLUKE ML8 188 B1
Raeswood Dr PLK/PH/NH G53 125 M1
Raeswood Rd PLK/PH/NH G53 125 M1
Raewell Crs BLSH ML4 132 F6 10
Rafford St GOV/IBX G51 104 A2 3
Raggithill Av RAYR/DAL KA6 226 F3 1
Raglan St ALEX/LLW G83 25 M6
COWCAD G4 5 G4
Raglan Street La
ALEX/LLW G83 25 M6 5
Raillies Av LARGS KA30 115 K3
Raillies Rd LARGS KA30 115 K3
Railway Rd AIRDRIE ML6 110 D2
Raise St SALT KA21 200 F1
Raith Av CSMK G45 128 D5 2
PSTWK KA9 225 L2
Raithburn Av CSMK G45 128 C5
KLMNKN/STW KA3 206 F5
Raithburn Rd CSMK G45 128 C6
Raith Dr BALLOCH G68 47 K8
BLSH ML4 133 H5
Raithhill AYRS KA7 229 H8
Raith Ter PSTWK KA9 225 L2
Ralston Av
CARD/HILL/MSPK G52 102 F5
PSLY PA1 102 F6
Ralston Ct
CARD/HILL/MSPK G52 102 F5
Ralston Dr
CARD/HILL/MSPK G52 102 F5
KLMNKN/STW KA3 212 D1
Ralston Pl
CARD/HILL/MSPK G52 102 F5
Ralston Rd BRHD/NEIL G78 125 J7
BSDN G61 61 L4
Ralston St AIRDRIE ML6 110 E2
PSLY PA1 9 L5
Ralstonyards Rd
KLMNKN/STW KA3 212 E2
Ramage Rd CARLUKE ML8 179 H8
Ramillies Ct CARLUKE ML8 179 G8
Ramoth LNK/LMHG ML11 198 D5
Rampart Av KNTSWD G13 81 G1
Ramsay Av JNSTN PA5 99 L8
Ramsay Ct NMRNS G77 150 E6
Ramsay Crs KLBCH PA10 99 H7
Ramsay Hl EKILN G74 154 A6 2
Ramsay Pl CTBR ML5 109 J4
JNSTN PA5 99 L8 1
Ramsay St CLYDBK G81 59 M6
Ramseyston Dr
RAYR/DAL KA6 231 H5 10
Ramstane Pl IRVSE KA11 204 C4
Ram St CAR/SHTL G32 106 F4 4
Ranald Gdns RUTH G73 129 K6
Randolph Av
CRMNK/CLK/EAG G76 128 A8 1
Randolph Dr
CRMNK/CLK/EAG G76 127 M8
Randolph Gdns
CRMNK/CLK/EAG G76 127 M8 2
Randolph La PTCK G11 81 M6
Randolph Rd PTCK G11 81 M5
Ranfurly Dr BALLOCH G68 48 E5
Ranfurly Pl BRWEIR PA11 98 D2
Ranfurly Rd BRWEIR PA11 98 E3
CARD/HILL/MSPK G52 102 F4
Range Av MTHW ML1 158 C6
Range Pl HMLTN ML3 156 E8
Rangerhouse Rd EKILS G75 171 M4
Range Rd MTHW ML1 158 B5
Range St MTHW ML1 158 B5
Ranken Crs IRV KA12 203 K6
Ranken Dr IRV KA12 203 K6
Rankin Ct KLMNKN/STW KA3 207 J6
Rankin Crs AIRDRIE ML6 69 M7
Rankin Dr LARGS KA30 115 K4
NMRNS G77 150 C3
Rankine Av EKILS G75 15 K7
Rankine Pl JNSTN PA5 99 M6
Rankine St JNSTN PA5 99 M6
Rankin Rd WISHAW ML2 159 L5
Rankin St CARLUKE ML8 178 F7
GRNKW/INVK PA16 32 C5
Rannoch Av BSHPBGS G64 64 B8
CTBR ML5 87 K8
HMLTN ML3 156 A8
NMRNS G77 150 D2
Rannoch Ct CUMB G67 68 B3
Rannoch Dr BSDN G61 62 A7
CUMB G67 68 B3
KKNTL G66 46 A8
RNFRW PA4 80 C5
WISHAW ML2 177 H1
Rannoch Gn EKILN G74 153 M6 5
Rannoch Pl IRV KA12 203 J3
PSLYS PA2 9 L7
SHOTTS ML7 137 L3 5
Rannoch Rd AIRDRIE ML6 88 F8
JNSTN PA5 99 M8
KLMCLM PA13 75 J2 3
UD/BTH/TAN G71 108 E8
WMYSB PA18 70 A1 4
Rannoch St LNPK/KPK G44 128 A3
Rannoch Ter LRKH ML9 176 C8 3
Raploch Av SCOT G14 81 H5
Raploch Crs CLYDBK G81 60 D2 4
Raploch La SCOT G14 81 H5
Raploch Rd LRKH ML9 175 M7
Raploch St LRKH ML9 175 M6
Rashielee ERSK PA8 59 G7
Rashielee Av ERSK PA8 59 H7
Rashielee Rd ERSK PA8 59 G7
Rashley Sq ARD KA22 191 K5
Rathlin Av KLMNK KA1 211 M5
Rathlin St GOV/IBX G51 104 A1
Rathlin Ter DMBTN G82 36 C4
Ratho Dr BALLOCH G68 48 E4
SPRGB/BLRNK G21 83 L5
Ratho Pk HMLTN ML3 174 B2
Ratho St GRNK PA15 3 K6
Rattray St CAR/SHTL G32 106 E6
Ravel Rw DEN/PKHD G31 13 L6
Ravelston Rd BSDN G61 61 L7
Ravelston St CAR/SHTL G32 13 M3
Ravel Wynd UD/BTH/TAN G71 132 A1
Raven Rd GRNKW/INVK PA16 32 B4 2
Ravenscliffe Dr GIF/THBK G46 127 H6
Ravenscourt EKILN G74 152 C6
Ravenscraig Av PSLYS PA2 8 D9
PSLYS PA2 101 J8 1
Ravenscraig Ct BLSH ML4 133 H4
Ravenscraig Dr
PLK/PH/NH G53 126 B3
Ravenscraig Rd
KLMNKN/STW KA3 197 K1
Ravenscraig Ter
PLK/PH/NH G53 126 C4 2
Ravenshall Rd PLKSD/SHW G41 127 J1
Ravenshill Dr MTHW ML1 135 J8
Ravenstone Dr GIF/THBK G46 127 J4
Ravenswood Av PSLYS PA2 123 L2 2
Ravenswood Dr
PLKSD/SHW G41 104 D8
Ravenswood Rd
BAIL/MDB/MHD G69 108 C5
Raven Wynd WISHAW ML2 159 H6
Rawyards Av AIRDRIE ML6 89 H7
Raymond Pl EKILS G75 14 B4
Rayne Pl DRUM G15 61 H5
Ream Av AIRDRIE ML6 111 M3
Reay Av DMBTN G82 35 G1
EKILN G74 153 H7
Reay Gdns EKILN G74 153 H7 2
Recawr Pk AYRS KA7 229 H6
Redan St DMNK/BRGTN G40 12 D5
Redbrae Rd KKNTL G66 45 K8
Redburn Av GIF/THBK G46 151 H1
Redburn Ct CUMB G67 49 M3 3
Redburn Pl CUMB G67 49 M4
IRV KA12 203 H4
Redburn Rd CUMB G67 49 M3
Redcastle Sq
STPS/GTHM/RID G33 85 K8 3
Redcliffe Dr EKILS G75 171 H1 3
Redclyffe Gdns HBR/GL G84 20 D5
Reddance Ter DALRY KA24 184 A1
Red Deer Rd EKILS G75 14 A5
Redding Av KLMNKN/STW KA3 206 F5
Rederech Crs HMLTN ML3 155 M7
Redford St STPS/GTHM/RID G33 7 L8
Red Fox Dr ALEX/LLW G83 25 L1
Red Gables Sq ARD KA22 191 H6
Redgate Pl SCOT G14 81 H5 5
Redgauntlet Rd HBR/GL G84 22 F1
Redgrave EKILN G74 154 C4
Redhill Rd BALLOCH G68 48 D6
Redhills Vw KKNTL G66 44 E2
Redhurst Crs PSLYS PA2 124 C2 4
Redhurst La PSLYS PA2 124 C2 5
Redhurst Wy PSLYS PA2 124 C2 6
Redlands La KVD/HLHD G12 82 C5 14
Redlands Rd KVD/HLHD G12 82 C5
Redlands Ter KVD/HLHD G12 82 C5 15
Redlands Terrace La
KVD/HLHD G12 82 C5 16
Redlawood Pl
BLTYR/CAMB G72 131 G3
Redlawood Rd
BLTYR/CAMB G72 131 G3
Redmire Crs SHOTTS ML7 161 H1
Redmoss Rd CLYDBK G81 59 M3
KKNTL G66 45 H4
Redmoss St PPK/MIL G22 83 H4 2
Rednock St PPK/MIL G22 5 K1
Redpath Dr
CARD/HILL/MSPK G52 103 H3
Red Rd DMBTN G82 23 M5
SPRGB/BLRNK G21 7 H1
Red Road Ct SPRGB/BLRNK G21 7 H2
Red Rw DMBTN G82 25 K7
Redstone Av KLWNG KA13 193 M5
Redwing Gdns WISHAW ML2 159 G8 2
Redwood Av EKILN G74 152 E8
Redwood Ct EKILN G74 152 E8
Redwood Crs BLTYR/CAMB G72 130 F5
BSHPTN PA7 58 C6
EKILN G74 152 E7
UD/BTH/TAN G71 132 C1
Redwood Dr EKILN G74 152 E6
SPRGB/BLRNK G21 6 E2 2
Redwood Gv CTBR ML5 110 B3
Redwood Pl EKILN G74 152 F7
UD/BTH/TAN G71 132 C1
Redwood Rd CUMB G67 49 K7
MTHW ML1 134 B4
Reedloch Dr TROON KA10 216 F2
Reek St BEITH KA15 168 E2
Reelick Av KNTSWD G13 80 E1 4
Reelick Qd KNTSWD G13 80 E1
Reema Rd BLSH ML4 133 J3
Reen Pl UD/BTH/TAN G71 132 B5
Reform St BEITH KA15 144 B8
Regal Gv SHOTTS ML7 137 L5
Regency Wy HMLTN ML3 157 G7 6
MTHW ML1 133 M5 1
Regent Dr RUTH G73 129 G1 7
Regent Moray St KVGV G3 82 D8
Regent Park Sq
PLKSD/SHW G41 104 F7
Regent Pl CLYDBK G81 59 L5
Regents Ct NMLNS KA16 215 J2 4
Regents Ga UD/BTH/TAN G71 131 L5 1
Regent Sq KKNTL G66 65 J5
Regent St CLYDBK G81 59 L5
GRNK PA15 2 D5
KKNTL G66 65 J1 5
PSLY PA1 102 B4
Register Av BLSH ML4 133 G6
Register Rd KSYTH G65 47 L1
Regwood St PLKSD/SHW G41 127 K1
Reid Av BSDN G61 62 A3
DALRY KA24 184 B3
PSLYN/LNWD PA3 100 B4
Reid Gv MTHW ML1 158 B5
Reid Pl DMNK/BRGTN G40 12 D8
Reid's Av SVSTN KA20 192 D7
Reid St AIRDRIE ML6 89 H8
CTBR ML5 110 A1
DMNK/BRGTN G40 12 D9
DMNK/BRGTN G40 105 M6
GTCI KA28 138 A7
HMLTN ML3 155 M4
RUTH G73 129 H1
SHOTTS ML7 113 G7
Reid Ter SALT KA21 201 G2
Reidvale St DEN/PKHD G31 12 D3
Reilly Rd CRG/CRSL/HOU PA6 77 J1
Reith Dr EKILS G75 14 C8
Remus Pl BLSH ML4 133 L4
Renfield La CGLW G2 11 H1
Renfield St CGLW G2 5 H8
RNFRW PA4 80 D5
Renfrew Ct CGLW G2 5 J8 1
Renfrew Rd GOV/IBX G51 81 J8
PSLYN/LNWD PA3 9 J1
PSLYN/LNWD PA3 101 M2
RNFRW PA4 81 G8
Renfrew St CGLW G2 4 F7
CTBR ML5 109 J5

Rennie Pl EKILN G74 153 G6
SALT KA21 200 F1
Rennie St KLMNK KA1 16 F5
Renshaw Dr
CARD/HILL/MSPK G52 103 H3
Renshaw Rd BSHPTN PA7 58 B6
JNSTN PA5 100 C8
Renton Pk IRVSE KA11 204 C2
Renton Rd DMBTN G82 36 D1
GRNK PA15 33 J8
Renton St COWCAD G4 5 J6
Renwick Wy PSTWK KA9 225 K4
Reservoir Rd GRK PA19 31 M3
Resipol Rd
STPS/GTHM/RID G33 85 L4
Reston Dr
CARD/HILL/MSPK G52 103 H3
Reuther Av RUTH G73 129 H2
Revoch Dr KNTSWD G13 81 G2
Reynolds Av EKILS G75 15 K7
Reynolds Pth WISHAW ML2 159 K8
Rhannan Rd LNPK/KPK G44 128 A4
Rhannan Ter LNPK/KPK G44 128 A4
Rhindhouse Pl
BAIL/MDB/MHD G69 108 D4
Rhindhouse Rd
BAIL/MDB/MHD G69 108 D4
Rhindmuir Av
BAIL/MDB/MHD G69 108 C4
Rhindmuir Ct
BAIL/MDB/MHD G69 108 C3
Rhindmuir Crs
BAIL/MDB/MHD G69 108 D3
Rhindmuir Dr
BAIL/MDB/MHD G69 108 C3
Rhindmuir Gdns
BAIL/MDB/MHD G69 108 C3
Rhindmuir Pth
BAIL/MDB/MHD G69 108 D3
Rhindmuir Pl
BAIL/MDB/MHD G69 108 D3
Rhindmuir Rd
BAIL/MDB/MHD G69 108 C3
Rhindmuir Wynd
BAIL/MDB/MHD G69 108 D3
Rhindsdale Crs
BAIL/MDB/MHD G69 108 C4
Rhinds St CTBR ML5 109 H5
Rhu Road Higher HBR/GL G84 20 A6
Rhu Road Lower HBR/GL G84 20 A7
Rhyber Av LNK/LMHG ML11 199 H4
Rhymer St SPRGB/BLRNK G21 6 B7
Rhymie Rd CAR/SHTL G32 107 K6
Rhynie Dr GOV/IBX G51 104 B4
Riach Gdns MTHW ML1 133 J8
Ribblesdale EKILN G74 153 J6
Riccarton EKILS G75 171 H2
Riccarton Rd KLMNK KA1 17 M9
KLMNK KA1 212 E3
Riccarton St GVH/MTFL G42 105 J7
Riccartsbar Av PSLYS PA2 8 D7
Rice Wy MTHW ML1 158 B5
Richardland Pl KLMNK KA1 17 G6
Richardson Av KLMNK KA1 213 G4
Richie Av DMBTN G82 35 G1
Richmond Av
CRMNK/CLK/EAG G76 151 L2
Richmond Ct RUTH G73 129 J1
Richmond Dr BLTYR/CAMB G72 129 L4
PSLYN/LNWD PA3 100 A2
RUTH G73 129 K2
Richmond Gdns
BAIL/MDB/MHD G69 66 B8
Richmond Gv RUTH G73 129 J2
Richmond Pl GLSTN KA4 214 C4
RUTH G73 129 J1
Richmond Rd RUTH G73 129 K2
Richmond St CGLE G1 11 L1
CLYDBK G81 60 C8
Riddell St CLYDBK G81 60 C6
CTBR ML5 110 C2
Riddon Av KNTSWD G13 80 E1
Riddon Pl KNTSWD G13 80 E1
Riddrie Crs
STPS/GTHM/RID G33 106 E1
Riddrie Knowes
STPS/GTHM/RID G33 106 E1
Riddrievale Ct
STPS/GTHM/RID G33 84 E8
Riddrievale St
STPS/GTHM/RID G33 84 E8
Ridgepark Dr LNK/LMHG ML11 198 F4
Ried Ct KLMNKN/STW KA3 212 E2
Rigby St CAR/SHTL G32 13 M3
Rigfoot IRVSE KA11 204 B4
Righead KLMNKN/STW KA3 197 J1
Rigghead Av CUMB G67 49 H4
Riggside Rd
STPS/GTHM/RID G33 85 J7
The Riggs MLNGV G62 42 A6
PSTWK KA9 221 J8
Riglaw Pl KNTSWD G13 81 G2
Rigmuir Rd GOV/IBX G51 103 J3
Rigwoodie Pl AYRS KA7 228 E8
Rimmon Crs SHOTTS ML7 137 L3
Rimsdale St DMNK/BRGTN G40 12 E6
Ringford St SPRGB/BLRNK G21 6 C2
Ripon Dr KVD/HLHD G12 82 A3
Risk St CLYDBK G81 59 M5
DMBTN G82 36 E6
Ritchie Ct KLMNKN/STW KA3 207 J6
Ritchie Crs JNSTN PA5 100 C6
Ritchie Pk JNSTN PA5 100 B5
Ritchie Pl NMRNS G77 150 C5
Ritchie St GBLS G5 10 F7
GTCI KA28 138 A7
WISHAW ML2 158 D6
WKIL KA23 181 J4
Riverbank Dr BLSH ML4 133 K6
Riverbank Pl KLMNK KA1 17 G7
Riverbank St NMLNS KA16 215 J2
PLKSW/MSWD G43 127 J2
River Ct CRMNK/CLK/EAG G76 151 M3
Riverdale Gdns HMLTN ML3 156 E8
River Dr RNFRW PA4 79 J4
Riverford Rd
PLKSW/MSWD G43 127 J2
RUTH G73 106 C8
River Rd CAR/SHTL G32 130 B2
Riversdale La SCOT G14 81 G5
Riverside ALEX/LLW G83 25 L1
CRG/CRSL/HOU PA6 77 L8
KKNTL G66 29 H7
MLNGV G62 42 A7
Riverside Ct LNPK/KPK G44 127 M7
Riverside Gdns
CRMNK/CLK/EAG G76 151 M4
Riverside La DMBTN G82 36 E6
Riverside Pl AYR KA8 19 G3
BLTYR/CAMB G72 130 E3
Riverside Rd GLSTN KA4 214 B3
GRNK PA15 2 F8
IRVSE KA11 204 D8
KBRN KA25 143 H8
KLMNKN/STW KA3 197 L1
LNK/LMHG ML11 198 B5
PLKSW/MSWD G43 127 L2
Riverside Ter
CRMNK/CLK/EAG G76 151 M3
Riverside Wk MTHW ML1 157 M1
Riverside Wy IRVSE KA11 208 F1
River St AYR KA8 18 F2
River Ter AYR KA8 18 F2
Riverton Dr EKILS G75 171 H1
River View Crs DMBTN G82 35 H1
Riverview Dr GBLS G5 10 E3
Riverview Gdns KVGV G3 10 F3
Riverview Pl GBLS G5 10 E3
River Wk KLWNG KA13 193 L4
Roaden Av PSLYS PA2 123 M2
Roaden Rd PSLYS PA2 123 M2
Roadside CUMB G67 49 G4
Roadside Pl AIRDRIE ML6 89 K1
Robert Burns Av CLYDBK G81 60 C6
MTHW ML1 134 E5
Robert Burns Ct BEITH KA15 144 B8
Robert Burns Qd BLSH ML4 132 F4
Robert Creighton Pl
KLMNKN/STW KA3 16 F2
Robert Gilson Gdns
CTBR ML5 110 B4
Robertland Rigg
KLMNKN/STW KA3 197 L1
Robert Noble Pl KLMNK KA1 16 B1
Roberton Av
PLKSD/SHW G41 104 C7
Roberton St AIRDRIE ML6 111 K6
Robert Smillie Crs LRKH ML9 176 A8
Robertson Crs AYR KA8 229 K1
BRHD/NEIL G78 148 D2
SALT KA21 201 G2
Robertson Dr BLSH ML4 133 G5
EKILN G74 15 M1
Robertson La CGLW G2 10 F2
Robertson Pl KLMNK KA1 16 F5
Robertson St AIRDRIE ML6 110 E1
BRHD/NEIL G78 125 H6
GRNKW/INVK PA16 32 D3
HMLTN ML3 155 M4
KVGV G3 11 G3
Roberts Qd BLSH ML4 133 H6
Roberts St WISHAW ML2 159 G6
Robert Stewart Pl
KLMNK KA1 16 C3
Robert St GOV/IBX G51 104 A2
PGL PA14 34 E8
SHOTTS ML7 137 L5
Robert Templeton Dr
BLTYR/CAMB G72 130 B4
Robert Wynd WISHAW ML2 160 A3
Robin Pl WISHAW ML2 159 H6
Robin Rd GRNKW/INVK PA16 32 B4
Robroyston Av
STPS/GTHM/RID G33 84 E6
Robroyston Rd BSHPBGS G64 64 F8
STPS/GTHM/RID G33 7 M2
STPS/GTHM/RID G33 84 F2
Robsland Av AYRS KA7 18 F9
Robslee Crs GIF/THBK G46 127 G6
Robslee Dr GIF/THBK G46 127 H6
Robslee Rd GIF/THBK G46 127 G6
Robson Gv GVH/MTFL G42 105 H6
Roche Wy DALRY KA24 184 C2
Rochsoles Crs AIRDRIE ML6 89 G7
Rochsoles Dr AIRDRIE ML6 88 F7
Rochsolloch Rd AIRDRIE ML6 110 D3
Rockall Dr LNPK/KPK G44 128 B5
Rockbank Pl DMNK/BRGTN G40 12 E5
Rockbank St DMNK/BRGTN G40 12 E5
Rockburn Crs BLSH ML4 133 G2
Rockburn Dr
CRMNK/CLK/EAG G76 151 J1
Rockcliffe Pth AIRDRIE ML6 111 M8
Rockcliffe St
DMNK/BRGTN G40 105 M6
Rock Dr KLBCH PA10 99 H7
Rockfield Pl
SPRGB/BLRNK G21 84 C4
Rockfield Rd SPRGB/BLRNK G21 84 C4
Rockhampton Av EKILS G75 171 H2
Rockland Pk LARGS KA30 139 K1
Rockmount Av BRHD/NEIL G78 125 K8
GIF/THBK G46 127 G6
Rockpark Ct SALT KA21 201 G2
Rock St PPK/MIL G22 5 J3
Rockwell Av PSLYS PA2 124 C1
Roddinghead Rd NMRNS G77 151 H6
The Rodding LNK/LMHG ML11 199 H4
Rodger Av NMRNS G77 150 C4
Rodger Dr RUTH G73 129 G3
Rodger Pl RUTH G73 129 G3
Rodil Av LNPK/KPK G44 128 C5
Rodney Pl HBR/GL G84 21 G7
Rodney Rd GRK PA19 31 M3
Rodney St COWCAD G4 5 G4
Roebank Dr BRHD/NEIL G78 125 J8
Roebank Rd BEITH KA15 144 C8
Roebank St DEN/PKHD G31 7 G9
Roffey Park Rd PSLY PA1 102 D4
Rogart St DMNK/BRGTN G40 12 D6
Rogerfield Rd
BAIL/MDB/MHD G69 108 C2
Rokeby La KVD/HLHD G12 4 A3
Roland Crs NMRNS G77 150 F6
Roman Av BSDN G61 61 M4
DRUM G15 61 G8
Roman Ct BSDN G61 61 L4
LNK/LMHG ML11 199 M2
Roman Crs OLDK G60 58 F2
Roman Dr BLSH ML4 133 H5
BSDN G61 61 M4
Roman Gdns BSDN G61 61 M4
Roman Hill Rd CLYDBK G81 60 A2
Roman Pl BLSH ML4 132 E6
Roman Rd AYRS KA7 229 J5
BSDN G61 61 M4
CLYDBK G81 60 A3
KKNTL G66 65 H1
MTHW ML1 157 L2
Roman Wy UD/BTH/TAN G71 132 C3
Romney Av LNPK/KPK G44 128 C4
Rona Av PGL PA14 55 H2
Ronaldsay Dr BSHPBGS G64 64 D7
Ronaldsay Pl CUMB G67 68 D1
Ronaldsay St PPK/MIL G22 83 J2
Ronaldshaw Pk AYRS KA7 18 D7
Rona Pl KLMNKN/STW KA3 207 H4
Rona St SPRGB/BLRNK G21 7 G4
Rona Ter BLTYR/CAMB G72 129 M6
Ronay St PPK/MIL G22 83 K2
WISHAW ML2 159 L4
Rook Rd GRNKW/INVK PA16 32 A4
Rooksdell Av PSLYS PA2 101 J8
Ropework La CGLE G1 11 J4
Rorison Pl LRKH ML9 176 F8
Rosa Burn Av EKILS G75 171 H5
Rosa Pl SALT KA21 191 M7
Rosebank Av BLTYR/CAMB G72 131 L8
KKNTL G66 45 L8
Rosebank Crs AYRS KA7 18 E9
Rosebank Dr BLTYR/CAMB G72 130 C5
UD/BTH/TAN G71 132 C2
Rosebank Gdns IRVSE KA11 203 M2
UD/BTH/TAN G71 108 B7
Rosebank Pl HMLTN ML3 156 A6
KLMNKN/STW KA3 206 F7
Rosebank Rd BLSH ML4 133 H1
WISHAW ML2 177 J3
Rosebank St AIRDRIE ML6 111 L1
Rosebank Ter
BAIL/MDB/MHD G69 108 F5
KLMCLM PA13 55 K8
Roseberry La AIRDRIE ML6 111 K6
Roseberry Pl HMLTN ML3 156 A5
Roseberry Rd AIRDRIE ML6 111 K5
Roseberry St GBLS G5 105 L7
Roseburn Ct CUMB G67 49 M4
Rose Crs GRK PA19 31 K3
HMLTN ML3 155 M5
Rose Dl BSHPBGS G64 84 B1
Rosedale EKILN G74 153 J6
Rosedale Av PSLYS PA2 123 K3
Rosedale Dr
BAIL/MDB/MHD G69 108 A5
Rosedale Gdns HBR/GL G84 20 F8
MRYH/FIRH G20 82 C1
Rosedale St LNK/LMHG ML11 198 F7
Rosedene Ter BLSH ML4 133 G3
Rosefield Gdns
UD/BTH/TAN G71 131 L2
Rosegreen Crs BLSH ML4 133 G1
Rosehall Av CTBR ML5 110 B5
Rosehall Rd SHOTTS ML7 137 K6
Rosehall Ter WISHAW ML2 158 E8
Rosehill Dr CUMB G67 68 A2
Rosehill Rd BSHPBGS G64 64 C1
Roseholm Av IRV KA12 203 L7
Rose Knowe Rd GVH/MTFL G42 128 D1
Roselea Dr MLNGV G62 42 B6
Roselea Gdns KNTSWD G13 81 M2
Roselea Pl BLTYR/CAMB G72 131 J8
Roselea Rd UD/BTH/TAN G71 131 L1
Roselea St LRKH ML9 176 B5
Rosemary Crs EKILN G74 153 K5
Rosemary Pl EKILN G74 153 K5
Rosemount BALLOCH G68 48 F4
Rosemount Av NMRNS G77 150 D7
Rose Mount Ct AIRDRIE ML6 111 J1
Rosemount Dr IRVSE KA11 216 D1
Rosemount Gdns PSTWK KA9 225 J3
Rosemount La BRWEIR PA11 98 B3
Rosemount Mdw
UD/BTH/TAN G71 131 L7
Rosemount Pl GRK PA19 31 G3
Rosemount St SPRGB/BLRNK G21 6 D7
Rosendale Wy
BLTYR/CAMB G72 155 L2
Roseneath Dr HBR/GL G84 20 B7
Roseneath St
GRNKW/INVK PA16 32 C1
Roseness Pl
STPS/GTHM/RID G33 107 G1
Rosenheath Ga EKILN G74 14 B1
Rosepark Av UD/BTH/TAN G71 132 C3
Rose St CGLW G2 5 G8
CUMB G67 68 B3
GRNKW/INVK PA16 32 C5
KKNTL G66 65 K1
MTHW ML1 158 A4
Rosevale Crs BLSH ML4 133 J5
HMLTN ML3 156 B7
Rosevale Rd BSDN G61 61 L5
Rosevale St PTCK G11 82 A7
Rosewood Av BLSH ML4 133 H2
PSLYS PA2 101 H8
Rosewood Pth BLSH ML4 132 E4
Rosewood St KNTSWD G13 81 L2
Roseyard Pl PGL PA14 34 C8
Roslea Dr DEN/PKHD G31 12 F2
Roslin Ct KLMCLM PA13 75 J2
Roslin St GRNK PA15 2 C2
Roslyn Dr BAIL/MDB/MHD G69 108 F4
Rosneath Rd PGL PA14 54 D1
Rosneath St GOV/IBX G51 104 A1
Ross Av KKNTL G66 65 M1
RNFRW PA4 80 A8
Rossbank Rd PGL PA14 34 A7
Ross Crs MTHW ML1 157 J4
Ross Dr AIRDRIE ML6 110 E5
MTHW ML1 157 J4
UD/BTH/TAN G71 109 J8
Rossendale Ct
PLKSW/MSWD G43 127 J1
Rossendale Rd
PLKSW/MSWD G43 127 J1
Ross Gdns MTHW ML1 157 J4
Rosshall Av PSLY PA1 102 C5
Ross Hall Pl RNFRW PA4 80 D6
Rosshill Av
CARD/HILL/MSPK G52 102 F4
Rosshill Rd
CARD/HILL/MSPK G52 102 F4
Rossie Crs BSHPBGS G64 84 C1
Rossie Gv NMRNS G77 150 B4
Rossland Crs BSHPTN PA7 58 A6
Rosslea Dr GIF/THBK G46 127 J7
Rosslyn Av EKILN G74 153 M6
RUTH G73 129 J2
Rosslyn Ct HMLTN ML3 156 A5
Rosslyn Pl AYR KA8 225 H6
Rosslyn Rd BSDN G61 61 H3
Rosslyn Ter KVD/HLHD G12 82 C5
Ross Pl RUTH G73 129 K5
Ross Rd SALT KA21 191 M7
Ross St AYR KA8 225 H7
CGLE G1 11 M4
CTBR ML5 110 A2
PSLY PA1 9 L6
Ross Ter HMLTN ML3 157 J8
Rostan Rd PLKSW/MSWD G43 127 J4
Rosyth Rd GBLS G5 105 L7
Rosyth St GBLS G5 105 L7
Rotherwick Dr PSLY PA1 102 E5
Rotherwood Av KNTSWD G13 61 J8
PSLYS PA2 123 M1
Rotherwood La KNTSWD G13 61 J7
Rotherwood Pl KNTSWD G13 81 K1
Rothesay Crs CTBR ML5 110 B6
Rothesay Pl CTBR ML5 110 B5
EKILN G74 14 E5
KLMNKN/STW KA3 206 F6
Rothesay Rd GRNKW/INVK PA16 31 M6
Rothesay St EKILS G75 14 E5
Rothes Dr SMSTN G23 82 D1
Rothes Pl MRYH/FIRH G20 62 C8
Rottenburn Br
GRNKW/INVK PA16 71 M3
Rottenrow CGLE G1 5 L9
COWCAD G4 12 A1
Rottenrow East COWCAD G4 11 M1
Roughcraig St AIRDRIE ML6 89 G7
Roughlea Pl TROON KA10 216 F3
Roughrigg Rd AIRDRIE ML6 112 A3
Roukenburn St GIF/THBK G46 126 E5
Rouken Glen Rd GIF/THBK G46 127 G8
The Roundel LARGS KA30 115 L5
WISHAW ML2 159 J7
Roundhill Dr JNSTN PA5 100 E6
Roundknowe Rd
UD/BTH/TAN G71 108 C8
Round Riding Rd DMBTN G82 37 G5
Routenburn Rd LARGS KA30 115 H1
Rowallan Crs PSTWK KA9 225 K2
Rowallan Dr KLMNKN/STW KA3 207 G5
Rowallan Gdns
KLMNKN/STW KA3 207 H3
PTCK G11 81 M6
Rowallan La
CRMNK/CLK/EAG G76 151 L2
PTCK G11 81 M6
Rowallan La East PTCK G11 82 A6
Rowallan Rd GIF/THBK G46 126 F7
Rowallan St HBR/GL G84 20 B6
Rowallan Ter
STPS/GTHM/RID G33 85 H5
Rowan Av KKNTL G66 45 H4
RNFRW PA4 80 C5
Rowanbank Pl CTBR ML5 110 D1
Rowanbank Rd PSTWK KA9 225 L2
Rowan Ct BLTYR/CAMB G72 130 F5
Rowan Crs AYRS KA7 19 L9
KKNTL G66 65 J4
Rowandale Av
BAIL/MDB/MHD G69 108 A5
Rowand Av GIF/THBK G46 127 J7
Rowanden Av BLSH ML4 133 G3
Rowan Dr BSDN G61 61 M2
CLYDBK G81 59 M5
DMBTN G82 36 A5
Rowan Gdns PLKSD/SHW G41 104 B5
Rowan Ga PSLYS PA2 9 J9
Rowan Gv HMLTN ML3 174 F6
Rowanhill Pl KLMNK KA1 16 B6
Rowanlea Av PSLYS PA2 123 K2
Rowanlea Dr GIF/THBK G46 127 K5
Rowanpark Dr BRHD/NEIL G78 125 G4
Rowan Pl BLTYR/CAMB G72 130 C3
BLTYR/CAMB G72 155 K1
CTBR ML5 109 L5
KLMNK KA1 16 A6
Rowan Ri HMLTN ML3 156 E7
Rowan Rd CUMB G67 49 K6
PLKSD/SHW G41 104 B5
PSLYN/LNWD PA3 99 M2
Rowans Gdns UD/BTH/TAN G71 132 B5
Rowanside Ter ARD KA22 191 J6
The Rowans BSHPBGS G64 63 M7
Rowan St BEITH KA15 168 C1
GRNKW/INVK PA16 32 C4
PSLYS PA2 9 J9
WISHAW ML2 159 H4
Rowan Ter IRV KA12 203 K5
Rowantree Av MTHW ML1 134 D2
RUTH G73 129 H4
UD/BTH/TAN G71 132 C2
Rowantree Gv ALEX/LLW G83 25 L5
Rowantreehill Rd KLMCLM PA13 75 K1
Rowantree Pl JNSTN PA5 99 M8
KKNTL G66 44 E2
LRKH ML9 176 D7
Rowantree Rd JNSTN PA5 99 M8
Rowantree Ter KKNTL G66 44 E2
MTHW ML1 134 B4
Rowanwood Crs CTBR ML5 109 K4
Rowena Av KNTSWD G13 61 K8
Roxburgh Av GRNK PA15 2 B5
Roxburgh Dr BSDN G61 61 L2
CTBR ML5 110 D5
Roxburgh Pk EKILN G74 15 H4
Roxburgh Rd KLMNK KA1 212 E3
PSLYS PA2 123 K2
Roxburgh St GRNK PA15 2 B4
KVD/HLHD G12 82 D6
Royal Av LARGS KA30 115 K5
Royal Crs KVGV G3 4 A8
Royal Dr HMLTN ML3 157 G7
Royal Exchange Ct CGLE G1 11 J1
Royal Exchange Sq CGLE G1 11 J1
Royal Inch Ter RNFRW PA4 80 D4
Royal St GRK PA19 31 L1
Royal Ter KVGV G3 4 A7
WISHAW ML2 159 J2
Royal Terrace La KVGV G3 4 A7
Royellen Av HMLTN ML3 155 M7
Roystonhill SPRGB/BLRNK G21 6 C7
Royston Rd COWCAD G4 6 B7
SPRGB/BLRNK G21 6 D6
STPS/GTHM/RID G33 7 L3
Royston Sq SPRGB/BLRNK G21 6 B6
Roy St SPRGB/BLRNK G21 5 L3
Rozelle Av DRUM G15 61 H6
NMRNS G77 150 B5
Rozelle Dr NMRNS G77 150 B5
Rozelle Pl NMRNS G77 150 B5
Rozelle Ter AYRS KA7 229 H8
Rubie Crs IRV KA12 208 C1
Rubislaw Dr BSDN G61 61 L6
Ruby St DMNK/BRGTN G40 12 E8
Ruchazie Pl
STPS/GTHM/RID G33 106 F1
Ruchazie Rd
STPS/GTHM/RID G33 106 F1
Ruchill Pl MRYH/FIRH G20 82 F4
Ruchill St MRYH/FIRH G20 82 E4
Rue End St GRNK PA15 2 F5
Ruel St LNPK/KPK G44 128 A2
Rufflees Av BRHD/NEIL G78 125 K6
Rugby Av KNTSWD G13 81 H1
Rugby Crs KLMNK KA1 16 B6
Rugby Rd KLMNK KA1 16 B6
Rullion Pl
STPS/GTHM/RID G33 106 F1
Rumford St DMNK/BRGTN G40 12 C9
Runciman Pl EKILN G74 154 B5
Rupert St COWCAD G4 4 D5
Rushyhill St
SPRGB/BLRNK G21 84 A5
Ruskin La KVD/HLHD G12 4 A2
Ruskin Pl KSYTH G65 47 K1
Ruskin Ter KVD/HLHD G12 4 A3
Russell Colt St CTBR ML5 110 A1
Russell Ct KLMNKN/STW KA3 207 J6
Russell Dr ALEX/LLW G83 25 J2
AYR KA8 19 G1
BSDN G61 61 L3
DALRY KA24 184 D1
Russell Gdns
UD/BTH/TAN G71 132 A1
Russell La WISHAW ML2 159 G7
Russell Pl CRMNK/CLK/EAG G76 152 A4
EKILS G75 14 A8
PSLYN/LNWD PA3 99 M3
Russell Rd CLYDBK G81 59 L2
LNK/LMHG ML11 199 H4
Russell St AIRDRIE ML6 111 L7
AYR KA8 19 H1
BLSH ML4 133 K4
HMLTN ML3 155 M4
JNSTN PA5 100 A6
PSLYN/LNWD PA3 101 K2
WISHAW ML2 159 G7
Rutherford Av BSDN G61 61 H1
Rutherford Ct CLYDBK G81 60 A7
Rutherford La EKILS G75 15 G7
Rutherford Sq EKILS G75 15 G6
Ruthven Av GIF/THBK G46 127 K8
Ruthven La KVD/HLHD G12 82 C6
Ruthven Pl BSHPBGS G64 84 C1
Ruthven St KVD/HLHD G12 82 C6
Rutland Crs GOV/IBX G51 10 B4
Rutland Pl GOV/IBX G51 10 A4
Ryan Rd BSHPBGS G64 64 B8
WMYSB PA18 70 A1
Ryan Wy RUTH G73 129 J6
Ryat Dr NMRNS G77 150 C3
Ryat Gn NMRNS G77 150 C4
Ryatt Linn ERSK PA8 58 F8
Rydal Gv EKILS G75 170 F3
Rydal Pl EKILS G75 170 F3
Ryden Mains Rd AIRDRIE ML6 88 D5
Ryde Rd WISHAW ML2 159 J6
Rye Crs SPRGB/BLRNK G21 84 B4
Ryecroft Dr
BAIL/MDB/MHD G69 108 B4
Ryedale Pl DRUM G15 61 G5
Ryefield Av CTBR ML5 109 K2
JNSTN PA5 99 K8
Ryefield Pl JNSTN PA5 99 K8
Ryefield Rd
SPRGB/BLRNK G21 84 B4
Ryehill Pl SPRGB/BLRNK G21 84 C4
Ryehill Rd SPRGB/BLRNK G21 7 J1
SPRGB/BLRNK G21 84 C4
Ryemount Rd
SPRGB/BLRNK G21 84 C4
Rye Rd SPRGB/BLRNK G21 84 B4
Ryeside Pl DALRY KA24 166 C8
Ryeside Rd SPRGB/BLRNK G21 84 B5
Ryewraes Rd
PSLYN/LNWD PA3 100 B4
Rylands PSTWK KA9 225 J3
Rylands Dr CAR/SHTL G32 107 K5
Rylands Gdns CAR/SHTL G32 107 L5
Rylees Crs
CARD/HILL/MSPK G52 102 E2
Rylees Rd
CARD/HILL/MSPK G52 102 E3
Rysland Av NMRNS G77 150 E4
Rysland Crs NMRNS G77 150 E4
Ryvra Rd KNTSWD G13 81 K3

S

Sachelcourt Av BSHPTN PA7 58 B7
Sackville Av KNTSWD G13 81 M4
Sackville La KNTSWD G13 81 M4
Saddell Rd DRUM G15 61 H5

Saffron Crs WISHAW ML2 158 D8
Saffronhall Crs HMLTN ML3 156 D5
Saffronhall La HMLTN ML3 156 D5
St Abb's Dr PSLYS PA2 101 G8
St Aidan's Pth WISHAW ML2 159 J3
St Andrew's Av BSHPBGS G64 63 L7
PSTWK KA9 225 J3
UD/BTH/TAN G71 132 A8
St Andrew's Brae DMBTN G82 37 H3
St Andrews Ct EKILS G75 171 J3
St Andrew's Crs DMBTN G82 37 H4
PLKSD/SHW G41 10 B7
PSLYN/LNWD PA3 79 J8
St Andrews Dr BALLOCH G68 49 H3
BRWEIR PA11 98 B3
BSDN G61 61 K2
GRK PA19 31 G3
HMLTN ML3 155 K5
PLKSD/SHW G41 104 C7
PSLYN/LNWD PA3 101 K1
St Andrew's Dr West
PSLYN/LNWD PA3 101 J1
St Andrew's Gdns AIRDRIE ML6 111 H1
DALRY KA24 184 B3
St Andrew's La CGLE G1 11 L3
GRK PA19 31 G3
St Andrews Pl BEITH KA15 168 A2
St Andrew's Rd ARD KA22 191 K5
PLKSD/SHW G41 10 C8
RNFRW PA4 80 C6
St Andrew's Sq CGLE G1 11 L4
St Andrew's St AYRS KA7 19 G6
CGLE G1 11 L3
KLMNK KA1 16 F7
MTHW ML1 134 A4
St Andrew St GRNK PA15 3 G6
St Andrews Wy IRVSE KA11 208 D1
WISHAW ML2 159 J3
St Andrews Wynd HBR/GL G84 20 E6
St Annes Av ERSK PA8 79 K1
St Annes Wynd ERSK PA8 79 J1
St Ann's Dr GIF/THBK G46 127 J7
St Barchan's Rd KLBCH PA10 99 H7
St Blane's Dr RUTH G73 128 E3
St Boswell's Crs PSLYS PA2 101 G8
St Boswells Dr CTBR ML5 110 D5
St Bride's Av UD/BTH/TAN G71 132 C2
St Bride's Dr WKIL KA23 181 K4
St Bride's Rd
PLKSW/MSWD G43 127 K3
WKIL KA23 181 J3
St Brides Wy UD/BTH/TAN G71 132 A5
St Bryde St EKILN G74 15 G2
St Catherines Crs SHOTTS ML7 137 K3
St Catherines Rd AYR KA8 225 M7
GIF/THBK G46 127 J7
St Clair Av GIF/THBK G46 127 J6
St Clair St MRYH/FIRH G20 4 D4
St Clair Ter TROON KA10 216 A7
St Columba Dr KKNTL G66 65 L2
St Cuthbert's Rd PSTWK KA9 225 J3
St Cyrus Gdns BSHPBGS G64 64 C8
St Cyrus Rd BSHPBGS G64 64 C8
St Davids Dr AIRDRIE ML6 111 J5
St David's Pl LRKH ML9 176 A6
St Denis Wy CTBR ML5 109 M1
St Edmunds Gv MLNGV G62 42 A6
St Enoch Av UD/BTH/TAN G71 132 C1
St Enoch Pl CGLE G1 11 H3
St Fillans Dr CRG/CRSL/HOU PA6 77 G7
St Fillans Rd
STPS/GTHM/RID G33 85 J4
St Flanan Rd KKNTL G66 46 D7
St George's Rd AYR KA8 225 H6
CGLW G2 4 D8
COWCAD G4 4 E5
KVGV G3 4 D7
St Germains BSDN G61 61 L5
St Giles Pk HMLTN ML3 156 B7
St Giles Wy HMLTN ML3 156 B7
St Helena Crs CLYDBK G81 60 C3
St Inan Av IRV KA12 203 K6
St Inan's Dr BEITH KA15 144 C8
St Ives Rd BAIL/MDB/MHD G69 66 F6
St James Av PSLYN/LNWD PA3 101 H2
St James Ct CTBR ML5 109 L6
St James Rd COWCAD G4 5 M9
St James' St PSLYN/LNWD PA3 8 F2
St James Wy CTBR ML5 109 L6
St Joan's Crs KLWNG KA13 193 L7
St John's Ct PLKSD/SHW G41 10 A8
St John's Qd PLKSD/SHW G41 10 B8
St John's Rd GRK PA19 31 L1
PLKSD/SHW G41 104 D6
St John St AYRS KA7 18 E2
CTBR ML5 110 A2
PSTWK KA9 225 J1
St Joseph's Ct SPRGB/BLRNK G21 6 D7
St Joseph's Vw
SPRGB/BLRNK G21 6 D8
St Kenneth Dr GOV/IBX G51 103 K1
St Kentigerns Rd
LNK/LMHG ML11 199 H4
St Kilda Bank IRVSE KA11 203 M7
St Kilda Dr SCOT G14 81 L5
St Kilda Pl IRVSE KA11 204 A7
St Kilda Wy WISHAW ML2 159 L4
St Lawrence Pk EKILS G75 14 B4
St Lawrence Pl SALT KA21 192 A8
St Lawrence St GRNK PA15 3 H6
St Leonard's Ct AYRS KA7 19 G9
St Leonard's Dr
GIF/THBK G46 127 J6
St Leonard's Rd AYRS KA7 18 F9
EKILN G74 15 L3
LNK/LMHG ML11 199 H5
St Leonard St LNK/LMHG ML11 199 H5
St Leonards Wk CTBR ML5 110 C6
St Luke's Av CARLUKE ML8 188 E1
St Machan's Wy KKNTL G66 29 K8
St Machars Rd BRWEIR PA11 98 E2
St Margaret Av DALRY KA24 184 A2
St Margaret's Dr
WISHAW ML2 158 E8
St Margaret's Pl CGLE G1 11 K4
St Margaret's Rd ARD KA22 191 K6
St Mark Gdns CAR/SHTL G32 106 F4
St Mark's Ct WISHAW ML2 159 J3
St Mark St CAR/SHTL G32 106 E4
St Marnock St
DMNK/BRGTN G40 12 E5
KLMNK KA1 16 E5
St Martins Ga CTBR ML5 110 A5
St Mary's Crs BRHD/NEIL G78 125 J7
St Marys Gdns
BRHD/NEIL G78 125 K7
St Mary's La CGLW G2 11 H1
St Mary's Pl SALT KA21 191 L8
St Mary's Rd BLSH ML4 132 E4
BSHPBGS G64 63 L7
St Mary's Wy DMBTN G82 36 F6
St Maur's Crs
KLMNKN/STW KA3 206 E5
St Maur's Pl KLMNKN/STW KA3 206 E6
St Medan's Pl SALT KA21 191 M8
St Meddans Crs TROON KA10 216 D6
St Meddans St TROON KA10 216 C7
St Michael Dr HBR/GL G84 20 E7
St Michael Rd WISHAW ML2 158 B8
St Mirren's Rd KSYTH G65 47 L1
St Mirren St PSLY PA1 9 H4
St Monance St
SPRGB/BLRNK G21 83 M4
St Mungo Av CGLE G1 5 K8
COWCAD G4 5 M8
Saint Mungo Ct BRWEIR PA11 98 E1
St Mungo Pl COWCAD G4 5 M8
HMLTN ML3 155 K5
St Mungo's LNK/LMHG ML11 199 G6
St Mungo's Rd CUMB G67 48 F8
St Mungo St BSHPBGS G64 83 M1
St Nicholas Rd LNK/LMHG ML11 199 H4
PSTWK KA9 225 H2
St Ninian's LNK/LMHG ML11 199 H4
St Ninian's Crs PSLYS PA2 9 K9
St Ninian's Dr ARD KA22 191 K5
St Ninian's Pl HMLTN ML3 155 M6
St Ninian's Rd HMLTN ML3 155 M6
PSLYS PA2 9 J8
PSTWK KA9 225 H3
St Ninian Ter GBLS G5 11 J6
St Palladius Ter DALRY KA24 184 D1
St Patrick's Ct LNK/LMHG ML11 198 F5
St Patrick's Rd
LNK/LMHG ML11 198 E5
St Peter's La CGLW G2 10 F1
St Phillans Av AYRS KA7 19 H7
St Quivox Rd PSTWK KA9 225 J1
St Ronan's Dr HMLTN ML3 174 C1
PLKSD/SHW G41 104 D8
RUTH G73 129 J3
St Stephens Av RUTH G73 129 J6
St Stephen's Crs RUTH G73 129 K6
St Stephen's Pl SVSTN KA20 192 F7
St Teiling LNK/LMHG ML11 199 H3
St Vigeans Av NMRNS G77 150 B5
St Vincent Crs AYRS KA7 228 F7
KVGV G3 104 D1
St Vincent Crescent La KVGV G3 4 A8
St Vincent La CGLW G2 4 F9
St Vincent Pl CGLE G1 11 J1
EKILS G75 171 G1
LNK/LMHG ML11 199 H5
MTHW ML1 157 L2
St Vincent St CGLW G2 4 F9
KVGV G3 4 C9
St Vincent Ter KVGV G3 4 D9
St Winifred's Wy
WISHAW ML2 159 G5
St Winning's La KLWNG KA13 193 K6
St Winning's Rd KLWNG KA13 193 K6
St Winning's Well
KLWNG KA13 193 K6
St Winnoc Rd LOCHW PA12 120 D6
Salamanca St DEN/PKHD G31 13 M5
Salasaig Ct
STPS/GTHM/RID G33 107 G2
Salen St CARD/HILL/MSPK G52 103 M4
Saline St AIRDRIE ML6 110 D3
Salisbury EKILN G74 154 D5
Salisbury Av KLMNK KA1 212 F2
Salisbury Crs MTHW ML1 133 H8
Salisbury Pl CLYDBK G81 59 K4
PSTWK KA9 225 J1
Salisbury St GBLS G5 11 H7
Salkeld St GBLS G5 11 G7
Salmona St PPK/MIL G22 5 G1
Salmon St GRNK PA15 2 B4
Saltaire Av UD/BTH/TAN G71 132 A4
Saltcoats Rd SVSTN KA20 201 J1
Salterland Rd BRHD/NEIL G78 125 L4
Saltfield La AYR KA8 224 F7
Saltire Crs LRKH ML9 176 C7
Saltmarket CGLE G1 11 K4
Saltmarket Pl CGLE G1 11 K4
Saltoun La KVD/HLHD G12 82 D6
Saltoun St KVD/HLHD G12 82 D6
Saltpans Rd AYR KA8 224 F6
Salvia St BLTYR/CAMB G72 129 L3
Samson Av KLMNK KA1 17 J6
Sandaig Rd
STPS/GTHM/RID G33 107 L4
Sandalwood Av EKILN G74 153 K5
Sandalwood Ct EKILN G74 153 K5
Sanda Pl KLMNKN/STW KA3 207 G4
SALT KA21 191 M7
Sanda St MRYH/FIRH G20 4 A1
Sandbank Av MRYH/FIRH G20 82 D2
Sandbank Crs ALEX/LLW G83 25 M4
MRYH/FIRH G20 82 D3
Sandbank Dr MRYH/FIRH G20 82 D2
Sandbank St MRYH/FIRH G20 82 D3
Sandbank Ter MRYH/FIRH G20 82 D2
Sandbed St KLMNK KA1 16 F4
Sandend Rd PLK/PH/NH G53 126 A2
Sanderling Pl JNSTN PA5 122 D3
Sanderling Rd
PSLYN/LNWD PA3 101 K1
Sanderson Av IRV KA12 203 H8
UD/BTH/TAN G71 132 D3
Sandfield Av MLNGV G62 42 A6
Sandfield Rd PSTWK KA9 225 J2
Sandfield St MRYH/FIRH G20 82 E4
Sandgate AYRS KA7 18 E3
Sandgate Av CAR/SHTL G32 107 K6
Sandhaven Pl
PLK/PH/NH G53 126 A2
Sandhaven Rd PLK/PH/NH G53 126 A2
Sandhead Crs AIRDRIE ML6 111 L8
Sandhill Gdns TROON KA10 216 F6
Sandholes Rd JNSTN PA5 99 J4
Sandholes St PSLY PA1 8 D4
Sandholm Pl SCOT G14 80 F4
Sandholm Ter SCOT G14 80 F4
Sandiefield Rd GBLS G5 11 J7
Sandielands Av ERSK PA8 79 K2
Sandilands Crs MTHW ML1 157 H4
Sandilands St CAR/SHTL G32 107 H4
Sandmill St SPRGB/BLRNK G21 6 E6
Sandpiper Dr EKILS G75 171 G4
Sandpiper Pl EKILS G75 171 G4
Sandpiper Rd LOCHW PA12 120 C7
Sandpiper Wy BLSH ML4 132 E1
Sandra Rd BSHPBGS G64 64 C7
Sandray Av PGL PA14 55 H3
Sandringham Av NMRNS G77 151 G3
Sandringham Dr JNSTN PA5 100 B8
Sandringham La
KVD/HLHD G12 82 D6
Sandwood Rd
CARD/HILL/MSPK G52 103 G3
Sandybrae Rd SKLM PA17 70 B5
Sandy Ct WKIL KA23 181 J6
Sandyfaulds Sq GBLS G5 11 K7
Sandyfaulds St GBLS G5 11 L8
Sandyford Av MTHW ML1 134 D1
Sandyford Pl MTHW ML1 134 D2
Sandyford Place La KVGV G3 4 B8
Sandyford Rd MTHW ML1 134 D2
PSLYN/LNWD PA3 101 M1
PSTWK KA9 222 B8
RAYR/DAL KA6 226 F3
Sandyford St KVGV G3 104 C1
Sandyhills Crs CAR/SHTL G32 107 H6
Sandyhills Dr CAR/SHTL G32 107 H6
Sandyhills Gv CAR/SHTL G32 107 J7
Sandyhills Pl CAR/SHTL G32 107 H6
Sandyhills Rd CAR/SHTL G32 107 H6
Sandyknowes Rd CUMB G67 68 F1
Sandylands Prom SALT KA21 200 F2
Sandy Rd CARLUKE ML8 178 F7
IRV KA12 203 G4
PTCK G11 82 A8
RNFRW PA4 80 C8
WKIL KA23 181 J6
Sannox Dr MTHW ML1 157 H2
SALT KA21 191 M7
Sannox Gdns DEN/PKHD G31 7 H9
Sannox Pl HBR/GL G84 20 F6
Sannox Vw AYR KA8 225 L7
Sanquhar Av PSTWK KA9 225 K2
Sanquhar Dr PLK/PH/NH G53 126 A1
Sanquhar Farm Rd AYR KA8 225 K5
Sanquhar Gdns
BLTYR/CAMB G72 131 H7
PLK/PH/NH G53 126 A1
Sanquhar Pl PLK/PH/NH G53 126 A1
Sapphire Rd BLSH ML4 133 G6
Saracen Head Rd COWCAD G4 12 A3
Saracen St PPK/MIL G22 83 J4
Sarazen Ct MTHW ML1 158 E1
Sarazen Dr TROON KA10 216 E8
Sardinia La KVD/HLHD G12 82 D6
Sark Dr TROON KA10 216 F4
Saskatoon Pl EKILS G75 153 H8
Saturn Av PSLYN/LNWD PA3 100 E5
Saucel Hill Ter PSLYS PA2 9 H7
Saucel St PSLY PA1 9 H5
Sauchiehall La CGLW G2 4 E8
Sauchiehall St CGLW G2 5 G8
KVGV G3 82 D8
Sauchiesmoor Rd
CARLUKE ML8 189 G1
Saughs Av STPS/GTHM/RID G33 84 F3
Saughs Dr STPS/GTHM/RID G33 84 F3
Saughs Ga STPS/GTHM/RID G33 84 F3
Saughs Pl
STPS/GTHM/RID G33 84 F3
Saughs Rd STPS/GTHM/RID G33 84 F3
Saughton St CAR/SHTL G32 106 E2
Saughtree Av SALT KA21 191 M7
Saunterne Rd PSTWK KA9 221 J8
Savoy Pk AYRS KA7 18 C6
Savoy St DMNK/BRGTN G40 12 C8
Sawmillfield St COWCAD G4 5 G4
Saxon Rd KNTSWD G13 81 K2
Scadlock Rd PSLYN/LNWD PA3 8 A1
Scalpay EKILN G74 154 C8
Scalpay Pl KLMNKN/STW KA3 207 G4
PPK/MIL G22 83 K2
Scalpay St PPK/MIL G22 83 K2
Scapa St SMSTN G23 82 E1
Scaraway Dr PPK/MIL G22 83 K1
Scaraway Pl PPK/MIL G22 83 K1
Scaraway St PPK/MIL G22 83 J1
Scaraway Ter PPK/MIL G22 83 K1
Scarba Dr PLKSW/MSWD G43 127 H3
Scarba Qd WISHAW ML2 158 E8
Scarffe Av PSLYN/LNWD PA3 99 M4
Scargie Rd KLMNK KA1 211 L5
Scarhill Av AIRDRIE ML6 110 F4
Scarhill La AIRDRIE ML6 111 G4
Scarhill St CTBR ML5 109 M6
MTHW ML1 135 H7
Scarletmuir LNK/LMHG ML11 198 F4
Scarlow St PGL PA14 34 C7
Scarrel Dr CSMK G45 129 G5
Scarrel Rd CSMK G45 129 G5
Scarrel Ter CSMK G45 129 G5
Scaur O' Doon Rd AYRS KA7 228 C6
Schaw Dr BSDN G61 61 L3
CLYDBK G81 60 D3
Schaw Rd PSLYN/LNWD PA3 102 A3
Scholar's Ga EKILS G75 171 K3
School Av BLTYR/CAMB G72 130 B4
School Brae FAIRLIE KA29 139 L6
Schoolhouse La
BLTYR/CAMB G72 155 J3
School La CARLUKE ML8 178 E7
DMBTN G82 36 D5
IRV KA12 203 J8
KKNTL G66 44 D1
School Pl ARD KA22 191 J7
School Qd AIRDRIE ML6 88 F7
School Rd BSHPBGS G64 44 C8
KBRN KA25 143 G7
NMRNS G77 150 D5
PSLY PA1 102 E4
SHOTTS ML7 113 K6
STPS/GTHM/RID G33 85 L3
WISHAW ML2 160 A5
School St AIRDRIE ML6 111 K7
CTBR ML5 110 A5
HMLTN ML3 156 D8
LARGS KA30 115 J5
SHOTTS ML7 137 M5
Schoolwell St SVSTN KA20 192 C8
School Wynd KBRN KA25 143 G7
PSLY PA1 9 G3
Scioncroft Av RUTH G73 129 J2
Scone Pl EKILN G74 153 K6
NMRNS G77 151 H5
Scone St PPK/MIL G22 5 K3
Sconser St SMSTN G23 62 E8
Scorton Gdns CAR/SHTL G32 107 M5
Scotia Crs LRKH ML9 176 A8
Scotia Gdns HMLTN ML3 174 C2
Scotia St MTHW ML1 157 J2
Scotland St GBLS G5 10 D6
Scotland St West
GOV/IBX G51 104 D4
PLKSD/SHW G41 10 A5
PLKSD/SHW G41 104 D4
Scotlaw Dr LARGS KA30 115 K5
Scotsblair Av KKNTL G66 65 J2
Scotsburn Rd
SPRGB/BLRNK G21 84 C5
Scotstoun St SCOT G14 81 J6
Scott Av JNSTN PA5 122 E1
KKNTL G66 45 J3
OLDK G60 58 D1
Scott Ct HBR/GL G84 20 C8
Scott Crs CUMB G67 68 D2
KLMNK KA1 16 C7
LARGS KA30 115 L7
TROON KA10 216 E5
Scott Dr BSDN G61 61 J3
CUMB G67 68 D2
LARGS KA30 115 L7
Scott Gv HMLTN ML3 156 D7
Scott Hl EKILN G74 154 A6
Scott Pl BLSH ML4 133 H2
TROON KA10 216 D5
Scott Rd CARD/HILL/MSPK G52 102 F1
IRV KA12 203 J8
KLMNK KA1 16 C7
Scott's Pl AIRDRIE ML6 111 H1
Scott's Rd PSLYS PA2 102 C6
Scott St ALEX/LLW G83 25 M4
ALEX/LLW G83 25 M5
BAIL/MDB/MHD G69 108 B5
CLYDBK G81 59 L5
GRNK PA15 2 E6
HMLTN ML3 156 D8
KVGV G3 4 F7
LARGS KA30 115 K7
LRKH ML9 176 B7
MTHW ML1 157 L2
Seabank Av LARGS KA30 115 K8
Seabank Rd AYRS KA7 18 C2
PSTWK KA9 221 H8
Seabank St SALT KA21 201 G2
Seafar Rd CUMB G67 48 F7
Seafield Av BSDN G61 61 M2
Seafield Cottage La
GRNKW/INVK PA16 32 D1
Seafield Ct ARD KA22 191 H6
Seafield Crs AYRS KA7 18 B8
BALLOCH G68 47 L8
Seafield Dr ARD KA22 191 J6
AYRS KA7 228 D4
RUTH G73 129 K6
Seafield Rd AYRS KA7 18 C8
Seaford St KLMNK KA1 16 D5
Seaforth Crs AYR KA8 225 H5
BRHD/NEIL G78 125 H4
Seaforth Pl BLSH ML4 132 F7
Seaforth Rd AYR KA8 225 H5
CARD/HILL/MSPK G52 103 G2
CLYDBK G81 60 B8
Seaforth Rd North
CARD/HILL/MSPK G52 103 G2
Seaforth Rd South
CARD/HILL/MSPK G52 103 G2
Seagate IRV KA12 203 H6
PSTWK KA9 221 J7
Seagrove St CAR/SHTL G32 13 M3
CAR/SHTL G32 106 E3
Seamill Gdns EKILN G74 14 D1
Seamill St PLK/PH/NH G53 125 M4
Seamore St LARGS KA30 115 J5
MRYH/FIRH G20 4 D4
Seath Av AIRDRIE ML6 110 E1
PGL PA14 56 C3
Seath Rd RUTH G73 106 A8
Seath St GVH/MTFL G42 105 J7
Seaton Ter HMLTN ML3 156 A5
IRV KA12 203 J4
Seaview Rd SALT KA21 200 F2
Seaview Ter TROON KA10 217 G5
Seaward La PLKSD/SHW G41 10 B4
Seaward Pl PLKSD/SHW G41 10 B6
Seaward St GOV/IBX G51 10 C3
PLKSD/SHW G41 10 C5
Second Av ALEX/LLW G83 25 M4
BSDN G61 62 A6
CLYDBK G81 59 M6
DMBTN G82 37 J7
IRV KA12 208 C1
KKNTL G66 65 J8
LNPK/KPK G44 128 B3
RNFRW PA4 80 C8
STPS/GTHM/RID G33 85 H4
UD/BTH/TAN G71 108 E8
Second Gdns
PLKSD/SHW G41 104 A5
Second Rd BLTYR/CAMB G72 155 L4
Second St UD/BTH/TAN G71 131 M1
Seedhill PSLY PA1 9 J5
Seedhill Rd PSLY PA1 9 K4
Seggielea La KNTSWD G13 81 K3
Seggielea Rd KNTSWD G13 81 K3
Segton Av KLWNG KA13 193 J6
Seil Dr LNPK/KPK G44 128 B5
Selborne Pl KNTSWD G13 81 L4
Selborne Place La
KNTSWD G13 81 L4
Selborne Rd KNTSWD G13 81 L4
Selby Gdns CAR/SHTL G32 107 K5
Selby Pl CTBR ML5 87 K7
Selby St CTBR ML5 87 K7
Selkirk Av
CARD/HILL/MSPK G52 103 J5
PSLYS PA2 101 G8
Selkirk Dr RUTH G73 129 J2
Selkirk Pl EKILN G74 154 D6
HMLTN ML3 156 E7
Selkirk Rd PGL PA14 54 D1
Selkirk St BLTYR/CAMB G72 155 K2
HMLTN ML3 156 E7
WISHAW ML2 159 J4
Selkirk Wy CTBR ML5 110 E6
Sella Rd BSHPBGS G64 64 D7
Selvieland Rd
CARD/HILL/MSPK G52 102 E4
Semphill Gdns EKILN G74 15 L2
Sempie St HMLTN ML3 155 M5
Sempill Av ERSK PA8 58 F7
Semple Av BSHPTN PA7 58 B6
LOCHW PA12 120 C6
Semple Crs FAIRLIE KA29 139 K8
Semple Pl PSLYN/LNWD PA3 100 B2
Semple Rd PSTWK KA9 225 K4
Semple Vw HWWD PA9 121 M4
Senga Crs BLSH ML4 133 G2
Seres Rd CRMNK/CLK/EAG G76 151 K1
Sergeant Law Rd
BRHD/NEIL G78 147 J1
PSLYS PA2 123 M4
Seright Crs
KLMNKN/STW KA3 212 D2
Seright Sq KLMNKN/STW KA3 212 D1
Serpentine Wk GRNK PA15 3 H7
Sersley Dr KBRN KA25 142 F8
Service St KKNTL G66 29 J8
Seton La ARD KA22 191 J7
Seton St ARD KA22 191 J7
Seton Ter DEN/PKHD G31 12 D2
SKLM PA17 70 B5
Settle Gdns CAR/SHTL G32 107 M5
Seven Sisters KKNTL G66 65 L4
Seventh Av
UD/BTH/TAN G71 131 M1
Seventh Rd
BLTYR/CAMB G72 155 L4
Severn Rd EKILS G75 170 E2
Seymour Av KLWNG KA13 193 M7
Seymour Gn EKILS G75 171 H1
Seyton Av GIF/THBK G46 127 J8
Seyton La EKILN G74 153 L6
Shaftesbury St CLYDBK G81 59 M7
KVGV G3 4 D9
Shafton Pl KNTSWD G13 81 L1
Shafton Rd KNTSWD G13 81 L1
Shakespeare Av CLYDBK G81 59 M5
Shakespeare St
MRYH/FIRH G20 82 E4
Shalloch Pk AYRS KA7 228 B7
Shalloch Pl IRVSE KA11 204 B7
Shamrock St COWCAD G4 4 F6
KKNTL G66 65 K1
Shandon Brae ALEX/LLW G83 25 M1
Shandon Crs ALEX/LLW G83 25 M1
BLSH ML4 133 G2
Shandon Pl GRNK PA15 33 J7
Shandon Ter HMLTN ML3 155 M6
Shand St WISHAW ML2 159 H6
Shandwick St ESTRH G34 108 A1
Shankland La GRNK PA15 33 M7
Shankland Rd GRNK PA15 33 M7
Shanks Av BRHD/NEIL G78 125 J7
Shanks Ct KLMNKN/STW KA3 206 F7
Shanks Crs JNSTN PA5 99 L7
Shanks St AIRDRIE ML6 89 G8
MRYH/FIRH G20 82 E4
Shanks Wy BRHD/NEIL G78 125 J4
Shannon St MRYH/FIRH G20 82 F4
Shanter Pl KLMNKN/STW KA3 17 M4
Shanter Wy AYRS KA7 228 E8
Shantron Rd ALEX/LLW G83 25 L3
Shapinsay St PPK/MIL G22 83 K1
Sharon St DALRY KA24 184 B2
Sharp Av CTBR ML5 109 J5
Sharpe Av IRVSE KA11 209 K1
Sharphill Rd SALT KA21 200 F1
Sharp St GRK PA19 31 M2
MTHW ML1 157 H2
Shavian Ter KLWNG KA13 193 L6
Shavin Brae AYRS KA7 229 K3
Shaw Av BSHPTN PA7 58 C6
Shawbank Pl KLMNK KA1 17 G6
Shaw Br KLMNKN/STW KA3 206 E1
Shawbridge St
PLKSW/MSWD G43 127 J2
Shawburn St HMLTN ML3 156 A5
Shaw Ct ERSK PA8 58 F6
Shawfarm Ct PSTWK KA9 221 K8
Shawfarm Pl PSTWK KA9 221 K8
Shawfarm Rd PSTWK KA9 221 K8
Shawfield Av AYRS KA7 229 G5
Shawfield Crs CARLUKE ML8 177 M4
Shawfield Dr GBLS G5 105 L7
Shawfield Rd GBLS G5 105 M7
Shawgill Ct CARLUKE ML8 177 M5
Shawhead Av CTBR ML5 110 B5
Shawhill Ct PLKSD/SHW G41 127 K1
Shawhill Crs NMRNS G77 150 E6
Shawhill Rd PLKSW/MSWD G43 127 K1
Shawholm Crs
PLKSW/MSWD G43 127 H2
Shawmoss Rd PLKSD/SHW G41 104 C8
Shawpark St MRYH/FIRH G20 82 E3
Shaw Pl DALRY KA24 184 B2
GRNK PA15 2 D4
PSLYN/LNWD PA3 100 B4
SALT KA21 192 A7
Shawrigg Rd LRKH ML9 176 C7
Shaw Rd MLNGV G62 62 A1
NMRNS G77 150 E5

PSTWK KA9 221 K8
Shaws Rd LRKH ML9 176 D8
Shawstonfoot Rd MTHW ML1 136 A8
Shaw St GOV/IBX G51 104 A1
Shawwood Crs NMRNS G77 150 E6
Shearer Dr HMLTN ML3 174 C2
Sheddens Pl CAR/SHTL G32 106 F3
Sheena Dr ALEX/LLW G83 25 M7
Sheepburn Rd
UD/BTH/TAN G71 131 L2
Sheila St STPS/GTHM/RID G33 84 E5
Sheiling Hl HMLTN ML3 156 E5
Sheldaig Rd PPK/MIL G22 83 J1
Sheldrake Pl JNSTN PA5 122 D3
Shellbridge Wy ARD KA22 191 J7
Shelley Dr CLYDBK G81 60 A5
UD/BTH/TAN G71 132 B7
Shelley Rd KVD/HLHD G12 81 M4
Shells Rd KKNTL G66 45 L8
Sherbrooke Av
PLKSD/SHW G41 104 C6
Sherbrooke Dr
PLKSD/SHW G41 104 C5
Sherbrooke Gdns
PLKSD/SHW G41 104 C6
Sherbrooke Pl EKILS G75 14 B4
Sherburn Gdns CAR/SHTL G32 107 M5
Sherdale Av AIRDRIE ML6 111 K7
Sheriff Park Av RUTH G73 129 G2
Sherry Av MTHW ML1 133 M4
Sherry Dr HMLTN ML3 156 A8
Sherwood Av PSLY PA1 9 M1
UD/BTH/TAN G71 132 A4
Sherwood Dr GIF/THBK G46 127 G6
Sherwood Pl DRUM G15 61 H6
Sherwood Rd KLMNK KA1 212 F3
PSTWK KA9 225 L1
Shetland Dr KLMNKN/STW KA3 207 G3
LNPK/KPK G44 128 B5
Shettleston Rd DEN/PKHD G31 13 M5
DEN/PKHD G31 106 E4
Shewalton Rd IRVSE KA11 208 E3
Shiel Av EKILN G74 153 M6
Shielbridge Gdns SMSTN G23 62 E8
Shiel Ct BRHD/NEIL G78 125 H4
Shieldaig Dr RUTH G73 129 H5
Shieldburn Rd GOV/IBX G51 103 J3
Shieldhall Gdns GOV/IBX G51 103 J2
Shieldhall Rd GOV/IBX G51 103 H1
Shieldhill Rd CARLUKE ML8 188 F1
Shieldmuir St WISHAW ML2 158 C5
Shiel Dr LRKH ML9 175 M4
Shield Rd GLSTN KA4 214 A4
Shields Ct MTHW ML1 158 B6
Shields Dr MTHW ML1 158 B6
Shields Loan
LNK/LMHG ML11 198 F4
Shields Rd EKILS G75 170 E7
MTHW ML1 158 A5
NMLNS KA16 215 J2
PLKSD/SHW G41 10 C6
Shield Ter GLSTN KA4 214 A3
Shiel Hl AYRS KA7 229 H7
Shiel Pl CTBR ML5 110 D4
EKILN G74 153 M6
IRV KA12 203 J3
Shiel Rd BSHPBGS G64 64 B8
Shiel Ter WISHAW ML2 159 M3
Shilford Av KNTSWD G13 81 G2
Shilford Rd BRHD/NEIL G78 123 H8
Shillay St PPK/MIL G22 83 L1
Shilliaw Dr PSTWK KA9 225 K4
Shilliaw Pl PSTWK KA9 225 K4
Shillingworth Pl BRWEIR PA11 98 D3
Shilton Dr PLK/PH/NH G53 126 C4
Shilton La BSHPTN PA7 58 E5
Shinwell Av CLYDBK G81 60 D8
Shira Ter EKILN G74 15 L3
Shirley Qd MTHW ML1 157 K6
Shirrel Av BLSH ML4 133 G2
Shirrel Rd MTHW ML1 134 A5
Shirva Lea KSYTH G65 46 F5
Shiskine Dr
KLMNKN/STW KA3 206 E5
MRYH/FIRH G20 82 C1
Shiskine Pl HBR/GL G84 20 F7
MRYH/FIRH G20 82 C1
Shiskine St MRYH/FIRH G20 82 C1
Shore Rd SKLM PA17 70 A6
SVSTN KA20 201 K2
TROON KA10 216 B7
Shore St DMNK/BRGTN G40 105 M7
GRK PA19 31 L1
PGL PA14 34 B7
Shortlees Crs KLMNK KA1 211 M6
Shortlees Rd KLMNK KA1 211 M7
Shortridge St MRYH/FIRH G20 82 E4
Shortroods Av
PSLYN/LNWD PA3 101 K2
Shortroods Crs
PSLYN/LNWD PA3 101 K2
Shortroods Rd
PSLYN/LNWD PA3 101 K2
Shottskirk Rd SHOTTS ML7 137 K4
Shotts St STPS/GTHM/RID G33 107 K1
Shuna Pl MRYH/FIRH G20 82 E4
NMRNS G77 150 B3
Shuna St MRYH/FIRH G20 82 E3
Shuttle St CGLE G1 11 M1
KLBCH PA10 99 G5
KSYTH G65 47 K1
PSLY PA1 9 G4
Sidland Rd SPRGB/BLRNK G21 84 C4
Sidlaw Av BRHD/NEIL G78 125 J8
HMLTN ML3 155 M7
PGL PA14 54 F3
Sidlaw Dr WISHAW ML2 158 F6
Sidlaw Foot IRVSE KA11 204 C7
Sidlaw Pl KLMNK KA1 212 A6
Sidlaw Rd BSDN G61 61 H3
Sidlaw Wy LRKH ML9 175 M4
Sidney St SALT KA21 200 E2
Sielga Pl ESTRH G34 108 A1
Siemens Pl SPRGB/BLRNK G21 7 G5
Siemens St SPRGB/BLRNK G21 7 G5
Sievewright St RUTH G73 106 C8
Sighthill Ter SHOTTS ML7 113 H7
Sikeside Pl CTBR ML5 110 D4
Sikeside St CTBR ML5 110 D4
Silkin Av CLYDBK G81 60 D8
Silk St PSLY PA1 9 J3
Sillars Meadow IRV KA12 203 K7
Silvan Pl
CRMNK/CLK/EAG G76 152 A4
Silverae Ct LARGS KA30 115 K7
Silverburn Crs MTHW ML1 134 D6
Silverburn St
STPS/GTHM/RID G33 106 E1
Silverdale EKILN G74 153 J6
Silverdale Crs LNK/LMHG ML11 198 F5
Silverdale Gdns LARGS KA30 115 K6
Silverdale St DEN/PKHD G31 13 K8
Silverdale Ter AIRDRIE ML6 89 M6
Silver Firs MTHW ML1 134 B6
Silverfir St GBLS G5 11 L9
Silvergrove St
DMNK/BRGTN G40 12 B7
Silvermuir Av
LNK/LMHG ML11 199 M2
Silverton Av DMBTN G82 37 H6
Silvertonhill Av HMLTN ML3 174 E1
Silvertonhill La DMBTN G82 37 H6
Silvertonhill Pl HMLTN ML3 174 D2
Silverwells UD/BTH/TAN G71 132 A8
Silverwells Crs
UD/BTH/TAN G71 132 A8
Silverwood Rd
KLMNKN/STW KA3 212 D1
Simonsburn Rd KLMNK KA1 211 L6
Simons Crs KLMNK KA1 211 L5
RNFRW PA4 80 D4
Simpson Ct CLYDBK G81 60 A7
UD/BTH/TAN G71 131 M3
Simpson Dr EKILS G75 14 C7
SALT KA21 191 M6
Simpson Pl KLWNG KA13 193 M8
Simpson St CRH/DND KA2 206 A8
MRYH/FIRH G20 4 D3
Simpson Wy BLSH ML4 133 J2
Simshill Rd LNPK/KPK G44 128 B6
Simson Av WKIL KA23 181 L5
Sim St KLMNKN/STW KA3 197 J1
Sinclair Av BSDN G61 61 L3
Sinclair Ct KLMNKN/STW KA3 207 J6
Sinclair Dr CTBR ML5 109 K2
GVH/MTFL G42 127 M2
HBR/GL G84 20 E6
LARGS KA30 115 K4
Sinclair Gdns BSHPBGS G64 84 B1
Sinclair Gv BLSH ML4 132 F7
Sinclair La HBR/GL G84 20 E5
Sinclair Pk EKILS G75 15 G5
Sinclair Pl EKILS G75 15 G6
Sinclair St CLYDBK G81 80 D1
GRNK PA15 3 L9
HBR/GL G84 20 D7
MLNGV G62 42 A7
SVSTN KA20 192 C8
Sinclair Ter LARGS KA30 115 K4
Singer Rd CLYDBK G81 59 M6
EKILS G75 171 M3
Singer St CLYDBK G81 60 B6
Sir Michael Pl GRNK PA15 2 C4
PSLY PA1 8 F5
Sir Michael St GRNK PA15 2 C4
Sixth Av RNFRW PA4 80 C8
Sixth St UD/BTH/TAN G71 108 E8
Skaethorn Rd MRYH/FIRH G20 82 B2
Skaterigg La KNTSWD G13 81 L4
Skelbo Pl ESTRH G34 86 D8
Skellyton Crs LRKH ML9 176 B7
Skelmorlie Castle Rd SKLM PA17 70 A4
Skelmorlie Cross SKLM PA17 70 B5
Skelmorlie Pl KLWNG KA13 193 K6
Skene Rd GOV/IBX G51 104 A4
KLMNKN/STW KA3 207 J7
Skerne Gv EKILS G75 170 F3
Skerray Qd PPK/MIL G22 83 J1
Skerray St PPK/MIL G22 83 J1
Skerryvore Pl
STPS/GTHM/RID G33 107 H1
Skerryvore Rd
STPS/GTHM/RID G33 107 H1
Skipness Av CARLUKE ML8 189 G1
Skipness Dr GOV/IBX G51 103 K1
Skirsa Ct SMSTN G23 83 G1
Skirsa Pl SMSTN G23 82 F2
Skirsa Sq SMSTN G23 83 G2
Skirsa St SMSTN G23 82 F1
Skirving St PLKSD/SHW G41 127 L1
Skovlunde Wy EKILS G75 171 L3
Skye EKILN G74 153 M5
Skye Av RNFRW PA4 80 C8
Skye Ct CUMB G67 68 D1
Skye Crs GRK PA19 31 K3
OLDK G60 59 J4
PSLYS PA2 124 D2
Skye Dr CUMB G67 68 D1
OLDK G60 59 J4
Skye Gdns BSDN G61 61 H3
Skye Pl CUMB G67 68 D1
SVSTN KA20 192 F7
Skye Qd WISHAW ML2 159 L4
Skye Rd CUMB G67 68 D1
PGL PA14 55 H3
PSTWK KA9 221 J8
RUTH G73 129 K6
Skye St GRNKW/INVK PA16 32 C5
Slaemuir Av PGL PA14 54 F3
Slakiewood Av
BAIL/MDB/MHD G69 86 E2
Slatefield KKNTL G66 44 D1
Slatefield St DEN/PKHD G31 12 E4
Sleaford Av MTHW ML1 157 K5
Slenavon Av RUTH G73 129 K5
Slessor Dr EKILS G75 14 F8
Sloan Av IRV KA12 203 K7
RAYR/DAL KA6 227 H3
Sloan Pl AYR KA8 225 K7
Sloan St AYR KA8 225 K7
Sloy St PPK/MIL G22 83 M5
WISHAW ML2 159 G8
Small Crs BLTYR/CAMB G72 155 K2
Smeaton Av BSHPBGS G64 64 B1
Smeaton St MRYH/FIRH G20 82 F3
Smiddy Ct LNK/LMHG ML11 199 G5
Smillie Pl CRH/DND KA2 211 J3
Smillie St GRNK PA15 33 L7
Smith Av GLGNK KA14 167 K3
WISHAW ML2 177 G2
Smith Crs CLYDBK G81 60 B4
Smith Dr SALT KA21 201 G1
Smithhills St PSLY PA1 9 H3
Smith Qd CTBR ML5 110 C2
Smith's La PSLYN/LNWD PA3 9 H1
Smithstone Ct IRV KA12 203 M4
Smithstone Crs KSYTH G65 47 L4
Smithstone Rd BALLOCH G68 47 M7
Smithstone Wy IRVSE KA11 203 M3
Smith St AYRS KA7 18 F5
DALRY KA24 184 C2
GRNK PA15 2 D4
PSTWK KA9 225 J1
SCOT G14 81 L7
Smithview WISHAW ML2 177 J2
Smithy Ct DMBTN G82 35 G1
Smithycroft HMLTN ML3 157 G7
Smithycroft Rd
STPS/GTHM/RID G33 84 E8
Smithyends CUMB G67 49 H4
Smithy Rd DMBTN G82 35 G1
Smollett Rd DMBTN G82 37 H6
Smollett St ALEX/LLW G83 25 K4
Smugglers Brig Rd
CARLUKE ML8 188 B7
Smyllum Pk LNK/LMHG ML11 199 J5
Smyllum Rd LNK/LMHG ML11 199 J5
Snaefell Av RUTH G73 129 J4
RUTH G73 129 J5
Snaefell Crs RUTH G73 129 J4
Sneddon Av WISHAW ML2 159 J8
Sneddon St HMLTN ML3 156 A3
Sneddon Ter HMLTN ML3 155 M3
Snowdon St GBLS G5 11 L8
Snowdon Ter WKIL KA23 181 H4
Snuff Mill Rd LNPK/KPK G44 128 A4
LNPK/KPK G44 128 B4
Society St DEN/PKHD G31 13 H5
Sollas Pl KNTSWD G13 80 E1
Solway Ct HMLTN ML3 174 B1
Solway Pl BAIL/MDB/MHD G69 66 D8
KLMNK KA1 212 B5
TROON KA10 216 E4
Solway Rd BSHPBGS G64 64 D7
Solway St DMNK/BRGTN G40 105 M7
Somerford Rd BSDN G61 61 M8
Somerled Av PSLYN/LNWD PA3 79 M8
Somerset Av HMLTN ML3 156 B5
Somerset Pl KVGV G3 4 C7
Somerset Place Ms KVGV G3 4 C7
Somerset Rd AYR KA8 225 H7
Somervell St BLTYR/CAMB G72 129 M3
Somerville Ct BEITH KA15 144 B8
Somerville Dr EKILS G75 15 G8
GVH/MTFL G42 128 B1
Somerville La EKILS G75 15 G8
Somerville Pl HBR/GL G84 22 E1
Somerville Wy IRVSE KA11 204 B2
Sommerville Dr SVSTN KA20 201 L3
Sophia Crs IRV KA12 203 H3
Sorbie Rd ARD KA22 191 L7
Sorby St DEN/PKHD G31 13 L6
Sorley St PTCK G11 81 M7
Sorn Pl GLSTN KA4 214 C4
Sorn St DMNK/BRGTN G40 13 G9
Sorrel Dr AYRS KA7 229 J6
Soulis St KLMNKN/STW KA3 16 F3
Sourlie Ter IRVSE KA11 203 M4
Souter Dr KLMNKN/STW KA3 17 M5
Souterhouse Pth CTBR ML5 109 M4
Souterhouse Rd CTBR ML5 109 M4
Souter Pl AYRS KA7 19 J9
Southampton Dr KVD/HLHD G12 82 B3
Southampton La KVD/HLHD G12 82 B3
South Annandale St
GVH/MTFL G42 105 H7
Southannan Rd FAIRLIE KA29 139 K8
South Av BLTYR/CAMB G72 155 K4
CARLUKE ML8 178 E8
CLYDBK G81 60 A7
PSLYS PA2 124 F1
RNFRW PA4 80 D6
Southbank Dr KKNTL G66 65 J1
Southbank Rd KKNTL G66 65 H2
South Bank St CLYDBK G81 80 C2
Southbank St DEN/PKHD G31 13 L6
Southbar Av KNTSWD G13 81 G2
Southbar Rd ERSK PA8 79 G2
South Barrwood Rd KSYTH G65 47 L2
South Beach TROON KA10 216 C7
South Beach Esp TROON KA10 216 C8
South Beach La TROON KA10 216 C7
South Beach Rd ARD KA22 191 K8
AYRS KA7 18 C1
South Biggar Rd AIRDRIE ML6 111 H2
South Brae KKNTL G66 44 C2
Southbrae Av BRWEIR PA11 98 B2
Southbrae Dr KNTSWD G13 81 K5
Southbrae La KNTSWD G13 81 L4
South Bridge St AIRDRIE ML6 111 G1
South Burn Rd AIRDRIE ML6 110 D2
Southburn Rd CMPF/LLE G63 27 J6
South Caldeen Rd CTBR ML5 110 B4
South Campbell St PSLYS PA2 9 H7
South Carbrain Rd CUMB G67 69 G1
South Chester St
CAR/SHTL G32 107 G4
South Church Pl
ALEX/LLW G83 25 M6
South Circular Rd CTBR ML5 110 A2
South Claremont La
MLNGV G62 42 A8
South Commonhead Av
AIRDRIE ML6 88 F8
South Crescent Rd ARD KA22 191 K8
Southcroft Rd RUTH G73 105 L8
Southcroft St GOV/IBX G51 104 B2
South Crosshill Rd BSHPBGS G64 64 A8
South Dean Park Av
UD/BTH/TAN G71 132 A7
Southdeen Av DRUM G15 61 H6
Southdeen Rd DRUM G15 61 G6
South Douglas St CLYDBK G81 80 C1
South Dr KBRN KA25 166 F1
PSLYN/LNWD PA3 100 B3
TROON KA10 216 F6
South Dumbreck Rd KSYTH G65 47 H1
South Elgin Pl CLYDBK G81 80 C2
South Elgin St CLYDBK G81 80 C2
Southend Pl BLSH ML4 132 F5
Southend Rd CLYDBK G81 60 B4
Southern Av RUTH G73 129 H4
Southerness Dr BALLOCH G68 49 G4
South Erskine Pk BSDN G61 61 K4
Southesk Av BSHPBGS G64 63 M6
South Exchange Ct CGLE G1 11 J2
Southfield CTBR ML5 110 C4
Southfield Av PGL PA14 54 F1
PSLYS PA2 124 E1
Southfield Crs CTBR ML5 110 C4
PLK/PH/NH G53 126 C1
Southfield Pk AYRS KA7 19 G9
Southfield Rd BALLOCH G68 48 C8
South Frederick St CGLE G1 11 K2
South Gargieston Dr
CRH/DND KA2 211 J3
Southgate MLNGV G62 42 A8
South Glassford St MLNGV G62 42 B8
South Hamilton Pl KLMNK KA1 16 C6
South Hamilton St KLMNK KA1 16 C6
South Harbour St AYRS KA7 18 D1
Southhill Av RUTH G73 129 J4
Southhook Rd KLMNK KA1 16 A1
Southinch Av KNTSWD G13 80 E3
Southinch La SCOT G14 80 E3
South Isle Rd ARD KA22 191 J4
South King St HBR/GL G84 20 F8
Southlea Av GIF/THBK G46 127 G6
Southloch Gdns
SPRGB/BLRNK G21 6 D3
Southloch St SPRGB/BLRNK G21 6 D3
South Lodge Ct AYRS KA7 18 D7
South Mains Rd MLNGV G62 41 M8
South Medrox St CTBR ML5 87 J2
South Mound
CRG/CRSL/HOU PA6 77 G7
South Muirhead Rd CUMB G67 49 G7
Southmuir Pl MRYH/FIRH G20 82 D4
South Neuk KBRN KA25 167 G2
South Newmoor Av
IRVSE KA11 203 L8
South Nimmo St
AIRDRIE ML6 111 H2
South Park Av
BRHD/NEIL G78 125 H6
BRHD/NEIL G78 125 J6
Southpark Av KVD/HLHD G12 4 A3
PSTWK KA9 225 H2
South Park Dr PSLYS PA2 9 G9
South Park Gv HMLTN ML3 156 D6
Southpark La KVD/HLHD G12 4 A4
Southpark Rd AYRS KA7 18 D8
South Park Rd HMLTN ML3 156 D7
South Pl BLSH ML4 132 F5
South Portland St GBLS G5 11 H5
South Rd CRMNK/CLK/EAG G76 152 A4
PGL PA14 54 E1
WKIL KA23 181 J5
South Robertson Pl
AIRDRIE ML6 110 E2
South Scott St
BAIL/MDB/MHD G69 108 B5
Southside Av RAYR/DAL KA6 227 G3
South St CRG/CRSL/HOU PA6 77 H7
GRNKW/INVK PA16 32 C3
RNFRW PA4 79 H5
SCOT G14 81 G5
South Vennel LNK/LMHG ML11 199 G5
South Vesalius St
CAR/SHTL G32 107 G4
South Vw BLSH ML4 132 E5
BLTYR/CAMB G72 131 J8
CLYDBK G81 59 M6
Southview BSDN G61 61 J4
Southview Av
CRMNK/CLK/EAG G76 151 L4
Southview Ct
SPRGB/BLRNK G21 83 M2
Southview Crs BRWEIR PA11 76 D8
Southview Dr CMPF/LLE G63 27 H6
Southview Pl
BAIL/MDB/MHD G69 86 E3
Southview Rd CMPF/LLE G63 27 H6
Southview Ter
SPRGB/BLRNK G21 83 M2
Southward Wy TROON KA10 216 F2
South William St JNSTN PA5 99 M7
Southwold Rd PSLY PA1 102 E4
Southwood Dr LNPK/KPK G44 128 C4
Southwood Rd TROON KA10 220 F1
South Woodside Rd COWCAD G4 4 B4
MRYH/FIRH G20 4 C3
Soutra Pl STPS/GTHM/RID G33 107 H1
Spairdrum Rd CUMB G67 69 G5
Spalding Dr LARGS KA30 115 K4
Spalehall Dr MTHW ML1 134 F6
Spallander Rd TROON KA10 216 F3
Sparrow Gdns KLMNK KA1 17 L6
Spateston Rd HWWD PA9 122 C3
JNSTN PA5 122 D2
Spean Av EKILN G74 15 L3
Spean St LNPK/KPK G44 128 A2
Speirsfield Gdns PSLYS PA2 8 F6
Speirshall Cl SCOT G14 80 F4
Speirshall Ter SCOT G14 80 E3
Speirs Pl PSLYN/LNWD PA3 100 C2
Speirs Rd BSDN G61 62 A6
Spencer Dr PSLYS PA2 123 K2
Spencer Field Gdns
HMLTN ML3 156 F6
Spencer St CLYDBK G81 60 A6
KNTSWD G13 81 M2
Spence St MRYH/FIRH G20 82 C1
Spey Av KLMNK KA1 212 A4
PSLYS PA2 100 E8
Speyburn Pl IRVSE KA11 203 M3
Spey Ct AIRDRIE ML6 111 J4
Spey Dr RNFRW PA4 80 E7
Spey Gdns HMLTN ML3 174 B1
Spey Gv EKILS G75 170 F2
Spey Pl JNSTN PA5 122 C1
Spey Rd BSDN G61 61 J7
PSTWK KA9 221 K7
TROON KA10 216 F5
Spey St STPS/GTHM/RID G33 106 F1
Spey Ter EKILS G75 170 F2
Spiersbridge Av
GIF/THBK G46 126 E6
Spiersbridge La GIF/THBK G46 126 E6
Spiersbridge Rd GIF/THBK G46 126 F7
Spiersbridge Ter GIF/THBK G46 126 E6
Spiers Gv GIF/THBK G46 126 F6
Spiersland Wy BEITH KA15 168 C2
Spiers Pl BEITH KA15 168 A2
Spiers Rd CRG/CRSL/HOU PA6 77 H7
JNSTN PA5 100 B6
LOCHW PA12 120 B6
Spindlehowe Rd
UD/BTH/TAN G71 131 M4
Spindleside Rd MTHW ML1 135 K8
Spinners Gdns PSLY PA1 8 A7
Spinners La CLYDBK G81 60 B2
Spittal Rd CSMK G45 128 F5
Spoolers Rd PSLY PA1 8 B6
Spoutmouth CGLE G1 11 M3
Springbank Gdns IRVSE KA11 204 A2
Springbank Rd AYR KA8 225 H5
PSLYN/LNWD PA3 101 K2
SHOTTS ML7 137 J3
Springbank St MRYH/FIRH G20 4 D1
Springbank Ter
PSLYN/LNWD PA3 101 K2
Springboig Av CAR/SHTL G32 107 J3
Springboig Rd CAR/SHTL G32 107 J2
Springburn Pl EKILN G74 153 G6
Springburn Rd COWCAD G4 6 A8
SPRGB/BLRNK G21 6 B2
Springburn Wy
SPRGB/BLRNK G21 6 C1
Springcroft Av
BAIL/MDB/MHD G69 108 B3
Springcroft Crs
BAIL/MDB/MHD G69 108 B3
Springcroft Dr
BAIL/MDB/MHD G69 108 A3
Springcroft Gdns
BAIL/MDB/MHD G69 108 C3
Springcroft Gv ALEX/LLW G83 25 M6
BAIL/MDB/MHD G69 108 B3
Springcroft Rd
BAIL/MDB/MHD G69 108 B3
Springfield Av BSHPBGS G64 84 A1
PSLY PA1 102 B5
PSTWK KA9 225 K2
UD/BTH/TAN G71 131 M4
Springfield Ct CGLE G1 11 J2
Springfield Crs
BLTYR/CAMB G72 155 J2
BSHPBGS G64 84 A1
CARLUKE ML8 188 F1
UD/BTH/TAN G71 131 M4
Springfield Dr BRHD/NEIL G78 125 L8
Springfield Gdns
LNK/LMHG ML11 198 F4
Springfield Pk JNSTN PA5 100 A7
Springfield Park Rd RUTH G73 129 J3
Springfield Quay GOV/IBX G51 10 D3
Springfield Rd AIRDRIE ML6 111 L1
BRHD/NEIL G78 148 F2
BRHD/NEIL G78 149 J1
BSHPBGS G64 64 A8
CUMB G67 49 G5
DEN/PKHD G31 13 K7
MAUCH/CAT KA5 223 M6
SHOTTS ML7 113 G7
Springfields Gdns LARGS KA30 115 K8
Springfield Sq BSHPBGS G64 84 A1
Springfield Woods
JNSTN PA5 100 A7
Springhead Rd SHOTTS ML7 161 G1
Springhill Av AIRDRIE ML6 111 H1
CRH/DND KA2 210 E1
CTBR ML5 109 J5
Springhill Dr South
BAIL/MDB/MHD G69 108 A3
Springhill Gdns
PLKSD/SHW G41 104 E8
Springhill Pkwy
BAIL/MDB/MHD G69 108 B2
Springhill Pl CTBR ML5 109 J5
KLMNK KA1 16 C5
Springhill Rd
BAIL/MDB/MHD G69 107 M4
BRHD/NEIL G78 149 G4
CRMNK/CLK/EAG G76 151 M2
PGL PA14 34 C8
Springhill Ter IRVSE KA11 204 F7
Springholm Dr AIRDRIE ML6 88 F7
Springkell Av
PLKSD/SHW G41 104 D8
Springkell Dr PLKSD/SHW G41 104 B7
Springkell Gdns
PLKSD/SHW G41 104 C7
Springkell Ga
PLKSD/SHW G41 104 D7
Springkell St GRNK PA15 2 F6
Springside Pl DRUM G15 61 G5
Springs Pk RAYR/DAL KA6 231 J6
Springvale Dr PSLYS PA2 100 F7
Springvale Pk AYRS KA7 18 E7
Springvale Pl SALT KA21 200 F1
Springvale Rd AYRS KA7 18 E7
Springvale St SALT KA21 200 F2
Springwell Crs
BLTYR/CAMB G72 155 M2
Springwell Pl
KLMNKN/STW KA3 197 L1
Springwells Av AIRDRIE ML6 111 J1
Springwells Crs AIRDRIE ML6 111 J1
Springwood Dr KLMCLM PA13 55 K7
Spruce Av BLTYR/CAMB G72 155 J1
HMLTN ML3 156 E8
JNSTN PA5 100 A8
Spruce Ct HMLTN ML3 156 E8
Spruce Dr BLTYR/CAMB G72 130 F5
KKNTL G66 65 G4
Spruce Pk AYRS KA7 229 K1
Spruce Rd CUMB G67 49 K5
UD/BTH/TAN G71 109 J8
Spruce St PPK/MIL G22 83 K4

Squire St SCOT G14 81 K7
Stable Gv PSLY PA1 8 A5
Stable Pl MLNGV G62 41 M6
Stable Rd MLNGV G62 41 M6
Stable Wynd TROON KA10 217 H5
Staffa EKILN G74 172 C1
Staffa Av PGL PA14 55 G2
RNFRW PA4 80 C8
Staffa Dr AIRDRIE ML6 111 M2
KKNTL G66 66 B1
PSLYS PA2 124 E2
Staffa Rd BLTYR/CAMB G72 129 M6
Staffa St DEN/PKHD G31 7 G9
GRK PA19 31 K3
Staffin Dr SMSTN G23 62 D8
Staffin Rd TROON KA10 216 F4
Staffin St SMSTN G23 62 E8
Stafflar Dr KLMNK KA1 211 L6
Stafford Crs
GRNKW/INVK PA16 31 M5
Stafford Rd GRNKW/INVK PA16 31 M5
Stafford St BLSH ML4 132 F5
COWCAD G4 5 L7
HBR/GL G84 20 D7
KLMNKN/STW KA3 206 F7
Stafford St West HBR/GL G84 20 C6
Staffordway South
GRNKW/INVK PA16 31 L5
Stag Ct UD/BTH/TAN G71 132 C3
Stag St GOV/IBX G51 104 B2
Staig Wynd MTHW ML1 158 A5
Staikhill LNK/LMHG ML11 198 F4
Staineybraes Pl AIRDRIE ML6 88 F7
Stairlie Crs WKIL KA23 181 K4
Stakehill LARGS KA30 115 K6
Stalker St WISHAW ML2 158 C5
Stamford St DEN/PKHD G31 13 G6
Stamperland Av
CRMNK/CLK/EAG G76 151 M1
Stamperland Dr
CRMNK/CLK/EAG G76 151 M2
Stamperland Gdns
CRMNK/CLK/EAG G76 151 M2
Stamperland Hl
CRMNK/CLK/EAG G76 127 M8
Stanalane St GIF/THBK G46 126 F5
Standalane KLMNKN/STW KA3 197 K1
KLMNKN/STW KA3 206 B1
Standburn Rd
SPRGB/BLRNK G21 84 C3
Staneacre Pk HMLTN ML3 156 F6
Stanecastle Dr IRV KA12 203 L4
Stanecastle Rd IRVSE KA11 203 M5
Stanecraigs Pl WISHAW ML2 159 M3
Stanefield Dr MTHW ML1 134 E5
Stanely Av PSLYS PA2 101 H8
Stanely Ct PSLYS PA2 124 B1
Stanely Crs PSLYS PA2 124 B1
Stanely Dr PSLYS PA2 101 J8
Stanely Rd PSLYS PA2 101 J8
Stane Rd PGL PA14 54 E1
Stanford St CLYDBK G81 60 C8
Stanhope Dr RUTH G73 129 K4
Stanhope Pl WISHAW ML2 177 G1
Stanistone Rd CARLUKE ML8 179 G7
Stanlane Pl LARGS KA30 115 J6
Stanley Av ARD KA22 191 J6
Stanley Dr ARD KA22 191 J6
BLSH ML4 133 G3
BSHPBGS G64 64 B7
JNSTN PA5 99 J4
Stanley La JNSTN PA5 99 J4
Stanley Pl BLTYR/CAMB G72 131 K8
SALT KA21 191 L8
Stanley Rd ARD KA22 191 K6
SALT KA21 200 E1
Stanley St HMLTN ML3 155 M5
PLKSD/SHW G41 10 B5
Stanley Street La
PLKSD/SHW G41 10 B5
Stanmore Av LNK/LMHG ML11 199 H5
Stanmore Crs LNK/LMHG ML11 199 J4
Stanmore Rd GVH/MTFL G42 128 B1
LNK/LMHG ML11 199 K4
Stanners La GRNK PA15 3 G6
Stanrigg St AIRDRIE ML6 90 A7
Stark Av CLYDBK G81 59 L3
Starling Wy UD/BTH/TAN G71 132 E1
Starryshaw Rd SHOTTS ML7 137 L3
Startpoint St
STPS/GTHM/RID G33 107 G1
Station Av GRNK PA15 2 E5
GRNKW/INVK PA16 50 D5
HWWD PA9 121 M4
Station Brae BRHD/NEIL G78 148 C1
IRVSE KA11 204 C8
Station Br AYRS KA7 18 F5
Station Crs RNFRW PA4 80 E5
Station Dr IRVSE KA11 204 F6
KLMNK KA1 212 D3
PSTWK KA9 221 J8
Station Pl CARLUKE ML8 178 A3
Station Ri LOCHW PA12 120 C7
Station Rd AIRDRIE ML6 90 B7
AIRDRIE ML6 90 F5
AIRDRIE ML6 111 L1
AYRS KA7 19 G5
BAIL/MDB/MHD G69 86 C2
BAIL/MDB/MHD G69 108 C5
BLTYR/CAMB G72 155 L1
BRHD/NEIL G78 148 D2
BSDN G61 61 K5
BSHPTN PA7 58 B7
CARLUKE ML8 178 A3
CARLUKE ML8 178 D8
CMPF/LLE G63 26 F5
CRMNK/CLK/EAG G76 152 A4
DMBTN G82 35 G2
DMBTN G82 36 F5
FAIRLIE KA29 139 K7
GIF/THBK G46 127 J6
GLSTN KA4 214 C3
GRK PA19 31 L1
GRNKW/INVK PA16 50 D4
HBR/GL G84 22 F1
IRVSE KA11 204 F7
KKNTL G66 44 D1
KLBCH PA10 99 G7
KLBCH PA10 121 L3
LRKH ML9 176 B5
MLNGV G62 42 B8
MLNGV G62 63 G2
MRYH/FIRH G20 82 C1
MTHW ML1 134 B6
MTHW ML1 135 H8
OLDK G60 59 H3
PGL PA14 34 C8
PGL PA14 56 D2
PSLY PA1 8 A6
PSTWK KA9 221 J5
RAYR/DAL KA6 227 G3
RNFRW PA4 80 D5
SHOTTS ML7 137 M5
SKLM PA17 70 A4
STPS/GTHM/RID G33 85 G4
SVSTN KA20 201 K2
UD/BTH/TAN G71 131 L3
UD/BTH/TAN G71 132 A7
WISHAW ML2 159 G7
Station Rw CARLUKE ML8 178 A3
IRVSE KA11 209 L3
Station St DMBTN G82 25 K8
Station Wynd KLBCH PA10 99 H7
Steading Dr ALEX/LLW G83 25 M3
The Steading WISHAW ML2 159 H4
Steel St CGLE G1 11 L4
GRK PA19 31 M2
WISHAW ML2 159 H7
Steeple St KLBCH PA10 99 G6
Steeples Vw TROON KA10 216 E2
Stenhouse Av
BAIL/MDB/MHD G69 86 C2
Stenton Crs WISHAW ML2 158 D7
Stenton Pl WISHAW ML2 158 D8
Stenton St CAR/SHTL G32 106 E2
Stepends Rd AIRDRIE ML6 90 D6
AIRDRIE ML6 112 B3
Stepford Pl
STPS/GTHM/RID G33 107 M2
Stepford Rd
STPS/GTHM/RID G33 107 M2
Stephen Crs
BAIL/MDB/MHD G69 107 M4
Stephens Av AIRDRIE ML6 90 F5
Stephenson Pl EKILS G75 14 C6
Stephenson St
CARD/HILL/MSPK G52 102 E1
Stephenson Ter EKILS G75 14 C6
Stepps Rd KKNTL G66 65 L7
STPS/GTHM/RID G33 85 J8
STPS/GTHM/RID G33 107 J1
Steps Rd IRV KA12 203 J4
Stevenson Pl BLSH ML4 133 H2
Stevenson St CARLUKE ML8 178 E7
CLYDBK G81 59 M5
DMNK/BRGTN G40 12 A4
KLMNK KA1 16 B3
PSLYS PA2 9 G6
Stevens Pl GRK PA19 31 L3
Stevenston Ct MTHW ML1 134 A5
Stevenston Rd KLWNG KA13 193 J6
Stevenston St MTHW ML1 134 A5
Steven St ALEX/LLW G83 25 L4
Stewart Av BLTYR/CAMB G72 155 J2
NMRNS G77 150 E3
RNFRW PA4 80 A8
Stewart Ct BRHD/NEIL G78 125 J5
Stewart Crs BRHD/NEIL G78 125 K5
WISHAW ML2 160 A3
Stewart Dr CLYDBK G81 60 B3
CRMNK/CLK/EAG G76 151 K1
CTBR ML5 109 H3
IRV KA12 203 K5
Stewartfield Crs EKILN G74 153 J6
Stewartfield Dr EKILN G74 153 K5
Stewartfield Rd EKILN G74 153 J6
Stewartfield Wy EKILN G74 152 F5
EKILN G74 153 J5
Stewartgill Pl LRKH ML9 176 F8
Stewarton Crs
KLMNKN/STW KA3 207 H3
Stewarton Dr
BLTYR/CAMB G72 129 L4
Stewarton Rd NMRNS G77 150 C2
Stewarton St WISHAW ML2 159 J7
Stewart Pl BRHD/NEIL G78 125 K5
CARLUKE ML8 178 F7
Stewart Qd MTHW ML1 134 B3
Stewart Rd AYR KA8 225 J5
PSLYS PA2 124 F1
Stewarts La WISHAW ML2 159 J6
Stewart St BLSH ML4 133 J4
BRHD/NEIL G78 125 K5
CARLUKE ML8 178 F7
CLYDBK G81 59 L6
COWCAD G4 5 H6
CTBR ML5 110 A1
HMLTN ML3 156 A4
MLNGV G62 42 A8
Stewartville St PTCK G11 82 B7
Stinchar Rd PSTWK KA9 221 K7
Stirling Av BSDN G61 61 L7
EKILN G74 154 A6
Stirling Crs KLMNK KA1 206 C8
Stirling Dr BSDN G61 61 J3
BSHPBGS G64 63 L6
GRK PA19 30 F4
HMLTN ML3 155 L5
JNSTN PA5 99 K7
PSLYN/LNWD PA3 99 M4
RUTH G73 129 H4
Stirlingfauld Pl GBLS G5 11 H7
Stirling Gdns BSHPBGS G64 63 L6
Stirling Pl KKNTL G66 44 E1
Stirling Rd AIRDRIE ML6 69 G7
AIRDRIE ML6 89 H5
AIRDRIE ML6 111 K5
COWCAD G4 5 M9
CUMB G67 69 G3
DMBTN G82 37 G2
Stirling St AIRDRIE ML6 110 F2
CTBR ML5 109 K5
CUMB G67 49 H5
DMBTN G82 25 K7
MTHW ML1 158 B5
Stirrat St MRYH/FIRH G20 82 C3
PSLYN/LNWD PA3 101 H2
Stobbs Crs KLWNG KA13 193 L7
Stobbs Ter KLWNG KA13 193 L7
Stobcross Rd KVGV G3 10 A1
KVGV G3 104 C1
Stobcross St CTBR ML5 110 A3
Stobcross Wynd KVGV G3 104 D1
Stobhill Crs AYRS KA7 229 J4
Stobhill Rd SPRGB/BLRNK G21 83 M2
Stobo EKILN G74 154 C5
Stobo Ct EKILN G74 154 C5
Stobo St WISHAW ML2 159 J4
Stobs Dr BRHD/NEIL G78 125 H5
Stock Av PSLYS PA2 9 H8
Stockbridge Crs KBRN KA25 143 G5
Stockholm Crs PSLYS PA2 9 J7
Stockiemuir Av BSDN G61 61 L2
Stockiemuir Rd BSDN G61 41 J8
BSDN G61 61 K2
Stocks Rd MTHW ML1 135 M8
Stock St PSLYS PA2 9 G8
Stockwell Pl CGLE G1 11 J3
Stockwell St CGLE G1 11 K4
Stonebyres Ct HMLTN ML3 156 A6
Stonecraig Rd WISHAW ML2 159 J7
Stonedyke Crs CARLUKE ML8 179 G6
Stonedyke Gv DRUM G15 61 H7
Stonedyke Rd CARLUKE ML8 179 G6
Stonefield Av KVD/HLHD G12 82 C3
PSLYS PA2 101 M8
Stonefield Crs
BLTYR/CAMB G72 155 J3
CRMNK/CLK/EAG G76 151 J1
PSLYS PA2 101 M8
Stonefield Dr PSLYS PA2 101 M8
Stonefield Gdns PSLYS PA2 101 L8
Stonefield Pk AYRS KA7 228 C8
PSLYS PA2 101 L8
Stonefield Park Gdns
BLTYR/CAMB G72 155 L1
Stonefield Pl BLTYR/CAMB G72 155 H2
Stonefield Rd
BLTYR/CAMB G72 155 J2
Stonefield St AIRDRIE ML6 89 G8
Stonehall Av HMLTN ML3 156 B7
Stonehaven Crs AIRDRIE ML6 110 E4
Stonehaven Rd
GRNKW/INVK PA16 31 M6
Stonelaw Dr RUTH G73 129 H2
Stonelaw Rd RUTH G73 129 H2
Stoneleigh Rd
GRNKW/INVK PA16 32 C2
Stoneside Dr
PLKSW/MSWD G43 127 H3
Stoneside Sq
PLKSW/MSWD G43 127 G3
Stoney Brae PSLY PA1 9 G2
PSLYS PA2 124 E1
Stoneyetts Rd
BAIL/MDB/MHD G69 66 F7
Stoneygate Rd NMLNS KA16 215 H3
Stoneyholm Rd KBRN KA25 143 H7
Stoneymeadow Rd
BLTYR/CAMB G72 154 F4
EKILN G74 154 B4
Stoneymollan Rd DMBTN G82 24 A4
Stonyflatt Av DMBTN G82 37 H4
Stonyflatt Rd DMBTN G82 37 H4
Stonyhill Av KLMNK KA1 211 L5
Stonyhurst St PPK/MIL G22 5 G1
Stonylee Rd CUMB G67 49 G8
Stoopshill Crs DALRY KA24 184 E2
Storie St PSLY PA1 9 G4
Stormyland Wy
BRHD/NEIL G78 125 J7
Stornoway Crs WISHAW ML2 159 L5
Stornoway St PPK/MIL G22 83 J1
Stow Brae PSLY PA1 9 G6
Stow St PSLY PA1 9 G5
Strachan St BLSH ML4 133 G5
Strachur St PPK/MIL G22 83 G2
Strain Crs AIRDRIE ML6 111 H3
Straiton Dr HMLTN ML3 155 K7
Straiton St CAR/SHTL G32 106 E2
Strandhead KLMNKN/STW KA3 197 J1
Strand St KLMNK KA1 16 E3
Strang Pl PSTWK KA9 225 K4
Stranka Av PSLYS PA2 8 C7
Stranraer Dr DRUM G15 61 J7
Stratford EKILN G74 154 D4
Stratford St MRYH/FIRH G20 82 D4
Strathallan Crs AIRDRIE ML6 89 G6
Strathallon Pl RUTH G73 129 K5
Strathaven Rd HMLTN ML3 174 B6
Strathavon Crs AIRDRIE ML6 89 G7
Strathayr Pl AYR KA8 18 F2
Strathblane Crs AIRDRIE ML6 89 G6
Strathblane Dr EKILS G75 170 E1
Strathblane Rd CMPF/LLE G63 27 K6
KKNTL G66 28 E7
MLNGV G62 42 B7
Strathbran St DEN/PKHD G31 13 L8
Strathcairn Crs AIRDRIE ML6 89 G6
Strath Carron CARLUKE ML8 178 A3
Strathcarron Dr PSLYS PA2 102 B8
Strathcarron Pl
MRYH/FIRH G20 82 D3
Strathcarron Rd PSLYS PA2 125 H1
Strathcarron Wy PSLYS PA2 102 B8
Strathclyde Av ARD KA22 191 K6
Strathclyde Dr RUTH G73 129 G2
Strathclyde Pl HBR/GL G84 20 A7
Strathclyde Rd DMBTN G82 37 G4
MTHW ML1 157 H3
Strathclyde St
DMNK/BRGTN G40 106 A7
Strathclyde Vw
UD/BTH/TAN G71 132 B8
Strathclyde Wy BLSH ML4 133 J2
Strathcona Dr KNTSWD G13 81 M2
Strathcona Gdns
MRYH/FIRH G20 82 A2
Strathcona La EKILS G75 14 E8
Strathcona Pl EKILS G75 14 E8
RUTH G73 129 K5
Strathcona St KNTSWD G13 81 M3
Strathconon Gdns EKILS G75 170 E1
Strath Crs NMLNS KA16 215 H3
Strath Dearn CARLUKE ML8 178 A4
Strathdearn Gv EKILS G75 170 E1
Strathdee Av CLYDBK G81 60 B4
Strathdee Rd LNPK/KPK G44 127 L7
Strathdon Av LNPK/KPK G44 127 L7
PSLYS PA2 8 C8
Strathdon Dr LNPK/KPK G44 127 M7
Strathdon Pl EKILS G75 170 E1
Strathdoon Pl AYRS KA7 228 D7
Strathearn Gv KKNTL G66 46 B7
Strathearn Rd
CRMNK/CLK/EAG G76 151 L3
Strath Elgin CARLUKE ML8 177 M4
Strathendrick Dr
PLKSW/MSWD G43 127 L5
Strathfillan Rd EKILN G74 14 D2
Strathgoil Crs AIRDRIE ML6 89 G6
Strathgryffe Crs BRWEIR PA11 76 C8
Strath Halladale
CARLUKE ML8 178 A4
Strathkelvin Av
SPRGB/BLRNK G21 83 M2
Strathlachlan Av
CARLUKE ML8 179 G8
Strathleven Dr ALEX/LLW G83 25 M7
DMBTN G82 25 M8
Strathmore Av
BLTYR/CAMB G72 131 J8
PSLY PA1 102 D5
Strathmore Crs AIRDRIE ML6 89 G7
Strathmore Gdns RUTH G73 129 K5
Strathmore Gv EKILS G75 170 E1
Strathmore Pk IRVSE KA11 204 B3
Strathmore Pl CTBR ML5 110 D4
Strathmore Rd HMLTN ML3 156 E6
PPK/MIL G22 83 H2
Strathmore Wk CTBR ML5 110 D4
Strathmungo Crs
AIRDRIE ML6 88 F7
Strath Nairn CARLUKE ML8 178 A4
Strathnairn Av EKILS G75 170 E1
Strathnairn Ct EKILS G75 170 E1
Strathnairn Dr EKILS G75 170 E1
Strathnairn Wy EKILS G75 170 E1
Strath Naver CARLUKE ML8 178 A4
Strathnaver Crs AIRDRIE ML6 89 G6
Strathnaver Gdns EKILS G75 170 F1
Stratholm Ter NMLNS KA16 215 G3
Strathord Pl
BAIL/MDB/MHD G69 67 G5
Strathord St CAR/SHTL G32 107 G6
Strath Peffer CARLUKE ML8 177 M4
Strathpeffer Crs AIRDRIE ML6 89 G7
Strathspey Crs AIRDRIE ML6 89 G6
Strathtay Av EKILS G75 170 E1
LNPK/KPK G44 127 L7
Strathtummel Crs
AIRDRIE ML6 89 G6
Strathview Gv
LNPK/KPK G44 127 L7
Strathview Pk LNPK/KPK G44 127 L7
Strathview Rd BLSH ML4 132 E7
Strathy Pl KLMNK KA1 212 B4
MRYH/FIRH G20 82 D3
Strathyre Gdns AIRDRIE ML6 88 F4
BSDN G61 62 B4
Strathyre Rd BLTYR/CAMB G72 155 M3
Strathyre St PLKSD/SHW G41 127 L1
Stratton Dr GIF/THBK G46 127 H7
Strauss Av CLYDBK G81 60 E8
Stravaig Pth PSLYS PA2 124 A2
Stravaig Wk PSLYS PA2 124 A2
Stravanan Ct CSMK G45 128 E7
Stravanan Rd CSMK G45 128 D7
Stravanan St CSMK G45 128 D7
Stravanan Ter CSMK G45 128 D7
Stravenhouse Rd
CARLUKE ML8 177 L5
Strawberrybank Rd
KLMNKN/STW KA3 17 H1
Strawberry Field Rd
CRG/CRSL/HOU PA6 77 H8
Strawhill Rd
CRMNK/CLK/EAG G76 151 L2
Strenabey Av RUTH G73 129 K5
Striven Crs WISHAW ML2 159 G8
Striven Gdns MRYH/FIRH G20 4 C2
Striven Rd WMYSB PA18 70 A1
Striven Ter HMLTN ML3 156 A8
Stroma Av PGL PA14 55 G3
Stroma St SPRGB/BLRNK G21 7 H4
Stromness St GBLS G5 10 F7
Strone Crs GRNK PA15 3 G8
Strone Gdns KSYTH G65 47 H1
Stronend St PPK/MIL G22 83 H4
Strone Rd ALEX/LLW G83 25 L2
STPS/GTHM/RID G33 107 H2
Stronsay Pl
KLMNKN/STW KA3 207 G4
Stronsay St SPRGB/BLRNK G21 7 H4
Stronsay Wy IRVSE KA11 204 A7
Stronvar Dr SCOT G14 81 H5
Stroud Rd EKILS G75 15 K9
EKILS G75 171 J4
Strowan Crs CAR/SHTL G32 107 H5
Strowan's Rd DMBTN G82 37 J6
Strowan St CAR/SHTL G32 107 H5
Strowan's Well Rd DMBTN G82 37 J6
Struan Av GIF/THBK G46 127 J6
Struan Gdns LNPK/KPK G44 128 A4
Struan Rd LNPK/KPK G44 128 A4
Struie St ESTRH G34 108 A1
Struma Dr
CRMNK/CLK/EAG G76 151 J1
Struthers Av KLMNKN/STW KA3 212 D1
Struthers Crs EKILN G74 154 B5
Struthers Pl TROON KA10 216 F1
Stuart Av OLDK G60 59 H4
RUTH G73 129 H4
Stuart Dr BSHPBGS G64 83 L1
LNK/LMHG ML11 199 H4
LRKH ML9 176 C8
Stuart Mount Dr WMYSB PA18 50 A8
Stuarton Pk EKILN G74 14 F1
Stuart Qd WISHAW ML2 158 D8
Stuart Rd BSHPTN PA7 58 B5
CRMNK/CLK/EAG G76 152 D1
DMBTN G82 37 J5
Stuart St EKILN G74 15 G2
GTCI KA28 138 A7
OLDK G60 59 H4
Stuckleckie Rd HBR/GL G84 20 F8
Sturrock St KLMNK KA1 16 F5
Succoth St KNTSWD G13 81 M2
Sudbury Crs EKILS G75 153 H8
Suffolk Rd GRNKW/INVK PA16 31 L5
Suffolk St CGLE G1 11 M4
HBR/GL G84 20 B7
Sugworth Av
BAIL/MDB/MHD G69 108 B4
Sumburgh St
STPS/GTHM/RID G33 106 F2
Summerfield Rd CUMB G67 68 A3
Summerfield St
DMNK/BRGTN G40 106 B7
Summerhill & Garngibbock Rd
CUMB G67 68 C6
Summerhill Av LRKH ML9 176 A7
Summerhill Dr DRUM G15 61 H5
Summerhill Gdns DRUM G15 61 H5
Summerhill Pl DRUM G15 61 H5
Summerhill Rd
CRMNK/CLK/EAG G76 151 M2
DRUM G15 61 H5
Summerlea Rd GIF/THBK G46 126 F5
WKIL KA23 181 H5
Summerlee Rd LRKH ML9 175 M4
WISHAW ML2 158 C5
Summerlee St CTBR ML5 109 M2
STPS/GTHM/RID G33 107 J2
Summer St DMNK/BRGTN G40 12 D6
Summertown Rd GOV/IBX G51 104 B2
Sunart Av RNFRW PA4 80 B5
Sunart Gdns BSHPBGS G64 64 C8
Sunart Rd BSHPBGS G64 64 C8
CARD/HILL/MSPK G52 103 L4
WMYSB PA18 50 A8
Sunart St WISHAW ML2 159 G8
Sunbury Av
CRMNK/CLK/EAG G76 151 J2
Sundale Av
CRMNK/CLK/EAG G76 151 K3
Sunderland Av DMBTN G82 36 C5
Sundrum Pk RAYR/DAL KA6 231 H4
Sundrum Pl KLWNG KA13 193 K7
Sunflower Gdns MTHW ML1 157 K1
Sunningdale Av AYRS KA7 229 G6
NMRNS G77 150 F4
Sunningdale Dr BRWEIR PA11 98 C3
Sunningdale Rd SMSTN G23 82 D1
Sunningdale Sq KLWNG KA13 193 J5
Sunningdale Wynd
UD/BTH/TAN G71 131 L6
Sunnybank Dr
CRMNK/CLK/EAG G76 151 K3
Sunnybank Gv
CRMNK/CLK/EAG G76 151 K3
Sunnyhill KSYTH G65 46 F6
Sunnylaw Dr PSLYS PA2 8 A9
Sunnylaw St PPK/MIL G22 83 H5
Sunnyside KLMNKN/STW KA3 206 B2
Sunnyside Av MTHW ML1 134 B4
PGL PA14 55 G1
UD/BTH/TAN G71 131 M4
Sunnyside Crs MTHW ML1 134 A4
Sunnyside Dr
BAIL/MDB/MHD G69 108 F4
CRMNK/CLK/EAG G76 151 K1
DRUM G15 61 G8
Sunnyside Ov PSLYS PA2 101 L8
Sunnyside Pl
BRHD/NEIL G78 125 H7
DRUM G15 61 G8
MTHW ML1 134 A4
Sunnyside Rd CTBR ML5 110 A2
HMLTN ML3 175 G5
KLMNK KA1 211 M7
LNK/LMHG ML11 198 D4
MTHW ML1 159 H1
PSLYS PA2 101 K8
Sunnyside Sq East KLMNK KA1 211 M7
Sunnyside Sq West KLMNK KA1 211 M7
Sunnyside St LRKH ML9 175 M5
Sunnyside Ter MTHW ML1 134 A4
Surrey La GBLS G5 11 H7
Surrey St GBLS G5 11 H7
Susannah St ALEX/LLW G83 25 L4
Sussex St PLKSD/SHW G41 10 A5
Sutcliffe Ct KNTSWD G13 81 L2
Sutcliffe Rd KNTSWD G13 81 M2
Sutherland Av BSDN G61 61 L2
PLKSD/SHW G41 104 C6
Sutherland Crs HMLTN ML3 156 A5
Sutherland Dr AIRDRIE ML6 110 F4
GIF/THBK G46 127 K8
KLMNKN/STW KA3 207 K8
Sutherland La PTCK G11 82 C7
Sutherland Pl BLSH ML4 132 F7
Sutherland Rd CLYDBK G81 60 B7
GRNKW/INVK PA16 32 A5
Sutherland St
BLTYR/CAMB G72 155 J4
HBR/GL G84 20 B7
PSLY PA1 8 E3
Sutherland Ter GLSTN KA4 214 D3
Sutherland Wy EKILN G74 154 C6
Sutherness Dr
STPS/GTHM/RID G33 107 G2
Sutton Ct KLWNG KA13 193 H6
Swaledale EKILN G74 153 J6
Swallow Brae
GRNKW/INVK PA16 50 E4
Swallow Gdns KNTSWD G13 80 F2
Swallow Rd CLYDBK G81 60 D2
WISHAW ML2 159 H6
Swan Pl JNSTN PA5 122 C2
Swanson Rd ALEX/LLW G83 25 K2
Swanston St
DMNK/BRGTN G40 106 A7
Swan St CLYDBK G81 59 M6
COWCAD G4 5 K6
Swan Wy CARLUKE ML8 177 M5
Sween Av LNPK/KPK G44 128 A5
Sween Dr HMLTN ML3 156 A8
Sweethope Gdns
UD/BTH/TAN G71 132 B7

Sweethope Pl
UD/BTH/TAN G71 132 A6
Swift Av GRNKW/INVK PA16 50 F4
Swift Bank HMLTN ML3 155 L8
Swift Cl WISHAW ML2 159 H6
Swift Crs KNTSWD G13 80 F2
Swift Pl EKILS G75 170 E3
JNSTN PA5 122 D2
Swindon St CLYDBK G81 59 L6
Swinstie Rd MTHW ML1 159 J1
Swinstie Vw MTHW ML1 135 J8
Swinton Av
BAIL/MDB/MHD G69 108 D4
Swinton Crs
BAIL/MDB/MHD G69 108 C4
CTBR ML5 109 H5
Swinton Dr
CARD/HILL/MSPK G52 103 H4
Swinton Gdns
BAIL/MDB/MHD G69 108 D4
Swinton Pth
BAIL/MDB/MHD G69 108 D4
Swinton Pl
CARD/HILL/MSPK G52 103 H4
Swinton Rd
BAIL/MDB/MHD G69 108 C3
Swinton Vw
BAIL/MDB/MHD G69 108 C4
Swisscot Av HMLTN ML3 174 B1
Swisscot Wk HMLTN ML3 174 B1
Switchback Rd BSDN G61 61 M7
Swordale Pl ESTRH G34 108 A1
Sword St AIRDRIE ML6 110 F2
DEN/PKHD G31 12 D3
Sycamore Av BEITH KA15 144 B7
JNSTN PA5 100 A8
KKNTL G66 65 K4
UD/BTH/TAN G71 132 C2
Sycamore Ct EKILS G75 171 K3
Sycamore Crs AIRDRIE ML6 111 K3
AYRS KA7 229 K3
EKILS G75 171 K3
Sycamore Dr AIRDRIE ML6 111 K3
CLYDBK G81 59 M5
HMLTN ML3 156 F7
Sycamore Gv
BLTYR/CAMB G72 155 J1
Sycamore Pl EKILS G75 171 K3
GRK PA19 31 J3
MTHW ML1 134 C6
Sycamore Wy
BLTYR/CAMB G72 130 F5
KKNTL G66 45 H4
Sydenham Rd KVD/HLHD G12 82 C6
Sydes Brae BLTYR/CAMB G72 155 G6
Sydney Dr EKILS G75 14 B7
Sydney Pl EKILS G75 14 B6
Sydney St CLYDBK G81 59 K5
DEN/PKHD G31 12 B3
Sykehead Av BLSH ML4 133 H4
Sykeside Rd AIRDRIE ML6 110 E5
Symington Pl IRVSE KA11 208 F3
Symington Rd North
KLMNK KA1 218 C6
Symington Rd South
KLMNK KA1 218 C7
Syms La AYR KA8 19 G2
Syriam Pl SPRGB/BLRNK G21 83 M5
Syriam St SPRGB/BLRNK G21 83 M4

T

Tabard Pl KNTSWD G13 81 J1
Tabard Rd KNTSWD G13 81 J1
Tabernacle La
BLTYR/CAMB G72 130 A4
Tabernacle St BLTYR/CAMB G72 130 A4
Taggart Rd KSYTH G65 47 M6
Taig Rd KKNTL G66 66 B2
Tait Av BRHD/NEIL G78 125 K5
Tait Wk CARLUKE ML8 188 B8
Talbot EKILN G74 154 C5
Talbot Ct SCOT G14 81 H4
Talbot Dr KNTSWD G13 81 H4
Talbot Pl SCOT G14 81 H4
Talbot Ter SCOT G14 81 H4
UD/BTH/TAN G71 131 L1
Talisman Av DMBTN G82 36 C5
Talisman Crs HBR/GL G84 22 F1
MTHW ML1 133 K7
Talisman Rd KNTSWD G13 81 J3
PSLYS PA2 123 L2
Tallant Rd DRUM G15 61 H6
Tallant Ter DRUM G15 61 J6
Talla Rd CARD/HILL/MSPK G52 103 H4
Tamarack Crs UD/BTH/TAN G71 109 J8
Tamar Dr EKILS G75 170 F3
Tambowie Av MLNGV G62 41 M7
Tambowie Crs MLNGV G62 41 M7
Tambowie St KNTSWD G13 81 L2
Tamshill St MRYH/FIRH G20 82 F3
Tanar Av RNFRW PA4 80 F8
Tandlehill Rd KLBCH PA10 99 G8
Tanera Av LNPK/KPK G44 128 C4
Tanfield Pl CAR/SHTL G32 107 J2
Tanfield St CAR/SHTL G32 107 J2
Tankerland Rd
PLKSW/MSWD G43 128 A3
Tannadice Av
CARD/HILL/MSPK G52 103 J6
Tanna Dr CARD/HILL/MSPK G52 103 M6
Tannahill Crs JNSTN PA5 122 E1
Tannahill Dr EKILN G74 154 C6
Tannahill Rd
PLKSW/MSWD G43 127 M3
PSLYN/LNWD PA3 8 B1
Tannahill Ter PSLYN/LNWD PA3 8 B1
Tannoch Dr CUMB G67 68 F2
MLNGV G62 42 B6
Tannoch Pl CUMB G67 68 F2
Tannoch Rd BRHD/NEIL G78 147 H6
Tannochside Dr
UD/BTH/TAN G71 109 G8
Tannock St KLMNK KA1 16 E8
PPK/MIL G22 5 H1
Tantallon Av GRK PA19 30 F4
Tantallon Ct CARLUKE ML8 178 E6
Tantallon Dr CTBR ML5 87 J8
PSLYS PA2 101 G8
Tantallon Pk EKILN G74 14 C2
Tantallon Rd
BAIL/MDB/MHD G69 108 A6
PLKSD/SHW G41 127 L2
Tanzieknowe Av
BLTYR/CAMB G72 130 B6
Tanzieknowe Dr
BLTYR/CAMB G72 130 B6
Tanzieknowe Pl
BLTYR/CAMB G72 130 B6
Tanzieknowe Rd
BLTYR/CAMB G72 130 B6
Taransay St GOV/IBX G51 103 M1
Tarbert Av BLTYR/CAMB G72 131 J7
WISHAW ML2 159 G8
WKIL KA23 181 L4
Tarbert Ct HMLTN ML3 156 A8
Tarbert Pl CARLUKE ML8 179 G8
Tarbet St GRK PA19 31 M2
Tarbolton EKILN G74 154 D6
Tarbolton Crs AIRDRIE ML6 134 D1
Tarbolton Dr CLYDBK G81 60 C6
Tarbolton Pth LRKH ML9 175 M6
Tarbolton Pl
KLMNKN/STW KA3 207 J3
Tarbolton Rd CRH/DND KA2 209 M8
CUMB G67 49 H7
KLMNK KA1 218 F4
PLKSW/MSWD G43 127 K3
PSTWK KA9 221 K5
Tarbrax Wy HMLTN ML3 156 A6
Tarfside Av
CARD/HILL/MSPK G52 103 K5
Tarfside Gdns
CARD/HILL/MSPK G52 103 K5
Tarfside Ov
CARD/HILL/MSPK G52 103 K5
Target Rd AIRDRIE ML6 111 H3
Tarland St GOV/IBX G51 103 M3
Tarras Dr RNFRW PA4 80 E8
Tarryholme Dr IRV KA12 203 J7
Tasker St GRNKW/INVK PA16 32 B4
Tasman Dr EKILS G75 171 H2
Tasmania Qd WISHAW ML2 159 L6
Tassie Pl EKILN G74 15 K2
Tassie St PLKSW/MSWD G43 127 K1
Tattershall Rd
STPS/GTHM/RID G33 85 J7
Tavistock Dr
PLKSW/MSWD G43 127 K4
Tay Av PSLYS PA2 100 F8
RNFRW PA4 80 E6
Taybank Dr AYRS KA7 229 G6
Tay Ct EKILS G75 170 E1
Tay Crs BSHPBGS G64 64 B8
STPS/GTHM/RID G33 84 E8
Tay Gv EKILS G75 170 E2
Tayinloan Dr CARLUKE ML8 189 H1
Taylor Av KLBCH PA10 98 F6
MTHW ML1 134 D7
Taylor Brown Cl
KLMNKN/STW KA3 197 M1
Taylor Pl COWCAD G4 5 M9
Taylor St ALEX/LLW G83 25 J2
AYR KA8 224 F7
CLYDBK G81 80 C1
COWCAD G4 11 M1
Taymouth Dr GRK PA19 30 F4
Taymouth St CAR/SHTL G32 107 H6
Taynish Dr LNPK/KPK G44 128 B5
Tay Pl DMBTN G82 37 H2
EKILS G75 170 E2
JNSTN PA5 122 C1
KLMNK KA1 212 A4
SHOTTS ML7 137 L3
Tay Rd BSDN G61 61 K7
BSHPBGS G64 64 B8
PSTWK KA9 221 J6
TROON KA10 216 F4
Tayside AIRDRIE ML6 88 F8
Tay St CTBR ML5 87 J8
GRNKW/INVK PA16 32 B4
Tay Ter EKILS G75 170 E1
Teak Pl UD/BTH/TAN G71 109 K8
Teal Ct BLSH ML4 132 E1
Teal Crs EKILS G75 170 F4
Teal Dr KNTSWD G13 81 G2
Tealing Av
CARD/HILL/MSPK G52 103 J5
Tealing Crs
CARD/HILL/MSPK G52 103 J5
Teasel Av PLK/PH/NH G53 126 B6
Teawell Rd NMRNS G77 150 D4
Technology Av
BLTYR/CAMB G72 155 J4
Teesdale EKILN G74 153 J6
Teign Gv EKILS G75 170 F3
Teith Av RNFRW PA4 80 F7
Teith Dr BSDN G61 61 J6
Teith Pl KLMNK KA1 212 B4
Teith St STPS/GTHM/RID G33 84 E8
Telegraph Rd AIRDRIE ML6 91 H1
Telephone La KVD/HLHD G12 82 C7
Telford Pl CUMB G67 69 G2
IRVSE KA11 203 M8
Telford Rd CUMB G67 69 G1
EKILS G75 14 D5
Telford St BLSH ML4 133 G3
Teme Pl EKILS G75 170 F2
Templand Crs DALRY KA24 184 C1
Templand Rd DALRY KA24 184 B1
Templar Av KNTSWD G13 81 K1
Temple Gdns KNTSWD G13 81 M2
Templehill TROON KA10 216 B6
Templeland Rd PLK/PH/NH G53 103 J7
Temple Locks Ct
KNTSWD G13 81 M2
Temple Locks Pl KNTSWD G13 81 M2
Templerigg Ct PSTWK KA9 221 J8
Templerigg St PSTWK KA9 221 J8
Temple Rd MRYH/FIRH G20 82 A2
Templeton Crs PSTWK KA9 225 K1
Templeton St DMNK/BRGTN G40 12 B6
Tennant Av EKILN G74 153 G8
Tennant St RNFRW PA4 80 D5
Tennent St CTBR ML5 110 B4
Tennyson Dr DEN/PKHD G31 106 E5
Tenters Wy PSLY PA1 8 B6
Tern Pl JNSTN PA5 122 D2
Terrace Rd GRNK PA15 2 E4
Terregles Av PLKSD/SHW G41 104 C7
Terregles Crs PLKSD/SHW G41 104 B7
Terregles Dr PLKSD/SHW G41 104 C7
Teviot Av BSHPBGS G64 64 A6
PSLYS PA2 123 L1
Teviot Crs BSDN G61 61 K7
Teviot Dr BSHPTN PA7 58 C7
Teviot Pl TROON KA10 216 E5
Teviot Rd PGL PA14 54 F3
Teviot St AYR KA8 225 H6
CTBR ML5 87 K7
KVGV G3 104 C1
Teviot Ter JNSTN PA5 122 C1
Tewkesbury Rd EKILN G74 154 D4
Thane Rd KNTSWD G13 81 J3
Thanes Ga UD/BTH/TAN G71 131 L4
Thankerton Av BLSH ML4 133 M4
Thankerton Rd LRKH ML9 176 B8
Tharsis St SPRGB/BLRNK G21 6 D7
The Loaning KKNTL G66 65 J2
Thimble St DMBTN G82 25 K7
Third Av ALEX/LLW G83 25 M4
DMBTN G82 37 J7
IRV KA12 208 B1
KKNTL G66 65 K8
LNPK/KPK G44 128 B2
RNFRW PA4 80 C7
STPS/GTHM/RID G33 85 H4
Third Gdns PLKSD/SHW G41 104 A5
Thirdpart Crs KNTSWD G13 80 E2
Thirdpart Pl KLMNK KA1 16 B6
Third Rd BLTYR/CAMB G72 155 L4
Third St UD/BTH/TAN G71 131 M1
Thirlmere EKILS G75 170 F4
Thistle Bank KKNTL G66 65 K5
Thistle Crs LRKH ML9 176 B7
Thistledown Gv CTBR ML5 110 C3
Thistle Gdns MTHW ML1 134 A5
Thistle Pl EKILN G74 153 K6
Thistle Qd AIRDRIE ML6 89 H8
Thistle Rd MTHW ML1 134 A5
Thistle St AIRDRIE ML6 89 H8
GBLS G5 11 J6
KKNTL G66 65 K2
MTHW ML1 135 J8
PSLYS PA2 8 C8
Thistle Ter GBLS G5 11 H7
Thomas Campbell St
SALT KA21 201 G1
Thomas Muir Av
BSHPBGS G64 84 A1
Thomas Muir La GRNK PA15 33 M7
Thomas Muir St GRNK PA15 33 M7
Thomas St ALEX/LLW G83 25 L5
PSLY PA1 8 B5
Thompson Av KKNTL G66 65 L1
Thompson Pl CLYDBK G81 60 C3
Thompson St DEN/PKHD G31 12 E3
Thomson Av JNSTN PA5 99 L6
WISHAW ML2 158 D8
Thomson Dr AIRDRIE ML6 110 F3
BSDN G61 61 M3
UD/BTH/TAN G71 132 D4
Thomson Gv
BLTYR/CAMB G72 130 A2
Thomson St AYR KA8 225 J7
CARLUKE ML8 178 F8
JNSTN PA5 99 L7
KLMNKN/STW KA3 16 F1
RNFRW PA4 80 C7
Thomson Ter
KLMNKN/STW KA3 197 J1
SHOTTS ML7 137 K4
Thom St GRNKW/INVK PA16 32 C5
Thorn Av EKILN G74 152 C6
RAYR/DAL KA6 231 H5
Thornbank St KVGV G3 104 C1
Thorn Brae JNSTN PA5 100 A6
Thornbridge Av
BAIL/MDB/MHD G69 108 B4
KVD/HLHD G12 82 C4
Thornbridge Gdns
BAIL/MDB/MHD G69 108 A4
Thornbridge Rd
BAIL/MDB/MHD G69 108 A4
Thorncliffe Gdns
PLKSD/SHW G41 104 E7
Thorncroft Dr LNPK/KPK G44 128 C5
Thorndean Av BLSH ML4 133 H5
Thorndean Crs BLSH ML4 133 H5
Thorndene JNSTN PA5 100 B6
Thorndene Av MTHW ML1 134 C7
Thornden La SCOT G14 81 G5
Thorn Dr BSDN G61 61 K4
RUTH G73 129 J5
Thorndyke EKILN G74 154 C4
Thornhill JNSTN PA5 100 A7
Thornhill Av BLTYR/CAMB G72 155 K1
JNSTN PA5 100 B7
Thornhill Ct KLWNG KA13 193 H6
Thornhill Dr JNSTN PA5 100 B7
Thornhill Gdns JNSTN PA5 100 A6
NMRNS G77 150 D7
Thornhill Pl KLMNK KA1 211 L6
Thornhill Rd HMLTN ML3 155 L5
Thornhill Wy CTBR ML5 110 D5
Thornhouse Av IRV KA12 203 K6
Thorniecroft Dr CUMB G67 68 C3
Thorniecroft Pl CUMB G67 68 C3
Thorniewood Gdns
UD/BTH/TAN G71 132 A3
Thorniewood Rd
UD/BTH/TAN G71 131 M1
Thornkip Pl CTBR ML5 110 D4
Thornlea Dr GIF/THBK G46 127 K5
Thornlea Pl LNK/LMHG ML11 199 M2
Thornlea St CARLUKE ML8 189 G1
Thornley Av KNTSWD G13 81 H3
Thornliebank Rd GIF/THBK G46 127 G5
PLKSW/MSWD G43 127 G4
Thornlie Gill WISHAW ML2 159 H7
Thornly Park Av PSLYS PA2 124 F1
Thornly Park Dr PSLYS PA2 124 F1
Thornly Park Gdns
PSLYS PA2 101 L8
Thornly Park Rd PSLYS PA2 101 M8
Thorn Rd BLSH ML4 133 H4
BSDN G61 61 J4
Thornside Rd JNSTN PA5 100 A6
Thorn Ter KLMNKN/STW KA3 207 G5
Thornton Av CRH/DND KA2 205 L8
Thornton Pl HMLTN ML3 174 D3
Thornton Rd EKILN G74 152 C6
Thornton St CTBR ML5 87 K7
MRYH/FIRH G20 82 D2
Thorntree Av BEITH KA15 144 B7
BLTYR/CAMB G72 155 M4
HMLTN ML3 155 M4
Thorntree Wy
UD/BTH/TAN G71 132 B6
Thornwood Av AYR KA8 225 L7
KKNTL G66 65 G4
PTCK G11 82 A7
Thornwood Crs PTCK G11 81 M6
Thornwood Dr BRWEIR PA11 98 B2
IRV KA12 203 J7
PTCK G11 81 M6
Thornwood Gdns PTCK G11 82 A7
Thornwood Pl PTCK G11 81 M6
Thornwood Qd PTCK G11 81 M6
Thornwood Rd PTCK G11 81 M7
Thornwood Ter PTCK G11 81 M7
Thornyburn Dr
BAIL/MDB/MHD G69 108 D5
Thornyburn Pl
BAIL/MDB/MHD G69 108 C5
Thornyflat Crs AYR KA8 225 M7
Thornyflat Dr AYR KA8 225 L7
Thornyflat Pl AYR KA8 225 M7
Thornyflat Rd AYR KA8 225 L7
Thornyflat St AYR KA8 225 L7
Thrashbush Av WISHAW ML2 159 K5
Thrashbush Crs WISHAW ML2 159 K5
Thrashbush Rd WISHAW ML2 159 K6
Threave Ct CARLUKE ML8 178 E5
Threave Pl NMRNS G77 150 B4
Threepwood Rd BEITH KA15 144 D8
Threestonehill Av
CAR/SHTL G32 107 H3
Threshold EKILN G74 15 J2
Threshold Pk EKILN G74 15 J2
Thriplee Rd BRWEIR PA11 98 C1
Thrums EKILN G74 154 D4
Thrums Av BSHPBGS G64 64 C8
Thrushbush La AIRDRIE ML6 89 H7
Thrushbush Qd AIRDRIE ML6 89 G7
Thrushbush Rd AIRDRIE ML6 89 G7
Thrushcraig Crs PSLYS PA2 9 J9
Thrush Pl JNSTN PA5 122 D2
Thurso St PTCK G11 82 C8
Thurston Rd
CARD/HILL/MSPK G52 103 G4
Thyme Sq MTHW ML1 157 L1
Tibbermore Rd PTCK G11 82 A6
Tig Rd AYR KA8 225 G6
Tillanburn Rd MTHW ML1 134 F6
Tillet Ov PSLYN/LNWD PA3 101 K2
Tillie St MRYH/FIRH G20 4 C3
Till St WISHAW ML2 159 H3
Tillycairn Dr
STPS/GTHM/RID G33 85 K7
Tillycairn Rd
STPS/GTHM/RID G33 85 K7
Tillycairn St
STPS/GTHM/RID G33 85 L7
Tilt Rd WISHAW ML2 159 M3
Tilt St STPS/GTHM/RID G33 84 E7
Timmons Gv BLSH ML4 133 K4
Timmons Ter AIRDRIE ML6 111 K8
Tinker's La MTHW ML1 157 J3
Tintagel Gdns
BAIL/MDB/MHD G69 66 F6
Tinto Av KLMNK KA1 212 A5
Tintock Rd KKNTL G66 46 B7
Tinto Crs WISHAW ML2 159 J7
Tinto Dr BRHD/NEIL G78 149 J1
Tinto Rd AIRDRIE ML6 111 H3
BSDN G61 61 H3
PLKSW/MSWD G43 127 J4
Tinto St WISHAW ML2 159 J7
Tinto Vw HMLTN ML3 174 E1
Tinto Wy EKILS G75 171 H4
Tinwald Pth
CARD/HILL/MSPK G52 103 G4
Tiree EKILN G74 172 C2
Tiree Av PGL PA14 55 G2
RNFRW PA4 102 C1
Tiree Ct CUMB G67 68 D1
Tiree Crs WISHAW ML2 159 M2
Tiree Dr CUMB G67 68 D1
Tiree Gdns AIRDRIE ML6 88 F4
BSDN G61 61 H3
OLDK G60 59 J3
Tiree Gra HMLTN ML3 155 M8
Tiree Pl CTBR ML5 109 L5
NMRNS G77 150 B3
OLDK G60 59 J3
SVSTN KA20 192 F8
Tiree Rd CUMB G67 68 D1
Tiree St SPRGB/BLRNK G21 7 J4
Tirry Av RNFRW PA4 80 F7
Titchfield Rd TROON KA10 216 A7
Titchfield St GLSTN KA4 214 B3
KLMNK KA1 16 F6
Titchfield Wy IRVSE KA11 204 A4
Titwood Dr KLMNKN/STW KA3 206 F5
Titwood Rd NMRNS G77 150 D8
PLKSD/SHW G41 104 C7
Tiverton Av CAR/SHTL G32 107 K6
Tivoli Ct EKILS G75 14 F9
EKILS G75 171 L3
Tobago Pl DMNK/BRGTN G40 12 C5
EKILS G75 153 G8
Tobago St DMNK/BRGTN G40 12 B5
GRNK PA15 2 C4
Tobermory Rd RUTH G73 129 K6
Todburn Dr PSLYS PA2 124 F2
Todd St DEN/PKHD G31 13 K1
Todhill Av KLMNKN/STW KA3 206 F5
Todhills North EKILS G75 15 G6
Todhills South EKILS G75 15 G6
Todholm Crs PSLYS PA2 102 B7
Todholm Rd PSLYS PA2 102 B7
Todholm Ter PSLYS PA2 9 M8
PSLYS PA2 102 B7
Todrig Dr KLMNK KA1 211 K5
Tofthill Av BSHPBGS G64 63 M7
Tofthill Gdns BSHPBGS G64 63 L7
Tofts DALRY KA24 184 D2
Togo Pl GRNK PA15 2 B6
Tollbrae Av AIRDRIE ML6 111 H2
Tollcross Park Gdns
CAR/SHTL G32 106 E6
Tollcross Park Gv
CAR/SHTL G32 106 F6
Tollcross Park Vw
CAR/SHTL G32 106 F6
Tollcross Rd CAR/SHTL G32 107 H6
DEN/PKHD G31 13 L6
Tollerton Dr IRV KA12 203 K5
Tollhouse Gdns BLSH ML4 133 J6
Tollhouse Wy IRVSE KA11 204 A4
Toll La GOV/IBX G51 10 B4
Tollpark Crs WISHAW ML2 160 A4
Tollpark Pl BALLOCH G68 49 L1
Tollpark Rd BALLOCH G68 49 L1
Toll St MTHW ML1 157 M4
Toll Wynd HMLTN ML3 174 C2
Tolsta St SMSTN G23 62 E8
Tomtain Brae BALLOCH G68 67 M2
Tomtain Ct BALLOCH G68 67 M2
Toner Gdns WISHAW ML2 177 H2
Tontine Crs DMBTN G82 36 D1
Tontine La CGLE G1 11 L3
Tontine Pl RUTH G73 129 L5
Topaz Ter BLSH ML4 133 G6
Toponthank La
KLMNKN/STW KA3 207 G3
Toppersfield KLBCH PA10 99 J7
Torbeg Gdns EKILS G75 171 H5
Torbracken HWWD PA9 122 A3
Torbreck St
CARD/HILL/MSPK G52 103 M4
Torbrex Rd CUMB G67 49 G8
Torburn Av GIF/THBK G46 127 H5
Tordene Pth BALLOCH G68 48 D6
Torgyle St SMSTN G23 62 D8
Tormeadow Rd NMRNS G77 150 D4
Tormore St GOV/IBX G51 103 K3
Tormusk Dr CSMK G45 129 G5
Tormusk Gdns CSMK G45 129 G5
Tormusk Gv CSMK G45 129 G5
Tormusk Rd CSMK G45 129 G5
Torness St PTCK G11 82 C7
Torogay Pl PPK/MIL G22 83 L1
Torogay St PPK/MIL G22 83 J2
Torogay Ter PPK/MIL G22 83 J1
Torphin Crs CAR/SHTL G32 107 G2
Torphin Wk CAR/SHTL G32 107 H2
Torrance Av AIRDRIE ML6 111 K2
Torrance Rd BSHPBGS G64 64 C2
EKILN G74 14 E2
GRNK PA15 33 H8
Torrance St
SPRGB/BLRNK G21 83 M5
Torran Dr RNFRW PA4 79 L2
Torran Rd STPS/GTHM/RID G33 107 M2
Torranyard Ter HMLTN ML3 155 L8
Torr Av BRWEIR PA11 75 L7
Torriden Pl CTBR ML5 109 L4
Torriden St CTBR ML5 109 K4
Torridon Av MTHW ML1 134 D6
PLKSD/SHW G41 104 B6
Torridon Gdns NMRNS G77 151 H5
Torrington Av GIF/THBK G46 151 G1
Torrington Crs CAR/SHTL G32 107 K6
Torrin Rd SMSTN G23 62 D8
Torrisdale Pl CTBR ML5 109 L2
Torrisdale St CTBR ML5 109 L2
GVH/MTFL G42 104 F7
Torr La BRWEIR PA11 75 L7
Torr Rd BRWEIR PA11 98 C1
BSHPBGS G64 64 D8
Torr St PPK/MIL G22 83 K5
Torryburn Rd SPRGB/BLRNK G21 7 J1
SPRGB/BLRNK G21 84 C5
Torwood Brae HMLTN ML3 155 M7
Toryglen Rd RUTH G73 128 E1
Toryglen St GBLS G5 105 L7
Tourhill Rd KLMNKN/STW KA3 206 F4
Tourmaline Ter BLSH ML4 133 H6
Toward Ct BLTYR/CAMB G72 131 L8
Toward Rd
STPS/GTHM/RID G33 107 J2
WMYSB PA18 50 A8
Toward Vw SKLM PA17 70 B5
Tower Av BRHD/NEIL G78 125 K5
Tower Crs RNFRW PA4 80 B7
Tower Dr GRK PA19 31 K3
RNFRW PA4 80 B7
Towerhill Av KLMNKN/STW KA3 206 B3
Towerhill Rd KNTSWD G13 61 J8
Towerlands Farm Rd
IRVSE KA11 204 A6
Towerlands Rd IRVSE KA11 204 A6
Tower Pl JNSTN PA5 100 A8
KLMNK KA1 211 K6
MLNGV G62 42 B7
Tower Rd BSHPBGS G64 43 J6
CUMB G67 69 G3
JNSTN PA5 99 M8
Towerside Crs PLK/PH/NH G53 103 G7
Towerside Rd PLK/PH/NH G53 103 G7
Towers Rd AIRDRIE ML6 111 L1
Tower St PLKSD/SHW G41 10 A5
Tower Ter PSLY PA1 8 E5
Towie Pl MRYH/FIRH G20 82 D4
UD/BTH/TAN G71 131 M3
Townend KLMNKN/STW KA3 206 C2
Townend La DALRY KA24 184 C2
Townend Rd DMBTN G82 37 G4
KLMNK KA1 211 L6
Townend St DALRY KA24 184 C2
Townend Ter KLMNK KA1 218 C5
Townfoot IRVSE KA11 209 H1
Townhead IRV KA12 203 K7
KBRN KA25 143 H7
KLMNKN/STW KA3 206 C2
KLWNG KA13 193 K5

Townhead Av *BLSH* ML4 .... 133 L1
Townhead Cl *LARGS* KA30 .... 115 J6 10
Townhead Dr *MTHW* ML1 .... 134 F6
Townhead Pl
UD/BTH/TAN G71 .... 132 A1 10
Townhead Rd *CTBR* ML5 .... 87 G8
NMRNS G77 .... 150 D5 3
SALT KA21 .... 201 G1
Townhead St *BEITH* KA15 .... 168 B1 3
HMLTN ML3 .... 156 F6 6
KSYTH G65 .... 47 K2
SVSTN KA20 .... 192 D8
Townhead Ter *PSLY* PA1 .... 8 F4
Townhill Rd *HMLTN* ML3 .... 155 L6
Townhill Ter *HMLTN* ML3 .... 155 L6 3
Townholm *KLMNKN/STW* KA3 .... 17 G1
Townmill Rd *DEN/PKHD* G31 .... 6 E8
Townsend St *COWCAD* G4 .... 5 J6
Tradeston St *GBLS* G5 .... 10 F4
Trafalgar St *CLYDBK* G81 .... 59 M6
DMNK/BRGTN G40 .... 105 M6 5
GRNK PA15 .... 2 C6
Trainard Av *CAR/SHTL* G32 .... 106 F5
Tramore Crs *PSTWK* KA9 .... 225 J1 7
Tranent Pl *MTHW* ML1 .... 135 J7
STPS/GTHM/RID G33 .... 106 E1 4
Traquair Av *WISHAW* ML2 .... 159 J4
Traquair Dr
CARD/HILL/MSPK G52 .... 103 H5
Treebank Crs *AYRS* KA7 .... 19 M9
Treeburn Av *GIF/THBK* G46 .... 127 H6
Treemain Rd *GIF/THBK* G46 .... 151 G1
Treesbank Rd *KLMNK* KA1 .... 211 M6
Trees Park Av *BRHD/NEIL* G78 .... 125 H5
Treeswoodhead Rd
KLMNK KA1 .... 212 A5
Trefoil Av *PLKSD/SHW* G41 .... 127 K1
Trelawney Ter *SVSTN* KA20 .... 201 L3
Trent Pl *EKILS* G75 .... 170 E3
Trent St *CTBR* ML5 .... 87 K7
Tresta Rd *SMSTN* G23 .... 82 F1
Tribboch St *LRKH* ML9 .... 175 M6 3
Trigoni Ct *LARGS* KA30 .... 115 K8 2
Trinidad Gn *EKILS* G75 .... 153 G8 3
Trinity Av
CARD/HILL/MSPK G52 .... 103 J5
Trinity Crs *BEITH* KA15 .... 144 C8 3
Trinity Dr *BLTYR/CAMB* G72 .... 130 C6 1
DALRY KA24 .... 184 B3
Trinley Rd *KNTSWD* G13 .... 61 K8
Triton Pl *BLSH* ML4 .... 133 M4
Trondra Pth *ESTRH* G34 .... 107 M1 3
Trondra Pl *ESTRH* G34 .... 107 M1
Trongate *CGLE* G1 .... 11 L3
Tron Pl *LARGS* KA30 .... 115 J6 11
Troon Av *EKILS* G75 .... 170 C3
Troon Ct *EKILS* G75 .... 171 H3
Troon Dr *BRWEIR* PA11 .... 98 C2
Troon Gdns *BALLOCH* G68 .... 48 F3
Troon Pl *NMRNS* G77 .... 151 G5
Troon Rd *TROON* KA10 .... 217 G6
Troon St *DMNK/BRGTN* G40 .... 13 G9
Trossachs Av *MTHW* ML1 .... 134 A4 3
Trossachs Ct *MRYH/FIRH* G20 .... 4 E3
Trossachs Rd *RUTH* G73 .... 129 K7
Trossachs St *MRYH/FIRH* G20 .... 4 E3
Troubridge Av *KLBCH* PA10 .... 99 J8 1
Troubridge Crs *KLBCH* PA10 .... 99 H7
Trows Rd *WISHAW* ML2 .... 177 H3
Truce Rd *KNTSWD* G13 .... 81 H1
Truro Av *BAIL/MDB/MHD* G69 .... 66 F6
Tryfield Pl *AYR* KA8 .... 225 G7
Tryst Rd *CUMB* G67 .... 48 F8
Tudor La South *SCOT* G14 .... 81 L6 3
Tudor Rd *SCOT* G14 .... 81 L6 4
Tudor St
BAIL/MDB/MHD G69 .... 107 M6 4
Tulley Wynd *MTHW* ML1 .... 133 K7 3
Tulliallan Pl *EKILN* G74 .... 15 K5
Tullichewan Crs
ALEX/LLW G83 .... 25 K2 3
Tullichewan Dr *ALEX/LLW* G83 .... 25 J2
Tullichewan Rd *ALEX/LLW* G83 .. 25 K1 3
Tullis St *DMNK/BRGTN* G40 .... 12 B8
Tulloch-ard Pl *RUTH* G73 .... 129 K6 3
Tulloch Gdns *MTHW* ML1 .... 158 B5
Tulloch St *LNPK/KPK* G44 .... 128 A3 4
Tullymet Rd *HMLTN* ML3 .... 174 D1
Tummel Dr *AIRDRIE* ML6 .... 88 F7
Tummel Gn *EKILN* G74 .... 153 L6 4
Tummel Rd *WMYSB* PA18 .... 70 A1 3
Tummel St *STPS/GTHM/RID* G33 .. 84 E8
Tummel Wy *CUMB* G67 .... 49 G7
Tunnel St *KVGV* G3 .... 10 A2
Tuphall Rd *HMLTN* ML3 .... 156 D7
Turnberry Av *GRK* PA19 .... 31 H3
PTCK G11 .... 82 B6 5
Turnberry Ct *KLWNG* KA13 .... 193 H6 10
Turnberry Crs *CTBR* ML5 .... 109 L5
Turnberry Dr *BRWEIR* PA11 .... 98 C3 4
HMLTN ML3 .... 155 K7
KLMNK KA1 .... 211 M5
NMRNS G77 .... 151 G5
RUTH G73 .... 128 F5
Turnberry Gdns *AIRDRIE* ML6 .... 111 L8 2
BALLOCH G68 .... 49 G4 1
Turnberry Pl *CSMK* G45 .... 128 F5 1
EKILS G75 .... 171 H3
Turnberry Rd *PTCK* G11 .... 82 A6
Turnberry Wynd *IRVSE* KA11 .... 208 D1
UD/BTH/TAN G71 .... 131 L6
Turnbull Av *ALEX/LLW* G83 .... 25 K6
Turnbull Crs *ALEX/LLW* G83 .... 25 K6 1
Turnbull St *CGLE* G1 .... 11 L4
Turner Pl *KLMNKN/STW* KA3 .... 207 G6
Turner Rd *PSLYN/LNWD* PA3 .... 101 M1
Turners Av *PSLY* PA1 .... 8 A6
Turner St *CTBR* ML5 .... 109 M3
Turnhill Av *ERSK* PA8 .... 79 H2 1
Turnhill Crs *ERSK* PA8 .... 79 H2 2
Turnhill Dr *ERSK* PA8 .... 79 H2
Turnhill Gdns *ERSK* PA8 .... 79 H2 3
Turningshaw Rd
CRG/CRSL/HOU PA6 .... 77 L3
Turnlaw *EKILS* G75 .... 171 K4
Turnlaw Rd *BLTYR/CAMB* G72 .... 130 A7
Turnlaw St *GBLS* G5 .... 11 M8
Turnyland Mdw *ERSK* PA8 .... 79 H2
Turnyland Wy *ERSK* PA8 .... 79 H2 4
Turquoise Ter *BLSH* ML4 .... 133 G6 5
Turret Crs *KNTSWD* G13 .... 81 J1
Turret Rd *KNTSWD* G13 .... 81 J1
Turriff St *GBLS* G5 .... 11 G8
Tweed Av *PSLYS* PA2 .... 100 F7
Tweed Ct *AIRDRIE* ML6 .... 111 J4 2
Tweed Crs *KLMNK* KA1 .... 212 A4 3
RNFRW PA4 .... 80 E7
WISHAW ML2 .... 159 J4
Tweed Dr *BSDN* G61 .... 61 K6
Tweedmuir Pl *CTBR* ML5 .... 110 C6
Tweed Pl *JNSTN* PA5 .... 122 C1
Tweed Rd *PSTWK* KA9 .... 221 J7 2
Tweedsmuir *BSHPBGS* G64 .... 64 C7
Tweedsmuir Crs *BSDN* G61 .... 61 L2
Tweedsmuir Pk *HMLTN* ML3 .... 174 C1 2
Tweedsmuir Rd
CARD/HILL/MSPK G52 .... 103 H5
Tweed St *AYR* KA8 .... 225 H5
CTBR ML5 .... 110 A6
EKILS G75 .... 170 E2
GRNKW/INVK PA16 .... 32 B4
LRKH ML9 .... 176 A8
Tweedvale Av *SCOT* G14 .... 80 E3
Tweedvale Pl *SCOT* G14 .... 80 E3 2
Twinlaw St *ESTRH* G34 .... 86 D8
Tylney Rd *PSLY* PA1 .... 102 D4 1
Tyndrum Rd *BSDN* G61 .... 62 B4 2
Tyndrum St *COWCAD* G4 .... 5 J6
Tynecastle Crs *CAR/SHTL* G32 .... 107 H2
Tynecastle Pl *CAR/SHTL* G32 .... 107 H2 5
Tynecastle St *CAR/SHTL* G32 .... 107 H2
Tyne Pl *EKILS* G75 .... 170 E3
Tynron Ct *HMLTN* ML3 .... 155 K8
Tynwald Av *RUTH* G73 .... 129 J5

U

Udston Rd *HMLTN* ML3 .... 155 L5
Udston Ter *HMLTN* ML3 .... 155 M4 1
Uig Pl *STPS/GTHM/RID* G33 .... 107 L4 1
Uist Av *PGL* PA14 .... 55 G2
Uist Crs *STPS/GTHM/RID* G33 .... 107 L4
Uist Dr *KKNTL* G66 .... 66 A1
Uist Pl *AIRDRIE* ML6 .... 111 K3
Uist St *GOV/IBX* G51 .... 103 M2
Uist Wy *WISHAW* ML2 .... 159 L4
Ullswater *EKILS* G75 .... 170 F4 2
Ulundi Rd *JNSTN* PA5 .... 99 L7
Ulva St *CARD/HILL/MSPK* G52 .... 103 M4
Ulverston Ter *HMLTN* ML3 .... 174 C3
Umberly Rd *KLMNK* KA1 .... 211 L6
Underbank *LARGS* KA30 .... 115 H2
Underwood *KLWNG* KA13 .... 193 K5
Underwood La *PSLY* PA1 .... 8 E3
Underwood Pl *KLMNK* KA1 .... 212 A6
Underwood Rd *PSLY* PA1 .... 8 E2
PSTWK KA9 .... 225 K2
RUTH G73 .... 129 J3
Underwood St
PLKSD/SHW G41 .... 127 L1 3
Union Ar *AYRS* KA7 .... 18 F5
Union Av *AYR* KA8 .... 225 G6
Union Pl *CGLE* G1 .... 11 H1
Union St *ALEX/LLW* G83 .... 25 M5
CARLUKE ML8 .... 178 F8
CGLE G1 .... 11 H2
HMLTN ML3 .... 156 D6
KKNTL G66 .... 65 J1 3
KLMNKN/STW KA3 .... 16 F2
LARGS KA30 .... 115 J6
LRKH ML9 .... 176 A6
MTHW ML1 .... 134 A5
NMLNS KA16 .... 215 L2
PSLYS PA2 .... 9 G8
SALT KA21 .... 200 F2
SHOTTS ML7 .... 137 K4
Union Street La
ALEX/LLW G83 .... 25 M5 3
Unitas Crs *CARLUKE* ML8 .... 188 E1
Unitas Rd *BLSH* ML4 .... 133 J4
Unity Pk *SHOTTS* ML7 .... 137 K5
Unity Pl *COWCAD* G4 .... 4 F5
University Av *KVD/HLHD* G12 .... 82 D7
University Gdns *KVD/HLHD* G12 .... 82 D7
University Pl *KVD/HLHD* G12 .... 82 D7
Unsted Pl *PSLY* PA1 .... 9 L4
Unthank Rd *BLSH* ML4 .... 133 J4
Uphall Pl
STPS/GTHM/RID G33 .... 106 E2 13
Upland La *SCOT* G14 .... 81 J5 15
Upland Rd *SCOT* G14 .... 81 J5 16
U P La *KSYTH* G65 .... 47 K1 10
Uplawmoor Rd *BRHD/NEIL* G78 .... 147 J5
Upper Adelaide St
HBR/GL G84 .... 20 F8 3
Upper Arthur St
ALEX/LLW G83 .... 25 K5 1
Upper Bourtree Ct *RUTH* G73 .. 129 J5 4
Upper Bourtree Dr *RUTH* G73 .... 129 H5
Upper Bridge St *ALEX/LLW* G83 .... 25 K5
Upper Cartsburn St *GRNK* PA15 .... 2 F8
Upper Colquhoun St
HBR/GL G84 .... 20 D6
Upper Crofts *AYRS* KA7 .... 228 F8
Upper Glenburn Rd *BSDN* G61 .... 61 K4
Upper Glenfinlas St *HBR/GL* G84 .. 20 E7
Upper Loaning *AYRS* KA7 .... 228 F8
Upper Mill St *AIRDRIE* ML6 .... 111 G1
Upper Smollett St
ALEX/LLW G83 .... 25 K5
Upper Stoneymollan Rd
ALEX/LLW G83 .... 25 G1
Upper Sutherland Crs
HBR/GL G84 .... 20 B6
Upper Sutherland St
HBR/GL G84 .... 20 B6 2
U P Rd *KSYTH* G65 .... 47 K1 11
Urquhart Crs *RNFRW* PA4 .... 80 C7
Urquhart Dr *EKILN* G74 .... 154 A6
GRK PA19 .... 30 F4 5
Urquhart Pl *HBR/GL* G84 .... 20 D5 1
Urquhart Rd
KLMNKN/STW KA3 .... 207 K7 1
Urrdale Rd *PLKSD/SHW* G41 .... 104 B4
Usmore Pl
STPS/GTHM/RID G33 .... 107 L4 2

V

Vaila St *SMSTN* G23 .... 82 F2
Valerio Ct *BLTYR/CAMB* G72 .... 155 K1 3
Valetta Pl *CLYDBK* G81 .... 59 K6
Valeview Ter *DMBTN* G82 .... 37 G3
GVH/MTFL G42 .... 128 A1
Vallantine Crs
UD/BTH/TAN G71 .... 132 A1
Vallay St *PPK/MIL* G22 .... 83 K1
Valley Ct *HMLTN* ML3 .... 156 C7
Valleyfield *EKILS* G75 .... 14 C4
KKNTL G66 .... 45 G3
Valleyfield Dr *BALLOCH* G68 .... 47 L8 2
Valleyfield St *SPRGB/BLRNK* G21 .... 6 B2
Valley Vw *BLTYR/CAMB* G72 .... 130 C3 2
MTHW ML1 .... 158 B6
Vancouver Dr *EKILS* G75 .... 153 H8
Vancouver La *SCOT* G14 .... 81 J5 17
SCOT G14 .... 81 K5 4
Vancouver Pl *CLYDBK* G81 .... 59 K5 2
Vancouver Rd *SCOT* G14 .... 81 J6
Vanguard St *CLYDBK* G81 .... 60 D7
Vardar Av *CRMNK/CLK/EAG* G76 .. 151 K2
Vardon Lea *MTHW* ML1 .... 134 E8
Varna La *SCOT* G14 .... 81 L6
Varna Rd *SCOT* G14 .... 81 L5
Varnsdorf Wy *AIRDRIE* ML6 .... 111 K3
Vassart Pl *MRYH/FIRH* G20 .... 82 F4
Vaults La *KLWNG* KA13 .... 193 L6
Veir Ter *DMBTN* G82 .... 36 E6
Veitches Ct *CLYDBK* G81 .... 60 A3 2
Veitch Pl *KKNTL* G66 .... 44 D1
Vennachar St *SHOTTS* ML7 .... 137 L3
Vennacher Rd *RNFRW* PA4 .... 80 A5
Vennal St *DALRY* KA24 .... 184 B2
Vennard Gdns *PLKSD/SHW* G41 .. 104 F7
Vennel La *KLMNKN/STW* KA3 .... 197 L1
Vennel St *KLMNKN/STW* KA3 .... 197 L1
Vermont Av *RUTH* G73 .... 129 G2 10
Vermont St *PLKSD/SHW* G41 .... 104 D4
Vernon Bank *EKILN* G74 .... 153 L6
Vernon Dr *PSLYN/LNWD* PA3 .... 100 A3
Vernon Pl *CRH/DND* KA2 .... 209 L7
Vernon St *SALT* KA21 .... 200 F2
Verona Av *SCOT* G14 .... 81 J5
Verona Gdns *SCOT* G14 .... 81 J5 18
Verona La *SCOT* G14 .... 81 J5
Vesalius St *CAR/SHTL* G32 .... 107 G4 10
Viaduct Cir *KLWNG* KA13 .... 193 L4
Viaduct Rd
CRMNK/CLK/EAG G76 .... 151 M3
Vicarfield St *GOV/IBX* G51 .... 104 B2
Vicarland Rd *BLTYR/CAMB* G72 .. 130 A4
Vicars Wk *BLTYR/CAMB* G72 .... 130 B4
Vickers St *MTHW* ML1 .... 157 H1
Victoria Av *CARLUKE* ML8 .... 178 E8
Victoria Circ *KVD/HLHD* G12 .... 82 C6 10
Victoria Crs *AIRDRIE* ML6 .... 110 E3
CRMNK/CLK/EAG G76 .... 151 M2
IRV KA12 .... 203 H8
KSYTH G65 .... 47 H1
WISHAW ML2 .... 158 D5 4
Victoria Crescent La
KVD/HLHD G12 .... 82 C6
Victoria Crescent Pl
KVD/HLHD G12 .... 82 C6 11
Victoria Crescent Rd
KVD/HLHD G12 .... 82 C6 12
Victoria Dr *BRHD/NEIL* G78 .... 125 H5 3
TROON KA10 .... 216 C7
Victoria Dr East *RNFRW* PA4 .... 80 C7 3
Victoria Dr West *RNFRW* PA4 .... 80 B6
Victoria Gdns
BRHD/NEIL G78 .... 125 H5 6
KLMCLM PA13 .... 55 J8
Victoria La *NMRNS* G77 .... 150 D7
Victoria Pk *AYRS* KA7 .... 18 D8
KSYTH G65 .... 47 H1
Victoria Park Cnr *SCOT* G14 .... 81 K5
Victoria Park Dr North
SCOT G14 .... 81 L6
Victoria Park Dr South
SCOT G14 .... 81 K6 3
Victoria Park Gdns North
PTCK G11 .... 81 M6
Victoria Park Gdns South
PTCK G11 .... 81 M6
Victoria Park La South
SCOT G14 .... 81 K6
Victoria Park St *SCOT* G14 .... 81 K6 6
Victoria Pl *AIRDRIE* ML6 .... 110 F3
BLSH ML4 .... 132 F5 3
BRHD/NEIL G78 .... 125 J5
KSYTH G65 .... 47 J1
MLNGV G62 .... 42 B8 3
Victoria Qd *MTHW* ML1 .... 133 M4
Victoria Rd *BALLOCH* G68 .... 48 D3
BRHD/NEIL G78 .... 125 H5
GRK PA19 .... 31 J2
HBR/GL G84 .... 20 E7
JNSTN PA5 .... 99 K4
KKNTL G66 .... 65 J5
PSLYS PA2 .... 8 D9
RUTH G73 .... 129 H3
SALT KA21 .... 200 F1
STPS/GTHM/RID G33 .... 85 K4
Victoria St *ALEX/LLW* G83 .... 25 L5 3
AYR KA8 .... 19 H2
BLTYR/CAMB G72 .... 155 K3
DMBTN G82 .... 37 G7
HMLTN ML3 .... 156 B3
KKNTL G66 .... 65 J1
LRKH ML9 .... 176 A6
RUTH G73 .... 129 G1
WISHAW ML2 .... 160 A5
Victor St *AIRDRIE* ML6 .... 90 A7
Victory Dr *KLBCH* PA10 .... 99 G5 2
Viewbank *GIF/THBK* G46 .... 127 G6 3
Viewbank Av *AIRDRIE* ML6 .... 111 H7
Viewbank St *CTBR* ML5 .... 87 M4
Viewfield *AIRDRIE* ML6 .... 110 E2
Viewfield Av
BAIL/MDB/MHD G69 .... 107 M4
BLTYR/CAMB G72 .... 131 L8
BSHPBGS G64 .... 83 L1 3
KKNTL G66 .... 45 H4
KKNTL G66 .... 65 J4
LOCHW PA12 .... 120 B7 1
Viewfield Dr
BAIL/MDB/MHD G69 .... 107 L4
Viewfield La *KVD/HLHD* G12 .... 4 A5
Viewfield Rd *AYR* KA8 .... 225 G7
BLSH ML4 .... 132 F6
BSHPBGS G64 .... 83 L1
CTBR ML5 .... 109 J5
Viewglen Ct *CSMK* G45 .... 128 D8
Viewmount Dr *MRYH/FIRH* G20 .... 82 D2
Viewpark Av *DEN/PKHD* G31 .... 7 G8
Viewpark Dr *RUTH* G73 .... 129 H3
Viewpark Gdns *RNFRW* PA4 .... 80 B7 4
Viewpark Pl *MTHW* ML1 .... 157 J3
Viewpark Rd *MTHW* ML1 .... 157 J3
Viewpoint Rd
SPRGB/BLRNK G21 .... 83 M3
Viking Crs *CRG/CRSL/HOU* PA6 .... 99 K1
Viking Rd *AIRDRIE* ML6 .... 111 H4
Viking Ter *EKILS* G75 .... 171 L3
Viking Wy *GIF/THBK* G46 .... 126 F4
LARGS KA30 .... 115 L6
Villafield Av *BSHPBGS* G64 .... 64 A6
Villafield Dr *BSHPBGS* G64 .... 64 A6
Village Gdns
BLTYR/CAMB G72 .... 131 L8 3
Village Rd *BLTYR/CAMB* G72 .... 130 E4
Vineburgh Av *IRV* KA12 .... 203 J5
Vineburgh Ct *IRV* KA12 .... 203 H5
Vine Park Av *KLMNKN/STW* KA3 .. 206 B2
Vine Park Dr
KLMNKN/STW KA3 .... 206 B2 4
Vine St *PTCK* G11 .... 82 B7 3
Vinicombe La
KVD/HLHD G12 .... 82 D6 11
Vinicombe St *KVD/HLHD* G12 .... 82 D6
Vintner St *COWCAD* G4 .... 5 J4
Viola Pl *BSHPBGS* G64 .... 64 C1
Violet Gdns *CARLUKE* ML8 .... 188 E1 2
Violet Pl *MTHW* ML1 .... 134 B3
Violet St *PSLY* PA1 .... 9 L4
Virginia Ct *CGLE* G1 .... 11 J2
Virginia Gdns *AYR* KA8 .... 225 G7
MLNGV G62 .... 62 C1 4
Virginia Pl *CGLE* G1 .... 11 K2
Virginia St *CGLE* G1 .... 11 K2
GRNK PA15 .... 2 F5
Viscount Av *RNFRW* PA4 .... 80 C8
Viscount Ga *UD/BTH/TAN* G71 .... 131 L4
Vivian Av *MLNGV* G62 .... 41 M8
Voil Dr *LNPK/KPK* G44 .... 128 A5
Vorlich Ct *BRHD/NEIL* G78 .... 125 J8 3
Vorlich Gdns *BSDN* G61 .... 61 J2
Vorlich Pl *KLMNK* KA1 .... 212 A5
Vrackie Pl *KLMNK* KA1 .... 212 A5
Vulcan St *MTHW* ML1 .... 157 L1
SPRGB/BLRNK G21 .... 6 B1 1

W

Waddell Av *AIRDRIE* ML6 .... 88 D5
Waddell Ct *KLMNKN/STW* KA3 .... 206 F5
Waddell St *AIRDRIE* ML6 .... 89 G8
GBLS G5 .... 11 L7
Waggon Rd *AYR* KA8 .... 224 F7
Waid Av *NMRNS* G77 .... 150 C3
Waldemar Rd *KNTSWD* G13 .... 81 J2
Walden Rd *KLMNK* KA1 .... 212 E3
Waldo St *KNTSWD* G13 .... 81 M2 3
Walker Av *KLMNKN/STW* KA3 .... 17 J5
TROON KA10 .... 216 D4
Walkerburn Dr *WISHAW* ML2 .... 159 J3
Walkerburn Rd
CARD/HILL/MSPK G52 .... 103 H5
Walker Ct *PTCK* G11 .... 82 B8 2
Walker Dr *JNSTN* PA5 .... 100 B7
Walker Pth
UD/BTH/TAN G71 .... 132 A1 11
Walker Rd *AYR* KA8 .... 225 H7
Walkerston Av *LARGS* KA30 .... 115 K8 3
Walker St *GRNKW/INVK* PA16 .... 32 C4 3
KBRN KA25 .... 143 G8
PSLY PA1 .... 8 E4
PTCK G11 .... 82 B8
Walkinshaw Crs
PSLYN/LNWD PA3 .... 101 H3
Walkinshaw Rd
PSLYN/LNWD PA3 .... 79 H6
Walkinshaw St
DMNK/BRGTN G40 .... 12 E7
JNSTN PA5 .... 99 M6
Wallace Av *BSHPTN* PA7 .... 58 B6
CRH/DND KA2 .... 209 M7
JNSTN PA5 .... 100 C7
SVSTN KA20 .... 192 D8
TROON KA10 .... 216 D3
Wallace Ct *KLMNK* KA1 .... 212 E3 2
Wallace Dr *LRKH* ML9 .... 176 C7 3
Wallacefield Rd *TROON* KA10 .... 216 D6
Wallacehill Rd *KLMNK* KA1 .... 211 M5
Wallace Pl *BLTYR/CAMB* G72 .... 131 L8
GRNK PA15 .... 2 D4
HMLTN ML3 .... 157 G7
Wallace Rd *IRV* KA12 .... 203 J5
MTHW ML1 .... 134 B7 1
PSLYN/LNWD PA3 .... 80 A8
WMYSB PA18 .... 70 A1
Wallace St *AIRDRIE* ML6 .... 90 A7
CLYDBK G81 .... 80 B1
CTBR ML5 .... 110 A4
DMBTN G82 .... 37 G7
GBLS G5 .... 11 G5 1
GLSTN KA4 .... 214 C3
GRNKW/INVK PA16 .... 32 D5
KLMNK KA1 .... 16 D7
MTHW ML1 .... 157 K2
PGL PA14 .... 34 E8
PSLYN/LNWD PA3 .... 9 G1
RUTH G73 .... 129 G2 11
Wallacetown Av
KLMNKN/STW KA3 .... 207 H3 4
Wallace Vw *KLMNK* KA1 .... 211 M4
Wallace Wy *LNK/LMHG* ML11 .... 199 J5
Wallacewell Crs
SPRGB/BLRNK G21 .... 84 B4
Wallacewell Pl
SPRGB/BLRNK G21 .... 84 B4 2
Wallacewell Qd
SPRGB/BLRNK G21 .... 84 C3
Wallacewell Rd
SPRGB/BLRNK G21 .... 84 B4
Wallbrae Rd *CUMB* G67 .... 68 F1
Wallneuk *PSLY* PA1 .... 9 J2
Wallneuk Rd *PSLYN/LNWD* PA3 .... 9 K2
Walls St *CGLE* G1 .... 11 L2
Walmer Crs *GOV/IBX* G51 .... 104 C4
Walnut Crs *JNSTN* PA5 .... 123 H1
PPK/MIL G22 .... 83 K4
Walnut Dr *KKNTL* G66 .... 65 H3 3
Walnut Pl *PPK/MIL* G22 .... 83 K4 3
UD/BTH/TAN G71 .... 109 J8 1
Walnut Rd *KLMNK* KA1 .... 211 J2
PPK/MIL G22 .... 83 J4
Walpole Pl *JNSTN* PA5 .... 122 C2
Walter St *DEN/PKHD* G31 .... 13 H1
WISHAW ML2 .... 159 K6
Walton Av *NMRNS* G77 .... 150 C3
Walton St *BRHD/NEIL* G78 .... 125 J6
PLKSD/SHW G41 .... 127 L1 1
Wamba Av *KNTSWD* G13 .... 81 L1
Wamphray Pl *EKILS* G75 .... 170 D2
Wandilla Av *CLYDBK* G81 .... 60 D7 2
Wanlock St *GOV/IBX* G51 .... 82 A8
Wards Ct *AYR* KA8 .... 225 H5
Wardend Rd *BSHPBGS* G64 .... 44 B8
Warden Rd *KNTSWD* G13 .... 81 K2
Wardhill Rd *SPRGB/BLRNK* G21 .... 84 B4
Wardhouse Rd *PSLYS* PA2 .... 124 C2
Wardie Pl
STPS/GTHM/RID G33 .... 107 M2 3
Wardie Rd *BAIL/MDB/MHD* G69 .. 108 A2
Wardlaw Av *RUTH* G73 .... 129 H2
Wardlaw Crs *EKILS* G75 .... 15 H9
TROON KA10 .... 217 G5
Wardlaw Dr *RUTH* G73 .... 129 H2 2
Wardlaw Gdns *IRVSE* KA11 .... 204 B2
Wardlaw Rd *BSDN* G61 .... 61 M8
KLMNKN/STW KA3 .... 207 L4
Wardneuk *PSTWK* KA9 .... 225 J3 4
Wardneuk Dr
KLMNKN/STW KA3 .... 207 G5
Wardpark Ct *CUMB* G67 .... 49 K3
Wardpark Pl *CUMB* G67 .... 49 K3
Wardpark Rd *CUMB* G67 .... 49 J3
Ward Rd *AYR* KA8 .... 225 H5
Wardrop Pl *EKILN* G74 .... 153 M6 3
Wardrop St *BEITH* KA15 .... 168 C1
GOV/IBX G51 .... 104 A1 3
PSLY PA1 .... 9 G5
Wards Crs *CTBR* ML5 .... 109 L4
Wards Pl *KLMNK* KA1 .... 16 E6
Ware Rd *STPS/GTHM/RID* G33 .... 107 M2
Warilda Av *CLYDBK* G81 .... 60 C7 2
Warlock Dr *BRWEIR* PA11 .... 76 D8 3
Warlock Rd *BRWEIR* PA11 .... 76 D7
Warly Dr *CRH/DND* KA2 .... 209 M8
Warly Pl *CRH/DND* KA2 .... 209 M8
Warner St *SVSTN* KA20 .... 201 K2
Warnock Crs *BLSH* ML4 .... 133 H5
Warnock Rd *NMRNS* G77 .... 150 C2
Warnock St *COWCAD* G4 .... 6 B9
Warren Park Ms *LARGS* KA30 .... 115 K8
Warrenpark Rd *LARGS* KA30 .... 115 K8
Warren Rd *HMLTN* ML3 .... 174 D1
Warren St *GVH/MTFL* G42 .... 105 H8
Warren Wk *KKNTL* G66 .... 44 E2
Warriston Crs
STPS/GTHM/RID G33 .... 7 M9
Warriston Pl *CAR/SHTL* G32 .... 107 H2 3
Warriston St
STPS/GTHM/RID G33 .... 7 L9
Warrix Av *IRV* KA12 .... 203 K7
Warrix Gdns *TROON* KA10 .... 220 E1
Warroch St *KVGV* G3 .... 10 D2
Warwick *EKILN* G74 .... 154 C5
Warwick Gv
BLTYR/CAMB G72 .... 155 L4 3
Warwickhill Rd *KLMNK* KA1 .... 16 B2
Warwick Rd *GRNKW/INVK* PA16 .... 31 L5
Washington Rd *KKNTL* G66 .... 45 H8
PSLYN/LNWD PA3 .... 101 M1
Washington St *KVGV* G3 .... 10 E3
Watchmeal Crs *CLYDBK* G81 .... 60 C2
Waterbank Rd
CRMNK/CLK/EAG G76 .... 152 D3
Watercut Rd *IRV* KA12 .... 202 F1
Waterfoot Av *PLK/PH/NH* G53 .... 126 C1
Waterfoot Rd *NMRNS* G77 .... 150 F6
Waterfoot Rw
CRMNK/CLK/EAG G76 .... 151 L6
Waterfoot Ter
PLK/PH/NH G53 .... 126 C1 4
Waterford Rd *GIF/THBK* G46 .... 127 H6
Waterlands Gdns
CARLUKE ML8 .... 179 G6 2
Waterlands Pl *CARLUKE* ML8 .... 178 A5 3
Waterlands Rd *CARLUKE* ML8 .... 178 B3
Waterloo Dr
LNK/LMHG ML11 .... 199 G4 1
Waterloo La *CGLW* G2 .... 11 G1
Waterloo Rd *LNK/LMHG* ML11 .... 198 F3
PSTWK KA9 .... 225 H4
Waterloo St *CGLW* G2 .... 10 F1
Watermill Av *KKNTL* G66 .... 65 K5
Water Rd *BRHD/NEIL* G78 .... 125 J6
Water Rw *GOV/IBX* G51 .... 104 A1
Watersaugh Dr *MTHW* ML1 .... 135 H7
Waterside *IRV* KA12 .... 203 H6
Waterside Av *NMRNS* G77 .... 150 C5
Waterside Ct *KLMNK* KA1 .... 16 E5
Waterside Dr *NMRNS* G77 .... 150 C5
Waterside Gdns
CRMNK/CLK/EAG G76 .... 152 D2
HMLTN ML3 .... 156 E8 3
Waterside Rd *CRMNK/CLK/EAG* G76 152 D1 2
KKNTL G66 .... 65 L2

KLWNG KA13 193 L5
Waterside St GBLS G5 11 L8
KLMNK KA1 16 E5
LARGS KA30 115 K6
Waterston Wy LOCHW PA12 120 C6
Water St PGL PA14 34 C7
Wateryetts Dr KLMCLM PA13 55 K8
Watling Pl EKILS G75 153 G8
Watling St MTHW ML1 133 H8
UD/BTH/TAN G71 108 E8
Watson Av PSLYN/LNWD PA3 100 B4
RUTH G73 128 F2
Watson Crs KSYTH G65 47 L1
Watson Pl BLTYR/CAMB G72 155 H2
Watson St BLTYR/CAMB G72 155 J2
CGLE G1 11 L3
KLMNKN/STW KA3 17 J5
LRKH ML9 175 M6
MTHW ML1 157 L4
UD/BTH/TAN G71 131 M4
Watson Ter IRV KA12 203 K7
Watsonville Pk MTHW ML1 157 L3
Watt Crs BLSH ML4 133 H2
Wattfield Rd AYRS KA7 18 D8
Watt La BRWEIR PA11 98 E2
Watt Low Av RUTH G73 128 F3
RUTH G73 129 G3
Watt Pl GRNK PA15 2 E4
MLNGV G62 41 M6
Watt Rd BRWEIR PA11 98 D2
CARD/HILL/MSPK G52 102 F2
Watt St AIRDRIE ML6 89 J8
GBLS G5 10 C5
GRNKW/INVK PA16 2 B2
Waukglen Av PLK/PH/NH G53 126 B7
Waukglen Crs PLK/PH/NH G53 126 C6
Waukglen Dr PLK/PH/NH G53 126 B6
Waukglen Gdns
PLK/PH/NH G53 126 B6
Waukglen Pth
PLK/PH/NH G53 126 B6
Waukglen Pl PLK/PH/NH G53 126 B6
Waukglen Rd PLK/PH/NH G53 126 B6
Waulking Mill Rd CLYDBK G81 60 C2
Waulkmill Av BRHD/NEIL G78 125 J5
Waulkmill Pl KLMNK KA1 17 G6
Waulkmill St GIF/THBK G46 126 E5
Waulkmill Wy
BRHD/NEIL G78 125 K5
Waverley EKILN G74 154 D5
Waverley Av HBR/GL G84 23 G1
KLMNK KA1 206 C8
Waverley Ct UD/BTH/TAN G71 132 A7
Waverley Crs CUMB G67 68 D2
HMLTN ML3 155 M5
KKNTL G66 65 K1
LNK/LMHG ML11 199 J4
Waverley Dr AIRDRIE ML6 89 H8
RUTH G73 129 J2
WISHAW ML2 159 H5
Waverley Gdns JNSTN PA5 100 D7
PLKSD/SHW G41 104 E8
Waverley Pl SALT KA21 191 L8
Waverley Rd PSLYS PA2 123 M1
Waverley St CTBR ML5 88 B8
GRNKW/INVK PA16 32 C6
HMLTN ML3 155 M5
PLKSD/SHW G41 104 E8
Waverley Ter BLTYR/CAMB G72 155 J4
DMBTN G82 36 B5
Weardale La
STPS/GTHM/RID G33 107 J1
Weardale St
STPS/GTHM/RID G33 107 J1
Weaver Av NMRNS G77 150 D3
Weaver Crs AIRDRIE ML6 111 G4
Weaver La KLBCH PA10 99 G5
Weaver Pl EKILS G75 170 E2
Weavers Av PSLY PA1 8 B7
Weavers Pl NMLNS KA16 215 L2
Weavers Rd PSLY PA1 8 B7
Weaver St AYR KA8 224 F7
COWCAD G4 11 M1
Weavers Wk LNK/LMHG ML11 199 G6
Weaver Ter PSLYS PA2 9 L7
Webster Groves WISHAW ML2 159 K4
Webster St
DMNK/BRGTN G40 106 A6
KNTSWD G13 80 E1
Wedderlea Dr
CARD/HILL/MSPK G52 103 H4
Wee Cl BEITH KA15 144 B8
Weensmoor Rd
PLK/PH/NH G53 125 M5
Weeple Dr PSLYN/LNWD PA3 100 A3
Wee Sunnyside Rd HMLTN ML3 175 H7
Weighhouse Cl PSLY PA1 9 G4
Weighhouse Rd CARLUKE ML8 178 E6
Weir Av BRHD/NEIL G78 125 J7
PSTWK KA9 221 K8
Weir Pl CARLUKE ML8 177 M5
GRNK PA15 3 M9
Weir Rd ARD KA22 191 K5
AYR KA8 224 F7
Weirston Rd KLWNG KA13 194 A6
Weir St CTBR ML5 110 A2
GRNK PA15 33 L7
PSLY PA1 9 J3
Weirwood Av
BAIL/MDB/MHD G69 107 M5
Weirwood Gdns
BAIL/MDB/MHD G69 107 M5
Welbeck Crs TROON KA10 216 A7
Welbeck Rd GLSTN KA4 214 B4
PLK/PH/NH G53 126 B4
Welbeck St
GRNKW/INVK PA16 32 C1
KLMNK KA1 17 H7
Weldon Pl KSYTH G65 47 M6
Welfare Av BLTYR/CAMB G72 130 D5
Welland Pl EKILS G75 170 E2
Wellbank Gdns WKIL KA23 181 J4
Wellbank Pl
UD/BTH/TAN G71 131 M4
Wellbrae LRKH ML9 176 A7
Wellbrae Rd HMLTN ML3 156 B8
Wellcroft Pl GBLS G5 11 G7
Wellcroft Rd HMLTN ML3 155 L6
Wellcroft Ter HMLTN ML3 155 L6
Well Dr LNK/LMHG ML11 198 E6
Wellesley Crs BALLOCH G68 47 L8
EKILS G75 170 F2
Wellesley Dr BALLOCH G68 47 K8
EKILS G75 170 F1
Wellfield Av GIF/THBK G46 127 H6
Wellgatehead LNK/LMHG ML11 199 G6
Wellgate St LRKH ML9 176 A5
Well Gn PLKSW/MSWD G43 127 J1
Wellhall Ct HMLTN ML3 156 B5
Wellhall Rd HMLTN ML3 155 M7
Wellhead Ct
LNK/LMHG ML11 199 H5
Wellhouse Crs
STPS/GTHM/RID G33 107 L2
Wellhouse Rd
STPS/GTHM/RID G33 107 M1
Wellington EKILS G75 171 H2
Wellington Av
KLMNKN/STW KA3 212 D1
Wellington La AYRS KA7 18 D4
CGLW G2 10 F1
Wellington Pl CLYDBK G81 59 K6
CTBR ML5 109 J4
KLMNKN/STW KA3 16 F1
WISHAW ML2 177 K1
Wellington Rd BSHPBGS G64 64 B5
Wellington Sq AYRS KA7 18 D3
Wellington St AIRDRIE ML6 89 G8
CGLW G2 11 G1
GRNK PA15 2 B5
KLMNKN/STW KA3 16 F2
PSLYN/LNWD PA3 8 F2
PSTWK KA9 225 H4
WISHAW ML2 158 C4
Wellington Ter
LNK/LMHG ML11 198 F4
Wellknowe Av EKILN G74 152 C6
Wellknowe Pl EKILN G74 152 B6
Wellknowe Rd EKILN G74 152 C6
Well La KKNTL G66 44 D1
Wellmeadow Cl NMRNS G77 150 D4
Wellmeadow Gn
NMRNS G77 150 D4
Wellmeadow Rd
PLKSW/MSWD G43 127 G3
Wellmeadow St PSLY PA1 8 E4
Wellmeadow Wy NMRNS G77 150 D4
Wellpark AYRS KA7 228 F8
Wellpark Av KLMNKN/STW KA3 17 L5
Wellpark Gv KLMNKN/STW KA3 17 L4
Wellpark La SALT KA21 200 F1
Wellpark Pl KLMNKN/STW KA3 17 L5
Wellpark Rd MTHW ML1 157 J3
SALT KA21 200 F2
Wellpark St COWCAD G4 12 B2
Wellpark Ter BRHD/NEIL G78 148 D3
Well Rd KLBCH PA10 99 G6
LNK/LMHG ML11 199 G6
Wellshot Dr BLTYR/CAMB G72 129 M4
Wellshot Rd CAR/SHTL G32 106 F5
Wellside Av AIRDRIE ML6 89 G8
Wellside Dr BLTYR/CAMB G72 130 C5
Wellside La AIRDRIE ML6 89 G8
Wellside Qd AIRDRIE ML6 89 G7
Wellsquarry Rd EKILN G74 153 J5
Wells St CLYDBK G81 59 M6
Well St PSLY PA1 8 C2
WKIL KA23 181 J4
Wellview Dr MTHW ML1 157 K2
Wellwood Av
LNK/LMHG ML11 199 H4
Wellwynd AIRDRIE ML6 110 F1
Wellyard La
GRNKW/INVK PA16 31 J6
Wellyard Wy GRNKW/INVK PA16 31 J7
Wellyard Wynd
GRNKW/INVK PA16 31 J7
Welsh Dr BLTYR/CAMB G72 155 K3
HMLTN ML3 174 C2
Wemyss Av NMRNS G77 150 C2
Wemyss Bay Rd WMYSB PA18 70 A1
Wemyss Bay St GRNK PA15 2 A7
Wemyss Dr BALLOCH G68 47 L8
Wemyss Gdns
BAIL/MDB/MHD G69 108 A6
Wenlock Rd PSLYS PA2 9 K8
Wensleydale EKILN G74 153 J6
Wentworth Dr SMSTN G23 62 E8
Wentworth Sq KLWNG KA13 193 J5
Wesley St AIRDRIE ML6 110 F2
West Abercromby St
HBR/GL G84 20 D6
West Academy St WISHAW ML2 158 E6
Westacres Rd NMRNS G77 150 B5
West Av AIRDRIE ML6 90 A6
BLTYR/CAMB G72 155 L4
CARLUKE ML8 178 D8
MTHW ML1 134 A7
RNFRW PA4 80 C6
STPS/GTHM/RID G33 85 K4
UD/BTH/TAN G71 132 B3
West Balgrochan Rd
BSHPBGS G64 44 B8
Westbank La KVD/HLHD G12 4 A5
Westbank Qd KVD/HLHD G12 4 A5
West Barmoss Av PGL PA14 54 F2
West Blackhall St GRNK PA15 2 C2
GRNKW/INVK PA16 2 C1
Westbourne Av PSTWK KA9 225 K1
Westbourne Crs BSDN G61 61 J4
Westbourne Dr BSDN G61 61 J4
Westbourne Gdns
PSTWK KA9 225 K1
Westbourne Gardens La
KVD/HLHD G12 82 C5
Westbourne Gdns South
KVD/HLHD G12 82 C5
Westbourne Gdns West
KVD/HLHD G12 82 C5
Westbourne Rd
KVD/HLHD G12 82 B5
Westbourne Terrace La North
KVD/HLHD G12 82 C5
Westbourne Terrace La South
KVD/HLHD G12 82 B5
West Bowhouse Gdn IRVSE KA11 204 A4
West Bowhouse Wy IRVSE KA11 204 A4
West Brae PSLY PA1 8 E4
Westbrae Dr SCOT G14 81 L5
Westbrae Rd NMRNS G77 150 F3
West Bridgend DMBTN G82 36 E5
Westburn Av
BLTYR/CAMB G72 130 D3
PSLYN/LNWD PA3 101 G4
Westburn Crs CLYDBK G81 60 B2
RUTH G73 128 F2
Westburn Farm Rd
BLTYR/CAMB G72 130 B3
Westburn Rd BLTYR/CAMB G72 130 B3
West Burnside St KSYTH G65 47 K1
West Burn St GRNK PA15 2 C3
West Campbell St CGLW G2 10 F2
NMLNS KA16 215 L2
PSLY PA1 8 B5
West Canal St CTBR ML5 109 M3
Westcastle Crs CSMK G45 128 D6
Westcastle Gdns CSMK G45 128 D6
Westcastle Gv CSMK G45 128 D6
West Chapelton Av BSDN G61 61 M5
West Chapelton Crs BSDN G61 61 M5
West Chapelton Dr BSDN G61 61 M5
West Church St NMLNS KA16 215 K2
Westcliff DMBTN G82 36 B5
West Clyde St HBR/GL G84 20 B8
LRKH ML9 176 B7
Westclyffe St
PLKSD/SHW G41 104 E8
West Coats Rd
BLTYR/CAMB G72 129 M5
Westcott Pl LNK/LMHG ML11 199 J4
West Crs TROON KA10 216 F5
West Dhuhill Dr HBR/GL G84 20 D5
West Doura Av SALT KA21 191 M8
West Doura Wy
KLWNG KA13 193 H6
West Dr AIRDRIE ML6 111 L3
West End DALRY KA24 184 B2
Westend Ct CARLUKE ML8 177 M5
West End Dr BLSH ML4 132 F5
Westend Park St KVGV G3 4 C6
West End Pl BLSH ML4 132 F5
Westerburn St CAR/SHTL G32 106 F3
Wester Carriagehill PSLYS PA2 9 G9
Wester Cleddens Rd
BSHPBGS G64 64 A7
Wester Common Dr
PPK/MIL G22 83 G5
Wester Common Rd
PPK/MIL G22 83 G5
Westercraigs DEN/PKHD G31 12 D2
Westerdale EKILN G74 153 J6
Westerfield Rd
CRMNK/CLK/EAG G76 152 D5
Westergill Av AIRDRIE ML6 111 L3
Westergreens Av KKNTL G66 65 J3
Westerhill Rd BSHPBGS G64 64 B5
Westerhouse Ct
CARLUKE ML8 178 D7
Westerhouse Rd ESTRH G34 108 A1
Westerkirk Dr SMSTN G23 62 E8
Westerlands KVD/HLHD G12 82 A3
Westerlands Dr NMRNS G77 150 B5
Westerlands Gv NMRNS G77 150 B5
Westerlands Pl NMRNS G77 150 B4
Wester Leddriegreen Rd
CMPF/LLE G63 27 H5
Westermains Av KKNTL G66 65 H2
Wester Mavisbank Av
AIRDRIE ML6 110 E1
Wester Moffat Av AIRDRIE ML6 111 L1
Wester Moffat Crs
AIRDRIE ML6 111 L2
Wester Myvot Rd CUMB G67 68 A5
Western Av RUTH G73 129 G1
Western Crs KBRN KA25 167 G2
Western Isles Rd OLDK G60 59 J4
Western Rd BLTYR/CAMB G72 129 M6
GLSTN KA4 214 A3
KLMNKN/STW KA3 206 F6
Wester Rd CAR/SHTL G32 107 K6
Westerton KKNTL G66 44 E1
Westerton Av
CRMNK/CLK/EAG G76 152 A4
KNTSWD G13 81 M1
LRKH ML9 176 A8
Westerton La
CRMNK/CLK/EAG G76 152 A4
West Fairholm St LRKH ML9 175 M4
West Faulds Rd
LNK/LMHG ML11 199 L4
Westfield DMBTN G82 36 C5
GLGNK KA14 167 H1
Westfield Av RUTH G73 128 F2
Westfield Crs BSDN G61 61 L7
Westfield Dr BALLOCH G68 67 M2
BSDN G61 61 L7
CARD/HILL/MSPK G52 103 G4
GRNKW/INVK PA16 32 C1
KLMCLM PA13 75 H1
Westfield Pl BALLOCH G68 67 K3
Westfield Rd AYRS KA7 18 C8
BALLOCH G68 67 M1
GIF/THBK G46 127 G7
MTHW ML1 134 C2
PGL PA14 54 F1
Westfields BSHPBGS G64 63 L6
West Fullarton St KLMNK KA1 16 C3
Westgarth Pl EKILN G74 153 G6
West Ga WISHAW ML2 159 K6
West George La CGLW G2 11 H1
West George St CGLE G1 11 J1
CGLW G2 4 E9
CTBR ML5 110 A1
West Glebe Ter HMLTN ML3 156 C7
West Glen Rd KLMCLM PA13 55 L8
West Graham St KVGV G3 4 F7
West Greenhill Pl KVGV G3 4 A9
West Gv TROON KA10 216 F6
West Highland Wy
CMPF/LLE G63 26 C7
West High St KKNTL G66 45 J8
Westhouse Av RUTH G73 128 E2
Westhouse Gdns RUTH G73 128 E2
West Kilbride Rd DALRY KA24 184 B2
West King St HBR/GL G84 20 B7
West Kirklands Pl DALRY KA24 184 B2
West Kirk St AIRDRIE ML6 110 F2
Westland Dr SCOT G14 81 K6
Westlands Gdns PSLYS PA2 8 F8
West La PSLY PA1 8 A5
West Langlands St KLMNK KA1 16 D3
Westlea Pl AIRDRIE ML6 111 G3
West Lennox Dr HBR/GL G84 20 D6
West Lodge Rd RNFRW PA4 80 B5
West Mains Rd EKILN G74 14 F2
EKILN G74 153 H7
West Montrose St HBR/GL G84 20 C7
Westmoor Crs KLMNK KA1 16 B7
Westmoreland St
GVH/MTFL G42 105 G7
Westmorland Rd
GRNKW/INVK PA16 31 L5
Westmuir Pl RUTH G73 128 E1
Westmuir St DEN/PKHD G31 13 L6
West Nemphlar Rd
LNK/LMHG ML11 198 C3
West Netherton St KLMNK KA1 16 E7
West Nile St CGLE G1 11 H1
Weston Av RAYR/DAL KA6 227 H7
Weston Brae RAYR/DAL KA6 227 H6
Weston Pl PSTWK KA9 225 J3
Weston Ter WKIL KA23 181 J4
Westpark Ct SVSTN KA20 201 J1
West Park Crs
KLMNKN/STW KA3 206 B1
West Park Dr
KLMNKN/STW KA3 206 B1
Westpark Dr PSLYN/LNWD PA3 8 A2
West Pl WISHAW ML2 160 A4
Westport EKILS G75 152 F8
West Port LNK/LMHG ML11 198 F5
Westport MAUCH/CAT KA5 223 L6
Westport St KSYTH G65 47 K1
West Prince's La COWCAD G4 4 B4
West Prince's St COWCAD G4 4 C4
HBR/GL G84 20 B7
KVGV G3 4 D6
West Quay PGL PA14 34 C7
Westray Av NMRNS G77 150 C2
PGL PA14 55 H3
Westray Circ PPK/MIL G22 83 K3
Westray Ct CUMB G67 68 D1
Westray Pl PPK/MIL G22 83 K2
Westray Rd CUMB G67 68 D1
Westray Sq PPK/MIL G22 83 J2
Westray St PPK/MIL G22 83 J2
West Regent La CGLW G2 5 G9
West Regent St CGLW G2 4 E8
West Rd BSHPBGS G64 44 B8
IRV KA12 203 H6
KLBCH PA10 99 G5
PGL PA14 54 E1
West Rossdhu Dr HBR/GL G84 20 D6
West Sanquhar Rd AYR KA8 225 H7
West Scott Ter HMLTN ML3 156 D8
West Shaw St GRNK PA15 2 B3
KLMNK KA1 16 E8
West Stewart St GRNK PA15 2 C2
HMLTN ML3 156 C5
West St CLYDBK G81 80 E1
GBLS G5 10 E6
PSLY PA1 8 C5
West Thomson St CLYDBK G81 60 A6
West Thornlie St WISHAW ML2 159 G7
Westward Wy TROON KA10 216 E2
West Wellbrae Crs HMLTN ML3 174 B1
West Whitby St DEN/PKHD G31 13 K7
Westwood Av AYR KA8 225 L8
GIF/THBK G46 127 H6
Westwood Crs AYR KA8 225 L8
HMLTN ML3 156 C7
Westwood Dr MTHW ML1 135 L8
Westwood Gdns
PSLYN/LNWD PA3 8 A2
Westwood Hl EKILS G75 171 H2
Westwood Qd CLYDBK G81 60 D8
Westwood Rd EKILS G75 153 H8
PLKSW/MSWD G43 127 H3
WISHAW ML2 159 M2
West Woodside Av PGL PA14 54 F3
West Woodstock St KLMNK KA1 16 C4
Weymouth Crs
GRNKW/INVK PA16 31 L4
Weymouth Dr KVD/HLHD G12 82 A3
Whamflet Av
BAIL/MDB/MHD G69 108 C2
Wheatfield Rd AYRS KA7 18 C6
BSDN G61 61 K7
Wheatholm St AIRDRIE ML6 89 H8
Wheating Br KLMNKN/STW KA3 197 H8
Wheatland Av
BLTYR/CAMB G72 155 J1
Wheatland Dr LNK/LMHG ML11 198 F5
Wheatlandhead Ct
BLTYR/CAMB G72 155 J1
Wheatlands Dr KLBCH PA10 99 G5
Wheatlands Farm Rd
KLBCH PA10 99 G5
Wheatlandside
LNK/LMHG ML11 198 F4
Wheatley Crs KSYTH G65 47 K2
Wheatley Loan BSHPBGS G64 84 C1
Wheatley Rd SALT KA21 192 A7
SVSTN KA20 192 E8
Wheatpark Rd
LNK/LMHG ML11 198 F5
Whifflet St CTBR ML5 110 A6
Whin Av BRHD/NEIL G78 125 G5
Whinfell Dr EKILS G75 171 G3
Whinfell Gdns EKILS G75 171 G3
Whinfield Av PSTWK KA9 225 H3
Whinfield Rd
PLK/PH/NH G53 126 A5
PSTWK KA9 225 H3
Whinhall Av AIRDRIE ML6 88 E8
Whinhall Rd AIRDRIE ML6 88 E8
Whin Hl EKILN G74 154 B5
Whinhill Av LARGS KA30 115 K6
Whinhill Crs GRNK PA15 2 F9
Whin Hill Rd AYRS KA7 229 G7
Whinhill Rd GRNK PA15 2 F8
PLK/PH/NH G53 103 G6
PSLYS PA2 102 B7
Whin Loan KSYTH G65 46 D1
Whinney Gv WISHAW ML2 159 L5
Whinnie Knowe LRKH ML9 175 M8
Whinpark Av BLSH ML4 132 F6
Whin Pl EKILN G74 154 B4
Whins Rd PLKSD/SHW G41 104 C8
TROON KA10 216 E2
Whin St CLYDBK G81 60 A5
Whirlie Dr
CRG/CRSL/HOU PA6 99 H1
Whirlie Rd CRG/CRSL/HOU PA6 77 H8
Whirlow Gdns
BAIL/MDB/MHD G69 108 A4
Whirlow Rd
BAIL/MDB/MHD G69 108 A4
Whiskeyhall RAYR/DAL KA6 227 G3
Whistleberry Crs HMLTN ML3 156 A2
Whistleberry Dr HMLTN ML3 156 B3
Whistleberry Pk HMLTN ML3 156 A2
Whistleberry Rd HMLTN ML3 156 A2
Whistlefield Ct BSDN G61 61 L6
Whitacres Rd PLK/PH/NH G53 125 M5
Whitburn St CAR/SHTL G32 106 F2
Whiteadder Pl EKILS G75 170 D2
White Av DMBTN G82 37 H6
White Cart Rd
PSLYN/LNWD PA3 101 L1
White Craig Rd ARD KA22 191 K5
Whitecraigs Pl SMSTN G23 82 E1
Whitecrook Sreet CLYDBK G81 80 C1
Whitecrook St CLYDBK G81 80 B1
Whitefield Av BLTYR/CAMB G72 130 A5
Whitefield Rd GOV/IBX G51 104 C3
Whitefield Ter KKNTL G66 29 J8
Whiteford Av DMBTN G82 37 H3
Whiteford Ct HMLTN ML3 174 C3
Whiteford Crs DMBTN G82 37 J4
Whiteford Pl DMBTN G82 37 J4
Whiteford Rd PSLYS PA2 9 M8
Whiteford Vw AYRS KA7 229 K2
Whitehall Av PSTWK KA9 225 K1
Whitehall St KVGV G3 10 D2
Whitehaugh Av PSLY PA1 102 B4
Whitehaugh Crs
PLK/PH/NH G53 126 A5
Whitehaugh Dr PSLY PA1 102 B4
Whitehaugh Rd
PLK/PH/NH G53 126 A5
Whitehill Av AIRDRIE ML6 89 G7
BALLOCH G68 48 D7
KKNTL G66 45 L8
STPS/GTHM/RID G33 85 K3
Whitehill Crs CARLUKE ML8 178 F6
CLYDBK G81 60 E2
KKNTL G66 45 M8
LNK/LMHG ML11 198 F5
RAYR/DAL KA6 227 G7
Whitehill Dr RAYR/DAL KA6 227 H7
Whitehill Farm Rd
STPS/GTHM/RID G33 85 K3
Whitehill Gdns DEN/PKHD G31 12 F2
Whitehill Gv NMRNS G77 150 F7
Whitehill Rd BSDN G61 61 K5
HMLTN ML3 156 B4
Whitehills Dr EKILS G75 14 E8
Whitehills Pl EKILS G75 14 E8
Whitehills Ter EKILS G75 14 E9
Whitehill St DEN/PKHD G31 6 E9
Whitehill Street La
DEN/PKHD G31 12 E2
Whitehill Ter LNK/LMHG ML11 198 F5
Whitehill Wy
RAYR/DAL KA6 231 H5
Whitehirst Park Rd
KLWNG KA13 193 H6
Whitehurst BSDN G61 61 J3
Whitekirk Pl DRUM G15 61 G7
Whitelaw Av CTBR ML5 87 M4
Whitelaw Crs BLSH ML4 133 K5
Whitelaw St MRYH/FIRH G20 82 C2
Whitelaw Ter KSYTH G65 46 F5
Whitelea Av KLMCLM PA13 75 J1
Whitelea Crs KLMCLM PA13 75 K1
Whitelea Rd KLMCLM PA13 75 J1
Whitelee EKILS G75 171 K4
Whitelee Crs NMRNS G77 150 B3
Whitelee Ga NMRNS G77 150 B3
Whitelees Rd CUMB G67 49 M3
GRNK PA15 33 M7
LNK/LMHG ML11 199 K6
Whiteloans UD/BTH/TAN G71 132 B6
Whitemoss Av EKILN G74 15 H3
LNPK/KPK G44 127 M5
Whitemoss Gv EKILN G74 15 J2
Whitemoss Rd EKILN G74 15 H3
Whitepond Av BLSH ML4 132 F6
Whites Bridge Av PSLY PA1 100 F5
PSLYN/LNWD PA3 100 F4
PSLYN/LNWD PA3 100 F5
Whiteshaw Av CARLUKE ML8 178 D8
Whiteshaw Dr CARLUKE ML8 178 D7
Whiteshaw Rd CARLUKE ML8 178 B6
Whiteside Rd PSTWK KA9 225 K2
Whiteside Ter PSTWK KA9 225 K2
White St AYR KA8 225 H5
CLYDBK G81 80 D2
PTCK G11 82 B7
Whitevale St DEN/PKHD G31 12 F4
Whitewisp Ct IRVSE KA11 204 A5
Whitfield Dr AYR KA8 225 K6
Whithope Rd PLK/PH/NH G53 125 M5
Whithorn Crs
BAIL/MDB/MHD G69 66 F6
Whiting Rd WMYSB PA18 50 A8
Whitlawburn Av
BLTYR/CAMB G72 129 L5
Whitlawburn Rd
BLTYR/CAMB G72 129 L5
Whitlawburn Ter
BLTYR/CAMB G72 129 L5
Whitlees Crs ARD KA22 191 K7
Whitletts Ct AYR KA8 225 L7
Whitletts Rd AYR KA8 19 J1
Whitriggs Rd PLK/PH/NH G53 125 M5
Whitslade Pl ESTRH G34 86 A8
Whitslade St ESTRH G34 86 A8
Whitsun Dl EKILN G74 153 J6

Whittagreen Av MTHW ML1 134 D6
Whittagreen Crs MTHW ML1 134 D6
Whittingehame Dr
KVD/HLHD G12 81 M4
Whittingehame La
KNTSWD G13 81 M4 4
Whittington St CTBR ML5 110 A3 1
Whittlemuir Av LNPK/KPK G44 127 M5
Whittle Pl IRVSE KA11 203 M7
Whittle Rd AYR KA8 225 J6
Whitton Dr GIF/THBK G46 127 K5
Whitton St MRYH/FIRH G20 82 C1
Whitworth St
MRYH/FIRH G20 83 G3 5
Whyte Av BLTYR/CAMB G72 129 L3
IRV KA12 203 K8
Wick Av AIRDRIE ML6 110 E5
The Wickets PSLY PA1 9 M6
Wickham Av NMRNS G77 150 D3
Wide Cl LNK/LMHG ML11 199 G5 7
Wigton Av NMRNS G77 150 C2
Wigtoun Pl CUMB G67 49 H5
Wildcat Rd WKIL KA23 181 H5
Wildman Rd CARLUKE ML8 178 B2
Wilfred Av KNTSWD G13 81 K2
Wilkie Crs LRKH ML9 176 B7
Wilkie Rd UD/BTH/TAN G71 132 A4
William Dr HMLTN ML3 174 D2
Williamfield Gv IRV KA12 203 H5 2
Williamfield Pk IRV KA12 203 H5 3
William Mann Dr NMRNS G77 150 B5
Williamsburgh Ter PSLY PA1 9 M3 1
Williamson Av DMBTN G82 37 G5
Williamson Dr HBR/GL G84 20 F8
Williamson Pl JNSTN PA5 100 B7
Williamson St CLYDBK G81 60 B5
DMNK/BRGTN G40 13 J8
William Spiers Pl LRKH ML9 176 B8
William St CLYDBK G81 60 A3
CTBR ML5 110 B5
HBR/GL G84 20 C8
HMLTN ML3 156 B4
JNSTN PA5 99 M7 4
KLMNKN/STW KA3 16 F1
KSYTH G65 47 K1
KVGV G3 4 D9
PGL PA14 34 B8
PSLY PA1 8 C4
William Ure Pl BSHPBGS G64 64 B4
Williamwood Dr LNPK/KPK G44 127 L7
Williamwood Pk
LNPK/KPK G44 127 M7 2
Williamwood Pk West
LNPK/KPK G44 127 M7 3
Willie Ross Pl
KLMNKN/STW KA3 207 K5
Willison's La PGL PA14 34 C8 2
Willock Pl MRYH/FIRH G20 82 E2
Willockston Rd TROON KA10 216 E7
Willoughby Dr KNTSWD G13 81 M3 5
Willoughby La KNTSWD G13 81 M3 6
Willow Av BSHPBGS G64 84 A1 4
JNSTN PA5 100 C7 2
KKNTL G66 65 J4
MTHW ML1 134 A7
Willowbank Crs KVGV G3 4 C5 1
Willowbank Gdns KKNTL G66 65 K1
Willowbank St KVGV G3 4 C6
Willowburn Rd BEITH KA15 167 M2
Willow Ct EKILS G75 14 A9
Willow Crs CTBR ML5 109 M5
Willowdale Crs
BAIL/MDB/MHD G69 108 A5
Willowdale Gdns
BAIL/MDB/MHD G69 108 A5 3
Willow Dr AIRDRIE ML6 111 K2
BLTYR/CAMB G72 155 J1
JNSTN PA5 99 M8
KKNTL G66 45 J4
Willowford Rd PLK/PH/NH G53 125 M5
Willow Gv MTHW ML1 134 B4
Willow La CAR/SHTL G32 107 H7
Willow Pk AYRS KA7 229 J5
Willow Pl GRNKW/INVK PA16 50 D5 1
JNSTN PA5 100 A7 2
UD/BTH/TAN G71 132 D1 2
Willow Rd KLMNK KA1 16 A5
The Willows
CRMNK/CLK/EAG G76 152 E1 3
Willow St KNTSWD G13 81 M2
Willow Wy HMLTN ML3 156 E8
Willowyard Rd BEITH KA15 167 M1
Wills Rd AYR KA8 225 J7
Willwood Dr WISHAW ML2 159 J2 2
Wilmot Rd KNTSWD G13 81 K3 3
Wilsgait St MTHW ML1 135 J7
Wilson Av IRV KA12 203 J5
KLMNKN/STW KA3 17 H4
PSLYN/LNWD PA3 100 A3
TROON KA10 216 F7
Wilson Ct BLSH ML4 132 F4 4
Wilson Pl CRH/DND KA2 209 L7
EKILN G74 154 A5
NMRNS G77 150 C5
Wilson Rd SHOTTS ML7 160 F1
Wilsons Rd MTHW ML1 135 L2
Wilson St AIRDRIE ML6 110 F1
ALEX/LLW G83 25 K4
AYR KA8 225 H7
BEITH KA15 144 B8 11
CGLE G1 11 K2
CTBR ML5 110 C2
HMLTN ML3 156 A4 3
LARGS KA30 115 K6
LRKH ML9 176 B8
MTHW ML1 157 M2
PGL PA14 34 D8
RNFRW PA4 80 D5
Wiltonburn Rd PLK/PH/NH G53 126 A5
Wilton Crescent La
MRYH/FIRH G20 4 C2
Wilton Dr MRYH/FIRH G20 4 D2
Wilton Rd CARLUKE ML8 179 H8
Wilton St CTBR ML5 87 K7
MRYH/FIRH G20 4 C2
Wilverton Rd KNTSWD G13 81 L1
Winburne Crs HMLTN ML3 156 B5 3
Winchester Dr KVD/HLHD G12 82 B3
Windemere Gdns
HMLTN ML3 174 C3 3
Winderemere St BLSH ML4 132 F5 3
Windermere EKILS G75 170 F4
Windhill Crs PLKSW/MSWD G43 127 H4
Windhill Rd PLKSW/MSWD G43 127 H4
Windlaw Gdns LNPK/KPK G44 127 M5
Windlaw Park Gdns
LNPK/KPK G44 127 M5 3
Windlaw Rd CSMK G45 128 D8
Windmill Ct MTHW ML1 157 M4 4
Windmillhill St MTHW ML1 157 M4
Windmill Rd HMLTN ML3 156 D5
Windmill St SALT KA21 200 E2
Windrow Ter WISHAW ML2 159 J2
Windsor Av NMRNS G77 150 F4
Windsor Ct CARLUKE ML8 178 F7 5
Windsor Crs CLYDBK G81 60 A6
JNSTN PA5 100 B8
PSLY PA1 9 M1
Windsor Dr AIRDRIE ML6 88 F5
Windsor Gdns HMLTN ML3 156 A4 10
LARGS KA30 115 K3
Windsor Qd CARLUKE ML8 178 F7 6
Windsor Rd MTHW ML1 134 A4
RNFRW PA4 80 C7
Windsor St CAR/SHTL G32 107 J3 5
CTBR ML5 109 L6
MRYH/FIRH G20 4 E4
SHOTTS ML7 137 L4
Windsor Ter MRYH/FIRH G20 4 E4
Windward Pk AYRS KA7 229 G8
Windward Rd EKILS G75 153 G8
Windyedge Crs KNTSWD G13 81 J4 5
Windyedge Pl KNTSWD G13 81 J4 6
Windyedge Rd MTHW ML1 135 J6
Windyhill Pk
CRMNK/CLK/EAG G76 151 K7
Windyhill Rd NMLNS KA16 215 H4
Windyridge Pl
BLTYR/CAMB G72 155 J2 1
Windy Yetts KSYTH G65 46 F6
Winehouse Yett CRH/DND KA2 209 L7
Winfield Av BLTYR/CAMB G72 129 L2 4
Wingate Av DALRY KA24 184 B2
Wingate Crs EKILN G74 154 C5
Wingate Dr EKILN G74 154 C5
Wingate Pk EKILN G74 154 C5 2
Wingate St WISHAW ML2 158 D5
Wingfaulds Av DALRY KA24 184 A1
Wingfield Gdns
UD/BTH/TAN G71 132 B8 5
Winifred St STPS/GTHM/RID G33 7 L1
Winning Ct BLTYR/CAMB G72 131 L8
Winning Rw DEN/PKHD G31 13 M5
Winnipeg Dr EKILS G75 171 H1
Winstanley Wynd KLWNG KA13 193 J4
Winston Av PSTWK KA9 225 K2
Winston Crs KKNTL G66 29 J8
Winston Rd HBR/GL G84 21 G7
Wintergreen Ct EKILN G74 153 K5 7
Wintergreen Dr EKILN G74 153 K5 8
Winton Av GIF/THBK G46 127 J7
KLWNG KA13 193 J6
Winton Circ SALT KA21 200 E2
Winton Ct ARD KA22 191 J8
Winton Crs BLTYR/CAMB G72 155 K2
Winton Dr KVD/HLHD G12 82 C4
Winton La SKLM PA17 70 A4
Winton Gdns
UD/BTH/TAN G71 131 M2 4
Winton La ARD KA22 191 J7 5
KVD/HLHD G12 82 C4
Winton Pk EKILS G75 152 F8
Winton Pl ARD KA22 191 J7 7
Winton St ARD KA22 191 J7
SALT KA21 200 E1
Wirran Pl KNTSWD G13 80 E1
Wishart Av CLYDBK G81 60 C2
Wishart Pl GLSTN KA4 214 B4
Wishart St DEN/PKHD G31 6 B9
Wishaw High Rd MTHW ML1 159 J1
Wishawhill St WISHAW ML2 158 F5 2
Wishaw Low Rd MTHW ML1 159 H2
Wishaw Rd WISHAW ML2 177 M1
Wisner Ct GIF/THBK G46 126 F6 2
Wisteria La CARLUKE ML8 188 F1 7
Wiston St BLTYR/CAMB G72 130 D4
Witches Linn ARD KA22 191 H5
Witchill Pl KLMNKN/STW KA3 16 E1
Witchknowe Ct KLMNK KA1 212 A5 4
Witchknowe Rd KLMNK KA1 211 M5
Witch Rd KLMNKN/STW KA3 16 E1
Woddrop St DMNK/BRGTN G40 106 B7
Wolcott Dr BLTYR/CAMB G72 155 K1 3
Wolfe Av NMRNS G77 150 C2
Wolseley St GBLS G5 11 L9
Wood Aven Dr EKILN G74 153 K5
Woodbank Crs
CRMNK/CLK/EAG G76 151 L3
JNSTN PA5 99 M7 3
Woodbank Gdns
ALEX/LLW G83 25 J2 2
LARGS KA30 115 H3 5
Woodbank Rd CRH/DND KA2 205 M8
Woodburn Av AIRDRIE ML6 110 F3
BLTYR/CAMB G72 155 L1
CRMNK/CLK/EAG G76 151 L3
KLWNG KA13 193 L5
Woodburn Pl
CRG/CRSL/HOU PA6 99 L2
Woodburn Rd BEITH KA15 168 C1 5
MTHW ML1 134 D2
PLKSW/MSWD G43 127 K4
Woodburn St MTHW ML1 157 L1
Woodburn Ter LRKH ML9 176 C7 5
Woodburn Wy BALLOCH G68 48 C7
MLNGV G62 42 A8
Wood Crs KLWNG KA13 193 L5
MTHW ML1 157 L1
Woodcroft Av LARGS KA30 115 L6
PTCK G11 81 M5
Wooddale MTHW ML1 157 K5
Woodend Ct CAR/SHTL G32 107 L7 2
Woodend Dr AIRDRIE ML6 89 J8
KNTSWD G13 81 L4
PSLY PA1 102 D5
Woodend Gdns
CAR/SHTL G32 107 K7 2
Woodend La KNTSWD G13 81 L4
Woodend Ov RAYR/DAL KA6 229 L7
Woodend Pl JNSTN PA5 100 B7 1
Woodend Rd AYRS KA7 228 F8
CAR/SHTL G32 107 K7
CARLUKE ML8 179 G7
RUTH G73 129 H5
Woodend St HBR/GL G84 20 B7
Wood Farm Rd GIF/THBK G46 127 G8
Woodfield UD/BTH/TAN G71 132 C3 5
Woodfield Av AYR KA8 225 G4
Woodfield Crs AYR KA8 225 G5
Woodfield Rd AYR KA8 225 G5
Woodfoot Pl
PLK/PH/NH G53 126 A5 4
Woodfoot Qd PLK/PH/NH G53 126 B5
Woodfoot Rd HMLTN ML3 156 A7
PLK/PH/NH G53 126 A5
Woodford Pl
PSLYN/LNWD PA3 100 A3 3
Woodford St
PLKSW/MSWD G43 127 K2
Woodgreen Av LNPK/KPK G44 128 B3
Woodgreen Wynd
KLWNG KA13 193 J4
Wood Gv UD/BTH/TAN G71 109 J8
Woodhall MTHW ML1 134 A1 1
Woodhall Av AIRDRIE ML6 111 H7
CTBR ML5 109 M6
HMLTN ML3 156 B5
MTHW ML1 133 M4
Woodhall Cottage Rd
AIRDRIE ML6 111 J8
Woodhall Mill Rd AIRDRIE ML6 134 C1
Woodhall Pl CTBR ML5 109 M6
Woodhall Rd AIRDRIE ML6 111 H7
CARLUKE ML8 188 D6
WISHAW ML2 159 M6
Woodhall St AIRDRIE ML6 111 K8
DMNK/BRGTN G40 106 B7 3
Woodhall Ter PGL PA14 55 H1
Woodhead Av BALLOCH G68 67 M2
KKNTL G66 65 K2
UD/BTH/TAN G71 132 B8 7
Woodhead Ct BALLOCH G68 67 M2
Woodhead Crs HMLTN ML3 174 A1
UD/BTH/TAN G71 131 M1
Woodhead Gdns
UD/BTH/TAN G71 156 B1
Woodhead Gv BALLOCH G68 67 M2 10
Woodhead Pl BALLOCH G68 67 M2 11
Woodhead Rd
BAIL/MDB/MHD G69 86 B3
BALLOCH G68 67 M2 12
PLK/PH/NH G53 125 M4
RAYR/DAL KA6 231 H4
Woodhead Ter
BAIL/MDB/MHD G69 86 B2 5
Woodhead Vw
BALLOCH G68 67 M2 13
Woodhill Crs IRVSE KA11 204 B3
Woodhill Pl
KLMNKN/STW KA3 206 B3 1
Woodhill Rd BSHPBGS G64 64 C8
KLMNKN/STW KA3 206 E6
SPRGB/BLRNK G21 84 B3 2
Woodholm Av LNPK/KPK G44 128 C3
Woodhouse St KNTSWD G13 81 L2
Woodilee Rd KKNTL G66 65 L3
MTHW ML1 134 E5
Woodland Av AIRDRIE ML6 111 J5
KKNTL G66 65 H1
PSLYS PA2 124 E1
Woodland Crs
BLTYR/CAMB G72 130 B5
Woodland Gdns
CRMNK/CLK/EAG G76 152 D2
HMLTN ML3 156 E7
Woodland Pl ARD KA22 191 J6 6
Woodlands Av
BAIL/MDB/MHD G69 86 E2
CARLUKE ML8 177 M3
IRV KA12 203 J5
UD/BTH/TAN G71 132 A6 5
Woodlands Ct ALEX/LLW G83 25 J2 3
GIF/THBK G46 126 F7 2
Woodlands Crs AYRS KA7 229 H5
GIF/THBK G46 126 F6
JNSTN PA5 99 K8
UD/BTH/TAN G71 132 A6
Woodlands Dr COWCAD G4 4 C5
CTBR ML5 109 K2
KVGV G3 4 C5
MTHW ML1 133 M4
Woodlands Gdns
UD/BTH/TAN G71 131 M6
Woodlands Ga GIF/THBK G46 126 F6
KVGV G3 4 C6
Woodlands Gv
KLMNKN/STW KA3 207 H5
MLNGV G62 42 A6
Woodlands Pk GIF/THBK G46 126 F7
Woodlands Pl CTBR ML5 109 K2
KLMNKN/STW KA3 207 H5 1
Woodlands Rd GIF/THBK G46 126 F7
KVGV G3 4 C6
MTHW ML1 134 D2
MTHW ML1 157 M6
Woodlands St GTCI KA28 138 B6 3
MLNGV G62 42 A7
MTHW ML1 157 M5 1
PSTWK KA9 225 H1
Woodlands Ter KVGV G3 4 B7
The Woodlands BLSH ML4 133 K6 2
Woodland Ter LRKH ML9 176 C8
Woodland Wy CUMB G67 49 H6
Woodlea Av AIRDRIE ML6 111 J5
Woodlea Ct CRH/DND KA2 205 M7
Woodlea Crs CRH/DND KA2 205 M7
Woodlea Dr GIF/THBK G46 127 K5
HMLTN ML3 174 D1
Woodlea La GRK PA19 32 A2 2
Woodlea Pl AIRDRIE ML6 89 J8 1
AYRS KA7 229 H7
Woodlinn Av LNPK/KPK G44 128 B4
Woodmill KLWNG KA13 193 M8
Woodmill Dr BSHPBGS G64 44 C8
Woodmill Gdns CUMB G67 67 M3 5
Woodneuk Rd
BAIL/MDB/MHD G69 86 F4 2
PLK/PH/NH G53 126 B5
Woodneuk St AIRDRIE ML6 111 K8
Woodneuk Ter
BAIL/MDB/MHD G69 86 F4
Wood Pk AYRS KA7 229 H5
Wood Qd CLYDBK G81 80 E1
Wood Rd TROON KA10 216 A7
Woodrow MTHW ML1 134 B1
Woodrow Av KLMCLM PA13 55 K8
MTHW ML1 134 B7
Woodrow Circ PLKSD/SHW G41 104 D5
Woodrow Pl PLKSD/SHW G41 104 C5
Woodrow Rd PLKSD/SHW G41 104 D5
Woodside BLSH ML4 133 L1
CRG/CRSL/HOU PA6 77 K8
WKIL KA23 181 J6
Woodside Av BRWEIR PA11 76 D8 5
BRWEIR PA11 98 D1 3
GIF/THBK G46 127 G6
HMLTN ML3 156 E7 11
KKNTL G66 65 K4
KSYTH G65 47 M1
RUTH G73 129 J2
Woodside Crs BRHD/NEIL G78 125 K7
KVGV G3 4 D7
PSLY PA1 8 C4
WISHAW ML2 160 B3
Woodside Dr AIRDRIE ML6 111 G7
CRMNK/CLK/EAG G76 151 K7
Woodside Gdns
CRMNK/CLK/EAG G76 151 J2 2
CRMNK/CLK/EAG G76 152 D2
CTBR ML5 109 K5 2
Woodside La JNSTN PA5 99 J3
Woodside Pl KVGV G3 4 C7
UD/BTH/TAN G71 132 C1 5
Woodside Place La KVGV G3 4 C7
Woodside Rd BEITH KA15 144 B8 12
CRMNK/CLK/EAG G76 152 D2
JNSTN PA5 99 K3
KLWNG KA13 193 J5 9
Woodside St AIRDRIE ML6 111 K7 2
CTBR ML5 109 K6
MTHW ML1 134 A6
MTHW ML1 158 B5
Woodside Ter KVGV G3 4 C7
Woodside Terrace La KVGV G3 4 C7
Woodside Wk HMLTN ML3 156 E7
Woodside Wy RUTH G73 129 J2 3
Woodstock Av KKNTL G66 65 M1
LNK/LMHG ML11 199 H5 5
PLKSD/SHW G41 127 K1
PSLYS PA2 123 L1
Woodstock Dr WISHAW ML2 159 J6 6
Woodstock Pl KLMNK KA1 16 D4
Woodstock Rd
GRNKW/INVK PA16 32 C6
LNK/LMHG ML11 199 H5
Woodstock St KLMNK KA1 16 D4
Wood St AIRDRIE ML6 89 H8
CTBR ML5 109 L2
DEN/PKHD G31 7 G9
GRNKW/INVK PA16 32 B1
KLWNG KA13 193 L5
MTHW ML1 133 M8
PSLYS PA2 102 B6
Woodvale Av AIRDRIE ML6 111 J5
BSDN G61 62 B7
GIF/THBK G46 151 H1
Woodvale Dr PSLYN/LNWD PA3 101 G4
Woodview UD/BTH/TAN G71 132 D1
Woodview Dr AIRDRIE ML6 111 G4
BLSH ML4 133 J2 4
Woodview Ter HMLTN ML3 156 B5 4
Woodville Pk GOV/IBX G51 104 B3
Woodville St GOV/IBX G51 104 B3
Woodwynd KLWNG KA13 193 L5
Woodyard Rd DMBTN G82 36 E6
Woodyett Pk
CRMNK/CLK/EAG G76 151 M4
Woodyett Rd
CRMNK/CLK/EAG G76 151 M4
Wordsworth Wy
UD/BTH/TAN G71 132 B6
Worsley Crs NMRNS G77 150 C3
Wotherspoon Dr BEITH KA15 144 B7 1
Wraes Av BRHD/NEIL G78 125 K5
Wraes Vw BRHD/NEIL G78 124 F8
Wraisland Crs BSHPTN PA7 57 M5 1
Wrangholm Crs MTHW ML1 134 B6 3
Wrangholm Dr MTHW ML1 134 A6
Wren Ct BLSH ML4 132 E1
Wren Pl JNSTN PA5 122 D2
Wren Rd GRNKW/INVK PA16 32 A4
Wright Av BRHD/NEIL G78 125 G7
Wrightfield Pl AYRS KA7 228 E7
Wrightlands Crs ERSK PA8 79 L1
Wright St RNFRW PA4 79 M8
Wyburn Pl AYR KA8 225 G6 3
Wye Crs CTBR ML5 87 K8
Wykeham Pl KNTSWD G13 81 J3
Wykeham Rd KNTSWD G13 81 J3
Wylie EKILN G74 154 D4
Wylie Av ALEX/LLW G83 25 K6 2
NMRNS G77 150 D2
Wylie Pl DMBTN G82 25 L7 2
Wylie St HMLTN ML3 156 D7 4
Wyllie Rd SALT KA21 201 G1 3
Wynd Beatson
UD/BTH/TAN G71 109 G8 5
Wyndford Dr MRYH/FIRH G20 82 D4
Wyndford Pl
MRYH/FIRH G20 82 D4 11
Wyndford Rd MRYH/FIRH G20 82 D4
Wyndford Ter
UD/BTH/TAN G71 132 B2
Wyndham Ct KVD/HLHD G12 82 D5 3
Wyndham St KVD/HLHD G12 82 D5
The Wynd CUMB G67 49 H4
Wynyard Gn EKILS G75 171 H1
Wyper Pl DMNK/BRGTN G40 12 E4
Wyvil Av KNTSWD G13 61 L8
Wyvis Av BSDN G61 61 J2
KNTSWD G13 80 E1
Wyvis Pl IRVSE KA11 204 A5
KNTSWD G13 80 F1
Wyvis Qd CLYDBK G81 80 F1 5
Wyvis Rd KLMNK KA1 212 A6 4

Y

Yair Dr CARD/HILL/MSPK G52 103 G3
Yardside Rd KLMNKN/STW KA3 206 B2
Yarrow Crs BSHPTN PA7 58 C7
WISHAW ML2 159 H5
Yarrow Gdns MRYH/FIRH G20 4 C2
Yarrow Gardens La
MRYH/FIRH G20 4 C2
Yarrow Pk EKILN G74 15 K4
Yarrow Rd BSHPBGS G64 64 A5
Yate St DEN/PKHD G31 13 G6
Yerton Brae WKIL KA23 181 J5
Yetholm St SCOT G14 80 E3 3
Yetholm Ter HMLTN ML3 155 L6
Yett Rd MTHW ML1 134 D6
Yetts Av KLMCLM PA13 55 K8
Yetts Crs KKNTL G66 65 M1
Yetts Hole Rd AIRDRIE ML6 88 C1
Yew Dr SPRGB/BLRNK G21 6 F2
Yew Pl JNSTN PA5 99 M8
Yews Crs HMLTN ML3 156 B4
Yieldshields Rd CARLUKE ML8 179 L7
CARLUKE ML8 189 K1
Yokerburn Pl KNTSWD G13 80 E2 2
Yokerburn Ter CLYDBK G81 80 D2 3
Yoker Ferry Rd RNFRW PA4 80 E4
Yoker Mill Gdns KNTSWD G13 80 E2 3
Yoker Mill Rd KNTSWD G13 80 E2
Yonderton Pl WKIL KA23 181 K5 3
York Dr RUTH G73 129 K4
Yorke Pl KLMNK KA1 16 B2
Yorke Rd TROON KA10 216 D8
Yorkhill Pde KVGV G3 82 C8
Yorkhill St KVGV G3 104 D1
York Rd GRNKW/INVK PA16 31 L4
York St CLYDBK G81 60 D7
KVGV G3 10 F2
WISHAW ML2 159 H7
York Street La AYR KA8 18 E1
Young Av TROON KA10 216 D3
Younger Dr PSTWK KA9 221 J6 1
Young Pl EKILS G75 172 A4
UD/BTH/TAN G71 132 A1 12
WISHAW ML2 160 B4 2
Young Rd LNK/LMHG ML11 199 L4
Young St ARD KA22 191 J7
AYR KA8 225 H4
CLYDBK G81 60 B5
WISHAW ML2 159 H6
Young Ter SPRGB/BLRNK G21 6 E1
Young Wynd BLSH ML4 133 G1
Yukon Ter EKILS G75 171 H1
Yvetot Av LNK/LMHG ML11 199 H5 7
Yvetot Ct CARLUKE ML8 178 E6 5

Z

Zambesi Dr
BLTYR/CAMB G72 131 J8 10
Zena Crs STPS/GTHM/RID G33 7 L1
Zena Pl STPS/GTHM/RID G33 7 L1
Zena St STPS/GTHM/RID G33 7 L1
Zetland Rd
CARD/HILL/MSPK G52 102 F1

Abbey Medical Centre PSLY PA1 9 J5
Abbey Primary School KLWNG KA13 193 K5
Abercorn Industrial Estate PSLYN/LNWD PA3 9 H2
Abercorn Secondary School COWCAD G4 5 G5
Abronhill Health Centre CUMB G67 49 L5
Abronhill High School CUMB G67 49 L5
Abronhill Primary School CUMB G67 49 K6
Acredyke School SPRGB/BLRNK G21 84 C2
Agricultural Museum CRMNK/CLK/EAG G76 152 F4
Ailsa Hospital RAYR/DAL KA6 229 L7
Airdrie Acadamy AIRDRIE ML6 88 F8
Airdrie Health Centre AIRDRIE ML6 110 E2
Airdrieonians Football Club AIRDRIE ML6 111 J3
Air Link Industrial Estate PSLYN/LNWD PA3 101 L1
Aitkenbar Primary School DMBTN G82 37 J4
Aitkenhead Primary School UD/BTH/TAN G71 108 F8
Aiton Primary School BLTYR/CAMB G72 130 A3
Albert Primary School AIRDRIE ML6 111 H1
Albert Primary School SPRGB/BLRNK G21 83 M4
Albion Rovers Football Club CTBR ML5 110 C3
Alexander Hospital CTBR ML5 109 L1
The Alexander Kerr Practice WISHAW ML2 159 H7
Alexandra Parade Primary School DEN/PKHD G31 6 F9
Alexandra Primary School AIRDRIE ML6 111 G2
Alexandria Medical Centre ALEX/LLW G83 25 L4
Alexandria Swimming Pool ALEX/LLW G83 25 K3
Alison Lea Medical Centre EKILN G74 154 C6
Allanshaw Industrial Estate HMLTN ML3 156 C5
Allanton Primary School SHOTTS ML7 161 H1
Alloway Primary School AYRS KA7 228 F8
All Saints RC Secondary School SPRGB/BLRNK G21 84 C5
AMF Bowling KVGV G3 10 C1
The Anderson Doe Podiatry Clinic PTCK G11 81 M5
Anderston Medical Centre KVGV G3 4 B8
Anderston Primary School KVGV G3 10 C1
Annanhill Primary School KLMNK KA1 16 B4
Annette Street Primary School GVH/MTFL G42 105 G7
Annfield Medical Centre DEN/PKHD G31 12 D2
Annick Primary School IRVSE KA11 203 M4
Anniesland College CLYDBK G81 80 C1
Anniesland College of Further Education PTCK G11 81 M7
Anniesland Industrial Estate KNTSWD G13 81 L1
The Antonine Sports Centre CLYDBK G81 60 A3
Aquatec Leisure Centre MTHW ML1 157 L2
Arcadia Business Centre CLYDBK G81 60 A8
Arches Theatre CGLE G1 11 G3
Ardeer Golf Club SVSTN KA20 192 E5
Ardeer Primary School SVSTN KA20 201 K2
Arden Primary School GIF/THBK G46 126 D5
Ardgowan Bowling & Tennis Club GRNKW/INVK PA16 2 A2
Ardgowan Medical Practice GRNKW/INVK PA16 2 B3
Ardgowan Primary School GRNKW/INVK PA16 32 D3
Ardoch Medical Centre BLTYR/CAMB G72 129 M3
Ardrossan Rugby Football Club ARD KA22 191 L8
Argo Sports Centre DRUM G15 60 E6
Argyle Indoor Market CGLE G1 11 J2
Arkleston Primary School RNFRW PA4 80 D8
Arran Surgery PLKSD/SHW G41 10 B5
Art Exposure Gallery CGLE G1 11 K3
Arts Guild Theatre GRNKW/INVK PA16 2 A1
Ashcraig School STPS/GTHM/RID G33 85 H6
Ashfield Greyhound Racing Co PPK/MIL G22 83 K4
Ashfield Medical Practicett MLNGV G62 42 A8
Ashley Street School KVGV G3 4 D6
Atholl Preparatory School MLNGV G62 42 A6
Auchenback Primary School BRHD/NEIL G78 125 K8
Auchenlodment Primary School JNSTN PA5 100 A8
Auchenraith Primary School BLTYR/CAMB G72 155 L2
Auchinairn Primary School BSHPBGS G64 84 B1
Auchincruive Agricultural College RAYR/DAL KA6 226 C6
Auchinloch School KKNTL G66 65 K7
Auldhouse Primary School EKILS G75 171 J8
Auldhouse Retail Park PLKSW/MSWD G43 127 J2
Auld Kirk Museum KKNTL G66 45 J8
Ayr Acadamie AYRS KA7 18 D2
Ayr College AYR KA8 19 H4
Ayr Grammar School AYRS KA7 18 F6
Ayr Hospital RAYR/DAL KA6 229 K8
Ayr Ice Rink AYR KA8 225 G6
Ayrshire Central Hospital IRV KA12 203 H3
Ayr United Football Club AYR KA8 225 H7
Baillieston Football Club BAIL/MDB/MHD G69 108 C5
Baillieston Health Centre BAIL/MDB/MHD G69 108 B5
Baird Memorial Primary School CUMB G67 68 C2
Baldernock School BSHPBGS G64 43 H7
Baljaffray School BSDN G61 61 J1
Baljaffray Shopping Centre BSDN G61 61 J2
Ballerup High School EKILS G75 171 H4
Balmore Surgery PPK/MIL G22 83 H4
Balmuildy Primary School BSHPBGS G64 63 M6
Balornock Primary School SPRGB/BLRNK G21 84 A5
Balrossie School KLMCLM PA13 75 G2
Bankhead School RUTH G73 128 F2
Bannerman High School BAIL/MDB/MHD G69 108 A5
Baras Market DMNK/BRGTN G40 12 A4
Barassie Primary School TROON KA10 216 D4
Bargarran Primary School ERSK PA8 58 F6
Bargeddie Primary School CTBR ML5 109 G3
Barmulloch Primary School SPRGB/BLRNK G21 7 K1
Barncluith Business Centre HMLTN ML3 156 F6
Barras Market DMNK/BRGTN G40 12 A4
Barratt Trading Estate COWCAD G4 5 G5
Barrhead Bowling Club BRHD/NEIL G78 125 J6
Barrhead High School BRHD/NEIL G78 125 K6
Barrhead Sports Centre BRHD/NEIL G78 125 J6
Barrowfield School DMNK/BRGTN G40 13 G7
Barr Thomson Business Park KLMNK KA1 17 G9
Battlefield Primary School GVH/MTFL G42 127 M2
Bearsden Primary School BSDN G61 61 L4
Beckford Street Business Centre HMLTN ML3 156 D4
The Beechwood Gallery MLNGV G62 42 A7
Beith Golf Club BEITH KA15 144 F6
Beith Health Centre BEITH KA15 144 B8
Bell College of Technology HMLTN ML3 156 D4
Bellfield Primary School KLMNK KA1 212 A5
The Bell Leisure Centre DMBTN G82 36 E6
Belmont House School NMRNS G77 150 F3
Belvidere Primary School BLSH ML4 133 G5
Benburb Football Club GOV/IBX G51 103 L3
Berryhill Primary School WISHAW ML2 158 E6
Biggart Hospital PSTWK KA9 225 K2
Bishopbriggs High School BSHPBGS G64 64 A8
Bishoploch School ESTRH G34 86 D8
Bishopton Health Centre BSHPTN PA7 58 B7
Bishoptown Primary School BSHPTN PA7 58 B6
Blackfriars Primary School GBLS G5 11 K7
Blacklands Primary School KLWNG KA13 193 K7
Blacklaw Primary School EKILN G74 15 M4
Blackwoods Medical Centre BAIL/MDB/MHD G69 66 F6
Blairtummock Primary School ESTRH G34 108 B1
Blantyre High School BLTYR/CAMB G72 155 K2
Blantyre Victoria Football Club BLTYR/CAMB G72 155 M2
Blawarthill Hospital KNTSWD G13 81 G3
Blood Transfusion Service CARLUKE ML8 178 D2
Bluebird Gallery LOCHW PA12 120 C7
Blythswood Estate RNFRW PA4 80 B5
Bobbys Leisure Centre CUMB G67 48 F7
Boglestone Primary School PGL PA14 54 F1
Bonhill Primary School ALEX/LLW G83 25 L6
Bonnyholm Primary School PLK/PH/NH G53 103 G6
Bonnyton Industrial Estate KLMNK KA1 16 C2
Borderline Theatre Co AYR KA8 18 E1
Bothwell Castle UD/BTH/TAN G71 131 K5
Bothwell Medical Centre UD/BTH/TAN G71 132 A7
Bothwell Primary School UD/BTH/TAN G71 131 M7
Bourtreehill Health Centre IRVSE KA11 204 A6
Bowfield Hotel & Country Club HWWD PA9 121 K7
Boyd Street Health Centre PSTWK KA9 225 J1
Braehead Industrial Estate RNFRW PA4 80 F6
Braehead Primary School AYR KA8 225 J7
Brae Head Primary School DMBTN G82 37 G4
Braeside School CSMK G45 128 F5
Braidbar School GIF/THBK G46 127 K6
Braidcraft Medical Centre PLK/PH/NH G53 103 K8
Braidfield High School CLYDBK G81 60 C7
Braidhurst Business Centre MTHW ML1 133 J6
Braidhurst High School MTHW ML1 133 K8
Braidwood Primary School CARLUKE ML8 188 F5
Branch Surgery CARLUKE ML8 177 M4
Brannock High School MTHW ML1 134 C6
Brediland Primary School PSLYS PA2 101 G8
Brenda Temple CGLE G1 11 K3
Bridge of Weir Primary School BRWEIR PA11 76 D8
Bridge of Weir Surgery BRWEIR PA11 98 D2
Bridgeton Business Centre DMNK/BRGTN G40 12 C5
Bridgeton Health Centre DMNK/BRGTN G40 12 C5
Brisbane Primary School LARGS KA30 115 L4
Broadway Leisure Centre PSTWK KA9 225 J1
Broomhill Industrial Estate KKNTL G66 45 M7
Broomhill Primary School PTCK G11 81 M5
Broomlands Primary School IRVSE KA11 204 A7
Bruce Medical Centre BLSH ML4 133 H4
Buchanan Business Park STPS/GTHM/RID G33 85 M3
Buchanan Galleries CGLE G1 5 J9
Buckingham Clinic KVD/HLHD G12 82 D6
Budhill Medical Practice CAR/SHTL G32 107 H4
Burmah Doctors Surgeryt PTCK G11 82 B7
Burnbank Medical Centre HMLTN ML3 156 A4
Burnbrae School PLK/PH/NH G53 126 D4
Burnhead Primary School UD/BTH/TAN G71 132 D1
Burnhill Sports Centre RUTH G73 128 F1
Burns Cottage AYRS KA7 228 E7
Burnside Clinic IRV KA12 203 H5
Burnside Primary School RUTH G73 129 H4
Busby District Primary School CRMNK/CLK/EAG G76 151 M3
Bushes Primary School PSLYS PA2 124 D1
Butterbiggins Medical Centre GVH/MTFL G42 105 H6
The Byre Gallery KVD/HLHD G12 82 D6
Byres Road Market PTCK G11 82 C7
Cadder Primary School SMSTN G23 82 F2
Cadzow Business Centre HMLTN ML3 156 D5
Cadzow Health Centre HMLTN ML3 174 D1
Cairnbrook Industrial Estate ESTRH G34 108 C1
Cairnhill Industrial Estate AIRDRIE ML6 111 G3
Cairnhill Trading Estate AIRDRIE ML6 111 G3
The Cairns Primary School BLTYR/CAMB G72 130 C5
Calderbank Primary School AIRDRIE ML6 111 J6
Caldercuilt Primary School SMSTN G23 62 D8
Calderhead High School SHOTTS ML7 137 L4
Calder Primary School MTHW ML1 157 M2
Caldervale High School AIRDRIE ML6 111 M2
Calderwood Lodge Primary School PLKSW/MSWD G43 127 K4
Calderwood Primary School RUTH G73 129 J3
Caldwell Golf Club BRHD/NEIL G78 146 F6
Caldwell House Hospital BRHD/NEIL G78 146 D8
Caledonian University CGLW G2 5 H8
Caledonian University COWCAD G4 5 K7
Caledonia Primary School BAIL/MDB/MHD G69 108 B6
Callander Street Clinic MRYH/FIRH G20 4 F3
Cambuslang Avory Club BLTYR/CAMB G72 130 A5
Cambuslang Clinic BLTYR/CAMB G72 130 B4
Cambuslang College BLTYR/CAMB G72 130 B4
Cambuslang College EKILN G74 15 G1
Cambuslang Rangers FC BLTYR/CAMB G72 129 M3
Cambuslang Recreation Centre BLTYR/CAMB G72 130 D4
Cambuslang Rugby Club BLTYR/CAMB G72 129 K4
Cambusnethan Primary School WISHAW ML2 159 K6
Campsie Black Watch Football Club KKNTL G66 44 C1
Campsie Recreation Centre KKNTL G66 44 D1
Campsie View School KKNTL G66 65 G4
Canberra Primary School EKILS G75 171 H1
Canniesburn Hospital BSDN G61 61 L7
Caprington Golf Course KLMNK KA1 211 K6
Carbrain Primary School CUMB G67 49 H7
Cardinal Newman High School BLSH ML4 132 F4
Cardonald Clinic CARD/HILL/MSPK G52 103 J4
Cardonald Primary School CARD/HILL/MSPK G52 103 H5
Cardross Golf Club DMBTN G82 35 H2
Cardross Primary School DMBTN G82 24 A8
Carleith Primary School CLYDBK G81 59 L3
Carlibar Primary School BRHD/NEIL G78 125 J6
Carluke Health Centre CARLUKE ML8 178 E7
Carluke High School CARLUKE ML8 179 H7
Carluke Primary School CARLUKE ML8 179 G6
Carman Leisure Centre DMBTN G82 25 K7
Carmunnock Primary School CRMNK/CLK/EAG G76 152 D2
Carmyle Medical Centre CAR/SHTL G32 130 B1
Carmyle Primary School CAR/SHTL G32 107 J8
Carnbooth School CRMNK/CLK/EAG G76 152 B2
Carnbroe Primary School CTBR ML5 110 D5
Carntyne Primary School STPS/GTHM/RID G33 7 M9
Carntyne Surgery STPS/GTHM/RID G33 106 F1
Carnwadrick Primary School GIF/THBK G46 126 F5
Carolside Medical Centre CRMNK/CLK/EAG G76 151 L2
Carolside Primary School CRMNK/CLK/EAG G76 151 L3
Carsemeadow School BRWEIR PA11 75 M7
Carsemeadow School BRWEIR PA11 75 K7
Castlebank Industrial Estate PTCK G11 82 A8
Castlefield Primary School EKILS G75 171 H3
Castlehead High School PSLYS PA2 8 E6
Castlehill Primary School BSDN G61 61 H3
Castlehill Primary School WISHAW ML2 177 G1
Castlemilk Health Centre CSMK G45 128 E6
Castlemilk High School CSMK G45 128 E7
Castlepark Primary School IRV KA12 203 J3
Castle (Remains of) WKIL KA23 180 D3
Castle Semple Sailing Club LOCHW PA12 120 D6
Castleton Primary School CSMK G45 128 D6
Cathcart Street Surgery AYRS KA7 18 D2
Cathedral RC Primary School MTHW ML1 157 L2
Cathkin High School BLTYR/CAMB G72 129 L5
Cathkin Primary School RUTH G73 129 K6
Celtic Football Club DEN/PKHD G31 13 J6
Centenary Surgery CTBR ML5 110 A4
Central College of Commerce CGLE G1 5 K9
Central Health Centre CUMB G67 48 F8
Central Mosque GBLS G5 11 J5
Centre Gallery CGLW G2 4 E8
Chapel Green Primary School KSYTH G65 46 E2
Chapelhall Industrial Estate AIRDRIE ML6 111 K6
Chapelhall Secondary School AIRDRIE ML6 111 K6
Chapelside Primary School AIRDRIE ML6 89 G8
Charing Cross Clinic KVGV G3 4 D7
The Charleston Surgery PSLYS PA2 9 H6
Chatelherault Primary School HMLTN ML3 156 E8
Child Health Clinic PLKSW/MSWD G43 127 J1
Chinese Medical Centre KVD/HLHD G12 4 A3
Chirnsyde Primary School PPK/MIL G22 83 K3
Christie Park School ALEX/LLW G83 25 K4
Christ the King Primary School MTHW ML1 134 B3
Chryston Primary School BAIL/MDB/MHD G69 86 C1
Chryston Secondary School BAIL/MDB/MHD G69 86 C1
Chryston Valley Business Centre BAIL/MDB/MHD G69 86 C1
Citadel Leisure Centre AYRS KA7 18 C1
City Chambers CGLE G1 11 K1
City Council CGLW G2 5 G9
City Halls & Ticket Office CGLE G1 11 K2
City of Glasgow Council CGLE G1 5 J9
City of Glasgow Council CGLE G1 11 M4
City of Glasgow Council CSMK G45 128 F6
City of Glasgow Council GBLS G5 11 K6
Civic Centre EKILN G74 15 G3
Civic Centre HMLTN ML3 155 M6
Civic Centre MTHW ML1 158 A5
Civic Theatre AYR KA8 19 H4
Claremont High School EKILN G74 172 C1
Clarkston Primary School AIRDRIE ML6 111 K1
Cleland Hospital MTHW ML1 135 J8
Cleland Primary School MTHW ML1 135 J8
Cleveden Secondary School KVD/HLHD G12 82 B4
Cleveden Secondary School MRYH/FIRH G20 4 B1
Clober Golf Club House MLNGV G62 41 M6
Clober Primary School MLNGV G62 41 L7
Clune Park Primary School PGL PA14 34 D8
Clydebank Business Centre CLYDBK G81 80 C1
Clydebank College CLYDBK G81 60 B6
Clydebank College DMBTN G82 36 D5
Clydebank Health Centre CLYDBK G81 60 B5
Clydebank High School CLYDBK G81 60 A5
Clydebank Town Hall CLYDBK G81 60 A8
Clyde Football Club BALLOCH G68 47 M8
Clyde Industrial Estate RUTH G73 129 K1
Clydemuir Primary School CLYDBK G81 59 K5
Clydesdale Business Centre LNK/LMHC ML11 199 J6
Clyde Valley High School WISHAW ML2 177 H2

Clydeview School *MTHW* ML1 157 J2
Clydeway Business Centre *KVGV* G3 10 B1
Coatbridge Business Centre *CTBR* ML5 110 C3
Coatbridge College *CTBR* ML5 110 C2
Coatbridge Health Centre *CTBR* ML5 110 A3
Coatbridge High School *CTBR* ML5 110 A2
Coathill Hospital *CTBR* ML5 110 A5
Cochrane Castle Primary School *JNSTN* PA5 122 D1
Colgrain Primary School *HBR/GL* G84 21 G8
The College & Cathedral College *GTCI* KA28 138 B6
College of Art *CGLW* G2 4 F8
College of Building & Printing *CGLE* G1 5 K9
College of Food & Technology *CGLE* G1 5 K9
Colquhoun Park Primary School *BSDN* G61 61 J6
Coltness High School *WISHAW* ML2 159 K5
Coltness Primary School *WISHAW* ML2 159 J3
Columba High School *CTBR* ML5 110 A5
Compass Gallery *CGLW* G2 4 F9
Condorrat Health Centre *CUMB* G67 68 A3
Condorrat Primary School *CUMB* G67 68 B2
Corpus Christi RC School *AIRDRIE* ML6 111 H7
Corsehill Primary School *KLWNG* KA13 193 M5
Cotton Street Business Park *DMNK/BRGTN* G40 106 A7
Council Chambers *GLSTN* KA4 214 C3
Country Club Hotel *CMPF/LLE* G63 27 J7
The Country Estate Gallery *CARLUKE* ML8 188 C8
Courthill Clinic *BSDN* G61 61 J3
Cowglen Golf Club *BEITH* KA15 168 B1
Cowglen Hospital *PLK/PH/NH* G53 126 D2
Coylton Health Clinic *RAYR/DAL* KA6 231 H6
Coylton Primary School *RAYR/DAL* KA6 231 J6
Craigbank Secondary School *PLK/PH/NH* G53 126 D1
Craigdhu Primary School *MLNGV* G62 61 M1
Craighead Primary School *KKNTL* G66 45 H3
Craighead School *HMLTN* ML3 156 B2
Craigholme School *PLKSD/SHW* G41 104 D6
Craigie College of Education *AYR* KA8 19 M5
Craigilea Primary School *PSLYN/LNWD* PA3 101 G3
Craigpark Park *AYR* KA8 225 K8
Crawforddyke Primary School *CARLUKE* ML8 189 G1
Croftcroighn School *STPS/GTHM/RID* G33 85 L8
Crofthead Industrial Estate *BRHD/NEIL* G78 148 C2
Crookfur Primary School *NMRNS* G77 150 D2
Crookston (NT) *PLK/PH/NH* G53 103 H7
Cross Arthurlie Primary School *BRHD/NEIL* G78 125 G5
Crosshouse Hospital *CRH/DND* KA2 206 A7
Crosshouse Primary School *CRH/DND* KA2 205 L8
Crosshouse Primary School *EKILS* G75 171 G4
Crowngate Business Centre *DMNK/BRGTN* G40 12 D6
Cumbernauld Airport *BALLOCH* G68 49 J1
Cumbernauld College *CUMB* G67 48 F8
Cumbernauld High School *CUMB* G67 49 J8
Cumbernauld Primary School *CUMB* G67 49 H5
Cumbernauld Theatre *CUMB* G67 49 H5
Cumbrae Primary School *GTCI* KA28 138 A6
Cuthbertson Primary School *PLKSD/SHW* G41 105 G6
The Cutting Gallery *SHOTTS* ML7 137 K4
Cyril Gerber Gallery *CGLW* G2 5 G9
Daily Record & Sunday Mail Offices *KVGV* G3 10 C2
Dalgarven Mill Museum *KLWNG* KA13 193 K1
Dalmarnock Primary School *DMNK/BRGTN* G40 12 E8
Dalmarnock Trading Estate *RUTH* G73 106 B8
Dalmilling Golf Club *AYR* KA8 225 L8
Dalmilling Primary School *AYR* KA8 225 L7
Dalreoch Primary School *DMBTN* G82 36 C4
Dalry Primary School *DALRY* KA24 184 B2
Dalsholm Industrial Estate *MRYH/FIRH* G20 82 B2
Dalziel Business Centre *MTHW* ML1 157 L3
Dalziel High School *MTHW* ML1 157 K3
Darrows Estate *UD/BTH/TAN* G71 132 D3
David Dale College *DMNK/BRGTN* G40 12 D5
David Livingston Centre *BLTYR/CAMB* G72 131 L7
David Livingstone Memorial Primary School *BLTYR/CAMB* G72 131 K8
Dental Hospital & School *CGLW* G2 4 F8
Department of General Practice *KVD/HLHD* G12 82 C5
Devol Industrial Estate *PGL* PA14 54 D1
Dinmont Doctors Surgery *PLKSD/SHW* G41 104 D8
Doonfoot Primary School *AYRS* KA7 228 B6
Douglas Inch Clinic *KVGV* G3 4 D7
Dowanhill Primary School *PTCK* G11 82 C7
Dr D'silva & Partners *UD/BTH/TAN* G71 132 C2
Dreghorn Primary School *IRVSE* KA11 204 D8
Dr Huq *CTBR* ML5 109 M3
Drs M Agnew & P Mckillop *CTBR* ML5 109 M3
Drumchapel Health Centre *DRUM* G15 60 F6
Drumchapel High School *DRUM* G15 61 G5
Drummore School *DRUM* G15 61 J5
Drumoyne Industrial Estate *GOV/IBX* G51 103 L3
Drumoyne Primary School *GOV/IBX* G51 103 L3
Drumpark Special School *CTBR* ML5 109 G3
Drumpellier Cricket Club *CTBR* ML5 109 K3
Duchess Industrial Estate *RUTH* G73 106 C8
Dumbarton Football Club *DMBTN* G82 37 H5
Dumbarton Health Centre *DMBTN* G82 36 E5
Dumbarton Joint Hospital *DMBTN* G82 36 C5
Dumbarton Peoples Theatre *DMBTN* G82 37 H6
Dunard Primary School *MRYH/FIRH* G20 4 C1
Dunbartonshire & Lomond Council *BSHPBGS* G64 63 M7
Duncanrig Secondary School *EKILS* G75 153 H8
Duncanrig Sports Centre *EKILS* G75 171 H1
Dundas Business Centre *COWCAD* G4 5 G6
Dundonald Castle *CRH/DND* KA2 209 L7
Dundonald Health Centre *CRH/DND* KA2 209 M7
Dundonald Medical Practice *CRH/DND* KA2 209 M7
Dundonald Primary School *CRH/DND* KA2 209 M7
Dunrobin Primary School *AIRDRIE* ML6 111 L2
Duntreath Castle *CMPF/LLE* G63 26 D2
Dykehead Primary School *SHOTTS* ML7 137 K4
Dykesmains Primary School *SALT* KA21 191 M6
Earnock Secondary School *HMLTN* ML3 156 A7
East Bank Primary School *CAR/SHTL* G32 107 J4
East Dunbartonshire Council *BAIL/MDB/MHD* G69 86 C1
East Dunbartonshire Council *BAIL/MDB/MHD* G69 108 A4
East Dunbartonshire Council *BSDN* G61 61 K3
East Dunbartonshire Council *BSDN* G61 62 A5
East Dunbartonshire Council *BSHPBGS* G64 63 L5
East Dunbartonshire Council *BSHPBGS* G64 83 M1
East Dunbartonshire Council *KKNTL* G66 44 D1
East Dunbartonshire Council *KKNTL* G66 65 J2
East Dunbartonshire Council *KSYTH* G65 46 F5
East Dunbartonshire Council *MLNGV* G62 42 A7
Easter Moffat Golf Club *AIRDRIE* ML6 90 B8
Eastfield Primary School *BALLOCH* G68 48 B8
East Fulton Primary School *PSLYN/LNWD* PA3 99 M3
East Kilbride Ice Rink *EKILN* G74 14 F4
East Kilbride Sports Club *EKILN* G74 172 C3
East Milton Primary School *EKILS* G75 14 A4
Eastmuir Surgery *CAR/SHTL* G32 107 J4
East Renfrewshire Council *BRHD/NEIL* G78 125 H6
East Renfrewshire Council *CRMNK/CLK/EAG* G76 151 L2
East Renfrewshire Council *GIF/THBK* G46 127 J8
Eastside Industrial Estate *KKNTL* G66 45 K8
Eastwood High School *NMRNS* G77 150 E2
Edenkiln Surgery *CMPF/LLE* G63 27 J6
Edinbarnet Primary School *CLYDBK* G81 60 C1
Eglinton Castle *KLWNG* KA13 194 C8
Elderpark Clinic *GOV/IBX* G51 103 M2
Elder Park Primary School *GOV/IBX* G51 103 L1
Elderslie Cottage Hospital *JNSTN* PA5 100 C7
Elise Hospital *BRWEIR* PA11 75 K7
Elmvale Primary School *PPK/MIL* G22 83 L4
Elmwood Medical Centre *NMRNS* G77 150 E3
Elmwood Special School *DMBTN* G82 37 G5
Empire Theatre *LRKH* ML9 175 M6
Erskine Health Centre *ERSK* PA8 59 G6
Erskine Hospital *BSHPTN* PA7 58 E3
Erskine Swimming Pool *ERSK* PA8 59 J7
Erskine View Clinic *OLDK* G60 59 G3
Fallside Secondary School *UD/BTH/TAN* G71 132 D3
Family Planning Clinic *KVGV* G3 4 C7
Farm Castle Industrial Estate *RUTH* G73 129 J1
Farmeloan Industrial Estate *RUTH* G73 129 H1
Fencedyke Primary School *IRVSE* KA11 204 A6
Ferguslie Cricket Club *PSLYS* PA2 8 D7
Ferguslie Primary School *PSLYN/LNWD* PA3 8 A1
Ferry Terminal *GRK* PA19 31 L1
Ferry Terminal *GRK* PA19 31 G3
Ferry Terminal *TROON* KA10 216 B6
Festival Business Centre *GOV/IBX* G51 104 C3
Fiddle Gallery *MRYH/FIRH* G20 4 B1
Film Theatre *CGLW* G2 5 G8
The Fireplace & Furnisher Gallery *KVGV* G3 82 D8
Fire Service Training Station *COWCAD* G4 5 H6
Fire Station *CGLW* G2 5 H7
Fire Station *COWCAD* G4 12 A3
Firhill Business Centre *MRYH/FIRH* G20 4 E1
Flemington Industrial Estate *BLTYR/CAMB* G72 130 E5
Florence Street Clinic *GBLS* G5 11 K5
The Flower Gallery *DEN/PKHD* G31 12 E2
The Flower Gallery *PSLY* PA1 9 M3
The Food Gallery *KVGV* G3 4 C7
Fordbank Primary School *JNSTN* PA5 122 C1
Forehill Primary School *AYRS* KA7 19 L8
Forge Industrial Estate *KLMNK* KA1 16 C2
Fort Matilda Industrial Estate *GRNKW/INVK* PA16 32 A1
The Fort Theatre *BSHPBGS* G64 63 M8
Fountain Business Centre *CTBR* ML5 110 A2
The Framework Gallery *TROON* KA10 216 C6
French Street Industrial Estate *RNFRW* PA4 80 B7
Fullwood Health Centre *MTHW* ML1 134 A5
Fullwood Industrial Estate *HMLTN* ML3 156 B4
Gadburn School *SPRGB/BLRNK* G21 84 C4
Gaiety Theatre *AYRS* KA7 18 E2
Galleon Leisure Centre *KLMNK* KA1 16 E6
The Gallery at Home Creations *RUTH* G73 129 J3
Gallery of Modern Art *CGLE* G1 11 J1
The Gallery *DEN/PKHD* G31 13 L6
The Gallery *WKIL* KA23 181 J4
Gallowgate Market *CGLE* G1 11 L3
Gallowhill Primary School *PSLYN/LNWD* PA3 102 B2
Galston Clinic *GLSTN* KA4 214 C3
Galston Primary School *GLSTN* KA4 214 C3
Gargieston Primary School *KLMNK* KA1 211 J3
Garnetbank Primary School *KVGV* G3 4 E7
Garnock Business Park *SVSTN* KA20 201 K1
Garrell Business Centre *KSYTH* G65 47 J1
Garrowhill Primary School *BAIL/MDB/MHD* G69 108 A4
Gartconner Primary School *KKNTL* G66 66 C1
Gartcosh Primary School *BAIL/MDB/MHD* G69 86 F4
Gartcosh Works Sports Club *BAIL/MDB/MHD* G69 87 G4
Garthamlock Secondary School *STPS/GTHM/RID* G33 85 L7
Gartnavel General Hospital *KVD/HLHD* G12 82 B5
Gartnavel Royal Hospital *KVD/HLHD* G12 82 A5
Gartsherrie Industrial Estate *CTBR* ML5 87 M8
Gartsherrie Primary School *CTBR* ML5 109 L1
Gask House School *BSHPBGS* G64 83 M2
The Gatehouse Gallery *GIF/THBK* G46 126 F7
Gavinburn School *OLDK* G60 58 F2
GHK Rugby Football Club *KNTSWD* G13 81 M3
Giffnock Primary School *GIF/THBK* G46 127 J6
Giffnock Synagogue *GIF/THBK* G46 127 J7
Giffnock Theatre Player *GIF/THBK* G46 127 J7
Glasgow Airport *PSLYN/LNWD* PA3 79 L8
Glasgow Art Gallery & Museum *KVGV* G3 82 D8
Glasgow Caledonian University *KVD/HLHD* G12 82 A3
Glasgow Caledonian University *KVGV* G3 4 B5
Glasgow Cathedral *COWCAD* G4 6 A9
Glasgow City Council *BAIL/MDB/MHD* G69 108 B5
Glasgow City Council *CAR/SHTL* G32 13 L1
Glasgow City Council *CAR/SHTL* G32 106 F4
Glasgow City Council *CAR/SHTL* G32 107 H4
Glasgow City Council *CARD/HILL/MSPK* G52 102 F4
Glasgow City Council *CARD/HILL/MSPK* G52 103 K5
Glasgow City Council *CGLE* G1 5 J9
Glasgow City Council *CGLE* G1 11 L2
Glasgow City Council *CGLE* G1 11 J2
Glasgow City Council *CGLW* G2 4 E8
Glasgow City Council *CGLW* G2 5 G8
Glasgow City Council *CGLW* G2 10 E1
Glasgow City Council *COWCAD* G4 5 L8
Glasgow City Council *COWCAD* G4 5 G3
Glasgow City Council *COWCAD* G4 5 K4
Glasgow City Council *CSMK* G45 128 D6
Glasgow City Council *DEN/PKHD* G31 7 H8
Glasgow City Council *DEN/PKHD* G31 13 L6
Glasgow City Council *DMBTN* G82 36 E6
Glasgow City Council *DMNK/BRGTN* G40 12 E6
Glasgow City Council *DMNK/BRGTN* G40 13 G6
Glasgow City Council *DMNK/BRGTN* G40 106 A6
Glasgow City Council *DRUM* G15 60 F5
Glasgow City Council *ESTRH* G34 108 A1
Glasgow City Council *GBLS* G5 10 E4
Glasgow City Council *GBLS* G5 10 F5
Glasgow City Council *GBLS* G5 11 H5
Glasgow City Council *GBLS* G5 11 L7
Glasgow City Council *GIF/THBK* G46 126 C5
Glasgow City Council *GOV/IBX* G51 103 L3
Glasgow City Council *GOV/IBX* G51 104 A1
Glasgow City Council *GOV/IBX* G51 104 C3
Glasgow City Council *GVH/MTFL* G42 105 H7
Glasgow City Council *GVH/MTFL* G42 128 D1
Glasgow City Council *KNTSWD* G13 81 M3
Glasgow City Council *KNTSWD* G13 81 H3
Glasgow City Council *KVD/HLHD* G12 82 C3
Glasgow City Council *KVGV* G3 4 A8
Glasgow City Council *LNPK/KPK* G44 128 B3
Glasgow City Council *MRYH/FIRH* G20 4 E4
Glasgow City Council *MRYH/FIRH* G20 4 E2
Glasgow City Council *MRYH/FIRH* G20 82 A2
Glasgow City Council *MRYH/FIRH* G20 82 D2
Glasgow City Council *MRYH/FIRH* G20 82 E4
Glasgow City Council *PLK/PH/NH* G53 103 H8
Glasgow City Council *PLK/PH/NH* G53 125 M5
Glasgow City Council *PLK/PH/NH* G53 126 B2
Glasgow City Council *PLKSD/SHW* G41 10 D7
Glasgow City Council *PLKSD/SHW* G41 104 D6
Glasgow City Council *PLKSW/MSWD* G43 127 J1
Glasgow City Council *PPK/MIL* G22 83 L2
Glasgow City Council *PPK/MIL* G22 83 H5
Glasgow City Council *PTCK* G11 82 B8
Glasgow City Council *SPRGB/BLRNK* G21 6 A3
Glasgow City Council *SPRGB/BLRNK* G21 6 C3
Glasgow City Council *SPRGB/BLRNK* G21 6 C7
Glasgow City Council *SPRGB/BLRNK* G21 6 A1
Glasgow City Council *SPRGB/BLRNK* G21 7 G3
Glasgow City Council *SPRGB/BLRNK* G21 83 M3
Glasgow City Council *SPRGB/BLRNK* G21 84 C3
Glasgow City Council *STPS/GTHM/RID* G33 106 F1
Glasgow City Council *STPS/GTHM/RID* G33 107 K3
Glasgow City Council *STPS/GTHM/RID* G33 107 M3
Glasgow City Council *STPS/GTHM/RID* G33 107 H1
Glasgow City Council *STPS/GTHM/RID* G33 107 J1
Glasgow Cricket Club *PLKSD/SHW* G41 104 D7
Glasgow Golf Club *IRVSE* KA11 208 C4
Glasgow Nuffield Hospital *KVD/HLHD* G12 82 B4
Glasgow Royal Infirmary *DEN/PKHD* G31 6 C8
Glasgow School of Art *KVGV* G3 5 G7
Glasgow Steiner School *KVGV* G3 104 D1
Glasgow Western Post Graduate Medical Centre *KVD/HLHD* G12 82 D4
Glasgow Zoo *UD/BTH/TAN* G71 108 B7
Glebe Primary School *IRV* KA12 203 J7
Glenboig Primary School *CTBR* ML5 87 M4
Glenburn Clinic *PSLYS* PA2 124 D1
Glenburn Primary School *PSTWK* KA9 221 L8
Glenburn School *GRNKW/INVK* PA16 31 L7
Glencairn Industrial Estate *KLMNK* KA1 16 F8
Glencairn Primary School *MTHW* ML1 157 L4
Glencairn Primary School *SVSTN* KA20 201 K1
Glencryan School *CUMB* G67 68 E2
Glendale Primary School *PLKSD/SHW* G41 10 D8
Glengarnock Primary School *GLGNK* KA14 167 H2
Glengowan Primary School *AIRDRIE* ML6 91 G5
Glenhead Primary School *CUMB* G67 49 L4
Gleniffer High School *PSLYS* PA2 124 A1
Glenlee Primary School *HMLTN* ML3 156 A4
Glenmanor Primary School *BAIL/MDB/MHD* G69 66 F7
Glenmill Surgery *STPS/GTHM/RID* G33 7 M2
Glenpark Industrial Estate *DEN/PKHD* G31 13 G3
Glenvale Football Club *PSLY* PA1 8 D4
Glenwood Business Centre *CSMK* G45 128 E6
Glenwood Business Park *CSMK* G45 128 E6
Golden Hill Primary School *CLYDBK* G81 60 B3
Golfhill Primary School *AIRDRIE* ML6 88 E7
Golfhill Primary School *DEN/PKHD* G31 6 C9
Gorbals Health Centre *GBLS* G5 11 K7
Gourock Central Junior School *GRK* PA19 31 K1

Gourock Golf Club *GRK* PA19 ... 31 H3
Gourock Health Centre *GRK* PA19 ... 31 L1
Gourock High School *GRK* PA19 ... 31 K2
Govan Health Centre *GOV/IBX* G51 ... 103 L1
Govan High Secondary School *GOV/IBX* G51 ... 103 L2
Govanhill Health Centre *GVH/MTFL* G42 ... 105 H7
Greater Glasgow Health Board *DEN/PKHD* G31 ... 13 L5
Greenan Gallery *AYRS* KA7 ... 18 D3
Greenfaulds High School *CUMB* G67 ... 68 D2
Greenfield Street School *GOV/IBX* G51 ... 103 M2
Greengairs Primary School *AIRDRIE* ML6 ... 69 L7
Greenhill Primary School *CTBR* ML5 ... 110 A1
Greenhills Health Centre *EKILS* G75 ... 171 G3
Greenhills Primary School *EKILS* G75 ... 171 J3
Greenock Cricket Club *GRNKW/INVK* PA16 ... 32 D2
Greenock Golf Club House *GRNKW/INVK* PA16 ... 32 C3
Greenock Health Centre *GRNK* PA15 ... 2 B4
Greenock High School *GRNKW/INVK* PA16 ... 31 K7
Greenock Wanderers Rugby Football Club *GRNKW/INVK* PA16 ... 32 B1
Greenwood Acadamy *IRVSE* KA11 ... 204 A8
Grovewood Business Centre *BLSH* ML4 ... 132 E1
Gryffe High School *CRG/CRSL/HOU* PA6 ... 77 G8
Haghill School *DEN/PKHD* G31 ... 13 H1
Hairmyres & Stonehouse Hospitals NHS Trust *EKILS* G75 ... 152 F8
Haldane Primary School *ALEX/LLW* G83 ... 25 M1
Halfmerke Primary School *EKILN* G74 ... 154 A6
Hallside Primary School *BLTYR/CAMB* G72 ... 130 E5
Hamilton Academical Football Club Ltd *HMLTN* ML3 ... 156 C4
Hamilton Business Park *HMLTN* ML3 ... 156 D4
Hamilton College *HMLTN* ML3 ... 156 D4
Hamilton District Council *LRKH* ML9 ... 176 A6
Hamilton Grammar School *HMLTN* ML3 ... 156 D6
Hamiltonhill Industrial Estate *PPK/MIL* G22 ... 5 H2
Hamilton Race Course *HMLTN* ML3 ... 156 D2
Hampden School *GVH/MTFL* G42 ... 128 E2
Harbour Industrial Estate *ARD* KA22 ... 191 J7
Hareleeshill Primary School *LRKH* ML9 ... 176 C7
Harestanes Primary School *KKNTL* G66 ... 46 A8
Hartfield Clinic *DMBTN* G82 ... 37 G5
Hartwood Hospital *MTHW* ML1 ... 136 E7
Hartwood Hospital *SHOTTS* ML7 ... 136 F7
The Harvest Clinic *COWCAD* G4 ... 4 E6
Haughney Doctors Surgery *NMRNS* G77 ... 150 F4
Hawkhead Hospital *PSLYS* PA2 ... 102 C7
Haycocks Primary School *SVSTN* KA20 ... 192 E7
Haysholm School *IRV* KA12 ... 203 L5
Healthcare International (HCI) *CLYDBK* G81 ... 59 M7
Health & Welfare Clinic *BAIL/MDB/MHD* G69 ... 86 D1
Heatherbank Museum of Social Work Trust *KVD/HLHD* G12 ... 4 B5
Heathery Knowe Primary School *EKILS* G75 ... 14 D8
Heathfield Primary School *AYR* KA8 ... 225 H4
Helensburgh Golf Club *HBR/GL* G84 ... 20 F6
Helensburgh Medical Centre *HBR/GL* G84 ... 20 D8
Helensburgh Swimming Pool *HBR/GL* G84 ... 20 D8
The Henderson Theatre *SHOTTS* ML7 ... 137 M5
Heriot Primary School *PSLYS* PA2 ... 123 M1
Hermitage School *HBR/GL* G84 ... 20 D7
High Blantyre Primary School *BLTYR/CAMB* G72 ... 155 H2
High Court & Court of Justiciary *CGLE* G1 ... 11 K4
Highholm Primary School *PGL* PA14 ... 34 B8
Highlanders Academy Primary School *GRNKW/INVK* PA16 ... 32 D5
High School of Glasgow *KNTSWD* G13 ... 81 L3
High Street Industrial Estate *KKNTL* G66 ... 45 J8
Hillhead High School *KVD/HLHD* G12 ... 4 A4
Hillhead Primary School *KKNTL* G66 ... 65 L1
Hillhead Primary School *KLMNKN/STW* KA3 ... 206 E6
Hillhead Rugby Club *KVD/HLHD* G12 ... 82 B5
Hillington Industrial Estate *CARD/HILL/MSPK* G52 ... 102 F2
Hillington Primary School *CARD/HILL/MSPK* G52 ... 103 G3
Hillpark Secondary School *PLKSW/MSWD* G43 ... 127 J4
Hill Street Industrial Estate *ARD* KA22 ... 191 J8
Hillstrust Primary School *GOV/IBX* G51 ... 104 A1
Hindu Temple *KVD/HLHD* G12 ... 4 A4
Hollybrook School *GVH/MTFL* G42 ... 105 H7
Hollywood Bowl *BAIL/MDB/MHD* G69 ... 109 J6
Holm Industrial Estate *PSLYS* PA2 ... 9 J8
Holmlea Primary School *LNPK/KPK* G44 ... 128 A3
Holy Cross High School *HMLTN* ML3 ... 156 E5
Holycross RC Primary School *GRNKW/INVK* PA16 ... 32 B3
Holy Cross School *KSYTH* G65 ... 47 M5
Holy Family Primary School *BLSH* ML4 ... 133 J4
Holy Family Primary School *KKNTL* G66 ... 65 H3
Holy Family RC Primary School *PGL* PA14 ... 55 G1
Holy Reedemer RC School *CLYDBK* G81 ... 80 D2
Holyrood Secondary School *GVH/MTFL* G42 ... 105 J8
Holytown Primary School *MTHW* ML1 ... 134 B4
Homoeopaths Surgery *KVGV* G3 ... 4 D8
Househillmuir Road School *PLK/PH/NH* G53 ... 126 B4
Houston Primary School *CRG/CRSL/HOU* PA6 ... 77 H8
Houston Surgery *CRG/CRSL/HOU* PA6 ... 77 H6
Howford School *PLK/PH/NH* G53 ... 103 G7
Howwood Primary School *HWWD* PA9 ... 121 M4
The Hui Chun Clinic *KVGV* G3 ... 4 F7
The Hunter Health Centre *EKILN* G74 ... 15 G3
Hunter High School *EKILN* G74 ... 154 C7
Hunter House Museum *EKILN* G74 ... 154 C5
Hunter Primary School *EKILN* G74 ... 154 C6
Hunter Sport Centre *KLMNKN/STW* KA3 ... 206 F6
Hunterston Castle *WKIL* KA23 ... 163 G6
Hurlford Primary School *KLMNK* KA1 ... 212 E3
Hurlford Primary School *KLMNKN/STW* KA3 ... 207 K5
Hutchesons Grammar Junior School *PLKSD/SHW* G41 ... 105 G7
Hutchesons Grammar School *PLKSD/SHW* G41 ... 104 D7
Hutchesons St Aloysians Rugby Club *GIF/THBK* G46 ... 127 G4
Hyndland Primary School *PTCK* G11 ... 82 B7
Hyndland Senior Secondary School *KVD/HLHD* G12 ... 82 A6
Ian Kenny Gallery *LRKH* ML9 ... 175 M5
Ibh Carrick Glen Hospital *RAYR/DAL* KA6 ... 229 M8
Ibrox Industrial Estate *GOV/IBX* G51 ... 104 B3
Ibrox Primary School *GOV/IBX* G51 ... 104 A4
Inchinnan Primary School *RNFRW* PA4 ... 79 K2
Indoor Market *DRUM* G15 ... 60 F6
Insomnia Gallery *KVGV* G3 ... 4 D7
International Christian College *COWCAD* G4 ... 5 M9
Inverclyde Royal Hospital *GRNKW/INVK* PA16 ... 31 M5
Inverkip Primary School *GRNKW/INVK* PA16 ... 50 D4
Irvine Sports Club *IRV* KA12 ... 203 H7
Islamic Mosque *KVGV* G3 ... 4 D6
Isobel Mair School *CRMNK/CLK/EAG* G76 ... 127 K8
Jackton Business Centre *EKILS* G75 ... 170 C2
James Mcfarlane School *ARD* KA22 ... 191 J6
James Reid School *SVSTN* KA20 ... 192 B7
Jamestown Primary School *ALEX/LLW* G83 ... 25 M2
James Watt College *GRNK* PA15 ... 2 F3
James Watt College *GRNKW/INVK* PA16 ... 2 A3
John Galt Primary School *IRV* KA12 ... 203 J5
John Hillhouse Industrial Estate *BLTYR/CAMB* G72 ... 129 K1
John Logie Baird Primary School *HBR/GL* G84 ... 20 F7
John Ogilvie High School *HMLTN* ML3 ... 155 M5
Johnstone Health Centre *JNSTN* PA5 ... 99 M7
Johnstone High School *JNSTN* PA5 ... 122 D1
Johnstone Hospital *JNSTN* PA5 ... 100 A5
Johnstone Swimming Pool *JNSTN* PA5 ... 99 M6
John Street Clinic *DMBTN* G82 ... 36 D1
John Wheatley College *ESTRH* G34 ... 108 B1
The John Wright Sports Centre *EKILN* G74 ... 15 K2
Jordanhill College School *KNTSWD* G13 ... 81 K4
Junior High School of Glasgow *BSDN* G61 ... 61 K5
Junior Secondary School *MTHW* ML1 ... 133 M5
Keil School *DMBTN* G82 ... 36 D6
Keir Hardie Memorial Primary School *MTHW* ML1 ... 134 C6
Keir Hardie Sports Centre *MTHW* ML1 ... 134 A3
Kelburne Cricket Club *PSLY* PA1 ... 9 M2
Kelburn Primary School *LARGS* KA30 ... 115 K6
The Kelly Gallery *CGLW* G2 ... 4 F8
Kelvindale Primary School *KVD/HLHD* G12 ... 82 A4
Kelvin Gallery *CGLW* G2 ... 5 G8
Kendon Business Centre *AYRS* KA7 ... 18 D5
Kenilworth Medical Centre *CUMB* G67 ... 68 E1
Kennyhill School *DEN/PKHD* G31 ... 7 J9
Kerelaw School *SVSTN* KA20 ... 192 D7
Kerr Practice *DMNK/BRGTN* G40 ... 12 D6
The Kibble School *PSLYN/LNWD* PA3 ... 101 K1
Kilbarchan Primary School *KLBCH* PA10 ... 99 G5
Kilbirnie Golf Club *KBRN* KA25 ... 142 F8
Kilbowie Primary School *CLYDBK* G81 ... 60 B6
Kildrum Primary School *CUMB* G67 ... 49 J6
Kilmacolm Primary School *KLMCLM* PA13 ... 75 J2
Kilmarnock (Barassie) Golf Club *TROON* KA10 ... 216 D2
Kilmarnock College *IRV* KA12 ... 203 J6
Kilmarnock College *KLMNKN/STW* KA3 ... 17 H3
Kilmarnock Football Club *KLMNK* KA1 ... 16 C6
Kilmarnock Indoor Market *KLMNK* KA1 ... 16 F6
Kilmarnock Tennis Club *KLMNKN/STW* KA3 ... 17 G3
Kilmaurs Clinic *KLMNKN/STW* KA3 ... 206 B2
Kilmaurs Primary School *KLMNKN/STW* KA3 ... 206 B2
Kilpatrick Primary School *CLYDBK* G81 ... 59 L3
Kilsyth Health Centre *KSYTH* G65 ... 47 L1
Kilsyth Primary School *KSYTH* G65 ... 47 K1
Kilwinning Clinic *KLWNG* KA13 ... 193 M6
Kilwinning Medical Practice *KLWNG* KA13 ... 193 L6
Kincaidston Primary School *AYRS* KA7 ... 229 G4
Kingcase Primary School *PSTWK* KA9 ... 225 H3
Kingsgate Retail Park *EKILN* G74 ... 154 A3
Kings Glen Primary School *GRNK* PA15 ... 33 K8
Kings Park Secondary School *LNPK/KPK* G44 ... 128 C4
Kings Theatre *CGLW* G2 ... 4 E8
Kingston Business Park *PGL* PA14 ... 34 A7
Kingston Industrial Estate *PGL* PA14 ... 34 A7
Kinning Park Medical Centre *GOV/IBX* G51 ... 10 B4
Kirkfield Primary School *LNK/LMHG* ML11 ... 198 D5
Kirkhall Surgery *PSTWK* KA9 ... 221 J8
Kirkhill Primary School *NMRNS* G77 ... 151 H4
Kirkintilloch Foot Clinic *KKNTL* G66 ... 65 J1
Kirkintilloch High School *KKNTL* G66 ... 65 M1
Kirkintilloch Industrial Estate *KKNTL* G66 ... 45 K7
Kirklandeuk Primary School *RNFRW* PA4 ... 80 C5
Kirklandside Hospital *KLMNK* KA1 ... 212 C4
Kirkriggs School *CSMK* G45 ... 129 G4
Kirkshaws Primary School *CTBR* ML5 ... 109 L5
Kirkstyle Primary School *KLMNK* KA1 ... 17 H9
Kirktonholme Primary School *EKILN* G74 ... 14 C2
Kirkton Primary School *CARLUKE* ML8 ... 178 E8
Kirkwood Health Clinic *CTBR* ML5 ... 109 J5
Kittoch School *EKILS* G75 ... 14 D7
Knock Castle *LARGS* KA30 ... 92 A6
Knowetop Primary School *MTHW* ML1 ... 158 A5
Knoxland Primary School *DMBTN* G82 ... 37 G7
Kylie Acad *AYRS* KA7 ... 229 K2
Lady Alice Primary School *GRNKW/INVK* PA16 ... 32 C5
Ladyburn Business Park *GRNK* PA15 ... 33 L6
Lady Margaret Hospital *GTCI* KA28 ... 138 A6
Lady Octavia Recreation Centre *GRNK* PA15 ... 3 K9
Ladywell Primary School *MTHW* ML1 ... 157 J2
Lagoon Leisure Centre *PSLY* PA1 ... 9 K3
Laigh Bent Sports Club *HMLTN* ML3 ... 156 E6
Lainshaw Primary School *KLMNKN/STW* KA3 ... 197 K1
Laird Business Park *DMNK/BRGTN* G40 ... 106 A7
Lairdsland Primary School *KKNTL* G66 ... 65 J1
Lamlash Primary School *STPS/GTHM/RID* G33 ... 107 H1
Lammermoor Primary School *WISHAW* ML2 ... 159 H5
Lanark Gallery *LNK/LMHG* ML11 ... 199 G5
Lanark Golf Club *LNK/LMHG* ML11 ... 199 K6
Lanark Grammar School *LNK/LMHG* ML11 ... 199 G6
Lanark Primary School *LNK/LMHG* ML11 ... 199 H4
Lanarkshire County Council *LRKH* ML9 ... 176 A4
Lanarkshire Health Board *AIRDRIE* ML6 ... 111 M1
Lanarkshire Health Board *CARLUKE* ML8 ... 178 D2
Lanarkshire Health Board *HMLTN* ML3 ... 155 M5
Lanarkshire Health Board *UD/BTH/TAN* G71 ... 132 B6
Lanarkshire Health Board *WISHAW* ML2 ... 160 A5
Lanark Tennis Club *LNK/LMHG* ML11 ... 199 G4
Lanfauld School *DRUM* G15 ... 60 F5
Langbank Primary School *PGL* PA14 ... 56 B2
Langbrae School *KKNTL* G66 ... 65 G4
Langcraigs Primary School *PSLYS* PA2 ... 124 C2
Langlands Primary School *CUMB* G67 ... 68 F1
Langlands School *GOV/IBX* G51 ... 103 L2
Langloan Primary School *CTBR* ML5 ... 109 L3
Langside College *CSMK* G45 ... 128 F6
Langside College *GVH/MTFL* G42 ... 128 A1
Langside Galleries *GVH/MTFL* G42 ... 127 M1
Lansdowne Clinic *KVD/HLHD* G12 ... 82 A4
Largs Golf Club *LARGS* KA30 ... 115 L8
Largs Sailing Club *LARGS* KA30 ... 115 J7
Larkfield Primary School *GRNKW/INVK* PA16 ... 31 L5
Larkhall Leisure Centre & Baths *LRKH* ML9 ... 175 M7
Lawmuir Primary School *BLSH* ML4 ... 133 G6
Law Primary School *CARLUKE* ML8 ... 178 A4
Leisure Centre *PSTWK* KA9 ... 221 H8
Leithland Road Primary School *PLK/PH/NH* G53 ... 103 H8
Lennox Castle Hospital *KKNTL* G66 ... 28 F8
Lennoxtown Primary School *KKNTL* G66 ... 44 D1
Lenzie Hospital *KKNTL* G66 ... 65 L6
Lenzie Moss Primary School *KKNTL* G66 ... 65 H4
Lenzie Primary School *KKNTL* G66 ... 65 J4
Levenvale Primary School *ALEX/LLW* G83 ... 25 K2
Leverndale Hospital *PLK/PH/NH* G53 ... 102 F7
Lightburn Hospital *CAR/SHTL* G32 ... 107 H2
Lille Art Gallery *MLNGV* G62 ... 42 B7
Lillie Art Gallery *BSDN* G61 ... 61 L4
Lilybank School *PGL* PA14 ... 33 M7
Linburn School *CARD/HILL/MSPK* G52 ... 102 F3
Linnvale Primary School *CLYDBK* G81 ... 60 D8
Linwood Health Centre *PSLYN/LNWD* PA3 ... 100 C4
Linwood High School *PSLYN/LNWD* PA3 ... 99 M3
Linwood Moss Sports Centre *PSLYN/LNWD* PA3 ... 100 A2
Littlehill Primary School *STPS/GTHM/RID* G33 ... 7 L3
Loanhead Primary School *KLMNK* KA1 ... 17 G5
Lochend Secondary School *ESTRH* G34 ... 86 C8
Lochfield Primary School *PSLYS* PA2 ... 101 M8
Lochgoin Primary School *DRUM* G15 ... 60 F5
Lochinch Playing Fields & Sports Club *PLKSW/MSWD* G43 ... 103 M8
Lochpark Stadium *CARLUKE* ML8 ... 188 F1
Loch Primary School *RUTH* G73 ... 129 K5
Lochshore Industrial Estate *GLGNK* KA14 ... 167 J2
Lochwinnoch Community Museum *LOCHW* PA12 ... 120 C6
Lochwinnoch Golf Club *LOCHW* PA12 ... 120 B7
Lochwinnoch Junior Secondary School *LOCHW* PA12 ... 120 C6
Lockhart Hospital *LNK/LMHG* ML11 ... 199 J6
Logans Primary School *MTHW* ML1 ... 157 H1
Lomond Healthcare NHS Trust *ALEX/LLW* G83 ... 25 K3
Lomond School *HBR/GL* G84 ... 20 D6
London Road Primary School *DMNK/BRGTN* G40 ... 13 H7
Long Calderwood Primary School *EKILN* G74 ... 154 C4
Loudoun Golf Club *GLSTN* KA4 ... 214 E2
Loudoun Montgomery Primary School *IRV* KA12 ... 203 J8
Loudoun Sports Centre *GLSTN* KA4 ... 214 D2
Lourdes Primary School *CARD/HILL/MSPK* G52 ... 103 J5
Low Waters Medical Centre *HMLTN* ML3 ... 174 C1
M8 Trading Estate 81-83 *PLKSD/SHW* G41 ... 10 B6
Machanhill Primary School *LRKH* ML9 ... 176 B6
The Macinnes Practice *AIRDRIE* ML6 ... 111 K6
Madhok Medical Centre *GVH/MTFL* G42 ... 128 A2
Manse Road Medical Centre *WISHAW* ML2 ... 160 A4
Markets *SPRGB/BLRNK* G21 ... 7 G7
Marr College *TROON* KA10 ... 216 E5
Marr Rugby Football Club *TROON* KA10 ... 217 G8
Maryhill Football Club *MRYH/FIRH* G20 ... 82 D3
Maryhill Health Centre *MRYH/FIRH* G20 ... 82 E3
The Mary Russell School *PSLYS* PA2 ... 102 C7
Masonic Temple *BRHD/NEIL* G78 ... 125 H7
Mavisbank School *AIRDRIE* ML6 ... 110 F1
Maxwellton Primary School *EKILN* G74 ... 15 L1
Mayfield Industrial Estate *KLMNK* KA1 ... 213 G3
Mayfield Primary School *SVSTN* KA20 ... 192 B7
Mcdougall House *BLSH* ML4 ... 133 G1
Mcgill Primary School *PLK/PH/NH* G53 ... 103 J7
Mcinnes Doctors Surgery *MTHW* ML1 ... 134 E5
Mclean Museum & Art Gallery *GRNKW/INVK* PA16 ... 2 B2
Mclellan Galleries *CGLW* G2 ... 5 G8
Meadowburn Primary School *BSHPBGS* G64 ... 64 A6
Meadowhead Industrial Estate *IRVSE* KA11 ... 208 E5
Meadowside Industrial Estate *RNFRW* PA4 ... 80 D3
Mearns Castle High School *NMRNS* G77 ... 151 G6
Megabowl *CLYDBK* G81 ... 60 C8
Melrose Primary School *CUMB* G67 ... 68 E2
Merchiston Hospital *JNSTN* PA5 ... 99 L4

Merkland School *KKNTL* G66 45 M8
Merksworth High School *PSLYN/LNWD* PA3 101 K2
Merrylee Primary School *PLKSW/MSWD* G43 127 M4
Middlefield School *PTCK* G11 82 B7
Middlemuir School *CLYDBK* G81 59 M6
Midlock Medical Centre *GOV/IBX* G51 104 B4
Millersneuk Primary School *KKNTL* G66 65 L5
Milngavie & Bearsden Sports Club *MLNGV* G62 62 D2
Milngavie Business Centre *MLNGV* G62 42 A8
Milngavie Golf Club *MLNGV* G62 41 L4
Miltonbank Primary School *PPK/MIL* G22 83 J1
Milton Clinic *PPK/MIL* G22 83 J2
Milton Primary School *DMBTN* G82 37 M8
Milton School *PPK/MIL* G22 83 L2
Mitchell Theatre & Library *KVGV* G3 4 D8
Modryvale Medical Centre *MTHW* ML1 157 M4
Monklands & Bellshill Hospitals NHS Trust *BLSH* ML4 133 G1
Monklands District General Hospital *CTBR* ML5 110 D2
Monklands Industrial Estate *CTBR* ML5 109 M7
Monkton Primary School *PSTWK* KA9 221 K5
Moore & Dalziel Doctors Surgery *PTCK* G11 82 B7
Moorfoot Primary School *GRK* PA19 31 J3
Moorpark Industrial Estate *SVSTN* KA20 201 K2
Moorpark Primary School *RNFRW* PA4 80 B7
Morningside Primary School *WISHAW* ML2 160 B5
Mosque *GVH/MTFL* G42 105 G8
Mossblown Health Centre *RAYR/DAL* KA6 227 G3
Mossedge Industrial Estate *PSLYN/LNWD* PA3 100 C3
Mossend Primary School *BLSH* ML4 133 J5
Mossend Surgery *BLSH* ML4 133 J4
Mosshead Primary School *BSDN* G61 61 L2
Mossneuk Primary School *EKILS* G75 170 F2
Motherwell Business Centre *MTHW* ML1 157 M2
Motherwell College *MTHW* ML1 157 M5
Motherwell Cricket Club *MTHW* ML1 158 A6
Motherwell Football Club *MTHW* ML1 157 M5
Mount Cameron Primary School *EKILN* G74 15 M7
Mount Florida Medical Centre *GVH/MTFL* G42 128 A1
Mount Florida School *LNPK/KPK* G44 128 B2
Mount Manor Business Park *KVGV* G3 4 A9
Mount Vernon Primary School *CAR/SHTL* G32 107 K6
Mugdock Castle *MLNGV* G62 41 M2
Muiredge Primary School *UD/BTH/TAN* G71 132 A3
Muirhead Primary School *TROON* KA10 216 E5
Muirhouse Primary School *MTHW* ML1 158 C7
Muir Street Primary School *MTHW* ML1 157 K1
Munro Business Centre *KNTSWD* G13 81 L3
Murano Medical Centre *MRYH/FIRH* G20 82 F5
Murray Primary School *EKILS* G75 14 F6
The Murray Surgery *EKILS* G75 14 D8
Museum *LNK/LMHG* ML11 198 F5
Museum *RNFRW* PA4 80 D5
Museum of Royal Highland Fusilliers *CGLW* G2 4 D8
Museum of the Cumbraes *GTCI* KA28 138 A6
Museum of Transport *KVGV* G3 82 C8
Napiers Dispensary & Clinic *PTCK* G11 82 C7
Natural Therapy Clinic *CGLW* G2 4 F8
Neilsland Primary School *HMLTN* ML3 156 A8
Neilston Primary School *BRHD/NEIL* G78 148 E2
Neilston Swimming Pool *BRHD/NEIL* G78 148 E2
Nerston Residential School *EKILN* G74 154 A2
Nethercommon Industrial Estate *PSLYN/LNWD* PA3 101 L2
Nethercraigs Sports Centre *PLK/PH/NH* G53 103 K7
Netherlee Primary School *LNPK/KPK* G44 127 M7
Netherton Business Centre *KLMNK* KA1 16 E7
Netherton Primary School *WISHAW* ML2 158 E8
Netherton School *CSMK* G45 128 C7
New Albion Industrial Estate *KNTSWD* G13 80 E2
Newark Castle *PGL* PA14 34 D7
Newarthill Primary School *MTHW* ML1 134 E6
Newmains Primary School *RNFRW* PA4 80 C8
Newmains Primary School *WISHAW* ML2 159 M5
Newmilns Primary School *NMLNS* KA16 215 G2
New Monkland Primary School *AIRDRIE* ML6 88 E5
Newspaper Offices *CGLE* G1 11 L1
New Stage Theatre *PLKSD/SHW* G41 104 F7
Newton Mearns Primary School *NMRNS* G77 150 D5
Newton Primary School *AYR* KA8 19 G1
The Nicholas Geraghty Clinic *MTHW* ML1 157 M2
Nitshill Primary School *PLK/PH/NH* G53 126 A5
Noble Primary School *BLSH* ML4 133 G2
North Ayrshire Council *GTCI* KA28 138 A7
Northcote Surgery *KVD/HLHD* G12 82 C6
North Glasgow College *SPRGB/BLRNK* G21 6 B2
North Glasgow University Hospital NHS Trust *SPRGB/BLRNK* G21 83 M2
North Lanarkshire Council *AIRDRIE* ML6 110 F2
North Lanarkshire Council *BAIL/MDB/MHD* G69 66 E7
North Lanarkshire Council *BLSH* ML4 132 F4
North Lanarkshire Council *BLSH* ML4 133 H4
North Lanarkshire Council *BLSH* ML4 133 G3
North Lanarkshire Council *CTBR* ML5 109 M4
North Lanarkshire Council *CTBR* ML5 110 B2
North Lanarkshire Council *CUMB* G67 48 F8
North Lanarkshire Council *CUMB* G67 49 H6
North Lanarkshire Council *CUMB* G67 49 K3
North Lanarkshire Council *CUMB* G67 68 F3
North Lanarkshire Council *CUMB* G67 69 G1
North Lanarkshire Council *KSYTH* G65 47 J1
North Lanarkshire Council *MTHW* ML1 157 L2
North Lanarkshire Council *MTHW* ML1 158 B5
North Lanarkshire Council *STPS/GTHM/RID* G33 85 L3
North Lanarkshire Council *UD/BTH/TAN* G71 132 D3
North Lanarkshire Council *UD/BTH/TAN* G71 132 C1
North Lanarkshire Council *WISHAW* ML2 158 D6
North Lanarkshire Council *WISHAW* ML2 176 C1
North Woodside Swimming Pool *COWCAD* G4 4 F5
Notre Dame High School *GRNKW/INVK* PA16 32 D6
Notre Dame High School *KVD/HLHD* G12 82 C6
Notre Dame Primary School *KVD/HLHD* G12 82 C6
Nuneaton Industrial Estate *DMNK/BRGTN* G40 12 E9
Oakbank Industrial Estate *MRYH/FIRH* G20 4 F3
Oakfield Primary School *GRNK* PA15 3 K8
Oakgrove Primary School *COWCAD* G4 4 F5
Odeon Cinema *AYRS* KA7 18 F5
Odeon Cinema *CGLW* G2 5 H9
Odeon Cinema *GOV/IBX* G51 10 C4
Old Monkland Primary School *CTBR* ML5 109 J5
Onthank Primary School *KLMNKN/STW* KA3 206 F4
Open Air Market Stall *CGLE* G1 11 K4
Optimax Laser Eye Clinic *CGLW* G2 4 E7
Orbiston Business Centre *BLSH* ML4 133 G6
Our Lady of Assumption Primary School *MRYH/FIRH* G20 83 G3
Our Lady of Lourdes RC School *EKILS* G75 14 B6
Our Lady of Peace RC Primary School *PSLYN/LNWD* PA3 100 A4
Our Lady of the Annunciation Primary School *PLKSW/MSWD* G43 127 L4
Our Lady of the Missions Primary School *GIF/THBK* G46 127 H6
Our Lady & St Francis Primary School *MTHW* ML1 134 C7
Our Lady & St Patricks High School *DMBTN* G82 36 C5
Our Ladys High School *CUMB* G67 48 D8
Our Ladys High School *MTHW* ML1 158 A5
Outdoor Recreation Centre *BSHPBGS* G64 84 A1
Overton Primary School *GRNKW/INVK* PA16 32 D6
Overtown Primary School *WISHAW* ML2 177 J2
Oxgang Primary School *KKNTL* G66 65 M1
Paisley Abbey *PSLY* PA1 9 J4
Paisley Golf Club *PSLYS* PA2 124 B4
Paisley Grammar School *PSLY* PA1 9 L3
Paisley Maternity Hospital *PSLYS* PA2 8 D8
Paisley Museum & Art Galleries *PSLY* PA1 8 F3
Paisley Picture Framers & Gallery *PSLY* PA1 9 H5
Palace Theatre *KLMNKN/STW* KA3 17 G4
Parkhead Hospital *DEN/PKHD* G31 13 L5
Parkhouse School *PPK/MIL* G22 83 K3
Parklands School *HBR/GL* G84 20 E7
Park Lodge School *HBR/GL* G84 20 E8
Park Mains School *ERSK* PA8 59 H8
Park School *KLMNKN/STW* KA3 17 J2
Parkview Business Centre *KVGV* G3 4 D7
Partick Market *PTCK* G11 82 C7
Partick Thistle Football Club *MRYH/FIRH* G20 4 E1
The Pavilion Theatre *CGLW* G2 5 H8
Penilee Secondary School *CARD/HILL/MSPK* G52 102 F3
Pennyburn Primary School *KLWNG* KA13 193 J7
Pentagon Business Centre *KVGV* G3 10 E2
Peoples Palace Museum *DMNK/BRGTN* G40 12 A5
Peterburn Primary School *AIRDRIE* ML6 111 K4
Petershill Football Club *SPRGB/BLRNK* G21 6 D2
Petershill Recreation Centre *SPRGB/BLRNK* G21 7 H3
Phoenix Industrial Estate *PSLYN/LNWD* PA3 101 L1
Pierhead Clinic *GRK* PA19 31 L1
Pinewood Primary School *DRUM* G15 61 J5
Plains Primary School *AIRDRIE* ML6 90 A7
Pollokshields Primary School *PLKSD/SHW* G41 10 C9
Port Glasgow Baths *PGL* PA14 34 C8
Port Glasgow Golf Club *PGL* PA14 54 D2
Port Glasgow Health Centre *PGL* PA14 34 C7
Port Glasgow High School *PGL* PA14 55 G3
Port Glasgow Juniors Football Club *PGL* PA14 35 G8
Port Glasgow Protestant Athletic Club *PGL* PA14 34 A7
Portland Industrial Estate *SVSTN* KA20 201 K2
Portland Park Medical Centre *HMLTN* ML3 156 E7
Portland Surgery *TROON* KA10 216 B6
Possilpark Health Centre *PPK/MIL* G22 83 J5
Prestwick Acad *PSTWK* KA9 221 K8
Prestwick Golf Club *PSTWK* KA9 221 H8
Prestwick St Cuthbert Golf Club *PSTWK* KA9 225 K3
Prestwick St Nicholas Golf Club *PSTWK* KA9 225 H2
Primary School *RNFRW* PA4 80 D7
Primary School Wemyss Bay *WMYSB* PA18 50 A8
Pro Bowl *KKNTL* G66 45 J7
Pro Lane Bowl *EKILS* G75 15 J9
Provand's Lordship *COWCAD* G4 6 A9
Public Baths *HMLTN* ML3 156 D5
Public Baths *LNK/LMHG* ML11 199 G5
Quadrant Shopping Centre *CTBR* ML5 110 B2
Quarry Brae Primary School *DEN/PKHD* G31 13 M7
Queens Drive Retail Park *KLMNK* KA1 17 G7
Queen's Park FC *GVH/MTFL* G42 128 B2
Ralston Golf Club *PSLY* PA1 102 D5
Ralston Primary School *PSLY* PA1 102 E4
Ramgarhia Association Sikh Temple *KVD/HLHD* G12 4 B4
Ramoy Business Centre *PSLY* PA1 8 D4
Ramshorn Theatre *CGLE* G1 11 L1
Rangers Football Club *GOV/IBX* G51 104 B3
Rangers Football Club Plc *CGLE* G1 11 L3
Rank Leisure Odeon Cinema *KLMNK* KA1 17 G7
Rashielee Primary School *ERSK* PA8 59 H6
Ravenscraig Hospital *GRNKW/INVK* PA16 32 A6
Ravenscraig Primary School *GRNKW/INVK* PA16 31 L6
Ravenscraig Recreation Centre *GRNKW/INVK* PA16 31 L6
Ravenspark Golf Club *IRV* KA12 203 G3
Ravenspark Hospital *IRV* KA12 202 F3
Ravenswood Doctors Surgery *JNSTN* PA5 99 L6
Ravenswood Primary School *CUMB* G67 68 E1
Redburn Industrial Estate *IRV* KA12 203 H1
Redburn School *CUMB* G67 49 J7
Red Deer Day Hospital *EKILS* G75 14 A5
Regency Medical Clinic *KVGV* G3 4 C7
Reid Kerr College *PSLYN/LNWD* PA3 101 M3
Renfrew Council *PSLYS* PA2 124 E3
Renfrew Council *RNFRW* PA4 80 D5
Renfrew Council *RNFRW* PA4 80 B7
Renfrew District Welfare Clinic *PSLYS* PA2 100 F8
Renfrew Health Centre *RNFRW* PA4 80 C7
Renfrew High School *RNFRW* PA4 80 D7
Renfrewshire Council *JNSTN* PA5 99 L6
Renfrewshire Council *PSLY* PA1 9 K5
Renfrewshire Council *PSLY* PA1 9 G2
Renfrewshire Council *PSLY* PA1 9 J3
Renfrewshire Council *PSLYN/LNWD* PA3 8 E2
Renfrewshire Council *PSLYN/LNWD* PA3 8 B2
Renfrewshire Council *PSLYS* PA2 9 H8
Renfrewshire Healthcare NHS Trust *PSLYS* PA2 125 H1
Renfrewshire & Inverclyde Primary Care NHS Trust *PSLY* PA1 9 H3
Renton Primary School *DMBTN* G82 25 K8
Richmond Doctors Surgery *PTCK* G11 82 A7
Richmond Park School *GBLS* G5 105 K6
Ridge Park School *LNK/LMHG* ML11 198 F3
Riverbank Business Centre *KLMNK* KA1 17 H6
Riverview Medical Practice *JNSTN* PA5 99 M6
Riverway Retail Park *IRV* KA12 203 H8
Roadmeetings Hospital *CARLUKE* ML8 189 J1
Robert Smillie Memorial Primary School *LRKH* ML9 175 M8
Robertsons Sports Centre *PSLYS* PA2 124 F2
Rob Roy Football Club *KKNTL* G66 65 G1
Robslee School *GIF/THBK* G46 127 H7
Rochsolloch Primary School *AIRDRIE* ML6 110 E3
Rosebank School *AYRS* KA7 19 G8
Rosehall High School *CTBR* ML5 109 M6
Rosevale School *PPK/MIL* G22 83 K2
Ross Clinic *KVD/HLHD* G12 82 B6
Ross Hall Hospital *CARD/HILL/MSPK* G52 103 G6
Routenburn Golf Club *LARGS* KA30 115 J3
Rowallan Business Park *KLMNKN/STW* KA3 207 J2
Royal Alexandra Hospital NHS Trust *PSLYS* PA2 8 D8
Royal College of Nursing *KVGV* G3 4 C7
Royal Concert Hall *CGLE* G1 5 J8
Royal Gourock Yacht Club *GRK* PA19 31 J2
Royal Hospital for Sick Children *DRUM* G15 61 G7
Royal Infirmary *COWCAD* G4 5 L9
Royal Infirmary *COWCAD* G4 6 B8
Royal Maternity Hospital *CGLE* G1 11 L1
Royal Troon Golf Club *TROON* KA10 220 D1
Royston Primary School *SPRGB/BLRNK* G21 6 C7
RSAMD *CGLW* G2 5 H8
Rutherglen Health Centre *RUTH* G73 129 H2
Rutherglen High School *RUTH* G73 129 H1
Rutherglen Swimming Pool *RUTH* G73 129 G2
Sacred Heart Primary School *BLSH* ML4 133 G6
Sacred Heart Primary School *CUMB* G67 49 H7
Sacred Heart Primary School *DMNK/BRGTN* G40 12 D8
Sacred Heart Primary School *GRNKW/INVK* PA16 31 L5
SAE Technology College *PLKSD/SHW* G41 10 B5
Sailing Club *PSTWK* KA9 225 H2
St Agathas Primary School *KKNTL* G66 66 B1
St Agnes Primary School *SMSTN* G23 82 E1
St Aidans High School *WISHAW* ML2 159 H5
St Aidans RC Primary School *WISHAW* ML2 159 J4
St Aidans School *CAR/SHTL* G32 13 M3
St Alberts Primary School *PLKSD/SHW* G41 10 A7
St Alloyisious Primary School *SPRGB/BLRNK* G21 83 L4
St Aloysius College *KVGV* G3 4 F7
St Aloysius College Junior School *KVGV* G3 4 F7
St Aloysius Preparatory School *KVGV* G3 4 F7
St Aloysius RC School *AIRDRIE* ML6 111 L7
St Ambrose RC School *CTBR* ML5 109 L1
St Andrewes Cathedral *CGLE* G1 11 H3
St Andrews Business Centre *KLMNK* KA1 16 F7
St Andrews Clinics for Children *KVD/HLHD* G12 82 D6
St Andrews High School *CLYDBK* G81 80 C1
St Andrews High School *EKILS* G75 14 D9
St Andrews RC Primary School *AIRDRIE* ML6 88 E8
St Andrews RC School *BSDN* G61 61 J3
St Andrews Secondary RC School *CAR/SHTL* G32 107 G2
St Angelas Primary School *GIF/THBK* G46 126 D6
St Angustines RC Primary School *CTBR* ML5 109 M3
St Annes Primary School *DMNK/BRGTN* G40 12 F4
St Annes Primary School *ERSK* PA8 79 J1
St Annes Primary School *HMLTN* ML3 174 D1
St Anns Primary School *RAYR/DAL* KA6 227 G3
St Anthonys Football Club *GOV/IBX* G51 104 A3
St Anthonys RC Primary School *JNSTN* PA5 122 C2
St Anthonys RC School *RUTH* G73 129 K5
St Anthonys School *GOV/IBX* G51 103 M1
St Athanasuis Primary School *CARLUKE* ML8 178 F8
St Augustines Primary School *PPK/MIL* G22 83 J2
St Barbaras RC Secondary School *BAIL/MDB/MHD* G69 86 D2
St Bartholomews RC Primary School *CTBR* ML5 87 K8
St Batholemews Primary School *CSMK* G45 128 F5
St Benedicts RC School *ESTRH* G34 86 A8
St Bernadette Primary School *MTHW* ML1 157 H1
St Bernards RC Primary School *CTBR* ML5 110 B6
St Blanes Primary School *BLTYR/CAMB* G72 155 J1
St Blanes Primary School *SMSTN* G23 62 D8
St Brendans High School *PSLYN/LNWD* PA3 100 C3

St Brendans Primary School *MTHW* ML1 158 B7
St Brides Primary School *BLTYR/CAMB* G72 130 A4
St Brides Primary School *GVH/MTFL* G42 105 G7
St Brides RC Primary School *UD/BTH/TAN* G71 132 A5
St Brides RC School *EKILN* G74 15 J4
St Bridgets Primary School *BAIL/MDB/MHD* G69 108 B4
St Bridgets Primary School *KBRN* KA25 166 F1
St Bridgets School *GVH/MTFL* G42 128 E1
St Brigids Primary School *WISHAW* ML2 159 M4
St Cadocs Primary School *NMRNS* G77 150 C4
St Cadocs School *BLTYR/CAMB* G72 130 C5
St Catherines School *PSLYN/LNWD* PA3 101 M3
St Catherines School *SPRGB/BLRNK* G21 84 C4
St Charles RC Primary School *PSLYS* PA2 9 J9
St Charles RC School *BLTYR/CAMB* G72 130 F3
St Clares Primary School *ESTRH* G34 108 D1
St Columbas High School *CLYDBK* G81 60 C5
St Columbas Primary School *KLMCLM* PA13 75 J1
St Columbas Primary School *UD/BTH/TAN* G71 132 C2
St Columbas RC High School *GRK* PA19 32 A3
St Columbas RC Primary School *KLMNK* KA1 17 G5
St Columbas School *KLMCLM* PA13 75 K1
St Columbkilles RC School *RUTH* G73 129 H2
St Convals Primary School *PLKSW/MSWD* G43 127 K1
St Cuthberts Primary School *PPK/MIL* G22 83 G5
St Cuthberts RC School *JNSTN* PA5 122 C2
St Davids RC Primary School *JNSTN* PA5 99 K8
St Davids RC School *AIRDRIE* ML6 89 M7
St Denis's Primary School *DEN/PKHD* G31 13 G2
St Dominics Primary School *CSMK* G45 128 F7
St Dominnics RC Primary School *AIRDRIE* ML6 111 J3
St Edwards Primary School *AIRDRIE* ML6 111 J2
St Elizabeth RC Primary School *HMLTN* ML3 174 D2
St Enoch Business Centre *CGLE* G1 11 H3
St Enoch Shopping Centre *CGLE* G1 11 J3
St Fergus RC Primary School *PSLYN/LNWD* PA3 8 B2
St Fillans RC Primary School *CRG/CRSL/HOU* PA6 77 G7
St Flannans RC Primary School *KKNTL* G66 45 M8
St Francis of Assisi Primary School *BAIL/MDB/MHD* G69 107 M6
St Francis Primary School *GBLS* G5 11 L8
St Francis Primary School *PGL* PA14 54 F2
St Francis RC Primary School *BALLOCH* G68 68 A2
St Gabriels Primary School *UD/BTH/TAN* G71 132 D1
St Gabriels RC Primary School *GRNKW/INVK* PA16 31 K6
St Georges Medical Centre *KVGV* G3 4 E6
St Georges School *CARD/HILL/MSPK* G52 103 G4
St Gerards Primary School *BLSH* ML4 133 H2
St Gerards Secondary School *GOV/IBX* G51 104 B2
St Gilberts Primary School *SPRGB/BLRNK* G21 7 J3
St Helens Primary School *BSHPBGS* G64 64 C7
St Helens Primary School *CUMB* G67 68 B2
St Hilarys RC Primary School *EKILN* G74 15 M5
St Ignatius Primary School *WISHAW* ML2 159 H6
St James Primary School *DMNK/BRGTN* G40 12 A5
St James RC Primary School *RNFRW* PA4 80 C6
St James RC School *CTBR* ML5 109 L5
St James Street Health Centre *PSLY* PA1 8 F2
St Joachins RC Primary School *CAR/SHTL* G32 107 J8
St Joan of Arc School *PPK/MIL* G22 83 H2
St John Bosco Primary School *ERSK* PA8 58 F7
St John Ogilvie Primary School *IRVSE* KA11 204 B6
St John Ogilvie School *PSLY* PA1 102 B5
St Johns Approved School Springboig *CAR/SHTL* G32 107 K2
St Johns Primary School *AYR* KA8 19 H1
St Johns Primary School *BRHD/NEIL* G78 125 J5
St Johns Primary School *HMLTN* ML3 156 D6
St Johns Primary School *SVSTN* KA20 192 F8
St Johns RC Primary School *GBLS* G5 11 H5
St Johns RC Primary School *PGL* PA14 34 A7
St John the Baptist Primary School *UD/BTH/TAN* G71 132 A3
St Josephs Primary School *BLTYR/CAMB* G72 155 K1
St Josephs Primary School *CRMNK/CLK/EAG* G76 151 L4
St Josephs Primary School *STPS/GTHM/RID* G33 85 L4
St Josephs RC Primary School *COWCAD* G4 4 F5
St Josephs RC Primary School *GRNKW/INVK* PA16 32 A5
St Josephs RC School *CLYDBK* G81 60 D2
St Josephs RC School *CUMB* G67 68 F1
St Josephs School *CTBR* ML5 87 J2
St Josephs School *HBR/GL* G84 20 F7
St Josephs School *MLNGV* G62 41 M8
St Judes Primary School *STPS/GTHM/RID* G33 107 L3
St Julies School *CSMK* G45 128 D5
St Kenneth RC Primary School *EKILN* G74 14 E1
St Kenneths RC Primary School *GRNK* PA15 33 J7
St Kessogs RC School *ALEX/LLW* G83 25 M1
St Kevins Primary School *BAIL/MDB/MHD* G69 109 G4
St Lawrence Primary School *GRNK* PA15 3 G7
St Leonards Primary School *EKILN* G74 154 D6
St Louises Primary School *EKILS* G75 14 D8
St Lucys Primary School *CUMB* G67 49 M5
St Lukes High School *BRHD/NEIL* G78 149 J1
St Lukes Primary School *KLWNG* KA13 193 H7
St Machans RC Primary School *KKNTL* G66 29 K8
St Margaret Marys Primary School *CSMK* G45 128 C7
St Margaret Marys Secondary School *CSMK* G45 128 D6
St Margarets High School *AIRDRIE* ML6 111 H1
St Margarets Primary School *JNSTN* PA5 99 L7
St Marks Primary School *CAR/SHTL* G32 106 E4
St Marks Primary School *IRV* KA12 203 L5
St Marks RC Primary School *BRHD/NEIL* G78 125 J8
St Marks RC Primary School *RUTH* G73 129 H4
St Marnocks Primary School *PLK/PH/NH* G53 103 J8
St Marthas School *SPRGB/BLRNK* G21 84 B4
St Martins Primary School *CSMK* G45 128 F7
St Martins RC Primary School *ALEX/LLW* G83 25 L6
St Marys Cathedral *COWCAD* G4 4 C4
St Marys Hospital *LNK/LMHG* ML11 199 K4
St Marys Primary School *ALEX/LLW* G83 25 L5
St Marys Primary School *KKNTL* G66 65 G1
St Marys Primary School *LARGS* KA30 115 K5
St Marys Primary School *LRKH* ML9 175 M7
St Marys Primary School *MRYH/FIRH* G20 82 C2
St Marys Primary School *MTHW* ML1 135 H8
St Marys Primary School *PSLY* PA1 8 C6
St Marys RC Primary School *AIRDRIE* ML6 90 F4
St Marys RC Primary School *CUMB* G67 48 E8
St Marys RC Primary School *HMLTN* ML3 156 D5
St Marys RC School *CLYDBK* G81 59 M3
St Marys RC School *LNK/LMHG* ML11 199 J5
St Marys RC Secondary School *GRNKW/INVK* PA16 2 B2
St Marys School *CTBR* ML5 110 A4
St Matthews Primary School *BSHPBGS* G64 64 B7
St Matthews Primary School *KLMNKN/STW* KA3 17 M3
St Matthews RC Primary School *WISHAW* ML2 158 E5
St Maurices Secondary School *BALLOCH* G68 68 A1
St Michaels Primary School *BAIL/MDB/MHD* G69 67 G7
St Michaels Primary School *DEN/PKHD* G31 13 K6
St Michael's Primary School *DMBTN* G82 36 D5
St Mirins High School *PSLY* PA1 8 A5
St Mirins Primary School *LNPK/KPK* G44 128 C4
St Modans School *STPS/GTHM/RID* G33 107 G1
St Monicas RC School *CTBR* ML5 109 J5
St Monicas School *PLK/PH/NH* G53 103 H8
The St Mungo Museum of Religious Life & Art *COWCAD* G4 6 A9
St Mungo's Primary School *COWCAD* G4 5 M8
St Mungos Primary School *GRNK* PA15 3 L8
St Ninians High School *GIF/THBK* G46 126 F7
St Ninians High School *KKNTL* G66 65 H1
St Ninians Primary School *KNTSWD* G13 61 J8
St Ninians Primary School *PSTWK* KA9 225 K1
St Ninians RC Primary School *GRK* PA19 31 K3
St Ninians RC Primary School *HMLTN* ML3 155 L5
St Oswalds School *LNPK/KPK* G44 127 M4
St Patricks High School *CTBR* ML5 110 B2
St Patricks Primary School *DMBTN* G82 37 G5
St Patricks Primary School *GRNK* PA15 2 A6
St Patricks Primary School *MTHW* ML1 133 M6
St Patricks Primary School *SHOTTS* ML7 137 M5
St Patricks Primary School *TROON* KA10 216 C7
St Patricks RC Primary School *CTBR* ML5 110 B2
St Patricks RC School *KSYTH* G65 47 K2
St Patricks School RC Primary School *KVGV* G3 10 D1
St Pauls Primary School *CAR/SHTL* G32 107 G6
St Pauls Primary School *SCOT* G14 81 J6
St Pauls RC Primary School *HMLTN* ML3 156 B3
St Peters RC Primary School *DMBTN* G82 37 H3
St Peters RC Primary School *PSLYS* PA2 124 D1
St Peters School *PTCK* G11 82 C7
St Philips School *AIRDRIE* ML6 89 M8
St Philomenas Primary School *STPS/GTHM/RID* G33 7 M2
St Pius Primary School *DRUM* G15 61 G5
St Raymonds School *LNPK/KPK* G44 128 B7
St Rochs Secondary School *SPRGB/BLRNK* G21 6 B7
St Rose of Lima Primary School *STPS/GTHM/RID* G33 85 J7
St Saviours School *GOV/IBX* G51 104 B2
St Serfs RC Primary School *AIRDRIE* ML6 89 H7
St Sophias Primary School *GLSTN* KA4 214 A3
St Stephens High School *PGL* PA14 54 F2
St Stephens Primary School *COWCAD* G4 6 A5
St Stephens RC Primary School *CTBR* ML5 110 E4
St Stephens School *CLYDBK* G81 59 M6
St Teresas Primary School *PPK/MIL* G22 5 K2
St Theresas RC Primary School *MTHW* ML1 134 D6
St Thomas Aquinas RC Secondary School *SCOT* G14 81 K5
St Thomas RC Primary School *BRHD/NEIL* G78 148 D2
St Thomas RC Primary School *WISHAW* ML2 159 G7
St Timothys Primary School *CAR/SHTL* G32 107 G3
St Timothys RC School *CTBR* ML5 109 M5
St Vincents Primary School *EKILS* G75 171 H4
St Winnings Primary School *KLWNG* KA13 193 K6
Saltcoats Health Centre *SALT* KA21 200 F2
Sandaig Primary School *STPS/GTHM/RID* G33 107 M3
Sanderson High School *EKILN* G74 172 C1
Sandwood School *CARD/HILL/MSPK* G52 103 G4
Saracen Health Centre *PPK/MIL* G22 83 H5
Saracen Primary School *PPK/MIL* G22 5 G1
Sauchiehall Shopping Centre *CGLW* G2 5 H8
School & Leisure Wear *TROON* KA10 216 C6
School of Art *KVGV* G3 4 F7
Scotland Street School Museum *GBLS* G5 10 D6
Scottish Exhibition and Conference Centre *KVGV* G3 104 D2
Scottish Maritime Museum *DMBTN* G82 37 G6
Scottish Maritime Museum *IRV* KA12 203 G8
Scottish Youth Theatre *CGLE* G1 11 H1
Scott Practice *ALEX/LLW* G83 25 L4
Scotus College *BSDN* G61 61 J5
Seafiled School *ARD* KA22 191 H5
Shaftesbury Medical Practice *SCOT* G14 81 K6
Sharmanka Gallery & Workshop *CGLE* G1 11 K3
Shawbridge Industrial Estate *PLKSW/MSWD* G43 127 H2
Shawhead Primary School *CTBR* ML5 110 B6
Shawlands Primary School *PLKSD/SHW* G41 104 D8
Shawlands Surgery *PLKSD/SHW* G41 127 K1
Sheriff Court *GBLS* G5 11 J4
Shettleston Day Hospital *CAR/SHTL* G32 106 F5
Shettleston Health Centre *CAR/SHTL* G32 107 G4
Shortlees Primary School *KLMNK* KA1 211 M6
Shotts Bon Accord Football & Social Club *SHOTTS* ML7 137 K3
Showcase Cinema *BAIL/MDB/MHD* G69 109 H5
Showcase Cinemas *PSLYN/LNWD* PA3 100 E4
Sighthill Primary School *SPRGB/BLRNK* G21 5 M3
Sikeside Primary School *CTBR* ML5 110 D4
Simshill Primary School *LNPK/KPK* G44 128 B5
Sir John Maxwell School *PLKSW/MSWD* G43 127 J2
Skelmorlie Castle *SKLM* PA17 92 A1
Skelmorlie Golf Club *SKLM* PA17 70 C6
Skelmorlie Primary School *SKLM* PA17 70 B4
Slamuir Primary School *PGL* PA14 55 G3
Smithycroft Secondary School *STPS/GTHM/RID* G33 84 E8
Somerset Eye Clinic *KVGV* G3 4 B7
Southbank Surgery *KKNTL* G66 65 J1
South Beach Practice *ARD* KA22 191 K8
Southern General Hospital NHS Trust *GOV/IBX* G51 103 K1
South Lanarkshire Council *BLTYR/CAMB* G72 130 E5
South Lanarkshire Council *BLTYR/CAMB* G72 130 A3
South Lanarkshire Council *BLTYR/CAMB* G72 155 L4
South Lanarkshire Council *BLTYR/CAMB* G72 155 K2
South Lanarkshire Council *CARLUKE* ML8 178 E7
South Lanarkshire Council *EKILN* G74 14 F4
South Lanarkshire Council *EKILN* G74 14 F2
South Lanarkshire Council *EKILN* G74 15 G1
South Lanarkshire Council *EKILN* G74 15 H3
South Lanarkshire Council *EKILN* G74 152 F8
South Lanarkshire Council *EKILN* G74 153 G6
South Lanarkshire Council *EKILS* G75 15 K9
South Lanarkshire Council *EKILS* G75 171 L4
South Lanarkshire Council *HMLTN* ML3 155 M6
South Lanarkshire Council *HMLTN* ML3 156 B5
South Lanarkshire Council *HMLTN* ML3 156 C2
South Lanarkshire Council *HMLTN* ML3 156 C5
South Lanarkshire Council *HMLTN* ML3 156 E6
South Lanarkshire Council *LRKH* ML9 176 A6
South Lanarkshire Council *LRKH* ML9 176 A3
South Lanarkshire Council *RUTH* G73 129 H1
Southpark Primary School *EKILS* G75 14 A9
South Park School *AYRS* KA7 19 G9
South Primary School *PSLYS* PA2 9 H9
Spectrum Business Centre *RUTH* G73 129 H1
Spiersbridge Business Park *GIF/THBK* G46 126 E6
Spittal School *RUTH* G73 128 F4
Sports Centre *BSDN* G61 62 B2
Springburn Museum *SPRGB/BLRNK* G21 6 C1
Springburn Sports Centre *SPRGB/BLRNK* G21 83 M5
Springfield Primary School *DMNK/BRGTN* G40 106 B7
Springfield Primary School *GRK* PA19 31 J5
Springhill Primary School *BRHD/NEIL* G78 125 H8
Springside Primary School *IRVSE* KA11 204 F7
Stakis Glasgow Airport *RNFRW* PA4 80 A5
Stanecastle School *IRVSE* KA11 204 A4
Stanley Primary School *ARD* KA22 191 J6
Stathclyde Regional Council *SPRGB/BLRNK* G21 7 H1
Stepps Primary School *STPS/GTHM/RID* G33 85 L3
Steunans Primary School *CLYDBK* G81 60 C7
Stirling's Library *CGLE* G1 11 J2
Stobcross Street Industrial Estate *CTBR* ML5 110 A3
Stobhill General Hospital *SPRGB/BLRNK* G21 84 A3
Stock Exchange *CGLE* G1 11 H1
Stonedyke Primary School *DRUM* G15 61 H7
Stonelaw High School *RUTH* G73 129 H2
Stow College *KVGV* G3 4 F6
Strathblane Primary School *CMPF/LLE* G63 27 H6
Strathclyde Art Centre *KVGV* G3 10 E2
Strathclyde Business Centre *GOV/IBX* G51 104 D3
Strathclyde Business Centre *GRNK* PA15 33 L6
Strathclyde Business Centre *MTHW* ML1 133 M5
Strathclyde Business Centre *PLKSD/SHW* G41 10 A5
Strathclyde Hospital *MTHW* ML1 157 J4
Strathclyde Regional Council *HMLTN* ML3 156 C5
Strathclyde Regional Council *LRKH* ML9 176 A5
Strathclyde Regional Council *PSLY* PA1 9 M4
Strathmore Surgery *EKILN* G74 14 F4
Street Level Gallery *CGLE* G1 11 K3
Struthers Primary School *TROON* KA10 216 F4
Summerhill School *DRUM* G15 61 H5
Sunnyside School *STPS/GTHM/RID* G33 85 J6
Swinton Primary School *BAIL/MDB/MHD* G69 108 D3
Symington Health Centre *KLMNK* KA1 218 C5
Symington Primary School *KLMNK* KA1 218 D5
Synagogue *GVH/MTFL* G42 104 F7
Tam O'shanter Experience *AYRS* KA7 228 F8
Tams Brig Surgery *AYR* KA8 224 F7
Tannochside Primary School *UD/BTH/TAN* G71 132 B2
Taylor High School *MTHW* ML1 134 A6
Templehill Surgery *TROON* KA10 216 B6
Temple School *KNTSWD* G13 81 M2
Templeton Business Centre *DMNK/BRGTN* G40 12 A6
Thames Open College *CGLW* G2 11 G1
Thomas Muir High School *BSHPBGS* G64 64 C7
Thorniewood Football Club *UD/BTH/TAN* G71 132 B2
Thornliebank Health Centre *GIF/THBK* G46 126 F5
Thornliebank Industrial Estate *GIF/THBK* G46 126 E7
Thornlie Primary School *WISHAW* ML2 159 G7
Thorntree Primary School *CAR/SHTL* G32 107 G3
Thornwood School *PTCK* G11 81 M7
Tinto Primary School *PLKSW/MSWD* G43 127 J3
Todholm Infants School *PSLYS* PA2 102 B7
Tollbrae Primary School *AIRDRIE* ML6 111 H2
Tollcross Industrial Estate *CAR/SHTL* G32 107 G6
The Toonspeak Young Peoples Theatre *SPRGB/BLRNK* G21 6 D5
Tormusk Primary School *CSMK* G45 129 G6
Torrance Primary School *BSHPBGS* G64 44 B8
Toryglen School *RUTH* G73 128 E1

Toss Theatre
BLSH ML4 .... 133 J4
Tourhill Industrial Estate
KLMNKN/STW KA3 .... 206 B3
Towerlands Primary School
IRVSE KA11 .... 204 C7
Town Hall Business Centre
MTHW ML1 .... 157 K3
Townhead Clinic
CTBR ML5 .... 109 L1
Townhead Clinic
KKNTL G66 .... 65 K2
Townhead Health Centre
COWCAD G4 .... 6 B8
Townhead Primary School
CTBR ML5 .... 87 K7
Townhead Surgery
IRV KA12 .... 203 J7
Townhill Primary School
HMLTN ML3 .... 155 L7
Transmission Gallery
CGLE G1 .... 11 K3
Trees Riding School
RAYR/DAL KA6 .... 230 D7
Treeswoodhead Clinic
KLMNK KA1 .... 212 A5
Triangle Shopping Mall
KLWNG KA13 .... 193 L6
Trinity High School
BLTYR/CAMB G72 .... 129 L2
Trinity High School
RNFRW PA4 .... 80 D5
Tron Theatre
CGLE G1 .... 11 L3
Turnbull High School
BSHPBGS G64 .... 63 L7
The Turret Surgery
KKNTL G66 .... 65 J1
Turret Theatre
KKNTL G66 .... 45 J8
Twechar Primary School
KSYTH G65 .... 46 F6
UCI Cinema
CLYDBK G81 .... 60 B7
UCI Cinema
EKILN G74 .... 15 G4
Uddingston Cricket & Sports Club
UD/BTH/TAN G71 .... 131 L4
Uddingston Grammar School
UD/BTH/TAN G71 .... 131 L3
Udston Primary School
HMLTN ML3 .... 155 L5
Underground Gallery
KVD/HLHD G12 .... 82 D6
University of Glasgow
BSDN G61 .... 61 K2
University of Glasgow
BSDN G61 .... 82 A1
University of Glasgow
KVD/HLHD G12 .... 82 C4
University of Glasgow
KVD/HLHD G12 .... 82 D7
University of Glasgow
KVGV G3 .... 4 B6
University of Glasgow
PTCK G11 .... 82 C8
University of Paisley
PSLY PA1 .... 8 F4
University of Paisley
PSLYS PA2 .... 8 F6
University of Strathclyde
CGLE G1 .... 5 K9
University of Strathclyde
CGLE G1 .... 11 M1
University of Strathclyde
COWCAD G4 .... 5 L9
University of Strathclyde
KNTSWD G13 .... 81 K4
University of Strathclyde
STPS/GTHM/RID G33 .... 85 H5
Victoria Buildings Business Centre
PSLY PA1 .... 9 M4
Victoria Industrial Estate
PSLY PA1 .... 9 M4
Victoria Infirmary
HBR/GL G84 .... 20 F8
Victoria Infirmary
PLKSD/SHW G41 .... 127 M1
Victoria Memorial Cottage Hospital
KSYTH G65 .... 47 H1
Victoria Park School
CARLUKE ML8 .... 178 F7
Victory Baths
RNFRW PA4 .... 80 D5
Viewfield Business Centre
AYR KA8 .... 225 G7
Village Theatre
EKILN G74 .... 15 H2
Virgin Cinema
DEN/PKHD G31 .... 13 K5
Walker Clinic
KVGV G3 .... 4 C8
Wallace Primary School
JNSTN PA5 .... 100 D7
The Waverley Gallery
PSTWK KA9 .... 225 J1
Waverley Park Day Hospital
KKNTL G66 .... 45 K8
Welbeck Golf Club
TROON KA10 .... 216 D7
Welfare Clinic
CUMB G67 .... 49 H6
Welhouse Primary School
STPS/GTHM/RID G33 .... 107 L2
Wellgreen Health Centre
PLKSW/MSWD G43 .... 127 J1
Wellhall Medical Centre
HMLTN ML3 .... 156 A6
Wellpark Clinic
GRNK PA15 .... 2 D5
Wellshot Primary School
CAR/SHTL G32 .... 106 F5
West Coats Primary School
BLTYR/CAMB G72 .... 129 M4
West Dunbartonshire Council
ALEX/LLW G83 .... 25 K4
West Dunbartonshire Council
CLYDBK G81 .... 59 M7
West Dunbartonshire Council
CLYDBK G81 .... 60 C8
West Dunbartonshire Council
DMBTN G82 .... 36 F6
West Dunbartonshire Council
OLDK G60 .... 59 G2
Wester Cleddens Primary School
BSHPBGS G64 .... 64 A7
Western Gailes Golf Club
IRVSE KA11 .... 208 C6
Western Infirmary, A&E
PTCK G11 .... 82 C7
Westerton Primary School
BSDN G61 .... 61 L7
Westfield Health Clinic
CARD/HILL/MSPK G52 .... 103 G4
Westfield Primary School
BALLOCH G68 .... 67 M2
Westfield Surgery
JNSTN PA5 .... 99 L6
West Kilbride Golf Club
WKIL KA23 .... 181 H5
West Kilbride Primary School
WKIL KA23 .... 181 J4
Westmuir Medical Centre
DEN/PKHD G31 .... 13 M6
West of Scotland Cricket Club
PTCK G11 .... 82 B7
West Park School
CRH/DND KA2 .... 205 M8
West Primary School
PSLY PA1 .... 8 C5
Westwood Business Centre
ESTRH G34 .... 108 B1
Whinhill Golf Club
GRNK PA15 .... 2 C9
Whitecraigs Rugby Club
NMRNS G77 .... 150 A4
Whitecrook Business Centre
CLYDBK G81 .... 60 C8
Whitecrook Primary School
CLYDBK G81 .... 60 C8
Whitehill School
DEN/PKHD G31 .... 13 G1
Whitehill Swimming Pool
DEN/PKHD G31 .... 12 F1
Whitehirst Park Primary School
KLWNG KA13 .... 193 J6
Whiteinch Business Park
SCOT G14 .... 81 K7
Whiteinch Indoor Bowling Stadium
SCOT G14 .... 81 L7
Whiteinch Medical Practice
SCOT G14 .... 81 K6
Whiteinch Primary School
SCOT G14 .... 81 L6
Whitlawburn Shopping Centre
BLTYR/CAMB G72 .... 129 L6
Whitletts Clinic
AYR KA8 .... 225 K6
Whitletts Primary School
AYR KA8 .... 225 L6
Williamsburgh Primary School
PSLY PA1 .... 9 M4
William Street Clinic
KVGV G3 .... 4 D9
William Temple Chemist
GOV/IBX G51 .... 104 D4
Williamwood High School
CRMNK/CLK/EAG G76 .... 151 K1
Williamwood Medical Centre
CRMNK/CLK/EAG G76 .... 151 K1
Willowbank Primary School
KVGV G3 .... 4 C5
Willowbank School
CTBR ML5 .... 109 L3
Windlaw Primary School
CSMK G45 .... 128 E8
Windyhill Golf Clubhouse
BSDN G61 .... 61 G1
Winton Primary School
ARD KA22 .... 191 J7
Wishaw Business Centre
WISHAW ML2 .... 159 H6
Wishaw Health Centre
WISHAW ML2 .... 159 H6
Wishaw Sports Centre
WISHAW ML2 .... 158 F7
Witchhill School
KLMNKN/STW KA3 .... 16 E1
Woodfarm Secondary School
GIF/THBK G46 .... 127 G6
Woodhill Primary School
BSHPBGS G64 .... 64 C8
Woodilee Industrial Estate
KKNTL G66 .... 65 L3
Woodlands Primary School
IRV KA12 .... 203 K6
Woodside Place Business Centre
KVGV G3 .... 4 D7
Woodside Primary School
HMLTN ML3 .... 156 E7
Woodside Secondary School
KVGV G3 .... 4 B8
Woodstock Primary School
KLMNK KA1 .... 16 C4
Woodville Park Industrial Estate
GOV/IBX G51 .... 104 B3
The Wool Gallery
MLNGV G62 .... 42 A7
Wyndford Recreation Centre
KVD/HLHD G12 .... 82 D4
Wynd Gallery
LNK/LMHG ML11 .... 199 G5
XS Superbowl
PSLYN/LNWD PA3 .... 9 K1
Yoker Primary School
SCOT G14 .... 80 F3
Yoker Sports Centre
SCOT G14 .... 80 F3
York Place Surgery
KKNTL G66 .... 65 J1

C4
1 North Gower St
2 Percy St
3 Porter St

C5
1 Laburnum Rd

C7
1 Roberton Av

D1
1 Kelvinhaugh Ga
2 Kelvinhaugh Pl
3 Lumsden St
4 Overnewton Pl
5 Overnewton Sq
6 Palmerston Pl
7 Stobcross Wynd

D3
1 Clutha St
2 Lendel Pl
3 Mavisbank Rd

D4
1 Clifford La
2 Clifford Pl
3 Langshot St
4 Plantation Park Gdns
5 Scotland St West

D7
1 Springkell Ga

D8
1 Midlothian Dr
2 Springkell Av

E1
1 Claremont St
2 Clifton Pl
3 St Vincent Crescent La

E2
1 Congress Wy
2 Finnieston Sq
3 Stobcross Rd

E3
1 Eaglesham Ct
2 Eaglesham Pl
3 Middlesex Gdns
4 Plantation Sq
5 Rutland Crs
6 Seaward La
7 Toll La

E4
1 Lambhill Quadrant
2 Middlesex St
3 Sussex St

E5
1 Maxwell La
2 St John's Quadrant

E7
1 Darnley Pl
2 Mariscat Rd
3 Pollokshields Sq

E8
1 Abbot St
2 Lochside St
3 Springhill Gdns
4 Westclyffe St

F1
1 Beltane St
2 Berkeley Terrace La
3 Breadalbane St
4 Cleveland La
5 Cleveland St
6 Newton Terrace La
7 Pembroke St
8 Shaftesbury St

F2
1 Cranston St
2 Macintyre St
3 Perth St
4 Piccadilly St

F3
1 Marine Gdns

F4
1 Carnoustie St
2 Seaward Pl

F5
1 Maxwell Ov

F6
1 Knowehead Gdns
2 Nithsdale Pl

F7
1 Barbreck Rd
2 Douglas Ter
3 Kildrostan St
4 Marywood Sq
5 Nithsdale Rd
6 Nithsdale St
7 Torrisdale St

F8
1 Niddrie Sq

Page 105

G1
1 Bath La
2 Blythswood Sq
3 Dalhousie St
4 Douglas La
5 Douglas St
6 Elmbank Crs
7 Elmbank Street La
8 Sauchiehall St
9 Scott St
10 West Regent St

G2
1 Anthony St
2 Balaclava St
3 Blythswood St
4 Bothwell St
5 Oak St
6 St Peter's La
7 Washington St
8 Wellington La
9 West Campbell St

G3
1 James Watt La
2 Laidlaw St
3 Morrison St
4 Riverview Gdns
5 Tradeston St

G4
1 Dalintober St

G5
1 Cardwell St
2 Francis St
3 Gourock St
4 Lauder St
5 Mauchline St
6 Stromness St

G6
1 Butterfield Pl
2 Muirhouse St
3 Nursery St

G7
1 Bowman St
2 Chapman St
3 Kingarth La

G8
1 Burton La
2 Maybank St

H1
1 Bath La
2 Renfield St
3 Renfrew St
4 Rose St
5 Sauchiehall La
6 Sauchiehall St
7 West Nile St

H2
1 Adams Court La
2 Argyle St
3 Buchanan St
4 Gordon St
5 Hope St
6 Midland St
7 Mitchell St
8 National Bank La
9 Robertson La
10 St Enoch Pl
11 St Mary's La
12 St Vincent La
13 Waterloo La
14 West George La

H3
1 Coburg St
2 Dixon St
3 Nicholson St
4 Oswald St
5 South Portland St

H4
1 Bedford La
2 Kilbarchan St
3 Nicholson St
4 Stirlingfauld Pl
5 Wallace St

H5
1 Abbotsford Pl
2 Salisbury St
3 Surrey La
4 Surrey St

H6
1 Annandale St
2 Larkfield St
3 Robson Gv

H7
1 Cathcart Rd
2 Covanhill St
3 Inglefield St
4 Jamieson Ct
5 Jamieson St
6 South Annandale St

H8
1 Belleisle St
2 Crosshill Av
3 Eskdale St
4 Kingsley Av

J1
1 Cowcaddens St
2 Dundas St
3 Martha St
4 North Frederick St
5 Renfrew Ct
6 St Mungo Av

J2
1 Anchor La
2 Brunswick La
3 Citizen La
4 Garth St
5 George Sq
6 John St
7 Maxwell St
8 Miller St
9 Nelson Mandela Pl
10 North Ct
11 North Frederick St
12 Royal Exchange Ct
13 Royal Exchange Sq
14 St Vincent Pl
15 South Exchange Ct
16 South Frederick St
17 Springfield Ct
18 Virginia Ct
19 Virginia Pl
20 Virginia St
21 Wilson St

J3
1 Aird's La
2 Dunlop St
3 Goosedubbs
4 Jocelyn Sq
5 Mart St
6 Maxwell St
7 Melville Ct
8 Metropole La
9 Old Wynd
10 Ropework La
11 St Margaret's Pl
12 Saltmarket Pl

J4
1 Cleland St
2 Old Rutherglen Rd
3 St Ninian Ter
4 Thistle St

J5
1 Alexander Crs
2 Commercial Rd
3 Cumberland Pl
4 Cumberland St
5 Gilmour Pl
6 Hallside Pl
7 Oregon Pl
8 Pine Pl
9 Sandiefield Rd

J7
1 Bennan Sq
2 Hairmyres St
3 Hickman Ter
4 Lawmoor Pl

K1
1 Cathedral St
2 Dobbie's Loan Pl
3 Rottenrow
4 St Mungo Pl
5 Taylor Pl

K2
1 Albion St
2 Blackfriars St
3 Candleriggs
4 College La
5 Montrose St
6 North Portland St
7 Parsonage Rw
8 Richmond St
9 Shuttle St
10 Weaver St

K3
1 Bridgegate Pth
2 Chisolm St
3 Great Dovehill
4 James Morrison St
5 Little Dovehill
6 Molendinar St
7 Monteith Rw
8 St Andrew's La
9 St Andrew's Sq
10 St Andrew's St
11 Spoutmouth
12 Tontine La
13 Trongate

K5
1 Ballater Pl
2 Cumberland St
3 Hayfield St
4 Old Rutherglen Rd
5 Sandyfaulds St
6 Snowdon St
7 Waddell St
8 Waterside St

K6
1 Birch St
2 Braehead St

K8
1 Crossbank Dr
2 Crossbank Rd

L1
1 Warnock St

L2
1 Cathedral Sq
2 Macleod St
3 Rottenrow
4 Wellpark St

L3
1 Chalmers Ga
2 Claythorn Circ
3 Claythorn Ct
4 Claythorn Ter
5 East Campbell St
6 Gibson St
7 Mcfarlane St
8 Moncur St
9 Stevenson St
10 Sydney St

L4
1 Arcadia St
2 Claythorn Pk
3 Drake St
4 Graignestock Pl
5 Greenhead St
6 Monteith Pl
7 Silvergrove St
8 Tobago St

L5
1 Annes Ct

L7
1 Dalmeny St
2 Granton St
3 Queensferry St

M2
1 Broompark Circ
2 Broompark La
3 Broompark St
4 Clayton Ter
5 Dunchattan Pl
6 Oakley Ter
7 Seton Ter

M3
1 Annbank Pl
2 Annbank St
3 Brandon St

M4
1 Anson St
2 Brook St
3 Dornoch St
4 Forbes Dr
5 Kerr Dr
6 Kerr Pl
7 Landressy St
8 Olympia St
9 Park La
10 Redan St
11 Tobago Pl

M5
1 Acorn St
2 Dale St
3 Mackeith St
4 Megan St
5 Old Dalmarnock Rd
6 Reid Pl

M6
1 Madras St
2 Martin St
3 Poplin St
4 Rockcliffe St
5 Trafalgar St

M7
1 Shawfield Rd

Page 106

A1
1 Ballindalloch Dr
2 Ballindalloch La

A2
1 Craigielea St
2 Hillfoot St
3 Onslow Sq
4 Whitehill Gdns
5 Whitehill Street La

A3
1 Inglis St
2 Wyper Pl

A4
1 Avenue St
2 Barrowfield St
3 Brookside St
4 Camlachie St
5 Crownpoint Rd
6 David St
7 Fielden Pl
8 Forrest St
9 Kirkpatrick St
10 Overtown St
11 Rimsdale St
12 Rockbank Pl
13 Rockbank St
14 St Marnock St

A5
1 Albany St
2 Bernard Ter
3 Montgomery St
4 Walkinshaw St

A6
1 Baltic Ct
2 Bartholomew St
3 Bonnar St
4 Old Dalmarnock Rd
5 Playfair St
6 Webster St

B1
1 Alexandra Ct
2 Crinan St
3 Culloden St
4 Duntroon St
5 Easter Craigs
6 Harcourt Dr
7 Kennyhill Sq
8 Meadowpark St
9 Staffa St
10 Wood St

B2
1 Alexandra Park St
2 Birkenshaw St
3 Ingleby Dr
4 Marne St
5 Meadowpark St

B3
1 Fleming St
2 Gateside St
3 Glendale Pl

B4
1 Camlachie St
2 Coalhill St
3 Dunrobin St
4 Janefield St

B5
1 Boness St
2 Davaar St
3 Kerrydale St
4 Mauldslie St

B6
1 Ardenlea St
2 Baltic St
3 Connal St

B7
1 Beechgrove St
2 Birkwood St
3 Woodhall St

C2
1 Aberdour St
2 Aberfeldy St
3 Abernethy St
4 Balure St
5 Dreghorn St

C3
1 Lightburn Rd
2 Netherfield St

C4
1 Burgher St

C5
1 Buddon St
2 Janefield St
3 Kinloch St
4 West Whitby St

C8
1 Hunter Rd
2 Montraive St
3 Riverford Rd
4 Slevewright St

D1
1 Findhorn St
2 Grierson La
3 Grierson St
4 Lomax St
5 Longford St

D3
1 Myreside Pl
2 Penicuik St

D4
1 Back Cswy
2 East Wellington St
3 Helenvale Ct
4 Nisbet St
5 Pharonhill St
6 Powfoot St
7 Ravel Rw
8 Salamanca St
9 Sorby St
10 Southbank St
11 Winning Rw

D5
1 Canmore Pl
2 Dunning St
3 Helenvale St
4 Macbeth Pl
5 Macduff Pl
6 Ogilvie Pl
7 Strathbran St

D6
1 Birnam Rd
2 Glenisla St
3 Maukinfauld Ct

E1
1 Dunsyre St
2 Gogar St
3 Silverburn St
4 Tranent Pl

E2
1 Barnton St
2 Conniston St
3 Dalmahoy St
4 Edinburgh Rd
5 Gorebridge St
6 Harwood St
7 Joppa St
8 Leadburn St
9 Murrayfield St
10 Saughton St
11 Stenton St
12 Straiton St
13 Uphall Pl

E3
1 Craigleith St
2 Seagrove St

E4
1 Edenwood St
2 Quarryknowe Gdns

E5
1 Cuthelton Dr
2 Pitcairn St

E6
1 Lundie St
2 Potter Cl
3 Potter Gv
4 Potter Pl

F1
1 Fidra St
2 Loretto Pl
3 Ruchazie Pl
4 Rullion Pl

F2
1 Benhar Pl
2 Carntynehall Rd
3 Loanhead St
4 Piershill St

F3
1 Brockville St
2 Kirkliston St

F4
1 Blair St
2 Dalveen St
3 Kilmany Gdns
4 Ram St
5 St Mark Gdns

F5
1 Enterkin St
2 Fairholm St

F6
1 Benholm St
2 Colgrave Crs
3 Corbett Ct
4 Easterhill Pl
5 Tollcross Park Gv
6 Tollcross Park Vw

F7
1 Braidfauld Pl

Page 107

G1
1 Cloch St
2 Eyrepoint Ct
3 Roseness Pl

G2
1 Addiewell St
2 Neistpoint Dr
3 Newhaven St

G4
1 Ardholm St
2 Balintore St
3 Chester St
4 Culrain Gdns
5 Mcnair St
6 Obiston Gdns
7 Pettigrew St
8 South Chester St
9 South Vesalius St
10 Vesalius St

G5
1 Amulree Pl
2 Ard St
3 Eckford St

G6
1 Causewayside Crs
2 Eversley St
3 Luncarty Pl
4 Luncarty St
5 Pencaitland Gv

G7
1 Archerfield Av
2 Archerfield Crs
3 Archerfield Gv
4 Lloyd Av

H1
1 Lamlash Pl
2 Skerryvore Pl

H2
1 Carntyne Rd
2 Inchkeith Pl
3 Lightburn Pl
4 Torphin Wk
5 Tynecastle Pl
6 Warriston Pl

H3
1 Castlelaw Gdns
2 Castlelaw St
3 Kirknewton St

H4
1 Balgair Ter
2 Cramond Ter
3 Earnside St
4 Fenella St
5 Meadowwell St

H5
1 Grampian Pl

H6
1 Sandyhills Crs
2 Sandyhills Pl

H7
1 Newbattle Ct
2 Newbattle Gdns
3 Newbattle Pl
4 Newtongrange Gdns

H8
1 Buckingham Dr
2 Carmyle Av
3 Douglas Av

J1
1 Consett La
2 Heathfield St

J2
1 Greenend Pl
2 Larchgrove Pl
3 Tanfield Pl

J3
1 Barlanark Av
2 Davidson Pl
3 Hermiston Pl
4 Larchgrove Av
5 Windsor St

J4
1 Crownhall Rd
2 Eastbank Dr

J5
1 Dodside Gdns
2 Dodside Pl
3 Dodside St

J8
1 Cross St
2 Foxley St

K1
1 Burntbroom St

K2
1 Bartiebeith Rd
2 Mossend St

K3
1 Blythe Pl
2 Duncansby Rd
3 Kerrera Pl

K4
1 Cambuskenneth Gdns
2 Carroglen Gv
3 Farmington Gdns
4 Farmington Gv
5 Linacre Gdns
6 Linlithgow Gdns
7 Mayberry Gv

K5
1 Blackcroft Gdns
2 Craigvicar Gdns
3 Culzean Dr
4 Duncryne Rd
5 Farmington Av
6 Grantlea Ter
7 Loch Voil St
8 Selby Gdns

K6
1 Criffell Gdns
2 Daldowie Av
3 Durris Gdns
4 Links Rd
5 Meryon Rd
6 Penryn Gdns
7 Rhymie Rd

K7
1 Dornford Rd
2 Woodend Gdns

L2
1 Barlanark Pl
2 Burnett Rd
3 Delny Pl
4 Dunan Pl

L3
1 Carvel Crs
2 Halhill Crs

L4
1 Uig Pl
2 Usmore Pl

L5
1 Allean Gdns
2 Baillieston Rd
3 Birchwood Pl
4 Carrick Gv
5 Despard Gdns
6 Duncryne Gdns
7 Rylands Gdns

L6
1 Corsewall Av
2 Mansionhouse Gv

L7
1 Briarwood Ct
2 Woodend Ct

M1
1 Trondra Pth

M2
1 Arnol Pl
2 Easthall Pl
3 Eddlewood Pth
4 Glenburnie Pl
5 Halliburton Crs
6 Kiltearn Rd
7 Langbar Crs
8 Stepford Pl
9 Wardie Pl

M3
1 Pendeen Pl

M4
1 Barrachnie Ct
2 Barrachnie Crs
3 Millbeg Crs

M5
1 Allerton Gdns
2 Cayton Gdns
3 Halton Gdns
4 Juniper Ct
5 Langton Gdns
6 Scorton Gdns
7 Settle Gdns
8 Weirwood Gdns

M6
1 Crombie Gdns
2 Crown St
3 Orchard St
4 Tudor St

M7
1 Burntbroom Rd

Page 108

A2
1 Edderton Pl
2 Eddlewood Ct
3 Halliburton Ter
4 Lochbridge Rd

A4
1 Bannercross Av
2 Bannercross Gdns
3 Florida Gdns
4 Quinton Gdns
5 Thornbridge Gdns

A5
1 Culzean Crs
2 Oak Crs
3 Willowdale Gdns

A6
1 Blair Crs
2 Calderwood Gdns
3 Fir Pl
4 Kelburne Gdns
5 Wemyss Gdns

B3
1 Barony Wynd
2 Micklehouse Ov
3 Micklehouse Pl
4 Micklehouse Wynd
5 Springcroft Gv

B5
1 Calder Pl
2 Drumpellier Pl
3 Longlee
4 Maxwell St
5 Muiredge Ter
6 Scott St
7 South Scott St

C1
1 Duntarvie Cl
2 Duntarvie Crs
3 Duntarvie Gdns
4 Duntarvie Quandrant
5 Easterhouse Pl

C2
1 Easterhouse Quadrant
2 Ervie St
3 Finlarig St
4 Whamflet Av

C3
1 Forteviot Av
2 Queensby Pl
3 Rhindmuir Ct
4 Rhindmuir Gdns
5 Springcroft Gdns
6 Swinton Rd

C4
1 Faulds Gdns
2 Forteviot Av
3 Forteviot Pl
4 Swinton Vw

C5
1 Blaven Ct
2 Bracadale Gv
3 Ellismuir Pl
4 Muirhead Gdns
5 Muirhead Gv
6 Thornyburn Pl

D1
1 Dalswinton Pth
2 Drumlanrig Pl
3 Fordoun St

D3
1 Rhindmuir Crs
2 Rhindmuir Pth
3 Rhindmuir Pl
4 Rhindmuir Wynd

D4
1 Crossview Av
2 Mainhill Av
3 Rhindhouse Pl
4 Rhindhouse Rd
5 Swinton Gdns
6 Swinton Pth

D5
1 Bracadale Dr
2 Bracadale Gdns
3 Ellismuir Farm Rd

E8
1 Cathkin Rd
2 Dechmont Rd

F4
1 Melrose Av

F8
1 Atholl Ter
2 Balmoral Gdns
3 Broomfield Ter
4 Laidlaw Gdns
5 Lomond Rd
6 Monroe Pl

Page 109

J8
1 Crowflat Vw
2 Mulberry Rd
3 Spruce Rd
4 Walnut Pl

K2
1 Carrick Pl

K4
1 Oakwood Dr

K5
1 Kellock Crs
2 Woodside Gdns

M1
1 St Denis Wy

Page 110

D4
1 Glen Luss Pl
2 Glenspean Pl
3 Greenlees Gv
4 Hawthorn Dr
5 Strathmore Pl
6 Strathmore Wk
7 Thornkip Pl

D5
1 Arran Pl
2 Dunavon Pl
3 Roxburgh Dr

D6
1 Deanstone Pl
2 Earlston Crs

E2
1 South Robertson Pl

E5
1 Cumbrae Pl
2 Methlick Av

F1
1 Aitchison Ct
2 Burnbank Quadrant
3 Burniebrae

F3
1 Devonview Pl

F4
1 Dornoch Wy

Page 111

G2
1 Baillies La
2 Broomknoll St
3 Buchanan St

J1
1 Craiglea Pl

K2
1 Castle Quadrant
2 Meadowside Gdns
3 Meadowside Pl
4 Pine St

K7
1 Glen Fruin Pl
2 Woodside St

K8
1 Doune Crs
2 Drumore Av
3 Glen Affric Dr
4 Glen Affric Wy
5 Glen Orchy Pl
6 Glen Shee Crs

L1
1 Springfield Rd

L2
1 Finlayson Quadrant
2 Fyvie Crs
3 Moorpark Av
4 Wester Moffat Crs

L3
1 Bramley Pl

L8
1 Sandhead Crs
2 Turnberry Gdns

M2
1 Moorfield Crs

M3
1 Gimmerscroft Crs

M8
1 Castlehill Crs
2 Grampian Crs
3 Kippford Pl
4 Rockcliffe Pth

Page 115

J8
1 Bath St
2 Bellman's Cl
3 Green
4 Lade St
5 Lindon Aisle
6 Lindon Ct
7 Manse Ct
8 Morris St
9 Stanlane Pl
10 Townhead Cl
11 Tron Pl

Page 125

H5
1 Aline Ct
2 Burnside Av
3 Moidart Ct
4 Quarry Rd
5 Victoria Dr
6 Victoria Gdns

H6
1 Chappell St
2 Connor Rd
3 George St
4 Levern Gdns
5 South Park Av

H7
1 Cogan Pl
2 Sunnyside Pl

H8
1 Deanston Pk

J7
1 Alasdair Ct
2 Cloth St
3 Dougray Pl
4 Foundry La
5 Lomond Ct

J8
1 Beechwood Gv
2 Fintry Crs
3 Nevis Ct
4 Sidlaw Av
5 Vorlich Ct

K5
1 Stewart Pl
2 Waulkmill Wy

Page 126

A6
1 Colwood Gdns

B6
1 Bruntsfield Gdns
2 Flowerdale Pl
3 Langford Pl
4 Waukglen Pth

B7
1 Barberry Gdns
2 Barberry Pl

C1
1 Braidcraft Pl
2 Brockburn Ter
3 Leverndale Av
4 Waterfoot Ter

C2
1 Househillmuir Pl

C3
1 Freeland Ct
2 Priesthill Av

C4
1 Glen Moriston Rd
2 Ravenscraig Ter

C5
1 Glen Alby Pl
2 Glen Clunie Pl
3 Glen Livet Pl

C6
1 Bellflower Pl
2 Nitshill Rd

C7
1 Haberlea Gdns

D5
1 Ben Garrisdale Pl
2 Ben Laga Pl
3 Ben Lui Pl
4 Ben Macdui Gdns

D6
1 Kilmaluag Ter

D8
1 Deaconsbank Crs

E5
1 Cona St

E6
1 Spiersbridge Av

E7
1 Invergarry Pl
2 Loganswell Dr
3 Loganswell Pl
4 Nitshill Rd

F4
1 Brent Wy
2 Forties Ct

F5
1 Drumpark St
2 Eastwood Crs
3 Kennishead Rd
4 North Park Av
5 Stanalane St

F6
1 Hillside Ct
2 Wisner Ct

F7
1 Newfield Pl
2 Woodlands Ct

Page 127

H2
1 Shawholm Crs

H3
1 Auldhouse Av
2 Cartcraigs Rd
3 Greenknowe Rd
4 Harriet Pl
5 Pitcaple Dr

J1
1 Dovecot
2 Greenview St
3 Leckie St
4 Mannering Ct
5 Rossendale Ct
6 Rossendale Rd
7 Well Gn

J2
1 Ashtree Rd
2 Bengal Pl
3 Johnshaven St
4 Macdougall St
5 Mcarthur St

J3
1 Cogan Rd
2 Fersit St

J4
1 Brooklea Dr
2 Merrylee Crs
3 Merrylee Pk

J5
1 Carleton Ct

J6
1 Elliot Dr
2 May Ter
3 Orchard Pk
4 St Leonard's Dr
5 Station Rd

J7
1 Egidia Av
2 Maryville Gdns

J8
1 Montgomery Dr

K1
1 Prospect Rd
2 Shawhill Ct

K3
1 Auldhouse Ter
2 Craigellan Rd
3 Tarbolton Rd

K4
1 Briar Gv
2 Merryvale Pl

K6
1 Heathside Rd

K8
1 Kensington Dr

L1
1 James Gray St
2 Strathyre St
3 Underwood St
4 Walton St

L4
1 Letham Ct

L5
1 Crathes Ct
2 Strathendrick Dr

L7
1 Strathdee Rd
2 Strathview Gv

M1
1 Camphill Av
2 Overdale Av
3 Overdale Gdns

M2
1 Boswell Ct
2 Braemar St
3 Millbrae Gdns
4 Millbrae Rd

M3
1 Muirskeith Pl
2 Tannahill Rd

M4
1 Glasserton Pl

M5
1 Brenfield Dr
2 Cairndow Av
3 Cairndow Avenue La
4 Dairsie St
5 Gartly St
6 Hazel Av
7 Muirfield Ct
8 Whitemoss Av
9 Windlaw Park Gdns

M7
1 Leefield Dr
2 Williamwood Pk
3 Williamwood Pk West

M8
1 Netherway
2 Randolph Gdns

Page 128

A1
1 Annan St
2 Florida Dr
3 Hanover Cl

A2
1 Arundel Dr
2 Battlefield Gdns
3 Craigmillar Rd
4 Langside Gdns
5 Lochleven La

A3
1 Holmhead Pl
2 Muirskeith Crs
3 Old Castle Rd
4 Tulloch St

A4
1 Ailort Av
2 Bowling Green Rd
3 Kildary Av
4 Rhannan Ter
5 Snuff Mill Rd
6 Struan Gdns

A7
1 Leewood Dr

A8
1 Randolph Av

B1
1 Advie Pl
2 Brownlie St
3 Clincart Rd
4 Lindores St
5 Mclennan St

B2
1 Ballogie Rd
2 Cathcart Rd
3 Cathkinview Pl
4 Cordiner St
5 Knockhill Dr

B3
1 Greenholme St

B4
1 Snuff Mill Rd

B8
1 Blaeloch Ter

C1
1 Myrtle Pl
2 Prospecthill Dr

C2
1 Kingsdale Av

C3
1 Kingsbridge Dr

C4
1 Romney Av

C7
1 Downcraig Gv
2 Holmbyre Ter

C8
1 Ardencraig La
2 Blaeloch Av

D1
1 Ardnahoe Pl
2 Kerrycroy Pl
3 Prospecthill Sq

D2
1 Kerrylamont Av

D3
1 Kingscourt Av

D5
1 Lawhill Av
2 Raith Av

D6
1 Arnprior Crs
2 Westcastle Gv

D7
1 Ardmaleish St
2 Birgidale Ter
3 Cassiltoun Gdns
4 Stravanan St
5 Stravanan Ter

E1
1 Edinbeg Pl

E2
1 Ardmory Pl
2 Greenan Av
3 Westhouse Gdns

E4
1 Highcroft Av
2 Lugar Pl

E5
1 Crofthill Rd
2 Crofthouse Dr

E6
1 Barlia St
2 Glenwood Pth

E7
1 Ardmaleish Crs
2 Ardmaleish Ter
3 Lenihall Ter
4 Stravanan Ct

E8
1 Dunagoil Ter

F1
1 Burnhill Quadrant
2 Chapel Ct
3 Drummond Av
4 Glebe Pl
5 Glencairn Ct
6 Kildale Wy

F2
1 Avonbank Rd
2 Bellscroft Av
3 Cathcart Rd
4 Muirbank Gdns
5 Orchard Dr

F3
1 Watt Low Av

F4
1 Ailsa Dr
2 Arran Ter
3 Castlemilk Rd
4 Croftend La
5 Ellisland Crs
6 Kyle Sq

F5
1 Turnberry Pl

F6
1 Machrie St

Page 129

G1
1 Castle St
2 High St
3 King Street La
4 Kirkwood St
5 Mill Ct
6 Princes Ga
7 Regent Dr
8 Western Av

G2
1 Balvaird Crs
2 Balvaird Dr
3 Bankhead Dr
4 Chesters Pl
5 Clincarthill Rd
6 Greenhill St
7 Hillfoot Av
8 Macdonald St
9 Sheriff Park Av
10 Vermont Av
11 Wallace St

G3
1 Broomieknowe Gdns
2 Rodger Pl
3 Watt Low Av

G4
1 Drumlaw Wy
2 Mossgiel Pl

G5
1 Croftfoot Crs
2 Croftfoot St
3 George Mann Ter
4 Launeston Wy
5 Tormusk Gv

G7
1 Aster Dr
2 Bluebell Gdns

H1
1 Caledonia Av
2 Gallowflat St
3 Mccallum Av

H2
1 Belmont Dr
2 Clincarthill Rd
3 Kelso Av
4 Lindores Av
5 Reuther Av
6 Wardlaw Dr

H3
1 Broomieknowe Dr
2 Mitchell Dr

H4
1 Glenlui Av
2 Rowantree Av

H5
1 Barrisdale Wy
2 Hillhead Pl
3 Muirbrae Wy

H6
1 Arnisdale Wy
2 Colvend Dr
3 Fernbrae Wy
4 Kenmure Wy
5 Merrick Wy

J1
1 Richmond Ct

J2
1 Cathkin Av
2 Limeside Gdns
3 Sciencroft Av
4 Selkirk Dr
5 Waverley Dr
6 Woodside Gv

J4
1 Blairbeth Ter
2 Burnside Ct
3 Burnside Ga
4 Burnside Rd
5 Church Av
6 Snaefell Av
7 Southhill Av

J5
1 Fishescoates Av
2 Hazelwood Gdns
3 Snaefell Av
4 Upper Bourtree Ct

K2
1 Broomfield Av
2 Lauder Dr
3 Richmond Rd

K3
1 Hillary Av
2 Lauder Dr

K4
1 Burnbrae Dr
2 Cornwall Av
3 Fishescoates Av
4 Fishescoates Gdns
5 Gloucester Av
6 Ingerbreck Av
7 Stanhope Dr

K5
1 Breadalbane Gdns
2 Lovat Pl
3 Mar Gdns
4 Minto Av
5 Morar Ter
6 Strathallon Pl
7 Strathcona Pl
8 Strathmore Gdns
9 Strenabey Av

K6
1 Glencoe Rd
2 Tulloch-ard Pl

K7
1 Inchmurrin Gdns
2 Inchmurrin Pl

L2
1 Burn Pl
2 Glenpark Gdns
3 Glenpark Ter
4 Winfield Av

L3
1 Cathkin Pl

L4
1 Brandon Gdns
2 Brownside Av
3 Chatelherault Av
4 Langlea Gdns

L5
1 Atholl Gdns
2 Whitlawburn Ter

L6
1 Bowmore Gdns
2 Hilton Ter
3 Iona Rd

L7
1 Glen Etive Pl

M3
1 Beech Av
2 Library Gdns
3 North Av

M5
1 Holmhills Pl

Page 130

A3
1 Arnott Wy
2 Brown Pl
3 Colebrooke St
4 Katrine Pl
5 Mansion Ct
6 Mcintyre Ter
7 Orion Wy

B1
1 Broomhill Av
2 Dornie Dr
3 Gardenside Pl
4 Hillcrest Av
5 Orchard Ct

B5
1 Hollybank Pl

C1
1 Ardargie Gv
2 Ardargie Pl
3 Clydeview Ter
4 Duisdale Rd
5 Estate Quadrant
6 Hillcrest Rd
7 Laurelbank Rd
8 Naismith St
9 Noldrum Gdns
10 Quebec Wynd

D5
1 Branchock Av
2 Dean Park Dr
3 Glen St
4 Welfare Av

D6
1 Dechmont Av

E3
1 Eastwood Vw
2 Greenwood Av
3 Riverside Pl

E4
1 Aspen Pl
2 Hallside Crs
3 Hallside Dr
4 Montgomery St

E5
1 Cherrytree Dr
2 Helenslea

E6
1 Campsie Vw

F5
1 Rowan Ct

F6
1 Poplar Wy

Page 131

J8
1 Aldersyde Pl
2 Annfield Gdns
3 Bellairs Pl
4 Burns Gdns
5 Cedar Pl
6 Cloudhowe Ter
7 Dechmont Gdns
8 Melrose Pl
9 South Vw
10 Zambesi Dr

K8
1 Abiegail Pl
2 Crawford Crs
3 Glenview Pl
4 Stanley Pl

L1
1 Bowmore Gdns
2 Cartmore Gdns
3 Kenmar Gdns
4 Kirkview Gdns
5 Roselea Rd

L3
1 Crowflats Rd
2 Knowehead Gdns
3 Station Rd

M3
1 Angela Wy
2 Deanbrae St
3 Greenrigg St
4 Muiredge Ct
5 Simpson Ct
6 Towie Pl

M4
1 Castlecroft Gdns
2 Loancroft Gdns
3 Spindlehowe Rd
4 Springfield Crs
5 Sunnyside Av
6 Wellbank Pl

M7
1 Birkdale Ct
2 Carnoustie Ct
3 Gleneagles Pk

Page 132

A1
1 Cameron Dr
2 Campsie Vw
3 Chrighton Gn
4 Cullen Pl
5 Donaldson Gn
6 Kilpatrick Wy
7 Ochil Vw
8 Prentice La
9 Russell Gdns
10 Townhead Pl
11 Walker Pth
12 Young Pl

A2
1 Almond V
2 Baillie Wynd
3 Copperfield La
4 Craigpark Wy
5 Dechmont Vw
6 Howe Gdns
7 Kilbride Vw
8 Minard Wy
9 Pandora Wy

A6
1 Belstane Pl
2 Homeston Av
3 Kirkfield Rd
4 Pinwherry Pl
5 Sweethope Pl
6 Woodlands Av

A7
1 Dean Park Av
2 North Dean Park Av
3 South Dean Park Av

B8
1 Blairston Gdns
2 Clydevale
3 Croftbank Crs
4 Grange Gdns
5 Langside Ct
6 Wingfield Gdns
7 Woodhead Av

C3
1 Alexander Av
2 Quarrybrae Gdns
3 Woodfield

D3
1 Bothwellpark Pl
2 Cockhill Wy
3 New Edinburgh Rd

D4
1 Crighton Wynd

E4
1 Lauranne Pl
2 Lysa Vale Pl
3 Margaret Pl
4 Rosewood Pth

E6
1 Bellshill Rd
2 Combe Quadrant
3 Park Pl

F1
1 Phoenix Crs

F3
1 Abbotsford La
2 Bowyer Vennel

F4
1 Gilmour Pl
2 Ida Quadrant
3 Kelbourne Crs
4 Wilson Ct

F5
1 Blackmoss Dr
2 Braehead Pl
3 Caledonian Av
4 Helenslea Pl
5 Mansfield Rd
6 Queens Crs
7 Southend Pl
8 Victoria Pl
9 Windermere St

F6
1 Bothwellhaugh Quadrant
2 Broomhill Crs
3 Crofthead Pl
4 Dechmont Vw
5 Farm La
6 Kenmuiraid Pl
7 Knivysbridge Pl
8 Oakview Quadrant
9 Orbiston Sq
10 Raewell Crs
11 Whinpark Av
12 Whitepond Av

F7
1 Gordon Pl
2 Lesley Quadrant
3 Macdonald Gv
4 Mcintosh Quadrant
5 Seaforth Pl
6 Sutherland Pl

Page 133

G2
1 Ettrick Av
2 Limegrove St
3 Marifield Gdns
4 Senga Crs

G5
1 Elmbank St
2 Emerald Ter
3 Gardenside
4 Hallside Av
5 Mauldslie St
6 Robertson Dr

H3
1 Mcmahon Gv

H4
1 Academy Ter
2 Anderson Ct
3 Bowling Green St
4 East Dean St
5 Gladstone St
6 Sykehead Av

H6
1 Community Pl
2 Pearl St
3 Roberts Quadrant
4 Tourmaline Ter

J4
1 Barty's Rd

J8
1 Arnott Quadrant
2 Blackwood Gdns
3 Cassels Gv
4 Gibson Quadrant

K5
1 Archiebald Pl
2 Beveridge Ter
3 Eastfield Ter
4 Elm View Ct

K6
1 Riverbank Dr
2 The Woodlands

K7
1 Ashton St
2 Davies Quadrant
3 Flaxfield Gv
4 Graeme Ct
5 Kylemore Crs
6 Tulley Wynd

K8
1 Breadalbane Crs
2 Duncan Ct
3 Elliot Ct
4 Glenallan Ter
5 Kylemore Crs
6 Montrose St

M4
1 Allbany Crs
2 Central Av
3 Elizabeth Quadrant
4 Thankerton Av

M5
1 Regency Wy

M6
1 James Vw
2 Laidlaw Av
3 Murdoch Pl
4 Queens Crs

Page 134

A4
1 Alexandria Quadrant
2 Beechgrove Quadrant
3 Burnside Quadrant
4 Centenary Quadrant
5 Diana Quadrant
6 Mcdonald Pl
7 St Andrews St
8 Trossachs Av

A6
1 Blackmoor Pl
2 Esdaile Ct
3 Ivy Pl
4 Phoenix Pl

A7
1 Bannockburn Pl
2 Cromdale Wy
3 Elm Rd
4 Hillhead Crs
5 North Av

B8
1 Byresknowe La
2 Coalhall Av
3 Eastend Av
4 Motherwell Rd

E5
1 Caledonia Dr
2 Clockerhill Pl
3 Mccormack Gdns
4 Pickerstonhill

E8
1 Jones Wynd

F4
1 Allandale Av
2 Innermanse Quadrant

F5
1 Church St
2 Greenfield Quadrant
3 Greenside St

Page 144

B8
1 Bellman's Cl
2 Caledonia Rd
3 King's Ct
4 Kirk Vw
5 Laigh Ct
6 Main St
7 Medine Ct
8 Muirpark Rd
9 Somerville Ct
10 Wee Cl
11 Wilson St
12 Woodside Rd

Page 150

B4
1 Blair Gdns
2 Craigievar Pl
3 Craig Pl
4 Crarea Pl
5 Easdale Pl
6 Raasay Gdns
7 Rossie Gv
8 Threave Pl
9 Westerlands Pl

B5
1 Kilkerran Ct
2 Kilkerran Pk
3 Kilkerran Wy
4 Rozelle Dr
5 Rozelle Pl
6 Westerlands Gv

F4
1 Cedarwood Av

F5
1 Blackhouse Gdns
2 Blackhouse Rd
3 Broomhill Gdns

F6
1 Castlemount Av

Page 151

H5
1 Abernethy Pl
2 Bankfoot Pl
3 Birnam Pl
4 Blairatholl Crs
5 Crathie Pl
6 Gleneagles Ga
7 Scone Pl

Page 153

G8
1 Antigua Wy
2 Bahamas Wy
3 Barbados Gn
4 Dominica Gn
5 Tobago Pl
6 Trinidad Gn
7 Watling Pl

J5
1 Brooklime Gdns
2 Burnet Rose Ct
3 Burnet Rose Gdns
4 Burnet Rose Pl
5 Macarthur Crs

J6
1 Bellflower Ct
2 Carmunnock Rd
3 Dunnottar Ct
4 Dunnottar Crs
5 Esk Dl
6 Macarthur Ct
7 Macarthur Gdns
8 Macpherson Pk
9 Silverdale
10 Wensleydale

J7
1 Methven Pl
2 Mitchell Ct
3 Mitchell Gv
4 Rosenheath Ga
5 West Ga

K6
1 Barassie
2 Cawdor Wy
3 Croy
4 Duart Dr
5 Dunrobin Ct
6 Dunrobin Crs
7 Dunvegan Pl
8 Fulmar Pk
9 Kildrummy Pl
10 Pennyroyal Ct
11 Scone Pl
12 Thistle Pl

K7
1 Cadzow Gn
2 Dalmellington Ct
3 Dalmellington Dr
4 Doonfoot Gdns

K8
1 Falkland Pl
2 Valleyfield

L7
1 Ashton Gn
2 Kirkton Ga
3 Ladybank Ct
4 Ladybank Gdns
5 Stuarton Pk

L8
1 Brouster Pl
2 Cloverhill Ter
3 Creighton Gv
4 Cunninghame Rd
5 Holm La
6 Newlands Pl

M6
1 Bosfield Cnr
2 Dunglass Sq
3 Lochaber Pl
4 Manse La
5 Rannoch Gn
6 Wardrop Pl

M7
1 Dunblane Pl
2 Guthrie Pl
3 Jedburgh Pl
4 Kittoch Pl
5 Ladybank Pl
6 Lindsay Gv
7 Montgomery Pl
8 Montgomery St
9 Pankhurst Pl
10 St Bryde St

Page 154

B5
1 Lauder Gn

B6
1 Abercromby Pl
2 Ayton Pk South
3 Drummond Pl
4 Maxwellton Pl
5 Munro Pl
6 Pollok Pl

B8
1 Garnock Pk
2 Glen Urquhart

C8
1 Davaar

Page 155

J1
1 Broad Sq
2 Columba Pth
3 Dyfrig St
4 Kintyre Rd
5 Oaklea Crs
6 Sycamore Gv
7 Wheatlandhead Ct

J2
1 Windyridge Pl

K1
1 Birch Pl
2 Cameron Wy
3 Valerio Ct
4 Wolcott Dr

K2
1 Coldstream St
2 Selkirk St

K3
1 Braehead
2 Carrick Gdns
3 Mossbank

K4
1 Loanfoot Rd

M4
1 Udston Ter

M5
1 Stanley St

M6
1 Hillhouse Ter
2 St Ninian's Pl
3 St Ninian's Rd
4 Shandon Ter

M7
1 Campsie Vw

Page 156

A4
1 Burnbank Centre
2 Crawford St
3 Gladstone Ct
4 Holyrood St
5 Limetree Ct
6 Mcgowan Pl
7 Queen St
8 Stewart St
9 Wilson St
10 Windsor Gdns

B3
1 Abbotsford Crs
2 Atholl St
3 Backmuir Pl
4 Dryburgh St

B6
1 Cameron Crs
2 Chantinghall Ter

C5
1 Douglas Park La
2 Douglas St
3 Peacock Dr
4 West Stewart St

C7
1 Arden Ter
2 Hillside La
3 West Glebe Ter

D5
1 Almada La
2 Guthrie St
3 Saffronhall Crs
4 Saffronhall La

D7
1 Alness Ter
2 Dalmeny Rd
3 Gardenside Rd
4 Wylie St

D8
1 Alexander Balfour Gdns
2 Arden Ter
3 Croftwood Rd
4 Hutchison St

E5
1 Back O' Barns
2 Cadzow Pk
3 Common Gn
4 Fore Rw
5 Lower Auchingramont Rd
6 Portwell
7 Shelling Hl

E6
1 Avon St
2 Gateside St
3 Lamb St
4 Strathmore Rd

E7
1 Burnside La
2 Centenary Gdns
3 Cypress Ct
4 Johnstone Rd
5 Neilson Ct
6 Portland Pk
7 Portland Sq
8 Rowan Ri
9 Selkirk Pl
10 Selkirk St
11 Woodside Av

E8
1 Allanton Pl
2 Riverdale Gdns
3 Waterside Gdns

F5
1 Back O'barns

F6
1 Bourne St
2 Landsdowne Gdns
3 Miller Field Pl
4 Spencer Field Gdns
5 Staneacre Pk
6 Townhead St

F7
1 Castlehill Gdns
2 Juniper Gv

Page 157

H1
1 Lismore Av

H3
1 Devon Wy
2 Haughview Rd
3 Kay Gdns

J3
1 Wellpark Rd

J4
1 Crawford Gdns
2 Kenneth Rd
3 Ross Dr

K1
1 Lantana Gv
2 Sunflower Gdns

K5
1 Grenadier Gdns

L2
1 Hope St
2 Menteith Rd
3 Paterson St
4 Roman Rd
5 St Vincent Pl
6 Scott St

L4
1 Aster Gdns
2 Factory Rd
3 Glencairn St

M1
1 Calderbank Ter

M2
1 Albert St
2 Calder Vw
3 Coursington Gdns
4 Coursington Pl
5 Coursington Rd
6 Draffen St

M4
1 Blair Pth
2 Macdonald St
3 Toll St
4 Windmill Ct

M5
1 Woodlands St

Page 158

B5
1 Burnside St
2 Finnie Wynd
3 Howson Lea
4 Money Gv
5 Rice Wy

E6
1 New Ashtree St

Page 159

H4
1 Applecross Quadrant
2 Berriedale Quadrant
3 Forres Quadrant
4 Laburnum Crs
5 Nairn Quadrant
6 The Steading

H6
1 The Clachan
2 Library Rd
3 Robin Pl
4 Shand St
5 Swallow Rd

H7
1 Mcalpine St
2 Mcinnes Ct

J4
1 Stobo St

J7
1 Bush Crs
2 Knowehead Rd
3 The Roundel

J8
1 Conservation Pl
2 Dimsdale Crs
3 Perchy Vw
4 Sneddon Av

K2
1 Larchfield Gv

M3
1 Barrisdale Rd
2 Muirside Pl
3 Queen St
4 Shiel Ter
5 Stanecraigs Pl

Page 171

H1
1 Algoma Pl
2 Columbia Pl
3 Redcliffe Dr
4 Riverton Dr

H5
1 Invercloy Ct
2 Machrie Gn
3 Pirnmill Av
4 Torbeg Gdns

H6
1 Moorfoot Gdns

J1
1 Alberta Crs
2 Barkly Ter
3 Bunbury Ter
4 Hudson Wy
5 Le Froy La
6 Lethbridge Pl
7 Melbourne Gn
8 Sydney Pl

J3
1 St Andrews Ct

K2
1 Armstrong Gv
2 Livingstone Crs
3 Simpson Pl

K3
1 Sycamore Ct

K4
1 Drumduff
2 Laurel Pl
3 Whitelee

L1
1 Bell Gn West
2 Caledonian Ct
3 Denholm Crs
4 Fleming Pl
5 Hill Vw
6 Macadam Pl
7 Muirhouse La
8 Rutherford Sq

L2
1 Cullen La
2 Heathery Knowe
3 Lairshill Rd
4 The Murray Sq
5 Strathcona La

L3
1 Andersen Ct
2 Grantoften Pth
3 Odense Ct
4 Tivoli Ct

L4
1 Anderside
2 Broughton
3 Drumloch Gdns
4 Mosslingal
5 Mountherrick
6 Powbrone

M1
1 Denholm Gn
2 Sinclair Pk
3 Todhills North
4 Todhills South

M2
1 Somerville La

Page 176

A8
1 Bemersyde Pl
2 Loch Park Pl
3 Robert Smillie Crs

C7
1 Afton St
2 Catrine St
3 Cheviot Rd
4 Chillin Pl
5 Doon St
6 Hareleeshill Rd
7 Landsdowne Rd
8 Wallace Dr
9 Woodburn Ter

C8
1 Bannockburn Dr
2 Bertram St
3 Blair Atholl Dr
4 Dickson St
5 Glen Fruin Dr
6 Howard St
7 Pitlochry Dr
8 Rannoch Ter

Page 178

E6
1 Cooper Av
2 Hemmingen Ct
3 Neidpath Rd
4 Nimmo Pl
5 Tantallon Ct
6 Yvetot Ct

Page 191

J5
1 Armour Pl
2 Dalry Rd
3 Garthland Dr
4 Hazel Av

J6
1 Birch Ter
2 Central Quadrant
3 Cuninghame Rd
4 Eglinton Sq
5 Harvey St
6 Woodland Pl

J7
1 Anderson Ter
2 Fullerton Sq
3 School Pl
4 Seton La
5 Seton St
6 Winton La
7 Winton Pl

Page 193

H6
1 Braid Ct
2 Carnoustie Ct
3 Dalmahoy Wy
4 Dornoch Ct
5 Eden Ct
6 Ganton Ct
7 Nairn Ct
8 Sutton Ct
9 Thornhill Ct
10 Turnberry Ct
11 West Doura Wy

Page 199

G6
1 St Mungo's

Page 206

E8
1 David Orr St
2 Inkerman Pl
3 North Hamilton St
4 Robert Stewart Pl
5 Warwickhill Rd
6 West Fullarton St

Page 207

G8
1 Boyd Ct
2 Morris La
3 Union St

J8
1 Macallister Pl
2 Macauley Pl
3 Macbeth Gdns
4 Macdonald Pl
5 Macdougall Pl
6 Macinnes Pl
7 Macintosh Pl
8 Mackie Pl
9 Macnicol Pl

Page 211

K2
1 Fir Pl
2 Galrigside Rd
3 Heather Pl
4 Laurel Pl
5 Thirdpart Pl

K3
1 East Gargieston Av
2 Holmes Crs

Page 212

A5
1 Broomhill Rd East
2 Lawers Crs
3 Lawers Rd
4 Witchknowe Ct

A6
1 Cheviot Pl
2 Dumgoyne Rd
3 Peatland Rd
4 Wyvis Rd

Page 225

G8
1 Content St
2 Limonds Wynd
3 Philip Sq
4 Queen's Quadrant
5 Russell St

J1
1 Boyd St
2 Briarhill St
3 Broompark Crs
4 Duart Crs
5 Hunter St
6 Salisbury Pl
7 Tramore Crs

J2
1 Craigneil Dr
2 Cunninghame Rd
3 Hawthorn Av
4 Hawthorn Gdns

J4
1 Benmore
2 Creran Ct
3 Devilla Ct
4 Fearnoch
5 Laighland

K5
1 Boundary Rd

L7
1 Drummond Crs
2 Main Rd
3 Sannox Vw
4 Whitletts Ct

M7
1 Thornyflat Crs

Page 231

H5
1 Arthurston Ter
2 Barngore Dr
3 Burgoyne Dr
4 Carnell Dr
5 Chestnut Gv
6 Douglas Rd
7 Gadgirth Ct
8 Meadow Pk
9 Milton Pk
10 Ramseyston Dr
11 Whitehill Wy

Notes

Notes